Less managing. More teaching. Greater learning.

 INSTRUCTORS...

Would you like your **students** to show up for class more **prepared**? *(Let's face it, class is much more fun if everyone is engaged and prepared...)*

Want ready-made application-level **interactive assignments,** student progress reporting, and auto-assignment grading? *(Less time grading means more time teaching...)*

Want an **instant view of student or class performance** relative to learning objectives? *(No more wondering if students understand...)*

Need to **collect data and generate reports** required for administration or accreditation? *(Say goodbye to manually tracking student learning outcomes...)*

Want to **record and post your lectures** for students to view online?

 With **McGraw-Hill's** *Connect*® **Management,**

INSTRUCTORS GET:

- Interactive Applications – **book-specific interactive assignments** that require students to APPLY what they've learned.

- Simple **assignment management**, allowing you to spend more time teaching.

- **Auto-graded** assignments, quizzes, and tests.

- **Detailed Visual Reporting** where student and section results can be viewed and analyzed.

- Sophisticated **online testing** capability.

- A **filtering and reporting** function that allows you to easily assign and report on materials that are correlated to accreditation standards, learning outcomes, and Bloom's taxonomy.

- An easy-to-use **lecture capture** tool.

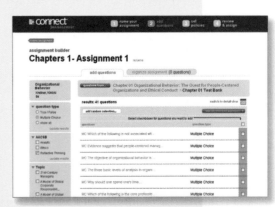

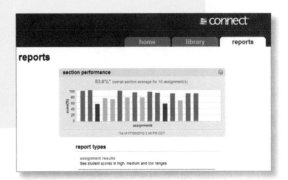

Want an online, **searchable version** of your textbook?

 Wish your textbook could be **available online** while you're doing your assignments?

 ## *Connect® Plus Management* eBook

If you choose to use *Connect® Plus Management*, you have an affordable and searchable online version of your book integrated with your other online tools.

Connect® Plus Management eBook offers features like:

- Topic search
- Direct links from assignments
- Adjustable text size
- Jump to page number
- Print by section

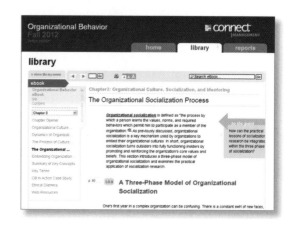

 Want to get more **value** from your textbook purchase?

Think learning management should be a bit more **interesting**?

 ## Check out the STUDENT RESOURCES section under the *Connect®* Library tab.

Here you'll find a wealth of resources designed to help you achieve your goals in the course. You'll find things like **quizzes, PowerPoints, and Internet activities** to help you study. Every student has different needs, so explore the STUDENT RESOURCES to find the materials best suited to you.

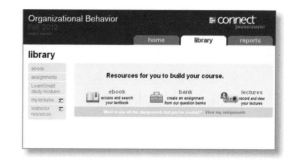

Organizational Behavior tenth edition

Organizational Behavior tenth edition

Robert Kreitner
Angelo Kinicki

Both of Arizona State University

 McGraw-Hill Irwin

5 6 7 8 9 0 DOW/DOW 1 0 9 8 7 6 5 4

ISBN 978-0-07-802936-3
MHID 0-07-802936-8

Vice president and editor-in-chief: *Brent Gordon*
Editorial director: *Paul Ducham*
Executive editor: *Michael Ablassmeir*
Executive director of development: *Ann Torbert*
Development editor: *Kelly I. Pekelder*
Editorial coordinator: *Andrea Heirendt*
Vice president and director of marketing: *Robin J. Zwettler*
Marketing director: *Amee Mosley*
Senior marketing manager: *Michelle Heaster*
Marketing specialist: *Elizabeth Steiner*
Vice president of editing, design, and production: *Sesha Bolisetty*
Senior project manager: *Dana M. Pauley*
Senior buyer: *Michael R. McCormick*
Senior designer: *Matt Diamond*
Senior photo research coordinator: *Jeremy Cheshareck*
Photo researcher: *Editorial Image, LLC*
Senior media project manager: *Bruce Gin*
Media project manager: *Balaji Sundararaman, Hurix Systems Pvt. Ltd.*
Cover and interior design: *Cara Hawthorne, cara david DESIGN*
Typeface: *10.5/12 Times Roman*
Compositor: *MPS Limited, a Macmillan Company*
Printer: *R. R. Donnelley*

Library of Congress Cataloging-in-Publication Data

Kreitner, Robert.
    Organizational behavior / Robert Kreitner, Angelo Kinicki. -- 10th ed.
        p. cm.
    Includes index.
    ISBN-13: 978-0-07-802936-3 (alk. paper)
    ISBN-10: 0-07-802936-8 (alk. paper)
    1. Organizational behavior. I. Kinicki, Angelo. II. Title.
HD58.7.K766 2013
658.3--dc23

                                             2011043477

About the Authors

Bob and his wife Margaret atop 13,140-foot Boundary Peak (Nevada's highest point).

Robert (Bob) Kreitner, PhD, is professor emeritus of management at Arizona State University and a member of ASU's W P Carey School of Business Faculty Hall of Fame. Prior to joining ASU in 1975, Bob taught at Western Illinois University. He also taught organizational behavior at Thunderbird. Bob has addressed a diverse array of audiences worldwide on management topics. He has authored articles for journals such as *Organizational Dynamics, Business Horizons, Educational and Psychological Measurement, Journal of Organizational Behavior Management,* and *Journal of Business Ethics.* He also is coauthor (with Fred Luthans) of the award-winning book *Organizational Behavior Modification and Beyond: An Operant and Social Learning Approach* and coauthor (with Carlene Cassidy) of *Management,* 12th edition, an introductory management text. His textbooks collectively have been through 31 editions.

Among his consulting and executive development clients have been American Express, SABRE Computer Services, Honeywell, Motorola, Amdahl, the Hopi Indian Tribe, State Farm Insurance, Goodyear Aerospace, Doubletree Hotels, Bank One–Arizona, Nazarene School of Large Church Management, Ford Motor Company, US Steel, and Allied-Signal. In 1981–82 he served as chairman of the Academy of Management's Management Education and Development Division.

Bob was born in Buffalo, New York. After a four-year enlistment in the US Coast Guard, including service on the icebreaker *EASTWIND* in Antarctica, Bob attended the University of Nebraska–Omaha on a football scholarship. Bob also holds an MBA from the University of Nebraska–Omaha and a PhD from the University of Nebraska–Lincoln. While working on his PhD in business at Nebraska, he spent six months teaching management courses for the university in Micronesia. In 1996, Bob taught two courses in Albania's first-ever MBA program. He taught a summer leadership program in Switzerland from 1995 to 1998. Bob and his wife Margaret, a retired Intel Corp manager, live in Phoenix with their two cats Yahoo and Sweetie Pie. They enjoy world travel, lots of hiking, and fishing in Alaska.

Angelo with Na'vi at the Colorado Wolf and Wildlife center. Na'vi is a 40-pound Black Phase Timber Wolf.

Angelo Kinicki, DBA, is a professor, author, and consultant. He is a professor of management and has held the Weatherup/Overby Chair in Leadership since 2005. He also is a Dean's Council of 100 Distinguished Scholar at the W P Carey School of Business. He joined the faculty in 1982, the year he received his doctorate in business administration from Kent State University. His primary research interests include leadership, organizational culture, organizational change, and multilevel issues associated with predicting organizational effectiveness. Angelo has published more than 90 articles in a variety of academic journals and is coauthor of seven textbooks (25 including revisions) that are used by hundreds of universities around the world. Several of his books have been translated into multiple languages.

Angelo is an award-winning researcher and teacher. He has received several awards, including a best research paper award from the Organizational Behavior (OB) division of the Academy of Management, the All Time Best Reviewer Award (1996–99) and the Excellent Reviewer Award (1997–98) from the *Academy of Management Journal,* and six teaching awards from Arizona State University [Outstanding Teaching Award—MBA and Master's Program, John W Teets Outstanding Graduate Teacher Award (twice), Outstanding Undergraduate Teaching Excellence Award, Outstanding Graduate Teaching Excellence Award, and Outstanding Executive Development Teaching Excellence Award].

Angelo also has served on the editorial review boards for the *Academy of Management Journal, Personnel Psychology,* the *Journal of Management,* and the *Journal of Vocational Behavior.* Angelo has been an active member of the Academy of Management, including service as a representative at large for the Organizational Behavior division, member of the Best Paper Award committee for both the OB and Human Resources (HR) divisions, chair of the committee to select the best publication in the *Academy of Management Journal,* and program committee reviewer for the OB and HR divisions.

Angelo also is a busy international consultant and is a principal at Kinicki and Associates Inc, a management consulting firm that works with top management teams to create organizational change aimed at increasing organizational effectiveness and profitability. He has worked with many *Fortune* 500 firms as well as numerous entrepreneurial organizations in diverse industries. His expertise includes facilitating strategic/operational planning sessions, diagnosing the causes of organizational and work-unit problems, conducting organizational culture interventions, implementing performance management systems, designing and implementing performance appraisal systems, developing and administering surveys to assess employee attitudes, and leading management/executive education programs. He developed a 360-degree leadership feedback instrument called the Performance Management Leadership Survey (PMLS) that is used by companies throughout the United States and Europe. The survey is used to assess an individual's leadership style and to coach individuals interested in developing their leadership skills.

Angelo and his wife Joyce have enjoyed living in the beautiful Arizona desert for 30 years and are natives of Cleveland, Ohio. They enjoy traveling, golfing, hiking, spending time in the White Mountains, and spoiling Nala, their golden retriever.

With love to my precious little family, Margaret and our cats Yahoo and Sweetie Pie.

—B.K.

With respect and admiration to Dr William Spears. His work has reduced the carbon footprint of many schools, hospitals, and churches. He also is a role model for educators and entrepreneurs everywhere. I am proud to be his friend.

—A.K.

Preface

Whatever the size and purpose of the organization and the technology involved, *people* are the common denominator when facing today's immense challenges. Success or failure hinges on the ability to attract, develop, retain, motivate, and lead a diverse array of appropriately skilled people (and to do so in an ethical manner). *The human factor drives everything.* To know more about workplace behavior is to gain a valuable competitive edge. The purpose of this textbook is to help present and future organizational participants better understand and manage people at work.

Although this tenth edition of *Organizational Behavior* is aimed at undergraduate business students in similarly named courses, previous editions have proven highly versatile. *Organizational Behavior* has been used effectively in MBA programs, executive education and management development programs, and industrial and organizational psychology programs around the world. (Note: Special Canadian and European editions are available.) This textbook is the culmination of our combined 65+ years of teaching experience and research of organizational behavior and management in the United States, Pacific Rim, and Europe. Thanks to detailed feedback from students, professors, and practicing managers, this tenth edition is state-of-the-art in both content and delivery. Many new changes have been made in this edition, reflecting new research evidence, new management techniques, new media, and the fruits of our own learning process.

Organizational Behavior, tenth edition, is *user driven* (as a result of carefully listening to our readers). It was developed through close *teamwork* between the authors and the publisher, and is the product of *continuous improvement.* This approach has helped us achieve a difficult combination of balances. Among them are balances between theory and practice, solid content and interesting coverage, and instructive detail and readability. Students and instructors say they want an up-to-date, relevant, and interesting textbook that actively involves the reader in the learning process. Our efforts toward this end are evidenced by dozens of new topics, many new real-life examples, a stimulating art program, and timely new cases and boxed features. A Legal/Ethical Challenge exercise at the end of each chapter (13 new; 2 updated) is instructive and useful for either individual consideration or team discussion. We realize that reading a comprehensive textbook is hard work, but we also firmly believe the process should be interesting (and sometimes fun).

New and Improved Coverage

Our readers and reviewers have kindly told us how much they appreciate our efforts to keep this textbook up-to-date and relevant. Toward that end, you will find the following important new and significantly improved coverage in the tenth edition:

Chapter 1

New chapter-opening case about Zappos.com. New discussion of employee engagement, as a preview of comprehensive coverage in Chapter 6. New discussion of Internet/social media revolution as a preview of comprehensive coverage in Chapter 14. Four new Real World/Real People boxed features. New chapter-closing case about Whole Foods' CEO John Mackey. New Legal/Ethical Challenge, at the end of the chapter, about education reform.

Chapter 2

New chapter-opening case about sexual harassment. Expanded discussion of sexual harassment. New discussion of electronic harassment. Updated workforce demographics pertaining to gender, race, age, and education. Table 2-1 about generational differences expanded and revised. Five new Real World/Real People boxed features. New Legal/Ethical Challenge about workplace drug policies.

Chapter 3

New discussion of ethical cultures in organizations. New key term, *PE fit,* and discussion of how students can determine the PE fit of potential jobs. Updated example of the functions of culture at Southwest Airlines. New examples to illustrate the culture types within the Competing Values Framework. New Figure 3-4 to summarize research on relationships between organizational culture and measures of organizational effectiveness. New examples of the 11 ways companies can change organizational culture. New discussion about using social media for networking. Three new and one updated Real World/Real People boxed features. New chapter-closing case about Chrysler's Sergio Marchionne.

Chapter 4

New chapter-opening case about conducting training in Israel. New Table 4-1 depicting the United States as a nation of immigrants. New research evidence about how multicultural experiences improve creative performance. New data on foreign students in the United States and U.S. students studying abroad. Expanded coverage of cultural intelligence (knowledge, mindfulness, and skills) from book by David C Thomas and Kerr Inkson, *Cultural Intelligence: Living and Working Globally*, 2009. New subhead section and new Table 4-4: Countries Achieve High Overall Management Scores by Emphasizing Different Practices. Detailed new coverage of cross-cultural training research. One new and one updated Real World/Real People boxed features. New chapter-closing case about China. Updated Legal/Ethical Challenge about corruption in Russia.

Chapter 5

New chapter-opening case about Facebook's CEO Mark Zuckerberg during his Harvard days. New section on changes in self-esteem during adulthood. New discussion of napping rooms at Nike and Google. New research evidence about emotional intelligence from two recent meta-analyses. Three new Real World/Real People boxed features. New Legal/Ethical Challenge that discusses how some managers play the guilt card.

Chapter 6

New chapter-opening case. Updated research and examples on managing work–family balance with a focus on generational differences. New section on employee engagement. New key term, *employee engagement,* and new discussion identifying the causes and consequences of employee engagement and the practical takeaways. Updated research on generational differences in job satisfaction and consequences of job satisfaction. Three new Real World/Real People boxed features. New Legal/Ethical Challenge about spying on students with Web cameras.

Chapter 7

New chapter-opening case on vulnerability. Updated material on sex-role stereotypes. New examples of the fundamental attribution bias and the self-serving bias. Two new Real World/Real People boxed features. New Legal/Ethical Challenge about people walking away from their mortgages.

Chapter 8

New chapter-opening case about Michelle Rhee and teacher evaluation. Chapter learning objectives simplified. Major overhaul of section on job design, now organized around three categories of job design: top-down approaches, bottom-up approaches, and idiosyncratic deals (i-deals). Two new key terms, *job crafting* and *idiosyncratic deals.* New Table 8-3 with examples of job crafting. Five new Real World/Real People boxed features. New chapter-closing case about how managers need to handle tough employment decisions.

Chapter 9

New chapter-opening case about NuStar Energy. Rewritten section on three-step goal-setting process. New research on goal ladders. New key term: *goal ladders.* New example of 360-degree feedback at BlackRock. New example for variable reinforcement. Two new Real World/Real People boxed features. New chapter-closing case about DineEquity's CEO Julia A Stewart (leaders as teachers). New Legal/Ethical Challenge about staffing.

Chapter 10

New chapter-opening case about how Intel's Pat McDonald handled a plant closing. New social capital example. New section about social loafing. New key term, *cyberloafing.* New Table 10–6: Dealing with Social Loafing in the Internet Age. Four new Real World/Real People boxed features. Updated Legal/Ethical Challenge about being an online "friend" with the boss.

Chapter 11

New chapter-opening case about customer service being like a team sport at Wynn Resorts. New data on lack of trust in government and business leaders. Expanded definition and explanation of trust. Recent research evidence about shared intense emotional experiences and socioemotional cohesiveness. New example of managing virtual teams at Ernst & Young. New example of Stephanie Thanos' 20-person cross-functional team at Lifespan Hospitals. Expanded discussion of team leadership with findings from three recent studies. Four new Real World/Real People boxed features. New chapter-closing case about Google's "Three-Thirds" HR team. New Legal/Ethical Challenge about working from the beach.

Chapter 12

New chapter-opening cases about decision making at Google. New key terms, *opportunity* (relative to rational model of decision making) and *evidence-based decision making.* Major new section about evidence-based decision making with new model in Figure 12-2. Revised and improved model of intuition in Figure 12-4. New section titled "Contextual Characteristics Associated with Creativity." Five new Real World/Real People boxed features. New chapter-closing case about BP Gulf of Mexico oil disaster. New Legal/Ethical Challenge about keeping your colleagues honest.

Chapter 13

New data on workplace bullying. New union-management cooperation example for desired conflict outcomes. Stephen Covey on finding "a third way" when resolving conflict. New data on how long it takes to become a top-notch negotiator, plus the Golden Rule of Negotiation. New section on the five emotional elements of negotiation. Three new Real World/Real People boxed features. New chapter-closing case about conflict.

Chapter 14

Improved chapter learning objectives. New chapter-opening case about Best Buy's CEO Brian Dunn. How iPads are used at Medtronic. Major new section: How social media are changing the communication landscape. New discussion of two important impacts of social media. New example of mismatched words and body language. Condensed and revamped section on linguistic styles and gender. New research evidence on employees' self-censorship. New material on listening to and involving middle managers. New research evidence about positive aspects of gossip. New section titled: Needed: A Policy for Social Media Use in the Workplace. IBM's social computing guidelines. New Table 14-9: Workplace Policy Guidelines for Using Social Media. Four new Real World/Real People boxed features. New chapter-closing case about Soraya Darabi's social media world. New Legal/Ethical Challenge about electronic monitoring of employees.

Chapter 15

New chapter-opening case about Deborah Dunsire's use of power. Expanded discussion of reward power (importance of shaping behavior with recognition and positive reinforcement). How Hilton's Homewood Suites hotel chain empowers its employees. New research data on nonmanagerial employees' trust for supervisors. New research data on perceived empowerment and intrinsic motivation, creativity, and openness to change. New material on 4 Ps of political success. Four new Real World/Real People boxed features. New chapter-closing case about Trader Joe's retired president Doug Rauch. New Legal/Ethical Challenge about getting even with a coworker.

Chapter 16

New chapter-opening case about the exit of Time Inc.'s CEO Jack Griffin. Expanded coverage of traits possessed by bad leaders. New section titled "Caveat When Applying Situational Theories." New illustration of transactional leadership with Stephen Green, founder of Hartwell Pacific. New illustration of transformational leadership with GE CEO Jeff Immelt. Three new Real World/Real People boxed features. New chapter-closing case on Lynn Tilton, founder and CEO of Patriarch. New Legal/Ethical Challenge revolving around James O'Keefe's use of subversive techniques to make NPR look bad.

Chapter 17

New chapter-opening case on office technology and innovation. Expanded coverage of learning organizations including learning from success and failure. New key term, *team mental model*. Three new Real World/Real People boxed features. New chapter-closing case about innovation communities. New Legal/Ethical Challenge about tracking Internet browsing.

Chapter 18

New chapter-opening case about Nokia's need to change. New key term, *telepresence*, discussed as a technological force for change. New example of Esquel making changes related to sustainability due to social and political forces for change. New coverage of US Army's resilience training. New discussion and new key term, *psychological detachment*. New coverage of Martin Seligman's ABCDE model of cognitive restructuring, a stress reduction technique. Updated statistics on wellness programs. Five new Real World/Real People boxed features. New chapter-closing case about organizational change at HCL Technologies.

AACSB Coverage

In keeping with the curriculum recommendations for AACSB International (the Association to Advance Collegiate Schools of Business, www.aacsb.edu) for greater attention to managing in a global economy, managing cultural diversity, improving product/service quality, and making ethical decisions, we feature this coverage:

- A full chapter on international organizational behavior and cross-cultural management (Chapter 4). Comprehensive coverage from the landmark GLOBE project and a new 17-country study about how management practices differ across countries. To ensure integrated coverage of international topics, several of the Real World/Real People boxed features have a global theme.

- A full chapter on managing diversity (Chapter 2) offers comprehensive and up-to-date coverage of managing diversity. Many of the Real World/Real People boxed features also have a diversity theme.

- Principles of total quality management (TQM) and the legacy of W Edwards Deming are discussed in Chapter 1 to establish a quality-improvement context for the entire textbook.

Also, many quality-related examples have been integrated into the textual presentation.

- As outlined next, the tenth edition includes comprehensive coverage of ethics-related concepts, cases, and issues. Many of the Real World/Real People boxed features have an ethics theme, with specific attention called out by an ethics label.

- The tenth edition test bank available on the OLC has each question tagged to the AACSB knowledge category it covers.

Integrative Topics (with specific page references)

CHAPTER	ETHICS	DIVERSITY	INTERNATIONAL OB	INTERNET/ SOCIAL MEDIA	TEAMS/ TEAMWORK
1	5, 13, 16, 20–26, 25, 29–30		20–22	14–16	17
2	33, 38, 46, 56, 58–59	Entire Chapter		53	51
3	64–65, 71, 74, 87	82	70, 74, 79, 86	76, 77, 78, 83, 84	60, 67–68, 76, 79
4	105	90, 91, 93, 96–97, 98, 99–101, 110–11, 112	Entire Chapter		114
5	126, 129–130, 133–134, 139, 146–147, 149	122, 123, 131, 137–138, 139	124, 132, 144	121	
6	154, 155, 161, 173–174, 177	157, 168, 170		167, 176	163, 166, 167, 169
7	179, 180, 185, 191–194, 200, 203	184, 188, 190–191, 194, 200		187	179, 182, 196
8	205, 210, 213, 217, 222, 225, 234–235	208–209, 221	227	216	211–212, 220, 227–228, 229, 231, 232, 234
9	241, 253, 257, 258, 263	246, 250	240, 243, 246		255
10	267, 268, 279, 281, 283, 289, 290, 291, 292, 297	279, 283, 286–289, 296–297	270–271, 276, 280, 284, 285, 287, 291, 293	272, 294–295	269–271
11	310, 312–313, 327	311	299, 301, 303, 309–310, 311–312, 322, 323	316–319	Entire Chapter
12	331–332, 337, 346–348, 361–363	343, 348–351, 353–356	343, 351, 359	331, 354–356, 358	329, 340, 341, 343, 348, 352, 353–356, 361–363

CHAPTER	ETHICS	DIVERSITY	INTERNATIONAL OB	INTERNET/ SOCIAL MEDIA	TEAMS/ TEAMWORK
13	368, 369, 372–373, 374–375, 386–388, 391	372, 373–374, 381	376–378, 383, 385, 386, 388	369	367–368, 369–370, 371
14	406, 411, 414, 415, 418, 420, 424–425, 429	398, 399, 406, 408–411, 421	398, 401, 406, 418	395–396, 402–403, 416–417, 421–422, 425–427, 428–429	414, 423
15	434, 439, 440–441, 448, 452, 453, 454, 455, 458–459	435–436, 438, 440, 453, 457	431–432, 436, 438, 440, 446, 455–456	438	435, 441, 447
16	467, 475, 482, 492	469, 480–481, 484–485	480–481, 487		461, 469, 475, 478, 480–481
17	526–527	512	498, 505–506, 508, 509, 510, 512–513, 514–515, 516, 518, 519, 520	495, 507–508, 521, 526–527	495, 498, 501, 507–508, 525–526
18	533, 534, 564	531, 533	529, 531, 532, 533, 534, 540, 542, 563	532, 542, 563	532, 536, 538, 563

Comprehensive Ethics Coverage

Ethics is covered early and completely in Chapter 1 to set a proper moral tone for managing people at work. Ethical issues are raised throughout the text, with additional significant coverage of the Ethical Decision-Making Tree in Chapter 12 and a discussion of the moral aspect of leadership in Chapter 16. In nearly every chapter, one or two of the Real World/ Real People boxed features are ethically based and are highlighted with an ethics label. Also in this tenth edition are 18 Legal/Ethical Challenges (one following each chapter). They raise hard-hitting ethical issues and ask tough questions, virtually guaranteeing a lively discussion/debate for cooperative learning. These Legal/Ethical Challenges (13 are new to this edition; 2 have been updated), along with the Real World/Real People boxes, are constant reminders of the importance of ethical management.

Pedagogical Features

The tenth edition of *Organizational Behavior* is designed to be a complete teaching/learning tool that captures the reader's interest and imparts useful knowledge. Some of the most significant pedagogical features of this text are the following:

- Classic and modern topics are given balanced treatment in terms of the latest and best available theoretical models, research evidence, and practical applications. Each chapter follows a Theory-Research-Practice approach. Students reading each chapter will gain an understanding of the basic theories about OB, learn whether or not the theories are valid by drawing on research to make summary conclusions, and will see how the theories and research apply in real-world examples.

- Several concise learning objectives open each chapter to focus the reader's attention and serve as a comprehension check. Look for a wolf paw print icon calling attention to each learning objective within the text. Additionally, the chapter summary is written to correlate with chapter learning objectives.

- Every major section in all 18 chapters is accompanied by a feature in the margin called "To the Point." The integrative questions in this key pedagogical feature focus the student's attention on test-relevant material, with the goal of improving their grade.

- A colorful and lively art program includes captioned photographs and figures.
- Hundreds of real-world examples involving large and small, public and private organizations have been incorporated into the textual material to make this edition up-to-date, interesting, and relevant.

Streamlined End-of-Chapter Materials

The end-of-chapter materials for the tenth edition of *Organizational Behavior* were carefully selected for their use as a study guide for students. Each chapter contains

- A Summary of Key Concepts correlating with the Learning Objectives for that chapter.
- A list of Key Terms (with text page notations).
- An OB in Action Case Study (16 are new in this edition).
- A Legal/Ethical Challenge (13 are new in this edition).
- A reminder about the resources available on the Web.

Fresh Cases, Updated Research, and New Examples

Our continuing commitment to a timely and relevant textbook is evidenced by the 16 (89%) new chapter-opening cases and 13 (72%) new chapter-closing cases. These cases highlight male and female role models and large and small public and private organizations. Among the diverse array of organizations featured are Zappos.com, Walmart, Williams-Sonoma, Chrysler, Facebook, NuStar Energy, DineEquity, Intel, Wynn Resorts, Google, BP, Best Buy, Takeda, Trader Joe's, Time Inc, and Patriarch.

Every chapter opens with a real-name, real-world short case to provide a practical context for the material at hand. All of the chapter-opening vignettes are new.

This tenth edition is filled with current and relevant examples from both research and practice perspectives. In fact, you will find several hundred source material references dated 2010 and 2011.

Real World/Real People

While theory and research are important to the study of OB, current examples of real people in real organizational situations are needed to bring OB to life for the reader. The tenth edition contains 69 Real World/Real People boxed features strategically located throughout the text. Sixty-three (91%) are new to this edition. They are up-to-date (mostly drawn from 2010 and 2011 sources), often provocative, and definitely interesting. The Real World/Real People features tend to be short, designed for quick reading, and tightly linked to the accompanying textual discussion. They show real people and organizations in action at their best and sometimes at their worst. Among the diverse selection of organizations featured are American Express, Sodexo, Card-First BlueCross BlueShield, CVS Caremark, BMW, UnitedHealthcare, Apple, AT&T, GlaxoSmithKline, McDonald's, United Health Group, Nutrisystem, Unilever, Home Depot, Satyam Computers, General Motors, Starwood, Ford, Sky Factory, Tyson Foods, Facebook, College Hunks Hauling Junk, Netflix, BP, Whole Foods, 37signals, Toro, Republic Airways, Johnson & Johnson, New York Philharmonic, BAE Systems, Cascade Engineering, US Coast Guard, Toyota, IBM, and Ohio Health.

Real World/Real People features that involve ethical issues are highlighted with an ethics label. In response to reviewer feedback, we've also included a discussion question with each box that ties it to the chapter content, to serve as a learning aid and class discussion starter.

Words of Appreciation

This textbook is the fruit of many people's labor. Our colleagues at Arizona State University have been supportive from the start. Through the years, our organizational behavior students at ASU, Thunderbird, and the University of Tirana (Albania) were enthusiastic and candid academic "customers." We are grateful for their feedback and we hope we have done it justice in this new edition. Sincere appreciation goes to Mindy West, of Arizona State University, for her skillful and dedicated work on the *Instructor's Resource Manual.* Thank you to Brad Cox of Midland Tech for creating the unique and dynamic PowerPoint presentations and Floyd Ormsbee of Clarkson University for his work on Connect. Thank you to Terri Lawson for a very professional job of managing our permissions.

To the manuscript reviewers spanning the prior nine editions go our gratitude and thanks. Their feedback was thoughtful, rigorous, constructive, and, above all, essential to our goal of *kaizen* (continuous improvement). Our reviewers for this edition were

Grace Auyang, Ph.D.
University of Cincinnati

M. Suzanne Clinton
University of Central Oklahoma

Elizabeth Cooper
University of Rhode Island

Tim DeGroot
Midwestern State University

Kathy Edwards
University of Texas at Austin

Leslie Elrod
University of Cincinnati RWC

Sean D. Jasso, Ph.D.
University of California, Riverside

Dr. Christopher McChesney, Ph.D.
Indian River State College

Ellen J. Mullen, Ph.D.
Iowa State University

Jeff Peterson
Woodbury School of Business, Utah Valley University

Mary Pisnar
Baldwin-Wallace College

Consuelo M. Ramirez, Ph.D.
University of Texas at San Antonio

Donald R Schreiber
Baylor University

Jerry Stevens
Texas Tech University

Jerald T Storey
Western Governors University

Ethan P. Waples
University of Central Oklahoma

Special thanks go to our dedicated "pack" at McGraw-Hill/Irwin: our editors Mike Ablassmeir and Kelly Pekelder; our marketing manager Anke Weekes; and our design and production team Matt Diamond, Dana Pauley, Michael McCormick, and Jeremy Cheshareck.

Finally, we would like to thank our wives, Margaret and Joyce, for being tough and caring "first customers" of our work. This book has been greatly enhanced by their common sense, reality testing, and hands-on managerial experience. Thanks in large measure to their love, moral support, and patience, this project once again was completed ahead of schedule and it strengthened rather than strained a treasured possession—our friendship.

We hope you enjoy this textbook. Best wishes for success and happiness!

Bob Kreitner

Angelo Kinicki

Guided Tour

The perfect balance of theory, research and practice

"This edition of Kreitner/Kinicki is a good marriage of research and applications of organizational behavior. Utilizing story telling, experiential activities, on-line technology as well as traditional materials, this text will appeal both to the student and the professor." Elizabeth Cooper, University of Rhode Island

Up-to-date, interesting and relevant—Filled with current and relevant examples involving large and small, public and private organizations from both research and practice perspectives (several hundred source material references dated 2010 and 2011).

*"Kreitner/Kinicki provides **solid coverage of key OB topics** and gives **real examples** of how the topics relate to managerial and organizational reality. The text and supplements provide good tools to communicate with students and **engage them in the learning process.**"* Mary Pisnar, Baldwin-Wallace College

Cites meta-analysis studies—When citing research many competitors will summarize only a few research studies and then draw a conclusion. Instead, Kreitner and Kinicki cite meta-analysis studies, which statistically summarize numerous studies before arriving at conclusions—a more efficient and statistically accurate process.

*"**The writing is excellent.** Kreitner and Kinicki explain constructs, theories, and models effectively, while also making the material interesting to read (not dry)!"* Ellen Mullen, Iowa State University

Provocative and interesting—Each chapter opens with a real-name, real-world short case to provide a practical context for the material at hand. All of the chapter-opening vignettes are new (16) or updated (2) for this edition.

*"The book itself is interesting and informative; it is **thought-provoking yet reader-friendly.** The authors have incorporated many tools to effectively reach all types of learners and make the course very manageable for the instructor."* Ellen Mullen, Iowa State University

Back to the Opening Case—Throughout the chapter, students are asked to apply what they've learned to the opening case via thoughtfully crafted questions. This enables students to see the practical application of chapter material and actively involves them in the learning process.

*"Absolutely, **the book emphasizes practicality!** As a former manager, I believe it is critical that the students be able to apply the theory in OB textbooks. Your textbook is a 'dream come true' for me!"* Consuelo M. Ramirez, University of Texas at San Antonio

> *Back to the* Chapter-Opening Case
>
> What evidence of a 21st-century organization, based on Table 1–3, can you find in the Zappos.com case?

real WORLD/real PEOPLE—In addition to the vast number of examples throughout the text, this boxed feature highlights male and female role models and large and small public and private organizations.

"K&K provides excellent real-world sections and applications through case studies, individual and group activities, etc.—these are great for providing student hand-on experience with the chapter material." Suzanne Clinton, University of Central Oklahoma

Connect®   Integration—Assignable, auto-graded Interactive Application exercises found in McGraw-Hill Connect® allow students to apply chapter concepts and practice what they have learned, while saving instructors time grading. Icons in the margin indicate what topics can be practiced online.

real WORLD // real PEOPLE

Will Happy Employees Mean Happy Customers for American Express?

[L]ast year when [American Express] gave its global customer service division a makeover, it decided to focus on making life better for its 26,000 call-center employees. The theory: Happier employees mean happier customers. "We've learned the importance of the attitude of the employee," says Jim Bush, EVP of world service. AmEx started by asking customer service employees what they wanted to see—and then delivered better pay, flexible schedules, and more career development. It also switched from a directive to keep calls short and transaction-oriented to engaging customers in longer conversations. Collectively, the moves have boosted service margins by 10%. "Great service starts with the people who deliver it," says [CEO Ken] Chenault. "We want American Express to be the company people recommend to their friends."

Based on Table 1–3, what evidence of 21st-century management can you find here?

SOURCE: Excerpted from C Tkaczyk, "American Express," *Fortune*, August 16, 2010, p 14.

American Express CEO Kenneth I Chenault.

Legal/Ethical Challenge exercise at the end of each chapter (13 new; 2 updated) is instructive and useful for either individual consideration or team discussion.

Ethics integrated throughout—Highlighted with an ethics label, Real World/Real People features with discussion questions get the reader actively involved in the learning process and serve as a learning aid and class discussion starter.

*"Kreitner/Kinicki has an applied approach that is relevant to today's student. The embedded charts make material easier to understand. **The strong ethics influence** is a critical focus to organizational behavior."* Leslie Elrod, University of Cincinnati, Raymond Walters College

"To the Point."—The integrative questions in this key pedagogical feature focus the student's attention on test-relevant material, with the goal of improving their grade.

TO THE POINT

How does organizational culture influence organizational outcomes?

Comprehensive Supplements for Instructors and Students

"The depth of supplementary materials is astounding and I had no idea of this fact." Tim DeGroot, Midwestern State University

Instructor's Manual
Prepared by Professor Mindy West of Arizona State University, each chapter includes a chapter summary, back to the chapter-opening case solution, lecture outline, Legal/Ethical Challenge interpretation, OB in Action case solutions, video resources, and much more.

Test Bank
The test bank includes more than 100 test questions per chapter, including true-false, multiple choice, and essay with answers, page references, and Bloom's Taxonomy level coding. Each test question is also tagged to the Learning Objective it covers in the chapter and the AACSB Learning Standard it falls under.

EZ Test
McGraw-Hill's flexible and easy-to-use electronic testing program allows instructors to create tests from book-specific items. It accommodates a wide range of question types, and instructors may add their own questions. Multiple versions of the test can be created, and any test can be exported for use with course management systems such as WebCT or Blackboard. EZ Test Online allows you to administer EZ Test-created exams and quizzes online.

PowerPoint
The PowerPoint slides have been prepared by Professor Brad Cox of Midlands Technical College and are designed to be meaningful lessons for students that encourage active thinking and participation and allow the instructor to have at his or her fingertips the information he or she wants to convey for each slide.

McGraw-Hill *Connect Management*
Less Managing. More Teaching. Greater Learning
McGraw-Hill *Connect Management* is an online assignment and assessment solution that connects students with the tools and resources they'll need to achieve success.
McGraw-Hill *Connect Management* helps prepare students for their future by enabling faster learning, more efficient studying, and higher retention of knowledge.

McGraw-Hill *Connect Management* features
Connect Management offers a number of powerful tools and features to make managing assignments easier, so faculty can spend more time teaching. With *Connect Management* students can engage with their coursework anytime and anywhere, making the learning process more accessible and efficient. *Connect Management* offers you the features described below.

Online Interactives Online Interactives are engaging tools that teach students to apply key concepts in practice. These Interactives provide them with immersive, experiential learning opportunities. Students will engage in a variety of interactive scenarios to deepen critical knowledge on key course topics. They receive immediate feedback at intermediate steps throughout each exercise, as well as comprehensive feedback at the end of the assignment. All Interactives are automatically scored and entered into the instructor gradebook.

Student progress tracking *Connect Management* keeps instructors informed about how each student, section, and class is performing, allowing for more productive use of lecture and office hours. The progress-tracking function enables you to:

- View scored work immediately and track individual or group performance with assignment and grade reports.
- Access an instant view of student or class performance relative to learning objectives.
- Collect data and generate reports required by many accreditation organizations, such as AACSB.

Smart grading When it comes to studying, time is precious. *Connect Management* helps students learn more efficiently by providing feedback and practice material when they need it, where they need it. When it comes to teaching, your time also is precious. The grading function enables you to:

- Have assignments scored automatically, giving students immediate feedback on their work and side-by-side comparisons with correct answers.
- Access and review each response; manually change grades or leave comments for students to review.
- Reinforce classroom concepts with practice tests and instant quizzes.

Simple assignment management With *Connect Management,* creating assignments is easier than ever, so you can spend more time teaching and less time managing. The assignment management function enables you to:

- Create and deliver assignments easily with selectable end-of-chapter questions and test bank items.
- Streamline lesson planning, student progress reporting, and assignment grading to make classroom management more efficient than ever.
- Go paperless with the eBook and online submission and grading of student assignments.

Instructor library The *Connect Management* Instructor Library is your repository for additional resources to improve student engagement in and out of class. You can select and use any asset that enhances your lecture. The *Connect Management* Instructor Library includes:

- Instructor Manual
- PowerPoint files
- TestBank
- Management Asset Gallery
- eBook

Student study center The *Connect Management* Student Study Center is the place for students to access additional resources. The Student Study Center:

- Offers students quick access to lectures, practice materials, eBooks, and more.
- Provides instant practice material and study questions, easily accessible on the go.
- Gives students access to the Personalized Learning Plan described below.

Lecture capture via Tegrity Campus Increase the attention paid to lecture discussion by decreasing the attention paid to note taking. For an additional charge, Lecture Capture offers new ways for students to focus on the in-class discussion, knowing they can revisit important topics later. See page xviii for further information.

McGraw-Hill Connect Plus Management McGraw-Hill reinvents the textbook learning experience for the modern student with *Connect Plus Management.* A seamless integration of an eBook and *Connect Management, Connect Plus Management* provides all of the *Connect Management* features plus the following:

- An integrated eBook, allowing for anytime, anywhere access to the textbook.
- Dynamic links between the problems or questions you assign to your students and the location in the eBook where that problem or question is covered.
- A powerful search function to pinpoint and connect key concepts in a snap.

In short, *Connect Management* offers you and your students powerful tools and features that optimize your time and energies, enabling you to focus on course content, teaching, and student learning. *Connect Management* also offers a wealth of content resources for both instructors and students. This state-of-the-art, thoroughly tested system supports you in preparing students for the world that awaits.

For more information about Connect, go to **www.mcgrawhillconnect.com,** or contact your local McGraw-Hill sales representative.

Tegrity Campus: Lectures 24/7

Tegrity Campus is a service that makes class time available 24/7 by automatically capturing every lecture in a searchable format for students to review when they study and complete assignments. With a simple one-click start-and-stop process, you capture all computer screens and corresponding audio. Students can replay any part of any class with easy-to-use browser-based viewing on a PC or Mac.

Educators know that the more students can see, hear, and experience class resources, the better they learn. In fact, studies prove it. With Tegrity Campus, students quickly recall key moments by using Tegrity Campus's unique search feature. This search helps students efficiently find what they need, when they need it, across an entire semester of class recordings. Help turn all your students' study time into learning moments immediately supported by your lecture.

Lecture Capture enables you to

- Record and distribute your lecture with the click of a button.
- Record and index PowerPoint® presentations and anything shown on your computer so it is easily searchable, frame by frame.
- Offer access to lectures anytime and anywhere by computer, iPod, or mobile device.
- Increase listening and class participation by easing students' concerns about note taking. Lecture Capture will make it more likely you will see students' faces, not the tops of their heads.

To learn more about Tegrity, watch a 2-minute Flash demo at **http://tegritycampus.mhhe.com.**

Assurance of Learning Ready

Many educational institutions today are focused on the notion of *assurance of learning*, an important element of some accreditation standards. *Organizational Behavior* is designed specifically to support your assurance of learning initiatives with a simple, yet powerful solution.

Each test bank question for *Organizational Behavior* maps to a specific chapter learning outcome/objective listed in the text. You can use our test bank software, EZ Test and EZ Test Online, or in *Connect Management* to easily query for learning outcomes/objectives that directly relate to the learning objectives for your course. You can then use the reporting features of EZ Test to aggregate student results in similar fashion, making the collection and presentation of assurance of learning data simple and easy.

AACSB Statement

The McGraw-Hill Companies is a proud corporate member of AACSB International. Understanding the importance and value of AACSB accreditation, *Organizational Behavior*, 10e recognizes the curricula guidelines detailed in the AACSB standards for business accreditation by connecting selected questions in [the text and/or the test bank] to the six general knowledge and skill guidelines in the AACSB standards.

The statements contained in *Organizational Behavior*, 10e are provided only as a guide for the users of this textbook. The AACSB leaves content coverage and assessment within the purview of individual schools, the mission of the school, and the faculty. While *Organizational Behavior*, 10e and the teaching package make no claim of any specific AACSB qualification or evaluation, we have within *Organizational Behavior*, 10e labeled selected questions according to the six general knowledge and skills areas.

McGraw-Hill and Blackboard

McGraw-Hill Higher Education and Blackboard have teamed up. What does this mean for you?

1. **Your life, simplified.** Now you and your students can access McGraw-Hill's Connect™ and Create™ right from within your Blackboard course—all with one single sign-on. Say goodbye to the days of logging in to multiple applications.

2. **Deep integration of content and tools.** Not only do you get single sign-on with Connect™ and Create™, you also get deep integration of McGraw-Hill content and content engines right in Blackboard. Whether you're choosing a book for your course or building Connect™ assignments, all the tools you need are right where you want them—inside of Blackboard.

3. **Seamless Gradebooks.** Are you tired of keeping multiple gradebooks and manually synchronizing grades into Blackboard? We thought so. When a student completes an integrated Connect™ assignment, the grade for that assignment automatically (and instantly) feeds your Blackboard grade center.

4. **A solution for everyone.** Whether your institution is already using Blackboard or you just want to try Blackboard on your own, we have a solution for you. McGraw-Hill and Blackboard can now offer you easy access to industry leading technology and content, whether your campus hosts it, or we do. Be sure to ask your local McGraw-Hill representative for details.

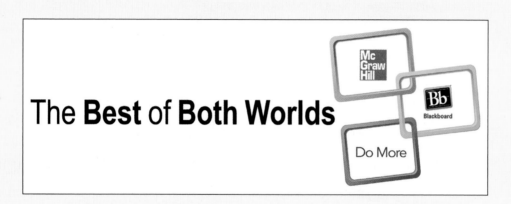

McGraw-Hill Customer Care Contact Information

At McGraw-Hill, we understand that getting the most from new technology can be challenging. That's why our services don't stop after you purchase our products. You can e-mail our Product Specialists 24 hours a day to get product-training online. Or you can search our knowledge bank of Frequently Asked Questions on our support website. For Customer Support, call **800-331-5094,** e-mail **hmsupport@mcgraw-hill.com,** or visit **www.mhhe.com/support.** One of our Technical Support Analysts will be able to assist you in a timely fashion.

McGraw-Hill's Expanded Management Asset Gallery!

McGraw-Hill/Irwin Management is excited to now provide a one-stop shop for our wealth of teaching/learning assets, making it quick and easy for instructors to locate specific materials to enhance their courses.

All of the following can be accessed within the Management Asset Gallery:

Manager's Hot Seat

This interactive, video-based application puts students in the manager's hot seat, builds critical thinking and decision-making skills, and allows students to apply concepts to real managerial challenges. Students watch as 15 real managers apply their years of experience when confronting unscripted issues such as bullying in the workplace, cyber loafing, globalization, intergenerational work conflicts, workplace violence, and leadership versus management.

Self-Assessment Gallery

Unique among publisher-provided self-assessments, our 23 self-assessments give students background information to ensure that they understand the purpose of the assessment. Students test their values, beliefs, skills, and interests in a wide variety of areas, allowing them to personally apply chapter content to their own lives and careers.

Every self-assessment is supported with PowerPoints® and an instructor manual in the Management Asset Gallery, making it easy for the instructor to create an engaging classroom discussion surrounding the assessments.

Test Your Knowledge

To help reinforce students' understanding of key management concepts, Test Your Knowledge activities give students a review of the conceptual materials followed by application-based questions to work through. Students can choose practice mode, which gives them detailed feedback after each question, or test mode, which provides feedback after the entire test has been completed. Every Test Your Knowledge activity is supported by instructor notes in the Management Asset Gallery to make it easy for the instructor to create engaging classroom discussions surrounding that materials that students have completed.

Management History Timeline

This Web application allows instructors to present and students to learn the history of management in an engaging and interactive way. Management history is presented along an intuitive timeline that can be traveled through sequentially or by selected decade. With the click of a mouse, students learn the important dates, see the people who influenced the field, and understand the general management theories that have molded and shaped management as we know it today.

Video Library DVDs

McGraw-Hill/Irwin offers the most comprehensive video support for the Organizational Behavior classroom through a course library video DVD. This discipline has a library volume DVD tailored to integrate and visually reinforce chapter concepts. The library volume DVD contains more than 40 clips! The rich video material, organized by topic, comes from sources such as PBS, NBC, BBC, SHRM, and McGraw-Hill. Video cases and video guides are provided for some clips.

Destination CEO Videos

Video clips featuring CEOs on a variety of topics. Accompanying each clip are multiple-choice questions and discussion questions to use in the classroom or assign as a quiz.

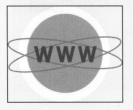

Online Learning Center (OLC)

www.mhhe.com/kreitner10e Find a variety of online teaching and learning tools that are designed to reinforce and build on the text content. Students will have direct access to the learning tools while instructor materials are password protected.

eBook Options

eBooks are an innovative way for students to save money and to "go green." McGraw-Hill's eBooks are typically 40% off the bookstore price. Students have the choice between an online and a downloadable CourseSmart eBook.

Through CourseSmart, students have the flexibility to access an exact replica of their textbook from any computer that has Internet service without plug-ins or special software via the online version, or to create a library of books on their hard drive via the downloadable version. Access to the CourseSmart eBooks lasts for one year.

Features   CourseSmart eBooks allow students to highlight, take notes, organize notes, and share the notes with other CourseSmart users. Students can also search for terms across all eBooks in their purchased CourseSmart library. CourseSmart eBooks can be printed (five pages at a time).

More info and to purchase   Please visit **www.coursesmart.com** for more information and to purchase access to our eBooks. CourseSmart allows students to try one chapter of the eBook, free of charge, before purchase.

Create

Craft your teaching resources to match the way you teach! With McGraw-Hill Create, **www.mcgrawhillcreate .com,** you can easily rearrange chapters, combine material from other content sources, and quickly upload content you have written, like your course syllabus or teaching notes. Find the content you need in Create by searching through thousands of leading McGraw-Hill textbooks. Arrange your book to fit your teaching style. Create even allows you to personalize your book's appearance by selecting the cover and adding your name, school, and course information. Order a Create book and you'll receive a complimentary print review copy in three to five business days or a complimentary electronic review copy (eComp) via e-mail in about one hour. Go to **www. mcgrawhillcreate.com** today and register. Experience how McGraw-Hill Create empowers you to teach *your* students *your* way.

Brief Contents

Contents

part two
Individual Behavior in Organizations 119

chapter five
Key Individual Differences and the Road to Success 120

chapter six
Values, Attitudes, Job Satisfaction, and Counterproductive Work Behaviors 150

part one

The World of Organizational Behavior

chapter 1

Organizational Behavior: The Quest for People-Centered Organizations and Ethical Conduct

 Learning Objectives

When you finish studying the material in this chapter, you should be able to:

LO.1   Define the term *organizational behavior,* and contrast McGregor's Theory X and Theory Y assumptions about employees.

LO.2   Identify the four principles of total quality management (TQM).

LO.3   Define the term *e-business,* and describe the Net Generation.

LO.4   Contrast human and social capital, and explain why we need to build both.

LO.5   Define the term *management,* and identify at least five of the eleven managerial skills in Wilson's profile of effective managers.

LO.6   Characterize 21st-century managers.

LO.7   Describe Carroll's global corporate social responsibility pyramid, and discuss the problem of moral erosion.

LO.8   Identify four of the seven general ethical principles, and explain how to improve an organization's ethical climate.

LO.9   Describe the sources of organizational behavior research evidence.

Why Is Zappos.com So Good at Zapping the Competition?

There's a good chance you have never heard of Tony Hsieh (pronounced "Shay"), CEO of Zappos.com. But if you are among the legions of satisfied and loyal customers of the online retailer of footwear and other goods, you owe him an enthusiastic high five. Initially as an investor/adviser and eventually CEO, Hsieh guided Zappos from a struggling Internet start-up to a merger with Amazon.com in 2009 for $1.2 billion. Along the way, he helped Zappos develop a zany corporate culture of close-knit employees obsessed with great 24/7 customer service. "Customer Service Isn't Just a Department!" trumpets the firm's website. When the Amazon deal was announced, Hsieh told an all-hands meeting of employees that each of them would receive a free Kindle e-book reader and a retention bonus equal to 40% of their annual salary. Most importantly, he vowed to maintain the company's cherished culture. The following excerpt from Hsieh's new book, *Delivering Happiness: A Path to Profits, Passion, and Purpose*, highlights how Zappos.com came to put people—customers and employees—first.

> I e-mailed the entire company several times and got a lot of suggestions and feedback on which core values were the most important to our employees.
>
> I was surprised the process took so long, but we wanted to make sure not to rush through the process because whatever core values we eventually came up with, we wanted to be ones that we could truly embrace. . . .
>
> We eventually came up with our final list of ten core values [from an initial list of 37], which we still use today:
>
> 1. Deliver WOW Through Service
> 2. Embrace and Drive Change
> 3. Create Fun and a Little Weirdness
> 4. Be Adventurous, Creative, and Open-Minded
> 5. Pursue Growth and Learning
> 6. Build Open and Honest Relationships with Communication
> 7. Build a Positive Team and Family Spirit
> 8. Do More with Less
> 9. Be Passionate and Determined
> 10. Be Humble. . . .
>
> *Be Humble* is probably the core value that ends up affecting our hiring decisions the most. There are a lot of experienced, smart and talented people we interview that we know can make an immediate impact on our top or bottom line. But a lot of them are also really egotistical, so we end up not hiring them.
>
> Our philosophy at Zappos is that we're willing to make short-term sacrifices (including lost revenue or profits) if we believe that the long-term benefits are worth it. Protecting the company culture and sticking to core values is a long-term benefit.[1]

Zappos's CEO Tony Hsieh likes to mix hard work and fun at the online retailer.

Tony Hsieh does more than just talk about the importance of his company's people; he trusts, empowers, and listens to them. No surprise then that Zappos.com ranked number 6 on *Fortune*'s 2011 "100 Best Companies to Work For" list.[2] Hsieh helped create what Stanford University's Jeffrey Pfeffer calls a "people-centered" organization. Research evidence from companies in both the United States and Germany shows the following seven *people-centered practices* to be strongly associated with much higher profits and significantly lower employee turnover:

1. Job security (to eliminate fear of layoffs).
2. Careful hiring (emphasizing a good fit with the company culture).
3. Power to the people (via decentralization and self-managed teams).
4. Generous pay for performance.
5. Lots of training.
6. Less emphasis on status (to build a "we" feeling).
7. Trust building (through the sharing of critical information).[3]

Importantly, these factors are a *package* deal, meaning they need to be installed in a coordinated and systematic manner—not in bits and pieces.

According to Pfeffer, only 12% of today's organizations have the systematic approaches and persistence to qualify as true people-centered organizations, thus giving them a competitive advantage.[4] To us, an 88% shortfall in the quest for people-centered organizations represents a tragic waste of human and economic potential. Pfeffer recently couched his call for greater people-centeredness in the "green management" term *sustainability*: "Just as there is concern for protecting natural resources, there could be a similar level of concern for protecting human resources."[5] There are profound ethical implications as well, especially during the recent deep recession with millions of layoffs. At people-centered organizations (see Real World/Real People for an inspiring example), layoffs are a very last resort, not a knee-jerk first response to bad news. Both practical experience and research tell us that layoffs hurt everyone, including the "survivors" who keep their jobs. A recent study of 318 companies led to this conclusion: "Three-fourths of 4,172 workers who have kept their jobs say their productivity has dropped since their organizations let people go."[6] Of course, layoffs are sometimes unavoidable. But imaginative people-centered organizations can make layoffs a last resort with tactics such as across-the-board pay cuts and/or reduced hours and voluntary unpaid leaves of absence. Additionally, consider these unique people-centered tactics:

Example. Vermont's Rhino Foods, which makes the cookie dough for Ben & Jerry's ice cream, recently sent 15 factory workers to nearby lip balm manufacturer Autumn Harp for a week to help it handle a holiday rush. The employees were paid by Rhino, which then invoiced its neighbor for the hours worked. President Ted Castle is looking to adopt a similar approach with salaried managers, too. "It's a lot easier to just do the layoff," says Castle. "But in the long term, it's not easier for the business."

Matt Cooper, vice-president of Larkspur (Calif.) recruiting firm Accolo, asked employees to take five days of unpaid leave this quarter but won't dock paychecks until March. If big deals come through, he'll lift the pay cut.[7]

Each of us needs to accept the challenge to do a better job of creating and maintaining people-centered organizations, whatever our role(s) in society—employer/

real WORLD // real PEOPLE: ethics

Lola Gonzalez Laid Herself Off First!

Like countless small-business owners, Lola Gonzalez agonizingly resolved to trim her firm's nine-person staff when the economic recovery began to sputter . . . [in early 2010].

Unlike other entrepreneurs, she picked an unlikely employee to lay off: herself.

The owner of Accurate Background Check in Ocala, Fla., says she couldn't bear to fire employees who have worked there for years. So she stopped paying herself a six-figure salary and got a job for less than half the pay as a social worker.

"How could you let somebody go that you trusted and that trusted you?" says Gonzalez, 51, who's still a social worker. . . .

Employees initially froze in fear [during her announcement], then erupted in laughter. Until they realized she was serious. . . .

Besides putting in a 40-hour week, . . . Gonzalez gets twice-weekly phone updates on goings-on at her business and still does certain background checks herself without getting paid.

What are the broader, long-term benefits of this people-centered practice?

SOURCE: Excerpted from P Davidson, "How a Boss Saved Jobs: She Laid Herself Off," *USA Today,* November 26, 2010, p 1B.

---

entrepreneur, employee, manager, stockholder, student, teacher, voter, elected official, social/political activist. Toward that end, the mission of this book is to help increase the number of people-centered and ethically managed organizations around the world to improve the general quality of life.[8]

The purpose of this first chapter is to define organizational behavior (OB); examine its contemporary relevance; explore its historical, managerial, and ethical contexts; and introduce a topical road map for the balance of this book.

Welcome to the World of OB

Organizational behavior deals with how people act and react in organizations of all kinds. Think of the many organizations that touch your life on a regular basis; organizations that employ, educate, connect, inform, feed, heal, protect, and entertain you. Cradle to grave, we interface with organizations at every turn. According to Chester I Barnard's classic definition, an **organization** is "a system of consciously coordinated activities or forces of two or more persons."[9] Organizations are a social invention helping us to achieve things collectively that we could not achieve alone. For better or for worse, they extend our reach. Consider the inspiring example of the World Health Organization (WHO):

◀ ··

TO THE POINT

Why is it important to study organizational behavior, regardless of one's organizational level or specialty?

··

Example. In 1967, 10 to 15 million people around the globe were struck annually by smallpox. That year, the World Health Organization set up its smallpox-eradication unit. In 13 years it was able to declare the world free of the disease. In 1988, 350,000 people were afflicted by polio when the WHO set up a similar eradication unit. Since then it has spent $3 billion and received the help of 20 million volunteers from around the world. The result: in 2003 there were only 784 reported cases of polio.[10]

On the other hand, organizations such as al-Qaeda kill and terrorize, and others such as failed banks and businesses squander our resources. Organizations are

organization System of consciously coordinated activities of two or more people.

the chessboard on which the game of life is played. To know more about *organizational* behavior—life within organizations—is to know more about the nature, possibilities, and rules of that game.

 LO.1 Organizational Behavior: An Interdisciplinary Field

Organizational behavior, commonly referred to as OB, is an interdisciplinary field dedicated to better understanding and managing people at work. By definition, organizational behavior is both research and application oriented. Three basic levels of analysis in OB are individual, group, and organizational. OB draws upon a diverse array of disciplines, including psychology, management, sociology, organization theory, social psychology, statistics, anthropology, general systems theory, economics, information technology, political science, vocational counseling, human stress management, psychometrics, ergonomics, decision theory, and ethics.[11] This rich heritage has spawned many competing perspectives and theories about human work behavior. By 2003, one researcher had identified 73 distinct theories about behavior within the field of OB.[12]

Some FAQs about Studying OB

Through the years we (and our colleagues) have fielded some frequently asked questions (FAQs) from our students about our field. Here are the most common ones, along with our answers.

Why Study OB?   If you thoughtfully study this book, you will learn more about yourself, how to interact effectively with others, and how to thrive (not just survive) in organizations. Lots of insights about your own personality, emotions, values, job satisfaction, perceptions, needs, and goals are available in Part 2. Relative to your interpersonal effectiveness, you will learn about being a team player, building trust, managing conflict, negotiating, communicating, and influencing and leading others. We conclude virtually every major topic with practical how-to-do-it instructions. The idea is to build your skills in areas such as self-management, making ethical decisions, avoiding groupthink, listening, coping with organizational politics, handling change, and managing stress. Respected OB scholar Edward E Lawler III created the "virtuous career spiral" in Figure 1–1 to illustrate how OB-related skills point you toward career success. "It shows that increased skills and performance can lead to better jobs and higher rewards."[13]

If I'm an Accounting (or Other Technical) Major, Why Should I Study OB?   Many students in technical fields such as accounting, finance, computer science, and engineering consider OB to be a "soft" discipline with little or no relevance. You may indeed start out in a narrow specialty, but eventually your hard-won success will catch up with you and you will be tapped for some sort of supervisory or leadership position. Your so-called soft people skills will make or break your career at that point. Also, in today's team-oriented and globalized workplace, your teamwork, cross-cultural, communication, conflict handling, and negotiation skills and your powers of persuasion will be needed early and often. Jack Welch, the legendary CEO of General Electric, and Suzy Welch, the former editor of *Harvard Business Review,* offered this answer to a business school professor's question about how best to prepare students for today's global business environment:

Example. We'd make the case that the nitty-gritty of managing people should rank higher in the educational hierarchy. In the past two years we've visited 35 B-schools around the world and have been repeatedly surprised by how little classroom attention is paid to hiring, motivating, team-building, and firing. Instead, B-schools seem far more invested in teaching braniac concepts—disruptive technologies,

figure 1–1 OB-Related Skills Are the Ticket to Ride the Virtuous Career Spiral

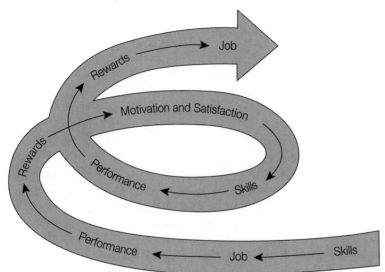

SOURCE: Edward E Lawler III, *Treat People Right! How Organizations and Individuals Can Propel Each Other into a Virtual Spiral of Success,* Jossey-Bass, 2003, p 21. Reprinted with permission of John Wiley & Sons, Inc.

complexity modeling, and the like. Those may be useful, particularly if you join a consulting firm, but real managers need to know how to get the most out of people.

We hope you have the clout to make sure people management is front and center at your university. If you do, you'll launch your students' careers with a real head start.[14]

Can I Get a Job in OB? Organizational behavior is an academic designation. With the exception of teaching/research positions, OB is not an everyday job category such as accounting, marketing, information technology, or finance. Students of OB typically do not get jobs in organizational behavior, per se. This reality in no way demeans OB or lessens its importance in effective organizational management. OB is a *horizontal* discipline cutting across virtually every job category, business function, and professional specialty. Anyone who plans to make a living in a large or small, public or private, organization needs to study organizational behavior.

A Historical Perspective of OB

A historical perspective of the study of people at work helps in studying organizational behavior. According to a management history expert, this is important because:

Example. Historical perspective is the study of a subject in light of its earliest phases and subsequent evolution. Historical perspective differs from history in that the object of historical perspective is to sharpen one's vision of the present, not the past.[15]

◄·························
TO THE POINT
What lessons from McGregor and Deming can help managers build human and social capital?
·························

organizational behavior Interdisciplinary field dedicated to better understanding and managing people at work.

In other words, we can better understand where the field of OB is today and where it appears to be headed by appreciating where it has been and how it is being redirected.[16] Let us examine four significant landmarks in the understanding and management of people in the workplace.

1. The human relations movement.
2. The quality movement.
3. The Internet and social media revolution.
4. The age of human and social capital.

The Human Relations Movement

Go to www.mcgrawhillconnect.com for an interactive exercise to test your knowledge on the history of organizational behavior.

A unique combination of factors during the 1930s fostered the human relations movement. First, following legalization of union–management collective bargaining in the United States in 1935, management began looking for new ways of handling employees. Second, behavioral scientists conducting on-the-job research started calling for more attention to the "human" factor. Managers who had lost the battle to keep unions out of their factories heeded the call for better human relations and improved working conditions. One such study, conducted at Western Electric's Chicago-area Hawthorne plant, was a prime stimulus for the human relations movement. Ironically, many of the Hawthorne findings have turned out to be more myth than fact.

The Hawthorne Legacy   Interviews conducted decades later with three subjects of the Hawthorne studies and reanalysis of the original data with modern statistical techniques do not support initial conclusions about the positive effect of supportive supervision. Specifically, money, fear of unemployment during the Great Depression, managerial discipline, and high-quality raw materials—not supportive supervision—turned out to be responsible for high output in the relay assembly test room experiments.[17] Nonetheless, the human relations movement gathered momentum through the 1950s, as academics and managers alike made stirring claims about the powerful effect that individual needs, supportive supervision, and group dynamics apparently had on job performance.

These relay assembly test room employees in the classic Hawthorne Western Electric studies turned in record performance. Why? No one knows for certain, and debate continues today. Supportive supervision was long believed to be the key factor. Whatever the reason, Hawthorne gave the budding human relations movement needed research credibility.

The Writings of Mayo and Follett   Essential to the human relations movement were the writings of Elton Mayo and Mary Parker Follett. Australian-born Mayo, who headed the Harvard researchers at Hawthorne, advised managers to attend to employees' emotional needs in his 1933 classic *The Human Problems of an Industrial Civilization.* Follett was a true pioneer, not only as a woman management consultant in the male-dominated industrial world of the 1920s, but also as a writer who saw employees as complex combinations of attitudes, beliefs, and needs. Mary Parker Follett was way ahead of her time in telling managers to motivate job performance instead of merely demanding it, a "pull" rather than "push" strategy. She also built a logical bridge between political democracy and a cooperative spirit in the workplace.[18]

McGregor's Theory Y   In 1960, Douglas McGregor wrote a book entitled *The Human Side of Enterprise,* which has become an important philosophical base for the modern view of people at work.[19] Drawing on his experience as a management consultant, McGregor formulated

table 1–1 McGregor's Theory X and Theory Y

OUTDATED (THEORY X) ASSUMPTIONS ABOUT PEOPLE AT WORK	MODERN (THEORY Y) ASSUMPTIONS ABOUT PEOPLE AT WORK
1. Most people dislike work; they avoid it when they can.	1. Work is a natural activity, like play or rest.
2. Most people must be coerced and threatened with punishment before they will work. People require close direction when they are working.	2. People are capable of self-direction and self-control if they are committed to objectives.
3. Most people actually prefer to be directed. They tend to avoid responsibility and exhibit little ambition. They are interested only in security.	3. People generally become committed to organizational objectives if they are rewarded for doing so.
	4. The typical employee can learn to accept and seek responsibility.
	5. The typical member of the general population has imagination, ingenuity, and creativity.

SOURCE: From D McGregor, *The Human Side of Enterprise*, McGraw-Hill, 1960, Ch 4. Copyright © 2008 The McGraw-Hill Companies. Reprinted with permission.

two sharply contrasting sets of assumptions about human nature (see Table 1–1). His Theory X assumptions were pessimistic and negative and, according to McGregor's interpretation, typical of how managers traditionally perceived employees. To help managers break with this negative tradition, McGregor formulated his **Theory Y,** a modern and positive set of assumptions about people. McGregor believed managers could accomplish more through others by viewing them as self-energized, committed, responsible, and creative beings.

Unfortunately, according to ongoing research on *employee engagement*, McGregor's Theory Y is still a distant vision in the American workplace:

Example. The August 2009 Gallup Employee Engagement Index reported that only 33 percent of workers are engaged in their jobs, 49 percent are not engaged, and 18 percent are actively disengaged. The Gallup Organization defines the categories as follows:

Engaged employees work with passion and feel a profound connection to their company. They drive innovation and move the organization forward.

Non-engaged employees have essentially "checked out." They sleepwalk through workdays. They put in time but don't approach their work with energy or passion.

Actively disengaged employees aren't just unhappy at work; they're busy acting out their unhappiness. Every day, these workers undermine what engaged coworkers accomplish.

Theory Y McGregor's modern and positive assumptions about employees being responsible and creative.

Gallup researchers, who base the Employee Engagement Index on a survey of nearly 42,000 randomly selected adults, estimate that disengaged workers cost US businesses as much as $350 billion a year.[20]

Employee engagement, and many ways to improve it, are discussed in later chapters.

New Assumptions about Human Nature   Unfortunately, unsophisticated behavioral research methods caused the human relationists to embrace some naive and misleading conclusions.[21] For example, human relationists believed in the axiom, "A satisfied employee is a hardworking employee." Subsequent research, as discussed later in this book, shows the satisfaction → performance linkage to be more complex than originally thought.

Despite its shortcomings, the human relations movement opened the door to more progressive thinking about human nature. Rather than continuing to view employees as passive economic beings, managers began to see them as active social beings and took steps to create more humane work environments.

The Quality Movement

In 1980, NBC aired a television documentary titled "If Japan Can . . . Why Can't We?" It was a wake-up call for North American companies to dramatically improve product quality or continue losing market share to Japanese electronics and automobile companies. A full-fledged movement ensued during the 1980s and 1990s. Much was written, said, and done about improving the quality of both goods and services.[22]

Thanks to the concept of *total quality management* (TQM) and Six Sigma programs, the quality of the goods and services we purchase today is significantly better than in years past. Six Sigma was developed in 1986 at Motorola by engineer Bill Smith to achieve an astounding 99.9997% quality target by eliminating defects and cutting waste. It was licensed to companies such as General Electric that became avid users. An estimated 35% of US companies have adopted Six Sigma.

Example. Six Sigma, broadly speaking, expresses a way of thinking about business problems that encourages precision and predictability. The mantra of Six Sigma "black belts" is DMAIC, for "define, measure, analyze, improve, control." The "sigma" refers to the Greek letter, which in statistics is used to measure how far something deviates from perfection. The "six" comes from the goal to be no more than six standard deviations away from that perfect measure.[23]

The underlying principles of TQM and Six Sigma are more important than ever given customers' steadily rising expectations:

Example. Establish a reputation for great value, top quality, or pulling late-night miracles in time for crucial client meetings, and soon enough, the goalposts move. "Greatness" lasts only as long as someone fails to imagine something better. Inevitably, the exceptional becomes the expected.

Call it the performance paradox: If you deliver, you only qualify to deliver more. Great companies and their employees have always endured this treadmill of expectations. But these days, the brewing forces of technology, productivity, and transparency have accelerated the cycle to breakneck speed.[24]

The quality movement has profound practical implications for managing people today.

What Is TQM?   Experts on the subject offered this definition of **total quality management:**

Example. TQM means that the organization's culture is defined by and supports the constant attainment of customer satisfaction through an integrated system of tools, techniques, and training. This involves the continuous improvement of organizational processes, resulting in high-quality products and services.[25]

Quality consultant Richard J Schonberger sums up TQM as "continuous, customer-centered, employee-driven improvement."[26] TQM is necessarily employee driven because product or service quality cannot be continuously improved without the active learning and participation of *every* employee. Thus, in successful quality improvement programs, TQM principles are embedded in the organization's culture. In fact, according to the results of a field experiment, bank customers had higher satisfaction after interacting with bank employees who had been trained to provide excellent service.[27]

The Deming Legacy   Quality is in the corporate DNA today thanks in large part to the pioneering work of W Edwards Deming.[28] Ironically, the mathematician credited with Japan's post–World War II quality revolution rarely talked in terms of quality. He instead preferred to discuss "good management" during the hard-hitting seminars he delivered right up until his death at age 93 in 1993.[29] Although Deming's passion was the statistical measurement and reduction of variations in industrial processes, he had much to say about how employees should be treated. Regarding the human side of quality improvement, Deming called for the following:

- Formal training in statistical process control techniques and teamwork.
- Helpful leadership, rather than order giving and punishment.
- Elimination of fear so employees will feel free to ask questions.
- Emphasis on continuous process improvements rather than on numerical quotas.
- Teamwork.
- Elimination of barriers to good workmanship.[30]

One of Deming's most enduring lessons for managers is his 85–15 rule.[31] Specifically, when things go wrong, there is roughly an 85% chance the *system* (including management, machinery, and rules) is at fault. Only about 15% of the time is the individual employee at fault. Unfortunately, as Deming observed, the typical manager spends most of his or her time wrongly blaming and punishing individuals for system failures. Statistical analysis is required to uncover system failures.

total quality management An organizational culture dedicated to training, continuous improvement, and customer satisfaction.

LO.2 Principles of TQM   Despite variations in the language and scope of TQM programs, it is possible to identify four common TQM principles:

1. Do it right the first time to eliminate costly rework and product recalls.
2. Listen to and learn from customers and employees.
3. Make continuous improvement an everyday matter.
4. Build teamwork, trust, and mutual respect.[32]

Deming's influence is clearly evident in this list. Once again, as with the human relations movement, we see *people* as the key factor in organizational success.

In summary, TQM advocates have made a valuable contribution to the field of OB by providing a *practical* context for managing people. The case for TQM is strong because, as discovered in two comprehensive studies, *it works*.[33] When people are managed according to TQM principles, more of us are likely to get the employment opportunities and high-quality goods and services we demand. Organizations that lose sight of the TQM principle of continuous improvement do so at their own peril. When Chrysler's once-popular PT Cruiser went out of production in 2010, one observer noted, "It's a car that, initially, people loved. But the company then tried to squeeze as much profit as it could out of the car, refusing to properly redesign it and eventually fitting it with cheaper radios and interior materials to save a few pennies."[34]

As you will see many times in later chapters, this book is anchored to Deming's philosophy and TQM principles—especially the idea of continuous improvement.

Back to the Chapter-Opening Case

What TQM principles are embedded in Zappos.com's values and culture?

 LO.3 The Internet and Social Media Revolution

Connect Go to www.mcgrawhillconnect.com for an interactive exercise to test your knowledge on The Net Generation.

In the early 1990s, when Internet start-ups were the rage, advocates said the Internet would change everything. Then came the tech crash of 2001 and the Internet promise was ridiculed as pure hype. But after some adolescent growing pains, *the now-mobile Internet has in fact changed everything.* Raw numbers are impressive: Internet users worldwide grew from 361 million in 2001 to nearly 2 billion by 2010.[35] What was once *e-commerce* (buying and selling goods and services over the Internet) has evolved into **e-business,** using the Internet to facilitate *every* aspect of running a business, including the management of virtual teams.[36] Said one industry observer: "Strip away the highfalutin talk, and at bottom, the Internet is a tool that dramatically lowers the cost of communication. That means it can radically alter any industry or activity that depends heavily on the flow of information."[37]

Another important shift in the Internet—enabled by social media innovations such as Facebook, LinkedIn, and Twitter—is the growing importance of *user-generated* content. Passive consumers of mass content (e.g., watching TV and movies and reading print media) have become creators and distributors of individualized content who blog, Facebook, and tweet whatever they like to whomever they like whenever they like.[38] This is hugely empowering for the individual consumer, employee, citizen, student, etc.

Example. [Social media entrepreneur] Amit Kapur envisions a Web that's more about him. When he visits a news site, the headlines will be heavy on technology,

real WORLD // real PEOPLE: ethics

Is Your Robot Watching Me?

In a 2007 issue of *Scientific American,* [Microsoft co-founder] Bill Gates predicted that the future would bring a "robot in every home." In the foreseeable future, though, it may be a robot in every cubicle—or at least every third cubicle.

Industrial and technological companies across the globe are already hard at work trying to make this a reality. The QB, a "remote presence robot" created by Anybots, based in Mountain View, California, is basically a video-conferencing system on wheels. The QB, which looks a little like Wall-E, is controlled remotely through a Web browser and keyboard, allowing managers to virtually visit satellite branches from the comfort of their offices. The $15,000 QB was unveiled in May, and according to Any-bots' founder, Trevor Blackwell, sales are in the hundreds. "Everyone already has videoconferencing," says Blackwell. "Yet planes are still full of people traveling for business."

Where should managers draw the line between proper managerial oversight of remote workers and invading their privacy with electronic monitoring technology?

SOURCE: Excerpted from E Spitznagel, "The Robot Revolution Is Coming," *Bloomberg Businessweek*, January 17–23, 2011, p 70.

---

his passion; when we opens Yelp on his iPhone, the restaurant review app will already know about his upcoming trip to San Francisco and recommend restaurants there. "I imagine this future where everywhere you go online or any application you open on your mobile device is in some way personalized to you and your interests," says Kapur, 29.[39]

New technologies such as smart phones, cloud computing, and augmented reality are important change drivers.[40] But relative to OB, we need to focus on how the evolving Internet has changed the *behavior* of those who have grown up with the Internet and take Google, Facebook, YouTube, and tweeting for granted. Don Tapscott, author of the intriguing book *Grown Up Digital: How the Net Generation Is Changing the World*, says the 81 million Americans born between January 1977 and December 1997 have a unique worldview shaped by the Internet:

Example. These are the eight norms of the Net Generation. They value freedom—freedom to be who they are, freedom of choice. They want to customize everything, even their jobs. They learn to be skeptical, to scrutinize what they see and read in the media, including the Internet. They value integrity—being honest, considerate, transparent, and abiding by their commitment. They're great collaborators, with friends online and at work. They thrive on speed. They love to innovate.

. . . [I]f you understand these norms, you can change your company, school or university, government, or family for the twenty-first century.[41]

(Tapscott's ideas about the Net Generation are expanded upon in Chapter 14.) In short, organizations and organizational life will never be the same because of the virtual world of the Internet[42] (see Real World/Real People).

e-business Running the *entire* business via the Internet and managing virtual teams.

Managers are challenged to effectively communicate with, supervise, and lead widely dispersed individuals and teams linked via modern telecommunications and Internet technology. The creation and management of virtual teams is covered in detail in Chapter 11 and virtual organizations are explored in Chapter 17.

 LO.4 The Need to Build Human and Social Capital

Knowledge workers, those who add value by using their brains rather than the sweat off their backs, are more important than ever in today's global economy. What you know and who you know increasingly are the keys to both personal and organizational success (see Figure 1–2). In the United States, the following "perfect storm" of current and emerging trends heightens the importance and urgency of building human capital:

- Spread of advanced technology to developing countries with rapidly growing middle classes (e.g., China, India, Russia, and Brazil).
- Offshoring of increasingly sophisticated jobs (e.g., product design, architecture, medical diagnosis).
- Comparatively poor math and science skills among America's youth.
- Massive brain drain caused by retiring post–World War II baby-boom generation.[43]

figure 1–2 The Strategic Importance and Dimensions of Human and Social Capital

What Is Human Capital? (Hint: Think BIG)   A team of human resource management authors offered this perspective: "We're living in a time when a new economic paradigm—characterized by speed, innovation, short cycle times, quality, and customer satisfaction—is highlighting the importance of intangible assets, such as brand recognition, knowledge, innovation, and particularly human capital."[44]

Human capital is the productive potential of an individual's knowledge and actions. *Potential* is the operative word in this intentionally broad definition. When you are hungry, money in your pocket is good because it has the potential to buy a meal. Likewise, a present or future employee with the right combination of knowledge, skills, and motivation to excel represents human capital with the potential to give the organization a competitive advantage. In a 2010 poll of 449 human resource professionals, "Obtaining human capital and optimizing human capital investments" was identified as the number-one challenge for companies over the next 10 years.[45] Intel, a high-tech computer-chip manufacturer, is proactive in this area because its future depends on innovative engineering. It takes years of math and science studies to make world-class engineers. Not wanting to leave the future supply of engineers to chance, Intel annually spends $100 million funding education initiatives at all levels worldwide.[46] The company encourages youngsters to study math and science and sponsors rigorous science competitions with scholarships up to $100,000 for the winners.[47] Will all of the students end up working for Intel? No. That's not the point. The point is much bigger—namely, to build the *world's* human capital.

Thanks to Intel's deep commitment to education and building human capital, these select students got a pat on the back from President Obama.

What Is Social Capital?   Our focus now shifts from the individual to social units (e.g., friends, family, company, group or club, nation). Think *relationships*. **Social capital** is productive potential resulting from strong relationships, goodwill, trust, and cooperative effort.[48] Again, the word *potential* is key. According to experts on the subject: "It's true: the social capital that used to be a given in organizations is now rare and endangered. But the social capital we can build will allow us to capitalize on the volatile, virtual possibilities of today's business environment."[49] Relationships do matter. In a general survey, 77% of the women and 63% of the men rated "Good relationship with boss" extremely important. Other factors—including good equipment, resources, easy commute, and flexible hours—received lower ratings.[50] Moreover, research indicates the favorable impacts positive social interactions can have on cardiovascular health and the immune system.[51]

Building Human and Social Capital   Various dimensions of human and social capital are listed in Figure 1–2. They are a preview of what lies ahead in this book, including our discussion of organizational learning in Chapter 17. Formal organizational learning and *knowledge management* programs, as discussed in Chapter 12, need social capital to leverage individual human capital for the greater good. It is a straightforward formula for success. Growth depends on the timely sharing of valuable knowledge. After all, what good are bright employees who do not network, teach, and inspire?

---

human capital The productive potential of one's knowledge and actions.

social capital The productive potential of strong, trusting, and cooperative relationships.

Back to the Chapter-Opening Case

How does Zappos.com build human and social capital?

TO THE POINT
Which of Wilson's managerial skills are most important for 21st-century managers?

LO.5 The Managerial Context: Getting Things Done with and through Others

Like the organizations they run, managers touch our lives in many ways. Schools, hospitals, government agencies, and large and small businesses all require systematic management. Formally defined, **management** is the process of working with and through others to achieve organizational objectives, efficiently and ethically, in the face of constant change. For students of OB, the central feature of this definition is *working with and through others*. Managers play a constantly evolving role. Today's successful managers are no longer the I've-got-everything-under-control order givers of yesteryear. Rather, they need to creatively envision and actively sell bold new directions in an ethical and people-friendly manner. Effective managers are team players empowered by the willing and active support of others who are driven by conflicting self-interests. Each of us has a huge stake in how well managers carry out their evolving role. A recent review of 30 years of business literature led to this conclusion about what good management involves: "Find a clear purpose. Be aware that past experience and a mass of information can interfere with wise decisions. Maintain a bias toward action. Be open to change. Seek feedback."[52] A good managerial role model is Walmart's CEO Mike Duke. His predecessor Lee Scott recently had this to say in a *Fortune* magazine interview:

Example. "Mike is not only a good leader but a really good manager. There's so much said today about leadership. But I don't think in business you can forget the fact that you don't just have to lead, you have to manage." . . .

"Yeah, he's a better manager than I am," says Scott. "I think it's his ability to deal with data, his ability to set a schedule and follow that schedule, and to get all of the things done that he needs to get done. Mike is disciplined, and I think that causes him to be able to accomplish a great deal—how he manages his time, how he manages his people, and the effectiveness of the time he spends with people."[53]

Quality of management can make a big difference for employees and customers, alike.

Let us take a closer look at the skills managers need to perform and the future direction of management.

What Do Managers Do? A Skills Profile

Observational studies by Henry Mintzberg and others have found the typical manager's day to be a fragmented collection of brief episodes.[54] Interruptions are commonplace, while large blocks of time for planning and reflective thinking are not. In one particular study, four top-level managers spent 63% of their time on activities lasting less than nine minutes each. Only 5% of the managers' time was devoted to activities lasting more than an hour.[55] But what specific skills do effective managers perform during their hectic and fragmented workdays?

Many attempts have been made over the years to paint a realistic picture of what managers do. Diverse and confusing lists of managerial functions and roles

table 1–2 Skills Exhibited by an Effective Manager

1. **Clarifies goals and objectives** for everyone involved.

2. **Encourages participation,** upward communication, and suggestions.

3. **Plans and organizes** for an orderly work flow.

4. Has **technical and administrative expertise** to answer organization-related questions.

5. **Facilitates work** through team building, training, coaching, and support.

6. **Provides feedback** honestly and constructively.

7. **Keeps things moving** by relying on schedules, deadlines, and helpful reminders.

8. **Controls details** without being overbearing.

9. Applies reasonable **pressure for goal accomplishment.**

10. **Empowers and delegates** key duties to others while maintaining goal clarity and commitment.

11. **Recognizes good performance** with rewards and positive reinforcement.

SOURCES: Adapted from material in F Shipper, "A Study of the Psychometric Properties of the Managerial Skill Scales of the Survey of Management Practices,"*Educational and Psychological Measurement,* June 1995, pp 468–79; and C L Wilson, *How and Why Effective Managers Balance Their Skills: Technical, Teambuilding, Drive* (Columbia, MD: Rockatech Multimedia Publishing, 2003).

have been suggested. Fortunately, a stream of research over the past 20 years by Clark Wilson and others has given us a practical and statistically validated profile of managerial *skills*[56] (see Table 1–2). Wilson's managerial skills profile focuses on 11 observable categories of managerial behavior. This is very much in tune with today's emphasis on managerial competency. Wilson's unique skills-assessment technique goes beyond the usual self-report approach with its natural bias. In addition to surveying a given manager about his or her 11 skills, the Wilson approach also asks those who report directly to the manager to answer questions about their boss's skills. According to Wilson and his colleagues, the result is an assessment of skill *mastery,* not simply skill awareness.[57] The logic behind Wilson's approach is both simple and compelling. Who better to assess a manager's skills than the people who experience those behaviors on a day-to-day basis—those who report directly to the manager?

According to Lee Scott, Mike Duke's predecessor as CEO of Walmart, Duke is both a good leader *and* a good manager because of his discipline, ability to handle lots of data, people skills, and focus on getting timely results.

The Wilson managerial skills research yields four useful lessons:

1. Dealing effectively with *people* is what management is all about. The 11 skills in Table 1–2 constitute a goal creation/commitment/feedback/reward/accomplishment cycle with human interaction at every turn.

management Process of working with and through others to achieve organizational objectives, efficiently and ethically, amid constant change.

2. Managers with high skills mastery tend to have better subunit performance and employee morale than managers with low skills mastery.[58]

3. *Effective* female and male managers *do not* have significantly different skill profiles,[59] contrary to claims in the popular business press in recent years.[60]

4. At all career stages, *derailed* managers (those who failed to achieve their potential) tended to be the ones who *overestimated* their skill mastery (rated themselves higher than their employees did).[61] This prompted the following conclusion from the researcher: "[W]hen selecting individuals for promotion to managerial positions, those who are arrogant, aloof, insensitive, and defensive should be avoided."[62]

 LO.6 21st-Century Managers

Today's workplace is indeed undergoing immense and permanent changes.[63] Organizations have been "reengineered" for greater speed, efficiency, and flexibility. Teams are pushing aside the individual as the primary building block of organizations.[64] Command-and-control management is giving way to participative management and empowerment. Ego-centered leaders are being replaced by customer-centered leaders. Employees increasingly are being viewed as internal customers. A 2008 summit of 35 executives and management scholars prompted a call for a *reinvention* of management. Lead researcher Gary Hamel framed the challenge this way:

Example. [Historically,] the problems were efficiency and scale, and the solution was bureaucracy, with its hierarchical structure, cascading goals, precise role definitions, and elaborate rules and procedures.

Managers today face a new set of problems, products of a volatile and unforgiving environment. Some of the most critical: How in an age of rapid change do you create organizations that are as adaptable and resilient as they are focused and efficient? How in a world where the winds of creative destruction blow at gale force can a company innovate quickly and boldly enough to stay relevant and profitable? How in a creative economy where entrepreneurial genius is the secret to success do you inspire employees to bring the gifts of initiative, imagination, and passion to work every day? How . . . do you encourage executives to fulfill their responsibilities to all stakeholders?[65]

All this creates a mandate for more flexible, innovative, and responsive organizations and a new kind of manager in the 21st century (see Table 1–3).

Back to the **Chapter-Opening Case**

What evidence of a 21st-century organization, based on Table 1–3, can you find in the Zappos.com case?

The Contingency Approach to Management

Scholars have wrestled for many years with the problem of how best to apply the diverse and growing collection of management tools and techniques. Their answer is the contingency approach. The **contingency approach** calls for using management techniques in a situationally appropriate manner, instead of trying to rely on "one best way" or "one size fits all."

table 1–3   Evolution of the 21st-Century Manager

	PAST MANAGERS	FUTURE MANAGERS
Primary role	Order giver, privileged elite, manipulator, controller	Facilitator, team member, teacher, advocate, sponsor, coach
Learning and knowledge	Periodic learning, narrow specialist	Continuous life-long learning, generalist with multiple specialties
Compensation criteria	Time, effort, rank	Skills, results
Cultural orientation	Monocultural, monolingual	Multicultural, multilingual
Primary source of influence	Formal authority	Knowledge (technical and interpersonal)
View of people	Potential problem	Primary resource; human capital
Primary communication pattern	Vertical	Multidirectional
Decision-making style	Limited input for individual decisions	Broad-based input for joint decisions
Ethical considerations	Afterthought	Forethought
Nature of interpersonal relationships	Competitive (win–lose)	Cooperative (win–win)
Handling of power and key information	Hoard and restrict access	Share and broaden access for greater transparency
Approach to change	Resist	Facilitate

The contingency approach encourages managers to view organizational behavior within a situational context. According to this modern perspective, evolving situations, not hard-and-fast rules, determine when and where various management techniques are appropriate. Harvard's Clayton Christensen put it this way: "Many of the widely accepted principles of good management are only situationally appropriate."[66] For example, as discussed in Chapter 16, contingency researchers have determined that there is no single best style of leadership. Organizational behavior specialists embrace the contingency approach because it helps them realistically interrelate individuals, groups, and evolving circumstances inside and outside the organization. Moreover, the contingency approach sends a clear message to managers in today's global economy: Carefully read the situation and then be flexible enough to adapt (see Real World/Real People on page 20).

contingency approach Using management tools and techniques in a situationally appropriate manner; avoiding the one-best-way mentality.

real WORLD // real PEOPLE

Will Happy Employees Mean Happy Customers for American Express?

[L]ast year when [American Express] gave its global customer service division a makeover, it decided to focus on making life better for its 26,000 call-center employees. The theory: Happier employees mean happier customers. "We've learned the importance of the attitude of the employee," says Jim Bush, EVP of world service. AmEx started by asking customer service employees what they wanted to see—and then delivered better pay, flexible schedules, and more career development. It also switched from a directive to keep calls short and transaction-oriented to engaging customers in longer conversations. Collectively, the moves have boosted service margins by 10%. "Great service starts with the people who deliver it," says [CEO Ken] Chenault. "We want American Express to be the company people recommend to their friends."

Based on Table 1–3, what evidence of 21st-century management can you find here?

SOURCE: Excerpted from C Tkaczyk, "American Express," *Fortune*, August 16, 2010, p 14.

American Express CEO Kenneth I Chenault.

The Ethics Challenge

TO THE POINT

How can an understanding of Carroll's social responsibility pyramid and the seven moral principles lead to more ethical conduct in the workplace?

Thanks to highly publicized criminal acts of now-jailed executives from the likes of Enron, Tyco, and WorldCom,[67] corporate officers in the United States became subject to high accountability standards and harsh penalties under the Sarbanes-Oxley Act of 2002.[68] Sadly, instead of improving, business ethics continued to hit new lows, as symbolized by Ponzi schemer Bernard Madoff's 150-year prison sentence in 2009 and Goldman Sachs's record $550 million fine to settle fraud charges in 2010.[69] The general public and elected officials (who have their own criminal hall of shame) continue to call for greater attention to ethical conduct.[70]

Clearly, *everyone* needs to join in the effort to stem this tide of unethical conduct. There are a variety of individual and organizational factors that contribute to unethical behavior. OB is an excellent vantage point for better understanding and improving workplace ethics. If OB can provide insights about managing human work behavior, then it can teach us something about avoiding *misbehavior*.

Ethics involves the study of moral issues and choices. It is concerned with right versus wrong, good versus bad, and the many shades of gray in supposedly black-and-white issues. Moral implications spring from virtually every decision, both on and off the job. Managers are challenged to have more imagination and the courage to do the right thing to make the world a better place.

To enhance our understanding of ethics within an OB context, we will discuss (1) a corporate social responsibility model, (2) the general erosion of morality, (3) seven moral principles for managers, (4) how to improve an organization's ethical climate, and (5) a personal call to action.

 LO.7 A Model of Global Corporate Social Responsibility and Ethics

Corporate social responsibility (CSR) is defined as "the notion that corporations have an obligation to constituent groups in society other than stockholders and beyond that prescribed by law or union contract."[71] CSR challenges businesses to go above and beyond just making a profit to serve the interests and needs of

figure 1–3   Carroll's Global Corporate Social Responsibility Pyramid

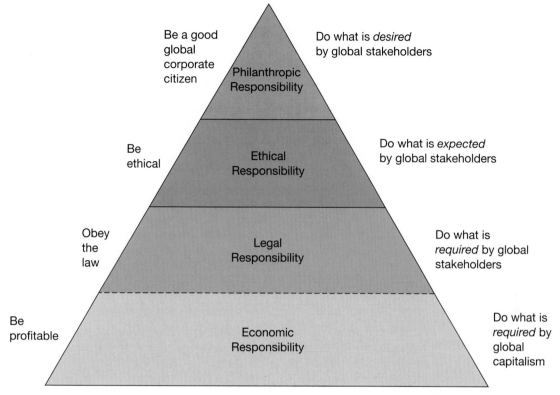

SOURCE: A B Carroll, *Academy of Management Executive: The Thinking Manager's Source.* Copyright © 2004 by The Academy of Management. Reproduced by permission of The Academy of Management via Copyright Clearance Center.

"stakeholders," including past and present employees, customers, suppliers, and countries and communities where facilities are located.[72] A good deal of controversy surrounds the drive for greater CSR because classical economic theory says businesses are responsible for producing goods and services to make profits, not solving the world's social, political, and environmental ills.[73] What is your opinion?

University of Georgia business ethics scholar Archie B Carroll views CSR in broad terms. So broad, in fact, that he created a model of CSR/business ethics with the global economy and multinational corporations in mind (see Figure 1–3). This model is very timely because it effectively triangulates three major trends: (1) economic globalization, (2) expanding CSR expectations, and (3) the call for improved business ethics. Carroll's global CSR pyramid, from the bottom up, advises organizations in the global economy to

- *Make a profit* consistent with expectations for international businesses.
- *Obey the law* of host countries as well as international law.
- *Be ethical in its practices,* taking host-country and global standards into consideration.
- *Be a good corporate citizen,* especially as defined by the host country's expectations.[74]

 Go to www.mcgrawhillconnect.com for a video case on Patagonia and their philosophy concerning corporate social responsibility.

ethics Study of moral issues and choices.

corporate social responsibility Corporations are expected to go above and beyond following the law and making a profit.

In keeping with the pyramid idea, Carroll emphasizes that each level needs to be solid if the structure is to stand. A pick-and-choose approach to CSR is inappropriate. The top level of the pyramid, according to Carroll, reflects "global society's expectations that business will engage in social activities that are not mandated by law nor generally expected of business in an ethical sense."[75] The spirit of Carroll's global corporate social responsibility pyramid is evident in Nike's ongoing quest to shake its sweatshop image:

Example. Progress has been slow in coming to Nike's global supply chain, which employs nearly 800,000 workers in 52 countries. Still, Nike . . . has made strides since it embraced corporate responsibility. What started as a massive PR shield has evolved into a broader mandate for the way it makes and sells products. Nike has been particularly inventive at weaving environmental awareness into its design process, rating each sneaker according to a sustainability index. On labor, the company admits that its initial efforts—setting a code of conduct and monitoring compliance—haven't ended abuses across the hundreds of factories that produce its goods. But the lessons from the 1990s—to own up to problems, then find companywide solutions—are helping the world's biggest shoemaker . . . with labor issues. "I'm proud of what we've accomplished, but we're still not where we need to be," says Nike's current CEO, Mark Parker.[76]

Our OB in Action Case Study on Whole Foods at the end of this chapter is a good CSR example. With this global CSR perspective in mind, we now narrow the focus to individual moral behavior.

Back to the Chapter-Opening Case

Where does Zappos.com belong on Carroll's Corporate Social Responsibility Pyramid in Figure 1–3? Explain.

Go to www.mcgrawhillconnect.com for an interactive comprehension case exercise to learn about ethics.

An Erosion of Morality?

David Callahan, in his book *The Cheating Culture: Why More Americans Are Doing Wrong to Get Ahead,* paints this disturbing picture of modern society:

Example. [T]he character of Americans has changed. Those values associated with the market hold sway in their most caricatured form: individualism and self-reliance have morphed into selfishness and self-absorption; competitiveness has become social Darwinism; desire for the good life has turned into materialism; aspiration has become envy. There is a growing gap between the life that many Americans want and the life they can afford—a problem that bedevils even those who would seem to have everything. Other values in our culture have been sidelined; belief in community, social responsibility, compassion for the less able or less fortunate.[77]

Bolstering this negative view is a 2010 survey in which 72% of Americans polled said corruption had increased in the United States during the past three years.[78] Does this portrayal of a "cheating culture" have merit and, if so, to what extent? Let us examine the OB research evidence for relevant insights.

Taking Local Norms and Conduct into Consideration

National culture, as discussed in Chapter 4, affects how people think and act about everything, including ethical issues. This reality was supported in a multination study (including the United States, Great Britain, France, Germany, Spain, Switzerland, India, China, and Australia) of management ethics. Managers from each country were asked to judge the ethicality of 12 questionable behaviors, including such things as giving and accepting gifts, passing blame, sharing confidential information, and concealing errors. Results revealed significant differences across the 10 nations in the study. That is, managers in some countries approved of practices that were frowned upon in other countries.[79] Consequently, care needs to be taken when extrapolating Callahan's characterization of American morality to other cultures. Each culture requires its own ethical analysis, taking local norms into consideration.

Ethical Lapses in the Workplace

A nationwide survey of 581 human resource professionals revealed that 62% of the respondents occasionally observed unethical behavior at their companies.[80] Unethical behavior occurs at all organizational levels, although recent research indicates that senior executives tend to have significantly more positive perceptions of ethics in their organizations than do lower-level employees.[81] Perhaps that is because lower-level employees regularly witness common ethical lapses such as lying about being sick, fudging a report, bullying and sexual harassment, personal use of company equipment, and stealing company property or funds. Executives are not immune to being victims of unethical conduct, however. For example, a survey of job applicants for executive positions indicated that 64% had been misinformed about the financial condition of potential employers, and 58% of these individuals were negatively affected by this misinformation.[82] It is very likely that some of those affected individuals moved their families and left their friends only to discover the promise of a great job in a financially stable organization was a lie. Job applicants, for their part, also have ethical lapses. An analysis of 2.6 million background checks by ADP Screening and Selection Services, revealed that "44% of applicants lied about their work histories, 41% lied about their education, and 23% falsified credentials or licenses."[83]

Experts estimate that US companies lost about $994 billion to fraud in 2008, much of it at the hands of insiders.[84] On a global scale, the World Bank says, "bribery has become a $1 trillion industry."[85]

connect Go to www.mcgrawhillconnect.com for a self-assessment to determine your ethical decision-making skills.

Intense Pressure for Results Starts Early

Lower-level managers generally want to "look good" for their bosses. In support of this conclusion, many studies have found a tendency among middle- and lower-level managers to act unethically in the face of perceived pressure for results. Further, this tendency is particularly pronounced when individuals are significantly rewarded for accomplishing their goals.[86] By fostering a pressure-cooker atmosphere for results, managers can unwittingly set the stage for unethical shortcuts by employees who seek to please the boss, protect their jobs, and be loyal to the company.[87]

Unfortunately, the seeds of this problem are planted early in life. A survey of 787 youngsters ages 13 to 18 found "that 44% of teens feel they're under strong pressure to succeed in school, no matter the cost. Of those, 81% believe the pressure will be the same or worse in the workplace."[88] Sixty-nine percent of the students admitted to lying in the past year (with 27% confessing they even lied on the survey!).[89] Anonymous surveys by the Josephson Institute of Ethics of 43,321 students ages 15 to 18 from private and public high schools across the United States found 60% admittedly had cheated on a test in 2010 "and 34% did so twice or more. Students at non-religious private schools cited the lowest percentage (33%), while 56% at religious schools said they cheated."[90]

Some believe intense pressure for results by BP managers ultimately was responsible for the 11 deaths and environmental disaster when Transocean's Deepwater Horizon drilling rig exploded and sank into the Gulf of Mexico in 2010.

table 1–4   The Magnificent Seven: General Moral Principles for Managers

1. *Dignity of human life:* The lives of people are to be respected. Human beings, by the fact of their existence, have value and dignity. We may not act in ways that directly intend to harm or kill an innocent person. Human beings have a right to live; we have an obligation to respect that right to life. Human life is to be preserved and treated as sacred.

2. *Autonomy:* All persons are intrinsically valuable and have the right to self-determination. We should act in ways that demonstrate each person's worth, dignity, and right to free choice. We have a right to act in ways that assert our own worth and legitimate needs. We should not use others as mere "things" or only as means to an end. Each person has an equal right to basic human liberty, compatible with a similar liberty for others.

3. *Honesty:* The truth should be told to those who have a right to know it. Honesty is also known as integrity, truth telling, and honor. One should speak and act so as to reflect the reality of the situation. Speaking and acting should mirror the way things really are. There are times when others have the right to hear the truth from us; there are times when they do not.

4. *Loyalty:* Promises, contracts, and commitments should be honored. Loyalty includes fidelity, promise keeping, keeping the public trust, good citizenship, excellence in quality of work, reliability, commitment, and honoring just laws, rules, and policies.

5. *Fairness:* People should be treated justly. One has the right to be treated fairly, impartially, and equitably. One has the obligation to treat others fairly and justly. All have the right to the necessities of life—especially those in deep need and the helpless. Justice includes equal, impartial, unbiased treatment. Fairness tolerates diversity and accepts differences in people and their ideas.

6. *Humaneness:* There are two parts: (a) Our actions ought to accomplish good, and (b) we should avoid doing evil. We should do good to others and to ourselves. We should have concern for the well-being of others; usually, we show this concern in the form of compassion, giving, kindness, serving, and caring.

7. *The common good:* Actions should accomplish the "greatest good for the greatest number" of people. One should act and speak in ways that benefit the welfare of the largest number of people, while trying to protect the rights of individuals.

SOURCE: From Kent Hodgson, *A Rock and a Hard Place: How to Make Ethical Business Decisions When the Choices Are Tough* © 1992. Reprinted with permission of the author.

In summary, Callahan's earlier characterization of America's cheating culture is an appropriate wake-up call. The challenge to improve is immense because unethical behavior is pervasive.

 LO.8 General Moral Principles

Management consultant and writer Kent Hodgson has helpfully taken managers a step closer to ethical decisions by identifying seven general moral principles (see Table 1–4). Hodgson calls them "the magnificent seven" to emphasize their timeless and worldwide relevance. Notions of both justice and care are clearly evident in the magnificent seven, which are detailed and, hence, more practical. Importantly, according to Hodgson, there are no absolute ethical answers for decision makers. The goal for managers should be to rely on moral principles so their decisions are *principled, appropriate,* and *defensible.*[91] (See Real World/Real People.)

How to Improve the Organization's Ethical Climate

Improving workplace ethics is not just a nice thing to do; it also can have a positive impact on the bottom line. Studies in the United States and the United Kingdom demonstrated that corporate commitment to ethics can be profitable. Evidence

real WORLD // real PEOPLE: **ethics**

Do Billionaire Businesspeople Have an Obligation to "Give Back" to Society?

Bill Gates and Warren Buffett announced . . . [in 2010] that 40 of America's richest people have agreed to sign a "Giving Pledge" to donate at least half their wealth to charity. With a collective net worth said to total $230 billion, that promise translates to at least $115 billion. . . .

Successful entrepreneurs-turned-philanthropists typically say they feel a responsibility to "give back" to society. But "giving back" implies they have taken something. What, exactly, have they taken? Yes, they have amassed great sums of wealth. But that wealth is the reward they have earned for investing their time and talent in creating products and services that others value. They haven't taken from society, but rather enriched us in ways that were previously unimaginable.

What do you think about the issue of giving back? Explain the ethics and general moral principles of your position.

SOURCE: Excerpted from K O Dennis, "Gates and Buffett Take the Pledge," *The Wall Street Journal,* August 20, 2010, p A15.

---

suggested that profitability is enhanced by a reputation for honesty and corporate citizenship.[92] Ethics also can impact the quality of people who apply to work in an organization. An online survey of 1,020 individuals indicated that 83% rated a company's record of business ethics as "very important" when deciding to accept a job offer. Only 2% rated it as "unimportant."[93]

A team of management researchers recommended the following actions for improving on-the-job ethics.[94]

- *Behave ethically yourself.* Managers are potent role models whose habits and actual behavior send clear signals about the importance of ethical conduct. Ethical behavior is a top-to-bottom proposition and executives are challenged "to simultaneously maximize the so-called triple bottom line, or 'People, Planet, Profit.'"[95]

- *Screen potential employees.* Surprisingly, employers are generally lax when it comes to checking references, credentials, transcripts, and other information on applicant résumés. More diligent action in this area can screen out those given to fraud and misrepresentation. Integrity testing is fairly valid but is no panacea.[96]

- *Develop a meaningful code of ethics.* Codes of ethics can have a positive impact if they satisfy these four criteria:
  1. They are *distributed* to every employee.
  2. They are firmly *supported* by top management.
  3. They refer to *specific* practices and ethical dilemmas likely to be encountered by target employees (e.g., salespersons paying kickbacks, purchasing agents receiving payoffs, laboratory scientists doctoring data, or accountants "cooking the books").
  4. They are evenly *enforced* with rewards for compliance and strict penalties for noncompliance.[97]

- *Provide ethics training.* Employees can be trained to identify and deal with ethical issues during orientation and through seminar, video, and Internet training sessions.[98]

- *Reinforce ethical behavior.* Behavior that is reinforced tends to be repeated, whereas behavior that is not reinforced tends to disappear. Ethical conduct too often is ignored or even punished while unethical behavior is rewarded.

Mc Graw Hill connect ™ Go to www.mcgrawhillconnect.com for an interactive exercise to test your knowledge on the model of global corporate social responsibility.

- *Create positions, units, and other structural mechanisms to deal with ethics.* Ethics needs to be an everyday affair, not a one-time announcement of a new ethical code that gets filed away and forgotten. A growing number of large companies in the United States have chief ethics officers who report directly to the CEO, thus making ethical conduct and accountability priority issues.

- *Create a climate in which whistle-blowing becomes unnecessary.* **Whistle-blowing** occurs when an employee reports a perceived unethical and/or illegal activity to a third party such as government agencies, news media, or public-interest groups. Enron's Sherron Watkins was a highly publicized whistle-blower.[99] Organizations can reduce the need for whistle-blowing by encouraging free and open expression of dissenting viewpoints and giving employees a voice through fair grievance procedures and/or anonymous ethics hot lines.

A Personal Call to Action

 Go to www.mcgrawhillconnect.com for an interactive exercise to test your knowledge on improving the ethical climate in your organization.

In the final analysis, ethics comes down to individual perception and motivation. Organizational climate, role models, structure, training, and rewards all can point employees in the right direction. But individuals first must be **morally attentive,** meaning they faithfully consider the ethical implications of their actions and circumstances.[100]

Second, they must *want* to do the right thing and have the courage to act. Bill George, the respected former CEO of Medtronic, the maker of life-saving devices such as heart pacemakers, gave us this call to action: "Each of us needs to determine . . . where our ethical boundaries are and, if asked to violate (them), refuse. . . . If this means refusing a direct order, we must be prepared to resign."[101] Rising to this challenge requires strong personal *values* (more about values in Chapter 6) and the *courage* to adhere to them during adversity.

Learning about OB: Research and a Road Map

TO THE POINT
Which of the five research methodologies is likely to provide the best insights about OB?

OB is a broad and growing field. We have a lot of ground to cover. To make the trip as instructive and efficient as possible, we use a theory→research→practice strategy. For virtually all major topics in this book, we begin by presenting the underlying theoretical framework (often with graphical models showing how key variables are related) and defining key terms. Next, we tap the latest research findings for valuable insights. Finally, we round out the discussion with illustrative practical examples and, when applicable, how-to-do-it advice.

LO.9 Five Sources of OB Research Insights

OB gains its credibility as an academic discipline by being research driven. Scientific rigor pushes aside speculation, prejudice, and untested assumptions about workplace behavior. We systematically cite "hard" evidence from five different categories. Worthwhile evidence was obtained by drawing on the following *priority* of research methodologies:

- *Meta-analyses.* A **meta-analysis** is a statistical pooling technique that permits behavioral scientists to draw general conclusions about certain variables from many different studies.[102] It typically encompasses a vast number of subjects, often reaching the thousands. Meta-analyses are instructive because they focus on general patterns of research evidence, not fragmented bits and pieces or isolated studies.[103]

- *Field studies.* In OB, a **field study** probes individual or group processes in an organizational setting. Because field studies involve real-life situations, their results often have immediate and practical relevance for managers.

- *Laboratory studies.* In a **laboratory study**, variables are manipulated and measured in contrived situations. College students are commonly used as subjects. The highly controlled nature of laboratory studies enhances research precision. But generalizing the results to organizational management requires caution.

- *Sample surveys.* In a **sample survey,** samples of people from specified populations respond to questionnaires. The researchers then draw conclusions about the relevant population. Generalizability of the results depends on the quality of the sampling and questioning techniques.

- *Case studies.* A **case study** is an in-depth analysis of a single individual, group, or organization, Because of their limited scope, case studies yield realistic but not very generalizable results.

connect™ Go to www.mcgrawhillconnect.com for an interactive exercise to test your knowledge on the sources of organizational behavior research.

A Topical Model for Understanding and Managing OB

Figure 1–4 is a topical road map for our journey through this book. Our destination is organizational effectiveness through continuous improvement. Four different criteria for determining whether or not an organization is effective are discussed in Chapter 17. The study of OB can be a wandering and pointless trip if we overlook the need to translate OB lessons into an effective and efficient organized endeavor.

At the far left side of our topical road map are managers and team leaders, those who are responsible for accomplishing organizational results with and through others. The three circles at the center of our road map correspond to Parts 2, 3, and 4 of this text. Logically, the flow of topical coverage in this book (following introductory Part 1) goes from individuals, to group processes, to organizational processes. Around the core of our topical road map in Figure 1–4 is the organization. Accordingly, we end our journey with organization-related material in Part 4. Organizational structure and design are covered there in Chapter 17 to establish and develop the *organizational* context of organizational behavior. Rounding out our organizational context is a discussion of organizational change in Chapter 18. Chapters 3 and 4 provide a *cultural* context for OB.

The dotted line represents a permeable boundary between the organization and its environment. Energy and influence flow both ways across this permeable boundary. Truly, no organization is an island in today's highly interactive and interdependent world. Relative to the *external* environment, international cultures

whistle-blowing Reporting unethical/illegal acts to outside third parties.

morally attentive Faithfully considering the ethical implications of one's actions.

meta-analysis Pools the results of many studies through statistical procedure.

field study Examination of variables in real-life settings.

laboratory study Manipulation and measurement of variables in contrived situations.

sample survey Questionnaire responses from a sample of people.

case study In-depth study of a single person, group, or organization.

figure 1–4 A Topical Model for What Lies Ahead

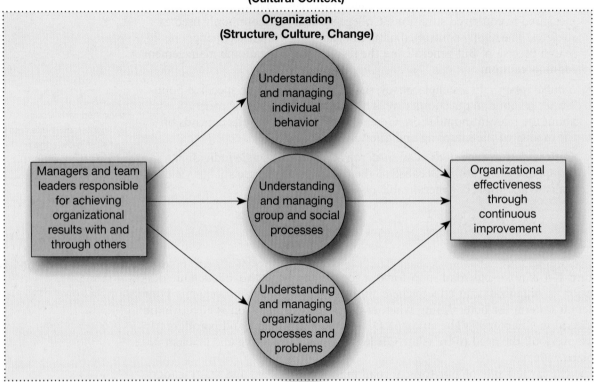

are explored in Chapter 4. Organization–environment contingencies are examined in Chapter 17.

Chapter 2 examines the OB implications of significant demographic and social trends. These discussions provide a realistic context for studying and managing people at work.

Bon voyage! Enjoy your trip through the challenging, interesting, and often surprising world of OB.

Summary of Key Concepts

1. *Define the term* organizational behavior, *and contrast McGregor's Theory X and Theory Y assumptions about employees.* Organizational behavior (OB) is an interdisciplinary field dedicated to better understanding and managing people at work. It is both research and application oriented. Theory X employees, according to traditional thinking, dislike work, require close supervision, and are primarily interested in security. According to the modern Theory Y view, employees are capable of self-direction, of seeking responsibility, and of being creative.

2. *Identify the four principles of total quality management (TQM).* (*a*) Do it right the first time to eliminate costly rework. (*b*) Listen to and learn from customers and employees. (*c*) Make continuous improvement an everyday matter. (*d*) Build teamwork, trust, and mutual respect.

3. *Define the term* e-business, *and describe the Net Generation.* E-business involves using the Internet to more effectively and efficiently manage every aspect of a business, including virtual teams. Tapscott describes the Net Generation—the 81 million Americans born between the start of 1977 and the end of 1997 who grew up with the Internet—in terms of eight norms: (*a*) value freedom, (*b*) customize everything, (*c*) be skeptical, (*d*) value integrity, (*e*) abide by commitments, (*f*) be a great collaborator, (*g*) thrive on speed, (*h*) love to innovate.

4. *Contrast human and social capital, and explain why we need to build both.* The first involves *individual* characteristics; the second involves *social* relationships. Human capital is the productive potential of an individual's knowledge and actions. Dimensions include such things as intelligence,

visions, skills, self-esteem, creativity, motivation, eth-ics, and emotional maturity. Social capital is productive potential resulting from strong relationships, goodwill, trust, and cooperative effort. Dimensions include such things as shared visions and goals, trust, mutual respect, friendships, empowerment, teamwork, win–win negotia-tions, and volunteering. Social capital is necessary to tap individual human capital for the good of the organization through knowledge sharing and networking.

5. *Define the term* management, *and identify at least five of the eleven managerial skills in Wilson's profile of effective managers.* Management is the process of working with and through others to achieve organizational objectives in an efficient and ethical manner. According to the Wilson skills profile, an effective manager (*a*) clarifies goals and objectives, (*b*) encourages participation, (*c*) plans and organizes, (*d*) has technical and administrative expertise, (*e*) facilitates work through team building and coach-ing, (*f*) provides feedback, (*g*) keeps things moving, (*h*) controls details, (*i*) applies reasonable pressure for goal accomplishment, (*j*) empowers and delegates, and (*k*) recognizes and rewards good performance.

6. *Characterize 21st-century managers.* They will be team players who will get things done cooperatively by rely-ing on joint decision making, their knowledge instead of formal authority, and their multicultural skills. They will engage in life-long learning and be compensated on the basis of their skills and results. They will facilitate rather than resist change, share rather than hoard power and key information, and be multidirectional communicators. Ethics will be a forethought instead of an afterthought. They will be generalists with multiple specialties.

7. *Describe Carroll's global corporate social responsibility pyramid, and discuss the problem of moral erosion.* From

bottom to top, the four levels of corporate responsibility in Carroll's pyramid are: *economic* (make a profit); *legal* (obey the law); *ethical* (be ethical in its practices); and *philanthropic* (be a good corporate citizen). Progress needs to be made on all levels. Callahan's claim that America has developed a "cheating culture" is supported by unethi-cal conduct at all organizational levels. An unintended but serious consequence of excessive pressure for results, beginning in school and carrying over to the workplace, is expedient unethical behavior. Moral erosion is evident in high school and workplace surveys about misconduct.

8. *Identify four of the seven general ethical principles, and explain how to improve an organization's ethical climate.* The "magnificent seven" moral principles are (*a*) dignity of human life, (*b*) autonomy, (*c*) honesty, (*d*) loyalty, (*e*) fairness, (*f*) humaneness (by doing good and avoiding evil), and (*g*) the common good (accomplishing the great-est good for the greatest number of people). An organiza-tion's ethical climate can be improved by managers being good role models, carefully screening job applicants, creat-ing and firmly enforcing a code of ethics mentioning spe-cific practices, providing ethics training, rewarding ethical behavior, creating ethics-related positions and structures, and reducing the need for whistle-blowing (reporting unethical conduct to outside third parties) through open and honest debate.

9. *Describe the sources of organizational behavior research evidence.* Five sources of OB research evidence are meta-analyses (statistically pooled evidence from several studies), field studies (evidence from real-life situations), laboratory studies (evidence from contrived situations), sample surveys (questionnaire data), and case studies (observation of a single person, group, or organization).

Key Terms

Organization, 5	Social capital, 15	Morally attentive, 26
Organizational behavior, 6	Management, 16	Meta-analysis, 26
Theory Y, 9	Contingency approach, 18	Field study, 27
Total quality management, 11	Ethics, 20	Laboratory study, 27
E-business, 12	Corporate social responsibility, 20	Sample survey, 27
Human capital, 15	Whistle-blowing, 26	Case study, 27

OB in Action Case Study

John Mackey, Cofounder and Co-CEO of Whole Foods Market, Believes in "Conscious Capitalism"[104]

What is conscious capitalism?

First, you have to understand the basic principles that help capitalism flourish. One is property rights. You need the ability to trade your property, and to trade it

to pretty much whomever you want. Another is the rule of law—laws and regulations that are well understood so that you can factor them into your business decisions. The rule of law has to be applied equally to everyone. . . . You also need to have conscious businesses—that is, businesses that become conscious of their higher purpose, which is not just about maximizing profits and shareholder value.

Second, you have to recognize the stakeholder model: Customers, employees, investors, suppliers, larger communities, and the environment are all interdependent. You operate the business in such a way that it's not a zero-sum game.

Third, you need what we call conscious leadership. You could also call it servant leadership. Leaders identify their own flourishing with the flourishing of the organization. They're trying to serve the organization and its purpose.

Fourth, you have to create a conscious culture—a culture that allows the organization to fulfill its higher purpose, implements the stakeholder model, and enables conscious leadership to flourish.

So, what are the core principles of Whole Foods, and where do they come from?

I think business enterprises are like any other communities. They can aspire to the highest values that have inspired humans throughout time. You can use different value models, but I like Plato's the good, the true, and the beautiful. Add the heroic to that—meaning changing and improving the world and standing up for what you believe is true and right and good. I think Whole Foods' highest purpose is a heroic one: to try to change and improve our world. That is what animates me personally. That is what animates the company. I resisted that purpose for a long time, by the way. I actually thought we were in some variant of service—that it was really about fulfilling the good. The team members consistently told me I was wrong, that we had a different purpose. It was this more heroic purpose.

In terms of the age-old debate about whether companies exist for the shareholders or for something else, is there one group? Is it customers? Is it employees? Or is it this purpose?

That gets back to the second principle of conscious capitalism—the stakeholder model. I think it's kind of deep in human nature to think in terms of the zero sum. If one stakeholder is winning, someone else must be losing. It comes from sports, where there is one winner and lots of losers, and this idea of a fixed pie, where if someone is getting a bigger piece, someone else has to be getting a smaller piece, and what's needed for social justice is to make sure people get equal pieces. But a conscious business recognizes that you can have an expanding pie, and potentially everyone can get a larger piece.

I'll give you a simple example: Management's job at Whole Foods is to make sure that we hire good people, that they are well trained, and that they flourish in the workplace, because we found that when people are really happy in their jobs, they provide much higher degrees of service to the customers. Happy team members result in happy customers. Happy customers do more business with you. They become advocates for your enterprise, which results in happy investors. That is a win, win, win, win strategy. You can expand it to include your suppliers and the communities where you do business, which are tied in to this prosperity circle. A metaphor I like is the spiral, which tends to move upward but doesn't move in a straight line.

Questions for Discussion

1. What role, if any, does McGregor's Theory Y play at Whole Foods? Explain.
2. How does Whole Foods build human and social capital?
3. How does this case bring the profile of the 21st-century manager (Table 1–3) to life? Explain.
4. Where would you locate Whole Foods on Carroll's global corporate social responsibility pyramid in Figure 1–3? Explain.
5. Which of the seven moral principles in Table 1–4 appear to be in force at Whole Foods? Explain.
6. What appeals to you (or does not appeal to you) about working at Whole Foods? Explain.

Legal/Ethical Challenge

School Reform Advocate Michelle Rhee Wants to Put Students First

"There are lots of problems with seniority-based layoffs. The *L.A. Times* looked at which teachers were recently laid off in Los Angeles and bumped that list up against the teacher-performance data they have there. Many who were laid off were in the top quartile. That's just insane! The union president says this is the only way to do it that's fair. But it's in direct contradiction to what's right for kids. If they had done it by quality, not seniority, it would have been more cost effective and better for stability; you would have laid off fewer teachers. Those are the kinds of policies we're going after—and they exist everywhere."[105]

As a parent, school board member, or school administrator, what position would you take on this ethics-laden issue?

1. By virtue of their many years of service, senior teachers have earned the right to be protected from a layoff. (What is your ethical reasoning for this view?)
2. Like students, teachers should be graded and rewarded in terms of documented performance. (What general

criteria should be applied to determine who gets laid off? What is your ethical argument?)

3. Younger, lower-paid teachers are in a better position to survive a layoff than their longer-tenured colleagues. (What is your ethical argument?)

4. The only truly fair approach is to have a lottery drawing to determine who gets laid off. (What are the ethical arguments for and against this approach?)

5. Invent other interpretations or options. Discuss.

Web Resources

For study material and exercises that apply to this chapter, visit our website, **www.mhhe.com/kreitner10e**

chapter 2

Managing Diversity: Releasing Every Employee's Potential

 Learning Objectives

When you finish studying the material in this chapter, you should be able to:

LO.1   Define diversity and review the four layers of diversity.

LO.2   Explain the difference between affirmative action and managing diversity.

LO.3   Explain why Alice Eagly and Linda Carli believe that a woman's career is best viewed as traveling through a labyrinth.

LO.4   Review the demographic trends pertaining to racial groups, educational mismatches, and an aging workforce.

LO.5   Highlight the managerial implications of increasing diversity in the workforce.

LO.6   Describe the positive and negative effects of diversity by using social categorization theory and information/decision-making theory.

LO.7   Identify the barriers and challenges to managing diversity.

LO.8   Discuss the organizational practices used to effectively manage diversity as identified by R Roosevelt Thomas Jr.

Why Did Management Ignore Complaints of Sexual Harassment?

Michelle Barfield was prepared for prisoners to harass her when she started her new job as an Arizona Department of Corrections officer at the maximum-security unit in Florence two years ago.

What Barfield did not count on was receiving worse treatment from her co-workers.

A federal jury found the treatment Barfield endured from a group of male co-workers, including vulgar comments about sexual acts and references to her interracial marriage, was unacceptable. The jury awarded her more than $600,000 in U.S. District Court last week. . . .

Corrections Director Charles Ryan said the agency is taking harassment claims seriously and has implemented an additional training program for supervisors since Barfield's allegations came to light. . . .

Barfield said her allegations of harassment were ignored or minimized by supervisors at the prison in Florence, so she remains skeptical about the agency's commitment to dismantling the corrections officers' "boys clubs" that she said dominate some units around the state. . . .

Barfield claims the harassment began almost as soon as she started working in Florence's Central Unit in November 2008, with her co-workers making comments about her looks, her body, and her motivations for working in a prison.

"They said, 'No girl wants to work here unless they want to (have sex with) an inmate or another officer,' Barfield recalled in a recent interview.

At first, Barfield said, she told the other corrections officers not to speak to her that way. Then she tried ignoring it.

Her fellow officers told Barfield that their behavior—including handcuffing Barfield to an inmate's cell and tearing her rotator cuff in an unsolicited wrestling match—were part of an initiation into the unit.

As time went on without her co-workers changing their behavior, Barfield brought the situation to the attention of a commander.

The commander, Sgt. David Wall, initially encouraged her to not file a report "so it wouldn't become a (human resources) issue," Barfield said.

Wall was later reprimanded by a deputy warden in Florence. . . .

One officer was fired, but the situation hardly improved. Other officers responded by not communicating with her, a danger in that work environment.

Word also got out in the prison yard of Barfield's interracial marriage. Soon, suspected members of a White supremacist prison gang began making remarks about her marriage.[1]

The chapter-opening vignette illustrates sexual harassment. **Sexual harassment** reflects unwanted sexual attention that creates an adverse or hostile work environment and it is more widespread than you might think. A recent poll of 12,000 people in 24 countries showed that 10% were sexually or physically harassed.[2] Sexual harassment is a violation of Equal Employment Opportunity laws in the United States, and it negatively affects victims like Michelle Barfield in multiple ways.

Effectively managing diversity is important because it affects employees' satisfaction, productivity, turnover, and safety, but it also makes good business sense. Unfortunately, some organizations like the Arizona Department of Corrections and Walmart are missing the mark when it comes to managing diversity, and the result can be costly lawsuits. Michelle Barfield received more than $600,000 from the Arizona Department of Corrections, and Walmart settled a class-action discrimination case for $12 million in 2010. Walmart is currently facing another class-action lawsuit that involves 1.5 million female employees who claim they were paid less than men for doing similar work and that they were given fewer promotional opportunities than men. The US Supreme Court is planning to hear the case.[3]

Managing diversity is a sensitive, potentially volatile, and sometimes uncomfortable issue. Yet managers are required to deal with it in the name of organizational survival. Accordingly, the purpose of this chapter is to help you get a better understanding of this important context for organizational behavior. We begin by defining diversity. Next, we build the business case for diversity and then discuss the barriers and challenges associated with managing diversity. The chapter concludes by describing the organizational practices used to manage diversity effectively.

LO.1 Defining Diversity

TO THE POINT

Why is it important for managers to focus on managing diversity?

Diversity represents the multitude of individual differences and similarities that exist among people. It is not an issue of age, race, or gender. It is not an issue of being heterosexual, gay, or lesbian or of being Catholic, Jewish, Protestant, Muslim, or Buddhist. Diversity also does not pit white males against all other groups of people. Diversity pertains to the host of individual differences that make all of us unique and different from others.

This section begins our journey into managing diversity by first reviewing the key dimensions of diversity. Because many people associate diversity with affirmative action, this section compares affirmative action with managing diversity. They are not the same.

Layers of Diversity

Like seashells on a beach, people come in a variety of shapes, sizes, and colors. This variety represents the essence of diversity. Lee Gardenswartz and Anita Rowe, a team of diversity experts, identified four layers of diversity to help distinguish the important ways in which people differ (see Figure 2–1). Taken together, these layers define your personal identity and influence how each of us sees the world.

Figure 2–1 shows that personality is at the center of the diversity wheel. Personality is at the center because it represents a stable set of characteristics that is responsible for a person's identity. The dimensions of personality are discussed later in Chapter 5. The next layer of diversity consists of a set of internal dimensions that are referred to as surface-level dimensions of diversity. These dimensions, for the most part, are not within our control, but they strongly influence our attitudes and expectations and assumptions about others, which, in turn, influence our behavior. Take the encounter experienced by an African American woman in middle management while vacationing at a resort:

figure 2-1   The Four Layers of Diversity

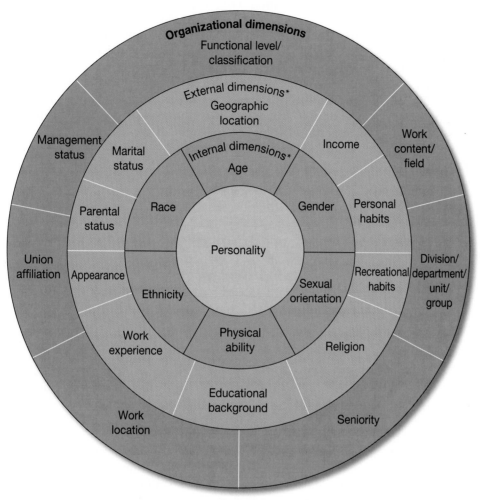

*Internal dimensions and external dimensions are adapted from Marilyn Loden and Judy B Rosener, *Workforce America!* (Homewood, IL: Business One Irwin, 1991).

SOURCE: L Gardenswartz and A Rowe, *Diverse Teams at Work: Capitalizing on the Power of Diversity* (New York: McGraw-Hill, 1994), p 33. © 1994.

Example. While I was sitting by the pool, "a large 50-ish white male approached me and demanded that I get him extra towels. I said, 'Excuse me?' He then said, 'Oh, you don't work here,' with no shred of embarrassment or apology in his voice."[4]

Stereotypes regarding one or more of the surface-level dimensions of diversity most likely influenced this man's behavior toward the woman.

Figure 2–1 reveals that the next layer of diversity is composed of external influences, which are referred to as secondary dimensions of diversity. They represent individual differences that we have a greater ability to influence or control. Examples include where you grew up and live today, your religious affiliation, whether

connect™ Go to www.mcgrawhillconnect.com for an interactive exercise to test your knowledge of the layers of diversity.

sexual harassment Unwanted sexual attention that creates an adverse or hostile work environment.

diversity The host of individual differences that make people different from and similar to each other.

you are married and have children, and your work experiences. These dimensions also exert a significant influence on our perceptions, behavior, and attitudes.

Consider religion as an illustration. Organizations are paying more attention to religious discrimination in light of the fact that the frequency of religious discrimination claims has doubled in the last 15 years. Employment laws require organizations to "reasonably accommodate employees' sincerely held religious practices unless doing so would impose an undue hardship on the employer. A reasonable religious accommodation is any adjustment to the work environment that will allow the employee to practice his religion. Examples of reasonable accommodation include: flexible scheduling, voluntary substitutions or swaps, job reassignments and lateral transfers, and modification of grooming requirements."[5]

Back to the Chapter-Opening Case

Which layers of diversity from Figure 2–1 contributed to the sexual harassment experienced by Michelle Barfield?

The final layer of diversity includes organizational dimensions such as seniority, job title and function, and work location.

LO.2   Affirmative Action and Managing Diversity

Effectively managing diversity requires organizations to adopt a new way of thinking about differences among people. Rather than pitting one group against another, managing diversity entails recognition of the unique contribution every employee can make. Companies should not try to manage diversity because it is the "socially acceptable" thing to do. Rather, managing diversity is the right thing to do because it helps organizations to achieve their business goals. For example, Cisco, Whole Foods Market, Container Store, Adobe Systems, and Zappos.com focus on hiring and promoting diverse employees as part of a strategy to create and market products appealing to a broader and more diverse customer base.[6] This section highlights the differences between affirmative action and managing diversity.

Go to www.mcgrawhillconnect.com for a self-assessment on appreciating and valuing diversity.

Affirmative Action   Affirmative action is an outgrowth of equal employment opportunity (EEO) legislation. The goal of this legislation is to outlaw discrimination and to encourage organizations to proactively prevent discrimination. **Discrimination** occurs when employment decisions about an individual are due to reasons not associated with performance or are not related to the job. For example, organizations cannot discriminate on the basis of race, color, religion, national origin, sex, age, physical and mental disabilities, and pregnancy.

In contrast to the proactive perspective of EEO legislation, **affirmative action** is an artificial intervention aimed at giving management a chance to correct an imbalance, an injustice, a mistake, or outright discrimination that occurred in the past. Affirmative action does not legitimize quotas. Quotas are illegal. They can only be imposed by judges who conclude that a company has engaged in discriminatory practices. It also is important to note that under no circumstances does affirmative action require companies to hire unqualified people.

Although affirmative action created tremendous opportunities for women and minorities, it does not foster the type of thinking that is needed to effectively manage diversity. For example, a meta-analysis summarizing 35 years of research involving 29,000 people uncovered the following results: (1) affirmative action plans are perceived more negatively by white males than women and minorities because it is perceived to work against their own self-interests; (2) affirmative action plans are viewed more positively by people who are liberals and Democrats than conservatives and Republicans; and (3) affirmative action plans are not supported by people who possess racist or sexist attitudes.[7]

Affirmative action programs also were found to negatively affect the women and minorities expected to benefit from them. Research demonstrated that women and minorities, supposedly hired on the basis of affirmative action, felt negatively stigmatized as unqualified or incompetent. They also experienced lower job satisfaction and more stress than employees supposedly selected on the basis of merit.[8] Another study, however, showed that these negative consequences were reduced for women when a merit criterion was included in hiring decisions. In other words, women hired under affirmative action programs felt better about themselves and exhibited higher performance when they believed they were hired because of their competence rather than their gender.[9]

Managing Diversity   **Managing diversity** entails enabling people to perform up to their maximum potential. It focuses on changing an organization's culture and infrastructure such that people provide the highest productivity possible. Sodexo, a firm in the hospitality industry with 380,000 employees in 80 countries, is a good example of a company that effectively manages diversity. Sodexo was rated by DiversityInc in 2010 as the very best company for diversity based on its annual 200-question survey of 449 firms (see Real World/Real People on page 38).[10] Ann Morrison, a diversity expert, conducted a study of 16 organizations that successfully managed diversity. Her results uncovered three key strategies for success: education, enforcement, and exposure.

She describes them as follows:

Example. The education component of the strategy has two thrusts: one is to prepare nontraditional managers for increasingly responsible posts, and the other is to help traditional managers overcome their prejudice in thinking about and interacting with people who are of a different sex or ethnicity. The second component of the strategy, enforcement, puts teeth in diversity goals and encourages behavior change. The third component, exposure to people with different backgrounds and characteristics, adds a more personal approach to diversity by helping managers get to know and respect others who are different.[11]

You can see from this description that Sodexo uses all of these diversity strategies.

In summary, both consultants and academics believe that organizations should strive to manage diversity rather than simply using affirmative action. More is said about managing diversity later in this chapter.

Building the Business Case for Managing Diversity

The rationale for managing diversity goes well beyond legal, social, and moral reasons. Quite simply, the primary reason for managing diversity is the ability to grow and maintain a business in an increasingly competitive marketplace. Consider what William Weldon, Chairman and CEO of Johnson & Johnson, had to say about managing diversity.

TO THE POINT
Which of the managerial implications of diversity are consistent with recommendations for reconciling the effects of diverse work environments?

---

discrimination Occurs when employment decisions are based on factors that are not job related.

affirmative action Focuses on achieving equality of opportunity in an organization.

managing diversity Creating organizational changes that enable all people to perform up to their maximum potential.

real WORLD // real PEOPLE

Sodexo Ranked as Best Company for Managing Diversity

The deep leadership commitment to diversity is an integral part of Sodexo's moral fiber and strong ethics. Global CEO Michel Landel, U.S. President and CEO George Chavel, and Senior Vice President and Global Chief Diversity Officer Dr. Rohini Anand are constantly on the front lines of new and expanded diversity initiatives.

Sodexo has led every other company in its ability to implement, measure and assess strong internal diversity initiatives. Its Spirit of Mentoring program is an example for all organizations of a focused, practical and extremely comprehensive mentoring effort that includes advance training and benchmarks at regular intervals to examine how mentoring pairs are relating to each other and accomplishing goals.

Sodexo is at the forefront of creative ways to examine the ROI of diversity initiatives. Recently, for example, the company undertook a comprehensive study of more than 1,700 members of employee-resource groups to understand their perceived benefits of group participation.

The company's diversity training, mandatory for its entire work force, offers an example to others. Over the past five years, Sodexo has developed an integrated metrics tool that assesses behavior at all levels of the organization, including the C-suite. The company measures its progress with its Sodexo Diversity Index, an innovative scorecard that tracks both quantitative and qualitative results.

Sodexo also reaches out externally, holding forums and meetings with clients to improve their diversity initiatives and to help them understand how critical diversity is to everyone's success. Sodexo's strong reputation and proven success in diversity has led many of its clients to tell DiversityInc that's why they enhanced their business relationship with the food-service company.

How did Sodexo use the diversity strategies of education, enforcement, and exposure?

SOURCE: Excerpted from "No. 1: Sodexo." Retrieved December 27, 2010, from http://www.diversityinc.com/article/7252/.

Part of Sodexo's success is attributed to its progressive approach toward managing diversity. Would you like to work at the company?

Example. Diversity and inclusion are part of the fabric of our businesses and are vital to our future success worldwide. The principles of diversity and inclusion are rooted in Our Credo [the company's values] and enhance our ability to deliver products and services to advance the health and well-being of people throughout the world. We cannot afford to reduce our focus on these critical areas in any business climate.[12]

Many companies understand and endorse this proposition. Research also indirectly supports the logic of this strategy. For example, a study of 207 companies in 11 industries demonstrated that financial performance was higher when the organization's top management team (TMT) was diverse and collocated in the same location.[13]

Organizations cannot use diversity as a strategic advantage if employees fail to contribute their full talents, abilities, motivation, and commitment. It is thus essential for an organization to create an environment or culture that allows all employees to reach their full potential. Managing diversity is a critical component of creating such an environment.

This section explores the business need to manage diversity by first reviewing the demographic trends that are creating an increasingly diverse workforce. We then summarize the managerial implications of demographic diversity and review evidence pertaining to the positive and negative effects associated with diverse work environments.

Increasing Diversity in the Workforce

Workforce demographics, which are statistical profiles of the characteristics and composition of the adult working population, are an invaluable human-resource planning aid. They enable managers to anticipate and adjust for surpluses or shortages of appropriately skilled individuals. Consider the implications associated with an aging population that will be retiring in record numbers over the next decade, a US birthrate that is too low to provide enough workers to meet future demands, a workforce in 2050 that is composed of 55% minority employees, a labor shortage caused by a population that does not possess the knowledge and skills needed in a knowledge economy, and one in seven US adults who lack the literacy skills to read anything beyond a child's picture book.[14] Experts predict that these demographic trends will create a serious shortage of skilled workers in the future.

Moreover, general population demographics give managers a preview of the values and motives of current and future employees. Demographic changes in the US workforce during the last two or three decades have immense implications for organizational behavior. This section explores the managerial implications of four demographic-based characteristics of the workforce: (1) women navigate a labyrinth after breaking the glass ceiling, (2) racial groups are encountering a glass ceiling and perceived discrimination, (3) there is a mismatch between workers' educational attainment and occupational requirements, and (4) generational differences in an aging workforce.

LO.3 Women Navigate a Labyrinth after Breaking the Glass Ceiling   *The Wall Street Journal* journalists—Carol Hymowitz and Timothy Schellhardt—coined the term **glass ceiling** in 1986. The term *glass ceiling* was used to represent an absolute barrier or solid roadblock that prevented women from advancing to higher-level positions. This ceiling resulted in women finding themselves stuck in lower-level jobs, ones that do not have profit-and-loss responsibility, and those with less visibility, power, and influence. There are a variety of statistics that support the prior existence of a glass ceiling. For example, women earned 77 cents on the dollar relative to men's earnings in 2010, and women received fewer stock options than male executives, even after controlling for level of education, performance, and job function.[15] A recent longitudinal study of 4,100 MBA students from leading business schools also revealed four key trends: (1) men started their careers at higher levels than women even after controlling for work experience, industry, and region; (2) men reported higher starting salaries after controlling for job levels and industry; (3) men moved up the career ladder further and faster than women; and (4) men had higher career satisfaction over time than women.[16] These differences are a function of several potential causes:[17]

- Women face discrimination.
- Women spend more time handling domestic and child care issues than men.
- Women encounter more obstacles to their leadership and authority than men (e.g., negative stereotypes).
- Women accumulate less continuous work experience than men because they periodically exit the workforce for family or motherhood.

workforce demographics Statistical profiles of adult workers.

glass ceiling Invisible barrier blocking women and minorities from top management positions.

- Women have less social capital and lower breadth of personal networks than men.
- Organizations have increased demands for longer hours, travel, and relocation and these demands conflict with the domestic roles held by many married women.

Back to the Chapter-Opening Case

Which of the potential causes of discrimination played a role in Barfield's experience at the Arizona Department of Corrections?

Carol Hymowitz, the same journalist who initially introduced the metaphor of a glass ceiling, wrote an article in *The Wall Street Journal* in 2004 that concluded women had broken through the glass ceiling. This led renowned researcher Alice Eagly and her colleague Linda Carli to conduct a thorough investigation into the organizational life of women. They summarized their findings in a 2007 book titled *Through the Labyrinth.* These authors agreed with Hymowitz after analyzing many types of longitudinal data. We arrived at the following results after updating data reported in Eagly and Carli's book. There were many more female CEOs in 2010 (12 and 26 female CEOs within *Fortune* 500 and *Fortune* 1000 firms, respectively) and more women in managerial, professional, and related occupations (51% in 2009) than there were in the 1980s and 1990s.[18] Statistics further showed that women made great strides in terms of (1) educational attainment (women earned the majority of bachelor's, master's, professional, and PhD degrees from 2006 through 2010); (2) holding seats on boards of directors of *Fortune* 500 firms (a 6.1% increase between 1995 and 2010); (3) obtaining leadership positions in educational institutions (in 2010, women represented 18.7% of college presidents and 29.9% of board members); and (4) receiving federal court appointments (in 2010, 22% and 28% of federal district court judges and US circuit court judges, respectively, were women).[19]

You can interpret the above statistics in one of two ways. On the one hand, you might believe that women are underpaid and underrepresented in leadership positions and that they are victims of discriminatory organizational practices. Alternatively, you can agree with Alice Eagly and Linda Carli's conclusion that

Example. women have made substantial progress but still have quite far to go to achieve equal representation as leaders. . . . These statistics demonstrate considerable social change and show that women's careers have become far more successful than they were in the past. Men still have more authority and higher wages, but women have been catching up. Because some women have moved into the most elite leadership roles, absolute barriers are a thing of the past.[20]

Indra Nooyi, CEO of Pepsi, is a good example of someone who has successfully moved through a career labyrinth. She was rated as the most powerful woman in business in 2009 and 2010 by *Fortune*. She is very focused on growing Pepsi's revenues by offering healthier food and beverages.

These authors believe that women are not victims. Rather, they propose that a woman's career follows a pattern more characteristic of traveling through a labyrinth.

A labyrinth is represented by a maze and is defined as "an intricate structure of interconnecting passages through which it is difficult to find one's way."[21] Eagly and Carli used the labyrinth metaphor because they believe that a woman's path to success is

real WORLD // real PEOPLE

CareFirst BlueCross BlueShield Helps Employees Move Up the Career Ladder

Julie Fisher began working for the company about 25 years ago as a claims examiner. "It's such a big company with so much opportunity," It helped, too, that Fisher's immediate bosses focused heavily on development and often acted as mentors, both formally and informally.

In fact, their mere presence was inspirational. "I would see different women here in the company being very successful and progressing and being valued," says Fisher. "There are a number of females in significant roles here and they are very accessible."

In fact, 62 percent of CareFirst's management team is female. And the organization has long had family-friendly policies in place—like flexible scheduling. "I've always had management that was very flexible," says Fisher, who had four children while working at CareFirst and at times had to take advantage of that flexibility. "In turn, I've made it a practice to ensure that flexibility was there as well" for other employees.

And now that her children are in college, Fisher is equally grateful for the company's benefits, including its retirement and saving plans.

SOURCE: Excerpted from C B Antoniades, "Best Places to Work 2010," *Baltimore Magazine.net,* February 2010, http://www.baltimoremagazine.net/features/2010/02/best-places-to-work-2010.

Julie Fisher is very happy with her employer's approach toward managing diversity.

---

not direct or simple, but rather contains twists, turns, and obstructions, particularly for married women with children. Managers and organizations thus are advised to develop policies, procedures, and programs aimed at helping women to navigate their way through the maze of career success (see Real World/Real People featuring Julie Fisher at CareFirst BlueCross Blueshield above). More will be said about this later in this section.

LO.4 **Racial Groups Are Encountering a Glass Ceiling and Perceived Discrimination** Historically, the United States has been a black-and-white country. The percentage change in US population between 2000 and 2050 by race reveals that this pattern no longer exists (see Figure 2–2). Figure 2–2 shows that Asians and Hispanics are expected to have the largest growth in population between 2000 and 2050. The Asian population will triple to 33 million by 2050, and the Hispanics will increase their ranks by 118% to 102.6 million. Hispanics will account for 25% of the population in 2050. All told, the so-called minority groups will constitute approximately 55% of the workforce in 2050 according to the Census Bureau.

Unfortunately, three additional trends suggest that current-day minority groups are experiencing their own glass ceiling. First, minorities in general are advancing less in the managerial and professional ranks than whites. For example, whites, blacks, Asians, and Hispanics or Latinos held 38%, 29.21%, 48.8%, and 19.4% of all managerial, professional, and related occupations in the United States in 2009.[22] Second, the number of race-based charges of discrimination that were deemed to show reasonable cause by the US Equal Employment Opportunity Commission increased from 294 in 1995 to 1,061 in 2008. Companies paid a total of $79.3 million to resolve these claims outside of litigation in 2008.[23] Third, minorities also

figure 2–2 Percentage Change in US Population by Race

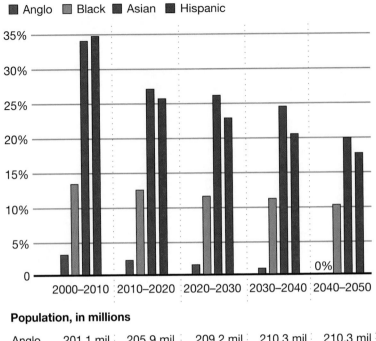

Population, in millions

	2000–2010	2010–2020	2020–2030	2030–2040	2040–2050
Anglo	201.1 mil	205.9 mil	209.2 mil	210.3 mil	210.3 mil
Black	40.5	45.4	50.4	55.9	61.4
Asian	14.2	18.0	22.6	28.0	33.4
Hispanic	47.8	59.8	73.1	87.6	102.6

Source: US Census Bureau   Associated Press

SOURCE: G C Armas, "Almost Half of US Likely to Be Minorities by 2050," *Arizona Republic,* March 18, 2004, p A5. US Census Bureau, Table 1a, "Projected Population of the US by Race and Hispanic Origin: 2000–2050," www.census.gov/ipc/www/usinterimproj/. Used by permission of the Associated Press.

tend to earn less personal income than whites. Median annual earnings in 2009 were $51,861, $32,584, $65,469, and $38,039 for whites, blacks, Asians, and Hispanics, respectively. Interestingly, Asians had the highest median income.[24] Finally, a number of studies showed that minorities experienced more perceived discrimination, racism-related stress, and less psychological support than whites.[25]

Mismatch between Educational Attainment and Occupational Requirements Approximately 28% of the labor force has a college degree, and college graduates earn substantially more than workers with less education.[26] At the same time, however, three trends suggest a mismatch between educational attainment and the knowledge and skills needed by employers. First, recent studies show that college graduates, while technically and functionally competent, are lacking in terms of teamwork skills, critical thinking, and analytic reasoning. Second, there is a shortage of college graduates in technical fields related to science, math, and engineering. Third, organizations are finding that high-school graduates working in entry-level positions do not possess the basic skills needed to perform effectively. This latter trend is partly due to a national high-school graduation rate of only 75% and the existence of about 32 million adults in the United States that are functionally illiterate.[27] Literacy is defined as "an individual's ability to read, write, and speak English, compute and solve problems at levels of proficiency necessary to function on the job and in society, to achieve one's goals, and develop one's knowledge and potential."[28] Illiteracy costs corporate America around $60 billion a year in lost productivity. These statistics are worrisome to both government officials and business leaders.

The key issue confronting organizations in the United States, and any country that wants to compete in a global economy, is whether or not the population has the skills and abilities needed to drive economic growth. Unfortunately, results from a study commissioned by the National Center on Education and the Economy suggests that the United States is losing ground on this issue. Findings were summarized in a book titled *Tough Choice or Tough Times: The Report of the New Commission on the Skills of the American Workforce.* The authors arrived at the following conclusions based on their analysis.

Example. Whereas for most of the 20th century the United States could take pride in having the best-educated workforce in the world, that is no longer true. Over the past 30 years, one country after another has surpassed us in the proportion of their entering workforce with the equivalent of a high-school diploma, and many more are on the verge of doing so. Thirty years ago, the United States could lay claim to having 30 percent of the world's population of college students. Today that proportion has fallen to 14 percent and is continuing to fall.

While our international counterparts are increasingly getting more education, their young people are getting a better education as well. American students and young adults place anywhere from the middle to the bottom of the back in all three continuing comparative studies of achievement in mathematics, science, and general literacy in the advanced industrial nations.

While our relative position in the world's education league tables has continued its long slow decline, the structure of the global economy has continued to evolve. Every day, more and more of the work that people do ends up in a digitized form. From X rays used for medical diagnostic purposes, to songs, movies, architectural drawings, technical papers, and novels, that work is saved on a hard disk and transmitted instantly over the Internet to someone near or far who makes use of it in an endless variety of ways. Because this is so, employers everywhere have access to a worldwide workforce composed of people who do not have to move to participate in work teams that are truly global. Because this is so, a swiftly rising number of American workers at every skill level are in direct competition with workers in every corner of the globe.[29]

These conclusions underscore the fact that the mismatch between educational attainment and occupational requirements have both short- and long-term implications for organizations and countries alike. American companies are more likely to outsource technical work to countries like India and China, to hire more immigrants to fill entry-level positions, to spend more money on employee training, and to use phased retirement programs that encourage skilled employees to work beyond retirement age.

Generational Differences in an Aging Workforce

America's population and workforce are getting older. By 2011, half of the US workforce will be over 50 years of age, and 80% will be over 50 by 2018.[30] Life expectancy is increasing as well. The number of people living into their 80s is increasing rapidly, and this group disproportionately suffers from chronic illness. The United States is not the only country with an aging population. The United Nations estimates that 33% of the population in developed countries will be over the age of 60 by 2050, and one in three people will be pensioners. These statistics led some experts to conclude that the global financial crises in 2009–2010 "will be nothing compared with the costs of an aging global population."[31]

An aging population in the United States underscores a potential skill gap in the future. As those employees in the Baby-Boom generation retire—the

real WORLD // real PEOPLE

CVS Caremark Implements Programs to Retain and Transfer Knowledge of Older Employees

CVS decided to implement a program aimed at transferring knowledge from older workers to younger ones upon learning that 7 percent of its employees were over 50.

Part of CVS's success stems from providing flexible programs and benefits that particularly appeal to older workers. A prime example is its "Snowbird" program, which allows older workers to transfer to different CVS/pharmacy locations on a seasonal basis. . . . "The retention rate of the snowbirds is significantly higher than the industry average," says David L. Casey, vice president, diversity officer for CVS Caremark. The program enables CVS to manage the swell of business in warm-climate stores during the winter, and the snowbirds drive customer loyalty. . . .

Another program CVS is piloting in Chicago has older pharmacists—some still working, some retired—mentor pharmacy technicians and high school students. It has proven to be as much a learning experience for the mentors as the mentees.

How does the Snowbird program drive customer loyalty?

SOURCE: Excerpted from J Mullich, "Coming of Age," *The Wall Street Journal,* October 7, 2010, p B6.

CVS Caremark operates more pharmacies than any other company in the United States. The company credits part of its success to its progressive approach toward diversity.

---

78 million people born between 1946 and 1964—the US workforce will lose the skills, knowledge, experience, and relationships possessed by the more than a quarter of all Americans. This situation will likely create skill shortages in fast-growing technical fields. Proactive companies like CVS Caremark have already implemented programs aimed at overcoming this knowledge transfer problem (see Real World/Real People above).

In addition to the challenges associated with an aging workforce, the four generations of employees working together underscores the need for managers to effectively deal with generational differences in values, attitudes, and behaviors among the workforce: A fifth generation will enter the workforce around 2020. For example, companies such as IBM, Lockheed Martin, Ernst & Young LLP, and Aetna have addressed this issue by providing training workshops on generational diversity.

Table 2–1 presents a summary of generational differences that exist across commonly labeled groups of people: Traditionalists, Baby Boomers, Gen Xers, Millennials (also knows as Gen Ys), and the forthcoming Gen 2020 group. Before examining these proposed differences, it is important to note that these labels and distinctions are generalizations and are used for the sake of discussion. There are always exceptions to the characterizations shown in Table 2–1 and all conclusions should be interpreted with caution.[32]

Table 2–1 reveals that Millennials account for the largest block of employees in the workforce, followed by Baby Boomers. This is important because many Millennials are being managed by Boomers who possess a very different set of personal traits. Traits, which are discussed in Chapter 5, represent stable physical and mental characteristics that form an individual's identity. Conflicting traits are likely to create friction between people. For example, the workaholic and

table 2–1   Generational Differences

	TRADITIONALISTS	BABY BOOMERS	GEN XERS	MILLENNIALS (GEN YS)	GEN 2020
Birth Time Span	1925–1945	1946–1964	1965–1979	1980–2001	2002–
Current Population	38.6 million	78.3 million	62 million	92 million	23 million
Key Historical Events	Great Depression, World War II, Korean War, Cold War era, Rise of suburbs	Vietnam War, Watergate, assassinations of John and Robert Kennedy and Martin Luther King, women's rights, Kent State killings, first man on the moon	MTV, AIDS epidemic, Gulf War, fall of Berlin Wall, Oklahoma City bombing, 1987 stock market crash, Bill Clinton-Monica Lewinsky scandal	September 11th terrorist attack, Google, Columbine High School shootings, Enron and other corporate scandals, wars in Iraq and Afghanistan, Hurricane Katrina, financial crisis of 2008 and high unemployment	Social media, election of Barack Obama, financial crisis of 2008 and high unemployment
Broad Traits	Patriotic, loyalty, discipline, conformist, high work ethic, respect for authority	Workaholic, idealistic, work ethic, competitive, materialistic, seeks personal fulfillment	Self-reliance, work/life balance, adaptable, cynical, distrust authority, independent, technologically savvy	Entitled, civic minded, close parental involvement, cyberliteracy, appreciate diversity, multitasking, work/life balance technologically savvy	Multitasking, online life, cyberliteracy, communicate fast and online
Defining Invention	Fax machine	Personal computer	Mobile phone	Google and Facebook	Social media and iPhone apps

SOURCE: Adapted from J C Meister and K Willyerd, *The 2020 Workplace* (NewYork: Harper Collins, 2010), pp 54–55; and R Alsop, *The Trophy Kids Grow Up* (San Francisco: Jossey-Bass, 2008) p. 5.

competitive nature of Boomers is likely to conflict with the entitled and work/life balance perspective of Millennials. As discussed in the next section, managers and employees alike will need to be sensitive to the generational differences highlighted in Table 2–1 in the pursuit of effectively managing diversity.

We would like to close our discussion about age by highlighting results from two recent meta-analyses. Researchers in the first study wanted to investigate the relationship between age and 10 dimensions of performance: core task performance, creativity, performance in training workshops, helping behavior at work, safety performance, counterproductive work behaviors, aggression at work, substance abuse, tardiness, and absenteeism. Results demonstrated that older workers displayed more helping and safety-oriented behavior. Older workers also exhibited less workplace aggression, substance abuse, tardiness, and absenteeism. Age was predominantly unrelated to core task performance, creativity, and performance in training workshops.[33] The second meta-analysis summarized research from over 800 studies. Results revealed that age was positively related to job attitudes toward work tasks, colleagues, supervisors, and organizations as a whole.[34] These two meta-analyses suggest that older employees can make valuable contributions in today's organizations.

LO.5 Managerial Implications of Demographic Diversity

It is important for organizations to draw the best talents and motivation from employees given the globally based and technologically connected nature of business. Organizations simply cannot afford to alienate segments of the workforce. Consider the issue of sexual orientation. A 2010 National Survey of Health and Behavior in the United States revealed that approximately 7% of women and 8% of men identify themselves as lesbian, gay, or bisexual. It also is currently legal in 30 states to fire employees who are lesbian or gay, and it is legal in 37 states to fire transgender individuals.[35] This situation is likely to create negative job attitudes and feelings of marginalization for lesbian, gay, bisexual, and transgender (LGBT) people.[36] Corporate law firm Bingham McCutchen and software developer Adobe Systems have tried to overcome this problem by instituting programs such as additional benefits for transgender employees and same-sex partner benefits.[37]

Regardless of sexual orientation, gender, race, or age, all organizations need to hire, retain, and develop a diverse workforce that provides a deeper pool of talent and unique perspectives that help the organization identify and meet the needs of a diverse customer base. For example, a Citizens Union Bank branch in Louisville, Kentucky, designed and staffed the branch with the goal of attracting more Latin American customers. The interior contains "bright, colorful walls of yellows and blues, large-scale photos of Latin American countries, comfortable couches, sit-down desks, a children's play area, a television tuned to Hispanic programming and even a vending area stocked with popular Latin American brand soft drinks and snacks. Along with its interior design, this branch has a different name: 'Nuestro Banco,' Spanish for 'Our Bank.'"[38] Branch deposits are setting records, and the CEO is planning to use this same model in other locations. The point to remember is that companies need to adopt policies and procedures that meet the needs of all employees. As such, programs such as day care, elder care, flexible work schedules, and benefits such as paternal leaves, less-rigid relocation policies, concierge services, and mentoring programs are likely to become more popular. In addition to this general conclusion, this section summarizes some unique managerial implications associated with effectively managing diversity in regards to demographic trends related to gender, race, education, and age.

Managing Gender-Based Diversity Special effort is needed to help women navigate through the labyrinth of career success. Organizations can do this by providing women the developmental assignments that prepare them for promotional opportunities.[39] Laura Desmond, CEO of Starcom Media Vest/The Americas, suggests that women need to help themselves advance to senior-level positions. She believes that "getting to the top requires setting goals and persevering—along with a willingness to seek stretch assignments that challenge and yield broader experiences." Andrea Jung, chair and CEO of Avon Products, further recommends that women should find a company or industry that they love because "the hard work and sacrifices required are only possible if you are fully engaged in your company and enjoy what you do."[40]

Women also can help their own cause by following seven recommendations proposed by Alice Eagly and Linda Carli, authors of *Through the Labyrinth*.[41] First, focus on being exceptionally competent and seek mentors or sponsors: Mentoring is discussed in Chapter 3. Research shows that men get promoted more frequently than women because they are more likely to get sponsored by their bosses and informal mentors.[42] Second, network to build social capital. Social capital, as you may recall from Chapter 1, represents the totality of one's professional and personal relationships. Learning to play the game of golf may

connect™ Go to www.mcgrawhillconnect.com for an interactive exercise to test your knowledge of generational differences in the workplace.

represent one viable strategy in this pursuit. For example, Susan Reed, editor-in-chief of *Golf for Women,* concluded that "[w]omen are just now learning what men have known for years: that golf may be one of the best relationship-building tools there is—both for business and for pleasure. Women resist going out for the afternoon because they're generally too responsible, shortsightedly so. Like men, they need to realize that leaving the work on the desk (which will be there anyway) and going out to play golf with a valuable business prospect is a good decision."[43] Third, seek work/life balance by delegating housework or hiring domestic help. Fourth, improve your negotiating skills. Fifth, take credit for your accomplishments; men do. Sixth, work toward creating a partnership with your spouse that leads to a mutually supportive relationship. Interviews with female executives suggest that a supportive spouse is a key factor in their career success. For example, the spouse of Indra Nooyi, CEO of PepsiCo, quit his job so that he could take on more responsibility for raising their children and running the house.[44] Finally, develop an interpersonal style that balances the need to be assertive and communal.

Managing Racially Based Diversity   Organizations are encouraged to educate employees about negative stereotyping regarding people of color, particularly when it comes to selecting and promoting leaders. Negative stereotypes not only block qualified people from obtaining promotions, but they can undermine a person's confidence in their ability to lead.[45] Given the projected increase in the number of Hispanics entering the workforce over the next 25 years, managers should consider progressive methods to recruit, retain, and integrate this segment of the population into their organizations. For example, Miami Children's Hospital and Shaw Industries in Dalton, Georgia, attempted to improve employee productivity, satisfaction, and motivation by developing customized training programs to improve the communication skills of their Spanish-speaking employees.[46] Research further reveals that the retention and career progression of minorities can be significantly enhanced through effective mentoring.

David Thomas, a researcher from Harvard University, conducted a three-year study of mentoring practices at three US corporations: a manufacturer, an electronics company, and a high-tech firm. His results revealed that successful people of color who advanced the furthest had a strong network of mentors and sponsors who nurtured their professional development. Findings also demonstrated that people of color should be mentored differently than their white counterparts. He recommended that organizations

---

Example. should provide a range of career paths, all uncorrelated with race, that lead to the executive suite . . . . Achieving this system, however, would require integrating the principles of opportunity, development, and diversity into the fabric of the organization's management practices and human resource systems. And an important element in the process would be to identify potential mentors, train them, and ensure that they are paired with promising professionals of color.[47]

Managing Education–Based Diversity   Mismatches between the amount of education needed to perform current jobs and the amount of education possessed by members of the workforce are growing. This trend creates two potential problems for organizations. First, there will be a shortage of qualified people in technical fields. To combat this issue, both Lockheed Martin and Agilent Technologies offer some type of paid apprenticeship or internship to attract high-school students interested in the sciences. Other companies such as State Street, Fidelity, and Cisco are attempting to overcome skill gaps by encouraging employees to participate in skills-based volunteering projects. The goal of these projects is to increase targeted skills through volunteer activities.[48]

real WORLD // real PEOPLE

BMW Effectively Redesigns Its Plant in Bavaria

Many of the ideas implemented in the 2017 line were physical changes to the workplace that would reduce wear and tear on workers' bodies and thus the likelihood that workers would call in sick. The new wooden flooring together with weight-adapted footwear, for example, reduced joint strain and exposure to static electricity jolts. The line workers also installed special chairs at several workstations, which allowed them to work sitting down or to relax for short periods during breaks . . . .

Design and equipment changes were complemented by changes in work practices. The line introduced job rotation across workstations during a shift in order to balance the load on workers' bodies . . . .

In addition, a physiotherapist developed strength and stretching exercises, which he did with the workers every day for the first few weeks.

Why does this example represent effective management of diversity?

SOURCE: Excerpted from C H Loch, F J Sting, N Bauer, and H Mauermann, "How BMW Is Defusing the Demographic Time Bomb," *Harvard Business Review*, March 2010, pp 101–2.

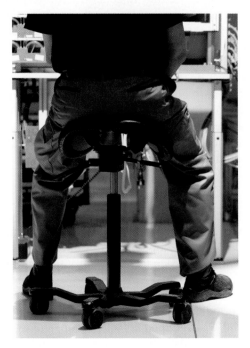

BWM designed chairs like this one to help employees do their jobs more effectively and comfortably. Would you like to sit on this chair throughout the work day?

Second, underemployment among college graduates threatens to erode job satisfaction and work motivation. As well-educated workers begin to look for jobs commensurate with their qualifications and expectations, absenteeism and turnover likely will increase. This problem underscores the need for job redesign (see the discussion in Chapter 8). In addition, organizations will need to consider interventions, such as realistic job previews and positive reinforcement programs (discussed in Chapter 9), to reduce absenteeism and turnover. On-the-job remedial skills and literacy training will be necessary to help the growing number of dropouts and illiterates cope with job demands.

Managing Age-Related Diversity   Organizations can take advantage of the human and social capital possessed by older employees by implementing programs that encourage employees to stay employed and transfer their knowledge to others. For example, BMW redesigned a plant's production line in Lower Bavaria in order to help older employees cope with the demands of physically demanding jobs and to reduce absenteeism (see Real World/Real People above). BMW experienced a 7% increase in productivity and a significant reduction in absenteeism based on these changes.[49] In order to make this type of strategy work, however, organizations will need to encourage Baby Boomers to remain in the workforce in lieu of retiring. The following seven initiatives can help to keep older workers engaged and committed to working.[50]

1. Provide challenging work assignments that make a difference to the firm.
2. Give the employee considerable autonomy and latitude in completing a task.

3. Provide equal access to training and learning opportunities when it comes to new technology.

4. Provide frequent recognition for skills, experience, and wisdom gained over the years.

5. Provide mentoring opportunities whereby older workers can pass on accumulated knowledge to younger employees.

6. Ensure that older workers receive sensitive, high-quality supervision.

7. Design a work environment that is both stimulating and fun.

Generational differences outlined in Table 2–1 can affect employee motivation and productivity, thereby necessitating a need to educate employees about working with diverse employees. For example, in-depth interviews with 50 workers over the age of 50 revealed that older workers felt blocked from important communication networks by younger employees and that their experience and skills were not valued. One respondent commented that "when older colleagues spoke during company meetings, younger colleagues would yawn, avoid eye contact with the speaker, doodle, or send text or instant messages under the table.[51] In contrast, some Gen Y employees believe that Baby Boomers want to be rewarded for the amount of time they spend at work rather than productivity. Best Buy's headquarters has attempted to reconcile this concern by creating an evaluation system that judges people only on task completion and performance. People are encouraged to work only as many hours as needed to get the job done.[52]

Go to www.mcgrawhillconnect.com for an interactive comprehension case exercise to learn how Leaseplan manages diversity.

Further, Gen X employees also report feeling "stuck in the middle." A Gen Xer named Michael noted, "I have an executive management team who are 8 to 12 years older than I am, with no plans for retirement in the near future. This leaves me stuck. I have been searching for business opportunities due to my distrust of Corporate America's motives."[53] Companies clearly need to find ways to motivate and retain Gen X employees who may be stuck in organizational hierarchies.

Traditional and Boomer managers also need to consider their approach toward managing the technologically savvy Gen Xers and Gen Ys. For example, Gen Xers and Ys are more likely to visit social networking sites during the workday, often perceiving this activity as a "virtual coffee break." In contrast, Traditional and Boomer managers are more likely to view this as wasted time, thereby leading to policies that attempt to shut down such activity. Experts suggest that restricting access to social media will not work in the long run if one wants to motivate younger employees.[54]

Finally, the shortage of skilled employees in the future underscores the need for organizations to recruit Millennials. Not only do Gen Ys represent the largest block of employees in the workforce (see Table 2–1), but they possess traits and skills needed in an increasingly technologically advanced economy. Organizations are responding to this issue by trying to create work environments that meet the needs of this segment of the workforce. For example, Growth Works Capital, Ernst & Young, Philip Morris USA, IBM, and Bearing Point implemented new rewards programs and job design interventions aimed at attracting and retaining Gen Y employees. Unilever similarly created a "consumerization architect" position that focuses on helping employees use popular technology after learning that Gen Y employees were dissatisfied with the company's use of information technology.[55]

Age-related diversity can cause unnecessary friction in the workplace. How can managers help facilitate helpful interactions across all generations?

LO.6 The Positive and Negative Effects of Diverse Work Environments

Earlier in this chapter we stated that effectively managing diversity is not only a good thing to do in order to attract and retain the most talented employees, but it makes good business sense. Although one can easily find testimonials from managers and organizations supporting this conclusion, we need to examine the validity of this claim by considering the evidence provided by OB research. As you will learn shortly, this research reveals that there are both positive and negative effects of diversity on important work outcomes. Organizational behavior researchers have explained these conflicting results by integrating two competing explanations of how diversity impacts employee attitudes, behavior, and performance. These explanations are based on what is called *social categorization theory* and *information/decision-making* theory. This section focuses on helping you understand how to garner the positive benefits of diversity by presenting a process model of diversity that integrates these two explanations.

Social Categorization Theory   A team of OB researchers describe the **social categorization theory** of diversity as follows:

Example. The social categorization perspective holds that similarities and differences are used as a basis for categorizing self and others into groups, with ensuing categorizations distinguishing between one's own in-group and one or more out-groups. People tend to like and trust in-group members more than out-group members and thus generally tend to favor in-groups over out-groups . . . . [W]ork group members are more positively inclined toward their group and the people within it if fellow group members are similar rather than dissimilar to the self.[56]

This perspective further implies that similarity leads to liking and attraction, thereby fostering a host of positive outcomes. If this were the case, one would expect that the more homogeneous a work group, the higher the member commitment and group cohesion, and the lower the amount of interpersonal conflicts. There is a large body of research supporting propositions derived from the social categorization model.[57]

For example, past research revealed that people who were different from their work units in racial or ethnic background were less psychologically committed to their organizations and less satisfied with their careers.[58] Additional studies showed that demographic diversity was associated with less cooperation among team members and more negative impressions toward people who were demographically different.[59] Finally, recent studies demonstrated that demographic diversity was associated with higher levels of employee depression, turnover, and deviance (i.e., exhibiting behavior that violates norms and threatens the well-being of the organization) and lower profits.[60] All told then, the social categorization model supports the idea that homogeneity is better than heterogeneity in terms of affecting work-related attitudes, behavior, and performance.

Information/Decision-Making Theory   The second theoretical point of view, referred to as **information/decision-making theory,** arrives at opposite predictions, proposing that diverse groups should outperform homogenous groups. The logic of this theory was described as follows:

Example. The idea is that diverse groups are more likely to possess a broader range of task-relevant knowledge, skills, and abilities that are distinct and nonredundant and to have different opinions and perspectives on the task at hand. This not only gives diverse groups a larger pool of resources, but may also have other beneficial effects.[61]

This perspective highlights three positive effects of diverse work groups.[62] First, diverse groups are expected to do a better job in earlier phases of problem solving because they are more likely to use their diverse backgrounds to generate a more comprehensive view of a problem. For example, gender and ethnic diversity can help work teams to better understand the needs and perspectives of a multicultural customer base. Second, the existence of diverse perspectives can help groups to brainstorm or uncover more novel alternatives during problem-solving activities. Finally, diversity can enhance the number of contacts a group or work unit has at its disposal. This broad network enables groups to gain access to new information and expertise, which results in more support for decisions than homogenous groups. Research supports this theory of diversity.

Team performance was positively related to a team's diversity in gender, ethnicity, age, and education.[63] Heterogeneous groups also were found to produce better-quality decisions and demonstrated higher productivity than homogenous groups.[64] Preliminary research also supports the idea that workforce diversity promotes creativity and innovation. This occurs through the sharing of diverse ideas and perspectives. Rosabeth Moss-Kanter, a management expert, was one of the first to investigate this relationship. Her results indicated that innovative companies deliberately used heterogeneous teams to solve problems, and they employed more women and minorities than less innovative companies. She also noted that innovative companies did a better job of eliminating racism, sexism, and classism.[65] A summary of 40 years of diversity research supported Moss-Kanter's conclusion that diversity can promote creativity and improve a team's decision making.[66]

Reconciling the Effects of Diverse Work Environments

Our previous discussion about social categorization theory and information/decision-making theory revealed that there are both positive and negative effects associated with diversity. The model in Figure 2–3 summarizes the process underlying these effects. Consistent with social categorization theory, there is a negative relationship between the amount of diversity in a work group and the quality of interpersonal processes and group dynamics within a work group (path A in Figure 2–3). This negative relationship ultimately results in negative outcomes because of the positive relationship between the quality of interpersonal processes and group dynamics and outcomes (path C). For example, gender and racial diversity in a work group foster more interpersonal conflict, which in turn results in lower job satisfaction, higher turnover, and lower productivity. Recent research shows that this type of negative pattern is more pronounced when groups have salient demographic fault-lines.[67] A **demographic fault line** is defined as "hypothetical dividing lines that may split a group into subgroups based on one or more attributes."[68] Fault lines form when work-group members possess varying demographic characteristics (e.g., gender, age, ethnicity), and negative interpersonal processes occur when people align themselves based on salient fault lines or demographic characteristics.

In contrast, research regarding the information/decision-making theory tells us that the amount of diversity in a work group is positively associated with

connect™ Go to www.mcgrawhillconnect.com for a video case on Andre Thornton and how he deals with diversity issues in his business.

---

social categorization theory Similarity leads to liking and attraction.

information/decision-making theory Diversity leads to better task-relevant processes and decision making.

demographic fault line A hypothetical dividing line that splits groups into demographically based subgroups.

figure 2–3 A Process Model of Diversity

A Process Model of Diversity

Dimensions of Diversity

Surface level
- Age
- Gender
- Physical ability
- Ethnicity
- Race

Deep level
- Value
- Attitudes
- Beliefs
- Personality

−(A) →

Interpersonal Processes and Group Dynamics

+(C) →

+(B) →

Task-Relevent Processes and Decision Making

+(D) →

Outcomes

Work attitudes
Work behavior
Performance

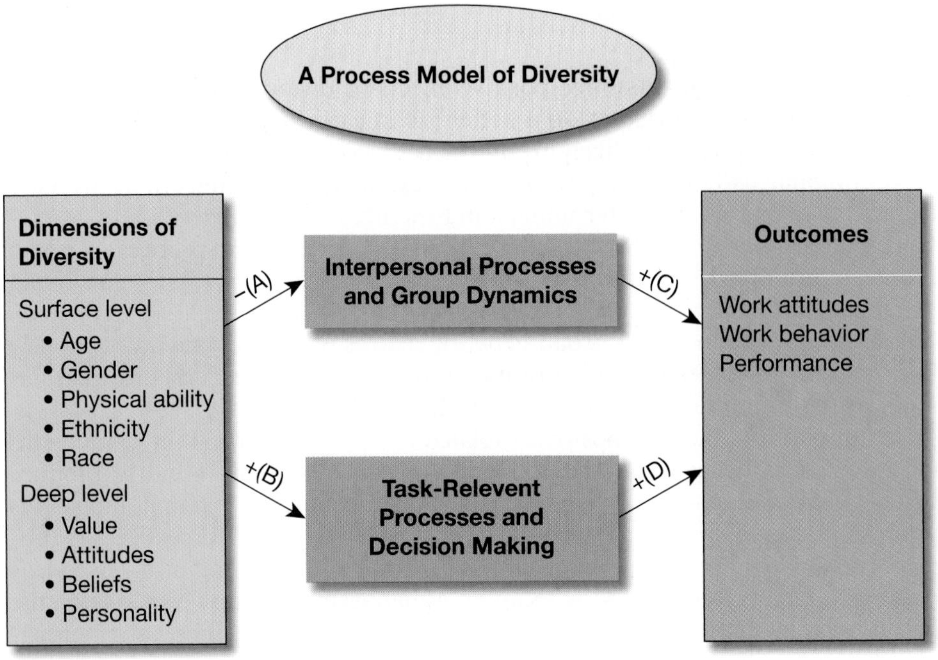

task-relevant processes and decision making (path B), which in turn fosters positive outcomes (path D). Gender and racial diversity in this case lead to positive outcomes because they lead to improved task-related processes and decision making. Two studies further demonstrated that the positive effects of diversity were stronger when work groups were open-minded, more readily discussed and shared information, and displayed more integrative behavior.[69]

Given that work-group diversity is associated with positive and negative outcomes, we need to consider what management can do to reduce the potential negative effects of diversity. First, organizations can target training to improve the inherent negative relationship between a work group's diversity and its interpersonal processes and group dynamics (path A in Figure 2–3). For example, training can be used to help employees understand demographic differences and to develop interpersonal skills that foster integrative and collaborative behavior.[70] This training might focus on conflict management, interpersonal influence, giving feedback, communication, and valuing differences. Second, managers can seek ways to help employees ease the tensions of working in diverse groups. Such efforts might include the creation of support groups. Finally, steps could be taken to reduce the negative effects of unconscious stereotyping, which is discussed in Chapter 7, and increase the use of group goals in heterogeneous groups. Rewarding groups to accomplish group goals might encourage group members to focus on their common objectives rather than on demographic fault lines that are unrelated to performance.

Back to the Chapter-Opening Case

Based on the process model of diversity, what should management at the Arizona Department of Corrections do to reduce future incidents of sexual harassment?

LO.7 Barriers and Challenges to Managing Diversity

▶ ·

TO THE POINT
What are the most
common barriers to
implementing successful
diversity programs?

· ·

We introduced this chapter by noting that diversity is a sensitive, potentially vola-tile, and sometimes uncomfortable issue. It is therefore not surprising that organi-zations encounter significant barriers when trying to move forward with managing diversity. The following is a list of the most common barriers to implementing successful diversity programs:[71]

1. *Inaccurate stereotypes and prejudice.* This barrier manifests itself in the belief that differences are viewed as weaknesses. In turn, this promotes the view that diversity hiring will mean sacrificing competence and quality.

2. *Ethnocentrism.* The ethnocentrism barrier represents the feeling that one's cultural rules and norms are superior or more appropriate than the rules and norms of another culture. This barrier is thoroughly discussed in Chapter 4.

3. *Poor career planning.* This barrier is associated with the lack of opportunities for diverse employees to get the type of work assignments that qualify them for senior management positions.

4. *A negative diversity climate.* Climate is generally viewed as employee percep-tions about an organization's formal and informal policies, practices, and procedures. **Diversity climate** is a subcomponent of an organization's overall climate and is defined as the employees' aggregate "perceptions about the organization's diversity-related formal structure characteristics and informal values."[72] Diversity climate is positive when employees view the organization as being fair to all types of employees; the concept of organizational fairness is discussed in Chapter 8. Recent research revealed that a positive diversity climate enhanced the positive effects of diversity while a negative diversity climate reduced the positive aspects of employee diversity.[73]

5. *An unsupportive and hostile working environment for diverse employees.* Sex-ual, racial, and age harassment are common examples of hostile work envi-ronments. Whether perpetrated against women, men, older individuals, or LGBT people, hostile environments are demeaning, unethical, and appro-priately called "work environment pollution." You certainly won't get em-ployees' best work if they believe that the work environment is hostile toward them. Remember, a hostile work environment is perceptual. This means that people have different perceptions of what entails "hostility." The perception process is discussed in Chapter 7.

   It also is important to note that harassment can take place via e-mail, texting, and other forms of social media. For example, a recent study of 220 employees revealed that the initial harassment began by e-mail or phone.[74] Managers are encouraged to treat electronic harassment the same as any other type of harassment.

6. *Lack of political savvy on the part of diverse employees.* Diverse employ-ees may not get promoted because they do not know how to "play the game" of getting along and getting ahead in an organization. Research reveals that women and people of color are excluded from organizational networks.[75]

diversity climate Employees' aggregate perceptions about an organization's policies, practices, and procedures pertaining to diversity.

7. *Difficulty in balancing career and family issues.* Women still assume the majority of the responsibilities associated with raising children. This makes it harder for women to work evenings and weekends or to frequently travel once they have children. Even without children in the picture, household chores take more of a woman's time than a man's time.

8. *Fears of reverse discrimination.* Some employees believe that managing diversity is a smoke screen for reverse discrimination. This belief leads to very strong resistance because people feel that one person's gain is another's loss.

This photo highlights a diverse workforce at GE. The company is proud of its approach toward managing diversity.

9. *Diversity is not seen as an organizational priority.* This leads to subtle resistance that shows up in the form of complaints and negative attitudes. Employees may complain about the time, energy, and resources devoted to diversity that could have been spent doing "real work."

10. *The need to revamp the organization's performance appraisal and reward system.* Performance appraisals and reward systems must reinforce the need to effectively manage diversity. This means that success will be based on a new set of criteria. For example, General Electric evaluates the extent to which its managers are inclusive of employees with different backgrounds. These evaluations are used in salary and promotion decisions.[76]

11. *Resistance to change.* Effectively managing diversity entails significant organizational and personal change. As discussed in Chapter 18, people resist change for many different reasons.

In summary, managing diversity is a critical component of organizational success.

Back to the Chapter-Opening Case

Which barriers and challenges to managing diversity played a role in what happened to Michelle Barfield?

TO THE POINT

Why is fostering mutual adaptation the best action option for managing diversity?

LO.8 Organizational Practices Used to Effectively Manage Diversity

So what are organizations doing to effectively manage diversity? Answering this question requires that we provide a framework for categorizing organizational initiatives. Researchers and practitioners have developed relevant frameworks. One was developed by R Roosevelt Thomas Jr, a diversity expert. He identified eight generic action options that can be used to address any type of diversity issue. This section reviews Thomas's framework in order to provide you with a broad understanding about how organizations are effectively managing diversity.

R Roosevelt Thomas Jr's Generic Action Options

Thomas identified eight basic responses for handling any diversity issue. After describing each action option, we discuss relationships among them.[77]

Option 1: Include/Exclude   This choice is an outgrowth of affirmative action programs. Its primary goal is to either increase or decrease the number of diverse people at all levels of the organizations. Shoney's restaurant represents a good example of a company that attempted to include diverse employees after settling a discrimination lawsuit. The company subsequently hired African Americans into positions of dining-room supervisors and vice presidents, added more franchises owned by African Americans, and purchased more goods and services from minority-owned companies.[78]

Option 2: Deny   People using this option deny that differences exist. Denial may manifest itself in proclamations that all decisions are color, gender, and age blind and that success is solely determined by merit and performance. Consider State Farm Insurance, for example. "Although it was traditional for male agents and their regional managers to hire male relatives, State Farm Insurance avoided change and denied any alleged effects in a nine-year gender-bias suit that the company lost."[79]

Option 3: Assimilate   The basic premise behind this alternative is that all diverse people will learn to fit in or become like the dominant group. It only takes time and reinforcement for people to see the light. Organizations initially assimilate employees through their recruitment practices and the use of company orientation programs. New hires generally are put through orientation programs that aim to provide employees with the organization's preferred values and a set of standard operating procedures. Employees then are encouraged to refer to the policies and procedures manual when they are confused about what to do in a specific situation. These practices create homogeneity among employees.

Option 4: Suppress   Differences are squelched or discouraged when using this approach. This can be done by telling or reinforcing others to quit whining and complaining about issues. The old "you've got to pay your dues" line is another frequently used way to promote the status quo.

Option 5: Isolate   This option maintains the current way of doing things by setting the diverse person off to the side. In this way the individual is unable to influence organizational change. Managers can isolate people by putting them on special projects. Entire work groups or departments are isolated by creating functionally independent entities, frequently referred to as "silos." Shoney's employees commented to a *Wall Street Journal* reporter about isolation practices formerly used by the company:

Example. White managers told of how Mr. Danner [previous chairman of the company] told them to fire blacks if they became too numerous in restaurants in white neighborhoods; if they refused, they would lose their jobs, too. Some also said that when Mr. Danner was expected to visit their restaurant, they scheduled black employees off that day or, in one case, hid them in the bathroom. Others said blacks' applications were coded and discarded.[80]

---

connect™ Go to www.mcgrawhillconnect.com for an interactive exercise to test your knowledge of Thomas's generic action options.

Option 6: Tolerate   Toleration entails acknowledging differences but not valuing or accepting them. It represents a live-and-let-live approach that superficially allows organizations to give lip service to the issue of managing diversity. Toleration is different from isolation in that it allows for the inclusion of diverse people. However, differences are not really valued or accepted when an organization uses this option.

Option 7: Build Relationships   This approach is based on the premise that good relationships can overcome differences. It addresses diversity by fostering quality relationships—characterized by acceptance and understanding—among

real WORLD // real PEOPLE

UnitedHealthcare Fosters Mutual Adaptation

Shortly after she'd [Lois Quam] had twins Will and Steve, Quam was offered another high-profile opportunity. Her boss wanted her to run UnitedHealthcare's public-sector services division. . . . "It was so overwhelming with twins. You can't pretend it doesn't make a difference. So I said, 'I'd really like to do this, but my primary focus for this period of my life is my sons.'" She remembers thinking, "This is going badly! It isn't strategic to be so blunt." But her boss surprised her. "He said, 'It's not a job that pays by the hour. You do it in a way that works for you, and if it doesn't work for me, I'll tell you.'"

Looking back, Quam describes her reaction as an "amazing gift" . . . because it affirmed her instincts about the best way to balance career and family.

How does this example illustrate mutual adaptation?

SOURCE: A Beard, "Surviving Twin Challenges—At Home and Work," *Harvard Business Review*, January–February 2011, p 164.

---

diverse groups. Rockwell Collins, a producer of aviation electronics in Cedar Rapids, Iowa, is a good example of a company attempting to use this diversity option. Rockwell is motivated to pursue this option because it has a shortage of qualified employees in a state that is about 6% nonwhite. To attract minority candidates the company "is building closer relationships with schools that have strong engineering programs as well as sizable minority populations. It also is working more closely with minority-focused professional societies."[81] The city of Cedar Rapids is also getting involved in the effort by trying to offer more cultural activities and ethnic-food stores that cater to a more diverse population base.

Option 8: Foster Mutual Adaptation   In this option, people are willing to adapt or change their views for the sake of creating positive relationships with others. This implies that employees and management alike must be willing to accept differences and, most important, agree that everyone and everything is open for change. Lois Quam's experience at UnitedHealthcare is a good example of mutual adaptation (see Real World/Real People above).

Conclusions about Action Options   Although the action options can be used alone or in combination, some are clearly better than others. Exclusion, denial, assimilation, suppression, isolation, and toleration are among the least preferred options. Inclusion, building relationships, and mutual adaptation are the preferred strategies. That said, Thomas reminds us that mutual adaptation is the only approach that unquestionably endorses the philosophy behind managing diversity. In closing this discussion, it is important to note that choosing how to best manage diversity is a dynamic process that is determined by the context at hand. For instance, some organizations are not ready for mutual adaptation. The best one might hope for in this case is the inclusion of diverse people.

Summary of Key Concepts

1. *Define diversity and review the four layers of diversity.* Diversity represents the individual differences that make people different from and similar to each other. Diversity pertains to everybody. It is not simply an issue of age, race, gender, or sexual orientation. The layers of diversity define an individual's personal identity and constitute a perceptual filter that influences how we interpret the world. Personality is at the center of the diversity wheel. The second layer of diversity consists of a set of internal dimensions that are referred to as surface-level dimensions of diversity. The third layer is composed of external influences and is called secondary dimensions of diversity. The final layer of diversity includes organizational dimensions.

2. *Explain the difference between affirmative action and managing diversity.* Affirmative action is an outgrowth of equal employment opportunity legislation and is an artificial intervention aimed at giving management a chance to correct past discrimination. Managing diversity entails creating a host of organizational changes that enable all people to perform up to their maximum potential.

3. *Explain why Alice Eagly and Linda Carli believe that a woman's career is best viewed as traveling through a labyrinth.* Eagly and Carli believe that women were barred from achieving high-level managerial positions in the past, but that women now have busted through these barriers. Eagly and Carli propose that women have made these strides by successfully navigating a labyrinth of twists, turns, and obstacles.

4. *Review the demographic trends pertaining to racial groups, educational mismatches, and an aging workforce.* With respect to racial groups, Asians and Hispanics are expected to have the largest growth in the population between 2000 and 2050, and minority groups will constitute 49.9% of the population in 2050. Minority groups also are experiencing a glass ceiling. There is a mismatch between workers' educational attainment and occupational requirements. The workforce is aging.

5. *Highlight the managerial implications of increasing diversity in the workforce.* There are seven broad managerial implications: (*a*) To attract the best workers, companies need to adopt policies and programs that meet the needs of all employees; (*b*) companies can help women and people of color enhance their promotability by helping them find mentors and sponsors; (*c*) companies should educate employees about negative stereotyping, particularly when it comes to selecting and promoting leaders; (*d*) companies should consider using progressive methods to recruit, retain, and integrate Hispanic workers into organizations; (*e*) there will be a shortage of qualified people in technical fields and on-the-job remedial skills, and literacy training will be needed to help the number of high-school dropouts and illiterates

cope with job demands; (*f*) organizations will need to provide tangible support to school systems if the United States is to remain globally competitive; and (*g*) there are three broad recommendations for managing an aging workforce.

6. *Describe the positive and negative effects of diversity by using social categorization theory and information/decision-making theory.* Social categorization theory implies that similarity leads to liking and attraction, thereby fostering a host of positive outcomes. This theory supports the idea that homogeneity is better than heterogeneity because diversity causes negative interpersonal processes and group dynamics. The information/decision-making theory is based on the notion that diverse groups should outperform homogenous groups because diversity is positively associated with task-relevant processes and decision making.

7. *Identify the barriers and challenges to managing diversity.* There are 10 barriers to successfully implementing diversity initiatives: (*a*) inaccurate stereotypes and prejudice, (*b*) ethnocentrism, (*c*) poor career planning, (*d*) an unsupportive and hostile working environment for diverse employees, (*e*) lack of political savvy on the part of diverse employees, (*f*) difficulty in balancing career and family issues, (*g*) fears of reverse discrimination, (*h*) diversity is not seen as an organizational priority, (*i*) the need to revamp the organization's performance appraisal and reward system, and (*j*) resistance to change.

8. *Discuss the organizational practices used to effectively manage diversity as identified by R Roosevelt Thomas Jr.* There are many different practices organizations can use to manage diversity. R Roosevelt Thomas Jr identified eight basic responses for handling any diversity issue: include/exclude, deny, assimilate, suppress, isolate, tolerate, build relationships, and foster mutual adaptation. Exclusion, denial, assimilation, suppression, isolation, and toleration are among the least preferred options. Inclusion, building relationships, and mutual adaptation are the preferred strategies.

Key Terms

Sexual harassment, 34	Managing diversity, 37	Information/decision-making theory, 50
Diversity, 34	Workforce demographics, 39	
Discrimination, 36	Glass ceiling, 39	Demographic fault line, 51
Affirmative action, 36	Social categorization theory, 50	Diversity climate, 53

OB in Action Case Study

LeasePlan Effectively Manages Diversity[82]

Shortly after joining LeasePlan USA as its head of sales and marketing in 2003, Mike Pitcher met with representatives of the vehicle-leasing company's top customers. To his surprise, most were women.

Women also outnumbered men among LeasePlan's 450 employees. Yet the vast majority of top managers at the company, a subsidiary of Netherlands-based Lease-Plan Corp., were men.

Soon after, LeasePlan began an effort to transform its corporate culture—rooted in the old-boy network of fleet managers—and promote more women. Executives hired a consultant to offer women career counseling, revised the company's pay plan to stress performance over longevity, and displaced some longtime managers. Today, three of the eight top executives are women, up from one in seven two years ago.

Women employees say LeasePlan is a more supportive and collaborative employer. Mr. Pitcher, now the company's chief executive, calls the initiative a strategic investment rather than the "the politically correct thing to do."

"LeasePlan doesn't build anything," he says. "Our sustainable competitive advantage is our people."

Such efforts require sustained commitment at the top, says Sheila Wellington, clinical professor of management at New York University's Stern School of Business. Executives "need to make it very clear that this isn't the flavor of the month," says Ms. Wellington, a former president of Catalyst, a research firm for focusing on women's workplace issues.

Ms. Wellington says executives must hold middle managers accountable for supporting and promoting female subordinates, particularly at smaller companies. . . .

LeasePlan executives launched their initiative in 2006. They hired Pathbuilders, Inc., an Atlanta human-resources consultancy that focuses on women, to craft a program that includes a skills assessment, career guidance, and tips on communicating and building a "brand." The program, which taps about 30 women each year, also features networking events and a panel discussion with female executives from other firms.

The broader effort to transform the corporate culture distinguishes LeasePlan from other companies trying to promote women, says Maria Goldsholl, chief operating officer of Mom Corps, a staffing company specializing in flexible employment for women . . . .

The program also appears to be boosting job satisfaction and engagement among LeasePlan's women employees. In a 2006 survey, 35% of women agreed the "management supports my efforts to manage my career." The following year, 47% of all female employees and 71% of program participants agreed. The percentage of women who said they think positions at LeasePlan are awarded fairly increased to 30% from 22%.

Gerri Patton, director of client activation, says the program helped her become more confident and outspoken. The 23-year LeasePlan veteran encourages her female subordinates to apply. "I wish I would have done that program 10 or 15 years ago," she says. "There's no telling where I would be . . . The sky would have been the limit."

Questions for Discussion

1. What is the business case that is driving LeasePlan's interest in managing diversity? Discuss.

2. Compare and contrast the extent to which LeasePlan is using principles from affirmative action and managing diversity. Explain your rationale.

3. To what extent are LeasePlan's efforts consistent with recommendations derived from Alice Eagly and Linda Carli? Discuss.

4. Which of R Roosevelt Thomas Jr's eight generic diversity options is LeasePlan using to manage diversity? Explain.

5. While LeasePlan's diversity initiative is clearly working, what recommendations would you make for improving their program? Explain.

Legal/Ethical Challenge

Should Joseph Casias Be Fired by Walmart?[83]

This case takes place in Michigan, a state that allows the use of medical marijuana.

Joseph Casias, a 30-year-old father of two, began work in 2004 as an entry-level grocery stocker at the Walmart in Battle Creek, Mich. By 2008, he had progressed to inventory control manager and was recognized as Associate of the Year, an honor given to only 2 of 400 employees.

In November 2009, Casias twisted his knee at work; because Walmart policy requires drug testing after a workplace injury, he underwent a urine test. Before the test, he showed the testing staff a registry card stating that he was a medical marijuana patient under Michigan law. He explained that he had been diagnosed with inoperable brain cancer at age 17, and the marijuana, prescribed by his oncologist, helped alleviate daily pain.

When the drug test revealed marijuana metabolites in Casias's system, the store manager told him that Walmart would not honor his registry card—and Casias was terminated.

What would you do if you were an executive at Walmart?

1. Give Casias his job back. He is a great employee and is not violating state law about using marijuana for medical conditions.

2. Zero tolerance should be applied and he should be fired. Regardless of what state law says, it is illegal under federal laws to use marijuana. Standards for marijuana should be the same as any other drug.

3. He should be fired because he presents a safety hazard to himself and others. The company must protect all employees from people who use drugs.

4. Invent other options. Discuss.

Web Resources

For study material and exercises that apply to this chapter, visit our website, **www.mhhe.com/kreitner10e**

chapter 3

Organizational Culture, Socialization, and Mentoring

 Learning Objectives

When you finish studying the material in this chapter, you should be able to:

LO.1   Define organizational culture and discuss its three layers.

LO.2   Discuss the difference between espoused and enacted values.

LO.3   Describe the four functions of organizational culture.

LO.4   Discuss the four types of organizational culture associated with the competing values framework.

LO.5   Summarize the five conclusions derived from research about the outcomes associated with organizational culture.

LO.6   Review the four caveats about culture change.

LO.7   Summarize the methods used by organizations to change organizational culture.

LO.8   Describe the three phases in Feldman's model of organizational socialization.

LO.9   Discuss the various socialization tactics used to socialize employees.

LO.10   Explain the four developmental networks associated with mentoring.

Would You Like to Work at Southwest Airlines?

Southwest Airline's Culture permeates every aspect of our company. It is our essence, our DNA, our past, our present, and our future. It is so important, in fact, that I wish I had more space to discuss it.

We often say that other airlines can copy our business plan from top to bottom but Southwest stands apart from the clones because of our People. But I would still wager that if another company somehow managed to hire all our fantastic Employees, that company wouldn't match up to Southwest.

Why? The new employer wouldn't possess the Southwest Culture, the secret sauce, if you will, of our organization. That Culture motivates and sustains us. For many of us, being part of Southwest is not just a vocation, but a mission. I don't dictate the Culture; neither do our other Officers. Rather, it stems from the collective personality of our Employees. It took us more than 30 years just to establish some definitions of our Culture upon which we could all agree. Those definitions are laid out in what we call "Living the Southwest Way." That creed consists of three values: A Warrior Spirit that recognizes courage, hard work, and desire to be the best; a Servant's Heart that follows the Golden Rule and treats others with respect; and a Fun-LUVing Attitude that includes FUN, of course, but also passion and celebration.

In January, we observed the 18th anniversary of the founding of our Corporate Culture Committee, a group dedicated to preserving our Culture for the present and the future. This Committee stresses that the Southwest Culture resides in each Employee, no matter the Employee's title. But the Culture Committee also recognizes how fragile Culture can be. I've talked with some of our Employees who have come to us from other airlines and firms that, long ago, maintained a strong culture. These Employees often said that they witnessed how a little benign neglect was able to destroy that culture almost overnight.

Their experiences confirm what I have always believed: Lip service can be a great danger. It's easy to write columns like this bragging about our Culture; the hard work is living up to it every day. Thus, the Committee Members act as examples for all of our other Employees to see. They show that Culture comes from the heart, not from the memo. As you might imagine, they have a difficult job, but we are fortunate to have the dedication of these Culture Warriors who battle indifference and complacency on a daily basis. With their help, our Culture continues to fly high.[1]

The chapter-opening vignette highlights three key conclusions about organizational culture. First, an organization's culture can impact employee motivation, satisfaction, and turnover. Southwest is able to maintain low employee turnover and high job satisfaction by creating a positive, employee-focused culture. The same can be said about the top five companies to work for in America in 2009 according to *Fortune*—SAS, Edward Jones, Wegman Food Markets, Google, and Nugget Market.[2] Second, organizational culture can be a source of competitive advantage. A recent study of 194 retail and service stores confirmed this conclusion. As is true for Southwest Airlines, results showed that market performance was higher for firms with cultures that showed a joint concern for employees and customers.[3] Finally, managers can influence organizational culture. Southwest uses its culture committee as a vehicle to shape and reinforce the values desired by senior management.

This chapter will help you better understand how managers can use organizational culture as a competitive advantage. After defining and discussing the context of organizational culture, we examine (1) the dynamics of organizational culture, (2) the process of culture change, (3) the organization socialization process, and (4) the embedding of organizational culture through mentoring.

TO THE POINT

How does organizational culture influence organizational outcomes?

LO.1 Organizational Culture: Definition and Context

Organizational culture is "the set of shared, taken-for-granted implicit assumptions that a group holds and that determines how it perceives, thinks about, and reacts to its various environments."[4] This definition highlights three important characteristics of organizational culture. First, organizational culture is passed on to new employees through the process of socialization, a topic discussed later in this chapter. Second, organizational culture influences our behavior at work. Finally, organizational culture operates at different levels.

Figure 3–1 provides a conceptual framework for reviewing the widespread impact organizational culture has on organizational behavior. It also shows the linkage between this chapter—culture, socialization, and mentoring—and other key topics in this book. Figure 3–1 reveals organizational culture is shaped by four key components: the founder's values, the industry and business environment, the national culture, and the senior leaders' vision and behavior: The impact of

figure 3–1 A Conceptual Framework for Understanding Organizational Culture

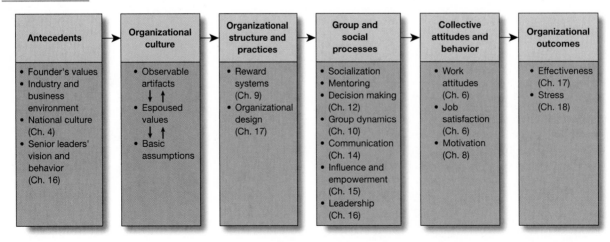

SOURCE: From C Ostroff, A Kinicki, and M Tamkins, "Organizational Culture and Climate," *Handbook of Psychology,* vol 12, edited by Walter C Borman, Daniel R Ilgen, Richard J Klimoski, and Irving B Weiner, pp 565–93, Copyright © 2003. Reprinted with permission of John Wiley & Sons.

national culture on organizational behavior is discussed in detail in Chapter 4. In turn, organizational culture influences the type of organizational structure adopted by a company and a host of practices, policies, and procedures implemented in pursuit of organizational goals. These organizational characteristics then affect a variety of group and social processes. This sequence ultimately affects employees' attitudes and behavior and a variety of organizational outcomes. All told, Figure 3–1 reveals that organizational culture is a contextual variable influencing individual, group, and organizational behavior. This is why we are discussing organizational culture as the third chapter in your textbook.

Dynamics of Organizational Culture

To gain a better understanding of how organizational culture is formed and used by employees, this section begins by discussing the layers of organizational culture. We then review the four functions of organizational culture, types of organizational culture, and outcomes associated with organizational culture.

Layers of Organizational Culture

Figure 3–1 shows the three fundamental layers of organizational culture: observable artifacts, espoused values, and basic assumptions. Each level varies in terms of outward visibility and resistance to change, and each level influences another level.

Observable Artifacts
At the more visible level, culture represents observable artifacts. Artifacts consist of the physical manifestation of an organization's culture. Organizational examples include acronyms, manner of dress, awards, myths and stories told about the organization, published lists of values, observable rituals and ceremonies, special parking spaces, decorations, and so on. For example, the Ritz-Carlton hotel uses storytelling to reinforce a culture that is focused on exceeding customers' expectations. The company shares "wow stories" at meetings each week that relay guests' tales of staff members going above and beyond the call of duty. Each "wow" winner, such as a laundry attendant who dove into a dumpster to retrieve one young guest's stuffed gingerbread man, gets $100.[5] This level also includes visible behaviors exhibited by people and groups. At Google, for example, the core design team of 16 employees have daily "stand-up" meetings. "Everyone working on the project gathers standing up, to make sure no one gets too comfortable and no time is wasted during the rapid-fire update."[6] These stand-up meetings are an artifact of Google's desire to work hard and get things done in a timely manner. Artifacts are easier to change than the less visible aspects of organizational culture.

LO.2 **Espoused Values**   Values possess five key components. "**Values** (1) are concepts or beliefs, (2) pertain to desirable end-states or behaviors, (3) transcend situations, (4) guide selection or evaluation of behavior and events, and (5) are ordered by relative importance."[7] It is important to distinguish between values that are espoused versus those that are enacted.

Espoused values represent the explicitly stated values and norms that are preferred by an organization. They are generally established by the founder of a new or small company and by the top management team in a larger organization.

TO THE POINT
What are the key conclusions regarding layers of culture, functions of culture, types of culture, and outcomes associated with organizational culture?

connect Go to www.mcgrawhillconnect.com for an interactive exercise to test your knowledge of the conceptual framework.

organizational culture Shared values and beliefs that underlie a company's identity.

values Enduring belief in a mode of conduct or end-state.

espoused values The stated values and norms that are preferred by an organization.

real WORLD // real PEOPLE: ethics

Williams-Sonoma's Espoused Values Focus on Employees, Customers, Shareholders, and Ethical Behavior

People First We believe the potential of our company has no limit and is driven by our associates and their imagination. We are committed to an environment that attracts, motivates and recognizes high performance.

Customers We are here to please our customers— without them nothing else matters.

Quality We must take pride in everything we do. From our people, to our products and in our relationships with business partners and our community, quality is our signature.

Shareholders We must provide a superior return to our shareholders. It's everyone's job.

Ethical Sourcing Williams-Sonoma, Inc., and all of its brands are committed to maintaining the highest level of integrity and honesty throughout all aspects of our business. We work to ensure that our business associates, including agents, vendors and suppliers,

share our commitment to socially responsible employment conditions.

Wood Product Sourcing Williams-Sonoma, Inc., is committed to environmental stewardship, and more specifically, to responsible wood sourcing to protect and conserve this vital natural resource integral to the health of the environment and the communities from which we source.

Paper Procurement Policy Equally important to Williams-Sonoma, Inc.'s commitment to responsible wood sourcing, is our commitment to sound paper procurement practices that also ensure the sustainability of forests and other natural resources.

To what extent are these values consistent with your own values? Would you like to work at Williams-Sonoma?

SOURCE: Excerpted from "Corporate Values," www .williams-sonomainc.com/careers/corporate-values.html, accessed January 2, 2011.

Consider, for example, the espoused values of Williams-Sonoma (see Real World/Real People above). This specialty retailer of home furnishings was founded in 1956 and has experienced substantial growth since its inception.

On a positive note, Williams-Sonoma and many more companies are espousing the value of sustainability. **Sustainability** represents "a company's ability to make a profit without sacrificing the resources of its people, the community, and the planet."[8] Sustainability also is referred to as "being green," and Pulitzer Prize winner Thomas Friedman believes that "outgreening" other nations can renew America and defeat al-Qaeda.[9] Others believe that outgreening can produce a competitive advantage for organizations. For example, insurer Safeco and Microsoft have significantly cut costs and increased productivity by implementing employer-subsidized transportation that reinforces the idea that people be encouraged not to drive to work.

Because espoused values represent aspirations that are explicitly communicated to employees, managers hope that those values will directly influence employee behavior. Unfortunately, aspirations do not automatically produce the desired behaviors because people do not always "walk the talk." BP, for instance, has long claimed that it values safety, yet the company had a refinery fire in Texas City, Texas, that killed 15 people in 2005, a 2006 pipeline leak in Alaska that lost over 200,000 gallons of crude, and

The Deepwater Horizon spill was one of the worst environmental disasters in U.S. history. This worker is using a vacuum hose to collect oil that washed on shore in the Gulf of Mexico. The oil spill damaged marine and wildlife habitats and cost billions to cleanup.

the 2010 Deepwater Horizon spill in the Gulf lost more than 200 million gallons according to the U.S. government.[10]

Enacted values, on the other hand, represent the values and norms that actually are exhibited or converted into employee behavior. They represent the values that employees ascribe to an organization based on their observations of what occurs on a daily basis. For example, Starbucks CEO, Howard Schultz, is trying hard to enact the company value of providing quality products and great service in response to the financial problems faced by the company in 2009. He told an interviewer in 2010 that "I shut our stores for three and a half hours of retraining. People said, 'How much is that going to cost?' I had shareholders calling me and saying, 'Are you out of your mind?' I said, 'I'm doing the right thing. We are retraining our people because we have forgotten what we stand for, and that is the pursuit of an unequivocal, absolute commitment to quality.'"[11] Schultz is obviously hoping that these artifacts encourage employees to provide good service.

It is important for managers to reduce gaps between espoused and enacted values because they can significantly influence employee attitudes and organizational performance. For example, a survey administered by the Ethics Resource Center showed that employees were more likely to behave ethically when management behaved in a way that set a good ethical example and kept its promises and commitments. This finding is underscored by another recent study of 500,000 employees from more than 85 countries. Results revealed that companies experienced 10 times more misconduct when they had weak rather than strong ethical cultures.[12] Managers clearly need to walk the talk when it comes to behaving ethically.

Basic Assumptions   Basic underlying assumptions are unobservable and represent the core of organizational culture. They constitute organizational values that have become so taken for granted over time that they become assumptions that guide organizational behavior. They thus are highly resistant to change. When basic assumptions are widely held among employees, people will find behavior based on an inconsistent value inconceivable. Southwest Airlines, for example, is noted for operating according to basic assumptions that value employees' welfare and providing high-quality service. Employees at Southwest Airlines would be shocked to see management act in ways that did not value employees' and customers' needs.

connect™ Go to www.mcgrawhillconnect.com for a self-assessment to learn what your preferred corporate culture type is.

Back to the Chapter-Opening Case

What observable artifacts, espoused values, and basic assumptions are displayed in the case?

What Are the Takeaways from Research on Levels of Culture?   The key takeaway involves the consequences of what is called PE fit. **PE fit** is defined "as the compatibility between an individual and a work environment that occurs when their characteristics are well matched."[13] Results from a meta-analysis of over 170 studies and 40,000 workers demonstrated that people have higher job satisfaction and commitment to their organizations and lower intentions to quit when their personal characteristics (e.g., skills, abilities, and personalities) and values (e.g., integrity) match or fit the job requirements,

sustainability Meeting humanity's needs without harming future generations.

Enacted values The values and norms that are exhibited by employees.

PE Fit Extent to which personal characteristics match those from a work environment.

real WORLD // real PEOPLE

Lack of PE Fit Leads Apple Employee to Leave the Company

The Apple Inc. executive in charge of the iPhone has left the company following a string of stumbles with the device, and what people familiar with the situation said was a falling out with then Chief Executive Steve Jobs. . . .

Several people familiar with Mr. Papermaster's situation said his departure was driven by a broader cultural incompatibility with the company.

Mr. Papermaster had lost the confidence of Mr. Jobs months ago and hasn't been part of the decision-making process for some time, these people said. They added that Mr. Papermaster didn't appear to have the type of creative thinking expected at Apple and wasn't used to Apple's corporate culture, where even senior executives are expected to keep on top of the smallest details of their areas of responsibility and often have to handle many tasks directly, as opposed to delegating them.

What could Mr. Papermaster have done to increase his PE fit?

SOURCE: Excerpted from Y I Kane and I Sherr, "IPhone Executive Is Out at Apple," *The Wall Street Journal*, August 9, 2010, p B1.

---

organizational values, and the values of the workgroup.[14] These results highlight that PE fit is important for your future job and career satisfaction. As a case in point, Mark Papermaster, Apple's former senior vice president for mobile devices, left the company partly because of low PE fit (see Real World/Real People above).

You may be wondering how to determine PE fit prior to accepting a job or promotion. It can be done, but it takes some work on your part. You first must conduct an evaluation of your strengths, weaknesses, and values. Next, do the same for the company or department at hand by doing research about the company on the Internet or talking with current employees. This information will now enable you to prepare a set of diagnostic questions to ask during the interview process. These questions need to focus on determining your level of fit. For example, if you value recognition for hard work, then ask a recruiter how the company rewards performance. If the answer does not support a strong link between performance and rewards, you probably will have a low PE fit and will not be happy working at this company.

Some companies understand the importance of PE fit and have designed methods within the recruiting process to encourage its accomplishment. Consider the selection process used by ReThink Rewards, a Toronto-based company, when hiring salespeople.

Example. The process includes group interviews, each with 10 candidates and two employees—a sales representative and a human resource representative. The interviewers then select 10 finalist candidates and ask each to review one of the company's case studies and give a 20-minute PowerPoint presentation to two other employees. The presentations are followed by 10-minute question-and-answer sessions. Finalists are interviewed by the hiring manager and HR representative, who use "Topgrading" methods—an approach that involves an extensive interview with each candidate about his or her experiences in high school, college and the workplace. . . . During the Topgrading interview, the candidate is asked 15 questions about each job he or she has held in the past 10 years, including opportunities, challenges, mistakes and accomplishments.[15]

 LO.3 Four Functions of Organizational Culture

As illustrated in Figure 3–2, an organization's culture fulfills four functions. To help bring these four functions to life, let us consider how each of them has taken

figure 3–2 Four Functions of Organizational Culture

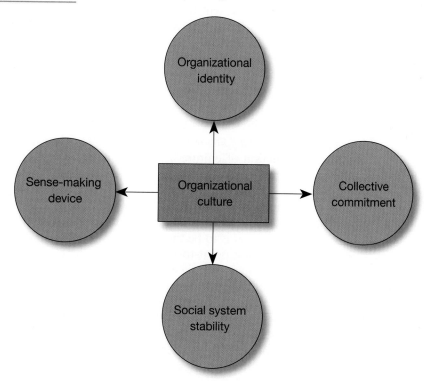

SOURCE: Adapted from discussion in L Smircich, "Concepts of Culture and Organizational Analysis," *Administrative Science Quarterly,* September 1983, pp 339–58. Reprinted with permission.

shape at Southwest Airlines. Southwest is a particularly instructive example because it has grown to become the largest carrier in the United States based on scheduled departures since its inception in 1971 and has achieved 38 consecutive years of profitability. *Fortune* has ranked Southwest in the top five of the Best Companies to Work For in America from 1997 to 2000; Southwest has chosen not to participate in this ranking process since 2000. Southwest also was ranked as one of the Top 50 Companies committed to corporate social responsibility in 2010.[16]

1. *Give members an organizational identity.* Southwest Airlines is known as a fun place to work that values employee satisfaction and customer loyalty over corporate profits. Gary Kelly, Southwest's CEO, highlighted this theme by noting that "our people are our single greatest strength and our most enduring long-term competitive advantage. "[17]

    The company also has a catastrophe fund based on voluntary contributions for distribution to employees who are experiencing serious personal difficulties. Southwest's people-focused identity is reinforced by the fact that it is an employer of choice. For example, Southwest received 90,043 résumés and hired 831 new employees in 2009. The company also was rated as providing outstanding opportunities for women and Hispanics by *Professional Women* magazine and *Hispanic* magazine, respectively, and *Business Ethics* ranked Southwest among the 100 Best Corporate Citizens seven years in a row.

2. *Facilitate collective commitment.* The mission of Southwest Airlines "is dedication to the highest quality of Customer Service delivered with a sense of warmth, friendliness, individual pride, and Company Spirit."[18] Southwest's nearly 35,000 employees are committed to this mission. The Department of Transportation's Air Travel Consumer Report reported Southwest was ranked number one in fewest customer complaints since 1987.

connect™ Go to www.mcgrawhillconnect.com for a video case on the organizational culture at Pike Place Fish Market.

The smile on this Southwest Airlines employee demonstrates the four functions of culture. Southwest employees have high job satisfaction and low employee turnover, in part attributable to its philosophy of having fun and celebrating. Would you like to work at Southwest?

3. *Promote social system stability.* Social system stability reflects the extent to which the work environment is perceived as positive and reinforcing, and the extent to which conflict and change are effectively managed. Southwest is noted for its philosophy of having fun, having parties, and celebrating. For example, each city in which the firm operates is given a budget for parties. Southwest also uses a variety of performance-based awards and service awards to reinforce employees. The company's positive and enriching environment is supported by the lowest turnover rates in the airline industry and the employment of 1,164 married couples.

4. *Shape behavior by helping members make sense of their surroundings.* This function of culture helps employees understand why the organization does what it does and how it intends to accomplish its long-term goals. Keeping in mind that Southwest's leadership originally viewed ground transportation as their main competitor in 1971, employees come to understand why the airline's primary vision is to be the best primarily short-haul, low-fare, high-frequency, point-to-point carrier in the United States.

Employees understand they must achieve exceptional performance, such as turning a plane in 20 minutes, because they must keep costs down in order to compete against Greyhound and the use of automobiles. In turn, the company reinforces the importance of outstanding customer service and high performance expectations by using performance-based awards and profit sharing. Employees own about 5% of the company stock.

 LO.4 Types of Organizational Culture

Organizational behavior researchers have proposed three different frameworks to capture the various types of organizational culture: the organizational culture inventory, the competing values framework, and the organizational culture profile. This section discusses the competing values framework because it is the most widely used approach for classifying organizational culture. It also was named as one of the 40 most important frameworks in the study of organizations and has been shown to be a valid approach for classifying organizational culture.[19]

The **competing values framework (CVF)** provides a practical way for managers to understand, measure, and change organizational culture. It was originally developed by a team of researchers who were trying to classify different ways to assess organizational effectiveness. This research showed that measures of organizational effectiveness vary along two fundamental dimensions or axes. One axis pertains to whether an organization focuses its attention and efforts on internal dynamics and employees or outward toward its external environment and its customers and shareholders. The second is concerned with an organization's preference for flexibility and discretion or control and stability. Combining these two axes creates four types of organizational culture that are based on different core values and different sets of criteria for accessing organizational effectiveness. The CVF is shown in Figure 3–3.[20]

Figure 3–3 shows the strategic thrust associated with each cultural type along with the means used to accomplish this thrust and the resulting ends or goals pursued by each cultural type. Before beginning our exploration of the CVF, it is important to note that organizations can possess characteristics associated with each culture type. That said, however, organizations tend to have one type of culture that is more dominant than the others. Let us begin our discussion of culture types by starting in the upper-left-hand quadrant of the CVF.

Clan Culture   A **clan culture** has an internal focus and values flexibility rather than stability and control. It resembles a family-type organization in which

figure 3–3   Competing Values Framework

Flexibility and discretion

Clan	**Adhocracy**
Thrust: Collaborate	**Thrust:** Create
Means: Cohesion, participation, communication, empowerment	**Means:** Adaptability, creativity, agility
Ends: Morale, people development, commitment	**Ends:** Innovation, growth, cutting-edge output
Hierarchy	**Market**
Thrust: Control	**Thrust:** Compete
Means: Capable processes, consistency, process control, measurement	**Means:** Customer focus, productivity, enhancing competitiveness
Ends: Efficiency, timeliness, smooth functioning	**Ends:** Market share, profitability, goal achievement

Internal focus and integration (left)   **External focus and differentiation** (right)

Stability and control

SOURCE: Adapted from K S Cameron, R E Quinn, J Degraff, and A V Thakor, *Competing Values Leadership* (Northampton, MA: Edward Elgar, 2006), p 32.

effectiveness is achieved by encouraging collaboration between employees. This type of culture is very "employee-focused" and strives to instill cohesion through consensus and job satisfaction and commitment through employee involvement.

Clan organizations devote considerable resources to hiring and developing their employees, and they view customers as partners.

A company with a strong clan culture is Decagon Devices in Pullman, Washington. The company may be small, but senior management tries to maintain a family atmosphere at work. The company's CEO, Tamsin Jolley, noted that "the way that we like to see it is that as we add employees we're just adding members to the family." This feeling starts with a profit-sharing program that distributes 20% of pretax profits to employees on a quarterly basis.

connect™ Go to www.mcgrawhillconnect.com for an interactive exercise to test your knowledge of the competing values framework.

Example. Then there are day-to-day activities that bring workers closer together. Each Wednesday, some employees take turns bringing home-cooked meals to work for their colleagues. Then, all the workers eat lunch together. The weekly meal is an opportunity for managers to share news about the company, introduce new employees, and teach workers how to read the company's financial statements. The company also encourages employees to socialize at work. The office has a ping-pong table and slot-car track, and there's a long tradition of employees playing soccer on their breaks.[21]

Decagon Devices also provides generous employee health benefits and hosts annual catered family picnics and holiday parties.

competing values framework (CVF) A framework for categorizing organizational culture.

clan culture A culture that has an internal focus and values flexibility rather than stability and control.

SAS, rated as the number one best company to work for in America in 2009 by *Fortune,* as well as Zappos and Discount Tire represent other good examples of successful companies with clan cultures.[22] Zappos, for example, encourages managers to spend up to 20% of their spare time engaging in teambuilding outside of work.[23]

Adhocracy Culture   An **adhocracy culture** has an external focus and values flexibility. This type of culture fosters the creation of innovative products and services by being adaptable, creative, and fast to respond to changes in the marketplace. Adhocracy cultures do not rely on the type of centralized power and authority relationships that are part of market and hierarchical cultures. They empower and encourage employees to take risks, think outside the box, and experiment with new ways of getting things done. This type of culture is well suited for start-up companies, those in industries undergoing constant change, and those in mature industries that are in need of innovation to enhance growth. Consider how these cultural characteristics are reinforced at the biopharmaceutical firm AstraZeneca. "AstraZeneca is experimenting with new ways to organize research to improve productivity. Scientists now are responsible for candidate drugs until they begin the final human trials, ending a culture of handing off early-stage products to other researchers as if on an assembly line."[24] India-based Tata group, with over 90 operating companies in more than 80 countries is another company with an adhocracy culture. "Known for its ultracheap minicar, the Nano, Tata takes innovation so seriously that it's developed an 'Innometer.' The conglomerate measures creative goals and accomplishments vs. domestic or global benchmarks while instilling a 'sense of urgency' among employees."[25] Tata was ranked as the 17th most innovative firm in the world in 2010 by *Bloomberg Businessweek*. W. L. Gore, Intel, and Google are other companies that possess cultural characteristics consistent with an adhocracy.

Market Culture   A **market culture** has a strong external focus and values stability and control. Organizations with this culture are driven by competition and a strong desire to deliver results and accomplish goals. Because this type of culture is focused on the external environment, customers and profits take precedence over employee development and satisfaction. The major goal of managers is to drive toward productivity, profits, and customer satisfaction. Consider Richard Branson's new Virgin America airline. Branson believes that "American carriers are all very much the same, and the people who run them do not think of the customers at all." "It's become a bus service." To meet customer needs, Branson's new airline uses Airbus A319 and A320 jets that are roomier, contain in-flight entertainment at every seat, Wi-Fi Internet access, and special lighting that displays 12 shades of pink, purple, and blue.[26] Time will tell whether this market culture will lead to sustainable profits.

Employees in market cultures also are expected to react fast, work hard, and deliver quality work on time. Organizations with this culture tend to reward people who deliver results. Byung Mo Ahn, president of Kia Motors, is a good example of a leader who desires to promote a market culture. He fired two senior executives from Kia Motors America in February 2008 because they were not meeting their expected sales goals. Employees from North America note that Mr. Ahn has created a very aggressive and competitive work environment. Some describe the environment as militaristic.[27]

Hierarchy Culture   Control is the driving force within a hierarchy culture. The **hierarchy culture** has an internal focus, which produces a more formalized and structured work environment, and values stability and control over flexibility. This orientation leads to the development of reliable internal processes, extensive measurement, and the implementation of a variety of control mechanisms. Effectiveness in a company with this type of culture is likely to be assessed with measures of efficiency, timeliness, quality, safety, and reliability of producing and delivering products and services. Johnson & Johnson (J&J) is a good example of why some organizations desire a hierarchical culture. J&J had serious manufacturing problems in 2010 that led to recalls of children's Tylenol and other over-the-counter drugs. "A Food and Drug Administration inspection report, dated April 30, cites incidents of mishandling of materials, lax documentation and inadequate investigation of consumer complaints." The company estimates a loss of $600 million in 2010 and a hit to its reputation. To correct the problem, the company created "a company-wide quality team and is upgrading plants," improving plants, and training employees.[28] Time will tell if a focus on creating a hierarchical culture in its manufacturing operations will correct J&J's problems.

Back to the Chapter-Opening Case

How would you categorize Southwest Airline's Culture based on the competing values framework?

Cultural Types Represent Competing Values   It is important to note that certain cultural types reflect opposing core values. These contradicting cultures are found along the two diagonals in Figure 3–3. For example, the clan culture—upper-left quadrant—is represented by values that emphasize an internal focus and flexibility, whereas the market culture—bottom-right quadrant—has an external focus and concern for stability and control. You can see the same conflict between an adhocracy culture that values flexibility and an external focus and a hierarchy culture that endorses stability and control along with an internal focus. Why are these contradictions important?

They are important because an organization's success may depend on its ability to possess core values that are associated with competing cultural types. While this is difficult to pull off, it can be done. 3M is a good example. The company is trying to merge competing cultural characteristics from an adhocracy with those from a hierarchy. Reflecting an adhocracy culture, 3M released 1,000 new products in 2009, and it "awards annual Genesis Grants, worth as much as $100,000, to company scientists for research. The money is allocated by their peers and is spent on projects for which 'no sensible, conventional person in the company would give money,' " says Chris Holmes, a 3M division vice president. The company has a goal to generate 30% of its revenue from products developed in the last five years. In contrast, 3M pursued a hierarchical culture by implementing quality management techniques to reduce waste and defects and increase efficiency. Although 3M achieved better efficiency and earnings in the short run, new product revenue decreased and scientists complained that the quality initiatives were choking off innovation. One engineer quipped that "it's really tough to schedule invention." 3M's CEO, George Buckley, was made aware of these cultural conflicts and decided to reduce the conflict within company labs by decreasing hierarchical policies/procedures

3M is one of the most innnovative firms in the world. Even during the recent recession, the company released over 1,000 new products in one year.

---

adhocracy culture A culture that has an external focus and values flexibility.

market culture A culture that has a strong external focus and values stability and control.

hierarchy culture A culture that has an internal focus and values stability and control over flexibility.

while simultaneously increasing those related to adhocracy. The company continues to emphasize quality and reliability in its factories. To date, results indicate a successful transition as the company achieved both its efficiency and new product revenue goals in 2010.[29]

 LO.5 Outcomes Associated
with Organizational Culture

Both managers and academic researchers believe that organizational culture can be a driver of employee attitudes, performance, and organizational effectiveness. To test this possibility, various measures of organizational culture have been correlated with a variety of individual and organizational outcomes. So what have we learned? A team of researchers recently conducted a meta-analysis to answer this question. Their results were based on 93 studies involving over 1,100 companies. Figure 3–4 summarizes results from this study.[30]

Figure 3–4 shows the strength of relationships between eight different organizational outcomes and the culture types of clan, adhocracy, and market: Hierarchy was not included due to a lack of research on this type. Results reveal that the eight types of organizational outcomes had significant and positive relationships with clan, adhocracy, and market cultures. The majority of these relationships were of moderate strength, indicating that they are important to today's managers. Closer examination of Figure 3–4 leads to the following five conclusions:

1. Organizational culture is clearly related to measures of organizational effectiveness. This reinforces the conclusion that an organization's culture can be a source of competitive advantage.

2. Employees are more satisfied and committed to organizations with clan cultures. These results suggest that employees prefer to work in organizations

figure 3–4 Correlates of Organizational Culture

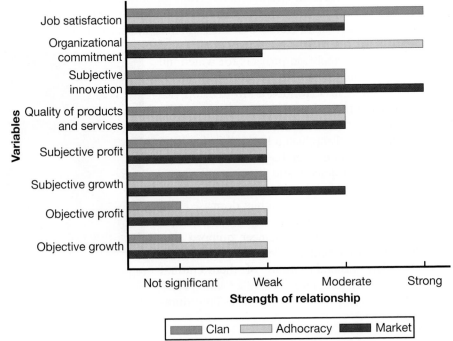

SOURCE: Data for this Figure were obtained from C A Hartnell, A Y Ou, and A J Kinicki, "Organizational Culture and Organizational Effectiveness: A Meta-Analytic Investigation of the Competing Values Framework's Theoretical Suppositions," Journal of Applied Psychology, July 2011, pp 677–694.

that value flexibility over stability and control and those that are more concerned with satisfying employees' needs than customer or shareholder desires.

3. Innovation and quality can be increased by building characteristics associated with clan, adhocracy, and market cultures into the organization.

4. An organization's financial performance (i.e., growth in profit and growth in revenue) is not very strongly related to organizational culture. Managers should not expect to increase financial performance by trying to change their organization's culture.

5. Companies with market cultures tend to have more positive organizational outcomes. Managers are encouraged to consider how they might make their cultures more market oriented.

Researchers also have investigated the importance of organizational culture within the context of a merger. These studies indicate that mergers frequently failed due to incompatible cultures. Owing to the increasing number of corporate mergers around the world, and the conclusion that 7 out of 10 mergers and acquisitions failed to meet their financial promise, managers within merged companies would be well advised to consider the role of organizational culture in creating a new organization.[31]

In summary, research underscores the significance of organizational culture. It also reinforces the need to learn more about the process of cultivating and changing an organization's culture. An organization's culture is not determined by fate. It is formed and shaped by the combination and integration of everyone who works in the organization. A change-resistant culture, for instance, can undermine the effectiveness of any type of organizational change. Although it is not an easy task to change an organization's culture, the next section provides a preliminary overview of how to create cultural change.

LO.6 The Process of Culture Change

TO THE POINT
What are the specific methods or techniques managers can use to change an organization's culture?

Before describing the specific ways in which managers can change organizational culture, let us review four caveats about culture change. First, we agree with the notion that leaders are the architects and developers of organizational culture, and managing organizational culture is one of the most important functions of leadership.[32] Second, the process of culture change essentially begins with targeting one of the three layers of organizational culture previously discussed—observable artifacts, espoused values, and basic assumptions. That said, culture will not change in a significant way unless managers are able to change basic underlying assumptions.[33] Third, it is important to consider the extent to which the current culture is aligned with the organization's vision and strategic plan before attempting to change any aspect of organizational culture. A **vision** represents a long-term goal that describes "what" an organization wants to become. For example, Walt Disney's original vision for Disneyland included the following components:

Example. Disneyland will be something of a fair, an exhibition, a playground, a community center, a museum of living facts, and a showplace of beauty and magic. It will be filled with the accomplishments, the joys and hopes of the world we live in. And it will remind and show us how to make those wonders part of our lives.[34]

---

vision Long-term goal describing "what" an organization wants to become.

A **strategic plan** outlines an organization's long-term goals and the actions necessary to achieve these goals. Mark Fields, executive vice president, Ford Motor Company, and president, The Americas, firmly believes that culture, vision, and strategic plans should be aligned. According to Fields, "Culture eats strategy for breakfast. You can have the best plan in the world, and if the culture isn't going to let it happen, it's going to die on the vine."[35]

Finally, it is important to use a structured approach when implementing culture change. Chapter 18 can help you in this regard as it presents several models that provide specific steps to follow when implementing any type of organizational change. Let us now consider the specific methods or techniques that managers can use to change an organization's culture.

 LO.7   Edgar Schein, a well-known OB scholar, notes that changing organizational culture involves a teaching process. That is, organizational members teach each other about the organization's preferred values, beliefs, norms, expectations, and behaviors. This is accomplished by using one or more of the following mechanisms:[36]

1. *Formal statements of organizational philosophy, mission, vision, values, and materials used for recruiting, selection, and socialization.* Sam Walton, the founder of Walmart, established three basic beliefs or values that represent the core of the organization's culture. They are (a) respect for the individual, (b) service to our customer, and (c) striving for excellence. Further, Nucor Corporation attempts to emphasize the value it places on its people by including every employee's name on the cover of the annual report. This practice also reinforces the clan type of culture the company wants to encourage.[37] Would you like to work at Nucor?

2. *The design of physical space, work environments, and buildings.* Novartis AG in Basel, Switzerland, designed its offices to foster collaboration. This was done by using "common workspaces, sofas, soft lighting and cappuccino machines to encourage people to talk, share ideas and build relationships." They also invested in laptops for employees so that they would not be tied down to cubicles.[38]

3. *Slogans, language, acronyms, and sayings.* For example, Robert Mittelstaedt, dean of the W. P. Carey School of Business at Arizona State University, promotes his vision of having one of the best business schools in the world through the slogan "Top-of-mind business school." Employees are encouraged to engage in activities that promote the quality and reputation of the school's academic programs.

4. *Deliberate role modeling, training programs, teaching, and coaching by managers and supervisors.* Fluor Corporation, one of the leading design, engineering, and contracting firms in the world, desires an ethical culture that fights corruption within the construction industry. The company, which derives more than half of its $17 billion in revenues overseas, puts all its employees through online anticorruption training sessions and teaches specialized workers, such as field operators, in person. Executives promote an open-door policy and a hotline for reporting crimes—as well as tough penalties for violators, who receive zero tolerance for infractions.[39]

5. *Explicit rewards, status symbols (e.g., titles), and promotion criteria.* At Triage Consulting Group, employees at the same level of their career earn the same pay, but employees are eligible for merit bonuses, reinforcing the culture of achievement. The merit bonuses are partly based on coworkers' votes for who contributed most to the company's success, and the employees who received the most votes are recognized each year at the company's "State of Triage" meeting.[40]

6. *Stories, legends, or myths about key people and events.* Baptist Health Care uses a combination of storytelling and recognition to embed clan- and market-based cultures that focus on employees and patients.

Example. We've been able to do more and different things because of our culture, which starts with the executives who carry it to the front-line and staff," says BHC Director of People Development Scott Ginnette. . . . For example, throughout the year we celebrate Champions, people who have done extraordinary things in service, by sharing their stories with all employees. Every facility has its own Champions, and at the end of the year, a committee decides which Champions will be named Legends, a higher honor. The Legends are taken by limo to an offsite dinner with board members where stories are shared and the Legends are recognized.[41]

Marriott also uses stories to reinforce its culture. For example, Ed Fuller, head of international lodging for Marriott International, teaches employees about fairness in career advancement by telling the story of how he and another senior executive started their careers as a security guard and a waiter.[42] Managers can develop and tell motivating stories by noticing relevant actions and tying them to values. Good stories also can come from listening to customers. It is important when telling stories that you are factual and authentic because someone may check out the story.

7. *The organizational activities, processes, or outcomes that leaders pay attention to, measure, and control.* When Ron Sargent took over as chief executive of Staples, he wanted to increase the focus on customer service. He started by investigating what values the office supply retailer's employees already held, and they told him they cared about helping others. Sargent used that value as the basis for developing their skill in serving customers. Staples began teaching employees more about the products they sell and now offers bonuses for team performance. Sargent also pays frequent visits to stores so he can talk directly to employees about what customers like and dislike.[43]

8. *Leader reactions to critical incidents and organizational crises.* BP's new CEO after the Gulf oil spill—Bob Dudley—responded quickly to criticism that the company valued profit and efficiency more than safety. He sent a memo to all employees indicating "that safety would be the sole criterion for rewarding employee performance in its operating business for the fourth quarter."[44] These types of rewards will need to be offered long term if the company truly wants to change employees' basic underlying assumptions.

9. *The workflow and organizational structure.* Hierarchical structures are more likely to embed an orientation toward control and authority than a flatter organization. This partly explains why leaders from many organizations are increasingly reducing the number of organizational layers in an attempt to empower employees (see Chapter 17) and increase employee involvement. Novartis AG is a prime example. The company changed its organizational structure to foster the creativity and productivity associated with adhocracy and market cultures. "Leaders are seeing results from cross-functional

strategic plan A long term plan outlining actions needed to achieve desired results.

real WORLD // real PEOPLE

Zappos Works Hard to Recruit and Select People Who Fit Its Culture

Here is what Rebecca Ratner, Zappos HR director, had to say about the company's approach to recruitment and selection. "We spend seven to 10 hours over four occasions at happy hours, team building events, or other things outside the office. We can see them, and they can us." The process seems to be good for retention. "In 2009, we had a 20 percent turnover rate," says Ratner. That is impressive for call centers. What keeps people at Zappos? "We pay 100 percent of employee benefits," . . . and then there's the wow factor.

"We can't ask people to wow a customer if they haven't been wowed by us," says Ratner. Zappos is so eager to wow employees and make sure who they hire is committed that they offer people $3,000 after they've been trained to walk away if they feel they and Zappos aren't a good fit. Almost no one takes the $3,000 walk-away money. But many trainees return for more Zappos training to become managers.

Why would Zappos's approach to recruiting result in greater PE fit?

SOURCE: Excerpted from J Larrere, "Develop Great Leaders," *Leadership Excellence,* April 2010, p 12.

The "Wow" factor at Zappos is partly created by encouraging employees to have fun at work. These employees are enjoying a game of Nerf basketball.

---

product development teams. Job rotation and cross-training are also successful. Creating informal networking opportunities sounds trivial, but the evidence is strong that relationships heavily impact productivity and creativity."[45]

10. *Organizational systems and procedures.* Companies are increasingly using electronic networks to enhance collaboration among employees in order to achieve innovation, quality, and efficiency. For example, Serena Software, a California-based company with 800 employees located in 29 offices across 14 countries, encouraged its employees to sign up for Facebook for free, and to use the network as a vehicle for getting to know each other. In contrast to using a public site for networking, Dow Chemical launched its own internal social network in order to create relationships between current, past, and temporary employees.[46]

11. *Organizational goals and the associated criteria used for recruitment, selection, development, promotion, layoffs, and retirement of people.* Zappos, which was ranked as the 15th best place to work by *Fortune* in 2009, spends a great deal of time trying to hire people who will fit into its clan-based culture (see Real World/Real People above). As you read this box keep in mind what you read earlier about PE fit.

Back to the Chapter-Opening Case

Which of the 11 methods or techniques for changing organizational culture were used by Southwest Airlines?

The Organizational Socialization Process

◀ ·····················
TO THE POINT
How can the practical lessons of socialization research be integrated within the three phases of socialization?
·····················

Organizational socialization is defined as "the process by which a person learns the values, norms, and required behaviors which permit him to participate as a member of the organization."[47] As previously discussed, organizational socialization is a key mechanism used by organizations to embed their organizational cultures. In short, organizational socialization turns outsiders into fully functioning insiders by promoting and reinforcing the organization's core values and beliefs. This section introduces a three-phase model of organizational socialization and examines the practical application of socialization research.

 LO.8 A Three-Phase Model of Organizational Socialization

One's first year in a complex organization can be confusing. There is a constant swirl of new faces, strange jargon, conflicting expectations, and apparently unrelated events. Some organizations treat new members in a rather haphazard, sink-or-swim manner. More typically, though, the socialization process is characterized by a sequence of identifiable steps.

Organizational behavior researcher Daniel Feldman has proposed a three-phase model of organizational socialization that promotes deeper understanding of this important process. As illustrated in Figure 3–5, the three phases are (1) anticipatory socialization, (2) encounter, and (3) change and acquisition. Each phase has its associated perceptual and social processes. Feldman's model also specifies behavioral and affective outcomes that can be used to judge how well an individual has been socialized. The entire three-phase sequence may take from a few weeks to a year to complete, depending on individual differences and the complexity of the situation.

These onlookers gathered outside the Hyderabad offices of PriceWaterhouseCoopers as police officers worked inside the building. The company was responsible for auditing Satyam Computers, and the former chairman was imprisoned after admitting to a $1 billion fraud.

Phase 1: Anticipatory Socialization The **anticipatory socialization phase** occurs before an individual actually joins an organization. It is represented by the information people have learned about different careers, occupations, professions, and organizations. Anticipatory socialization information comes from many sources. An organization's current employees are a powerful source of anticipatory socialization. So are the Internet and social media. For example, PricewaterhouseCoopers (PwC), the largest professional services firm in the world, uses several web-based sources to attract potential employees. "PwC's early identification strategy is supported by the pwc.tv Website, *Feed Your Future* magazine (downloadable through pwc.tv; it showcases the lives/careers of PwC professionals), and Leadership Adventure (face-to-face learning programs that emphasize the PwC Behaviors)."[48]

organizational socialization Process by which employees learn an organization's values, norms, and required behaviors.

anticipatory socialization phase Occurs before an individual joins an organization, and involves the information people learn about different careers, occupations, professions, and organizations.

figure 3–5   A Model of Organizational Socialization

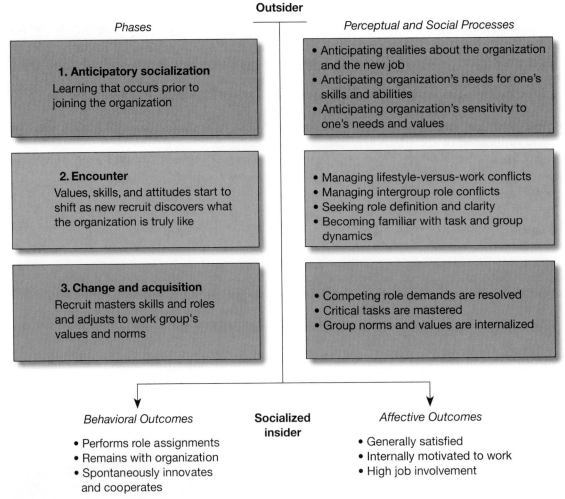

Outsider

Phases

1. Anticipatory socialization
Learning that occurs prior to joining the organization

2. Encounter
Values, skills, and attitudes start to shift as new recruit discovers what the organization is truly like

3. Change and acquisition
Recruit masters skills and roles and adjusts to work group's values and norms

Perceptual and Social Processes

- Anticipating realities about the organization and the new job
- Anticipating organization's needs for one's skills and abilities
- Anticipating organization's sensitivity to one's needs and values

- Managing lifestyle-versus-work conflicts
- Managing intergroup role conflicts
- Seeking role definition and clarity
- Becoming familiar with task and group dynamics

- Competing role demands are resolved
- Critical tasks are mastered
- Group norms and values are internalized

Behavioral Outcomes

- Performs role assignments
- Remains with organization
- Spontaneously innovates and cooperates

Socialized insider

Affective Outcomes

- Generally satisfied
- Internally motivated to work
- High job involvement

SOURCE: Adapted from material in D C Feldman, "The Multiple Socialization of Organization Members," *Academy of Management Review*, April 1981, pp 309–18. Copyright © 1981 by The Academy of Management. Reproduced by permission of The Academy of Management via Copyright Clearance Center.

connect™ Go to
www.mcgrawhillconnect.com
for an interactive exercise to
test your knowledge of the
organizational socialization
process.

Unrealistic expectations about the nature of the work, pay, and promotions are often formulated during phase 1. Because employees with unrealistic expectations are more likely to quit their jobs in the future, organizations may want to use realistic job previews. A **realistic job preview** (RJP) involves giving recruits a realistic idea of what lies ahead by presenting both positive and negative aspects of the job. Whirlpool, for example, uses its career website to post candid comments from employees about what it is like to work at the company.[49] RJPs may be electronic, verbal, in booklet form, audiovisual, or hands on. Research supports the practical benefits of using RJPs. A meta-analysis of 40 studies revealed that RJPs were related to higher performance and to lower attrition from the recruitment process. Results also demonstrated that RJPs lowered job applicants' initial expectations and led to lower turnover among those applicants who were hired.[50]

Phase 2: Encounter   This second phase begins when the employment contract has been signed. During the **encounter phase** employees come to learn what the organization is really like. It is a time for reconciling unmet expectations and making sense of a new work environment. Many companies use a combination of orientation and training programs to socialize employees during the encounter phase. Onboarding is one such technique. **Onboarding** programs help employees to integrate, assimilate, and transition to new jobs by making them familiar with corporate policies, procedures, culture, and politics and by clarifying work-role expectations and responsibilities.[51] Automatic Data Processing's (ADP) onboarding program consists of a combination of online training, classroom training, meetings with employees, written materials containing guidelines on what to expect in the first 90 days, an assimilation guide, and social networking. The company believes that these efforts are helping it to turn newcomers into fully functioning employees.[52]

Phase 3: Change and Acquisition   The **change and acquisition phase** requires employees to master important tasks and roles and to adjust to their work group's values and norms. This will only occur when employees have a clear understanding about their roles—role clarity is discussed in Chapter 10—and they are effectively integrated within the work unit. Being successful in phase 3 also necessitates that employees have a clear understanding regarding the use of social media. It is easy for you to create problems for yourself by not being aware of expectations regarding surfing, texting during meetings, and sending personal messages on company equipment. Experts suggest setting ground rules on the first day of employment, coaching employees on norms, and discussing how guidelines have changed over time.[53] Additionally, organizations such as Schlumberger, a large multinational oil company, use incentives and social gatherings to reinforce the new behaviors expected of employees.

Example. The company is gradually changing its old Soviet culture of blame. Luc Ollivier, a 50-year-old Frenchman, was installed as the boss of regional operations Siberian Geophysical. He's trying to reward performance and, more critical, systematically eliminate mistakes rather than simply punish the people who make them. Ollivier says the company's veteran drillers have immense experience, "but they don't like to teach the young people." So he is working to forge better ties through daylong get-togethers that conclude with a beer bash. Ollivier says the pace of work is up by more than 30% in the past two years., and Siberian Geophysical's drilling revenues reached about $250 million last year [2007], about double their level in 2006.[54]

Table 3–1 presents a list of socialization processes or tactics used by organizations to help employees through this adjustment process. Returning to Table 3–1, can you identify the socialization tactics used by Schlumberger?

Practical Application of Socialization Research

Past research suggests five practical guidelines for managing organizational socialization.

1. A recent survey showed that effective onboarding programs resulted in increased retention, productivity, and rates of task completion for new hires.[55] This reinforces the conclusion that managers should avoid a haphazard, sink-or-swim approach to organizational socialization because formalized socialization tactics positively affect new hires. Formalized or institutionalized socialization tactics were found to positively help employees in both domestic and international operations.[56]

realistic job preview Presents both positive and negative aspects of a job.

encounter phase Employees learn what the organization is really like and reconcile unmet expectations.

onboarding Programs aimed at helping employees integrate, assimilate, and transition to new jobs.

change and acquisition phase Requires employees to master tasks and roles and to adjust to work group values and norms.

LO.9 table 3–1 Socialization Tactics

TACTIC	DESCRIPTION
Collective vs. individual	Collective socialization consists of grouping newcomers and exposing them to a common set of experiences rather than treating each newcomer individually and exposing him or her to more or less unique experiences.
Formal vs. informal	Formal socialization is the practice of segregating a newcomer from regular organization members during a defined socialization period versus not clearly distinguishing a newcomer from more experienced members. Army recruits must attend boot camp before they are allowed to work alongside established soldiers.
Sequential vs. random	Sequential socialization refers to a fixed progression of steps that culminate in the new role, compared to an ambiguous or dynamic progression. The socialization of doctors involves a lock-step sequence from medical school, to internship, to residency before they are allowed to practice on their own.
Fixed vs. variable	Fixed socialization provides a timetable for the assumption of the role, whereas a variable process does not. American university students typically spend one year apiece as freshmen, sophomores, juniors, and seniors.
Serial vs. disjunctive	A serial process is one in which the newcomer is socialized by an experienced member, whereas a disjunctive process does not use a role model.
Investiture vs. divestiture	Investiture refers to the affirmation of a newcomer's incoming global and specific role identities and attributes. Divestiture is the denial and stripping away of the newcomer's existing sense of self and the reconstruction of self in the organization's image. During police training, cadets are required to wear uniforms and maintain an immaculate appearance; they are addressed as "officer" and told they are no longer ordinary citizens but representatives of the police force.

SOURCE: Descriptions were taken from B E Ashforth, *Role Transitions in Organizational Life: An Identity-Based Perspective* (Mahwah, NJ: Lawrence Erlbaum Associates, 2001), pp 149–83.

2. Organizations like the U.S. Military Academy at West Point use socialization tactics to reinforce a culture that promotes ethical behavior. Managers are encouraged to consider how they might best set expectations regarding ethical behavior during all three phases of the socialization process.[57]

3. The type of orientation program used to socialize employees affects their expectations and behavior. A recent study of 72 new Asian international graduate students revealed that they had more accurate expectations, felt less stress, reported better adjustment, and had higher retention rates when the orientation program focused on coping with new entry stress.[58] Managers need to help new hires integrate within the organizational culture and overcome the stress associated with working in a new environment. Consider the approach used by John Chambers, CEO of Cisco Systems: "He meets with groups of new hires to welcome them soon after they start, and at monthly breakfast meetings workers are encouraged to ask him tough questions."[59]

4. Support for stage models is mixed. Although there are different stages of socialization, they are not identical in order, length, or content for all people or jobs.[60] Managers are advised to use a contingency approach toward organizational socialization. In other words, different techniques are appropriate for different people at different times.

5. Managers should pay attention to the socialization of diverse employees. Research demonstrated that diverse employees, particularly those with disabilities, experienced different socialization activities than other newcomers. In turn, these different experiences affected their long-term success and job satisfaction.[61]

Embedding Organizational Culture through Mentoring

The modern word *mentor* derives from Mentor, the name of a wise and trusted counselor in Greek mythology. Terms typically used in connection with mentoring are *teacher, coach, sponsor,* and *peer*. **Mentoring** is defined as the process of forming and maintaining intensive and lasting developmental relationships between a variety of developers (i.e., people who provide career and psychosocial support) and a junior person (the protégé, if male; or protégée, if female).[62] Mentoring can serve to embed an organization's culture when developers and the protégé/protégée work in the same organization for two reasons. First, mentoring contributes to creating a sense of oneness by promoting the acceptance of the organization's core values throughout the organization. Second, the socialization aspect of mentoring also promotes a sense of membership.

Not only is mentoring important as a tactic for embedding organizational culture, but research suggests it can significantly influence the protégé/protégée's future career. For example, a meta-analysis revealed that mentored employees had higher compensation and more promotions than nonmentored employees. Mentored employees also were found to have higher organizational knowledge, job performance, and salary over time.[63] This section focuses on how people can use mentoring to their advantage. We discuss the functions of mentoring, the developmental networks underlying mentoring, and the personal and organizational implications of mentoring.

► **TO THE POINT**
What are the four developmental networks and how can you use them to advance your career?

Functions of Mentoring

Kathy Kram, a Boston University researcher, conducted in-depth interviews with both members of 18 pairs of senior and junior managers. As a by-product of this study, Kram identified two general functions—career and psychosocial—of the mentoring process. Five *career functions* that enhanced career development were sponsorship, exposure-and-visibility, coaching, protection, and challenging assignments. Four *psychosocial functions* were role modeling, acceptance-and-confirmation, counseling, and friendship. The psychosocial functions clarified the participants' identities and enhanced their feelings of competence.[64]

LO.10 Developmental Networks Underlying Mentoring

Historically, it was thought that mentoring was primarily provided by one person who was called a mentor. Today, however, the changing nature of technology, organizational structures, and marketplace dynamics require that people seek career information and support from many sources. Mentoring is currently viewed as a process in which protégés and protégées seek developmental guidance from a network of people, who are referred to as *developers*. McKinsey & Company tells its associates, "Build your own McKinsey." This slogan means the consulting firm expects its people to identify partners, colleagues, and

mentoring Process of forming and maintaining developmental relationships between a mentor and a junior person.

figure 3–6 Developmental Networks Associated with Mentoring

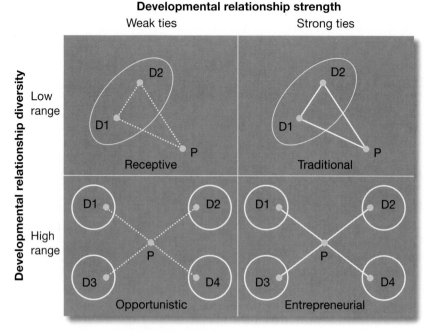

Key: D, developer; P, protégé

SOURCE: From M Higgins and K Kram, "Reconceptualizing Mentoring at Work: A Developmental Network Perspective," *Academy of Management Review,* April 2001, p 270. Copyright © 2001 by The Academy of Management. Reproduced by permission of The Academy of Management via Copyright Clearance Center.

subordinates who have related goals and interests so that they can help one another develop their expertise. Each McKinsey associate is thus responsible for his or her own career development—and for mentoring others. As McKinsey's approach recognizes, the diversity and strength of a person's network of relationships is instrumental in obtaining the type of career assistance needed to manage his or her career.[65] Figure 3–6 presents a developmental network typology based on integrating the diversity and strength of developmental relationships.[66]

The **diversity of developmental relationships** reflects the variety of people within the network an individual uses for developmental assistance. There are two sub-components associated with network diversity: (1) the number of different people the person is networked with and (2) the various social systems from which the networked relationships stem (e.g., employer, school, family, community, professional associations, and religious affiliations). As shown in Figure 3–6, developmental relationship diversity ranges from low (few people or social systems) to high (multiple people or social systems).

Developmental relationship strength reflects the quality of relationships among the individual and those involved in his or her developmental network. For example, strong ties are reflective of relationships based on frequent interactions, reciprocity, and positive affect. Weak ties, in contrast, are based more on superficial relationships. Together, the diversity and strength of developmental relationships result in four types of developmental networks (see Figure 3–5): receptive, traditional, entrepreneurial, and opportunistic.

A *receptive* developmental network is composed of a few weak ties from one social system such as an employer or a professional association. The single oval around D1 and D2 in Figure 3–6 is indicative of two developers who come from one social system. In contrast, a *traditional* network contains a few strong ties between an employee and developers that all come from one social system. An entrepreneurial network, which is the strongest type of developmental network, is made up of strong ties among several developers (D1–D4) who come from four different social systems. Finally, an opportunistic network is associated with having weak ties with multiple developers from different social systems.

Personal and Organizational Implications

There are five key personal implications to consider. First, it is important to foster a broad developmental network because the number and quality of your contacts will influence your career success. Second, job and career satisfaction are likely to be influenced by the consistency between your career goals and the type of developmental network at your disposal. For example, people with an entrepreneurial developmental network are more likely to experience change in their careers and to benefit from personal learning than people with receptive, traditional, and opportunistic networks. If this sounds attractive to you, you should try to increase the diversity and strength of your developmental relationships. In contrast, lower levels of job satisfaction are expected when employees have receptive developmental networks and they desire to experience career advancement in multiple organizations. Receptive developmental networks, however, can be satisfying to someone who does not desire to be promoted up the career ladder.[67]

Third, a developer's willingness to provide career and psychosocial assistance is a function of the protégé/protégée's ability and potential and the quality of the interpersonal relationship.[68] Research also shows that the quality of the mentoring relationship is likely to be higher when the parties have common values and personality characteristics.[69] This implies that you must take ownership for enhancing your skills, abilities, and developmental networks as well as your interpersonal relationships if you desire to experience career advancement throughout your life. Fourth, it is important to become proficient at using social networking tools such as Twitter, LinkedIn, and Facebook. Companies such as AT&T are increasingly using online tools to conduct mentoring across geographical boundaries (see Real World/Real People on page 84). These tools not only enable you to increase the breadth of your social network, but they also can increase your productivity. Finally, you should develop a mentoring plan. Experts suggest that this plan should include the following components:[70]

- Identify and prioritize your mentoring goals. These goals should be based on a determination of what you want to learn.
- Identify people who are skilled or experienced in areas you want to improve. Don't overlook your peers as they are a good source of functional, technical, and organizational knowledge.
- Determine how best to build a relationship with these "targeted" individuals.
- Determine how you can provide value to your mentor. Because mentoring is a two-way street, others are more likely to help you if they see some value in assisting you in the pursuit of your career goals.

diversity of developmental relationships The variety of people in a network used for developmental assistance.

developmental relationship strength The quality of relationships among people in a network.

real WORLD // real PEOPLE

AT&T Conducts Mentoring Online

At AT&T mentoring takes place in self-organizing, topic-based groups, which AT&T calls leadership circles. The self-organizing approach allows them to reach far more employees than programs run by HR. Using an online platform, one mentor can work with several mentees at a time—sometimes in different locations—on skills like generating sales leads or leading teams. The circles take advantage of platform features such as community forums, document-sharing spaces, group polling, and calendars that announce events and mentor availability. Since the supporting software has some built-in social-networking capability, mentees are able to connect to others with very little hands-on assistance from HR; peer-to-peer mentoring often starts to take place within a circle as it matures. Managers frequently share mentoring responsibilities within a circle—for instance, three executives might work together to advise a group of nine employees. Face-to-face meetings, conference calls, and webcast supplement the online coaching.

How would you like to be mentored online instead of face to face?

SOURCE: Excerpted from J C Meister and K Willyerd, "Mentoring Millennials," *Harvard Business Review*, May 2010, p 71.

- Determine when it is time to move on. Mentors are not forever. If you believe that your mentor is ineffective, or worse yet, causing more harm than benefit, find a new mentor.

Research also supports the organizational benefits of mentoring. For example, mentoring enhances the effectiveness of organizational communication. Specifically, mentoring increases the amount of vertical communication both up and down an organization, and it provides a mechanism for modifying or reinforcing organizational culture. Benefits such as these are leading more and more companies to set up formal mentoring programs. A survey found that 6 out of 10 companies already have programs for coaching or mentoring, and of the remaining companies, 8 out of 10 are planning such a program.[71]

Summary of Key Concepts

1. *Define organizational culture and discuss its three layers.* Organizational culture represents the shared assumptions that a group holds. It influences employees' perceptions and behavior at work. The three layers of organizational culture include observable artifacts, espoused values, and basic assumptions. Artifacts are the physical manifestations of an organization's culture. Espoused values represent the explicitly stated values and norms that are preferred by an organization. Basic underlying assumptions are unobservable and represent the core of organizational culture.

2. *Discuss the difference between espoused and enacted values.* Espoused values represent the explicitly stated values and norms that are preferred by an organization. Enacted values, in contrast, reflect the values and norms that actually are exhibited or converted into employee behavior.

3. *Describe the four functions of organizational culture.* Four functions of organizational culture are organizational identity, collective commitment, social system stability, and sense-making device.

4. *Discuss the four types of organizational culture associated with the competing values framework.* The competing values framework identifies four different types of organizational culture. A clan culture has an internal focus and values flexibility rather than stability and control. An adhocracy culture has an external focus and values flexibility. A market culture has a strong external focus and values stability and control. A hierarchy culture has an internal focus and values stability and control over flexibility.

5. *Summarize the five conclusions derived from research about the outcomes associated with organizational culture.* Organizational culture is related to measures of organizational effectiveness. Employees are more satisfied and committed to organizations with clan cultures. An organization's financial performance is not very strongly related to organizational culture. Innovation and quality can be increased by building characteristics associated with clan, adhocracy, and market cultures into the organization. Culture is not strongly related to financial performance, and companies with market cultures tend to have more positive organizational outcomes.

6. *Review the four caveats about culture change.* First, managing organizational culture is one of the most important functions of leadership. Second, the process of culture change begins by targeting one of the three layers of organizational culture. Third, it is important to consider the extent to which the current culture is aligned with the organization's vision and strategic plans before attempting to change any aspect of organizational culture. Finally, it is important to use a structured approach when implementing culture change.

7. *Summarize the methods used by organizations to change organizational culture.* Changing culture amounts to teaching employees about the organization's preferred values, beliefs, expectations, and behaviors. This is accomplished by using one or more of the following 11 mechanisms: (*a*) formal statements of organizational philosophy, mission, vision, values, and materials used for recruiting, selection, and socialization; (*b*) the design of physical space, work environments, and

buildings; (*c*) slogans, language, acronyms, and sayings; (*d*) deliberate role modeling, training programs, teaching, and coaching by managers and supervisors; (*e*) explicit rewards, status symbols, and promotion criteria; (*f*) stories, legends, and myths about key people and events; (*g*) the organizational activities, processes, or outcomes that leaders pay attention to, measure, and control; (*h*) leader reactions to critical incidents and organizational crises; (*i*) the workflow and organizational structure; (*j*) organizational systems and procedures; and (*k*) organizational goals and associated criteria used for recruitment, selection, development, promotion, layoffs, and retirement of people.

8. *Describe the three phases in Feldman's model of organizational socialization.* The three phases of Feldman's model are anticipatory socialization, encounter, and change and acquisition. Anticipatory socialization begins before an individual actually joins the organization. The encounter phase begins when the employment contract has been signed. Phase 3 involves the period in which employees master important tasks and resolve any role conflicts.

9. *Discuss the various socialization tactics used to socialize employees.* There are six key socialization tactics. They are collective versus individual, formal versus informal, sequential versus random, fixed versus variable, serial versus disjunctive, and investiture versus divestiture (see Table 3–1). Each tactic provides organizations with two opposing options for socializing employees.

10. *Explain the four developmental networks associated with mentoring.* The four developmental networks are based on integrating the diversity and strength of an individual's developmental relationships. The four resulting developmental networks are receptive, traditional, entrepreneurial, and opportunistic. A receptive network is composed of a few weak ties from one social system. Having a few strong ties with developers from one social system is referred to as a traditional network. An entrepreneurial network is made up of strong ties among several developers; and an opportunistic network is associated with having weak ties from different social systems.

Key Terms

Organizational culture, 62

Values, 63

Espoused values, 63

Sustainability, 64

Enacted values, 65

PE Fit, 65

Competing values framework (CVF), 68

Clan culture, 68

Adhocracy culture, 70

Market culture, 70

Hierarchy culture, 70

Vision, 73

Strategic plan, 74

Organizational socialization, 77

Anticipatory socialization phase, 77

Realistic job preview, 78

Encounter phase, 78

Onboarding, 78

Change and acquisition phase, 79

Mentoring, 81

Diversity of developmental relationships, 82

Developmental relationship strength, 82

OB in Action Case Study

Sergio Marchionne Undertakes Major Strategic and Culture Change at Chrysler Group[72]

A decline in sales isn't the only big problem facing Chrysler Group LLC. Another, according to Chief Executive Sergio Marchionne, is the almost ingrained tendency to react to falling sales by slashing prices.

In Detroit, "there's almost a fanatical, maniacal interest in (market) share," Mr. Marchionne told reporters Monday on the opening day of the North American International Auto Show. But rarely, he added, has heavy discounting in pursuit of high volumes helped auto makers generate profits in the long term. . . .

For the past seven months, the 57-year-old Italian-born Canadian has been working to shake up Chrysler and move the company away from old ways that forced it into bankruptcy reorganization last year. He has ousted several veteran executives, flattened its bureaucracy and, according to people who have worked closely with Mr. Marchionne, injected an element of fear into its ranks.

One of the more frustrating problems for Mr. Marchionne has been the use of heavy rebates and other incentives to maintain sales—an issue that has plagued General Motors Co. and Ford Motor Co. over the years.

Last July, for example, when the U.S. government offered as much as $4,500 in "cash for clunkers" rebates, Chrysler's sales chief at the time, Peter Fong, drew up a plan to offer an additional $4,500 from Chrysler, two people familiar with the matter said. . . .

But when Mr. Marchionne found out about it, he was furious, these people said. In an August meeting with Mr. Fong and his sales team, the CEO excoriated them, saying doubling discounts amounted to "giving away margin" at a time when Chrysler was scrambling for profits, one person familiar with the details of the meeting said. "Sergio was ballistic," this person said. . . .

Several weeks later, in September, Mr. Fong was summoned to the office of Nancy Rae, Chrysler's head of human resources, and was told his services were no longer needed, these people said. . . .

Mr. Marchionne took the helm at Chrysler in June, when the company exited bankruptcy protection and formed an alliance with Italy's FIAT SpA, where he also serves as CEO and which owns about 20% of Chrysler. In November, he laid out a turn-around plan that calls for Chrysler to launch a series of small cars designed by Fiat, and envisions Chrysler breaking even in 2010 and returning to profitability by 2011.

Besides working out ways for the two companies to work together, Mr. Marchionne has tried to shake up Chrysler's plodding corporate culture. . . .

To select his new management team, Mr. Marchionne held dozens of 15-minute interviews with Chrysler executives over several days to evaluate which ones to keep and which to push out, according to people who participated in the process.

When the process was over, Mr. Marchionne had 23 people reporting to him. Some were junior executives who had been moved up a level or two in the organization. . . .

Many in the industry believe Mr. Machionne has no option but to shock Chrysler out of its old ways. "The culture in Detroit is so insular, and he's going to have to throw some china against the wall," said Michael J. Jackson, chairman and CEO of AutoNation Inc., a large dealership chain. . . .

Mr. Marchionne took an office on the fourth floor of the technology center at Chrysler's headquarters in Auburn Hills, Mich., among Chrysler's engineers, instead of an office in its adjoining executive tower. His management team began meeting weekly in a nearby conference room equipped with video gear so that Fiat executives in Italy could take part.

In these meetings, Mr. Marchionne often spelled out what he saw as Chrysler's many deficiencies: margins and vehicle quality needed to improve and better control over pricing was imperative, according to one person who has been in the sessions. Details of the discussions weren't to leave the room. Security officers even called senior executives over the summer to make sure no one was talking to reporters about the company's plans.

Mr. Marchionne, a notorious workaholic, carries five BlackBerrys and works seven days a week. He spends about one full week a month in Michigan and flies back for weekend meetings when he isn't in town.

Questions for Discussion

1. What are the observable artifacts, espoused values, and basic assumptions associated with Chrysler's culture? Explain.

2. How is Mr. Machionne trying to improve the PE fit of his direct reports?

3. Use the competing values framework to diagnose Chrysler's culture. To what extent does it possess characteristics associated with clan, adhocracy, market, and hierarchy cultures? Discuss.

4. Begin by looking up Chrysler's mission or vision statement on the company's website. Now answer the following question: To what extent is the culture type you identified in question 2 consistent with the accomplishment of this mission or vision? Explain.

5. Which of the mechanisms for changing organizational culture did Mr. Marchionne use at Chrysler? Explain.

6. Would you like to work at Chrysler? Explain your rationale.

Legal/Ethical Challenge

Credit-Card Issuers Have Cultures That Focus on Growth by Targeting Financially Strapped People[73]

The troubles sound familiar. Borrowers falling behind on their payments. Defaults rising. Huge swaths of loans souring. Investors getting burned. But forget the now-familiar tales of mortgages gone bad. The next horror for beaten-down financial firms is the $950 billion worth of outstanding credit-card debt—much of it toxic. . . . The consumer debt bomb is already beginning to spray shrapnel throughout the financial markets, further weakening the U.S. economy. "The next meltdown will be in credit cards," says Gregory Larkin, senior analyst at research firm Innovest Strategic Value Advisors. . . .

But some banks and credit-card companies may be exacerbating their problems. To boost profits and get ahead of coming regulation, they're hiking interest rates. But that's making it harder for consumers to keep up. . . .? Sure the credit-card market is just a fraction of the $11.9 trillion mortgage market. But sometimes the losses can be more painful. That's because most credit-card debt is unsecured, meaning consumers don't have to make down payments when opening up their accounts. If they stop making monthly payments and the account goes bad, there are no underlying assets for credit-card companies to recoup. With mortgages, in contrast, some banks are protected both by down payments and by the ability to recover at least some of the money by selling the property. . . .

The industry's practices during the lending boom are coming back to haunt many credit-card lenders now. Cate Colombo, a former call center staffer at MBNA, the big

issuer bought by Bank of America in 2005, says her job was to develop a rapport with credit-card customers and advise them to use more of their available credit. Colleagues would often gather around her chair when she was on the phone with a customer and chant: "Sell, sell." "It was like *Boiler Room*," says Colombo, referring to the 2000 movie about unscrupulous stock brokers. "I knew that they would probably be in debt for the rest of their lives." Unless, of course, they default.

Assume that you are member of Congress. What would you do in light of the facts in this case?

1. Create legislation that does not allow credit-card issuers to raise interest rates for those who cannot pay their bills.

2. Create legislation that makes it a crime for people like Cate Columbo to entice people to spend money on a credit card when they can't afford it.

3. I would not create any legislation. Credit-card issuers and people like Cate Columbo are not to blame for our financial problems. People must be responsible for their own behavior.

4. Invent other options.

Web Resources

Additional tools and resources are available to help you master the content of this chapter on the website at
www.mhhe.com/kreitner10e

chapter 4

International OB: Managing across Cultures

 Learning Objectives

When you finish studying the material in this chapter, you should be able to:

LO.1 Define the term *culture,* and explain how societal culture and organizational culture combine to influence on-the-job behavior.

LO.2 Define *ethnocentrism,* and explain how to develop cultural intelligence.

LO.3 Distinguish between high-context and low-context cultures, and identify and describe the nine cultural dimensions from Project GLOBE.

LO.4 Distinguish between individualistic and collectivist cultures, and explain the difference between monochronic and polychronic cultures.

LO.5 Specify the practical lesson from the Hofstede cross-cultural study, and explain what Project GLOBE researchers discovered about leadership.

LO.6 Discuss the results and practical significance of the recent Bloom and Van Reenen study of national management styles.

LO.7 Explain why US managers have a comparatively high failure rate on foreign assignments.

LO.8 Summarize the research findings about North American women on foreign assignments.

LO.9 Identify four stages of the foreign assignment cycle and the OB trouble spot associated with each stage.

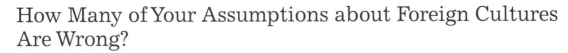

How Many of Your Assumptions about Foreign Cultures Are Wrong?

Sue, an American time management expert, attributes her consistent training success to her grounding in a well-planned, structured PowerPoint presentation. When she is sent to the Israeli site of a US company, she does diligent homework, adds content slides, expands the objectives, and learns some words in Hebrew.

What she doesn't expect is attendees showing up late or engaged in lively conversations, or absent participants who reportedly are attending an urgent meeting. Even more unexpected is participants e-mailing during her presentation. Someone even challenges the wording of her carefully thought-out objectives.

After an hour of questions on every slide, loud debates, and lapses into Hebrew, Sue is only on slide 7 of 60! She calls a break.

What went wrong?

Culture interfered. . . .

In spite of surface similarities, there are significant differences with tremendous gaps in the ways Americans and Israelis perceive and approach learning, communication, work, and professionalism.

The cultural reality is that Israelis are very good at handling change and improvising amid fast-moving events. They generally have a relaxed attitude about time and schedules. They value spontaneity, flexibility, and spirited debate rather than making and adhering to rigid plans. Multitasking and just-in-time action, hallmarks of Israeli culture, are seen as being practical and efficient. When Israelis greet authority figures and visitors with lots of challenging questions, they are showing interest, not necessarily being critical. Normal conversation in Israel can be loud with plenty of interruptions, but with no disrespect intended.[1]

We hear a lot about globalization and the global economy these days. Cultural misalignments, such as those Sue encountered while working in Israel, are a growing challenge. Cross-cultural skills can spell the difference between success and disappointment in today's global economy. Signs and symptoms of economic globalization making headlines in recent years have been the controversial North American Free Trade Agreement, riots at World Trade Organization meetings, complaints about the offshoring of jobs, trade imbalances, foreign sweatshops, and intellectual property abuses.[2] These are legitimate concerns, but some have been exaggerated out of proportion as circumstances evolve. For instance, take the offshoring of jobs—replacing domestic employees with lower-paid workers in foreign countries. According to a recent research report, "About half of offshore service work arrangements fail, and often it's because executives don't take into account the 'invisible costs' of communication and cultural friction."[3] Rising wages and quality problems in India, China, and elsewhere also are making offshoring less attractive.[4] Still, a global economic earthquake is underway:

Example. For more than half a century, Americans could take for granted that the world economy would orbit around them. No longer. . . .

"The change is from globalization going one way to globalization going every way. It's as much about what developing countries are doing as developed countries," said Mark Foster, a London-based Accenture consultant.

Assuming continued economic growth in the developing world, the ranks of the global middle class are expected to triple by 2030 to 1.2 billion, according to the World Bank. Today, a bit more than half of that free-spending group resides in developing countries. By 2030, almost all of it, 92%, will call the developing world home.

For multinational corporations, that means paying ever more attention to what's happening outside the United States and especially in Asia, Latin America, parts of the Middle East and Africa.[5]

Global managers, who can move comfortably from one culture to another while conducting business, have an advantage in the new global economy. Consider, for example, this recent *Harvard Business Review* research report:

Example. Travel and living abroad have long been seen as good for the soul. What's perhaps less well-known is that they're also good for the company. People who have international experience or identify with more than one nationality are better problem solvers and display more creativity, our research suggests. What's more, we found that people with this international experience are more likely to create new businesses and products and to be promoted.[6]

According to another study, US multinational companies headed by CEOs with international assignments on their résumés tended to outperform the competition.[7] Even managers and employees who stay in their native country will find it hard to escape today's global economy and cross-cultural interactions. For example, at Nestlé's headquarters in Vevey, Switzerland, people of 100 different nationalities work for the world's biggest food company. Nestlé's CEO Paul Bulcke was born in Belgium and speaks six languages.[8] Cross-cultural dealings are particularly common in countries such as the United States, Canada, and Brazil—culturally diverse nations populated by both indigenous people and generations of immigrants (see Table 4–1).[9] (In fact, you will learn some interesting things about Navajo culture later in this chapter.) Employees who do stay

American tourists arriving in far away Auckland, New Zealand, on cruise ships have little trouble fitting in thanks to a common language. Yet both countries have unique cultures and a good deal of diversity because of a rich blend of indigenous people and immigrants. Global managers cannot afford to ignore those differences.

table 4–1   The United States, a Nation of Immigrants, Has Diverse Cultural Roots

If the 312+ million people in America could be reduced proportionately to a village of 100 people, their ancestry would have the following profile:

German	15 people
Irish	11 people
African	9 people
English	9 people
Mexican	7 people
Italian	6 people
Polish	3 people
French	3 people
Native American	3 people
Scottish	2 people
Dutch	2 people
Norwegian	2 people
Scotch-Irish	1 person
Swedish	1 person
All other immigrants	26 people

SOURCES: David J. Smith, *If America Were a Village* (Toronto: Kids Can Press, 2009); and Greg Toppo, "Counting to 100 in 'America,'" *USA Today,* September 3, 2009, p 7D.

home will be thrust into international relationships by working for foreign-owned companies or by dealing with foreign suppliers, customers, and co-workers.[10] Perhaps they will be offered an unexpected foreign assignment.[11]

The global economy is a rich mix of opportunities, problems, and cultures, and now is the time to prepare to thrive in it. Accordingly, the purpose of this chapter is to help you take a step in that direction by exploring the impacts of culture in today's increasingly internationalized organizations. This chapter draws on the area of cultural anthropology.[12] We begin with a model that shows how societal culture and organizational culture (covered in Chapter 3) combine to influence work behavior. Next, we discuss how to develop *cultural intelligence.* Key dimensions of societal culture are presented with the goal of enhancing cross-cultural awareness. Practical lessons from cross-cultural management research are then reviewed. The chapter concludes by exploring the challenge of accepting a foreign assignment and avoiding *culture shock.*

connect Go to www.mcgrawhillconnect.com for an interactive comprehension case exercise to test your knowledge of personal interaction in different cultures.

LO.1 Culture and Organizational Behavior

How would you, as a manager, interpret the following situations?

TO THE POINT

What does culture involve and how are societal and organizational culture related?

Example. An Asian executive for a multinational company, transferred from Taiwan to the Midwest, appears aloof and autocratic to his peers.

A West Coast bank embarks on a "friendly teller" campaign, but its Filipino female tellers won't cooperate.

A white manager criticizes a black male employee's work. Instead of getting an explanation, the manager is met with silence and a firm stare.[13]

If you attribute the behavior in these situations to personalities, three descriptions come to mind: arrogant, unfriendly, and hostile. These are reasonable conclusions. Unfortunately, they are probably wrong, being based more on prejudice and stereotypes than on actual fact. However, if you attribute the behavioral outcomes to *cultural* differences, you stand a better chance of making the following more valid interpretations: "As it turns out, Asian culture encourages a more distant managing style, Filipinos associate overly friendly behavior in women with prostitution, and blacks as a group act more deliberately, studying visual cues, than most white men."[14] One cannot afford to overlook relevant cultural contexts when trying to understand and manage organizational behavior.

Societal Culture Is Complex and Multilayered

In Chapter 3, we discussed *organizational* culture. Here, the focus is more broadly on *societal* culture. "**Culture** is a set of beliefs and values about what is desirable and undesirable in a community of people, and a set of formal or informal practices to support the values."[15] So culture has both prescriptive (what people should do) and descriptive (what they actually do) elements. Culture is passed from one generation to the next by family, friends, teachers, and relevant others. Most cultural lessons are learned by observing and imitating role models as they go about their daily affairs or as observed in the media.[16]

Culture is difficult to grasp because it is multilayered. International management experts Fons Trompenaars (from the Netherlands) and Charles Hampden-Turner (from Britain) offered this instructive analogy in their landmark book, *Riding the Waves of Culture:*

Example. Culture comes in layers, like an onion. To understand it you have to unpeel it layer by layer.

On the outer layer are the products of culture, like the soaring skyscrapers of Manhattan, pillars of private power, with congested public streets between them. These are expressions of deeper values and norms in a society that are not directly visible (values such as upward mobility, "the more-the-better," status, material success). The layers of values and norms are deeper within the "onion," and are more difficult to identify.[17]

The best way to "peel the cultural onion" is to be proactive and get to know people from different cultures. IBM's CEO, Samuel Palmisano, put it this way: "I enjoy spending time in many countries, especially in the developing world. There is tremendous optimism and excitement about their future. You can't learn about these diverse cultures and immense opportunities by staying in your corporate headquarters."[18] The same goes for students in classrooms. Recent research with college students documented how multicultural experiences improved creative performance.[19] (Hmmm, a good argument for students trying to get their parents to pay for a summer in Europe after graduation?)

Culture Is a Subtle but Pervasive Force

Culture generally remains below the threshold of conscious awareness because it involves *taken-for-granted assumptions* about how one should perceive, think, act, and feel. Pioneering cultural anthropologist Edward T Hall put it this way:

Example. Since much of culture operates outside our awareness, frequently we don't even know what we know. We pick. . . [expectations and assumptions] up in the cradle. We unconsciously learn what to notice and what not to notice, how to divide time and space, how to walk and talk and use our bodies, how to behave as men or women, how to relate to other people, how to handle responsibility, whether experience is seen as whole or fragmented. This applies to all people. The Chinese or the Japanese or the Arabs are as unaware of their assumptions as we are of our own. We each assume that they're part of human nature. What we think of as "mind" is really internalized culture.[20]

In sum, it has been said: "you are your culture, and your culture is you." As part of the growing sophistication of marketing practices in the global economy, companies are hiring cultural anthropologists to decipher the cultural roots of customer needs and preferences.[21]

A Model of Societal and Organizational Cultures

As illustrated in Figure 4–1, culture influences organizational behavior in two ways. Employees bring their societal culture to work with them in the form of customs and language. Organizational culture, a by-product of societal culture, in turn affects the individual's values, ethics, attitudes, assumptions, and expectations. Societal culture is shaped by the various environmental factors listed in the left-hand side of Figure 4–1.

Once inside the organization's sphere of influence, the individual is further affected by the *organization's* culture. Mixing of societal and organizational cultures can produce interesting dynamics in multinational companies. For example, with French and American employees working side by side at General Electric's medical imaging production facility in Waukesha, Wisconsin, unit head Claude Benchimol has witnessed some culture shock:

Example. The French are surprised the American parking lots empty out as early as 5 PM; the Americans are surprised the French don't start work at 8 AM. Benchimol feels the French are more talkative and candid. Americans have more

figure 4–1   Cultural Influences on Organizational Behavior

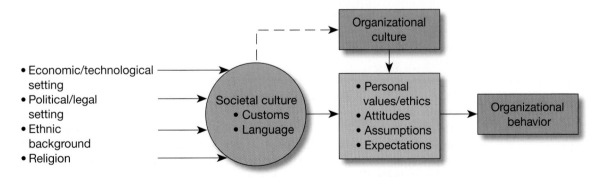

culture Beliefs and values about how a community of people should and do act.

of a sense of hierarchy and are less likely to criticize. But they may be growing closer to the French. Says Benchimol: "It's taken a year to get across the idea that we are all entitled to say what we don't like to become more productive and work better."[22]

Same company, same company culture, yet GE's French and American co-workers have different attitudes about time, hierarchy, and communication. They are the products of different societal cultures.

When managing people at work, the individual's societal culture, the organizational culture, and any interaction between the two need to be taken into consideration. For example, American workers' cultural orientation toward quality improvement differs significantly from the Japanese cultural pattern. "Unlike Japanese workers, Americans aren't interested in making small step-by-step improvements to increase quality. They want to achieve the breakthrough, the impossible dream. The way to motivate them: Ask for the big leap, rather than for tiny steps."[23]

TO THE POINT

Can cultural intelligence reduce ethnocentrism?

Developing Cultural Intelligence

What is your readiness to interact effectively with people from other cultures? To help answer that question, imagine a continuum with *ethnocentrism* on the low-readiness end and *cultural intelligence* on the high-readiness end. Let's explore these two extremes, with the goal of decreasing ethnocentrism and increasing cultural intelligence.

LO.2   Ethnocentrism: A Cross-Cultural Roadblock

Ethnocentrism, the belief that one's native country, culture, language, and modes of behavior are superior to all others, has its roots in the dawn of civilization. First identified as a behavioral science concept in 1906, involving the tendency of groups to reject outsiders,[24] the term *ethnocentrism* generally has a more encompassing (national or societal) meaning today. Worldwide evidence of ethnocentrism is plentiful. As a case in point, listen to Hiwa Assad, a former Kurdish guerilla fighter who lives in the city of Kirkuk in the Kurdish region of northern Iraq. "People in Kirkuk have two faces. . . . They sit with you and talk as if they're angels. They say, 'I have no enemies and don't hate other religions and nationalities.' But the minute they are alone with their own sect, they are the first ones to insult and hate."[25] Militant ethnocentrism led to deadly "ethnic cleansing" in Bosnia and Kosovo and genocide in the African nations of Rwanda, Burundi, and the Darfur region of Sudan.

Less dramatic, but still troublesome, is ethnocentrism within managerial and organizational contexts. Experts on the subject framed the problem this way:

Example. [Ethnocentric managers have] a preference for putting home-country people in key positions everywhere in the world and rewarding them more handsomely for work, along with a tendency to feel that this group is more intelligent, more capable, or more reliable. . . . Ethnocentrism is often not attributable to prejudice as much as to inexperience or lack of knowledge about foreign persons and situations. This is not too surprising, since most executives know far more about employees in their home environments. As one executive put it, "At least I understand why our own managers make mistakes. With our foreigners, I never know. The foreign managers may be better. But if I can't trust a person, should I hire him or her just to prove we're multinational?"[26]

Research suggests ethnocentrism is bad for business. A survey of 918 companies with home offices in the United States (272 companies), Japan (309), and Europe (337) found ethnocentric staffing and human resource policies to be associated with increased personnel problems. Those problems included recruiting difficulties, high turnover rates, and lawsuits over personnel policies. Among the three regional samples, Japanese companies had the most ethnocentric human resource practices and the most international human resource problems.[27]

Current and future managers—and people in general—can effectively deal with ethnocentrism through education, greater cross-cultural awareness, international experience, and a conscious effort to value cultural diversity. Fareed Zakaria, a CNN correspondent born in India, recently offered this wake-up call about the risks of ethnocentrism:

CNN correspondent Fareed Zakaria, who was born in India, worries that the average American's narrow view of the world will hurt the country's competitiveness.

Example. Americans speak few languages, know little about foreign cultures, and remain unconvinced that they need to rectify this. Americans rarely benchmark to global standards because they are sure that their way must be the best and most advanced. The result is that they are increasingly suspicious of the emerging global era. There is a growing gap between America's worldly business elite and cosmopolitan class, on the one hand, and the majority of the American people, on the other. Without real efforts to bridge it, this divide could destroy America's competitive edge and its political future.[28]

Here are a couple of positive signs regarding college students: According to the latest available figures, there were 690,923 foreign students studying in the United States (boosting the US economy by $20 billion) and 260,327 US students studying abroad in 2009.[29]

Cultural Paradoxes Require Cultural Intelligence

An important qualification needs to be offered at this juncture. All of the cultural differences in this chapter and elsewhere need to be viewed as *tendencies* and *patterns* rather than as absolutes.[30] As soon as one falls into the trap of assuming *all* Italians are this, and *all* Koreans will do that, and so on, potentially instructive generalizations become mindless stereotypes. Two professors with extensive foreign work experience offer this advice: "As teachers, researchers, and managers in cross-cultural contexts, we need to recognize that our original characterizations of other cultures are best guesses that we need to modify as we gain more experience."[31] Consequently, they contend, we will be better prepared to deal with inevitable *cultural paradoxes.* By paradox, they mean there are always exceptions to the rule; individuals who do not fit the expected cultural pattern. A good example is the head of Canon. "By Japanese CEO standards, Canon Inc.'s Fujio Mitarai is something of an anomaly. For starters, he's fast and decisive—a far cry from the consensus builders who typically run Japan Inc."[32] One also encounters lots of cultural paradoxes in large and culturally diverse nations such as the United States and Australia. This is where the need for cultural intelligence arises.

Cultural intelligence, the ability to accurately interpret ambiguous cross-cultural situations, is an important skill in today's diverse workplaces.[33] David C

ethnocentrism Belief that one's native country, culture, language, and behavior are superior.

cultural intelligence The ability to interpret ambiguous cross-cultural situations accurately.

real WORLD // real PEOPLE

Details Count When Doing Business in Germany

- *Titles.* Always use titles, like Doctor, Frau, or Herr. Don't use first names unless invited.
- *Birthdays.* When it's your birthday, it's your responsibility to provide food and drinks.
- *Punctuality.* Always be on time. Be direct and detail oriented.
- *Meetings.* Expect business meetings to be longer than in other countries.
- *Hierarchy.* Make your status known. Hierarchy is considered important.
- *Toasting.* Make eye contact when toasting. Not doing so is said to bring bad luck.
- *Utensils.* Crossing your utensils means you're still eating. Laying them parallel means you're finished.

- *Talking.* Avoid exaggerations and high-pressure talk.
- *Visits.* When invited to someone's home, always arrive on time and bring a small gift.
- *Hands.* Keep your hands on the table when eating. To do otherwise is considered rude.

What does an awareness of such seemingly small details have to do with cultural intelligence? What would you put on your list of cultural tips for foreigners doing business in the United States to help them be culturally intelligent?

SOURCE: Excerpted from "How Not to Embarrass Yourself in Germany," *Bloomberg Businessweek*, October 4–10, 2010, p 82.

Thomas and Kerr Inkson, authors of the book *Cultural Intelligence: Living and Working Globally*, say cultural intelligence has three parts:

Example.

1. First, the culturally intelligent person requires *knowledge* of culture and of the fundamental principles of cross-cultural interactions. This means knowing what culture is, how cultures vary, and how culture affects behavior.

2. Second, the culturally intelligent person needs to practice *mindfulness*, the ability to pay attention in a reflective and creative way to cues in the cross-cultural situations encountered and to one's own knowledge and feelings.

3. Third, based on knowledge and mindfulness, the culturally intelligent person develops cross-cultural *skills* and becomes competent across a wide range of situations. These skills involve choosing the appropriate behavior from a well-developed repertoire of behaviors that are correct for different intercultural situations.[34]

Those interested in developing their cultural intelligence need to first polish their *emotional* intelligence, discussed in detail in Chapter 5, and then practice in unfamiliar cross-cultural situations.[35] Of course, as in all human interaction, there is no adequate substitute for really getting to know, listen to, and care about others (see Real World/Real People). Imagine the opportunities for students to build cultural intelligence at the IE Business School in Madrid, Spain, a highly ranked international MBA program:

Example. [L]ast year's class of 287 included 55 nationalities. . . . IE's student body is among the most diverse in the world. Rodrigo Sanchez Hidalgo, who graduated from the program in December, worked with classmates from 15 countries, including Kazakhstan and El Salvador. To help attract an even more international mix of students, IE recently opened marketing and admissions offices in Singapore, Dubai, Berlin, and Lisbon. The goal: producing graduates adept at navigating a multicultural business environment. "This is not a melting pot where participants share a common culture," says Santiago Iñiguez de Ozoño, dean of the business school.[36]

Back to the Chapter-Opening Case

What should Sue do to increase her cultural intelligence?

 LO.3 Understanding Cultural Differences

► **TO THE POINT**
How can knowing about high-context cultures and the GLOBE dimensions improve managerial effectiveness?

This section explores basic ways of describing and comparing cultures. As a foundation, we contrast high-context and low-context cultures and introduce nine cultural dimensions identified in the GLOBE project. Then our attention turns to examining cross-cultural differences in terms of individualism, time, space, and religion.

High-Context and Low-Context Cultures

This is a broadly applicable and very useful cultural distinction[37] (see Figure 4–2). People from **high-context cultures**—including China, Korea, Japan, Vietnam, Mexico, and Arab cultures—rely heavily on situational cues for meaning when perceiving and communicating with others. Nonverbal cues such as one's official position, status, or family connections convey messages more powerfully than do spoken words. Take, for example, Arif M Naqvi, a native of Pakistan doing business in Dubai, United Arab Emirates:

figure 4–2 Contrasting High-Context and Low-Context Cultures

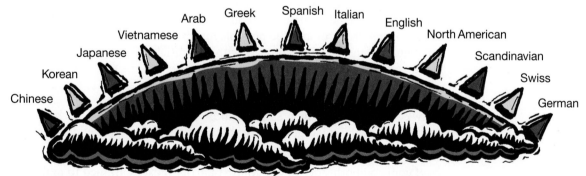

High-Context
- Establish social trust first
- Value personal relations and goodwill
- Agreement by general trust
- Negotiations slow and ritualistic

Low-Context
- Get down to business first
- Value expertise and performance
- Agreement by specific, legalistic contract
- Negotiations as efficient as possible

SOURCE: Reprinted from M Munter, "Cross-Cultural Communication for Managers," *Business Horizons*, vol 36, no 3, p 72, © 1993, with permission from Elsevier.

high-context cultures Primary meaning derived from nonverbal situational cues.

Example. Naqvi is an insider, doing business with some of the most influential people in the region, including Khalid bin Sultan, the son of Saudi Crown Prince Sultan. His contacts and experience are crucial when it comes to making deals happen; relationships are often more important than money in the Middle East. . . .

It takes finesse to close a deal, as it did for Naqvi with Aramex International, a courier company. Fadi Ghandour, founder and CEO of Aramex, recalls a series of . . . [long, drawn-out] lunches and dinners over several months with Naqvi.[38]

Reading the Fine Print in Low-Context Cultures   In **low-context cultures,** written and spoken words carry the burden of shared meanings. Low-context cultures include those found in Germany, Switzerland, Scandinavia, North America, and Great Britain. True to form, Germany has precise written rules for even the smallest details of daily life.[39] In *high*-context cultures, agreements tend to be made on the basis of someone's word or a handshake, after a prolonged get-acquainted and trust-building period. Low-context Americans and Canadians, at least those with cultural roots in Northern Europe, see the handshake as a signal to get a signature on a detailed, lawyer-approved, ironclad contract.

Avoiding Cultural Collisions   Misunderstanding and miscommunication often are problems in international business dealings when the parties are from high- versus low-context cultures. A Mexican business professor made this instructive observation:

Example. Over the years, I have noticed that across cultures there are different opinions on what is expected from a business report. US managers, for instance, take a pragmatic, get-to-the-point approach, and expect reports to be concise and action-oriented. They don't have time to read long explanations: "Just the facts, ma'am."

Latin American managers will usually provide long explanations that go beyond the simple facts. . . .

I have a friend who is the Latin America representative for a United States firm and has been asked by his boss to provide regular reports on sales activities. His reports are long, including detailed explanations on the context in which the events he is reporting on occur and the possible interpretations that they might have. His boss regularly answers these reports with very brief messages, telling him to "cut the crap and get to the point!"[40]

Awkward situations such as this can be avoided when those on both sides of the context divide make good-faith attempts to understand and accommodate their counterparts. Here are some practical tips:

- People on both sides of the context barrier must be trained to make adjustments.
- A new employee should be greeted by a group consisting of his or her boss, several colleagues who have similar duties, and an individual located near the newcomer.
- Background information is essential when explaining anything. Include the history and personalities involved.
- Do not assume the newcomer is self-reliant. Give explicit instructions not only about objectives, but also about the process involved.
- High-context workers from abroad need to learn to ask questions outside their department and function.
- Foreign workers must make an effort to become more self-reliant.[41]

Nine Cultural Dimensions from the GLOBE Project

Project GLOBE (Global Leadership and Organizational Behavior Effectiveness) is the brainchild of University of Pennsylvania professor Robert J House.[42] It is a massive and ongoing attempt to "develop an empirically based theory to describe, understand, and predict the impact of specific cultural variables on leadership and organizational processes and the effectiveness of these processes."[43] GLOBE has evolved into a network of more than 150 scholars from 62 societies since the project was launched in Calgary, Canada, in 1994. Most of the researchers are native to the particular cultures they study, thus greatly enhancing the credibility of the project. During the first two phases of the GLOBE project, a list of nine basic cultural dimensions was developed and statistically validated. Translated questionnaires based on the nine dimensions were administered to thousands of managers in the banking, food, and telecommunications industries around the world to build a database. Results are being published on a regular basis. Much work and many years are needed if the project's goal, as stated above, is to be achieved. In the meantime, we have been given a comprehensive, valid, and up-to-date tool for better understanding cross-cultural similarities and differences.

McGraw Hill **connect** Go to www.mcgrawhillconnect.com for an interactive exercise to test your knowledge of the cultural dimensions identified in the GLOBE Project.

The nine cultural dimensions from the GLOBE project are

- *Power distance.* How much unequal distribution of power should there be in organizations and society?
- *Uncertainty avoidance.* How much should people rely on social norms and rules to avoid uncertainty and limit unpredictability?
- *Institutional collectivism.* How much should leaders encourage and reward loyalty to the social unit, as opposed to the pursuit of individual goals?
- *In-group collectivism.* How much pride and loyalty should individuals have for their family or organization?
- *Gender egalitarianism.* How much effort should be put into minimizing gender discrimination and role inequalities?
- *Assertiveness.* How confrontational and dominant should individuals be in social relationships?
- *Future orientation.* How much should people delay gratification by planning and saving for the future?
- *Performance orientation.* How much should individuals be rewarded for improvement and excellence?
- *Humane orientation.* How much should society encourage and reward people for being kind, fair, friendly, and generous?[44]

What about Your Culture?   Take a short break from your reading and rate your beliefs on a scale from 1 to 10 (with 1 = little or none and 10 = a great deal) on the nine GLOBE dimensions above. It will help you better comprehend the GLOBE cultural concepts. Can you trace your cultural profile to family history and country of origin of your ancestors? For example, one of your author's German roots are evident in his cultural profile.

Country Profiles and Practical Implications   How do different countries score on the GLOBE cultural dimensions? Data from 18,000 managers yielded the profiles in Table 4–2. A quick overview shows a great deal of cultural diversity around the world. But thanks to the nine GLOBE dimensions, we have

low-context cultures Primary meaning derived from written and spoken words.

table 4–2 Countries Ranking Highest and Lowest on the GLOBE Cultural Dimensions

DIMENSION	HIGHEST	LOWEST
Power distance	Morocco, Argentina, Thailand, Spain, Russia	Denmark, Netherlands, South Africa (black sample), Israel, Costa Rica
Uncertainty avoidance	Switzerland, Sweden, Germany (former West), Denmark, Austria	Russia, Hungary, Bolivia, Greece, Venezuela
Institutional collectivism	Sweden, South Korea, Japan, Singapore, Denmark	Greece, Hungary, Germany (former East), Argentina, Italy
In-group collectivism	Iran, India, Morocco, China, Egypt	Denmark, Sweden, New Zealand, Netherlands, Finland
Gender egalitarianism	Hungary, Poland, Slovenia, Denmark, Sweden	South Korea, Egypt, Morocco, India, China
Assertiveness	Germany (former East), Austria, Greece, United States, Spain	Sweden, New Zealand, Switzerland, Japan, Kuwait
Future orientation	Singapore, Switzerland, Netherlands, Canada (English-speaking), Denmark	Russia, Argentina, Poland, Italy, Kuwait
Performance orientation	Singapore, Hong Kong, New Zealand, Taiwan, United States	Russia, Argentina, Greece, Venezuela, Italy
Humane orientation	Philippines, Ireland, Malaysia, Egypt, Indonesia	Germany (former West), Spain, France, Singapore, Brazil

SOURCE: Adapted from M Javidan, R J House, and P W Dorfman, "A Nontechnical Summary of GLOBE Findings," in *Culture, Leadership, and Organizations: The GLOBE Study of 62 Societies*, ed R J House, P J Hanges, M Javidan, P W Dorfman, and V Gupta (Thousand Oaks, CA: Sage, 2004), pp 29–48.

a more precise understanding of *how* cultures vary. Closer study reveals telling cultural *patterns*, or cultural fingerprints for nations. The US managerial sample, for instance, scored high on assertiveness and performance orientation. Accordingly, Americans are widely perceived as pushy and hardworking. Switzerland's high scores on uncertainty avoidance and future orientation help explain its centuries of political neutrality and world-renowned banking industry. Singapore is known as a great place to do business because it is clean and safe and its people are well educated and hardworking. This is no surprise, considering Singapore's high scores on social collectivism, future orientation, and performance orientation.[45]

In contrast, Russia's low scores on future orientation and performance orientation could foreshadow a slower-than-hoped-for transition from a centrally planned economy to free-enterprise capitalism.

As explained by business and science author Malcolm Gladwell, cultural tendencies can become a life-and-death matter in hazardous occupations. Despite having modern aircraft and well-trained pilots, Korean Air experienced too many crashes during the 1990s.

Example. What they were struggling with was a cultural legacy, that Korean culture is hierarchical. You are obliged to be deferential toward your elders and superiors in a way that would be unimaginable in the United States. But Boeing and Airbus design modern, complex airplanes to be flown by two equals. That works beautifully in low-power-distance cultures [like the United States, where hierarchies aren't as relevant]. But in cultures that have high power distance, it's very difficult. I use the case study of a very famous plane crash in Guam of Korean Air. They're flying along, and they run into a little bit of trouble, the weather's bad.

The pilot makes an error, and the co-pilot doesn't correct him. But once Korean Air figured out that their problem was cultural, they fixed it.[46]

These illustrations bring us to an important practical lesson: *Knowing the cultural tendencies of your co-workers, foreign business partners, and competitors can give you a strategic competitive advantage (and even save lives in hazardous occupations).*

LO.4 Individualism versus Collectivism

Have you ever been torn between what you personally wanted and what the group, organization, or society expected of you? If so, you have firsthand experience with a fundamental and important cultural distinction: individualism versus collectivism. This source of cultural variation—represented by two of the nine GLOBE dimensions—deserves a closer look. As might be expected with an extensively researched topic, individualism versus collectivism has many interpretations.[47] Let us examine the basic concept for greater cultural awareness.

Individualistic cultures, characterized as "I" and "me" cultures, give priority to individual freedom and choice. Accordingly, they emphasize *personal* responsibility for one's affairs. This is no small matter in an aging society:

Example. A strong feeling of "social solidarity," as [Johns Hopkins University professor Gerald F] Anderson sees it, makes Europeans inclined to be generous to older people, more willing to support them. "Their attitude is, we're older and we'll need some help," he says. "The US attitude is, we're all rugged individualists and we're going to take care of ourselves, not others."[48]

This cultural distinction was borne out in a recent survey of the quality of life among senior citizens in 16 industrialized nations. The Netherlands was number one and the United States ranked number 13.[49]

Collectivist cultures, oppositely called "we" and "us" cultures, rank shared goals higher than individual desires and goals. People in collectivist cultures are expected to subordinate their own wishes and goals to those of the relevant social unit. A worldwide survey of 30,000 managers by Trompenaars and Hampden-Turner, who prefer the term *communitarianism* to *collectivism*, found the highest degree of individualism in Israel, Romania, Nigeria, Canada, and the United States. Countries ranking lowest in individualism—thus qualifying as collectivist cultures—were Egypt, Nepal, Mexico, India, and Japan. Brazil, China, and France also ended up toward the collectivist end of the scale.[50]

A Business Success Factor   Of course, one can expect to encounter both individualists and collectivists in culturally diverse countries such as the United States. For example, imagine the frustration of Dave Murphy, a Boston-based mutual fund salesperson, when he tried to get Navajo Indians in Arizona interested in saving money for their retirement. After several fruitless meetings with groups of Navajo employees, he was given this cultural insight by a local official: "If you come to this environment, you have to understand that money is different. It's there to be spent. If you have some, you help your family."[51] (This suggests Navajos generally would score high on in-group collectivism and low on future orientation on the GLOBE scale.) To traditional Navajos, enculturated as collectivists,

---

individualistic culture Primary emphasis on personal freedom and choice.

collectivist culture Personal goals less important than community goals and interests.

saving money is an unworthy act of selfishness. Subsequently, the sales pitch was tailored to emphasize the *family* benefits of individual retirement savings plans.

Allegiance to Whom?   The Navajo example brings up an important point about collectivist cultures. Specifically, which unit of society predominates? For the Navajos, family is the key reference group. But, as Trompenaars and Hampden-Turner observe, important differences exist among collectivist (or communitarian) cultures:

Example. For each single society, it is necessary to determine the group with which individuals have the closest identification. They could be keen to identify with their trade union, their family, their corporation, their religion, their profession, their nation, or the state apparatus. The French tend to identify with *la France, la famille, le cadre;* the Japanese with the corporation; the former eastern bloc with the Communist Party; and Ireland with the Roman Catholic Church. Communitarian goals may be good or bad for industry depending on the community concerned, its attitude and relevance to business development.[52]

This observation validates GLOBE's distinction between institutional and in-group collectivism.

Cultural Perceptions of Time

Go to www.mcgrawhillconnect.com for a video case on Disney Imagineering.

In North American and Northern European cultures, time seems to be a simple matter. It is linear, relentlessly marching forward, never backward, in standardized chunks. Time-crunched Americans believe in Ben Franklin's advice that "time is money." It is spent, saved, or wasted.[53] A prime example is William P Lauder, CEO of Esteé Lauder Companies, the cosmetics giant. Lauder declared in a recent interview: "When I see people waste time, I call them on it immediately. Time is their greatest resource, and when it's gone, it's lost forever."[54] Lauder's opposite is actor Johnny Depp. According to a *Newsweek* reporter, "He seems like a man who has never rushed to, or from, anywhere in his life. He is chronically late for interviews—sometimes four or five hours, sometimes days—but this time around a gentlemanly 50 minutes."[55] Kentucky-born Depp certainly doesn't fit the stereotypical American who shows up 10 minutes early for appointments. When working across cultures, time becomes a very complex matter. Imagine a New Yorker's chagrin when left in a waiting room for 45 minutes, only to find a Latin American government official dealing with three other people at once. The North American resents the lack of prompt and undivided attention. The Latin American official resents the North American's impatience and apparent self-centeredness. This vicious cycle of resentment can be explained by the distinction between **monochronic time** and **polychronic time:**

Example. The former is revealed in the ordered, precise, schedule-driven use of public time that typifies and even caricatures efficient Northern Europeans and North Americans. The latter is seen in the multiple and cyclical activities and concurrent involvement with different people in Mediterranean, Latin American, and especially Arab cultures.[56]

While the people of Dubai, United Arab Emirates, are generally polychronic, this courier service follows a monochronic schedule for an increasingly Westernized business scene.

Low-context cultures, such as in the United States, tend to run on monochronic time, while higher-context cultures, such as in Central America's Costa Rica, tend to run on polychronic time. People in polychronic cultures view time as flexible, fluid, and multidimensional. For example, imagine yourself doing business in the Persian Gulf nation of Qatar:

Example. Qataris continue to cherish the old custom of the *majlis*, the evening get-togethers where men (and only men) sip tea, smoke *shisha* tobacco, and solve the problems of the world through endless discussion. Grahame Maher, head of the local Vodafone operation, had to master this age-old routine before he could win over the Qataris. Says Maher: "I learned a way to do business that we have forgotten in the West because it takes too much time.[57]

Of course, economic globalization has spawned monochronic global business practices that create exceptions in traditional polychromic cultures.

Example. Travel guides about Spain warn tourists that because of the siesta—the tradition of a long break for lunch and a nap—shops and businesses may be closed for a good part of the afternoon. But at least in Spain's major cities, the siesta gradually is giving way to the influences of globalization and work/life balance.

Employers in Spain have been re-thinking their practice of permitting long afternoon breaks that extend the Spanish workday far into the evening. The siesta can interrupt Spanish companies' dealings with other European businesses for a large portion of the workday. Moreover, it is becoming impractical for employees in the larger cities to travel home for lunch, and the length of the workday is becoming an issue for many employees.[58]

Managers need to adjust their mental clocks when doing business across cultures.

Back to the Chapter-Opening Case

What role does the distinction between monochronic and polychronic time play in this case?

Interpersonal Space

Anthropologist Edward T Hall noticed a connection between culture and preferred interpersonal distance. People from high-context cultures were observed standing close when talking to someone. Low-context cultures appeared to dictate a greater amount of interpersonal space. Hall applied the term **proxemics** to the study of cultural expectations about interpersonal space.[59] He specified four interpersonal distance zones. Some call them space bubbles. They are *intimate* distance, *personal* distance, *social* distance, and *public* distance. Ranges for the four interpersonal distance zones are illustrated in Figure 4–3, along with selected cultural differences.

North American business conversations normally are conducted at about a three- to four-foot range, within the personal zone in Figure 4–3. A range of approximately one foot is common in Latin American and Asian cultures, uncomfortably close for Northern Europeans and North Americans. Some Arab

monochronic time Belief that time is limited, precisely segmented, and schedule driven.

polychronic time Belief that time is flexible, multidimensional, and based on relationships and situations.

proxemics Hall's term for the study of cultural expectations about interpersonal space.

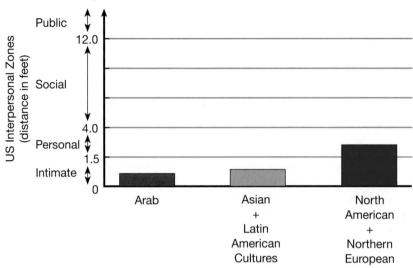

figure 4–3 Interpersonal Distance Zones for Business Conversations Vary from Culture to Culture

traditionalists like to get even closer. Mismatches in culturally dictated interpersonal space zones can prove very distracting for the unprepared. Hall explains,

---

Example. Arabs tend to get very close and breathe on you. It's part of the high sensory involvement of a high-context culture. . . .

The American on the receiving end can't identify all the sources of his discomfort but feels that the Arab is pushy. The Arab comes close, the American backs up. The Arab follows, because he can only interact at certain distances. Once the American learns that Arabs handle space differently and that breathing on people is a form of communication, the situation can sometimes be redefined so the American relaxes.[60]

Asian and Middle-Eastern hosts grow weary of having to seemingly chase their low-context guests around at social gatherings to maintain what they feel is proper conversational range. Backing up all evening to keep conversational partners at a proper distance is an awkward experience as well. Awareness of cultural differences, along with skillful accommodation, are essential to productive cross-cultural business dealings.

Religion

Religious beliefs and practices can have a profound effect on cross-cultural relations (see Real World/Real People). A comprehensive treatment of different religions is beyond the scope of our current discussion.[61] However, we can examine the relationship between religious affiliation and work-related values. A study of 484 international students at a midwestern US university uncovered wide variability. The following list gives the most important work-related value for each of five religious affiliations:

Catholic. Consideration ("Concern that employees be taken seriously, be kept informed, and that their judgments be used.")

Protestant. Employer effectiveness ("Desire to work for a company that is efficient, successful, and a technological leader.")

Buddhist. Social responsibility ("Concern that the employer be a responsible part of society.")

real WORLD // real PEOPLE: ethics

Arizona Hospital Blends Modern Medicine with Navajo Traditions

When a Navajo woman delivers a baby at Banner Page Hospital in northern Arizona, she invites her entire family—often more than 10 people—into the birthing room. She may give birth squatting, as is custom among Native Americans. A medicine man will offer ancient prayers and herbs for the mother to ease childbirth. After the baby is delivered, nurses will save the placenta so the family can take it home and bury it in a sacred place.

In this desert town flanked by canyons and Lake Powell, traditional Navajo healing is merging with modern medicine. The hospital's Native American Cultural Committee, formed in 2002, is working toward an inclusive medical community by tackling the cultural sensitivities of the Navajo people, many of whom are wary of modern medicine.

[According to the head of the hospital's Native American Cultural Committee] "[y]ou have to consider the entire person, family and culture."

As a hospital administrator, what business and ethical arguments would you offer to defend this accommodation to Navajo traditions?

SOURCE: Excerpted from A Haupt, "Hospital Honors Its Navajo Ties," *USA Today*, August 18, 2008, p 10B.

Muslim. Continuity ("Desire for stable environment, job longevity, reduction of uncertainty.")

No religious preference. Professional challenge ("Concern with having a job that provides learning opportunities and opportunities to use skills well.")[62]

Thus, there was virtually *no agreement* across religions about the primary work value. This led the researchers to conclude: "Employers might be wise to consider the impact that religious differences (and more broadly, cultural factors) appear to have on the values of employee groups."[63] Of course, in the United States and other selected countries, equal employment opportunity laws forbid managers from basing employment-related decisions on an applicant's religious preference.

Practical Insights from Cross-Cultural Management Research

◄ ⋯⋯⋯⋯⋯⋯⋯

TO THE POINT
Is American-style leadership effective worldwide?
⋯⋯⋯⋯⋯⋯⋯

Nancy Adler, an international OB specialist at Canada's McGill University, has offered the following definition: "**Cross-cultural management** explains the behavior of people in organizations around the world and shows people how to work in organizations with employee and client populations from many different cultures."[64] Historically, cross-cultural management research has focused almost exclusively on cultural differences. One researcher, troubled by inappropriate cross-cultural comparisons, recently called this approach "comparing chopsticks with forks."[65]

cross-cultural management
Understanding and teaching behavioral patterns in different cultures.

But GLOBE researchers Mansour Javidan and Robert J House recommend studying *similarities* as well as differences. They believe tracking cultural similarities will help us judge how applicable specific management practices are in foreign cultures. "For example, leadership theories developed in the US are probably more easily generalizable to UK managers (another member of the Anglo cluster) than to managers in an Arab country."[66] In this section we will examine three different streams of cross-cultural management research. All three offer useful lessons for managers in today's global economy.

The Hofstede Study: How Well Do US Management Theories Apply in Other Countries?

The short answer to this important question: *not very well*. This answer derives from a landmark study conducted 30 years ago by Dutch researcher Geert Hofstede. His unique cross-cultural comparison of 116,000 IBM employees from 53 countries worldwide focused on four cultural dimensions:

- *Power distance.* How much inequality does someone expect in social situations?
- *Individualism–collectivism.* How loosely or closely is the person socially bonded?

- *Masculinity–femininity.* Does the person embrace stereotypically competitive, performance-oriented masculine traits or nurturing, relationship-oriented feminine traits?
- *Uncertainty avoidance.* How strongly does the person desire highly structured situations?

The US sample ranked relatively low on power distance, very high on individualism, moderately high on masculinity, and low on uncertainty avoidance.[67]

The high degree of variation among cultures led Hofstede to two major conclusions: (1) Management theories and practices need to be adapted to local cultures. This is particularly true for made-in-America management theories (e.g., Maslow's need hierarchy) and Japanese team management practices. *There is no one best way to manage across cultures.*[68] (2) Cultural arrogance is a luxury individuals, companies, and nations can no longer afford in a global economy.

Welcome to the Gateway Language Village, a total-immersion English-language school in Zhuhai, China. Students from China and elsewhere are forbidden to converse in anything but English when they set foot on campus. GLV was founded by Ping Hong, who grew up in China and holds a master's degree from Purdue University in the United States. He and his Colombian wife have a boy and a girl who speak Chinese, Spanish, and English. They will be well-equipped to succeed in the global economy.

 LO.5 Leadership Lessons from the GLOBE Project

In phase 2, the GLOBE researchers set out to discover which, if any, attributes of leadership were universally liked or disliked. They surveyed 17,000 middle managers working for 951 organizations across 62 countries. Their results, summarized in Table 4–3, have important implications for trainers and present and future global managers.[69] Visionary and inspirational *charismatic leaders* who are good team builders generally do the best. On the other hand, *self-centered leaders* seen

| table 4–3 | Leadership Attributes Universally Liked and Disliked across 62 Nations |

UNIVERSALLY POSITIVE LEADER ATTRIBUTES	UNIVERSALLY NEGATIVE LEADER ATTRIBUTES
Trustworthy	Loner
Just	Asocial
Honest	Noncooperative
Foresight	Irritable
Plans ahead	Nonexplicit
Encouraging	Egocentric
Positive	Ruthless
Dynamic	Dictatorial
Motive arouser	
Confidence builder	
Motivational	
Dependable	
Intelligent	
Decisive	
Effective bargainer	
Win–win problem solver	
Administrative skilled	
Communicative	
Informed	
Coordinator	
Team builder	
Excellence oriented	

SOURCE: Excerpted and adapted from P W Dorfman, P J Hanges, and F C Brodbeck, "Leadership and Cultural Variation: The Identification of Culturally Endorsed Leadership Profiles," in *Culture, Leadership, and Organizations: The GLOBE Study of 62 Societies*, ed R J House, P J Hanges, M Javidan, P W Dorfman, and V Gupta (Thousand Oaks, CA: Sage, 2004), Tables 21.2 and 21.3, pp 677–78.

as loners or face-savers generally receive a poor reception worldwide. (See Chapter 16 for a comprehensive treatment of leadership.) Local and foreign managers who heed these results are still advised to use a contingency approach to leadership after using their cultural intelligence to read the local people and culture. David Whitwam, the longtime CEO of appliance maker Whirlpool, framed the challenge this way:

Example. Leading a company today is different from the 1980s and '90s, especially in a global company. It requires a new set of competencies. Bureaucratic structures don't work anymore. You have to take the command-and-control types out of the system. You need to allow and encourage broad-based involvement in the company. Especially in consumer kinds of companies, we need a diverse work-force with diverse leadership. You need strong regional leadership that lives in the culture. We have a North American running the North American business, and a Latin American running the Latin American business.[70]

LO.6 Countries Have Differing Management Styles

Results of a recent comprehensive 17-country study validate and build upon Hof-stede's conclusion: Management practices are indeed country and culture specific. The study involved 5,922 randomly selected factories with 100 to 5,000 employees. Interviewers rated factory managers from low to high on their use of 18 effective management practices. According to the lead researchers Nicholas Bloom and John Van Reenen, the 18 practices fall into three categories:

1. *Monitoring.* How well do companies monitor what goes on inside their firms and use this for continuous improvement?
2. *Targets.* Do companies set the right targets, track the right outcomes, and take appropriate actions if the two are inconsistent?
3. *Incentives.* Are companies promoting and rewarding employees based on performance, and trying to hire and keep their best employees?[71]

Responses for managers in each country were pooled to determine a character-istic national management style. Among the key findings:

- Countries ranked from highest to lowest on the quality of combined man-agement practices were the United States, Germany and Sweden (tied for second), Japan, Canada, France, Italy, Great Britain, Australia, Northern Ireland, Poland, Republic of Ireland, Portugal, Brazil, India, China, and Greece.
- The 17 countries each have their own distinctive mix of emphasis on "mon-itoring," "targets," and "incentives." For example, see the profiles for the five overall highest ranked countries in Table 4–4.
- There is no one best worldwide style of management.

Go to www.mcgrawhillconnect.com for an interactive exercise to test your knowledge of the varying management styles found in different countries.

table 4–4   Countries Achieve High Overall Management Scores by Emphasizing Different Practices

Rank among 17 countries

	MONITORING	TARGETS	INCENTIVES
United States	2	3	**1**
Germany	3	**2**	3
Sweden	**1**	4	5
Japan	7	**1**	4
Canada	4	5	**2**

SOURCE: Adapted from data in N Bloom and J Van Reenen, "Why Do Management Practices Differ Across Firms and Countries?" *Journal of Economic Perspectives*, Winter 2010, Table 2, p 210.

- Foreign multinational companies are better managed than local ones. Thus, multinational companies are in a good position to role model and teach sound management practices.

The key practical lesson from this study tells managers working in a foreign country to be flexible and adapt their style to local preferences. For example, as indicated in Table 4–4, incentives are very appropriate in the United States and Canada, but less so in Sweden where monitoring is commonplace. Targets (goals) are the preferred practice in Japan and Germany. A culturally appropriate *balance* of emphasis on monitoring, targets, and incentives will yield the best results. This requires background research, cultural intelligence, and patience, rather than rushing to implement an alien style of management.

Preparing Employees for Successful Foreign Assignments

◀ ....

TO THE POINT
What does it take to succeed on a foreign assignment?
....

As the reach of global companies continues to grow, many opportunities for living and working in foreign countries will arise. Imagine, for example, the opportunities for foreign duty and cross-cultural experiences at Siemens, the German electronics and industrial equipment giant. Based in Munich, Siemens has 405,000 employees in 190 countries. More than 61,000 of those employees work in the United States.[72] Siemens and other global players need a vibrant and growing cadre of employees who are willing and able to do business across cultures.[73] Business columnists Jack and Suzy Welch recently offered this view of the next 10 years: "There's gold in them-thar hills for any experienced manager who's got the ambition, interest, and global mind-set to work abroad for several years."[74] Thus, the purpose of this final section is to help you prepare yourself and others to work successfully in foreign countries, because a foreign assignment can be a real résumé builder these days.

LO.7 Why Do US Expatriates Fail on Foreign Assignments?

As we use the term here, **expatriate** refers to anyone living or working outside their home country. Hence, they are said to be *expatriated* when transferred to another country and *repatriated* when transferred back home. Reliable statistics of how many Americans, both civilian and military, are presently working outside the country are not available, although it is certainly in the millions. We do know that only 27% of US citizens hold a valid passport (compared to 40% in Canada, 64% in the United Kingdom, and 90% in Germany).[75] This rough indicator of low global engagement helps explain why Americans are commonly characterized as cross-culturally inept and prone to failure on international assignments. Research supports this view. A pair of international management experts offered this assessment:

Example. Over the past decade, we have studied the management of expatriates at about 750 US, European, and Japanese companies. We asked both the expatriates themselves and the executives who sent them abroad to evaluate their experiences. In addition, we looked at what happened after expatriates returned home. . . .

expatriate Anyone living or working in a foreign country.

Overall, the results of our research were alarming. We found that between 10% and 20% of all US managers sent abroad returned early because of job dissatisfaction or difficulties in adjusting to a foreign country. Of those who stayed for the duration, nearly one-third did not perform up to the expectations of their superiors. And perhaps most problematic, one-fourth of those who completed an assignment left their company, often to join a competitor, within one year after repatriation. That's a turnover rate double that of managers who did not go abroad.[76]

A more recent study of why expatriate employees returned home early found the situation to be slowly improving. Still, *personal and family adjustment problems* (36.6%) and *homesickness* (31%) were found to be major stumbling blocks for American managers working in foreign countries.[77] A survey asking 72 human resource managers at multinational corporations to identify the most important success factor in a foreign assignment provided this insight: "Nearly 35% said cultural adaptability: patience, flexibility, and tolerance for others' beliefs."[78]

US multinational companies clearly need to do a better job of preparing employees and their families for foreign assignments, particularly in light of the high costs involved: The tab for sending an executive who earns $160,000 in the United States, plus a spouse and two children, to India for two years is about $900,000, says Jacqui Hauser, vice president of consulting services for Cendant Mobility, a relocation-services firm in Danbury, Connecticut. This includes housing and cost-of-living allowances, foreign- and hardship-pay premiums, tax assistance, education and car allowances, and paid transportation home each year for the entire family.[79]

LO.8   A Bright Spot: North American Women on Foreign Assignments

Kraft Foods' CEO Irene Rosenfeld believes her decision to accept a foreign assignment in Canada was a great career booster.

Historically, a woman from the United States or Canada on a foreign assignment was a rarity. Things are changing, albeit slowly. A review of research evidence and anecdotal accounts uncovered these insights:

- The proportion of corporate women from North America on foreign assignments grew from about 3% in the early 1980s to between 11% and 15% in recent years.

- Self-disqualification and management's assumption that women would not be welcome in foreign cultures—not foreign prejudice, itself—are the primary barriers for potential female expatriates.

- Expatriate North American women are viewed first and foremost by their hosts as being foreigners, and only secondarily as being female.

- North American women have a very high success rate on foreign assignments.[80]

Considering the rapidly growing demand for global managers today, self-disqualification by women and management's prejudicial policies are counterproductive. For their part, women and others who desire a foreign assignment need to be proactive by becoming culturally intelligent and announcing their desire for a foreign assignment. The CEO of tobacco giant Reynolds American is a good case in point: "Susan Ivey says her big break came in 1990, when she was asked to take an overseas assignment and given 48 hours to decide. She went for it. The experience, Ivey says, was 'broadening in every way.'"[81] When Irene Rosenfeld, CEO of Kraft Foods, was asked about her best decision, she said: "My move to Canada in 1996 was a terrific growth opportunity. All my direct reports were very experienced men who had never worked for a woman before. The team was not wild about Americans either. . . . I really learned the difference between managing and leading."[82]

LO.9 Avoiding OB Trouble Spots in Foreign Assignments

Finding the right person (often along with a supportive and adventurous family) for a foreign position is a complex, time-consuming, and costly process. For our purposes, it is sufficient to narrow the focus to common OB trouble spots in the foreign assignment cycle. As illustrated in Figure 4–4, the first and last stages of the cycle occur at home. The middle two stages occur in the foreign or host country. Each stage hides an OB-related trouble spot that needs to be anticipated and neutralized. Otherwise, the bill for another failed foreign assignment will grow.

Avoiding Unrealistic Expectations with Cross-Cultural Training

Realistic job previews (RJPs) have proven effective at bringing people's unrealistic expectations about a pending job assignment down to earth by providing a realistic balance of good and bad news. People with realistic expectations tend to quit less often and be more satisfied than those with unrealistic expectations. RJPs are a must for future expatriates. In addition, cross-cultural training is required. (For training tips in different cultures, see Real World/Real People.)

Cross-cultural training is any type of structured experience designed to help departing employees (and their families) adjust to a foreign culture. The trend is toward more such training in the United States. But there is a great deal of room for improvement, in both quantity and quality. Experts believe that cross-cultural training, although costly, is less expensive than failed foreign assignments.

connect Go to www.mcgrawhillconnect.com for an interactive exercise to test your knowledge of the foreign assignment cycle.

figure 4–4   The Foreign Assignment Cycle (with OB Trouble Spots)

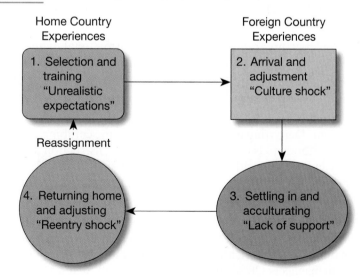

cross-cultural training Structured experiences to help people adjust to a new culture/country.

real WORLD // real PEOPLE

Training Needs to Fit the Local Culture

Brazil
- Building personal relationships is key in Brazilian culture, so talk about yourself.
- Time is much more event oriented in Brazil. In terms of personal space, program participants who approach you during class activities may stand much closer to you than you are used to. Power is accepted and respected. Those who have high status positions are not questioned, even when the individual has doubts about a stance taken. . . . What may seem like fighting or arguing to a trainer [during group discussions] is normal communication behavior in Brazil.[a]

United Arab Emirates (UAE)
- The official business language is English.
- Accommodate prayer times for Muslim participants. It is not necessary to adjust the training schedule or draw attention to it, as prayer is a personal choice.
- Most people working in the UAE come from group-oriented societies and often like to work in small groups, discussing and comparing ideas. Role plays and case studies work well to demonstrate practical examples of what is being taught. However, be careful to avoid any activity that would place members of the opposite gender in uncomfortable situations with each other (e.g., standing close or touching).

- Realize that people in the UAE operate on a more elastic time frame than in the West.[b]

Vietnam
- This is a traditional country that expects a formal type of training. The trainer is front and center lecturing. Working in groups is not expected.
- As in most Asian countries, harmony is desired—especially in the classroom. Never put a student on the spot or single him or her out. Older participants are greatly respected.
- The training should be short and to the point. Practical information is highly valued.
- After asking the group a question, silence often may ensue. The students do not want to challenge you or present their opinions. In the Vietnamese culture, teachers are highly respected.[c]

What cultural dimensions discussed in this chapter are evident in these training tips? Explain.

SOURCES: [a]Excerpted from N Orkin, "Focus on Brazil," *Training*, May 2008, p 20

[b]Excerpted from S Kaleel and K Blanchard-Cattarossi, "Focus on UAE," *Training*, September 2008, p. 20.

[c]Excerpted from N Orkin, "Focus on Vietnam," *Training*, September 2009, p 16.

Programs vary widely in type and also in rigor. Of course, the greater the difficulty, the greater the time and expense:

- *Easiest.* Predeparture training is limited to informational materials, including books, lectures, films, videos, and Internet searches.
- *Moderately difficult.* Experiential training is conducted through case studies, role playing, simulations, and introductory language instruction.
- *Most difficult.* Departing employees are given some combination of the preceding methods plus comprehensive language instruction and field experience in the target culture. As an example of the latter, PepsiCo transfers "about 25 young foreign managers a year to the US for one-year assignments in bottling plants."[83]

Which approach is the best? Research to date offers helpful insights. One study involving US employees in South Korea led the researcher to recommend a *combination* of informational and experiential predeparture training.[84] Another recent study of 226 expatriate managers (30% female) from the United States, United Kingdom, France, and Germany working in Nigeria, Africa, documented that both predeparture and in-host country cross-cultural training are needed. Other significant findings:

- Prior international experience aids adjustment to a foreign culture.
- All types of cross-cultural training help adjustment, but in-host country training is best.

table 4–5 Key Cross-Cultural Competencies

CROSS-CULTURAL COMPETENCY CLUSTER	KNOWLEDGE OR SKILL REQUIRED
Building relationships	Ability to gain access to and maintain relationships with members of host culture
Valuing people of different cultures	Empathy for difference; sensitivity to diversity
Listening and observation	Knows cultural history and reasons for certain cultural actions and customs
Coping with ambiguity	Recognizes and interprets implicit behavior, especially nonverbal cues
Translating complex information	Knowledge of local language, symbols or other forms of verbal language, and written language
Taking action and initiative	Understands intended and potentially unintended consequences of actions
Managing others	Ability to manage details of a job including maintaining cohesion in a group
Adaptability and flexibility	Views change from multiple perspectives
Managing stress	Understands own and other's mood, emotions, and personality

SOURCE: Excerpted from Y Yamazaki and D C Kayes, "An Experiential Approach to Cross-Cultural Learning: A Review and Integration of Competencies for Successful Expatriate Adaptation," *Academy of Management Learning and Education,* December 2004, Table 2, p 372.

- Technical positions need less cross-cultural training than high-social contact positions in management, marketing, and public relations.
- Experiential training focused on the host country culture, involving active participation in real-life simulations, enhances adjustment more than one-way presentations about cultures in general.[85]

As a general rule of thumb, the more rigorous the cross-cultural training, the better. Ideally, trainees should walk away with the nine cross-cultural competencies in Table 4–5.

Our personal experience with teaching OB to foreign students both in the United States and around the world reminds us there really is no substitute for an intimate knowledge of the local culture, language, customs, and etiquette. A good example is Jeremy Shepherd, owner of Pearl Paradise, a Santa Monica, California, online jewelry business. "[He] speaks the Chinese Mandarin dialect, buys directly from pearl farmers in China and cuts out the middleman. That lets him sell high-quality pearls at lower prices to everyone from college students to investment bankers."[86] Who will likely have the language advantage as the global economy evolves, given these recent figures? According to the US Department of Education, 24,000 American children are studying Chinese, while 200 million Chinese are studying English.[87] Spanish is by far the most common foreign language offering in US public middle and high schools.[88] Meanwhile, nearly 81% of all Americans speak only English.[89]

connect Go to www.mcgrawhillconnect.com for an interactive exercise to test your knowledge of the key cross cultural competencies.

Back to the Chapter-Opening Case

What does Sue need to do right now, following the break, to salvage this day of training? What does she need to do to be better prepared for her next training session in Israel in three months?

Avoiding Culture Shock   Have you ever been in a totally unfamiliar situation and felt disoriented and perhaps a bit frightened? If so, you already know something about culture shock. According to anthropologists, **culture shock** involves anxiety and doubt caused by an overload of unfamiliar expectations and social cues.[90] College freshmen often experience a variation of culture shock. An expatriate manager, or family member, may be thrown off balance by an avalanche of strange sights, sounds, and behaviors. Among them may be unreadable road signs, strange-tasting food, inability to use your left hand for social activities (in traditional Arab cultures, the left hand is the toilet hand), or failure to get a laugh with your surefire joke. For the expatriate manager trying to concentrate on the fine details of a business negotiation, culture shock is more than an embarrassing inconvenience. It is a disaster! Like the confused college freshman who quits and goes home, culture-shocked employees often panic and go home early.

The best defense against culture shock is comprehensive cross-cultural training, including intensive language study. Once again, the best way to pick up subtle—yet important—social cues is via the local language.

Support during the Foreign Assignment   Especially during the first six months, when everything is so new to the expatriate, a support system needs to be in place.[91] *Host-country sponsors*, assigned to individual managers or families, are recommended because they serve as "cultural seeing-eye dogs." In a foreign country, where even the smallest errand can turn into an utterly exhausting production, sponsors can get things done quickly because they know the cultural and geographical landscape. Honda's Ohio employees, for example, enjoyed the help of family sponsors when training in Japan:

Example. Honda smoothed the way with Japanese wives who once lived in the US. They handled emergencies such as when Diana Jett's daughter Ashley needed stitches in her chin. When task force senior manager Kim Smalley's daughter, desperate to fit in at elementary school, had to have a precisely shaped bag for her harmonica, a Japanese volunteer stayed up late to make it.[92]

Avoiding Reentry Shock   Strange as it may seem, many otherwise successful expatriate managers encounter their first major difficulty only after their foreign assignment is over. Why? Returning to one's native culture is taken for granted because it seems so routine and ordinary. But having adjusted to another country's way of doing things for an extended period of time can put one's own culture and surroundings in a strange new light. Three areas for potential reentry shock are work, social activities, and general environment (e.g., politics, climate, transportation, food). Ira Caplan's return to New York City exemplifies reentry shock:

Example. During the past 12 years, living mostly in Japan, he and his wife had spent their vacations cruising the Nile or trekking in Nepal. They hadn't seen much of the US. They are getting an eyeful now. . . .

Prices astonish him. The obsession with crime unnerves him. What unsettles Mr. Caplan more, though, is how much of himself he has left behind.

In a syndrome of return no less stressful than that of departure, he feels displaced, disregarded, and diminished. . . .

In an Italian restaurant, crowded at lunchtime, the waiter sets a bowl of linguine in front of him. Mr. Caplan stares at it. "In Asia, we have smaller portions and smaller people," he says.

Asia is on his mind. He has spent years cultivating an expertise in a region of huge importance. So what? This is New York.[93]

Mc Graw Hill connect Go to www.mcgrawhillconnect.com for a self-assessment to learn how prepared you are for a foreign assignment.

Work-related adjustments were found to be a major problem for samples of repatriated Finnish, Japanese, and American employees.[94] Upon being repatriated, a 12-year veteran of one US company said: "Our organizational culture was turned upside down. We now have a different strategic focus, different 'tools' to get the job done, and different buzzwords to make it happen. I had to learn a whole new corporate 'language.'"[95] Reentry shock can be reduced through employee career counseling and home-country sponsors. Simply being aware of the problem of reentry shock is a big step toward effectively dealing with it.[96]

Overall, the key to a successful foreign assignment is making it a well-integrated link in a career chain rather than treating it as an isolated adventure.

culture shock Anxiety and doubt caused by an overload of new expectations and cues.

Summary of Key Concepts

1. *Define the term* culture, *and explain how societal culture and organizational culture combine to influence on-the-job behavior.* Culture is a set of beliefs and values about what is desirable and undesirable in a community of people, and a set of formal or informal practices to support the values. Culture has both prescriptive and descriptive elements and involves taken-for-granted assumptions about how to think, act, and feel. Culture overrides national boundaries. Key aspects of societal culture, such as customs and language, are brought to work by the individual. Working together, societal and organizational culture influence the person's values, ethics, attitudes, and expectations.

2. *Define* ethnocentrism, *and explain how to develop cultural intelligence.* Ethnocentrism is the belief that one's native culture, language, and ways of doing things are superior to all others. Cultural intelligence, the ability to interpret ambiguous cross-cultural situations, is an extension of emotional intelligence (discussed in Chapter 5). It can be developed through comprehensive experience with foreign people and cultures.

3. *Distinguish between high-context and low-context cultures and identify and describe the nine cultural dimensions from Project GLOBE.* People from low-context cultures infer relatively less from situational cues and extract more meaning from spoken and written words. In high-context cultures such as China and Japan, managers prefer slow negotiations and trust-building meetings, which tend to

frustrate low-context Northern Europeans and North Americans who prefer to get right down to business. The nine GLOBE cultural dimensions are: (*a*) Power distance—How equally should power be distributed? (*b*) Uncertainty avoidance—How much should social norms and rules reduce uncertainty and unpredictability? (*c*) Institutional collectivism—How much should loyalty to the social unit override individual interests? (*d*) Ingroup collectivism—How strong should one's loyalty be to family or organization? (*e*) Gender egalitarianism—How much should gender discrimination and role inequalities be minimized? (*f*) Assertiveness—How confrontational and dominant should one be in social relationships? (*g*) Future orientation—How much should one delay gratification by planning and saving for the future? (*h*) Performance orientation—How much should individuals be rewarded for improvement and excellence? (*i*) Humane orientation—How much should individuals be rewarded for being kind, fair, friendly, and generous?

4. *Distinguish between individualistic and collectivist cultures, and explain the difference between monochronic and polychronic cultures.* People in individualistic cultures think primarily in terms of "I" and "me" and place a high value on freedom and personal choice. Collectivist cultures teach people to be "we" and "us" oriented and to subordinate personal wishes and goals to the interests of the relevant social unit (such as family, group, organization, or society). People in monochronic cultures are schedule driven and prefer to do one thing at a time. To them, time is like money; it is spent wisely or wasted. In polychronic cultures, there is a tendency to do many things at once and to perceive time as flexible and multidimensional. Polychronic people view monochronic people as being too preoccupied with time.

5. *Specify the practical lesson from the Hofstede cross-cultural study, and explain what Project GLOBE researchers discovered about leadership.* There is no one best way to manage across cultures. Management theories and practices need to be adapted to the local culture. Across 62 cultures, the GLOBE researchers identified leader attributes that are universally liked and universally disliked. The universally liked leader attributes—including trustworthy, dynamic, motive arouser, decisive, and intelligent—are associated with the charismatic/transformational leadership style that is widely applicable. Universally disliked leader attributes—such as noncooperative, irritable, egocentric, and dictatorial—should be avoided in all cultures.

6. *Discuss the results and practical significance of the recent Bloom and Van Reenen study of national management styles.* Their 17-country study of effective management practices involving monitoring, targets, and incentives found distinct management styles for each country, no one-best worldwide style of management, and foreign multinational companies being better managed than local ones. Foreign managers need to adapt their style to local preferences and prevailing management practices. With cultural intelligence and patience, managers of multinational companies can role-model and teach good management practices worldwide.

7. *Explain why US managers have a comparatively high failure rate on foreign assignments.* American expatriates are troubled by personal and family adjustment problems and homesickness. A great deal of money is wasted when expatriates come home early. More extensive cross-cultural training is needed.

8. *Summarize the research findings about North American women on foreign assignments.* The number of North American women on foreign assignments is still small, but growing. Self-disqualification and prejudicial home-country supervisors and staffing policies are largely to blame. Foreigners tend to view North American women primarily as foreigners and secondarily as women. North American women have a high success rate on foreign assignments. Foreign language skills, a strong and formally announced desire, foreign experience, networking, family and supervisory support, and visibility with upper management can increase the chances of getting a desired foreign assignment for both women and men.

9. *Identify four stages of the foreign assignment cycle and the OB trouble spot associated with each stage.* Stages of the foreign assignment cycle (with OB trouble spots) are (1) selection and training (unrealistic expectations); (2) arrival and adjustment (culture shock); (3) settling in and acculturating (lack of support); and (4) returning home and adjusting (reentry shock).

Key Terms

OB in Action Case Study

China Myths, China Facts[97]

Chinese business culture is unique, but not in all the ways outsiders tend to assume. To identify the most common myths, we interviewed dozens of North American and European expats ["expatriots" who work in a foreign country] as well as some Chinese managers now working in the West, all of whom have spent at least three years doing business in China. Our research uncovered three principal myths, perpetuated informally through stereotypes and formally through management-training programs.

Anyone working with the Chinese will find a multi-faceted, fast-changing culture. As one respondent notes, managers can tap Eastern and Western strengths alike by learning the nuances of both business cultures and developing the flexibility to work in either one. "The Chinese will often pop in to see you with no appointment," says one executive. "I've learned I can do this, too. If I have 30 minutes to spare, I just make a quick call from a taxi and visit someone working in the area."

Myth 1: Collectivism
Reality: Individualism

Wei Chen, a Chinese manager in Paris's luxury goods sector, attributes the rise in individualism to citizens' suppression for many generations: "As a child I was punished for stepping out of the box and told to 'be average.' But we have left this mentality with a passion. In China, we are so eager to move ahead. Westerners often feel our style is pushy and aggressive." An executive at a Canadian pharmaceutical company points out, "There is an intense self-interest [in China]—more important than company, community, or nation. It is like nothing I have experienced in the West. The US is generally considered the most individualistic part of the world, but it has nothing on China." Interview subjects cited the Cultural Revolution, the one-child policy, and mass migration to big cities as factors in the unraveling collective spirit.

The part of the myth that's true: Decisions are often made in groups, and the Chinese are highly skilled at working in teams.

Myth 2: Long-term deliberation
Reality: Real-time reaction

Managers unanimously indicated that the speed of decision making and execution in China is extraordinary compared with the West, where "we spend time trying to predict the future and getting it wrong," says Frédéric Maury, a French executive in technical services. "In China no one thinks about the future." That's hyperbole, perhaps, but a manager who has worked for the World Bank in China for a decade agrees with the sentiment, saying that ad hoc logistics are quite common but amazingly well executed. "I've attended dozens if not hundreds of workshops in China, and not one has gone according to plan. Things change the night before: speakers, topics, even venues. But it all always ends up working out fine."

The part of the myth that's true: Business relationships and government policies are both built for the long term.

Myth 3: Risk aversion
Reality: Risk tolerance

"In the West we like to debate something, print it out, debate it again, do some analysis," says British logistics executive Michael Drake. "But in China it's, 'Right, we've decided, boom, off we go!'" Many participants believe the appetite for risk is tied to growth. Edith Coron, a French intercultural consultant and coach, says, "In an environment where GDP is growing at over 10% a year, it's understandable that the level of entrepreneurship and risk taking should be so high." Chinese manager Wei Chen confirms, "We don't want to lose a single minute. We have a lot of confidence, and we are very comfortable with risk."

The part of the myth that's true: Chinese workers often hesitate to give individual opinions or brainstorm openly when more-senior people are present.

Questions for Discussion

1. Has this presentation challenged any assumptions you had about China and the Chinese people? Explain.
2. Using your best cultural intelligence, how would you adjust your behavior on a business trip to China?
3. What cultural adjustments will Chinese managers need to make if they want to effectively manage Americans in the rapidly growing number of Chinese-owned businesses in the United States?
4. Based on what you just learned in this chapter, are you more or less interested in getting a foreign assignment some day? Explain.

Legal/Ethical Challenge

3M Tries to Make a Difference in Russia

Background fact: Russia is the world's most corrupt major economy, according to Berlin-based Transparency International's 2010 Corruption Perceptions Index, . . . sliding to 154th among 178 countries and placing it alongside Tajikistan and Kenya.[98]

3M's Situation: Russian managers aren't inclined . . . to reward people for improved performance. They spurn making investments for the future in favor of realizing immediate gains. They avoid establishing consistent business practices that can reduce uncertainty. Add in the country's high political risk and level of corruption, and it's no wonder that many multinationals have all but given up on Russia. . . .

The Russian business environment can be corrupt and dangerous; bribes and protection money are facts of life. But unlike many international companies, which try to distance themselves from such practices by simply banning them, 3M Russia actively promotes not only ethical behavior but also the personal security of its employees. . . .

3M Russia also strives to differentiate itself from competitors by being an ethical leader. For example, it holds training courses in business ethics for its customers.[99]

Should 3M Export Its American Ethical Standards to Russia?

1. If 3M doesn't like the way things are done in Russia, it shouldn't do business there. Explain your rationale.

2. 3M should do business in Russia but not meddle in Russian culture. "When in Russia, do things the Russian way." Explain your rationale.

3. 3M has a basic moral responsibility to improve the ethical climate in foreign countries where it does business. Explain your rationale.

4. 3M should find a practical middle ground between the American and Russian ways of doing business. How should that happen?

5. Invent other options. Discuss.

Web Resources

For study material and exercises that apply to this chapter, visit our website at **www.mhhe.com/kreitner10e**

part two

Individual Behavior in Organizations

chapter 5

Key Individual Differences and the Road to Success

 ## Learning Objectives

When you finish studying the material in this chapter, you should be able to:

LO.1   Define *self-esteem,* and explain how it can be improved with Branden's six pillars of self-esteem.

LO.2   Define *self-efficacy,* and explain its sources.

LO.3   Contrast high and low self-monitoring individuals, and discuss the ethical implications of organizational identification.

LO.4   Identify and describe the Big Five personality dimensions, and specify which one is correlated most strongly with job performance.

LO.5   Describe the proactive personality and an internal locus of control.

LO.6   Identify at least five of Gardner's eight multiple intelligences.

LO.7   Distinguish between positive and negative emotions, and explain how they can be judged.

LO.8   Identify the four key components of emotional intelligence, and discuss the practical significance of emotional contagion and emotional labor.

LO.9   Explain how psychological capital, deliberate practice, luck, and humility can pave your road to success.

Can an Introvert Guide Facebook to Long-Term Success?

In his book, *The Facebook Effect: The Inside Story of the Company That Is Connecting the World,* David Kirkpatrick provides instructive insights into the personality and character of the company's founder and CEO. This excerpt looks back at Mark Zuckerberg as a college computer whiz on his way to becoming CEO of an Internet giant. By early 2011, Facebook's more than 500 million active users (over 70% from outside the United States) shared 30 billion pieces of content each month.[1]

Mark Zuckerberg was a short, slender, intense introvert with curly brown hair whose fresh freckled face made him look closer to fifteen than the nineteen he was [at Harvard]. His uniform was baggy jeans, rubber sandals—even in winter—and a T-shirt that usually had some sort of clever picture or phrase. One he was partial to during this period portrayed a little monkey and read "Code Monkey." He could be quiet around strangers, but that was deceiving. When he did speak, he was wry. His tendency was to say nothing until others fully had their say. He stared. He would stare at you while you were talking, and stay absolutely silent. If you said something stimulating, he'd finally fire up his own ideas and the words would come cascading out. But if you went on too long or said something obvious, he would start looking through you. When you finished, he'd quietly mutter "yeah," then change the subject or turn away. Zuckerberg is a highly deliberate thinker and rational to the extreme. His handwriting is well ordered, meticulous, and tiny, and he sometimes uses it to fill notebooks with lengthy deliberations.

Girls were drawn to his mischievous smile. . . . They liked his confidence, his humor, and his irreverence. He typically wore a contented expression on his face that seemed to say "I know what I'm doing." Zuck, as he was known, had an air about him that everything would turn out fine, no matter what he did.[2]

CEO Mark Zuckerberg shares a laugh with Facebook co-workers, despite his history of being an introvert.

From a biological standpoint, people are more alike than different. How much alike and to what extent?

Example. [Answers can be found in] each human's 100 million cells. Coiled in each cell are 46 bundles of DNA, 23 from each parent. Each bundle of DNA is made up of four chemicals—adenosine, thymine, cytosine, and guanine—paired two by two in a twisted ladder called a double helix.

The Human Genome Project yielded the precise sequence of these so-called base pairs, packaged in roughly 20,500 genes, about the same number found in chimpanzees and dogs. Genetically speaking, the planet's 7 billion people are 99.5% identical. Individual genomes vary by just one pair of bases for every 5,000 found along the genome.

That's a tiny number, considering the genome is made up of 3 billion base pairs. Yet the variations are all-important, accounting for all of the traits that make one person different from another, whether it's height, weight, hair and eye color or heart disease and cancer risk.[3]

Dealing with individual differences—the genetic half-percent that makes you a unique being—is an endless challenge for managers. For instance, how do you express yourself in the workplace? Are you a go-getter, like Mark Zuckerberg in the opening case, or a slacker? Are you a loner or highly social? Do you see yourself as master of your own fate, or a victim of circumstances? Are you emotional or calm and cool? Is your job satisfaction through the roof or stuck in the basement? Thanks to a vast array of individual differences such as these, modern organizations have a rich and interesting human texture. In fact, according to research, "variability among workers is substantial at all levels but increases dramatically with job complexity. In life insurance sales, for example, variability in performance is around six times as great as in routine clerical jobs."[4]

Growing workforce diversity compels managers to view individual differences in a fresh new way. Rather than stifling diversity, as in the past, today's managers need to better understand and accommodate employee diversity and individual differences.[5] Both this chapter and the next explore the key individual differences portrayed in Figure 5–1. The figure is intended to be an instructional road map showing the bridges between self-concept and self-expression. This chapter focuses on self-concept, personality, abilities, and emotions. Personal values, attitudes, and job satisfaction are covered in Chapter 6. Taken as an integrated whole, all these factors provide a foundation for better understanding each organizational contributor (including yourself) as a unique and special individual. This chapter ends with a practical capstone section about achieving *success*, however you choose to define that form of self-expression.

Self-Concept

TO THE POINT

What can managers do to build their employees' self-esteem and self-efficacy?

When you look in the mirror, you recognize who it is. You see your*self*.[6] This is a remarkable talent in the animal kingdom, according to scientists. Only humans, apes, dolphins, and elephants can recognize themselves in a mirror.[7] But what exactly do you know about that person in the mirror? People ages 16 to 70 were asked what they would do differently if they could live life over again; 48% chose the response category "Get in touch with self."[8] Toward that end, this section

figure 5–1   An Instructional Road Map for the Study of Individual
             Differences in Chapters 5 and 6

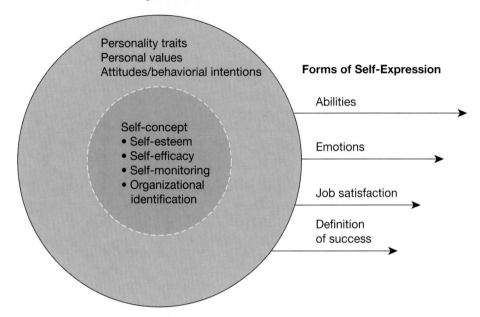

The Unique Individual

Personality traits
Personal values
Attitudes/behaviorial intentions

Forms of Self-Expression

Self-concept
• Self-esteem
• Self-efficacy
• Self-monitoring
• Organizational
  identification

Abilities

Emotions

Job satisfaction

Definition
of success

helps you get in better touch with yourself on the way to better understanding and managing yourself and others in the workplace. Former General Electric CEO Jack Welch tells us: "You've got to be comfortable with yourself to make a good boss."[9]

Sociologist Viktor Gecas defines **self-concept** as "the concept the individual has of himself as a physical, social, and spiritual or moral being."[10] In other words, because you have a self-concept, you recognize yourself as a distinct human being. A self-concept would be impossible without the capacity to think about complex things and processes. This brings us to the role of cognitions. **Cognitions** represent "any knowledge, opinion, or belief about the environment, about oneself, or about one's behavior."[11] Among many different types of cognitions, those involving anticipation, introspection, planning, goal setting, evaluating, and setting personal standards are particularly relevant to OB.

Our attention now turns to three topics invariably mentioned when behavioral scientists discuss self-concept. They are self-esteem, self-efficacy, and self-monitoring. We also consider the ethical implications of organizational identification, a social aspect of self. A practical social learning model of self-management can be found in Learning Module A (Learning Module A is located on our website at www.mhhe.com/kreitner10e). Each of these areas deserves a closer look by those who want to better understand and effectively manage themselves and others.

 Go
to www.mcgrawhillconnect.
com for a self-assessment
to determine your core self-
evaluation.

self-concept Person's self-
perception as a physical, social,
spiritual being.

cognitions A person's knowledge,
opinions, or beliefs.

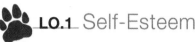 **LO.1** Self-Esteem

Self-esteem is a belief about one's own self-worth based on an overall self-evaluation.[12] Personal achievements and praise tend to bolster one's self-esteem. Prolonged unemployment, soured relationships, and even "bad hair" days can erode it.[13] Self-esteem is measured by having survey respondents indicate their agreement or disagreement with both positive and negative statements. A positive statement on one general self-esteem survey is "I feel I am a person of worth, the equal of other people."[14]

Among the negative items is "I feel I do not have much to be proud of."[15] Those who agree with the positive statements and disagree with the negative statements have high self-esteem. They see themselves as worthwhile, capable, and acceptable. People with low self-esteem view themselves in negative terms, do not feel good about themselves, and experience self-doubts. Research shows they tend to have health problems and low-quality social relationships, as well as being vulnerable to depression.[16]

connect Go to www.mcgrawhillconnect.com for an interactive exercise to test your knowledge of core self-evaluation.

Changes in Self-Esteem during Adulthood A recently reported study that followed a nationally representative sample of 3,617 Americans ages 25 to 104 over a 16-year period documented a general pattern of changes in self-esteem during adulthood. For all demographic groups, self-esteem followed the same trajectory, "increasing during young and middle adulthood, reaching a peak at about age 60 years, and then declining in old age."[17] Not surprisingly, more educated people were found to have higher self-esteem. Declining self-esteem in old age was attributed to socioeconomic changes and health issues.

Self-Esteem across Cultures What are the cross-cultural implications for self-esteem, a concept that has been called uniquely Western? In a survey of 13,118 students from 31 countries worldwide, a moderate positive correlation was found between self-esteem and life satisfaction. But the relationship was stronger in individualistic cultures (e.g., United States, Canada, New Zealand, Netherlands) than in collectivist cultures (e.g., Korea, Kenya, Japan). The researchers concluded that individualistic cultures socialize people to focus more on themselves, while people in collectivist cultures "are socialized to fit into the community and to do their duty. Thus, how a collectivist feels about him- or herself is less relevant to . . . life satisfaction."[18] Global managers need to remember to deemphasize self-esteem when doing business in collectivist ("we") cultures, as opposed to emphasizing it in individualistic ("me") cultures.

Can General Self-Esteem Be Improved? The short answer is yes (see Table 5–1). More detailed answers come from research. In one study, youth-league baseball coaches who were trained in supportive teaching techniques had a positive effect on the self-esteem of young boys. A control group of untrained coaches had no such positive effect.[19] Another study led to this conclusion: "Low self-esteem can be raised more by having the person think of desirable characteristics possessed rather than of undesirable characteristics from which he or she is free."[20] This approach can help neutralize the self-defeating negative thoughts among those with low self-esteem. Meanwhile, a lively debate continues among educational policy makers over the relative importance of boosting students' self-esteem versus making sure they master the basics of reading, writing, and math. When researchers reviewed data from 1975 through 2006, they found that the self-esteem movement had carried the day. But at what cost? Results showed that while self-esteem among high-school seniors had risen over the years, self-perceptions of *competence* had not. This left the researchers worried that "over-praised" kids who were confident about becoming "very good" spouses, parents,

table 5–1 Branden's Six Pillars of Self-Esteem

What nurtures and sustains self-esteem in grown-ups is not how others deal with us but how we ourselves operate in the face of life's challenges—the choices we make and the actions we take.

This leads us to the six pillars of self-esteem.

1. *Live consciously.* Be actively and fully engaged in what you do and with whom you interact.

2. *Be self-accepting.* Don't be overly judgmental or critical of your thoughts and actions.

3. *Take personal responsibility.* Take full responsibility for your decisions and actions in life's journey.

4. *Be self-assertive.* Be authentic and willing to defend your beliefs when interacting with others, rather than bending to their will to be accepted or liked.

5. *Live purposefully.* Have clear near-term and long-term goals and realistic plans for achieving them to create a sense of control over your life.

6. *Have personal integrity.* Be true to your word and your values.

Between self-esteem and the practices that support it, there is reciprocal causation. This means that the behaviors that generate good self-esteem are also expressions of good self-esteem.

SOURCE: From Nathaniel Branden, *Self-Esteem at Work: How Confident People Make Powerful Companies,* 1998, pp 33–36. Reprinted with permission of John Wiley & Sons.

and employees could be primed for a big letdown in real life.[21] What are your thoughts on this?

LO.2 Self-Efficacy

Self-confidence that leads to results is important in today's demanding workplaces. In fact, when 2,500 managers and executives in the United States were polled, 72% of the women and 66% of the men said *self-confidence* was the most important quality for succeeding in business.[22] Self-confidence that can be backed up with real results involves more than high self-esteem; it also requires self-efficacy.[23] **Self-efficacy** is a person's belief about his or her chances of successfully accomplishing a specific task. According to one organizational behavior writer, "Self-efficacy arises from the gradual acquisition of complex cognitive, social, linguistic, and/or physical skills through experience."[24] Role models can inspire us to build self-efficacy (see Real World/Real People on page 126).

The relationship between self-efficacy and performance is a cyclical one. Efficacy → performance cycles can spiral upward toward success or downward toward failure.[25] Researchers have documented strong linkages between high self-efficacy expectations and success in widely varied physical and mental tasks, anxiety reduction, addiction control, pain tolerance, illness recovery, avoidance of seasickness in naval cadets, physical exercise, stress avoidance, and trainee learning.[26] Oppositely, those with low self-efficacy expectations tend to have lower success rates. Although self-efficacy sounds like some sort of mental magic, it operates in a very straightforward manner, as a model will show.

self-esteem One's overall self-evaluation.

self-efficacy Belief in one's ability to do a task.

real WORLD // real PEOPLE: ethics

Military Veterans Bring High Self-Efficacy to MBA Programs

Ryan McDermott, a second-year student at Darden [the University of Virginia's School of Business], led a combat mission down the most dangerous road in Baghdad, fought four battles, and wrote a plan for training and deploying 3,600 soldiers, all by the age of 26. Summer Jones, a former naval officer, by 26 had launched Tomahawk missiles off a ship in the Persian Gulf, commanded 200 sailors, and delivered the news of September 11 Pentagon casualties to their families. When her Georgetown University evening MBA classmates wonder how the 32-year-old maintains a full-time job, raises two children, supports her husband in law school, and earns her MBA at the same time, she tells them: "When you've been in a wartime environment, you step back and say, 'This is easy.'" As if to prove it, she gave birth to her second son just after the first week of the MBA program without missing a day of class.

What is the ethical argument for hiring military veterans?

SOURCE: J Porter, "From the Battlefield to B-School," *BusinessWeek*, March 24, 2008, p 80.

Summer Jones and her growing family.

What Are the Mechanisms of Self-Efficacy?   A basic model of self-efficacy is displayed in Figure 5–2. It draws upon the work of Stanford psychologist Albert Bandura. Let us explore this model with a simple illustrative task. Imagine you have been told to prepare and deliver a 10-minute talk to an OB class of 50 students on the workings of the self-efficacy model in Figure 5–2.

Your self-efficacy calculation would involve cognitive appraisal of the interaction between your perceived capability and situational opportunities and obstacles. As you begin to prepare for your presentation, the four sources of self-efficacy beliefs would come into play. Because prior experience is the most potent source, according to Bandura, it is listed first and connected to self-efficacy beliefs with a solid line. Past success in public speaking would boost your self-efficacy. But bad experiences with delivering speeches would foster low self-efficacy. Regarding behavior models as a source of self-efficacy beliefs, you would be influenced by the success or failure of your classmates in delivering similar talks. Their successes would tend to bolster you (or perhaps their failure would if you were very competitive and had high self-esteem). Likewise, any supportive persuasion from your classmates that you will do a good job would enhance your self-efficacy. Physical and emotional factors also might affect your self-confidence. A sudden case of laryngitis or a bout of stage fright could cause your self-efficacy expectations to plunge. Your cognitive evaluation of the situation then would yield a self-efficacy belief—ranging from high to low expectations for success. Importantly, self-efficacy beliefs are not merely boastful statements based on bravado; they are deep convictions supported by experience.

figure 5–2 A Model of How Self-Efficacy Beliefs Can Pave the Way for Success or Failure

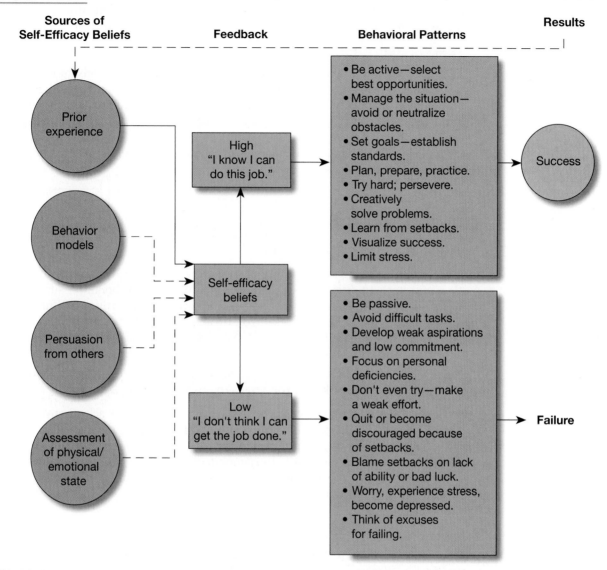

SOURCES: Adapted from discussion in A Bandura, "Regulation of Cognitive Processes through Perceived Self-Efficacy," *Developmental Psychology,* September 1989, pp 729–35; and R Wood and A Bandura, "Social Cognitive Theory of Organizational Management," *Academy of Management Review,* July 1989, pp 361–84.

Moving to the *behavioral patterns* portion of Figure 5–2, we see how self-efficacy beliefs are acted out. In short, if you have high self-efficacy about giving your 10-minute speech, you will work harder, more creatively, and longer when preparing for your talk than will your low-self-efficacy classmates. The results would then take shape accordingly. People program themselves for success or failure by enacting their self-efficacy expectations. Positive or negative results subsequently become feedback for one's base of personal experience. Along those lines, a national panel of scholars convened to discover why American students don't do better in math concluded, "Effort counts. Students who believe that working hard will make them smarter in math actually do achieve better."[27]

Self-Efficacy Implications for Managers   On-the-job research evidence encourages managers to nurture self-efficacy, both in themselves and in others. In fact, a meta-analysis encompassing 21,616 subjects found a significant positive correlation between self-efficacy and job performance.[28] Self-efficacy can be boosted in the workplace through careful hiring, challenging assignments, training and coaching, goal setting, supportive leadership and mentoring, and rewards for improvement. Boeing's CEO, James McNerney, offered this perspective:

Example. Success and achievement can feed on themselves. It feels good to keep succeeding. It feels great to see the people you work with grow and achieve. Maybe the ignition happens when you're younger, and then it feeds on itself. The next question is how you give it to people who weren't fortunate enough to have it given to them when they were young. It gets back to leadership attributes—expect a lot, inspire people, ask them to take the values that are important to them at home or at church and bring them to work.[29]

LO.3 Self-Monitoring

Consider these contrasting scenarios:

1. You are rushing to an important meeting when a co-worker pulls you aside and starts to discuss a personal problem. You want to break off the conversation, so you glance up at the clock. He keeps talking. You say, "I'm late for a big meeting." He continues. You turn and start to walk away. The person keeps talking as if he never received any of your verbal and nonverbal signals that the conversation was over.
2. Same situation. Only this time, when you glance at the clock, the person immediately says, "I know, you've got to go. Sorry. We'll talk later."

In the first all-too-familiar scenario, you are talking to a "low self-monitor." The second scenario involves a "high self-monitor." But more is involved here than a potentially irritating situation. A significant and measurable individual difference in self-expression behavior, called self-monitoring, is highlighted. **Self-monitoring** is the extent to which a person observes his or her own self-expressive behavior and adapts it to the demands of the situation. Experts on the subject offer this explanation:

Example. Individuals high in self-monitoring are thought to regulate their expressive self-presentation for the sake of desired public appearances, and thus be highly responsive to social and interpersonal cues of situationally appropriate performances. Individuals low in self-monitoring are thought to lack either the ability or the motivation to so regulate their expressive self-presentations. Their expressive behaviors, instead, are thought to functionally reflect their own enduring and momentary inner states, including their attitudes, traits, and feelings.[30]

In organizational life, both high and low monitors are subject to criticism. High self-monitors are sometimes called *chameleons*, who readily adapt their self-presentation to their surroundings. Low self-monitors, on the other hand, often are criticized for being on their own planet and insensitive to others.

Back to the Chapter-Opening Case

Would you call Mark Zuckerberg a high or low self-monitor? Explain. How can you deal effectively in the workplace with such a person?

A Matter of Degree   Self-monitoring is not a precise either-or proposition. It is a matter of degree; a matter of being relatively high or low in terms of related patterns of self-expression. For instance, consider this description of a relatively low self-monitoring individual: "We have an employee who turns every interaction—work-related or not—into a conversation about her. She's otherwise good at her job, but folks are beginning to avoid meetings with her or task forces on which she serves. 'She sucks the air out of the room,' a co-worker complained."[31] What are your self-monitoring tendencies?

Research Findings and Practical Recommendations   A meta-analysis encompassing 23,191 subjects in 136 samples found self-monitoring to be relevant and useful when dealing with job performance and emerging leaders.[32] According to field research, there is a positive relationship between high self-monitoring and career success. Among 139 MBA graduates who were tracked for five years, high self-monitors enjoyed more internal and external promotions than did their low self-monitoring classmates.[33] Another study of 147 managers and professionals found that high self-monitors had a better record of acquiring a mentor (someone to act as a personal career coach and professional sponsor).[34] These results mesh well with an earlier study that found managerial success (in terms of speed of promotions) tied to political savvy (knowing how to socialize, network, and engage in organizational politics).[35]

The foregoing evidence and everyday experience lead us to make these practical recommendations:

For high, moderate, and low self-monitors: Become more consciously aware of your self-image and how it affects others.

For high self-monitors: Don't overdo it by evolving from a successful chameleon into someone who is widely perceived as insincere, dishonest, phony, and untrustworthy. You cannot be everything to everyone.

For low self-monitors: You can bend without breaking, so try to be a bit more accommodating while being true to your basic beliefs. Don't wear out your welcome when communicating. Practice reading and adjusting to nonverbal cues in various public situations. If your conversation partner is bored or distracted, stop—because they are not really listening.

Organizational Identification: A *Social* Aspect of Self-Concept with Ethical Implications

The dividing line between self and others is not a neat and precise one. A certain amount of blurring occurs, for example, when an employee comes to define him- or herself with a *specific* organization—a psychological process called *organizational identification.* According to an expert on this evolving OB topic, "**organizational identification** occurs when one comes to integrate beliefs about one's organization into one's identity."[36] Organizational identification

Are you willing to get a tattoo of your employer's corporate logo? As an extreme case of organizational and product identification, many Harley-Davidson employees have done it.

self-monitoring Observing one's own behavior and adapting it to the situation.

organizational identification Organizational values or beliefs become part of one's self-identity.

goes to the heart of organizational culture and socialization (recall our discussion in Chapter 3).

Managers put a good deal of emphasis today on organizational mission, philosophy, and values with the express intent of integrating the company into each employee's self-identity. Hopefully, as the logic goes, employees who identify closely with the organization will be more loyal, more committed, and harder working. For example, consider this snapshot of American Express. "Credit card behemoth breeds loyalty: Nearly a quarter of employees have been with the company more than 15 years. 'It is my honor to serve my brand, my creed, my company,' says one."[37] As an extreme case in point, organizational identification among employees at Harley-Davidson's motorcycle factories is so strong that many sport tattoos with the company's logo. Working at Harley is not just a job, it's a lifestyle. (Somehow, your authors have a hard time imagining an employee with a General Motors or a Burger King tattoo!) A company tattoo may be a bit extreme, but the ethical implications of identifying too closely with one's employer are profound. Phyllis Anzalone, a former Enron employee, is a good case in point. She admitted that Enron *was* her self-identity and she ended up with emotional scars:

Example. What did working at Enron do for Anzalone? For one thing, it made her a lot of money, so much that the company's failure cost her about $1 million. More important, it made her. It took her from being a reasonably successful facilities management salesperson from rural Louisiana and propelled her into the ranks of sales superstars. It changed her view of herself; it confirmed what she thought she could achieve. "Enron had a profound effect on my life," she says. As devastating as it was, I'm glad I did it. It was like being on steroids every day."

And what does Anzalone think of the executives who ran Enron—and then ran it into the ground? "They are scum," she says, "They are crooks, and they are traitors. They betrayed many people's trust, including mine."[38]

Anzalone distanced herself from Enron's most unsavory characters during her years with the company. But some of her colleagues, with equally strong organizational identification, evidently turned their backs on their personal ethical standards and values when working on clearly illegal deals. When employees suspend their critical thinking and lose their objectivity, unhealthy groupthink can occur and needed constructive conflict does *not* occur. (Groupthink is covered in Chapter 10 and functional conflict is discussed in Chapter 13.) Whistle-blowing, as defined in Chapter 1, is unlikely to occur when organizational identification is excessive. Company loyalty and dedication are one thing; blind obedience to unethical leaders or a twisted sense of duty are quite another. Recent research places part of the blame on vulnerable employees believing they will be rewarded eventually for doing wrong in the name of the company."[39]

•••••••••••••••••••••▶
TO THE POINT
How would someone with a proactive personality likely score on the Big Five dimensions?
•••••••••••••••••••••

Personality: Concepts and Controversy

Individuals have their own way of thinking and acting, their own unique style or *personality*. **Personality** is defined as the combination of stable physical and mental characteristics that give the individual his or her identity.[40] These characteristics or traits—including how one looks, thinks, acts, and feels—are the product of interacting genetic and environmental influences.[41] In this section, we introduce the Big Five personality dimensions, explore the proactive personality, and issue some cautions about workplace personality testing.

table 5–2   The Big Five Personality Dimensions

PERSONALITY DIMENSION	CHARACTERISTICS OF A PERSON SCORING POSITIVELY ON THE DIMENSION
1. **Extraversion**	Outgoing, talkative, sociable, assertive
2. **Agreeableness**	Trusting, good-natured, cooperative, softhearted
3. **Conscientiousness**	Dependable, responsible, achievement oriented, persistent
4. **Emotional stability**	Relaxed, secure, unworried
5. **Openness to experience**	Intellectual, imaginative, curious, broad-minded

SOURCE: Adapted from M R Barrick and M K Mount, "Autonomy as a Moderator of the Relationships between the Big Five Personality Dimensions and Job Performance," *Journal of Applied Psychology,* February 1993, pp 111–18.

 LO.4 The Big Five Personality Dimensions

 Go to www.mcgrawhillconnect.com for an interactive comprehension case exercise on individual behavior in organizations.

Decades of research produced cumbersome lists of personality traits. In fact, one recent study identified 1,710 English-language adjectives used to describe aspects of personality.[42] Fortunately, this confusing situation has been statistically distilled to the Big Five.[43] They are extraversion, agreeableness, conscientiousness, emotional stability, and openness to experience (see Table 5–2 for descriptions).

Standardized personality tests determine how positively or negatively a person scores on each of the Big Five. For example, someone scoring negatively on extraversion would be an introverted person prone to shy and withdrawn behavior. Someone scoring negatively on emotional security would be nervous, tense, angry, and worried. Appropriately, the negative end of the emotional stability scale is labeled neuroticism.

A person's scores on the Big Five reveal a personality profile as unique as his or her fingerprints. One's personality profile tends to be stable and durable. A recent meta-analysis concluded that "both normal personality and personality disorders were highly stable across the life span, and patients in therapy experienced no more personality change than did nonpatients."[44] Extraversion and conscientiousness were found to be the most stable of the Big Five, according to data on 799 people covering the 40 years between their elementary-school days and midlife.[45] So don't be surprised when many of your high-school classmates seem pretty much the same at your 20th reunion, except perhaps for some extra pounds and thinning hair, of course.

Back to the Chapter-Opening Case

Will being an introvert as a young college student help or hinder Mark Zuckerberg as CEO of Facebook as it continues to grow into a global social media giant? Explain.

personality Stable physical and mental characteristics responsible for a person's identity.

But one important question lingers: Are personality models ethnocentric and unique to the culture in which they were developed? At least as far as the Big Five model goes, cross-cultural research evidence points in the direction of no. Specifically, the Big Five personality structure held up very well in one study of women and men from Russia, Canada, Hong Kong, Poland, Germany, and Finland and a second study (85% male) of South Korean managers and stockbrokers.[46] A more recent comprehensive analysis of Big Five studies led the researchers to this conclusion: "To date, there is no compelling evidence that culture affects personality structure."[47] However, a new study found only 3 out of 14 personality dimensions were consistent across 12 different languages.[48] This casts a shadow of doubt over cross-cultural studies of personality because unique language structures can make precise translations of survey questionnaires difficult.

Those interested in workplace behavior want to know the connection between the Big Five and job performance. Ideally, Big Five personality dimensions that correlate positively and strongly with job performance would be helpful in the selection, training, and appraisal of employees. A meta-analysis of 117 studies involving 23,994 subjects from many professions offers guidance.[49] Among the Big Five, *conscientiousness* had the strongest positive correlation with job performance and training performance. According to the researchers, "those individuals who exhibit traits associated with a strong sense of purpose, obligation, and persistence generally perform better than those who do not."[50] Recent research studies shed practical light on how to help conscientious employees perform well. Specifically, they prefer goal-focused leadership, like high-complexity jobs, and need valid feedback that will help them learn and not frustrate their pursuit of goals.[51] Not surprisingly, entrepreneurs score high on conscientiousness.[52] Another relevant finding: Extraversion (an outgoing personality) correlated positively with promotions, salary level, and career satisfaction. And, as one might expect, neuroticism (low emotional stability) was associated with low career satisfaction.[53]

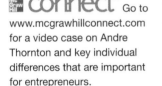 Go to www.mcgrawhillconnect.com for a video case on Andre Thornton and key individual differences that are important for entrepreneurs.

LO.5   The Proactive Personality

As suggested by the previous discussion, someone who scores high on the Big Five dimension of conscientiousness is probably a good worker. Thomas S Bateman and J Michael Crant took this important linkage an additional step by formulating the concept of the proactive personality. They define and characterize the **proactive personality** in these terms: "someone who is relatively unconstrained by situational forces and who effects environmental change. Proactive people identify opportunities and act on them, show initiative, take action, and persevere until meaningful change occurs."[54] They have what researchers have long called an **internal locus of control**, the belief that one controls the events and consequences affecting one's life.[55] For example, an "internal" tends to attribute positive outcomes, such as getting a passing grade on an exam, to her or his own abilities. Accordingly, an "internal" tends to blame negative events, such as failing an exam, on personal shortcomings—not studying hard enough, perhaps. Oppositely, people with an **external locus of control** tend to attribute key outcomes in their lives to environmental causes, such as luck or fate.[56] In a review of relevant studies, Crant found the proactive personality to be positively associated with individual, team, and organizational success.[57]

Successful entrepreneurs exemplify the proactive personality. People with proactive personalities truly are valuable *human capital*, as defined in Chapter 1. Those wanting to get ahead would do well to cultivate the initiative, drive, courage, and perseverance of someone with a proactive personality—and managers would do well to hire them (see Real World/Real People). Once hired, proactive

real WORLD // real PEOPLE: ethics

Julie Markham Is Making the World a Better Place

Julie Markham is the kind of person who refuses to give up on a dream—even if some people think it's an impossible dream. And that has made a world of difference to the University of Denver student, who graduated [in 2010]. . . .

It has taken her to Cambodia, India, Bangladesh, the Middle East, and, most recently, Kenya, where she is consulting with a local bank that is developing an eco-friendly village designed to move slum-dwellers into sustainable, affordable housing.

Markham, a real estate and finance major, has ignored naysayers who say microfinancing—sometimes called "barefoot banking"—won't lead to long-term social good. Or who think a college student could never play a role in transforming the lives of people across the globe.

Based on what you have just read about personality, what characteristics make Julie Markham an excellent role model for college students?

SOURCE: Excerpted from M B Marklein, "Students Defy Expectations," *USA Today,* June 9, 2010, p 1D.

---

employees need to be managed carefully. For example, a recent field study of employees and their managers at 130 pizza delivery stores in the United States led to this contingency management conclusion:

Example. While it's often true that extroverts make the best bosses and proactive employees make the best workers, combining the two can be a recipe for failure. Soft-spoken leaders may get the most out of proactive employees—so save the outgoing, talkative managers for teams that function best when they're told what to do.[58]

Issue: What about Personality Testing in the Workplace?

Personality testing as a tool for making decisions about hiring, training, and promotion is commonplace. Unfortunately, there is the major issue of *sloppy administration.* Annie Murphy Paul, author of *The Cult of Personality,*[59] explains:

Example. You hear a lot from psychologists who are supportive of personality testing, and sometimes from testing companies, that there are ideal ways to use these tests. An example would be to bring in a psychologist to do a study of the job itself and design or tailor a test specifically for that position, and then have it administered by a psychologist, and have the results remain confidential. I think the way these tests are actually used is that they're usually bought off the shelf, they're given indiscriminately, often by people who aren't trained or qualified, and then the results aren't kept confidential or private at all. For all the talk about standards on how [these tests] should be used, the way they're used in the real world is more hit-or-miss.[60]

---

proactive personality Action-oriented person who shows initiative and perseveres to change things.

internal locus of control Attributing outcomes to one's own actions.

external locus of control Attributing outcomes to circumstances beyond one's control.

Faking, cheating, and illegal discrimination also are potential problems with on-the-job personality testing. A computer simulation revealed the potential for faking conscientiousness, a key Big Five factor.[61] More recently, a field study of 32,311 applicants for managerial positions at a large US retailer uncovered systematic faking on an online personality test.[62] Regarding the problem of cheating, the case of Anton Smith is a cautionary tale: Prior to taking a 130-item personality test when applying for a job at an athletic footwear store in North Carolina, Smith got an edge when a friend found a pirated answer key on the Internet. Smith, who got the job but later left when the store went out of business, had this to say about the test: "It isn't useful. People are hip to it."[63] The problem of illegal discrimination was summed up by Dallas employment attorney Allan King when he told a group of human resource professionals that, because society is so diverse, "every test has an adverse impact against somebody."[64] A meta-analysis of personality testing across five racial groups in the United States came to essentially the same conclusion.[65]

The practical tips in Table 5–3 can help managers avoid abuses and costly discrimination lawsuits when using personality and psychological testing for employment-related decisions. Job-related skills testing and behavioral interviewing are workable alternatives to personality testing.

We now shift our focus to abilities and intelligence.

table 5–3 Advice and Words of Caution about Personality Testing in the Workplace

Researchers, test developers, and organizations that administer personality assessments offer the following suggestions for getting started or for evaluating whether tests already in use are appropriate for forecasting job performance:

• Determine what you hope to accomplish. If you are looking to find the best fit of job and applicant, analyze the aspects of the position that are most critical for it.

• Look for outside help to determine if a test exists or can be developed to screen applicants for the traits that best fit the position. Industrial psychologists, professional organizations, and a number of Internet sites provide resources.

• Insist that any test recommended by a consultant or vendor be validated scientifically for the specific purpose that you have defined. Vendors should be able to cite some independent, credible research supporting a test's correlation with job performance.

• Ask the test provider to document the legal basis for any assessment: Is it fair? Is it job related? Is it biased against any racial or ethnic group? Does it violate an applicant's right to privacy under state or federal laws? Vendors should provide a lawyer's statement that a test does not adversely affect any protected class, and employers may want to get their own lawyer's opinion, as well.

• Make sure that every staff member who will be administering tests or analyzing results is educated about how to do so properly and keeps results confidential. Use the scores on personality tests in tandem with other factors that you believe are essential to the job—such as skills and experience—to create a comprehensive evaluation of the merits of each candidate, and apply those criteria identically to each applicant.

Abilities (Intelligence) and Performance

◀ ······················
TO THE POINT
What are the major abilities and eight multiple intelligences?
······················

Individual differences in abilities and accompanying skills are a central concern for managers because nothing can be accomplished without appropriately skilled personnel. An **ability** represents a broad and stable characteristic responsible for a person's maximum—as opposed to typical—performance on mental and physical tasks. A **skill**, on the other hand, is the specific capacity to physically manipulate objects. Consider this difference as you imagine yourself being the only passenger on a small commuter airplane in which the pilot has just passed out. As the plane nose-dives, your effort and abilities will not be enough to save yourself and the pilot if you do not possess flying skills. As shown in Figure 5–3 successful performance (be it landing an airplane or performing any other job) depends on the right combination of effort, ability, and skill.

Abilities and skills are being developed in some unique ways today, thanks to modern technology. For example, a biomedical professor at Arizona State University and a Phoenix surgeon "conducted studies in which trainee surgeons played a Nintendo Wii video game called Marble Mania, which requires players to develop dexterity in their hand movements to succeed at the game.... The Wii game players showed 48 percent more improvement in their surgical techniques than the non-players."[66] Video game–obsessed youngsters can now tell their worried parents and teachers, "I'm just refining my surgical technique."

Among the many desirable skills and competencies in organizational life are written and spoken communication, initiative, decisiveness, tolerance, problem solving, adaptability, and resilience. Importantly, our cautions about on-the-job personality testing extend to ability, intelligence, and skill testing and certification.

Before moving on, we need to say something about a modern-day threat to abilities, skills, and general competence. That threat, according to public health officials, is *sleep deprivation.*

Abilities and the Need for Sleep

A 2010 survey of 1,007 adults from all major ethnic groups in the United States found that "Fewer than half—only about four in 10—of the respondents from each ethnic group say they get a good night's sleep on most nights."[67] Sad to

figure 5–3   Performance Depends on the Right Combination of Effort, Ability, and Skill

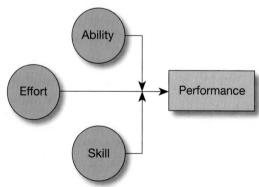

---

ability Stable characteristic responsible for a person's maximum physical or mental performance.

skill Specific capacity to manipulate objects.

say, sleep deprivation is an equal opportunity problem. In another survey, *job-related stress* was the number-one response (42%) to the question "What's robbing you of a good night's sleep?"[68] If your basic sleep needs are being routinely shortchanged, you are likely to be a less effective decision maker and problem solver, more stressed (see Chapter 18), and more prone to health problems than you should be.[69] "Adults typically need seven to nine hours of sleep each night to feel fully rested and function at their best."[70] Habitually sleep-deprived people need to be aware of this stunning fact: "Staying awake 24 hours impairs cognitive psychomotor performance to the same degree as having a 0.1 percent blood alcohol level."[71] That exceeds the 0.08 percent blood alcohol limit for drivers in the United States. In fact, experts estimate "that sleep-deprived drivers cause more than 100,000 automobile crashes a year and more than 1,500 deaths."[72] According to sleep researcher Sara Mednick:

Example. Without sleep you don't learn. My research shows that people deteriorate during the day. It's difficult to sustain productivity. Naps can add back to the sleep you're deprived of at night. And a nap enhances productivity even if you have enough nocturnal sleep. . . .

A 20-minute nap in the afternoon, between 1 PM and 3 PM, right after lunch, would be ideal. You don't want to get into deep sleep, because you need to be alert. This nap will allow you to be as productive right after the nap as you were before. That's what a lot of businesspeople need for on-your-feet thinking.[73]

Okay, this approach may be a bit over the top, but sleep experts recommend napping accommodations for today's overloaded and sleep-deprived workers.

Employers have taken note and are making changes:

Example. Following the rise of workplace perks like lactation rooms, gyms, and child-care facilities, Nike workers now have access to nap-friendly "quiet rooms" that can also be used for meditation. Google, a forerunner in employee perks, has a number of futuristic napping pods scattered throughout its Mountain View (California) campus.

Jawa, a small mobile technology company in Scottsdale, Arizona, has two resting rooms—one with a similar pod, the other with an old-fashioned couch—that are popular among programmers working long hours.[74]

The balance of this section explores intelligence, specific cognitive abilities, and the controversial idea of multiple intelligences.

Intelligence and Cognitive Abilities

Although experts do not agree on a specific definition, **intelligence** represents an individual's capacity for constructive thinking, reasoning, and problem solving.[75] Historically, intelligence was believed to be an innate capacity, passed genetically from one generation to the next. Research since has shown, however, that intelligence (like personality) also is a function of environmental influences.[76] Organic factors have more recently been added to the formula as a result of mounting evidence of the connection between alcohol and drug abuse and poor eating habits among pregnant women and intellectual development problems in their children.[77]

Researchers have produced some interesting findings about intelligence in recent years. A steady and significant rise in average intelligence among those in developed countries has been observed over the last 70 years. Why? Experts at an American Psychological Association conference concluded, "Some combination of better schooling, improved socioeconomic status, healthier nutrition, and a more technologically complex society might account for the gains in IQ scores."[78] If you think you're smarter than your parents and your teachers, despite being criticized for not knowing a lot of facts they think are important, you're probably right!

Two Types of Abilities   Human intelligence has been studied predominantly through the empirical approach. By examining the relationships between measures of mental abilities and behavior, researchers have statistically isolated major components of intelligence. Using this empirical procedure, pioneering psychologist Charles Spearman proposed in 1927 that all cognitive performance is determined by two types of abilities. The first can be characterized as a general mental ability needed for *all* cognitive tasks. The second is unique to the task at hand.[79] For example, an individual's ability to complete crossword puzzles is a function of his or her broad mental abilities as well as the specific ability to perceive patterns in partially completed words.

Seven Major Mental Abilities   Through the years, much research has been devoted to developing and expanding Spearman's ideas on the relationship between cognitive abilities and intelligence. One research psychologist listed 120 distinct mental abilities. Table 5–4 contains definitions of the seven most

table 5–4 Mental Abilities Underlying Performance

ABILITY	DESCRIPTION
1. Verbal comprehension	The ability to understand what words mean and to readily comprehend what is read.
2. Word fluency	The ability to produce isolated words that fulfill specific symbolic or structural requirements (such as all words that begin with the letter *b* and have two vowels).
3. Numerical	The ability to make quick and accurate arithmetic computations such as adding and subtracting.
4. Spatial	Being able to perceive spatial patterns and to visualize how geometric shapes would look if transformed in shape or position.
5. Memory	Having good rote memory for paired words, symbols, lists of numbers, or other associated items.
6. Perceptual speed	The ability to perceive figures, identify similarities and differences, and carry out tasks involving visual perception.
7. Inductive reasoning	The ability to reason from specifics to general conclusions.

SOURCE: From M D Dunnette, "Aptitudes, Abilities, and Skills," in *Handbook of Industrial and Organizational Psychology,* ed M D Dunnette, Rand McNally, 1976, pp 478–83. Reprinted with permission.

intelligence Capacity for constructive thinking, reasoning, problem solving.

frequently cited mental abilities. Of the seven abilities, personnel selection researchers have found verbal ability, numerical ability, spatial ability, and inductive reasoning to be valid predictors of job performance for both minority and majority applicants.[80]

LO.6 Do We Have Multiple Intelligences?

Howard Gardner, a professor at Harvard's Graduate School of Education, offered a new paradigm for human intelligence in his 1983 book *Frames of Mind: The Theory of Multiple Intelligences.*[81] He has subsequently identified eight different intelligences that vastly broaden the long-standing concept of intelligence. Gardner's concept of multiple intelligences (MI) includes not only cognitive abilities but social and physical abilities and skills as well:

- *Linguistic intelligence:* Potential to learn and use spoken and written languages.
- *Logical-mathematical intelligence:* Potential for deductive reasoning, problem analysis, and mathematical calculation.
- *Musical intelligence:* Potential to appreciate, compose, and perform music.
- *Bodily-kinesthetic intelligence:* Potential to use mind and body to coordinate physical movement.
- *Spatial intelligence:* Potential to recognize and use patterns.
- *Interpersonal intelligence:* Potential to understand, connect with, and effectively work with others.
- *Intrapersonal intelligence:* Potential to understand and regulate oneself.
- *Naturalist intelligence:* Potential to live in harmony with one's environment.[82]

Many educators and parents have embraced MI because it helps explain how a child could score poorly on a standard IQ test yet be obviously gifted in one or more ways (e.g., music, sports, relationship building). Moreover, according to advocates, the concept of MI underscores the need to help children develop their own unique mental and physical gifts at their own pace. They say standard IQ tests deal only with the first two intelligences on Gardner's list and a low IQ score can become a life-long burden because of stereotyping and prejudice (see Real World/Real People). Meanwhile, most academic psychologists and intelligence specialists continue to criticize Gardner's model as too subjective and poorly integrated. They prefer the traditional model of intelligence as a unified variable measured by a single test. We keep an open mind about MI, as evidenced by our coverage of cultural intelligence and emotional intelligence in this textbook.

.............................▶
TO THE POINT

What is the meaning of emotional intelligence, emotional contagion, and emotional labor?
....

Emotions in the Workplace

In the ideal world of management theory, employees pursue organizational goals in a logical and rational manner. Emotional behavior seldom is factored into the equation. Yet day-to-day organizational life shows us how prevalent and powerful emotions can be.[83] Anger and jealousy, both potent emotions, often push aside logic and rationality in the workplace. Managers use fear and other emotions to both motivate and intimidate. Sadness and anxiety creep in, too. For example, consider this 2008 meeting at Microsoft:

Example. Steve Ballmer was sobbing. He repeatedly tried to speak and couldn't get the words out. Minutes passed as he tried to regain his composure. But the

real WORLD // real PEOPLE: ethics

The Americans with Disabilities Act Falls Short on Employment

People with disabilities say they "expected more" employment gains after the Americans with Disabilities Act was signed into law July 26, 1990. Twenty years later, their expectations still aren't being met. . . .

The Kessler Foundation and the National Organization on Disability report that employment "is still the area where people with disabilities seem to be at the greatest disadvantage compared to the rest of the population."

Their poll, conducted by Harris Interactive, found that:

- Among all working-age people with disabilities, 21 percent said they were employed full time or part time compared with 59 percent of working-age people without disabilities.
- Among those with disabilities who described themselves as unemployed, 73 percent cited their disability as one of the reasons.

Why is it important for all of us, especially managers, to focus on the word *ability* in disability?

SOURCE: Excerpted from S Taylor, "Surveys Highlight Gap in Disability Employment," *HR Magazine,* September 2010, p 16.

audience of 130 of Microsoft's senior leaders waited patiently, many of them crying too. They knew that the CEO was choked up because this executive retreat, held in late March at a resort north of Seattle, was the last ever for company co-founder Bill Gates, as well as for Jeff Raikes, one of the company's longest-tenured executives. "I've spent more time with these two human beings than with anyone else in my life," Ballmer finally said. "Bill and Jeff have been my North Star and kept me going. Now I'm going to count on all of you to be there for me."[84]

Less dramatic, but still emotion-laden, is John Chambers's tightrope act as CEO of Cisco Systems:

Example. Any company that thinks it's utterly unbeatable is already beaten. So when I begin to think we're getting a little bit too confident, you'll see me emphasizing the paranoia side. And then when I feel that there's a little bit too much fear and apprehension, I'll just jump back to the other side. My job is to keep those scales perfectly balanced.[85]

These admired corporate leaders would not have achieved what they have without the ability to be logical and rational decision makers *and* be emotionally charged. In this section, our examination of individual differences turns to defining emotions, reviewing a typology of 10 positive and negative emotions, exploring emotional intelligence and maturity, and focusing on the interesting topics of emotional contagion and emotional labor.

LO.7 Positive and Negative Emotions

Richard S Lazarus, a leading authority on the subject, defines **emotions** as "complex, patterned, organismic reactions to how we think we are doing in our lifelong efforts to survive and flourish and to achieve what we wish for ourselves."[86] The word *organismic* is appropriate because emotions involve the *whole* person—biological, psychological, and social. Importantly, psychologists draw a distinction between *felt* and *displayed* emotions.[87] For example, a person might feel angry (felt emotion) at a rude co-worker but not make a nasty remark in return (displayed emotion). As discussed in Chapter 18, emotions play roles in both causing and adapting to stress and its associated biological and psychological problems. The destructive effect of emotional behavior on social relationships is all too obvious in daily life. On the other hand, research demonstrates how people tend to form tight social bonds when they share an intense emotional experience.[88] It is common for survivors of horrific events such as airplane crashes, for instance, to have reunions years later.

Lazarus's definition of emotions centers on a person's goals. Accordingly, his distinction between positive and negative emotions is goal oriented. Some emotions are triggered by frustration and failure when pursuing one's goals. Lazarus calls these *negative* emotions. They are said to be goal incongruent. For example, which of the six negative emotions in Figure 5–4 are you likely to experience if you fail the final exam in a required course? Failing the exam would be incongruent with your goal of graduating on time. On the other hand, which of the four *positive* emotions in Figure 5–4 would you probably experience if you graduated on time and with honors? The emotions you would experience in this situation are positive because they are congruent (or consistent) with an important lifetime goal. The individual's goals, it is important to note, may or may not be socially

figure 5–4 Positive and Negative Emotions

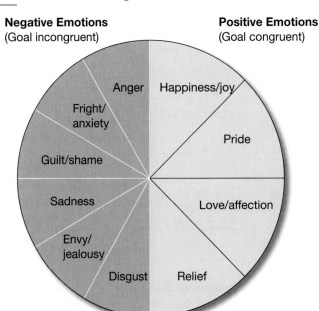

SOURCE: Adapted from discussion in R S Lazarus, *Emotion and Adaptation* (New York: Oxford University Press, 1991), chaps. 6, 7.

acceptable. Thus, a positive emotion, such as love/affection, may be undesirable if associated with sexual harassment. Oppositely, slight pangs of guilt, anxiety, and envy can motivate extra effort. On balance, the constructive or destructive nature of a particular emotion must be judged in terms of both its intensity and the person's relevant goal.

For a dramatic real-life example of the interplay between negative and positive emotions, consider the situation Kenneth I Chenault faced just 10 months after becoming CEO of American Express. The September 11, 2001, terrorist attacks claimed the lives of 11 employees, and the firm's headquarters building, across the street from ground zero in Lower Manhattan, had to be abandoned for what turned out to be eight months of repairs.

Example. Chenault gathered 5,000 American Express employees at the Paramount Theater in New York on September 20 for a highly emotional "town hall meeting." During the session, Chenault demonstrated the poise, compassion, and decisiveness that vaulted him to the top. He told employees that he had been filled with such despair, sadness, and anger that he had seen a counselor. Twice, he rushed to spontaneously embrace grief-stricken employees. Chenault said he would donate $1 million of the company's profits to the families of the AmEx victims. "I represent the best company and the best people in the world," he concluded." In fact, you are my strength, and I love you."[89]

Thus, Chenault masterfully used positive emotions to cope with profound negative emotions.

LO.8 Developing Emotional Intelligence

People cope with powerful emotions in lots of different ways. Take Taryn Rose, for example. She followed in her physician father's footsteps by attending medical school. However, near the end of her residency, she was bitten by the entrepreneurial bug and set her sights on developing and selling stylish shoes that would not ruin women's feet. But she did not want to disappoint her family. "I feared regret more than I feared failure,"[90] she recalled for *Fast Company* magazine, so she followed her dream. Now that she is the CEO of her own $20-million-a-year company, her family understands. For Taryn Rose, it took a good idea and determination to conquer her fears. Another way to deal effectively with fear and other emotions is to become more emotionally mature by developing emotional intelligence.

In 1995, Daniel Goleman, a psychologist turned journalist, created a stir in education and management circles with the publication of his book *Emotional Intelligence*. Hence, an obscure topic among psychologists became mainstream. Building upon Howard Gardner's concept of interpersonal intelligence, Goleman criticizes the traditional model of intelligence (IQ) for being too narrow, thus failing to consider interpersonal competence. Goleman's broader agenda includes "abilities such as being able to motivate oneself and persist in the face of frustrations; to control impulse and delay gratification; to regulate one's moods and keep distress from swamping the ability to think; to empathize and to hope."[91]

Mc Graw Hill **connect**™ Go to www.mcgrawhillconnect.com for an interactive exercise to test your knowledge of emotional intelligence.

emotions Complex human reactions to personal achievements and setbacks that may be felt and displayed.

table 5–5 Developing Personal and Social Competence through Emotional Intelligence

Personal Competence: These capabilities determine how we manage ourselves.

Self-Awareness

- *Emotional self-awareness:* Reading one's own emotions and recognizing their impact; using "gut sense" to guide decisions.
- *Accurate self-assessment:* Knowing one's strengths and limits.
- *Self-confidence:* A sound sense of one's self-worth and capabilities.

Self-Management

- *Emotional self-control:* Keeping disruptive emotions and impulses under control.
- *Transparency:* Displaying honesty and integrity; trustworthiness.
- *Adaptability:* Flexibility in adapting to changing situations or overcoming obstacles.
- *Achievement:* The drive to improve performance to meet inner standards of excellence.
- *Initiative:* Readiness to act and seize opportunities.
- *Optimism:* Seeing the upside in events.

Social Competence: These capabilities determine how we manage relationships.

Social Awareness

- *Empathy:* Sensing others' emotions, understanding their perspective, and taking active interest in their concerns.
- *Organizational awareness:* Reading the currents, decision networks, and politics at the organizational level.
- *Service:* Recognizing and meeting follower, client, or customer needs.

Relationship Management

- *Inspirational leadership:* Guiding and motivating with a compelling vision.
- *Influence:* Wielding a range of tactics for persuasion.
- *Developing others:* Bolstering others' abilities through feedback and guidance.
- *Change catalyst:* Initiating, managing, and leading in a new direction.
- *Conflict management:* Resolving disagreements.
- *Building bonds:* Cultivating and maintaining a web of relationships.
- *Teamwork and collaboration:* Cooperation and team building.

SOURCE: Reprinted by permission of Harvard Business School Publishing. Exhibit from D Goleman, R Boyatzis, and A McKee, *Primal Leadership: Realizing the Power of Emotional Intelligence,* 2002, p 398. Copyright 2002 by the Harvard Business School Publishing Corporation; all rights reserved.

Thus, **emotional intelligence** is the ability to manage oneself and one's relationships in mature and constructive ways. Referred to by some as EI and others as EQ, emotional intelligence is said to have four key components: self-awareness, self-management, social awareness, and relationship management. The first two constitute *personal competence;* the second two feed into *social competence* (see Table 5–5).

Researchers have flashed a caution light about using emotional intelligence as an employee selection and evaluation tool. The central issues, according to behavioral scientists who conducted a recent meta-analysis, are inconsistent theory and invalid measurement. They concluded that EI scores do not improve on the basic Big Five dimensions when it comes to predicting job performance.[92] Thus, using one of the many available EI questionnaires to assess job applicants or evaluate employee performance is an open invitation to unfair discrimination lawsuits. Another recent meta-analysis disputed the generous claims by advocates that EI is the core of visionary and charismatic leadership (called *transformational* leadership in Chapter 16).[93] Still, EI does appear to have a place in employee personal growth and development programs. As an integrated package, the proactive personality discussed earlier and the characteristics listed in Table 5–5 constitute an inspiring self-development agenda for each of us.

Back to the Chapter-Opening Case

Suppose you were an executive coach, how would you coach Mark Zuckerberg to have the emotional intelligence to handle being the head of a giant corporation?

Practical Research Insights about Emotional Contagion and Emotional Labor

Two streams of OB research on emotions are beginning to yield interesting and instructive insights.

Emotional Contagion   Have you ever had someone's bad mood sour your mood? That person could have been a parent, supervisor, co-worker, friend, or someone serving you in a store or restaurant. Appropriately, researchers call this emotional contagion. We, quite literally, can catch another person's bad mood or displayed negative emotions. This effect was documented in a study of 131 bank tellers (92% female) and 220 exit interviews with their customers. Tellers who expressed positive emotions tended to have more satisfied customers. Two field studies with nurses and accountants as subjects found a strong linkage between the work group's collective mood and the individual's mood.[94] Both foul moods and good moods turned out to be contagious.

Emotional Labor   Generations of managers have known about the power of emotional contagion in the marketplace. "Smile, look happy for the customers," employees are told over and over. But what if the employee is having a rotten day? What if they have to mask their true feelings and emotions? What if they have to fake it? Researchers have begun studying the dynamics of what they call emotional labor. A pair of authors, one from Australia, the other from the United States, summarized the research lessons to date:

Example. Emotional labor can be particularly detrimental to the employee performing the labor and can take its toll both psychologically and physically. Employees . . . may bottle up feelings of frustration, resentment, and anger, which are not appropriate to express. These feelings result, in part, from the constant requirement to monitor one's negative emotions and express positive ones. If not

emotional intelligence Ability to manage oneself and interact with others in mature and constructive ways.

real WORLD // real PEOPLE

One Chinese Student's Life Plan

On a recent trip to China, I met with a group of students at Beijing's Tsinghua University—the Harvard of [China]. . . . These young people were among the best and brightest that their country produces, which, considering the diligence of Chinese students, says a lot. I asked one physics genius what her plans were after graduation. She had already lined up a scholarship to pursue an MBA at Stanford. After that, she said, "I'll probably stay in the US for a while and work at McKinsey or a venture-capital firm in Silicon Valley." Then, she continued, "I'll come back to China and start a company. After I make my money, I will retire and move to Europe, where I'll take my parents traveling."

Is it a good or a bad idea to have your entire life planned out in detail? Explain. If yes, what is your vision for the future? What roles will hard work, luck, or fate play?

SOURCE: R Foroohar, "The World's Their Oyster," *Newsweek*, October 18, 2010, p 18.

---

given a healthy expressive outlet, this emotional repression can lead to a syndrome of emotional exhaustion and burnout.[95]

Steven Slater became an odd sort of folk hero for victims of excessive emotional labor in 2010. He was the JetBlue flight attendant who cursed the passengers and slid down the plane's emergency chute with a beer in hand after being banged in the head once too often by a piece of luggage.[96]

Interestingly, a pair of laboratory studies with US college students as subjects found no gender difference in *felt* emotions. But the women were more emotionally *expressive* than the men.[97] Managers clearly need to be attuned to (and responsive to) the emotional states and needs of their people. This requires some emotional intelligence.

·············▶
TO THE POINT
What do psychological capital and deliberate practice involve and how can we make our own luck?
·····················

 Go to www.mcgrawhillconnect.com for an interactive exercise to test your knowledge of how to pave your road to success using the lessons from OB.

Paving Your Road to Success with Lessons from OB

Let's put your new knowledge about yourself and others to practical use by exploring the road to success. Of course, we cannot define *success* for you—it depends on your own history, expectations, goals and dreams, and opportunities. We can share a couple of helpful perspectives, however. The first comes from legendary Omaha investor Warren Buffett: "They say success is getting what you want and happiness is wanting what you get."[98] The second comes from College Football Hall of Fame coach Lou Holtz: "Make sure you always have four things in your life: Something to do, someone to love, something to hope for and something to believe in."[99] With these inspirational words in mind, we explore four key paving stones for your road to success: psychological capital, deliberate practice, luck, and humility (see Real World/Real People).

LO.9 Psychological Capital

In Chapter 1, we introduced the concepts of human and social capital. To those we now add psychological capital (PsyCap). PsyCap is derived from the positive psychology movement that emphasizes what is *right* with people rather than what is wrong or dysfunctional. This approach focuses on human strengths and potential as a way to possibly *prevent* mental and behavioral problems and improve the general quality of life. University of Nebraska OB scholar Fred Luthans and his colleagues offer this definition of **psychological capital**:

Example. [PsyCap is] an individual's positive psychological state of development and is characterized by (1) having confidence (*self-efficacy*) to take on and put in the necessary effort to succeed at challenging tasks; (2) making a positive attribution (*optimism*) about succeeding now and in the future; (3) persevering toward goals, and when necessary, redirecting paths to goals (*hope*) in order to succeed; and (4) when beset by problems and adversity, sustaining and bouncing back and even beyond (*resiliency*) to attain success.[100]

Importantly, you can build your own PsyCap by applying lessons from this textbook relating to self-efficacy, positive attributions (Chapter 7), and goal setting (Chapter 9). **Resiliency**, the ability to bounce back from major blows in life, can be developed through deliberate practice, discussed below, and being inspired by role models such as Carol Tomé, Home Depot's chief financial officer:

Example. The oldest of four children, Tomé first learned about finance in Jackson, Wyoming, where her father ran the family-owned Jackson State Bank. She assumed that one day she would become Jackson State's first female CEO. When she was studying for an MBA at the University of Denver, however, her father called with news that upset her plans. He was divorcing her mother after 27 years of marriage and selling Jackson State.

"When I calmed down, I said to myself, 'Carol, you are going to be a banker. So be a banker,'" Tomé recalls. "As I sit here today, the best thing that ever happened to me, personally and professionally, was the fact that he sold the bank." Setting off on her own, she joined United Bank of Denver, and that led to a series of corporate finance jobs that landed her at Home Depot in 1995.[101]

Home Depot's Carol Tomé demonstrated resiliency on her road to success as the giant retailer's chief financial officer.

Deliberate Practice

Is there something you want to become really, *really* good at—world-class good? Maybe a sport, a musical instrument, speaking in public, writing a blog, playing a video game, designing products, coding software, singing and dancing, or woodworking. Then take this good advice from an old New York City joke: *Tourist*: "How do I get to Carnegie Hall?" *New Yorker*: "Practice, practice, practice." Okay, so how much practice? Try the 10,000-hour rule. After studying relevant research evidence, Malcolm Gladwell came to this conclusion in his best-seller *Outliers: The Story of Success*: "[T]he closer psychologists look at the careers of the gifted, the smaller the role innate talent seems to play and the bigger the role preparation seems to play. . . . [T]he people at the very top don't work just harder or even much harder than everyone else. They work much, *much* harder. . . . Ten thousand hours

psychological capital Striving for success by developing one's self-efficacy, optimism, hope, and resiliency.

resiliency The ability to handle pressure and quickly bounce back from personal and career setbacks.

is the magic number of greatness."[102] Generally, that works out to about 10 years of "deliberate" practice.

Fortune magazine's Geoff Colvin, in his interesting book *Talent Is Overrated: What* Really *Separates World-Class Performers from Everybody Else*, identifies the key elements of **deliberate practice**: "It is activity designed specifically to improve performance, often with a teacher's help; it can be repeated a lot; feedback on results is continuously available; it's highly demanding mentally, whether the activity is purely intellectual, such as chess or business-related activities, or heavily physical, such as sports; and it isn't much fun."[103]

Tiger Woods, who has relentlessly polished every aspect of his golf game since he was a toddler—first under his father's tutelage and later with the best coaches—shows the power of deliberate practice (despite his recent troubles). This situation, in addition to his titles and trophies, illustrates Tiger's uncanny "feel" for the game of golf:

Example. A few years ago, Nike was developing a driver and had Woods test the prototype. He hit three and said he liked the light one. The clubs weighed the same, Woods was told. No they don't, he replied. Nike's research crew put the drivers on a scale and discovered Woods was right. The club he liked weighed 2 grams less than the others.[104]

Luck

If you want to know about luck, then talk to lucky and unlucky people to see how they differ. That simple premise is behind more than a decade of innovative research by Richard Wiseman, a psychology professor in the United Kingdom. It turns out that luck involves much more than simply random chance or coincidence. Lucky people, through how they think and behave, make their own good fortune. Here are Wiseman's four guidelines for improving your luck:

1. *Be active and involved.* Be open to new experiences and networking with others to encounter more lucky chance opportunities.
2. *Listen to your hunches about luck.* Learn when to listen to your intuitive gut feelings. Meditation and mind-clearing activities can help.
3. *Expect to be lucky no matter how bad the situation.* Remain optimistic and work to make your expectations a self-fulfilling prophecy.
4. *Turn your bad luck into good fortune.* Take control of bad situations by remaining calm, positive, and focused on a better future.[105]

Many successful people made their own luck by making the best of life's hard knocks.

Humility

Before you declare yourself Grade A executive material, here is one more thing to toss into your tool kit: a touch of humility. **Humility** is "a realistic assessment of one's own contribution and the recognition of the contribution of others, along with luck and good fortune that made one's own success possible."[106] Humility has been called the silent virtue. How many truly humble people brag about being humble? Two OB experts offered this instructive perspective:

Example. Humble individuals have a down-to-earth perspective of themselves and of the events and relationships in their lives. Humility involves a capability to evaluate success, failure, work, and life without exaggeration. Furthermore, humility enables leaders to distinguish the delicate line between such characteristics as healthy self-confidence, self-esteem, and self-assessment, and those of over-confidence, narcissism, and stubbornness. Humility is the mid-point between the two negative extremes of arrogance and lack of self-esteem. This depiction allows one to see that a person can be humble and competitive or humble and ambitious at the same time, which contradicts common—but mistaken—views about humility.[107]

deliberate practice
A demanding, repetitive, and assisted program to improve one's performance.

humility Considering the contributions of others and good fortune when gauging one's success.

There you have it. The closest thing we can give you to a formula for success. Go for it!

Summary of Key Concepts

1. *Define* self-esteem, *and explain how it can be improved with Branden's six pillars of self-esteem.* Self-esteem is how people perceive themselves as physical, social, and spiritual beings. Branden's six pillars of self-esteem are to live consciously, be self-accepting, take personal responsibility, be self-assertive, live purposefully, and have personal integrity.

2. *Define* self-efficacy, *and explain its sources.* Self-efficacy involves one's belief about his or her ability to accomplish specific tasks. Those extremely low in self-efficacy suffer from learned helplessness. Four sources of self-efficacy beliefs are prior experience, behavior models, persuasion from others, and assessment of one's physical and emotional states. High self-efficacy beliefs foster constructive and goal-oriented action, whereas low self-efficacy fosters passive, failure-prone activities and emotions.

3. *Contrast high and low self-monitoring individuals, and discuss the ethical implications of organizational identification.* A high self-monitor strives to make a good public impression by closely monitoring his or her behavior and adapting it to the situation. Very high self-monitoring can create a "chameleon" who is seen as insincere and dishonest. Low self-monitors do the opposite by acting out their momentary feelings, regardless of their surroundings. Very low self-monitoring can lead to a one-way communicator who seems to ignore verbal and nonverbal cues from others. People who supplant their own identity with that of their organization run the risk of blind obedience and groupthink because of a failure to engage in critical thinking and not being objective about what they are asked to do.

4. *Identify and describe the Big Five personality dimensions, and specify which one is correlated most strongly with job performance.* The Big Five personality dimensions are extraversion (social and talkative), agreeableness (trusting and cooperative), conscientiousness (responsible and persistent), emotional stability (relaxed and unworried), and openness to experience (intellectual and curious). Conscientiousness is the best predictor of job performance.

5. *Describe the proactive personality and an internal locus of control.* Someone with a proactive personality shows initiative, takes action, and perseveres to bring about change. People with an internal locus of control, such as entrepreneurs, believe they are masters of their own fate.

6. *Identify at least five of Gardner's eight multiple intelligences.* Harvard's Howard Gardner broadens the traditional cognitive abilities model of intelligence to include social and physical abilities. His eight multiple intelligences include linguistic, logical-mathematical, musical, bodily-kinesthetic, spatial, interpersonal, intrapersonal, and naturalist.

7. *Distinguish between positive and negative emotions, and explain how they can be judged.* Positive emotions—happiness/joy, pride, love/affection, and relief—are personal reactions to circumstances congruent with one's goals. Negative emotions—anger, fright/anxiety, guilt/shame, sadness, envy/jealousy, and disgust—are personal reactions to circumstances incongruent with one's goals. Both types of emotions need to be judged in terms of intensity and the appropriateness of the person's relevant goal.

8. *Identify the four key components of emotional intelligence, and discuss the practical significance of emotional contagion and emotional labor.* Goleman's model says the four components are self-awareness, self-management, social awareness, and relationship management. People can, in fact, catch another person's good or bad moods and expressed emotions, much as they would catch a contagious disease. Managers and others in the workplace need to avoid spreading counterproductive emotions. People in service jobs who are asked to suppress their own negative emotions and display positive emotions, regardless of their true feelings at the time, pay a physical and mental price for their emotional labor. Managers who are not mindful of emotional labor may experience lower productivity, reduced job satisfaction, and possibly aggression and even violence.

9. *Explain how psychological capital, deliberate practice, luck, and humility can pave your road to success.* Psychological capital (PsyCap) can be built through self-efficacy, optimism (positive attributions), hope (goal setting), and resiliency. Deliberate practice involves following the 10,000-hour rule with a demanding, repetitive, and assisted program of improvement. Lucky people stay involved to maximize their chance opportunities, follow their lucky hunches, expect to be lucky no matter the circumstances, and turn bad luck into good fortune. Humble people factor the contributions of others and good fortune into their perceived success.

Key Terms

Self-concept, 123

Cognitions, 123

Self-esteem, 124

Self-efficacy, 125

Self-monitoring, 128

Organizational identification, 129

Personality, 130

Proactive personality, 132

Internal locus of control, 132

External locus of control, 132

Ability, 135

Skill, 135

Intelligence, 136

Emotions, 140

Emotional intelligence, 142

Psychological capital, 144

Resiliency, 145

Deliberate practice, 146

Humility, 146

OB in Action Case Study

The Best Advice I Ever Got

Stephen A. Schwarzman, Chairman and Chief Executive Officer, the Blackstone Group

I grew up in a small town outside Philadelphia and went to the local high school, where I ran track all four years. Our team practiced outdoors, and in the winter, in the bitter cold, the experience was pretty miserable. The school was set on a hill, and as we ran around the parking lot the wind would come whipping around the building and hit us. We had to watch our steps carefully so as not to slip and fall on the ice. While we were doing our laps, the coach—a 50-year-old named Jack Armstrong—would stand against one wall protected from the wind, bundled up in a huge coat and wool hat and gloves, clapping and smiling cheerfully. Every time the pack shuffled past, he'd shout, "Remember—you've got to make your deposits before you can make a withdrawal!"

Now, this was a public school with no special facilities, and the team was made up of average athletes with differing levels of intelligence and motivation. But we never lost one single meet. And because of that success, and maybe because of the way in which the advice itself was delivered—I remember it when people yell at me—Coach Armstrong's words resonated. I've thought of them a million times throughout my career in finance, and they've guided this firm, too.

Coach Armstrong came to mind in one of my first weeks on Wall Street, 35 years ago. I'd stayed up all night building a massive spreadsheet to be ready for a morning meeting. These were the days before Excel, and it was a huge feat for someone as bad at statistical stuff as I was to do this all by hand; I was pretty proud of myself. The partner on the deal, however, took one look at my work, spotted a tiny error, and went ballistic. As I sat there while he yelled at me, I realized I was getting the MBA version of Coach Armstrong's words. Making an effort and meeting the deadline simply weren't enough. To put it in Coach Armstrong's terms, it wasn't sufficient to make some deposits; I had to be certain that the deposits would cover any withdrawal 100% before we made a decision or did a deal. If I hadn't done all the up-front work and made completely

sure that my analysis was correct, I shouldn't have put anything forth. Inaccurate analysis produces faulty insights and bad decisions—which lead to losing a tremendous amount of money.

Today, whenever I'm under pressure to make a decision on a transaction but I don't know what the right one is, I try desperately to postpone it. I'll insist on more information—on doing extra laps around the intellectual parking lot—before committing. . . .

Every year I speak to our new associates and give them this advice, although in my own words. This isn't like school, I tell them, where you want to get your hand in the air and give an answer quickly. The only grade here is 100. Deadlines are important, but at Blackstone you can always get help in meeting them. As a firm, we can always figure out how to do another lap around the parking lot. Because what's true when running track is true when doing deals: The person who's the most ready for game day will be the one who wins.[108]

Questions for Discussion

1. How would you describe Stephen Schwarzman's personality?
2. Relative to the concepts you have just read about, what traits and characteristics would describe the "ideal" Blackstone job candidate? Explain your rationale for selecting each characteristic.
3. Ranked 1 = most important to 8 = least important, which of Gardner's eight multiple intelligences are most critical to being successful at a major investment company like Blackstone? Explain your ranking.
4. Using Table 5–5 as a guide, how important are the various emotional intelligence competencies for making good investment decisions? Explain.
5. Do you have what it takes to work for someone like Stephen Schwarzman? Explain in terms of the concepts in this chapter.

Legal/Ethical Challenge

Should Managers Play the Guilt Card?

[Recent research report out of Stanford] . . . the link between guilt and performance is clearly there. Not only that—in a follow-up study we found that more guilt equaled more commitment. Those who felt guilty worked harder and were more likely to promote the organization to others. . . .

In another study, we had 200 or so MBA students take the TOSCA survey [Test of Self-Conscious Affect that measures guilt-proneness] and had their former co-workers rate them on leadership behaviors, such as the ability to lead teams. The students who were more guilt-prone were considered better leaders. Our take is that guilt activates a keen sense of responsibility for one's actions. What I wonder is, Does guilt make people better leaders but, at the same time, make them averse to taking on leadership positions because they feel that responsibility? We don't know yet. . . .

Inducing guilt can sometimes backfire by eliciting resentment, but it can also be highly effective. If it weren't, then why is my mother so good at it?[109]

Is guilt a legitimate management tool for improving job performance?

1. Yes, guilt is one of many potentially productive characteristics people bring to the job that should be channeled for the good of the organization. What is your ethical justification?
2. A little guilt can be a powerful motivator, so it is okay for managers to selectively use guilt to enhance performance. The trick is to strike a humane balance—not too much, not too little. What is your ethical justification?
3. People generally are neurotic enough without managers throwing another brick on their emotional load. Give your ethical argument.
4. Invent other options. Discuss.

Web Resources

For study material and exercises that apply to this chapter, visit our website at **www.mhhe.com/kreitner10e**

chapter 6

Values, Attitudes, Job Satisfaction, and Counterproductive Work Behaviors

 Learning Objectives

When you finish studying the material in this chapter, you should be able to:

LO.1 Explain Schwartz's value theory, and describe three types of value conflict.

LO.2 Describe the values model of work–family conflict, and specify at least three practical lessons from work–family conflict research.

LO.3 Identify the three components of attitudes and discuss cognitive dissonance.

LO.4 Explain how attitudes affect behavior in terms of Ajzen's theory of planned behavior.

LO.5 Describe the model of organizational commitment.

LO.6 Define the work attitudes of employee engagement and job satisfaction.

LO.7 Identify and briefly describe five alternative causes of job satisfaction.

LO.8 Identify eight important correlates/consequences of job satisfaction, and summarize how each one relates to job satisfaction.

LO.9 Identify the causes of counterproductive work behaviors and the measures used to prevent them.

Why Does Jennifer Simonetti-Bryan Love Her Work?

Jennifer Simonetti-Bryan is 37 and has a hard-driving and achievement-oriented personality. She graduated from the University of Denver in 1995 and accepted a job with Citicorp (now Citigroup) as a management associate. Her work involved "loan syndication and corporate finance." Unfortunately, her love for the job began to wane after a few years. She told an interviewer from *Fortune* that "working nights and weekends, staring at models on a computer screen, she felt bored and unsatisfied. Only 10 more years, a colleague told her, and she'd make managing director."

Jennifer continued to devote herself to her job until a business lunch in the corporate dining room in the company's London office caused her to stop and reflect on the direction of her life. Interestingly, it was the meal itself that led Simonetti-Bryan to pursue a new career. She was "served an herb-crusted salmon paired with a Sancerre, a crisp white wine from France's Loire Valley. The way the acid in the wine cut right through the oil from the fish sparked her curiosity. She began taking classes in wine

appreciation, and in the wake of Citi's merger with Smith Barney in 1998, she took the plunge, abandoning her six-figure salary for a wine shop, then becoming brand manager for Cakebread Cellars and Domaine Carneros while collecting industry certifications."

In 2008 Jennifer became the fourth woman in the United States to obtain the Master of Wine title, which is the wine industry's highest honor. This accomplishment took months of hard work and studying. She ultimately had to pass a four-day exam that entailed identifying 36 different wines. She also had to complete a research project that led to advances within the wine industry. She now runs her own company, JSB Consulting. The company trains and educates people in the wine and spirits industry. She also judges international wine competitions and serves as a spokesperson for the industry.

Is Simonetti-Bryan happy? She said that "if I had all the money in the world . . . I would be doing exactly what I'm doing right now."[1]

The chapter-opening vignette highlights that people get engaged, satisfied, and motivated by their work for different reasons. While we do not want to be wine experts traveling the world teaching people about wine, we love to teach and write about organizational behavior. Why? Because our work is meaningful given our values and attitudes, just as her work is for Jennifer Simonetti-Bryan. The point to remember is that individual differences influence our values, attitudes, job satisfaction, and tendency to exhibit productive or counterproductive behaviors at work.

The overall goal of this chapter is to continue our investigation of individual differences from Chapter 5 so that you can get a better idea of how managers and organizations can use knowledge of individual differences to attract, motivate, and retain quality employees. We explore and discuss the impact of personal values and attitudes on important outcomes such as job satisfaction, performance, turnover, and counterproductive work behaviors.

Personal Values

TO THE POINT

Why is it important for managers to understand an employee's values?

When discussing organizational culture in Chapter 3, we defined *values* as desired ways of behaving or desired end-states. Our focus in Chapter 3 was on collective or shared values; here the focus shifts to *personal* values. Personal values essentially represent the things that have meaning to us in our lives. Values are important to your understanding of organizational behavior because they influence our behavior across different settings.

Shalom Schwartz has developed a comprehensive and well-accepted theory of personal values.[2] Let us learn more about personal values by exploring Schwartz's theory, discussing value conflicts, and examining the timely value-related topic of work versus family life conflicts.

LO.1 Schwartz's Value Theory

 Go to www.mcgrawhillconnect.com for an interactive exercise to test your knowledge of Schwartz's Value Theory.

Schwartz believes that values are motivational in that they "represent broad goals that apply across contexts and time."[3] For example, valuing achievement will likely result in your working hard to earn a promotion at work just as it will drive you to compete against friends in a weekly golf game. Values also are relatively stable and can influence behavior outside of our awareness.

Schwartz proposed that there are 10 broad values that guide behavior. He also identified the motivational mechanisms that underlie each value (see Table 6–1). It is these motivational mechanisms that give values their ability to influence our behavior. For example, Table 6–1 shows that the desire for social power, authority, and wealth drive someone who values power. In contrast, the value of conformity is driven by motives related to politeness, obedience, self-discipline, and honoring one's parents and elders. Not only have these 10 values been found to predict behavior as outlined in the theory, but they also generalize across cultures.[4]

Figure 6–1 shows the proposed relationships among the 10 values. The circular pattern reveals which values are most strongly related and which ones are in conflict. In general, adjacent values like self-direction and universalism are positively related, whereas values that are further apart (e.g., self-direction and power) are less strongly related. Taking this one step further, Schwartz proposes that values that are in opposing directions from the center conflict with each other. Examples are power and universalism or stimulation and conformity/tradition. For instance, the drive to live a stimulating life by engaging in activities like skydiving or mountain climbing would conflict with the desire to live a moderate or traditional life. Research provides partial support for these predictions.[5]

Nelson Mandella is strongly driven by his values. He served as president of South Africa from 1994–1999 and was an active anti-apartheid activist before his presidency. His activist activities resulted in his being imprisoned for 27 years.

table 6–1   Definition of Values and Motives in Schwartz's Theory

VALUE	DEFINITION AND UNDERLYING MOTIVES
Power	Social status and prestige, control or dominance over people and resources (social power, authority, wealth)
Achievement	Personal success through demonstrating competence according to social standards (successful, capable, ambitious, influential)
Hedonism	Pleasure and sensuous gratification for oneself (pleasure, enjoying life)
Stimulation	Excitement, novelty, and challenge in life (daring, a varied life, an exciting life)
Self-direction	Independent thought and action choosing, creating, exploring (creativity, freedom, independent, curious, choosing own goals)
Universalism	Understanding, appreciation, tolerance and protection of the welfare of all people and of nature (broadminded, wisdom, social justice, equality, a world at peace, a world of beauty, unity with nature, protecting the environment)
Benevolence	Preservation and enhancement of the welfare of people with whom one is in frequent personal contact (helpful, honest, forgiving, loyal, responsible)
Tradition	Respect, commitment, and acceptance of the customs and ideas that traditional culture or religion provides the self (humble, accepting my portion in life, devout, respect for tradition, moderate)
Conformity	Restraint of actions, inclinations, and impulses likely to upset or harm others and violate social expectations or norms (politeness, obedient, self-discipline, honoring parents and elders)
Security	Safety, harmony, and stability of society, of relationships, and of self (family security, national security, social order, clean, reciprocation of favors)

SOURCE: From Anat Bardi and Shalom H Schwartz, "Values and Behavior: Strength and Structure of Relations," *Personality & Social Psychology Bulletin*, October 2003, p 1208. Copyright © 2003 by Sage Publications.

figure 6–1   Relationship among Schwartz's Values

SOURCE: Anat Bardi and Shalom H Schwartz, "Values and Behavior: Strength and Structure of Relations," *Personality and Social Psychology Bulletin*, October 2003, p 1208. Copyright © 2003 by Sage Publications.

Go to www.mcgrawhillconnect.com for a video case on the values at Patagonia.

Back to the Chapter-Opening Case

How would you rate Jennifer Simonetti-Bryan in terms of Schwartz's 10 values? Which ones contributed to her decision to change careers?

Value Conflicts

There are three types of value conflict that are related to an individual's attitudes, job satisfaction, turnover, performance, and counterproductive behavior. They are *intra*personal value conflict, *inter*personal value conflict, and individual–organization value conflict. These sources of conflict are, respectively, from inside the person, between people, and between the person and the organization.

Intrapersonal Value Conflict   Our discussion of Schwartz's theory of values revealed that people are likely to experience inner conflict and stress when personal values conflict with each other. For employees who want balance in their lives, a stressful conflict can arise when one values, for example, "achievement" and "tradition." Paul Wenske, a former investigative reporter for the *Kansas City Star,* is experiencing intrapersonal value conflict after being forced to take a buy-out from his employer. He was an award-winning journalist for 30 years who strongly identified with his work role. He told *The Wall Street Journal* that "Suddenly you're not the same person you used to be. You look in the mirror. Who are you?" Therapists suggest that this type of value conflict can be reduced by "taking pride in characteristics that can't be stripped away—virtue, integrity, honesty, generosity. They also recommend investing more time and pride in relationships with family, friends, and community."[6] In general, people are happier and less stressed when their personal values are aligned.

Interpersonal Value Conflict   This type of value conflict often is at the core of personality conflicts, and such conflicts can negatively affect one's career.

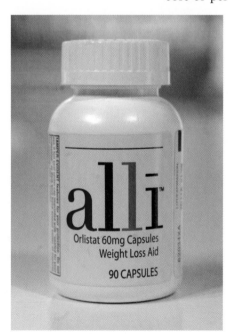

This GlaxoSmith Kline weight loss product has been a big seller since its 2007 launch. Researchers have been examining the possibility that this drug is associated with kidney and liver damage.

Consider the case of Jeffrey Johnson. He was fired by the owner of the *Los Angeles Times*—the Tribune Company—when his values collided with those of senior management. Senior management wanted Johnson to improve the paper's financial results by cutting costs. Johnson then was asked to eliminate employees from the payroll. The conflict for Johnson was that he did not believe that the newspaper's problems would be solved by employee layoffs. He wanted to improve the newspaper's financial status by exploring creative ways to generate revenue as opposed to cutting costs.[7] This example highlights how important it is to carefully evaluate the pros and cons of handling interpersonal value conflicts with our superiors.

Individual–Organization Value Conflict   As we saw in Chapter 3, companies actively seek to embed certain values into their corporate cultures. Conflict can occur when values espoused and enacted by the organization collide with employees' personal values. We defined this type of conflict as PE fit in Chapter 3: PE fit represents the extent to which personal characteristics match those from a work environment.[8] The Real World/Real People on page 155 highlights how a conflict between Cheryl Eckard's personal values and those of GlaxoSmithKline led to a lawsuit that was settled for $750 million. Individual-organizational values conflicts are not only important because they might lead to lawsuits, but this type of conflict is related to positive outcomes such as satisfaction, commitment, performance, career success, reduced stress, and lower turnover intentions.[9] It is important to consider the PE fit of your future job prospects before accepting a job.

real WORLD // real PEOPLE

Whistle-Blower at GlaxoSmithKline Receives $96 Million Payout

Cheryl Eckard, 51 years old, was a global quality assurance manager for GlaxoSmithKline (GSK). She sued the company under the False Claims Act: The Act allows US citizens to sue a company that is committing fraud against the government and to receive proceeds of what is recovered. GSK settled the suit for $750 million, and Eckard was awarded $96 million.

"The case centered on a factory in Cidra, Puerto Rico, where GSK made a range of products including an antibiotic ointment for babies, and drugs to treat nausea, depression and diabetes. In August 2002, Eckard . . . led a team sent to the plant to investigate manufacturing violations that had been identified by the US Federal Drugs Administration (FDA)."

"Ms. Eckard made some strong recommendations to her supervisors: Stop shipping all products from the plant, suspend manufacturing for two weeks to allow time to resolve the problems, and notify the FDA about the product mix-ups." She told her boss that "she would not participate in a cover-up of the quality assurance and compliance problems at Cidra," according to the lawsuit.

Eckard's ex-husband noted that she was a company person and not a malcontent. He indicated that she really cared about her job and worked very hard for the company. Eckard was terminated in 2003 "in what the company called a 'redundancy' related to the merger of Glaxo Wellcome and SmithKline Beecham PLC a couple years before, according to her suit."

"Eckard tried to alert GSK's management to the situation in Cidra even after she left the company. According to the lawsuit . . . Eckard tried to call GSK's chief executive JP Garnier in July 2003, but he declined to speak to her. She took her concerns to the FDA in August 2003 after concluding that GSK's compliance department lacked the authority to address her concerns."

The eight-year case finally ended in 2010 and Eckard concluded that "it's very difficult to survive this financially, emotionally you lose all your friends, because all your friends are people you have at work. . . . You really do have to understand that it's a very difficult process but very well worth it."

What was the source of Cheryl Eckard's value conflict?

SOURCE: Extracted from G Wearden, "GlaxoSmithKline Whistleblower Awarded $96m Payout," *Guardian.co.uk*, October 27, 2010, http://www.guardian.co.uk/business/2010/oct/27/glaxosmithkline-whistleblower-awarded; and P Loftus, "Whistleblower's Long Journey," *The Wall Street Journal*, October 28, 2010, pp B1, B2.

 LO.2 Work versus Family Life Conflict

A complex web of demographic and economic factors makes the balancing act between job and life very challenging for most of us. This is particularly true during a recessionary period of higher unemployment. In this section, we seek to better understand work versus family life conflict by introducing a values-based model and discussing practical research insights.

A Values-Based Model of Work–Family Conflict   Pamela L Perrewé and Wayne A Hochwarter proposed a model of work–family conflict (see Figure 6–2). On the left, we see one's general life values feeding into one's family-related values and work-related values. Family values involve enduring beliefs about the importance of family and who should play key family roles (e.g., child rearing, housekeeping, and income earning). Work values center on the relative importance of work and career goals in one's life. *Value similarity* relates to the degree of consensus among family members about family values. When a housewife launches a business venture despite her husband's desire to be the sole bread winner, lack of family value similarity causes work–family conflict. *Value congruence,* on the other hand, involves the amount of value agreement between employee and employer. If, for example, refusing to go on a business trip to stay home for a child's birthday is viewed as disloyalty to the company, lack of value congruence can trigger work–family conflict.

In turn, "work–family conflict can take two distinct forms: work interference with family and family interference with work."[10] For example, suppose two managers in the same department have daughters playing on the same soccer team.

figure 6–2 A Values Model of Work–Family Conflict

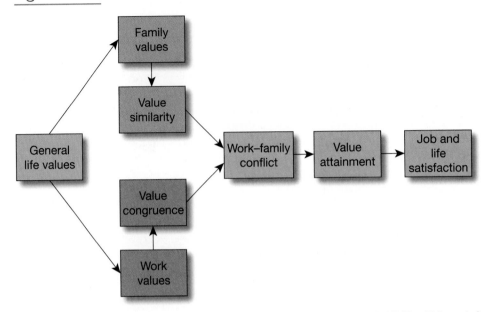

SOURCE: From Pamela L Perrewé and Wayne A Hochwarter, "Can We Really Have It All? The Attainment of Work and Family Values," *Current Directions in Psychological Science*, February 2001, p 30. Reprinted with permission of Wiley-Blackwell.

One manager misses the big soccer game to attend a last-minute department meeting; the other manager skips the meeting to attend the game. Both may experience work–family conflict, but for different reasons.[11]

The last two boxes in the model—value attainment and job and life satisfaction—are a package deal. Satisfaction tends to be higher for those who live according to their values and lower for those who do not. Overall, this model reflects much common sense. How does *your* life track through the model? Sadly, it is a painful trip for many these days.

Practical Research Insights about Work–Family Conflict This is a new but very active area of OB research. Let us consider six practical conclusions derived from this research.

- *Work–family balance begins at home.* Case studies of successful executives reveal that family and spousal support is critical for reaching senior level positions.[12] This in turn suggests that both men and women need help with domestic responsibilities if there is any chance of achieving work–family balance. You are encouraged to hire domestic help if you need and can afford it.

- *An employer's family-supportive philosophy is more important than specific programs.* Many employers offer family-friendly programs today, including child and elder day care assistance, parental leave, telecommuting, and flexible work schedules. However, if employees are afraid or reluctant to take advantage of those programs because the organization's culture values hard work and long hours above all else, families will inevitably suffer. To be truly family-friendly, the organization needs to provide programs and back them up with a family-supportive philosophy, culture, and resources. For example, Baptist Health South Florida invested more than $2 million in new benefits targeted toward helping employees with work–family balance issues.[13]

- *Informal flexibility in work hours and in allowing people to work at home is essential to promoting work–family balance.* Quite simply, flexibility allows people to cope more effectively with competing demands across their personal and work lives. This conclusion was supported by a recent study of 511 HR professionals. Ninety-one percent of respondents indicated that flexible work arrangements positively influenced morale, and 58 percent said that work–family balance "is the most effective tactic for attracting, rewarding and retaining top employees."[14]

- *Supportive bosses and colleagues can help.* Research demonstrated that work–family conflict was lower when employees had good relationships with their direct supervisor and work colleagues.[15] It is important that you proactively discuss potential work–family conflicts with your boss and colleagues prior to their occurrence as opposed to after the fact.

Great companies recognize that the ability to take care of family concerns is an important part of an employee's job satisfaction. How can a company's policies reflect a family-supportive philosophy?

- *The importance of work–family balance varies across generations.* A recent longitudinal study of work values across 16,000 people from different generational groups demonstrated that (1) Gen Ys and Gen Xs preferred more leisure time and had higher extrinsic values (e.g., desire for salary) than Baby Boomers, and (2) Gen Ys had lower altruistic values (e.g., desire to help others) and intrinsic values (e.g., desire to have an interesting job) than Boomers.[16] These results suggest that organizations should consider implementing work policies that are targeted toward different generational groups. For example, flextime and compressed work programs may be used to attract and retain both Gen Ys and Gen Xers while job enrichment, which is discussed in Chapter 8, may be used to motivate Baby Boomers.

- *Take a proactive approach to managing work–family conflict.* A recent meta-analysis of research involving more than 32,000 people demonstrated that an individual's personal life spills over to his or her work life and vice versa. This means that employees' job satisfaction, organizational commitment, and intentions to quit are significantly related to the amount of work–family conflict that exists in their lives.[17] Organizations thus are encouraged to train managers to use family-supportive supervisory behaviors because research shows that managers can be taught to help employees reduce their levels of work–family conflict.[18]

Organizational Response to Work–Family Issues   Organizations have implemented a variety of family-friendly programs and services aimed at helping employees to balance the interplay between their work and personal lives. For example, General Mills increased the size of its infant-care center at corporate headquarters by 43%, and it subsidized 25% of the cost. Intuit provided a $650 match of funds for dependent care accounts and made a $65 contribution for in-home care when a child is sick.[19] Although these programs are positively received by employees, experts now believe that such efforts are partially misguided because they focus on balancing work–family issues rather than integrating them. Balance is needed for opposites, and work and family are not opposites. Rather, our work and personal lives should be a well-integrated whole.

LO.3 Attitudes

Hardly a day goes by without the popular media reporting the results of another attitude survey. The idea is to take the pulse of public opinion. What do we think about President Obama, terrorism, the war on drugs, gun control, or taxes? In the workplace, meanwhile, managers conduct attitude surveys to monitor such things as job satisfaction and employee engagement. All this attention to attitudes is based on the realization that our attitudes influence our behavior. For example, research demonstrated that seniors with a positive attitude about aging had better memory, had better hearing, and lived longer than those with negative attitudes.[20]

TO THE POINT

Why is it important for managers to understand an employee's attitudes, and how do attitudes influence employee behavior?

In a work setting, meta-analytic studies revealed that job attitudes were positively related to performance and negatively associated with indicators of withdrawal—lateness, absenteeism, and turnover.[21] In this section, we discuss the components of attitudes and examine the connection between attitudes and behavior.

The Nature of Attitudes

An **attitude** is defined as "a learned predisposition to respond in a consistently favorable or unfavorable manner with respect to a given object."[22] Consider your attitude toward chocolate ice cream. You are more likely to purchase a chocolate ice cream cone if you have a positive attitude toward chocolate ice cream. In contrast, you are more likely to purchase some other flavor, say vanilla caramel swirl, if you have a positive attitude toward vanilla and a neutral or negative attitude toward chocolate ice cream. Let us consider a work example. If you have a positive attitude about your job (i.e., you like what you are doing), you would be more willing to extend yourself at work by working longer and harder. These examples illustrate that attitudes propel us to act in a specific way in a specific context. That is, attitudes affect behavior at a different level than do values. While values represent global beliefs that influence behavior across *all* situations, attitudes relate only to behavior directed toward *specific* objects, persons, or situations. Values and attitudes generally, but not always, are in harmony. A manager who strongly values helpful behavior may have a negative attitude toward helping an unethical co-worker. The difference between attitudes and values is clarified by considering the three components of attitudes: affective, cognitive, and behavioral. It is important to note that your overall attitude toward someone or something is a function of the combined influence of all three components.

Affective Component   The **affective component** of an attitude contains the feelings or emotions one has about a given object or situation. For example, how do you *feel* about people who talk on cell phones in restaurants? If you feel annoyed or angry with such people, you are expressing negative affect or feelings toward people who talk on cell phones in restaurants. In contrast, the affective component of your attitude is neutral if you are indifferent about people talking on cell phones in restaurants.

Cognitive Component   What do you *think* about people who talk on cell phones in restaurants? Do you believe this behavior is inconsiderate, productive, completely acceptable, or rude? Your answer represents the cognitive component of your attitude toward people talking on cell phones in restaurants. The **cognitive component** of an attitude reflects the beliefs or ideas one has about an object or situation.

Behavioral Component   The **behavioral component** refers to how one intends or expects to act toward someone or something. For example, how would you intend to respond to someone talking on a cell phone during dinner at a restaurant if this individual were sitting in close proximity to you and your guest? Attitude theory suggests that your ultimate behavior in this situation is a function of all three attitudinal components. You are unlikely to say anything to someone using a cell phone in a restaurant if you are not irritated by this behavior (affective), if you believe cell phone use helps people to manage their lives (cognitive), and you have no intention of confronting this individual (behavioral). [23]

What Happens When Attitudes and Reality Collide? Cognitive Dissonance

What happens when a strongly held attitude is contradicted by reality? Suppose you are extremely concerned about getting AIDS, which you believe is transferred from contact with body fluids, including blood. Then you find yourself in a life-threatening accident in a foreign country and need surgery and blood transfusions—including transfusions of blood (possibly AIDS-infected) from a blood bank with unknown quality control. Would you reject the blood to remain consistent with your beliefs about getting AIDS? According to social psychologist Leon Festinger, this situation would create cognitive dissonance.

Cognitive dissonance represents the psychological discomfort a person experiences when his or her attitudes or beliefs are incompatible with his or her behavior.[24] Festinger proposed that people are motivated to maintain consistency between their attitudes and beliefs and their behavior. He therefore theorized that people will seek to reduce the "dissonance," or psychological tension, through one of three main methods:

1. *Change your attitude or behavior, or both.* This is the simplest solution when confronted with cognitive dissonance. Returning to our example about needing a blood transfusion, this would amount to either (a) telling yourself that you can't get AIDS through blood and take the transfusion or (b) simply refusing to take the transfusion.
2. *Belittle the importance of the inconsistent behavior.* This happens all the time. In our example, you could belittle the belief that you can get AIDS from the foreign blood bank. (The doctor said she regularly uses blood from that blood bank.)
3. *Find consonant elements that outweigh dissonant ones.* This approach entails rationalizing away the dissonance. You can tell yourself that you are taking the transfusion because you have no other options. After all, you could die if you don't get the required surgery.

Back to the Chapter-Opening Case

Why was Jennifer Simonetti-Bryan experiencing cognitive dissonance, and how did she resolve it?

How Stable Are Attitudes?

In one landmark study, researchers found the *job* attitudes of 5,000 middle-aged male employees to be very stable over a five-year period. Positive job attitudes remained positive; negative ones remained negative. Even those who changed jobs or occupations tended to maintain their prior job attitudes.[25]

More recent research suggests the foregoing study may have overstated the stability of attitudes because it was restricted to a middle-aged sample. This time, researchers asked, What happens to attitudes over the entire span of adulthood? *General* attitudes were found to be more susceptible to change during early and late adulthood than during middle adulthood. Three factors accounted for middle-age attitude stability: (1) greater personal certainty, (2) perceived abundance of knowledge, and (3) a need for strong attitudes. Thus, the conventional notion that general attitudes become less likely to change as the person ages was rejected.

---

attitude Learned predisposition toward a given object.

affective component The feelings or emotions one has about an object or situation.

cognitive component The beliefs or ideas one has about an object or situation.

behavioral component How one intends to act or behave toward someone or something.

cognitive dissonance Psychological discomfort experienced when attitudes and behavior are inconsistent.

Elderly people, along with young adults, can and do change their general attitudes because they are more open and less self-assured.[26]

Because our cultural backgrounds and experiences vary, our attitudes and behavior vary. Attitudes are translated into behavior via behavioral intentions. Let us examine an established model of this important process.

 LO.4 Attitudes Affect Behavior via Intentions

Building on Leon Festinger's work on cognitive dissonance, Icek Ajzen and Martin Fishbein further delved into understanding the reason for discrepancies between individuals' attitudes and behavior. Ajzen ultimately developed and refined a model focusing on intentions as the key link between attitudes and planned behavior. His theory of planned behavior in Figure 6–3 shows three separate but interacting determinants of one's intention (a person's readiness to perform a given behavior) to exhibit a specific behavior.

Importantly, this model only predicts behavior under an individual's control, not behavior due to circumstances beyond one's control. For example, this model can predict the likelihood that Egyptian citizens would protest against President Hosni Mubarak in 2011. But it would be a poor model for predicting whether or not a specific individual would arrive at a specific protesting site at a designated time and date because of uncontrolled circumstances such as traffic delays or the amount of military blocking the route to the site.[27]

Determinants of Intention   Ajzen has explained the nature and roles of the three determinants of intention as follows:

The first is the *attitude toward the behavior* and refers to the degree to which a person has a favorable or unfavorable evaluation or appraisal of the behavior in question. The second predictor is a social factor termed *subjective norm;* it refers to the perceived social pressure to perform or not to perform the behavior. The third antecedent of intention is the degree of *perceived behavior control,* which . . . refers to the perceived ease or difficulty of performing the behavior and it is assumed to reflect past experience as well as anticipated impediments and obstacles.[28]

figure 6–3 Ajzen's Theory of Planned Behavior

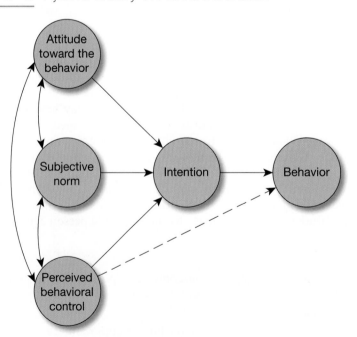

SOURCE: From I Ajzen, "The Theory of Planned Behavior," *Organizational Behavior and Human Decision Processes,* Figure 1, p 182. Copyright © 1991, with permission from Elsevier Science.

real WORLD // real PEOPLE

The Physicians Committee for Responsible Medicine Creates an Ad to Change People's Attitudes about Eating at McDonald's

Attitudes among members of the Physicians Committee for Responsible Medicine (PCRM) prompt the organization to make negative ads about McDonald's. The PCRM released a television commercial that "blames the burger giant for heart disease." The commercial features a woman crying "over a dead man lying in a morgue. In his hand is a hamburger. At the end, the golden arches appear over his feet, followed by the words, 'I was lovin' it,' a play on McDonald's long-time ad slogan, 'I'm lovin' it.' A voiceover says, 'High cholesterol, high blood pressure, heart attacks. Tonight, make it vegetarian.'"

"PCRM is airing the commercial to draw attention to heart-disease-related deaths in Washington. It says that the city has the second-highest rate of such deaths in the country . . . and that heart disease kills more than 1,500 Washingtonians each year. It also says the district has more McDonald's, Burger King and KFC restaurants per square mile than eight other similar-sized cities."

The PCRM is considering running the ad in other cities such as Los Angeles and Chicago and is planning to write Washington's Mayor Adrian Fenty about creating a moratorium on building any more fast-food restaurants in the city. A member of the city council is taking the charge one step further by proposing an ordinance that limits fast-food restaurants from being within a quarter mile of another restaurant.

A McDonald's spokesperson responded by saying that McDonald's "is committed to providing balanced menu choices and a variety of options to meet our customers' needs and preferences." Scott DeFife, an executive at the National Restaurant Association, stated that the ad was " 'irresponsible' and that it focused on scaring consumers into making bad choices based on "a limited view of good nutrition."

What beliefs are driving the PCRM's actions?

SOURCE: Excerpted from J Jargon, "New Ad Targets McDonald's," *The Wall Street Journal,* September 14, 2010, p B8.

To bring these three determinants of intention to life, let us consider the example of an advertisement made by the nonprofit Physicians Committee for Responsible Medicine (PCRM). The ad targeted McDonald's as a bad place to eat (see Real World/Real People above). PCRM members have a positive attitude about making and showing the ad because they believe McDonald's food contributes to heart disease. There also appears to be a strong subjective norm within the PCRM to promote healthy eating and to discourage people from eating at fast-food restaurants. Regarding perceived behavior control, the PCRM has control of how it spends its money.

Intentions and Behavior Research Lessons and Implications   According to the model of planned behavior, someone's intention to engage in a given behavior is a strong predictor of that behavior. For example, the quickest and possibly most accurate way of determining whether an individual will quit his or her job is to have an objective third party ask if he or she intends to quit. A meta-analysis of 34 studies of employee turnover involving more than 83,000 employees validated this direct approach. The researchers found stated behavioral intentions to be a better predictor of employee turnover than job satisfaction, satisfaction with the work itself, or organizational commitment.[29] Another study took these findings one step further by considering whether or not job applicants' intention to quit a job before they were hired would predict voluntary turnover six months after being hired. Results demonstrated that intentions to quit significantly predicted turnover.[30]

Volunteer Duane Dixon, on the left, cuts through a stud while other volunteers look on. These individuals volunteered to help build and furnish a home in five days for a wheelchair-bound woman in Alabama.

Research has demonstrated that Ajzen's model accurately predicted intentions to buy consumer products, to search for a new job, to have children, to vote for specific political candidates, to recycle, and engage in volunteer activities. Attitudes and behaviors regarding affirmative action programs, weight-loss intentions, and behavior, using Internet services to facilitate the shipping of products, nurses' willingness to work with older patients, and reenlisting in the National Guard also have been predicted successfully by the model.[31] From a practical standpoint, the theory of planned behavior has important managerial implications. Managers are encouraged to use prescriptions derived from the model to implement interventions aimed at changing employees' behavior.

According to this model, changing behavior starts with the recognition that behavior is modified through intentions, which in turn are influenced by three different determinants (see Figure 6–3). Managers can thus influence behavioral change by doing or saying things that affect the three determinants of employees' intentions to exhibit a specific behavior: attitude toward the behavior, subjective norms, and perceived behavioral control.[32]

It is important to remember that employee beliefs can be influenced through the information management provides on a day-by-day basis, the organization's culture, the content of training programs, the behavior of key employees, and the rewards that are targeted to reinforce certain beliefs. Consider how H C Jackson, founder of Jackson's Hardware in San Rafael, California, used these ideas to change employees' beliefs about taking over ownership of the company.

Example. As part of creating an ownership culture, Jackson's spends ample time teaching employees about the benefits of ownership. . . . The company has a committee whose role is to educate employees about stock ownership and how their work is directly related to the success of the business—and thus their own financial well-being. Jackson's also puts out an annual ownership plan newsletter and selects an "Employee Owner for the Month" who receives a gas card and $600 toward a weekend getaway and dinner or store purchase.[33]

On a personal level, you also can use this model to influence your own behavior.

If you want to increase the amount of time you spend studying, for example, you might begin by trying to influence your attitude toward studying. You could tell yourself that more studying leads to better grades, which in turn can help you find a rewarding job after graduation. You also can reward yourself for reaching a target score on the next exam. Subjective norms to study can be influenced by arranging to study with other students who are doing well in the class or by talking with your parents about what is going on in the class. Finally, it is important to remember that the amount of time you have for studying might be somewhat outside of your control. Our advice: control what you can and plan for contingencies.

TO THE POINT

What is the meaning of organizational commitment, job involvement, and employee engagement?

Key Work Attitudes

Work attitudes such as organizational commitment, employee engagement, and job satisfaction have a dual interest to managers. On the one hand, they represent important outcomes that managers may want to enhance. On the other hand, they are symptomatic of other potential problems. For example, low employee engagement or job satisfaction may be a symptom of an employee's intention to quit. It thus is important for managers to understand the causes and consequences of key work attitudes.

What is your attitude toward work? Is work something meaningful that defines and fulfills you, or is it just a way to pay the bills? Interestingly, attitudes toward work have changed significantly throughout recorded history. For the early Greeks, for instance, work was something done by enslaved people. Today, in contrast, work is viewed by many as a source of satisfaction and enjoyment, and there is growing sentiment that work should be fun. While everyone does not agree about having fun at work, organizations such as Southwest Airlines have turned it into a strategic competitive advantage. Key employee selection factors at Southwest Airlines are a keen sense of humor and a general positive attitude. Consider how CEO Bob Pike's positive attitude toward work would set the tone for his employees at Creative Training Techniques International:

Example. It is not a choice between fun and work, it is a choice for fun and work. I find it depressing that so many people spend 8 hours a day at work and 16 hours trying to forget that they did! It's time for us to replace the common definition of work: if it is not dull and boring then it can't be work! Work should be about passion, it should have a sense of purpose, it should be about involvement and participation. High-performing teams who do challenging work also know how to have fun. They have an attitude that says they enjoy what they do and that they belong to a diverse group of committed individuals who know the mission, values, and vision of the team. And they look forward to making a contribution.

Understand that there will always be both fun-loving and fun-killing people. Fun-killers don't actually object to the fun; they feel that the fun isn't relevant to the work and therefore not important.[34]

How would you like to work for Bob Pike?

People have a multitude of attitudes about things that happen to them at work, but OB researchers have focused on a limited number of them. This section specifically examines two work attitudes—organizational commitment and employee engagement—that have important practical implications. Job satisfaction, the most frequently studied work attitude, is thoroughly discussed in the next section of this chapter.

LO.5 Organizational Commitment

Before discussing a model of organizational commitment, it is important to consider the meaning of the term *commitment*. What does it mean to commit? Common sense suggests that commitment is an agreement to do something for yourself, another individual, group, or organization. Formally, OB researchers define commitment as "a force that binds an individual to a course of action of relevance to one or more targets."[35] This definition highlights that commitment is associated with behavior and that commitment can be aimed at multiple targets or entities. For example, an individual can be committed to his or her job, family, girl- or boyfriend, faith, friends, career, organization, or a variety of professional associations. Let us now consider the application of commitment to a work organization.

Organizational commitment reflects the extent to which an individual identifies with an organization and is committed to its goals. It is an important work attitude because committed individuals are expected to display a willingness to work harder to achieve organizational goals and a greater desire to stay employed at an organization. Figure 6–4 presents a model of organizational commitment that identifies its causes and consequences.

A Model of Organizational Commitment   Figure 6–4 shows that organizational commitment is composed of three separate but related components: affective commitment, normative commitment, and continuance commitment. John

---

organizational commitment
Extent to which an individual identifies with an organization and its goals.

figure 6–4 A Model of Organizational Commitment

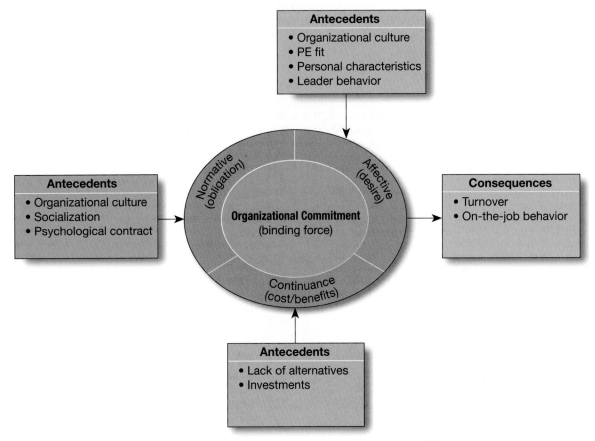

SOURCE: Adapted from J P Meyer and L Herscovitch, "Commitment in the Workplace: Toward a General Model," *Human Resource Management Review,* Autumn 2001, p 317.

Meyer and Natalie Allen, a pair of commitment experts, define these components as follows:

Example. *Affective commitment* refers to the employee's emotional attachment to, identification with, and involvement in the organization. Employees with a strong affective commitment continue employment with an organization because they *want* to do so. *Continuance commitment* refers to an awareness of the costs associated with leaving the organization. Employees whose primary link to the organization is based on continuance commitment remain because they *need* to do so. Finally, *normative commitment* reflects a feeling of obligation to continue employment. Employees with a high level of normative commitment feel that they *ought* to remain with the organization.[36]

Figure 6–4 also reveals that these three components combine to produce a binding force that influences the consequences of employee turnover and on-the-job behavior such as performance, absenteeism, and organizational citizenship, which is discussed later in this chapter.

Each component of commitment is influenced by a separate set of antecedents (see Figure 6–4). In the current context, an antecedent is something that causes the component of commitment to occur. For example, affective commitment is related to organizational culture and PE fit, which were discussed in Chapter 3, a variety of personal characteristics such as personality (recall our discussion in

Chapter 5), and leader behavior, which is reviewed in Chapter 16.[37] Because continuance commitment reflects a ratio of the costs and benefits associated with leaving an organization, antecedents are anything that affects the costs and benefits of leaving. Examples are a lack of job/career alternatives and the amount of real and psychological investments a person has in a particular organization or community. Continuance commitment would be high if an individual has no job alternatives, is actively involved in his or her church, has many friends in the community, owns shares of the company stock, and needs medical benefits for a family of five. Nancy Kramer, CEO of Resource Interactive, implemented a creative approach toward enhancing employees' continuance commitment.

Example. She launched the Resource Employee Equity Fund, or Reef. Here's how it works: The company buys stock in each of its 20 or so publicly held company clients. On employees' first anniversary, they each get one share of the Reef, which includes one share of each client's stock and 1/100th of a share of Warren Buffett's Berkshire Hathaway Inc. Class A shares. Each Reef share is worth about $1,900 right now, she says.[38]

Finally, normative commitment is influenced by organizational culture and the socialization process discussed in Chapter 3, as well as what is termed a psychological contracts. **Psychological contracts** represent an individual's perception about the terms and conditions of a reciprocal exchange between him- or herself and another party.[39] In a work environment, the psychological contract represents an employee's beliefs about what he or she is entitled to receive in return for what he or she provides to the organization. Research shows that an employer breach of the psychological contract is associated with lower organizational commitment, job satisfaction, and performance, and greater intentions to quit.[40]

Back to the Chapter-Opening Case

How would you evaluate Jennifer Simonetti-Bryan's commitment to Citicorp based on Figure 6–4?

Research and Practical Applications   Organizational commitment matters. A meta-analysis of 183 studies uncovered a significant and strong positive relationship between organizational commitment and job satisfaction.[41] This finding encourages managers to increase job satisfaction in order to elicit higher levels of commitment. In turn, another meta-analysis involving 26,344 individuals revealed organizational commitment was significantly correlated with job performance.[42] This is an important finding because it implies managers can increase productivity by enhancing employees' organizational commitment.

Finally, a third meta-analysis summarizing results across 27,500 people uncovered a significant, negative relationship between organizational commitment and turnover.[43] This finding underscores the importance of paying attention to employees' organizational commitment because high commitment helps reduce the costs of employee turnover. In summary, managers are encouraged to focus on improving employees' organizational commitment.

psychological contract An individual's perception about the terms and conditions of a reciprocal exchange with another party.

Interestingly, companies use a variety of methods to increase employees' organizational commitment. KPMG offers employees a sabbatical that allows them to take a leave of absence of 4 to 12 weeks at 20% of their pay. Google encourages engineers to spend 20% of their time on projects of their choosing.[44] All told, people are more likely to be committed to their organizations when they believe that the organization truly cares about their welfare and well-being. Managers also can increase the components of employee commitment through the following activities:

- Affective commitment is enhanced by hiring people whose personal values are consistent with the organization's values. A positive, satisfying work environment also should increase employees' desire to stay. Harley-Davidson is following this advice. "Employee surveys show 90% strongly identify with the company's riding culture. Some employees get to work at biker rallies at Harley's expense."[45]

- Continuance commitment is enhanced by offering employees a variety of progressive benefits and human resource programs. At Mattel, for instance, perks include "13 paid holidays, two paid days to volunteer in schools, two onsite child-care centers, five paid days of parental leave . . . half-days on Fridays all year long, and onsite toy stores that offer discounts."[46]

- Normative commitment can be increased by making sure that management does not breach its psychological contracts and by trying to enhance the level of trust throughout the organization. We provide specific recommendation for building and maintaining trust in Chapter 11.

LO.6 Employee Engagement

Bill Gates, chairman of Microsoft, is a good example of someone engaged with his work. His engagement has also spilled over into his personal life as he now focuses much time and effort into philanthropic activities. He is co-chair of the Bill & Melinda Gates Foundation.

Employee engagement is a relatively new concept to the field of organizational behavior. It was defined in 1990 by William Kahn on the basis of two qualitative studies of people at work. Based on his observations of workers at a summer camp and architecture firm, Kahn defined **employee engagement** as "the harnessing of organization members' selves to their work roles; in engagement, people employ and express themselves physically, cognitively, and emotionally during role performance."[47] The essence of this definition is the idea that engaged employees "give it their all" at work. Further study of this attitudinal variable reveals that it contains four components: (1) feelings of urgency, (2) feelings of being focused, (3) feelings of intensity, and (4) feelings of enthusiasm.[48] Have you ever felt like this at work or school? If yes, then you understand why academics, consultants, and managers want to understand how they can harness the power of employee engagement. We now unravel the performance-enhancing potential of employee engagement by considering its causes and consequences.

What Contributes to Employee Engagement? Employee engagement is caused by a host of variables that can be separated into two categories: personal factors and contextual or work-environment factors. Personal characteristics found or thought to influence employee engagement include positive or optimistic personalities, proactive personality, conscientiousness, PE fit, and being present or mindful.[49] Mindfulness represents the extent to which someone is focused on a moment in time and what is happening rather than daydreaming about something or somewhere else.

There are a broad set of contextual factors that potentially impact employee engagement. One clearly involves organizational culture. For example, employees are more likely to be engaged when an organization has a clan culture (see Chapter 3) that promotes employee development, recognition, and trust between management and employees.[50] For example, Scripps Health, ranked by *Fortune* as the 37th best place to work in the United States in 2011, provides all employees with

real WORLD // real PEOPLE

UnitedHealth Group Focuses on Improving Employee Engagement

Lori Sweere, executive vice president of human capital at the Minneapolis-based headquarters, was given the charge of developing a strategy to boost employee engagement. She began the effort by studying results from an employee engagement survey and conducting focus groups with managers and employees. She decided to implement the following initiatives based on this input.

"Manager's performance, communication and understanding of how each employee's job contributes to the business strategy were identified as areas for improvement that could enhance employee engagement. Now, 'I have personal and monthly communications with our 6,000 managers about how to engage employees, such as how to talk to employees about personal and business challenges in the economic downturn,'" according to Sweere.

"Another way United Health Group drives engagement is by using a Facebook-style tool called U-Link to help people connect. Employees form groups, and Sweere writes a blog and answers questions. 'People become engaged by promoting their brands and having access to people they never had access to before,' Sweere says. 'We have 15,000 telecommuters who need this technology to connect with others. We list name, title, where they work. People can volunteer to add more to their profiles. And people can search for expertise.'"

The above initiates were successful. Employee engagement scores from the survey increased over time, employee turnover decreased, customer satisfaction increased, and revenues were higher.

What contextual factors contributed to employee engagement?

SOURCE: Excerpted from A. Fox, "Raising Engagement," *HR Magazine,* May 2010, p 38.

---

at least one training class per year. The company spent $30 million in training and development programs in 2010.[51]

Job security and feelings of psychological safety also propel employee engagement. Psychological safety occurs when people feel safe to display engagement. In other words, employees must be free of any fears associated with trying new, innovative ideas or behaviors at work.[52] Leader behavior is another key contextual variable, particularly transformational leadership.[53] Transformational leadership is discussed in Chapter 16. Finally, employee engagement is higher when people feel that they are being supported by both their direct supervisor and the company as a whole and when they have a line of sight with the organization's vision, strategies, and goals: Line of sight represents the extent to which employees understand how their jobs influence the achievement of broader strategic goals.[54] Consider how AtlantiCare creates line of sight.

Mc Graw Hill **connect**™ Go to www.mcgrawhillconnect.com for an interactive exercise to test your knowledge of employee engagement.

Example. New hires at AtlantiCare receive a strategy map showing how specific corporate goals such as building customer loyalty, increasing patient volume and maintaining a favorable bond rating related to corporate values that include safety, team spirit and treating others with respect. All employees are urged to review the map frequently and to jot down ways they can personally contribute to performance excellence."[55]

UnitedHealth Group is a good example of a company that is using several contextual factors to increase employee engagement (see Real World/Real People above).

employee engagement Extent to which employees give it their all at work.

What Are the Consequences of Employee Engagement?   Consulting firms such as Gallup, Hewitt Associates, and Watson Wyatt have been in the forefront of collecting proprietary data supporting the practical value of employee engagement. For example, Gallup researchers conducted a meta-analysis involving 198,514 individuals from 7,930 business units and found that employee engagement was significantly associated with organizational-level customer satisfaction/loyalty, profitability, productivity, turnover, and safety outcomes.[56] Gallup estimates that organizations can achieve 12% higher customer satisfaction/loyalty, 18% more productivity, and 12% greater profitability when their employees are highly engaged.[57] Other recent studies similarly showed a positive relationship between employee engagement and employees' performance and physical and psychological well-being, and corporate-level financial performance and customer satisfaction.[58]

Practical Takeaways   While academic research still is needed to validate measures of employee engagement, we believe that organizations can find value in measuring, tracking, and responding to surveys of employee engagement. The Ritz-Carlton, for instance, was able to significantly lower employee turnover (18% versus an industry average of 158%) and increase both customer satisfaction and customer spending by following this recommendation.[59]

· · · · · · · · · · · · · · · · · · · ▶

TO THE POINT

What are the causes, correlates, and consequences of job satisfaction?

· · · · · · · · · · · · · · · · · · · ·

Job Satisfaction

Job satisfaction essentially reflects the extent to which an individual likes his or her job. Formally defined, **job satisfaction** is an affective or emotional response toward various facets of one's job. This definition implies job satisfaction is not a unitary concept. Rather, a person can be relatively satisfied with one aspect of his or her job and dissatisfied with one or more other aspects. For example, a recent survey of 11,000 people indicated that Gen Ys were more satisfied with their managers than Gen Xers or Boomers. In contrast, overall job satisfaction was higher for Boomers than it was for Gen Ys and Gen Xers.[60]

Researchers at Cornell University developed the Job Descriptive Index (JDI) to assess one's satisfaction with the following job dimensions: work, pay, promotions, co-workers, and supervision.[61] Researchers at the University of Minnesota concluded there are 20 different dimensions underlying job satisfaction. Although researchers do not have consensus about the exact number of dimensions that constitute job satisfaction, they do agree that it has five predominant causes. We believe that knowledge about the causes of job satisfaction can assist managers in trying to increase this key work attitude. Let us now examine the causes of job satisfaction.

 LO.7 The Causes of Job Satisfaction

Five predominant models of job satisfaction focus on different causes. They are need fulfillment, discrepancy, value attainment, equity, and dispositional/genetic components. A brief review of these models provides insight into the variety of methods that can be used to increase employees' job satisfaction.

Need Fulfillment   These models propose that satisfaction is determined by the extent to which the characteristics of a job allow an individual to fulfill his or her needs. For example, a survey by the Society for Human Resource Management asked employees to choose the aspects of their job that were very important to their job satisfaction. Their top four choices were compensation, benefits, job security, and work–life balance—all directly related to employees' ability to meet a variety of basic needs.[62] We suspect that the need for job security will become more important for employees during our current recession. Although need fulfillment models generated a great degree of controversy, it is generally accepted that need fulfillment is correlated with job satisfaction.[63]

Discrepancies   These models propose that satisfaction is a result of met expectations. **Met expectations** represent the difference between what an individual expects to receive from a job, such as good pay and promotional opportunities, and what he or she actually receives. When expectations are greater than what is received, a person will be dissatisfied. In contrast, this model predicts that an individual will be satisfied when he or she attains outcomes above and beyond expectations. A meta-analysis that included 17,241 people demonstrated that met expectations were significantly related to job satisfaction.[64] Many companies use employee attitude or opinion surveys to assess employees' expectations and concerns, even during bad economic conditions.

Value Attainment   The idea underlying **value attainment** is that satisfaction results from the perception that a job allows for fulfillment of an individual's important work values. For example, New Belgium Brewing Company, brewers of Fat Tire, attracts employees who value bicycling and environmental sustainability. The company gives each employee a cruiser bike after working for the company for one year and it established on-site recycling centers. Almost 50% of employees working at the corporate headquarters in Fort Collins, Colorado, commute by bike during the summer.[65] In general, research consistently supports the prediction that value fulfillment is positively related to job satisfaction. Managers can thus enhance employee satisfaction by structuring the work environment and its associated rewards and recognition to reinforce employees' values.

connect™ Go to www.mcgrawhillconnect.com for an interactive exercise to test your knowledge of the causes of job satisfaction.

Equity   In this model, satisfaction is a function of how "fairly" an individual is treated at work. Satisfaction results from one's perception that work outcomes, relative to inputs, compare favorably with a significant other's outcomes/inputs. A meta-analysis involving 64,757 people supported this model. Employees' perceptions of being treated fairly at work were highly related to overall job satisfaction.[66] Managers thus are encouraged to monitor employees' fairness perceptions and to interact with employees in such a way that they feel equitably treated. Chapter 8 explores how this can be accomplished.

Dispositional/Genetic Components   Have you ever noticed that some of your co-workers or friends appear to be satisfied across a variety of job circumstances, whereas others always seem dissatisfied? This model of satisfaction attempts to explain this pattern. Specifically, the dispositional/genetic model is based on the belief that job satisfaction is partly a function of both personal traits and genetic factors. As such, this model implies that stable individual differences are just as important in explaining job satisfaction as are characteristics of the work environment. Although there are a limited number of studies that tested these propositions, a recent meta-analysis revealed that dispositional factors were not significantly associated with all aspects of job satisfaction. Dispositions had stronger relationships with intrinsic aspects of a job (e.g., having autonomy) than with extrinsic aspects of work (e.g., receipt of rewards).[67] Genetic factors also were found to significantly predict life satisfaction, well-being, and general job satisfaction.[68] Overall, researchers estimate that 30% of an individual's job satisfaction is associated with dispositional and genetic components.[69] Pete and Laura Wakeman, founders of Great Harvest Bread Company, have used this model of job satisfaction while running their company for more than 25 years.

---

job satisfaction An affective or emotional response to one's job.

met expectations The extent to which one receives what he or she expects from a job.

value attainment The extent to which a job allows fulfillment of one's work values.

Example. Our hiring ads say clearly that we need people with "strong personal loves as important as their work." This is not a little thing. You can't have a great life unless you have a buffer of like-minded people all around you. If you want to be nice, you can't surround yourself with crabby people and expect it to work. You might stay nice for a while, just because—but it isn't sustainable over years. If you want a happy company, you can do it only by hiring naturally happy people. You'll never build a happy company by "making people happy"—you can't really "make" people any way that they aren't already. Laura and I want to be in love with life, and our business has been a good thing for us in that journey.[70]

Although Pete and Laura's hiring approach is consistent with the dispositional and genetic model of job satisfaction, it is important to note that hiring "like-minded" people can potentially lead to discriminatory decisions. Managers are advised not to discriminate on the basis of race, gender, religion, color, national origin, and age.

Example. These employees appear to be enjoying their jobs. Research suggests that they are more likely to enjoy their job based on genetic factors and personal traits.

Back to the Chapter-Opening Case

Which of the five models of job satisfaction best explains Jennifer Simonetti-Bryan's job satisfaction at Citicorp?

 LO.8 Major Correlates and Consequences of Job Satisfaction

This topic has significant managerial implications because thousands of studies have examined the relationship between job satisfaction and other organizational variables. Because it is impossible to examine them all, we will consider a subset of the more important variables from the standpoint of managerial relevance.

Table 6–2 summarizes the pattern of results. The relationship between job satisfaction and these other variables is either positive or negative. The strength of the relationship ranges from weak (very little relationship) to strong. Strong relationships imply that managers can significantly influence the variable of interest by increasing job satisfaction. Let us now consider seven key correlates of job satisfaction.

Motivation   A recent meta-analysis of nine studies and 1,739 workers revealed a significant positive relationship between motivation and job satisfaction. Because satisfaction with supervision also was significantly correlated with motivation, managers are advised to consider how their behavior affects employee satisfaction.[71] Managers can potentially enhance employees' motivation through various attempts to increase job satisfaction.

Job Involvement   Job involvement, which is a component of employee engagement, represents the extent to which an individual is personally involved with his or her work role. A meta-analysis involving 27,925 individuals demonstrated that job involvement was moderately related with job satisfaction.[72] Managers are thus encouraged to foster satisfying work environments in order to fuel employees' job involvement.

table 6–2   Correlates of Job Satisfaction

VARIABLES RELATED WITH SATISFACTION	DIRECTION OF RELATIONSHIP	STRENGTH OF RELATIONSHIP
Motivation	Positive	Moderate
Job involvement	Positive	Moderate
Organizational commitment	Positive	Moderate
Organizational citizenship behavior	Positive	Moderate
Withdrawal cognitions	Negative	Strong
Turnover	Negative	Moderate
Heart disease	Negative	Moderate
Perceived stress	Negative	Strong
Pro-union voting	Negative	Moderate
Job performance	Positive	Moderate
Life satisfaction	Positive	Moderate
Mental health	Positive	Moderate
Customer satisfaction	Positive	Moderate

Organizational Citizenship Behavior **Organizational citizenship behaviors (OCBs)** consist of employee behaviors that are beyond the call of duty. Examples include "such gestures as constructive statements about the department, expression of personal interest in the work of others, suggestions for improvement, training new people, respect for the spirit as well as the letter of housekeeping rules, care for organizational property, and punctuality and attendance well beyond standard or enforceable levels."[73] Managers certainly would like employees to exhibit these behaviors. A meta-analysis involving 21 separate studies revealed a significant and moderately positive correlation between organizational citizenship behaviors and job satisfaction.[74] Moreover, two recent and more extensive meta-analytic studies indicated that OCBs were significantly related to both individual-level consequences (e.g., performance appraisal ratings, intentions to quit, absenteeism, and turnover) and organizational-level outcomes (e.g., productivity, efficiency, lower costs, customer satisfaction, and unit-level satisfaction and turnover).[75] These results are important for two reasons. First, exhibiting OCBs is likely to create positive impressions about you among your colleagues and manager. In turn, these impressions affect your ability to work with others, your manager's evaluation of your performance, and ultimately your promotability. Second, the aggregate amount of employees' OCBs affects important organizational outcomes. It thus is important for managers to foster an environment that promotes OCBs. Managers are encouraged to make and implement employee-related decisions in an equitable fashion in order to foster OCBs. More is said about this in Chapter 8.

 Go to www.mcgrawhillconnect.com for a self-assessment to determine how satisfied you are with your present job.

organizational citizenship behaviors (OCBs) Employee behaviors that exceed work-role requirements.

Withdrawal Cognitions   Although some people quit their jobs impulsively or in a fit of anger, most go through a process of thinking about whether or not they should quit. **Withdrawal cognitions** encapsulate this thought process by representing an individual's overall thoughts and feelings about quitting. What causes an individual to think about quitting his or her job? Job satisfaction is believed to be one of the most significant contributors. For example, a study of managers, salespersons, and auto mechanics from a national automotive retail store chain demonstrated that job dissatisfaction caused employees to begin the process of thinking about quitting. In turn, withdrawal cognitions had a greater impact on employee turnover than job satisfaction in this sample.[76] Results from this study imply that managers can indirectly help to reduce employee turnover by enhancing employee job satisfaction.

Turnover   Let us consider the pros and cons of turnover before discussing the relationship between job satisfaction and turnover. Yes, turnover can be a good thing when a low-performing person like George Costanza from the *Seinfeld* show quits or is fired. This situation enables managers to replace the Georges of the world with better or more diverse individuals or to realign the budget. In contrast, losing a good employee is bad because the organization loses valuable human and social capital (recall our discussion in Chapter 1) and it can be costly.[77] Costs of turnover fall into two categories: separation costs and replacement costs.

Example. Separation costs may include severance pay, costs associated with an exit interview, outplacement fees, and possible litigation costs, particularly for involuntary separation. Replacement costs are the well-known costs of a hire, including sourcing expenses, HR processing costs for screening and assessing candidates, the time spent by hiring managers interviewing candidates, travel and relocation expenses, signing bonuses, if applicable, and orientation and training costs.[78]

Experts estimate that the cost of turnover for an hourly employee is roughly 30% of annual salary, whereas the cost can range up to 150% of yearly salary for professional employees.[79]

Although there are various things a manager can do to reduce employee turnover, many of them revolve around attempts to improve employees' job satisfaction. This trend is supported by results from a meta-analysis of 67 studies covering 24,556 people. Job satisfaction obtained a moderate negative relationship with employee turnover.[80] Given the strength of this relationship, managers are advised to try to reduce employee turnover by increasing employee job satisfaction. This recommendation is even more important for high performers.[81] For example, a recent survey of 20,000 high-potential employees indicated that 27% plan to find another job within a year.[82] Google seems to be aware of this issue in light of its decision to give all employees a 10% raise in 2010 despite a poor economy. Google obviously wanted to reduce defections of its talented workforce.[83]

Perceived Stress   Stress can have very negative effects on organizational behavior and an individual's health. Stress is positively related to absenteeism, turnover, coronary heart disease, and viral infections. Based on a meta-analysis covering 11,063 individuals, Table 6–2 reveals that perceived stress has a strong, negative relationship with job satisfaction.[84] Perceived stress also was found to be negatively associated with employee engagement. We recommend that managers attempt to reduce the negative effects of stress by improving job satisfaction and encouraging employees to detach from work during off-job time (i.e., stop thinking about work).[85]

Job Performance   One of the biggest controversies within OB research centers on the relationship between job satisfaction and job performance. Although researchers have identified eight different ways in which these variables are related, the dominant beliefs are either that satisfaction causes performance or performance causes satisfaction.[86] A team of researchers recently attempted to resolve this controversy through a meta-analysis of data from 312 samples involving 54,417 individuals.[87] There were two key findings from this study. First, job satisfaction and performance were moderately related. This is an important finding because it supports the belief that employee job satisfaction is a key work attitude managers should consider when attempting to increase employees' job performance. Second, the relationship between job satisfaction and performance was much more complex than originally thought. It is not as simple as satisfaction causing performance or performance causing satisfaction. Rather, researchers now believe both variables indirectly influence each other through a host of individual differences and work-environment characteristics. There is one additional consideration to keep in mind regarding the relationship between job satisfaction and job performance.

Researchers believe the relationship between satisfaction and performance is understated due to incomplete measures of individual-level performance. For example, if performance ratings used in past research did not reflect the actual interactions and interdependencies at work, inaccurate measures of performance served to lower the reported correlations between satisfaction and performance. Examining the relationship between *aggregate* measures of job satisfaction and organizational performance is one solution to correct this problem. In support of these ideas, a team of researchers conducted a recent meta-analysis of more than 5,000 business units. Results uncovered significant positive relationships between business-unit-level employee satisfaction and business-unit outcomes of productivity, turnover, absenteeism, and customer satisfaction.[88] It thus appears managers can positively affect a variety of important organizational outcomes such as performance and customer satisfaction by increasing employee job satisfaction.

Example. Occurrences of counterproductive work behavior like this generally increase during a recession.

 **LO.9** Counterproductive Work Behaviors

◀ ················

TO THE POINT
What are the causes of counterproductive work behaviors and how can managers prevent them?
················

In our discussion of job satisfaction, we noted that an absence of satisfaction may be associated with some types of undesirable behavior, such as low employee engagement and higher employee turnover. These costly behaviors, along with some that are even more disturbing, are part of a category of behavior known as **counterproductive work behaviors (CWBs),** types of behavior that harm employees, the organization as a whole, or organizational stakeholders such as customers and shareholder. Examples of CWBs include theft, gossiping, backstabbing, drug and alcohol abuse, destroying organizational property, violence, purposely doing bad or incorrect work, surfing the Net for personal use, excessive socializing, tardiness, sabotage, and sexual harassment.[89] Consider the following three examples:

Example. Recently, a Maryland man swiped 32 laptops from his nonprofit healthcare employer and put them on eBay. A chief financial officer changed the color of the type on some spreadsheet data from black to white so as to render the fake

---

withdrawal cognitions Overall thoughts and feelings about quitting a job.

counterproductive work behaviors (CWBs) Types of behavior

that harm employees and the organization as a whole.

numbers invisible while juicing the totals—and his bonus. One regional vice president for sales billed his corporate card $4,000 for Victoria's Secret lingerie—and not for his wife, either.[90]

Experts expect incidents like this to increase during the current recession.

Mistreatment of Others

Most forms of CWBs involve mistreatment of co-workers, subordinates, or even customers. For example, employees engage in harassment, bullying, or blatant unfairness. Unfortunately, a recent Zogby poll indicated that more than 50% of American adults had been bullied or witnessed bullying at work. Another poll of 12,000 people from 24 countries indicated that about 10% were harassed either sexually or physically at work.[91] Abuse by supervisors is especially toxic because employees report that when they feel they have been intimidated, humiliated, or undermined by an abusive supervisor, they are more likely to retaliate with counterproductive behavior aimed at the supervisor or their co-workers.[92] This type of response is especially likely when the organization does not provide channels through which employees can complain and find a resolution to the problem of mistreatment.

Violence at Work

Terrifying images of the shootings at Virginia Tech and that of US Representative Gabrielle "Gabby" Giffords and innocent bystanders in Tucson, Arizona, have brought home the urgency of protecting people in organizations from sudden acts of violence committed by insiders or outsiders. Often, co-workers are first to notice that an employee explodes in anger or seems depressed or troubled. Psychiatrist and consultant Roger Brunswick says, "Violence rarely begins with someone walking in and shooting others. Violence usually builds slowly and starts with bullying, intimidation and threats."[93] A first line of defense should be for the organization to set up and publicize how employees can report troubling behavior to their supervisor or human resource department. Pitney Bowes set up a hotline that employees can call anonymously to report any concerns, and it has trained managers to identify signs that something is wrong with an employee.[94]

Causes and Prevention of CWBs

Employers obviously want to prevent CWBs, so they need to know the causes of such behavior. A study that followed the work behaviors of more than 900 young adults for 23 years found that a diagnosis of conduct disorder in adolescence was associated with CWBs, but criminal convictions before entering the workforce were not associated with CWBs.[95] Personality traits and job conditions also could make CWBs more likely.[96] For example, young adults who scored higher on compulsion to adhere to norms, control their impulses, and avoid hostility tended not to use CWBs. They also were less likely to engage in CWBs if they had satisfying jobs that offered autonomy—and more likely to engage in CWBs if they had more resource power (such as more people to supervise). Intelligence may play a role, too. A study of applicants for law enforcement jobs found that higher scores for cognitive ability were associated with fewer reports of CWBs such as violence and destruction of property after candidates were hired.[97]

These findings suggest the following implications for management:

- Organizations can limit CWBs by hiring individuals who are less prone to engage in this type of behavior. Cognitive ability is associated with many measures of success, so it is a logical quality to screen for in-hiring decisions. Personality tests also may be relevant.

- Organizations should ensure they are motivating desired behaviors and not CWBs, for example, by designing jobs that promote satisfaction and by preventing abusive supervision. A study of 265 restaurants found that CWBs were greater in restaurants where employees reported abuse by supervisors and where managers had more employees to supervise.[98] CWBs in these restaurants were associated with lower profits and lower levels of customer satisfaction, so adequate staffing and management development could not only make employees' lives more pleasant but also improve the bottom line.

- If an employee does engage in CWBs, the organization should respond quickly and appropriately, defining the specific behaviors that are unacceptable and the requirements for acceptable behavior. Chapter 9 describes guidelines for giving effective feedback.

Summary of Key Concepts

1. *Explain Schwartz's value theory, and describe three types of value conflict.* Schwartz proposed that 10 core values guide our behavior across contexts and time (see Table 6–1). Each value possesses motivational mechanisms that drive behavior. Figure 6–1 further shows the relationships among the 10 values. Some are consistent and positively related, whereas others are inconsistent and conflict with each other. Three types of value conflict are intrapersonal, interpersonal, and individual–organization.

2. *Describe the values model of work–family conflict, and specify at least three practical lessons from work–family conflict research.* General life values determine one's values about family and work. Work–family conflict can occur when there is a lack of value similarity with family members. Likewise, work–family conflict can occur when one's own work values are not congruent with the company's values. When someone does not attain his or her values because of work–family conflicts, job or life satisfaction, or both, can suffer. Six practical lessons from work–family conflict research are the following: (a) work–family balance begins at home, (b) an employer's family-supportive philosophy is more important than specific programs, (c) informal flexibility in work hours and in allowing people to work at home is essential to promoting work–family balance, (d) supportive bosses and colleagues can help, (e) the importance of work–family balance varies across generations, and (f) one should take a proactive approach to managing work–family conflict.

3. *Identify the three components of attitudes and discuss cognitive dissonance.* The three components of attitudes are affective, cognitive, and behavioral. The affective component represents the feelings or emotions one has about a given object or situation. The cognitive component reflects the beliefs or ideas one has about an object or situation. The behavioral component refers to how one intends or expects to act toward someone or something. Cognitive dissonance represents the psychological discomfort an individual experiences when his or her attitudes or beliefs are incompatible with his or her behavior. There are three main methods for reducing cognitive dissonance: change an attitude or behavior, belittle the importance of the inconsistent behavior, and find consonant elements that outweigh dissonant ones.

4. *Explain how attitudes affect behavior in terms of Ajzen's theory of planned behavior.* Intentions are the key link between attitudes and behavior in Ajzen's model. Three determinants of the strength of an intention are one's attitude toward the behavior, subjective norm (social expectations and role models), and the perceived degree of one's control over the behavior. Intentions, in turn, are powerful determinants of behavior.

5. *Describe the model of organizational commitment.* Organizational commitment reflects how strongly a person identifies with an organization and is committed to its goals. Organizational commitment is composed of three related components: affective commitment, continuance commitment, and normative commitment. In turn, each of these components is influenced by a separate set of antecedents: An antecedent is something that causes the component of commitment to occur.

6. *Define the work attitudes of employee engagement and job satisfaction.* Employee engagement occurs when employees give it their all at work. It contains feelings of urgency, feelings of being focused, feelings of intensity, and feelings of enthusiasm. Job satisfaction reflects how much people like or dislike their jobs.

7. *Identify and briefly describe five alternative causes of job satisfaction.* They are need fulfillment (the degree to which one's own needs are met), discrepancies (satisfaction depends on the extent to which one's expectations are met), value attainment (satisfaction depends on the degree to which one's work values are fulfilled), equity (perceived fairness of input/outcomes determines one's level of satisfaction), and dispositional/genetic (job satisfaction is dictated by one's personal traits and genetic makeup).

8. *Identify eight important correlates/consequences of job cognitive dissonance, satisfaction, and summarize how each one relates to job satisfaction.* Table 6–2 reviews the correlates of job satisfaction.

9. *Identify the causes of counterproductive work behaviors and the measures used to prevent them.* Counterproductive

work behaviors (CWBs) may result from personal characteristics coupled with a lack of autonomy and job satisfaction. CWBs are more likely in situations where supervisors are abusive and responsible for many employees. Organizations can limit CWBs by hiring individuals with appropriate cognitive skills and personality traits. They can design jobs to promote satisfaction. They can develop managers to supervise effectively without abuse and should deliver immediate feedback and discipline if anyone engages in CWBs.

Key Terms

Attitude, 158

Affective component, 158

Cognitive component, 158

Behavioral component, 158

Cognitive dissonance, 159

Organizational commitment, 163

Psychological contract, 165

Employee engagement, 166

Job satisfaction, 168

Met expectations, 169

Value attainment, 169

Organizational citizenship behaviors (OCBs), 171

Withdrawal cognitions, 172

Counterproductive work behaviors (CWBs), 173

OB in Action Case Study

Companies Are Trying to Improve Employee Attitudes during the Recession[99]

CEOs may have cut back sharply on management consulting in the last downturn, but that's not stopping Bain & Company's worldwide managing director, Steve Ellis, from doing the same thing Bain did during the dot-com bust: hiring. He's adding consultants in hot-growth areas such as emerging markets and corporate turnarounds, and he's more aggressively targeting former consultants who went to financial-services firms and are now "stranded." "This is a huge opportunity to grab very talented people," says Ellis.

For many managers, recessions prompt a near-autonomic reflex: Hunker down, reduce head count, and cut every cost you can. While a certain dose of those bitter pills is unavoidable, smart leaders see downturns as having plenty of upside, too. Talent is cheaper. Companies can gain market share as others cut back. And savvy investments give bold players a head start when the economy picks up.

Nowhere is that more true than in the care and feeding of employees. Even amid a hiring freeze or a workforce reduction, there are ways to engage top workers. As the housing market crumbled, Home Depot cut jobs in its corporate offices. It also closed 15 locations. Still, Chairman and Chief Executive Frank Blake wanted to boost morale and set realistic goals. In addition to extending restricted stock grants to assistant store managers, he lowered sales and profit targets that hourly employees have to meet to receive bonuses. As a result, says Marvin Ellison, Home Depot's new executive vice president for US stores, the highest percentage ever of in-store employees got bonuses in the first half of this year. "We still challenged people to hit some pretty tough numbers," Ellison says.

Keeping people focused amid mounting layoffs often requires a more emotional approach. Talking about the company's nonfinancial goals can help prevent productivity from grinding to a halt as anxious employees await their fate. And once cuts are made, managers need to take time to discuss them and why they happened. Ignoring the matter, says Christopher Rice, president and CEO of leadership consulting firm BlessingWhite, creates an atmosphere that's "like the most awkward Thanksgiving dinner. And it doesn't go away."

Amid pressure to downsize, it's easy to forget that talent retention is a critical concern during a recession. Michael Kesner, a principal at Deloitte Consulting's human capital practice, notes that "companies who took advantage of employees in past downturns were rewarded with people bailing when things turned around." To avoid that, some of Kesner's clients are adding more weight to factors employees can control—such as customer satisfaction scores or production levels—when deciding on bonuses. Others are creating discretionary bonus pools to reward poachable stars. And with some 63% of companies reporting that all or most of the stock options they've been granted in the past five years are underwater, according to a Deloitte survey of 151 companies, a few are considering the controversial step of repricing or exchanging them. Compensation research firm Equilar reports that 23 companies have done so since the beginning of the year, including R. H. Donnelley and software maker VMware.

Plain, Unvarnished Communication

There are other ways to make employees feel valued. Consider Best Buy, which has watched its stock plummet 40% over the past month and announced it will hire fewer seasonal employees amid a dismal holiday shopping outlook. One way the company has also tried to keep employees engaged is by setting up online surveys to solicit ideas for cutting costs. Some 900 ideas have emerged since the surveys were sent out three weeks ago. A couple of them: save shipping costs by consolidating distribution of in-store signs and use a computerized phone system to schedule service calls. As John Pershing, Best Buy's executive vice president for human capital, says: "When you know you can make a difference and you're part of a solution, it can change your mind completely."

Indeed the best strategy for managing talent, in good times and bad, remains plain, unvarnished communication. "People are looking for reassurances, for transparency, and they're not looking for surprises," says Edward E. Lawler III, director of the Center for Effective Organizations at the University of Southern California. A CEO town hall meeting is fine, but it's no substitute for reassurances from managers further down the line. Says Jon R. Katzenbach, a senior partner and founder at consultant Katzenbach Partners: "If you're scared and you're worried about your job, hearing the CEO telling you things are good isn't nearly as effective as (hearing it from) the person you have respect for because you've worked with them all along."

That said, symbolic gestures from CEOs can help employees feel that everyone is sharing the pain. JetBlue Airways CEO David Barger has cut back across the board over the past year—delaying aircraft orders, trimming head count through voluntary unpaid leaves, even shedding the free pillows from his planes. In July he cut his own salary, from $500,000 to $375,000 for the year. "There's an awful lot of pain that's taking place across the industry," says Barger. "It was just the right thing to do."

Questions for Discussion

1. Which of Schwartz's 10 values are driving the behavior of managers at Bain & Company, Home Depot, and Best Buy? Provide examples to support your conclusions.

2. How would you describe Steve Ellis's affective, cognitive, and behavioral components of his attitude toward managing in a recession? Be specific.

3. How are Home Depot and Best Buy trying to increase employee involvement?

4. Use Ajzen's theory of planned behavior (Figure 6–3) to analyze how managers can increase employee performance during a recession. Be sure to explain what managers can do to affect each aspect of the theory.

5. Based on what you learned in this chapter, what advice would you give to managers trying increase employees' organizational commitment and job satisfaction in a recession? Be specific.

Legal/Ethical Challenge

How Would You Handle a School District That May Have Used Webcams to Spy on Students?[100]

A recent lawsuit claimed that a Philadelphia school district "used the webcams in school-issued laptops to spy on students at home." School-district officials have not commented on the allegations. "Plaintiffs Michael and Holly Robbins suspect the cameras captured students and family members as they undressed and in other embarrassing situations, according to the suit."

District spokesperson Doug Young said that "we can categorically state that we are and have always been committed to protecting the privacy of our students."

"The Robbinses said they learned of the alleged webcam images when Lindy Matsko, an assistant principal at Harriton High School, told their son Blake that school officials thought he had engaged in improper behavior at home."

"'(Matsko) cited as evidence a photograph from the webcam embedded in minor plaintiff's personal laptop issued by the school district,' the suit states." The Robbinses, however, have not actually seen any photographs that may have been captured by school officials.

"Matsko later confirmed to Michael Robbins that the school had the ability to activate the webcams remotely."

What would you do if you were an educational official for the State of Pennsylvania?

1. Take a proactive approach and fire the superintendent of the school district and the principal at Harriton High School.

2. Get ahead of this case by putting the superintendent of the school district and the principal at Harriton High School on administrative leave until the case is resolved.

3. Admitting guilt could cost the school district a lot of needed money. Deny that you knew anything about spying on students with webcams and let the case run its course in the courts.

4. Invent other options.

Web Resources

chapter 7

Social Perception and Attributions

 Learning Objectives

When you finish studying the material in this chapter, you should be able to:

LO.1   Describe perception in terms of the information-processing model.

LO.2   Summarize the key managerial implications of social perception.

LO.3   Discuss the process of stereotype formation.

LO.4   Summarize the managerial challenges and recommendations of sex role, age, racial, ethnic, and disability stereotypes.

LO.5   Describe and contrast the Pygmalion effect, the Galatea effect, and the Golem effect.

LO.6   Discuss how the model of the self-fulfilling prophecy is expected to work.

LO.7   Explain, according to Kelley's model, how external and internal causal attributions are formulated.

LO.8   Contrast the fundamental attribution bias and the self-serving bias.

Is It Good or Bad to Show Vulnerability?

A recent article in *Bloomberg Businessweek* reviewed the pros of showing vulnerability (i.e., discussing one's weaknesses or limitations) when advertising products and services and when trying to create more effective teams. The author—Patrick Lencioni—proposed that organizations and individuals create positive perceptions when they admit vulnerabilities, as long as companies and individuals mean it. "Vulnerability is often seen as weakness; it's actually a sign of strength. People who are genuinely open and transparent prove that they have confidence and self-esteem to allow others to see them as they really are, warts and all. There's something undeniably magnetic about people who can do that," according to Lencioni.

Lencioni also believes that showing vulnerability with your co-workers can help build teamwork. "When teammates feel free to admit mistakes, ask for help, and acknowledge their own weaknesses, they reduce divisive politics and build a bond of trust more valuable than almost any strategic advantage," said Lencioni.

Lencioni used examples of Domino's Pizza and the Chicago Bears football team to support his position. The Domino's Pizza ad "opens with customers describing Domino's pizza using words like ketchup and cardboard. Then, Domino's President J. Patrick Doyle matter-of-factly explains the importance of acknowledging how customers see his pizza. Finally he outlines the company's response: 40% more herbs in its sauce, better cheese, a special glaze on the crust." Similarly, the Chicago Bears "capped off a miserable season by buying a full-page ad admitting to a subpar attempt at professional football and thanking fans for their support in spite of the team's mediocrity."[1]

The chapter-opening case underscores an important aspect of the perception process: People do not have the same perceptions about ads, events, people, and things we encounter in our daily lives. For example, Domino's CEO obviously believes that positive impressions and increased sales will occur as a result of being vulnerable, whereas someone else might be turned off by pizza described as cardboard. We certainly would not buy season tickets to a mediocre football team just because ownership admitted that it had put a poor product on the field. How about you?

Our perceptions and feelings are influenced by information we receive from newspapers, magazines, television, radio, family, and friends. You see, we all use information stored in our memories to interpret the world around us, and our interpretations, in turn, influence how we respond and interact with others. As human beings, we constantly strive to make sense of our surroundings. The resulting knowledge influences our behavior and helps us navigate our way through life. Think of the perceptual process that occurs when meeting someone for the first time. Your attention is drawn to the individual's physical appearance, mannerisms, actions, and reactions to what you say and do. You ultimately arrive at conclusions based on your perceptions of this social interaction. The brown-haired, green-eyed individual turns out to be friendly and fond of outdoor activities. You further conclude that you like this person and then ask him or her to go to a concert, calling the person by the name you stored in memory.

The reciprocal process of perception, interpretation, and behavioral response also applies at work. Bernie Madoff, for example, used the perception process to help orchestrate a $50-billion Ponzi scheme against unsuspecting investors. Madoff, who was described as "entrepreneurial, rich, and charming," used the success of his company in the 1980s and 1990s to create an image of a can't-lose investment strategist. His offices "oozed success" and the trading room looked "very profitable—and totally legitimate." He was active in social circles and charitable organizations. All told, these perceptions helped Madoff to recruit wealthy investors and money managers and to maintain the perception that he was running one of the most exclusive and successful investment firms in the world. Unfortunately, it was a lie that continued to exist partly because of the perception process.[2]

The perception process influences much more than the impressions people make about each other. For example, companies use knowledge about perceptions when designing and marketing their products, and political candidates use it to get elected. The Transportation Security Administration also uses research about perception to design training programs aimed at helping airport security screeners to detect threatening objects more accurately.[3] An error in the perception process in this context can lead to catastrophic consequences! The point we are trying to make is that the perception process influences a host of managerial activities, organizational processes, and quality-of-life issues. We have written this chapter with this conclusion in mind. You will gain a thorough understanding of how perception works and how you can use it to enhance your future personal and professional success.

Let us now begin our exploration of the perceptual process and its associated outcomes. In this chapter we focus on (1) an information-processing model of perception, (2) stereotypes, (3) the self-fulfilling prophecy, and (4) how causal attributions are used to interpret behavior.

TO THE POINT

How can the information-processing model of perception explain poor hiring decisions, inaccurate performance appraisals, perceptions of leaders, and poor physical and psychological well-being?

LO.1 An Information-Processing Model of Perception

Perception is a cognitive process that enables us to interpret and understand our surroundings. Recognition of objects is one of this process's major functions. For example, both people and animals recognize familiar objects in their environments. You would recognize a picture of your best friend; dogs and cats can recognize their food dishes or a favorite toy. Reading involves recognition of visual patterns representing letters in the alphabet. People must recognize objects to meaningfully interact with their environment. But since organizational behavior's (OB's) principal focus is on people, the following discussion emphasizes *social* perception rather than object perception.

The study of how people perceive one another has been labeled *social cognition* and *social information processing.* In contrast to the perception of objects, social cognition is the study of how people make sense of other people and themselves. It focuses on how ordinary people think about people and how they think they think about people. . . .

Example. Research on social cognition also goes beyond naive psychology. The study of social cognition entails a fine-grained analysis of how people think about themselves and others, and it leans heavily on the theory and methods of cognitive psychology.[4]

Let us now examine the fundamental processes underlying perception.

Four-Stage Sequence and a Working Example

Perception involves a four-stage information-processing sequence (hence, the label "information processing"). Figure 7–1 illustrates a basic information-processing model of perception. Three of the stages in this model—selective attention/comprehension, encoding and simplification, and storage and retention—describe how specific information and environmental stimuli are observed and stored in memory. The fourth and final stage, retrieval and response, involves turning mental representations into real-world judgments and decisions.

Keep the following everyday example in mind as we look at the four stages of perception. Suppose you were thinking of taking a course in, say, personal finance. Three professors teach the same course, using different types of instruction and testing procedures. Through personal experience, you have come to prefer good professors who rely on the case method of instruction and essay tests. According to the information-processing model of perception, you would likely arrive at a decision regarding which professor to take as follows:

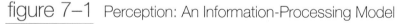

figure 7–1   Perception: An Information-Processing Model

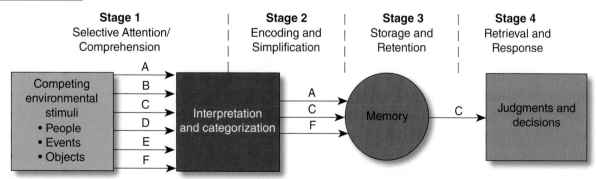

---

perception Process of interpreting one's environment.

Stage 1: Selective Attention/Comprehension

People are constantly bombarded by physical and social stimuli in the environment. Since they do not have the mental capacity to fully comprehend all this information, they selectively perceive subsets of environmental stimuli. This is where attention plays a role. **Attention** is the process of becoming consciously aware of something or someone. Attention can be focused on information either from the environment or from memory. Regarding the latter situation, if you sometimes find yourself thinking about totally unrelated events or people while reading a textbook, your memory is the focus of your attention. Research has shown that people tend to pay attention to salient stimuli.

Salient Stimuli   Something is salient when it stands out from its context. For example, a 250-pound man would certainly be salient in a women's aerobics class but not at a meeting of the National Football League Players' Association. One's needs and goals often dictate which stimuli are salient. For a driver whose gas gauge is on empty, an Exxon or Mobil sign is more salient than a McDonald's or Burger King sign. The reverse would be true for a hungry driver with a full gas tank. Moreover, research shows that people have a tendency to pay more attention to negative than positive information. This leads to a negativity bias.[5] This bias helps explain the gawking factor that slows traffic to a crawl following a car accident, and it can affect employee behavior at work. Consider the case of Falcon Containers. At Austin-based Falcon Containers, CEO Stephen Shang suggested in 2009 that his sales team quit watching economic news for two weeks and spend more time connecting with customers. Result: The company, which leases repurposed shipping containers as storage units, made a deal to create an Iraqi "village" out of the containers for an anti-IED effort by the U.S. Air Force. That led to more military business—fostering a 20% sales increase.[6] Shang was able to increase revenue by getting his employees to stop paying attention to negative economic news and focus on spending more time with customers.

Go to www.mcgrawhillconnect.com for an interactive exercise to test your knowledge of the information processing model.

Back to Our Example   You begin your search for the "right" personal finance professor by asking friends who have taken classes from the three professors. You also may interview the various professors who teach the class to gather still more relevant information. Returning to Figure 7–1, all the information you obtain represents competing environmental stimuli labeled A through F. Because you are concerned about the method of instruction (e.g., line A in Figure 7–1), testing procedures (e.g., line C), and past grade distributions (e.g., line F), information in those areas is particularly salient to you. Figure 7–1 shows that these three salient pieces of information thus are perceived, and you then progress to the second stage of information processing. Meanwhile, competing stimuli represented by lines B, D, and E in Figure 7–1 fail to get your attention and are discarded from further consideration.

Stage 2: Encoding and Simplification

Observed information is not stored in memory in its original form. Encoding is required; raw information is interpreted or translated into mental representations. To accomplish this, perceivers assign pieces of information to **cognitive categories.** "By *category* we mean a number of objects that are considered equivalent. Categories are generally designated by names, e.g., *dog, animal.*"[7] People, events, and objects are interpreted and evaluated by comparing their characteristics with information contained in schemata (or schema in singular form).

Schemata   A **schema** represents a person's mental picture or summary of a particular event or type of stimulus. A schema for an event, like going out to

table 7–1   Restaurant Schema

Schema: **Restaurant.**
Characters: **Customers, hostess, waiter, chef, cashier.**
Scene 1: **Entering.**
    Customer goes into restaurant.
    Customer finds a place to sit.
      He may find it himself.
      He may be seated by a hostess.
        He asks the hostess for a table.
        She gives him permission to go to the table.

Scene 2: **Ordering.**
    Customer receives a menu.
    Customer reads it.
    Customer decides what to order.
    Waiter takes the order.
      Waiter sees the customer.
      Waiter goes to the customer.
      Customer orders what he wants.
    Chef cooks the meal.

Scene 3: **Eating.**
    After some time the waiter brings the meal from the chef.
    Customer eats the meal.

Scene 4: **Exiting.**
    Customer asks the waiter for the check.
    Waiter gives the check to the customer.
    Customer leaves a tip.
      The size of the tip depends on the goodness of the service.
    Customer pays the cashier.
    Customer leaves the restaurant.

SOURCE: From D Rumelhart, *Introduction to Human Information Processing* (New York: John Wiley & Sons, Inc., 1977). Reprinted with permission of John Wiley & Sons, Inc.

dinner in a restaurant, is called a **script.** Your memory for going out to dinner probably is quite similar to the restaurant script shown in Table 7–1.

Back to the Chapter-Opening Case

What are the characteristics of a "good" pizza in your schema? Do they contain "tastes like cardboard"?

Cognitive-category labels are needed to make schemata meaningful. For example, you have a category label for "going to dinner" and another titled "sports car." Each schema contains information. Let us consider what you have stored in memory about sports cars. Does your schema contain a smaller vehicle with two

attention Being consciously aware of something or someone.

cognitive categories Mental depositories for storing information.

schema Mental picture of an event or object.

script A mental picture of an event.

Is this photo consistent with your "sports car schema"? If it is, you'll likely classify all small, two-door, red vehicles as sports cars. Can you think of another example of a common schema in today's culture?

doors? Is it red? If you answered yes, you would tend to classify all small, two-door, fire-engine-red vehicles as sports cars because this type of car possesses characteristics that are consistent with your "sports car schema."

Encoding Outcomes   We use the encoding process to interpret and evaluate our environment. Interestingly, this process can result in differing interpretations and evaluations of the same person or event. Varying interpretations of what we observe occur due to four key reasons.

First, people possess different information in the schemata used for interpretation. For instance, a meta-analysis of 62 studies revealed women and men had different opinions about what type of behaviors constituted sexual harassment. Women defined a broader range of behaviors as harassing.[8] Second, our moods and emotions influence our focus of attention and evaluations of others. Third, people tend to apply recently used cognitive categories during encoding. For example, you are more likely to interpret a neutral behavior exhibited by a professor as positive if you were recently thinking about positive categories and events. Fourth, individual differences influence encoding. Pessimistic or depressed individuals, for instance, tend to interpret their surroundings more negatively than optimistic and happy people. The point is that we should not be surprised when people interpret and evaluate the same situation or event differently. Researchers are currently trying to identify the host of factors that influence the encoding process.

Back to Our Example   Having collected relevant information about the three personal finance professors and their approaches, you compare this information with other details contained in schemata. This leads you to form an impression and evaluation of what it would be like to take a course from each professor. In turn, the relevant information contained on paths A, C, and F in Figure 7–1 are passed along to the third stage of information processing.

Stage 3: Storage and Retention

This phase involves storage of information in long-term memory. Long-term memory is like an apartment complex consisting of separate units connected to one another. Although different people live in each apartment, they sometimes interact. In addition, large apartment complexes have different wings (such as A, B, and C). Long-term memory similarly consists of separate but related categories. Like the individual apartments inhabited by unique residents, the connected categories contain different types of information. Information also passes among these categories. Finally, long-term memory is made up of three compartments (or wings) containing categories of information about events, semantic materials, and people.[9]

Event Memory   This compartment is composed of categories containing information about both specific and general events. These memories describe appropriate sequences of events in well-known situations, such as going to a restaurant (refer back to Table 7–1), going on a job interview, going to a food store, or going to a movie.

Semantic Memory   Semantic memory refers to general knowledge about the world. In so doing, it functions as a mental dictionary of concepts. Each

real WORLD // real PEOPLE

Nutrisystem and Unilever Use Everyday People Instead of Celebrities in Their Ads

Nutrisystem sent flip video cameras to customers in search of stories to use in its advertising. Here is what Charlotte Husser, 54, had to say.

> "What you're hearing from me has to come from the heart; there's no script," says Husser, who says she shed 32 pounds to become a size six after eating Nutrisystem's meals for five months.... Nutrisystem's CEO, Joe Redling, noted that "Nutrisystem wants to convey how they're helping people lose weight and how it's affecting lives of people that are noncelebrities."...

The Campaign for Real Beauty used by Unilever to promote its Dove soap is the classic case of using regular folk in ads.... Dove's marketing blitz, which began in 2004 and has featured women from age 20 to 95, aims to boost the self esteem of girls by showcasing real people instead of models. Although the company won't provide numbers, Unilever spokesman David Perez says "response to our campaigns featuring real women has been overwhelming positive."

Would you remember an ad if it contained information that reminded you of a family member?

SOURCE: Excerpted from L Patton, "Nutrisystem Gets Real with Its Diet Ads," *Bloomberg Businessweek,* January 10–16, 2011, pp 19–20.

sleeveless-ready in just 7 days. Dove has asked real women to try out our new improved Dove Deodorant for seven days. The result: visibly softer and smoother underarms. Thanks to 1/4 moisturising cream Dove Deodorant helps your underarm skin recover itself after shaving. See for yourself, try New Dove Deodorant. Approved by Real Woman.

---

concept contains a definition (e.g., a good leader) and associated traits (outgoing), emotional states (happy), physical characteristics (tall), and behaviors (works hard). Just as there are schemata for general events, concepts in semantic memory are stored as schemata. Given our previous discussion of managing diversity in Chapter 2 and international OB in Chapter 4, it should come as no surprise that there are cultural differences in the type of information stored in semantic memory.

Person Memory   Categories within this compartment contain information about a single individual (your professor) or groups of people (professors). You are more likely to remember information about a person, event, or an advertisement if it contains characteristics that are similar to something stored in the compartments of memory. For example, companies such as Nutrisystem and Unilever are increasingly using "regular" individuals rather than celebrities in their ads because people don't identify with celebrities (see Real World/Real People above).

Back to Our Example   As the time draws near for you to decide which personal finance professor to take, your schemata of them are stored in the three categories of long-term memory. These schemata are available for immediate comparison or retrieval.

Stage 4: Retrieval and Response

People retrieve information from memory when they make judgments and decisions. Our ultimate judgments and decisions are either based on the process of drawing on, interpreting, and integrating categorical information stored in long-term memory or on retrieving a summary judgment that was already made.

Concluding our example, it is registration day and you have to choose which professor to take for personal finance. After retrieving from memory your schemata-based impressions of the three professors, you select a good one who uses the case method and gives essay tests (line C in Figure 7–1). In contrast, you may choose your preferred professor by simply recalling the decision you made two weeks ago.

 LO.2 ## Managerial Implications

Social cognition is the window through which we all observe, interpret, and prepare our responses to people and events. A wide variety of managerial activities, organizational processes, and quality-of-life issues are thus affected by perception. Consider, for example, the following seven implications.

Hiring   Interviewers make hiring decisions based on their impression of how an applicant fits the perceived requirements of a job.[10] Unfortunately, many of these decisions are made on the basis of implicit cognition. **Implicit cognition** represents any thoughts or beliefs that are automatically activated from memory without our conscious awareness. The existence of implicit cognition leads people to make biased decisions without an understanding that it is occurring.[11] This tendency has been used as an explanation of alleged discriminatory behavior at Walmart, FedEx, Johnson & Johnson, and Cargill. Experts recommend two solutions for reducing this problem.[12] First, managers can be trained to understand and reduce this type of hidden bias. For example, one study demonstrated that training improved interviewers' ability to obtain high-quality, job-related information and to stay focused on the interview task. Trained interviewers provide more balanced judgments about applicants than nontrained interviewers.[13] Second, bias can be reduced by using structured as opposed to unstructured interviews, and by relying on evaluations from multiple interviewers rather than just one or two people.

Performance Appraisal   Faulty schemata about what constitutes good versus poor performance can lead to inaccurate performance appraisals, which erode work motivation, commitment, and loyalty. For example, a study of 166 production employees indicated that they had greater trust in management when they perceived that the performance appraisal process provided accurate evaluations of their performance.[14] Therefore, it is important for managers to accurately identify the behavioral characteristics and results indicative of good performance at the beginning of a performance review cycle. These characteristics then can serve as the standards for evaluating employee performance. The importance of using objective rather than subjective measures of employee performance was highlighted in a meta-analysis involving 50 studies and 8,341 individuals. Results revealed that objective and subjective measures of employee performance were only moderately related. The researchers concluded that objective and subjective measures of performance are not interchangeable.[15] Managers are thus advised to use more objectively based measures of performance as much as possible because subjective indicators are prone to bias and inaccuracy. In those cases where the job does not possess objective measures of performance, however, managers should still use subjective evaluations. Furthermore, because memory for specific instances of employee performance deteriorates over time, managers need a mechanism for accurately recalling employee behavior. Research reveals that individuals can be trained to be more accurate raters of performance.[16]

Leadership   Research demonstrated that employees' evaluations of leader effectiveness were influenced strongly by their schemata of good and poor leaders. A leader will have a difficult time influencing employees when he or she exhibits behaviors contained in employees' schemata of poor leaders. A team of researchers investigated the behaviors contained in our schemata of good and poor leaders. Good leaders were perceived as exhibiting the following behaviors: (1) assigning specific tasks to group members, (2) telling others that they had done well, (3) setting specific goals for the group, (4) letting other group members make decisions, (5) trying to get the group to work as a team, and (6) maintaining definite standards of performance. Another recent study found that good leaders were perceived as those who consistently treated all members of a work unit in a fair manner.[17]

Back to the Chapter-Opening Case

Do you think that Domino's CEO Patrick Doyle demonstrated leadership qualities by being vulnerable? Explain.

Communication and Interpersonal Influence   Managers need to remember that social perception is a screening process that can distort communication, both coming and going. Because people interpret oral and written communications by using schemata developed through past experiences, your ability to influence others is affected by information contained in others' schemata regarding age, gender, ethnicity, appearance, speech, mannerisms, personality, and other personal characteristics. It is important to keep this in mind when trying to influence others or when trying to sell your ideas.

Counterproductive Work Behaviors   Past research showed that employees exhibited a variety of counterproductive work behaviors (recall our discussion in Chapter 6) when they perceived that they were treated unfairly. It is very important for managers to treat employees fairly, remembering that perceptions of fairness are in the eye of the beholder. Chapter 8 discusses how this can be done in greater detail.

Physical and Psychological Well-Being   The negativity bias can lead to both physical and psychological problems. Specifically, research shows that perceptions of fear, harm, and anxiety are associated with the onset of illnesses, absenteeism, and intentions to quit.[18] We should all attempt to avoid the tendency of giving negative thoughts too much attention. Try to let negative thoughts roll off yourself just like water off a duck.

Designing Web Pages   Researchers have recently begun to explore what catches viewers' attention on Web pages by using sophisticated eye-tracking equipment. This research can help organizations to spend their money wisely when designing Web pages. Kara Pernice Coyne, director of a research project studying Web page design, praised the Web pages of JetBlue Airways and Sears while noting problems with the one used by Agere Systems.[19]

implicit cognition Any thought or belief that is automatically activated without conscious awareness.

TO THE POINT

How can managers
use knowledge of
stereotypes and
stereotype formation to
more effectively reduce
problems associated
with sex role, age,
racial, and disability
stereotypes?

LO.3 Stereotypes: Perceptions about Groups of People

While it is often true that beauty is in the eye of the beholder, perception does result in some predictable outcomes. Managers aware of the perception process and its outcomes enjoy a competitive edge. The Walt Disney Company, for instance, takes full advantage of perceptual tendencies to influence customers' reactions to waiting in long lines at its theme parks:

Example. In Orlando, at Disney-MGM Studios, visitors waiting to get into a Muppet attraction watch tapes of Kermit the Frog on TV monitors. At the Magic Kingdom, visitors to the Extra Terrestrial Alien Encounter attraction are entertained by a talking robot before the show. At some rides, the company uses simple toys, like blocks, to help parents keep small children busy and happy during the wait.[20]

This example illustrates how the focus of one's attention influences the perception of standing in long lines.

Likewise, managers can use knowledge of perceptual outcomes to help them interact more effectively with employees. For example, Table 7–2 describes five common perceptual errors. Since these perceptual errors often distort the evaluation of job applicants and of employee performance, managers need to guard against them. This section examines one of the most important and potentially harmful perceptual outcomes associated with person perception: stereotypes. After exploring the process of stereotype formation and maintenance, we discuss sex-role stereotypes, age stereotypes, race stereotypes, disability stereotypes, and the managerial challenge to avoid stereotypical biases.

Stereotype Formation and Maintenance

"A **stereotype** is an individual's set of beliefs about the characteristics or attributes of a group."[21] Stereotypes are not always negative. For example, the belief that engineers are good at math is certainly part of a stereotype. Stereotypes may or may not be accurate. Engineers may in fact be better at math than the general population. In general, stereotypic characteristics are used to differentiate a particular group of people from other groups.[22]

It is important to remember that stereotypes are a fundamental component of the perception process and we use them to help process the large amount of information that bombards us daily. As such, it is not immoral or bad to possess stereotypes. That said, however, inappropriate use of stereotypes can lead to poor decisions; can create barriers for women, older individuals, people of color, and people with disabilities; and can undermine loyalty and job satisfaction.

Stereotyping is a four-step process. It begins by categorizing people into groups according to various criteria, such as gender, age, race, and occupation. Next, we infer that all people within a particular category possess the same traits or characteristics (e.g., all women are nurturing, older people have more job-related accidents, all African Americans are good athletes, all professors are absentminded). Then, we form expectations of others and interpret their behavior according to our stereotypes. Finally, stereotypes are maintained by (1) overestimating the frequency of stereotypic behaviors exhibited by others, (2) incorrectly explaining expected and unexpected behaviors, and (3) differentiating minority individuals from oneself.[23] It is hard to stop people from using stereotypes because these four steps are self-reinforcing. The good news,

table 7–2   Commonly Found Perceptual Errors

PERCEPTUAL ERROR	DESCRIPTION	EXAMPLE	RECOMMENDED SOLUTION
Halo	A rater forms an overall impression about an object and then uses that impression to bias ratings about the object.	Rating a professor high on the teaching dimensions of ability to motivate students, knowledge, and communication because we like him or her.	Remember that an employee's behavior tends to vary across different dimensions of performance. Keep a file or diary to record examples of positive and negative employee performance throughout the year.
Leniency	A personal characteristic that leads an individual to consistently evaluate other people or objects in an extremely positive fashion.	Rating a professor high on all dimensions of performance regardless of his or her actual performance. The rater that hates to say negative things about others.	It does not help employees when they are given positive feedback that is inaccurate. Try to be fair and realistic when evaluating others.
Central tendency	The tendency to avoid all extreme judgments and rate people and objects as average or neutral.	Rating a professor average on all dimensions of performance regardless of his or her actual performance.	It is normal to provide feedback that contains both positive and negative information. The use of a performance diary can help to remember examples of employee performance.
Recency effects	The tendency to remember recent information. If the recent information is negative, the person or object is evaluated negatively.	Although a professor has given good lectures for 12 to 15 weeks, he or she is evaluated negatively because lectures over the last 3 weeks were done poorly.	It is critical to accumulate examples of performance that span the entire rating period. Keep a file or diary to record examples of performance throughout the year.
Contrast effects	The tendency to evaluate people or objects by comparing them with characteristics of recently observed people or objects.	Rating a good professor as average because you compared his or her performance with three of the best professors you have ever had in college. You are currently taking courses from the three excellent professors.	It is important to evaluate employees against a standard rather than your memory of the best or worst person in a particular job.

however, is that researchers have identified a few ways to break the chain of stereotyping.

Research shows that the use of stereotypes is influenced by the amount and type of information available to an individual and his or her motivation to accurately process information.[24] People are less apt to use stereotypes to judge others when they encounter salient information that is highly inconsistent with a stereotype. For instance, you are unlikely to assign stereotypic "professor" traits to a

 Go to www.mcgrawhillconnect.com for an interactive exercise to test your knowledge of the commonly found perceptual errors.

stereotype Beliefs about the characteristics of a group.

new professor you have this semester if he or she rides a Harley-Davidson, wears leather pants to class, and has a pierced nose. People also are less likely to rely on stereotypes when they are motivated to avoid using them. That is, accurate information processing requires mental effort. Stereotyping is generally viewed as a less effortful strategy of information processing. Let us now take a look at different types of stereotypes and consider additional methods for reducing their biasing effects.

LO.4 Sex-Role Stereotypes

A **sex-role stereotype** is the belief that differing traits and abilities make men and women particularly well suited to different roles. These stereotypes have been found to influence our perceptions of women as leaders. A recent summary of this research, for example, revealed that (1) people often prefer male bosses, (2) women have a harder time being perceived as an effective leader (e.g., women were seen as more effective than men only when the organization faced a crisis and turnaround), and (3) women of color are more negatively affected by sex-role stereotypes than white women or men in general.[25] Researchers believe that sex-role stereotypes are related to gender-based expectations that people use without any conscious awareness. The key question, however, is whether or not these stereotypes influence the hiring, evaluation, and promotion of people at work.

A meta-analysis of 19 studies found no significant relationships between applicant gender and hiring recommendations.[26] A second meta-analysis involving 24 experimental studies revealed that men and women received similar performance ratings for the same level of task performance. Stated differently, there was no pro-male bias. These experimental results were further supported in a field study of female and male professors.[27] Unfortunately, results pertaining to promotion decisions are not as promising. A field study of 682 employees in a multinational *Fortune* 500 company demonstrated that gender was significantly related to promotion potential ratings. Men received more favorable evaluations than women in spite of controlling for age, education, organizational tenure, salary grade, and type of job.[28] Biases against women also were found to be more prevalent when they worked in nontraditional jobs.[29]

Go to www.mcgrawhillconnect.com for a video case on Todd McFarlane.

Age Stereotypes

Age stereotypes reinforce age discrimination because of their negative orientation. For example, long-standing age stereotypes depict older workers as less satisfied, not as involved with their work, less motivated, not as committed, less productive than their younger co-workers, and more apt to be absent from work. Older employees are also perceived as being more accident prone. As with sex-role stereotypes, these age stereotypes are based more on fiction than fact.[30]

OB researcher Susan Rhodes sought to determine whether age stereotypes were supported by data from 185 different studies. She discovered that as age increases so does employees' job satisfaction, job involvement, internal work motivation, and organizational commitment. Moreover, older workers were not more accident prone.[31] With respect to performance, a meta-analysis involving over 52,000 people showed that age was unrelated to task performance, creativity, and performance in training workshops.[32] Some OB researchers, however, believe that this finding does not reflect the true relationship between age and performance. For example, one study of 24,210 people demonstrated that age and experience predicted performance better for complex jobs than other types of jobs.[33] Another study of 1,000 doctors, ages 25 to 92, and 600 other adults revealed "that a large proportion of older individuals scored as well or better on aptitude tests as those in the prime of life."[34]

What about turnover and absenteeism? One meta-analysis showed that age and turnover were negatively related.[35] That is, older employees quit less often than did younger employees. Similarly, a second meta-analysis indicated that age was inversely related to both voluntary (a day at the beach) and involuntary (sick day) absenteeism.[36] Results from these two meta-analyses suggest managers should focus more attention on the turnover and absenteeism among younger workers than among older workers.

Racial and Ethnic Stereotypes

Many different racial and ethnic stereotypes exist. For instance, African Americans have been viewed as athletic, aggressive, and angry; Asians, as quiet, introverted, smarter, and more quantitatively oriented; Hispanics, as family oriented and religious; and Arabs, as angry. Racial and ethnic stereotypes are particularly problematic because they are automatically triggered and lead to what researchers call *micro aggressions*. **Micro aggressions** represent "biased thoughts, attitudes, and feelings" that exist at an unconscious level.[37] Unfortunately, they can affect our behavior and negatively affect people of color. Consider the following scenario:

Example. Two colleagues—one Asian American, the other African American—board a small plane. A flight attendant tells them they can sit anywhere, so they choose seats near the front of the plane and across the aisle from each other so they can talk. At the last minute, three white men enter the plane and take the seats in front of them. Just before takeoff, the flight attendant, who is white, asks the two colleagues if they would mind moving to the back of the plane to better balance the plane's load. Both react with anger, sharing the same sense that they are being singled out to symbolically "sit at the back of the bus." When they express these feelings to the attendant, she indignantly denies the charge, saying she was merely trying to ensure the flight's safety and give the two some privacy.[38]

What do you think, was the flight attendant exhibiting a micro aggression or were the colleagues being too sensitive?

Negative racial and ethnic stereotypes are still apparent in many aspects of life and in many organizations.[39] Consider the experience of Eldrick (Tiger) Woods. Tiger was raised in two different cultures. His mother was from Thailand and his father was African American. Since becoming a professional golfer in 1996, Tiger has won 95 tournaments and has more career victories than any other active player on the PGA Tour. He also has the lowest career scoring average and greatest amount of career earnings than any other golfer in the history of the game. He also is the only golfer in history to hold the title for all four major tournaments at the same time.[40] Unfortunately, Tiger has experienced a host of racial stereotypes and biases (see Real World/Real People on page 192). Let us now consider the following evidence regarding racial and ethnic stereotypes in organizations.

A meta-analysis of interview decisions involving samples of 4,169 African Americans and 6,307 whites revealed that whites received higher interviewer evaluations. Another study of 2,805 interviews uncovered a same-race bias for

sex-role stereotype Beliefs about appropriate roles for men and women.

micro aggressions Biased thoughts, attitudes, and feelings that exist at an unconscious level.

real WORLD // real PEOPLE

Tiger Woods's Experiences with Racial Bias

"I became aware of my racial identity on my first day of school, on my first day of kindergarten. A group of sixth graders tied me to a tree, spray-painted the word 'nigger' on me, and threw rocks at me. That was my first day at school. And the teacher really didn't do much of anything. I used to live across the street from school and kind of down the way a little bit. The teacher said, 'Okay, just go home.' So I had to outrun all these kids going home, which I was able to do. It was certainly an eye-opening experience, you know, being five years old. We were the only minority family in all of Cypress, California.

"When my parents moved in, before I was born, they used to have these oranges come through the window all the time. And it could have not been racially initiated or it could have been. We don't know. But it was very interesting, though people don't necessarily know it, that I grew up in the 1980s and still had incidents. I had a racial incident even in the 1990s at my home course where I grew up, the Navy golf course. And right before the 1994 US Amateur, I was 18 years old, I was out practicing, just hitting pitch shots and some guy just yelled over the fence and used the N word numerous times at me. That's in 1994."

Despite his international acclaim and reputation, Tiger Woods battled racial stereotypes into the mid-1990s. What can be done to stop the spread of racism and racial stereotypes?

SOURCE: C Barkley, *Who's Afraid of a Large Black Man?* (New York: Penguin Press, 2005), p 7.

Hispanics and African Americans but not for whites. That is, Hispanics and African American interviewers evaluated applicants of their own race more favorably than applicants of other races. White interviewers did not exhibit any such bias.[41]

Performance ratings were found to be unbiased in two studies that used large samples of 21,547 and 39,537 rater–ratee pairs of African American and white employees, respectively, from throughout the United States. These findings revealed that African American and white managers did not differentially evaluate their employees based on race.[42]

Given the increasing number of people of color who will enter the workforce over the next 10 years (recall our discussion in Chapter 2), employers should focus on nurturing and developing women and people of color as well as increasing managers' sensitivities to invalid racial stereotypes and what is called *stereotype threat*. **Stereotype threat** "refers to the 'predicament' in which members of a social group (e.g., African Americans, women) 'must deal with the possibility of being judged or treated stereotypically, or of doing something that would confirm the stereotype.'"[43] Research has documented that stereotype threat was associated with lower performance on evaluative tasks for women and nonwhites. For example, African Americans and women performed worse on academic tests when something primed them to think about race or gender. The drop in performance was higher when people experienced a race/ethnicity-based stereotype.[44] These results suggest that it is important for teachers and managers to avoid activating any race/ethnicity or gender stereotypes (e.g., asking people about their race or gender) when people are taking evaluative tests such as an academic test, an employment test, or a graduate school admissions test.

Disability Stereotypes

People with disabilities not only face negative stereotypes that affect their employability, but they also can be stigmatized by the general population. These trends create a host of problems for people with disabilities. For example, people with disabilities are more likely to be unemployed—the unemployment rate in December 2010 was 15.6% for people with disabilities and 9.4% for those without disabilities—and to make less money than those without disabilities.[45] People with disabilities also were found to be two-and-a half times as likely to live in poverty as people without disabilities.[46] The problem is even more pronounced for people with serious mental illness. The Americans with Disabilities Act (ADA) was created in 1990 in response to these statistics. This act prohibits discrimination against qualified employees with physical or mental disabilities or chronic illness and requires "reasonable accommodation" of employees with disabilities.[47]

Managerial Challenges and Recommendations

The key managerial challenge is to reduce the extent to which stereotypes influence decision making and interpersonal processes throughout the organization.

We recommend that an organization first needs to inform its workforce about the problem of stereotyping through employee education and training. Training also can be used to equip managers with the skills needed to handle situations associated with managing employees with disabilities. The next step entails engaging in a broad effort to reduce stereotypes throughout the organization. Social scientists believe that "quality" interpersonal contact among mixed groups is the best way to reduce stereotypes because it provides people with more accurate data about the characteristics of other groups of people. As such, organizations should create opportunities for diverse employees to meet and work together in cooperative groups of equal status.

Another recommendation is for managers to identify valid individual differences (discussed in Chapter 5) that differentiate between successful and unsuccessful performers. As previously discussed, for instance, research reveals experience is a better predictor of performance than age. Research also shows that managers can be trained to use these valid criteria when hiring applicants and evaluating employee performance.[48]

Removing promotional barriers for men and women, people of color, and persons with disabilities is another viable solution to alleviating the stereotyping problem. Home Depot's participation in the "Ken's Kids" program is a good example of how companies can assist people with disabilities to obtain meaningful work. The Ken's Kids program helps disabled individuals find work by providing vocational training and job placement services (see Real World/Real People on page 194). Home Depot personnel believe that the program is a success.[49]

In conclusion, it is important to obtain top management's commitment and support to eliminate the organizational practices that support or reinforce stereotyping and discriminatory decisions. Research clearly demonstrates that top management support is essential to successful implementation of the types of organizational changes being recommended.

stereotype threat The predicament in which members of a social group (e.g., African Americans, women) must deal with the possibility of being judged or treated stereotypically, or of doing something that would confirm the stereotype.

real WORLD // real PEOPLE

Home Depot Participates in the Ken's Kids Program in Attempt to Hire People with Disabilities

Ken's Kids carefully assess potential trainees using a five-step selection process—application, interview, observation, store assessment, and parent interview—explains Deborah Callaghan, the Pennsylvania state coordinator. She oversees 45 Home Depot associates with disabilities....

Coaches "work side by side with trainees for three months in stores, reviewing tasks and things like product knowledge," explains Callaghan.... "Store managers receive sensitivity training as well."

Home Depot's district manager Debbie Kiedeisch commented on key aspects of the program's success. "You must have the support and buy-in from store management and store associates." Ken's Kids works to build that support by meeting with managers. The Home Depot's district managers conduct orientation and training so store managers can uphold company policies and explain procedures to new associates. Another reason the program is viable, she adds, is the level of support workers get from their coaches along the way.

Why wouldn't all companies endorse a program like Ken's Kids?

SOURCE: Excerpted from D M Owens, "Hiring Employees with Autism," *HR Magazine,* June 2010, pp 84–90.

Maurice Baynard is a participant in the Ken's Kids program.

TO THE POINT

What is the self-fulfilling prophecy, and how can managers use it to bolster individual and organizational productivity?

LO.5 Self-Fulfilling Prophecy: The Pygmalion Effect

Historical roots of the self-fulfilling prophecy are found in Greek mythology. According to mythology, Pygmalion was a sculptor who hated women yet fell in love with an ivory statue he carved of a beautiful woman. He became so infatuated with the statue that he prayed to the goddess Aphrodite to bring her to life. The goddess heard his prayer, granted his wish, and Pygmalion's statue came to life. The essence of the **self-fulfilling prophecy,** or Pygmalion effect, is that someone's high expectations for another person result in high performance for that person. A related self-fulfilling prophecy effect is referred to as the Galatea effect. The **Galatea effect** occurs when an individual's high self-expectations for him- or herself lead to high performance. The key process underlying both the Pygmalion and Galatea effects is the idea that people's expectations or beliefs determine their behavior and performance, thus serving to make their expectations come true. In other words, we strive to validate our perceptions of reality, no matter how faulty they may be. Thus, the self-fulfilling prophecy is an important perceptual outcome we need to better understand.

Research and an Explanatory Model

The self-fulfilling prophecy was first demonstrated in an academic environment. After giving a bogus test of academic potential to students from grades 1 to 6, researchers informed teachers that certain students had high potential for achievement. In reality, students were randomly assigned to the "high potential" and "control" (normal potential) groups. Results showed that children designated as having high potential obtained significantly greater increases in both IQ scores and reading ability than did the control students.[50] The teachers of the supposedly high potential group got better results because their high expectations caused them to give harder assignments, more feedback, and more recognition of achievement. Students in the normal potential group did not excel because their teachers did not expect outstanding results.

Research similarly has shown that by raising instructors' and managers' expectations for individuals performing a wide variety of tasks, higher levels of achievement/productivity can be obtained. Results from a meta-analysis involving 2,874 people working in a variety of industries and occupations demonstrated the Pygmalion effect was quite strong.[51] This finding implies that higher levels of achievement and productivity can be obtained by raising managers' performance expectations of their employees. Further, the performance-enhancing Pygmalion effect was stronger in the military, with men, and for people possessing low performance expectations. Extending these results, a recent study confirmed that female leaders can produce the Pygmalion effect on male subordinates.[52] This is an important finding in light of the increasing number of women in managerial roles (recall our discussion in Chapter 2).

Figure 7–2 presents a model that integrates the self-fulfilling prophecy, the Galatea effect, and self-efficacy, which was discussed in Chapter 5. The model shows that the self-fulfilling process begins with a manager's expectations for his or her direct reports. In turn, these expectations influence the type of leadership used by a leader (linkage 1). Positive expectations beget positive and supportive leadership, which subsequently leads employees to develop higher self-expectations

figure 7–2   A Model of the Self-Fulfilling Prophecy

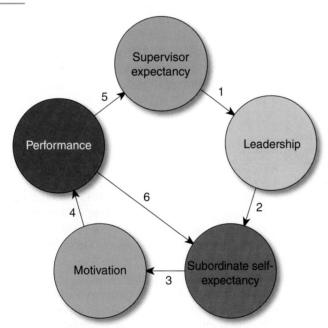

SOURCE: From D Eden, "Self-Fulfilling Prophecy as a Management Tool: Harnessing Pygmalion," *Academy of Management Review,* January 1984, p 67. Copyright © 1984 by The Academy of Management. Reproduced by permission of The Academy of Management via Copyright Clearance Center.

self-fulfilling prophecy Someone's high expectations for another person result in high performance.

Galatea effect An individual's high self-expectations lead to high performance.

THIS ISN'T ONE OF THOSE DUMPS I'VE HEARD ABOUT WHERE THE COOK SPITS ON THE FOOD OF OBNOXIOUS CUSTOMERS, IS IT?

BERT'S SELF-FULFILLING PROPHECY...

Oprah Winfrey is a great example of the Galatea effect. Born in Kosciusko, Mississippi, where she lived on a farm and was raised by her grandmother, she has evolved into one of the 100 most influential people of the 20th century as determined by *Time* magazine.

(linkage 2). The positive Galatea effect created by these higher expectations then motivates employees to exert more effort (linkage 3), ultimately increasing performance (linkage 4) and supervisory expectations (linkage 5). Successful performance also improves an employee's self-efficacy, which then fuels additional self-expectations of success (linkage 6). Research provides support for this model.[53] Researchers coined the term *Golem effect* to represent the negative side of the performance-enhancing process depicted in Figure 7–2. The **Golem effect** is a loss in performance resulting from low leader expectations.[54] Let us consider how it works.

Assume that an employee makes a mistake such as losing notes during a meeting or exhibits poor performance on a task—turning in a report a day late. A manager then begins to wonder if this person has what it takes to be successful in the organization. This doubt leads the manager to watch this person more carefully. The employee, of course, notices this doubt and begins to sense a loss of trust. The suspect employee then responds in one of two ways. He or she may doubt his or her own judgment and competence. This in turn leads the individual to become more risk averse and to decrease the amount of ideas and suggestions for the manager's critical review. The manager notices this behavior and interprets it as an example of less initiative. Oppositely, the employee may take on more and more responsibility so that he or she can demonstrate his or her competence and worth. This is likely to cause the employee to screw up on something, which in turn reinforces the manager's suspicions. You can see that this process results in a destructive relationship that is fueled by negative expectations. The point to remember is that the self-fulfilling prophecy works in both directions. The next section discusses ideas for enhancing the Pygmalion effect and reducing the Golem effect.

LO.6 Putting the Self-Fulfilling Prophecy to Work

Largely owing to the Pygmalion effect, managerial expectations powerfully influence employee behavior and performance. Consequently, managers need to harness the Pygmalion effect by building a hierarchical framework that reinforces positive performance expectations throughout the organization.

Employees' self-expectations are the foundation of this framework. In turn, positive self-expectations improve interpersonal expectations by encouraging people to work toward common goals. This cooperation enhances group-level productivity and promotes positive performance expectations within the work group. At Google, for example, employees routinely work long hours, especially when work groups are trying to meet deadlines for the launch of new products. Because Google is known for creating innovative products in a timely fashion, positive group-level expectations help create and reinforce an organizational culture of high expectancy for success. This process then excites people about working for the organization, thereby reducing turnover.[55]

Because positive self-expectations are the foundation for creating an organizationwide Pygmalion effect, let us consider how managers can create positive performance expectations. This task may be accomplished by using various combinations of the following:

1. Recognize that everyone has the potential to increase his or her performance.
2. Set high performance goals.
3. Positively reinforce employees for a job well done.
4. Provide frequent feedback that conveys a belief in employees' ability to complete their tasks.
5. Give employees the opportunity to experience increasingly challenging tasks and projects.
6. Communicate by using facial expressions, voice intonations, body language, and encouraging comments that reflect high expectations.
7. Provide employees with the input, information, and resources they need to achieve their goals.
8. Introduce new employees as if they have outstanding potential.
9. Encourage employees to stay focused on the present moment and not to worry about negative past events.
10. Help employees master key skills and tasks.[56]

Causal Attributions

Attribution theory is based on the premise that people attempt to infer causes for observed behavior. Rightly or wrongly, we constantly formulate cause-and-effect explanations for our own and others' behavior. Attributional statements such as the following are common: "Joe drinks too much because he has no willpower; but I need a couple of drinks after work because I'm under a lot of pressure." Formally defined, **causal attributions** are suspected or inferred causes of behavior. Even though our causal attributions tend to be self-serving and are often invalid, it is important to understand how people formulate attributions because they profoundly affect organizational behavior. For example, a supervisor who attributes an employee's poor performance to a lack of effort might reprimand that individual. However, training might be deemed necessary if the supervisor attributes the poor performance to a lack of ability.

Back to the Chapter-Opening Case

What attribution would you make about a sporting team that loses most games and then apologizes in an ad?

Generally speaking, people formulate causal attributions by considering the events preceding an observed behavior. This section explores Harold Kelley's model of attribution, two important attributional tendencies, and related managerial implications.

Connect™ Go to www.mcgrawhillconnect.com for an interactive exercise to test your knowledge of causal attributions.

Golem effect Loss in performance due to low leader expectations.

causal attributions Suspected or inferred causes of behavior.

....

TO THE POINT

How does Kelley's
model of attribution, the
fundamental attribution
bias, and the self-
serving bias explain
how managers tend
to manage both good
and poor-performing
employees?

....

LO.7 Kelley's Model of Attribution

Current models of attribution, such as Kelley's, are based on the pioneering work of the late Fritz Heider. Heider, the founder of attribution theory, proposed that behavior can be attributed either to **internal factors** within a person (such as ability and effort) or to **external factors** within the environment (such as task difficulty, help from others, and good/bad luck). This line of thought parallels the idea of an internal versus external locus of control, as discussed in Chapter 5. Building on Heider's work, Kelley attempted to pinpoint major antecedents of internal and external attributions. Kelley hypothesized that people make causal attributions after gathering information about three dimensions of behavior: consensus, distinctiveness, and consistency.[57] These dimensions vary independently, thus forming various combinations and leading to differing attributions.

Figure 7–3 presents performance charts showing low versus high consensus, distinctiveness, and consistency. These charts are now used to help develop a working knowledge of all three dimensions in Kelley's model.

1. *Consensus* involves a comparison of an individual's behavior with that of his or her peers. There is high consensus when one acts like the rest of the group and low consensus when one acts differently. As shown in Figure 7–3, high consensus is indicated when persons A, B, C, D, and E obtain similar levels of individual performance. In contrast, person C's performance is low in consensus because it significantly varies from the performance of persons A, B, D, and E.

2. *Distinctiveness* is determined by comparing a person's behavior on one task with his or her behavior on other tasks. High distinctiveness means the individual has performed the task in question in a significantly different manner than he or she has performed other tasks. Low distinctiveness means stable performance or quality from one task to another. Figure 7–3 reveals that the employee's performance on task 4 is highly distinctive because it significantly varies from his or her performance on tasks 1, 2, 3, and 5.

3. *Consistency* is determined by judging if the individual's performance on a given task is consistent over time. High consistency implies that a person performs a certain task the same, time after time. Unstable performance of a given task over time would mean low consistency. The downward spike in performance depicted in the consistency graph of Figure 7–3 represents low consistency. In this case, the employee's performance on a given task varied over time.

figure 7–3 Performance Charts Showing Low and High Consensus, Distinctiveness, and Consistency Information

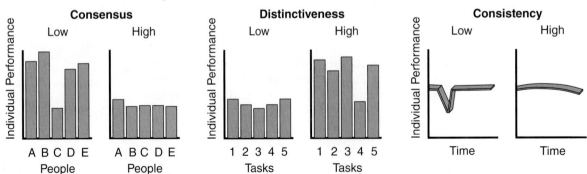

It is important to remember that consensus relates to other *people,* distinctiveness relates to other *tasks,* and consistency relates to *time.* The question now is: How does information about these three dimensions of behavior lead to internal or external attributions?

Kelley hypothesized that people attribute behavior to *external* causes (environmental factors) when they perceive high consensus, high distinctiveness, and low consistency. *Internal* attributions (personal factors) tend to be made when observed behavior is characterized by low consensus, low distinctiveness, and high consistency. So, for example, when all employees are performing poorly (high consensus), when the poor performance occurs on only one of several tasks (high distinctiveness), and the poor performance occurs during only one time period (low consistency), a supervisor will probably attribute an employee's poor performance to an external source such as peer pressure or an overly difficult task. In contrast, performance will be attributed to an employee's personal characteristics (an internal attribution) when only the individual in question is performing poorly (low consensus), when the inferior performance is found across several tasks (low distinctiveness), and when the low performance has persisted over time (high consistency). Many studies have supported this predicted pattern of attributions in a work setting.[58] The attribution process also has been extended by marketing researchers to examine consumers' attributions about customer service, product characteristics, and advertising and by OB researchers to study employees' response to workplace aggression and sexual harassment.[59]

LO.8 Attributional Tendencies

Researchers have uncovered two attributional tendencies that distort one's interpretation of observed behavior—*fundamental attribution bias* and *self-serving bias.*

Fundamental Attribution Bias   The **fundamental attribution bias** reflects one's tendency to attribute another person's behavior to his or her personal characteristics, as opposed to situational factors. This bias causes perceivers to ignore important environmental forces that often significantly affect behavior. For example, a woman was fired from her job on the night shift at a poultry plant for falling asleep. Although management may have thought that she was lazy, it turns out "that she paid for child care during the night while she was working, but she didn't earn enough to pay someone to watch her baby during the day. So, she would come home from the night shift and be greeted with a wide-awake kid."[60] A more likely attribution is that she fell asleep because of issues in her personal life and low wages paid by the poultry firm. Interestingly, research also shows that people from Westernized cultures tend to exhibit the fundamental attribution bias more than individuals from East Asia.[61] A recent study of shareholders similarly showed that shareholders attributed the price of stocks more to CEO behavior and less to market fluctuations.[62]

Self-Serving Bias   The **self-serving bias** represents one's tendency to take more personal responsibility for success than for failure. The self-serving bias suggests employees will attribute their success to internal factors (high ability or hard work) and their failures to uncontrollable external factors (tough job, bad luck, unproductive co-workers, or an unsympathetic boss). This tendency plays out in all

McGraw Hill **connect** Go to www.mcgrawhillconnect.com for an interactive comprehension case exercise to help you learn more about causal attributions.

McGraw Hill **connect** Go to www.mcgrawhillconnect.com for a self-assessment to learn about using attribution theory to resolve performance problems.

internal factors Personal characteristics that cause behavior.

external factors Environmental characteristics that cause behavior.

fundamental attribution bias Ignoring environmental factors that affect behavior.

self-serving bias Taking more personal responsibility for success than failure.

Pat Murphy, former head coach of men's baseball at Arizona State University. His very successful career at the university came to end when the program violated NCAA rules. Do you think it's natural to use the self-serving bias when faced with allegations of exhibiting inappropriate behavior or violating a formal policy?

aspects of life. For example, Bob Poznanovich was a vice president for sales and marketing for Zenith, now LG Electronics, before he was fired for using drugs. He admits to spending $1,000 per day getting high with other employees and customers, and was also frequently coming in late to work and missing many days of work. Poznanovich blames the company for his continued use of drugs. He says he "would have run out and gotten help" if management had warned him about his bad behavior.[63]

Pat Murphy, former head baseball coach at Arizona State University (ASU), similarly blames management for his department's violation of NCAA rules regarding phone calls with prospective student athletes. He believes that management did not properly instruct his staff on how to complete telephone logs. Management, on the other hand, blames Murphy for not making record keeping of phone calls a priority and concluded that "Murphy gave every impression of promoting a program of compliance while at the same time, unbeknownst to ASU, he was not following all of ASU's policies himself and was providing inaccurate telephone logs and representations to ASU's compliance staff."[64] The NCAA banned the baseball program from any postseason play in 2011.[65]

Many researchers have investigated the self-serving bias. Two studies, for instance, examined whether or not senior executives fell prey to the self-serving bias when communicating with stockholders in their annual letter to shareholders. Results revealed executives in the United States and Singapore took the credit themselves when their companies did well but blamed negative outcomes on the environment.[66] Overall, however, research on the self-serving bias has produced inconsistent results. Two general patterns of attributions have been observed in past research. The first reveals that individuals make internal attributions for success as predicted by a self-serving bias. In contrast, people make both internal and external attributions for failure.[67] This means people do not automatically blame failure on external factors, as would originally be expected from a self-serving bias. A team of researchers concluded, "When highly self-focused people feel that failure can be rapidly remedied, they will attribute failure to self; when the likelihood of improvement seems low, however, failure will be attributed externally."[68]

Managerial Application and Implications

Attribution models can be used to explain how managers handle poorly performing employees. One study revealed that managers gave employees more immediate, frequent, and negative feedback when they attributed their performance to low effort. This reaction was even more pronounced when the manager's success was dependent on an employee's performance. A second study indicated that managers tended to transfer employees whose poor performance was attributed to a lack of ability. These same managers also decided to take no immediate action when poor performance was attributed to external factors beyond an individual's control.[69]

The preceding discussion has several important implications for managers. First, men and women have different attributions regarding the causes of being promoted. Results from a recent survey of 140,000 people from 80 countries revealed that men and women had different attributions about what it takes to be promoted to a senior-level position. Men concluded that promotions were based on hard work whereas women reported that promotions were based more on luck and connections. As discussed in Chapter 2, these results, which were consistent across countries, suggest that a woman's promotional track resembles more of a labyrinth than a straight upward path. Managers thus are encouraged to help women develop social capital and to promote people on the basis of job-related criteria that are accurately measured.[70]

Second, managers tend to disproportionately attribute behavior to *internal* causes.[71] This can result in inaccurate evaluations of performance, leading to reduced employee motivation. No one likes to be blamed because of factors they perceive to be beyond their control. Further, because managers' responses to employee performance vary according to their attributions, attributional biases may lead to inappropriate managerial actions, including promotions, transfers, layoffs, and so forth. This can dampen motivation and performance. Attributional training sessions for managers are in order. Basic attributional processes can be explained, and managers can be taught to detect and avoid attributional biases. Finally, an employee's attributions for his or her own performance have dramatic effects on subsequent motivation, performance, and personal attitudes such as self-esteem. For instance, people tend to give up, develop lower expectations for future success, and experience decreased self-esteem when they attribute failure to a lack of ability. Fortunately, attributional retraining can improve both motivation and performance. Research shows that employees can be taught to attribute their failures to a lack of effort rather than to a lack of ability.[72] This attributional realignment paves the way for improved motivation and performance. It also is important to remember the implications of the self-serving bias. If managers want employees to accept personal responsibility for failure and correspondingly modify their effort and behavior, it is essential for employees to believe that they can improve upon their performance in the future. Otherwise, employees are likely to attribute failure to external causes and they will not change their behavior.

Summary of Key Concepts

1. *Describe perception in terms of the information processing model.* Perception is a mental and cognitive process that enables us to interpret and understand our surroundings. Social perception, also known as social cognition and social information processing, is a four-stage process. The four stages are selective attention/comprehension, encoding and simplification, storage and retention, and retrieval and response. During social cognition, salient stimuli are matched with schemata, assigned to cognitive categories, and stored in long-term memory for events, semantic materials, or people.

2. *Summarize the key managerial implications of social perception.* Social perception affects hiring decisions, performance appraisals, leadership perceptions, communication and interpersonal influence, counterproductive work behaviors, physical and psychological well-being, and the design of Web pages. Inaccurate schemata or racist and sexist schemata may be used to evaluate job applicants. Similarly, faulty schemata about what constitutes good versus poor performance can lead to inaccurate performance appraisals. Invalid schemata need to be identified and replaced with appropriate schemata through coaching and training. Further, managers are advised to use objective rather than subjective measures of performance. With respect to leadership, a leader will have a difficult time influencing employees when he or she exhibits behaviors contained in employees' schemata of poor leaders. Because people interpret oral and written communications by using schemata developed through past experiences, an individual's ability to influence others is affected by information contained in others' schemata regarding age, gender, ethnicity, appearance, speech, mannerisms, personality, and other personal characteristics. It is very important to treat employees fairly, as perceptions of unfairness are associated with counterproductive work behaviors. Try to let negative thoughts roll off yourself like water off a duck to avoid the physical and psychological effects of negative thoughts.

3. *Discuss the process of stereotype formation.* Stereotyping is a four-step process that begins by categorizing people into groups according to various criteria. Next, we infer that all people within a particular group possess the same traits or characteristics. Then, we form expectations of others and interpret their behavior according to our stereotypes. Finally, stereotypes are maintained by (*a*) overestimating the frequency of stereotypic behaviors exhibited by others, (*b*) incorrectly explaining expected and unexpected behaviors, and (*c*) differentiating minority individuals from oneself. The use of stereotypes is influenced by the amount and type of information available to an individual and his or her motivation to accurately process information.

4. *Summarize the managerial challenges and recommendations of sex-role, age, racial, ethnic, and disability stereotypes.* The key managerial challenge is to reduce the extent to which stereotypes influence decision making and interpersonal processes throughout the organization. Training can be used to educate employees about the problem of stereotyping and to equip managers with the skills needed to handle situations associated with managing employees with disabilities. Because mixed-group contact reduces stereotyping, organizations should create opportunities for diverse employees to meet and work together in cooperative groups of equal status. Hiring decisions should be based on valid individual differences, and managers can be trained to use valid criteria when evaluating employee

performance. Minimizing differences in job opportunities and experiences across groups of people can help alleviate promotional barriers. It is critical to obtain top management's commitment and support to eliminate stereotyping and discriminatory decisions.

5. *Describe and contrast the Pygmalion effect, the Galatea effect, and the Golem effect.* The Pygmalion effect, also known as the self-fulfilling prophecy, describes how someone's high expectations for another person result in high performance for that person. The Galatea effect occurs when an individual's high self-expectations lead to high self-performance. The Golem effect is a loss of performance resulting from low leader expectations.

6. *Discuss how the model of the self-fulfilling prophecy is expected to work.* According to the self-fulfilling prophecy, high managerial expectations foster high employee

self-expectations. These expectations in turn lead to greater effort and better performance and yet higher expectations.

7. *Explain, according to Kelley's model, how external and internal causal attributions are formulated.* Attribution theory attempts to describe how people infer causes for observed behavior. According to Kelley's model of causal attribution, external attributions tend to be made when consensus and distinctiveness are high and consistency is low. Internal (personal responsibility) attributions tend to be made when consensus and distinctiveness are low and consistency is high.

8. *Contrast the fundamental attribution bias and the self-serving bias.* Fundamental attribution bias involves emphasizing personal factors more than situational factors while formulating causal attributions for the behavior of others. Self-serving bias involves personalizing the causes of one's successes and externalizing the causes of one's failures.

Key Terms

Perception, 180

Attention, 182

Cognitive categories, 182

Schema, 182

Script, 183

Implicit cognition, 186

Stereotype, 188

Sex-role stereotype, 190

Micro aggressions, 191

Stereotype threat, 192

Self-fulfilling prophecy, 194

Galatea effect, 194

Golem effect, 196

Causal attributions, 197

Internal factors, 198

External factors, 198

Fundamental attribution bias, 199

Self-serving bias, 199

OB in Action Case Study

Job Offers Are Won and Lost Based on Interviewers' Perceptions of Responses to the Question "What Are Your Weaknesses"[73]

Worldwide Panel LLC, a small market-research firm, is getting flooded with résumés for four vacancies in sales and information technology.

However, officials expect to reject numerous applicants after asking them: "What is your greatest weakness?" Candidates often respond "with something that is not a weakness," says Christopher Morrow, senior vice president of the Calabasas, California, concern. "It is a deal breaker."

The weakness question represents the most common and most stressful one posed during interviews. Yet in today's weak job market, the wrong answer weakens your chances of winning employment.

Some people offer replies that they mistakenly assume the bosses love, such as "I am a perfectionist." That response "will be used against you" because you appear incapable of delegating, warns Joshua Ehrlich, dean of a master's program in executive coaching sponsored by BeamPines, a New York coaching firm, and Middlesex University in London.

A careful game plan could help you with the shortcoming query in a way that highlights your fit for a desired position. Job seekers who field the question well demonstrate that they can "take initiative and improve themselves," Mr Morrow says...

It's equally important that you consider an employer's corporate culture. While being interviewed by a start-up, "you could say, 'My weakness is I get bored by routine,'" says Ben Dattner, a New York industrial psychologist.

Last month, an aspiring executive director of a nonprofit group in suburban San Francisco nearly jeopardized his selection because his reply to a variation of the weakness question ignored one of its core values, according to Ms Klaus, a board member there. Near the end of his interview, she wondered whether he might have problems with any aspects of the job. "No, I am confident I could do it all," the prospect declared. His flip comment dismayed Ms Klaus, because she felt he lacked awareness of his weakness. She says his response raises doubts among board members that "he would be able to take critical feedback," an attribute the organization values highly.

Because the man was well qualified, the board gave him a second interview—and demanded a fuller explanation of his weak spots. He said he had been "unprepared for that question and nervous about coming out with a big fatal flaw," then described his tendency to make decisions too fast during workplace crises. Board members' doubts disappeared, and they picked him for the nonprofit's top job.

Ideally, your reply also should exclude the word "weakness" and cover your corrective steps. Dubbing your greatest fault a "window of opportunity" signals your improvement efforts should benefit the workplace, says Oscar Adler, a retired Maidenform Brands sales executive and author of the book *Sell Yourself in Any Interview.* For instance, he suggests, a salesman might note that he sold more after strengthening his facility with numbers.

When an interviewer pops this nerve-wracking query, your body language counts as well. The wrong nonverbal cues undercut your credibility. Certain candidates hunch over, glance furtively around the room or wring their sweaty palms. "They sort of look like they're being asked a question they can't handle," says Mr Adler.

Maintaining eye contact, regular breathing, and a broad smile impress employers that "you're prepared for the weakness question," says psychotherapist Pat Pearson, author of *Stop Self-Sabotage!*

For the same reason, you seem thoughtful if you pause before responding. But don't wait too long. "If you're going to take a minute," Mr Morrow cautions, "I've just identified your weakness."

Questions for Discussion

1. Which of the perceptual errors listed in Table 7–2 are affecting recruiters' perceptions in this case? Discuss.
2. What negative stereotypes are fueling recruiters' perceptions?
3. To what extent do the Pygmalion effect, the Galatea effect, and the Golem effect play a role in this case? Explain.
4. What lessons about perception did you learn from this case? Explain.
5. How would you answer the "weakness" question? Explain how it might be perceived by recruiters.

Legal/Ethical Challenge

Is It Okay to Walk Away from a Mortgage When You Can Afford to Pay?[74]

The dilemma deals with a situation facing many homeowners and focuses on the case of Chris Hanson. Hanson runs a real-estate investment firm, and he purchased a luxury condominium in Arizona for $875,000. He had no problem paying the down payment of $90,000 or making the monthly payments of $5,000. That said, he decided to miss his first monthly payment and to walk away from the property because the condominium is now worth about 50 percent of what he initially paid. He believes that it will take 10 years for the property to recover its value.

> He plans to let the lender foreclose on the home and rent an even nicer unit in either the same complex or one nearby, which he figures will cost less than half of his monthly mortgage payment.
>
> Mr Hanson's case illustrates the growing risk that borrowers in hard-hit housing markets will 'strategically' default, even when they can afford to stay in the homes...
>
> Mr Hanson said that he felt little moral obligation to make his payments because he felt banks' shoddy lending practices were primarily responsible for fueling the housing boom and bust.

Should we allow people to walk away from mortgages when they have enough income to pay?

1. Absolutely not! Chris Hanson signed a contract and he should uphold his end of the deal. After all, he still makes enough money to pay the bill.
2. Yes. Why should someone continue to pay a mortgage when a home is worth substantially less than the original purchase price? The banks should refinance the original loan based on the current value of the property.
3. No. Chris Hanson obviously understands the housing market and he simply is avoiding his responsibility and shirking the debt to financial institutions. Financial institutions will ultimately try to recover these losses, which in turn will affect consumers at large.
4. Invent other options.

Web Resources

For study material and exercises that apply to this chapter, visit our website at **www.mhhe.com/kreitner10e**

chapter 8

Foundations of Motivation

 Learning Objectives

When you finish studying the material in this chapter, you should be able to:

LO.1   Contrast Maslow's, Alderfer's, and McClelland's need theories.

LO.2   Explain the practical significance of Herzberg's distinction between motivators and hygiene factors.

LO.3   Discuss the role of perceived inequity in employee motivation.

LO.4   Explain the differences among distributive, procedural, and interactional justice.

LO.5   Describe the practical lessons derived from equity theory.

LO.6   Explain Vroom's expectancy theory.

LO.7   Explain how goal setting motivates an individual.

LO.8   Review the five practical lessons from goal-setting research.

LO.9   Discuss the three conceptually different approaches to job design.

Should Teacher Pay Be Tied to Student Achievement?

Michelle Rhee, former chancellor of Washington, D.C. schools, attempted to implement components of several motivation theories in order to increase teacher performance. She was driven to create change because past practice revealed that 95% of the school system's teachers were evaluated as excellent and nobody was fired for poor performance. At the same time, student test scores were among the lowest in the nation. In 2010 she fired 241 teachers, which amounted to roughly 6% of all teachers in the system. Seven hundred thirty-seven additional teachers were told that they were minimally effective.

Rhee made these changes after creating a new teacher evaluation system and negotiating a new compensation agreement with the Washington Teachers Union (WTU). The evaluation system is noted to be one of the most rigorous in the United States.

> It requires numerous classroom observations of teacher performance and measures teachers against student achievement. . . . Teachers are evaluated five times a year by school administrators and master teachers on such things as creating coherent lesson plans and engaging students. After an initial observation, teachers receive a plan detailing weaknesses and are offered coaching for improvement. . . . Teachers are ranked into four categories. This year, 16% reached the highest ranking, compared with 45% in past years. Some 20% landed in the bottom rating, compared with 4% in years past.

The new compensation system stipulated that "good teachers would get more money (including 21.6% pay increase through 2012 and opportunities for merit pay). In exchange, bad teachers could be shown the door."

George Parker, president of the WTU, was unhappy about the firings and indicated that the union would appeal the dismissals. He also threatened to file an unfair labor charge against the school district.

Richard Whitmire, author of *The Bee Eater: Michelle Rhee Takes on the Nation's Worst School District,* acknowledged that Rhee needed to take a tough approach toward motivating teachers because "only about a third of D.C. teachers were capable of carrying out" high-quality instruction.[1]

As you will learn later in this chapter, expectancy theory is based on the principle that an individual's pay should be tied to his or her performance. The fundamental concept underlying this theory is that employee motivation is higher when people are rewarded with rewards they value, such as higher pay. Contrary to this theory, the chapter-opening vignette illustrates that the teachers union was fighting Michelle Rhee's attempt to use expectancy theory. Why? Because there are many factors that influence employee motivation that go beyond the receipt of rewards. This chapter aims to help you understand these factors.

You will learn that an employee's motivation is a function of several components, including an individual's needs, the extent to which a work environment is positive and supportive, perceptions of being treated fairly, creating a strong relationship between performance and the receipt of valued rewards, the use of accurate measures of performance, and the setting of specific goals.

The term *motivation* derives from the Latin word *movere*, meaning "to move." In the present context, **motivation** represents "those psychological processes that cause the arousal, direction, and persistence of voluntary actions that are goal directed."[2] Researchers have proposed two general categories of motivation theories to explain the psychological processes underlying employee motivation: content theories and process theories. **Content theories of motivation** focus on identifying internal factors such as instincts, needs, satisfaction, and job characteristics that energize employee motivation. These theories do not explain how motivation is influenced by the dynamic interaction between an individual and the environment in which he or she works. This limitation led to the creation of process theories of motivation. **Process theories of motivation** focus on explaining the process by which internal factors and cognitions influence employee motivation.[3] Process theories are more dynamic than content theories.

Table 8–1 provides an overview of the various content and process theories discussed in this chapter. As you study these seven theories, remember that they offer different recommendations about how to motivate employees because they are based on different sets of assumptions regarding the causes of motivation. We help you to integrate and apply these varying recommendations by summarizing the managerial implications for each theory before discussing an alternative perspective.

After discussing the major content and process theories of motivation, this chapter provides an overview of job design methods used to motivate employees and concludes by focusing on practical recommendations for putting motivational theories to work.

TO THE POINT

How would you contrast the content theories of motivation proposed by Maslow, Alderfer, McClelland, and Herzberg?

LO.1 Content Theories of Motivation

Most content theories of motivation revolve around the notion that an employee's needs influence motivation. **Needs** are physiological or psychological deficiencies that arouse behavior. They can be strong or weak and are influenced by environmental factors. Thus, human needs vary over time and place. The general idea behind need theories of motivation is that unmet needs motivate people to

table 8–1 Overview of Motivation Theories

CONTENT THEORIES	PROCESS THEORIES
Maslow's need hierarchy theory	Adam's equity theory
Alderfer's ERG theory	Vroom's expectancy theory
McClelland's need theory	Goal-setting theory
Herzberg's motivator–hygiene theory	

satisfy them. Conversely, people are not motivated to pursue a satisfied need. Let us now consider four popular content theories of motivation: Maslow's need hierarchy theory, Alderfer's ERG theory, McClelland's need theory, and Herzberg's motivator–hygiene model.

Maslow's Need Hierarchy Theory

In 1943, psychologist Abraham Maslow published his now-famous **need hierarchy theory** of motivation. Although the theory was based on his clinical observation of a few neurotic individuals, it has subsequently been used to explain the entire spectrum of human behavior. Maslow proposed that motivation is a function of five basic needs. These needs are

1. *Physiological.* Most basic need. Entails having enough food, air, and water to survive.
2. *Safety.* Consists of the need to be safe from physical and psychological harm.
3. *Love.* The desire to be loved and to love. Contains the needs for affection and belonging.
4. *Esteem.* Need for reputation, prestige, and recognition from others. Also contains need for self-confidence and strength.
5. *Self-actualization.* Desire for self-fulfillment—to become the best one is capable of becoming.

Maslow said these five needs are arranged in the prepotent hierarchy shown in Figure 8–1. In other words, he believed human needs generally emerge in a predictable stair-step fashion. Accordingly, when one's physiological needs are relatively satisfied, one's safety needs emerge, and so on up the need hierarchy, one step at a time. Once a need is satisfied, it activates the next higher need in the hierarchy. This process continues until the need for self-actualization is activated.[4]

Although research does not clearly support this theory of motivation, two key managerial implications of Maslow's theory are worth noting. First, it is

Mc Graw Hill connect™ Go to www.mcgrawhillconnect.com for an interactive exercise to test your knowledge of Maslow's hierarchy of needs.

figure 8–1   Maslow's Need Hierarchy

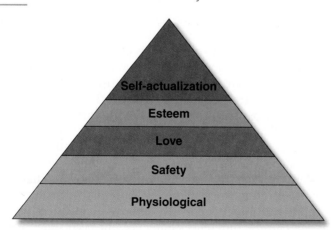

Self-actualization
Esteem
Love
Safety
Physiological

motivation Psychological processes that arouse and direct goal-directed behavior.

content theories of motivation Identify internal factors influencing motivation.

process theories of motivation Identify the process by which internal factors and cognitions influence motivation.

needs Physiological or psychological deficiencies that arouse behavior.

need hierarchy theory Five basic needs—physiological, safety, love, esteem, and self-actualization—influence behavior.

Michelle Rhee, former chancellor of Washington, D.C. public schools, has a career focused on self-actualization. She began her career teaching in an inner-city school for three years. She then founded and directed the New Teacher Project: an organization dedicated to training teachers to teach in urban schools. After working as chancellor of public schools in Washington for three years, she again founded an organization—StudentsFirst—that was devoted to educational reform.

important for managers to focus on satisfying employee needs related to self concepts—self-esteem and self-actualization—because their satisfaction is significantly associated with a host of important outcomes such as academic achievement, physical illness, psychological well-being (e.g., anxiety disorders, depression), criminal convictions, drug abuse, marital satisfaction, money and work problems, and performance at work.[5]

Second, a satisfied need may lose its motivational potential. Therefore, managers are advised to motivate employees by devising programs or practices aimed at satisfying emerging or unmet needs. Many companies have responded to this recommendation by offering employees targeted benefits that meet their specific needs. Consider Joie de Vivre, a hotel chain in California's Bay Area. Management uses Maslow's principles to verify that the company is building employee satisfaction and loyalty in a variety of ways. For example, Joie de Vivre managers provide recognition with formal processes to identify and comment on occasions when employees have provided exceptional service. They try to help housekeepers derive meaning from their jobs by bringing them together to talk about what the guests' experience would be like if the housekeepers weren't making their stay more comfortable.[6] Managers also can use customized surveys in order to assess the specific needs of their employees. In conclusion, managers are more likely to fuel employee motivation by offering benefits and rewards that meet individual needs.

Alderfer's ERG Theory

Clayton Alderfer developed an alternative theory of human needs in the late 1960s. Alderfer's theory differs from Maslow's in three major respects. First, a smaller set of core needs is used to explain behavior. From lowest to highest level they are *existence needs* (E)—the desire for physiological and materialistic well-being; *relatedness needs* (R)—the desire to have meaningful relationships with significant others; and *growth needs* (G)—the desire to grow as a human being and to use one's abilities to their fullest potential; hence, the label **ERG theory**. Second, ERG theory does not assume needs are related to each other in a stair-step hierarchy as does Maslow. Alderfer believes that more than one need may be activated at a time. Finally, ERG theory contains a frustration-regression component. That is, frustration of higher-order needs can influence the desire for lower-order needs.[7] For example, employees may demand higher pay or better benefits (existence needs) when they are frustrated or dissatisfied with the quality of their interpersonal relationships (relatedness needs) at work.

Research on ERG theory has provided mixed support for some of the theory's key propositions. That said, however, there are two key managerial implications associated with ERG. The first revolves around the frustration-regression aspect of the theory. Managers should keep in mind that employees may be motivated to pursue lower-level needs because they are frustrated with a higher-order need. For instance, the solution for a stifling work environment may be a request for higher pay or better benefits. Second, ERG theory is consistent with the finding that individual and cultural differences influence our need states. People are motivated by different needs at different times in their lives. This implies that managers should customize their reward and recognition programs to meet employees' varying needs. Consider how Marc Albin, CEO of Albin Engineering Services, handles this recommendation.

Example. To identify which parts of individual employees' egos need scratching, Albin takes an unconventional approach. "My experience in managing people is, they're all different," says Albin. "Some people want to be recognized for their cheerful attitude and their ability to spread their cheerful attitude. Some want to be recognized for the quality of their work, some for the quantity of their work. Some like to be recognized individually; others want to be recognized in groups." Consequently, at the end of each employee-orientation session Albin e-mails his new hires and asks them how and in what form they prefer their strokes. "It helps me understand what they think of themselves and their abilities, and I make a mental note to pay special attention to them when they're working in that particular arena," he says. "No one has ever said, 'Just recognize me for anything I do well.'"[8]

McClelland's Need Theory

David McClelland, a well-known psychologist, has been studying the relationship between needs and behavior since the late 1940s. Although he is most recognized for his research on the need for achievement, he also investigated the needs for affiliation and power. Let us consider each of these needs.

The Need for Achievement The **need for achievement** is defined by the following desires:

Example. To accomplish something difficult. To master, manipulate, or organize physical objects, human beings, or ideas. To do this as rapidly and as independently as possible. To overcome obstacles and attain a high standard. To excel one's self. To rival and surpass others. To increase self-regard by the successful exercise of talent.[9]

Achievement-motivated people share three common characteristics: (1) they prefer working on tasks of moderate difficulty; (2) they prefer situations in which performance is due to their efforts rather than to other factors, such as luck; and (3) they desire more feedback on their successes and failures than do low achievers. A review of research on the "entrepreneurial" personality showed that entrepreneurs were found to have a higher need for achievement than nonentrepreneurs.[10] James Dyson, inventor and manufacturer of the Dual Cyclone bagless vacuum cleaner is a good example. He went through 5,127 different prototypes of the vacuum's design before finding the model that would dominate the market. Dyson told an interviewer that the death of his father when he was nine was instrumental in his achievement orientation. "Not having a father, particularly at that time, was very unusual. I felt different. I was on my own. I can't quite explain it, but I think subconsciously I felt a need to prove myself."[11]

The Need for Affiliation People with a high **need for affiliation** prefer to spend more time maintaining social relationships, joining groups, and wanting to be loved. Individuals high in this need are not the most effective managers or leaders because they tend to avoid conflict, have a hard time making difficult decisions without worrying about being disliked, and avoid giving others negative feedback.[12]

ERG theory Three basic needs—existence, relatedness, and growth—influence behavior.

need for achievement Desire to accomplish something difficult.

need for affiliation Desire to spend time in social relationships and activities.

real WORLD // real PEOPLE

High Achievement Needs Can Lead to Negative Outcomes

"Ramalinga Raju founded Satyam Computers in 1987 and was its Chairman until January 7, 2009 when he resigned from the Satyam board after admitting to cheating six million shareholders. . . . In his letter of resignation, Raju described how an initial cover-up for a poor quarterly performance escalated: 'It was like riding a tiger, not knowing how to get off without being eaten.'". . . "Raju had also used dummy accounts to trade in Satyam's shares, violating the insider trading norm. It has not been alleged that these accounts may have been the means of siphoning off the missing funds. Raju has admitted to overstating the company's case reserves by USD $1.5 billion."

Raju was released on bail in August 2010, but was recently remanded back to prison.

Why would high achievement lead Ramalinga Raju to commit these crimes?

SOURCE: Excerpted from "Byrraju Ramalinga Raju," Wikipedia, last updated January 27, 2011, http:wikipedia.org.

The Need for Power   The **need for power** reflects an individual's desire to influence, coach, teach, or encourage others to achieve. People with a high need for power like to work and are concerned with discipline and self-respect. There are positive and negative sides to this need. The negative face of power is characterized by an "if I win, you lose" mentality. In contrast, people with a positive orientation to power focus on accomplishing group goals and helping employees obtain the feeling of competence. More is said about the two faces of power in Chapter 13. Because effective managers must positively influence others, McClelland proposes that top managers should have a high need for power coupled with a low need for affiliation.

Managerial Implications   Given that adults can be trained to increase their achievement motivation,[13] organizations should consider the benefits of providing achievement training for employees. Moreover, achievement, affiliation, and power needs can be considered during the selection process, for better placement. For example, a study revealed that individuals' need for achievement affected their preference to work in different companies. People with a high need for achievement were more attracted to companies that had a pay-for-performance environment than were those with a low achievement motivation.[14] Finally, it is important to balance the above recommendations with the downside of high achievement. McClelland noted that people with high achievement might be more prone to "cheat and cut corners and to leave people out of the loop." He also noted that some high achievers "are so fixated on finding a shortcut to the goal that they may not be too particular about the means they use to reach it."[15] Byrraju Ramalinga Raju, former founder and chairman of Satyam Computers, is a good example. Raju was known as a highly driven executive who had a grand vision for using technology to help develop rural India. He also was highly involved with several foundations in India. Unfortunately, Raju apparently took some illegal shortcuts to meet Satyam's short-term financial goals (see Real World/Real People above).[16]

Back to the Chapter-Opening Case

George Parker is trying to support the teachers in WTU by satisfying their needs. What needs is he focusing on by appealing the dismissals of teachers and threatening to file a lawsuit?

LO.2 Herzberg's Motivator–Hygiene Theory

Frederick Herzberg's theory is based on a landmark study in which he interviewed 203 accountants and engineers.[17] These interviews sought to determine the factors responsible for job satisfaction and dissatisfaction. Herzberg found separate and distinct clusters of factors associated with job satisfaction and dissatisfaction. Job satisfaction was more frequently associated with achievement, recognition, characteristics of the work, responsibility, and advancement. These factors were all related to outcomes associated with the *content* of the task being performed. Herzberg labeled these factors **motivators** because each was associated with strong effort and good performance. He hypothesized that motivators cause a person to move from a state of no satisfaction to satisfaction (see Figure 8–2). Therefore, Herzberg's theory predicts managers can motivate individuals by incorporating "motivators" into an individual's job.

Herzberg found job *dissatisfaction* to be associated primarily with factors in the work *context* or environment. Specifically, company policy and administration, technical supervision, salary, interpersonal relations with one's supervisor, and working conditions were most frequently mentioned by employees expressing job dissatisfaction. Herzberg labeled this second cluster of factors **hygiene factors**. He further proposed that they were not motivational. At best, Herzberg proposed that individuals will experience no job dissatisfaction when he or she has no grievances about hygiene factors (refer to Figure 8–2). Electronic Arts, an international developer, publisher, and distributor of video games, does not agree

figure 8–2   Herzberg's Motivator–Hygiene Model

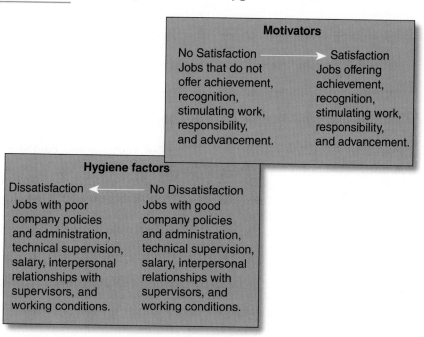

Motivators

No Satisfaction ⟶ Satisfaction
Jobs that do not offer achievement, recognition, stimulating work, responsibility, and advancement.
Jobs offering achievement, recognition, stimulating work, responsibility, and advancement.

Hygiene factors

Dissatisfaction ⟵ No Dissatisfaction
Jobs with poor company policies and administration, technical supervision, salary, interpersonal relationships with supervisors, and working conditions.
Jobs with good company policies and administration, technical supervision, salary, interpersonal relationships with supervisors, and working conditions.

SOURCE: Adapted in part from D A Whitsett and E K Winslow, "An Analysis of Studies Critical of the Motivator–Hygiene Theory," *Personnel Psychology,* Winter 1967, pp 391–415.

need for power Desire to influence, coach, teach, or encourage others to achieve.

motivators Job characteristics associated with job satisfaction.

hygiene factors Job characteristics associated with job dissatisfaction.

This exercise facility at Electronic Arts is a motivational factor for employees. The company, with over 8,000 employees worldwide, is the number one publisher of video games in Western markets.

with this aspect of Herzberg's theory. Management is attempting to increase employees' job satisfaction and reduce turnover by creating positive hygiene factors. These initiatives include the following: (1) allowing employees to bring pets to work; (2) creating workday intramural sporting events like basketball, soccer, and beach volleyball; (3) creating arcades where employees can play ping-pong, pool, and video games; (4) establishing an information resource center in which employees can borrow the latest video games, movies, books, and magazines for free; and (5) providing a gym with group fitness classes.[18]

The key to adequately understanding Herzberg's motivator–hygiene theory is recognizing that he believes that satisfaction is not the opposite of dissatisfaction. Herzberg concludes that "the opposite of job satisfaction is not job dissatisfaction, but rather no job satisfaction; and similarly, the opposite of job dissatisfaction is not job satisfaction, but no dissatisfaction."[19] Herzberg thus asserts that the dissatisfaction–satisfaction continuum contains a zero midpoint at which dissatisfaction and satisfaction are absent. Conceivably, an organization member who has good supervision, pay, and working conditions but a tedious and unchallenging task with little chance of advancement would be at the zero midpoint. That person would have no dissatisfaction (because of good hygiene factors) and no satisfaction (because of a lack of motivators).

Back to the Chapter-Opening Case

1. How do Michelle Rhee's changes in the Washington, D.C. school system affect Herzberg's hygiene factors and motivators?
2. Is the net result of these impacts positive or negative? Explain.

Herzberg's theory has generated a great deal of research and controversy.[20] Research does not support the two-factor aspect of his theory nor the proposition that hygiene factors are unrelated to job satisfaction. Just the same, there are two key implications associated with this theory. First, managers are encouraged to pay attention to hygiene factors and motivators because they both are related to employees' job satisfaction. This is precisely what Lauren Dixon, CEO of Dixon Schawbl, is doing to maintain employee motivation and satisfaction (see Real World/Real People on page 213): Dixon Schawbl was rated as the number one best small-business workplace in 2010. Second, recognizing good performance is important, particularly in a down economy when raises are sparse. It is important to recognize behaviors and results that are linked to the organization's goals.

Process Theories of Motivation

⋯⋯⋯⋯⋯▶

TO THE POINT

What is the difference between a content and a process theory of motivation?
⋯⋯⋯⋯⋯

Earlier in the chapter we discussed the difference between content theories of motivation, which focus on the impact of internal factors on motivation, and process theories. Process theories go one step further in explaining motivation by identifying the process by which various internal factors influence motivation. These models also are cognitive in nature. That is, they are based on the premise that motivation is a function of employees' perceptions, thoughts, and beliefs. We now

real WORLD // real PEOPLE: ethics

Dixon Schawbl Increases Employee Satisfaction by Improving Hygiene Factors

Advertising agency Dixon Schawbl built its office based on input from employees. "The result is a space that features a koi pond, a pair of waterfalls, a slide that employees can take from floor to floor instead of the stairwell, a fireplace, faux-finish walls covered in quirky artwork, contemporary furniture and a padded primal scream room."

CEO Lauren Dixon was amazed about the simple things that employees requested for the new offices. "You'd be surprised by how many people said that they wanted windows that they could open, non-traditional lighting or even just walls that weren't painted white," Dixon says. . . .

"Another reason job satisfaction has remained so high, Dixon believes, is the many opportunities employees

have to give back to their community. . . . Not surprisingly, Dixon Schawbl regularly receives a flood of job applicants from around the world. Those who make the cut enjoy a benefits package that includes vacation time, PTO, regular paid holidays, time off for birthdays, 401(k), health care, profit-sharing, maternity leave and flex time."

Which of the hygiene factors and motivators shown in Figure 8–2 were used by Dixon Schawbl?

SOURCE: Excerpted from J Cooper, "Best Small-Business Workplaces 2010," *Entrepreneur,* September 8, 2010, http://www. entrepreneur.com/article/priintthis/217278.html.

---

explore the three most common process theories of motivation: equity theory, expectancy theory, and goal-setting theory.

 LO.3 Adams's Equity Theory of Motivation

◄ ·

TO THE POINT

How does the concept of organizational justice expand Adams's theory of equity, and what are the practical lessons derived from equity theory?

· · · · · · · · · · · · · · · · · · · ·

Defined generally, **equity theory** is a model of motivation that explains how people strive for fairness and justice in social exchanges or give-and-take relationships. As a process theory of motivation, equity theory explains how an individual's motivation to behave in a certain way is fueled by feelings of inequity or a lack of justice. For example, supporters of WikiLeaks conducted cyberattacks against MasterCard and Visa because they felt these companies were unfairly trying to stifle WikiLeaks' dissemination of secret US diplomatic communications. Both MasterCard and Visa were temporarily down as a result of these attacks.[21]

Psychologist J Stacey Adams pioneered application of the equity principle to the workplace. Central to understanding Adams's equity theory of motivation is an awareness of key components of the individual–organization exchange relationship. This relationship is pivotal in the formation of employees' perceptions of equity and inequity and the manner in which people respond to these perceptions.

The Individual–Organization Exchange Relationship

Adams points out that two primary components are involved in the employee–employer exchange, *inputs* and *outcomes.* An employee's inputs, for which he or she expects a just return, include education/training, skills, creativity, seniority, age, personality traits, effort expended, and personal appearance. On the outcome

equity theory Holds that motivation is a function of fairness in social exchanges.

side of the exchange, the organization provides such things as pay/bonuses, medical benefits, challenging assignments, job security, promotions, status symbols, and participation in important decisions.

Negative and Positive Inequity

![McGraw Hill connect] Go to www.mcgrawhillconnect.com for a video case on employee motivation at Hot Topic.

On the job, feelings of inequity revolve around a person's evaluation of whether he or she receives adequate rewards to compensate for his or her contributive inputs. People perform these evaluations by comparing the perceived fairness of their employment exchange to that of relevant others.[22] This comparative process, which is based on an equity norm, was found to vary across personalities and countries.[23] People tend to compare themselves to other individuals with whom they have close interpersonalities—such as friends—or to similar others—such as people performing the same job or individuals of the same gender or educational level—rather than dissimilar others. For example, we do not compare our salaries to that of the head football coach at Arizona State University. But we do consider our pay relative to other college of business professors. This brings up an interesting trend within the legal profession. Big law firms have taken to paying "outsize salaries to star attorneys, in some cases 10 times what they give other partners, in a strategy that is stretching compensation gaps and testing morale at firms. . . . While there has always been a pay gap at big firms, in the past partners with ownership stakes were paid relatively similar amounts to encourage a team approach and to ward off possible resentment."[24] Do you think that this practice will negatively affect people's work attitudes and levels of engagement?

Three different equity relationships are illustrated in Figure 8–3: equity, negative inequity, and positive inequity. Assume the two people in each of the equity

figure 8–3   Negative and Positive Inequity

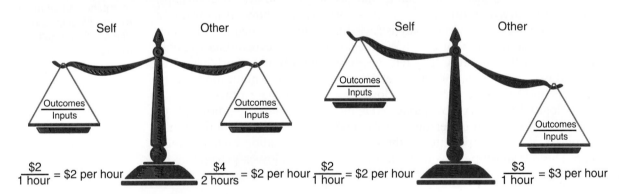

A. An Equitable Situation

Self   Other

$$\frac{\$2}{1 \text{ hour}} = \$2 \text{ per hour} \qquad \frac{\$4}{2 \text{ hours}} = \$2 \text{ per hour}$$

B. Negative Inequity

Self   Other

$$\frac{\$2}{1 \text{ hour}} = \$2 \text{ per hour} \qquad \frac{\$3}{1 \text{ hour}} = \$3 \text{ per hour}$$

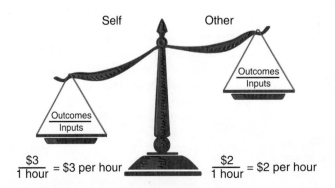

C. Positive Inequity

Self   Other

$$\frac{\$3}{1 \text{ hour}} = \$3 \text{ per hour} \qquad \frac{\$2}{1 \text{ hour}} = \$2 \text{ per hour}$$

relationships in Figure 8–3 have equivalent backgrounds (equal education, seniority, and so forth) and perform identical tasks. Only their hourly pay rates differ. Equity exists for an individual when his or her ratio of perceived outcomes to inputs is equal to the ratio of outcomes to inputs for a relevant co-worker (part A in Figure 8–3). Because equity is based on comparing *ratios* of outcomes to inputs, inequity will not necessarily be perceived just because someone else receives greater rewards. If the other person's additional outcomes are due to his or her greater inputs, a sense of equity may still exist. However, if the comparison person enjoys greater outcomes for similar inputs, **negative inequity** will be perceived (part B in Figure 8–3). On the other hand, a person will experience **positive inequity** when his or her outcome to input ratio is greater than that of a relevant co-worker (part C in Figure 8–3). Interestingly, the current economy can create positive inequity for layoff survivors because they feel fortunate to still have a job.

These protestors in Cairo were surely motivated by feelings of inequity. This predominantly non-violent uprising led to the resignation of Egyptian President Hosni Mubarak.

Reducing Inequity   Equity ratios can be changed by attempting to alter one's outcomes or adjusting one's inputs. For example, negative inequity might be resolved by asking for a raise or a promotion (i.e., raising outputs) or by reducing inputs (i.e., working fewer hours or exerting less effort). It also is important to note that equity can be restored by altering one's equity ratios behaviorally or cognitively, or both. A cognitive strategy entails psychologically distorting perceptions of one's own or one's comparison person's outcomes and inputs (e.g., conclude that comparison other has more experience or works harder).[25]

It is important to note that people also seek equity in a consumer context. The Real World/Real People on page 216 illustrates how consumers are increasingly using social media to complain about perceptions of inequity. Such complaints can become viral, ultimately resulting in negative views of a company's brand. Organizations now monitor and respond to items that are posted on-line in order to combat this trend.[26]

 LO.4 Expanding the Concept of Equity: Organizational Justice

Beginning in the late 1970s, researchers began to expand the role of equity theory in explaining employee attitudes and behavior. This led to a domain of research called *organizational justice*. Organizational justice reflects the extent to which people perceive that they are treated fairly at work. This, in turn, led to the identification of three different components of organizational justice: distributive, procedural, and interactional.[27] **Distributive justice** reflects the perceived fairness of how resources and rewards are distributed or allocated. **Procedural justice** is defined as the perceived fairness of the process and procedures used to make allocation

---

negative inequity Comparison in which another person receives greater outcomes for similar inputs.

positive inequity Comparison in which another person receives lesser outcomes for similar inputs.

distributive justice The perceived fairness of how resources and rewards are distributed.

procedural justice The perceived fairness of the process and procedures used to make allocation decisions.

real WORLD // real PEOPLE

Feelings of Consumer Inequity Can Go Viral

Maybe you've heard about the musician Dave Carroll and his experience as a United Airlines customer. He was so incensed that the company rejected his damage claim after its baggage handlers broke his guitar that he made a catchy YouTube video, "United Breaks Guitars." Eight million people have already viewed this decidedly negative take on the United brand.

Carroll's reaction is hardly unique. The popular mommy blogger Heather Armstrong was so upset over the failure of her Maytag washer and the company's ensuing service missteps that, using her mobile phone, she told her million-plus followers on Twitter they should never buy a Maytag. As another example, Greenpeace supporters barraged Nestlé's Facebook page with complaints about how the company's sourcing policies led to environmental damage.

Would you complain online if you received poor treatment from a company?

SOURCE: Excerpted from J Bernoff and T Schadler, "Empowered," *Harvard Business Review,* July–August 2010, p 95.

---

decisions. Research shows that positive perceptions of distributive and procedural justice are enhanced by giving employees a "voice" in decisions that affect them. Voice represents the extent to which employees who are affected by a decision can present relevant information about the decision to others. Voice is analogous to asking employees for their input into the decision-making process.

The last justice component, **interactional justice,** relates to the "quality of the interpersonal treatment people receive when procedures are implemented."[28] This form of justice does not pertain to the outcomes or procedures associated with decision making, but rather it focuses on whether or not people feel they are treated fairly when decisions are implemented. Fair interpersonal treatment necessitates that managers communicate truthfully and treat people with courtesy and respect.

Many studies of organizational justice have been conducted over the last two decades. Fortunately, four meta-analyses of more than 200 studies help summarize what has been learned from this research.[29] The following trends were uncovered: (1) job performance was positively associated with both distributive and procedural justice, but procedural justice was the best predictor of this outcome; (2) all three forms of justice were positively correlated with job satisfaction, organizational commitment, organizational citizenship behaviors, and employees' trust, and negatively with employees' withdrawal cognitions and turnover; (3) distributive and procedural injustice were negatively related to negative emotions such as anger; and all three forms of justice were negatively associated with aggressive behavior at work.[30] These results suggest a host of practical lessons for managers.

 LO.5 Practical Lessons from Equity Theory

Equity theory has at least six important practical implications. First, research on equity theory emphasizes the need for managers to pay attention to employees' perceptions of what is fair and equitable. No matter how fair management thinks the organization's policies, procedures, and reward system are, each employee's *perception* of the equity of those factors is what counts. For example, a nationwide study of 3,000 US workers revealed that 39% felt underpaid and only 37% reported feeling valued by their employer.[31] Managers thus are encouraged to make hiring decisions on merit-based, job-related information, and to make more attempts at providing positive recognition about employee behavior and performance. Moreover, because justice perceptions are influenced by the extent to which managers explain their decisions, managers are encouraged to explain the rationale behind their decisions.

Second, managers benefit by allowing employees to participate in making decisions about important work outcomes. In general, employees' perceptions of procedural justice are enhanced when they have a voice in the decision-making process. Managers are encouraged to seek employee input on organizational changes that are likely to impact the workforce. For instance, managers at Shell Refining decided to ask top-performing supervisors at its Port Arthur, Texas, refinery for input on how to improve plant performance. The result of this action was higher employee morale and a 30% reduction in unplanned maintenance repairs.[32]

Third, employees should be given the opportunity to appeal decisions that affect their welfare. Being able to appeal a decision fosters perceptions of distributive and procedural justice. Fourth, managers can promote cooperation and teamwork among group members by treating them equitably. Research reveals that people are just as concerned with fairness in group settings as they are with their own personal interests.[33] Fifth, employees' perceptions of justice are strongly influenced by the leadership behavior exhibited by their managers (leadership is discussed in Chapter 16). It thus is important for managers to consider the justice-related implications of their decisions, actions, and public communications. Consider the lawsuit being filed by the Equal Employment Opportunity Commission (EEOC) on behalf of three women who worked for FedEx.

Mc Graw Hill **connect**™ Go to www.mcgrawhillconnect.com for a self-assessment to test your perceptions of the fairness of interpersonal treatment at your organization.

Example. Federal officials filed a discrimination lawsuit on behalf of three women who say that FedEx Freight, Inc. gave a human-resources job at its Phoenix facility to a less-qualified male candidate.

All three women had prior human-resources experience and were recommended for the position. . . . Two of the women had earned bachelor's degrees, and one had a degree in human-resource management.

FedEx officials hired a male dock worker to be a human-resources field representative. The man did not have a bachelor's degree, according to the EEOC.[34]

The three women were clearly motivated to file a lawsuit based on their feelings of inequity regarding FedEx's hiring decision.

Finally, managers need to pay attention to the organization's climate for justice. For example, an organization's climate for justice was found to significantly influence employees' organizational commitment and job satisfaction.[35] Researchers also believe a climate of justice can significantly influence the type of customer service provided by employees. In turn, this level of service is likely to influence customers' perceptions of "fair service" and their subsequent loyalty and satisfaction.

Managers can attempt to follow these practical implications by monitoring equity and justice perceptions through informal conversations, interviews, or attitude surveys. Researchers have developed and validated a host of surveys that can be used for this purpose.

Back to the Chapter-Opening Case

To what extent are Michelle Rhee's changes consistent with the practical lessons derived from equity theory?

interactional justice Extent to which people feel fairly treated when procedures are implemented.

LO.6 Vroom's Expectancy Theory

Expectancy theory holds that people are motivated to behave in ways that produce desired combinations of expected outcomes. Generally, expectancy theory can be used to predict motivation and behavior in any situation in which a choice between two or more alternatives must be made. For instance, it can be used to predict whether to quit or stay at a job; whether to exert substantial or minimal effort at a task; and whether to major in management, finance, marketing, psychology, or communication.

Victor Vroom formulated a mathematical model of expectancy in his 1964 book *Work and Motivation*.[36] Vroom's theory has been summarized as follows: "The strength of a tendency to act in a certain way depends on the strength of an expectancy that the act will be followed by a given consequence (or outcome) and on the value or attractiveness of that consequence (or outcome) to the actor."[37]

Motivation, according to Vroom, boils down to the decision of how much effort to exert in a specific task situation. This choice is based on a two-stage sequence of expectations (effort→performance and performance→outcome). First, motivation is affected by an individual's expectation that a certain level of effort will produce the intended performance goal. For example, if you do not believe increasing the amount of time you spend studying will significantly raise your grade on an exam, you probably will not study any harder than usual. Motivation also is influenced by the employee's perceived chances of getting various outcomes as a result of accomplishing his or her performance goal. Finally, individuals are motivated to the extent that they value the outcomes received.

Vroom used a mathematical equation to integrate the above concepts into a predictive model of motivational force or strength. For our purposes, however, it is sufficient to define and explain the three key concepts within Vroom's model—*expectancy, instrumentality*, and *valence*.

Expectancy

An **expectancy**, according to Vroom's terminology, represents an individual's belief that a particular degree of effort will be followed by a particular level of performance. In other words, it is an effort→performance expectation. Expectancies take the form of subjective probabilities. As you may recall from a course in statistics, probabilities range from 0 to 1. An expectancy of 0 indicates effort has no anticipated impact on performance.

For example, suppose you have not memorized the keys on a keyboard. No matter how much effort you exert, your perceived probability of typing 30 error-free words per minute likely would be 0. An expectancy of 1 suggests that performance is totally dependent on effort. If you decided to memorize the letters on a keyboard as well as practice a couple of hours a day for a few weeks (high effort), you should be able to type 30 words per minute without any errors. In contrast, if you do not memorize the letters on a keyboard and only practice an hour or two per week (low effort), there is a very low probability (say, a 20% chance) of being able to type 30 words per minute without any errors.

The following factors influence an employee's expectancy perceptions:

1. Self-esteem
2. Self-efficacy (recall the discussion in Chapter 5)
3. Previous success at the task
4. Help received from a supervisor and subordinates

5. Information necessary to complete the task
6. Good materials and equipment to work with[38]

Instrumentality

An **instrumentality** is a performance→outcome perception. It represents a person's belief that a particular outcome is contingent on accomplishing a specific level of performance. Performance is instrumental when it leads to something else. For example, passing exams is instrumental to graduating from college.

Instrumentalities range from -1.0 to 1.0. An instrumentality of 1.0 indicates attainment of a particular outcome is totally dependent on task performance. An instrumentality of 0 indicates there is no relationship between performance and outcome. For example, most companies link the number of vacation days to seniority, not job performance. Finally, an instrumentality of -1.0 reveals that high performance reduces the chance of obtaining an outcome while low performance increases the chance. For example, the more time you spend studying to get an A on an exam (high performance), the less time you will have for enjoying leisure activities. Similarly, as you lower the amount of time spent studying (low performance), you increase the amount of time that may be devoted to leisure activities.

The concept of instrumentality is illustrated by the pay practices being used at household cleaning products company Reckitt Benckiser. The pay plan has three parts: base salary, and both short- and long-term bonuses/incentives.

Example. Base salaries are set near the median for competitors' pay. The real benefit comes in the form of bonuses. A manager who meets all targets will typically receive 40% of his or her base salary as a bonus that year. A manager who blows the targets out of the water (usually that means doubling the target numbers) can earn a bonus of up to 144%. Long-term compensation, in the form of options and performance-related restricted stock, depends on meeting three-year corporate growth targets for earnings per share. New long-term goals are put into place each year.[39]

Reckitt Benckiser clearly makes bonuses contingent on performance.

Valence

As Vroom used the term, **valence** refers to the positive or negative value people place on outcomes. Valence mirrors our personal preferences. For example, most employees have a positive valence for receiving additional money or recognition. In contrast, job stress and being laid off would likely result in negative valence for most individuals. In Vroom's expectancy model, *outcome*s refer to different consequences that are contingent on performance, such as pay, promotions, or recognition. An outcome's valence depends on an individual's needs and can be measured for research purposes with scales ranging from a negative value to a positive value. For example, an individual's valence toward more recognition can be assessed on a scale ranging from -2 (very undesirable) to 0 (neutral) to $+2$ (very desirable).

expectancy theory Holds that people are motivated to behave in ways that produce valued outcomes.

expectancy Belief that effort leads to a specific level of performance.

instrumentality A performance outcome perception.

valence The value of a reward or outcome.

Vroom's Expectancy Theory in Action

Vroom's expectancy model of motivation can be used to analyze a real-life motivation program. Consider the following performance problem described by Frederick W Smith, founder and chief executive officer of Federal Express Corporation:

Example. [W]e were having a helluva problem keeping things running on time. The airplanes would come in and everything would get backed up. We tried every kind of control mechanism that you could think of, and none of them worked. Finally, it became obvious that the underlying problem was that it was in the interest of the employees at the cargo terminal—they were college kids, mostly—to run late, because it meant that they made more money. So what we did was give them all a minimum guarantee and say, "Look, if you get through before a certain time, just go home, and you will have beat the system." Well, it was unbelievable. I mean, in the space of about 45 days, the place was way ahead of schedule. And I don't even think it was a conscious thing on their part.[40]

How did Federal Express get its college-age cargo handlers to switch from low effort to high effort? According to Vroom's model, the student workers originally exerted low effort because they were paid on the basis of time, not output. It was in their best interest to work slowly and accumulate as many hours as possible. By offering to let the student workers *go home early if and when they completed their assigned duties,* Federal Express prompted high effort. This new arrangement created two positively valued outcomes: guaranteed pay plus the opportunity to leave early. The motivation to exert high effort became greater than the motivation to exert low effort. Judging from the impressive results, the student workers had both high effort→performance expectancies and positive performance→outcome instrumentalities. Moreover, the guaranteed pay and early departure opportunity evidently had strongly positive valences for the student workers.

Back to the Chapter-Opening Case

To what extent is Michelle Rhee's motivation program consistent with the managerial and organizational implications of expectancy theory? Explain.

Research on Expectancy Theory and Managerial Implications

Many researchers have tested expectancy theory. In support of the theory, a meta-analysis of 77 studies indicated that expectancy theory significantly predicted performance, effort, intentions, preferences, and choice.[41] All told, there is widespread agreement that behavior and attitudes are influenced when organizations link rewards to targeted behaviors.[42] This relationship is discussed in more detail in Chapter 9.

Nonetheless, expectancy theory has been criticized for a variety of reasons. For example, the theory is difficult to test, and the measures used to assess expectancy, instrumentality, and valence have questionable validity. In the final analysis, however, expectancy theory has important practical implications for individual managers and organizations as a whole (see Table 8–2).

Managers are advised to enhance effort→performance expectancies by helping employees accomplish their performance goals. Managers can do this by providing support and coaching and by increasing employees' self-efficacy. It also is

table 8–2 Managerial and Organizational Implications
of Expectancy Theory

IMPLICATIONS FOR MANAGERS	IMPLICATIONS FOR ORGANIZATIONS
Determine the outcomes employees value.	Reward people for desired performance; and do not keep pay decisions secret.
Identify good performance so appropriate behaviors can be rewarded.	Design challenging jobs.
Make sure employees can achieve targeted performance levels.	Tie some rewards to group accomplishments to build teamwork and encourage cooperation.
Link desired outcomes to targeted levels of performance.	Reward managers for creating, monitoring, and maintaining expectancies, instrumentalities, and outcomes that lead to high effort and goal attainment.
Make sure changes in outcomes are large enough to motivate high effort.	Monitor employee motivation through interviews or anonymous questionnaires.
Monitor the reward system for inequities.	Accommodate individual differences by building flexibility into the motivation program.

important for managers to influence employees' instrumentalities and to monitor valences for various rewards.

In summary, there is no one best type of reward. Individual differences and need theories tell us that people are motivated by different rewards. For example, a recent survey of 1,047 employees from a variety of industries revealed that nonfinancial incentives such as praise, attention from leaders, and opportunity to lead projects were more effective at motivating respondents than financial incentives.[43] Is this true for you? We suspect that some people prefer nonfinancial rewards while others want money. The point is that managers should focus on linking employee performance to valued rewards regardless of the type of reward used to enhance motivation. The Real World/Real People on page 222 illustrates how General Motors is trying to implement this recommendation. Hourly workers at GM historically received pay raises based on seniority and job descriptions. The new approach is designed to directly link pay with performance. GM executives are hoping this new incentive system will lead to higher levels of productivity and profitability. It seems the plan may be working as GM is likely to report its first profitable year since 2004. The company also is planning to pay about $3,000 to each hourly worker in a profit-sharing payout: This is the largest payout in GM history.[44]

LO.7 Motivation through Goal Setting

Regardless of the nature of their specific achievements, successful people tend to have one thing in common. Their lives are goal oriented. Consider Mike Proulx, for example. "When Mike Proulx was bagging groceries as a teenager in the 1960s, he decided he would become president of Bashas. [Bashas is a privately held grocery chain in Arizona with more than 150 stores.] That's the job he has now held for three years. . . . When I was 18 I made a series of goals that included by age such and such I would be a store manager, and by a certain age, I was going to be district manager and then vice president and then president."[45] As a process model

◄ •

TO THE POINT

What is the process by which goals affect employee performance, and what are the practical lessons from goal-setting research?

• •

real WORLD // real PEOPLE

GM's Incentive System Is Consistent with Expectancy Theory

General Motors wants pay for union-represented workers tied to employees' work performance and the company's financial health—much like the way its salaried workers are paid. . . .

GM wants more flexible pay levels for workers as a way to encourage better performance and avoid locking the company into handing out big raises when the company isn't performing well, the company executives say.

"They are trying to give hourly workers the same metrics as salaried workers," GM Vice Chairman Stephen Girsky said Tuesday at the Detroit auto show. "There is a big pay-for-performance element going through the company and there is going to be more of it."

In addition to the performance-based pay, the union and US auto makers are exploring the idea of a profit-sharing formula as a way for workers to cash in on the industry's improving fortunes.

How do you think the union will respond to GM's changes in pay practices?

SOURCE: Excerpted from S Terlep, "GM Rethinks Pay for Unionized Workers," *The Wall Street Journal*, January 12, 2011, p B6.

Bold managerial moves like those described here helped GM to achieve six consecutive profitable quarters over 2010–2011.

of motivation, goal-setting theory explains how the simple behavior of setting goals activates a powerful motivational process that leads to sustained, high performance. This section explores the theory and research pertaining to goal setting, and Chapter 9 continues the discussion by focusing on the practical application of goal setting.

Goals: Definition and Background

Edwin Locke, a leading authority on goal setting, and his colleagues define a **goal** as "what an individual is trying to accomplish; it is the object or aim of an action."[46] The motivational effect of performance goals and goal-based reward plans has been recognized for a long time. At the turn of the 20th century, Frederick Taylor attempted to scientifically establish how much work of a specified quality an individual should be assigned each day. He proposed that bonuses be based on accomplishing those output standards: Taylor's theory is discussed in the next section of this chapter. More recently, goal setting has been promoted through a widely used management technique called management by objectives (MBO). The application of MBO is outlined in Chapter 9.

How Does Goal Setting Work?

Despite abundant goal-setting research and practice, goal-setting theories are surprisingly scarce. An instructive model was formulated by Locke and his associates. According to Locke's model, goal setting has four motivational mechanisms.

Goals Direct Attention
Goals direct one's attention and effort toward goal-relevant activities and away from goal-irrelevant activities. If, for example,

you have a term project due in a few days, your thoughts and actions tend to revolve around completing that project. In reality, however, we often work on multiple goals at once. This highlights the importance of prioritizing your goals so that you effectively allocate your efforts over time.[47]

Goals Regulate Effort   Not only do goals make us selectively perceptive, they also motivate us to act. The instructor's deadline for turning in your term project would prompt you to complete it, as opposed to going out with friends, watching television, or studying for another course. Generally, the level of effort expended is proportionate to the difficulty of the goal.

Goals Increase Persistence   Within the context of goal setting, persistence represents the effort expended on a task over an extended period of time: It takes effort to run 100 meters; it takes persistence to run a 26-mile marathon. Persistent people tend to see obstacles as challenges to be overcome rather than as reasons to fail. A difficult goal that is important to an individual is a constant reminder to keep exerting effort in the appropriate direction. Peter Löscher, CEO of Siemens, wanted to build on the power of persistence by setting goals associated with "green consciousness" and increased wind-energy sales. To do this he hired Peter Solmssen from GE because "the one thing GE does better than anybody is execution," said Solmssen. "They set a target, and they achieve it. That's it." With Solmssen's help, Löscher's new-goal driven approach led to increased wind-energy sales and a 48 percent increase in stock price.[48]

Goals Foster the Development and Application of Task Strategies and Action Plans   If you are here and your goal is out there somewhere, you face the problem of getting from here to there. For example, think about the challenge of starting a business. Do you want to earn profits, grow larger, or make the world a better place? To get there, you have to make a tremendous number of decisions and complete a myriad of tasks. Goals can help because they encourage people to develop strategies and action plans that enable them to achieve their goals. A series of studies conducted in South Africa, Zimbabwe, and Namibia found that small businesses were more likely to grow and succeed if their owners engaged in "elaborate and proactive planning."[49] The power of action plans also was used by Chris Liddell, chief financial officer for General Motors, when he was charged with executing the company's IPO in 2010 (see Real World/Real People on page 224).

 LO.8 Practical Lessons from Goal-Setting Research

Research consistently has supported goal setting as a motivational technique. Setting performance goals increases individual, group, and organizational performance. Further, the positive effects of goal setting were found in six other countries or regions: Australia, Canada, the Caribbean, England, West Germany, and Japan. Goal setting works in different cultures. Reviews of the many

Steve Jobs, holding the widely popular iPad, died in October 2011. His inventive and innovative traits helped Apple to become one of the largest and most valuable companies in the world.

goal What an individual is trying to accomplish.

real WORLD // real PEOPLE

Chris Liddell Executed Detailed Plans to Complete GM's IPO

General Motors's historic IPO was a trial by fire for Chief Financial Officer Chris Liddell. The 52-year-old had to please the auto maker's largest shareholder—the U.S. government—while managing a $23.1 billion offering that spanned three continents, 35 underwriting banks, and 90 promotional meetings. Mr Liddell, a top-flight rugby player in his native New Zealand, started planning the initial offering in March [2010]. "One of the disciplines he learned as a rugby player was the level of preparation that you need to accomplish something great," says James B Lee, Jr, vice chairman of underwriter, J P Morgan Chase & Co.

Mr Liddell told a *Wall Street Journal* reporter that "this thing was planned like a military campaign. Nine months of preparation went into those last two weeks. We knew exactly what we were going to say, how we were going to run the whole demand, bookbuilding process. It was incredibly well executed."

Why is action planning such a key component of goal setting?

SOURCE: Excerpted from D K Berman and S Terlep, "GM's IPO Point Man: Planning Is All," *The Wall Street Journal,* December 4–5, 2010, pp B1, B2.

---

goal-setting studies conducted over the past few decades have given managers five practical insights:

1. *Specific high goals lead to greater performance.* **Goal specificity** pertains to the quantifiability of a goal. For example, a goal of selling nine cars a month is more specific than telling a salesperson to do his or her best. Results from more than 1,000 studies entailing over 88 different tasks and 40,000 people demonstrated that performance was greater when people had specific high goals.[50]

2. *Feedback enhances the effect of specific, difficult goals.* Feedback plays a key role in all of our lives. Feedback lets people know if they are headed toward their goals or if they are off course and need to redirect their efforts. Goals plus feedback is the recommended approach. Goals inform people about performance standards and expectations so that they can channel their energies accordingly. In turn, feedback provides the information needed to adjust direction, effort, and strategies for goal accomplishment.

3. *Participative goals, assigned goals, and self-set goals are equally effective.* Both managers and researchers are interested in identifying the best way to set goals. Should goals be participatively set, assigned, or set by the employee him- or herself? A summary of goal-setting research indicated that no single approach was consistently more effective than others in increasing performance.[51] Managers are advised to use a contingency approach by picking a method that seems best suited for the individual and situation at hand.

4. *Action planning facilitates goal accomplishment.* An **action plan** outlines the activities or tasks that need to be accomplished in order to obtain a goal. They can also include dates associated with completing each task, resources needed, and obstacles that must be overcome. Managers can use action plans as a vehicle to have performance discussions with employees, and employees can use them to monitor progress toward goal achievement. An action plan also serves as a cue to remind us of what we should be working on, which in turn was found to lead to goal-relevant behavior and success. As a case in point, research shows that goal setting and action planning helped college students increase their academic performance.[52] Finally, managers are encouraged to allow employees to develop their own action plans because this autonomy fuels higher goal commitment and a sense of doing meaningful work.[53]

5. *Goal commitment and monetary incentives affect goal-setting outcomes.* **Goal commitment** is the extent to which an individual is personally committed to achieving a goal. In general, an individual is expected to persist in attempts to accomplish a goal when he or she is committed to it. Researchers believe that goal commitment moderates the relationship between the difficulty of a goal and performance. That is, difficult goals lead to higher performance only when employees are committed to their goals. Conversely, difficult goals are hypothesized to lead to lower performance when people are not committed to their goals. A meta-analysis of 21 studies supported these predictions.[54] It also is important to note that people are more likely to commit to high goals when they have high self-efficacy about successfully accomplishing their goals.

Like goal setting, the use of monetary incentives to motivate employees is seldom questioned. Unfortunately, research uncovered some negative consequences when goal achievement is linked to individual incentives. Empirical studies demonstrated that goal-based bonus incentives produced higher commitment to easy goals and lower commitment to difficult goals. People were reluctant to commit to high goals that were tied to monetary incentives. People with high goal commitment also offered less help to their co-workers when they received goal-based bonus incentives to accomplish difficult individual goals. Individuals also neglected aspects of the job that were not covered in the performance goals.[55] Finally, a recent survey of 227 executives from multiple industries revealed that 51 percent "bent the rules" in order to accomplish goals.[56] These results suggest that blind pursuit of goal accomplishment can foster unethical behavior.

The above discussion underscores some of the dangers of using goal-based incentives, particularly for employees in complex, interdependent jobs requiring cooperation. Managers need to consider the advantages, disadvantages, and dilemmas of goal-based incentives prior to implementation.

LO.9 Motivating Employees through Job Design

◀ ....

TO THE POINT

What are the similarities and differences between how top-down, bottom-up, and idiosyncratic deals approach job design?
....

Completing tasks is the core of any job, and job design focuses on increasing employee motivation by changing the type of tasks we complete in the course of doing our jobs. **Job design**, also referred to as *job redesign*, "refers to any set of activities that involve the alteration of specific jobs or interdependent systems of jobs with the intent of improving the quality of employee job experience and their on the-job productivity."[57] Historically, job design was viewed as a top-down approach in which managers changed employees' tasks with the intent of increasing motivation and productivity. In other words, job design was management led. In the last 10 years, this perspective gave way to what have been called bottom-up processes. This approach is based on the idea that employees can proactively change or redesign their own jobs, thereby boosting their own motivation and engagement. Job design is driven by employees rather than managers according to bottom-up processes. The latest approach to job design attempts to merge these two historical perspectives and is referred to as idiosyncratic deals. This view envisions job design as a process in which employees and individual managers jointly

---

goal specificity Quantifiability of a goal.

action plan Activities or tasks to be accomplished to obtain a goal.

goal commitment Amount of commitment to achieving a goal.

job design Changing the content or process of a specific job to increase job satisfaction and performance.

negotiate the types of tasks employees complete at work. In other words, the process of job design is jointly owned by employees and managers. This section provides an overview of these three conceptually different approaches to job design.[58] More coverage is given to top-down techniques and models because they have been used for longer periods of time and more research is available to evaluate their effectiveness.

Top-Down Approaches

The fundamental premise of top-down approaches is that management is responsible for creating efficient and meaningful combinations of work tasks for employees. If done correctly, the theory is that employees will display higher performance, job satisfaction, and employee engagement, and lower absenteeism and turnover. Let us now consider the five principal top-down approaches: scientific management, job enlargement, job rotation, job enrichment, and the job characteristics model.

Scientific Management   Scientific management draws from research in industrial engineering and is most heavily influenced by the work of Frederick Taylor. Taylor, a mechanical engineer, developed the principles of scientific management while working at both Midvale Steel Works and Bethlehem Steel in Pennsylvania. He observed very little cooperation between management and workers and found that employees were underachieving by engaging in output restriction, which Taylor called "systematic soldiering." Taylor's interest in scientific management grew from his desire to improve upon this situation.

Scientific management is "that kind of management which conducts a business or affairs by *standards* established by facts or truths gained through *systematic* observation, experiment, or reasoning."[59] Taylor's approach focused on using research and experimentation to determine the most efficient way to perform jobs. The application of scientific management involves the following five steps: (1) develop standard methods for performing jobs by using time and motion studies, (2) carefully select employees with the appropriate abilities, (3) train workers to use the standard methods and procedures, (4) support workers and reduce interruptions, and (5) provide incentives to reinforce performance.[60] Because jobs are highly specialized and standardized when they are designed according to the principles of scientific management, this approach to job design focuses on increasing efficiency, flexibility, and employee productivity.

Designing jobs according to the principles of scientific management has both positive and negative consequences. Positively, employee efficiency and productivity are increased. On the other hand, research reveals that simplified, repetitive jobs also lead to job dissatisfaction, poor mental health, higher levels of stress, and low sense of accomplishment and personal growth.[61] These negative consequences paved the way for the next four top-down approaches.

Job Enlargement   This technique was first used in the late 1940s in response to complaints about tedious and overspecialized jobs. **Job enlargement** involves putting more variety into a worker's job by combining specialized tasks of comparable difficulty. Some call this *horizontally loading* the job. Researchers recommend using job enlargement as part of a broader approach that uses multiple motivational methods because it does not have a significant and lasting positive effect on job performance by itself.[62]

Job Rotation   As with job enlargement, job rotation's purpose is to give employees greater variety in their work. **Job rotation** calls for moving employees from one specialized job to another. Rather than performing only one job, workers are trained and given the opportunity to perform two or more separate jobs on

real WORLD // real PEOPLE

Tata Consultancy Services Uses Job Rotation

India-based Tata Consultancy Services (TCS), a software services and consulting company, considers job rotation a key strategy for developing its workforce and delivering added value to customers. The overseas program sends employees native to India to contribute to TCS operations in countries such as China, Hungary, and South America, among others. With offices in 42 countries globally and customers spread throughout the world, the ability to send skilled workers overseas is a must. But it also helps TCS provide better service since it draws on the strength of its entire workforce, rather than simply relying on whatever talent can be found in the office located closest to the customer. "It gives us the opportunity to offer a value proposition to our customers from the point of view of quality and knowledge," says Ajoy Mukherjee, vice president, head, global human resources.

Overseas assignments at TCS usually span 18 to 24 months, with employees learning both from their work

with the customer, as well as from fellow TCS employees who are based permanently at that location. When the employee returns to India, he or she usually will continue working on the same kind of projects that were worked on abroad, thereby transferring the knowledge gained overseas to the home office. "The rotation is essential in building the competency of our people," says Mukherjee. "They were able to go onsite and meet face-to-face with our customers, and see how things work in another country." In addition to enhancing technical skills, the international people skills of those on overseas assignments are boosted.

Why would this rotation program increase employee satisfaction and performance?

SOURCE: Excerpted from M Weinstein, "Foreign but Familiar," *Training*, January 2009, p 22. Used with permission of Nielsen Business Media.

a rotating basis. By rotating employees from job to job, managers believe they can stimulate interest and motivation while providing employees with a broader perspective of the organization. Tata Consultancy Services (TCS), for example, uses job rotation as a way to develop its workforce and provide employees with exposure to international operations (see Real World/Real People above). Other proposed advantages of job rotation include increased worker flexibility and easier scheduling because employees are cross-trained to perform different jobs. Organizations also use job rotation as a vehicle to place new employees into the jobs of their choice. The idea is that turnover is reduced and performance increases because people self-select their jobs.

Despite positive experiences from companies such as TCS, it is not possible to draw firm conclusions about the value of job rotation programs because they have not been adequately researched.

Job Enrichment   Job enrichment is the practical application of Frederick Herzberg's motivator–hygiene theory of job satisfaction which we discussed earlier in this chapter. Specifically, **job enrichment** entails modifying a job such that an employee has the opportunity to experience achievement, recognition, stimulating work, responsibility, and advancement. These characteristics are incorporated into a job through vertical loading. Rather than giving employees additional tasks of similar difficulty (horizontal loading), *vertical loading* consists of giving

connect™ Go to www.mcgrawhillconnect.com for an interactive exercise to test your knowledge of motivating employees through job design.

scientific management Using research and experimentation to find the most efficient way to perform a job.

job enlargement Putting more variety into a job.

job rotation Moving employees from one specialized job to another.

job enrichment Building achievement, recognition, stimulating work, responsibility, and advancement into a job.

workers more autonomy and responsibility. Intuit, for example, attempts to do this by "encouraging workers to take four hours a week of 'unstructured time' for their own projects and hosting 'idea jams,' where teams present new concepts for prizes."[63]

The Job Characteristics Model   Two OB researchers, J Richard Hackman and Greg Oldham, played a central role in developing the job characteristics approach. These researchers tried to determine how work can be structured so that employees are internally or intrinsically motivated. **Intrinsic motivation** occurs when an individual is "turned on to one's work because of the positive internal feelings that are generated by doing well, rather than being dependent on external factors (such as incentive pay or compliments from the boss) for the motivation to work effectively."[64] Intrinsic motivation is closely aligned with the concept of employee engagement, which was discussed in Chapter 6. These positive feelings power a self-perpetuating cycle of motivation. As shown in Figure 8–4, internal work motivation is determined by three psychological states. In turn, these psychological states are fostered by the presence of five core job dimensions. The object of this approach is to promote high intrinsic motivation by designing jobs that possess the five core job characteristics shown in Figure 8–4. Let us examine the core job dimensions.

In general terms, **core job dimensions** are common characteristics found to a varying degree in all jobs. Three of the job characteristics shown in Figure 8–4 combine to determine experienced meaningfulness of work:

- *Skill variety.* The extent to which the job requires an individual to perform a variety of tasks that require him or her to use different skills and abilities.
- *Task identity.* The extent to which the job requires an individual to perform a whole or completely identifiable piece of work. In other words, task

figure 8–4   The Job Characteristics Model

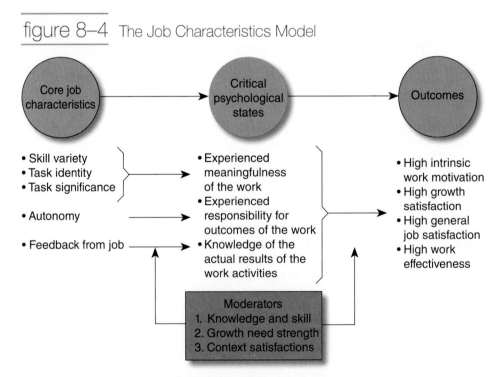

SOURCE: From J Richard Hackman and Greg R Oldham, *Work Redesign* (Prentice Hall Organizational Development Series), 1st ed © 1980, p 90. Reproduced by permission of Pearson Education, Upper Saddle River, NJ.

identity is high when a person works on a product or project from beginning to end and sees a tangible result.

- *Task significance.* The extent to which the job affects the lives of other people within or outside the organization.

Experienced responsibility is elicited by the job characteristic of autonomy, defined as follows:

- *Autonomy.* The extent to which the job enables an individual to experience freedom, independence, and discretion in both scheduling and determining the procedures used in completing the job.

Finally, knowledge of results is fostered by the job characteristic of feedback, defined as follows:

- *Feedback.* The extent to which an individual receives direct and clear information about how effectively he or she is performing the job.[65]

Hackman and Oldham recognized that everyone does not want a job containing high amounts of the five core job characteristics. They incorporated this conclusion into their model by identifying three attributes that affect how individuals respond to job enrichment. These attributes are concerned with the individual's knowledge and skill, growth need strength (representing the desire to grow and develop as an individual), and context satisfactions (see the box labeled Moderators in Figure 8–4). Context satisfactions represent the extent to which employees are satisfied with various aspects of their job, such as satisfaction with pay, co-workers, and supervision.

Jobs on an assembly line like this are generally low in the five core job characteristics that drive positive psychological states. Auto manufactures try to enrich these jobs by giving employees more responsibility and decision-making latitude.

Research underscores three practical implications of the job characteristics model. First, managers may want to use this model to also increase employee job satisfaction. A meta-analysis involving over 75,000 people demonstrated a moderately strong relationship between job characteristics and satisfaction.[66] Second, this same large-scale meta-analysis showed that managers can enhance employees' intrinsic motivation, job involvement, and performance, while reducing absenteeism and stress by increasing the core job characteristics.[67] Consistent with this finding, Nugget Market, rated as the eighth best place to work for by *Fortune* in 2010, uses a creative recognition program to enhance the motivation and performance. "Employee rallies are an everyday event at this nine-store supermarket chain, where a big flat-screen monitor in each store delivers awards and pumps up the troops. Workers who watch diligently can get \$20–\$1,500 bonuses."[68] Finally, managers are likely to find noticeable increases in the quality of performance after a job redesign program. Results from 21 experimental studies revealed that job redesign resulted in a median increase of 28% in the quality of performance.[69]

intrinsic motivation Motivation caused by positive internal feelings.

core job dimensions Job characteristics found to various degrees in all jobs.

More and more people are crafting jobs that entail doing work from home. What are the challenges of managing people who work from home?

Bottom-Up Approaches

As the term *bottom-up* suggests, this approach to job design is driven by employees rather than managers and is referred to as job crafting. **Job crafting** is defined as "the physical and cognitive changes individuals make in the task or relational boundaries of their work."[70] Employees are viewed as "job crafters" according to this model because they are expected to define and create their own job boundaries. As such, this approach to job design represents proactive and adaptive employee behavior aimed at changing tasks, relationships, and cognitions associated with one's job. Table 8–3 defines and illustrates the three key forms of job crating.

The first form of job crafting involves changing one's task boundaries. You can do this by altering the scope or nature of tasks you complete at work or you can take on fewer or more tasks. This is illustrated by the example of engineers taking on more relationship-oriented activities in order to complete projects. The second form of job crafting, shown in Table 8–3, entails changing the relational nature of one's job. Specifically, you can alter the quantity or quality of interactions you have with others at work, or you can establish new relationships. An example of this is a hospital janitorial employee interacting with patients, ultimately making this employee feels like he or she can impact patient care. Cognitive crafting is the final form of job crafting. It encompasses a change in how you perceive or think about the tasks and relationships associated with your job. For example, a nurse can view accurate record keeping as a key component of providing high-quality health care as opposed to a chore that detracts from helping patients.

The final column in Table 8–3 outlines the potential impact of job crafting on employee motivation and performance. You can see that job crafting is expected to change how employees perceive their jobs. Job crafting is expected to result in more positive attitudes about one's job, which in turn is expected to increases employee motivation, engagement, and performance. Preliminary research supports this proposition.[71]

table 8–3 Forms of Job Crafting

FORM	EXAMPLE	EFFECT ON MEANING OF WORK
Changing number, scope, and type of job tasks	Design engineers engaging in relational tasks that move a project to completion	Work is completed in a more timely fashion; engineers change the meaning of their jobs to be guardians or movers of projects
Changing quality and/or amount of interaction with others encountered in a job	Hospital cleaners actively caring for patients and families, integrating themselves into the workflow of their floor units	Cleaners change the meaning of their jobs to be helpers of the sick; see the work of the floor unit as an integrated whole of which they are a vital part
Changing cognitive task boundaries	Nurses taking responsibility for all information and "insignificant" tasks that may help them to care more appropriately for a patient	Nurses change the way they see the work to be more about patient advocacy, as well as high-quality technical care

SOURCE: A Wrzesniewski and J E Dutton, "Crafting a Job: Revisioning Employees As Active Crafters of Their Work," *Academy of Management Review,* April 2001, p 185.

Idiosyncratic Deals (I-Deals)

This last approach to job design represents a middle ground between top-down and bottom-up methods and attempts to overcome their limitations. For example, top-down approaches are constrained by the fact that managers cannot always create changes in task characteristics that are optimum for everyone. Similarly, job crafting is limited by the amount of latitude people have in changing their own jobs. **Idiosyncratic deals (i-deals)** represent "employment terms individuals negotiate for themselves, taking myriad forms from flexible schedules to career development."[72] Although "star performers" have long negotiated special employment contracts or deals, demographic trends and the changing nature of work have created increased opportunities for more employees to negotiate i-deals.

I-deals tend to involve personal flexibility, developmental needs, and task-related content. The goal of such deals is to increase employee motivation and productivity by allowing employees the flexibility to negotiate employment relationships that meet their needs and values. RSM McGladrey is a great example. The company promotes and encourages the creation of i-deals among its 8,000 employees. The focus of RSM McGladrey's program is to create innovative and flexible ways of working. The company believes that this approach to job design fuels employee engagement, satisfaction, productivity, and customer satisfaction while reducing employee turnover. This belief may prove convincing if one considers the many awards the company has received in the last few years. It was named to *Working Mother*'s list of top 100 companies for the third time in 2009, ranked fifth by *Accounting Today* in its list of top 100 firms in 2010, and one of the best places to launch a career by *BusinessWeek* in 2009.[73] The Real World/Real People on page 232 explains how these i-deals are negotiated.

Although this approach to job design is too new to have generated much research, preliminary evidence is positive. A recent study of hospitals in both the United States and Germany shows that i-deals are associated with less stress and more opportunities to perform meaningful work, which in turn leads to higher levels of employee engagement.[74] Future research is needed to determine the generalizability of these encouraging results.

Putting Motivational Theories to Work

◄ ·······················

TO THE POINT

What are the challenges managers face when implementing motivational programs?
·······················

We started this chapter by noting that motivating employees is a key aspect of being an effective manager. That said, managers face two key challenges when devising motivational programs. First, many managers are stretched in their job duties. They feel pulled in multiple directions and spend far too much time fighting fires instead of proactively focusing on employees' needs. This situation is frustrating and can lead to lower job satisfaction and motivation for managers. It still is imperative, however, for managers to find the time, and a positive attitude, to apply to the task of employee motivation. Jack and Suzy Welch commented on this issue and concluded that "no boss is doing his job properly if he's not letting each of his people know where they stand in constructive detail" and delivering "outsize rewards for outsize performance."[75] Second, managers may not know how to motivate people beyond the simple use of monetary rewards. It is

job crafting Proactive and adaptive employee behavior aimed at changing the nature of one's job.

idiosyncratic deals (i-deals) Process by which employees and managers negotiate tasks completed by employees.

real WORLD // real PEOPLE

RSM McGladrey Encourages I-Deals

[The program allows] employees across the nation to take a portion of the year off, while working full-time or part-time the remainder of the year and receiving a pro-rated paycheck and full benefits all year. . . .

McGladrey employees have been taking advantage of FlexYear schedules for years. . . . The design is simple and focuses on business impact. It makes sense for the company, employees and clients.

First, an interested employee who has been with the firm a minimum of three months and has a performance rating of "achieving expectations" or better initiates a request for one of the firm's seven flexible work options by completing an eight-question business proposal that requires him or her to assess the impact of the request on the firm, its clients and his or her coworkers—and to propose solutions to issues that could arise as a result.

Second, managers evaluate proposals based on the impact on the business. Employees' personal reasons for pursuing the flexible work option are not considered. . . . Typically, employees take about two months off during the summer, but the duration and time of year may vary.

Third, if a proposal will create a neutral or positive impact, managers are encouraged to approve the request, at least on a pilot basis, to keep the employee on board. If there is a negative impact on the business, managers

are encouraged to decline the request—even if that means having a difficult conversation with an employee.

Finally, once approved, flexible work options are continually monitored to ensure that they still work for the employee, firm and our clients. They can be modified or ended—by the firm or the employee—at any time, based on individual and business needs.

By making FlexYear part of this business-based approach to flexibility, we were able to position it as a strategic tool that helps leaders manage the cyclical nature of our business while responding to the diverse needs of employees. . . .

Michelle Hickox, a partner in our Dallas office, has been on a FlexYear schedule for eight years and has seen firsthand the positive impact on her family and the firm. Through FlexYear, Hickox has enjoyed taking June and July off each year to make invaluable memories with her two girls. This option also allows her to develop deep relationship with her clients through open conversations about her schedule. And, FlexYear provides stretch opportunities for employees on Hickox's team who work with her clients while she is out.

What problems do you see with creating i-deals?

SOURCE: Excerpted from T Hopke, "Go Ahead, Take a Few Months Off," *HR Magazine,* September 2010, pp 72, 74.

important for managers to use a broader or more integrated approach when trying to motivate employees. This approach should consider the various theories and models discussed in this chapter as well as concepts covered in previous chapters. Organizations can help managers by providing them with training and coaching that focuses on how they can improve their ability to motivate others.

Summary of Key Concepts

1. *Contrast Maslow's, Alderfer's, and McClelland's need theories.* Maslow proposed that motivation is a function of five basic needs arranged in a prepotent hierarchy. The concept of a stair-step hierarchy has not stood up well under research. Alderfer concluded that three core needs explain behavior—existence, relatedness, and growth. He proposed that more than one need can be activated at a time and frustration of higher-order needs can influence the desire for lower-level needs. McClelland argued that motivation and performance vary according to the strength of an individual's need for achievement. High achievers prefer tasks of moderate difficulty, situations under their control, and a desire for more performance

feedback than low achievers. Top managers should have a high need for power coupled with a low need for affiliation.

2. *Explain the practical significance of Herzberg's distinction between motivators and hygiene factors.* Herzberg believes job satisfaction motivates better job performance. His hygiene factors, such as policies, supervision, and salary, erase sources of dissatisfaction. On the other hand, his motivators, such as achievement, responsibility, and recognition, foster job satisfaction. Although Herzberg's motivator–hygiene theory of job satisfaction has been criticized on methodological

grounds, it offers practical advice for motivating employees.

3. *Discuss the role of perceived inequity in employee motivation.* Equity theory is a model of motivation that explains how people strive for fairness and justice in social exchanges. On the job, feelings of inequity revolve around a person's evaluation of whether he or she receives adequate rewards to compensate for his or her contributive inputs. People perform these evaluations by comparing the perceived fairness of their employment exchange with that of relevant others. Perceived inequity creates motivation to restore equity.

4. *Explain the differences among distributive, procedural, and interactional justice.* Distributive, procedural, and interactional justice are the three key components underlying organizational justice. Distributive justice reflects the perceived fairness of how resources and rewards are distributed. Procedural justice represents the perceived fairness of the process and procedures used to make allocation decisions. Interactional justice entails the perceived fairness of a decision maker's behavior in the process of decision making.

5. *Describe the practical lessons derived from equity and interactional justice.* Equity theory has at least six practical implications. First, managers should pay attention to employees' perceptions of what is fair and equitable. It is the employee's view of reality that counts when trying to motivate someone, according to equity theory. Second, employees should be given a voice in decisions that affect them. Third, employees should be given the opportunity to appeal decisions that affect their welfare. Fourth, managers can promote cooperation and teamwork among group members by treating them equitably. Fifth, employees' perceptions of justice are strongly influenced by the leadership behavior exhibited by managers. Finally, managers need to pay attention to the organization's climate for justice because it influences employee attitudes and behavior.

6. *Explain Vroom's expectancy theory.* Expectancy theory assumes motivation is determined by one's perceived chances of achieving valued outcomes. Vroom's expectancy model of motivation reveals how effort→performance expectancies and performance→outcome instrumentalities influence the degree of effort expended to achieve desired (positively valent) outcomes. Managers are advised to enhance effort→performance expectancies by helping employees accomplish their performance goals.

7. *Explain how goal setting motivates an individual.* Four motivational mechanisms of goal setting are as follows: (*a*) Goals direct one's attention, (*b*) goals regulate effort, (*c*) goals increase one's persistence, and (*d*) goals encourage development of goal-attainment strategies and action plans.

8. *Review the five practical lessons from goal-setting research.* First, specific high goals lead to greater performance. Second, feedback enhances the effect of specific, difficult goals. Third, participative goals, assigned goals, and self-set goals are equally effective. Fourth, action planning facilitates goal accomplishment. Fifth, goal commitment and monetary incentives affect goal-setting outcomes.

9. *Discuss the three conceptually different approaches to job design.* The premise of top-down approaches is that management is responsible for creating efficient and meaningful combinations of work tasks for employees. There are five principal top-down approaches: scientific management, job enlargement, job enrichment, job rotation, and a contingency approach called the job characteristics model. Bottom-up approaches, which are referred to as job crafting, are driven by employees rather than managers. Employees are viewed as job crafters who define and create their own job boundaries. Idiosyncratic deals (i-deals) view job design as a process in which employees and managers jointly negotiate the types of tasks employees complete at work.

Key Terms

Motivation, 206

Content theories of motivation, 206

Process theories of motivation, 206

Needs, 206

Need hierarchy theory, 207

ERG theory, 208

Need for achievement, 209

Need for affiliation, 209

Need for power, 210

Motivators, 211

Hygiene factors, 211

Equity theory, 213

Negative inequity, 215

Positive inequity, 215

Distributive justice, 215

Procedural justice, 215

Interactional justice, 216

Expectancy theory, 218

Expectancy, 218

Instrumentality, 219

Valence, 219

Goal, 222

Goal specificity, 224

Action plan, 224

Goal commitment, 225

Job design, 225

Scientific management, 226

Job enlargement, 226

Job rotation, 226

Job enrichment, 227

Intrinsic motivation, 228

Core job dimensions, 228

Job crafting, 230

Idiosyncratic deals (i-deals), 231

OB in Action Case Study

How Should Managers Handle Tough Employment Decisions?[76]

Here is what Bill Conaty, former senior vice president of human resources at General Electric had to say.

> Restructurings, consolidation, salary freezes, a shifting health-care cost burden, furloughs, 401(k) match eliminations . . . this list, as you know, goes on and on. Did your company cancel this year's Christmas party? . . .

My concern is that, cumulatively, these negative actions are tugging at and fraying the delicate bonds of loyalty that tie employees to their employers. I believe it will be the companies that manage to deftly balance the necessary tough competitive actions with genuine compassion for their employees that will win big in the future.

People have long memories. What they don't have right now are a whole lot of career options. And they will judge their employer by how equitably they feel they were treated during the down market. So how exactly do you steer your company through this in a way that won't drive your people into the arms of the first headhunter who calls? . . .

As counterintuitive as it may sound, consider going deeper than you might on staff reductions, rather than nibbling around the edges hoping for a quick market turnaround. . . . When you are ready to make those cuts, deal compassionately with the casualties, financially and emotionally, to provide them as soft a landing as possible. Career transition centers, training opportunities, and a sincere interest in helping those who are moving on become more marketable will genuinely help.

Many companies don't need to be told that. Instead, managers often spend a disproportionate amount of time managing the layoff process and not enough attention on the surviving talent. Those survivors need to be recognized and rewarded. Yes, they'll pay close attention to how humanely layoffs are carried out, but they're also aware that their own workload and stress level has just been stepped up. You want this group to play offense, not to fret over when the next shoe will drop or feel that they're being overburdened.

With financial rewards temporarily off the screen, an astonishingly powerful form of recognition is a genuine pat on the back, along with words along these lines: "I think you're doing a great job under tough circumstances, and you're an essential part of my team.". . .

There's a strong tendency for executives in tight spots to simply clam up, fearing they don't have the answers people want to hear. To avoid appearing inadequate, they'll issue the occasional all-employee e-mail or canned Webcast. But you'll find that you don't need to have all the answers. You'll discover that the rumor mill has painted the most pessimistic picture imaginable, and you will quickly be able to dispel numerous falsehoods and present a clearer and more optimistic view. These times call for a personal touch. Employees who get to see and hear their leaders are far more likely to buy into a future beyond the crisis.

Now back to the subject of holiday parties: It's a mistake to legislate fun out of the workplace. You need to continue to celebrate, especially in tough times. . . . We need to dial down how we celebrate, yes, but it's not natural to have to continuously wear a deadly serious game face.

Questions for Discussion

1. Why is it important to focus on motivating employees who survive a layoff?

2. To what extent is Conaty's advice consistent with equity and expectancy theory?

3. Do you believe that recognition will motivate layoff survivors? Explain.

4. Do you agree that managers should find ways to have fun in the work environment after a layoff? Why or why not?

5. What is the biggest takeaway you get from trying to link content in this chapter to this case?

Legal/Ethical Challenge

Should Retrocessions Be Allowed in the United States?[77]

A retrocession is a kickback that "asset managers may be skimming off investments." While it is little known in the United States, the practice has been an open secret in European private banking for decades—and it recently surfaced as a perk that Zurich-based Credit Suisse may have received from Bernie Madoff's feeder funds.

"How does this work? Essentially, bankers get rebates from fund managers they park money with—and pocket the commissions instead of passing the savings on to clients. Retrocessions typically match 25% of a fund's management fee, says British hedge fund manager Fabien

Pictet. So on a $2 billion investment, a management fee of 2%, or $40 million, would yield a $10 million kickback."

What Is Your Opinion about Retrocessions?

1. A retrocession is like getting a sales commission and thus should be allowed.

2. A retrocession is another way that bankers are taking advantage of investors. Commissions should be passed

to investors and not kept by bankers. This practice should be against the law.

3. Bankers should be required to disclose this issue to potential investors and then let individuals decide for themselves. A bank customer may be okay with this practice because they have a long-term relationship with the banker.

4. Invent other options.

Web Resources

For study material and exercises that apply to this chapter, visit our website at **www.mhhe.com/kreitner10e**

chapter 9

Improving Job Performance with Goals, Feedback, Rewards, and Positive Reinforcement

Learning Objectives

When you finish studying the material in this chapter, you should be able to:

LO.1   Define the term *performance management,* distinguish between learning goals and performance outcome goals, and explain the three-step goal-setting process.

LO.2   Identify the two basic functions of feedback, and specify at least three practical lessons from feedback research.

LO.3   Define 360-degree feedback, and summarize how to give good feedback in a performance management program.

LO.4   Distinguish between extrinsic and intrinsic rewards, and explain the four building blocks of intrinsic rewards and motivation.

LO.5   Summarize the reasons why extrinsic rewards often fail to motivate employees.

LO.6   Discuss how managers can generally improve extrinsic reward and pay-for-performance plans.

LO.7   State Thorndike's law of effect, and explain Skinner's distinction between respondent and operant behavior.

LO.8   Define positive reinforcement, negative reinforcement, punishment, and extinction, and distinguish between continuous and intermittent schedules of reinforcement.

LO.9   Demonstrate your knowledge of behavior shaping.

How Does NuStar Do Right by Its Employees by "Doing It Wrong"?

San Antonio-based NuStar Energy is in the unglamorous business of refining, shipping, and storing petroleum products. Some of the firm's 1,400 US employees flirt with danger as they process loads of molten asphalt ultimately used in paving roads. So how did NuStar end up being number 30 on *Fortune* magazine's 2011 list of the 100 best companies to work for? In short, NuStar takes good care of its people. Employee safety is a top priority for CEO Curt Anastasio, who boasts that his company has never had a layoff. When business was bad in the summer of 2010, for example, NuStar management resorted to an employee-driven efficiency program in lieu of a 10% layoff. No wonder NuStar enjoys a meager 2% turnover rate. Fairness is one of Anastasio's trademark traits. "If employees don't get a bonus, the CEO doesn't either."[1] Community service also is in NuStar's corporate DNA, with the firm's employees tallying over 75,000 volunteer hours in 2010. NuStar's stockholders are happy, too, enjoying a nearly 65% total return over the last three years.

That's "a direct result of our employee-focused culture," Anastasio says. "If you take care of the employees, they'll take care of their communities and the investors."

NuStar surely takes care of employees. . . . Health and dental insurance are free. Everybody gets a bonus—or nobody does; recent bonuses ranged from 4% to 35%, or about $1,100 for a mailroom clerk to about $70,000 for a vice president. (Unionized workers, about one-tenth of the company, have their own bonus deal.) There's also merit pay; in 2010 the average was 3%. And there are equity grants. Last year half the company got them, with amounts ranging from $2,000 to $113,000. Of the $13.6 million awarded, $12 million went to employees below the executive level. A compensation consultant told NuStar's human resources vice president: "You guys are doing it wrong!"[2]

Time to find a new compensation consultant.

LO.1 This final chapter of Part 2 serves as a practical capstone for what we have learned so far in Parts 1 and 2. Our focus here is on improving individual job performance. We need to put to work what we have learned about cultural and individual differences, perception, and motivation. Some companies, such as NuStar Energy in the chapter-opening case, do a good job in this regard. A rewarding and employee-friendly culture, with lots of personal touches, creates loyal and motivated employees. Unfortunately, research shows that most managers fall far short when it comes to carefully nurturing job performance. A consulting firm's ongoing study of more than 500 managers since 1993 led to this conclusion:

Example. Only 1 out of 100 managers provides every direct report with these five basics every day:

1. Performance requirements and standard operating procedures related to tasks and responsibilities.
2. Defined parameters, measurable goals, and concrete deadlines for all work assignments for which the direct report will be held accountable.
3. Accurate monitoring, evaluation, and documentation of work performance.
4. Specific feedback on work performance with guidance for improvement.
5. Fairly distributed rewards and detriments [penalties].[3]

The researchers call this situation "under-management." The consequences of under-management are not good. According to the Society for Human Resource Management, "a new survey finds that only one in seven employees worldwide is fully engaged with their work. There is a vast, largely untapped reserve of employee performance potential."[4] (Recall our discussions of *employee engagement* in Chapters 1 and 6.) A comprehensive approach to tapping this vast potential is performance management. **Performance management** is an organizationwide system whereby managers integrate the activities of goal setting, monitoring and evaluating, providing feedback and coaching, and rewarding employees on a continuous basis.[5] This contrasts with the haphazard tradition of annual performance appraisals,[6] a generally unsatisfying experience for everyone involved.[7] (See Learning Module B, on the book's website, for more on performance appraisal.) Organizational behavior (OB) can shed valuable light on key aspects of performance management—namely, goal setting, feedback and coaching, and rewards and positive reinforcement.

As indicated in Figure 9–1, job performance needs a life-support system. Like an astronaut drifting in space without the protection and support of a space suit, job performance will not thrive without a support system. First, people with the requisite abilities, skills, and job knowledge need to be hired. Joe Kraus, co-founder and CEO of Jotspot, a Web page hosting service, offers this blunt advice:

Example. **Never compromise on hiring.** Every time I've compromised, I've come to regret it. You have to be tough, even if that means not hiring people who could turn out to be great, because of the damage one person who isn't great can do.

Nothing demotivates people like the equal treatment of unequals. When you hire a bozo and treat him the same as a rock star, it deflates the rock star.[8]

Next, training is required to correct any job knowledge shortfalls.[9] The organization's structure, culture, and job design and supervisory practices also can facilitate or hinder job performance. At the heart of the model in Figure 9–1 are the key aspects of the performance improvement cycle that we explore in depth in this chapter. Importantly, it is a dynamic and continuous cycle requiring top management's strategic oversight, followed up with day-to-day attention.

figure 9–1   Improving Individual Job Performance: A Continuous Process

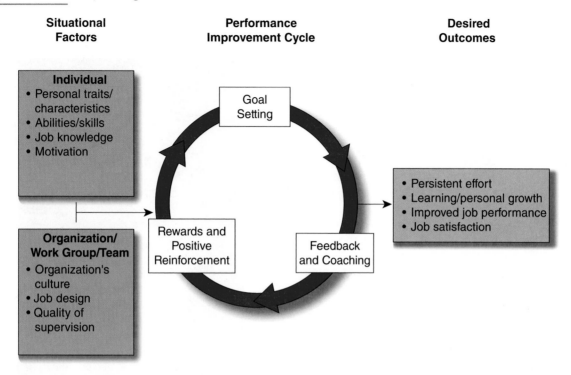

Goal Setting

Goal setting in the workplace could use an extreme makeover. According to a Franklin Covey survey of workers in the United States, 56% don't "clearly understand their organization's most important goals" and an astounding 81% "don't have clearly defined goals."[10] These figures could be cut in half and still represent a very unproductive situation. The missing element here is what goal-setting experts call line of sight. Employees with a clear **line of sight** understand the organization's strategic goals and know what actions they need to take, both individually and as team members.[11] A good case in point is Bloomberg LP, the 9,400-employee financial information services company founded by New York City Mayor Michael Bloomberg:

Example. The company has a highly unusual compensation system that ties employee pay directly to the sale of terminals—or more precisely, to net installations, or "net installs." The concept behind this system is that *everyone* at the company should be driving toward only one goal: selling more Bloombergs. To underscore that point, large electronic signs hanging from the ceilings in the Bloomberg offices report progress on both sales and installations. Bells ring to mark a sale—multiple times if the news justifies it.[12]

TO THE POINT
What are the keys to an effective goal-setting process?

connect™ Go to www.mcgrawhillconnect.com for an interactive exercise to test your knowledge of improving individual job performance.

---

performance management Continuous cycle of improving job performance with goal setting, feedback and coaching, and rewards and positive reinforcement.

line of sight Employees know the organization's strategic goals and how they need to contribute.

real WORLD // **real** PEOPLE

Starwood's CEO Frits van Paasschen Runs on Goals

[Chairman of the board Bruce] Duncan says that van Paasschen (pronounced "van passion"), 47, stood out because of his "intellectual firepower," success-shaping global strategies for consumer products at Disney, Nike, and Coors, his likable personality and the aggressive way he promised to tackle the job. Because he lacked hotel experience, he vowed to immerse himself in the industry. Since joining, he's visited 132 hotels in 20 countries and 45 cities. [He is fluent in English, Dutch, German, Italian, and Spanish.]

Van Paasschen's passion for running didn't hurt, either. "That shows someone who has a plan and gets it done," Duncan says. "It shows he'll do whatever it takes."

Van Paasschen credits running with much of his management style. Business, he says, is about conquering personal fears, setting high goals for yourself, and breaking barriers, which in many ways meshes with Starwood's culture.

What role have goals played in your life? Explain.

SOURCE: B De Lollis, "Starwood's CEO Takes an Idea and Runs with It," *USA Today*, June 23, 2008, pp 1B–2B.

Getting in shape for marathons helps Starwood's CEO Frits van Paasschen set tough goals to keep pace in the competitive hotel business.

To help you fully comprehend the power of goal setting, this section distinguishes between two types of goals, discusses management by objectives, and explains how to manage the goal-setting process.

Two Types of Goals

connect™ Go to www.mcgrawhillconnect.com for an interactive exercise to test your knowledge of managing the goal-setting process.

Goal-setting researchers have drawn an instructive distinction between performance outcome goals and learning goals. A **performance outcome goal** targets a specific end result. A **learning goal,** in contrast, strives to improve creativity and develop skills (see Real World/Real People). Managers typically overemphasize the former and ignore the latter as they try to "motivate" greater effort and achieve final results. But for employees who lack the necessary skills, performance outcome goals are more frustrating than motivating. When skills are lacking, a developmental process is needed wherein learning goals precede performance outcome goals. Goal researchers Gerard Seijts and Gary Latham explain with a golfing analogy:

Example. A performance outcome goal often distracts attention from the discovery of task-relevant strategies. For example, focusing on a golf score of 95 by novices may prevent them from focusing on the mastery of the swing and weight transfer and using the proper clubs necessary for attaining that score . . . .

In short, the novice golfer must learn how to play the game before becoming concerned with attaining a challenging performance outcome (e.g., score equals 95).[13]

This also applies in college (and later in life). Given that about 25% of students who enroll in four-year colleges never finish, goal-setting skills need more attention. A recent study with randomly selected students who were struggling academically demonstrated the power of teaching students how to skillfully set and integrate both learning and performance outcome goals. An intensive online tutorial involving how to write and achieve personal goals led to significant improvement in academic achievement four months later. The researchers summed up the tutorial as "a quick, effective, and inexpensive intervention for struggling undergraduate students."[14]

Management by Objectives

The motivational impact of performance goals and goal-based reward plans has been known for a long time. More than a century ago, Frederick Taylor attempted to scientifically establish how much work of a specified quality an individual should be assigned each day. He proposed that bonuses be based on accomplishing specific output quotas. Since the 1950s, goal setting has been promoted through a widely used management technique called management by objectives (MBO). **Management by objectives** is a management system that incorporates participation into decision making, goal setting, and objective feedback.[15] The central idea of MBO, getting individual employees to "own" a piece of a collective effort, is evident in this recent bit of advice from Google executive Paul Russell:

Example. Help your people map out their goals. Ask them to apply those aspirations to what they do every day. You'll build their sense of affiliation with the company and make them feel they belong. And they'll believe that they don't have to leave to accomplish their ambitions.[16]

A meta-analysis of MBO programs showed productivity gains in 68 of 70 different organizations. Specifically, results uncovered an average gain in productivity of 56% when top-management commitment was high. The average gain was only 6% when commitment was low. A second meta-analysis of 18 studies further demonstrated that employees' job satisfaction was significantly related to top management's commitment to an MBO implementation.[17] These impressive results are tempered by reports of ethical problems stemming from *extreme* pressure for results. Such was the case at IndyMac Bancorp, a mortgage lender seized by the government during the financial meltdown of 2008. According to one investigator: "There was a culture of top-down pressure to push through as many loans as possible—and to ignore the problems."[18] Ethically sound MBO programs marry learning goals and performance outcome goals anchored to high ethical standards.

---

performance outcome goal Targets a specific end result.

learning goal Encourages learning, creativity, and skill development.

management by objectives Management system incorporating participation into decision making, goal setting, and feedback.

Back to the Chapter-Opening Case

Why would MBO work well at NuStar?

Managing the Goal-Setting Process

There are three general steps to follow when implementing a goal-setting program.[19] Serious deficiencies in one step cannot make up for strength in the other two. The three steps need to be implemented in a systematic fashion.

Step 1: Set Goals   Whether goals are imposed or, preferably, set participatively via a free exchange with one's manager, they should be "SMART." SMART is an acronym for *specific, measurable, attainable, results* oriented, and *time* bound. Table 9–1 lists practical guidelines for writing SMART goals. There are two additional recommendations for Step 1. First, for complex tasks, employees need to be trained in problem-solving techniques and developing performance action plans. An action plan specifies the strategies or tactics necessary to accomplish a goal. As an everyday example, a person could have a goal of losing 10 pounds in two months with an action plan involving daily 30-minute walks and avoiding desserts and late-night snacks.

Second, because of individual differences, it may be necessary to establish different goals for employees performing the same job. For example, a study of 103 undergraduate business students revealed that individuals high in conscientiousness had higher motivation, had greater goal commitment, and obtained higher grades than students low in conscientiousness.[20]

table 9–1   Guidelines for Writing SMART Goals

Specific	Goals should be stated in precise rather than vague terms. For example, a goal that provides for 20 hours of technical training for each employee is more specific than stating that a manager should send as many people as possible to training classes. Goals should be quantified when possible.
Measurable	A measurement device is needed to assess the extent to which a goal is accomplished. Goals thus need to be measurable. It also is critical to consider the quality aspect of the goal when establishing measurement criteria. For example, if the goal is to complete a managerial study of methods to increase productivity, one must consider how to measure the quality of this effort. Goals should not be set without considering the interplay between quantity and quality of output.
Attainable	Goals should be realistic, challenging, and attainable. Impossible goals reduce motivation because people do not like to fail. Remember, people have different levels of ability and skill.
Results oriented	Corporate goals should focus on desired end results that support the organization's vision. In turn, an individual's goals should directly support the accomplishment of corporate goals. Activities support the achievement of goals and are outlined in action plans. To focus goals on desired end results, goals should start with the word *to,* followed by verbs such as *complete, acquire, produce, increase,* and *decrease.* Verbs such as *develop, conduct, implement,* or *monitor* imply activities and should not be used in a goal statement.
Time bound	Goals specify target dates for completion.

SOURCE: From A J Kinicki, *Performance Management Systems* (Superstition Mt., AZ: Kinicki & Associates, 2011), pp 2–9. Reprinted with permission; all rights reserved.

An individual's *goal orientation* is another important individual difference to consider when setting goals. Three types of goal orientations are a learning goal orientation, a performance-prove goal orientation, and a performance-avoid goal orientation. A team of researchers described the differences and implications for goal setting in the following way:

Example. People with a high learning goal orientation view skills as malleable. They make efforts not only to achieve current tasks but also to develop the ability to accomplish future tasks. People with a high performance-prove goal orientation tend to focus on performance and try to demonstrate their ability by looking better than others. People with a high performance-avoid goal orientation also focus on performance, but this focus is grounded in trying to avoid negative outcomes.[21]

Although some studies showed that people set higher goals, exerted more effort, had higher self-efficacy, and achieved higher performance when they possessed a learning goal orientation as opposed to either a performance-prove or performance-avoid goal orientation, other research demonstrated a more complex series of relationships.[22] Our take-away lessons are that personal goal orientations matter and individual differences need to be factored in when setting goals.

Step 2: Promote Goal Commitment   Goal commitment is important because employees are more motivated to pursue goals they view as personally relevant, obtainable, and fair. Goal commitment can be enhanced by following these guidelines:

1. Explain why the organization is committed to a comprehensive goal-setting program.
2. Create clear lines of sight by clarifying the corporate goals and linking the individual's goals to them. Jeroen van der Veer, CEO of Royal Dutch Shell, advises: "The task of leaders is to simplify."[23] He says it should take no more than two minutes to communicate the direction of the organization.
3. Let employees participate in setting their own goals and creating their own action plans. Encourage them to set challenging "stretch" goals. Goals should be difficult, but not impossible.[24]
4. Foster personal growth by having employees build **goal ladders,** chains of progressively more difficult and challenging goals.

New research evidence on goal ladders shows the important difference between focusing on completed versus remaining goals. Specifically, focusing on completed goals in the ladder promotes a feeling of satisfaction. Focusing on remaining goals in the ladder tends to motivate a higher level of achievement. High achievers are good at strategically alternating their focus on what has been accomplished (for a feeling of satisfaction) and their focus on the

Thanks to her amazing talent, rigorous goal setting, and resilience, Maya Moore led her University of Connecticut women's basketball team to back-to-back national championships. She continues to excel in the WNBA.

goal ladder A chain of progressively more difficult and challenging goals that fosters personal growth.

challenges ahead (for motivation to work harder).[25] Do you have goal ladders and, if so, where is your primary focus—backward or forward?

Step 3: Provide Support and Feedback   This step involves helping employees achieve their goals. Practical guidelines include the following:

- Make sure each employee has the necessary skills and information to reach his or her goals. As a pair of goal-setting experts succinctly stated, "Motivation without knowledge is useless."[26] Training often is required to help employees achieve difficult goals and build goal ladders.

- Pay attention to employees' effort→performance expectations, perceived self-efficacy, and reward preferences and adjust accordingly.

- Be supportive and helpful. Empower employees as they grow. Do not use goals as a threat.

- Give employees timely and task-specific feedback (knowledge of results) about what they are doing right and wrong.

- Provide monetary and nonmonetary incentives and reward both significant progress and goal accomplishment.[27]

Feedback

TO THE POINT

Why is feedback important and how should it be given?

Employees' hearty appetite for feedback too often goes unfulfilled. For example, according to one survey, "43% of employees feel they don't get enough guidance to improve their performance."[28] Achievement-oriented students also want feedback.[29] Following a difficult exam, for instance, students want to know two things: how they did and how their peers did. By letting students know how their work measures up to grading and competitive standards, an instructor's feedback permits the students to adjust their study habits so they can reach their goals. Likewise, managers in well-run organizations follow up goal setting with a feedback program to provide a rational basis for adjustment and improvement. For instance, consider the following remarks by Fred Smith, the founder and CEO of FedEx, the overnight delivery pioneer with over $35 billion in annual revenues and more than 247,000 employees.[30] Smith's experience as a US Marine company commander during the Vietnam War helped shape his leadership style.

Example. My leadership philosophy is a synthesis of the principles taught by the Marines and every organization for the past 200 years.

When people walk in the door, they want to know: What do you expect out of me? What's in this deal for me? What do I have to do to get ahead? Where do I go in this organization to get justice if I'm not treated appropriately? They want to know how they're doing. They want some feedback. And they want to know that what they are doing is important.

If you take the basic principles of leadership and answer those questions over and over again, you can be successful dealing with people.[31]

Fred Smith, CEO of FedEx, believes strong leadership involves providing specific and steady feedback to all employees.

As the term is used here, **feedback** is objective information about individual or collective performance. Subjective assessments such as "You're doing a poor job," "You're lazy," or "We really appreciate everyone's hard work" do not qualify as objective feedback. But hard data such as units sold, days absent, dollars saved,

real WORLD // real PEOPLE

Feedback Is a Way of Life for Ford's CEO Alan Mulally

Mulally meets around a circular table with his 15 top executives every Thursday at 7 am. . . . At these 2½-hour meetings, known as BPR for business plan review, he requires his direct reports to post more than 300 charts, each of them color-coded red, yellow, or green to indicate problems, caution, or progress.

At the BPR, Ford Chief Financial Officer Lewis Booth might give an update on debt reduction, or Americas chief Mark Fields might go over the mix of red, yellow, and green on new model launches. (Fields is famous for being the first Ford executive to put up a red light four years ago when he delayed the launch of an SUV because of a balky tailgate, earning him applause from Mulally for his candor.) . . . As the CEO likes to say, "You can't manage a secret. When you do this every week, you can't hide."

From a motivational standpoint, what are the pros and cons of this sort of public display and discussion of key performance data?

SOURCE: K Naughton, "The Happiest Man in Detroit," *Bloomberg Businessweek*, February 7–13, 2011, p 68.

---

projects completed, customers satisfied, and quality rejects are all candidates for objective feedback programs. Christopher D Lee, author of the book *Performance Conversations: An Alternative to Appraisals,* clarifies the concept of feedback by contrasting it with performance appraisals:

Example. Feedback is the exchange of information about the status and quality of work products. It provides a road map to success. It is used to motivate, support, direct, correct and regulate work efforts and outcomes. Feedback ensures that the manager and employees are in sync and agree on the standards and expectations of the work to be performed.

Traditional appraisals, on the other hand, discourage two-way communication and treat employee involvement as a bad thing. Employees are discouraged from participating in a performance review, and when they do, their responses are often considered "rebuttals."

To reverse this, successful performance management must contain a healthy degree of feedback and employee involvement.[32]

 LO.2 Two Functions of Feedback

Experts say feedback serves two functions for those who receive it: one is *instructional* and the other *motivational* (see Real World/Real People). Feedback instructs when it clarifies roles or teaches new behavior. For example, an assistant accountant might be advised to handle a certain entry as a capital item rather than as an expense item. On the other hand, feedback motivates when it serves as a reward or promises a reward.[33]

Having the boss tell you that a grueling project you worked on earlier has just been completed can be a rewarding piece of news. As documented by researchers, the motivational function of feedback can be significantly enhanced by pairing *specific,* challenging goals with *specific* feedback about results.[34] With these two functions of feedback in mind, we now explore the vital role of feedback recipients, some practical lessons from feedback research, 360-degree feedback, and how to give feedback for coaching purposes.

feedback Objective information about performance.

Are the Feedback Recipients Ready, Willing, and Able?

Conventional wisdom says the more feedback organizational members get, the better. An underlying assumption is that feedback works automatically. Managers simply need to be motivated to give it. According to a meta-analysis of 23,663 feedback incidents, however, feedback is far from automatically effective. While feedback did, in fact, have a generally positive impact on performance, performance actually *declined* in more than 38% of the feedback incidents.[35] Feedback also can be warped by nontask factors, such as race. A laboratory study at Stanford University focused on cross-race feedback on the content (subjective feedback) and writing mechanics (objective feedback) of written essays. White students gave African American students *less* critical *subjective* feedback than they did to white students. This positive racial bias disappeared with objective feedback.[36] These results are a bright caution light for those interested in improving job performance with feedback. Subjective feedback is easily contaminated by situational factors. Moreover, if objective feedback is to work as intended, managers need to understand the interaction between feedback recipients and their environment.

The Recipient's Characteristics   Personality characteristics such as self-esteem and self-efficacy can help or hinder one's readiness for feedback. Those having low self-esteem and low self-efficacy generally do not actively seek feedback that, unfortunately, would tend to confirm those problems. Needs and goals also influence one's openness to feedback. In a laboratory study, Japanese psychology students who scored high on need for achievement responded more favorably to feedback than did their classmates who had low need for achievement.[37] This particular relationship likely exists in Western cultures as well. For example, 331 employees in the marketing department of a large public utility in the United States were found to seek feedback on important issues or when faced with uncertain situations. Long-tenured employees from this sample also were less likely to seek feedback than employees with little time on the job.[38] High self-monitors, those chameleon-like people we discussed in Chapter 5, are also more open to feedback because it helps them adapt their behavior to the situation. Recall from Chapter 5 that high self-monitoring employees were found to be better at initiating relationships with mentors (who typically provide feedback).[39] Low self-monitoring people, in contrast, are tuned into their own internal feelings more than they are to external cues. For example, someone observed that talking to media legend and CNN founder Ted Turner, a very low self-monitor, was like having a conversation with a radio!

Researchers have started to focus more directly on the recipient's actual desire for feedback, as opposed to indirectly on personality characteristics, needs, and goals. Everyday experience tells us that not everyone really wants the performance feedback they supposedly seek. Restaurant servers who ask, "How was everything?" while presenting the bill, typically are not interested in a detailed reply.

The Recipient's Perception of Feedback   The *sign* of feedback, a term used in feedback research, refers to whether it is positive or negative. Generally, people tend to perceive and recall positive feedback more accurately than they do negative feedback.[40] But feedback with a negative sign (e.g., being told your performance is below average) can have a positive motivational impact. In fact, in one study, those who were told they were below average on a creativity test subsequently outperformed those who were led to believe their results were above average. The subjects apparently took the negative feedback as a challenge and set and pursued higher goals. Those receiving positive feedback apparently were less motivated to do better.[41] Nonetheless, feedback with a negative sign or threatening content needs to be administered carefully to avoid creating insecurity and defensiveness. Self-efficacy also can be damaged by negative feedback, as discovered in a pair of experiments with business students. The researchers concluded, "To facilitate the development of strong efficacy beliefs, managers should be careful about the provision of negative feedback. Destructive criticism by managers which attributes the cause of poor performance to internal factors reduces both the beliefs of self-efficacy and the self-set goals of recipients."[42]

The Recipient's Cognitive Evaluation of Feedback   Upon receiving feedback, people cognitively evaluate factors such as its accuracy, the credibility of the source, the fairness of the system (e.g., performance appraisal system), their performance-reward expectancies, and the reasonableness of the standards. Any feedback that fails to clear one or more of these cognitive hurdles will be rejected or downplayed. Personal experience largely dictates how these factors are weighed. For instance, you would probably discount feedback from someone who exaggerates or from someone who performed poorly on the same task you have just successfully completed. In view of the "trust gap," discussed in Chapter 11, managerial credibility is an ethical matter of central importance today. According to the authors of the book *Credibility: How Leaders Gain and Lose It, Why People Demand It,* "without a solid foundation of personal credibility, leaders can have no hope of enlisting others in a common vision."[43] Managers who have proven untrustworthy and not credible have a hard time improving job performance through feedback.

Feedback from a source who apparently shows favoritism or relies on unreasonable behavior standards would be suspect.[44] Also, as predicted by expectancy motivation theory, feedback must foster high effort→performance expectations and performance→reward linkages if it is to motivate desired behavior.

Go to www.mcgrawhillconnect.com for a self-assessment to determine how strong your desire for performance feedback is.

Practical Lessons from Feedback Research

After reviewing dozens of laboratory and field studies of feedback, a trio of OB researchers cited the following practical implications for managers:

- The acceptance of feedback should not be treated as a given; it is often misperceived or rejected. This is especially true in intercultural situations.
- Managers can enhance their credibility as sources of feedback by developing their expertise and creating a climate of trust.
- Negative feedback is typically misperceived or rejected.
- Although very frequent feedback may erode one's sense of personal control and initiative, feedback is too *infrequent* in most work organizations. Feedback needs to be tailored to the recipient.
- While average and below-average performers need extrinsic rewards for performance, high performers respond to feedback that enhances their feelings of competence and personal control.[45]

More recent research insights about feedback include the following:

- Computer-based performance feedback leads to greater improvements in performance when it is received directly from the computer system rather than via an immediate supervisor.[46]
- Recipients of feedback perceive it to be more accurate when they actively participate in the feedback session versus passively receiving feedback.[47]
- Destructive criticism tends to cause conflict and reduce motivation.[48]
- "The higher one rises in an organization the less likely one is to receive quality feedback about job performance."[49]

table 9–2 Six Common Trouble Signs for Organizational Feedback Systems

1. Feedback is used to punish, embarrass, or put down employees.

2. Those receiving the feedback see it as irrelevant to their work.

3. Feedback information is provided too late to do any good.

4. People receiving feedback believe it relates to matters beyond their control.

5. Employees complain about wasting too much time collecting and recording feedback data.

6. Feedback recipients complain about feedback being too complex or difficult to understand.

SOURCE: Adapted from C. Bell and R. Zemke, "On-Target Feedback," *Training,* June 1992, pp 36–44.

Managers who act on these research implications and the trouble signs in Table 9–2 can build credible and effective feedback systems.

Our discussion to this point has focused on traditional downward feedback. Let us explore a newer and interesting approach to feedback in the workplace.

 LO.3 360-Degree Feedback

The concept of **360-degree feedback** involves letting individuals compare their own perceived performance with behaviorally specific (and usually anonymous) performance information from their manager, subordinates, and peers. Even outsiders may be involved in what is sometimes called full-circle feedback.[50]

A meta-analysis of twenty-four 360-degree feedback studies in which the recipients were rated two or more times prompted this helpful conclusion from the researchers:

Example. Improvement is most likely to occur when feedback indicates that change is necessary, recipients have a positive feedback orientation, perceive a need to change their behavior, react positively to the feedback, believe change is feasible, set appropriate goals to regulate their behavior, and take actions that lead to skill and performance improvement.[51]

Top management support and an organizational climate of openness can help 360-degree feedback programs succeed. A recent example involves Larry Fink, CEO of BlackRock, a Wall Street investment firm managing an astounding $3.45 trillion in assets including the state pension funds for California and New York:

Example. As he ruminates on the future, he jumps up to fetch a blue binder from his bookshelf. "We do a 360 review of every leader," he says, opening the book. "This is really intense stuff."

He starts to read an anonymous comment contributed by another BlackRock executive: "Overall, I'd give Larry a 96 out of 100," he begins. Then, "I worry about Larry. I love that he's client focused, but one day he's going to keel over. In flying all around the world, he insists on taking commercial transportation. We should probably get him a plane."[52]

Research evidence and personal experience lead us to *favor* anonymity and *discourage* linking 360-degree feedback to pay and promotion decisions. According to one expert, *trust* is the issue:

Example. Trust is at the core of using 360-degree feedback to enhance productivity. Trust determines how much an individual is willing to contribute for an employer. Using 360 confidentially, for developmental purposes, builds trust; using it to trigger pay and personnel decisions puts trust at risk.[53]

Thus, 360-degree feedback definitely has a place in the development of managerial skills, especially in today's team-based organizations.

How to Give Feedback for Coaching Purposes and Organizational Effectiveness

Managers need to keep the following tips in mind when giving feedback as part of a comprehensive performance management program:

- Focus on *performance,* not personalities.
- Give *specific* feedback linked to learning goals and performance outcome goals.
- Channel feedback toward *key result areas* for the organization.
- Give feedback as *soon* as possible.
- Give feedback to coach *improvement,* not just for final results.
- Base feedback on *accurate* and *credible* information.
- Pair feedback with *clear expectations* for improvement.[54]

Organizational Reward Systems

Rewards are an ever-present and always controversial feature of organizational life. (Think of the ongoing debate over CEO compensation packages in the hundreds of millions of dollars.)[55] Some employees see their jobs as the source of a paycheck and little else. Others derive great pleasure from their jobs and association with co-workers. In fact, according to a Gallup survey, 55% of American workers said "they would continue to work even if they won a lottery jackpot to the tune of $10 million."[56] (How about you?) Even volunteers who donate their time to charitable organizations, such as the Red Cross, walk away with rewards in the form of social recognition and pride of having given unselfishly of their time. Hence, the subject of organizational rewards includes, but goes far beyond, monetary compensation.[57] This section examines key components of organizational reward systems to provide a conceptual background for discussing the timely topic of pay for performance.

Despite the fact that reward systems vary widely, it is possible to identify and interrelate some common components. The model in Figure 9–2 focuses on three important components: (1) types of rewards, (2) distribution criteria, and (3) desired outcomes. Let us examine these components.

◀ ....
TO THE POINT
What should managers do to improve job performance with intrinsic and extrinsic rewards?
....

360-degree feedback Comparison of anonymous feedback from one's superior, subordinates, and peers with self-perceptions.

real WORLD // real PEOPLE

Seventy-one-Year-Old Judith Van Ginkel Loves 60-Hour Workweeks

Judith Van Ginkel is 71 years old and works 50 to 60 hours a week. And yet, "I'm the luckiest person I know," she says.

Here's why: Well beyond what many people consider retirement age, Van Ginkel (whose career has mostly been in medical administration) runs Every Child Succeeds, a home visitation program overseen by Cincinnati Children's Hospital. Over the past decade, the dozens of social workers on her team have checked in on 17,000 at-risk pregnant women and their children, ensuring that these growing families get proper medical care and support. As a result, the infant mortality rate among participant families is well below the national average, despite their poverty rates—an outcome that Van Ginkel finds more exciting than playing golf. And so, "I'm going to continue doing this as long as I can do it well," she tells me.

What role does intrinsic motivation play in this situation?

SOURCE: L Vanderkam, "This Isn't Grandpa's Retirement," *USA Today*, January 5, 2011, p 7A.

LO.4   Types of Rewards

Financial, material, and social rewards qualify as **extrinsic rewards** because they come from the environment. Psychic rewards, however, are **intrinsic rewards** because they are self-granted. An employee who works to obtain extrinsic rewards, such as money or praise, is said to be extrinsically motivated. One who derives pleasure from the task itself or experiences a sense of competence or self-determination is said to be intrinsically motivated (see Real World/Real People). The relative importance of extrinsic and intrinsic rewards is a matter of culture and personal tastes.[58]

Back to the Chapter-Opening Case

Why is volunteering so intrinsically rewarding?

figure 9–2 A General Model of Organizational Reward Systems

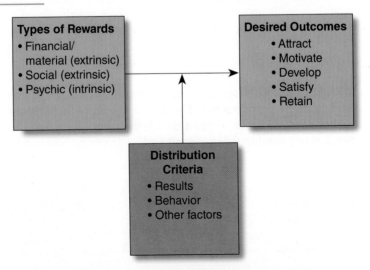

Reward Distribution Criteria

According to one expert on organizational reward systems, three general criteria for the distribution of rewards are as follows:

- *Performance: results.* Tangible outcomes such as individual, group, or organization performance; quantity and quality of performance.
- *Performance: actions and behaviors.* Such as teamwork, cooperation, risk taking, creativity.
- *Nonperformance considerations.* Customary or contractual, where the type of job, nature of the work, equity, tenure, level in hierarchy, and so forth are rewarded.[59]

One trend today is toward performance criteria and away from nonperformance criteria such as seniority. Another trend involves mixing reward distribution criteria: Westinghouse Electric is a recent case in point: "To ensure the rank and file get in gear, managers are now being graded not just on the dollars they generate but also on how many customers they've spoken to and how many proposals they've sent out."[60]

Desired Outcomes of the Reward System

As listed in Figure 9–2, a good reward system should attract talented people and motivate and satisfy them once they have joined the organization. Further, a good reward system should foster personal growth and development and keep talented people from leaving. A prime example is Tulsa-based QuikTrip: "Employees are treated so well at this 24-hour convenience chain—wages, benefits, and training—that they stay around for the long haul. More than 200 have been here more than 20 years."[61]

The Building Blocks of Intrinsic Rewards and Motivation

As defined earlier, intrinsic rewards are self-granted. But this does not leave management out of the picture. Indeed, there is a great deal managers can do to create situations in which employees are more likely to experience intrinsic rewards and be intrinsically motivated. Kenneth Thomas's model of intrinsic motivation provides helpful direction.[62] His model combines elements of job design (discussed in Chapter 8), the concept of empowerment (discussed in Chapter 15), and Edward Deci and Richard Ryan's cognitive evaluation theory. Deci and Ryan contend that people must satisfy their needs for autonomy and competence when completing a task for it to be intrinsically motivating.[63] Thomas uses the concept of *building blocks* to show managers how to construct the right conditions for four basic intrinsic rewards: meaningfulness, choice, competence, and progress (see Figure 9–3). Let us examine management's leadership challenges for each building block.

Unpaid community service volunteers are intrinsically rewarded with the satisfaction of expanding their comfort zone while helping others. Are you a volunteer?

Leading for Meaningfulness   Managers lead for meaningfulness by *inspiring* their employees and *modeling* desired behaviors.

---

extrinsic rewards Financial, material, or social rewards from the environment.

intrinsic rewards Self-granted, psychic rewards.

figure 9–3   Thomas's Building Blocks for Intrinsic Rewards and Motivation

Choice	Competence
• Delegated authority • Trust in workers • Security (no punishment) for honest mistakes • A clear purpose • Information	• Knowledge • Positive feedback • Skill recognition • Challenge • High, noncomparative standards
Meaningfulness	**Progress**
• A non-cynical climate • Clearly identified passions • An exciting vision • Relevant task purposes • Whole tasks	• A collaborative climate • Milestones • Celebrations • Access to customers • Measurement of improvement

SOURCE: Reprinted with permission of the publisher. From K Thomas, *Intrinsic Motivation at Work: Building Energy and Commitment.* Copyright © 2000 by K Thomas, Berrett-Koehler Publishers, San Francisco, CA. All rights reserved. www.bkconnection.com.

Figure 9–3 reveals how managers can accomplish this by helping employees to identify their passions at work and creating an exciting organizational vision employees feel connected to. In support of this recommendation, results from Gallup poll surveys show that employees are more engaged and productive when they see the connection between their work and the organization's vision.[64] This connection creates a sense of purpose for employees. Some jobs are so vital that they inherently foster a strong sense of meaningfulness. For example, consider this unique job at America's largest nuclear power plant near Phoenix:

Example. By 6 am, Michelle Catts is making her way to the office past guards armed with automatic weapons, ultrasensitive X-ray machines, electronic gates and sensors that sniff out explosives. . . .

Catts is one of four Nuclear Regulatory Commission inspectors at the plant serving as government watchdogs to make sure Arizona Public Service Co finds problems before they affect safety. . . .

"My job every day is to make sure this plant is operating safely," Catts said. "That's a pretty important job. It's a good feeling at the end of the day to know I found important things to ask about."[65]

Leading for Choice   Managers lead for choice by *empowering* employees and *delegating* meaningful assignments and tasks. This is how Gail Evans, an executive vice president at Atlanta-based CNN, feels about leading for choice.

Example. [She] says delegating is essential. If you refuse to let your staff handle their own projects, you're jeopardizing their advancement—because they aren't learning new skills and adding successes to their resume—and you're wasting your precious hours doing someone else's work.[66]

Leading for Competence   This involves *supporting* and *coaching* employees. Figure 9–3 lists key factors and actions for enhancing a sense of competence. Managers first need to make sure employees have the knowledge needed to successfully perform their jobs. Deficiencies can be handled through training and mentoring. Providing positive feedback and sincere recognition can also be coupled with the assignment of a challenging task to fuel employees' intrinsic motivation.

Leading for Progress   Managers lead for progress by *monitoring* and *rewarding* others. Douglas R Conant, CEO of Campbell Soup Company, has engineered a remarkable turnaround and is a good role model in this regard:

Example. The turnaround has been catalyzed by cost-cutting, smart innovations, and a concerted effort to reinvigorate the workforce. . . .

Conant hasn't shaken up a complacent 137-year-old company by being in-your-face. He happily gives others credit and deflects praise. He's not brash. . . . In his time at Campbell, he has sent out more than 16,000 hand-written thank-you notes to staffers, from the chief investment officer to the receptionist at headquarters—notes often found hanging in people's offices or above their desks. "[In business] we're trained to find things that are wrong, but I try to celebrate what's right," says Conant.[67]

We now direct our attention to *extrinsic* rewards—money, opportunities, and recognition granted by others.

 LO.5 Why Do Extrinsic Rewards Too Often Fail to Motivate?

Despite huge investments of time and money for monetary and nonmonetary compensation, the desired motivational impact often is not achieved. A management consultant/writer offers these eight reasons:

1. Too much emphasis on monetary rewards.
2. Rewards lack an "appreciation effect."
3. Extensive benefits become entitlements.
4. Counterproductive behavior is rewarded. (For example, "a pizza delivery company focused its rewards on the on-time performance of its drivers, only to discover that it was inadvertently rewarding reckless driving.")[68]
5. Too long a delay between performance and rewards.
6. Too many one-size-fits-all rewards.
7. Use of one-shot rewards with a short-lived motivational impact.
8. Continued use of demotivating practices such as layoffs, across-the-board raises and cuts, and excessive executive compensation.[69]

These stubborn problems have fostered a search for more effective extrinsic reward practices. While a thorough discussion of modern compensation practices is way beyond our present scope, we can explore a general approach to boosting the motivational impact of monetary rewards—pay for performance.

Pay for Performance

Pay for performance is the popular term for monetary incentives linking at least some portion of the paycheck directly to results or accomplishments. Many refer

pay for performance Monetary incentives tied to one's results or accomplishments.

These folks not only make really cool picnic baskets, they actually work *inside* one! Longaberger's headquarters building in Frazeyburg, Ohio, is a giant replica of the firm's famous maple wood baskets. Each day, 2,500 employees—who are paid on a piece-rate basis—weave 40,000 hand-crafted baskets. This team of Longaberger employees won a prestigious quality award for cutting waste and improving productivity.

to it simply as *incentive pay,* while others call it *variable pay.* "Broad-based variable pay programs are offered by 80% of US companies."[70] The general idea behind pay-for-performance schemes—including but not limited to merit pay, bonuses, and profit sharing—is to give employees an incentive for working harder or smarter. Pay for performance is something extra, compensation above and beyond basic wages and salaries. Proponents of incentive compensation say something extra is needed because hourly wages and fixed salaries do little more than motivate people to show up at work and put in the required hours.[71] The most basic form of pay for performance is the traditional piece-rate plan, whereby the employee is paid a specified amount of money for each unit of work. For example, 2,500 artisans at Longaberger's, in Frazeyburg, Ohio, are paid a fixed amount for each handcrafted wooden basket they weave. Together, they produce 40,000 of the prized maple baskets daily.[72] Sales commissions, whereby a salesperson receives a specified amount of money for each unit sold, is another long-standing example of pay for performance.[73] Today's service economy is forcing management to adapt creatively and go beyond piece rate and sales commission plans to accommodate greater emphasis on product and service quality, interdependence, and teamwork.

Modern Incentive Pay Plans   With everything from on-the-spot cash awards to team-based pay to skill-based pay, today's incentive compensation practices are still very much in the experimental stage. Much remains to be learned from research and practice. Meanwhile, the major take-away lesson is that it is foolish to even contemplate a one-size-fits-all approach to incentive compensation.

Research Insights   According to available expert opinion and research results, pay for performance too often falls short of its goal of improved job performance. "Experts say that roughly half the incentive plans they see don't work, victims of poor design and administration."[74] In fact, one study documented how incentive pay had a *negative* effect on the performance of 150,000 managers from 500 financially distressed companies.[75] A meta-analysis of 39 studies found only a modest positive correlation between financial incentives and performance *quantity* and no impact on performance *quality.*[76] Other researchers have found only a weak statistical link between large executive bonuses paid out in good years and subsequent improvement in corporate profitability.[77] Also, in a survey of small business owners, more than half said their commission plans failed to motivate extra effort from their salespeople.[78] Linking teachers' merit pay to student performance, a highly touted school reform idea, has had mixed results.

A study of variable pay plans by Hewitt Associates, a leading human resources consulting firm, uncovered this instructive pattern:

Example. [M]ore than one-third (41%) of the companies with single-digit revenue growth said the cost outweighed the benefits for them. Not only have the plans failed to improve business results for a quarter of these organizations, they have actually led to adverse results for 26% of those surveyed.

The situation was reversed, however, for companies experiencing double-digit revenue growth. These companies reported that their programs achieved positive outcomes and contributed to business results. "We've found that companies achieving high-revenue growth have successful programs because they provide the appropriate amount of administrative, communication and monetary support," says Paul Shafer, a business leader for Hewitt. If not implemented well, he says, variable pay "will be seen as an entitlement by employees and a substantial loss to employers."[79]

Clearly, the pay-for-performance area is still very much up in the air.

LO.6 Getting the Most Out of Extrinsic Rewards and Pay for Performance

Based on what we have learned to date, here is a workable plan for maximizing the motivational impact of extrinsic rewards:

- Tie praise, recognition, and noncash awards to *specific* results.
- Make pay for performance an integral part of the organization's basic strategy (e.g., pursuit of best-in-the-industry product or service quality).
- Base incentive determinations on objective performance data.
- Have all employees actively participate in the development, implementation, and revision of the performance-pay formulas.
- Encourage two-way communication so problems with the incentive plan will be detected early.
- Build pay-for-performance plans around participative structures such as suggestion systems or problem-solving teams.
- Reward teamwork and cooperation whenever possible.
- Actively sell the plan to supervisors and middle managers who may view employee participation as a threat to their traditional notion of authority.
- If annual cash bonuses are granted, pay them in a lump sum to maximize their motivational impact.
- Selectively use creative noncash rewards to create buzz and excitement.[80]

connect Go to www.mcgrawhillconnect.com for an interactive exercise to test your knowledge of the building blocks of an effective reward system.

Back to the **Chapter-Opening Case**

Why is NuStar's approach to incentive compensation so effective?

LO.7 Positive Reinforcement

Feedback and extrinsic reward programs too often are ineffective because they are administered in haphazard ways.[81] For example, consider these scenarios:

- A young programmer stops e-mailing creative suggestions to his boss because she never responds.
- The office politician gets a great promotion while her more skilled co-workers scratch their heads and gossip about the injustice.

In the first instance, a productive behavior faded away for lack of encouragement. In the second situation, unproductive behavior was unwittingly rewarded. Feedback and rewards need to be handled more precisely. Fortunately, the field of behavioral psychology can help. Thanks to the pioneering work of Edward L Thorndike, B F Skinner, and many others, a behavior modification technique called *positive reinforcement* helps managers achieve needed discipline and desired effect when providing feedback and granting extrinsic rewards.

Thorndike's Law of Effect

During the early 1900s, Edward L Thorndike observed in his psychology laboratory that a cat would behave randomly and wildly when placed in a small box with a secret trip lever that opened a door. However, once the cat accidentally tripped the lever and escaped, the animal would go straight to the lever when placed back in the box. Hence, Thorndike formulated his famous **law of effect,** which says *behavior with favorable consequences tends to be repeated, while behavior with unfavorable consequences tends to disappear.*[82] This was a dramatic departure from the prevailing notion a century ago that behavior was the product of inborn instincts.

Skinner's Operant Conditioning Model

Skinner refined Thorndike's conclusion that behavior is controlled by its consequences. Skinner's work became known as *behaviorism* because he dealt strictly with observable behavior.[83] As a behaviorist, Skinner believed it was pointless to explain behavior in terms of unobservable inner states such as needs, drives, attitudes, or thought processes.[84] He similarly put little stock in the idea of self-determination.

In his 1938 classic, *The Behavior of Organisms,* Skinner drew an important distinction between the two types of behavior: respondent and operant behavior.[85] He labeled unlearned reflexes, or stimulus–response (S–R) connections, **respondent behavior.** This category of behavior was said to describe a very small proportion of adult human behavior. Examples of respondent behavior would include shedding tears while peeling onions and reflexively withdrawing one's hand from a hot stove.[86] Skinner attached the label **operant behavior** to behavior that is learned when one "operates on" the environment to produce desired consequences. Some call this the response–stimulus (R–S) model. Years of controlled experiments with pigeons in "Skinner boxes" helped Skinner develop a sophisticated technology of behavior control, or operant conditioning. For example, he taught pigeons how to pace figure-eights and how to bowl by reinforcing the under-weight (and thus hungry) birds with food whenever they more closely approximated target behaviors. Skinner's work spawned the field of behavior modification and has significant implications for OB because the vast majority of organizational behavior falls into the operant category.[87]

Renowned behavioral psychologist B F Skinner and your co-author Bob Kreitner met and posed for a snapshot at an Academy of Management meeting in Boston. As a behaviorist, Skinner preferred to deal with observable behavior and its antecedents and consequences in the environment rather than with inner states such as attitudes and cognitive processes. Professor Skinner was a fascinating man who left a permanent mark on modern psychology.

Contingent Consequences

Contingent consequences, according to Skinner's operant theory, control behavior in four ways: positive reinforcement, negative reinforcement, punishment, and extinction. The term *contingent* means there is a systematic if-then linkage between the target behavior and the consequence. Remember Mom (and Pink Floyd) saying something to this effect: "If you don't finish your dinner, you don't get dessert"? (See Figure 9–4.) To avoid the all-too-common mislabeling of these consequences, let us review some formal definitions.

figure 9–4   Contingent Consequences in Operant Conditioning

Nature of Consequence

Behavior–Consequence Relationship

	Positive or Pleasing	Negative or Displeasing
Contingent Presentation	**Positive Reinforcement** *Behavioral outcome:* Target behavior occurs *more* often	**Punishment** *Behavioral outcome:* Target behavior occurs *less* often
Contingent Withdrawal	**Punishment (response cost)** *Behavioral outcome:* Target behavior occurs *less* often	**Negative Reinforcement** *Behavioral outcome:* Target behavior occurs *more* often

(no contingent consequence)
Extinction
Behavioral outcome:
Target behavior occurs *less* often

LO.8 Positive Reinforcement Strengthens Behavior   **Positive reinforcement** is the process of strengthening a behavior by contingently presenting something pleasing. (Importantly, a behavior is strengthened when it increases in frequency and weakened when it decreases in frequency.) A software engineer who volunteers for overtime because of praise and recognition from the boss is responding to positive reinforcement. In a recent field study, university fundraisers increased their number of calls after hearing a message of gratitude from their manager.[88] Indeed, busy managers need to be reminded about the powerful positive reinforcement effect of a simple "thank you," expressions of gratitude, and praise. When 388 administrative professionals were asked to rank their "most preferred forms of recognition in the workplace," verbal recognition came in number one at 42%. (Cash bonuses trailed at 19%.)[89]

A corporate culture built on positive reinforcement can foster loyalty, hard work, and creativity. This is especially true in hard economic times, as exemplified by JM Family Enterprises in Deerfield Beach, Florida:

Example. Amid falling sales, many intensely loyal employees at this privately held Toyota distributor volunteered to forgo bonuses. CEO Colin Brown rejected their offers and paid out bonuses, but asked for their support in cutting costs elsewhere in the company.[90]

Negative Reinforcement Also Strengthens Behavior   **Negative reinforcement** is the process of strengthening a behavior by contingently withdrawing something displeasing. For example, an army drill sergeant who stops yelling

law of effect Behavior with favorable consequences is repeated; behavior with unfavorable consequences disappears.

respondent behavior Skinner's term for unlearned stimulus–response reflexes.

operant behavior Skinner's term for learned, consequence-shaped behavior.

positive reinforcement Making behavior occur more often by contingently presenting something positive.

negative reinforcement Making behavior occur more often by contingently withdrawing something negative.

Go to www.mcgrawhillconnect.com for an interactive exercise to test your knowledge of positive reinforcement.

when a recruit jumps out of bed has negatively reinforced that particular behavior. Similarly, the behavior of clamping our hands over our ears when watching a jumbo jet take off is negatively reinforced by relief from the noise. Negative reinforcement is often confused with punishment. But the two strategies have opposite effects on behavior. Negative reinforcement, as the word *reinforcement* indicates, strengthens a behavior because it provides relief from an unpleasant situation.

Punishment Weakens Behavior   **Punishment** is the process of weakening behavior through either the contingent presentation of something displeasing or the contingent withdrawal of something positive. A manager assigning a tardy employee to a dirty job exemplifies the first type of punishment. Docking a tardy employee's pay is an example of the second type of punishment, called *response cost punishment*. Legal fines involve response cost punishment. Salespeople who must make up any cash register shortages out of their own pockets are being managed through response cost punishment. Ethical questions can and should be raised about this type of on-the-job punishment.[91]

Extinction Also Weakens Behavior   **Extinction** is the weakening of a behavior by ignoring it or making sure it is not reinforced. Getting rid of a former boyfriend or girlfriend by refusing to take his or her calls is an extinction strategy. A good analogy for extinction is to imagine what would happen to your houseplants if you stopped watering them. Like a plant without water, a behavior without occasional reinforcement eventually dies. Although very different processes, both punishment and extinction have the same weakening effect on behavior.

Schedules of Reinforcement

As just illustrated, contingent consequences are an important determinant of future behavior. The *timing* of behavioral consequences can be even more important. Based on years of tedious laboratory experiments with pigeons in highly controlled environments, Skinner and his colleagues discovered distinct patterns of responding for various schedules of reinforcement.[92]

Although some of their conclusions can be generalized to negative reinforcement, punishment, and extinction, it is best to think only of positive reinforcement when discussing schedules.

Continuous Reinforcement   Every instance of a target behavior is reinforced when a **continuous reinforcement** (CRF) schedule is in effect. For instance, when your iPhone is operating properly, you are reinforced with a screen display and sound every time you turn it on (a CRF schedule). But, as with any CRF schedule of reinforcement, the behavior of turning on the device will undergo rapid extinction if it is unresponsive.

Intermittent Reinforcement   Unlike CRF schedules, **intermittent reinforcement** involves reinforcement of *some* but not all instances of a target behavior. Four subcategories of intermittent schedules are fixed and variable ratio schedules and fixed and variable interval schedules. Reinforcement in *ratio* schedules is contingent on the number of responses observed. *Interval* reinforcement is tied to the passage of time. Some common examples of the four types of intermittent reinforcement are as follows:

1. *Fixed ratio.* Piece-rate pay; bonuses tied to the sale of a fixed number of units.
2. *Variable ratio.* Slot machines that pay off after a variable number of lever pulls; lotteries that pay off after the purchase of a variable number of tickets.
3. *Fixed interval.* Hourly pay; annual salary paid on a regular basis.

4. *Variable interval.* Random supervisory praise and pats on the back for employees who have been doing a good job.

Scheduling Is Critical   The schedule of reinforcement can more powerfully influence behavior than the magnitude of reinforcement. Although this proposition grew out of experiments with pigeons, subsequent on-the-job research confirmed it. Consider, for example, a field study of 12 unionized beaver trappers employed by a lumber company to keep the large rodents from eating newly planted tree seedlings.[93]

The beaver trappers were randomly divided into two groups that alternated weekly between two different bonus plans. Under the first schedule, each trapper earned his regular $7 per hour wage plus $1 for each beaver caught. Technically, this bonus was paid on a CRF schedule. The second bonus plan involved the regular $7 per hour wage plus a one-in-four chance (as determined by rolling the dice) of receiving $4 for each beaver trapped. This second bonus plan qualified as a variable ratio (VR-4) schedule. In the long run, both incentive schemes averaged out to a $1-per-beaver bonus. Surprisingly, however, when the trappers were under the VR-4 schedule, they were 58% more productive than under the CRF schedule, despite the fact that the net amount of pay averaged out the same for the two groups during the 12-week trapping season.

Work Organizations Typically Rely on the Weakest Schedule
Generally, variable ratio and variable interval schedules of reinforcement produce the strongest behavior that is most resistant to extinction. As gamblers will attest, variable schedules hold the promise of reinforcement after the next try. For example, the following drama at a Laughlin, Nevada, gambling casino is one more illustration of the potency of variable ratio reinforcement:

Example. An elderly woman with a walker had lost her grip on the slot [machine] handle and had collapsed on the floor.

"Help," she cried weakly.

The woman at the machine next to her interrupted her play for a few seconds to try to help her to her feet, but all around her the army of slot players continued feeding coins to the machines.

A security man arrived to soothe the woman and take her away.

"Thank you," she told him appreciatively. "But don't forget my winnings."[94]

Organizations without at least some variable reinforcement are less likely to prompt this type of dedication to task. A good example is Zappos, the Las Vegas–based online retailer, where "any employee can give any other employee a $50 bonus for a job well done."[95]

Unfortunately, time-based pay schemes such as hourly wages and yearly salaries that rely on the weakest schedule of reinforcement (fixed interval) are still the rule in today's workplaces. In fact, according to the US Bureau of Labor Statistics, "59 percent of US workers are paid by the hour."[96] While a steady paycheck is always welcome, it lacks the "surprise effect," something akin to drawing a winning

---

punishment Making behavior occur less often by contingently presenting something negative or withdrawing something positive.

extinction Making behavior occur less often by ignoring or not reinforcing it.

continuous reinforcement Reinforcing every instance of a behavior.

intermittent reinforcement Reinforcing some but not all instances of a behavior.

"full house" in a poker game. Creative managers know how to tap the power of variable reinforcement. For example,

---

Example. Ami Dar, who founded and runs idealist.org, picks one day a year to declare a Sun Day. He waits for the weatherman to alert him to a Tiffany-blue sky, cool breezes, and sunshine—and then he alerts his staff that the doors to the office will be closed and they'd better spend some time outside. A few people may panic at the thought of rescheduling meetings and missing emails, but Ami . . . [says] that they come back to work the next day with a little more . . . bounce in their steps. One of the keys to the success of a Sun Day? The element of surprise. It jars folks out of their routines and gives a (pleasant) shock to their senses. It also makes them feel doubly appreciated, in a way that you don't when a gift is expected.[97]

Back to the Chapter-Opening Case

Is there any form of variable reinforcement in NuStar's compensation plan that could boost employees' motivation with a surprise effect?

LO.9 Behavior Shaping

Have you ever wondered how trainers at aquarium parks manage to get bottle-nosed dolphins to do flips, killer whales to carry people on their backs, and seals to juggle balls? The results are seemingly magical. Actually, a mundane learning process called *shaping* is responsible for the animals' antics.

Two-ton killer whales, for example, have a big appetite, and they find buckets of fish very reinforcing. So if the trainer wants to ride a killer whale, he or she reinforces very basic behaviors that will eventually lead to the whale being ridden. The killer whale is contingently reinforced with a few fish for coming near the trainer, then for being touched, then for putting its nose in a harness, then for being straddled, and eventually for swimming with the trainer on its back. In effect, the trainer systematically raises the behavioral requirement for reinforcement.[98] Thus, **shaping** is defined as the process of reinforcing closer and closer approximations to a target behavior.

Shaping works very well with people, too, especially in training and quality programs involving continuous improvement. Praise, recognition, and instructive and credible feedback cost managers little more than moments of their time. Yet, when used in conjunction with learning goals and a behavior-shaping program, these consequences can efficiently foster significant improvements in job performance. The key to successful behavior shaping lies in reducing a complex target behavior to easily learned steps and then faithfully (and patiently) reinforcing any improvement. For example, Continental Airlines used a cash bonus program to improve its on-time arrival record from one of the worst in the industry to one of the best. Employees originally were promised a $65 bonus each month Continental earned a top-five ranking. Now it takes a second- or third-place ranking to earn the $65 bonus, and a $100 bonus awaits employees when they achieve a number one ranking.[99] (Table 9–3 lists practical tips on shaping.)

Okay, so what's the trick? Actually, a rather simple process called behavior shaping by trainers can get killer whales to eventually perform complex stunts. The whales like fish, lots of it. So they will learn progressively more difficult tasks to be positively reinforced with some fish.

table 9–3   Ten Practical Tips for Shaping Job Behavior

1. *Accommodate the process of behavioral change.* Behaviors change in gradual stages, not in broad, sweeping motions.

2. *Define new behavior patterns specifically.* State what you wish to accomplish in explicit terms and in small amounts that can be easily grasped.

3. *Give individuals feedback on their performance.* A once-a-year performance appraisal is not sufficient.

4. *Reinforce behavior as quickly as possible.*

5. *Use powerful reinforcement.* To be effective, rewards must be important to the employee—not to the manager.

6. *Use a continuous reinforcement schedule.* New behaviors should be reinforced every time they occur. This reinforcement should continue until these behaviors become habitual.

7. *Use a variable reinforcement schedule for maintenance.* Even after behavior has become habitual, it still needs to be rewarded, though not necessarily every time it occurs.

8. *Reward teamwork—not competition.* Group goals and group rewards are one way to encourage cooperation in situations in which jobs and performance are interdependent.

9. *Make all rewards contingent on performance.*

10. *Never take good performance for granted.* Even superior performance, if left unrewarded, will eventually deteriorate.

SOURCE: Adapted from A T Hollingsworth and D Tanquay Hoyer, "How Supervisors Can Shape Behavior," *Personnel Journal,* May 1985. pp 86–88.

shaping Reinforcing closer and closer approximations to a target behavior.

Summary of Key Concepts

1. *Define the term* performance management, *distinguish between learning goals and performance outcome goals, and explain the three-step goal-setting process.* Performance management is a continuous cycle of improving individual job performance with goal setting, feedback and coaching, and rewards and positive reinforcement. Learning goals encourage learning, creativity, and skill development. Performance outcome goals target specified end results. The three-step goal-setting process includes (*a*) set goals that are SMART—specific, measurable, attainable, results oriented, and time bound; (*b*) promote goal commitment with clear lines of sight to the organization's mission, participation, and goal ladders; (*c*) provide support and feedback with needed information and resources, training, and knowledge of results.

2. *Identify the two basic functions of feedback, and specify at least three practical lessons from feedback research.* Feedback, in the form of objective information about performance, both instructs and motivates. Feedback is not automatically accepted as intended, especially negative feedback. Managerial credibility can be enhanced through expertise and a climate of trust. Feedback must

not be too frequent or too scarce and must be tailored to the individual. Feedback directly from computers is effective. Active participation in the feedback session helps people perceive feedback as more accurate. The quality of feedback received decreases as one moves up the organizational hierarchy.

3. *Define 360-degree feedback, and summarize how to give good feedback in a performance management program.* A focal person receives anonymous 360-degree feedback from subordinates, the manager, peers, and selected others such as customers or suppliers. Good feedback is tied to performance goals and clear expectations, linked with specific behavior or results, reserved for key result areas, given as soon as possible, provided for improvement as well as for final results, focused on performance rather than on personalities, and based on accurate and credible information.

4. *Distinguish between extrinsic and intrinsic rewards, and explain the four building blocks of intrinsic rewards and motivation.* Extrinsic rewards—including pay, material goods, and social recognition—are granted by others. Intrinsic rewards are psychic rewards, such as a sense of competence or a feeling of accomplishment, that are self-granted and experienced internally. According to Thomas's model, the four basic intrinsic rewards are meaningfulness, choice, competence, and progress. Managers can boost intrinsic motivation by letting employees work on important whole tasks (meaningfulness), delegating and trusting (choice), providing challenge and feedback (competence), and collaboratively celebrating improvement (progress).

5. *Summarize the reasons why extrinsic rewards often fail to motivate employees.* Extrinsic reward systems can fail to motivate employees for these reasons: overemphasis on money, no appreciation effect, benefits become entitlements, wrong behavior is rewarded, rewards are delayed too long, use of one-size-fits-all rewards, one-shot rewards with temporary impact, and demotivating practices such as layoffs.

6. *Discuss how managers can generally improve extrinsic reward and pay-for-performance plans.* They need to be strategically anchored, based on quantified performance data, highly participative, actively sold to supervisors and middle managers, and teamwork oriented. Annual bonuses of significant size are helpful.

7. *State Thorndike's law of effect, and explain Skinner's distinction between respondent and operant behavior.* According to Edward L Thorndike's law of effect, behavior with favorable consequences tends to be repeated, while behavior with unfavorable consequences tends to disappear. B F Skinner called unlearned stimulus–response reflexes *respondent behavior.* He applied the term *operant behavior* to all behavior learned through experience with environmental consequences.

8. *Define positive reinforcement, negative reinforcement, punishment, and extinction, and distinguish between continuous and intermittent schedules of reinforcement.* Positive and negative reinforcement are consequence management strategies that strengthen behavior, whereas punishment and extinction weaken behavior. These strategies need to be defined objectively in terms of their actual impact on behavior frequency, not subjectively on the basis of intended impact.

Every instance of a behavior is reinforced with a continuous reinforcement (CRF) schedule. Under intermittent reinforcement schedules—fixed and variable ratio or fixed and variable interval—some, rather than all, instances of a target behavior are reinforced. Variable schedules produce the most extinction-resistant behavior.

9. *Demonstrate your knowledge of behavior shaping.* Behavior shaping occurs when closer and closer approximations of a target behavior are reinforced. In effect, the standard for reinforcement is made more difficult as the individual learns. The process begins with continuous reinforcement, which gives way to intermittent reinforcement when the target behavior becomes strong and habitual.

Key Terms

Performance management, 238	360-degree feedback, 248	Positive reinforcement, 257
Line of sight, 239	Extrinsic rewards, 250	Negative reinforcement, 257
Performance outcome goal, 240	Intrinsic rewards, 250	Punishment, 258
Learning goal, 240	Pay for performance, 253	Extinction, 258
Management by objectives, 241	Law of effect, 256	Continuous reinforcement, 258
Goal ladder, 243	Respondent behavior, 256	Intermittent reinforcement, 258
Feedback, 244	Operant behavior, 256	Shaping, 260

OB in Action Case Study

Why DineEquity's CEO Julia A Stewart Manages Like a Teacher[100]

Background: Stewart's restaurant business has 3,300 locations featuring the familiar IHOP and Applebee's brands.

My dad taught high school civics and US history, and throughout my life I learned from his example—from how he approached his students. If Dad was teaching a class on Abraham Lincoln, he'd work extremely hard to find some obscure details that would humanize Lincoln and pique the students' interest. . . .

He was convinced that teaching was the noblest profession and was livid and mortified when I decided to go into the restaurant business instead. But years later, when I'd hit the "big time" and was a VP at Taco Bell responsible for a thousand restaurants, I was able to show him how, as a businesswoman, I was using what he had taught.

One day we visited six or seven restaurants together in South Central LA. These were workplaces where employees typically didn't get a ton of praise or thank-you's. At each one, I'd go behind the counter, get on the food prep line, and catch an employee doing something right. I'd say, "Great job—that's the perfect way to portion that taco," and then turn to the next person down the line and ask, "Did you see how well this was done?" Or I'd stand in the middle of the kitchen and half-shout, "Who did the walk-in here today?" There would be silence, and then someone would confess, "I did." And I'd compliment him on the job and ask the people in the kitchen to gather around so they could see what had gone right and what could be done even better the next time. At the end of the day, Dad took me out for a drink and told me, "Julia, you teach and mentor, too—you just do it in a different classroom." . . .

If I'm on a plane with one of our top people, I'll ask a lot of questions about her work, ask for her expertise on a problem, and focus on coming up with a solution together. In other words, I coach—which is a kind of teaching. . . .

When employees feel like they're learning—in the office or in the kitchen—they become more enthusiastic about their work, and that shows through to the customer in a hundred different ways.

Questions for Discussion

1. What elements of the performance management cycle in Figure 9–1 are evident in Stewart's comments?
2. Is Julia Stewart a good role model for how to generate employee engagement and motivate the employees in her company's restaurants? Explain.
3. In terms of Thomas's four building blocks in Figure 9–3, how would you rate Stewart's "teaching" style of management for generating intrinsic motivation in her employees? Explain.
4. What role does positive reinforcement play in this case? Do you think Stewart uses it effectively? Explain.
5. Would you like to work as a restaurant manager for DineEquity under Stewart's leadership? Why or why not?

Legal/Ethical Challenge

Is Overtime the Right Way to Go?[101]

Quality Float Works of Schaumburg, Illinois, laid off three employees in 2009 and put its remaining 18 on a four-day workweek.

Now [mid-2010], sales are surging for the company, which makes metal balls that businesses use to signal when water levels get too high or low in tanks and troughs. Customers depleted their inventories in the slowdown and are panicked, says company president Sandra Westlund-Deenihan.

She's giving workers up to nine hours of overtime weekly. Although she hired two staffers recently, she's holding off on further additions. Existing employees "went through the hard times, and I felt I owed it to them first," she says.

Some workers are going straight from part-time to overtime duty.

What are the ethical implications of Westlund-Deenihan's decision?

1. This is a very fair deal based on the management principle of "share the pain, share the gain." It also gives Westlund-Deenihan some room to maneuver in case the economy softens again.
2. Rehiring the laid-off employees (those willing and able to return) for at least part-time work, before granting overtime to existing employees, would have better served the greater good. In all fairness, the laid-off employees probably suffered the most.
3. Westlund-Deenihan should have had the employees vote for overtime or for bringing back all laid-off employees, and acted accordingly.
4. Invent other options. Explain and discuss.

Web Resources

For study material and exercises that apply to this chapter, visit our website at **www.mhhe.com/kreitner10e**

part three

Group and Social Processes

chapter 10

Group Dynamics

 Learning Objectives

When you finish studying the material in this chapter, you should be able to:

LO.1   Identify the four sociological criteria of a group, and discuss the impact of social networking on group dynamics.

LO.2   Describe the five stages in Tuckman's theory of group development, and discuss the threat of group decay.

LO.3   Distinguish between role conflict and role ambiguity.

LO.4   Contrast roles and norms, and specify four reasons norms are enforced in organizations.

LO.5   Distinguish between task and maintenance roles in groups.

LO.6   Summarize the practical contingency management implications for group size.

LO.7   Discuss why managers need to carefully handle mixed-gender task groups.

LO.8   Describe groupthink, and identify at least four of its symptoms.

LO.9   Define social loafing, and explain how managers can prevent it.

How Can Managers Reduce the Pain of a Layoff?

As part of a company-wide reduction, several managers at an . . . [Intel factory in Hillsboro, Oregon,] lost jobs. An engineer who worked for Pat [McDonald, an Intel executive], Sumit Guha, told me how "she recounted the contributions of these employees in an open forum, wishing them luck, acknowledging that these employees were being let go for no fault of their own, and we all gave these employees a hand in appreciation of their contributions."

Things got worse in early 2009 when Intel announced the factory would cease production at year's end because it was using older technology—and approximately one thousand workers would lose their positions. Pat not only expressed concern and compassion, she took a stance that demonstrated she had her employees' backs. Pat quickly announced to her team that although output metrics would continue to be important, helping people get through the transition was a higher priority—especially finding affected employees new jobs inside and outside of Intel. Pat and her team not only provided extensive outplacement counseling and related services, they personally visited numerous local employers to campaign for new jobs for their people. Managers and employees emulated this behavior. For example, employees shared job search leads and helped each other prepare for interviews, even as they were vying for the same positions. . . .

Pat's emphasis on people and connection with them not only instilled calm, her priorities helped many find good new jobs. And plant performance didn't suffer a bit; productivity, efficiency, and quality reached record levels in 2009.[1]

Organizations, by definition, are collections of people constantly interacting to achieve something greater than individuals could accomplish on their own. Research consistently reveals the importance of social skills for both individual and organizational success. For example, a recent study of 1,040 managers employed by 100 manufacturing and service organizations in the United States found 15 reasons why managers fail in the face of rapid change. The top two reasons were "ineffective communication skills/practices" and "poor work relationships/interpersonal skills."[2] Relationships *do* matter in the workplace, as demonstrated by Pat McDonald's compassionate handling of the layoff at Intel. No surprise that Intel was number 51 on *Fortune* magazine's 2011 list of the 100 best companies to work for, up from 98 the year before.[3]

Management, as defined in Chapter 1, involves getting things done with and through others. Experts say managers need to build *social capital* with four key social skills: social perception, impression management, persuasion and social influence, and social adaptability (see Table 10–1).[4] How polished are your social skills? Where do you need improvement? Daniel Goleman recommends an expanded form of emotional intelligence he calls *social intelligence*, "being intelligent not just *about* our relationships but also *in* them."[5] For example, consider how this informal relationship evolved into both a win-win business relationship and a stronger community:

Example. A decade ago, Archie Williams, the founder of a small printer-toner distribution company in the impoverished Boston neighborhood of Roxbury, happened to play a round of golf with Tom Stemberg, the founder and then chief executive of office supply mega-retailer Staples. Through 18 holes, the pair pitched, putted, and chatted—and became fast friends. Soon, Stemberg started buying printer cartridges from Williams's company, Roxbury Technology.

The deal turned out to be a win for both Staples and Roxbury—the company and the neighborhood. The office supply giant found a reliable supplier for an important product and Roxbury got a partner that could distribute its goods nationally. Stemberg soon became a mentor to Williams's company, helping with strategic planning, finance, and legal advice. Roxbury Technology is now a preferred supplier to Staples . . . [with nearly $17 million in annual sales, and] almost all of Roxbury's 65 employees live in the neighborhood or nearby.[6]

table 10–1   Key Social Skills Managers Need for Building Social Capital

SOCIAL SKILL	DESCRIPTION	TOPICAL LINKAGES IN THIS TEXT
Social perception	Ability to perceive accurately the emotions, traits, motives, and intentions of others	• Individual differences, Chapters 5 and 6 • Emotional intelligence, Chapter 5 • Social perception, Chapter 7 • Employee motivation, Chapters 8 and 9
Impression management	Tactics designed to induce liking and a favorable first impression by others	• Impression management, Chapter 15
Persuasion and social influence	Ability to change others' attitudes or behavior in desired directions	• Influence tactics and social power, Chapter 15 • Leadership, Chapter 16
Social adaptability	Ability to adapt to, or feel comfortable in, a wide range of social situations	• Cultural intelligence, Chapter 4 • Managing change, Chapter 18

SOURCE: Columns 1 and 2 excerpted from R A Baron and G D Markman, "Beyond Social Capital: How Social Skills Can Enhance Entrepreneurs' Success," *Academy of Management Executive,* February 2000, table 1, p 110.

Back to the Chapter-Opening Case

How did Intel's Pat McDonald build social capital with the social skills listed in Table 10–1?

Let us begin by defining the term *group* as a prelude to examining types of groups, functions of group members, social networking in the workplace, and the group development process. Our attention then turns to group roles and norms, the basic building blocks of group dynamics. Effects of group structure and member characteristics on group outcomes are explored next. Finally, three serious threats to group effectiveness are discussed. (This chapter serves as a foundation for our discussion of teams and teamwork in the following chapter.)

LO.1 Groups in the Social Media Age

Groups and teams are inescapable features of modern life.[7] College students are often teamed with their peers for class projects. Parents serve on community advisory boards at their local schools. Managers find themselves on product planning committees and productivity task forces. Productive organizations simply cannot function without gathering individuals into groups and teams. But as personal experience shows, group effort can bring out both the best and the worst in people. A marketing department meeting, where several people excitedly brainstorm and refine a creative new advertising campaign, can yield results beyond the capabilities of individual contributors.

Conversely, committees have become the butt of jokes (e.g., a committee is a place where they take minutes and waste hours; a camel is a horse designed by a committee) because they all too often are plagued by lack of direction and by conflict. Modern managers need a solid understanding of groups and group processes to both avoid their pitfalls and tap their vast potential. Moreover, the huge and growing presence of the Internet and modern communication technologies—with their own unique networks of informal and formal social relationships—is a major challenge for profit-minded business managers.

Although other definitions of groups exist, we draw from the field of sociology and define a **group** as two or more freely interacting individuals who share collective norms and goals and have a common identity.[8] Figure 10–1 illustrates how the four criteria in this definition combine to form a conceptual whole. Organizational psychologist Edgar Schein shed additional light on this concept by drawing instructive distinctions between a group, a crowd, and an organization:

Example. The size of a group is thus limited by the possibilities of mutual interaction and mutual awareness. Mere aggregates of people do not fit this definition because they do not interact and do not perceive themselves to be a group even if they are aware of each other as, for instance, a crowd on a street corner watching some event. A total department, a union, or a whole organization would not be a group in spite of thinking of themselves as "we," because they generally do not all interact and are not all aware of each other. However, work teams, committees,

TO THE POINT
What can managers do about social networking technology blurring the line between formal and informal groups?

group Two or more freely interacting people with shared norms and goals and a common identity.

figure 10–1 Four Sociological Criteria of a Group

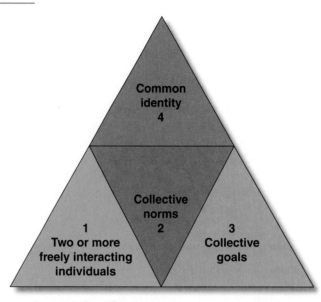

subparts of departments, cliques, and various other informal associations among organizational members would fit this definition of a group.[9]

connect Go to www.mcgrawhillconnect.com for an interactive exercise to test your knowledge of the four sociological criteria of a group.

Take a moment now to think of various groups of which you are a member. Does each of your groups satisfy the four criteria in Figure 10–1?

Formal and Informal Groups

Individuals join groups, or are assigned to groups, to accomplish various purposes. If the group is formed by a manager to help the organization accomplish its goals, then it qualifies as a **formal group**. Formal groups typically wear such labels as work group, project team, committee, corporate board, or task force. An **informal group** exists when the members' overriding purpose of getting together is friendship or common interests. Formal and informal groups may or may not overlap in the workplace. For instance, 23 percent of 1,050 women employees who had planned weddings did not plan to invite co-workers to their wedding.[10] Also, for better or for worse, family-run businesses and hiring family and friends can create overlapping formal and informal groups.[11]

Functions of Formal Groups

Researchers point out that formal groups fulfill two basic functions: *organizational* and *individual.* The various functions are listed in Table 10–2. Complex combinations of these functions can be found in formal groups at any given time.

For example, consider what Mazda's new American employees experienced when they spent a month working in Japan before the opening of the firm's Flat Rock, Michigan, plant:

Example. After a month of training in Mazda's factory methods, whipping their new Japanese buddies at softball and sampling local watering holes, the Americans were fired up. . . . [A maintenance manager] even faintly praised the Japanese

table 10–2 Formal Groups Fulfill Organizational and Individual Functions

ORGANIZATIONAL FUNCTIONS	INDIVIDUAL FUNCTIONS
1. Accomplish complex, interdependent tasks that are beyond the capabilities of individuals.	1. Satisfy the individual's need for affiliation.
2. Generate new or creative ideas and solutions.	2. Develop, enhance, and confirm the individual's self-esteem and sense of identity.
3. Coordinate interdepartmental efforts.	3. Give individuals an opportunity to test and share their perceptions of social reality.
4. Provide a problem-solving mechanism for complex problems requiring varied information and assessments.	4. Reduce the individual's anxieties and feelings of insecurity and powerlessness.
5. Implement complex decisions.	5. Provide a problem-solving mechanism for personal and interpersonal problems.
6. Socialize and train newcomers.	

SOURCE: Adapted from E H Schein, *Organizational Psychology*, 3rd ed (Englewood Cliffs, NJ: Prentice Hall, 1980), pp 149–51.

practice of holding group calisthenics at the start of each working day: "I didn't think I'd like doing exercises every morning, but I kind of like it."[12]

connect™ Go to www.mcgrawhillconnect.com for an interactive exercise to test your knowledge of the functions of formal groups.

While Mazda pursued the organizational functions it wanted—interdependent teamwork, creativity, coordination, problem solving, and training—the American workers benefited from the individual functions of formal groups. Among those benefits were affiliation with new friends, enhanced self-esteem, exposure to the Japanese social reality, and reduction of anxieties about working for a foreign-owned company. In short, Mazda created a workable blend of organizational and individual group functions by training its newly hired American employees in Japan.

Formal-Informal Boundaries Have Blurred in the Age of Social Media

Social relationships are complex, alive, and dynamic. They have little regard for arbitrary boundaries, especially with today's real-time social media. The desirability of overlapping formal and informal groups is problematic. Some managers firmly believe personal friendship fosters productive teamwork on the job while others view workplace "bull sessions" as a serious damper on productivity. In fact, a recent survey of workers 18 and older surfaced the major positives and negatives of workplace friendships. The positives were a more supportive workplace (selected by 70% of the employees) and increased teamwork (69%). The negatives were gossip (44%) and favoritism (37%).[13] Managers are responsible for

Some lively sports competition among co-workers can break down job boundaries, open lines of communication, build teamwork, and generate healthy group dynamics.

formal group Formed by the organization.

informal group Formed by friends or those with common interests.

real WORLD // real PEOPLE

Russian Culture Embraces Social Media

Facebook officially launched its [Russian] site in April [2010] and only ranks No. 5 so far, according to Internet tracker comScore, but its growth has been impressive. From January until August of 2010, its Russian operation has racked up a 376 percent increase in users, to 4.5 million.

. . . [T]here is a long tradition in Russia of relying on informal networks for simple day-to-day survival. "In Russia, there is no sense that you can rely on the public or the system, so you've traditionally had to rely on a network of friends," says Esther Dyson, a venture capitalist who has been investing in Russia's tech sector for

over a decade. In a country with weak institutions, "it's very natural for people to network for what they want." Even in these less oppressive, post-Soviet times, relationships are critical to everything from landing a job to wriggling out of a problem with authorities.

How are social media such as Facebook and Twitter empowering oppressed people around the world today?

SOURCE: Excerpted from J Ioffe, "In Russia, Facebook Is More Than a Social Network," *Bloomberg Businessweek,* January 3–9, 2011, pp 32–33.

---

striking a workable balance, based on the maturity and goals of the people involved. Additionally, there is the ethics-laden issue of managers being friends with the people they oversee.

The Social Media Revolution   For many years, the term *networking* simply meant building a modest list of personal and professional contacts and attempting to keep in touch on a regular basis. But thanks to Internet tools such as e-mail, blogs, Facebook, LinkedIn, YouTube, and Twitter, networking has gone hyper and global—with Facebook and Twitter even playing key roles in the Egyptian revolution.[14] (See Real World/Real People.) Why settle for a static list of contacts when you can have instant, comprehensive, and impactful interaction with countless thousands? *PC* magazine offers this working definition of a **social networking site (SNS):**

Example. A Web site that provides a virtual community for people interested in a particular subject or just to "hang out" together. Members create their own online "profile" with biographical data, pictures, likes, dislikes and any other information they choose to post. They communicate with each other by voice, chat, instant message, videoconference and blogs, and the service typically provides a way for members to contact friends of other members.[15]

Members of an SNS may or may not know each other on a face-to-face basis and SNS use is dominated by, but not restricted to, young people. According to a Pew Research Center survey, 75% of online users ages 18–24 and 30% of online users ages 35–44 have at least one profile on an SNS.[16]

As SNSs continue to mushroom and new applications emerge, organizational leaders generally have been left scratching their heads. Their unanswered questions abound: How can we profit from this? How can we embrace and/or control it? Is it a good or bad thing? What are the implications of this massive connectivity for productivity, privacy, harassment, confidentiality, protection of intellectual property, and information systems security? Networking via social media truly is the Wild West of organizational life, with mostly unanswered questions and unknown consequences.[17] (Corporate social media policies are discussed in Chapter 14.) Although the lines between formal and informal groups in the workplace have been blurred almost beyond recognition, managers still need to establish some boundaries.

Should Managers Be Friends with Those Who Report to Them?

A long-standing group dynamics dilemma magnified by social media involves manager–employee friendships (see the Legal/Ethical Challenge at the end of this chapter). In their business advice column, Jack and Suzy Welch offered this sound advice:

Example. [Y]ou don't need to be friends with your subordinates, as long as you share the same values for the business. But if you are friends with them, lucky you. Working with people you really like for 8 or 10 hours a day adds fun to everything.

That said, remember that boss-subordinate friendships live or die because of one thing: complete, unrelenting candor. Candor is imperative in any working relationship, but it's especially necessary when there's a social aspect involved. You don't want your liking someone's personality to automatically communicate that you like his or her performance. You may, but performance evaluations have to come in a distinct and separate set of conversations at work—as often as four times a year—in which you sit down with your subordinate, put the shared laughs from last weekend's barbecue in the corner, and talk about what's expected and what has been delivered.[18]

This requires a good deal of emotional and social intelligence.

🐾 LO.2 The Group Development Process

Groups and teams in the workplace go through a maturation process, such as one would find in any life-cycle situation (e.g., humans, organizations, products). While there is general agreement among theorists that the group development process occurs in identifiable stages, they disagree about the exact number, sequence, length, and nature of those stages.[19] One oft-cited model is the one proposed in 1965 by educational psychologist Bruce W Tuckman. His original model involved only four stages (forming, storming, norming, and performing).

The five-stage model in Figure 10–2 evolved when Tuckman and a doctoral student added "adjourning" in 1977.[20] A word of caution is in order. Somewhat akin to Maslow's need hierarchy theory, Tuckman's theory has been repeated and taught so often and for so long that many have come to view it as documented fact, not merely a theory. Even today, it is good to remember Tuckman's own caution that his group development model was derived more from group therapy sessions than from natural-life groups. Still, many in the organizational behavior (OB) field like Tuckman's five-stage model of group development because of its easy-to-remember labels and commonsense appeal.

Five Stages

Let us walk through the five stages in Tuckman's model. Notice in Figure 10–2 how individuals give up a measure of their independence when they join and participate in a group. Also, the various stages are not necessarily of the same duration or intensity. For instance, the storming stage may be practically nonexistent or painfully long, depending on the goal clarity and the commitment and maturity of the members. You can make this process come to life by relating the various stages

TO THE POINT

Why is it important to know the stages of group development when creating effective work groups and teams?

connect™ Go to www.mcgrawhillconnect.com for an interactive exercise to test your knowledge of the group development process.

social networking site (SNS) A Web-enabled community of people who share all types of information.

figure 10–2 Tuckman's Five-Stage Theory of Group Development

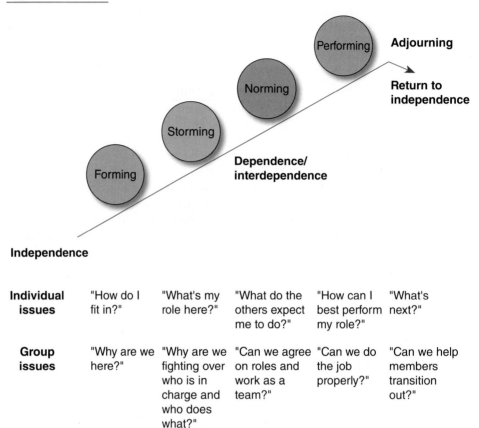

	Forming	Storming	Norming	Performing	Adjourning
Individual issues	"How do I fit in?"	"What's my role here?"	"What do the others expect me to do?"	"How can I best perform my role?"	"What's next?"
Group issues	"Why are we here?"	"Why are we fighting over who is in charge and who does what?"	"Can we agree on roles and work as a team?"	"Can we do the job properly?"	"Can we help members transition out?"

to your own experiences with work groups, committees, athletic teams, social or religious groups, or class project teams. Some group happenings that surprised you when they occurred may now make sense or strike you as inevitable when seen as part of a natural development process.

Stage 1: Forming   During this ice-breaking stage, group members tend to be uncertain and anxious about such things as their roles, who is in charge, and the group's goals. Also, prior experience between members of the group can create friction, according to a new study.[21] Mutual trust is low, and there is a good deal of holding back to see who takes charge and how. If the formal leader (e.g., a supervisor) does not assert his or her authority, an emergent leader will eventually step in to fulfill the group's need for leadership and direction. Leaders typically mistake this honeymoon period as a mandate for permanent control. But later problems may force a leadership change.

Recent research found improved communication among members of new problem-solving teams comprised of specialists possessing unique knowledge[22] (a common situation today). So teambuilding, discussed in the next chapter, can give new groups a helpful running start.

Stage 2: Storming   This is a time of testing. Individuals test the leader's policies and assumptions as they try to determine how they fit into the power structure. Subgroups take shape, and subtle forms of rebellion, such as procrastination, occur. Many groups stall in stage 2 because power politics erupts into open rebellion.[23]

Stage 3: Norming   Groups that make it through stage 2 generally do so because a respected member, other than the leader, challenges the group to resolve its power struggles so something can be accomplished. Questions about authority and power are resolved through unemotional, matter-of-fact group discussion. A feeling of team spirit is experienced because members believe they have found their proper roles. **Group cohesiveness**, defined as the "we feeling" that binds members of a group together, is the principal by-product of stage 3.[24] (For a good laugh, see the golfing explanation below the photo.)

Stage 4: Performing

Activity during this vital stage is focused on solving task problems. As members of a mature group, contributors get their work done without hampering others. There is a climate of open communication, strong cooperation, and lots of helping behavior. Conflicts and job boundary disputes are handled constructively and efficiently. Cohesiveness and personal commitment to group goals help the group achieve more than any one individual could acting alone. According to a pair of group development experts,

---

Example. the group structure can become flexible and adjust to fit the requirements of the situation without causing problems for the members. Influence can shift depending on who has the particular expertise or skills required for the group task or activity. Subgroups can work on special problems or subproblems without posing threats to the authority or cohesiveness of the rest of the group.[25]

Stage 5: Adjourning

The work is done; it is time to move on to other things. Having worked so hard to get along and get something done, many members feel a compelling sense of loss. The return to independence can be eased by rituals celebrating "the end" and "new beginnings." Parties, award ceremonies, graduations, or mock funerals can provide the needed punctuation at the end of a significant group project. Leaders need to emphasize valuable lessons learned in group dynamics to prepare everyone for future group and team efforts.

A *Fortune* article examined the question, Why do people love to mix golf and business? (Hint: It's all about group dynamics.):

Ask people why they golf with business associates, and the answer is always the same: It's a great way to build relationships. They say this far more about golf than about going to dinner or attending a baseball game, and for good reason. Indeed, this may be the central fact about corporate golf, though it's rarely said: When people golf together, they see one another humiliated. At least 95% of all golfers are terrible, which means that in 18 holes everyone in the foursome will hit a tree, take three strokes in one bunker, or four-putt, with everyone else watching. Bonding is simply a matter of people jointly going through adversity, and a round of golf will furnish plenty of it. Of course it's only a game, but of course it isn't, so the bonds can be surprisingly strong. And what's that worth?

SOURCE: G Colvin, "Why Execs Love Golf," *Fortune*, April 30, 2001, p 46.

Back to the Chapter-Opening Case

What evidence of stage 5 in Tuckman's group development model can you find in Pat McDonald's handling of the plant closing?

Group Development: Research and Practical Implications

A growing body of group development research provides managers with some practical insights.

---

group cohesiveness A "we feeling" binding group members together.

Extending the Tuckman Model: Group Decay

An interesting study of 10 software development teams, ranging in size from 5 to 16 members, enhanced the practical significance of Tuckman's model.[26] Unlike Tuckman's laboratory groups who worked together only briefly, the teams of software engineers worked on projects lasting *years*. Consequently, the researchers discovered more than simply a five-stage group development process. Groups were observed actually shifting into reverse once Tuckman's "performing" stage was reached, in what the researchers called *group decay*. In keeping with Tuckman's terminology, the three observed stages of group decay were labeled "de-norming," "de-storming," and "de-forming." These additional stages take shape as follows:

- *De-norming.* As the project evolves, there is a natural erosion of standards of conduct. Group members drift in different directions as their interests and expectations change.

- *De-storming.* This stage of group decay is a mirror opposite of the storming stage. Whereas disagreements and conflicts arise rather suddenly during the storming stage, an undercurrent of discontent slowly comes to the surface during the de-storming stage. Individual resistance increases and cohesiveness declines.

- *De-forming.* The work group literally falls apart as subgroups battle for control. Those pieces of the project that are not claimed by individuals or subgroups are abandoned. "Group members begin isolating themselves from each other and from their leaders. Performance declines rapidly because the whole job is no longer being done and group members little care what happens beyond their self-imposed borders."[27]

The primary management lesson from this study is that group leaders should not become complacent upon reaching the performing stage. According to the researchers, "The performing stage is a knife edge or saddle point, not a point of static equilibrium."[28] Awareness is the first line of defense. Beyond that, constructive steps need to be taken to reinforce norms, bolster cohesiveness, and reaffirm the common goal—*even when work groups seem to be doing their best.*

Feedback

Another fruitful study was carried out by a pair of Dutch social psychologists. They hypothesized that interpersonal feedback would vary systematically during the group development process. "The unit of feedback measured was a verbal message directed from one participant to another in which some aspect of behavior was addressed."[29] After collecting and categorizing 1,600 instances of feedback from four different eight-person groups, they concluded the following:

- Interpersonal feedback increases as the group develops through successive stages.

- Interpersonal feedback becomes more specific as the group develops.

- As the group develops, positive feedback increases and negative feedback decreases.

- The credibility of peer feedback increases as the group develops.[30]

These findings hold important lessons for managers. The content and delivery of interpersonal feedback among work group or committee members can be used as a gauge of whether the group is developing properly. For example, the onset of stage 2 (storming) will be signaled by a noticeable increase in *negative* feedback. Effort can then be directed at generating specific, positive feedback among the members so the group's development will not stall. Our discussion of feedback in Chapter 9 is helpful in this regard.

Deadlines

Field and laboratory studies found uncertainty about deadlines to be a major disruptive force in both group development and intergroup relations. The practical implications of this finding were summed up by the researcher as follows:

Example. Uncertain or shifting deadlines are a fact of life in many organizations. Interdependent organizational units and groups may keep each other waiting, may suddenly move deadlines forward or back, or may create deadlines that are known to be earlier than is necessary in efforts to control erratic workflows. The current research suggests that the consequences of such uncertainty may involve more than stress, wasted time, overtime work, and intergroup conflicts. Synchrony in group members' expectations about deadlines may be critical to groups' abilities to accomplish successful transitions in their work.[31]

Thus, effective group management involves clarifying not only tasks and goals, but schedules and deadlines as well. When group members accurately perceive important deadlines, the pacing of work and timing of interdependent tasks tend to be more efficient.

Leadership Styles   Along a somewhat different line, experts in the area of leadership contend that different leadership styles are needed as work groups develop.

Example. In general, it has been documented that leadership behavior that is active, aggressive, directive, structured, and task-oriented seems to have favorable results early in the group's history. However, when those behaviors are maintained throughout the life of the group, they seem to have a negative impact on cohesiveness and quality of work. Conversely, leadership behavior that is supportive, democratic, decentralized, and participative seems to be related to poorer functioning in the early group development stages. However, when these behaviors are maintained throughout the life of the group, more productivity, satisfaction, and creativity result.[32]

The practical punch line here is that managers are advised to shift from a directive and structured leadership style to a participative and supportive style as the group develops.[33]

Roles and Norms: Social Building Blocks for Group and Organizational Behavior

◀ ·······················
TO THE POINT
What are roles and norms and how do they affect workplace behavior?
·······················

Work groups transform individuals into functioning organizational members through subtle yet powerful social forces.[34] These social forces, in effect, turn "I" into "we" and "me" into "us." Group influence weaves individuals into the organization's social fabric by communicating and enforcing both role expectations and norms. We need to understand roles and norms if we are to effectively manage group and organizational behavior.

Roles

Four centuries have passed since William Shakespeare had his character Jaques speak the following memorable lines in Act II of *As You Like It:* "All the world's a stage, And all the men and women merely players; They have their exits and their entrances; And one man in his time plays many parts." This intriguing notion of

figure 10–3 A Role Episode

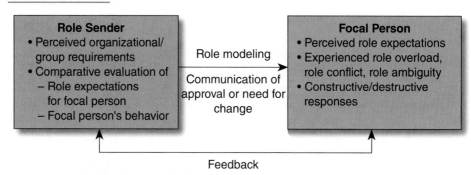

Role Sender		Focal Person
• Perceived organizational/ group requirements	Role modeling	• Perceived role expectations
• Comparative evaluation of	Communication of approval or need for change	• Experienced role overload, role conflict, role ambiguity
– Role expectations for focal person		• Constructive/destructive responses
– Focal person's behavior		

Feedback

SOURCE: Adapted in part from R L Kohn, D M Wolfe, R P Quinn, and J D Snoek, *Organizational Stress: Studies in Role Conflict and Ambiguity,* 1981 ed. (Malabar, FL: Robert E Krieger Publishing, 1964), p 26.

all people as actors in a universal play was not lost on 20th-century sociologists who developed a complex theory of human interaction based on roles. According to an OB scholar, "**roles** are sets of behaviors that persons expect of occupants of a position."[35] Role theory attempts to explain how these social expectations influence employee behavior. This section explores role theory by analyzing a role episode and defining the terms *role overload, role conflict,* and *role ambiguity.*

Role Episodes   A role episode, as illustrated in Figure 10–3, consists of a snapshot of the ongoing interaction between two people. In any given role episode, there is a role sender and a focal person who is expected to act out the role. Within a broader social context, one may be simultaneously a role sender and a focal person. For the sake of social analysis, however, it is instructive to deal with separate role episodes.

Role episodes begin with the role sender's perception of the relevant organization's or group's behavioral requirements. Those requirements serve as a standard for formulating expectations for the focal person's behavior. The role sender then cognitively evaluates the focal person's actual behavior against those expectations. Appropriate verbal and behavioral messages are then sent to the focal person to pressure him or her into behaving as expected. A meta-analysis of the results from 160 different studies involving 77,954 employees confirmed that positive and negative peer pressure powerfully influence role performance.[36] This is how Westinghouse used a carrot-and-stick approach to communicate role expectations:

Example. The carrot is a plan, that . . . rewarded 134 managers with options to buy 764,000 shares of stock for boosting the company's financial performance.

The stick is quarterly meetings that are used to rank managers by how much their operations contribute to earnings per share. The soft-spoken . . . [chairman of the board] doesn't scold. He just charts in green the results of the sectors that have met their goals and charts the laggards in red. Peer pressure does the rest. Shame "is a powerful tool," says one executive.[37]

Interestingly, only 10 percent strongly agreed and 31 percent agreed with the following statement in a new workplace survey: "Do you believe that individuals in your organization are held accountable for meeting performance expectations?"[38] Significant productivity improvement could be achieved if organizations did a better job of communicating and enforcing role expectations.

On the receiving end of the role episode, the focal person accurately or inaccurately perceives the communicated role expectations and modeled behavior.

Various combinations of role overload, role conflict, and role ambiguity are then experienced. (These three outcomes are defined and discussed in the following sections.) The focal person then responds constructively by engaging in problem solving, for example, or destructively because of undue tension, stress, and strain.

Role Overload According to organizational psychologist Edgar Schein, **role overload** occurs when "the sum total of what role senders expect of the focal person far exceeds what he or she is able to do."[39] Students who attempt to handle a full course load and maintain a decent social life while working 30 or more hours a week know full well the physical and emotional consequences of role overload. As the individual tries to do more and more in less and less time, stress mounts, personal effectiveness slips, and health may deteriorate.

"How did life suddenly get so complicated?" When tackling adulthood, with all its competing role expectations and pressures, it is good to have these three anchors: (1) I know who I am and what I can do, (2) I know what I want, and (3) I have sound goals and plans for getting there.

LO.3 Role Conflict Have you ever felt like you were being torn apart by the conflicting demands of those around you? If so, you were a victim of role conflict. **Role conflict** is experienced when "different members of the role set expect different things of the focal person." Job holders often face conflicting demands between work and family, as discussed in Chapter 6. Women tend to experience greater work-versus-family role conflict than men because they typically shoulder more of the household, child care, and elder care duties.

Example. The average wife still does roughly double the housework of the average husband: the equivalent of two full workdays of additional chores each week. Even when the man is unemployed, the woman handles a majority of the domestic workload, and it's the same story with child care. If both parents are working, women spend 400 percent more time with the kids. Meanwhile, the number of fatherless kids in America has nearly tripled since 1960, and the percentage of men who call themselves stay-at-home dads has stalled below 3 percent. The old roles, say sociologists, are hard to shake.[40]

connect Go to www.mcgrawhillconnect.com for a self-assessment to help determine your team role preference.

Employees in single-person and nontraditional households have their own versions of role conflict between work and outside interests.

Role conflict also may be experienced when internalized values, ethics, or personal standards collide with others' expectations. For instance, an otherwise ethical production supervisor may be told by a superior to "fudge a little" on the quality control reports so an important deadline will be met. The resulting role conflict forces the supervisor to choose between being loyal but unethical or ethical but disloyal. Tough ethical choices such as this mean personal turmoil, interpersonal conflict, and even resignation. Consequently, experts say business schools should do a better job of weaving ethics education into their course requirements.

roles Expected behaviors for a given position.

role overload Others' expectations exceed one's ability.

role conflict Others have conflicting or inconsistent expectations.

Role Ambiguity   Those who experience role conflict may have trouble complying with role demands, but they at least know what is expected of them. Such is not the case with **role ambiguity**, which occurs when "members of the role set fail to communicate to the focal person expectations they have or information needed to perform the role, either because they do not have the information or because they deliberately withhold it."[41] In short, people experience role ambiguity when they do not know what is expected of them. Organizational newcomers often complain about unclear job descriptions and vague promotion criteria. According to role theory, prolonged role ambiguity can foster job dissatisfaction, erode self-confidence, and hamper job performance. As the following situation illustrates, management can reduce workplace role ambiguity:

Example. Good leaders excel at converting something ambiguous into something behavioral. Take Terry Leahy, one of the leaders responsible for reversing the fortunes of Tesco, now the UK's No 1 grocer. One of Tesco's ambiguous goals was to do a better job "listening to customers." Leahy broke down that goal into a set of specific actions. For instance, cashiers were trained to call for help anytime more than one person was waiting in the checkout line. In addition, Tesco received 100,000 queries per week from customers. Leahy's team made sure that all Tesco managers had access to customer concerns. . . . As a result, they learned counterintuitive lessons, such as that customers dislike stainless-steel refrigerators, which remind people of a hospital—not an ideal association for a grocer.[42]

As might be expected, role ambiguity varies across cultures. In a 21-nation study, people in individualistic cultures were found to have higher role ambiguity than people in collectivist cultures.[43] In other words, people in collectivist or "we" cultures had a clearer idea of others' expectations. Collectivist cultures make sure everyone knows their proper place in society. People in individualistic "me" cultures, such as the United States, may enjoy more individual discretion, but comparatively less input from others has its price—namely, greater role ambiguity.

As mentioned earlier, these role outcomes typically are experienced in some combination, usually to the detriment of the individual and the organization. In fact, a study in Israel documented lower job performance when employees experienced a combination of role conflict and role ambiguity.[44]

 **LO.4** Norms

Norms are more encompassing than roles. While roles involve behavioral expectations for specific positions, norms help organizational members determine right from wrong and good from bad. According to one respected team of management consultants: "A **norm** is an attitude, opinion, feeling, or action—shared by two or more people—that guides their behavior."[45] Although norms are typically unwritten and seldom discussed openly, they have a powerful influence on group and organizational behavior. PepsiCo, for instance, has evolved a norm that equates corporate competitiveness with physical fitness. According to observers,

---

Example. Leanness and nimbleness are qualities that pervade the company. When Pepsi's brash young managers take a few minutes away from the office, they often head straight for the company's physical fitness center or for a jog around the museum-quality sculptures outside of PepsiCo's Purchase, New York, headquarters.[46]

At PepsiCo and elsewhere, group members positively reinforce those who adhere to current norms with friendship and acceptance. On the other hand,

real WORLD // real PEOPLE: ethics

How Founder Bill Witherspoon Made Helping Others the Norm at Sky Factory

I think of our factory as a community, and service is the core of the community. There are two kinds of service. One is: I do this for you, and I expect a return. For example, I provide good customer service, and I expect loyalty. The other kind of service is selfless. I do something for you without thought of a return. I help you spontaneously and without thinking about it. That second kind of service is powerful. When someone has a moment of free time, how wonderful if she automatically thinks,

Now, what can I do to help someone else? At the start of our Friday meetings, the leader for that week tells an appreciative story about someone at the company and presents the person with $25. Often, the story involves an unselfish, unsolicited offer of help.

Why is the concept of "community" a powerful group dynamics tool in today's workplaces?

SOURCE: L Buchanan, "The Art of Work," *Inc,* June 2010, p 80.

---

nonconformists experience criticism and even **ostracism**, or rejection by group members. Anyone who has experienced the "silent treatment" from a group of friends knows what a potent social weapon ostracism can be.[47] Norms can be put into proper perspective by understanding how they develop and why they are enforced.

How Norms Are Developed   Experts say norms evolve in an informal manner as the group or organization determines what it takes to be effective. Generally speaking, norms develop in various combinations of the following four ways:

1. *Explicit statements by supervisors or co-workers.* For instance, a group leader might explicitly set norms about not drinking (alcohol) at lunch. (See Real World/Real People.)

2. *Critical events in the group's history.* At times there is a critical event in the group's history that establishes an important precedent. (For example, a key recruit may have decided to work elsewhere because a group member said too many negative things about the organization. Hence, a norm against such "sour grapes" behavior might evolve.)

3. *Primacy.* The first behavior pattern that emerges in a group often sets group expectations. If the first group meeting is marked by very formal interaction between supervisors and employees, then the group often expects future meetings to be conducted in the same way.

4. *Carryover behaviors from past situations.* Such carryover of individual behaviors from past situations can increase the predictability of group members' behaviors in new settings and facilitate task accomplishment. For instance, students and professors carry fairly constant sets of expectations from class to class.[48]

We would like you to take a few moments and think about the norms that are currently in effect in your classroom. List the norms on a sheet of paper. Do these norms help or hinder your ability to learn? Norms can affect performance either positively or negatively.

---

role ambiguity Others' expectations are unknown.

norm Shared attitudes, opinions, feelings, or actions that guide social behavior.

ostracism Rejection by other group members.

table 10–3 Four Reasons Norms Are Enforced

NORM	REASON FOR ENFORCEMENT	EXAMPLE
"Make our department look good in top management's eyes."	Group/organization survival	After vigorously defending the vital role played by the Human Resources Management Department at a divisional meeting, a staff specialist is complimented by her boss.
"Success comes to those who work hard and don't make waves."	Clarification of behavioral expectations	A senior manager takes a young associate aside and cautions him to be a bit more patient with co-workers who see things differently.
"Be a team player, not a star."	Avoidance of embarrassment	A project team member is ridiculed by her peers for dominating the discussion during a progress report to top management.
"Customer service is our top priority."	Clarification of central values/ unique identity	Two sales representatives are given a surprise Friday afternoon party for having received prestigious best-in-the-industry customer service awards from an industry association.

Why Norms Are Enforced   Norms tend to be enforced by group members when they:

 Go to www.mcgrawhillconnect.com for an interactive video case on group dynamics at Pike Place Fish Market.

- Help the group or organization survive.
- Clarify or simplify behavioral expectations.
- Help individuals avoid embarrassing situations.
- Clarify the group's or organization's central values and/or unique identity.[49]

Working examples of each of these four situations are presented in Table 10–3.

Back to the Chapter-Opening Case

What corporate norms are evident in the Intel case?

Relevant Research Insights and Managerial Implications

Although instruments used to measure role conflict and role ambiguity have questionable validity,[50] two separate meta-analyses indicated that role conflict and role ambiguity negatively affected employees. Specifically, role conflict and role ambiguity were associated with job dissatisfaction, tension and anxiety, lack of organizational commitment, intentions to quit, and, to a lesser extent, poor job performance.[51]

The meta-analyses' results hold few surprises for managers. Generally, because of the negative association reported, it makes sense for management to reduce both role conflict and role ambiguity. In this endeavor, managers can use feedback, formal rules and procedures, directive leadership, challenging behaviorally specific goals, and participation. Managers also can use the mentoring process discussed in Chapter 3 to reduce role conflict and ambiguity.

Regarding norms, a set of laboratory studies involving a total of 1,504 college students as subjects has important implications for workplace diversity programs. Subjects in groups where the norm was to express prejudices, condone discrimination, and laugh at hostile jokes tended to engage in these undesirable behaviors. Conversely, subjects tended to disapprove of prejudicial and discriminatory conduct when exposed to groups with more socially acceptable norms.[52] So, once again, our parents and teachers were right when they warned us about the dangers of hanging out with the "wrong crowd." Managers who want to build strong diversity programs need to cultivate favorable role models and positive group norms. Poor role models and antisocial norms need to be identified and weeded out.

Group Structure and Composition

Work groups of various size are made up of individuals with varying personalities, abilities, and motivation.[53] Moreover, those individuals perform different roles, on either an assigned or voluntary basis. No wonder some work groups are more productive than others. No wonder some committees are tightly knit while others wallow in conflict. In this section, we examine three important dimensions of group structure and composition: (1) functional roles of group members, (2) group size, and (3) gender composition. Each of these dimensions alternatively can enhance or hinder group effectiveness, depending on how it is managed.

TO THE POINT

How do task and maintenance roles vary and what does research tell us about group size and mixed-gender groups?

Functional Roles Performed by Group Members

As described in Table 10–4, both task and maintenance roles need to be performed if a work group is to accomplish anything.[54]

LO.5 Task versus Maintenance Roles   **Task roles** enable the work group to define, clarify, and pursue a common purpose. Meanwhile, **maintenance roles** foster supportive and constructive interpersonal relationships. In short, task roles keep the group *on track* while maintenance roles keep the group *together*. A project team member is performing a task function at an update meeting when he or she says, "What is the real issue here? We don't seem to be getting anywhere." Another individual who says, "Let's hear from those who oppose this plan," is performing a maintenance function. Importantly, each of the various task and maintenance roles may be played in varying combinations and sequences by either the group's leader or any of its members.

Checklist for Managers   The task and maintenance roles listed in Table 10–4 can serve as a handy checklist for managers and group leaders who wish to ensure proper group development. Roles that are not always performed when needed, such as those of coordinator, evaluator, and gatekeeper, can be performed in a timely manner by the formal leader or assigned to other members. The task roles of initiator, orienter, and energizer are especially important because they are *goal-directed* roles. Research studies on group goal setting confirm the motivational power of challenging

In today's fast-paced, project-oriented workplaces, everyone needs to be adept at playing different roles and clarifying relevant norms. How are your skills in this area of group dynamics?

table 10–4 Functional Roles Performed by Group Members

TASK ROLES	DESCRIPTION
Initiator	Suggests new goals or ideas.
Information seeker/giver	Clarifies key issues.
Opinion seeker/giver	Clarifies pertinent values.
Elaborator	Promotes greater understanding through examples or exploration of implications.
Coordinator	Pulls together ideas and suggestions.
Orienter	Keeps group headed toward its stated goal(s).
Evaluator	Tests group's accomplishments with various criteria such as logic and practicality.
Energizer	Prods group to move along or to accomplish more.
Procedural technician	Performs routine duties (e.g., handing out materials or rearranging seats).
Recorder	Performs a "group memory" function by documenting discussion and outcomes.
MAINTENANCE ROLES	DESCRIPTION
Encourager	Fosters group solidarity by accepting and praising various points of view.
Harmonizer	Mediates conflict through reconciliation or humor.
Compromiser	Helps resolve conflict by meeting others half way.
Gatekeeper	Encourages all group members to participate.
Standard setter	Evaluates the quality of group processes.
Commentator	Records and comments on group processes/dynamics.
Follower	Serves as a passive audience.

SOURCE: Adapted from discussion in K D Benne and P Sheats, "Functional Roles of Group Members," *Journal of Social Issues,* Spring 1948, pp 41–49.

Mc Graw Hill connect™ Go to www.mcgrawhillconnect.com for a comprehension case to test your knowledge of masculine behavior and group dynamics.

goals. As with individual goal setting (in Chapter 9), difficult but achievable goals are associated with better group results.[55] Also in line with individual goal-setting theory and research, group goals are more effective if group members clearly understand them and are both individually and collectively committed to achieving them. Initiators, orienters, and energizers can be very helpful in this regard.

International managers need to be sensitive to cultural differences regarding the relative importance of task and maintenance roles. In Japan, for example, cultural tradition calls for more emphasis on maintenance roles, especially the roles of harmonizer and compromiser:

Example. Courtesy requires that members not be conspicuous or disputatious in a meeting or classroom. If two or more members discover that their views differ—a fact that is tactfully taken to be unfortunate—they adjourn to find more information and to work toward a stance that all can accept. They do not press their personal opinions through strong arguments, neat logic, or rewards and threats. And they do not hesitate to shift their beliefs if doing so will preserve smooth interpersonal relations. (To lose is to win.)[56]

Group Size

How many group members is too many? The answer to this deceptively simple question has intrigued managers and academics for years. Folk wisdom says "two heads are better than one" but warns that "too many cooks spoil the broth." Recent employee survey evidence shows three-person work groups to be the most popular (54%), followed by groups of four or more (27%) and then by two-person groups (9%).[57] So where should a manager draw the line when staffing a committee? At three? At five or six? At ten or more? Researchers have taken two different approaches to pinpointing optimum group size: mathematical modeling and laboratory simulations. Let us briefly review research evidence from these two approaches.

The Mathematical Modeling Approach   This approach involves building a mathematical model around certain desired outcomes of group action such as decision quality. Due to differing assumptions and statistical techniques, the results of this research are inconclusive. Statistical estimates of optimum group size have ranged from 3 to 13.[58]

The Laboratory Simulation Approach   This stream of research is based on the assumption that group behavior needs to be observed firsthand in controlled laboratory settings. A laboratory study by respected Australian researcher Philip Yetton and his colleague, Preston Bottger, provides useful insights about group size and performance.[59] A total of 555 subjects (330 managers and 225 graduate management students, of whom 20% were female) were assigned to task teams ranging in size from two to six. The teams worked on the National Aeronautics and Space Administration moon survival exercise. (This exercise involves the rank ordering of 15 pieces of equipment that would enable a spaceship crew on the moon to survive a 200-mile trip between a crash-landing site and home base.)[60] After analyzing the relationships between group size and group performance, Yetton and Bottger concluded the following:

Example. It would be difficult, at least with respect to decision quality, to justify groups larger than five members. . . . Of course, to meet needs other than high decision quality, organizations may employ groups significantly larger than four or five.[61]

More recent laboratory studies exploring the brainstorming productivity of various size groups (2 to 12 people), in face-to-face versus computer-mediated situations, proved fruitful. In the usual face-to-face brainstorming sessions, productivity of ideas did not increase as the size of the group increased. But brainstorming productivity increased as the size of the group increased when ideas were typed into networked computers.[62] These results suggest that computer networks are helping to deliver on the promise of productivity improvement through modern information technology.

LO.6 Managerial Implications   Within a contingency management framework, there is no hard-and-fast rule about group size. It depends on the manager's objective for the group. If a high-quality decision is the main objective, then a three- to five-member group would be appropriate. However, if the objective is to generate creative ideas, encourage participation, socialize new members, engage in training, or communicate policies, then groups much larger than five could be justified. But even in this developmental domain, researchers have found upward limits on group size. According to a meta-analysis, the positive effects of team-building activities diminished as group size increased.[63] Managers also need to be aware of *qualitative* changes that occur when group size increases. A meta-analysis of eight studies found the following relationships: As group size increased, group leaders tended to become more directive, and group member satisfaction tended to decline slightly.[64]

Odd-numbered groups (e.g., three, five, seven members) are recommended if the issue is to be settled by a majority vote. Voting deadlocks (e.g., 2–2, 3–3) can stall even-numbered groups.

LO.7 Effects of Men and Women Working Together in Groups

As pointed out in Chapter 2, the female portion of the US labor force has grown significantly in recent decades. This demographic shift has impacted attitudes. For example, in a report about a longitudinal study of US executives, the researchers observed:

Example. Men and women are . . . responding similarly to the statement "I would feel comfortable working for a woman." Most female respondents continue to say they would, though there's been a slight drop since 1985. Of the men, 71% say they would. That figure is up significantly from 1965 (27%) and 1985 (47%).[65]

With more committees and teams requiring collaboration between women and men, some profound effects on group dynamics might be expected. Let us see what researchers have found in the way of group gender composition effects and what managers can do about them.

Women Face an Uphill Battle in Mixed-Gender Task Groups

Laboratory and field studies paint a picture of inequality for women working in mixed-gender groups. Both women and men need to be aware of these often subtle but powerful group dynamics so corrective steps can be taken. Here is a prime example from a recent study of the link between handshake strength and job interview ratings. The researchers concluded:

Example. [W]e demonstrate that women overcome the effects of weaker handshakes, such that on average they do not receive lower interview performance ratings from interviewers, and that women may actually benefit more than do men if they present a strong and complete grip when they shake hands.[66]

Of course, the cultural context of this study (US university students as subjects) needs to be taken into consideration. Handshake etiquette varies across cultures.

In a laboratory study of six-person task groups, a clear pattern of gender inequality was found in the way group members interrupted each other. Men

One study suggests that females entering male-dominated fields, such as law enforcement, face greater challenges than do males entering female-dominated fields, such as nursing.

interrupted women significantly more often than they did other men. Women, who tended to interrupt less frequently and less successfully than men, interrupted men and women equally.[67] Another laboratory study involving Canadian college students found "both men and women exhibiting higher levels of interruption behavior in male-dominated groups."[68]

A field study of mixed-gender police and nursing teams in the Netherlands found another group dynamics disadvantage for women. These two particular professions—police work and nursing—were fruitful research areas because men dominate the former while women dominate the latter. As women move into male-dominated police forces and men gain employment opportunities in the female-dominated world of nursing, who faces the greatest resistance? The answer from this study was the women police officers. As the representation of the minority gender (either female police officers or male nurses) increased in the work groups, the following changes in attitude were observed:

Example. The attitude of the male majority changes from neutral to resistant, whereas the attitude of the female majority changes from favorable to neutral. In other words, men increasingly want to keep their domain for themselves, while women remain willing to share their domain with men.[69]

Again, managers are faced with the challenge of countering discriminatory tendencies in group dynamics.

The Issue of Sexual Harassment   According to an industry survey by a New York law firm specializing in workplace issues, the problem of sexual harassment refuses to go away:

Example. 63% of [234] respondents noted that they had handled a sexual harassment complaint at their company. That's up from 2003, when 57% said they had handled one. At least there was some good news here; that's way down from 1995, when 95% of respondents said that they'd handled one.[70]

The problem persists outside the business sector as well:

Example. About one out of seven female veterans of Afghanistan or Iraq who visit a Veterans Affairs center for medical care report being a victim of sexual assault or harassment during military duty.[71]

Making matters worse, a field study of five organizations found sexual harassment compounded by ethnic discrimination. According to the researchers, "Women experienced more sexual harassment than men, minorities experienced more ethnic harassment than whites, and minority women experienced more harassment overall than majority men, minority men, and majority women."[72] Thus, it was double jeopardy for the minority women. On-the-job harassment is persistent because it is rooted in widespread abusive behavior among teenagers (both face-to-face and electronically).[73]

Another study of social-sexual behavior among 1,232 working men ($n = 405$) and women ($n = 827$) in the Los Angeles area found *nonharassing* sexual behavior to be very common, with 80% of the total sample reporting experience with such behavior. Indeed, according to the researchers, increased social contact between women and men in work groups and organizations has led to increased sexualization (e.g., flirting and romance) in the workplace.[74]

table 10–5 Behavioral Categories of Sexual Harassment

CATEGORY	DESCRIPTION	BEHAVIORAL EXAMPLES
Derogatory attitudes— impersonal	Behaviors that reflect derogatory attitudes about men or women in general	Obscene gestures not directed at target Sex-stereotyped jokes
Derogatory attitudes— personal	Behaviors that are directed at the target that reflect derogatory attitudes about the target's gender	Obscene phone calls Belittling the target's competence
Unwanted dating pressure	Persistent requests for dates after the target has refused	Repeated requests to go out after work or school
Sexual propositions	Explicit requests for sexual encounters	Proposition for an affair
Physical sexual contact	Behaviors in which the harasser makes physical sexual contact with the target	Embracing the target Kissing the target
Physical nonsexual contact	Behaviors in which the harasser makes physical nonsexual contact with the target	Congratulatory hug
Sexual coercion	Requests for sexual encounters or forced encounters that are made a condition of employment or promotion	Threatening punishment unless sexual favors are given Sexual bribery

SOURCE: From M Rotundo, D Nguyen, and P R Sackett, "A Meta-Analytic Review of Gender Differences in Perceptions of Sexual Harassment," *Journal of Applied Psychology*, October 2001, Article 914–922. Copyright © 2001 by the American Psychological Association. Reprinted with permission.

From an OB research standpoint, sexual harassment is a complex and multifaceted problem. For example, a meta-analysis of 62 studies found women perceiving a broader range of behaviors as sexual harassment (see Table 10–5), as opposed to what men perceived. Women and men tended to agree that sexual propositions and coercion qualified as sexual harassment, but there was less agreement about other aspects of a hostile work environment.[75]

Constructive Managerial Action   Male and female employees can and often do work well together in groups. A survey of 387 male US government employees sought to determine how they were affected by the growing number of female co-workers. The researchers concluded, "Under many circumstances, including intergender interaction in work groups, frequent contact leads to cooperative and supportive social relations."[76] More recently, a field study of 1,158 US Air Force officers divided into mixed-gender teams for a five-week officer development program determined that "a higher female proportion within teams contributed to better team problem solving."[77] Still, managers need to take affirmative steps to ensure that the documented sexualization of work environments does not erode into sexual harassment. Whether perpetrated against women or men, sexual harassment is demeaning, unethical, and appropriately called "work environment pollution." Moreover, the US Equal Employment Opportunity Commission holds employers legally accountable for behavior it considers sexually harassing. An expert on the subject explains:

real WORLD // real PEOPLE: ethics

A Costly EEOC Violation for Tyson Foods

[Amanda] West told her trainer and her supervisor [at a Kentucky chicken processing plant] about sexual comments, stares and wolf-whistles as well as offensive touching and lewd gestures toward her by co-workers, whom she identified. The supervisor responded that she should not take offense—"that's just how they treat their women over there"—and said she was "hot." He then said he would look into it, asked her not to go to human resources and offered to move her to a different production line. She agreed. The only other action the supervisor took was to "observe her for a few days."

Two weeks passed while the harassment continued. . . . During her exit interview [when she quit after only five weeks], she told a human resource manager about the harassment and the complaint she had made. The manager said he would investigate but did not. West filed a charge with the Equal Employment Opportunity Commission (EEOC), followed by her lawsuit.

Outcome: A jury awarded West $1.2 million (punitive damages included). After an appeal, the 6th Circuit Court upheld the verdict in 2010.

What are the main ethical and strategic business arguments against sexual harassment? Based on your work experience, how common is sexual harassment? Explain.

SOURCE: Excerpted from S M Schaecher, "Five-Week Employee Wins $1.2 Million in Harassment Claim," *HR Magazine*, July 2010, p 66.

Example. What exactly is sexual harassment? The Equal Employment Opportunity Commission (EEOC) says that unwelcome sexual advances, requests for sexual favors, and other verbal or physical conduct of a sexual nature constitute sexual harassment when submission to such conduct is made a condition of employment; when submission to or rejection of sexual advances is used as a basis for employment decisions; or when such conduct creates an intimidating, hostile, or offensive work environment. These EEOC guidelines interpreting Title VII of the Civil Rights Act of 1964 further state that employers are responsible for the actions of their supervisors and agents and that employers are responsible for the actions of other employees if the employer knows or should have known about the sexual harassment.[78]

Importantly, ignorance of any sexual harassment in the organization is not a viable legal defense for employers (see Real World/Real People). Beyond avoiding lawsuits by establishing and enforcing antidiscrimination and sexual harassment policies, managers need to be proactive. Diversity workshops including how to identify and avoid sexual harassment are strongly recommended.[79]

Threats to Group Effectiveness

Even when managers carefully staff and organize task groups, group dynamics can still go haywire. Forehand knowledge of three major threats to group effectiveness—the Asch effect, groupthink, and social loafing—can help managers take necessary preventive steps. Because the first two problems relate to blind conformity, some brief background discussion is in order.

Very little would be accomplished in task groups and organizations without conformity to norms, role expectations, policies, and rules and regulations. After all, deadlines, commitments, and product/service quality standards need to be established and adhered to if the organization is to survive. But conformity is a two-edged sword. Excessive or blind conformity can stifle critical thinking,

◀ ·······················

TO THE POINT

What are the Asch effect, groupthink, and social loafing and how can they be prevented?

·······················

"I caught Barclay lip-synching when everyone else was saying yes."

SOURCE: *Harvard Business Review*, December 2006, p 122.

the first line of defense against unethical conduct. Almost daily accounts in the popular media of executive misdeeds, insider trading scandals, price fixing, illegal dumping of hazardous wastes, and other unethical practices make it imperative that future managers understand the mechanics of blind conformity.[80]

The Asch Effect

Nearly 60 years ago, social psychologist Solomon Asch conducted a series of laboratory experiments that revealed a negative side of group dynamics.[81] Under the guise of a "perception test," Asch had groups of seven to nine volunteer college students look at 12 pairs of cards such as the ones in Figure 10–4. The object was to identify the line that was the same length as the standard line. Each individual was told to announce his or her choice to the group. Since the differences among the comparison lines were obvious, there should have been unanimous agreement during each of the 12 rounds. But that was not the case.

A Minority of One   All but one member of each group were Asch's confederates who agreed to systematically select the wrong line during seven of the rounds (the other five rounds were control rounds for comparison purposes). The remaining individual was the naive subject who was being tricked. Group pressure was created by having the naive subject in each group be among the last to announce his or her choice. Thirty-one subjects were tested. Asch's research question was: "How often would the naive subjects conform to a majority opinion that was obviously wrong?"

Only 20% of Asch's subjects remained entirely independent; 80% yielded to the pressures of group opinion at least once! And 58% knuckled under to the "immoral majority" at least twice. Hence, the **Asch effect**, the distortion of individual judgment by a unanimous but incorrect opposition, was documented.

A Managerial Perspective   Asch's experiment has been widely replicated with mixed results. Both high and low degrees of blind conformity have been

figure 10–4 The Asch Experiment

Standard Line Card

Comparison Lines Card

1   2   3

observed with various situations and subjects. Replications in Japan and Kuwait have demonstrated that the Asch effect is not unique to the United States.[82] A 1996 meta-analysis of 133 Asch-line experiments from 17 countries found a *decline* in conformity among US subjects since the 1950s. Internationally, collectivist countries, where the group prevails over the individual, produced higher levels of conformity than individualistic countries.[83] The point is not precisely how great the Asch effect is in a given situation or culture, but rather, managers committed to ethical conduct need to be concerned that the Asch effect even exists.

For Jeffrey Skilling, the now-jailed former CEO of Enron, the Asch effect was something to cultivate and nurture. Consider this organizational climate for blind obedience:

Example. Skilling was filling headquarters with his own troops. He was not looking for "fuzzy skills," a former employee recalls. His recruits talked about a socialization process called "Enronizing." Family time? Quality of life? Forget it. Anybody who did not embrace the elbows-out culture "didn't get it." They were "damaged goods" and "shipwrecks," likely to be fired by their bosses at blistering annual job reviews known as rank-and-yank sessions. The culture turned paranoid: former CIA and FBI agents were hired to enforce security. Using "sniffer" programs, they would pounce on anyone e-mailing a potential competitor. The "spooks," as the former agents were called, were known to barge into offices and confiscate computers.[84]

Even isolated instances of blind, unthinking conformity seriously threaten the effectiveness and integrity of work groups and organizations. Robert I Sutton, a professor of management science at Stanford University, recently offered this blistering assessment of blind conformity:

Example. Mindless imitation is among the most dangerous and widespread forms of management idiocy. One of the dumbest excuses for screwing up is "everyone else does it." . . . When everyone else does nothing at all, or all do the same inane thing, such collective stupidity makes people feel far better than when they do the same, equally moronic things on their own.[85]

Functional conflict and assertiveness, discussed in Chapters 13 and 14, can help employees respond appropriately when they find themselves facing an immoral majority. Ethical codes focused on specific practices also can provide support and guidance.

LO.8 Groupthink

Why did President Lyndon B Johnson and his group of intelligent White House advisers make some very *unintelligent* decisions that escalated the Vietnam War? Those fateful decisions were made despite obvious warning signals, including stronger than expected resistance from the North Vietnamese and withering support at home and abroad. Systematic analysis of the decision-making processes underlying the war in Vietnam and other US foreign policy fiascoes

Asch effect Giving in to a unanimous but wrong opposition.

Group member diversity and an open discussion of the dangers of groupthink are major lines of defense against both blind conformity and groupthink. Do you have the courage to speak out when you believe things are going in the wrong direction?

prompted Yale University's Irving Janis to coin the term *groupthink*. Modern managers can all too easily become victims of groupthink, just like President Johnson's staff, if they passively ignore the danger.

Definition and Symptoms of Groupthink

Janis defines **groupthink** as "a mode of thinking that people engage in when they are deeply involved in a cohesive in-group, when members' strivings for unanimity override their motivation to realistically appraise alternative courses of action."[86] He adds, "Groupthink refers to a deterioration of mental efficiency, reality testing, and moral judgment that results from in-group pressures."[87] Unlike Asch's subjects, who were strangers to each other, members of groups victimized by groupthink are friendly, tightly knit, and cohesive.

The symptoms of groupthink listed in Figure 10–5 thrived in US corporate boardrooms of the past where cohesive directors too often caved in to strong-willed CEOs and signed off on bad decisions. But circumstances have taken a positive turn:

Example. A new era for directors dawned with the passage of the Sarbanes-Oxley Act of 2002. Then board members were hit with the frightening prospect of real financial liability in a smattering of lawsuits that followed the corporate crime wave. Now the heat on directors is growing more intense. Their reputations are increasingly at risk when the companies they watch over are tainted by scandal. Their judgment is being questioned by activist shareholders outraged by sky-high pay packages. And investors and regulators are subjecting their actions to higher scrutiny. Long gone are the days when a director could get away with a quick rubber-stamp of a CEO's plans. . . .

The old rules of civility that discouraged directors from asking managers tough or embarrassing questions are eroding.[88]

---

figure 10–5 Symptoms of Groupthink Lead to Defective Decision Making

Symptoms of Groupthink

1. Invulnerability: An illusion that breeds excessive optimism and risk taking.
2. Inherent morality: A belief that encourages the group to ignore ethical implications.
3. Rationalization: Protects pet assumptions.
4. Stereotyped views of opposition: Causes group to underestimate opponents.
5. Self-censorship: Stifles critical debate.
6. Illusion of unanimity: Silence interpreted to mean consent.
7. Peer pressure: Loyalty of dissenters is questioned.
8. Mindguards: Self-appointed protectors against adverse information.

Decision-making defects

1. Few alternatives.
2. No reexamination of preferred alternatives.
3. No reexamination of rejected alternatives.
4. Rejection of expert opinions.
5. Selective bias of new information.
6. No contingency plans.

SOURCES: Symptoms excerpted from I L Janis, *Groupthink: Psychological Studies of Policy, Decisions and Fiascoes,* 2E. Copyright © 1982 by Wadsworth, a part of Cengage Learning. Reproduced by permission. www.cengage.com/permission. Defects excerpted from G Moorhead, "Groupthink: Hypothesis in Need of Testing," *Group & Organization Studies,* December 1982, p 434. Copyright © 1982 by Sage Publications. Reprinted by permission of Sage Publications.

Groupthink Research and Prevention Laboratory studies using college students as subjects validate portions of Janis's groupthink concept. Specifically, it has been found that

- Groups with a moderate amount of cohesiveness produce better decisions than low- or high-cohesive groups.
- Highly cohesive groups victimized by groupthink make the poorest decisions, despite high confidence in those decisions.[89]

Janis believes prevention is better than cure when dealing with groupthink. He recommends the following preventive measures:

1. Each member of the group should be assigned the role of critical evaluator. This role involves actively voicing objections and doubts.
2. Top-level executives should not use policy committees to rubber-stamp decisions that have already been made.
3. Different groups with different leaders should explore the same policy questions.
4. Subgroup debates and outside experts should be used to introduce fresh perspectives.
5. Someone should be given the role of devil's advocate when discussing major alternatives. This person tries to uncover every conceivable negative factor.
6. Once a consensus has been reached, everyone should be encouraged to rethink their position to check for flaws.[90]

These antigroupthink measures can help cohesive groups produce sound recommendations and decisions.[91] Facebook has its own unique approach to avoiding groupthink (see Real World/Real People on page 294).

Avoiding groupthink is a powerful argument in favor of *diversity;* not only racial and gender diversity, but diversity in age, background, religion, education, and world views as well.

LO.9 Social Loafing

Is group performance less than, equal to, or greater than the sum of its parts? Can three people, for example, working together accomplish less than, the same as, or more than they would working separately? An interesting study conducted more than a half century ago by a French agricultural engineer named Ringelmann found the answer to be "less than."[92] In a rope-pulling exercise, Ringelmann reportedly found that three people pulling together could achieve only two-and-a-half times the average individual rate. Eight pullers achieved less than four times the individual rate. This tendency for individual effort to decline as group size increases has come to be called **social loafing.**[93] Let us briefly analyze this threat to group effectiveness and synergy with an eye toward avoiding it.

groupthink Janis's term for a cohesive in-group's unwillingness to realistically view alternatives.

social loafing Decrease in individual effort as group size increases.

real WORLD // **real** PEOPLE

How Groupthink Is "Hacked" at Facebook

At the heart of the process is the notion of "hacking," which [CEO Mark] Zuckerberg insists is not about breaking and entering: "It's about being unafraid to break things in order to make them better." . . .

Determined to keep that mind-set alive as the company grows, Facebook has raised the all-nighter to an art form. "Hackathons," which started when the site was just a handful of friends around a dining table, are now all-hands meetings held every month or so. Any project, any idea is on the table. If you can find some friends to work on it with you, go for it. The company provides food,

music, and beer. It sounds like so much code-boy BS, except that most everyone shows up, even the lawyers. Even Zuckerberg. And the sessions have produced an astonishing array of popular site features, including video messaging and chat.

What other steps can Facebook employees take to avoid groupthink as the company continues to grow?

SOURCE: Excerpted from E McGirt, "Most Innovative Companies: Facebook," *Fast Company,* March 2010, p 110.

Social Loafing Theory and Research   Among the theoretical explanations for the social loafing effect are (1) equity of effort ("Everyone else is goofing off, so why shouldn't I?"), (2) loss of personal accountability ("I'm lost in the crowd, so who cares?"), (3) motivational loss due to the sharing of rewards ("Why should I work harder than the others when everyone gets the same reward?"), and (4) coordination loss as more people perform the task ("We're getting in each other's way").

Laboratory studies refined these theories by identifying situational factors that moderated the social loafing effect. Social loafing occurred when

- The task was perceived to be unimportant, simple, or not interesting.[94]
- Group members thought their individual output was not identifiable.[95]
- Group members expected their co-workers to loaf.[96]

But social loafing did *not* occur when group members in two laboratory studies expected to be evaluated.[97] Also, research suggests that self-reliant "individualists" are more prone to social loafing than are group-oriented "collectivists." But individualists can be made more cooperative by keeping the group small and holding each member personally accountable for results.[98] Social loafing also was reduced in a recent study when a hybrid combination of individual and shared rewards were employed.[99]

Practical Implications in Today's Online Workplaces   These findings demonstrate that social loafing is not an inevitable part of group effort. Management can curb this threat to group effectiveness by making sure the task is challenging and perceived as important. It also is a good idea to hold group members personally accountable for identifiable portions of the group's task. Still, social loafing is a moving target requiring creative countermeasures in the Internet Age.

Today's digital workplaces are fertile ground for the growth of social loafing. **Cyberloafing**—defined as using the Internet for nonwork-related activities such as communicating with friends via e-mail and social media, Web surfing, shopping, and gaming—is commonplace. Virtual teams, discussed in the next chapter, have loosened traditional administrative oversight of employees.[100] Table 10–6 lists problems and remedies for managers seeking to reduce social loafing in today's online workplaces.

table 10–6 Dealing with Social Loafing in the Internet Age

PROBLEM	REMEDIES
Cyberloafing	
• Spending work time on the Internet for nonwork activities; this could include shopping, managing an online business, surfing the Web, e-mailing jokes, updating social media accounts, Twitter, etc.	• Fair and just employee computer monitoring • Internet, social media, and e-mail usage policies • Establishing norms of appropriate Internet use among employees
Lack of effort in virtual teams/knowledge work	
• Lowering effort levels because it is difficult to observe and identify the impact of individual efforts on team performance • Substituting potentially less valuable maintenance activities for task-related effort • Ambiguity in relationship between effort and performance	• Stress individual and mutual accountability for achieving team goals when establishing team norms and rewards • Ensuring mechanisms are in place to surface and confront team conflict • Focus on achieving both learning and performance goals

SOURCE: Excerpted from Table 1 in R E Kidwell, "Loafing in the 21st Century: Enhanced Opportunities—and Remedies—for Withholding Job Effort in the New Workplace," *Business Horizons,* November–December 2010, pp 543–52.

cyberloafing Employees using the Internet for nonwork activities.

Summary of Key Concepts

1. *Identify the four sociological criteria of a group, and discuss the impact of social networking on group dynamics.* Sociologically, a *group* is defined as two or more freely interacting individuals who share collective norms and goals and have a common identity. Social networking sites such as Facebook and Twitter have blurred the line between formal and informal groups by giving people unprecedented access to one's personal life. This has magnified the longstanding dilemma of how friendly managers should be with their direct reports. They are urged to compartmentalize their official and unofficial roles.

2. *Describe the five stages in Tuckman's theory of group development, and discuss the threat of group decay.* The five stages in Tuckman's theory are forming (the group comes together), storming (members test the limits and each other), norming (questions about authority and power are resolved as the group becomes more cohesive), performing (effective communication and cooperation help the group get things done), and adjourning (group members go their own way). According to recent research, group decay occurs when a work group achieves the "performing" stage and then shifts into reverse. Group decay occurs through de-norming (erosion of standards), de-storming (growing discontent and loss of cohesiveness), and de-forming (fragmentation and breakup of the group).

3. *Distinguish between role conflict and role ambiguity.* Organizational roles are sets of behaviors persons expect of occupants of a position. One may experience role overload (too much to do in too little time), role conflict (conflicting role expectations), or role ambiguity (unclear role expectations).

4. *Contrast roles and norms, and specify four reasons norms are enforced in organizations.* While roles are specific to the person's position, norms are shared attitudes that differentiate appropriate from inappropriate behavior in a variety of situations. Norms evolve informally and are enforced because they help the group or organization survive, clarify behavioral expectations, help people avoid embarrassing situations, and clarify the group's or organization's central values.

5. *Distinguish between task and maintenance roles in groups.* Members of formal groups need to perform both task (goal-oriented) and maintenance (relationship-oriented) roles if anything is to be accomplished.

6. *Summarize the practical contingency management implications for group size.* Laboratory simulation studies suggest decision-making groups should be limited to five or fewer members. Larger groups are appropriate when creativity, participation, and socialization are the main objectives. If majority votes are to be taken, odd-numbered groups are recommended to avoid deadlocks.

7. *Discuss why managers need to carefully handle mixed-gender task groups.* Women face special group dynamics

challenges in mixed-gender task groups. Steps need to be taken to make sure increased sexualization of work environments does not erode into illegal sexual harassment.

8. *Describe groupthink, and identify at least four of its symptoms.* Groupthink plagues cohesive in-groups that shortchange moral judgment while putting too much emphasis on unanimity. Symptoms of groupthink include invulnerability, inherent morality, rationalization, stereotyped views of opposition, self-censorship, illusion of unanimity, peer pressure, and mindguards. Critical evaluators, outside expertise, and devil's advocates are among the preventive measures recommended by Irving Janis, who coined the term *groupthink*.

9. *Define social loafing, and explain how managers can prevent it.* Social loafing involves the tendency for individual effort to decrease as group size increases. This problem can be contained if the task is challenging and important, individuals are held accountable for results, and group members expect everyone to work hard. The Internet and virtual teams are fertile ground for social loafing. Cyberloafing can be curbed with policies and norms covering e-mail, Internet, and social media use. Members of virtual teams need to be held personally and mutually accountable for team results, capable of handing team conflict, and focused on both learning and performance goals.

Key Terms

Group, 269

Formal group, 270

Informal group, 270

Social networking site (SNS), 272

Group cohesiveness, 275

Roles, 278

Role overload, 279

Role conflict, 279

Role ambiguity, 280

Norm, 280

Ostracism, 281

Task roles, 283

Maintenance roles, 283

Asch effect, 290

Groupthink, 292

Social loafing, 293

Cyberloafing, 294

OB in Action Case Study

Unmasking Manly Men

What can managers in white-collar firms learn from roughnecks and roustabouts on an offshore oil rig? That extinguishing macho behavior is vital to achieving top performance. That's a key finding from our study of life on two oil platforms, during which we spent several weeks over the course of 19 months living, eating, and working alongside crews offshore.

Oil rigs are dirty, dangerous, and demanding workplaces that have traditionally encouraged displays of masculine strength, daring, and technical prowess. But over the past 15 years or so the platforms we studied have deliberately jettisoned their hard-driving, macho cultures in favor of an environment in which men admit when they've made mistakes and explore how anxiety, stress, or lack of experience may have caused them; appreciate one another publicly; and routinely ask for and offer help. These workers shifted their focus from proving their masculinity to larger, more compelling goals: maximizing the safety and well-being of co-workers and doing their jobs effectively.

The shift required a new attitude toward work, which was pushed from the top down. If you can't expose errors and learn from them, management's thinking went, you can't be safe or effective. Workers came to appreciate that to improve safety and performance in a potentially deadly environment, they had to be open to new information that challenged their assumptions, and they had to acknowledge when they were wrong. Their altered stance revealed two

things: First, that much of their macho behavior was not only unnecessary but actually got in the way of doing their jobs; and second, that their notions about what constituted strong leadership needed to change. They discovered that the people who used to rise to the top—the "biggest, baddest roughnecks," as one worker described them—weren't necessarily the best at improving safety and effectiveness. Rather, the ones who excelled were mission-driven guys who cared about their fellow workers, were good listeners, and were willing to learn.

Over the 15-year period these changes in work practices, norms, perceptions, and behaviors were implemented companywide. The company's accident rate declined by 84%, while productivity (number of barrels produced), efficiency (cost per barrel), and reliability (production "up" time) increased beyond the industry's previous benchmark.

But the changes had an unintended effect as well. The men's willingness to risk a blow to their image—by, for example, exposing their incompetence or weakness when necessary in order to do their jobs well—profoundly influenced their sense of who they were and could be as men. No longer focused on affirming their masculinity, they felt able to behave in ways that conventional masculine norms would have precluded.

If men in the hypermasculine environment of oil rigs can let go of the macho ideal and improve their performance, then men in corporate America might be able to do likewise. Numerous studies have examined the costs of macho displays in contexts ranging from aeronautics to manufacturing to high tech to the law. They show that men's attempts to prove their masculinity interfere with the training of recruits, compromise decision quality, marginalize women workers, lead to civil- and human-rights violations, and alienate men from their health, feelings, and relationships with others. The price of men's striving to demonstrate their masculinity is high, and both individuals and organizations pay it.

The problem lies not in traditionally masculine attributes per se—many tasks require aggressiveness, strength, or emotional detachment—but in men's efforts to prove themselves on these dimensions, whether in the hazardous setting of an offshore oil platform or in the posh, protected surroundings of the executive suite. By creating conditions that focus people on the real requirements of the job, rather than on stereotypical images believed to equate with competence, organizations can free employees to do their best work.[101]

Questions for Discussion

1. How do the concepts of roles and norms figure into this case? Explain.
2. What are the implications for mixed-gender work groups? Is this a good way to combat sexual harassment? Explain.
3. Does this attitude shift make groupthink more or less likely? Explain.
4. What are the takeaway lessons for men?

Legal/Ethical Challenge

My Boss Wants to "Friend" Me Online

Paul Dyer always was able to hold off his boss's invitations to party by employing that arm's-length response: "We'll have to do that sometime," he'd say.

But when his boss, in his 30s, invited Dyer, 24, to be friends on the social-networking site . . . Facebook, dodging wasn't so easy.

On the one hand, accepting a person's request to be friends online grants them access to the kind of intimacy never meant for office consumption, such as recent photos of keggers. . . .

But declining a "friend" request from a colleague or a boss is a slight. So Dyer accepted the invitation, then removed any inappropriate or incriminating photos of himself. . . .

Dyer, it turns out, wasn't the one who had to be embarrassed. His boss had photos of himself attempting to imbibe two drinks at once, ostensibly, Dyer ventures, to send the message: "I'm a crazy, young party guy."[102]

If You Were Paul Dyer, What Would You do Now?

1. Big mistake. Unwind the situation as quickly and as graciously as possible, preferably in person. Explain how.
2. Don't panic. Let the online relationship wither away from lack of attention.
3. Play along for awhile in the hope that the boss has a short online attention span and will flit off to pester others.
4. You've made a bad decision; don't compound it by alienating your boss. Participate in the virtual relationship, applying your own ethical boundaries. Explain those boundaries.
5. Invent other interpretations or options. Discuss.

NOTE: In a recent survey of 1,017 workers 18 and older, 37% said yes and 63% said no to the following question: "Is it smart to keep personal and professional lives separate?"[103]

Web Resources

For study material and exercises that apply to this chapter, visit our website at **www.mhhe.com/kreitner10e**

chapter 11

Developing and Leading Effective Teams

 Learning Objectives

When you finish studying the material in this chapter, you should be able to:

LO.1   Explain how a work group becomes a team.

LO.2   Identify and describe four types of work teams.

LO.3   Explain the model of effective work teams, and specify the two criteria of team effectiveness.

LO.4   Identify five teamwork competencies team members need to possess.

LO.5   Discuss why teams fail.

LO.6   List at least four things managers can do to build trust.

LO.7   Distinguish two types of group cohesiveness, and summarize cohesiveness research findings.

LO.8   Define virtual teams and self-managed teams.

LO.9   Describe high-performance teams, and discuss team leadership.

Why Is Great Customer Service Like a Team Sport?

Team chemistry is something [Wynn Resort's human resources executive Arte] Nathan—and owner Steve Wynn for that matter—take very seriously. One legendary story in the organization is an experience Wynn and his family had when on vacation in Paris. They were staying at a Four Seasons, and breakfast had been delivered to the room. His daughter had ordered a croissant, but she only ate half of it, leaving the other half to nibble on later that day. Wynn and his family left the room to explore Paris. And, upon returning to the hotel, his daughter began thinking about that croissant. But when they entered the room, the pastry was gone, taken by housekeeping. She was disappointed. Housekeeping assumed the half croissant was trash. Or did they?

A light was blinking on the room's telephone. It was a message from the front desk . . . that housekeeping had informed them that they had removed the half croissant from the room, assuming that upon return the rightful owner of the croissant would prefer a fresh pastry. So the front desk contacted the kitchen to set aside a croissant, and room service was informed that upon request, they would need to deliver the pastry post haste.

"What makes this story so powerful?" asks Nathan. "The level of teamwork and communication between different departments is simply amazing. All participants understood the end game—customer satisfaction. And everyone accepted their role in making the experience fantastic."[1]

At first glance, this story may seem like no big deal because it revolves around a little girl's pastry. But think of it in terms of a sports metaphor in which the difference between winning and losing comes down to many opportunities for good or bad teamwork. In today's service-dominated economy, winning often hinges on employees being customer-focused team players. Steve Wynn wants his employees to team up for the kind of customer satisfaction he and his family experienced at the Paris Four Seasons. The concept of *social capital*, covered in Chapter 1, really comes to life when our attention turns to teams and teamwork in modern organizations. Business columnists Jack and Suzy Welch offered this perspective:

Example. It is the excitement of being part of something bigger than yourself and the thrill of building something—a product, a service, or a team. It is the fun of laughing, debating, sweating it out with fellow travelers—friends and allies in the never-ending competition for customers and profits. . . . It just doesn't get any better.[2]

Cooperation, trust, and camaraderie energize organizations. Judging from a recent survey that asked corporate leaders to look ahead five years, we all need to polish our teamwork skills: "Teamwork/collaboration" (74%) was among the top three most important knowledge/skill areas, just behind "critical thinking/problem solving" (78%) and "information technology application" (77%).[3] Jeff Vijungco, director of recruiting at Adobe Systems, tells how he finds team players: "I actually count the number of times a candidate says 'I' in an interview. We'd much rather hear 'we'."[4]

Emphasis in this chapter is on tapping the full and promising potential of work groups and teams. We will (1) identify different types of work teams; (2) look at what makes teams succeed or fail; (3) examine keys to effective teamwork, such as trust; (4) explore modern applications of the team concept, including virtual teams and self-managed teams; and (5) discuss team building and team leadership.

TO THE POINT

How can you help a work group evolve into an effective team?

LO.1 Work Teams: Types, Effectiveness, and Stumbling Blocks

Jon R Katzenbach and Douglas K Smith, management consultants at McKinsey & Company, say it is a mistake to use the terms *group* and *team* interchangeably. After studying many different kinds of teams—from athletic to corporate to military—they concluded that successful teams tend to take on a life of their own. Katzenbach and Smith define a **team** as "a small number of people with complementary skills who are committed to a common purpose, performance goals, and approach for which they hold themselves mutually accountable."[5] Relative to Tuckman's theory of group development in Chapter 10—forming, storming, norming, performing, and adjourning—teams are task groups that have matured to the *performing* stage (but not slipped into decay). Because of conflicts over power and authority and unstable interpersonal relations, many work groups never qualify as a real team.[6] Katzenbach and Smith clarified the distinction this way: "The essence of a team is *common commitment*. Without it, groups perform as individuals; with it, they become a powerful unit of collective performance."[7] (See Table 11–1.) A prime example of melding a group of individuals into a team is how coach Skip Holtz created a winning football program at East Carolina University. Holtz, now at the University of South Florida, sent a powerful signal when he first met with his new team on the Greenville, North Carolina, campus:

table 11–1   The Evolution of a Team

A work group becomes a team when
1. Leadership becomes a shared activity.
2. Accountability shifts from strictly individual to both individual and collective.
3. The group develops its own purpose or mission.
4. Problem solving becomes a way of life, not a part-time activity.
5. Effectiveness is measured by the group's collective outcomes and products.

SOURCE: Condensed and adapted from J R Katzenbach and D K Smith, *The Wisdom of Teams: Creating the High-Performance Organization* (New York: HarperBusiness, 1999), p 214.

Example. The first thing he did was take the players' names off the back of the jerseys.

"I came away from our first meeting with the feeling that this was a very selfish, self-centered team," Holtz says. "There weren't a lot of people talking about goals and the big picture. We needed to change the culture and the attitude and change it fast."

Defensive end Zack Slate was a freshman on a 2–9 team in 2004 and remembers the meeting.

Example. "We had a lot of guys split in a lot of different ways. There was no sense of team," Slate says. "Coach Holtz started building from the ground up with discipline and precision."[8]

When Katzenbach and Smith refer to "a small number of people" in their definition, they mean between 2 and 25 team members. They found effective teams to typically have fewer than 10 members. This conclusion was echoed in a survey of 400 workplace team members in the United States and Canada: "The average North American team consists of 10 members. Eight is the most common size."[9]

LO.2 A General Typology of Work Teams

Work teams are created for various purposes and thus face different challenges. Managers can deal more effectively with those challenges when they understand how teams differ. A helpful way of sorting things out is to consider a typology of work teams developed by Eric Sundstrom and his colleagues.[10] Four general types of work teams listed in Table 11–2 are (1) advice, (2) production, (3) project,

team Small group with complementary skills who hold themselves mutually accountable for common purpose, goals, and approach.

table 11–2   Four General Types of Work Teams and Their Outputs

TYPES AND EXAMPLES	DEGREE OF TECHNICAL SPECIALIZATION	DEGREE OF COORDINATION WITH OTHER WORK UNITS	WORK CYCLES	TYPICAL OUTPUTS
Advice Committees Review panels, boards Quality circles Employee involvement groups Advisory councils	Low	Low	Work cycles can be brief or long; one cycle can be team life span.	Decisions Selections Suggestions Proposals Recommendations
Production Assembly teams Manufacturing crews Mining teams Flight attendant crews Data processing groups Maintenance crews	Low	High	Work cycles typically repeated or continuous process; cycles often briefer than team life span.	Food, chemicals Components Assemblies Retail sales Customer service Equipment repairs
Project Research groups Planning teams Architect teams Engineering teams Development teams Task forces	High	Low (for traditional units) or High (for cross-functional units)	Work cycles typically differ for each new project; one cycle can be team life span.	Plans, designs Investigations Presentations Prototypes Reports, findings
Action Sports teams Entertainment groups Expeditions Negotiating teams Surgery teams Cockpit crews Military platoons and squads Police and fire teams	High	High	Brief performance events, often repeated under new conditions, requiring extended training or preparation.	Combat missions Expeditions Contracts, lawsuits Concerts Surgical operations Competitive events Disaster assistance

SOURCE: Excerpted and adapted from E Sundstrom, K P DeMeuse, and D Futrell, "Work Teams," *American Psychologist,* February 1990, p 125. Reprinted with permission of the author.

Go to www.mcgrawhillconnect.com for an interactive exercise to test your knowledge of the four general types of work teams.

and (4) action. Each of these labels identifies a basic *purpose.* For instance, advice teams generally make recommendations for managerial decisions. Less commonly do they actually make final decisions. In contrast, production and action teams carry out management's decisions.

Four key variables in Table 11–2 deal with technical specialization, coordination, work cycles, and outputs. Technical specialization is low when the team draws upon members' general experience and problem-solving ability. It is high when team members are required to apply technical skills acquired through higher education or extensive training. The degree of coordination with other work units is determined by the team's relative independence (low coordination) or interdependence (high coordination). Work cycles are the amount of time teams need to discharge their missions. The various outputs listed in Table 11–2 are intended to illustrate real-life impacts. A closer look at each type of work team is in order.[11]

Advice Teams   As their name implies, advice teams are created to broaden the information base for managerial decisions. Advice teams tend to have a low degree of technical specialization. Coordination also is low because advice teams work pretty much on their own. Ad hoc committees (e.g., the annual picnic committee) have shorter life cycles than standing committees (e.g., the grievance committee).

Production Teams   This second type of team is responsible for performing day-to-day operations. Minimal training for routine tasks accounts for the low degree of technical specialization. But coordination typically is high because work flows from one team to another. For example, railroad maintenance crews require fresh information about needed repairs from train crews, and the train crews, in turn, need to know exactly where maintenance crews are working.

Project Teams   Projects require creative problem solving, often involving the application of specialized knowledge. Since projects focus on a specific outcome (e.g., developing a new vaccine, producing a movie, or building a skyscraper), time is critical and the team may disband upon completion of the project. The trend in product development today is toward cross-functional teams that bring together specialists from production, marketing, and finance from around the world. Take Lenovo's ThinkPad X300 PC, for example:

Example.   Like most ThinkPads, this one got its start in the US. The planners, project leaders, and some of the designers are in North Carolina. The more detailed design and engineering work is done by a team in Yamato, Japan. Manufacturing and purchasing take place in Shenzhen, China.[12]

A high-tech global project team such as this requires a high degree of coordination and efficient communication. Project teams also can bring realism into academic settings.

Action Teams   This last type of team is best exemplified by a baseball team. High specialization is combined with high coordination. Nine highly trained athletes play specialized defensive positions. But good defensive play is not enough because hits are needed to score runs. Moreover, coordination between the manager, base runners, base coaches, and the bull pen needs to be precise. So it is with airline cockpit crews, firefighters, hospital surgery teams, mountain-climbing expeditions, rock music groups, labor-contract negotiating teams, and police SWAT teams, among others. A unique challenge for action teams is to exhibit peak performance on demand.[13]

This four-way typology of work teams is dynamic and changing, not static. Some teams evolve from one type to another. Other teams represent a combination of types. For example, consider the work of a team at General Foods: "The company launched a line of ready-to-eat desserts by setting up a team of nine people with the freedom to operate like entrepreneurs starting their own business. The team even had to oversee construction of a factory with the technology required to manufacture their product."[14] This particular team was a combination advice-project-action team. In short, the General Foods team did everything but manufacture the end product themselves (that was done by production teams).

These highly trained and versatile firefighters qualify as an action team because they are capable of synchronized peak performance at a moment's notice.

Back to the Chapter-Opening Case

What type of team, according to Table 11–2, delivered the excellent customer service at the Paris Four Seasons? Explain your choice. What are management's greatest challenges with this sort of team?

LO.3 Effective Work Teams

The effectiveness of athletic teams is a straightforward matter of wins and losses. Things become more complicated, however, when the focus shifts to work teams in today's complex organizations.[15] Figure 11–1 lists two effectiveness criteria for work teams: performance and viability. Conceptually, the first one is simple: Did the team get the job done? The second criterion is more subtle and easily ignored or overlooked, to the longer-term detriment of the organization. **Team viability** is defined as team members' satisfaction and continued willingness to contribute. Are the team members better or worse off for having contributed to the team effort? A work team is not truly effective if it gets the job done but self-destructs in the process and burns everyone out. In a recent five-year study of National Basketball Association players, low-status players who experienced uncooperative behavior from teammates tended to perform poorly and have physical health problems.[16]

Also, as indicated in Figure 11–1, work teams require a team-friendly organization if they are to be effective. Work teams need a support system. They have a much greater chance of success if they are nurtured and facilitated by the organization. The team's purpose needs to be in concert with the organization's strategy. Similarly, team participation and autonomy require an organizational culture that values those processes. A good role model is Linda Hunt, president of St. Joseph's Hospital and Medical Center in Phoenix, Arizona. She recently noted, "We live the model of collaboration. We promote it in our centers of excellence and in our teaching programs, and we incorporate teams into quality care wherever possible."[17]

figure 11–1 Effective Work Teams

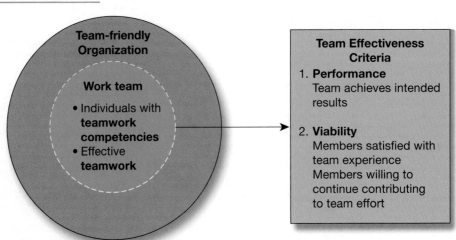

SOURCES: Adapted in part from E Sundstrom, K P DeMeuse, and D Futrell, "Work Teams," *American Psychologist,* February 1990, pp 120–33; and C A Beatty and B A Barker Scott, *Building Smart Teams: A Roadmap to High Performance* (Thousand Oaks, CA: Sage, 2004), pp 5–8.

Team members also need appropriate technological tools, *reasonable* schedules, and training. Teamwork needs to be rewarded by the organizational reward system.[18] Such is not the case when pay and bonuses are tied solely to individual output. For a positive example, consider what took place at Internet equipment maker Cisco Systems:

Example. [CEO John] Chambers . . . made teamwork a critical part of top execs' bonus plans. He told them 30% of their [annual] bonuses . . . would depend on how well they collaborated with others. "It tends to formalize the discussion around how can I help you and how can you help me," says Sue Bostrom, head of Cisco's Internet consulting group.[19]

LO.4 Contributors Need Teamwork Competencies Forming workplace teams and urging employees to be good team players are good starting points on the road to effective teams. But much more is needed today.[20] Jeff Zucker, president of NBC Universal Television Group, initially faced this situation:

connect™ Go to www.mcgrawhillconnect.com for an interactive exercise to test your knowledge of teamwork competencies.

Example. My biggest challenge is getting the new team to maximize our potential and combine together into one culture. We have a bunch of people with strong personalities who are extremely good at what they do. I want them to feel they are the best, and yet have us work together as a team.[21]

In short, Zucker's leadership group had not yet melded into a true team, as defined earlier. He needed to make sure his people possessed the teamwork competencies in Table 11–3. Teamwork skills and competencies need to be role modeled and taught. For example, when Jim Vesterman was an MBA student at the University of Pennsylvania's Wharton School, he recalled lifelong teamwork lessons he learned as a combat US Marine serving in Iraq:

Example. We were one team. Our platoon commander would often quote Kipling to describe Marines: "The strength of the pack is the wolf, and the strength of the wolf is the pack." The Marine Corps recruits wolves. But its strength comes from training them to fight as a pack . . .

When I'm working with a group now, I can honestly say that I think about the team first. The "I first" approach has been drilled out of me.[22]

Notice in Table 11–3 the importance of group problem solving, mentoring, and conflict management skills.

Military personnel, such as these US Army basic training graduates at Fort Leonard Wood in Missouri, know the wisdom behind the old saying that there is no letter "*i*" in the word *team*.

What Does Effective Teamwork Involve?

Unfortunately, the terms *team* and *teamwork* are

team viability Team members satisfied and willing to contribute.

table 11–3 How Strong Are Your Teamwork Competencies?

Orients Team to Problem-Solving Situation
Assists the team in arriving at a common understanding of the situation or problem. Determines the important elements of a problem situation. Seeks out relevant data related to the situation or problem.

Organizes and Manages Team Performance
Helps team establish specific, challenging, and accepted team goals. Monitors, evaluates, and provides feedback on team performance. Identifies alternative strategies or reallocates resources to address feedback on team performance.

Promotes a Positive Team Environment
Assists in creating and reinforcing norms of tolerance, respect, and excellence. Recognizes and praises other team members' efforts. Helps and supports other team members. Models desirable team member behavior.

Facilitates and Manages Task Conflict
Encourages desirable and discourages undesirable team conflict. Recognizes the type and source of conflict confronting the team and implements an appropriate resolution strategy. Employs "win–win" negotiation strategies to resolve team conflicts.

Appropriately Promotes Perspective
Defends stated preferences, argues for a particular point of view, and withstands pressure to change position for another that is not supported by logical or knowledge-based arguments. Changes or modifies position if a defensible argument is made by another team member. Projects courtesy and friendliness to others while arguing position.

SOURCE: From G Chen, L M Donahue, and R I Klimoski, "Training Undergraduates to Work in Organizational Teams," *Academy of Management Learning and Education,* March 2004, App. A, p 40. Copyright © 2004 by The Academy of Management. Reproduced by permission of The Academy of Management via Copyright Clearance Center.

tossed around rather casually today. Many work groups are called teams when they are far from it. Real teamwork requires a concerted collective effort (see Table 11–4). It requires lots of tolerance, practice, and trial-and-error learning.[23] Using Table 11–4 as a guide, have you ever personally experienced *real* teamwork?

LO.5 Why Do Work Teams Fail?

Advocates of the team approach to management paint a very optimistic and bright picture. Yet there is a dark side to teams.[24] While exact statistics are not available, they can and often do fail. Anyone contemplating the use of team structures in the workplace needs a balanced perspective of advantages and limitations.

Common Management Mistakes with Teams   The main threats to team effectiveness, according to the center of Figure 11–2, are *unrealistic expectations* leading to *frustration.* Frustration, in turn, encourages people to abandon teams. Both managers and team members can be victimized by unrealistic expectations.

On the left side of Figure 11–2 is a list of common management mistakes. These mistakes generally involve doing a poor job of creating a supportive environment for teams and teamwork.

Problems for Team Members   The lower-right portion of Figure 11–2 lists common problems for team members. Contrary to critics' Theory X contention about employees lacking the motivation and creativity for real teamwork, it is common for teams to take on too much too quickly and to drive themselves too hard for fast results. Important group dynamics and team skills get lost in the rush for results. Consequently, team members' expectations need to be given

table 11–4   Characteristics of Effective Teamwork

1. Clear purpose	The vision, mission, goal, or task of the team has been defined and is now accepted by everyone. There is an action plan.
2. Informality	The climate tends to be informal, comfortable, and relaxed. There are no obvious tensions or signs of boredom.
3. Participation	There is much discussion, and everyone is encouraged to participate.
4. Listening	The members use effective listening techniques such as questioning, paraphrasing, and summarizing to get out ideas.
5. Civilized disagreement	There is disagreement, but the team is comfortable with this and shows no signs of avoiding, smoothing over, or suppressing conflict.
6. Consensus decisions	For important decisions, the goal is substantial but not necessarily unanimous agreement through open discussion of everyone's ideas, avoidance of formal voting, or easy compromises.
7. Open communication	Team members feel free to express their feelings on the tasks as well as on the group's operation. There are few hidden agendas. Communication takes place outside of meetings.
8. Clear roles and work assignments	There are clear expectations about the roles played by each team member. When action is taken, clear assignments are made, accepted, and carried out. Work is fairly distributed among team members.
9. Shared leadership	While the team has a formal leader, leadership functions shift from time to time depending on the circumstances, the needs of the group, and the skills of the members. The formal leader models the appropriate behavior and helps establish positive norms.
10. External relations	The team spends time developing key outside relationships, mobilizing resources, and building credibility with important players in other parts of the organization.
11. Style diversity	The team has a broad spectrum of team-player types including members who emphasize attention to task, goal setting, focus on process, and questions about how the team is functioning.
12. Self-assessment	Periodically, the team stops to examine how well it is functioning and what may be interfering with its effectiveness.

SOURCE: From G M Parker, *Team Players and Teamwork: The New Competitive Business Strategy* (San Francisco: Jossey-Bass, 1990), table 2, p 33. Reprinted with permission of John Wiley & Sons, Inc.

a reality check by management and team members themselves. Also, teams need to be counseled against quitting when they run into an unanticipated obstacle. Failure is part of the learning process with teams, as it is elsewhere in life. Comprehensive training in interpersonal skills can prevent many common teamwork problems.

figure 11–2 Why Work Teams Fail

Mistakes typically made by management

- Teams cannot overcome weak strategies and poor business practices.
- Hostile environment for teams (command-and-control culture; competitive/individual reward plans; management resistance).
- Teams adopted as a fad, a quick-fix; no long-term commitment.
- Lessons from one team not transferred to others (limited experimentation with teams).
- Vague or conflicting team assignments.
- Inadequate team skills training.
- Poor staffing of teams.
- Lack of trust.

Unrealistic expectations resulting in frustration

Problems typically experienced by team members

- Team tries to do too much too soon.
- Conflict over differences in personal work styles (and/or personality conflicts).
- Too much emphasis on results, not enough on team processes and group dynamics.
- Unanticipated obstacle causes team to give up.
- Resistance to doing things differently.
- Poor interpersonal skills (aggressive rather than assertive communication, destructive conflict, win–lose negotiation).
- Poor interpersonal chemistry (loners, dominators, self-appointed experts do not fit in).
- Lack of trust.

TO THE POINT
What can be done to improve cooperation, trust, and cohesiveness in work teams?

Effective Teamwork through Cooperation, Trust, and Cohesiveness

As competitive pressures intensify, experts say organizational success increasingly will depend on teamwork rather than individual stars. Nowhere is this more true than in hospitals. Imagine yourself or a loved one being in this terrible situation:

Example. A 67-year-old woman was admitted to the hospital for treatment of cerebral aneurysms—weakened blood vessels in the brain. Doctors examined her and sent her to her room.

The next day, she was wheeled into cardiology, of all places, where a doctor had threaded a catheter into her heart before someone noticed he had the wrong patient. The procedure was stopped; the patient recovered.[25]

Analysis of this case by researchers revealed the need for better communication and teamwork (see Real World/Real People).

Whether in hospitals or the world of business, three components of teamwork receiving the greatest attention are cooperation, trust, and cohesiveness. Let us explore the contributions each can make to effective teamwork.

real WORLD // real PEOPLE

Surgeons and Nurses Learn Life-and-Death Teamwork Skills

Training doctors and nurses to work as teams—using safety techniques borrowed from the aviation industry—cut the death rate from surgery by 18%, a new study shows.

Surgical teams in the study, which included 108 hospitals around the country, focused on low-tech techniques, such as holding briefings and debriefings before and after each operation, says study author and former astronaut James Bagian, a professor at the University of Michigan's medical and engineering schools.

These briefings, which are routinely conducted before airplane flights, allow crews to anticipate and prepare for potential safety risks, Bagian says.

Briefings helped surgical teams make important discoveries, such as learning that patients were on blood thinners, which increase the risk for serious bleeding during surgery....

[Surgical] teams learned to recognize red flags, challenge each other when they found safety risks and develop presurgical checklists.... The more training surgical teams received, the safer they became.

If you were the dean of a university medical school, how would you incorporate teamwork training into the curriculum?

SOURCE: Excerpted from L Szabo, "Study: Teamwork Makes Surgery Safer," *USA Today*, October 20, 2010, p 5D.

Cooperation

Individuals are said to be cooperating when their efforts are systematically *integrated* to achieve a collective objective.[26] The greater the integration, the greater the degree of cooperation. Ritz-Carlton, the luxury hotel chain, effectively integrates cooperation into its service quality improvement strategy:

Example. The whole approach . . . depends upon identifying and correcting things that go wrong. To ensure that errors are reported rather than covered up, Ritz-Carlton tries hard to de-stigmatize them, shifting the focus from blame to correction. Mistakes are referred to as "Mr. BIVs," after a cartoon character whose name stands for breakdowns, inefficiencies, and variations. The point is that "a Mr. BIV occurred, and we want to surface it and get rid of it forever," explains [training director Diana] Oreck.

At the start of every shift, every day, at every Ritz-Carlton property, a 15-minute staff meeting takes place. Part of it is devoted to refresher training on one of the 12 "Service Values" incorporated into the company's Gold Standards. . . . Another part alerts the staff to Mr. BIVs that have arisen and the guests affected.[27]

Cooperation versus Competition A widely held assumption among managers is that "competition brings out the best in people." From an economic standpoint, business survival depends on staying ahead of the competition. But from an interpersonal standpoint, critics contend competition has been overemphasized, primarily at the expense of cooperation.[28] UK-born Sandra Dawson, an expert on organizational change who teaches management at the University of Cambridge, recently offered these helpful insights:

Example. I am a very strong advocate for collaboration. . . . [I tell my students,] "You need no lessons in competition. You will be as competitive as anyone, because you are here and because you are determined about where you want to go. But I am not sure how you will collaborate, though that may well differentiate you in tomorrow's global business world."

real WORLD // real PEOPLE: ethics

Internal Competition Drives College Hunks Hauling Junk

Nick Friedman had an idea. Suppose you could take the natural high spirits that compel college students to kidnap one another's team mascots and toilet-paper rival frat houses and harness it for good?

Friedman is president of College Hunks Hauling Junk,... headquartered in Tampa. The company's 23 franchises employ mostly college students and recent grads; even about half of the franchise owners are in their 20s. Friedman motivates employees almost exclusively through internal competition. Franchises and individuals vie for bragging rights and (generally modest) monetary rewards in contests over total revenue, average job sizes, customer loyalty, disposal costs, and a long list of other performance measures....

They developed a dashboard—available to the entire company over an intranet—and created competitions around the numbers tracked there. Most employees check the dashboard every day for their own and rivals' latest standings.

What are the major pros and cons of relying heavily on internal competition to motivate employees?

SOURCE: Excerpted from L Buchanan, "Managing a Little Friendly Competition: Egging on Employee Rivalries," *Inc,* October 2009, pp 99–100.

I found women likelier to agree initially that collaboration is important. I found men much more difficult to get to the door of collaboration. Men maybe have a tougher time looking beyond themselves and those like them. They have got to believe that there is value in the "Other," who will by definition have different interests and ways to see the world.

. . . [W]e teach collaboration by demonstrating its success in action [through group projects with local companies]. . . . The groups have to deliver on very tight deadlines they can meet only if they take the best from each member and do not allow one member to dominate in all respects.[29]

Meanwhile, a recent study of 260 retail employees documented positive impacts for a highly competitive work environment. Those impacts included less role ambiguity and higher job satisfaction.[30] While competitive people are likely attracted to retail sales, employees in other job categories such as health care or teaching may not thrive on competition. A contingency management approach is warranted when it comes to motivating employees with competition (see Real World/Real People).

Research Support for Cooperation   After conducting a meta-analysis of 122 studies encompassing a wide variety of subjects and settings, one team of researchers concluded that

1. Cooperation is superior to competition in promoting achievement and productivity.
2. Cooperation is superior to individualistic efforts in promoting achievement and productivity.
3. Cooperation without intergroup competition promotes higher achievement and productivity than cooperation with intergroup competition.[31]

Given the size and diversity of the research base, these findings strongly endorse cooperation in modern organizations. Cooperation can be encouraged by reward systems that reinforce teamwork, along with individual achievement.

Interestingly, cooperation can be encouraged by quite literally tearing down walls, or not building them in the first place. A study of 229 managers and professionals employed by eight small businesses proved insightful:

Example.   The researchers looked at the effects of private offices, shared private offices, cubicles, and team-oriented open offices on productivity, and found to their initial surprise that the small team, open-office configuration (desks scattered about in a small area with no partitions) to be significantly correlated with superior performance. In addition, they found that the open-office configuration was particularly favored by the youngest employees, who believe open offices provide them greater access to colleagues and the opportunity to learn from their more seasoned senior compatriots.[32]

There is a movement among architects and urban planners to design and build structures that encourage spontaneous interaction, cooperation, and teamwork.

A study involving 84 male US Air Force trainees uncovered an encouraging link between cooperation and favorable race relations. After observing the subjects interact in three-man teams during a management game, the researchers concluded: "[Helpful] teammates, both black and white, attract greater respect and liking than do teammates who have not helped. This is particularly true when the helping occurs voluntarily."[33] These findings suggest that managers can enhance equal employment opportunity and diversity programs by encouraging *voluntary* helping behavior in interracial work teams. Accordingly, it is reasonable to conclude that voluntary helping behavior could build cooperation in mixed-gender teams and groups as well.

Another study involving 72 health care professionals in a US Veterans Affairs Medical Center found a negative correlation between cooperation and team size. In other words, cooperation diminished as the health care team became larger.[34] Managers thus need to restrict the size of work teams if they desire to facilitate cooperation.

LO.6 Trust

These have not been good times for trust. Years of wasteful government spending, the financial meltdown, persistent high unemployment, bloated executive bonuses, corporate scandals, and broken promises have left many people justly cynical about trusting what leaders say and do.[35] A 2010 public opinion survey found "that only 22% of Americans said they trust the government in Washington most of the time, among the lowest measures in half a century."[36] So it is no surprise that an international survey found only about 50% of US, Canadian, and Mexican

connect™ Go to www.mcgrawhillconnect.com for a self-assessment exercise on measuring your work group's level of autonomy.

employees trusted top management. Significantly, 75% of those surveyed in all three countries reportedly trusted their immediate supervisors. This prompted the following observation: "The findings should matter to management because of the close link between trust and employee engagement: The more employees trust management, the more engaged and productive they will be—and vice versa."[37] This contention is reinforced by another survey: "In a study of 500 business professionals, conducted by MasterWorks, Annandale, Virginia, 95% said the main factor in deciding to stay or leave their job was whether they had a trusting relationship with their manager."[38] Clearly, remedial action is needed to close the trust gap, especially the huge one between employees and top management.

In this section, we examine the concept of trust and introduce six practical guidelines for building trust.

Reciprocal Faith and a Cognitive Leap

Trust is defined as reciprocal faith in others' intentions and behavior.[39] The word *reciprocal* emphasizes the give-and-take aspect of trust. In short, we tend to give what we get: trust begets trust; distrust begets distrust. While explaining specific steps 3M takes to build trust among its 75,000 employees in 200 countries, human resources experts recently observed:

Example. Trust is believing that you can count on others in a relationship—trust is all about relationships—to do what's right for you, regardless of whether you can confirm that they have. Trust permits parties to the relationship to take risks because they both believe that neither will act without first considering the action's impact on the relationship. Trust is what frees employees to put their full energy and commitment to work.[40]

Trust can be fragile, too. Syndicated business columnist Harvey Mackay reminds us that "[i]t takes years to build up trust, but only seconds to destroy it."[41] Appropriately, an interesting new line of management research centers on *trust repair*, both organizational and interpersonal.[42]

One model of organizational trust includes a personality trait called **propensity to trust.** The developers of the model explain:

Example. Propensity might be thought of as the *general willingness to trust others.* Propensity will influence how much trust one has for a trustee prior to data on that particular party being available. People with different developmental experiences, personality types, and cultural backgrounds vary in their propensity to trust. . . . An example of an extreme case of this is what is commonly called blind trust. Some individuals can be observed to repeatedly trust in situations that most people would agree do not warrant trust. Conversely, others are unwilling to trust in most situations, regardless of circumstances that would support doing so.[43]

What is your propensity to trust? How did you develop that personality trait? Trust involves "a cognitive 'leap' beyond the expectations that reason and experience alone would warrant"[44] (see Figure 11–3). For example, suppose a member of a newly formed class project team works hard, based on the assumption that her teammates also are working hard. That assumption, on which her trust is based, is a cognitive leap that goes beyond her actual experience with her new teammates. When you trust someone, you have *faith* in their good intentions. The act of trusting someone, however, carries with it the inherent risk of betrayal. Progressive managers believe that the benefits of interpersonal trust far outweigh any risks of betrayed trust. For example, Michael Powell, who founded the chain of

figure 11–3 Interpersonal Trust Involves a Cognitive Leap

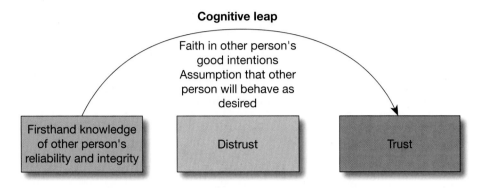

Cognitive leap

Faith in other person's
good intentions
Assumption that other
person will behave as
desired

| Firsthand knowledge of other person's reliability and integrity | Distrust | Trust |

bookstores bearing his name more than 25 years ago, built his business around the principles of open-book management, empowerment, and trust. Powell's propensity to trust was sorely tested when one of his employees stole more than $60,000 in a used-book purchasing scheme. After putting in some accounting safeguards, Powell's propensity to trust remains intact. He observed,

connect Go to www.mcgrawhillconnect.com for an interactive exercise to test your knowledge of how to build trust.

Example. The incident was a watershed for me and my staff, dispelling any naïveté we may have had about crime. We realized that not only *can* theft happen; it *will* happen. At the same time, dealing with the matter forced us to revisit our basic values and managerial philosophies. We believe that the modern demands of business call for an empowered and fully flexible staff, and we know that such a staff will often have to handle valuable commodities and money. We also believe that most people are not going to abuse our trust if they are put in a position with a reasonable amount of review and responsibility.[45]

How to Build Trust Management professor/consultant Fernando Bartolomé offers the following six guidelines for building and maintaining trust:

1. *Communication.* Keep team members and employees informed by explaining policies and decisions and providing accurate feedback. Be candid about one's own problems and limitations. Tell the truth.

2. *Support.* Be available and approachable. Provide help, advice, coaching, and support for team members' ideas.

3. *Respect.* Delegation, in the form of real decision-making authority, is the most important expression of managerial respect. Actively listening to the ideas of others is a close second. (Empowerment, discussed in Chapter 15, is not possible without trust.)

4. *Fairness.* Be quick to give credit and recognition to those who deserve it. Make sure all performance appraisals and evaluations are objective and impartial.

Talk about trust! This construction worker's life is in the hands of the crane operator. Many variables—including the worker's propensity to trust and the crane operator's reputation—factor into the trust calculation for this dangerous situation.

trust Reciprocal faith in others' intentions and behavior.

propensity to trust A personality trait involving one's general willingness to trust others.

5. *Predictability.* Be consistent and predictable in your daily affairs. Keep both expressed and implied promises.

6. *Competence.* Enhance your credibility by demonstrating good business sense, technical ability, and professionalism.[46]

Trust needs to be earned; it cannot be demanded. Trust is anchored to **credibility**—"developing the integrity, intent, capabilities, and results that make you *believable,* both to yourself and to others."[47] How credible and trustworthy are you? How about those in your personal and professional circles?

Back to the Chapter-Opening Case

What role does trust play in customer-service teams and how can management build that trust?

 LO.7 Cohesiveness

Cohesiveness is a process whereby "a sense of 'we-ness' emerges to transcend individual differences and motives."[48] Members of a cohesive group stick together. They are reluctant to leave the group. Cohesive group members stick together for one or both of the following reasons: (1) because they enjoy each others' company or (2) because they need each other to accomplish a common goal. Accordingly, two types of group cohesiveness, identified by sociologists, are socio-emotional cohesiveness and instrumental cohesiveness.[49]

 Go to www.mcgrawhillconnect.com for a comprehension case on how Xplane designs and manages teams effectively.

Socio-Emotional and Instrumental Cohesiveness   **Socio-emotional cohesiveness** is a sense of togetherness that develops when individuals derive emotional satisfaction from group participation. Accordingly, recent research shows that shared intense emotional experiences (such as going to the dentist) tend to bond people together.[50] Most general discussions of group cohesiveness are limited to the socio-emotional type. However, from the standpoint of getting things accomplished in task groups and teams, we cannot afford to ignore instrumental cohesiveness. **Instrumental cohesiveness** is a sense of togetherness that develops when group members are mutually dependent on one another because they believe they could not achieve the group's goal by acting separately. A feeling of "we-ness" is *instrumental* in achieving the common goal. Team advocates generally assume both types of cohesiveness are essential to productive teamwork. But is this really true?

Lessons from Group Cohesiveness Research   What is the connection between group cohesiveness and performance? A landmark meta-analysis of 49 studies involving 8,702 subjects provided these insights:

• There is a small but statistically significant cohesiveness→performance effect.

• The cohesiveness→performance effect was stronger for smaller and real groups (as opposed to contrived groups in laboratory studies).

• The cohesiveness→performance effect becomes stronger as one moves from nonmilitary real groups to military groups to sports teams.

• Commitment to the task at hand (meaning the individual sees the performance standards as legitimate) has the most powerful impact on the cohesiveness→performance linkage.

- The *performance→cohesiveness* linkage is stronger than the cohesiveness→performance linkage. Thus, success tends to bind group or team members together rather than closely knit groups being more successful.
- Contrary to the popular view, cohesiveness is not "a 'lubricant' that minimizes friction due to the human 'grit' in the system."[51]
- All this evidence led the researchers to this practical conclusion: "Efforts to enhance group performance by fostering interpersonal attraction or 'pumping up' group pride are not likely to be effective."[52]

A second meta-analysis found no significant relationship between cohesiveness and the quality of group decisions. However, support was found for Janis's contention that *groupthink* tends to afflict cohesive in-groups with strong leadership. Groups whose members liked each other a great deal tended to make poorer quality decisions.[53]

Getting Some Positive Impact from Group Cohesiveness   Research tells us that group cohesiveness is no secret weapon in the quest for improved group or team performance. The trick is to keep task groups small, make sure performance standards and goals are clear and accepted, achieve some early successes, and follow the tips in Table 11–5. A good example is Westinghouse's

table 11–5   Steps Managers Can Take to Enhance the Two Types of Group Cohesiveness

Socio-Emotional Cohesiveness

Keep the group relatively small.

Strive for a favorable public image to increase the status and prestige of belonging.

Encourage interaction and cooperation.

Emphasize members' common characteristics and interests.

Point out environmental threats (e.g., competitors' achievements) to rally the group.

Instrumental Cohesiveness

Regularly update and clarify the group's goal(s).

Give every group member a vital "piece of the action."

Channel each group member's special talents toward the common goal(s).

Recognize and equitably reinforce every member's contributions.

Frequently remind group members they need each other to get the job done.

credibility Being believable through integrity, intent, capabilities, and results.

cohesiveness A sense of "we-ness" helps group stick together.

socio-emotional cohesiveness Sense of togetherness based on emotional satisfaction.

instrumental cohesiveness Sense of togetherness based on mutual dependency needed to get the job done.

highly automated military radar electronics plant in College Station, Texas. Compared with their counterparts at a traditional factory in Baltimore, each of the Texas plant's 500 employees produces eight times more, at half the per-unit cost: The key, says Westinghouse, is not the robots but the people. Employees work in teams of 8 to 12. Members devise their own solutions to problems. Teams measure daily how each person's performance compares with that of other members and how the team's performance compares with the plant's. Joseph L Johnson, 28, a robotics technician, says that is a big change from a previous hourly factory job where he cared only about "picking up my paycheck." Here, peer pressure "makes sure you get the job done."[54]

connect Go to www.mcgrawhillconnect.com for a video case on Johnson & Johnson.

Self-selected work teams (in which people pick their own teammates) and off-the-job social events can stimulate socio-emotional cohesiveness.[55] The fostering of socio-emotional cohesiveness needs to be balanced with instrumental cohesiveness. The latter can be encouraged by making sure everyone in the group recognizes and appreciates each member's vital contribution to the group goal. While balancing the two types of cohesiveness, managers need to remember that groupthink theory and research cautions against too much cohesiveness.

TO THE POINT
What are the keys to success for virtual and self-managed teams?

LO.8 Teams in Action: Virtual Teams and Self-Managed Teams

All sorts of interesting approaches to teams and teamwork can be found in the workplace today. A great deal of experimentation is taking place as organizations struggle to be more flexible and responsive. New information technologies also have spurred experimentation with team formats. This section profiles two different approaches to teams: virtual teams and self-managed teams. We have selected these particular types of teams for three reasons: (1) they have recognizable labels, (2) they have at least some research evidence, (3) they vary in degree of empowerment (refer to Figure 15–2 in Chapter 15).

As indicated in Table 11–6, the two types of teams are distinct but not totally unique. Overlaps exist. For instance, computer-networked virtual teams may or may not have volunteer members and may or may not be self-managed. Another point of overlap involves the fifth variable in Table 11–6: relationship to organization structure. Teams are called *parallel* structures when they exist outside normal channels of authority and communication.[56] Self-managed teams, on the

table 11–6   Basic Distinctions between Virtual Teams and Self-Managed Teams

	VIRTUAL TEAMS	SELF-MANAGED TEAMS
Type of team (see Table 11–2)	Advice or project (usually project)	Production, project, or action
Type of empowerment (see Figure 15–2)	Consultation, participation, or delegation	Delegation
Members	Managers and technical specialists	Production/service, technical specialists
Basis of membership	Assigned (some voluntary)	Assigned
Relationship to organization structure	Parallel or integrated	Integrated
Amount of face-to-face communication	Periodic to none	Varies, depending on use of information technology

real WORLD // real PEOPLE

Far-flung IBM Employees Team Up with Mobile Apps

IBM engineer William Bodin needed a way to communicate securely with a team of developers halfway around the world. So he turned to an application, created by colleagues, that could be downloaded to his smartphone. It let him collaborate with teammates in Vietnam while he was sitting rink-side at his son's hockey practice.

Bodin . . . has since created an online storefront that gives employees across the company access to software that can help them get their work done. The store, called Whirlwind, has been used by more than 11,000 IBMers in the six weeks it's been open for business. There are apps for everything from scheduling conference rooms to approving purchasing orders to accessing IBM's internal social network. Previously, employees couldn't do most of this unless they were logged onto a desktop PC or a network-linked laptop. Now they can do it all from a smartphone or other mobile device.

What positive and/or negative unforeseen consequences could the extensive use of virtual teams have on individuals and organizations?

SOURCE: Excerpted from R King, "Mobile Apps Suit Up For the Office," *Bloomberg Businessweek,* November 8–14, 2010, pp 44–45.

The long-standing dream of working from the beach is now a reality, thanks to modern telecommunications and wireless Internet technology. Your virtual office on Hawaii's Waikiki Beach awaits. Interested?

---

other hand, are *integrated* into the basic organizational structure. Virtual teams vary in this regard, although they tend to be parallel because they are made up of functional specialists (engineers, accountants, marketers, etc.) who team up on temporary projects. Keeping these basic distinctions in mind, let us explore virtual teams and self-managed teams.

Virtual Teams

Virtual teams are a product of modern times. They take their name from *virtual reality* computer simulations, where "it's almost like the real thing." Thanks to information technologies such as the mobile Internet, e-mail, social media, videoconferencing, and groupware, you can be a member of a work team without really being there[57] (see Real World/Real People). Traditional team meetings are location specific. Team members are either physically present or absent. Virtual teams, in contrast, convene electronically with members reporting in from different locations, different organizations, and even different time zones.

Because virtual teams are relatively new, there is no consensual definition. Our working definition of a **virtual team** is a physically dispersed task group that conducts its business primarily through modern information technology. Advocates

virtual team Information technology allows group members in different locations to conduct business.

say virtual teams are very flexible and efficient because they are driven by information and skills, not by time and location. People with needed information or skills can be team members, regardless of where or when they actually do their work. Virtual teams are second nature to those who grew up with the Internet and social media.

On the negative side, lack of face-to-face interaction can weaken trust, communication, and accountability. Working remotely may also negatively impact how management perceives work quality. In a survey of 1,465 employees, 55% answered yes and 45% said no to the question: "Do you think your work quality is perceived the same when you work remotely as when you are physically in the office?"[58] Leading and managing from a distance can be very challenging. Billie Williamson, an Ernst & Young partner responsible for corporate diversity, has managed virtual teams for more than 10 years. She offers this instructive perspective:

Example. Managing virtually offers many benefits: It's easy to accommodate differing schedules, schedule meetings on short notice, reduce travel expenses, be more ecologically friendly, and decrease unproductive travel time. It also allows for the creation of more diverse teams that bring together broader experience and knowledge. But the most important thing for managers to remember is that the success of any team, virtual or not, depends on the people. Technology can bring you together, but it's the manager who must make sure the relationships stay vital, each team member is valued, and productivity is high.[59]

Research Insights   As one might expect with a new and ill-defined area, research evidence to date is a bit spotty. Here is what we have learned so far from recent studies of computer-mediated groups:

- Virtual groups formed over the Internet follow a group development process similar to that for face-to-face groups.[60] (Recall our discussion of Tuckman's model in Chapter 10.)
- Internet chat rooms create more work and yield poorer decisions than face-to-face meetings and telephone conferences.[61]
- Successful use of groupware (software that facilitates interaction among virtual group members) requires training and hands-on experience.[62]
- Inspirational leadership has a positive impact on creativity in electronic brainstorming groups.[63]
- Conflict management is particularly difficult for asynchronous virtual teams (those not interacting in real time) that have no opportunity for face-to-face interaction.[64]
- Having at least one member of a team working remotely "prompts the group to be more disciplined in its coordination and communication—yielding a better and more productive experience for all members. . . . But turn that isolate into a pair—by adding a coworker at the same location—and the team suffers."[65] The latter problem occurs because the remote pair tends to bond with each other, all too often against "headquarters."

Practical Considerations   Virtual teams may be in fashion, but they are not a cure-all. In fact, they may be a giant step backward for those not well versed in modern information technology. Managers who rely on virtual teams agree on one point: *Meaningful face-to-face contact, especially during early phases of the group development process, is absolutely essential.* Virtual group members need "faces" in their minds to go with names and electronic messages. Periodic face-to-face interaction not only fosters social bonding among virtual team members, it also facilitates conflict resolution. Additionally, virtual teams cannot succeed

table 11–7   How to Create and Manage a Virtual Team

Forming the Team

- Develop a team mission statement along with teamwork expectations and norms, project goals, and deadlines.
- Recruit team members with complementary skills and diverse backgrounds who have the ability and willingness to contribute.
- Get a high-level sponsor to champion the project.
- Post a skill, biographical sketch, contact information, and "local time" matrix to familiarize members with each other and their geographic dispersion.

Preparing the Team

- Make sure everyone has a broadband connection and is comfortable with virtual teamwork technologies (e.g., e-mail, instant messaging, conference calls, online meeting and collaboration programs such as WebEx, and videoconferencing).
- Establish hardware and software compatibility.
- Make sure everyone is comfortable with synchronous (interacting at the same time) and asynchronous (interacting at different times) teamwork.
- Get individuals to buy in on team goals, deadlines, and individual tasks.

Building Teamwork and Trust

- Make sure everyone is involved (during meetings and overall).
- Arrange periodic face-to-face work meetings, team-building exercises, and leisure activities.
- Encourage collaboration between and among team members on subtasks.
- Establish an early-warning system for conflict (e.g., gripe sessions).

Motivating and Leading the Team

- Post a scoreboard to mark team progress toward goals.
- Celebrate team accomplishments both virtually and face-to-face.
- Begin each virtual team meeting with praise and recognition for outstanding contributions.
- Keep team members' line managers informed of their accomplishments and progress.

SOURCE: From R Kreitner and C Cassidy, *Management*, 12th ed (Mason, OH: South-Western Cengage Learning, 2012), Table 13.3. Copyright © 2009 SouthWestern, a part of Cengage Learning. Reproduced by permission. www.cengage.com/permission.

without some old-fashioned factors such as top-management support, hands-on training, a clear mission and specific objectives, effective leadership, and schedules and deadlines. (See the practical tips listed in Table 11–7.)

Self-Managed Teams

Have you ever thought you could do a better job than your boss? Well, if the trend toward self-managed work teams continues to grow as predicted, you just may get your chance. For example, "[a]t a General Mills cereal plant in Lodi, California, teams . . . schedule, operate, and maintain machinery so effectively that the factory runs with no managers present during the night shift."[66] More typically, managers are present to serve as trainers and facilitators. Self-managed teams come in every conceivable format today, some more autonomous than others.

Self-managed teams are defined as groups of workers who are given administrative oversight for their task domains. Administrative oversight involves

self-managed teams Groups of employees granted administrative oversight for their work.

delegated activities such as planning, scheduling, monitoring, and staffing. These are chores normally performed by managers. In short, employees in these unique work groups act as their own supervisor. Accountability is maintained *indirectly* by outside managers and leaders. According to a study of a company with 300 self-managed teams, 66 "team advisers" relied on these four indirect influence tactics:

- *Relating.* Understanding the organization's power structure, building trust, showing concern for individual team members.
- *Scouting.* Seeking outside information, diagnosing teamwork problems, facilitating group problem solving.
- *Persuading.* Gathering outside support and resources, influencing team to be more effective and pursue organizational goals.
- *Empowering.* Delegating decision-making authority, facilitating team decision-making process, coaching.[67]

Self-managed teams are variously referred to as semiautonomous work groups, autonomous work groups, and super teams.

Managerial Resistance   Something much more complex is involved than this apparently simple label suggests. The term *self-managed* does not mean simply turning workers loose to do their own thing. Indeed, an organization embracing self-managed teams should be prepared to undergo revolutionary changes in management philosophy, structure, staffing and training practices, and reward systems. Moreover, the traditional notions of managerial authority and control are turned on their heads. Not surprisingly, many managers strongly resist giving up the reins of power to people they view as subordinates. They see self-managed teams as a threat to their job security.

Cross-Functionalism   A common feature of self-managed teams, particularly among those above the shop-floor or clerical level, is **cross-functionalism**.[68] In other words, specialists from different areas are put on the same team. For example, consider this cross-functional team of twenty members:

Example. The Lifespan organization [based in Providence, Rhode Island] consists of four hospitals, each with a separate strategy for delivering online annual mandatory training, with the majority of such online training related to patient safety. Stephanie Thanos' gap analysis in summer 2009 revealed a major opportunity to improve and consolidate this training. Thanos successfully launched an online patient safety curriculum committee, bringing together representatives of a wide array of clinical and operational functions, including nursing and physician leaders, risk management experts, and quality officers from all hospitals, to design a single online course that reduced the duplication of efforts and delivered a universal message to all employees across the organization.[69]

Mark Stefik, a manager at the world-renowned Palo Alto Research Center in California, explains the wisdom of cross-functionalism:

Example. Something magical happens when you bring together a group of people from different disciplines with a common purpose. It's a middle zone, the breakthrough zone. The idea is to start a team on a problem—a hard problem, to keep people motivated. When there's an obstacle, instead of dodging it, bring in another point of view: an electrical engineer, a user interface expert, a sociologist, whatever spin on the market is needed. Give people new eyeglasses to cross-pollinate ideas.[70]

Are Self-Managed Teams Effective? The Research Evidence

Among companies with self-managed teams, the most commonly delegated tasks are work scheduling and dealing directly with outside customers. The least common team chores are hiring and firing.[71] Most of today's self-managed teams remain bunched at the shop-floor level in factory settings. Experts predict growth of the practice in the managerial ranks and in service operations.[72]

Much of what we know about self-managed teams comes from testimonials and case studies. Fortunately, a body of higher quality field research is slowly developing. A review of three meta-analyses covering 70 individual studies concluded that self-managed teams had

- A positive effect on productivity.
- A positive effect on specific attitudes relating to self-management (e.g., responsibility and control).
- No significant effect on general attitudes (e.g., job satisfaction and organizational commitment).
- No significant effect on absenteeism or turnover.[73]

A recent study of 97 teams in a public safety organization found that self-managing behaviors tended to enhance team effectiveness when the job involved more than just routine tasks.[74]

Although encouraging, these results do not qualify as a sweeping endorsement of self-managed teams. Nonetheless, experts say the trend toward self-managed work teams will continue upward in North America because of a strong cultural bias in favor of direct participation (see Table 11–8). Managers need to be prepared for the resulting shift in organizational administration.[75]

Team Building and Team Leadership

◀ ·······················

TO THE POINT

How can team building and team leadership create a high-performance team?

·······················

Helping a work group evolve into a true team requires imaginative and cost-effective team building and a special set of leadership skills. Let us explore what these requirements entail.

Team Building

Team building is a catch-all term for a whole host of techniques aimed at improving the internal functioning of work groups. Whether conducted by company trainers or outside consultants, team-building activities and workshops strive for greater cooperation, better communication, and less dysfunctional conflict.

Rote memorization and lectures/discussions are discouraged by team-building experts who prefer *active* versus passive learning. Greater emphasis is placed on *how* work groups get the job done than on the job itself. Experiential learning techniques such as interpersonal trust exercises, conflict-handling

cross-functionalism Team made up of technical specialists from different areas.

team building Experiential learning aimed at better internal functioning of groups.

table 11–8 There Are Many Ways to Empower Self-Managed Teams

External Leader Behavior

1. Make team members responsible and accountable for the work they do.
2. Ask for and use team suggestions when making decisions.
3. Encourage team members to take control of their work.
4. Create an environment in which team members set their own team goals.
5. Stay out of the way when team members attempt to solve work-related problems.
6. Generate high team expectations.
7. Display trust and confidence in the team's abilities.

Production/Service Responsibilities

1. The team sets its own production/service goals and standards.
2. The team assigns jobs and tasks to its members.
3. Team members develop their own quality standards and measurement techniques.
4. Team members take on production/service learning and development opportunities.
5. Team members handle their own problems with internal and external customers.
6. The team works with a whole product or service, not just a part.

Human Resource Management System

1. The team gets paid, at least in part, as a team.
2. Team members are cross-trained on jobs within their team.
3. Team members are cross-trained on jobs in other teams.
4. Team members are responsible for hiring, training, punishment, and firing.
5. Team members use peer evaluations to formally evaluate each other.

Social Structure

1. The team gets support from other teams and departments when needed.
2. The team has access to and uses important and strategic information.
3. The team has access to and uses the resources of other teams.
4. The team has access to and uses resources inside and outside the organization.
5. The team frequently communicates with other teams.
6. The team makes its own rules and policies.

SOURCE: From B L Kirkman and B Rosen, "Powering Up Teams," *Organizational Dynamics,* Winter 2000, p 56. Copyright © 2000 with permission from Elsevier Science.

This office version of a garage band at M5 Networks turns team building into entertainment for the whole finance department. It's a good way to fight afternoon drowsiness, too.

role-play sessions, creative activities (see Real World/Real People), and competitive games are common. Outdoor activities can be a nice change of pace for office and factory dwellers. An extreme case in point: "Each year Seagate Technology spends $2 million for 200 employees to spend a week hiking, kayaking, and adventure racing in the mountains of New Zealand."[76] Company officials insist it's worth it. But ethical red flags were raised about lavish off-site events during the recent deep recession. Less costly team-building activities, such as volunteering to build a Habitat for Humanity home, can be both effective and socially responsible.[77] Jeffrey Katzenberg, CEO of DreamWorks Animation SKG, the studio that gave us *Shrek,* prefers celebrations for team building: "When a movie opens, when a DVD comes out, or when awards are won, all of those milestones are celebrated in a big way."[78]

Free online resources, such as www.businessballs.com (named for the art of juggling balls), are an excellent way to spark your imagination about how to go about building your team in a cost-effective manner.

real WORLD // real PEOPLE

McDonald's Uses Team Building to Develop Leaders in China

Zhou Xiaobu runs from one end of a table to another, grasping a piece of a jigsaw puzzle her team is assembling as part of a leadership training exercise for McDonald's managers. "Go, go, go!" yells their instructor, exhorting them to work for the prize, a box of Danish butter cookies that will go to the first group to build the company's trademark Golden Arches. Above their heads a sign reads: "Learning today, leading tomorrow." The thick green binders stuffed with paperwork on each of the 31 students' desks indicate this is no place for slackers.

Such is the seriousness of purpose found at McDonald's new Hamburger University near Shanghai,

where the chain aims to crank out a new generation of leaders to fuel big expansion plans in China.

If you were a management development trainer at McDonald's Hamburger University in the US, what specific team-building activity would you select and what would you do to make it an effective learning event?

SOURCE: M Wei, "East Meets West at Hamburger University," *Bloomberg Businessweek,* January 31–February 6, 2011, p 22.

The Bottom Line: Without clear goals, proper leadership, careful attention to details, and transfer of learning back to the job, both on-site and off-site team-building sessions can become an expensive disappointment.[79]

LO.9 The Goal of Team Building: High–Performance Teams

Team building allows team members to wrestle with simulated or real-life problems. Outcomes are then analyzed by the group to determine what group processes need improvement. Learning stems from recognizing and addressing faulty group dynamics. Perhaps one subgroup withheld key information from another, thereby hampering group progress. With cross-cultural teams becoming commonplace in today's global economy, team building is more important than ever.[80]

A nationwide survey of team members from many organizations, by Wilson Learning Corporation, provides a useful model or benchmark of what we should expect of teams. The researchers' question was simply: "What is a high-performance team?"[81] The respondents were asked to describe their peak experiences in work teams. Analysis of the survey results yielded the following eight attributes of high-performance teams:

1. *Participative leadership.* Creating an interdependency by empowering, freeing up, and serving others.

2. *Shared responsibility.* Establishing an environment in which all team members feel as responsible as the manager for the performance of the work unit.

3. *Aligned on purpose.* Having a sense of common purpose about why the team exists and the function it serves.

4. *High communication.* Creating a climate of trust and open, honest communication.

5. *Future focused.* Seeing change as an opportunity for growth.

6. *Focused on task.* Keeping meetings focused on results.

7. *Creative talents.* Applying individual talents and creativity.

8. *Rapid response.* Identifying and acting on opportunities.[82]

These eight attributes effectively combine many of today's most progressive ideas on management, among them being participation, empowerment, service ethic, individual responsibility and development, self-management, trust, active listening, and envisioning. But patience and diligence are required. According to a manager familiar with work teams, "high-performance teams may take three to five years to build."[83]

Back to the Chapter-Opening Case

If you worked at one of Steve Wynn's hotels or resorts, what sort of team building activities would you use for your employees to make sure each of your guests experienced great customer service?

Assessing the Effectiveness of Team Building   Managers are accountable for knowing if their team-building activities are effective. The most widely used assessment framework among corporate trainers was first developed in 1959 by University of Wisconsin professor Donald L Kirkpatrick. His four-level evaluation model, from most superficial to most comprehensive, consists of the following:

- *Reaction.* How did the participants feel about the activity?
- *Learning.* Did the experience increase knowledge or improve skills?
- *Behavior.* Did participants' on-the-job behavior improve as a result of the activity?
- *Results.* Did participants subsequently achieve better measurable results?[84]

Unfortunately, managers too often settle for a quick post-activity survey of participants (e.g., Did you enjoy the activity? Was it worthwhile?). Adequate assessment requires a more comprehensive approach. Tony Hsieh, CEO of online retailer Zappos, is headed in the right direction by quizzing managers responsible for team building:

Example. [He] polls managers after they've taken teams to dinner or on a hike, and they invariably talk about communication, greater trust, and budding friendships. "Then we ask, 'How much more efficient do you think your team is now?'" Hsieh says. "The range is anywhere from 20% to 100%."[85]

Leading Teams

Practical experience and a growing body of research have made it apparent that leading a team is not the same as leading individuals.[86] Leadership versatility is needed. This is somewhat akin to the difference between conducting a group exercise with a classroom full of students and discussing a problem with one student after class. Very different relationship dynamics are involved in the two situations. As a prelude to our comprehensive coverage of leadership in Chapter 16, this final section highlights the importance of being able to lead both individuals and teams. Harvard Business School professor Linda A Hill framed the challenge for new managers this way:

Example. [T]he new manager must figure out how to harness the power of a team. Simply focusing on one-on-one relationships with members of the team can undermine that process.

. . . [M]any new managers fail to recognize, much less address, their team-building responsibilities. Instead, they conceive of their people-management role as building the most effective relationships they can with each individual subordinate, erroneously equating the management of their team with managing the individuals on the team.

They attend primarily to individual performance and pay little or no attention to team culture and performance. They hardly ever rely on group forums for identifying and solving problems. Some spend too much time with a small number of trusted subordinates, often those who seem most supportive. New managers tend to handle issues, even those with teamwide implications, one-on-one. This leads them to make decisions based on unnecessarily limited information.[87]

Recent research provides these practical insights about team leadership:

- A study of 28 self-selected teams of business students with three to five members each found that team leadership aimed at building group cohesiveness and limiting conflict tended to enhance team performance.[88]

- Another study found a coaching style of leadership was effective for charismatic leaders (personal magnetism) when dealing with team members having low self-efficacy. A directive style worked better for leaders who lacked charisma and had team members with high self-efficacy.[89] (Recall from Chapter 5 that those with high self-efficacy have a strong "can do" attitude.)

- When individual-focused versus group-focused leadership behaviors were studied in 70 work teams from eight different companies, researchers found that "treating members as separate individuals and applying differentiated leadership may result in some loss of group effectiveness. This occurs because divergence in members' self-efficacy lowers the group's collective efficacy."[90]

These studies are just the beginning of what promises to be a fruitful area of leadership research. Meanwhile, the contingency approach to leading (covered in detail in Chapter 16) gets a strong vote of confidence. There clearly is no single one-size-fits-all leadership style for today's team-based organizations. Team leaders need to be versatile and flexible when adapting their style to the following dynamic web of relationships: leader↔each individual; leader↔team as a whole; team member↔team member; and subgroup↔subgroup. Present and future team leaders need to be well-versed in groupthink, group decision making, managing conflict, negotiation, communication, influence and power, leadership, and managing change (see Chapters 10, 12, 13, 14, 15, 16, and 18).

Summary of Key Concepts

1. *Explain how a work group becomes a team.* A team is a mature group where leadership is shared, accountability is both individual and collective, the members have developed their own purpose, problem solving is a way of life, and effectiveness is measured by collective outcomes.

2. *Identify and describe four types of work teams.* Advice teams provide information for managerial decisions. Production teams perform an organization's day-to-day operations. Project teams apply specialized knowledge to solve problems needed to complete a specific project. Action teams are highly skilled and highly coordinated to provide peak performance on demand.

3. *Explain the model of effective work teams, and specify the two criteria of team effectiveness.* Work teams need three things: (*a*) a team-friendly organization to provide a support system, (*b*) individuals with teamwork competencies, and (*c*) effective teamwork. The two team effectiveness criteria are performance (getting the job done) and team

viability (satisfied members who are willing to continue contributing to the team).

4. *Identify five teamwork competencies team members need to possess.* They are (*a*) orients team to problem-solving situation, (*b*) organizes and manages team performance, (*c*) promotes a positive team environment, (*d*) facilitates and manages task conflict, and (*e*) appropriately promotes perspective.

5. *Discuss why teams fail.* Teams fail because unrealistic expectations cause frustration and failure. Common management mistakes include weak strategies, creating a hostile environment for teams, faddish use of teams, not learning from team experience, vague team assignments, poor team staffing, inadequate training, and lack of trust. Team members typically try too much too soon, experience conflict over differing work styles and personalities, ignore important group dynamics, resist change, exhibit poor interpersonal skills and chemistry, and display a lack of trust.

6. *List at least four things managers can do to build trust.* Six recommended ways to build trust are through communication, support, respect (especially delegation), fairness, predictability, and competence.

7. *Distinguish two types of group cohesiveness, and summarize cohesiveness research findings.* Cohesive groups have a shared sense of togetherness or a "we" feeling. Socioemotional cohesiveness involves emotional satisfaction. Instrumental cohesiveness involves goal-directed togetherness. There is a small but significant relationship between cohesiveness and performance. The effect is stronger for smaller groups. Commitment to task among group members strengthens the cohesiveness-performance linkage. Success can build group cohesiveness. Cohesiveness is not a cure-all for group problems. Too much cohesiveness can lead to groupthink.

8. *Define virtual teams and self-managed teams.* Virtual teams are physically dispersed work groups that conduct their business via modern information technologies such as the Internet, e-mail, and videoconferences. Self-managed teams are work groups that perform their own administrative chores such as planning, scheduling, and staffing.

9. *Describe high-performance teams and discuss team leadership.* Eight attributes of high-performance teams are participative leadership, shared responsibility, aligned on purpose, high communication, future focused for growth, focused on task, creative talents applied, and rapid response. Leading a team is not the same as leading the individuals within it. A flexible and adaptable leadership style is required to manage the complex web of relationships in a work team. More emphasis is needed on team building, broader input, and group problem solving.

Key Terms

Team, 300

Team viability, 304

Trust, 312

Propensity to trust, 312

Credibility, 314

Cohesiveness, 314

Socio-emotional cohesiveness, 314

Instrumental cohesiveness, 314

Virtual team, 317

Self-managed teams, 319

Cross-functionalism, 320

Team building, 321

OB in Action Case Study

Google's "Three-Thirds" HR Team

If you've ever imagined a "dream team" of human resource professionals, a collection of diverse talent drawn up to have maximum impact on organizational results, it may have had similarities to the People Operations department at Google, the fast-growing technology company in Mountain View, California.

Google's HR team is built on what Laszlo Bock, vice president of global people operations, calls the "three-thirds" staffing model. Roughly one-third of the team's employees have HR backgrounds and bring expertise in client relations as well as specialty skill areas such as employment law and compensation and benefits. This group also has what Bock calls high-level "pattern recognition" skills, or the ability to identify organizational trends and anticipate issues even before they're on line units' radar. An example would be predicting ebbs and flows in hiring and attrition.

Another third have little or no human resource experience and were recruited from strategic consulting firms or Google line functions such as engineering or sales. Most in this group are embedded within business units. Staff in this subgroup have "tremendous problem-solving skills and knowledge about how everything *outside* of HR works," Bock says. "If you can find people with that skill set, plus an aptitude for people-related issues, we've found they partner very well with traditional HR employees."

The final third is a workforce analytics group featuring people who hold doctorates in statistics, finance, organizational psychology, and other areas. These analysts help make determinations on matters such as setting compensation levels that will retain top talent for maximum periods and conducting the right number of interviews to ensure selection of the best job candidate.

Subteams within this third group also conduct more esoteric research. For example, they explore cognitive heuristics—the mental shortcuts that people use in making decisions or solving problems but that can also lead to biases.

This group also examines ways to counter influences such as the halo effect—a job candidate considered good or bad in one category is assumed by hiring managers to be similarly good or bad in other categories—and the recency effect, in which too much weight is given to an employee's most recent performance in yearly evaluations.

Analytics specialists also focus on predictive modeling, or using principles of mathematics and psychology to determine the profiles of people who will be most successful at Google and those likely to leave the company prematurely based on their changing behavior patterns.

"This group helps us prove what we do in People Operations works and contributes directly to Google's business results," Bock says.

While the three-thirds model might appear to set up walled-off silos in the department, Bock encourages regular interaction and knowledge sharing among HR team members.[91]

Questions for Discussion

1. Using Table 11–1 as a guide, what needs to be done to turn Google's HR group into a true *team*?
2. Should Google's HR team members have been instructed ahead of time in the teamwork competencies in Table 11–3? Explain how it should have been done.
3. How important is trust with this sort of cross-functional team? Explain how to quickly build trust among cross-functional team members who bring a diverse array of backgrounds and perspectives to the table.
4. Which type of cohesiveness, socio-emotional or instrumental, is more important in this type of cross-functional team? Explain.
5. What advice would you give Google's Laszlo Bock about managing a cross-functional team, team building, and team leadership?

Legal/Ethical Challenge

You Can Reach Me at the Beach

Bill Kilburg, 48, is the chairman and chief executive of Scottsdale (Arizona)-based Hospitality Performance Network Global, a broker of group meetings. For six weeks each summer, he and his co-founder rent houses five blocks apart in Mission Beach, San Diego, and work from there. "My CFO [chief financial officer] gets my parking space, so she's happy," Kilburg says. He generally works from the shore on his BlackBerry until 1 p.m., then cracks a beer and heads into the ocean. He's philosophical about his ability to lead the 170-person company from the beach. "My job is the strategic growth of the company," he says. "It's not like I have to be sitting in my office to do that."[92]

What are the ethical implications of being a virtual boss?

1. The idea today is to work smarter, not harder. Kilburg is a good role model for using information technology to achieve a healthy work–life balance. Explain your ethical reasoning.
2. Virtual leadership may sound good in theory, but well-run businesses rely on trust built with lots of face-to-face teamwork. Electronic interaction cannot adequately replace face-to-face communication and problem solving. Explain your ethical reasoning.
3. This elitist style of leadership could breed resentment, damage employee morale, erode trust, and dampen team spirit. (Is going to the coast and leaving your employees to sweat out an Arizona summer a good way to build trust?) Explain your ethical reasoning.
4. Invent other options. Discuss.

Web Resources

For study material and exercises that apply to this chapter, visit our website at **www.mhhe.com/kreitner10e**

chapter 12

Individual and Group Decision Making

 Learning Objectives

When you finish studying the material in this chapter, you should be able to:

LO.1 Compare and contrast the rational model of decision making, Simon's normative model, and the garbage can model.

LO.2 Discuss eight decision-making biases.

LO.3 Discuss the thrust of evidence-based decision making and its implementation principles.

LO.4 Explain the model of decision-making styles.

LO.5 Explain the model of intuition and the ethical decision tree.

LO.6 Summarize the pros and cons of involving groups in the decision-making process.

LO.7 Contrast brainstorming, the nominal group technique, the Delphi technique, and computer-aided decision making.

LO.8 Describe the stages of the creative process.

LO.9 Discuss the practical recommendations for increasing creativity.

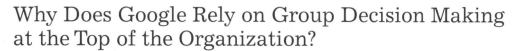

Why Does Google Rely on Group Decision Making at the Top of the Organization?

A group of Google executives meets every Monday afternoon in the corporate boardroom. "The weekly meeting, known as Execute, was launched last summer with a specific mission: to get the near-sovereign leaders of Google's far-flung product groups into a single room and harmonize their disparate initiatives." Google's co-founders Sergy Brin and Larry Page, who recently took over as CEO, and former CEO Eric Schmidt run the meetings. Attendees at the meeting include Andy Rubin, engineering VP for Android, Salar Kamangar, VP for Youtube, and Vic Gundotra, engineering VP for social networks. Page told a reporter from *Bloomberg Businessweek* that the goal of these meetings is "to get these different product leaders together to find time to talk through all the integration points. . . . Every time we increase the size of the company, we need to keep things going to make sure we keep our speed, pace, and passion."

Over the years, the decision-making process at Google led to a host of innovative products such as Gmail and Android, not to mention the company's heralded search engine. Unfortunately, the company has recently encountered several failed offerings, including Google Buzz, which is a Twitter clone, and Google Wave, a service that allows people to collaborate online.

"Page doesn't explicitly blame those missteps on the company's loosely knit management or the famous troika at the top. Yet he concedes, 'We do pay a price [for shared decision making], in terms of speed and people not necessarily knowing where they go to ask questions.' Page believes that his appointment as CEO will help the company to get things done faster.

People outside and inside Google note that Larry Page does not fit the profile of a traditional chief executive. He's an introvert who does not like public speaking or having a strict daily regimen. This is one reason why Google is holding the weekly Execute meetings. Attendees at these meetings will become spokespeople for the organization around the world. "Page says one of his goals is to take the decisive leadership style they have shown within their product groups, spread it across the company, and apply it to major decisions."

Page wants to increase the speed with which people make decisions and innovate at Google. He believes that the weekly Execute meetings are prime vehicles for making this happen.[1]

Time will tell whether or not Google's approach to decision making works in the long run. Individually, we all make decisions on a daily basis. From deciding what clothes to wear to whom we want to marry, our decisions impact our lives in many ways. Sometimes our choices are good and other times they are bad. At work, however, decision making is one of the primary responsibilities of being a manager, and the quality of one's decisions can have serious consequences. Consider the case of Ronald Shaich, chairman and CEO of Panera Bread Company. Despite objections from others around him, he relied on his own judgment and intuition and decided to sell off Au Bon Pain in 1998 in order to grow Panera Bread Company. At the time, Panera had 135 stores. He said it was a "bet-the-job kind of choice." The sale resulted in $73 million to invest in Panera, and the rest is history. Panera now operates 1,500 cafés around the country. He told a *Bloomberg Businessweek* reporter that "I make my best decisions when I'm on vacation. You're not focused on all the stuff that comes at you as CEO. I've moved into a chairman role and I'm now more productive than ever. My decisions are formed by where I want to go."[2]

The overall goal of this chapter is to provide you with a thorough understanding of decision making so that you can improve the quality of your personal and group-based decisions. Who knows, you may one day use material in this chapter to help make entrepreneurial decisions like Larry Page and Ronald Shaich. To help in this pursuit, this chapter focuses on (1) models of decision making, (2) decision-making biases, (3) evidence-based decision making, (4) the dynamics of decision making, (4) group decision making, and (5) creativity.

TO THE POINT

What are the key differences between rational and nonrational models of decision making and how can these models be integrated?

LO.1 Models of Decision Making

Decision making entails identifying and choosing alternative solutions that lead to a desired state of affairs. For example, you may be reading this book as part of an online course that you decided to take because you are working full time. Alternatively, you may be a full-time student reading this book as part of a course being taken on campus. Identifying and sorting out alternatives like when and how to take a course is the process of decision making.

You can use two broad approaches to make decisions. You can follow a *rational model* or various *nonrational models*. Let us now consider how each of these approaches works. We begin by examining the rational model of decision making.

The Rational Model

The **rational model** proposes that managers use a rational, four-stage sequence when making decisions (see Figure 12–1). According to this model, managers are completely objective and possess complete information to make a decision. Despite criticism for being unrealistic, the rational model is instructive because it analytically breaks down the decision-making process and serves as a conceptual anchor for newer models.[3] Let us now consider each of these four steps.

Stage 1: Identify the Problem or Opportunity—Determining the Actual versus the Desirable   A **problem** exists when the actual situation and the desired situation differ. As a manager, you will have no shortage of

figure 12–1   The Four Stages in Rational Decision Making

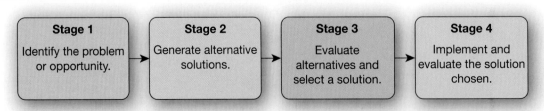

Stage 1	Stage 2	Stage 3	Stage 4
Identify the problem or opportunity.	Generate alternative solutions.	Evaluate alternatives and select a solution.	Implement and evaluate the solution chosen.

real WORLD // real PEOPLE

Reed Hastings Seizes Opportunities to Grow Netflix

Hastings anticipated, virtually from the moment he started Netflix, that consumers would eventually prefer to get movies instantly delivered via the Internet. (Hastings's foresight is amazing, considering that back in 2000, less than 7% of US homes had broadband.) And so rather than let any number of current and potential competitors—including premium cable channels like HBO . . . and some of the biggest companies in the tech world—swoop in and deliver a lethal blow, Hastings is now retooling Netflix as a streaming-video company, disrupting his own business before it gets disrupted.

For Hastings the decline of AOL is a reminder of what happens to companies unwilling to take risks. AOL, the dominant dial-up online service, struggled as broadband service proliferated. It had good e-mail and some unique content, but those services didn't buy AOL loyalty or make it synonymous with broadband, and ultimately AOL lost customers.

The opportunity faced by Hastings involved deciding how to get Netflix's 10 million subscribers to switch from DVD to streaming. Hastings decided in 2011 to separate its DVD-by-mail business from the online movie streaming business. The move angered customers and the stock price significantly dropped.

To what extent do you think an individual's personality plays a part in perceiving opportunity?

SOURCE: Excerpted from M V Copeland, "Reed Hastings: Leader of the Pack," *Fortune*, December 6, 2010, p 123; Updated with "Netflix Separates DVD, Streaming Businesses," Florida Today.com, http://www.floridatoday.com/article/20110920/BUSINESS/109200306/1003, September 20, 2011.

---

problems. Customer complaints. Employee turnover. Competitors' new products. Production problems. Consider the problems faced by Mattel's CEO, Bob Eckert. He concluded that his company had a problem when two of his top managers arrived in his office to tell him lead had been discovered in one of the company's toys. Around the same time, newspapers were publishing reports that magnets were becoming dislodged from other Mattel toys: If a small child swallowed them, they could cause serious damage by attaching themselves together in the child's intestines. Eckert had to decide whether his company had a publicity problem, a design problem, or a production problem—and if it were a production problem, where that problem was occurring and why.[4]

However, managers also have to make decisions regarding opportunities. An **opportunity** represents a situation in which there are possibilities to do things that lead to results that exceed goals and expectations. For example, Reed Hastings, founder, chairman, and CEO of Netflix, saw great opportunities in transforming his DVD-by-mail company into a streaming-video company (see Real World/Real People above). Financial results suggest that Reed clearly capitalized on opportunity: Netflix was the stock of the year in 2010, increasing 200% since January, as compared to the S&P 500's 7% gain.[5]

Whether you face a problem or an opportunity, the goal is always the same: to make improvements that change conditions from their current state to more desirable ones. This requires you to diagnose the causes of the problem.

Mattel CEO Bob Eckert quickly responded to a problem regarding finding lead in some of the company's toys. Failure to respond could have cost the company severe negative public relations.

---

decision making Identifying and choosing solutions that lead to a desired end result.

rational model Logical four-step approach to decision making.

problem Gap between an actual and a desired situation.

opportunity Situations that present possibilities for exceeding goals or expectations.

Stage 2: Generate Alternative Solutions—Both the Obvious and the Creative

After identifying a problem and its causes, the next logical step is generating alternative solutions. Later in this chapter we discuss several group problem-solving techniques that can be used during this stage. Unfortunately, a research study of 400 strategic decisions revealed that managers struggled during this stage because of three key decision-making blunders. These blunders were (1) rushing to judgment, (2) selecting readily available ideas or solutions, and (3) making poor allocation of resources to study alternative solutions. Decision makers thus are encouraged to slow down when making decisions, to evaluate a broader set of alternatives, and to invest in studying a greater number of potential solutions.[6]

Stage 3: Evaluate Alternatives and Select a Solution—Ethics, Feasibility, and Effectiveness

In this stage, you need to evaluate alternatives in terms of several criteria. Not only are costs and quality important, but you should consider the following questions: (1) Is it ethical? (If not, don't consider it.) Returning to the earlier example of Mattel's problems, CEO Eckert said, "How you achieve success is just as important as success itself."[7] He announced a recall of 18.2 million toys, the largest recall in Mattel's history. The company also announced that its magnet toys had been redesigned to make them safer and that it had investigated the Chinese contractor that had used the paint containing lead. (2) Is it feasible? (If time is an issue, costs are high, resources are limited, technology is needed, or customers are resistant, for instance, than the alternative is not feasible.) (3) Will it remove the causes and solve the problem?

connect Go to www.mcgrawhillconnect.com for an interactive exercise to test your knowledge of the rational model of decision making.

Stage 4: Implement and Evaluate the Solution Chosen

Once a solution is chosen, it needs to be implemented. After the solution is implemented, the evaluation phase assesses its effectiveness. If the solution is effective, it should reduce the difference between the actual and desired states that created the problem. If the gap is not closed, the implementation was not successful, and one of the following is true: Either the problem was incorrectly identified or the solution was inappropriate. Assuming the implementation was unsuccessful, management can return to the first step, problem identification. If the problem was correctly identified, management should consider implementing one of the previously identified, but untried, solutions. This process can continue until all feasible solutions have been tried or the problem has changed.

Summarizing the Rational Model

The rational model is prescriptive, outlining a logical process that managers should use when making decisions. As such, the rational model is based on the notion that managers optimize when making decisions. **Optimizing** involves solving problems by producing the best possible solution and is based on a set of highly desirable assumptions—having complete information, leaving emotions out of the decision-making process, honestly and accurately evaluating all alternatives, time and resources are abundant and accessible, and people are willing to implement and support decisions. Practical experience, of course, tells us that these assumptions are unrealistic. As noted by Herbert Simon, a decision theorist who in 1978 earned the Nobel Prize for his work on decision making, "The assumptions of perfect rationality are contrary to fact. It is not a question of approximation; they do not even remotely describe the processes that human beings use for making decisions in complex situations."[8]

That said, there are three benefits of trying to follow a rational process as much as realistically possible.

- The quality of decisions may be enhanced, in the sense that they follow more logically from all available knowledge and expertise.

- It makes the reasoning behind a decision transparent and available to scrutiny.

- If made public, it discourages the decider from acting on suspect considerations (such as personal advancement or avoiding bureaucratic embarrassment).[9]

Nonrational Models of Decision Making

In contrast to the rational model's focus on how decisions should be made, **nonrational models** attempt to explain how decisions actually are made. They are based on the assumption that decision making is uncertain, that decision makers do not possess complete information, and that it is difficult for managers to make optimal decisions. Two nonrational models are Herbert Simon's *normative* model and the *garbage can model*.

Simon's Normative Model   Herbert Simon proposed this model to describe the process that managers actually use when making decisions. The process is guided by a decision maker's bounded rationality. **Bounded rationality** represents the notion that decision makers are "bounded" or restricted by a variety of constraints when making decisions. These constraints include any personal characteristics or internal and external resources that reduce rational decision making. Personal characteristics include the limited capacity of the human mind, personality (a meta-analysis of 150 studies showed that males displayed more risk taking than females),[10] and time constraints. Examples of internal resources are the organization's human and social capital, financial resources, technology, plant and equipment, and internal processes and systems. External resources include things the organization cannot directly control such as employment levels in the community, capital availability, and government policies.[11]

Ultimately, these limitations result in the tendency to acquire manageable rather than optimal amounts of information. In turn, this practice makes it difficult for managers to identify all possible alternative solutions. In the long run, the constraints of bounded rationality cause decision makers to fail to evaluate all potential alternatives, thereby causing them to satisfice.

Satisficing consists of choosing a solution that meets some minimum qualifications, one that is "good enough." Satisficing resolves problems by producing solutions that are satisfactory, as opposed to optimal. Finding a radio station to listen to in your car is a good example of satisficing. You cannot optimize because it is impossible to listen to all stations at the same time. You thus stop searching for a station when you find one playing a song you like or do not mind hearing.

A recent national survey by the Business Performance Management Forum underscores the existence of satisficing: only 26% of respondents indicated that their companies had formal, well-understood decision-making processes. Respondents noted that the most frequent causes of poor decision making included:

- Poorly defined processes and practices.
- Unclear company vision, mission, and goals.
- Unwillingness of leaders to take responsibility.
- A lack of reliable, timely information.[12]

The Garbage Can Model   As is true of Simon's normative model, this approach grew from the rational model's inability to explain how decisions are actually made. It assumes that organizational decision making is a sloppy and haphazard process. This contrasts sharply with the rational model, which proposed that decision makers follow a sequential series of steps beginning with a problem and ending with a solution. According to the **garbage can model**, decisions result

optimizing Choosing the best possible solution.

nonrational models Explain how decisions actually are made.

bounded rationality Constraints that restrict rational decision making.

satisficing Choosing a solution that meets a minimum standard of acceptance.

garbage can model Holds that decision making is sloppy and haphazard.

from a complex interaction between four independent streams of events: problems, solutions, participants, and choice opportunities.[13] The interaction of these events creates "a collection of choices looking for problems, issues and feelings looking for decision situations in which they might be aired, solutions looking for issues to which they might be the answer, and decision makers looking for work."[14] A similar type of process occurs in your kitchen garbage basket. We randomly discard our trash and it gets mashed together based on chance interactions. Consider, for instance, going to your kitchen trash container and noticing that the used coffee grounds are stuck to a banana peel. Can you explain how this might occur? The answer is simple: because they both got thrown in around the same time. Just like the process of mixing garbage in a trash container, the garbage can model of decision making assumes that decision making does not follow an orderly series of steps. Rather, attractive solutions can get matched up with whatever handy problems exist at a given point in time or people get assigned to projects because their workload is low at that moment. This model of decision making thus attempts to explain how problems, solutions, participants, and choice opportunities interact and lead to a decision.

Campbell Soup Company invented a shelving system that neatly stacks its products on shelves like this one. The system is good for Campbell Soup and for grocery stores.

The garbage can model has four practical implications. First, this model of decision making is more pronounced in industries that rely on science-based innovations such as pharmaceutical companies.[15] Managers in these industries thus need to be more alert for the potential of haphazard decision making. Second, many decisions are made by oversight or by the presence of a salient opportunity. For example, managers from the Campbell Soup Company needed to find a way to motivate supermarkets to give them more space on the shelves. They thus decided to create a new shelving system that automatically slides soup cans to the front when a shopper picks up a can. The decision was a success. Customers bought more soup, increasing the revenue for both Campbell and the supermarkets, and the supermarkets reduced their restocking costs.[16]

Third, political motives frequently guide the process by which participants make decisions. It thus is important for you to consider the political ramifications of your decisions. Organizational politics are discussed in Chapter 15. Finally, important problems are more likely to be solved than unimportant ones because they are more salient to organizational participants.[17]

Integrating Rational and Nonrational Models

Applying the idea that decisions are shaped by characteristics of problems and decision makers, consultants David Snowden and Mary Boone have come up with their own approach that is not as haphazard as the garbage can model but acknowledges the challenges facing today's organizations. They essentially integrate rational and nonrational models by identifying four kinds of decision environments and an effective method of decision making for each.[18]

1. A simple context is stable, and clear cause-and-effect relationships can be discerned, so the best answer can be agreed on. This context calls for the rational model, where the decision maker gathers information, categorizes it, and responds in an established way.

2. In a complicated context, there is a clear relationship between cause and effect, but some people may not see it, and more than one solution may be effective. Here, too, the rational model applies, but it requires the investigation of options, along with analysis of them.

3. In a complex context, there is one right answer, but there are so many unknowns that decision makers don't understand cause-and-effect relationships. Decision makers therefore need to start out by experimenting, testing options, and probing to see what might happen as they look for a creative solution.

4. In a chaotic context, cause-and-effect relationships are changing so fast that no pattern emerges. In this context, decision makers have to act first to establish order and then find areas where it is possible to identify patterns so that aspects of the problem can be managed. The use of intuition and evidence-based decision making, both of which are discussed later in this chapter, may be helpful in this situation.[19]

Back to the Chapter-Opening Case

How does Google's Execute meetings attempt to integrate rational and nonrational models of decision making?

LO.2 Decision-Making Biases

TO THE POINT

How would you describe the eight decision-making biases?

People make a variety of systematic mistakes when making decisions. These mistakes are generally associated with a host of biases that occur when we use judgmental heuristics. **Judgmental heuristics** represent rules of thumb or shortcuts that people use to reduce information-processing demands.[20] We automatically use them without conscious awareness. The use of heuristics helps decision makers to reduce the uncertainty inherent within the decision-making process. Because these shortcuts represent knowledge gained from past experience, they can help decision makers evaluate current problems. But they also can lead to systematic errors that erode the quality of decisions, particularly for people facing time constraints such as primary health care doctors. For example, a recent study of medical malpractice claims showed that diagnostic errors, which are partly a function of judgmental heuristics, accounted for about 40% of such cases. Diagnostic errors kill 40,000 to 80,000 people a year in the United States. Experts suggest that we need to become more involved with our health care and follow up on lab results to help reduce such mistakes.[21]

connect™ Go to www.mcgrawhillconnect.com for an interactive exercise to test your knowledge of the biases involved in making decisions.

There are both pros and cons to the use of heuristics. In this section we focus on discussing eight biases that affect decision making: (1) availability, (2) representativeness, (3) confirmation, (4) anchoring, (5) overconfidence, (6) hindsight, (7) framing, and (8) escalation of commitment. Knowledge about these biases can help you to avoid using them in the wrong situation.

1. **Availability heuristic.** The availability heuristic represents a decision maker's tendency to base decisions on information that is readily available in memory. Information is more accessible in memory when it involves an event that recently occurred, when it is salient (e.g., a plane crash), and when it evokes strong emotions (e.g., a high-school student shooting other students). This heuristic is likely to cause people to overestimate the occurrence of unlikely events such as a plane crash or a high-school shooting. This bias also is partially responsible for the recency effect discussed in Chapter 7. For example, a manager is more likely to give an employee a positive performance evaluation if the employee exhibited excellent performance over the last few months.

judgmental heuristics Rules of thumb or shortcuts that people use to reduce information-processing demands.

2. **Representativeness heuristic.** The representativeness heuristic is used when people estimate the probability of an event occurring. It reflects the tendency to assess the likelihood of an event occurring based on one's impressions about similar occurrences. A manager, for example, may hire a graduate from a particular university because the past three people hired from this university turned out to be good performers. In this case, the "school attended" criterion is used to facilitate complex information processing associated with employment interviews. Unfortunately, this shortcut can result in a biased decision. Similarly, an individual may believe that he or she can master a new software package in a short period of time because a different type of software was easy to learn. This estimate may or may not be accurate. For example, it may take the individual a much longer period of time to learn the new software because it involves learning a new programming language.

3. **Confirmation bias.** The confirmation bias has two components. The first is to subconsciously decide something before investigating why it is the right decision, for example, deciding to purchase a particular type of PDA (personal digital assistant). This directly leads to the second component, which is to seek information that supports purchasing this PDA while discounting information that does not.

4. **Anchoring bias.** How would you answer the following two questions? Is the population of Iraq greater than 40 million? What's your best guess about the population of Iraq? Was your answer to the second question influenced by the number *40 million* suggested by the first question? If yes, you were affected by the anchoring bias. The anchoring bias occurs when decision makers are influenced by the first information received about a decision, even if it is irrelevant. This bias happens because initial information, impressions, data, feedback, or stereotypes anchor our subsequent judgments and decisions.

5. **Overconfidence bias.** The overconfidence bias relates to our tendency to be over-confident about estimates or forecasts. This bias is particularly strong when you are asked moderate to extremely difficult questions rather than easy ones. Imagine the problem this bias might create for a sales manager estimating sales revenue for the next year. Research shows that overoptimism significantly influences entrepreneurs' decisions to start and sustain new ventures.[22] To what extent do you think this bias affected the Deepwater Horizon oil rig explosion in 2010? A presidential oil-spill commission concluded that technological arrogance, hubris, and the overconfidence bias played major roles (see Real World/Real People on page 337).[23]

6. **Hindsight bias.** Imagine yourself in the following scenario: You are taking an OB course that meets Tuesday and Thursday, and your professor gives unannounced quizzes each week. It's the Monday before a class, and you are deciding whether to study for a potential quiz or to watch Monday night football. Two of your classmates have decided to watch the game rather than study because they don't think there will be a quiz the next day. The next morning you walk into class and the professor says, "Take out a sheet of paper for the quiz." You turn to your friends and say, "I knew we were going to have a quiz; why did I listen to you?" The hindsight bias occurs when knowledge of an outcome influences our belief about the probability that we could have predicted the outcome earlier. We are affected by this bias when we look back on a decision and try to reconstruct why we decided to do something.

7. **Framing bias.** This bias relates to the manner in which a question is posed. Consider the following scenario: Imagine that the United States is preparing for the outbreak of an unusual Asian disease that is expected to kill 600 people. Two alternative programs to combat the disease have been proposed.

real WORLD // real PEOPLE

Overconfidence Bias Partly to Blame for Oil-Rig Disaster

According to Bob Bea, an engineering professor at the University of California Berkely, "technological disasters, like the PB oil spill, follow a well-worn "trail of tears." Bea has investigated 630 different types of disasters and is an expert on offshore drilling.

"Bea categorizes disasters into four groups. One such group is when an organization simply ignores warning signs through overconfidence and incompetence. He thinks the BP spill falls into that category. Bea pointed to congressional testimony that BP ignored problems with a dead battery, leaky cement job, and loose hydraulic fittings."

"Disasters don't happen because of 'an evil empire,' Bea said. 'It's hubris, arrogance, and indolence.'"

"Cutting-edge technology often works flawlessly. At first, everyone worries about risk. Then people get lulled into complacency by success, and they forget that they are operating on the edge, say experts who study disasters. Corners get cut, problems ignored. Then boom."

Charles Perrow, a professor at Yale University, concluded that "there's nothing safe out there. We like to pretend there is and argue afterward, 'That's why we took the risks, because it hadn't failed before.'"

How could BP have overcome the overconfidence bias?

SOURCE: Excerpted from S Borenstein, "Disasters Often Stem from Hubris," *The Arizona Republic*, July 12, 2010, p A4.

The Deep Horizon oil rig disaster.

Assume that the exact scientific estimates of the consequences of the programs are as follows:

Program A: If Program A is adopted, 200 people will be saved.

Program B: If Program B is adopted, there is a one-third probability that 600 people will be saved and a two-thirds probability that no people will be saved.

Which of the two programs would you recommend?[24] Research shows that most people chose Program A even though the two programs produce the same results. This result is due to the framing bias. The framing bias is the tendency to consider risks about gains—saving lives–differently than risks pertaining to losses—losing lives. You are encouraged to frame decision questions in alternative ways in order to avoid this bias.

8. **Escalation of commitment bias.** The escalation of commitment bias refers to the tendency to stick to an ineffective course of action when it is unlikely that the bad situation can be reversed. Personal examples include investing more money into an old or broken car or putting more effort into improving a personal relationship that is filled with conflict. A business example pertains to Blockbuster "asking creditors to put up more money to help it exit bankruptcy protection, prompting a debate among bondholders about whether to invest further in the struggling video chain or put it up for sale."[25] Would you invest in Blockbuster? Researchers recommend the following actions to reduce the escalation of commitment:

• Set minimum targets for performance, and have decision makers compare their performance against these targets.

• Regularly rotate managers in key positions throughout a project.

- Encourage decision makers to become less ego-involved with a project.
- Make decision makers aware of the costs of persistence.[26]

TO THE POINT

What is thrust of evidence-based decision making, and what does it take to implement this approach in organizations?

LO.3 Evidence-Based Decision Making

Interest in the concept of evidence-based decision making stems from two sources. The first is the desire to avoid the decision-making biases discussed in the previous section, and the second is research done on evidence-based medicine. Dr David Sackett defines evidence-based medicine as "the conscientious, explicit and judicious use of current best evidence in making decisions about the care of individual patients." Researchers and practitioners are studying evidence-based medicine because research suggests that physicians make only 15% of their decisions based on evidence, and this approach helps determine the most efficient use of health care resources.[27] OB researchers have taken this framework and applied it to the context of managerial decision making.

Quite simply, **evidence-based decision making** (EBDM) represents a process of conscientiously using the best available data and evidence when making managerial decisions. We explore this new approach to decision making by beginning with a model of EBDM and then reviewing a set of implementation principles that can help companies to implement this model of decision making. We conclude by examining the reasons why it is hard to implement EBDM. Understanding this material will help you reduce the susceptibility to decision-making biases.

connect Go to www.mcgrawhillconnect.com for an interactive exercise to test your knowledge of evidence-based decision making.

A Model of Evidence-Based Decision Making (EBDM)

Figure 12–2 illustrates a five-step model of EBDM.[28] You can see that the process begins by gathering internal and external data and evidence about a problem at hand. This information is then integrated with views from stakeholders (e.g., employees, shareholders, customers) and ethical considerations to make a final decision. All told, the process shown in Figure 12–2 helps managers to face hard facts and avoid their personal biases when making decisions. EBDM's use of relevant and reliable data from different sources is clearly intended to make any decision-making context more explicit, critical, systematic, and fact based.

It is important to consider that evidence is used in three different ways within the process depicted in Figure 12–2: to make a decision, to inform a decision, and to support a decision.[29] "Evidence is used to *make* a decision whenever the decision follows directly from the evidence." For example, if you wanted to purchase a particular used car (e.g., Toyota Prius) based on price and color (e.g., red), you

figure 12–2 Evidence-Based Decision-Making Model

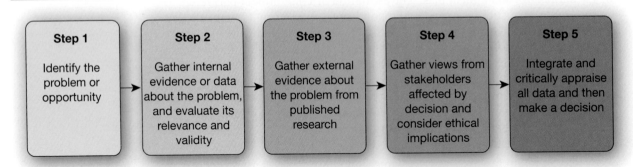

Step 1	Step 2	Step 3	Step 4	Step 5
Identify the problem or opportunity	Gather internal evidence or data about the problem, and evaluate its relevance and validity	Gather external evidence about the problem from published research	Gather views from stakeholders affected by decision and consider ethical implications	Integrate and critically appraise all data and then make a decision

SOURCE: Derived from R B Briner, D Denyer, and D M Rousseau. "Evidence-Based Management: Concept Cleanup Time?" *Academy of Management Perspectives*, November 2009, pp 19–32.

would obtain data from the Internet and classified ads and then choose the seller offering the lowest priced red Prius. "Evidence is used to inform a decision whenever the decision process combines hard, objective facts with qualitative inputs, such as intuition or bargaining with stakeholders." For instance, in hiring new college graduates, objective data about applicants' past experience, education, and participation in student organizations would be relevant input to making a hiring decision. Nonetheless, subjective impressions garnered from interviews and references would typically be combined with the objective data to make a final decision. These two uses of evidence are clearly positive and should be encouraged. The same cannot be said about using evidence to support a decision.

"Evidence is used to *support* a decision whenever the evidence is gathered or modified for the sole purpose of lending legitimacy to a decision that has already been made." This application of evidence has both positive and negative effects. On the positive side, manufactured evidence can be used to convince an external audience that the organization is following a sound course of action in response to a complex and ambiguous decision context. This can lead to confidence and goodwill about how a company is responding to environmental events. On the negative side, this practice can stifle employee involvement and input because people will come to believe that management is going to ignore evidence and just do what it wants. There are two takeaways about using evidence to support a decision. First, this practice should not always be avoided. Second, because this practice has both pros and cons, management needs to carefully consider when it "might" be appropriate to ignore disconfirming evidence and push its own agenda or decisions.

Seven Implementation Principles

Stanford professors Jeffrey Pfeffer and Robert Sutton have been studying evidence-based management for quite some time. Based on this experience, they offer seven implementation principles to help companies integrate EBDM into an organization's culture.[30]

1. **Treat your organization as an unfinished prototype.** The thrust of this principle involves creating a mindset that the organization is an unfinished prototype that may be broken and in need of repair, thus avoiding the hubris and arrogance of concluding that nothing needs to be changed in the organization. For example, the products QVC sells are chosen through a process of experimentation in which EBDM is used to understand why some products sell and others don't. The use of experiments, as done at QVC, is one recommendation for making this happen. The Real World/Real People on page 340 illustrates how one retailer uses experimentation to determine the best type of promotions.[31]

2. **No brag, just facts.** This slogan is used by DaVita, a company that operates 600 dialysis centers, to reinforce a culture that supports EBDM. The company measures, monitors, and rewards the effectiveness of its dialysis centers

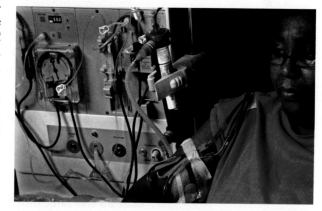

This dialysis patient is benefitting from DaVita's use of EBDM. The use of EBDM helps the company provide better service, and ultimately contributes to profitability.

evidence-based decision making
Conscientiously using the best data when making decisions.

real WORLD // real PEOPLE

A Retailer Experiments with Discount Promotions

The retailer designed six experimental conditions—a control and five discount levels that ranged from 0 to 35% for the private-label items. The retailer divided its stores into six groups, and the treatments were randomized across the groups. This meant each store had a mixture of the experimental conditions distributed across the different products in the study. For example, in Store A—label sugar was discounted 20%, and private-label mascara was full price, whereas in Store B mascara was discounted, but sugar was not. This experimental design allowed the retailer to control for variations in sales that occurred because the store groups were not identical.

The test revealed that matching the national brand promotions with moderate discounts on the private-label products generated 10% more profits than not promoting the private-label items. As a result, the retailer now automatically discounts private-label items when the competing national brands are under promotion.

Why don't more companies do experiments like this?

SOURCE: Excerpted from E T Anderson and D Simester, "Every Company Can Profit from Testing Customers' Reactions to Changes. Here's How to Get Started," *Harvard Business Review*, March 2011, p 103.

---

and patient well-being on a regular basis. In contrast, Hewlett-Packard's former CEO Carly Fiorina bragged to the press about the company's merger with Compaq but failed to do any research on consumers' opinions about Compaq products prior to the merger. These products were viewed as among the worst in the industry.

3. **See yourself and your organization as outsiders do.** Many managers are filled with optimism and inflated views of their talents and chances for success. This leads them to downplay risks and to commit an escalation of commitment bias. "Having a blunt friend, mentor, or counselor," Pfeffer and Sutton suggest, "can help you see and act on better evidence."

4. **Evidence-based management is not just for senior executives.** Research shows that the best organizations are those in which all employees, not just top managers, are committed to EBDM.[32] Pfeffer and Sutton encourage managers to "treat employees as if a big part of their job is to invent, find, test, and implement the best ideas." This implies that employees must be given the training and resources needed to engage in EBDM.

5. **Like everything else, you still need to sell it.** "Unfortunately, new and exciting ideas grab attention even when they are vastly inferior to old ideas," say Pfeffer and Sutton. "Vivid, juicy stories and case studies sell better than detailed, rigorous, and admittedly dull data—no matter how wrong the stories or how right the data." This means that you will need to similarly use vivid stories and case studies such as the DaVita example used earlier to sell the value of EBDM. You can also hire gurus to help sell the value of evidence-based practices.

6. **If all else fails, slow the spread of bad practice.** Because employees may face pressures to do things that are known to be ineffective, it may be necessary to engage in what Pfeffer and Sutton call "evidence-based misbehavior." This can include ignoring requests and delaying action. Be cautious if you use this principle.

7. **The best diagnostic question: what happens when people fail?** "Failure hurts, it is embarrassing, and we would rather live without it," say the Stanford professors. "Yet there is no learning without failure. . . . If you look at how the most effective systems in the world are managed, a hallmark is that when something goes wrong, people face the hard facts, learn what

happened and why, and keep using those facts to make the system better." The US civil aviation system is a good example. It has created the safest system in world through its accident and incident reporting system. Ford's CEO Alan Mulally is another example. He meets with his top 15 executives every Thursday morning at 7 A.M. for 2½ hours to conduct a business plan review. "He requires his direct reports to post more than 300 charts, each of them color-coded red, yellow, or green to indicate problems, caution, or progress. . . . Afterward, the adjoining Taurus and Continental rooms are papered with these charts so Mulally can study them. As the CEO likes to say, 'You can't manage a secret. When you do this every week, you can't hide.'"[33]

Why Is It Hard to be Evidenced Based?

Despite the known value of using EBDM, there are seven reasons why it is hard for anyone to bring the best evidence to bear when making decisions. They are: (1) There's too much evidence. (2) There's not enough good evidence. (3) The evidence doesn't quite apply. (4) People are trying to mislead you. (5) You are trying to mislead you. (6) The side effects outweigh the cure. (7) Stories are more persuasive, anyway.[34]

Dynamics of Decision Making

Decision making is part science and part art. Accordingly, this section examines decision-making styles, which is part of the "science" component. It is important to understand decision-making styles because they influence the manner in which people make decisions. We also examine the "art" side of the equation by discussing the role of intuition in decision making and a decision tree for making ethical decisions. An understanding of these dynamics can help managers make better decisions.

◀ ∙∙∙∙∙∙∙∙∙∙∙∙∙∙∙∙∙∙∙∙∙∙

TO THE POINT

What are the key conclusions regarding decision-making styles, intuition in decision making, and ethical decision making?

∙∙∙∙∙∙∙∙∙∙∙∙∙∙∙∙∙∙∙∙∙∙∙∙∙

 LO.4 General Decision-Making Styles

This section focuses on how an individual's decision-making style affects his or her approach to decision making. A **decision-making style** reflects the combination of how an individual perceives and comprehends stimuli and the general manner in which he or she chooses to respond to such information.[35] A team of researchers developed a model of decision-making styles that is based on the idea that styles vary along two different dimensions: value orientation and tolerance for ambiguity.[36] *Value orientation* reflects the extent to which an individual focuses on either task and technical concerns or people and social concerns when making decisions. Some people, for instance, are very task focused at work and do not pay much attention to people issues, whereas others are just the opposite. The second dimension pertains to a person's *tolerance for ambiguity*. This individual difference indicates the extent to which a person has a high need for structure or control in his or her life. Some people desire a lot of structure in their lives (a low tolerance for ambiguity) and find ambiguous situations stressful and psychologically uncomfortable. In contrast, others do not have a high need for structure and can thrive in uncertain situations (a high tolerance for ambiguity). Ambiguous

decision-making style A combination of how individuals perceive and respond to information.

figure 12–3 Decision-Making Styles

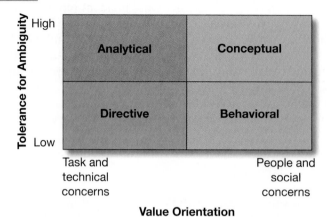

SOURCE: Based on discussion contained in A J Rowe and R O Mason, *Managing with Style: A Guide to Understanding, Assessing, and Improving Decision Making* (San Francisco: Jossey-Bass, 1987), pp 1–17.

situations can energize people with a high tolerance for ambiguity. When the dimensions of value orientation and tolerance for ambiguity are combined, they form four styles of decision making (see Figure 12–3): directive, analytical, conceptual, and behavioral.

Directive   People with a *directive* style have a low tolerance for ambiguity and are oriented toward task and technical concerns when making decisions. They are efficient, logical, practical, and systematic in their approach to solving problems. People with this style are action oriented and decisive and like to focus on facts. In their pursuit of speed and results, however, these individuals tend to be autocratic, exercise power and control, and focus on the short run.

Interestingly, a directive style seems well suited for an air-traffic controller. Here is what Paul Rinaldi had to say about his decision-making style to a reporter from *Fortune*.

Example. It's not so much analytical as it is making a decision quickly and sticking with it. You have to do that knowing that some of the decisions you're going to make are going to be wrong, but you're going to make that decision be right. You can't back out. You've constantly got to be taking into account the speed of the airplane, its characteristics, the climb rate, and how fast it's going to react to your instructions. You're taking all that in and processing it in a split second, hoping that it'll all work together. If it doesn't, then you go to plan B. . . . The percentage of us that make it to retirement is not real high. It takes a toll on you. We can't make mistakes.[37]

Analytical   This style has a much higher tolerance for ambiguity and is characterized by the tendency to overanalyze a situation. People with this style like to consider more information and alternatives than do directives. Analytic individuals are careful decision makers who take longer to make decisions but who also respond well to new or uncertain situations. They can often be autocratic.

Zhang Guangming is a good example of someone with an analytical style. "Zhang Guangming's car-buying synapses have been in overdrive for months. He has spent hours poring over Chinese car buff magazines, surfing Web sites to mine data on various models, and trekking out to a dozen dealerships across Beijing. Finally, Zhang settled on either a Volkswagen Bora or a Hyundai Sonata sedan. But with cutthroat competition forcing dealers to slash prices, he's not sure whether to buy now or wait."[38]

Conceptual   People with a conceptual style have a high tolerance for ambiguity and tend to focus on the people or social aspects of a work situation. They take a broad perspective to problem solving and like to consider many options and future possibilities. Conceptual types adopt a long-term perspective and rely on intuition and discussions with others to acquire information. They also are willing to take risks and are good at finding creative solutions to problems. On the downside, however, a conceptual style can foster an idealistic and indecisive approach to decision making. Howard Stringer, Sony Corporation's first foreign-born CEO, possesses characteristics of a conceptual style.

Example. Mr Stringer's dilemma is that he is caught between different management styles and cultures. He says he recognizes the risk of falling behind amid breakneck changes in electronics. But he says there's an equal risk of moving too aggressively. "I don't want to change Sony's culture to the point where it's unrecognizable from the founder's vision," he says. . . . Mr Stringer, 65 years old, stuck with [an] executive team he inherited. He tried gently persuading managers to cooperate with one another and urged them to think about developing products in a new way.[39]

Behavioral   This style is the most people oriented of the four styles. People with this style work well with others and enjoy social interactions in which opinions are openly exchanged. Behavioral types are supportive, receptive to suggestions, show warmth, and prefer verbal to written information. Although they like to hold meetings, people with this style have a tendency to avoid conflict and to be too concerned about others. This can lead behavioral types to adopt a wishy-washy approach to decision making and to have a hard time saying no to others and to have difficulty making difficult decisions.

Research and Practical Implications   Research shows that very few people have only one dominant decision-making style. Rather, most managers have characteristics that fall into two or three styles. Studies also show that decision-making styles vary by age, occupations, personality types, gender, and countries.[40] You can use knowledge of decision-making styles in four ways. First, knowledge of styles helps you to understand yourself. Awareness of your style assists you in identifying your strengths and weaknesses as a decision maker and facilitates the potential for self-improvement. Second, you can increase your ability to influence others by being aware of styles. For example, if you are dealing with an analytical person, you should provide as much information as possible to support your ideas. This same approach is more likely to frustrate a directive type. Third, knowledge of styles gives you an awareness of how people can take the same information and yet arrive at different decisions by using a variety of decision-making strategies. Different decision-making styles represent one likely source of interpersonal conflict at work (conflict is thoroughly discussed in Chapter 13). Finally, it is important to remember that there is not a single best decision-making style that applies in all situations. It is most beneficial to use a contingency approach in which you use a style that is best suited for the situation at hand. For example, if the context requires a quick decision, then a directive style might be best. In contrast, a behavioral approach would be more appropriate when making decisions that involve employees' welfare. At this point we cannot provide more detailed recommendations because researchers have not developed a complete contingency theory that outlines when to use the different decision-making styles.

LO.5 The Role of Intuition in Decision Making

Steve Jobs, former CEO of Apple, was a very intuitive person. Sadly, he died in October 2011. Part of Apple's success is related to employees like Jobs who somehow foresee the future demands of consumers. We encourage you to practice your intuitive skills.

In the book *How We Decide*, author Jonah Lehrer concluded that intuition is effectively used by many people when making decisions.[41] **Intuition** represents judgments, insights, or decisions that "come to mind on their own, without explicit awareness of the evoking cues and of course without explicit evaluation of the validity of these cues."[42] Research reveals that anyone can be intuitive, and its use is unrelated to gender.[43] It thus is important to understand the sources of intuition and to develop your intuitive skills because intuition is as important as rational analysis in many decisions. Consider the following examples:

Example. Ignoring recommendations from advisers, Ray Kroc purchased the McDonald's brand from the McDonald brothers: "I'm not a gambler and I didn't have that kind of money, but my funny bone instinct kept urging me on." Ignoring numerous naysayers and a lack of supporting market research, Bob Lutz, former president of Chrysler, made the Dodge Viper a reality. "It was this subconscious, visceral feeling. And it just felt right." Ignoring the fact that 24 publishing houses had rejected the book and her own publishing house was opposed, Eleanor Friede gambled on a "little nothing book," called *Jonathan Livingston Seagull:* "I felt there were truths in this simple story that would make it an international classic."[44]

Unfortunately, the use of intuition does not always lead to blockbuster decisions such as those by Ray Kroc or Eleanor Friede. To enhance your understanding of the role of intuition in decision making, this section reviews a model of intuition and discusses the pros and cons of using intuition to make decisions.

A Model of Intuition   Figure 12–4 presents a model of intuition. Starting at the far right, the model shows there are two types of intuition:

1. A holistic hunch represents a judgment that is based on a subconscious integration of information stored in memory. People using this form of intuition

figure 12–4 A Dual Model of Intuition

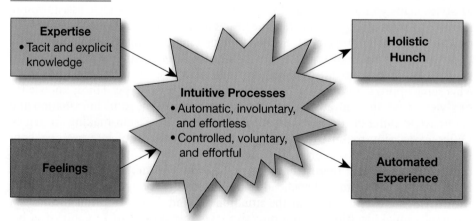

SOURCES: Based in part on D Kahneman and G Klein, "Conditions for Intuitive Expertise," *American Psychologist,* September 2009, pp 515–26; E Sadler-Smith and E Shefy, "The Intuitive Executive: Understanding and Applying 'Gut Feel' in Decision-Making," *Academy of Management Executive,* November 2004, pp 76–91; and C C Miller and R D Ireland, "Intuition in Strategic Decision Making: Friend or Foe in the Fast-Paced 21st Century," *Academy of Management Executive,* February 2005, pp 19–30.

may not be able to explain why they want to make a certain decision, except that the choice "feels right."

2. Automated experiences represent a choice that is based on a familiar situation and a partially subconscious application of previously learned information related to that situation. For example, when you have years of experience driving a car, you react to a variety of situations without conscious analysis.

Returning to Figure 12–4, you can see that intuition is represented by two distinct processes. One is automatic, involuntary and mostly effortless. The second is quite the opposite in that it is controlled, voluntary, and effortful. Research reveals that these two processes can operate separately or jointly to influence intuition.[45] For example, when trying to answer one of the "Back to Chapter-Opening Case" questions in this book, you may spontaneously have an answer pop into your mind based on your recollection of what you previously read (an automatic process). Upon further reflection (controlled process), however, you may decide your initial thought is wrong and that you need to go back and reread some material to arrive at another answer. This in turn may cause novel ideas to come to mind, and the two processes continue. These intuitive processes are influenced by two sources: expertise and feelings (see Figure 12–4). Expertise represents an individual's combined explicit knowledge (i.e., information that can easily be put into words) and tacit knowledge (i.e., information gained through experience that is difficult to express and formalize) regarding an object, person, situation, or decision opportunity. This source of intuition increases with age and experience. The feelings component reflects the automatic, underlying effect one experiences in response to an object, person, situation, or decision opportunity. An intuitive response is based on the interaction between one's expertise and feelings in a given situation.

Pros and Cons of Using Intuition When Making Decisions   On the positive side, intuition can speed up the decision-making process.[46] Intuition thus can be valuable in our complex and ever-changing world. Intuition may be a practical approach when resources are limited and deadlines are tight. For example, intuition based on deep knowledge and active preparation informs quick and complicated decisions in an effective hospital emergency department. Recalling her work as director of an emergency department, Kathleen Gallo says, "While the arrival of a helicopter with a whole family of car-wreck victims might look like a crisis and might be a crisis for the family, it is not a crisis for the staff . . . because they are prepared."[47]

On the downside, intuition is subject to the same types of biases associated with rational decision making. It is particularly susceptible to the availability and representativeness heuristics, as well as the anchoring, overconfidence, and hindsight biases.[48] In addition, the decision maker may have difficulty convincing others that the intuitive decision makes sense, so a good idea may be ignored.

Where does that leave us with respect to using intuition? We believe that intuition and rationality are complementary and that managers should attempt to use both when making decisions. We thus encourage you to use intuition when making decisions. You can develop your intuitive awareness by using the guidelines shown in Table 12–1.

intuition Judgments that come to mind without explicit awareness of the causes or an evaluation of their validity.

table 12–1 Guidelines for Developing Intuitive Awareness

RECOMMENDATION	DESCRIPTION
1. Open up the closet	To what extent do you experience intuition; trust your feelings; count on intuitive judgments; suppress hunches; covertly rely upon gut feel?
2. Don't mix up your I's	Instinct, insight, and intuition are not synonymous; practice distinguishing among your instincts, your insights, and your intuitions.
3. Elicit good feedback	Seek feedback on your intuitive judgments; build confidence in your gut feel; create a learning environment in which you can develop better intuitive awareness.
4. Get a feel for your batting average	Benchmark your intuitions; get a sense for how reliable your hunches are; ask yourself how your intuitive judgment might be improved.
5. Use imagery	Use imagery rather than words; literally visualize potential future scenarios that take your gut feelings into account.
6. Play devil's advocate	Test out intuitive judgments; raise objections to them; generate counter-arguments; probe how robust gut feel is when challenged.
7. Capture and validate your intuitions	Create the inner state to give your intuitive mind the freedom to roam; capture your creative intuitions; log them before they are censored by rational analysis.

SOURCE: From E Sadler-Smith and E Shefy, "The Intuitive Executive: Understanding and Applying 'Gut Feel' in Decision-Making," *Academy of Management Executive,* November 2004, p 88. Copyright © 2004 by The Academy of Management. Reproduced by permission of The Academy of Management via Copyright Clearance Center.

Back to the Chapter-Opening Case

How will Google's approach to decision making increase the use of intuition in making decisions?

Road Map to Ethical Decision Making: A Decision Tree

In Chapter 1 we discussed the importance of ethics and the growing concern about the lack of ethical behavior among business leaders. Unfortunately, research shows that many types of unethical behavior go unreported, and unethical behavior is negatively associated with employee engagement.[49] While these trends partially explain the passage of laws to regulate ethical behavior in corporate America, we believe that ethical acts ultimately involve individual or group decisions. It thus is important to consider the issue of ethical decision making. Harvard Business School professor Constance Bagley suggests that a decision tree can help managers to make more ethical decisions.[50]

figure 12-5 An Ethical Decision Tree

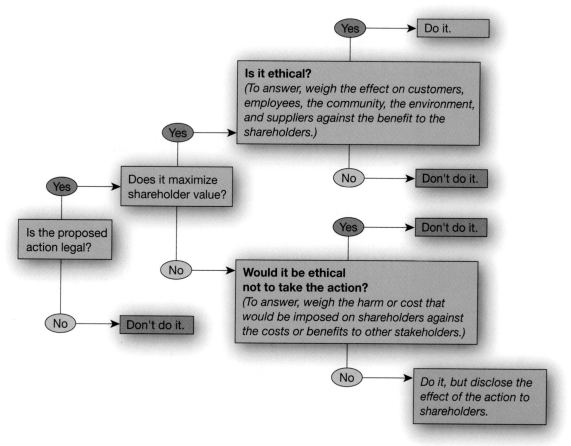

A **decision tree** is a graphical representation of the process underlying decisions and it shows the resulting consequences of making various choices. Decision trees are used as an aid in decision making. Ethical decision making frequently involves trade-offs, and a decision tree helps managers navigate through them. The decision tree shown in Figure 12–5 can be applied to any type of decision or action that an individual manager or corporation is contemplating. Looking at the tree, the first question to ask is whether or not the proposed action is legal. If the action is illegal, do not do it. If the action is legal, then consider the impact of the action on shareholder value. A decision maximizes shareholder value when it results in a more favorable financial position (e.g., increased profits) for an organization. Whether or not an action maximizes shareholder value, the decision tree shows that managers still need to consider the ethical implications of the decision or action. For example, if an action maximizes shareholder value, the next question to consider is whether or not the action is ethical. The answer to this question is based on considering the positive effect of the action on an organization's other key constituents (i.e., customers, employees, the community, the environment, and

decision tree Graphical representation of the process underlying decision making.

suppliers) against the benefit to the shareholders. According to the decision tree framework, managers should make the decision to engage in an action if the benefits to the shareholders exceed the benefits to the other key constituents. Managers should not engage in the action if the other key constituents would benefit more from the action than shareholders.

Figure 12–5 illustrates that managers use a slightly different perspective when their initial conclusion is that an action does not maximize shareholder value. In this case, the question becomes, Would it be ethical not to take action? This question necessitates that a manager consider the *harm or cost* of an action to shareholders against the *costs or benefits* to other key constituents. If the costs to shareholders from a managerial decision exceed the costs or benefits to other constituents, the manager or company should not engage in the action. Conversely, the manager or company should take action when the perceived costs or benefits to the other constituents are greater than the costs to shareholders. Let us apply this decision tree to IBM's decision to raise the amount of money it required retirees to contribute to their health benefits.[51] The company made this decision in order to save money.

Is it legal for a company to decrease its contribution to retiree health care benefits while simultaneously raising retirees' contributions? The answer is yes. Does an organization maximize shareholder value by decreasing its retiree health care expenses? Again, the answer is yes. We now have to consider the overall benefits to shareholders against the overall benefits to other key constituents. The answer to this question is more complex than it appears and is contingent on an organization's corporate values. Consider the following two examples. In company one, the organization is losing money and it needs cash in order to invest in new product development. Management believes that new products will fuel the company's economic growth and ultimate survival. This company's statement of corporate values also reveals that the organization values profits and shareholder return more than employee loyalty. In this case, the company should make the decision to increase retirees' health care contributions. Company two, in contrast, is profitable and has been experiencing increased market share with its products. This company's statement of corporate values also indicates that employees are the most important constituent it has, even more than shareholders: Southwest Airlines is a good example of a company with these corporate values. In this case, the company should not make the decision to decrease its contribution to retirees' benefits.

It is important to keep in mind that the decision tree cannot provide a quick formula that managers and organizations can use to evaluate every ethical question. Ethical decision making is not always clear-cut and it is affected by cross-cultural differences. Organizations are encouraged to conduct ethics training and to increase awareness about cross-cultural issues when the work involves people with mixed cultural backgrounds.[52] That said, the decision tree does provide a framework for considering the trade-offs between managerial and corporate actions and managerial and corporate ethics. Try using this decision tree the next time you are faced with a significant ethical question or problem.

TO THE POINT

What are the pros and cons of group decision making and the various problem-solving techniques?

Group Decision Making

Groups such as committees, task forces, project teams, or review panels often play a key role in the decision-making process. ATA Engineering Inc., for example, is committed to group decision making.

Example. At least eight to 10 ATA employees are involved in interviewing every job candidate. If one employee objects to the hire, the candidate may not be offered a job unless that employee changes his or her mind. Sometimes, even the biggest company decisions are made by workers. When the lease was up on the company's building, for instance, ATA formed a committee of employees to address the issue. The group decided to stay put, after determining the current location was convenient to the majority of employees.[53]

Is ATA right in assuming that two or more heads are always better than one? Do all employees desire to have a say in the decision-making process? To what extent are managers involving employees in the decision-making process? What techniques do groups use to improve their decision making? Are face-to-face meetings more effective than computer-aided decision making? This section provides the background for answering these questions. We discuss (1) group involvement in decision making, (2) advantages and disadvantages of group-aided decision making, and (3) group problem-solving techniques.

LO.6 Group Involvement in Decision Making

Whether groups assemble in face-to-face meetings or rely on other technologically based methods to communicate, they can contribute to each stage of the decision-making process. In order to maximize the value of group decision making, however, it is important to create an environment in which group members feel free to participate and express their opinions. Research sheds light on how managers can create such an environment.

A team of researchers conducted two studies to determine whether a group's innovativeness was related to *minority dissent*, defined as the extent to which group members feel comfortable disagreeing with other group members, and a group's level of participation in decision making. Results showed that the most innovative groups possessed high levels of both minority dissent and participation in decision making.[54] How can you apply these results to your own group meetings at school or work? One way is to foster more discussion among group members during meetings. Research also confirms a side benefit to this recommendation. Group members' job satisfaction and performance are increased through group discussion.[55] Another suggestion is to seek divergent views from group members during decision making, and do not ridicule or punish people who disagree with the majority opinion.

connect Go to www.mcgrawhillconnect.com for a self-assessment to learn about assessing your participation in group decision making.

Advantages and Disadvantages of Group Decision Making

Including groups in the decision-making process has both pros and cons (see Table 12–2). On the positive side, groups contain a greater pool of knowledge, provide more varied perspectives, create more comprehension of decisions, increase decision acceptance, and create a training ground for inexperienced employees. John Mackey, CEO of Whole Foods Market, reinforced some of these positive characteristics during an interview with the *Harvard Business Review* (see Real World/Real People on page 351). These advantages must be balanced, however, with the disadvantages listed in Table 12–2. In doing so, managers need to determine the extent to which the advantages and disadvantages apply to the decision situation. The following three guidelines may then be applied to help decide whether groups should be included in the decision-making process.

1. If additional information would increase the quality of the decision, managers should involve those people who can provide the needed information.

table 12–2   Advantages and Disadvantages of Group-Aided Decision Making

ADVANTAGES	DISADVANTAGES
1. **Greater pool of knowledge.** A group can bring much more information and experience to bear on a decision or problem than can an individual acting alone.	1. **Social pressure.** Unwillingness to "rock the boat" and pressure to conform may combine to stifle the creativity of individual contributors.
2. **Different perspectives.** Individuals with varied experience and interests help the group see decision situations and problems from different angles.	2. **Domination by a vocal few.** Sometimes the quality of group action is reduced when the group gives in to those who talk the loudest and longest.
3. **Greater comprehension.** Those who personally experience the give-and-take of group discussion about alternative courses of action tend to understand the rationale behind the final decision.	3. **Logrolling.** Political wheeling and dealing can displace sound thinking when an individual's pet project or vested interest is at stake.
4. **Increased acceptance.** Those who play an active role in group decision making and problem solving tend to view the outcome as "ours" rather than "theirs."	4. **Goal displacement.** Sometimes secondary considerations such as winning an argument, making a point, or getting back at a rival displace the primary task of making a sound decision or solving a problem.
5. **Training ground.** Less experienced participants in group action learn how to cope with group dynamics by actually being involved.	5. **Groupthink.** Sometimes cohesive in-groups let the desire for unanimity override sound judgment when generating and evaluating alternative courses of action. (Groupthink was discussed in Chapter 10.)

SOURCE: From R Kreitner, *Management*, 8th ed Copyright © 2001 by SouthWestern, a part of Cengage Learning. Reproduced by permission. www.cengage.com/permission.

2. If acceptance is important, managers need to involve those individuals whose acceptance and commitment are important.

3. If people can be developed through their participation, managers may want to involve those whose development is most important.[56]

Group versus Individual Performance

Before recommending that managers involve groups in decision making, it is important to examine whether groups perform better or worse than individuals. After reviewing 61 years of relevant research, a decision-making expert concluded that "[g]roup performance was generally qualitatively and quantitatively superior to the performance of the average individual."[57] Although subsequent research of small-group decision making generally supported this conclusion, there are five important issues to consider when using groups to make decisions:

1. Groups were less efficient than individuals. It thus is important to consider time constraints when determining whether to involve groups in decision making.

real WORLD // real PEOPLE

John Mackey, CEO of Whole Foods Market, Believes in Consensual Decision Making

Here is what Mr. Mackey had to say to an interviewer from *Harvard Business Review* about his emphasis on consensual making decisions.

"I found that when you make decisions by consensus, and you let all the disagreements get expressed, you make better decisions. If you don't do that, there is a natural human tendency on the part of whoever didn't get their way to want to be proved right. It's like "See, I told you that wasn't going to work.""

Mr. Mackey also was asked if gaining consensus takes a long time. He responded that "It can. Generally, if you're making decisions that really are going to impact the business, it's good to talk them over. It's a little bit like Japanese management decision-making—they spend a lot more time trying to develop consensus in the decision group. The virtue of it is that although it takes longer to make the decision, implementation goes a lot faster, because there isn't resistance or sabotage that works its way through the organization."

Do you think that it is always necessary to gain consensus when groups make decisions?

SOURCE: Excerpted from "What Is It That Only I Can Do?" *Harvard Business Review,* January–February 2011, pp 119–20.

John Mackey, CEO of Whole Foods Market, seems to be enjoying the stocking of apples in one of his stores.

---

2. Groups were more confident about their judgments and choices than individuals. Because group confidence is not a surrogate for group decision quality, this overconfidence can fuel groupthink—groupthink was discussed in Chapter 10—and a resistance to consider alternative solutions proposed by individuals outside the group.

3. Groups tend to make more moderate decisions. It appears that the need to reach consensus or compromise leads to less extreme decisions.[58]

4. Decision-making accuracy was higher when (*a*) groups knew a great deal about the issues at hand and (*b*) group leaders possessed the ability to effectively evaluate the group members' opinions and judgments. Groups need to give more weight to relevant and accurate judgments while downplaying irrelevant or inaccurate judgments made by its members.[59]

5. The composition of a group affects its decision-making processes and ultimately performance. For example, groups of familiar people are more likely to make better decisions when members share a lot of unique information. In contrast, unacquainted group members should outperform groups of friends when most group members possess common knowledge.[60]

These employees are conducting a brainstorming session. Brainstorming can be fun and is used to generate multiple ideas and solutions for solving problems.

Additional research suggests that managers should use a contingency approach when determining whether to include others in the decision-making process. Let us now consider these contingency recommendations.

Back to the Chapter-Opening Case

To what extent is Google's approach to decision making consistent with research and recommendations about group decision making?

Practical Contingency Recommendations   If the decision occurs frequently, such as deciding on promotions or who qualifies for a loan, use groups because they tend to produce more consistent decisions than do individuals. Given time constraints, let the most competent individual, rather than a group, make the decision. In the face of environmental threats such as time pressure and potential serious effects of a decision, groups use less information and fewer communication channels. This increases the probability of a bad decision. This conclusion underscores a general recommendation that managers should keep in mind: Because the quality of communication strongly affects a group's productivity, on complex tasks it is essential to devise mechanisms to enhance communication effectiveness.

 LO.7 Group Problem-Solving Techniques

Using groups to make decisions generally requires that they reach a consensus. According to a decision-making expert, a **consensus** "is reached when all members can say they either agree with the decision or have had their 'day in court' and were unable to convince the others of their viewpoint. In the final analysis, everyone agrees to support the outcome."[61] This definition indicates that consensus does not require unanimous agreement because group members may still disagree with the final decision but are willing to work toward its success.

Groups can experience roadblocks when trying to arrive at a consensus decision. For one, groups may not generate all relevant alternatives to a problem because an individual dominates or intimidates other group members. This can be overt or subtle. For instance, group members who possess power and authority, such as a CEO, can be intimidating, regardless of interpersonal style, simply by being present in the room. Moreover, shyness inhibits the generation of alternatives. Shy or socially anxious individuals may withhold their input for fear of embarrassment or lack of confidence. Satisficing is another hurdle to effective group decision making. As previously noted, groups satisfice due to limited time, information, or ability to handle large amounts of information. A management expert offered the following dos and don'ts for successfully achieving consensus: Groups should use active listening skills, involve as many members as possible, seek out the reasons behind arguments, and dig for the facts. At the same time, groups should not horse trade (I'll support you on this decision because you supported me on the last one), vote, or agree just to avoid "rocking the boat."[62] Voting is not encouraged because it can split the group into winners and losers.

Decision-making experts have developed three group problem-solving techniques—brainstorming, the nominal group technique, and the Delphi technique—to reduce the above roadblocks. Knowledge of these techniques can help you to more effectively use groups in the decision-making process. Further, the advent of computer-aided decision making enables managers to use these techniques to solve complex problems with large groups of people.

Brainstorming Brainstorming was developed by A F Osborn, an advertising executive, to increase creativity.[63] **Brainstorming** is used to help groups generate multiple ideas and alternatives for solving problems. For example, "Jim Albaugh, chief executive of Boeing's Commercial Airplanes business, tapped eight retired Boeing executives last fall to form a Senior Advisory Group."[64] The group's goal was to brainstorm with current engineers and project managers about how best to get the 787 Dreamliner program on track. Production of the plane experienced a series of setbacks and is currently more than three years behind its original delivery date.

When brainstorming, a group such as Boeing's Senior Advisory Group is convened, and the problem at hand is reviewed. Individual members then are asked to silently generate ideas/alternatives for solving the problem. Silent idea generation is recommended over the practice of having group members randomly shout out their ideas because it leads to a greater number of unique ideas. Groups tend to focus on a more limited number of ideas and get fixated on one idea when they don't conduct silent brainstorming before sharing in a group setting.[65] Next, these ideas/alternatives are solicited and shared in writing. Managers or team leaders may want to collect the brainstormed ideas anonymously, as research demonstrated that more controversial ideas and more nonredundant ideas were generated by anonymous than nonanonymous brainstorming groups.[66] Finally, a second session is used to critique and evaluate the alternatives. Managers are advised to follow the seven rules for brainstorming used by IDEO, a product design company:[67]

1. *Defer judgment.* Don't criticize during the initial stage of idea generation. Phrases such as "We've never done it that way," "It won't work," "It's too expensive," and "Our manager will never agree" should not be used.

2. *Build on the ideas of others.* Encourage participants to extend others' ideas by avoiding "buts" and using "ands."

3. *Encourage wild ideas.* Encourage out-of-the-box thinking. The wilder and more outrageous the ideas, the better.

4. *Go for quantity over quality.* Participants should try to generate and write down as many new ideas as possible. Focusing on quantity encourages people to think beyond their favorite ideas.

5. *Be visual.* Use different colored pens (e.g., red, purple, blue) to write on big sheets of flip chart paper, white boards, or poster board that are put on the wall.

6. *Stay focused on the topic.* A facilitator should be used for keeping the discussion on target.

7. *One conversation at a time.* The ground rules are that no one interrupts another person, no dismissing of someone's ideas, no disrespect, and no rudeness.

Brainstorming is an effective technique for generating new ideas/alternatives, and research reveals that people can be trained to improve their brainstorming skills. Brainstorming is not appropriate for evaluating alternatives or selecting solutions.

consensus Presenting opinions and gaining agreement to support a decision.

brainstorming Process to generate a quantity of ideas.

real WORLD // real PEOPLE

CKE Restaurants Combines Brainstorming, NGT, and Intuition to Make Decisions about New Products

At CKE Restaurants, which includes the Hardee's and Carl's Jr. quick-service restaurant chains, the process for new product introduction calls for rigorous testing at a certain stage. It starts with brainstorming, in which several cross-functional groups develop a variety of new product ideas. Only some of them make it past the next phase, judgmental screening, during which a group of marketing, product development, and operations people will evaluate ideas based on experience and intuition. Those that make the cut are actually developed and then tested in stores, with well-defined measures and control groups. At that point, executives decide whether to roll out a product systemwide, modify it for retesting, or kill the whole idea.

CKE has attained an enviable hit rate in new product introductions—about one in four new products is successful, versus one in 50 or 60 for consumer products.

How many different groups of people are involved in the decision-making process at CKE Restaurants?

SOURCE: Excerpted from T H Davenport, "How to Design Smart Business Experiments," *Harvard Business Review,* February 2009, pp 72–73.

The Nominal Group Technique   The **nominal group technique** (NGT) helps groups generate ideas and evaluate and select solutions. NGT is a structured group meeting that follows this format:[68] A group is convened to discuss a particular problem or issue. After the problem is understood, individuals silently generate ideas in writing. Each individual, in round-robin fashion, then offers one idea from his or her list. Ideas are recorded on a blackboard or flip chart; they are not discussed at this stage of the process. Once all ideas are elicited, the group discusses them.

Anyone may criticize or defend any item. During this step, clarification is provided as well as general agreement or disagreement with the idea. The "30-second soap box" technique, which entails giving each participant a maximum of 30 seconds to argue for or against any of the ideas under consideration, can be used to facilitate this discussion. Alternatively, groups can create an effort/benefit matrix to facilitate this discussion. This is done by identifying the amount of effort and the costs required to implement each idea and comparing these to the potential benefits associated with each idea. Finally, group members anonymously vote for their top choices. The group leader then adds the votes to determine the group's choice. Prior to making a final decision, the group may decide to discuss the top-ranked items and conduct a second round of voting.

The nominal group technique reduces the roadblocks to group decision making by (1) separating brainstorming from evaluation, (2) promoting balanced participation among group members, and (3) incorporating mathematical voting techniques in order to reach consensus. CKE Restaurants, for example, uses a combination of brainstorming and NGT in its new product development process (see Real World/Real People above). NGT has been successfully used in many different decision-making situations and has been found to generate more ideas than a standard brainstorming session.[69]

The Delphi Technique   This problem-solving method was originally developed by the Rand Corporation for technological forecasting.[70] It now is used as a multipurpose planning tool. The **Delphi technique** is a group process that anonymously generates ideas or judgments from physically dispersed experts. Unlike NGT, experts' ideas are obtained from questionnaires or via the Internet as opposed to face-to-face group discussions.

A manager begins the Delphi process by identifying the issue(s) he or she wants to investigate. For example, a manager might want to inquire about customer demand, customers' future preferences, or the effect of locating a plant in a certain region of the country. Next, participants are identified and a questionnaire is developed. The questionnaire is sent to participants and returned to the manager. In today's computer-networked environments, this often means that the questionnaires are e-mailed to participants. The manager then summarizes the responses and sends feedback to the participants. At this stage, participants are asked to (1) review the feedback, (2) prioritize the issues being considered, and (3) return the survey within a specified time period. This cycle repeats until the manager obtains the necessary information.

The Delphi technique is useful when face-to-face discussions are impractical, when disagreements and conflict are likely to impair communication, when certain individuals might severely dominate group discussion, and when groupthink is a probable outcome of the group process.[71]

Computer-Aided Decision Making   The increased globalization of organizations coupled with the advancement of information technology has led to the development of computer-aided decision-making systems. Computerization is being used in two general ways. First, many organizations are using a variety of computer, software, and electronic devices to improve decision making. Such systems allow managers to quickly obtain larger amounts of information from employees, customers, or suppliers around the world. For example, Best Buy, Google, GE, Intel, and Microsoft all use internal intranets to obtain input from employees. Both Best Buy and Google found that these systems were helpful in estimating the demand for new products and services.[72] Walmart also is well known for using computer-aided decision making to improve decision making. For example, Walmart stores are using a new computerized system to schedule its 1.3 million workers. The system creates staffing levels for each store based on the number of customers in the store at any given point in time.[73] These systems also were found to improve information processing and decision making within virtual teams— recall our discussion in Chapter 11.

The second general application of computer-aided decision making relates to running meetings. Two types of systems are used: chauffeur driven and group driven. Chauffeur-driven systems ask participants to answer predetermined questions on electronic keypads or dials. Live television audiences are frequently polled with this system. The computer system tabulates participants' responses in a matter of seconds.

Group-driven electronic meetings are conducted in one of two major ways. First, managers can use e-mail systems or the Internet to collect information or brainstorm about a decision that must be made. For example, Miami Children's Hospital uses a combination of the Internet and a conferencing software technology to make decisions about the design of its training programs. Here is what Loubna Noureddin, director of staff and community education, had to say about the organization's computer-aided decision making: "What I truly like about it is my connection to other hospitals," Noureddin says. "I'm able to understand what other hospitals are doing about specific things. I put my question out, and people can respond, and I can answer back." She explains, for instance, that using the system, she and her colleagues have received guidance from other corporate educators, and even subject-matter experts, on how to best train workers in such fields

nominal group technique Process to generate ideas and evaluate solutions.

Delphi technique Process to generate ideas from physically dispersed experts.

as critical care. "You get many other hospitals logging into the system, and telling us what they do," she says.[74]

Noureddin claims that the system has saved the company time and money. The second method of computer-aided, group-driven meetings is conducted in special facilities equipped with individual workstations that are networked to each other. Instead of talking, participants type their input, ideas, comments, reactions, or evaluations on their keyboards. The input simultaneously appears on a large projector screen at the front of the room, thereby enabling all participants to see all input. This computer-driven process reduces consensus roadblocks because input is anonymous, everyone gets a chance to contribute, and no one can dominate the process. Research demonstrated that computer-aided decision making produced greater quality and quantity of ideas than either traditional brainstorming or the nominal group technique for both small and large groups of people.[75]

In conclusion, we expect the use of computer-aided decision making to increase in the future. These systems are well suited for modern organizational life and for the large number of Millennials or Gen Ys entering the workforce.

..........................▶

TO THE POINT

How can managers
increase creativity
throughout each stage of
the creative process?

....

Creativity

In light of today's need for fast-paced decisions, an organization's ability to stimulate the creativity and innovation of its employees is becoming increasingly important. Many organizations believe that creativity and innovation, which is discussed in Chapter 17, are the seeds of success. Relative to our discussion in this chapter, creativity can be used in all four steps of rational decision making and anytime an individual or group is trying solve a problem, make a decision, or develop something new. Creativity is particularly important during brainstorming sessions.

To gain further insight into managing the creative process, we begin by defining creativity and highlighting the individual and contextual characteristics associated with creativity. We then review the stages underlying the creative process and conclude with practical recommendations for increasing creativity in organizations.

Definition and Individual Characteristics Associated with Creativity

Although many definitions have been proposed, **creativity** is defined here as the process of using imagination and skill to develop a new or unique product, object, process, or thought.[76] It can be as simple as locating a new place to hang your car keys or as complex as developing a pocket-size microcomputer. Creativity can also be applied to the context of cutting costs. For example, President Barack Obama and members of Congress are currently looking for creative ways to cut costs in the federal budget.[77] This definition highlights three broad types of creativity. One can create something new (creation), one can combine or synthesize things (synthesis), or one can improve or change things (modification).

Individual creative behavior is directly affected by a variety of individual characteristics. First off, creativity requires motivation. In other words, people make a decision whether or not they want to apply their knowledge and capabilities to create new ideas, things, or products. In addition to motivation, creative people typically march to the beat of a different drummer. They are highly motivated individuals who spend considerable time developing both tacit and explicit knowledge about their field of interest or occupation. But contrary to stereotypes, creative people are not necessarily geniuses or introverted nerds. In addition, they are not *adaptors*. "Adaptors are those who . . . prefer to resolve difficulties or make decisions in such a way as to have the least impact upon the assumptions, procedures, and values of the organization."[78] In contrast, creative individuals are dissatisfied

table 12–3 Individual Characteristics Associated with Creativity

Intellectual Abilities
- Ability to see problems in new ways and to escape bounds of conventional thinking.
- Ability to recognize which ideas are worth pursuing and which are not.
- Ability to persuade and influence others.

Tacit (Implied) and Explicit Knowledge (about field of interest, occupation, issue, product, service, etc.)

Styles of Thinking
- Preference for thinking in novel ways of one's own choosing.

Personality Traits
- Willingness to overcome obstacles.
- Willingness to take sensible risks.
- Willingness to tolerate ambiguity.
- Self-efficacy.
- Openness to experience and conscientiousness.

Intrinsic Task Motivation

SOURCES: Based on discussion in T Brown, "Thinking," *Harvard Business Review,* June 2008, pp 85–92; and R J Sternberg and R I Lubart, "Investing in Creativity," *American Psychologist,* July 1996, pp 677–78.

with the status quo. They look for new and exciting solutions to problems. Creative people tend to be curious.[79] Further, research indicates that male and female managers do not differ in levels of creativity, and there are a host of personality characteristics that are associated with creativity.[80] These characteristics include, but are not limited to, those shown in Table 12–3. This discussion comes to life by considering the following example.

The Post-it Notes story represents a good illustration of how the individual characteristics shown in Table 12–3 promote creative behavior/performance. Post-it Notes are a $200 million-a-year product for 3M Corporation:

Example. The idea originated with Art Fry, a 3M employee who used bits of paper to mark hymns when he sat in his church choir. These markers kept falling out of the hymnbooks. He decided that he needed an adhesive-backed paper that would stick as long as necessary but could be removed easily. He soon found what he wanted in the 3M laboratory, and the Post-it Note was born.

Fry saw the market potential of his invention, but others did not. Market-survey results were negative; major office-supply distributors were skeptical. So he began giving samples to 3M executives and their secretaries. Once they actually used the little pieces of adhesive paper, they were hooked. Having sold 3M on the project, Fry used the same approach with other executives throughout the United States.[81]

Notice how Fry had to influence others to try out his idea. Table 12–3 shows that creative people have the ability to persuade and influence others.

creativity Process of developing something new or unique.

Contextual Characteristics Associated with Creativity

We noted in Chapter 1 that contextual factors influence our behavior at work. This is certainly true when it comes to creativity. Returning to our discussion of organizational culture in Chapter 3, research reveals that organizations with an adhocracy culture tend to be more innovative.[82] This finding suggests that managers may want to follow the Google experience of allowing more flexibility, risk taking, and experimentation into the work environment in order to enhance creative behavior among employees. Creativity also is associated with time pressure and the level of stress in the work environment. Contrary to the belief that people are more creative under a crisis or severe time pressure, time pressure stifles creativity. So does stress. Creativity is highest when workers are under moderate stress.[83] Finally, leadership plays a big role in fostering creativity. Leaders can boost creative behavior by showing concern for others and by treating employees fairly—recall our discussion of equity theory in Chapter 8.[84]

LO.8   The Steps or Stages of Creativity

Researchers are not absolutely certain how creativity takes place. Nonetheless, we do know that creativity involves "making remote associations" between unconnected events, ideas, information stored in memory (recall our discussion in Chapter 7), or physical objects. Consider how Dr William Foege, then working for the US Centers for Disease Control and Prevention, led the effort to eradicate smallpox in Nigeria. Foege realized that his supply of vaccine was insufficient for the whole population. But he observed how people congregated to shop in markets, so he targeted his campaign to vaccinate the people in those crowded areas, even if they were merely visitors. In so doing, Foege (now a senior fellow with the Carter Center and the Bill and Melinda Gates Foundation) created a model for future vaccination campaigns that efficiently interrupt the paths by which a virus spreads.[85]

Go to www.mcgrawhillconnect.com for an interactive exercise to test your knowledge of the stages of creativity.

The idea of "remote associations" describes thinking such as Foege's connection of shopping behavior and a virus's spread. But it doesn't explain how Foege was able to make this creative link. Researchers, however, have identified five stages underlying the creative process: preparation, concentration, incubation, illumination, and verification. Let us consider these stages.

The preparation stage reflects the notion that creativity starts from a base of knowledge. Experts suggest that creativity involves a convergence between tacit and explicit knowledge. Renowned choreographer Twyla Tharp emphasizes the significance of preparation in the creative process: "I think everyone can be creative, but you have to prepare for it with routine." Tharp's creativity-feeding habits include reading literature, keeping physically active (which stimulates the brain as well as the rest of the body), and choosing new projects that are very different from whatever she has just completed. Even an activity as simple as looking up a word in the dictionary offers an opportunity for preparation: Tharp looks at the word before and after, too, just to see if it gives her an idea.[86]

During the concentration stage, an individual focuses on the problem at hand. Creative ideas at work are often triggered by work-related problems, incongruities, or failures. That said, research shows that when you focus too much on trying to come up with creative solutions it can actually block creativity. For example, daydreaming has been linked with creativity. Other research demonstrated that "Internet leisure browsing" increased creativity.[87] Allow yourself time to be distracted when searching for creative solutions as it can enhance the next stage of creativity—the incubation stage.

Incubation is done unconsciously. During this stage, people engage in daily activities while their minds simultaneously mull over information and make remote

real WORLD // real PEOPLE

Martha Beck's "Kitchen Sink" Technique Increases Creativity

This morning I sat down to write about how we can all learn to better use the right hemispheres of our brains. For 30 minutes, I tapped restlessly at a laptop. Nothing much happened, idea-wise. Flat beer.

Finally I resorted to a strategy I call the Kitchen Sink. I read bits of eight books: four accounts of brain research, one novel about India, one study of bat behavior, one biography of Theodore Roosevelt, and one memoir of motherhood. Next, I drove to my favorite Rollerblading location, listening en route to a stand-up comic, a mystery novel, and an Eckhart Tolle lecture. I yanked on my

Rollerblades and skated around, squinting slack-jawed into the middle distance. After a while, a tiny lightbulb went on. Well, I thought, I could write about this.

Duh.

The Kitchen Sink, you see, is one way to activate your brain's creative right hemisphere.

What activities would you include in your kitchen sink?

SOURCE: M Beck, "Half a Mind Is a Terrible Thing to Waste," *Oprah Magazine*, November 2009, p 57.

---

associations. Martha Beck, author of six book, uses a technique she calls the "kitchen sink" during this stage. The Real World/Real People above illustrates its application when she was trying to write an article on how to better use the creative side of our brains. Associations generated in this stage ultimately come to life in the *illumination* stage. Finally, *verification* entails going through the entire process to verify, modify, or try out the new idea.

Let us examine the stages of creativity to determine why Japanese organizations propose and implement more ideas than do American companies. To address this issue, a creativity expert visited and extensively interviewed employees from five major Japanese companies. He observed that Japanese firms have created a management infrastructure that encourages and reinforces creativity. People were taught to identify problems (discontents) on their first day of employment. In turn, discontents were referred to as "golden eggs" to reinforce the notion that it is good to identify problems.

These organizations also promoted the stages of incubation, illumination, and verification through teamwork and incentives. For example, some companies posted the golden eggs on large wall posters in the work area; employees were then encouraged to interact with each other to execute the final three stages of the creative process. Employees eventually received monetary awards for any suggestions that passed all five phases of this process.[88] This research underscores the conclusion that creativity can be enhanced by effectively managing the creativity process and by fostering a positive and supportive work environment.

 LO.9 Practical Recommendations for Increasing Creativity

While some consultants recommend hypnotism as a good way to increase employees' creativity, we prefer suggestions derived from research and three executives leading creative or innovative companies: Jeffrey Katzenberg, CEO of Dreamworks Animation; Ed Catmull, cofounder of Pixar; and David Kelley, founder of IDEO. Both research and practical experience underscore the conclusion that creativity can be enhanced by effectively managing the stages of creativity and by fostering a positive and supportive work environment. To that end, managers are encouraged to establish an organizational culture that emphasizes innovation, to establish innovation goals (e.g., develop five new patents), and to allocate rewards and resources to innovative activities. At a minimum, individuals need the time and space to reflect and think about whatever issues or problems need creative solutions.

All three executives further recommend that management should create a "safe" work environment that encourages risk taking, autonomy, collaboration, and trusting relationships among employees.[89] These executives suggest that it is important to develop a "peer environment" in which people are more concerned about working for the greater good than for their own personal success. This norm can be nurtured through the use of transformational leadership, which is discussed in Chapter 16.[90] The willingness to give and accept ongoing feedback in a nondefensive manner is another critical component of a culture dedicated to creativity. For example, Pixar uses daily reviews or "dailies" as a process of giving and receiving constant feedback. This will be most effective if organizations train managers in the process of providing effective feedback. Ed Catmull and David Kelly also emphasize the importance of hiring great people who possess some of the individual characteristics shown in Table 12–3. This can be done by asking job applicants "for a story, example or insight that reveals thinking, judgment and problem-solving skills." For example, you might ask an individual to describe a situation in which he or she improvised or how he or she handled a complex problem in a previous job.[91] Finally, these executives also suggest that management should stay connected with innovations taking place in the academic community. For example, Dreamworks invites academics to deliver lectures and Pixar encourages technical artists to publish and attend academic conferences. In summary, creativity is a process that can be managed, and it is built around the philosophy of hiring and retaining great people to work in a positive and supportive work environment.

Summary of Key Concepts

1. *Compare and contrast the rational model of decision making, Simon's normative model, and the garbage can model.* The rational decision-making model consists of identifying the problem or opportunity, generating alternative solutions, evaluating and selecting a solution, and implementing and evaluating the solution. Research indicates that decision makers do not follow the series of steps outlined in the rational model.

   Simon's normative model is guided by a decision maker's bounded rationality. Bounded rationality means that decision makers are bounded or restricted by a variety of constraints when making decisions. This leads to satisficing.

   The garbage can model is based on the assumption that decision making is sloppy and haphazard. Decisions result from an interaction between four independent streams of events: problems, solutions, participants, and choice opportunities.

2. *Discuss eight decision-making biases.* Decision-making bias occurs as the result of using judgmental heuristics. The eight biases that affect decision making include (*a*) availability, (*b*) representativeness, (*c*) confirmation, (*d*) anchoring, (*e*) overconfidence, (*f*) hindsight, (*g*) framing, and (*h*) escalation of commitment.

3. *Discuss the thrust of evidence-based decision making and its implementation principles.* The goal of evidence-based

decision making is to conscientiously use the best data when making decisions. Seven implementation principles help companies to integrate this process into an organization's culture: (*a*) treat your organization as an unfinished prototype, (*b*) no brag, just facts, (*c*) see yourself and your organization as outsiders do, (*d*) evidence-based management is not just for senior executives, (*e*) like everything else, you still need to sell it, (*f*) if all else fails, slow the spread of bad practices, and (*g*) the best diagnostic question: what happens when people fail?

4. *Explain the model of decision-making styles.* The model of decision-making styles is based on the idea that styles vary along two different dimensions: value orientation and tolerance for ambiguity. When these two dimensions are combined, they form four styles of decision making: directive, analytical, conceptual, and behavioral. People with a directive style have a low tolerance for ambiguity and are oriented toward task and technical concerns. Analytics have a higher tolerance for ambiguity and are characterized by a tendency to overanalyze a situation. People with a conceptual style have a high threshold for ambiguity and tend to focus on people or social aspects of a work situation. This behavioral style is the most people oriented of the four styles.

5. *Explain the model of intuition and the ethical decision tree.* Intuition consists of insight or knowledge that is obtained

without the use of rational thought or logical inference. There are two types of intuition: holistic hunches and automated experiences. Intuition is represented by two distinct process, one is automatic and the second is controlled, and there are two sources of intuition: expertise, which consists of an individual's combined explicit and tacit knowledge regarding an object, person, situation, or decision opportunity; and feelings. Intuition is based on the interaction between one's expertise and feelings in a given situation.

The ethical decision tree presents a structured approach for making ethical decisions. Managers work through the tree by answering a series of questions and the process leads to a recommended decision.

6. *Summarize the pros and cons of involving groups in the decision-making process.* There are both pros and cons to involving groups in the decision-making process. Although research shows that groups typically outperform the average individual, there are five important issues to consider when using groups to make decisions. (*a*) Groups are less efficient than individuals. (*b*) A group's overconfidence can fuel groupthink. (*c*) Groups tend to make more moderate decisions than individuals. (*d*) Groups are more accurate when they know a great deal about the issues at hand and when the leader possesses the ability to effectively evaluate the group members' opinions and judgments. (*e*) The composition of a group affects its decision-making processes and performance. In the final analysis, managers are encouraged to use a contingency approach when determining whether to include others in the decision-making process.

7. *Contrast brainstorming, the nominal group technique, the Delphi technique, and computer-aided decision making.* Group problem-solving techniques facilitate better decision making within groups. Brainstorming is used to help groups generate multiple ideas and alternatives for solving problems. The nominal group technique assists groups both to generate ideas and to evaluate and select solutions. The Delphi technique is a group process that anonymously generates ideas or judgments from physically dispersed experts. The purpose of computer-aided decision making is to reduce consensus roadblocks while collecting more information in a shorter period of time.

8. *Describe the stages of the creative process.* Creativity is defined as the process of using imagination and skill to develop a new or unique product, object, process, or thought. There are five stages of the creative process: preparation, concentration, incubation, illumination, and verification.

9. *Discuss practical recommendations for increasing creativity.* Creativity can be enhanced by effectively managing the stages of creativity and by fostering a positive and supportive work environment. People need the time and space to be creative. Managers are encouraged to create a "safe" work environment that encourages risk taking, autonomy, collaboration, and trusting relationships among employees. It also is important to develop a "peer environment" in which people are more concerned about working for the greater good than their own personal success.

Key Terms

Decision making, 330

Rational model, 330

Problem, 330

Opportunity, 331

Optimizing, 332

Nonrational models, 333

Bounded rationality, 333

Satisficing, 333

Garbage can model, 333

Judgmental heuristics, 335

Evidence-based decision making, 338

Decision-making style, 341

Intuition, 344

Decision tree, 347

Consensus, 352

Brainstorming, 353

Nominal group technique, 354

Delphi technique, 354

Creativity, 356

OB in Action Case Study

Faulty Decision Making Is a Cause of the Deepwater Horizon Disaster[92]

Federal authorities investigating BP PLC's oil spill in the Gulf of Mexico are zeroing in on bad decisions, missed warnings, and worker disagreements in the hours before the April 20 inferno aboard the *Deepwater Horizon* that spawned one of the worst environmental disasters in US history.

In particular, the panel is examining why rig workers missed telltale signs that the well was close to an uncontrolled blow-out, according to an internal document assembled by the investigators and reviewed by *The Wall Street Journal*. The document lists more than 20 "anomalies" in the well's behavior and the crew's response that particularly interest the investigators.

Investigators are also turning attention to decisions made by employees of Transocean Ltd., the rig's owner, in addition to those made by BP that day, the list indicates.

In particular, the list suggests investigators are looking at whether better coordination between the two companies might have prevented the disaster. The document includes several instances of unexpected pressure increases triggering disagreements among workers from the two firms. . . .

The list of 20 anomalies includes several irregularities in the well's behavior, some of which were already known. The list also includes instances where common well-control protocols weren't followed.

Aboard a rig, any single problem by itself might not be cause for alarm, according to industry officials with experience in deep-water drilling. But the cascade of problems on the *Deepwater Horizon* in the hours before it exploded should have been a warning to workers to try to shut the well or take other precautions to avoid potential disaster.

Eleven people died aboard the rig as it burned in April and sank.

In this week's planned testimony, the investigative panel is likely to ask rig workers why none of the signs led to a halt in work. Instead, workers from BP and Transocean kept taking steps to complete the well, including removing heavy fluid, known as drilling "mud," that is used to tamp down pressure within a well, according to documents previously released to congressional investigators.

It isn't clear if the crew noticed in the hours before the explosion that more fluid was leaving the well than workers were putting into it—a potential sign of a serious imbalance deep within a well that can lead to a catastrophe. These signs continued for several hours, until the well exploded shortly before 10 p.m., according to the list.

At noon on April 20—some 10 hours before the blowout occurred—more fluid left the pipe than was expected during routine test. And around 4 p.m., pressure on the drill pipe was higher than expected, the panel notes. Both are indications that workers were losing control.

Workers were having a tough time determining exactly how much fluid was entering and leaving the well because simultaneous operations were under way. The panel was critical of this. "Hard to track fluid volumes in the wellbore when you are pumping mud to boat . . . and also [pumping] saltwater into the hole," the list notes.

Shortly before 5 p.m., pressure built up unexpectedly on the section of pipe suspended in the well. Managers from BP and Transocean disagreed on what that meant. "Some employees recalled a disagreement between Transocean and BP on the rig floor about the negative test and pressure on the work string," the list notes.

At 7:10 p.m., BP's two top officials on the rig met near the spot where the pipe comes out of the water and through the rig's floor. They discussed the high pressure, according to the investigative panel, which has been gathering evidence for two months. Transocean rig workers, according to the panel, offered an explanation that didn't raise an alarm.

That employees of Transocean, the rig's owner, might not have realized the seriousness of the situation—and may have misunderstood the data from the well—could shift some scrutiny onto that company. Most of the spotlight so far has fallen on BP, which owned the well and hired Transocean to drill it.

BP has emerged as a target of criticism for, among other things, choosing a well design that was less costly to build than alternative designs, but which came with additional risks. The investigative panel's list of anomalies underscores how easy it can be to overlook signs that a deepwater well is in trouble and could turn deadly.

Questions for Discussion

1. Which model of decision making is represented in this case?

2. To what extent did decision-making biases impact the decisions made in this case? Identify the specific biases that were present. Is BP's and Transocean's approach more characteristic of the rational, normative, or garbage can models of decision making? Discuss your rationale.

3. How could evidence-based decision making been used to help avoid this disaster?

4. What do you think are the key causes of this disaster?

5. What are the key takeaways from this case? Explain.

Legal/Ethical Challenge

How Would You Handle the Early Reporting of Sales?[93]

Assume the role of Jonathan in this scenario.

Jonathan has a new job. Just promoted from the accounting group at headquarters, he is now the controller for a regional sales unit of a consumer electronics company. He is excited about this step up and wants to build a good relationship with his new team. However, when the quarterly numbers come due, he realizes that the next quarter's sales are being reported early to boost bonus compensation. The group manager's silence suggests that this sort of thing has probably happened before. Having dealt with such distortion when he sat in corporate, Jonathan is fully aware of its potential to cause major

damage. But this is the first time he is working with people who are creating the problem instead of those who are trying to fix it.

This may seem like a mundane accounting matter. But the consequences . . . are very serious.

What would you do if you were Jonathan?

1. Nothing. I need to get along with my new team, and this has been standard practice in the past. Further, this really isn't that much of a big deal.

2. Let it go for now, but I will speak to the group's manager about this practice. My goal would be to understand why this practice has been going on, and then I might attempt to put an end to it.

3. Confront the issue right now and put an end to this practice. If I get any resistance, I would immediately reach out to my contacts at corporate headquarters.

4. Invent other options.

Web Resources

For study material and exercises that apply to this chapter, visit our website at **www.mhhe.com/kreitner10e**

chapter 13

Managing Conflict and Negotiating

 Learning Objectives

When you finish studying the material in this chapter, you should be able to:

LO.1 Define the term *conflict,* and put the three metaphors of conflict into proper perspective for the workplace.

LO.2 Distinguish between functional and dysfunctional conflict, and discuss why people avoid conflict.

LO.3 List six antecedents of conflict, and identify the desired outcomes of conflict.

LO.4 Define *personality conflicts,* and explain how managers should handle them.

LO.5 Discuss the role of in-group thinking in intergroup conflict, and explain what management can do about intergroup conflict.

LO.6 Discuss what can be done about cross-cultural conflict.

LO.7 Explain how managers can stimulate functional conflict, and identify the five conflict-handling styles.

LO.8 Explain the nature and practical significance of conflict triangles and alternative dispute resolution for third-party conflict intervention.

LO.9 Explain the difference between distributive and integrative negotiation, and discuss the concept of added-value negotiation.

Can Managers Be Too Nice?

Lowrie Beacham didn't like confronting people or making decisions that favored one staffer over another, including the time two of his people were vying to be in charge of the new fitness center.

"Instead of having one bad day and getting over it, it went on for literally years," he recalls. "You just kick the can a little farther down the road—'Let's have a meeting on this next month'—anything you can try to keep from having that confrontation."

Anytime his employees bristled at his gentle criticisms, he'd change the subject: "You're getting to work on time; that's wonderful!" he'd say, "Never mind that your clients say you're difficult to work with."

What resulted was a dysfunctional department, he admits, "with no discipline, no confidence in where they stood, lots of scheming and kvetching, back-stabbing." He gave up his management role. "I'm extremely happy not managing," he says.

The bad manager tends to conjure images of the blood-vessel-bursting screamer looking for a handle to fly off. But these types are increasingly rare. Far more common, and more insidious, are the managers who won't say a critical word to the staffers who need to hear it. In avoiding an unpleasant conversation, they allow something worse to ferment in the delay. They achieve kindness in the short term but heartlessness in the long run, dooming the problem employee to nonimprovement. You can't fix what you can't say is broken.[1]

How would you handle the following situation?

Example. Your name is Annie and you are a product development manager for Amazon.com. As you were eating lunch today in your cubicle, Laura, a software project manager with an office nearby, asked if she could talk to you for a few minutes. You barely know Laura and you have heard both good and bad things about her work habits. Although your mind was more on how to meet Friday's deadline than on lunch, you waved her in.

She proceeded to pour out her woes about how she is having an impossible time partnering with Hans on a new special project. He is regarded as a top-notch software project manager, but Laura has found him to be ill-tempered and uncooperative. Laura thought you and Hans were friends because she has seen the two of you talking in the cafeteria and parking lot. You told Laura you have a good working relationship with Hans, but he's not really a friend. Still, Laura pressed on. "Would you straighten Hans out for me?" she asked. "We've got to get moving on this special project."

"Why this?" "Why now?" "Why me?!!" you thought as your eyes left Laura and drifted back to your desk.

Write down some ideas about how to handle this all-too-common conflict situation. Set it aside. We'll revisit your recommendation later in the chapter. In the meantime, we need to explore the world of conflict because, as indicated in the opening vignette, walking the tightrope between too much and too little conflict is a never-ending challenge in organizational life. After discussing a modern view of conflict and three major types of conflict, we learn how to manage conflict both as a participant and as a third party. The related topic of negotiation is examined next. We conclude with a contingency approach to conflict management and negotiation.

LO.1 Conflict: A Modern Perspective

TO THE POINT
What is the positive side of conflict, and what should managers know about the antecedents and positive outcomes of conflict?

Make no mistake about it. Conflict is an unavoidable aspect of organizational life. These major trends conspire to make *organizational* conflict inevitable:

- Constant change.
- Greater employee diversity.
- More teams (virtual and self-managed).
- Less face-to-face communication (more electronic interaction).
- A global economy with increased cross-cultural dealings.

Dean Tjosvold, at Hong Kong's Lingnan University, notes that "change begets conflict, conflict begets change"[2] and challenges us to do better with this sobering global perspective:

Example. Learning to manage conflict is a critical investment in improving how we, our families, and our organizations adapt and take advantage of change. Managing conflicts well does not insulate us from change, nor does it mean that we will always come out on top or get all that we want. However, effective conflict management helps us keep in touch with new developments and create solutions appropriate for new threats and opportunities.

Much evidence shows we have often failed to manage our conflicts and respond to change effectively. High divorce rates, disheartening examples of sexual and physical abuse of children, the expensive failures of international joint ventures, and bloody ethnic violence have convinced many people that we do not have the abilities to cope with our complex interpersonal, organizational, and global conflicts.[3]

But respond we must. As outlined in this chapter, tools and solutions are available, if only we develop the ability and will to use them persistently. The choice is ours: Be active managers of conflict, or be managed by conflict.

A comprehensive review of the conflict literature yielded this consensus definition: "**conflict** is a process in which one party perceives that its interests are being opposed or negatively affected by another party."[4] The word *perceives* reminds us that sources of conflict and issues can be real or imagined. The resulting conflict is the same. Conflict can escalate (strengthen) or deescalate (weaken) over time. "The conflict process unfolds in a context, and whenever conflict, escalated or not, occurs the disputants or third parties can attempt to manage it in some manner."[5] Consequently, current and future managers need to understand the dynamics of conflict and know how to handle it effectively (both as disputants and as third parties). This call to action is bolstered by a survey asking employees what their manager's New Year's resolution should be. The number-one response was "Deal with workplace conflicts faster."[6]

The Language of Conflict: Metaphors and Meaning

Conflict is a complex subject for several reasons.[7] Primary among them is the reality that conflict often carries a lot of emotional luggage. Fear of losing or fear of change quickly raises the emotional stakes in a conflict. Conflicts also vary widely in magnitude. Conflicts have both participants and observers. Some observers may be interested and active; others, disinterested and passive. Consequently, the term *conflict* can take on vastly different meanings, depending on the circumstances and one's involvement. For example, consider these three metaphors and accompanying workplace expressions:

- *Conflict as war:* "We shot down that idea."
- *Conflict as opportunity:* "What will it take to resolve this disagreement?"
- *Conflict as journey:* "Let's search for common ground and all learn something useful."[8]

Anyone viewing a conflict as war or a sports contest will try to win at all costs and wipe out the enemy. For example, Donald Trump has said, "In life, you have fighters and nonfighters. You have winners and losers. I am both a fighter and a winner."[9] Alternatively, those seeing a conflict as an opportunity and a journey will tend to be more positive, open-minded, and constructive. In a hostile world, combative and destructive warlike thinking often prevails. But typical daily workplace conflicts are *not* war. So when dealing with organizational conflicts, we are challenged to rely less on the metaphor and language of war and more on the metaphors and language of *opportunity* and *journey.* For instance, Christine Day, CEO of yoga apparel retailer Lululemon Athletica, offers this advice: "You might disagree with your co-workers on

If you think yoga is a tough stretch, try being a manager today. Christine Day, CEO of Lululemon Athletica, strives hard to work out goal-focused agreements among the employees of her rapidly growing yoga apparel company.

conflict One party perceives its interests are being opposed or set back by another party.

how to get there, but make sure you agree on what you're trying to accomplish."[10] We need to monitor our choice of words in conflict situations carefully.

While explaining the three metaphors, conflict experts Kenneth Cloke and Joan Goldsmith made this instructive observation that we want to keep in mind for the balance of this chapter:

Example. Conflict gives you an opportunity to deepen your capacity for empathy and intimacy with your opponent. Your anger transforms the "Other" into a stereotyped demon or villain. Similarly, defensiveness will prevent you from communicating openly with your opponents, or listening carefully to what they are saying. On the other hand, once you engage in dialogue with that person, you will resurrect the human side of their personality—and express your own as well.

Moreover, when you process your conflicts with integrity, they lead to growth, increased awareness, and self-improvement. Uncontrolled anger, defensiveness, and shame defeat these possibilities. Everyone feels better when they overcome their problems and reach resolution, and worse when they succumb and fail to resolve them. It is a bitter truth that victories won in anger lead to long-term defeat. Those defeated turn away, feeling betrayed and lost, and carry this feeling with them into their next conflict.

Conflict can be seen simply as a way of learning more about what is not working and discovering how to fix it. The usefulness of the solution depends on the depth of your understanding of the problem. This depends on your ability to listen to the issue as you would to a teacher, which depends on halting the cycle of escalation and searching for opportunities for improvement.[11]

In short, win–win beats win–lose in both conflict management and negotiation.

A Conflict Continuum

Ideas about managing conflict underwent an interesting evolution during the 20th century. Initially, scientific management experts such as Frederick W Taylor believed all conflict ultimately threatened management's authority and thus had to be avoided or quickly resolved. Later, human relationists recognized the inevitability of conflict and advised managers to learn to live with it. Emphasis remained on resolving conflict whenever possible, however. Beginning in the 1970s, organizational behavior specialists realized conflict had both positive and negative outcomes, depending on its nature and intensity. This perspective introduced the revolutionary idea that organizations could suffer from *too little* conflict. Figure 13–1 illustrates the relationship between conflict intensity and outcomes.

figure 13–1   The Relationship between Conflict Intensity and Outcomes

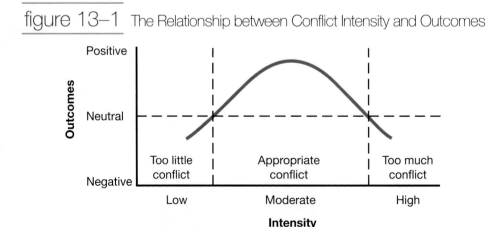

SOURCE: From L D Brown, *Managing Conflict at Organizational Interfaces,* 1st ed. Copyright © 1983. Reproduced by permission of Pearson Education, Upper Saddle River, NJ.

real WORLD // real PEOPLE

Software Maker 37signals Thrives on Functional Conflict

Jason Fried, co-founder of Chicago-based 37signals:

We're an opinionated bunch at 37signals. . . . That is true whether we're dealing with the outside world (in our blog posts, conference talks, interviews, etc.) or with one another. And since we're a semivirtual company with people in 12 different cities, we don't have the benefit of body language to help inform the subtleties of discussion. Because we can't see one another, we can't serve up a smile or a "You know what I mean" glance to defuse a conflict in the making.

So we've learned a few things about managing conflict. Conflict, of course, can be a downer. But managed conflict is a good thing—it's fertile ground for a great exchange of ideas. When people dig in and defend their positions, a deeper understanding of a problem is possible. As long as people are defending a genuine idea and not just their pride, much can be learned.

How comfortable would you be working in this sort of confrontational environment?

SOURCE: J Fried, "I Know You Are, But What Am I?" *Inc,* July–August 2010, p 39.

Work groups, departments, or organizations experiencing too little conflict tend to be plagued by apathy, lack of creativity, indecision, and missed deadlines. Excessive conflict, on the other hand, can erode organizational performance because of political infighting, dissatisfaction, lack of teamwork, and turnover. Workplace bullying, reportedly experienced by one-third of the employees in a recent survey,[12] is unhealthy conflict. Workplace aggression and violence also can be manifestations of excessive conflict.[13] Appropriate types and levels of conflict energize people in constructive directions.

 LO.2 Functional versus Dysfunctional Conflict

The distinction between **functional conflict** and **dysfunctional conflict** pivots on whether the organization's interests are served. According to one conflict expert,

---

Example. Some [types of conflict] support the goals of the organization and improve performance; these are functional, constructive forms of conflict. They benefit or support the main purposes of the organization. Additionally, there are those types of conflict that hinder organizational performance; these are dysfunctional or destructive forms. They are undesirable and the manager should seek their eradication.[14]

Functional conflict is commonly referred to in management circles as constructive or cooperative conflict. In terms of what we just discussed about the language of conflict, those engaging in functional conflict apply a win–win attitude to solve problems and find common ground (see Real World/Real People above). Organizational psychologist Kerry Sulkowicz draws an important distinction between aggressiveness and assertiveness when giving this advice about functional conflict:

Example. The best CEOs I work with know how to exert pressure, say no, and start and win a fight when necessary. So much for teamwork? Actually, collaboration

---

functional conflict Serves organization's interests.

dysfunctional conflict Threatens organization's interests.

and confrontation aren't mutually exclusive. There's aggression—a basic survival mechanism—and then there's its tamer, more socially adaptive cousin, assertiveness, which can be deployed usefully, including with people working on the "same side."

The need to be assertive comes up all the time. It's essential in negotiating contracts, rejecting bad work, criticizing a strategy, or firing (or defending) an employee. Yet some people will do almost anything to avoid confrontation. . . .

The key, oddly enough, is to empathize with the person you're confronting. To that end, marshal useful facts rather than impressions, offer alternatives along with your objections, and limit comments to the deed, not the doer. Your opponent won't hear anything you say after an attack on his or her character. And don't be self-righteous. Or gloat if you prevail. Nobody likes a poor winner.[15]

Why People Avoid Conflict

Are you uncomfortable in conflict situations? Do you go out of your way to avoid conflict? If so, you're not alone. Many of us avoid conflict for a variety of both good and bad reasons. Tim Ursiny, in his entertaining and instructive book *The Coward's Guide to Conflict,* contends that we avoid conflict because we fear various combinations of the following things: "harm," "rejection," "loss of relationship," "anger," "being seen as selfish," "saying the wrong thing," "failing," "hurting someone else," "getting what you want," and "intimacy."[16] This list is self-explanatory, except for the fear of "getting what you want." By this, Ursiny is referring to those who, for personal reasons, feel undeserving or fear the consequences of success, or both (so they tend to sabotage themselves).[17] For our present purposes, it is sufficient to become consciously aware of our fears and practice overcoming them. Reading, understanding, and acting on the material in this chapter are steps in a positive direction.

Back to the Chapter-Opening Case

Are you a conflict avoider like Lowrie Beacham? If yes, what problems does it cause, and what can you do to improve?

The 2011 disaster at Japan's Fukushima Daiichi nuclear power plants created a perfect storm of dysfunctional conflict as fingers pointed in all directions among Tokyo Electric Power Company officials, national and local government leaders, and an outraged public. How many antecedents of conflict in the accompanying list do you think played a contributing role?

 LO.3 Antecedents of Conflict

Certain situations produce more conflict than others. By knowing the antecedents of conflict, managers are better able to anticipate it and take steps to resolve it if it becomes dysfunctional. Among the situations tending to produce either functional or dysfunctional conflict are

- Incompatible personalities or value systems.
- Overlapping or unclear job boundaries.
- Interdepartment/intergroup competition.
- Competition for limited resources.
- Inadequate communication.
- Interdependent tasks (e.g., one person cannot complete his or her assignment until others have completed their work).
- Organizational complexity (conflict tends to increase as the number of hierarchical layers and specialized tasks increase).

- Unreasonable or unclear policies, standards, or rules.
- Unreasonable deadlines or extreme time pressure.
- Collective decision making (the greater the number of people participating in a decision, the greater the potential for conflict).
- Decision making by consensus.
- Unmet expectations (employees who have unrealistic expectations about job assignments, pay, or promotions are more prone to conflict).
- Unresolved or suppressed conflicts.[18]

Proactive managers carefully read these early warnings and take appropriate action.

Back to the Chapter-Opening Case

Which antecedents of conflict are primarily responsible for the problems in the opening case? What are the cause-and-effect relationships?

Desired Conflict Outcomes

Within organizations, conflict management is more than simply a quest for agreement. If progress is to be made and dysfunctional conflict minimized, a broader agenda is in order. Tjosvold's cooperative conflict model calls for three desired outcomes:

1. *Agreement.* But at what cost? Equitable and fair agreements are best. An agreement that leaves one party feeling exploited or defeated will tend to breed resentment and subsequent conflict.

2. *Stronger relationships.* Good agreements enable conflicting parties to build bridges of goodwill and trust for future use. Moreover, conflicting parties who trust each other are more likely to keep their end of the bargain.

3. *Learning.* Functional conflict can promote greater self-awareness and creative problem solving. Like the practice of management itself, successful conflict handling is learned primarily by doing. Knowledge of the concepts and techniques in this chapter is a necessary first step, but there is no substitute for hands-on practice. In a contentious world, there are plenty of opportunities to strive for better conflict outcomes.[19]

A prime example is education reform. As evidenced by recent headlines, school boards and administrators, teacher's unions, and parents too often wallow in unfruitful conflict to the detriment of students. A refreshing and instructive exception is Hillsborough County, with the eighth-largest US school district that encompasses Tampa and St Petersburg, Florida. Can you spot the three desired conflict outcomes in the following situation?

Example. In recent years, teamwork between the union and management has resulted in a longer, eight-hour school day; higher pay for the most effective teachers; and a comprehensive coaching program for struggling teachers. They have also worked together to refine a rigorous teacher-evaluation system that considers student-achievement gains along with the observations of principals and outside peer reviewers.[20]

TO THE POINT

What are the keys to effectively handling personality, intergroup, and cross-cultural conflict?

Types of Conflict

Certain antecedents of conflict, highlighted earlier, deserve a closer look. This section probes the nature and organizational implications of three basic types of conflict: personality conflict, intergroup conflict, and cross-cultural conflict. Our discussion of each type of conflict includes some practical tips and techniques.

LO.4 Personality Conflict

We visited the topic of personalities in our Chapter 2 discussion of diversity. Also, recall the Big Five personality dimensions introduced in Chapter 5. Once again, your *personality* is the package of stable traits and characteristics creating your unique identity. According to experts on the subject:

Example. Each of us has a unique way of interacting with others. Whether we are seen as charming, irritating, fascinating, nondescript, approachable, or intimidating depends in part on our personality, or what others might describe as our style.[21]

connect™ Go to www.mcgrawhillconnect.com for an interactive exercise to test your knowledge of how to deal with personality conflicts.

Given the many possible combinations of personality traits, it is clear why personality conflicts are inevitable. We define a **personality conflict** as interpersonal opposition based on personal dislike, disagreement, or different styles. For example, imagine the potential for a top-level personality conflict at EMC Corporation, a leading maker of data storage equipment and services. Michael C Ruettgers, executive chairman of the Massachusetts-based firm, gave up his CEO position to Joseph M Tucci in January 2001 after running the company for nine years. This is how the situation was reported in the business press in early 2002:

Example. [According to former employees], Tucci has wanted to move faster to cut costs, make acquisitions, and introduce new software, but Ruettgers and EMC have slowed the pace of change. And Ruettgers, who had planned to be less active in daily affairs, has continued to attend weekly meetings to review operations. . . .

The personal and management styles of Tucci, a salesman, and Ruettgers, who started at EMC as an operations expert, couldn't be more different. Tucci likes to build one-on-one relationships, while Ruettgers is more aloof. Tucci seems to be more willing than Ruettgers to make tough decisions quickly. Bill Scannell, EMC's senior vice president for global sales, says Tucci gives him an answer immediately when he asks for advice. Ruettgers tends to chew on things awhile. And Tucci praises and thanks his troops regularly, while Ruettgers once told a former executive that saying thank-you is a sign of weakness.[22]

A personality conflict with his former boss didn't keep EMC's CEO Joseph M Tucci from succeeding with a more people-friendly style of management.

Any way you look at it, Tucci was in a tough spot, and conflicting personalities only made it worse. How did things turn out? By 2006, Tucci's strategy and personal style were vindicated as EMC posted impressive results from hot new products.[23] Good guys don't always finish last!

Workplace Incivility: The Seeds of Personality Conflict   Somewhat akin to physical pain, chronic personality conflicts often begin with seemingly insignificant irritations. A pair of OB researchers offered this cautionary overview of the problem and its consequences:

Example. Incivility, or employees' lack of regard for one another, is costly to organizations in subtle and pervasive ways. Although uncivil behaviors occur commonly, many organizations fail to recognize them, few understand their harmful effects, and most managers and executives are ill-equipped to deal with them. Over the past eight years, as we have learned about this phenomenon through interviews, focus groups, questionnaires, experiments, and executive forums with more than 2,400 people across the US and Canada, we have found that incivility causes its targets, witnesses, and additional stake-holders to act in ways that erode organizational values and deplete organizational resources. Because of their experiences of workplace incivility, employees decrease work effort, time on the job, productivity, and performance. Where incivility is not curtailed, job satisfaction and organizational loyalty diminish as well. Some employees leave their jobs solely because of the impact of this subtle form of deviance.[24]

Vicious cycles of incivility need to be avoided, or broken early, with an organizational culture that places a high value on respect for co-workers. This requires managers and leaders to act as caring and courteous role models. A positive spirit of cooperation, as opposed to one based on negativism and aggression, also helps. Proactive steps need to be taken because of these troubling survey results:

- In a 2007 survey, "38% of women said they heard sexual innuendo, wise-cracks, or taunts at the office last year, up from 22%. . . . [M]en were more likely than women to hear all types of tasteless or questionable comments, with 44% saying they heard racial slurs, for instance, compared with 24% of women."[25]

- In a 2008 survey of 11,251 adults, 86% answered yes to the question, "Do you work with one or more annoying co-workers?"[26]

Some organizations have resorted to workplace etiquette training. More specifically, constructive feedback or skillful behavior shaping can keep a single irritating behavior from precipitating a full-blown personality conflict (or worse).[27] Another promising tool for nipping workplace incivility in the bud is a **day of contemplation,** defined as "a *paid* day off where an employee showing lack of dedication to the job is granted the opportunity to rethink his commitment to working at your company."[28] This tactic, also called *decision-making leave,* is not part of the organization's formal disciplinary process, nor is it a traditional suspension without pay. A day of contemplation is a one-time-only-per-employee option to get employees back on the right track.

Dealing with Personality Conflicts

Personality conflicts are a potential minefield for managers. Let us frame the situation. Personality traits, by definition, are stable and resistant to change. Moreover, according to the American Psychiatric Association's *Diagnostic and Statistical Manual of Mental Disorders,* there are 410 psychological disorders that can and do show up in the workplace.[29] This brings up legal issues. Employees in the United States suffering from psychological

personality conflict Interpersonal opposition driven by personal dislike or disagreement.

day of contemplation A one-time-only day off with pay to allow a problem employee to recommit to the organization's values and mission.

table 13–1 How to Deal with Personality Conflicts

TIPS FOR EMPLOYEES HAVING A PERSONALITY CONFLICT	TIPS FOR THIRD-PARTY OBSERVERS OF A PERSONALITY CONFLICT	TIPS FOR MANAGERS WHOSE EMPLOYEES ARE HAVING A PERSONALITY CONFLICT
• Communicate directly with the other person to resolve the perceived conflict (emphasize problem solving and common objectives, not personalities). • Avoid dragging co-workers into the conflict. • If dysfunctional conflict persists, seek help from direct supervisors or human resource specialists.	• Do not take sides in someone else's personality conflict. • Suggest the parties work things out themselves in a constructive and positive way. • If dysfunctional conflict persists, refer the problem to parties' direct supervisors.	• Investigate and document conflict. • If appropriate, take corrective action (e.g., feedback or behavior shaping). • If necessary, attempt informal dispute resolution. • Refer difficult conflicts to human resource specialists or hired counselors for formal resolution attempts and other interventions.

NOTE: All employees need to be familiar with and *follow* company policies for diversity, antidiscrimination, and sexual harassment.

disorders such as depression and mood-altering diseases such as alcoholism are protected from discrimination by the Americans with Disabilities Act.[30] (Other nations have similar laws.) Also, sexual harassment and other forms of discrimination can grow out of apparent personality conflicts. Finally, personality conflicts can spawn workplace aggression and violence.

Traditionally, managers dealt with personality conflicts by either ignoring them or transferring one party. In view of the legal implications, just discussed, both of these options may be open invitations to discrimination lawsuits. Table 13–1 presents practical tips for both nonmanagers and managers who are involved in or affected by personality conflicts. Our later discussions of handling dysfunctional conflict and alternative dispute resolution techniques also apply.

 LO.5 Intergroup Conflict

Conflict among work groups, teams, and departments is a common threat to organizational competitiveness. For example, when Michael Volkema became CEO of Herman Miller, he found an inward-focused company with divisions fighting over budgets. He curbed intergroup conflict at the Michigan-based furniture maker by emphasizing collaboration and redirecting everyone's attention outward, to the customer.[31] Managers who understand the mechanics of intergroup conflict are better equipped to face this sort of challenge.

In-Group Thinking: The Seeds of Intergroup Conflict   As we discussed in previous chapters, *cohesiveness*—a "we feeling" binding group members together—can be a good or bad thing. A certain amount of cohesiveness can turn a group of individuals into a smooth-running team. Too much cohesiveness, however, can breed groupthink because a desire to get along pushes aside critical thinking. The study of in-groups by small group researchers has revealed a whole package of changes associated with increased group cohesiveness. Specifically,

- Members of in-groups view themselves as a collection of unique individuals, while they stereotype members of other groups as being "all alike."
- In-group members see themselves positively and as morally correct, while they view members of other groups negatively and as immoral.
- In-groups view outsiders as a threat.
- In-group members exaggerate the differences between their group and other groups. This typically involves a distorted perception of reality.[32]

real WORLD // real PEOPLE: ethics

Has America Become the Land of Incivility?

You'd think that in our highly religious American ex-periment, our collection of Good Books and legions of prayerful people would cultivate a political world that reflected high-minded values. And you'd be wrong.

If there's anything about politics on which Americans might agree, it's probably that our pitched battles over elections, policy and power are not summoning our better angels. Truth telling? Be serious. Humility? Hah! Civility? Don't be a fool. . . .

Sadly, the vitriol and meanness are making it virtually impossible for those we elect to do their job and govern.

When the two sides of the aisle seem mainly interested in scoring political points and landing rhetorical punches, it's no wonder we have what pundit Thomas Friedman calls our national power failure—"the failure of our political system to unite, even in a crisis, to produce the policy responses America needs to thrive in the 21st century."

Are you part of the solution or part of the problem? How can we improve this state of affairs?

SOURCE: Excerpted from T Krattenmaker, "In God-Fearing USA, Where Is the Decency?" *USA Today,* October 25, 2010, p 11A.

Avid sports fans who simply can't imagine how someone would support the opposing team exemplify one form of in-group thinking. Also, this pattern of behavior is a form of ethnocentrism, discussed as a cross-cultural barrier in Chapter 4. Reflect for a moment on evidence of in-group behavior in your life. Does your circle of friends make fun of others because of their race, gender, nationality, religion, politics, sexual orientation, weight, or major in college? (See Real World/ Real People above).

In-group thinking is one more fact of organizational life that virtually guarantees conflict. Managers cannot eliminate in-group thinking, but they certainly should not ignore it when confronted with intergroup conflicts.

Research Lessons for Handling Intergroup Conflict   Sociologists have long recommended the contact hypothesis for reducing intergroup conflict. According to the *contact hypothesis,* the more the members of different groups interact, the less intergroup conflict they will experience. Those interested in improving race, international, and union–management relations typically encourage cross-group interaction. The hope is that *any* type of interaction, short of actual conflict, will reduce stereotyping and combat in-group thinking. But research evidence has been mixed. A meta-analysis of 515 different studies did indeed support the contact hypothesis, with greater intergroup contact associated with less prejudice.[33] On the other hand, a field study of 83 health center employees (83% female) at a midwestern US university probed the specific nature of intergroup relations and concluded that

Example. the number of *negative* relationships was significantly related to higher perceptions of intergroup conflict. Thus, it seems that negative relationships have a salience that overwhelms any possible positive effects from friendship links across groups.[34]

Intergroup contact and friendships are still desirable, as documented in many studies,[35] but they are readily overpowered by negative intergroup interactions. Thus, *priority number one for managers faced with intergroup conflict is to identify and root out specific negative linkages among groups.* A single personality conflict, for instance, may contaminate the entire intergroup experience. The same goes for an employee who voices negative opinions or spreads negative rumors about another group. Our updated contact model in Figure 13–2 is based on this and other research insights, such as the need to foster positive attitudes toward other groups.

figure 13–2 An Updated Contact Model for Minimizing Intergroup Conflict

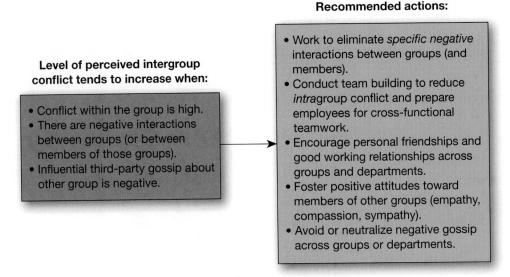

Level of perceived intergroup conflict tends to increase when:

- Conflict within the group is high.
- There are negative interactions between groups (or between members of those groups).
- Influential third-party gossip about other group is negative.

Recommended actions:

- Work to eliminate *specific negative* interactions between groups (and members).
- Conduct team building to reduce *intra*group conflict and prepare employees for cross-functional teamwork.
- Encourage personal friendships and good working relationships across groups and departments.
- Foster positive attitudes toward members of other groups (empathy, compassion, sympathy).
- Avoid or neutralize negative gossip across groups or departments.

SOURCES: Based on research evidence in G Labianca, D J Brass, and B Gray, "Social Networks and Perceptions of Intergroup Conflict: The Role of Negative Relationships and Third Parties," *Academy of Management Journal,* February 1998, pp 55–67; C D Batson et al., "Empathy and Attitudes: Can Feeling for a Member of a Stigmatized Group Improve Feelings toward the Group?" *Journal of Personality and Social Psychology,* January 1997, pp 105–18; and S C Wright et al., "The Extended Contact Effect: Knowledge of Cross-Group Friendships and Prejudice," *Journal of Personality and Social Psychology,* July 1997, pp 73–90.

Also, notice how conflict within the group and negative gossip from third parties are threats that need to be neutralized if intergroup conflict is to be minimized.[36]

 LO.6 Cross-Cultural Conflict

Doing business with people from different cultures is commonplace in our global economy where cross-border mergers, joint ventures, and alliances are the order of the day.[37] Because of differing assumptions about how to think and act, the potential for cross-cultural conflict is both immediate and huge.[38] Success or failure, when conducting business across cultures, often hinges on avoiding and minimizing actual or perceived conflict. For example, consider this cultural mismatch:

Example. Mexicans place great importance on saving face, so they tend to expect any conflicts that occur during negotiations to be downplayed or kept private. The prevailing attitude in the [United States], however, is that conflict should be dealt with directly and publicly to prevent hard feelings from developing on a personal level.[39]

This is not a matter of who is right and who is wrong; rather it is a matter of accommodating cultural differences for a successful business transaction. Awareness of the GLOBE project's cross-cultural dimensions, discussed in Chapter 4, is an important first step. Stereotypes also need to be identified and neutralized. Beyond that, cross-cultural conflict can be moderated by using international consultants and building cross-cultural relationships.

International Consultants   In response to broad demand, there is a growing army of management consultants specializing in cross-cultural relations. Competency and fees vary widely, of course. But a carefully selected cross-cultural consultant can be helpful, as this illustration shows:

Example. When electronics-maker Canon planned to set up a subsidiary in Dubai through its Netherlands division, it asked consultant Sahid Mirza of Glocom, based in Dubai, to find out how the two cultures would work together.

Mirza sent out the test questionnaires and got a sizeable response. "The findings were somewhat surprising," he recalls. "We found that, at the bedrock level, there were relatively few differences. Many of the Arab businessmen came from former British colonies and viewed business in much the same way as the Dutch."

But at the level of behavior, there was a real conflict. "The Dutch are blunt and honest in expression, and such expression is very offensive to Arab sensibilities." . . . As a result of Mirza's research, Canon did start the subsidiary in Dubai, but it trained both the Dutch and the Arab executives first.[40]

Consultants also can help untangle possible personality and intergroup conflicts from conflicts rooted in differing national cultures. *Note:* Although we have discussed these three basic types of conflict separately, they typically are encountered in complex, messy bundles.

Building Cross-Cultural Relationships to Avoid Dysfunctional Conflict

Rosalie L Tung's study of 409 expatriates from US and Canadian multinational firms is very instructive.[41] Her survey sought to pinpoint success factors for the expatriates (14% female) who were working in 51 different countries worldwide. Nine specific ways to facilitate interaction with host-country nationals, as ranked from most useful to least useful by the respondents, are listed in Table 13–2. Good listening skills topped the list, followed by sensitivity to others and cooperativeness rather than competitiveness. Interestingly, US managers are

During this session of a recent World Economic Forum in Switzerland, we see representatives from Japan, India, China, and France tackling the global economy. Conflict is inevitable in cross-cultural dealings such as this because of differing world views, cultures, languages, and political interests.

table 13–2 Ways to Build Cross-Cultural Relationships

BEHAVIOR	RANK
Be a good listener	1
Be sensitive to needs of others	2
Be cooperative, rather than overly competitive	2
Advocate inclusive (participative) leadership	3
Compromise rather than dominate	4
Build rapport through conversations	5
Be compassionate and understanding	6
Avoid conflict by emphasizing harmony	7
Nurture others (develop and mentor)	8

(The ranks 2 and 2 are marked as a Tie.)

SOURCE: Adapted from R L Tung, "American Expatriates Abroad: From Neophytes to Cosmopolitans," *Journal of World Business,* Summer 1998, table 6, p 136. © 1998, with permission from Elsevier.

culturally characterized as just the opposite: poor listeners, blunt to the point of insensitivity, and excessively competitive. Some managers need to add self-management and cultural intelligence to the list of ways to minimize cross-cultural conflict.[42]

TO THE POINT

How can managers stimulate functional conflict, manage dysfunctional conflict, and avoid conflict triangles?

Managing Conflict

As we have seen, conflict has many faces and is a constant challenge for managers who are responsible for reaching organizational goals. Our attention now turns to the active management of both functional and dysfunctional conflict. We discuss how to stimulate functional conflict, how to handle dysfunctional conflict, and how third parties can deal effectively with conflict. Relevant research lessons also are examined.

 LO.7 ## Stimulating Functional Conflict

Sometimes committees and decision-making groups become so bogged down in details and procedures that nothing useful is accomplished. Carefully monitored functional conflict can help get the creative juices flowing once again. Managers basically have two options. They can fan the fires of naturally occurring conflict—but this approach can be unreliable and slow. Alternatively, managers can resort to programmed conflict.[43] Experts in the field define **programmed conflict** as "conflict that raises different opinions *regardless of the personal feelings of the managers.*"[44] The trick is to get contributors to either defend or criticize ideas based on relevant facts rather than on the basis of personal preference or political interests. This requires disciplined role playing. Two programmed conflict techniques with proven track records are devil's advocacy and the dialectic method. Let us explore these two ways of stimulating functional conflict.

Devil's Advocacy   This technique gets its name from a traditional practice within the Roman Catholic Church. When someone's name came before the College of Cardinals for elevation to sainthood, it was absolutely essential to ensure that he or she had a spotless record. Consequently, one individual was assigned the role of *devil's advocate* to uncover and air all possible objections to the person's canonization. In accordance with this practice, **devil's advocacy** in today's organizations involves assigning someone the role of critic.[45] Recall from Chapter 10, Irving Janis recommended the devil's advocate role for preventing groupthink.

In the left half of Figure 13–3, note how devil's advocacy alters the usual decision-making process in steps 2 and 3. This approach to programmed conflict is intended to generate critical thinking and reality testing.[46] It is a good idea to rotate the job of devil's advocate so no one person or group develops a strictly negative reputation. Moreover, periodic devil's advocacy role-playing is good training for developing analytical and communication skills and emotional intelligence.

The Dialectic Method   Like devil's advocacy, the dialectic method is a time-honored practice. This particular approach to programmed conflict traces back to the dialectic school of philosophy in ancient Greece. Plato and his followers attempted to synthesize truths by exploring opposite positions (called *thesis* and *antithesis*). Court systems in the United States and elsewhere rely on directly opposing points of view for determining guilt or innocence. Accordingly, today's **dialectic method** calls for managers to foster a structured debate of opposing viewpoints prior to making a decision.[47] Steps 3 and 4 in the right half of Figure 13–3 set the dialectic approach apart from the normal decision-making process. For

figure 13–3   Techniques for Stimulating Functional Conflict: Devil's Advocacy and the Dialectic Method

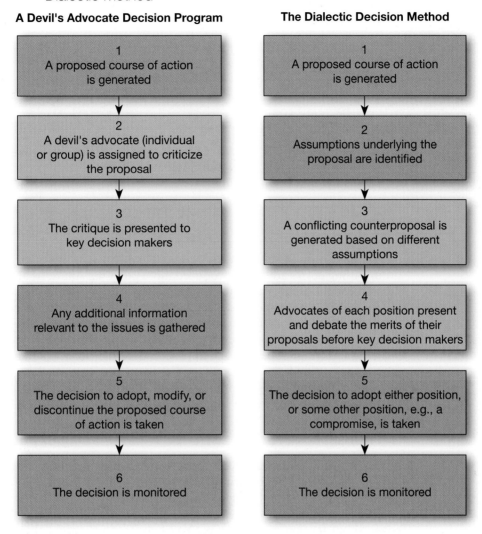

A Devil's Advocate Decision Program

1
A proposed course of action is generated

2
A devil's advocate (individual or group) is assigned to criticize the proposal

3
The critique is presented to key decision makers

4
Any additional information relevant to the issues is gathered

5
The decision to adopt, modify, or discontinue the proposed course of action is taken

6
The decision is monitored

The Dialectic Decision Method

1
A proposed course of action is generated

2
Assumptions underlying the proposal are identified

3
A conflicting counterproposal is generated based on different assumptions

4
Advocates of each position present and debate the merits of their proposals before key decision makers

5
The decision to adopt either position, or some other position, e.g., a compromise, is taken

6
The decision is monitored

SOURCE: From R A Cosier and C R Schwenk, "Agreement and Thinking Alike: Ingredients for Poor Decisions," *Academy of Management Executive,* February 1990, pp 72–73. Copyright © 1990 by The Academy of Management. Reproduced by permission of The Academy of Management via Copyright Clearance Center.

an example of the dialectic method in action, see Real World/Real People on page 380.

A major drawback of the dialectic method is that "winning the debate" may overshadow the issue at hand. Also, the dialectic method requires more skill training than does devil's advocacy. Regarding the comparative effectiveness of these two approaches to stimulating functional conflict, however, a laboratory study ended in a tie. Compared with groups that strived to reach a consensus, decision-making groups using either devil's advocacy or the dialectic method yielded equally higher quality decisions.[48] But in a more recent laboratory study,

programmed conflict Encourages different opinions without protecting management's personal feelings.

devil's advocacy Assigning someone the role of critic.

dialectic method Fostering a debate of opposing viewpoints to better understand an issue.

real WORLD // real PEOPLE

How Toro Mows Down Bad Ideas

Toro, the $1.8 billion lawn-mower giant, knows how to curb the urge to merge. Anytime an M&A [merger and acquisition] pitch reaches the desk of CEO Mike Hoffman, he asks a due-diligence group to make the case to the company's board. But he also turns to the "contra team"—half a dozen vice presidents and directors—to deliver the voice of dissent. According to chairman Ken Melrose . . . a few years ago the contras killed an eight-figure acquisition of a manufacturer that had pitched itself as a turnaround success. The contras' number crunching showed that its sector was facing a slump. The prospect's revenues have since tanked, while Toro has nearly doubled its sales. "Naysaying in corporate America isn't popular," Melrose says. "The contra team is a way to create negative views that are in the shareholders' best interest and the company's best interest."

What factors can limit the effectiveness of this technique?

SOURCE: Excerpted from P Kaihla, "Toro: The Contra Team," *Business 2.0,* April 2006, p 83.

---

groups using devil's advocacy produced more potential solutions and made better recommendations for a case problem than did groups using the dialectic method.[49]

In light of this mixed evidence, managers have some latitude in using either devil's advocacy or the dialectic method for pumping creative life back into stalled deliberations. Personal preference and the role players' experience may well be the deciding factors in choosing one approach over the other. The important thing is to actively stimulate functional conflict when necessary, such as when the risk of blind conformity or groupthink is high. Joseph M Tucci, the CEO of EMC introduced previously, fosters functional conflict by creating a supportive climate for dissent:

Example. Good leaders always leave room for debate and different opinions. . . .

The team has to be in harmony. But before you move out, there needs to be a debate. Leadership is not a right. You have to earn it. . . .

Every company needs a healthy paranoia. It's the CEO's job to keep it on the edge, to put tension in the system. You have to do the right thing for the right circumstances.[50]

This meshes well with the results of a pair of laboratory studies that found a positive relationship between the degree of minority dissent and team innovation, *but only when participative decision making was used.*[51]

Back to the Chapter-Opening Case

How could Lowrie Beacham have used programmed conflict to turn his employees' resistance to critical feedback into functional conflict?

Alternative Styles for Handling Dysfunctional Conflict

People tend to handle negative conflict in patterned ways referred to as *styles.* Several conflict styles have been categorized over the years. According to conflict

figure 13–4 Five Conflict-Handling Styles

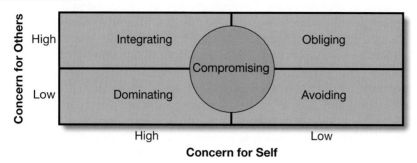

SOURCE: From M Afzalur Rahim, "A Strategy for Managing Conflict in Complex Organizations," *Human Relations,* January 1985, p 84. Copyright © 1985, The Tavistock Institute.

specialist Afzalur Rahim's model, five different conflict-handling styles can be plotted on a 2 × 2 grid. High to low concern for *self* is found on the horizontal axis of the grid, while low to high concern for *others* forms the vertical axis (see Figure 13–4). Various combinations of these variables produce the five different conflict-handling styles: integrating, obliging, dominating, avoiding, and compromising.[52] There is no single best style; each has strengths and limitations and is subject to situational constraints.

Integrating (Problem Solving)

In this style, interested parties confront the issue and cooperatively identify the problem, generate and weigh alternative solutions, and select a solution.[53] Integrating is appropriate for complex issues plagued by misunderstanding. However, it is inappropriate for resolving conflicts rooted in opposing value systems. Its primary strength is its longer lasting impact because it deals with the underlying problem rather than merely with symptoms. The primary weakness of this style is that it is very time consuming.

Obliging (Smoothing)

"An obliging person neglects his or her own concern to satisfy the concern of the other party."[54] This style, often called *smoothing,* involves playing down differences while emphasizing commonalities. Obliging may be an appropriate conflict-handling strategy when it is possible to eventually get something in return. But it is inappropriate for complex or worsening problems. Its primary strength is that it encourages cooperation.[55] Its main weakness is that it's a temporary fix that fails to confront the underlying problem.

Dominating (Forcing)

High concern for self and low concern for others encourages "I win, you lose" tactics. The other party's needs are largely ignored. This style is often called *forcing* because it relies on formal authority to force compliance. Dominating is appropriate when an unpopular solution must be implemented, the issue is minor, a deadline is near, or a crisis looms. It can be awkward in an open and participative climate. Speed is its primary strength. The primary weakness of this domineering style is that it often breeds resentment. Interestingly, the National Center for Women and Policing cites this particular conflict-handling style as a reason for hiring more women.

Example. Women are 12.7% of the personnel in large police departments but account for 2% of excessive-force cases that are upheld. . . . The findings support their contention that women's negotiating and communication skills should prompt police departments to hire more women.[56]

Avoiding This tactic may involve either passive withdrawal from the problem or active suppression of the issue. Avoidance is appropriate for trivial issues or when the costs of confrontation outweigh the benefits of resolving the conflict. It is inappropriate for difficult and worsening problems. The main strength of this style is that it buys time in unfolding or ambiguous situations. The primary weakness is that the tactic provides a temporary fix that sidesteps the underlying problem.

Compromising This is a give-and-take approach involving moderate concern for both self and others. Compromise is appropriate when parties have opposite goals or possess equal power. But compromise is inappropriate when overuse would lead to inconclusive action (e.g., failure to meet important deadlines). The primary strength of this tactic is that it has no disgruntled losers, but it's a temporary fix that can stifle creative problem solving.

 LO.8 Third-Party Interventions

In a perfect world, people would creatively avoid conflict and handle actual conflicts directly and positively. Dream on! Organizational politics being what they are, we can find ourselves as unwilling (and often unready) third parties to someone else's conflict. Thus, a working knowledge of conflict triangles and alternative dispute resolution techniques, the focus of this section, is essential to effective management today.

Conflict Triangles Remember Annie, the Amazon.com manager at the start of this chapter? Her busy day was interrupted by her co-worker Laura's tale of a conflict situation. Laura was recruiting Annie to help settle the situation. This is a classic conflict triangle. A **conflict triangle** "occurs when two people are having a problem and, instead of addressing the problem directly with each other, one of them gets a third person involved."[57] As discussed under the heading of organizational politics in Chapter 15, employees tend to form political *coalitions* because there is power in numbers. In Annie's case, Laura was engaged in a not-so-subtle attempt to gang up against her adversary Hans. Moreover, Laura was using Annie to vent her pent-up frustrations. This is a common and often very disruptive situation in today's organizations. The question is, What to do?

connect Go to www.mcgrawhillconnect.com for a comprehension case on managing conflict and negotiation.

Those finding themselves in conflict triangles have a wide range of options, according to experts on the subject. Figure 13–5 shows how responses can promote either functional or dysfunctional conflict. Preferred options 1 and 2, called *detriangling,* involve the third-party channeling the disputants' energy in a direct and positive manner toward each other. Importantly, the third party avoids becoming part of a political coalition in options 1 and 2. Options 3 through 8 can be a slippery slope toward further counterproductive triangling. Also, political and ethical implications multiply as the third party progresses to option 3 and beyond.

Alternative Dispute Resolution (ADR) Disputes between employees, between employees and their employer, and between companies too often end up in lengthy and costly court battles. For example, while discussing the steady rise in wrongful termination lawsuits, one business writer cited these figures: "A company can easily spend $100,000 to get a meritless lawsuit tossed out before trial. And if a case goes to a jury, the fees skyrocket to $300,000, and often much higher."[58] A more constructive, less expensive approach called *alternative dispute resolution* has enjoyed enthusiastic growth in recent years.[59] In fact, the widely imitated *People's Court*–type television shows operating outside the formal judicial system are part of this trend toward what one writer calls

The Three Stooges (Larry, Moe, and Curly) provided raucous laughs about how **not** to handle conflict triangles. Don't become a stooge by being drawn into someone else's conflict.

figure 13–5 Third-Party Intervention Options for Handling Conflict Triangles

Detriangling
(least political; low
risk of dysfunctional
conflict)

More triangling
(most political; high
risk of dysfunctional
conflict)

1. Reroute complaints by coaching the sender to find ways to constructively bring up the matter with the receiver. Do not carry messages for the sender.
2. Facilitate a meeting with the sender and receiver to coach them to speak directly and constructively with each other.
3. Transmit verbatim messages with the sender's name included and coach the receiver on constructive ways to discuss the message with the sender.
4. Carry the message verbatim but protect the sender's name.
5. Soften the message to protect the sender.
6. Add your spin to the message to protect the sender.
7. Do nothing. The participants will triangle in someone else.
8. Do nothing and spread the gossip. You will triangle in others.

SOURCE: List of options excerpted from P Ruzich, "Triangles: Tools for Untangling Interpersonal Messes," *HR Magazine*, July 1999, p 134.

"do-it-yourself justice."[60] **Alternative dispute resolution** (ADR), according to a pair of Canadian labor lawyers, "uses faster, more user-friendly methods of dispute resolution, instead of traditional, adversarial approaches (such as unilateral decision making or litigation)."[61] The following ADR techniques represent a progression of steps third parties can take to resolve organizational conflicts.[62] They are ranked from easiest and least expensive to most difficult and costly. A growing number of organizations have formal ADR policies involving an established sequence of various combinations of these techniques:

- *Facilitation.* A third party, usually a manager, informally urges disputing parties to deal directly with each other in a positive and constructive manner. This can be a form of detriangling, as discussed earlier.

- *Conciliation.* A neutral third party informally acts as a communication conduit between disputing parties. This is appropriate when conflicting parties refuse to meet face to face. The immediate goal is to establish direct communication, with the broader aim of finding common ground and a constructive solution.

- *Peer review.* A panel of trustworthy co-workers, selected for their ability to remain objective, hears both sides of a dispute in an informal and confidential meeting. Any decision by the review panel may or may not be binding, depending on the company's ADR policy. Membership on the peer review panel often is rotated among employees.

- *Ombudsman.* Someone who works for the organization, and is widely respected and trusted by his or her co-workers, hears grievances on a confidential basis, and attempts to arrange a solution. This approach, more common in Europe than North America, permits someone to get help from above without relying on the formal hierarchy chain.

- *Mediation.* "The mediator—a trained, third-party neutral—actively guides the disputing parties in exploring innovative solutions to the conflict. Although some companies have in-house mediators who have received

conflict triangle Conflicting parties involve a third person rather than dealing directly with each other.

alternative dispute resolution
Avoiding costly lawsuits by resolving conflicts informally or through mediation or arbitration.

ADR training, most also use external mediators who have no ties to the company."[63] Unlike an arbitrator, a mediator does *not* render a decision. It is up to the disputants to reach a mutually acceptable decision.

- *Arbitration.* Disputing parties agree ahead of time to accept the decision of a neutral arbitrator in a formal courtlike setting, often complete with evidence and witnesses. Participation in this form of ADR can be voluntary or mandatory, depending on company policy or union contracts.[64] Statements are confidential. Decisions are based on legal merits. Trained arbitrators, typically from outside agencies such as the American Arbitration Association, are versed in relevant laws and case precedents.[65]

Practical Lessons from Conflict Research

Laboratory studies, relying on college students as subjects, uncovered the following insights about organizational conflict:

- People with a high need for affiliation tended to rely on a smoothing (obliging) style while avoiding a forcing (dominating) style.[66] Thus, personality traits affect how people handle conflict.

- Disagreement expressed in an arrogant and demeaning manner produced significantly more negative effects than the same sort of disagreement expressed in a reasonable manner.[67] In other words, *how* you disagree with someone is very important in conflict situations.

- Threats and punishment, by one party in a disagreement, tended to produce intensifying threats and punishment from the other party.[68] In short, aggression breeds aggression.

- As conflict increased, group satisfaction decreased. An integrative style of handling conflict led to higher group satisfaction than did an avoidance style.[69]

- A recent study of 252 MBA students (27% female) broken up into 65 self-managing teams underscored the importance of taking a proactive rather than reactive approach to conflict resolution. Each team pooled their talents for 40% of their grade across four core courses during one semester. According to the researchers, the more successful teams were more proactive: "they make decisions about group resources (time, member skills, materials, etc.) in a way that integrates individual interests by identifying issues and creating solutions to potential conflicts before they arise."[70] The less successful teams tended to reactively make decisions looking backward instead of toward the future. Thus, the old saying "an ounce of prevention is worth a pound of cure" is true when it comes to dysfunctional conflict.

- Companies with mandatory or binding arbitration policies were viewed *less* favorably than companies without such policies.[71] Apparently, mandatory or binding arbitration policies are a turn-off for job applicants who dislike the idea of being forced to do something.

Field studies involving managers and real organizations have given us the following insights:

- Both intradepartmental and interdepartmental conflict decreased as goal difficulty and goal clarity increased. Thus, challenging and clear goals can defuse conflict.

- Higher levels of conflict tended to erode job satisfaction and internal work motivation.[72]

- Men and women at the same managerial level tended to handle conflict similarly. In short, there was no gender effect.[73]

- Conflict tended to move around the organization in a case study of a public school system.[74] Thus, managers need to be alerted to the fact that conflict often originates in one area or level and becomes evident somewhere else. Conflict needs to be traced back to its source if there is to be lasting improvement.

- Samples of Japanese, German, and American managers who were presented with the same conflict scenario preferred different resolution techniques. Japanese and German managers did not share the Americans' enthusiasm for integrating the interests of all parties. The Japanese tended to look upward to management for direction, whereas the Germans were more bound by rules and regulations. In cross-cultural conflict resolution, there is no one best approach. Culture-specific preferences need to be taken into consideration prior to beginning the conflict resolution process.[75]

As we transition from conflict to negotiation, take a short break from your reading and reflect on how you can better handle any conflicts in your daily life. Think win–win. Stephen Covey, author of the perennial best seller *The 7 Habits of Highly Effective People,* recently offered this advice:

Example. Opposing parties usually come to the table with two contrasting solutions. The gap between them could be immense. So I've always counseled parties to come up with a third solution that's better than those already proposed—one that can help both sides achieve at least a piece of what they want.[76]

LO.9 Negotiation

Formally defined, **negotiation** is a give-and-take decision-making process involving interdependent parties with different preferences.[77] Common examples include labor–management negotiations over wages, hours, and working conditions and negotiations between supply chain specialists and vendors involving price, delivery schedules, and credit terms. Self-managed work teams with overlapping task boundaries also need to rely on negotiated agreements. Negotiating skills are more important today than ever[78] (see Real World/Real People on page 386). In fact, in a recent survey of 3,600 professional employees in 18 countries, only 52% said yes to the question, "Have you ever asked for or negotiated a pay raise?"[79]

Two Basic Types of Negotiation

Negotiation experts distinguish between two types of negotiation—*distributive* and *integrative.* Understanding the difference requires a change in traditional fixed-pie thinking:

Example. A *distributive* negotiation usually involves a single issue—a "fixed-pie"—in which one person gains at the expense of the other. For example, haggling over the price of a rug in a bazaar is a distributive negotiation. In most conflicts, however, more than one issue is at stake, and each party values the issues differently. The outcomes available are no longer a fixed-pie divided among

TO THE POINT

What are the two types of negotiation, and what does added-value negotiation involve?

Legendary investor Warren Buffett, seen here chatting with his daughter Suzie during a Berkshire Hathaway annual stockholders' meeting in Omaha, is a world-class negotiator who prefers win–win outcomes.

negotiation Give-and-take process between conflicting interdependent parties.

real WORLD // real PEOPLE

Sallie Credille Believes Everything Is Negotiable

Whether it's buying a cell phone, setting up cable service, or even paying an electric bill, Credille says she almost always bargains to get a better deal.

Credille, a marketing specialist based in Auburn, Alabama, says she's probably saved about $500 in the last five years through her negotiations, which include landing a lower price on a BlackBerry Storm cell phone and getting a power supplier to eliminate a service-transfer fee when she switched apartments in her native Atlanta.

Credille says she thinks she's been able to work out a deal with service providers about 50% of the time. It takes persistence though. Credille says she often has to call multiple representatives at a company before getting the response she's looking for.

"I've had circumstances where they just will not budge."

But often providers will budge, because they don't want to lose your business to a competitor.

How good a negotiator are you on an everyday basis? What holds you back if you're not?

SOURCE: J Berman, "Negotiate Your Way to Savings," *USA Today*, July 30, 2010, p 3B.

---

all parties. An agreement can be found that is better for both parties than what they would have reached through distributive negotiation. This is an *integrative* negotiation.

However, parties in a negotiation often don't find these beneficial trade-offs because each *assumes* its interests *directly* conflict with those of the other party. "What is good for the other side must be bad for us" is a common and unfortunate perspective that most people have. This is the mind-set we call the *mythical* "fixed-pie."[80]

Distributive negotiation involves traditional win–lose thinking. Integrative negotiation calls for a progressive win–win strategy.[81] In a laboratory study of joint venture negotiations, teams trained in integrative tactics achieved better outcomes for *both* sides than did untrained teams.[82] North American negotiators too often are short-term oriented and inadequate relationship builders when negotiating in Asia, Latin America, and the Middle East.[83] The added-value negotiation technique illustrated in Figure 13–6 is an integrative approach that can correct these shortcomings.

Meanwhile, patience and persistence are needed because, according to a negotiation expert, it takes around 800 hours of practice to become a top-notch bargainer.[84] Another negotiation specialist recommends doing the necessary homework prior to negotiating, citing the "Golden Rule of Negotiation: Information Is Power—So Get It!"[85]

"Never, EVER purr during the negotiating process, Derwood!"

Ethical Pitfalls in Negotiation

The success of integrative negotiation, such as added-value negotiation, hinges to a large extent on the *quality* of information exchanged, as researchers have documented.[86] Telling lies, hiding key facts, and engaging in the other potentially unethical tactics listed in Table 13–3 erode trust and goodwill, both vital in win–win negotiations.[87] An

figure 13–6 An Integrative Approach: Added-Value Negotiation

Separately	**Jointly**
Step 1: Clarify interests	
• Identify tangible and intangible needs	• Discuss respective needs • Find *common ground* for negotiation
Step 2: Identify options	
• Identify *elements of value* (e.g., property, money, behavior, rights, risks)	• Create a *marketplace of value* by discussing respective elements of value
Step 3: Design alternative deal packages	
• Mix and match *elements of value* in various workable combinations • Think in terms of *multiple deals*	• Exchange *deal packages*
Step 4: Select a deal	
• Analyze deal packages proposed by other party	• Discuss and select from feasible deal packages • Think in terms of *creative agreement*
Step 5: Perfect the deal	
	• Discuss unresolved issues • Develop written agreement • *Build relationships* for future negotiations

SOURCE: From K Albrecht and S Albrecht, "Added Value Negotiating," *Training,* April 1993, pp 26–29. Used with permission of Nielsen Business Media.

awareness of these dirty tricks can keep good faith bargainers from being unfairly exploited.[88] Unethical negotiating tactics need to be factored into organizational codes of ethics.

Practical Lessons from Negotiation Research

Laboratory and field studies have yielded these insights:

- Negotiators with fixed-pie expectations produced poor joint outcomes because they restricted and mismanaged information.[89]

- A meta-analysis of 62 studies found a *slight* tendency for women to negotiate more cooperatively than men. But when faced with an "apples-for-apples" bargaining strategy (equivalent countermoves), women were significantly more competitive than men.[90]

- Personality characteristics can affect negotiating success. Negotiators who scored high on the Big Five personality dimensions of extraversion and agreeableness (refer back to Table 5–2) tended to do poorly with distributive (fixed-pie; win–lose) negotiations.[91]

- Good and bad moods can have positive and negative effects, respectively, on negotiators' plans and outcomes.[92] So wait until both you and your boss are in a good mood before you ask for a raise.

table 13-3 Questionable/Unethical Tactics in Negotiation

TACTIC	DESCRIPTION/CLARIFICATION/RANGE
Lies	Subject matter for lies can include limits, alternatives, the negotiator's intent, authority to bargain, other commitments, acceptability of the opponent's offers, time pressures, and available resources.
Puffery	Among the items that can be puffed up are the value of one's payoffs to the opponent, the negotiator's own alternatives, the costs of what one is giving up or is prepared to yield, importance of issues, and attributes of the products or services.
Deception	Acts and statements may include promises or threats, excessive initial demands, careless misstatements of facts, or asking for concessions not wanted.
Weakening the opponent	The negotiator here may cut off or eliminate some of the opponent's alternatives, blame the opponent for his own actions, use personally abrasive statements to or about the opponent, or undermine the opponent's alliances.
Strengthening one's own position	This tactic includes building one's own resources, including expertise, finances, and alliances. It also includes presentations of persuasive rationales to the opponent or third parties (e.g., the public, the media) or getting mandates for one's position.
Nondisclosure	Includes partial disclosure of facts, failure to disclose a hidden fact, failure to correct the opponents' misperceptions or ignorance, and concealment of the negotiator's own position or circumstances.
Information exploitation	Information provided by the opponent can be used to exploit his weaknesses, close off his alternatives, generate demands against him, or weaken his alliances.
Change of mind	Includes accepting offers one had claimed one would not accept, changing demands, withdrawing promised offers, and making threats one promised would not be made. Also includes the failure to behave as predicted.
Distraction	These acts or statements can be as simple as providing excessive information to the opponent, asking many questions, evading questions, or burying the issue. Or they can be more complex, such as feigning weakness in one area so that the opponent concentrates on it and ignores another.
Maximization	Includes demanding the opponent make concessions that result in the negotiator's gain and the opponent's equal or greater loss. Also entails converting a win–win situation into win–lose.

SOURCE: Reprinted from H J Reitz, J A Wall Jr, and M S Love, "Ethics in Negotiation: Oil and Water or Good Lubrication?" *Business Horizons*, May–June 1998, p 6. © 1998, with permission from Elsevier.

- Subjects in a study trained in goal setting and problem solving enjoyed more satisfying and optimistic dialogues on a controversial subject than did those with no particular strategy.[93] Practical implication: don't negotiate without being adequately prepared.
- Studies of negotiations between Japanese, between Americans, and between Japanese and Americans found less productive joint outcomes across cultures than within cultures.[94] Less understanding of the other party makes cross-cultural negotiation more difficult than negotiations at home.

Conflict Management and Negotiation: A Contingency Approach

◀ ....

TO THE POINT

What are the practical lessons from the contingency approach to conflict management and negotiation?

....

Three realities dictate how organizational conflict should be managed. First, various types of conflict are inevitable because they are triggered by a wide variety of antecedents. Second, too little conflict may be as counterproductive as too much. Third, there is no single best way of avoiding or resolving conflict. Consequently, conflict specialists recommend a contingency approach to managing conflict. Antecedents of conflict and actual conflict need to be monitored. If signs of too little conflict such as apathy or lack of creativity appear, then functional conflict needs to be stimulated. This can be done by nurturing appropriate antecedents of conflict or programming conflict with techniques such as devil's advocacy and the dialectic method. On the other hand, when conflict becomes dysfunctional, the appropriate conflict-handling style needs to be used. Realistic training involving role-playing can prepare managers to try alternative conflict-handling styles.

Managers can keep from getting too deeply embroiled in conflict by applying four lessons from recent research: (1) establish challenging and clear goals, (2) disagree in a constructive and reasonable manner, (3) do not get caught up in conflict triangles, and (4) refuse to get caught in the aggression-breeds-aggression spiral.

Third-party interventions are necessary when conflicting parties are unwilling or unable to engage in conflict resolution or integrative negotiation. Integrative or added-value negotiation is most appropriate for intergroup and interorganizational conflict. The key is to get the conflicting parties to abandon traditional fixed-pie thinking and their win–lose expectations. Moreover, Daniel Shapiro, founder and head of the Harvard International Negotiation Program, advises negotiators not to shy away from emotions and emotional issues because rationality is important but not enough. The following core emotional elements of negotiation need to be addressed:

McGraw Hill **connect**™ Go to
www.mcgrawhillconnect.com
for a video case on how
Starbucks manages conflict
and negotiation.

- *Appreciation*: acknowledge that each other's thoughts, feelings, and actions have merit.
- *Affiliation*: treat each other as colleagues rather than as adversaries to be kept at a distance.
- *Autonomy*: respect each other's freedom to make important decisions.
- *Status*: recognize each other's standing instead of viewing the other person as inferior.
- *Role*: define your roles and activities in a fulfilling way.[95]

Come to think of it, this is sound advice for everyday life!

Summary of Key Concepts

1. *Define the term* conflict, *and put the three metaphors of conflict into proper perspective for the workplace.* Conflict is a process in which one party perceives that its interests are being opposed or negatively affected by another party. Conflict is inevitable but not necessarily destructive. Metaphorically, conflict can be viewed as war (win at all costs), an opportunity (be creative, grow, and improve), or a journey (a search for common ground and a better way). Within organizations, we are challenged to see conflicts as win–win opportunities and journeys rather than as win–lose wars.

2. *Distinguish between functional and dysfunctional conflict, and discuss why people avoid conflict.* Functional conflict

enhances organizational interests while dysfunctional conflict is counterproductive. Three desired conflict outcomes are agreement, stronger relationships, and learning. People avoid conflict because of the following fears: harm, rejection, loss of relationship, anger, being seen as selfish, saying the wrong thing, failing, hurting someone else, getting what we want, and intimacy.

3. *List six antecedents of conflict, and identify the desired outcomes of conflict.* Among the many antecedents of conflict are incompatible personalities or value systems; competition for limited resources; inadequate communication; unreasonable or unclear policies, standards, or rules; unreasonable deadlines or extreme time pressure; collective decision making; unmet expectations; and unresolved or suppressed conflicts. The three desired outcomes of conflict are agreement, stronger relationships, and learning.

4. *Define* personality conflicts, *and explain how managers should handle them.* Personality conflicts involve interpersonal opposition based on personal dislike or disagreement (or as an outgrowth of workplace incivility). Care needs to be taken with personality conflicts in the workplace because of the legal implications of diversity, anti-discrimination, and sexual harassment. Managers should investigate and document personality conflict, take corrective actions such as feedback or behavior modification if appropriate, or attempt informal dispute resolution. Difficult or persistent personality conflicts need to be referred to human resource specialists or counselors.

5. *Discuss the role of in-group thinking in intergroup conflict, and explain what management can do about intergroup conflict.* Members of in-groups tend to see themselves as unique individuals who are more moral than outsiders, whom they view as a threat and stereotypically as all alike. In-group thinking is associated with ethnocentric behavior. According to the updated contact model, managers first must strive to eliminate negative relationships between conflicting groups. Beyond that, they need to provide team building, encourage personal friendships across groups, foster positive attitudes about other groups, and minimize negative gossip about groups.

6. *Discuss what can be done about cross-cultural conflict.* International consultants can prepare people from different cultures to work effectively together. Cross-cultural conflict can be minimized by having expatriates build strong cross-cultural relationships with their hosts (primarily by being good listeners, being sensitive to others, and being more cooperative than competitive).

7. *Explain how managers can stimulate functional conflict, and identify the five conflict-handling styles.* There are many antecedents of conflict—including incompatible personalities, competition for limited resources, and unrealized expectations—that need to be monitored. Functional conflict can be stimulated by permitting antecedents of conflict to persist or programming conflict during decision making with devil's advocates or the dialectic method. The five conflict-handling styles are integrating (problem solving), obliging (smoothing), dominating (forcing), avoiding, and compromising. There is no single best style.

8. *Explain the nature and practical significance of conflict triangles and alternative dispute resolution for third-party conflict intervention.* A conflict triangle occurs when one member of a conflict seeks the help of a third party rather than facing the opponent directly. Detriangling is advised, whereby the third party redirects the disputants' energy toward each other in a positive and constructive manner. Alternative dispute resolution involves avoiding costly court battles with more informal and user-friendly techniques such as facilitation, conciliation, peer review, ombudsman, mediation, and arbitration.

9. *Explain the difference between distributive and integrative negotiation, and discuss the concept of added-value negotiation.* Distributive negotiation involves fixed-pie and win–lose thinking. Integrative negotiation is a win–win approach to better results for both parties. The five steps in added-value negotiation are as follows: step 1, clarify interests; step 2, identify options; step 3, design alternative deal packages; step 4, select a deal; and step 5, perfect the deal. Elements of value, multiple deal packages, and creative agreement are central to this approach.

Key Terms

Conflict, 367	Day of contemplation, 373	Conflict triangle, 382
Functional conflict, 369	Programmed conflict, 378	Alternative dispute resolution, 383
Dysfunctional conflict, 369	Devil's advocacy, 378	Negotiation, 385
Personality conflict, 372	Dialectic method, 378	

OB in Action Case Study

Whitney Johnson: "I Lost the Friendship, Along with a Painful Amount of Money"[96]

I love hearing about—and investing in—other people's dreams. Unfortunately, my first foray into funding a fledgling dream became a living nightmare.

Several years ago, a friend came to me with her idea of starting a magazine. I thought she had a strong concept for an underrepresented topic in the women's lifestyle space—so much so that in addition to investing cash, I persuaded my husband to act as chief operating officer for the start-up.

As we negotiated the shareholder structure, I was fair to a fault. An entrepreneur friend had just watched his equity stake go through massive dilution when his venture backers increased the valuation of his company. With his experience fresh in my mind, I resolved not to become like those investors. So, notwithstanding my significantly larger contribution of cash (in both equity and unsecured loans) and my husband's contribution of effort, we agreed to be minority shareholders with limited rights. If the business worked, we had less upside. If it failed, we stood to lose far more. In retrospect, this was naive.

As we moved from idea to execution, I asked another friend to take a key role in the project. She told me repeatedly: You need to better articulate the business plan, especially the decision-making process. But I refused to listen. Pointing to the importance of discovery-driven planning, I told her that we would "figure it out." Because my husband and I were the providers of working capital, I had the luxury of being cavalier.

We got off to a great start: The magazine was written up in the *New York Times,* and after just a few months, circulation reached 100,000. But the success was short-lived. In neglecting to craft a detailed business plan, we had failed not only to chart a path to profitability but also to put in place the processes that would allow us to make tough decisions. Who had the final say on the strategic direction? Cover art? Budget? Print runs? Hiring? We were at loggerheads with our partner quite often, but thanks to the management and deal structure I had freely agreed to, my husband and I had little say in the critical decisions.

Because we hadn't hammered out exactly how we would operate, infighting distracted us, cash became a concern, and the business imploded. My husband and I lost the friendship, along with a painful amount of money.

Investing in an entrepreneur is a lot like falling in love. At first, we just see the best; only later do flaws and failings become apparent. No one's perfect, of course. But sometimes our partners' weaknesses in combination with our own constitute a deadly cocktail.

It would be disingenuous to say I have no regrets. This failure was dearly bought. It was a severe blow to both my ego and my bottom line. But the lessons I learned about setting boundaries and establishing rules of engagement were invaluable. I now invest more effectively in stocks and start-ups, as well as in people and their dreams.

Failure was worth every cent.

Questions for Discussion

1. Is this a case of too much dysfunctional conflict and not enough functional conflict? Explain.

2. Which antecedents of conflict are evident in this case? Which one likely caused the most problems? Explain.

3. What lessons about minimizing intergroup conflict (in Figure 13–2) could Whitney Johnson have applied to improve the situation?

4. Which conflict-handling style probably would have worked best for Whitney Johnson? Explain.

5. Would either mediation or arbitration have been appropriate in this case? Explain the process and implications.

6. How might the situation have been different if Johnson and her husband had used the added-value negotiation strategy in Figure 13–6 right from the start? Explain, step by step.

Legal/Ethical Challenge

Break It Up!

"At the company where I work—we make creative products for children—two of the top executives are at war with each other. They go off on rants, they use foul language, and from time to time they actually have shoving matches. Both of these men are top producers, I might add. What lies behind this behavior? And is there anything co-workers can do? We're appalled, but the boss won't step in."[97]

What is the right thing to do in this situation? What are the ethical implications for your choice?

1. These guys are simply high-spirited thoroughbreds who kick up some dust while helping us win the race. Just stay out of their way.

2. The good results these men get are more than offset by the negative impact their feud has on company productivity and morale. A coalition of employees needs to confront the boss with the facts and recommend corrective action.

3. In this obvious clash of personalities, one of these bullies must be fired. Or should the company fire both?

4. The boss is clueless, so someone needs to elevate the issue to the board of directors.

5. A brave co-worker who has the respect of these feuding men needs to take them aside for a little talk about workplace civility, to break the cycle of dysfunctional conflict. This would be a win–win option, where everyone could save face and upper management wouldn't be dragged into the fray.

6. Let's take sides in this feud and fight it out until there's a clear winner and loser.

7. Invent other options. Discuss.

Web Resources

For study material and exercises that apply to this chapter, visit our website at **www.mhhe.com/kreitner10e**

part four

Organizational Processes

chapter 14

Communicating in the Digital Age

 Learning Objectives

When you finish studying the material in this chapter, you should be able to:

LO.1 Explain the perceptual process model of communication, and describe the barriers to effective communication.

LO.2 Specify two major impacts of social media that are changing the general communication landscape.

LO.3 Contrast the communication styles of assertiveness, aggressiveness, and nonassertiveness.

LO.4 Discuss the primary sources of nonverbal communication.

LO.5 Review the five dominant listening styles and 10 keys to effective listening.

LO.6 Describe how linguistic styles vary for women and men and what can be done to improve everyone's communication effectiveness.

LO.7 Discuss the formal and informal communication channels.

LO.8 Explain the contingency approach to media selection.

LO.9 Describe the Internet generation, and discuss the pros and cons of teleworking.

LO.10 Specify practical tips for more effective e-mail and cell phone etiquette, and discuss policies for using social media Web sites in the workplace.

How Did Best Buy's CEO Brian Dunn Get Comfortable with Social Media?

A few years ago our chief marketing officer asked me to get into social media. He was ahead of the curve in realizing that a cultural transformation was happening. Best Buy has 180,000 employees, the majority of whom are 24 years old or younger—and so a lot of workers were on MySpace and other sites. I asked him how we could control it, and his answer was: You can't. You engage with it.

Soon, I began talking to employees and customers on Facebook every night at 10 o'clock. It was difficult to get over being self-conscious, since just tweeting about something I saw in a store opened myself up to vulnerability. The hardest part, though, was that once I decided to allocate the time to this, people started weighing in all over the place without context. Then, at one point last year, my Twitter account was hacked and one of my tweets basically said I'd been having a lot of great sex lately.

I felt violated, but it didn't diminish my enthusiasm. I learned a couple of lessons along the way. I can engage for 5 or 10 minutes and get a great sense of what's going on in our stores. But when I encounter someone online who's having a problem, I want to reach out and fix it myself. I did that once early on and suddenly I was inundated by others. I'd set myself up as an answer center, and that's not my job. We'll have more than 1.5 billion customer interactions this year, and we have great processes for helping customers. I realized the best thing I can do is point them to the resources. The same goes for my employees.

In my office, I now have a large monitor of all the activity where we're mentioned. I want to know what's out there. I don't have to respond to all of it, but I write everything on my Twitter and Facebook accounts myself—and I'm the one who's posting. I'm responsible for what I say online, and I expect the same of my employees. The only guideline is that they act within our values. You can engage with social media and get comfortable with the messiness of it. We're past the tipping point. You have to be where people are.[1]

Modern information technology is connecting us and transforming our lives in unprecedented ways. The experience of Best Buy's CEO Brian Dunn offers a glimpse of what is occurring in the workplace. There are positives, negatives, and unintended consequences of living in a 24/7 digitally connected world. So it is important for all of us to understand the underlying communication process and the dynamics of communicating as technology continues to evolve. For example, consider the organizational ripple effects of this recent mobile Internet deployment:

Example. Medical device maker Medtronic has given more than 5,000 iPads to its sales reps. And the day iPads came out, Medtronic bought 10, loaded them with product information and placed them at a booth during a cardiologist conference, stealing all the buzz that day. "We quickly realized the business value of enabling the sales force," says Medtronic chief information officer Mike Hedges.[2]

The study of communication is fundamentally important because every managerial function and activity involves some form of direct or indirect communication. Whether planning and organizing or directing and leading, managers find themselves communicating with and through others. This implies that everyone's communication skills affect both personal and organizational effectiveness.[3] For example, one study found that 70% of "preventable hospital mishaps" resulted from a lack of communication between employees, particularly during handoffs of patient care.[4] A survey of employees at 336 organizations revealed that 66% of the respondents did not know or understand their organization's mission and business strategy, which subsequently led them to feel disengaged at work. This sort of communication breakdown leads to lower productivity and product quality, and higher labor costs and turnover.[5] There is plenty of room for improvement, as evidenced by the American Management Association's 2010 Critical Skills Survey that polled 2,115 executives: "more than half (51.4%) . . . said their employees were only average in effective communications skills (versus 38.1% who rated them above average)."[6]

This chapter will help you to better understand how managers can both improve their communication skills and design more effective communication programs. We discuss (1) basic dimensions of the communication process, focusing on a perceptual process model, barriers to effective communication, and social media impacts; (2) interpersonal communication; (3) organizational communication; and (4) communicating in the digital information technology age.

••••••••••••••••••••▶

TO THE POINT
Why is knowledge of the basic communication process, barriers to communication, and impacts of social media essential for communicating more effectively in today's workplaces?
••••••••••••••••••••

Basic Dimensions of the Communication Process and Social Media Impacts

Communication is defined as "the exchange of information between a sender and a receiver, and the inference (perception) of meaning between the individuals involved."[7] Managers who understand this process can analyze their own communication patterns as well as design communication programs that fit organizational needs. This section reviews a perceptual process model of communication, discusses the barriers to effective communication, and explores how social media are affecting communication.

 LO.1 Perceptual Process Model of Communication

Historically, the communication process was described in terms of a conduit model. This model depicts communication as a pipeline in which information and meaning are transferred from person to person. Today, communication experts criticize the conduit model for being unrealistic. The conduit model assumes communication transfers *intended meanings* from person to person. If this assumption were true, miscommunication would not exist and there would be no need to worry about being misunderstood. We could simply say or write what we want and assume the listener or reader accurately understands our intended meaning.

As we all know, communicating is not that simple or clear-cut. Communication is fraught with misunderstanding. In recognition of this, researchers have begun to examine communication as a form of social information processing (recall the discussion in Chapter 7) in which receivers interpret messages by cognitively processing information. This view led to development of a **perceptual model of communication** that depicts communication as a process in which receivers create meaning in their own minds. Let us consider the parts of this process and then integrate them with an example.

Sender, Message, and Receiver   The sender is the person wanting to communicate information—the message—and the receiver is the person, group, or organization for whom the message is intended.

Encoding   Encoding entails translating thoughts into a code or language that can be understood by others. This forms the foundation of the message. For example, if a professor wants to inform students about an assignment, she must first think about what information she wants to communicate. Once the professor resolves this issue in her mind and encodes it into spoken or written words, she needs to select a medium for sharing the message. Word choice is very important because the English language, for one example, has upward of 1 million words.[8]

Selecting a Medium   Managers have a wide variety of media at their disposal. Typical media in organizations include face-to-face conversations, phone calls, e-mail, voice mail and text messages, videoconferencing, written memos or letters, photographs or drawings, live or virtual meetings, bulletin boards, computer output, social media exchanges, and charts or graphs. Choosing the appropriate medium depends on many factors, including the nature of the message, its intended purpose, the audience, proximity to the audience, time constraints, and personal skills and preferences.

All media have advantages and disadvantages. Face-to-face conversations, for instance, are useful for communicating about important or emotionally charged issues and those requiring immediate feedback and intensive interaction. Phones are convenient, fast, and sometimes private, but lack nonverbal information. Although writing memos or letters is time consuming, it is a good medium when it is difficult to meet with the other person, when formality and a written record are important, and when face-to-face interaction is not necessary to enhance understanding. We have more to say later about choosing media.

Decoding and Creating Meaning   Decoding occurs when receivers receive a message. It is the process of interpreting and making sense of a message (see Real World/Real People on page 398). Returning to our example of a professor communicating about an assignment, decoding would occur among students when they receive the message from the professor.

---

communication Interpersonal exchange of information and understanding.

perceptual model of communication Process in which receivers create their own meaning.

real WORLD // real PEOPLE

Navajo Language Became a WWII Secret Weapon in an Odd Twist of History

Keith Little and Frank Chee Willetto know time is no longer on their side.

That's why the men, World War II veterans who used a code based on the Navajo language to stump the Japanese in battles, spend their days reminding the world of their contribution to ending the war. . . .

The Japanese never broke the code [spoken by the 400 Navajo Code Talkers]. . . .

The irony that their language helped win the war is not lost on some of the men who attended government-run boarding schools where they were forbidden to speak Navajo.

"I had to chew yellow soap every time I got caught talking my own language," says Willetto. . . . "And then they used our language to come up with a code."

He says he isn't angry, though. He wants Americans to know the Navajo did their part and says a museum will show that.

Curse words aside, what code words and phrases do you use among friends that your parents and managers likely can't comprehend? Why does every new generation need to develop its own distinctive "lingo"?

SOURCE: Excerpted from M Bello, "Code Talkers' Legacy Decoded," *USA Today*, November 11, 2010, p 3A.

In contrast to the conduit model's assumption that senders give messages their meaning, the perceptual model says that *receivers* give messages their meaning. Intended meaning can be an elusive thing. Consider this cross-cultural experience of a *Wall Street Journal* reporter on assignment in China.

Example. I was riding the elevator a few weeks ago with a Chinese colleague here in the *Journal*'s Asian headquarters. I smiled and said, "Hi." She responded, "You've gained weight." I might have been appalled, but at least three other Chinese co-workers also have told me I'm fat. I probably should cut back on the pork dumplings. In China, such an intimate observation from a colleague isn't necessarily an insult. It's probably just friendliness.[9]

This example highlights how decoding and creating meaning are influenced by cultural norms and values.

Feedback   How often do you think you have lost your cell phone connection with the other person? Something like this usually occurs: "Hello, are you there?" "Can you hear me?" The other person may say back, "Yes, I can hear you, but you're fading in and out." This is an example of feedback; the sender gets a reaction from the receiver.

Noise   **Noise** represents anything that interferes with the transmission and understanding of a message. It can affect any part of the communication process. This broad definition of noise includes many situations such as a speech impairment or accent, poor telephone connection, illegible handwriting, bad photocopy, inaccurate statistics, lies, background sounds, poor hearing and eyesight, and physical distance between sender and receiver. Figure 14–1 provides an example of the perceptual communication process. Notice the cyclical nature of this exchange of meaning, as the sender becomes a receiver and so on.

figure 14–1 Communication Process in Action

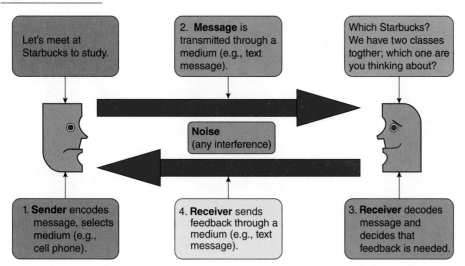

1. **Sender** encodes message, selects medium (e.g., cell phone).

2. **Message** is transmitted through a medium (e.g., text message).

3. **Receiver** decodes message and decides that feedback is needed.

4. **Receiver** sends feedback through a medium (e.g., text message).

Let's meet at Starbucks to study.

Which Starbucks? We have two classes togther; which one are you thinking about?

Noise (any interference)

Barriers to Effective Communication

There are two key components of effective communication. First, senders need to accurately communicate their intended message. Understanding is unlikely otherwise. Second, receivers need to correspondingly perceive and interpret the message accurately. Anything that gets in the way of the accurate transmission and reception of a message is a barrier to effective communication. It is important to be aware of and avoid these barriers when communicating.

Some barriers actually are part of the communication process itself (see Table 14–1). Communication will fail if any step in the communication process is disrupted or blocked. More broadly, three types of barriers are likely to impact communication effectiveness: (1) personal barriers, (2) physical barriers, and (3) semantic barriers.

Trying to communicate via cell phone while sitting in a café is likely to be affected by noise. The person's cell phone conversation can also represent noise to someone at the next table.

Personal Barriers   Have you ever communicated with someone and felt totally confused? This may have prompted you to wonder, "Is it him or is it me?" **Personal barriers** represent any individual attributes that hinder communication. Let us examine nine common personal barriers that foster miscommunication.

1. *Variable skills in communicating effectively.* Some people are simply better communicators than others. They may know one or more foreign languages.[10] They have the speaking and listening skills, the ability to use gestures for dramatic effect, the vocabulary to alter the message to fit the audience, the writing skills to convey concepts in simple and concise terms, and the social skills to make others feel comfortable. Others suffer for lack of these skills. Fortunately, practice and communication skills training can help.[11]

2. *Variations in how information is processed and interpreted.* Did you grow up in a rural setting, in the suburbs, or in a city? Did you attend private or public

table 14–1 Potential Breakdowns in the Communication Process Itself

- Sender barrier (e.g., forgetting to send a message, fearing to send a message, or procrastinating with a difficult message).

- Encoding barrier (e.g., poor language skills, poor word choice, or incomprehensible delivery).

- Medium barrier (e.g., faulty transmission, battery failure on wireless device, busy signal, shouting in a noisy place, or computer network failure).

- Decoding barrier (e.g., poor language skills; mixed signals from verbal and nonverbal messages; or failure to understand humor, slang, or technical jargon).

- Receiver barrier (e.g., no message received, unwillingness to receive message, or strong emotional reaction to message).

- Feedback barrier (e.g., blank stare, lack of verbal or written response, mixed signals from verbal and nonverbal messages).

school? What were your parents' attitudes about your doing chores and playing sports? Are you from a loving home or one marred with fighting, yelling, and lack of structure?

Answers to these questions are relevant because they make up the different frames of reference and experiences people use to interpret the world around them. As you may recall from Chapter 7, people selectively attend to various stimuli based on their unique frames of reference. This means that these differences affect our interpretations of what we see and hear.

3. *Variations in interpersonal trust.* Chapter 11 discussed the manner in which trust affects interpersonal relationships. Communication is more likely to be distorted when people do not trust each other.[12] Rather than focusing on the message, a lack of trust is likely to cause people to be defensive and question the accuracy of what is being communicated.

4. *Stereotypes and prejudices.* We noted in Chapter 7 that stereotypes are oversimplified beliefs about specific groups of people. They potentially distort communication because their use causes people to misperceive and filter information.[13] It is important for all of us to be aware of our stereotypes and to recognize that they may subconsciously affect the messages we send and how we interpret messages we receive.

5. *Big egos.* Our ego—whether due to pride, inflated self-esteem, superior ability, or arrogance—can be a major communication barrier. Inflated egos can cause political battles, turf wars, and overzealous pursuit of power, credit, and resources. Egos influence how we treat others as well as our receptiveness to being influenced by others. If you have ever been ridiculed or bullied in public, then you know how ego-related feelings can impact communication.

6. *Poor listening skills.* How many times have you been in class when one student asks the same question that was asked minutes earlier? How about going to a party and meeting a low self-monitoring person (as described in Chapter 5) who only talks about herself and shows little concern for you? This experience can be a major turnoff. Effective communication is unlikely when someone is not listening. Listening skills are discussed later in this chapter.

7. *Natural tendency to evaluate others' messages.* What do you say to someone after watching the latest movie in a theater? "What did you think of the movie?" He or she might reply, "It was great, best movie I've seen all year." You then may say, "I agree," or alternatively, "I disagree. I fell asleep three times." The point is that we all have a natural tendency, according to renowned psychologist Carl Rogers, to evaluate messages from our own point of view or frame of reference, particularly when we have strong feelings about the issue.[14]

8. *Inability to listen with understanding.* Listening with understanding occurs when a receiver can "see the expressed idea and attitude from the other person's point of view, to sense how it feels to him, to achieve his frame of reference in regard to the thing he is talking about."[15] Try to listen with understanding; it will make you less defensive and can improve your accuracy in perceiving messages.

9. *Nonverbal communication.* Communication accuracy is enhanced when one's facial expression and gestures are consistent with the intent of a message. Interestingly, people may not even be aware of their nonverbal messages. More is said about this important aspect of communication a bit later.

Physical Barriers: Sound, Time, Space, and More

Think about talking on a cell phone while standing in a busy area with traffic noise and people talking loudly next to you. Those are physical barriers. Other such barriers include time-zone differences, telephone-line static, distance from others, and crashed computers. Office design is another physical barrier, which is why more organizations are hiring experts to design facilities that promote open interactions, yet provide space for private meetings.

Semantic Barriers: When Words Matter

When your boss tells you, "We need to complete this project right away," what does it mean? Does "we" mean just you? You and your co-workers? Or you, your co-workers, and the boss? Does "right away" mean today, tomorrow, or next week? These are examples of semantic barriers. **Semantics** is the study of words.

Semantic barriers are more likely in today's global economy with its multicultural workforces. Their frequency also is fueled by foreign outsourcing, particularly to India. In response to complaints from American customers, Indian outsourcers such as Wipro have instituted training programs aimed at reducing cross-cultural semantic barriers:

Example. In an American-culture training class at Wipro, students identify Indian stereotypes (superstitious, religious, and helpful) and American stereotypes (sports-loving, punctual, not as knowledgeable about computers as they think). The point is to identify shallow images as barriers to good communication so they can be overcome.

The class reviews cultural differences—big and small. As a "high-context" culture where what is communicated is more internalized (say, in a family), Indians can seem to be beating around the bush to Americans, who are part of a low-context culture in which communications need to be more explicit. "If you like to talk and you're dealing with a low-context person," explains the instructor, Roger George, "you might want to keep it simple and get to the point."[16]

Jargon and buzzwords constitute another category of semantic barrier. **Jargon** represents language, acronyms, or terminology that is specific to a particular profession, group, or company. The use of acronyms has increased as our society has become more technologically oriented and pressed for time. (For example, "The CIO wants the RFP ASAP" means "The chief information officer wants to see the request for proposal as soon as possible.") *Buzzwords* are overused words or

semantics The study of words.

jargon Language or terminology that is specific to a particular profession, group, or company.

faddish phrases that become a form of verbal or written shorthand. (For example, an economist who says, "At the end of the day, the bottom line is that there's a lack of visibility" simply means, "I don't know what's going to happen.") Words or phrases that are ordinary to you may be mysterious to outsiders or nonspecialists. If we want to be clearly understood, it is important to choose our words and craft our messages with the receiver's situation and frame of reference in mind.[17]

🐾 LO.2 How Social Media Are Changing the Communication Landscape

Some called it Revolution 2.0. Egyptian protesters in Cairo's Tahrir Square kept tabs on each other and informed the outside world about toppling dictator Hosni Mubarak in 2011 with their cell phones and Web-linked social media.

Social media such as Facebook, Twitter, YouTube, and LinkedIn, as discussed in Chapter 10, are blurring the line between formal and informal groups in the workplace. More broadly, organizational communication and work life in general are being significantly altered by social media. For instance, "nearly 28% of college students plan to seek employment using LinkedIn, up from 5% [in 2010]. . . . Students get the lowdown on employers by viewing their websites, reading Facebook and Twitter updates and perusing LinkedIn profiles."[18] Two major impacts of social media, driven by user-generated content, are (1) immediate worldwide personal access to unfiltered information and (2) bottom-up empowerment. Let us briefly explore these dynamic intertwined impacts.

The revolutions in Tunisia and Egypt were a stunning demonstration of the speed and power of social media:

Example. The protests started when a 26-year-old fruit and vegetable seller, Mohamed Bouazizi, set fire to himself on December 17 [2010] in the town of Sidi Bouzid after the authorities ruled his cart illegal. As with the 2009 protests in Iran, word of this harrowing event instantly ricocheted around the country via Twitter, blogs, and other digital media.[19]

Tunisia's dictatorial government collapsed under the weight of widespread revolt and international support for the upheaval. A subsequent ripple effect of social media-fueled protests soon toppled Hosni Mubarak's oppressive regime in Egypt and sparked freedom protests across the Arab world.[20] Meanwhile, the experience of James Buck, an American graduate student, symbolized the personally empowering effect of social media:

Example. Egyptian police detained Buck for taking photographs of a protest in a city outside Cairo. Using his cell phone and his Twitter account, Buck broadcast a single word, "arrested." Buck's network alerted officials at the University of California at Berkeley, who ultimately got the US State Department and a local lawyer involved. Buck was out of jail in 24 hours.[21]

If social media are powerful enough to help force regime changes at the national level, imagine what they can do to reshape work organizations in the years to come.

Managerial Implications

Managers cannot afford to ignore or underestimate the speed and bottom-up power of social media (see Real World/Real People). Those who do will be caught unprepared for both internal and external

real WORLD // real PEOPLE: ethics

R$_x$: Social Media for Doctors?

Go into any obstetrician/gynecologist's office and you're likely to see a large bulletin board covered with snapshots of babies.

But the docs at one Irving, Texas, OB/GYN practice have taken that ubiquitous display of cute kids into the 21st century. Their patients can post photos on the MacArthur OB/GYN Facebook page, where the doctors post news about their practice and the medical world at large.

Jeff Livingston, who spearheaded the practice's venture into social media, also manages the @macobgyn Twitter account, which has about 1,600 followers. He sees Facebook as an educational and, perhaps just as

important, marketing tool. "People are looking for information online," Livingston says. "I wanted them to look at our page."

But few doctors have embraced social media as enthusiastically as he has. Concerns about time and patient privacy have deterred many.

Are there legitimate ethical issues here, or is this just good old-fashioned resistance to change on the part of doctors?

SOURCE: R Rubin, "Doctors Use Social Media to Connect with Patients," *USA Today,* July 8, 2010, p 6D.

---

crosscurrents. Internal social media content can provide early warnings about employee morale problems, human resource issues such as sexual harassment, privileged information leaks, Internet and social media abuse, ethical lapses, and simmering grievances. Monitoring external social media feeds and posts can help managers stay in front of customer complaints and backlashes, emerging competitive threats, and potential legal and public relations fiascos. Consequently, social media policies for organizations are discussed later in this chapter.

Back to the Chapter-Opening Case

How does the use of social media give Best Buy a strategic competitive advantage?

Interpersonal Communication

The quality of interpersonal communication within organizations is more important than ever. Researchers found that people with good communication skills helped groups to make more innovative decisions and were promoted more frequently than individuals with less developed abilities.[22] **Communication competence** is defined as the ability to communicate effectively in specific situations. Business etiquette, for example, is one component of communication competence.[23]

While there are a host of communication abilities and skills under the umbrella of communication competence, we focus on five you can control: assertiveness versus aggressiveness or nonassertiveness; nonverbal communication; and active listening. We conclude this section by discussing gender differences in communication.

> ◀ ....
> ## TO THE POINT
> What is involved in assertive communication, nonverbal communication, active listening, and genderflex communication?
> ....

communication competence
Ability to communicate effectively in specific situations.

table 14–2 Communication Styles

COMMUNICATION STYLE	DESCRIPTION	NONVERBAL BEHAVIOR PATTERN	VERBAL BEHAVIOR PATTERN
Assertive	Pushing hard without attacking; permits others to influence outcome; expressive and self-enhancing without intruding on others	Good eye contact Comfortable but firm posture Strong, steady, and audible voice Facial expressions matched to message Appropriately serious tone Selective interruptions to ensure understanding	Direct and unambiguous language No attributions or evaluations of other's behavior Use of "I" statements and cooperative "we" statements
Aggressive	Taking advantage of others; expressive and self-enhancing at other's expense	Glaring eye contact Moving or leaning too close Threatening gestures (pointed finger; clenched fist) Loud voice Frequent interruptions	Swear words and abusive language Attributions and evaluations of other's behavior Sexist or racist terms Explicit threats or put-downs
Nonassertive	Encouraging others to take advantage of us; inhibited; self-denying	Little eye contact Downward glances Slumped posture Constantly shifting weight Wringing hands Weak or whiny voice	Qualifiers ("maybe"; "kind of") Fillers ("uh," "you know," "well") Negaters ("It's not really that important"; "I'm not sure")

SOURCE: Adapted in part from J A Waters, "Managerial Assertiveness," *Business Horizons,* September–October 1982, pp 24–29.

LO.3 Assertiveness, Aggressiveness, and Nonassertiveness

Table 14–2 describes the styles of assertiveness, aggressiveness, and nonassertiveness and identifies nonverbal and verbal behavior patterns associated with each one. Here's a quick quiz to see if you understand the three contrasting communication styles. Which style did Carol Bartz, the very successful former CEO of Autodesk, display upon taking the top spot at struggling Yahoo! in 2009?

Example. Just a few minutes after being introduced at a hastily arranged conference call, the self-described straight shooter told analysts she intends to ensure Yahoo! gets "some friggin' breathing room" so the company can "kick some butt."[24]

Bartz's in-your-face aggressive communication style failed to turn things around at Yahoo!, but instead built resentment, mistrust, and resistance. She was fired in 2011. In general, you can improve your communication competence by trying to be more assertive and less aggressive or nonassertive. Let's apply this recommendation in the context of saying no to someone.

We all get asked to do things we really don't want to do. For example, you may have been asked by a lazy friend to share a homework assignment or, alternatively, to purchase a product you don't need. The communication goal in these cases is to say no in an assertive manner. Below are several tips for saying *no.*

Go to www.mcgrawhillconnect.com for an interactive exercise to test your knowledge of assertiveness, aggressiveness, and nonassertiveness.

- Don't feel like you have to provide a yes or no answer on the spot. You can ask for more time to think over the request.

- Be honest, and start your response with the word *no*. It's easier to be steadfast in your commitment to saying no if you start out by saying the word up front.
- Use nonverbal assertive behaviors to reinforce your words. For example, you can shake your head from side to side while saying no and you can look into the requester's eyes as you say no; but don't glare.
- Use verbal assertive behaviors. Say no with a firm, direct tone. Use "I" statements when necessary. For example, "I feel it's unfair to give you my homework so you can sleep in and skip class."[25]

It is okay to say no. Remember, the more you say yes to others, the less time you have to yourself. Saying yes when you want to say no can lead to guilt, anger, resentment, and potential failure.

LO.4 Nonverbal Communication

Nonverbal communication is "any message, sent or received independent of the written or spoken word . . . [It] includes such factors as use of time and space, distance between persons when conversing, use of color, dress, walking behavior, standing, positioning, seating arrangement, office locations and furnishing."[26]

Communication experts estimate that 65% of every conversation is partially interpreted through nonverbal communication.[27] It thus is important to ensure that your nonverbal signals are consistent with your intended verbal messages. Inconsistencies create noise and promote miscommunication.[28] Because of the prevalence of nonverbal communication and its significant impact on organizational behavior (including, but not limited to, perceptions of others, hiring decisions, work attitudes, and turnover), managers need to become consciously aware of the nonverbal signals they send and receive. Syndicated business columnist Harvey Mackay reminds us that "words whisper; body language roars."[29] Take this situation, for example:

Example. One of your employees, Sue, has been working with you for five years. She's reliable, effective in her job and has a cheery disposition that is appreciated by her co-workers. Today she comes in late, walks straight to her desk with her head hung low and doesn't greet her co-workers as she usually does. During the morning, she slams down her phone, loudly shuts her filing cabinet and sighs audibly. You ask gently if she is OK. She responds curtly, "Yes. Why do you ask?"[30]

---

connect™ Go to www.mcgrawhillconnect.com for an interactive exercise to test your knowledge of nonverbal communications.

Should you take her words at face value, or act in accordance with her nonverbal behavior?

Body Movements and Gestures   Body movements, such as leaning forward or backward, and gestures, such as pointing, provide additional nonverbal information that can either enhance or detract from the communication process. Open body positions such as leaning forward communicate *immediacy*, a term used to represent openness, warmth, closeness, and availability for communication. *Defensiveness* is communicated by gestures such as folding arms, crossing hands, and crossing one's legs. Judith Hall, a communication researcher, conducted a meta-analysis of gender differences in body movements and gestures. Results revealed

nonverbal communication Messages sent outside of the written or spoken word.

President Obama's well-intentioned thumbs-up sign at the 2009 G-20 economic summit in London is an insulting gesture in some countries and cultures. Nonverbal communication is problematic in cross-cultural situations.

Go to www.mcgrawhillconnect.com for a self-assessment to determine your level of business etiquette.

that women nodded their heads and moved their hands more than men. Leaning forward, large body shifts, and foot and leg movements were exhibited more frequently by men than women.[31]

Although it is fun to interpret body movements and gestures when playing charades, it is important to remember that body language is easily misinterpreted and highly dependent on context. Hand gestures are especially problematic in cross-cultural situations. For example, President Barack Obama's enthusiastic use of the thumbs-up sign at the 2009 G-20 meeting in London could have been interpreted as "great" in the US and China; the "number 1" in France; the "number 5" in Japan; and "up yours" in Australia, Italy, and many other places.[32]

Touch   Touching is another powerful nonverbal cue. People tend to touch those they like. A meta-analysis of gender differences in touching indicated that women do more touching during conversations than men.[33] Of particular note, however, is the fact that men and women interpret touching differently. Sexual harassment claims might be reduced by keeping this perceptual difference in mind.

Moreover, norms for touching vary significantly around the world. Consider the example of two males walking across campus holding hands. In the Middle East and many parts of Asia, this behavior would be common for males who are friends or have great respect for each other. In contrast, this behavior is not commonplace in the United States and Canada.

Facial Expressions   Facial expressions convey a wealth of information. Smiling at a business meeting in Kansas City, for instance, typically represents warmth, happiness, or friendship, whereas frowning conveys dissatisfaction or anger. But are these interpretations universal across cultures? The short answer is no. A summary of relevant research revealed that the association between facial expressions and emotions varies across cultures.[34] Smiling broadly and showing one's teeth, for example, conveys different emotions around the world. Once again, we need to be careful when using and reading facial expressions among diverse groups of employees and when working across cultures.

Eye Contact   Eye contact is a strong nonverbal cue that serves four functions in communication. First, eye contact regulates the flow of communication by signaling the beginning and end of conversation. There is a tendency to look away from others when beginning to speak and to look at them when done. Second, gazing (as opposed to glaring) facilitates and monitors feedback because it reflects interest and attention. Third, eye contact conveys emotion. People tend to avoid eye contact when discussing bad news or providing negative feedback. Fourth, gazing relates to the type of relationship between communicators.

As is true for body movements, gestures, and facial expressions, norms for eye contact vary across cultures. Westerners are taught at an early age to look at their parents when spoken to. In contrast, people from many Asian, Latin, and African cultures are taught to avoid eye contact with a parent or superior in order to show obedience and subservience.[35] Once again, managers should be sensitive to different orientations toward maintaining eye contact with diverse employees.

Practical Tips   Good nonverbal communication skills are essential for building positive interpersonal relationships. Communication experts offer the following advice to improve nonverbal skills:[36]

Positive Nonverbal Actions That Help Communication

- Maintaining appropriate eye contact.
- Occasionally using affirmative nods to indicate agreement.
- Smiling and showing interest.
- Leaning slightly toward the speaker.
- Keeping your voice low and relaxed.
- Being aware of your facial expressions.

Actions to Avoid

- Licking your lips or playing with your hair or mustache.
- Turning away from the person you are communicating with.
- Closing your eyes and displaying uninterested facial expressions such as yawning.
- Excessively moving in your chair or tapping your feet.
- Using an unpleasant tone and speaking too quickly or too slowly.
- Biting your nails, picking your teeth, and constantly adjusting your glasses.

Of course, these tips are culturally specific to conducting business in North America and need to be adjusted elsewhere.

 ## LO.5 Active Listening

Experts contend that listening is the keystone communication skill for employees involved in sales, customer service, or management. Brian Dunn, Best Buy's CEO profiled in the chapter-opening case, recently told a *Fortune* magazine interviewer: "One of my roles as CEO is to be the chief listener."[37] Researchers have found listening effectiveness to be positively associated with customer satisfaction and negatively associated with employee intentions to quit. Poor communication between employees and management also was cited as a primary cause of employee discontent and turnover.[38] Listening skills are particularly important for all of us because we spend a great deal of time listening to others.

Listening involves much more than hearing a message. Hearing is merely the physical component of listening. **Listening** is the process of *actively* decoding and interpreting verbal messages. Listening requires cognitive attention and information processing; hearing does not. With these distinctions in mind, we examine listening styles and offer some practical advice for becoming a more effective listener.

Listening Styles   Communication experts believe that people listen with a preferred listening style. While people may lean toward one dominant listening style, we tend to use a combination of two or three. There are five dominant listening styles: appreciative, empathetic, comprehensive, discerning, and evaluative.[39] Let us consider each style.

An *appreciative* listener listens in a relaxed manner, preferring to listen for pleasure, entertainment, or inspiration. He or she tends to tune out speakers who provide no amusement or humor in their communications. *Empathetic* listeners interpret messages by focusing on the emotions and body language being displayed by the speaker as well as the presentation media. They also tend to listen without judging. A *comprehensive* listener makes sense of a message by first organizing

listening Actively decoding and interpreting verbal messages.

specific thoughts and actions and then integrates this information by focusing on relationships among ideas. These listeners prefer logical presentations without interruptions. *Discerning* listeners attempt to understand the main message and determine important points. They like to take notes and prefer logical presentations. Finally, *evaluative* listeners listen analytically and continually formulate arguments and challenges to what is being said. They tend to accept or reject messages based on personal beliefs, ask a lot of questions, and can become interruptive.

You can improve your listening skills by first becoming aware of the effectiveness of the different listening styles you use in various situations. This awareness can then help you to modify your style to fit a specific situation. For example, if you are listening to a presidential debate, you may want to focus on using a comprehensive and discerning style. In contrast, an evaluative style may be more appropriate if you are listening to a sales presentation.

Becoming a More Effective Listener   Effective listening is a learned skill that requires effort and motivation. Patricia A Woertz, CEO of Archer Daniels Midland, the $44 billion-a-year agricultural commodities giant, recently offered this homespun advice: "My mom says we have two ears and one mouth for a reason. . . . We should be listening twice as much as we speak."[40] That's right; it takes energy and desire to really listen to others. Unfortunately, it may seem like there are no rewards for listening, but there are negative consequences when we don't. Think of a time, for example, when someone did not pay attention to you by looking at his or her watch or doing some other activity such as typing on a keyboard. How did you feel? You may have felt put down, unimportant, or offended. In turn, such feelings can erode the quality of interpersonal relationships as well as fuel job dissatisfaction, lower productivity, and result in poor customer service. Listening is an important skill that can be improved by avoiding the 10 habits of bad listeners while cultivating the 10 good listening habits (see Table 14–3).

In addition, a communication expert says we can improve our listening skills by adhering to the following three fundamental recommendations:[41]

1. Attend closely to what's being said, not to what you want to say next.
2. Allow others to finish speaking before taking your turn.
3. Repeat back what you've heard to give the speaker the opportunity to clarify the message.

 LO.6 Linguistic Styles and Gender

It is common knowledge that women and men communicate differently. These differences can create communication problems that undermine productivity and interpersonal communication. Gender-based differences in communication are partly caused by linguistic styles commonly used by women and men. Deborah Tannen, a communication researcher, defines **linguistic style** as follows:

Example. Linguistic style refers to a person's characteristic speaking pattern. It includes such features as directness or indirectness, pacing and pausing, word choice, and the use of such elements as jokes, figures of speech, stories, questions, and apologies. In other words, linguistic style is a set of culturally learned signals by which we not only communicate what we mean but also interpret others' meaning and evaluate one another as people.[42]

Linguistic style not only helps explain communication differences between women and men, it also influences our perceptions of others' confidence, competence, and abilities. Increased awareness of linguistic styles can enhance your communication competence.

table 14–3 The Keys to Effective Listening

KEYS TO EFFECTIVE LISTENING	THE BAD LISTENER	THE GOOD LISTENER
1. Capitalize on thought speed	Tends to daydream	Stays with the speaker, mentally summarizes the speaker, weighs evidence, and listens between the lines
2. Listen for ideas	Listens for facts	Listens for central or overall ideas
3. Find an area of interest	Tunes out dry speakers or subjects	Listens for any useful information
4. Judge content, not delivery	Tunes out dry or monotone speakers	Assesses content by listening to entire message before making judgments
5. Hold your fire	Gets too emotional or worked up by something said by the speaker and enters into an argument	Withholds judgment until comprehension is complete
6. Work at listening	Does not expend energy on listening	Gives the speaker full attention
7. Resist distractions	Is easily distracted	Fights distractions and concentrates on the speaker
8. Hear what is said	Shuts out or denies unfavorable information	Listens to both favorable and unfavorable information
9. Challenge yourself	Resists listening to presentations of difficult subject matter	Treats complex presentations as an exercise for the mind
10. Use handouts, overheads, or other visual aids	Does not take notes or pay attention to visual aids	Takes notes as required and uses visual aids to enhance understanding of the presentation

SOURCES: Derived from N Skinner, "Communication Skills," *Selling Power,* July–August 1999, pp 32–34; and G Manning, K Curtis, and S McMillen, *Building the Human Side of Work Community* (Cincinnati: Thomson Executive Press, 1996), pp 127–54.

Gender Differences in Communication   Research demonstrates that women and men tend to communicate differently in a number of ways.[43] Table 14–4 illustrates 10 gender-based communication differences. There are two important issues to keep in mind about the tendencies identified in Table 14–4. First, they are not stereotypes for all women and men. Some men are less likely to boast about their achievements, and some women are less likely to share the credit. There always are exceptions to the rule. Second, your linguistic style influences perceptions about your confidence, competence, and authority. These judgments may, in turn, affect your future job assignments and subsequent promotability. Consider, for instance, contrasting linguistic styles displayed by Greg and Mindy. Greg downplays any uncertainties he has about issues and asks very few questions. He does this even when he is unsure about an issue being discussed. In contrast, Mindy is more forthright at admitting when she does not understand something, and she tends to ask a lot of questions. People may perceive Greg as more competent than Mindy because he displays confidence and acts as if he understands the issues being discussed.

linguistic style A person's typical speaking pattern.

table 14–4   Communication Differences between Women and Men

1. Men are less likely to ask for information or directions in a public situation that would reveal their lack of knowledge.

2. In decision making, women are more likely to downplay their certainty; men are more likely to downplay their doubts.

3. Women tend to apologize even when they have done nothing wrong. Men tend to avoid apologies as signs of weakness or concession.

4. Women tend to accept blame as a way of smoothing awkward situations. Men tend to ignore blame and place it elsewhere.

5. Women tend to temper criticism with positive buffers. Men tend to give criticism directly.

6. Women tend to insert unnecessary and unwarranted thank-you's in conversations. Men may avoid thanks altogether as a sign of weakness.

7. Women tend to ask "What do you think?" to build consensus. Men often perceive that question to be a sign of incompetence and lack of confidence.

8. Women tend to give directions in indirect ways, a technique that may be perceived as confusing, less confident, or manipulative by men.

9. Men tend to usurp [take] ideas stated by women and claim them as their own. Women tend to allow this process to take place without protest.

10. Women use softer voice volume to encourage persuasion and approval. Men use louder voice volume to attract attention and maintain control.

SOURCE: From Dayle M Smith, *Women at Work: Leadership for the Next Century,* 1st. Copyright © 2000. Reproduced by permission of Pearson Education, Inc., Upper Saddle River, New Jersey.

Mc Graw Hill **connect**™ Go to www.mcgrawhillconnect.com for a video case on communication at 1154 Lil Studios.

Toward More Effective Linguistic Styles for Both Women and Men   Author Judith Tingley suggests that women and men should learn to genderflex. **Genderflex** entails the temporary use of communication behaviors typical of the other gender in order to increase the potential for influence.[44]

In contrast, Deborah Tannen recommends that *everyone* needs to become aware of how linguistic styles work and how they influence our perceptions and judgments. She believes that knowledge of linguistic styles helps to ensure that people with valuable insights or ideas get heard. Consider how gender-based linguistic differences affect who gets heard at a meeting:

Example. Those who are comfortable speaking up in groups, who need little or no silence before raising their hands, or who speak out easily without waiting to be recognized are far more likely to get heard at meetings. Those who refrain from talking until it's clear that the previous speaker is finished, who wait to be recognized, and who are inclined to link their comments to those of others will do fine at a meeting where everyone else is following the same rules but will have a hard time getting heard in a meeting with people whose styles are more like the first pattern. Given the socialization typical of boys and girls, men are more likely to have learned the first style and women the second, making meetings more congenial for men than for women.[45]

Knowledge of these linguistic differences can assist managers in devising methods to ensure that everyone's ideas are heard and given fair credit both in and out of meetings. Furthermore, it is useful to consider the organizational strengths and limitations of your linguistic style. You may want to consider modifying a linguistic characteristic that is a detriment to perceptions of your confidence, competence, and authority.

Organizational Communication

Looking through the lens of organizational communication is a good way to identify factors contributing to effective and ineffective management. We structure this discussion by focusing on the "who" and "how" of communication. For example, the first step in any type of communication is deciding who is going to be the recipient of the message. In work settings, you can communicate upward to your boss, downward to direct reports, horizontally with peers, and externally with customers and suppliers. We discuss the "who" of organizational communication by reviewing the various formal and informal channels. We then delve into the "how" of communication by reviewing a contingency model for selecting the appropriate medium. You will learn that communication effectiveness is determined by an appropriate match between the content of a message and the media used to communicate.

◀ ....
TO THE POINT
How should the grapevine and media selection be managed?
....

Formal Communication Channels:
Up, Down, Horizontal, and External

Formal communication channels follow the chain of command or organizational structure. Messages communicated on formal channels are viewed as official and are transmitted via one or more of three different routes: (1) vertical—either upward or downward, (2) horizontal, and (3) external.

LO.7 Vertical Communication: Communicating Up and Down
the Organization   *Vertical communication* involves the flow of information between people at different organizational levels.

- *Upward communication* involves communicating with someone at a higher organizational level. Employees may communicate upward about themselves, problems with co-workers, organizational practices and policies they do not understand or dislike, and results they have or have not achieved. Organizations and managers need vibrant upward communication to foster organizational fairness and ethical conduct, intrinsic motivation, and empowerment (more on empowerment in the next chapter). Upward communication also is a key component of organizational efforts to increase productivity and improve customer service. Frontline employees generally know first-hand what it takes to get the job done. Unfortunately, too many employees tend to hold back (engage in self-censorship). Researchers recently concluded:

Example. Surprisingly, the most common reason for withholding input is a sense of futility rather than fear of retribution.

　　In part because employees do sometimes speak up, bosses are often unaware of their workers' self-censorship. They imagine they're hearing what's

---

genderflex Temporarily using communication behaviors typical of the other gender.

formal communication channels
Follow the chain of command or organizational structure.

important when in fact they're being met with silence. . . . The combination of tight-lipped employees and oblivious bosses buries constructive criticism, not to mention the unvarnished truth. Most important, it prevents good ideas from bubbling up through the organization.[46]

Thus, managers need to do more than just listen to employees. They need to *act* on the input to be credible leaders and blunt cynical feelings of futility.

Managers can encourage upward communication via employee attitude and opinion surveys, suggestion systems, formal grievance procedures, open-door policies, informal chats, e-mail and social media, exit interviews, and town hall meetings.[47] Asking open-ended and nonjudgmental questions also is a good way to stimulate productive upward communication. Brad Smith, CEO of financial software firm Intuit, offers this tip: "Ask others, 'What would you have done differently if you were me?' to get more honest criticism."[48]

- *Downward communication* occurs when someone at a higher level in the organization conveys information or a message downward to one or more others. Managers generally provide five types of information through downward communication: strategies/goals, job instructions, job rationale, organizational policies and practices, and feedback about performance. Surveys highlight the need for improvement in this area. In a poll of 1,198 workers, the top-ranked workplace frustration was "poor communication by senior management about the business."[49] Seventy percent of 1,006 employees in a second survey answered no to the question: "Have your company's leaders communicated with employees about how the current economy might affect the company?"[50] Consider this school-of-hard-knocks management lesson:

Example. Doug Schukar was thrilled when USA Mortgage, his residential mortgage bank in St Louis, increased the loans it funded from $113 million in January 2009 to $1.2 billion by the end of the year. While other lenders struggled, he ramped up his sales efforts. Yet by failing to keep key middle managers informed of growth plans such as acquisitions, he let them get blindsided by the work that came from the company's rapid expansion. Result: Almost all resigned, and he hired replacements. Today he includes middle managers in annual and quarterly planning sessions.[51]

Because town hall meetings are increasingly used in organizations to facilitate vertical communication, tips for conducting them more effectively are offered below.

- The size of the meeting depends on the logistics of your workforce and the message being delivered. If you have good news to tell a number of employees, you can split them into more intimate groups if you like. But if the news is bad, it's better to have everyone hear it at the same time.
- Consider using speakers other than your senior executives.
- Broadcast town meetings so employees in other locations can participate. Taping allows absent employees to view the meeting later.
- When making a presentation, take the educational level of your audience into account.
- Don't make presentations too technical.
- Send invitations to all employees who are eligible to attend.

- Employees should be strongly encouraged to attend meetings, but attendance should not be mandatory. If your meeting is being held after business hours, consider paying employees for their time.[52]

Horizontal Communication: Communicating within and between Work Units   *Horizontal communication* flows among co-workers and between different work units, and its main purpose is coordination. During this sideways communication, employees share information and best practices, coordinate work activities and schedules, solve problems, offer advice and coaching, and resolve conflicts. Consider this life-and-death situation, for example:

Example. Eight hospitals reduced the number of deaths from surgeries by more than 40% by using a checklist that helps doctors and nurses avoid errors, according to a [recent] report. . . .

If all hospitals used the same checklist, they could save tens of thousands of lives and $20 billion in medical costs each year, says author Atul Gawande, a surgeon and associate professor at the Harvard School of Public Health. . . .

The study shows that an operation's success depends far more on teamwork and clear communication than the brilliance of individual doctors, says co-author Alex Haynes, also of Harvard. And that's good news, he says, because it means hospitals everywhere can improve.

Researchers modeled the checklist, which takes only two minutes to go through, after ones used by the aviation industry, which has dramatically reduced the number of crashes in recent years.[53]

In addition to using team checklists, horizontal communication is facilitated by project meetings, committees, team building (recall our discussion in Chapter 11), social gatherings, and matrix structures (discussed in Chapter 17).

Horizontal communication is impeded in three ways: (1) by specialization that causes people to work alone; (2) by encouraging competition that reduces information sharing; and (3) by an organizational culture that does not promote collaboration and cooperation.

External Communication: Communicating with Others outside the Organization   *External communication* is a two-way flow of information between employees and a variety of stakeholders outside the organization. External stakeholders include customers, suppliers, shareholders/owners, labor unions, government officials, community residents, and so on. Many organizations create formal departments, such as public or community relations, to coordinate their external communications. To protect competitive strategies, trade secrets, and the integrity of nondisclosure agreements, employees need to be fully informed about what they should *not* communicate to outsiders in everything from casual conversations to blogs and tweets.[54]

Informal Communication Channels

Informal communication channels do not follow the chain of command. They skip management levels and bypass lines of authority. Two commonly used informal channels are the grapevine and management by walking around.

informal communication channels
Do not follow the chain of command or organizational structure.

Is this conversation task-related, a bull session, or an intertwined combination of the two? It is hard to tell without actually listening in. Managers need to appreciate the positive and negative aspects of the grapevine and forget about trying to kill it.

The Grapevine The **grapevine** represents the unofficial communication system of the informal organization and encompasses all types of communication media. For example, an employee may share a bit of office gossip via e-mail, a face-to-face conversation, a text or Twitter message, or a phone call or voice mail. Although the grapevine can be a source of inaccurate or malicious rumors, it can function positively by facilitating organizational changes, embedding organizational culture, fostering group cohesiveness, and gathering employee and customer feedback.

People who consistently pass along grapevine information to others are called **liaison individuals** or gossips. Recent research of corporate social networks led to this positive assessment:

Example. The more staff members gossiped, the better their understanding of their social environment and the higher their peers rated their influence. . . .

Gossip can be very helpful to people in organizations, especially when the flow of information from the top gets choked off, as often happens when companies are in crisis or undergoing change. If a few people know what's really going on, gossip becomes the means of spreading that information to everyone else. . . .

It's true that gossip can sometimes crank up the fear level in an organization, but research shows it usually does the reverse. By sharing gossip, you make a personal connection, which gives you social and emotional support. Gossip also disseminates valuable information about a network—who's a free rider, who's a bully, and who's impossible to work with—and provides a means for censuring those who don't adhere to the group's norms.[55]

Some gossiping can provide a healthy emotional outlet, especially in uncertain times. Effective managers monitor the pulse of work groups by regularly communicating with known liaison gossips.

In contrast to liaison individuals, **organizational moles** use the grapevine for more devious purposes. They obtain information, often negative, in order to enhance their power and status. They do this by secretly reporting their perceptions and hearsay about the difficulties, conflicts, or failure of other employees to powerful members of management. Moles prefer to divert attention away from themselves and want to be seen as more competent than others. Managers are advised to create an open, trusting environment that discourages mole behavior because moles can destroy teamwork, create conflict, and impair productivity.

Researchers have provided the following insights about the grapevine over the years: (1) it is faster than formal channels; (2) it is about 75% accurate; (3) people rely on it when they are insecure, threatened, or faced with organizational changes; and (4) grapevine gossip is not an isolated form of communication, but instead embedded into all organizational sense-making communication.[56] Managers tend to view the grapevine negatively. In fact, when 250 advertising executives were asked in a recent survey, "Do you think office gossip has a positive or negative effect on the workplace?" 63% said negative.[57]

The key managerial recommendation is to *monitor* and *influence* the grapevine rather than wasting time trying to extinguish it. Effective managers can take a positive step by vigorously promoting upward communication, as just discussed. Information technology enables the following proactive approach to monitoring the grapevine:

Example. What if managers and employees could listen in on any gripe fests and hallway brainstorms taking place at the office, all at one time? That's the concept, in digital form, behind Hewlett-Packard's WaterCooler, a new tool from its research labs that indexes what employees say on their internal and external blogs.

real WORLD // real PEOPLE: ethics

Republic Airways' CEO Goes Undercover

For a recent episode of CBS's *Undercover Boss,* Bryan Bedford donned a wig, put on a pair of glasses and went to work on some of the least pleasant jobs his employees undertake daily.

The CEO of Republic Airways Holdings, which owns Frontier Airlines and four regional feeder carriers, cleaned planes, emptied human waste from aircraft holding tanks and sweated profusely unloading bags.

Typical of the show's narrative art—in which a CEO goes undercover as an employee and gains newfound respect and appreciation for his troops—Bedford also found himself stumped by mundane operational challenges and witness to testimonies from employees who

are struggling to get by on meager salaries. At the end of the episode, he announces a resolve to improve where he can, urges his direct reports to do the same and wraps it up with emotional huddles seemingly requisite of such reality shows.

How badly out of touch are today's executives with their own employees? Explain. Short of filming an episode of *Undercover Boss,* what specific MBWA practices would you recommend?

SOURCE: R Yu, "Republic Opens New Chapter," *USA Today,* January 20, 2011, p 1B.

Workers can opt in or out of the index, but many—about 11,000 at HP—choose to let their musings on everything from iPhone rumors to speculation about HP reorgs be aggregated on the site. Users can click on a "zeitgeist" link to see what's hot each week.[58]

Management by Walking Around (MBWA)   **Management by walking around** (MBWA) involves managers literally walking around the organization and informally talking to people from all departments and levels[59] (see Real World/ Real People). It is an effective way to communicate because employees prefer to get information directly from their manager. Linda Dulye, a communications specialist, concluded that employees "favor it more than e-mails, Web sites or intranet sites, or town hall meetings—even more than the grapevine. . . . The most effective channel for employees is the informal workplace 'walk-around'—having their manager come to their desk and sit and chat about work."[60] She offers the following tips for conducting MBWA:

1. Dedicate a certain amount of time each week for MBWA.

2. Don't take your cell phone. It is important to stay focused on the person/ people you are talking with and to avoid distractions.

3. Use active listening and don't take the approach that business is the only available topic for discussion. Employees may enjoy some amount of casual conversation.

4. The experience should be a two-way conversation. Show interest in your employees' issues and concerns.

5. Don't hesitate to take a notepad and record things requiring follow-up. Don't bring formal charts and graphs; the goal is to maintain an informal conversation.

6. Thank the individual or group for their time and feedback.[61]

---

grapevine Unofficial communication system of the informal organization.

liaison individuals Those who consistently pass along grapevine information to others.

organizational moles Those who use the grapevine to enhance their power and status.

management by walking around Managers walk around and informally talk to people from all areas and levels.

LO.8 Choosing Media: A Contingency Perspective

In this section, we turn our attention to discussing the overall "how" of the communication process. Specifically, we examine how managers can determine the best method or medium to use when communicating via the various formal and informal channels of communication.

Today's managers can choose from a dizzying array of communication media (telephone, e-mail, voice mail, cell phone, standard and express mail, text messaging, video, blogs and other social media, and so forth). Tony Hsieh, CEO of online retailer Zappos, reportedly has 30,000 people both inside and outside the company receiving his Twitter feeds.[62] Fortunately, research tells us that managers can help reduce information overload and improve communication effectiveness by more rigorously selecting communication media. If an inappropriate medium is used, managerial decisions may be based on inaccurate information, important messages may not reach the intended audience, and employees may become dissatisfied and unproductive. The recent recession severely tested management's ability to select appropriate communication media. Consider this positive example involving Johnson Financial Group, based in Racine, Wisconsin:

Example. Employees at the 63 locations of this financial services company were assured their jobs were safe and kept in the loop about the industry upheaval via town halls and voicemails from the CEO.[63]

Media selection is a key component of communication effectiveness. The following section explores a contingency model designed to help managers select communication media in a systematic and effective manner. Media selection in this model is based on the interaction between media richness and complexity of the problem/situation at hand.

Media Richness   Respected organizational theorists Richard Daft and Robert Lengel explain the communication concept of richness this way:

Example. Richness is defined as the potential information-carrying capacity of data. If the communication of an item of data, such as a wink, provides substantial new understanding, it would be considered rich. If the datum provides little understanding, it would be low in richness.[64]

Media richness involves the capacity of a given communication medium to convey information and promote understanding. Alternative media can vary from rich to lean.

Media richness is based on four factors: (1) feedback (ranging from fast to very slow), (2) channel (ranging from the combined visual and audio characteristics of a videoconference to the limited visual aspects of a computer report), (3) type of communication (ranging from personal to impersonal), and (4) language source (ranging from the natural body language and speech involved in a face-to-face conversation to the numbers contained in a financial statement).

A two-way face-to-face conversation is the richest form of communication. It provides immediate feedback and allows for the observation of multiple cues such as body language and tone of voice. Although relatively high in richness, telephone conversations and videoconferencing are not as informative as face-to-face exchanges. At the other end of the scale, newsletters, computer reports, and general e-mail blasts are lean media because feedback is very slow, the channels involve only limited visual information, and the information provided is generic or impersonal. E-mail and social media messages vary in media richness: leaner if they impersonally blanket a large audience and richer if they mix personal textual and video information that prompts quick conversational feedback.[65]

Complexity of the Managerial Problem/Situation   Managers face problems and situations that range from low to high in complexity. Low-complexity situations are routine, predictable, and managed by using objective or standard procedures. Calculating an employee's paycheck is an example of low complexity. Highly complex situations, such as a corporate reorganization, are ambiguous, unpredictable, hard to analyze, and often emotionally laden. Managers spend considerably more time analyzing these situations because they rely on more sources of information during their deliberations. There are no standard solutions to complex problems or situations.

Contingency Recommendations   The contingency model for selecting media is graphically shown in Figure 14–2. As indicated, there are three zones of communication effectiveness. Effective communication occurs when the richness of the medium is matched appropriately with the complexity of the problem or situation. Media low in richness—impersonal static and personal static—are better suited for simple problems; media high in richness—interactive media and face-to-face—are appropriate for complex problems or situations. Sun Microsystems, for example, followed this recommendation when communicating with employees

figure 14–2 A Contingency Model for Selecting Communication Media

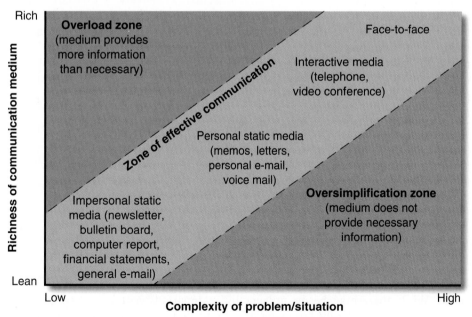

SOURCES: Adapted and updated from R Lengel and R L Daft, "The Selection of Communication Media as an Executive Skill," *Academy of Management Executive,* August 1988, p 226, and R L Daft and R H Lengel, "Information Richness: A New Approach to Managerial Behavior and Organization Design," in *Research in Organizational Behavior,* ed B M Staw and L L Cummings (Greenwich, CT: JAI Press, 1984), p 199.

media richness Capacity of a communication medium to

convey information and promote understanding.

about upcoming layoffs. The organization used a series of face-to-face sessions to deliver the bad news and provided managers with a set of slides and speaking points to help disseminate the necessary information.[66]

Conversely, ineffective communication occurs when the richness of the medium is either too high or too low for the complexity of the problem or situation. For example, a district sales manager would fall into the *overload zone* if she communicated monthly sales reports through richer media. Conducting face-to-face meetings or telephoning each salesperson would provide excessive information and take more time than necessary to communicate monthly sales data. The *oversimplification zone* represents another ineffective choice of communication media. In this situation, media with inadequate richness are used to communicate about complicated or emotional issues. For example, Radio Shack Corporation used e-mail to notify 400 employees at its Texas headquarters that they were being let go. Worse yet, a London-based body-piercing and jewelry store used a text message to fire an employee. This choice of medium is ineffective in this context because it does not preserve privacy and it does not allow employees to ask questions. Further, dismissing employees in this manner can lower morale among remaining employees and damage a company's image.[67]

Mc Graw Hill connect™ Go to www.mcgrawhillconnect.com for an interactive exercises to test your knowledge of organizational communication.

Back to the **Chapter-Opening Case**

How should Best Buy's CEO Brian Dunn make sure he remains in the zone of effective communication (in Figure 14–2) when using social media?

Research Evidence   The relationship between media richness and problem/situation complexity has not been researched extensively. Available evidence indicates that managers used richer sources when confronted with ambiguous and complicated events, and miscommunication increased when rich media were used to transmit information that was traditionally communicated through lean media.[68] These findings correspond to portions of the model in Figure 14–2. A meta-analysis of more than 40 studies revealed that media usage was significantly different across organizational levels. Upper-level executives/managers spent more time in face-to-face meetings than did lower-level managers.[69] That is a good thing if the executives have meetings with diverse inside and outside groups to broaden their perspective and promote upward communication. However, meeting over and over with the same executive team is a formula for groupthink.

TO THE POINT
What distinguishes the Internet generation and what are the keys to effective telecommuting, e-mail, and cell phone etiquette?

How Digital Communication Is Impacting Organizational Behavior

Imagine how a universal language would make worldwide communication much easier. While there may be no universally understood written and spoken languages, a universal *digital* language of 1s and 0s is reshaping the way we live, work, and play. Digitized words (wireless e-mail on a BlackBerry), pictures (video clips on YouTube), sounds (talking and listening to music on an iPhone), and motions (hitting and throwing on a Wii game) are conveniently packaged and readily shared communication content. In turn, the transmission of digitized content has been revolutionized by technologies such as the Internet, communication satellites, cell towers, and Wi-Fi. Put it all together and we have virtually immediate access to unprecedented amounts of information and globe-spanning communication opportunities.

real WORLD // **real** PEOPLE

How Entrepreneur Rashmi Sinha Deals with Information Overload

Background: After earning a PhD at Brown University, India-born Rashmi Sinha cofounded SlideShare, a Web site for sharing PowerPoint presentations.

When I get to the office, the first thing I do is look at my e-mail to make sure there are no pressing issues. I try to respond to most things immediately. It's something I learned from one of my graduate advisers. You'd e-mail him and he'd immediately reply, because, he said, "If I don't, I'm spending my time twice. Once when I see the e-mail, and again when I reply to it later on. And then in between, it's occupying mental space."

I never answer the phone or check my messages. I hate receiving random phone calls. I prefer to start a conversation by e-mail and then jump on the phone once I know what the conversation is about. Our office manager checks my voice mail messages . . . [and] lets me know if any messages are important. People who know me well call my cell phone, which I do answer.

Can the "one-touch" e-mail tactic lead to impulsive responses that might be regretted later? Overall, what are the pros and cons of Sinha's various information management practices? Explain.

SOURCE: C Pickens, "The Way I Work: Rashmi Sinha, SlideShare," *Inc*, April 2011, p 104.

The purpose of this concluding section is to explore how the digital communication revolution is affecting organizational behavior, both positively and negatively. Importantly, our focus here is not on the technological fine points of digital communication innovations (e.g., cloud computing, mobile Internet, augmented reality, and motion-controlled computers),[70] but rather on how digital communication affects how we act and interact in work settings. For instance, researchers wanted to know if "peers rate each other differently depending on what medium they use. It turns out people are far more likely to trash their colleagues via e-mail than when filling out a paper form."[71] Also, we are interested in assessing the impact of communication technology on employee productivity. For example,

---

Example. [a] recent MIT study found that in one organization the employees with the most extensive personal digital networks were 7% more productive than their colleagues—so Wikis and Web 2.0 tools may indeed improve productivity. In the same organization, however, the employees with the most cohesive face-to-face networks were 30% more productive. Electronic tools may well be suited to information discovery, but face-to-face communication . . . best supports information integration.[72]

More and faster digital communication does not necessarily mean *better* communication. Information overload (see Real World/Real People) in the workplace is a costly problem:

Example. People are drowning in a deluge of data. Corporate users received about 110 messages a day in 2010, says market researcher Radicati Group. There are 110 million tweets a day, Twitter says. Researcher Basex has pegged business productivity losses due to the "cost of unnecessary interruptions" at $650 billion in 2007.[73]

Hello, New York, Buy! Hello, Los Angeles, Sell! Being a Chicago Board Options Exchange trader is a study in how to handle information overload. Are you good at managing information overload, or does it manage you?

After highlighting two strategic concerns for management, we discuss eight norms of the Internet generation, the dynamics of work-connecting technologies, and some unintended consequences of today's communication/information technologies.

Strategic Concerns: Security and Privacy

Because much of today's communication involves complex Internet-linked computer systems, careless and malicious actions can wreak havoc in terms of costly downtime and lost or stolen data. Any discussion of digital communication and information technology must necessarily address the twin concerns of security and privacy. Failure in those areas compromises the integrity and reliability of the entire electronic communication process. Between 2000 and 2010, the FBI's Internet Crime Complaint Center received over 2 million complaints and a record $265 million in losses were recorded in 2008 alone.[74] Experts say the losses are much higher because companies report only a small fraction of Internet fraud for fear of bad publicity. The following specific cases are instructive and cautionary:

Example. Alpharetta, Georgia-based data broker ChoicePoint Inc . . . paid a record $10 million in civil penalties and $5 million in consumer redress in 2006 to settle Federal Trade Commission (FTC) charges that its security and record handling procedures violated consumers' privacy rights and various federal laws. And drug manufacturer Eli Lilly and Co. agreed to follow a four-stage information security program for 20 years to settle an FTC complaint lodged after an employee mistakenly released nearly 700 e-mail addresses collected through the company's Prozac.com website.[75]

For our present purposes, it is sufficient to review the Internet security and privacy protection tips in Table 14–5. *Prevention* is the key when it comes to protecting digital communication systems against hackers, identity theft, and fraud. How faithfully do you practice "safe computing"?[76]

table 14–5   Protecting against Security and Privacy Breaches on the Internet

- **Pick strong passwords.** Use a mix of letters, symbols, and numbers, following the guidelines at www.microsoft.com/protect/yourself/password/create.mspx.

- **Use different passwords** for different Web services. And never use your Web passwords for PIN codes on credit, debit, or ATM cards.

- **Don't reveal sensitive information**—not even in "private" areas of services such as Facebook or Flickr that offer public access to most material.

- **Don't share files** on services that offer optional sharing, such as Google Docs, unless there is a real need.

- **Keep data** whose disclosure would create legal liability or embarrassment on your personal hard drives and storage devices.

- **Avoid file-sharing services** such as Lime Wire that distribute pirated files. Both the services and the downloads can open your computer to prying eyes.

- **Apply the latest security updates** to all your software, including operating systems, browsers, and antivirus programs.

🐾 LO.9 Here Comes the Huge Internet Generation

The largest generation in US history, more than 81 million people born between the beginning of 1977 and the end of 1997, is unique for another reason other than its size: they grew up with the Internet as a central feature of their lives. Author, consultant, and University of Toronto professor Don Tapscott, in his book *Grown Up Digital: How the Net Generation Is Changing Your World*, calls them the Net Gen. Understanding their worldview, as shaped by the Internet and digital communication technologies, is a good preview of how workplaces are changing. Tapscott offers this overview:

Example. As talent, the Net Generation is already transforming the workforce. The biggest generation ever is flooding into a talent vortex being created by the expansion of the global economy, the mobility of labor, and the fastest and biggest generational retirement ever. They are bringing new approaches to collaboration, knowledge sharing, and innovation in businesses and governments around the world. There is strong evidence that the organizations that embrace these new ways of working experience better performance, growth, and success. To win the battle for talent, organizations need to rethink many aspects of how they recruit, compensate, develop, collaborate with, and supervise talent. I believe the very idea of management is changing.[77]

Years of focus groups and interviews with nearly 10,000 people worldwide (with an emphasis on young people) led Tapscott and his research team to identify eight Net Gen norms (see Table 14–6). These norms reflect general patterns

table 14–6 What Makes the Internet Generation Tick? Eight Norms

1. **Freedom.** A desire to experience new and different things takes precedence over long-term commitments. Flexible work hours and locations, a say in how things are done, and freedom of choice are desirable.

2. **Customization.** Everything from personalized cell phone ring tones to lifestyle choices to unique Facebook layouts make life interesting and fun.

3. **Scrutiny.** With both trash and treasure on the Internet, Net Geners have learned to be skeptical, check things out, and ask probing questions. Candor and straight talk are favored. Authority figures and "facts" are not taken at face value.

4. **Integrity.** "Net Geners care about integrity—being honest, considerate, transparent, and abiding by their commitments. This is also a generation with profound tolerance." Trust in employers, people, and products is important. Some ethical elasticity (e.g., pirating music and plagiarizing) when in cyberspace is an open issue.

5. **Collaboration.** Relationships are of key importance. They know how to work and play with others and are eager to offer up opinions and suggestions. Volunteering is valued.

6. **Entertainment.** A job should not be a life sentence; it should be both challenging and fun. The Internet is a productivity tool, personal communication device, information source, and "fun tool of choice." Multitasking is a way of life to keep things moving and interesting.

7. **Speed.** "They're used to instant response, 24/7. Video games give them instant feedback; Google answers their inquiries within nanoseconds." Rapid-fire texting, instant messaging, and tweeting are far faster and superior to e-mail and slow organizational decision making. Fast, accurate, and helpful feedback on job performance is demanded.

8. **Innovation.** An impatience for new and different user experiences is evident. "In the workplace, innovation means rejecting the traditional command-and-control hierarchy and devising work processes that encourage collaboration and creativity."

SOURCE: Quoted and adapted from discussion in D Tapscott, *Grown Up Digital: How the Net Generation Is Changing Your World* (New York: McGraw-Hill, 2009), pp 73–96.

of experiences, attitudes, preferences, and expectations. Net Gen members expect the same instant access to comprehensive information and people, and the accompanying empowerment, in their work lives as they had growing up and going to school. Change-resistant managers who stubbornly stand in the way of Net Gen's digital lifelines will get run over.

How many of the eight Net Gen norms in Table 14–6 are evident in this recent situation?

Example. Like just about every twentysomething, Jamie Varon, 23, had her heart set on working at Twitter. She had already applied for a position through the company's website. *And* asked a contact at Google to put in a good word for her. *And* showed up at the company's headquarters with a bag of cookies in an attempt to charm a recruiter into talking to her. But she still hadn't landed an interview. What Varon did next made her feel a little crazy. But then, it's a crazy time to be looking for a job. She created a website called twittershouldhireme.com, including her résumé, recommendations, and a blog tracking her quest. Within 24 hours the company contacted her. She had a lunch meeting set up at Twitter, and in the meantime got two job offers from tech companies that had noticed her site.[78]

The Two Faces of Telecommuting/Teleworking

Digital communication has significantly altered the traditional linkages between work, place, and time. This is especially true for knowledge workers who do not produce tangible products such as cars or provide hands-on services such as haircuts. Thanks to advanced telecommunications technology and Internet tools such as Facebook's SocialEyes that can link up to nine far-flung people for a video meeting, many variations of telecommuting are possible.[79] Rather than the person physically traveling to and from an office, **telecommuting** allows the work to travel electronically to and from the person's home. Wireless Internet access and cell phones have further evolved telecommuting into **teleworking** (connecting to the office from practically anywhere). All this has altered the traditional work and *place* connection, as employees can now perform their work in various locations rather than always physically gathering in one place. Because of computerized memory capabilities, the traditional work and *time* connection also has been altered. Employees in different locations and time zones can work simultaneously (called synchronous communication) and team members can work on the same project at different times (asynchronous communication).

Great parenting or major work distraction? The answer depends on how good this telecommuter is at getting the job done while multi-tasking at home. In terms of your own work future, what are the pros and cons of being a teleworker?

Use and Benefits Among US companies with at least 500 employees, 28% have some full-time telecommuters and 40% have some part-time telecommuters.[80] Behind the statistics are real people with altered lives:

Example. Eve Gelb's life was once a blur of hour-and-a-half commutes on the 405 Freeway in Los Angeles. What memories: The NPR fatigue. The stale minivan air. . . . But that's all in the past. Gelb, a project manager at a giant HMO, SCAN Health Plan, has given up her Ethan Allen-style office, yanked down the family photos, and moved into her home office. [Perhaps surprisingly,] it was her boss's idea.

SCAN is one of a growing number of companies encouraging workers to toil from home. Sure, employers have been doing this for years. But as the recession bites and companies look to save money on real estate costs, what was once a cushy perk is now deemed a business necessity. And that, along with a few choice enticements—voila!, a shiny new BlackBerry—is how companies are selling it to employees, whose emotions range from ecstasy to befuddlement.[81]

An expert recently listed the benefits of telecommuting: "(1) increases employee productivity, (2) increases the attractiveness of the employer, (3) decreases operating costs, (4) increases operationality during a crisis, and (5) contributes to green initiatives."[82] Additionally, telecommuting can bring homebound disabled people and prison inmates into the workforce.

Problems   The benefits of telecommuting/teleworking have been documented primarily through testimonial claims rather than through rigorous research. For example, IBM reported saving $100 million in capital facilities and equipment costs by letting 42% of its employees work from home. Teleworking reportedly resulted in productivity increases of 25 to 35% at FourGen Software and Continental Traffic Services, respectively.[83] Meanwhile, managerial doubts and negative research evidence have accumulated. One business journalist put it this way: "Well into the work-from-anywhere era, managers are beginning to ask: Are the underlings working remotely . . . or remotely working?"[84] Working from home, the grocery store, or the beach takes self-discipline. There also are career implications. A survey of 1,300 executives from 71 countries found a general belief that people who telework are less likely to get promoted.[85] This is the "out of sight, out of mind" dilemma. Another problem is a sense of professional isolation among teleworkers. In a recent study, "a matched sample of 261 professional-level teleworkers and their managers revealed that professional isolation negatively impacts job performance."[86] Finally, as the following summary of another recent study points out, the "freedom" of teleworking can create major work–life imbalance:

Example. Utilizing both surveys and follow-up focus group interactions, this study found that while work-connecting technologies permitted a greater range of options regarding when and where work was done, this same connectivity provided constant availability to work and often drove expectations that more must be done, thereby increasing the likelihood of longer work hours and—surprisingly— leading to a diminished sense of flexibility.[87]

Building on what we emphasized in our Chapter 11 discussion of virtual teams, regular professional or recreational face-to-face interaction is vital to group development, cohesiveness, and team spirit. Your authors, who have worked on this book in their home offices for many years, also recommend that teleworkers practice using the "off" switches in their heads and on their *electronic leashes*.

 LO.10 Dealing with Unintended Consequences of the Digital Age

An interesting thing happened on the way to our digital future. Convenient, speedy, and fun technologies spawned some unproductive, obnoxious, and even unsafe behaviors. For instance, language specialists lament how digital tools such

telecommuting/teleworking
Doing work generally performed in the office at home or in other convenient locations using advanced communication technologies.

as e-mail, text messaging, and Twitter have further eroded already poor writing skills. Teachers and managers are not pleased with research papers, formal documents, and official correspondence containing smiley faces and texting-style shorthand such as OMG & U R GR8.[88] Another digital-age bone of contention is what Microsoft vice president Linda Stone calls "continuous partial attention." Stone explains: "You're in a conference room, and all the people around the table are glancing—frequently and surreptitiously—at the cell phones or BlackBerrys they're holding just below the table. . . . This constant checking of handheld electronic devices has become epidemic."[89] Sound familiar? Let us explore the unintended behavioral consequences of e-mail and cell phones, two ubiquitous and vital forms of digital-age communication, with the goal of more effective communication. We conclude with a recommended workplace social media policy.

E-mail Overkill   People tend to have a love–hate relationship with e-mail because its speed and convenience has led to overload. In fact, a recent survey of 805 employees found 56% having three or more business and personal e-mail accounts.[90] Dealing with more than 100 e-mails a day is commonplace for busy managers. Mobile Internet smart phones and tablet computers such as iPads allow us to send and receive e-mail around the clock from practically anywhere—including, sometimes tragically, from behind the steering wheel. In addition to the hazards of distracted driving, unintended behavioral consequences of e-mail documented by researchers include (1) a decrease in all other forms of communication among co-workers—including greetings and informal conversations; (2) emotions often are poorly communicated or miscommunicated via e-mail messages; (3) the greater the use of e-mail, the less connected co-workers reportedly feel; and (4) people are more apt to lie via e-mail versus a pen and paper note.[91] While endorsing formal policy statements for technology use in organizations, one expert recently observed:

Example. E-mail continues to be fraught with legal, ethical and productivity issues. One problem: Users think of e-mail the way they think of oral communication—as informal, not as a medium that sticks if the wrong words come out. But written e-mail, stored on hard drives, is not like oral communication: A wrong word or phrase offered inadvertently, mischievously or angrily can have legal repercussions.[92]

Along with a formally written and communicated organizational e-mail policy, embracing the tips in Table 14–7, managers can curb e-mail overkill in creative ways. For example, an engineering group at computer chip maker Intel instituted e-mail-free Fridays.

Example. E-mail isn't forbidden, but everyone is encouraged to phone or meet face-to-face. The goal is more direct, free flowing communication and better exchange of ideas, Intel principal engineer Nathan Zeldes said in a company blog post.[93]

Cell Phone Use and Abuse   Over 90% of US households have a cell phone and the technology is deeply embedded in the culture. In fact, in a nationwide Pew survey, the majority of respondents said they would give up their landline phones, television, the Internet, and e-mail before they would surrender their cell phones.[94] As with e-mail, the widespread use of cell phones, about half with built-in cameras, has generated plenty of unintended behavioral consequences. Cell phone problems range from merely annoying (loud ring tones and conversations in public places) to unethical and illegal (sending pornographic photos and photographing restricted areas or materials) to deadly.[95] Regarding the controversial practice

table 14–7 Some Practical E-mail Tips

- **Do not assume e-mail is confidential.** Employers are increasingly monitoring all e-mail. Assume your messages will be a matter of permanent record and can be read by anyone.

- **Be professional and courteous.** Recommendations include delete trailing messages, don't send chain letters and jokes, don't type in all caps (it's equivalent to shouting), don't respond immediately to a nasty e-mail, refrain from using colored text and background, don't expose your contact list to strangers, and be patient about receiving replies.

- **Avoid sloppiness.** Use a spell checker or reread the message before sending.

- **Don't use e-mail for volatile or complex issues.** Use a medium that is appropriate for the situation at hand.

- **Keep messages brief and clear.** Use accurate subject headings and let the reader know what you want right up front. Use bullets, as in this table, for conciseness.

- **Save people time.** Type "no reply necessary" in the subject line or at the top of your message if appropriate. Write a descriptive subject line to help the receiver prioritize messages.

- **Be careful with attachments.** Large attachments can crash other systems and use up valuable time downloading. Send only what is necessary, and get permission to send multiple attachments.

SOURCES: Adapted from C Graham, "In-Box Overload," *Arizona Republic,* March 16, 2007, p A14; M Totty, "Rethinking the Inbox," *The Wall Street Journal,* March 26, 2007, p R8; F C Leffler and L Palais, "Filter Out Perilous Company E-Mails," SHRM Legal Report, *HR Magazine,* August 2008, pp 1–3; and P Kemp, "10 Ways to Reduce E-Mail Overload," Harvard Business Review, September 2009, p 88.

of texting while driving: "a study conducted by the Virginia Tech Transportation Institute using long-haul truck drivers concluded that when motorists texted while driving, their collision risk was 23 times greater."[96] Heeding this research and following the general cell phone etiquette tips in Table 14–8 can make for better and safer digital-age communication.

Needed: A Policy for Social Media Use in the Workplace In just a few short years, social media have significantly impacted life both inside and outside the workplace. Consider these telltale statistics, as of early 2011:

- Worldwide, Facebook has more than 610 million members who share 50,000 links every 60 seconds and LinkedIn has 90 million members.

McGraw Hill **connect**™ Go to www.mcgrawhillconnect.com for an interactive exercise to test your knowledge of the practical e-mail tips.

table 14–8 Five Commandments of Cell Phone Etiquette

1. **Thou shalt not subject defenseless others to cell phone conversations.** Cell phone etiquette, like all forms of etiquette, centers on having respect for others.

2. **Thou shalt not set thy ringer to play *La Cucaracha* every time thy phone rings.** It's a phone, not a public address system.

3. **Thou shalt turn thy cell phone off during public performances.** Set your phone on vibrate when in meetings or in the company of others and, if necessary, take or return calls at a polite distance.

4. **Thou shalt not dial while driving.** If you must engage in cell phone conversations while driving, use a hands-off device.

5. **Thou shalt not speak louder on thy cell phone than thou would on any other phone.** It's called "cell yell" and it's very annoying to others.

SOURCES: Five basic commandments in bold excerpted from D Brody, "The Ten Commandments of Cell Phone Etiquette," *Infoworld,* February 5, 2005, www.infoworld.com. Five interpretations quoted from R Kreitner and C Cassidy, *Management,* 12th ed (Mason, OH: South-Western Cengage Learning, 2012), page 319.

- YouTube users watch 2 billion videos a day. An average of 35 hours of video are uploaded to YouTube every minute.
- Twitter users send a billion tweets every week.
- A recent survey of 1,600 employees from the United States, Japan, the United Kingdom, and Germany revealed that 24% access social media sites on their employer's networks.
- In a survey of LinkedIn, Facebook, and Twitter users, 26% said they fib a little, 22% admitted they flat-out lie, and 21% resort to total fabrication. Only 31% claimed to be totally honest.
- When 7,200 managers were asked if their company monitors social media postings, 64% answered "No."[97]

Mc Graw Hill connect™ Go to www.mcgrawhillconnect.com for an interactive exercise to test your knowledge of social media use policies.

Conclusion: Social media use in the workplace is common, of questionable quality, and likely out of control. Employers can respond in a number of ways. They can simply block access to networking sites or, in a controversial assault on privacy, they can monitor employees' social media content on and/or off the job. IBM prefers a more proactive and cooperative approach:

Example. In 2005, seeing hundreds of its employees taking to blogging in their downtime, IBM drafted a set of "social computing guidelines" that has since grown to cover employee activity on sites like Twitter and Facebook. These guard-rails urge employees to be up-front about their identities, remember that they are personally responsible for what they publish, and to take a breath before hitting send. They also remind them to "stay away from controversial topics that aren't related to your IBM role," notes Gina Poole, vice-president for social software.

While many see Twitter as a place to indulge one's inner self, IBM wants employees to "add value" in all their online postings. "You're building your social reputation, so you don't want to be a frivolous or an uninteresting person," says Poole. "If you're just saying, 'I had pancakes for breakfast,' it doesn't really add value."[98]

Companies ultimately face twin challenges with social media: (1) tap the marketing, reputation-enhancing, team building and training, and customer and employee empowerment potential; (2) respect privacy rights and avoid legal and ethical abuses by employees. The policy guidelines in Table 14–9 (also applicable to the private use of company e-mail systems and phones) are a step in the right direction.

table 14–9   Workplace Policy Guidelines for Using Social Media

- Company approval is required for authors who use electronic resources of the company to send "tweets" or other public messages.

- Any identification of the author, including usernames, pictures or logos, or "profile" web pages should not use logos, trademarks, or other intellectual property of the company without approval from the company.

- If he or she is not providing an official message from the company, an employee who comments on any aspect of the business must include a disclaimer in his or her "profile" or "bio" that the views are his or her own and not those of the company.

- A message should not disclose any confidential or proprietary information of the company.

SOURCE: R Stephens, "In a Dither Over Twitter? Get a Policy," *HR Magazine,* June 2009, p 30.

Back to the **Chapter-Opening Case**

Putting yourself in Brian Dunn's position as CEO of Best Buy, what would your workplace social media policy specify?

Summary of Key Concepts

1. *Explain the perceptual process model of communication, and describe the barriers to effective communication.* Communication is a process of consecutively linked elements. Historically, this process was described in terms of a conduit model. Criticisms of this model led to development of a perceptual process model of communication that depicts receivers as information processors who create the meaning of messages in their own mind. Because receivers' interpretations of messages often differ from those intended by senders, miscommunication is a common occurrence. Every element of the perceptual model of communication is a potential process barrier. There are nine personal barriers that commonly influence communication: (*a*) variable skills in communicating effectively, (*b*) variations in how information is processed and interpreted, (*c*) variations in interpersonal trust, (*d*) stereotypes and prejudices, (*e*) big egos, (*f*) poor listening skills, (*g*) natural tendency to evaluate others' messages, (*h*) inability to listen with understanding, and (*i*) nonverbal communication. Physical barriers pertain to distance, physical objects, time, and work and office noise. Semantic barriers show up as encoding and decoding errors because these phases of communication involve transmitting and receiving words and symbols.

2. *Specify two major impacts of social media that are changing the general communication landscape.* Two major impacts of social media that managers cannot afford to ignore are (*a*) immediate worldwide personal access to unfiltered information and (*b*) bottom-up empowerment. Managers can stay in front of both internal and external changes and emerging opportunities and threats by monitoring social media content.

3. *Contrast the communication styles of assertiveness, aggressiveness, and nonassertiveness.* An assertive style is expressive and self-enhancing but does not violate others' basic human rights. In contrast, an aggressive style is expressive and self-enhancing but takes unfair advantage of others. A nonassertive style is characterized by timid and self-denying behavior. An assertive communication style is more effective than either an aggressive or nonassertive style.

4. *Discuss the primary sources of nonverbal communication.* There are several identifiable sources of nonverbal communication effectiveness. Body movements and gestures, touch, facial expressions, and eye contact are important nonverbal cues. The interpretation of these nonverbal cues significantly varies across cultures.

5. *Review the five dominant listening styles and 10 keys to effective listening.* The five dominant listening styles are

appreciative, empathetic, comprehensive, discerning, and evaluative. Good listeners use the following 10 listening habits: (*a*) capitalize on thought speed by staying with the speaker and listening between the lines, (*b*) listen for ideas rather than facts, (*c*) identify areas of interest between the speaker and listener, (*d*) judge content and not delivery, (*e*) do not judge until the speaker has completed his or her message, (*f*) put energy and effort into listening, (*g*) resist distractions, (*h*) listen to both favorable and unfavorable information, (*i*) read or listen to complex material to exercise the mind, and (*j*) take notes when necessary and use visual aids to enhance understanding.

6. *Describe how linguistic styles vary for women and men and what can be done to improve everyone's communication effectiveness.* Linguistic style is a person's characteristic culturally based speaking pattern (including such things as pacing, word choice, figures of speech, humor, and questions). The linguistic styles for women and men tend to vary in terms of how they ask for information, express certainty, apologize, accept blame, give criticism and praise, say thank you, build consensus, give directions, claim ownership of ideas, and use tone of voice. While acknowledging the risk of stereotypes, researchers say men tend to communicate more assertively, critically, and confidently and less apologetically. Genderflex communication calls for temporarily using the opposite gender's style for more effective communication. Knowledge of gender differences in linguistic styles can help everyone present themselves better and communicate more effectively in meetings and elsewhere.

7. *Discuss the formal and informal communication channels.* Formal communication channels follow the chain of command and include vertical, horizontal, and external routes. Vertical communication involves the flow of information up and down the organization. Horizontal communication flows within and between employees working in different work units. External communication flows between employees inside the organization and a variety of stakeholders outside the organization. Informal communication channels do not follow the chain of command. The grapevine and management by walking around represent the two most commonly used informal channels.

8. *Explain the contingency approach to media selection.* Selecting media is a key component of communication effectiveness. Media selection is based on the interaction between the information richness of a medium and the complexity of the problem/situation at hand. Information richness ranges from low to high and is a function of four

factors: speed of feedback, characteristics of the channel, type of communication, and language source. Problems/situations range from simple to complex. Effective communication occurs when the richness of the medium matches the complexity of the problem/situation. From a contingency perspective, richer media need to be used as problems/situations become more complex.

9. *Describe the Internet generation, and discuss the pros and cons of teleworking.* The 81 million people in the United States born between January 1977 and the end of 1997 were the first generation to grow up with the Internet. According to Don Tapscott, members of Net Gen are comfortable with advanced telecommunications and digital information technology and can be characterized by eight norms: freedom, customization, scrutiny, integrity, collaboration, entertainment, speed, and innovation. Teleworking involves doing work that is generally performed at a central office from various locations using advanced information technologies. It is called telecommuting when done from one's home. Employees who telework enjoy a measure of freedom and flexibility while their employers save on facilities. Telecommuting cuts travel expenses and reduces traffic congestion and pollution. On the downside, teleworkers can experience professional isolation, loss of informal interaction with colleagues, and the pressure of never being away from their work.

10. *Specify practical tips for more effective e-mail and cell phone etiquette, and discuss policies for using social media websites in the workplace.* E-mail can be more effectively managed by doing the following: (*a*) do not assume e-mail is confidential, (*b*) be professional and courteous, (*c*) avoid sloppiness, (*d*) don't use e-mail for volatile or complex issues, (*e*) keep messages brief and clear, (*f*) save people time, and (*g*) be careful with attachments. Basic cell phone etiquette involves having respect for others by avoiding annoying ring tones, loud conversations in public places, and unsafe dialing while driving. Recommended guidelines for using social media websites in the workplace include getting permission, not infringing on the employer's intellectual property rights, adding a company disclaimer for all personal opinions, and not disclosing the company's confidential or proprietary information.

Key Terms

OB in Action Case Study

Go Ahead, Use Facebook[99]

Wendy Wilkes was giving a presentation about Unilever's information technology to 30 new hires—most of them barely out of school—and they were not happy. They didn't like the company-issued mobile phones and laptops (or lack thereof). The employee Web site was so 1990s it didn't have interactive features, such as Facebook. And they couldn't download iTunes or instant-messaging software to communicate with people outside the company.

Wilkes can certainly identify with their gripes. The 27-year-old manager also joined the maker of such consumer staples as Lipton, Slim-Fast, and Vaseline right out of college. In school, she was accustomed to using her Hotmail account from any computer. But from her desktop at work she had access to corporate e-mail only. Not to mention that instant messaging—the foundation of her social life in college—was forbidden with anyone outside the company. "It was the amount of lockdown that surprised me the most," she says.

For anyone born after 1985, entering the workforce is a technological shock. Raised on MySpace.com and Wikipedia, these workers can't comprehend why they should have to wait 18 months for a company to build corporate software when they can download what they need instantly. "Technology is an important thing in my personal and work life, and I think the two of them should be connected," says Amy Johannigman, a 22-year-old college senior who worked at a company one summer where the use of social-networking sites was discouraged, camera phones verboten, and the interns were told to limit personal e-mails.

Revolt in the Ranks

Corporate policy isn't stopping Johannigman's contemporaries. Sure, there are official policies against using gear the tech department hasn't sanctioned, but the sheer number of workers who are flouting the rules makes enforcement nearly impossible. Consulting firm Forrester Research even coined a term for workers ignoring corporate policy and taking technology into their own hands: *Technology Populism.*

At Unilever, half of the desktop software and services used by employees comes from outside the company, and a lot of it shouldn't be there—Skype and iTunes, to name just a couple. "We can't stop them," says Chris Turner, Unilever's chief technology officer. "They're not accepting no as an answer."

Neither did Wilkes. She joined Unilever with a degree in information management and soon became a member of the marketing department's support team, where she experienced Unilever's rigid rules firsthand. So Wilkes put together some ideas about how employees could be more productive using consumer technology and sent her thoughts to Turner.

About six months ago, Turner offered Wilkes a new job, basically, in her words, to "get involved in trying to make a difference." Now Wilkes is one of 13 so-called "consumerization architects" whose job is to spread the use of popular—and in many cases free—technology. For example, Wilkes is looking into letting employees install webcams so they can confer by videoconference and cut down on travel time.

Unilever is still testing how to give employees more digital freedom. It may move users outside the corporate firewall and allow them to connect via their own computers, provided they're using certain security technologies. Anecdotal evidence suggests that the savings could be millions of dollars. "We see this as a real opportunity to start altering the cost model to deliver IT," says Turner.

Turner's ideas are unpopular with some people in his own department. But, as he points out, the social and economic forces are overwhelming.

Questions for Discussion

1. Have you ever been frustrated with out-of-date information technology in the workplace? If so, explain how it hampered your communication.

2. From a strategic standpoint, what are the arguments against uncontrolled information technology in the workplace?

3. As a top-level manager, what information technology policies would you put in place? What would you do to enforce those policies?

4. What is your personal stance on "Technology Populism"? What are the implications of your position for organizations?

5. What evidence of Net Gen norms (see Table 14–6) can you find in this case? Are they potentially positive or disruptive to organizational success? Explain.

6. How can Unilever's Wendy Wilkes give employees more digital freedom without endangering the company? Explain in terms of specific tools such as Skype, Webcam videoconferencing, iPods, Facebook, and Twitter.

Legal/Ethical Challenge

We Know Where You Are and What You're Doing[100]

Almost every worker has done it: gotten in a little Facebook updating, personal e-mailing, YouTube watching, and friend calling while on the clock.

Such indiscretions often went undetected by company management everywhere but the most secure and highly proprietary companies or governmental agencies. Not anymore.

Firms have become sharp-eyed, keenly eared watchdogs as they try to squeeze every penny's worth of their employees' salaries and to ensure they have the most professional and lawsuit-proof workplaces.

Managers use technological advances to capture workers' computer keystrokes, monitor the websites they frequent, even track their whereabouts through GPS-enabled cell phones. Some companies have gone as far as using webcams and minuscule video cameras to secretly record employees' movements.

What are the ethics of putting employees under constant electronic surveillance?

1. When employees are on company time they are fully accountable for their activities and whereabouts. Electronic surveillance is acceptable, with or without their knowledge.

2. Monitoring and geo-tracking your employees is acceptable if they are fully informed about the technology, procedures, and consequences.

3. If employees will be monitored by their employer, then the employees need to fully participate in formulating standards and limits of use. What standards and limits do you recommend?

4. Hello, Big Brother. Unacceptable infringements of personal privacy rights are being discussed here. Which forms of employee monitoring are the worst (and least) offensive? Explain.

5. Invent other options. Discuss.

Web Resources

For study material and exercises that apply to this chapter, visit our website at **www.mhhe.com/kreitner10e**

chapter 15

Influence, Empowerment, and Politics

 Learning Objectives

When you finish studying the material in this chapter, you should be able to:

LO.1   Explain the concept of mutuality of interest.

LO.2   Name at least three "soft" and two "hard" influence tactics, and summarize the practical lessons from influence research.

LO.3   Identify and briefly describe French and Raven's five bases of power, and discuss the responsible use of power.

LO.4   Define the term *empowerment,* and explain why it is a matter of degree.

LO.5   Explain why delegation is the highest form of empowerment, and discuss the connections among delegation, trust, and personal initiative.

LO.6   Define *organizational politics,* and explain what triggers it.

LO.7   Distinguish between favorable and unfavorable impression management tactics.

LO.8   Explain how to manage organizational politics.

How Did Deborah Dunsire Navigate Her Way to Power as a Cancer Fighter?

When Deborah Dunsire took over as chief executive officer at Millennium Pharmaceuticals in 2005, the Cambridge (Massachusetts) company had only one drug on the market—the blood-cancer treatment Velcade—and sales growth was slowing. Worse, the drug, an intravenous therapy used to treat multiple myeloma, was about to face competition from a pill made by Celgene. Dunsire boosted marketing and research and eventually got regulatory approval for broader use of Velcade. Over the next two years, sales of the drug jumped by 38 percent.

That performance drew plenty of attention in the industry. In 2008, Osaka-based Takeda Pharmaceutical acquired Millennium for $8.9 billion. . . . "She is a great asset" says Takeda CEO Yasuchika Hasegawa. "She has a proven track record and great leadership ability."

Dunsire's experience guiding new formulas through the US approval process and her blend of medical, marketing, and management skills are crucial to Takeda. . . . Takeda, Asia's largest drugmaker, had 2010 revenues of $15.8 billion.

Today, Dunsire, an MD who worked as a physician in South Africa for three years, is steering research on 15 compounds in development, including some Takeda turned over to her to oversee. The formulas represent about a third of Takeda's experimental drugs. . . .

Dunsire is one of just a handful of women heading biotech companies. When she was a child in Johannesburg, "things like that seemed out of my reach," she says. Neither her father, a carpenter, nor her mother, an office administrator, finished high school. From Lochgelly, a mining town in Scotland, the couple emigrated to Zimbabwe (then Rhodesia), where Dunsire was born, and then to South Africa. "Nobody ever moved from that town, but they did. They taught me to be curious and open to unexpected paths," she says.

After studying medicine at the University of Witwatersrand in Johannesburg and opening her own practice in that city, Dunsire answered an ad for a research job at Sandoz. One of the perks: a used Honda Civic. "I figured I could learn something completely new that I might be able to use later—and I got a car," she says. Though she missed working with patients, Dunsire says she quickly decided she could potentially save many more lives working in the pharmaceutical industry.

At Sandoz, Dunsire worked first in the medical-transplant unit and then trained the sales force. "We can bring forward new medicines that have real benefits, but if doctors don't know about them or how to use them . . . the patient isn't served," she says. Dunsire moved to Sandoz headquarters in Switzerland, and after the company merged with Ciba-Geigy to create Novartis in 1996, she helped persuade top executives to invest in cancer drugs.

Four years later she was tapped to lead Novartis's fledgling North American oncology business. Dunsire oversaw many launches, including Gleevec, Femara for breast cancer, and Zometa for metastatic bone diseases. The unit grew into one of Novartis's most profitable businesses and altered cancer treatment for millions of patients. Gleevec, which had sales of $4.3 billion last year, has turned once-lethal chronic myeloid leukemia into a manageable disease for many patients.

When Millennium came calling six years ago, Dunsire jumped at the chance to lead an entire company. "At Novartis I was maybe a lead violinist, but not having the overall vision a conductor has," she says. The acquisition by Takeda gives Millennium a global footprint, Dunsire says. She sits on an executive committee at Takeda that reviews possible acquisitions in the oncology field and travels to Japan six to eight times a year. Her passion, though, remains the lab. "I often hang out around [researchers'] cubicles just to see what's exciting and so I know what people are working on," she says. "They used to jump up when I showed up, but now they're used to me."

Dunsire says she doesn't necessarily want to run a bigger company. Before she joined Millennium, Novartis offered her management opportunities that she didn't find as interesting as heading a smaller company where she could be connected to research and to employees at every level. "I'm fulfilling my mission to work on illnesses we don't yet have adequate solutions for and to find cures," she says. "With cancer, I think we're at the beginning of the end of finding cures."[1]

Deborah Dunsire, MD, CEO, is a master of getting results in tough technical and cross-cultural situations.

LO.1 At the very heart of interpersonal dealings in today's work organizations is a constant struggle between individual and collective interests. For example, Sid wants a raise, but his company doesn't make enough money to both grant raises and buy needed capital equipment. The downside of such misalignment of interests was evident in the results of a recent survey of 150 senior executives who were asked, "What makes good employees quit?" "Unhappiness with management" was the number-one response category (35%), followed by "Limited opportunities for advancement" (33%) and "Lack of recognition" (13%).[2] Preoccupation with self-interest is understandable. After all, each of us was born, not as a cooperating organizational member, but as an individual with instincts for self-preservation. It took socialization in family, school, religious, sports, recreation, and employment settings to introduce us to the notion of mutuality of interest. Basically, **mutuality of interest** involves win–win situations in which one's self-interest is served by cooperating actively and creatively with potential adversaries. A pair of organization development consultants offered this managerial perspective of mutuality of interest:

Example. Nothing is more important than this sense of mutuality to the effectiveness and quality of an organization's products and services. Management must strive to stimulate a strong sense of shared ownership in every employee, because otherwise an organization cannot do its best in the long run. Employees who identify their own personal self-interest with the quality of their organization's output understand mutuality and strive to maintain it in their jobs and work relations.[3]

Figure 15–1 graphically portrays the constant tug-of-war between employees' self-interest and the organization's need for mutuality of interest. It also shows the linkage between this chapter—influence, empowerment, and politics—and other

figure 15–1   The Constant Tug-of-War between Self-Interest and Mutuality of Interest Requires Managerial Action

key topics in this book. Managers need a complete tool kit of techniques to guide diverse individuals, who are often powerfully motivated to put their own self-interests first, to pursue common objectives. At stake in this tug-of-war between individual and collective interests is no less than the ultimate survival of organizations such as Takeda Pharmaceuticals, featured in the opening case.

Organizational Influence Tactics

How do you get others to carry out your wishes? Do you simply tell them what to do? Or do you prefer a less direct approach, such as promising to return the favor? Whatever approach you use, the crux of the issue is *social influence*. A large measure of interpersonal interaction involves attempts to influence others, including parents, bosses, co-workers, spouses, children, teachers, friends, and customers. According to noted management author Gary Hamel: "Influence is like water, always flowing somewhere."[4] All of us need to sharpen our influence skills. A good starting point is familiarity with the following research insights.

◀ ·······················

TO THE POINT
What practical lessons
have researchers taught
us about influencing
others?

·······················

LO.2 Nine Generic Influence Tactics

A particularly fruitful stream of research, initiated by David Kipnis and his colleagues in 1980, reveals how people influence each other in organizations. The Kipnis methodology involved asking employees how they managed to get their bosses, co-workers, or subordinates to do what they wanted them to do.[5] Statistical refinements and replications by other researchers over a 13-year period eventually yielded nine influence tactics. The nine tactics, ranked in diminishing order of use in the workplace, are as follows:

1. *Rational persuasion.* Trying to convince someone with reason, logic, or facts.
2. *Inspirational appeals.* Trying to build enthusiasm by appealing to others' emotions, ideals, or values.
3. *Consultation.* Getting others to participate in planning, making decisions, and changes.
4. *Ingratiation.* Getting someone in a good mood prior to making a request; being friendly, helpful, and using praise or flattery (see Real World/Real People on page 434).
5. *Personal appeals.* Referring to friendship and loyalty when making a request.
6. *Exchange.* Making express or implied promises and trading favors.
7. *Coalition tactics.* Getting others to support your effort to persuade someone.
8. *Pressure.* Demanding compliance or using intimidation or threats.
9. *Legitimating tactics.* Basing a request on one's authority or right, organizational rules or policies, or express or implied support from superiors.[6]

These approaches can be considered *generic* influence tactics because they characterize social influence in all directions and in a wide variety of settings. Researchers have found this ranking to be fairly consistent regardless of whether the direction of influence is downward, upward, or lateral.[7]

Mc Graw Hill **connect**™ Go to
www.mcgrawhillconnect.com
for an interactive exercise to
test your knowledge of the
nine generic influence tactics.

mutuality of interest Balancing individual and organizational interests through win–win cooperation.

real WORLD // real PEOPLE: ethics

Should You Try to Charm the Boss?

Bosses now are told to praise down because the old-school days of a paycheck being enough to motivate employees are all but over, says Deloitte CEO Barry Salzberg. But praising up is a different animal. . . . Most CEOs say they appreciate an honest compliment if it passes the sincerity sniff test. Trouble is, bosses don't often have a good nose, at least not for the brown-noser.

CEOs do get a lot of opportunity to detect what's sincere and what isn't. University of Michigan business strategy professor James Westphal has researched ingratiation and says he finds that when someone is promoted to CEO, the compliments from below increase exponentially and spectacularly. But most CEOs aren't any better at detecting a snow job than the rest of us, he says, which raises the question: Should we be exercising discretion with the boss or should we be laying it on thick?

What is your attitude toward the use (or abuse) of ingratiation to get ahead in the workplace? What label would you affix to someone who overdoes it?

SOURCE: D Jones, "To Brown-Nose or Not to Brown-Nose?" *USA Today,* November 18, 2009, p 1B.

Back to the Chapter-Opening Case

Which influence tactics are evident in this case study? If you were Deborah Dunsire's mentor or personal coach, which tactic would you advise her to rely on the most? Explain.

Some call the first five influence tactics—rational persuasion, inspirational appeals, consultation, ingratiation, and personal appeals—*soft* tactics because they are friendlier and not as coercive as the last four tactics. Exchange, coalition, pressure, and legitimating tactics accordingly are called *hard* tactics because they involve more overt pressure. Margaret G McGlynn, president of Merck Vaccines, is a good role model for having made a career out of skillfully using rational persuasion:

Example. An ability to argue her case in a "relentlessly logical and wonderfully intense way," as ex-boss David Anstice puts it, helped McGlynn rise rapidly. . . .

McGlynn's powers of persuasion have also helped her achieve results on Capitol Hill. . . . After Merck won approval to market a vaccine for shingles—a painful disease that strikes the elderly—she started knocking on doors all over Capitol Hill. Turned out that the new Medicare Part D drug plan prevented doctors from getting fully paid to administer vaccines. "I explained to [policymakers] that shingles is a debilitating illness that causes a major impact on quality of life," she says. They seem to have listened: . . . Congress passed a bill that fixes the Medicare payment shortfall, which the President signed [in 2006].[8]

Three Possible Influence Outcomes

Put yourself in this familiar situation. It's Wednesday and a big project you've been working on for your project team is due Friday. You're behind on the preparation of your computer graphics for your final report and presentation. You catch a friend who is great at computer graphics as he heads out of the office at quitting time. You try this *exchange tactic* to get your friend to help you out: "I'm way behind. I need your help. If you could come back in for two to three hours tonight and help me with these graphics, I'll complete those spreadsheets you've been complaining about." According to researchers, your friend will engage in one of three possible influence outcomes:

1. *Commitment.* Your friend enthusiastically agrees and will demonstrate initiative and persistence while completing the assignment.

2. *Compliance.* Your friend grudgingly complies and will need prodding to satisfy minimum requirements.

3. *Resistance.* Your friend will say no, make excuses, stall, or put up an argument.[9]

The best outcome is commitment because the target person's intrinsic motivation will energize good performance. However, managers often have to settle for compliance in today's hectic workplace. Resistance means a failed influence attempt.

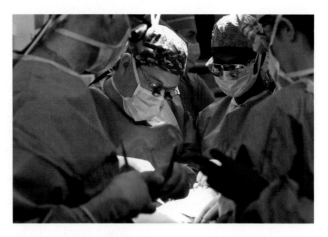

The success of the plastic surgery being performed here hinges partly on how well the surgeon listens to and is influenced by other specialists on the team. This requires a culture of empowerment in which everyone feels free to speak up if they spot a problem.

Practical Research Insights

Laboratory and field studies have taught us useful lessons about the relative effectiveness of influence tactics along with other instructive insights:

- Commitment is more likely when people rely on consultation, strong rational persuasion, and inspirational appeals and *do not* rely on pressure and coalition tactics.[10] Interestingly, in one study, managers were not very effective at *downward* influence. They relied most heavily on inspiration (an effective tactic), ingratiation (a moderately effective tactic), and pressure (an ineffective tactic).[11]

- A meta-analysis of 69 studies suggests ingratiation (making the boss feel good) can slightly improve your performance appraisal results and make your boss like you significantly more.[12] Another study, with diversity and ethical implications, found ingratiation to be an effective way for Caucasian men to get a seat on a corporate board of directors in the United States.[13]

- Commitment is more likely when the influence attempt involves something *important* and *enjoyable* and is based on a *friendly relationship.*[14]

- A field study of sales managers in the United States looked at how the quality of the working relationship between a manager and a team member affected willingness to help teammates. When the relationship was *not* good, inspirational appeals and exchange tactics actually *reduced* helping behavior, with lack of credibility being the likely culprit. On the other hand, exchange tactics increased helping behavior when the relationship was good. *Consultation* increased helping behavior, regardless of the quality of the relationship. This is a strong endorsement for participation, whereby managers and leaders solicit input from employees.[15]

- In a survey, 214 employed MBA students (55% female) tended to perceive their superiors' soft influence tactics as fair and hard influence tactics as unfair. Unfair influence tactics were associated with greater resistance among employees.[16]

- Another study probed male–female differences in influencing work group members. Many studies have found women to be perceived as less competent and less influential in work groups than men. The researchers had male and female work group leaders engage in either task behavior (demonstrating ability and task competence) or dominating behavior (relying on threats). For both women and men, task behavior was associated with perceived competence and effective influence. Dominating behavior was not effective. The following conclusion by the researchers has important practical implications for all current and future managers who desire to successfully influence others: "The display of task cues is an effective means to enhance one's status in groups and . . . the attempt to gain influence in task groups through dominance is an ineffective and poorly received strategy for both men and women."[17]

- Interpersonal influence is culture bound. The foregoing research evidence on influence tactics has a bias in favor of European-North Americans. Much remains to be learned about how to effectively influence others (without unintended insult) in today's diverse labor force and cross-cultural global economy.[18]

Finally, Barbara Moses, a Canadian consultant and author, offers this advice about influencing your boss:

Example. If your boss doesn't understand the need for change, this might be partly your fault. You can't make change; you have to sell it. And the key to selling anything is to understand where the other person is coming from—rather than to assume that your boss is a complete jerk. But most of us communicate from an egocentric place. We construct an idea or a project mainly in terms of what makes sense to us. Instead, ask yourself: "What's most important to my boss?" "What are his greatest concerns?" Go forward only after you've answered these questions.[19]

Social Power

TO THE POINT

Why do managers need to know about the two types and five bases of power?

The term *power* evokes mixed and often passionate reactions. Citing recent instances of government corruption and corporate misconduct, many observers view power as a sinister force. To these skeptics, Lord Acton's time-honored statement that "power corrupts and absolute power corrupts absolutely" is as true as ever.[20] However, organizational behavior (OB) specialists remind us that, like it or not, power is a fact of life in modern organizations. According to one management writer,

---

Example. Power must be used because managers must influence those they depend on. Power also is crucial in the development of managers' self-confidence and willingness to support subordinates. From this perspective, power should be accepted as a natural part of any organization. Managers should recognize and develop their own power to coordinate and support the work of subordinates; it is powerlessness, not power, that undermines organizational effectiveness.[21]

Thus, power is a necessary and generally positive force in organizations. As the term is used here, **social power** is defined as "the ability to marshal the human, informational, and material resources to get something done."[22]

Importantly, the exercise of social power in organizations is not necessarily a downward proposition. Employees can and do exercise power upward and laterally. An example of an upward power play occurred at Alberto-Culver Company, the personal care products firm. Leonard Lavin, founder of the company, was under pressure to revitalize the firm because key employees were departing for more innovative competitors such as Procter & Gamble. Lavin's daughter Carol Bernick and her husband Howard, both longtime employees, took things into their own hands:

Example. Even the Bernicks were thinking of jumping ship. Instead, . . . they marched into Lavin's office and presented him with an ultimatum: Either hand over the reins as CEO or run the company without them. It was a huge blow for Lavin, forcing him to face selling his company to outsiders or ceding control to the younger generation. Unwilling to sell, he reluctantly stepped down, though he remains chairman.

How does it feel to push aside your own father and wrest operating control of the company he created? "It isn't an easy thing to do with the founder of any company, whether he's your father or not," says Carol Bernick, 46, now vice chairman and president of Alberto-Culver North America.[23]

Howard Bernick became CEO, the firm's top-down management style was scrapped in favor of a more open culture, and Lavin reportedly was happy with how things turned out.[24]

LO.3 Dimensions of Power

While power may be an elusive concept to the casual observer, social scientists view power as having reasonably clear dimensions. Two dimensions of power that deserve our attention are (1) socialized versus personalized power and (2) the five bases of power.

Two Types of Power   Behavioral scientists such as David McClelland contend that one of the basic human needs is the need for power (n Pwr). Because this need is learned and not innate, the need for power has been extensively studied. Historically, need for power was said to be high when subjects interpreted TAT pictures in terms of one person attempting to influence, convince, persuade, or control another. More recently, however, researchers have drawn a distinction between **socialized power** and **personalized power**.

connect™ Go to www.mcgrawhillconnect.com for an interactive exercise to test your knowledge of the dimensions of power.

Example. There are two subscales or "faces" in n Pwr. One face is termed "socialized" (s Pwr) and is scored in the Thematic Apperception Test (TAT) as "plans, self-doubts, mixed outcomes and concerns for others, . . ." while the second face is "personalized" power (p Pwr), in which expressions of power for the sake of personal aggrandizement become paramount.[25]

Managers and others who pursue personalized power for their own selfish ends give power a bad name. According to research, personalized power is exhibited when managers

- Focus more on satisfying their own needs.
- Focus less on the needs of their underlings.
- Act like "the rules" others are expected to follow don't apply to them.[26]

---

social power Ability to get things done with human, informational, and material resources.

socialized power Directed at helping others.

personalized power Directed at helping oneself.

Sheryl Sandberg, the chief operating officer at Facebook, dedicated herself to socialized power as a result of working in less-developed parts of the world. What is your experience with personalized versus socialized power?

For example, Nancy Traversy, cofounder and CEO of the successful children's book publisher Barefoot Books, recently related this story about how she came to be an entrepreneur:

Example. I was born in Canada to a family of artists. I studied business, which made me the black sheep. After college I worked for the banking division of Pricewaterhouse in London. One day I was wearing a suit. One of the partners said to me, "Women don't wear trousers" and sent me home to change. It was a formative experience.[27]

A series of interviews with 25 American women elected to public office found a strong preference for socialized power.[28] A good case in point is Sheryl Sandberg, Facebook's chief operating officer, who recently wrote:

Example. My first job was at the World Bank, where I worked on health projects in India—leprosy, AIDS and blindness. During my first trip to India, I was taken on a tour of a village leprosy home, where I saw people in conditions that I would not have thought possible. I promised myself that going forward, I would work only on things that really mattered.

Facebook allows people to be their authentic selves online and therefore use the power of technology to discover each other and share who they really are. The connections they make have a real impact on their lives.[29]

Back to the Chapter-Opening Case

Which type of power, socialized or personalized, has Deborah Dunsire used most effectively in her professional life? Explain.

Five Bases of Power   A popular classification scheme for social power traces back more than 50 years to the work of John French and Bertram Raven. They proposed that power arises from five different bases: reward power, coercive power, legitimate power, expert power, and referent power.[30] Each involves a different approach to influencing others:

- *Reward power*. Managers have **reward power** when they obtain compliance by promising or granting rewards. Reward power is at the heart of shaping on-the-job behavior with verbal or written recognition and other forms of positive reinforcement. Training expert Roy Saunderson explains:

Example. Employees tell us one of the problems they have with rewards is they only receive them when the goal finally is accomplished. Their complaint is generally that no one ever says anything along the way to getting the results.

What a lost opportunity for acknowledging people for the many actions and behaviors leading up to the final outcome. And what a wonderful chance to draw upon the art and practice of recognition to validate the work done and the worth of the individual who did it.[31]

- *Coercive power*. Threats of punishment and actual punishment give an individual **coercive power**. For instance, consider this heavy-handed tactic by Wolfgang Bernhard, a Volkswagen executive: "A ruthless cost-cutter, Bernard, 46, has a favorite technique: He routinely locks staffers in meeting rooms, then refuses to open the doors until they've stripped $1,500 in costs from a future model."[32] Bathroom break, anyone?

- *Legitimate power*. This base of power is anchored to one's formal position or authority. Thus, individuals who obtain compliance primarily because of their formal authority to make decisions have **legitimate power**. Legitimate power may express itself in either a positive or negative manner in managing people. Positive legitimate power focuses constructively on job performance. Negative legitimate power tends to be threatening and demeaning to those being influenced. Its main purpose is to build the power holder's ego. Importantly, there is growing concern today about the limits of managers' legitimate power relative to privacy rights and off-the-job behavior.[33]

- *Expert power*. Valued knowledge or information gives an individual **expert power** over those who need such knowledge or information. The power of supervisors is enhanced because they know about work schedules and assignments before their employees do. Skillful use of expert power played a key role in the effectiveness of team leaders in a study of three physician medical diagnosis teams.[34] Knowledge *is* power in today's high-tech workplaces.

- *Referent power*. Also called charisma, **referent power** comes into play when one's personality becomes the reason for compliance. Role models have referent power over those who identify closely with them.[35]

Regarding charisma, Jack and Suzy Welch offered this instructive perspective in their business advice column:

Example. So how big is it? In the short term, very. In the long term, very again—but not alone.

Now, we're obviously not talking here about "bad" charisma, exuded without brains, vision, and character. That trait is useless, and even dangerous. In business, wow personalities with less-than-wow minds are called empty suits for good reason. Too many of these individuals manage to ho-ho-ho their way to the top, even to the CEO's office, but most self-destruct after looking great for a couple of years while achieving little. On a larger scale, darkly charismatic leaders have the power to wreck lives and nations. . . .

But good charismatic leaders are everywhere, too, leading with magnetism plus integrity and intelligence. And for them, charisma just makes the job a whole lot easier. Why? Because leaders have always had to energize their people.[36]

---

reward power Obtaining compliance with promised or actual rewards.

coercive power Obtaining compliance through threatened or actual punishment.

legitimate power Obtaining compliance through formal authority.

expert power Obtaining compliance through one's knowledge or information.

referent power Obtaining compliance through charisma or personal attraction.

Back to the Chapter-Opening Case

What specific power bases have played a role in Deborah Dunsire's career success? What is her strongest power base in her present position? Explain.

Research Insights about Social Power

In one study, a sample of 94 male and 84 female nonmanagerial and professional employees in Denver, Colorado, completed TAT tests. The researchers found that the male and female employees had similar needs for power (n Pwr) and personalized power (p Pwr). But the women had a significantly higher need for socialized power (s Pwr) than did their male counterparts.[37] This bodes well for today's work organizations where women are playing an ever greater administrative role. Unfortunately, as women gain power in the workplace, greater tension between men and women has been observed. *Training* magazine offered this perspective:

Example. Observers view the tension between women and men in the workplace as a natural outcome of power inequities between the genders. Their argument is that men still have most of the power and are resisting any change as a way to protect their power base. [Consultant Susan L] Webb asserts that sexual harassment has far more to do with exercising power in an unhealthy way than with sexual attraction. Likewise, the glass ceiling, a metaphor for the barriers women face in climbing the corporate ladder to management and executive positions, is about power and access to power.[38]

Accordingly, "powerful women were described more positively by women than by men" in a study of 140 female and 125 male college students in Sydney, Australia.[39]

A reanalysis of 18 field studies that measured French and Raven's five bases of power uncovered "severe methodological shortcomings."[40] After correcting for these problems, the researchers identified the following relationships between power bases and work outcomes such as job performance, job satisfaction, and turnover:

- Expert and referent power had a generally positive impact.
- Reward and legitimate power had a slightly positive impact.
- Coercive power had a slightly negative impact.

The same researcher, in a follow-up study involving 251 employed business college seniors, looked at the relationship between influence styles and bases of power. This was a bottom-up study. In other words, employee perceptions of managerial influence and power were examined. Rational persuasion was found to be a highly acceptable managerial influence tactic. Why? Because employees perceived it to be associated with the three bases of power they viewed positively: legitimate, expert, and referent.[41]

In summary, expert and referent power appear to get the best *combination* of results and favorable reactions from lower-level employees.

Using Power Responsibly and Ethically

As democracy continues to spread around the world, one reality is clear: Leaders who do not use their power responsibly risk losing it. This holds for corporations and nonprofit organizations as well as for government leaders and public figures.

real WORLD // real PEOPLE: ethics

A Heavy Hand at Johnson & Johnson

One day in 2005 a batch of more than 1 million bottles of St Joseph aspirin failed a quality test because a sample didn't dissolve properly, according to two employees involved in the testing process. Following company procedures, the employees blocked the batch from being shipped. Their manager then called the two into his office. "He said, 'You like working here?'" one of the workers recalls. "'This should pass. There's no reason this should fail.'" Ultimately the two quality workers were ordered to retest the drugs, then average the new scores to arrive at a passing grade so that the pills could ship. Says one of them: "You get to the point where, like me, you end up doing what you're told."

The manager they fingered denies knowledge of the incident. Tellingly, though, he acknowledges that there were ethical issues in the department and in turn blames another supervisor.

How would you have dealt with this abuse of power if you were one of the quality inspectors? Discuss the practical ramifications of your course of action.

SOURCE: M Kimes, "Why J&J's Headache Won't Go Away," *Fortune,* September 6, 2010, pp 104, 106.

A step in the right direction for managers who want to avoid such a turnaround and wield power responsibly is understanding the difference between commitment and mere compliance.

Responsible managers strive for socialized power while avoiding personalized power. Former NATO commander General Wesley Clark put it this way:

Example. Sometimes threatening works, but it usually brings with it adverse consequences—like resentment and a desire to get even in some way. People don't like to be reminded that they are inferior in power or status. And so, in business, it is important to motivate through the power of shared goals, shared objectives, and shared standards.[42]

In fact, in a survey, organizational commitment was higher among US federal government executives whose superiors exercised socialized power than among colleagues with "power-hungry" bosses. The researchers used the appropriate terms *uplifting power* versus *dominating power*.[43] How does this relate to the five bases of power? As with influence tactics, managerial power has three possible outcomes: commitment, compliance, or resistance. Reward, coercive, and negative legitimate power tend to produce *compliance* (and sometimes, resistance). On the other hand, positive legitimate power, expert power, and referent power tend to foster *commitment*. Once again, commitment is superior to compliance because it is driven by internal or intrinsic motivation. Employees who merely comply require frequent "jolts" of power from the boss to keep them going (see Real World/Real People). Committed employees tend to be self-starters who do not require close supervision—a key success factor in today's flatter, team-oriented organizations.

LO.4 Empowerment: From Power Sharing to Power Distribution

A promising trend in today's organizations centers on giving employees a greater say in the workplace. This trend wears various labels, including "high-involvement management," "participative management," and "open-book management." Regardless of the label one prefers, it is all about employees taking greater control of

◀ ....

TO THE POINT

How does empowerment occur, and why is effective delegation a difficult challenge?

....

Employee empowerment is a win-win situation for both employees and guests at Homewood Suites hotels. Of course, employees need to be carefully hired and properly trained to create a totally satisfying experience for customers who can demand their money back.

their work lives. Management consultant and writer W Alan Randolph offers this definition: "**Empowerment** is recognizing and releasing into the organization the power that people already have in their wealth of useful knowledge, experience, and internal motivation."[44] A core component of this process is pushing decision-making authority down to progressively lower levels. Steve Kerr, who has served as the "chief learning officer" at General Electric and Goldman Sachs, adds this important qualification: "We say empowerment is moving decision making down to the lowest level where a competent decision can be made."[45] This is how Hilton's Homewood Suites hotel chain empowers its employees:

Example. Empowerment is the key driver of engagement at Homewood Suites. The company offers a 100 percent money-back guarantee if a guest isn't satisfied. Any employee—from housekeeper to manager—can make good on that guarantee; they don't have to seek approval or argue. And, the guest doesn't have to go through a chain of command to have a complaint resolved.

"The return we get on every dollar refunded is 20 to 1," [executive Frank] Saitta says, based on repeat business and referrals from those refunded guests. The return on engaged employees "is much higher."[46]

Mc Graw Hill connect™ Go to www.mcgrawhillconnect.com for a comprehension case on how power is used at insurance and financial services firm J A Counter and Associates.

Of course, it is naive and counterproductive to hand power over to unwilling or unprepared employees. Let us explore the dynamics of employee empowerment, while keeping these cautionary words from Jack and Suzy Welch in mind: "empowerment is one of those concepts (like "creative destruction" and "collaborative work teams") that, as books are written and consultants move in, gets surrounded by more hype than honesty."[47]

A Matter of Degree

The concept of empowerment requires some adjustments in traditional thinking. First, power is not a zero-sum situation where one person's gain is another's loss. Social power is unlimited. This requires win–win thinking. Frances Hesselbein, the woman credited with modernizing the Girl Scouts of the USA, put it this way: "The more power you give away, the more you have."[48] Authoritarian managers who view employee empowerment as a threat to their personal power are missing the point because of their win–lose thinking.

The second adjustment to traditional thinking involves seeing empowerment as *a matter of degree* not as an either–or proposition.[49] Figure 15–2 illustrates how power can be shifted to the hands of nonmanagers step by step. The overriding goal is to increase productivity and competitiveness in leaner organizations. Each step in this evolution increases the power of organizational contributors who traditionally were told what, when, and how to do things. A good role model for the spirit of empowerment is Motorola executive Greg Brown:

Example. He boils his philosophy down to three words: listen, learn, lead. It means you need to understand your business down to the nuts and bolts, let your employees know you won't have all the answers, and focus on just a handful of truly crucial things, even though dozens seem as important.[50]

---

figure 15–2 The Evolution of Power: From Domination to Delegation

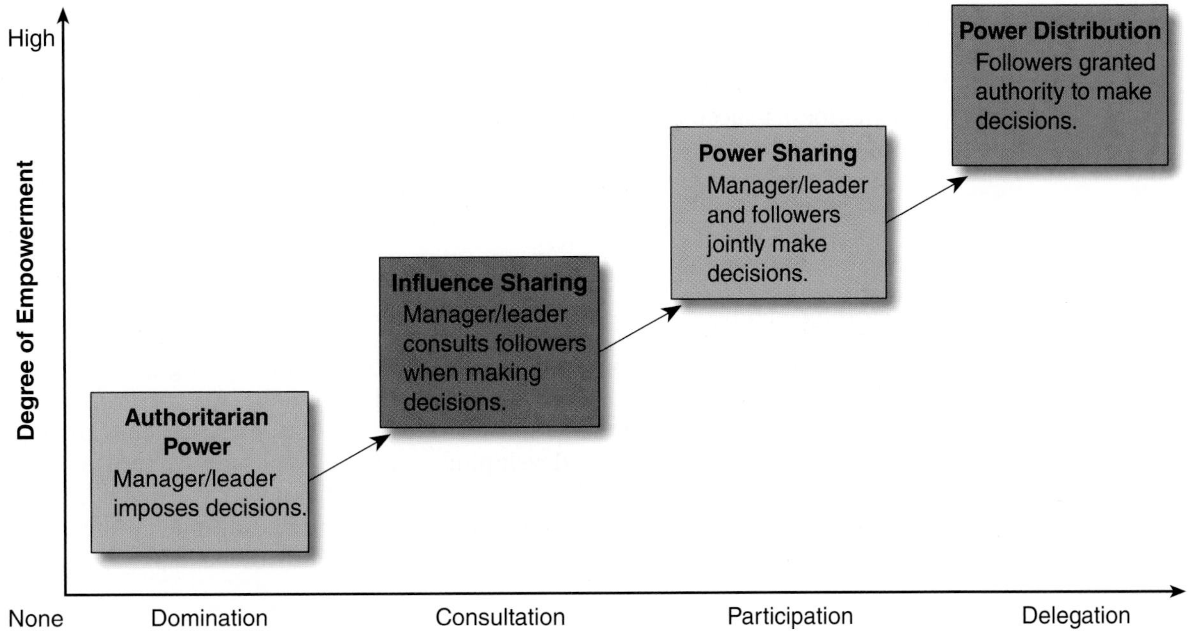

Participative Management

Confusion exists about the exact meaning of participative management (PM). Management experts have clarified this situation by defining **participative management** as the process whereby employees play a direct role in (1) setting goals, (2) making decisions, (3) solving problems, and (4) making changes in the organization. Participative management includes, but goes beyond, simply asking employees for their ideas or opinions.

Advocates of PM claim employee participation increases employee satisfaction, commitment, and performance. Consistent with both Maslow's need theory and the job characteristics model of job design (see Chapter 8), participative management is predicted to increase motivation because it helps employees fulfill three basic needs: (1) autonomy, (2) meaningfulness of work, and (3) interpersonal contact. Satisfaction of these needs enhances feelings of acceptance and commitment, security, challenge, and satisfaction. In turn, these positive feelings supposedly lead to increased innovation and performance.[51]

Participative management does not work in all situations. The design of work, the level of trust between management and employees, and the employees' competence and readiness to participate represent three factors that influence the effectiveness of PM. With respect to the design of work, individual participation is counterproductive when employees are highly interdependent on each other, as on an assembly line. The problem with individual participation in this case is that interdependent specialists generally do not have a broad understanding of the entire production process. Participative management also is less likely to succeed when employees do not trust management. Trusting one's supervisor was found to be particularly important for nonmanagerial employees in a recent study at a *Fortune* 500 company.[52] Finally, PM is more effective when employees are

connect™ Go to www.mcgrawhillconnect.com for an interactive exercise to test your knowledge of the evolution of power.

---

empowerment Sharing varying degrees of power with lower-level employees to tap their full potential.

participative management Involving employees in various forms of decision making.

competent, prepared, and interested in participating. Bonnie Hammer, president of NBC Universal Cable Entertainment, fosters participation by pushing her staff to the forefront:

Example. Although she has strong views about projects, she tries to ensure that the team doesn't succumb to groupthink. "I can't tell you how many meetings I open up with, 'My voice is last,'" she says. "I don't want anybody to hear my opinion before I hear everybody else's opinion. I give everyone the license to disagree."[53]

 LO.5 Delegation

The highest degree of empowerment is **delegation**, the process of granting decision-making authority to lower-level employees.[54] This amounts to *power distribution*. Delegation has long been the recommended way to lighten the busy manager's load while at the same time developing employees' abilities.[55] Importantly, delegation gives nonmanagerial employees more than simply a voice in decisions. It empowers them to make their own decisions. A prime example, in line with the Homewood Suites example above, is the Ritz-Carlton Hotel chain:

Example. At Ritz-Carlton, every worker is authorized to spend up to $2,000 to fix any problem a guest encounters. Employees do not abuse the privilege. "When you treat people responsibly, they act responsibly," said Patrick Mene, the hotel chain's director of quality.[56]

Not surprising, then, that Ritz-Carlton has won national service quality awards.

Barriers to Delegation   Delegation is easy to talk about, but many managers find it hard to actually do. A concerted effort to overcome the following common barriers to delegation needs to be made:

- Belief in the fallacy, "If you want it done right, do it yourself."
- Lack of confidence and trust in lower-level employees.
- Low self-confidence.
- Fear of being called lazy.
- Vague job definition.
- Fear of competition from those below.
- Reluctance to take the risks involved in depending on others.
- Lack of controls that provide early warning of problems with delegated duties.
- Poor example set by bosses who do not delegate.[57]

Delegation Research and Implications for Trust and Personal Initiative   Researchers at the State University of New York at Albany surveyed pairs of managers and employees and did follow-up interviews with the managers concerning their delegation habits. Their results confirmed some important commonsense notions about delegation. Greater delegation was associated with the following factors:

1. Employee was competent.
2. Employee shared manager's task objectives.

figure 15-3   Personal Initiative: The Other Side of Delegation

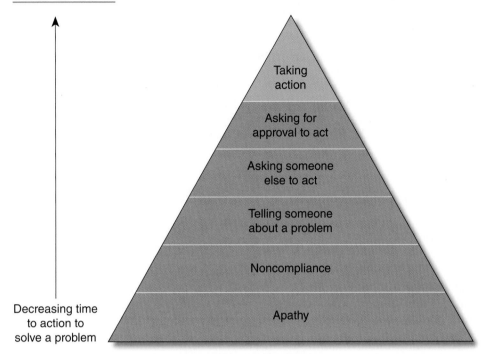

SOURCE: Figure from A L Frohman, "Igniting Organizational Change from Below: The Power of Personal Initiative," *Organizational Dynamics,* Winter 1997, p 46. © 1997, with permission from Elsevier.

3. Manager had a long-standing and positive relationship with employee.

4. The lower-level person also was a supervisor.[58]

This delegation scenario boils down to one pivotal factor, *trust*.[59]

Back to the Chapter-Opening Case

Which layer on the initiative pyramid in Figure 15–3 best characterizes Deborah Dunsire's management style? How has this helped her succeed?

    Managers prefer to delegate important tasks and decisions to the people they trust. As discussed in Chapter 11, it takes time and favorable experience to build trust. Of course, trust is fragile; it can be destroyed by a single remark, act, or omission. Ironically, managers cannot learn to trust someone without, initially at least, running the risk of betrayal. This is where the empowerment evolution in Figure 15–2 represents a three-step ladder to trust: consultation, participation, and delegation. In other words, managers need to start small and work up the empowerment ladder. They need to delegate small tasks and decisions and scale up as competence, confidence, and trust grow. Employees need to work on their side

delegation Granting decision-making authority to people at lower levels.

of the trust equation as well. One of the best ways to earn a manager's trust is to show *initiative* (see Figure 15–3) and then get results. Researchers in the area offer this instructive definition and characterization:

Example. **Personal initiative** is a behavior syndrome resulting in an individual's taking an active and self-starting approach to work and going beyond what is formally required in a given job. More specifically, personal initiative is characterized by the following aspects: it (1) is consistent with the organization's mission, (2) has a long-term focus, (3) is goal-directed and action-oriented, (4) is persistent in the face of barriers and setbacks, and (5) is self-starting and proactive.[60]

Recall our discussion of the *proactive personality* in Chapter 5.

Empowerment: The Research Record and Practical Advice

Like other widely heralded techniques—such as TQM, 360-degree reviews, teams, and learning organizations—empowerment has its fair share of critics and suffers from unrealistic expectations.[61] Research results to date are mixed, with a recent positive uptrend:

- A meta-analysis encompassing 27 studies and 6,732 individuals revealed that employee participation in the performance appraisal process was positively related to an employee's satisfaction with his or her performance review, perceived value of the appraisal, motivation to improve performance after the review, and perceived fairness of the appraisal process.[62]

- Another meta-analysis of 86 studies involving 18,872 people demonstrated that participation had a small statistically significant positive impact on job performance, but only a moderate positive effect on job satisfaction.[63]

- Relative to work teams, a field study of 102 hotels in the United States revealed that teams with empowering leadership tended to have more knowledge sharing, a greater sense of team efficacy, and better performance.[64]

- A study of 164 New Zealand companies employing at least 100 people found a positive correlation between high-involvement management practices and employee retention and company productivity.[65]

- A field study with 149 call center employees documented how "high-involvement work processes" more effectively boosted job performance (e.g., customer satisfaction), job satisfaction, and organizational commitment than did self-managed teams.[66]

- A study of 3,000 Canadian companies looked at the relationship between employee empowerment and layoffs. Productivity tended to drop after a layoff in high-involvement workplaces, except when the commitment to empowerment was continued during and after the layoff.[67]

- According to two new studies, employees who felt empowered had greater intrinsic motivation, attempted to be more creative, and were more supportive of organizational changes.[68]

We believe empowerment has good promise if managers go about it properly (see Real World/Real People). Empowerment is a sweeping concept with many different definitions and lots of moving parts. Consequently, researchers

real WORLD // real PEOPLE

Participation and Empowerment at the New York Philharmonic

In guiding the orchestra through a musical work, [music director and conductor Alan] Gilbert has his own ideas about how it should sound, from the volume to the tempo. But his musicians have worked with many conductors and have experience playing popular classical works.

"I'd be an idiot not to make use of the experience," he says. Gilbert gets them to buy in by asking them for help. He meets with senior musicians and section leaders, saying, "This is the kind of thing I'll be looking for over the next period of time from your section. Could you try to encourage that as well?" That gives the musicians a

sense of ownership and responsibility, while also "planting seeds," as Gilbert says, that will help him achieve the effect he is aiming for.

Gilbert carefully avoids the perception that he is imposing his will.

In the workplace, there is a fine line between participative management and manipulation to achieve one's own desired ends. How can you tell the difference?

SOURCE: J Shambora, "Advice From a Maestro," *Fortune*, April 11, 2011, p 38.

---

use inconsistent measurements, and cause-effect relationships are fuzzy. Managers committed to the idea of employee empowerment need to follow the path of continuous improvement, learning from their successes and failures. Eight years of research with 10 "empowered" companies led Randolph to formulate the three-pronged empowerment plan illustrated in Figure 15–4. Notice how open-book

figure 15–4   Randolph's Empowerment Model

The Empowerment Plan

Share Information
- Share company performance information.
- Help people understand the business.
- Build trust through sharing sensitive information.
- Create self-monitoring possibilities.

Create Autonomy through Structure	**Let Teams Become the Hierarchy**
• Create a clear vision and clarify the little pictures. • Create new decision-making rules that support empowerment. • Clarify goals and roles collaboratively. • Establish new empowering performance management processes. • Use heavy doses of training.	• Provide direction and training for new skills. • Provide encouragement and support for change. • Gradually have managers let go of control. • Work through the leadership vacuum stage. • Acknowledge the fear factor.

**Remember: Empowerment is not magic;
it consists of a few simple steps and a lot of persistence.**

SOURCE: W A Randolph, "Navigating the Journey to Empowerment," *Organizational Dynamics,* vol 24, no 3, p 46, © 1997, with permission from Elsevier.

personal initiative Going beyond formal job requirements and being an active self-starter.

Original characters Michael Scott (Steve Carell) and Dwight Schrute (Rainn Wilson) of *The Office* frequently engaged in office politics that quickly got out of hand. But when real life imitates art, it's not always so funny.

management and active information sharing are needed to build the necessary foundation of trust. Beyond that, clear goals and lots of relevant training are needed. Noting that the empowerment process can take several years to unfold, Randolph offered this perspective:

Example. While the keys to empowerment may be easy to understand, they are hard to implement. It takes tremendous courage to start sharing sensitive information. It takes true strength to build more structure just at the point when people want more freedom of action. It takes real growth to allow teams to take over the management decision-making process. And above all, it takes perseverance to complete the empowerment process.[69]

TO THE POINT

How can organizational politics and impression management be kept on a positive track?

connect Go to www.mcgrawhillconnect.com for a video case on power and influence during the Hurricane Katrina disaster.

LO.6 Organizational Politics and Impression Management

Most students of OB find the study of organizational politics intriguing. Perhaps this topic owes its appeal to the antics of Hollywood's corporate villains and TV shows such as *The Office*.[70] As we will see, however, organizational politics includes, but is certainly not limited to, dirty dealing. Organizational politics is an ever-present and sometimes annoying feature of modern work life. "Executives say that they spend 19% of their time dealing with political infighting with their staffs, according to a survey by OfficeTeam, a staffing services firm."[71] One expert recently observed, "Many 'new economy' companies use the acronym 'WOMBAT'—or waste of money, brains, and time—to describe office politics."[72] On the other hand, organizational politics can be a positive force in modern work organizations. Skillful and well-timed politics can help you get your point across, neutralize resistance to a key project, land a choice job assignment, or simply get the job done.

A recent Accountemps survey asked 572 workers, "How do you deal with office politics?" A majority (54%) chose the response "Know what's going on but do not participate," while 16% said "Participate directly" and 29% said they would not participate.[73] It's knowing how "the game" is played that really counts. Actively playing politics at work is a matter of personal preference and ethics. In her book *Secrets to Winning at Office Politics*, Marie G McIntyre lists the Four P's of political success:

- **Power assessment.** How can you improve your leverage position?

- **Performance.** How can your work make the business more successful?

- **Perception.** How can you enhance your reputation, especially with those who can achieve your goals?

- **Partnerships.** How can you increase your network of allies and supporters?[74]

To those ends, 32% of 3,447 middle and senior managers responding to an Internet survey said they needed coaching in how to be more politically savvy at work.[75]

We explore this important and interesting area by (1) defining the term *organizational politics*, (2) identifying three levels of political action, (3) discussing eight specific political tactics, (4) considering a related area called *impression management*, and (5) examining relevant research and practical implications.

Definition and Domain of Organizational Politics

"**Organizational politics** involves intentional acts of influence to enhance or protect the self-interest of individuals or groups."[76] An emphasis on *self-interest* distinguishes this form of social influence. Managers are constantly challenged to achieve a workable balance between employees' self-interests and organizational interests, as discussed at the beginning of this chapter. When a proper balance exists, the pursuit of self-interest may serve the organization's interests. Political behavior becomes a negative force when self-interests erode or defeat organizational interests. For example, researchers have documented the political tactic of filtering and distorting information flowing up to the boss. This self-serving practice put the reporting employees in the best possible light.[77]

Uncertainty Triggers Political Behavior   Political maneuvering is triggered primarily by *uncertainty*. Five common sources of uncertainty within organizations are

1. Unclear objectives.
2. Vague performance measures.
3. Ill-defined decision processes.
4. Strong individual or group competition.[78]
5. Any type of change.

Regarding this last source of uncertainty, organization development specialist Anthony Raia noted, "Whatever we attempt to change, the political subsystem becomes active. Vested interests are almost always at stake and the distribution of power is challenged."[79]

  Thus, we would expect a field sales representative, striving to achieve an assigned quota, to be less political than a management trainee working on a variety of projects. While some management trainees stake their career success on hard work, competence, and a bit of luck, many do not. These people attempt to gain a competitive edge through some combination of the political tactics discussed below. Meanwhile, the salesperson's performance is measured in actual sales, not in terms of being friends with the boss or taking credit for others' work. Thus, the management trainee would tend to be more political than the field salesperson because of greater uncertainty about management's expectations.

  Because employees generally experience greater uncertainty during the earlier stages of their careers, are junior employees more political than more senior ones? The answer is yes, according to a survey of 243 employed adults in upstate New York. In fact, one senior employee nearing retirement told the researcher: "I used to play political games when I was younger. Now I just do my job."[80]

Three Levels of Political Action   Although much political maneuvering occurs at the individual level, it also can involve group or collective action. Figure 15–5 illustrates three different levels of political action: the individual level, the coalition level, and the network level.[81] Each level has its distinguishing characteristics. At the individual level, personal self-interests are pursued by the individual. The political aspects of coalitions and networks are not so obvious, however.

  People with a common interest can become a political coalition by fitting the following definition. In an organizational context, a **coalition** is an informal group bound together by the *active* pursuit of a *single* issue. Coalitions may or may not

organizational politics Intentional enhancement of self-interest.

coalition Temporary groupings of people who actively pursue a single issue.

figure 15–5 Levels of Political Action in Organizations

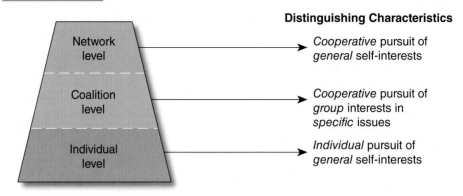

coincide with formal group membership. When the target issue is resolved (a sexual-harassing supervisor is fired, for example), the coalition disbands. Experts note that political coalitions have "fuzzy boundaries," meaning they are fluid in membership, flexible in structure, and temporary in duration.

Coalitions are a potent political force in organizations. Consider the situation Charles J Bradshaw faced in a finance committee meeting at Transworld Corporation. Bradshaw, president of the company, opposed the chairman's plan to acquire a $93 million nursing home company:

Example. [The senior vice president for finance] kicked off the meeting with a battery of facts and figures in support of the deal. "Within two or three minutes, I knew I had lost," Bradshaw concedes. "No one was talking directly to me, but all statements addressed my opposition. I could tell there was a general agreement around the board table." . . .

Then the vote was taken. Five hands went up. Only Bradshaw voted no.[82]

After the meeting, Bradshaw resigned his $530,000-a-year position, without as much as a handshake or good-bye from the chairman. In Bradshaw's case, the finance committee was a formal group that temporarily became a political coalition aimed at sealing his fate at Transworld. In recent years, coalitions on the corporate boards of Home Depot, Computer Associates, and Hewlett-Packard ousted the heads of those giant companies.

A third level of political action involves networks.[83] Unlike coalitions, which pivot on specific issues, networks are loose associations of individuals seeking social support for their general self-interests. Politically, networks are people oriented, while coalitions are issue oriented. Networks have broader and longer term agendas than do coalitions. For instance, Avon's Hispanic employees have built a network to enhance the members' career opportunities.[84]

Political Tactics

Anyone who has worked in an organization has firsthand knowledge of blatant politicking. Blaming someone else for your mistake is an obvious political ploy. But other political tactics are more subtle. Researchers have identified a range of political behavior.

One landmark study, involving in-depth interviews with 87 managers from 30 electronics companies in southern California, identified eight political tactics. Top-, middle-, and low-level managers were represented about equally in the sample. According to the researchers: "Respondents were asked to describe organizational political tactics and personal characteristics of effective political actors based on their accumulated experience in *all* organizations in which they had worked."[85] Listed in descending order of occurrence, the eight political tactics that emerged were

1. Attacking or blaming others.
2. Using information as a political tool.
3. Creating a favorable image. (Also known as *impression management.*)
4. Developing a base of support.
5. Praising others (ingratiation).
6. Forming power coalitions with strong allies.
7. Associating with influential people.
8. Creating obligations (reciprocity).

Table 15–1 describes these political tactics and indicates how often each reportedly was used by the interviewed managers.

Go to www.mcgrawhillconnect.com for an interactive exercise to test your knowledge of the eight common political tactics.

table 15–1 Eight Common Political Tactics in Organizations

POLITICAL TACTIC	PERCENTAGE OF MANAGERS MENTIONING TACTIC	BRIEF DESCRIPTION OF TACTIC
1. Attacking or blaming others	54%	Used to avoid or minimize association with failure. Reactive when scapegoating is involved. Proactive when goal is to reduce competition for limited resources.
2. Using information as a political tool	54	Involves the purposeful withholding or distortion of information. Obscuring an unfavorable situation by overwhelming superiors with information.
3. Creating a favorable image (impression management)	53	Dressing/grooming for success. Adhering to organizational norms and drawing attention to one's successes and influence. Taking credit for others' accomplishments.
4. Developing a base of support	37	Getting prior support for a decision. Building others' commitment to a decision through participation.
5. Praising others (ingratiation)	25	Making influential people feel good ("apple polishing").
6. Forming power coalitions with strong allies	25	Teaming up with powerful people who can get results.
7. Associating with influential people	24	Building a support network both inside and outside the organization.
8. Creating obligations (reciprocity)	13	Creating social debts ("I did you a favor, so you owe me a favor").

SOURCE: Adapted from R W Allen, D L Madison, L W Porter, P A Renwick, and B T Mayes, "Organizational Politics: Tactics and Characteristics of Its Actors," *California Management Review,* Fall 1979, pp 77–83.

table 15–2 Are You Politically Naive, Politically Sensible, or a Political Shark?

CHARACTERISTICS	NAIVE	SENSIBLE	SHARKS
Underlying attitude	Politics is unpleasant.	Politics is necessary.	Politics is an opportunity.
Intent	Avoid at all costs.	Further departmental goals.	Self-serving and predatory.
Techniques	Tell it like it is.	Network; expand connections; use system to give and receive favors.	Manipulate; use fraud and deceit when necessary.
Favorite tactics	None–the truth will win out.	Negotiate, bargain.	Bully; misuse information; cultivate and use "friends" and other contacts.

SOURCE: From J K Pinto and O P Kharbanda, "Lessons for an Accidental Profession," *Business Horizons,* Vol. 38, No. 2, p 45, © 1995, with permission from Elsevier.

The researchers distinguished between reactive and proactive political tactics. Some of the tactics, such as scapegoating, were *reactive* because the intent was to *defend* one's self-interest. Other tactics, such as developing a base of support, were *proactive* because they sought to *promote* the individual's self-interest.

What is your attitude toward organizational politics? How often do you rely on the various tactics in Table 15–1? You can get a general indication of your political tendencies by comparing your behavior with the characteristics in Table 15–2. Would you characterize yourself as politically *naive,* politically *sensible,* or a political *shark?* How do you think others view your political actions? What are the career, friendship, and ethical implications of your political tendencies?[86]

 LO.7 Impression Management

Impression management is defined as "the process by which people attempt to control or manipulate the reactions of others to images of themselves or their ideas."[87]

This encompasses how one talks, behaves, and looks. Most impression management attempts are directed at making a *good* impression on relevant others. But, as we will see, some employees strive to make a *bad* impression. For purposes of conceptual clarity, we will focus on *upward* impression management (trying to impress one's immediate supervisor) because it is most relevant for managers. Still, it is good to remember that *anyone* can be the intended target of impression management. Parents, teachers, peers, voters, employees, interviewers, and customers are all fair game when it comes to managing the impressions of others.

A Conceptual Crossroads Impression management is an interesting conceptual crossroads involving self-monitoring, attribution theory, and organizational politics. Perhaps this explains why impression management has gotten active research attention in recent years. High self-monitoring employees ("chameleons" who adjust to their surroundings) are likely to be more inclined to engage in impression management than would low self-monitors.[88] Impression management also involves the systematic manipulation of attributions. For example, a bank president will look good if the board of directors is encouraged to attribute organizational successes to her efforts and attribute problems and failures to factors beyond her control. Impression management definitely fits into the realm of organizational politics because of an overriding focus on furthering one's *self-interests*.

real WORLD // real PEOPLE: ethics

Linda Hudson Made Her Point with a Strong First Impression

The President and CEO of defense contractor BAE Systems offered this advice to women trying to climb the corporate ladder in male-dominated fields:

Challenge demeaning actions, but do it factually and professionally. Even far into my career at a management level, a vice president who was interviewing me for a role on his staff blatantly said, "I don't think a woman can do this job." I remember saying to him, "I don't expect to have to sit here and defend my gender. And if you aren't man enough to look at my credentials and conclude I'm the right person, then I'm wasting my time." I walked out on the interview. But I got the job.

What are the practical lessons here about influence, power, and impression management?

SOURCE: As quoted in B Kowitt, "Tips for Climbing the Corporate Ladder," *Fortune*, March 21, 2011, p 42.

Making a Good Impression   If you "dress for success," project an upbeat attitude at all times, and have polished a 15-second elevator speech for top executives, you are engaging in favorable impression management—particularly so if your motive is to improve your lot in life. Is it all worth the effort? In a survey of 2,198 employees, 56% said dressing for success paid off; 44% said no.[89] Too close to call. Creating a good first impression can be tricky, as this funny situation illustrates:

Job fairs, such as this one in Denver, Colorado, are a great place to practice impression management. How strong are you at creating a good first impression? What impressions do you think tattoos and body piercings make on job interviewers?

Example. On the first day of work unloading trucks for Wal-Mart Stores in 1984, Doug McMillon, then 17, drove his Honda Civic into his boss's car. It's lucky for Wal-Mart he wasn't fired. McMillon has spent much of the last 25 years working his way up to become CEO of Wal-Mart International.[90]

There are questionable ways to create a good impression, as well. Impression management can easily stray into unethical territory.

A statistical factor analysis of the influence attempts reported by a sample of 84 bank employees (including 74 women) identified three categories of favorable upward impression management tactics.[91] Favorable upward impression management tactics can be *job-focused* (manipulating information about one's job performance), *supervisor-focused* (praising and doing favors for one's supervisor), and *self-focused* (presenting oneself as a polite and nice person). A moderate amount of upward impression management is a necessity for the average employee today. Too little, and busy managers are liable to overlook some of your valuable contributions when they make job assignment, pay, and promotion decisions. Too much, and you run the risk of being branded a "schmoozer," a "phony," and other unflattering things by your co-workers. Excessive flattery and ingratiation can backfire by embarrassing the target person and damaging one's credibility. Also, the risk of unintended insult is very high when impression management tactics cross gender, racial, ethnic, and cultural lines (see Real World/Real People). International management experts warn:

impression management Getting others to see us in a certain manner.

Example. the impression management tactic is only as effective as its correlation to accepted norms about behavioral presentation. In other words, slapping a Japanese subordinate on the back with a rousing "Good work, Hiro!" will not create the desired impression in Hiro's mind that the expatriate intended. In fact, the behavior will likely create the opposite impression.[92]

Making a Poor Impression   At first glance, the idea of consciously trying to make a bad impression in the workplace seems absurd. But an interesting new line of impression management research has uncovered both motives and tactics for making oneself look *bad*. In a survey of the work experiences of business students at a large northwestern US university, more than half "reported witnessing a case of someone intentionally looking bad at work."[93] Why? Four motives came out of the study:

Example. (1) *Avoidance:* Employee seeks to avoid additional work, stress, burnout, or an unwanted transfer or promotion. (2) *Obtain concrete rewards:* Employee seeks to obtain a pay raise or a desired transfer, promotion, or demotion. (3) *Exit:* Employee seeks to get laid off, fired, or suspended, and perhaps also to collect unemployment or workers' compensation. (4) *Power:* Employee seeks to control, manipulate, or intimidate others, get revenge, or make someone else look bad.[94]

Within the context of these motives, *unfavorable* upward impression management makes sense.

Five unfavorable upward impression management tactics identified by the researchers are as follows:

1. *Decreasing performance*—restricting productivity, making more mistakes than usual, lowering quality, neglecting tasks.
2. *Not working to potential*—pretending ignorance, having unused capabilities.
3. *Withdrawing*—being tardy, taking excessive breaks, faking illness.
4. *Displaying a bad attitude*—complaining, getting upset and angry, acting strangely, not getting along with co-workers.
5. *Broadcasting limitations*—letting co-workers know about one's physical problems and mistakes, both verbally and nonverbally.[95]

The Wall Street Journal's Jared Sandberg explains what he calls "strategic incompetence":

Example. Strategic incompetence isn't about having a strategy that fails, but a failure that succeeds. It almost always works to deflect work one doesn't want to do—without ever having to admit it. For junior staffers, it's a way of attaining power through powerlessness. For managers, it can juice their status by pretending to be incapable of lowly tasks.[96]

Recommended ways to manage employees who try to make a bad impression can be found throughout this book. They include more challenging work, greater autonomy, better feedback, supportive leadership, clear and reasonable goals, and a less stressful work setting.

Back to the Chapter-Opening Case

If you were being interviewed by Deborah Dunsire for a managerial position, how would you go about making a good impression to land the job?

Research Evidence on Organizational Politics and Impression Management

Field research involving employees in real organizations rather than students in contrived laboratory settings has yielded these useful insights:

- In a study of 514 nonacademic university employees in the southwestern United States, white men had a greater understanding of organizational politics than did racial and ethnic minorities and white women. The researchers endorsed the practice of using mentors to help women and minorities develop their political skills.[97]

- Another study of 68 women and 84 men employed by five different service and industrial companies in the United States uncovered significant gender-based insights about organizational politics. In a version of gender wars,

Example. it was found that political behavior was perceived more favorably when it was performed against a target of the opposite gender. . . . Thus subjects of both sexes tend to relate to gender as a meaningful affiliation group. This finding presents a different picture from the one suggesting that women tend to accept male superiority at work and generally agree with sex stereotypes which are commonly discriminatory in nature.[98]

McGraw Hill **connect** Go to www.mcgrawhillconnect.com for a self-assessment to help you determine how political you are.

- In a survey of 172 team members in a large company's research and development unit, perceived higher levels of team politics were associated with lower organizational commitment, lower job satisfaction, poorer job performance, and lower unit effectiveness.[99]

- When 250 British managers were recently polled about organizational politics, political maneuvering was found to be commonplace and back-stabbing behavior reportedly triggered reciprocal back-stabbing. The researchers further concluded:

Example. Most managers viewed political behavior as ethical and necessary, and aspects of organizational effectiveness, change, resourcing and reputation were attributed to political tactics, although 80% had no training in this area. Tactics experienced frequently included networking, using "key players" to support initiatives, making friends with power brokers, bending the rules, and self-promotion. Tactics experienced as rare, but not unknown, included misinformation, spreading rumors, and keeping "dirt files" for blackmail.[100]

The results of a cross-cultural laboratory study are noteworthy. A unique study of 38 Japanese Americans and 39 European Americans at the University of

Utah showed how impression management can cause problems across cultures. Consistent with Japanese tradition, the Japanese Americans tended to publicly report their job performance in a self-effacing (or modest) way, *despite confiding in private that they had performed as well as the European Americans.* This Japanese cultural tendency toward understatement created a false impression for third-party European American evaluators (who were kept unaware of any cultural distinctions). According to the researchers, "Japanese American participants were seen as less competent and less likeable than their European American counterparts because of their tendency to downplay their performance."[101] The old American expression "It pays to toot your own horn" appears to be as true as ever. Too much tooting, however, can brand one as arrogant, self-centered, and overbearing. This sort of delicate cultural balancing act makes cross-cultural dealings very challenging.

LO.8 Managing Organizational Politics

Organizational politics cannot be eliminated. A manager would be naive to expect such an outcome. But political maneuvering can and should be managed to keep it constructive and within reasonable bounds. Harvard's Abraham Zaleznik put the issue this way: "People can focus their attention on only so many things. The more it lands on politics, the less energy—emotional and intellectual—is available to attend to the problems that fall under the heading of real work."[102] *Measurable objectives are management's first line of defense against counterproductive organizational politics.*

An individual's degree of politicalness is a matter of personal values, ethics, and temperament. People who are either strictly nonpolitical or highly political generally pay a price for their behavior. The former may experience slow promotions and feel left out, while the latter may run the risk of being called self-serving and lose their credibility. People at both ends of the political spectrum may be considered poor team players. A moderate amount of prudent political behavior generally is considered a survival tool in complex organizations. Meanwhile, managers are urged to follow the tips in Table 15–3 and everyone needs to

table 15–3 How to Keep Organizational Politics within Reasonable Bounds

- Screen out overly political individuals at hiring time.

- Create an open-book management system.

- Make sure every employee knows how the business works and has a personal line of sight to key results with corresponding measurable objectives for individual accountability.

- Have nonfinancial people interpret periodic financial and accounting statements for all employees.

- Establish formal conflict resolution and grievance processes.

- As an ethics filter, do only what you would feel comfortable doing on national television.

- Publicly recognize and reward people who get real results without political games.

SOURCE: Adapted in part from discussion in L B MacGregor Serven, *The End of Office Politics as Usual* (New York: American Management Association, 2002), pp 184–99.

follow Irene Rosenfeld's lead. The Brooklyn-born CEO of Kraft says this is the best advice she ever got:

Example. Be yourself. All too often, particularly in a corporate environment, there's a tendency to want to create a persona that's perceived to be what people are looking for. The opportunity to bring your whole self to work every day is a powerful idea, an inspiring idea, and it's a part of making one feel comfortable at a company.[103]

Summary of Key Concepts

1. *Explain the concept of mutuality of interest.* Managers are constantly challenged to foster mutuality of interest (a win–win situation) between individual and organizational interests. Organization members need to actively cooperate with actual and potential adversaries for the common good.

2. *Name at least three "soft" and two "hard" influence tactics, and summarize the practical lessons from influence research.* Five soft influence tactics are rational persuasion, inspirational appeals, consultation, ingratiation, and personal appeals. They are more friendly and less coercive than the four hard influence tactics: exchange, coalition tactics, pressure, and legitimating tactics. According to research, soft tactics are better for generating commitment and are perceived as more fair than hard tactics. Ingratiation—making the boss feel good through compliments and being helpful—can slightly improve performance appraisal results and make the boss like you a lot more. Influence through domination is a poor strategy for both men and women. Influence is a complicated and situational process that needs to be undertaken with care, especially across cultures.

3. *Identify and briefly describe French and Raven's five bases of power, and discuss the responsible use of power.* French and Raven's five bases of power are reward power (rewarding compliance), coercive power (punishing noncompliance), legitimate power (relying on formal authority), expert power (providing needed information), and referent power (relying on personal attraction). Responsible and ethical managers strive to use socialized power (primary concern is for others) rather than personalized power (primary concern for self). Research found higher organizational commitment among employees with bosses who used uplifting power than among those with power-hungry bosses who relied on dominating power.

4. *Define the term* empowerment, *and explain why it is a matter of degree.* Empowerment involves sharing varying degrees of power and decision-making authority with lower-level employees to tap their full potential. Empowerment is not an either–or, all-or-nothing proposition.

It can range from merely consulting with employees, to having them actively participate in making decisions, to granting them decision-making authority through delegation.

5. *Explain why delegation is the highest form of empowerment, and discuss the connections among delegation, trust, and personal initiative.* Delegation gives employees more than a participatory role in decision making. It allows them to make their own work-related decisions. Managers tend to delegate to employees they trust. Employees can get managers to trust them by demonstrating personal initiative (going beyond formal job requirements and being self-starters).

6. *Define* organizational politics, *and explain what triggers it.* Organizational politics is defined as intentional acts of influence to enhance or protect the self-interests of individuals or groups. Uncertainty triggers most politicking in organizations. Political action occurs at individual, coalition, and network levels. Coalitions are informal, temporary, and single-issue alliances.

7. *Distinguish between favorable and unfavorable impression management tactics.* Favorable upward impression management can be job-focused (manipulating information about one's job performance), supervisor-focused (praising or doing favors for the boss), or self-focused (being polite and nice). Unfavorable upward impression management tactics include decreasing performance, not working to potential, withdrawing, displaying a bad attitude, and broadcasting one's limitations.

8. *Explain how to manage organizational politics.* Since organizational politics cannot be eliminated, managers need to keep it within reasonable bounds. Measurable objectives for personal accountability are key. Participative management also helps, especially in the form of open-book management. Formal conflict resolution and grievance programs are helpful. Overly political people should not be hired, and employees who get results without playing political games should be publicly recognized and rewarded. The "how-would-it-look-on-TV" ethics test can limit political maneuvering.

Key Terms

Mutuality of interest, 432	Legitimate power, 439	Personal initiative, 446
Social power, 436	Expert power, 439	Organizational politics, 449
Socialized power, 437	Referent power, 439	Coalition, 449
Personalized power, 437	Empowerment, 442	Impression management, 452
Reward power, 438	Participative management, 443	
Coercive power, 439	Delegation, 444	

OB in Action Case Study

"You're Driving Us Crazy. You've Got to Back Off."[104]

Doug Rauch retired as president of Trader Joe's grocery store chain in 2008:

I'm a recovering controlaholic, as I suspect a lot of C-suite people are. My failure to recognize this problem nearly prevented Trader Joe's from successfully expanding.

Bringing Trader Joe's from the West Coast to the East meant we had to hire an entirely new staff. We had to teach everyone the Trader Joe's buying philosophy, the organizational culture, the details that made us successful. In my mind, no one could do that better than I could, because no one else had the knowledge I did. I happily micromanaged the expansion.

A year or so in, they'd gotten my message just fine. The culture was instilled, the philosophy bought into. Only I didn't see it. In my zeal to control everything, I failed to notice that it was time to take off the training wheels and let the new staff members grow into their roles. I kept micromanaging. The effect was stifling, especially on our buyers, the heart of our organization. I had always said that a buying team that doesn't make mistakes isn't worth a damn, yet I wasn't letting them make their own mistakes. They started to be afraid to take chances. It was beginning to affect the business.

Luckily for me, one intrepid senior buyer helped put a stop to all this. She approached me and said, "You're driving us crazy. You've got to back off. We'll make mistakes, but you've got to let us go."

It was a turning point. I went back to the buying team and admitted my problem. I told them I was "on the wagon" and that I needed them to give me regular feedback or I might fall off. We laughed about it—and the company flourished.

As I worked on letting go, I came to see micromanaging as a failure to let others shine or grow. So instead of fixing problems, I focused on nurturing problem solvers. I turned "Try this" into "What do you think we should try?" I replaced the satisfaction of doing something myself, the way I wanted it done, with the joy of watching others do something their way and succeed.

And that turns out to be far more rewarding.

Questions for Discussion

1. What influence tactics and power bases are evident in this case? Explain.
2. How does the distinction between socialized power and personalized factor into this case?
3. How would you describe Doug Rauch's behavior change in terms of Figure 15–2? Explain.
4. How does this case bolster the argument in favor of delegation?
5. What advice would you give to a manager who micromanages?
6. Do you think Doug Rauch's shift in management style made organizational politics more or less likely in the Trader Joe's organization? Explain.

Legal/Ethical Challenge

Payback Time?

"I'm a research assistant at a large consulting firm. Recently I noticed a significant error in a report prepared by a co-worker who's always acting superior to me. It's not my job to proof this report, so I've said nothing. The report's about to go out, and I hope Julie gets in trouble. My friends are appalled, but I don't think I owe this woman to bail her out. Am I right?"[105]

What are the ethical and practical implications of the following actions?

1. Don't say anything. What goes around comes around. Julie deserves to be taken down a peg or two. It's only fair.

2. Alert Julie's boss so the report gets corrected *and* Julie gets in trouble.

3. Privately tell Julie about the mistake in hopes of making her a political ally and possibly even a friend.

4. Grow up! It's not about you and your petty rivalries. Excellent customer service should be your top priority.

5. You have an obligation as an employee to speak up and help the entire company succeed.

6. Invent other options. Discuss.

Web Resources

For study material and exercises that apply to this chapter, visit our website at **www.mhhe.com/kreitner10e**

chapter 16

Leadership

Learning Objectives

When you finish studying the material in this chapter, you should be able to:

LO.1 Define the term *leadership*, and explain the difference between leading and managing.

LO.2 Review trait theory research and the takeaways from this theoretical perspective.

LO.3 Explain behavioral styles theory and its takeaways.

LO.4 Explain, according to Fiedler's contingency model, how leadership style interacts with situational control, and discuss the takeaways from this model.

LO.5 Discuss House's revised path–goal theory and its practical takeaways.

LO.6 Describe the difference between laissez-faire, transactional, and transformational leadership.

LO.7 Discuss how transformational leadership transforms followers and work groups.

LO.8 Explain the leader–member exchange model of leadership.

LO.9 Review the concept of shared leadership and the principles of servant-leadership.

LO.10 Describe the follower's role in the leadership process.

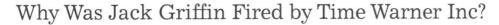

Why Was Jack Griffin Fired by Time Warner Inc?

Time Warner Inc. said it has forced out Jack Griffin, chief executive of the media company's Time Inc. publishing unit, after less than six months on the job.

In a memo to employees Thursday evening, Time Warner Chief Executive Jeff Bewkes said he had concluded that Mr. Griffin's leadership style "did not mesh with Time Inc. and Time Warner." . . .

A person familiar with the matter said Mr. Griffin exhibited "imperious behavior" that did not sit well with the ranks at Time Inc., which publishes *People, Sports Illustrated, Real Simple* and *Fortune* magazines, among others.

For example, Mr. Griffin insisted that every magazine include a masthead in each issue and that his name be on the top, bucking a long-standing tradition at the company of leaving it up to individual editors whether or not to run a masthead. The mandatory extra page cost the company as much as $6 million a year, said a senior executive, noting that the decision came after hundreds of employees were let go in recent years.

The senior executive also cited more minor examples of behavior that ruffled feathers, including his habit of calling 7:30 am meetings. "It was not a very family-friendly way to run things," the person said.

"It just came down to a clash of personalities and style," another person familiar with the matter said.

According to another person close to the situation, Mr. Griffin's over-reliance on outside consultants was a major factor in Time Warner's decision to fire him. Mr. Griffin often made major decisions in isolation from Time Inc., staff and top executives, turning to outsiders like consultants rather than the company's insiders, many who are veteran executives of Time Inc. . . .

Mr. Griffin's style stood in stark contrast to that of Mr. Bewkes, the Time Warner CEO, whose emphasis on teamwork and group decision making has become a hallmark of the conglomerate's corporate culture.

Mr. Griffin's hire came after a run at Meredith Corp. during which he received praise for moving the company beyond its roots as a magazine publisher and into other businesses like marketing services, a move that helped Meredith weather an advertising downturn that led to cuts and closures throughout the magazine industry.

In December, Mr. Griffin reorganized the company's corporate sales and marketing operations as part of an effort to refashion the company in the image of Meredith Corp.[1]

The chapter-opening case highlights a lesson we discussed in Chapter 1. Specifically, a contingency approach toward management is more likely to produce positive results for individuals and organizations: A contingency approach calls for using management tools and leadership styles in a situationally appropriate manner instead of relying on "one best way" or "one size fits all." Mr. Griffin did not follow this advice. His demise seems to be partly caused by his use of a leadership style that was successful at Meredith Corp. but did not fit with the culture and environment at Time Warner.

The overall goal of this chapter is to help you avoid the type of mistake made by Mr. Griffin by providing a thorough discussion of effective and ineffective leadership. After formally defining the term *leadership,* this chapter focuses on the following areas: (1) trait and behavioral approaches to leadership, (2) alternative situational theories of leadership, (3) the full-range theory of leadership, and (4) additional perspectives on leadership. Because there are many different leadership theories within each of these areas, it is impossible to discuss them all. This chapter reviews those theories with the most research support.

TO THE POINT

What is the difference between leading and managing?

LO.1 What Does Leadership Involve?

Because the topic of leadership has fascinated people for centuries, definitions abound. This section presents a definition of leadership, reviews the different approaches or perspectives used to study leadership, and highlights the similarities and differences between leading and managing.

Leadership Defined

Disagreement about the definition of leadership stems from the fact that it involves a complex interaction among the leader, the followers, and the situation. For example, some researchers define leadership in terms of personality and physical traits, while others believe leadership is represented by a set of prescribed behaviors. In contrast, other researchers define leadership in terms of the power relationship between leaders and followers. According to this perspective, leaders use their power to influence followers' behavior. Leadership also can be seen as an instrument of goal achievement. In other words, leaders are individuals who help others accomplish their goals. Still others view leadership from a skills perspective.

There are four commonalities among the many definitions of **leadership**: (1) leadership is a process between a leader and followers, (2) leadership involves social influence, (3) leadership occurs at multiple levels in an organization (at the individual level, for example, leadership involves mentoring, coaching, inspiring, and motivating; leaders also build teams, generate cohesion, and resolve conflicts at the group level; finally, leaders build culture and generate change at the organizational level), and (4) leadership focuses on goal accomplishment.[2] Based on these commonalities, leadership is defined as "a process whereby an individual influences a group of individuals to achieve a common goal."[3]

There are two components of leadership missing from the above definition: the moral and follower perspectives. Leadership is not a moral concept. History is filled with examples of effective leaders who were killers, corrupt, and morally bankrupt. Barbara Kellerman, a leadership expert, commented on this notion by concluding, "Leaders are like the rest of us: trustworthy and deceitful, cowardly and brave, greedy and generous. To assume that all good leaders are good people is to be willfully blind to the reality of the human condition, and it more severely limits our scope for becoming more effective at leadership."[4] The point is that good leaders develop a keen sense of their strengths and weaknesses and build on their positive attributes.

Moreover, research on leadership has only recently begun to recognize that the expectations, attitudes, and behavior of followers also affect how well the presumed leader can lead. "Followership" is discussed in the last section of this chapter.

Approaches to Leadership

Leadership is one of the most frequently investigated topics within the field of organizational behavior (OB) due to its importance to all organizations. As such, there are several different approaches or perspectives that have guided leadership research. While the popularity of these approaches has changed over time, knowledge of each one provides you with a better understanding of how the leadership process unfolds.

This chapter examines the different leadership approaches outlined in Table 16–1. OB researchers began their study of leadership in the early part of the

table 16–1 Approaches to Studying Leadership

1. Trait Approaches

- Stogdill and Mann's five traits—intelligence, dominance, self-confidence, level of energy, and task-relevant knowledge.
- Leadership prototypes—intelligence, masculinity, and dominance.
- Kouzes and Posner's four traits—honesty, forward-looking, inspiring, and competent.
- Goleman—emotional intelligence.
- Judge and colleagues—two meta-analyses: importance of extraversion, conscientiousness, and openness; importance of personality over intelligence.
- Kellerman's bad traits—incompetent, rigid, intemperate, callous, corrupt, insular, and evil.

2. Behavioral Approaches

- Ohio State studies—two dimensions: initiating structure behavior and consideration behavior.
- University of Michigan studies—two leadership styles: job centered and employee centered.

3. Contingency Approaches

- Fiedler's contingency model—task-oriented style and relationship-oriented style; and three dimensions of situational control: leader–member relations, task structure, and position power.
- House's path–goal revised theory—eight leadership behaviors clarify paths for followers' goals; and employee characteristics and environmental factors are contingency factors that influence the effectiveness of leadership behaviors.

4. Transformational Approaches

- Bass and Avolio's four transformational leadership behaviors—inspirational motivation, idealized influence, indivualized consideration, and intellectual stimulation.
- Full-range theory of leadership—leadership varies along a continuum from laissez-faire leadership to transactional leadership to transformational leadership.

5. Emerging Approaches

- Leader–member exchange (LMX) model—dyadic relationships between leaders and followers is critical.
- Shared leadership—mutual influence process in which people share responsibility for leading.
- Greenleaf's servant leadership—providing service to others, not oneself.
- Role of followers in leadership process—followers manage the leader–follower relationship.

SOURCE: Adapted from A Kinicki and B Williams, *Management: A Practical Introduction*, 5/e, p 443, McGraw-Hill, 2011. Copyright © 2011 The McGraw-Hill Companies. Reprinted with permission.

leadership Process whereby an individual influences others to achieve a common goal.

20th century by focusing on the traits associated with leadership effectiveness. This perspective was followed by attempts in the 1950s and 1960s to examine the behaviors or styles exhibited by effective leaders. This research led to the realization that there is not one best style of leadership, which in turn spawned various contingency approaches to leadership in the 1960s and 70s. Contingency approaches focused on identifying the types of leadership behaviors that are most effective in different settings. The transformational approach is the most popular perspective for studying leadership today. Research based on this approach began in the early 1980s and adheres to the idea that leaders transform employees to pursue organizational goals through a variety of leader behaviors. Finally, there are several emerging perspectives that examine leadership from new or novel points of view.

You would not believe how many different theories exist for each of these perspectives. There are literally a dozen or two. Moreover, the number of leadership theories exponentially increases if we count those proposed by managerial consultants. Rather than overwhelm you with all these theories of leadership, we focus on the historical ones that have received the most research support. We also discuss emerging perspectives that appear to have academic and practical application in the future. That said, we created a special learning module that contains descriptions of several leadership theories that are not covered in this chapter (see Learning Module C on the website for this book).

Leading versus Managing

It is important to appreciate the difference between leadership and management to fully understand what leadership is all about. Bernard Bass, a leadership expert, concluded that "leaders manage and managers lead, but the two activities are not synonymous."[5] Bass tells us that although leadership and management overlap, each entails a unique set of activities or functions. Broadly speaking, managers typically perform functions associated with planning, investigating, organizing, and control, and leaders deal with the interpersonal aspects of a manager's job. Leaders inspire others, provide emotional support, and try to get employees to rally around a common goal. Leaders also play a key role in creating a vision and strategic plan for an organization. Managers, in turn, are charged with implementing the vision and strategic plan. Table 16–2 summarizes the key characteristics associated with being a leader and a manager.[6]

There are several conclusions to be drawn from the information presented in Table 16–2. First, good leaders are not necessarily good managers, and good managers are not necessarily good leaders. Second, effective leadership requires effective managerial skills at some level. For example, JetBlue ex-CEO David Neeleman was let go after an ice storm revealed managerial deficiencies in how he handled the situation.[7] Good managerial skills turn a leader's vision into actionable tasks and successful implementation. Both Tim Cook, chief executive officer at Apple, who stepped in when Steve Jobs stepped down, and Alan Mulally, CEO of Ford Motor Company, endorsed this conclusion by noting that effective execution is a key driver of organizational success.[8] All told then, organizational success requires a combination of effective leadership and management. This in turn leads to the realization that today's leaders need to be effective at both leading and managing.

TO THE POINT

What are the key trait and behavioral approaches to leadership and what are their major takeaways?

LO.2 Trait and Behavioral Theories of Leadership

This section examines the two earliest approaches used to explain leadership. Trait theories focused on identifying the personal traits that differentiated leaders from followers. Behavioral theorists examined leadership from a different perspective. They tried to uncover the different kinds of leader behaviors that resulted in

table 16–2 Characteristics of Being a Leader and a Manager

BEING A LEADER MEANS	BEING A MANAGER MEANS
Motivating, influencing, and changing behavior.	Practicing stewardship, directing and being held accountable for resources.
Inspiring, setting the tone, and articulating a vision.	Executing plans, implementing, and delivering the goods and services.
Managing people.	Managing resources.
Being charismatic.	Being conscientious.
Being visionary.	Planning, organizing, directing, and controlling.
Understanding and using power and influence.	Understanding and using authority and responsibility.
Acting decisively.	Acting responsibly
Putting people first; the leader knows, responds to, and acts for his or her followers.	Putting customers first; the manager knows, responds to, and acts for his or her customers.
Leaders can make mistakes when 1. They choose the wrong goal, direction, or inspiration, due to incompetence or bad intentions; or 2. They overlead; or 3. They are unable to deliver on, implement the vision due to incompetence or a lack of follow-through commitment.	Managers can make mistakes when 1. They fail to grasp the importance of people as the key resource; or 2. They underlead; they treat people like other resources, numbers; or 3. They are eager to direct and to control but are unwilling to accept accountability.

SOURCE: Reprinted from P Lorenzi, "Managing for the Common Good: Prosocial Leadership," *Organizational Dynamics*, vol. 33, no. 3, p 286. © 2004, with permission from Elsevier.

higher work group performance. Both approaches to leadership can teach current and future managers valuable lessons about leading.

Trait Theory

Trait theory is the successor to what was called the "great man" theory of leadership. This approach was based on the assumption that leaders such as Abraham Lincoln, Martin Luther King Jr., or Mark Zuckerberg were born with some inborn ability to lead. In contrast, trait theorists believed that leadership traits were not innate but could be developed through experience and learning. A **leader trait** is a physical or personality characteristic that can be used to differentiate leaders from followers.

Before World War II, hundreds of studies were conducted to pinpoint the traits of successful leaders. Dozens of leadership traits were identified. During the postwar period, however, enthusiasm was replaced by widespread criticism. This section reviews a series of studies that provide a foundation for understanding leadership traits. We conclude by integrating results across the various studies and summarizing the practical recommendations of trait theory.

leader trait Personal characteristic that differentiates leaders from followers.

What Are the Core Traits Leaders Possess?   Ralph Stogdill in 1948 and Richard Mann in 1959 sought to summarize the impact of traits on leadership. Based on his review, Stogdill concluded that five traits tended to differentiate leaders from average followers: (1) intelligence, (2) dominance, (3) self-confidence, (4) level of energy and activity, and (5) task-relevant knowledge. Among the seven categories of personality traits examined by Mann, intelligence was the best predictor of leadership.[9] Vikram Pandit, CEO of Citigroup, is a good example of an intelligent person who has risen through the corporate ranks. He has a PhD from Columbia University and is known for his analytical skills.[10]

Do People Possess Prototypes about Preferred Leadership Traits?   The answer is yes based on implicit leadership theory (ILT). **Implicit leadership theory** is based on the idea that people have beliefs about how leaders should behave and what they should do for their followers. These beliefs are summarized in what is called a *leadership prototype.*[11] A **leadership prototype** is a mental representation of the traits and behaviors that people believe are possessed by leaders. It is important to understand the content of leadership prototypes because we tend to perceive that someone is a leader when he or she exhibits traits or behaviors that are consistent with our prototypes (recall our discussion of encoding and simplification in Chapter 7). Although past research demonstrated that people were perceived as leaders when they exhibited masculine-oriented traits and behaviors associated with masculinity, and dominance,[12] more recent studies showed an emphasis on more feminine traits and styles that emphasize empowerment, fairness, and supportiveness.[13] This change in prototypes bodes well for reducing bias and discrimination against women in leadership roles.

Is Honesty a Critical Leadership Trait?   James Kouzes and Barry Posner attempted to identify key leadership traits by asking the following open-ended question to more than 20,000 people around the world: "What values (personal traits or characteristics) do you look for and admire in your superiors?" The top four traits included honesty, forward-looking, inspiring, and competent.[14] The researchers concluded that these four traits constitute a leader's credibility. This research suggests that people want their leaders to be credible and to have a sense of direction. That said, our discussion in Chapter 3 revealed that an organization's culture significantly influences the extent to which leaders encourage and reinforce integrity at work. Consider how Tyson Foods CEO Donnie Smith regards the issue of honesty and integrity (see Real World Real People on page 467). Would you like to work at Tyson?

Is Emotional Intelligence a Key Leadership Trait?   We discussed Daniel Goleman's research on emotional intelligence in Chapter 5. Recall that *emotional intelligence* is the ability to manage oneself and one's relationships in mature and constructive ways: The six components of emotional intelligence are shown in Table 5–5. Given that leadership is an influence process between leaders and followers, it should come as no surprise that emotional intelligence is predicted to be associated with leadership effectiveness. While Goleman and other consultants contend that they have evidence to support this conclusion,[15] it has not been published in scientific journals. We agree with others who contend that there presently is not enough research published

Lynn Tilton, CEO of Patriarch Partners, possesses many of the leadership traits identified by trait researchers. Her company makes direct investments in distressed firms and it currently holds over 7 billion in equity in over 70 companies. She is featured in this chapter's closing case.

real WORLD // real PEOPLE

Tyson CEO, Donnie Smith, Believes in Behaving with Honesty and Integrity

Mr. Smith, who teaches a Sunday school class, says one of his most important jobs as CEO is to promote an ethical culture. The company employs 120 chaplains and he blogs about integrity.

Smith mentioned in an internal blog that the Bible was one of his favorite books. When asked by a reporter from the *Wall Street Journal* whether his faith affected his leadership style, he responded, "I don't think you can say, 'I do all my church stuff on Sunday between nine and noon, and the rest of the time I am either out for myself or running my business.'

My faith influences how I think, what I do, what I say. There are a lot of great biblical principles that are fundamental to operating a good business. Being fair and telling the truth are biblical principles."

Smith also was asked about the extent to which Tyson can be a moral company. He stated, "We are going to do what is right. And we're going to do what is right for one reason: because it's right. Now listen, we've got 117,000 people. There might be somebody that steps out of line occasionally. We will correct that."

Do you agree with Donnie Smith's philosophy about management?

SOURCE: Excerpted from S Kilman, "Tyson CEO Counts Chickens, Hatches Plan," *The Wall Street Journal*, September 7, 2010, pp B1, B9.

---

in OB journals to substantiate the conclusion that emotional intelligence is significantly associated with leadership effectiveness.[16]

Is Personality More Important Than Intelligence?   OB researcher Tim Judge and his colleagues completed two meta-analyses that bear on the subject of traits and leadership. The first examined the relationship among the Big Five personality traits (see Table 5–2 for a review of these traits) and leadership emergence and effectiveness in 94 studies. Results revealed that extraversion was most consistently and positively related to both leadership emergence and effectiveness. Conscientiousness and openness to experience also were positively correlated with leadership effectiveness.[17] Judge's second meta-analysis involved 151 samples and demonstrated that intelligence was modestly related to leadership effectiveness. Judge concluded that personality is more important than intelligence when selecting leaders.[18]

What Traits Are Possessed by Bad Leaders?   Thus far we have been discussing traits associated with "good leadership." Barbara Kellerman believes this approach is limiting because it fails to recognize that "bad leadership" is related to "good leadership." It also ignores the valuable insights that are gained by examining ineffective leaders. Kellerman thus set out to study hundreds of contemporary cases involving bad leadership and bad followers in search of the traits possessed by bad leaders. Her qualitative analysis uncovered seven key traits:[19]

1. *Incompetent.* The leader and at least some followers lack the will or skill (or both) to sustain effective action. With regard to at least one important leadership challenge, they do not create positive change. For example, James

---

implicit leadership theory Perceptual theory in which prototypes determine traits of effective leaders.

leadership prototype Mental representation of the traits and behaviors possessed by leaders.

Nokia's CEO, Stephen Elop, is working hard to help the company recover lost market share. How do companies like Nokia avoid the tendency to get rigid following past success?

Cayne, former CEO of Bear Stearns, was reportedly off playing golf and bridge as the company collapsed.

2. *Rigid.* The leader and at least some followers are stiff and unyielding. Although they may be competent, they are unable or unwilling to adapt to new ideas, new information, or changing times. Nokia's CEO, Stephen Elop, acknowledged that the company's significant drop in earnings in 2010 was partially due to this trait. He sent a letter to employees stating, "While competitors poured flames on our market share, what happened at Nokia? We fell behind, we missed big trends, and we lost time. At that time, we thought we were making the right decisions; but, with the benefit of hindsight, we now find ourselves years behind." For example, a lack of action on the company's part has allowed Apple's market share of $300 + phones to go from 25 percent in 2008 to 61 percent in 2010.[20]

3. *Intemperate.* The leader lacks self-control and is aided and abetted by followers who are unwilling or unable effectively to intervene. Tiger Woods represents a widely known example of someone who displayed this trait by not controlling his sexual urges.

4. *Callous.* The leader and at least some followers are uncaring and unkind. Ignored or discounted are the needs, wants, and desires of most members of the group or organization, especially subordinates. Steve Jobs was known for parking his car in handicapped spaces and for being so callous that he brought employees to tears.

5. *Corrupt.* The leader and at least some followers lie, cheat, or steal. To a degree that exceeds the norm, they put self-interest ahead of the public interest. Bernie Madoff, former head of Ascot Partners hedge firm, is a prime example. His misdeeds resulted in a Ponzi scheme that bilked over $50 billion from investors.

6. *Insular.* The leader and at least some followers minimize or disregard the health and welfare of "the other," that is, those outside the group or organization for which they are directly responsible. Philip Schoonover, former CEO of Circuit City, fired 3,400 of the most experienced employees because he felt they made too much money.

7. *Evil.* Evil leaders such as Adolf Hitler and Saddam Hussein encourage their followers to commit atrocities. They tend to use pain as an instrument of power. The harm done to men, women, and children is severe rather than slight. The harm can be physical, psychological, or both.[21]

The aforementioned traits are not the only ones associated with ineffective leadership. Additional negative traits include insensitivity to others, inability to get along with others, overemphasizing personal goals at the expense of others' success, arrogance, or hubris, focusing on self-promotion rather than on promotion of others, high need for control, building an empire by hoarding resources, making abrupt decisions without asking for input, and micromanaging others.[22] Do you know leaders who possess any of these traits? Unfortunately, we have seen many examples in our consulting experiences around the world.

Gender and Leadership   The increase of women in the workforce has generated much interest in understanding the similarities and differences in female and male leaders. Three separate meta-analyses and a series of studies conducted by consultants across the United States uncovered the following differences: (1) Men and women were seen as displaying more task and social leadership,

table 16–3 Key Positive Leadership Traits

Task competence (intelligence, knowledge, problem-solving skills).

Interpersonal competence (ability to communicate, demonstrate caring and empathy).

Intuition.

Traits of character (conscientiousness, discipline, moral reasoning, integrity, and honesty).

Biophysical traits (physical fitness, hardiness, and energy level).

Personal traits (self-confidence, sociability, self-monitoring, extraversion, self-regulating, and self-efficacy).

SOURCE: These traits were identified in B M Bass and R Bass, *The Bass Handbook of Leadership* (New York: Free Press, 2008), p 135.

respectively;[23] (2) women used a more democratic or participative style than men, and men used a more autocratic and directive style than women;[24] (3) men and women were equally assertive;[25] and (4) women executives, when rated by their peers, managers, and direct reports, scored higher than their male counterparts on a variety of effectiveness criteria.[26]

What Are the Takeaways from Trait Theory?

We can no longer afford to ignore the implications of leadership traits. Traits play a central role in how we perceive leaders, and they ultimately impact leadership effectiveness. This list of positive traits shown in Table 16–3, along with the negative traits identified by Kellerman, provides guidance regarding the leadership traits you should attempt to cultivate if you want to assume a leadership role in the future. Personality tests, which were discussed in Chapter 5, and other trait assessments can be used to evaluate your strengths and weaknesses vis-à-vis these traits: The website for this book contains a host of such tests that you can take for this purpose. Results of these tests can then be used to prepare a personal development plan. We encourage you to take advantage of this resource.

There are two organizational applications of trait theory. First, organizations may want to include personality and trait assessments into their selection and promotion processes. For example, Nina Brody, head of talent for Take Care Health Systems in Conshohocken, Pennsylvania, used an assessment tool to assist in hiring nurses, doctors, medical assistants, and others. She wanted to hire people with traits that fit or matched the organization's culture.[27] It is important to remember that this should only be done with valid measures of leadership traits. Second, management development programs can be used to build a pipeline of leadership talent. This is a particularly important recommendation in light of results from corporate surveys showing that the majority of companies do not possess adequate leadership talent to fill future needs.[28] For example, both small and large companies such as EMC, McDonald's, and KPMG send targeted groups of managers to developmental programs that include management classes, coaching sessions, trait assessments, and stretch assignments.[29]

Back to the Chapter-Opening Case

Which of the positive and negative leadership traits were displayed by Jack Griffin?

LO.3 Behavioral Styles Theory

This phase of leadership research began during World War II as part of an effort to develop better military leaders. It was an outgrowth of two events: the seeming inability of trait theory to explain leadership effectiveness and the human relations movement, an outgrowth of the Hawthorne studies. The thrust of early behavioral leadership theory was to focus on leader behavior, instead of on personality traits. It was believed that leader behavior directly affected work group effectiveness. This led researchers to identify patterns of behavior (called *leadership styles*) that enabled leaders to effectively influence others.

The Ohio State Studies   Researchers at Ohio State University began by generating a list of behaviors exhibited by leaders. At one point, the list contained 1,800 statements that described nine categories of leader behavior. Ultimately, the Ohio State researchers concluded there were only two independent dimensions of leader behavior: consideration and initiating structure. **Consideration** involves leader behavior associated with creating mutual respect or trust and focuses on a concern for group members' needs and desires. **Initiating structure** is leader behavior that organizes and defines what group members should be doing to maximize output. These two dimensions of leader behavior were oriented at right angles to yield four behavioral styles of leadership (see Figure 16–1).

It initially was hypothesized that a high-structure, high-consideration style would be the one best style of leadership. Through the years, the effectiveness of the high-high style has been tested many times.[30] Overall, results do not support this prediction, but findings from a meta-analysis of more than 20,000 individuals demonstrated that consideration and initiating structure had a moderately strong, significant relationship with leadership outcomes. Results revealed that followers performed more effectively for structuring leaders even though they preferred considerate leaders.[31] All told, results do not support the idea that there is one best style of leadership, but they do confirm the importance of considerate and structuring leader behaviors. Follower satisfaction, motivation, and performance are significantly associated with these two leader behaviors.

figure 16–1   Four Leadership Styles Derived from the Ohio State Studies

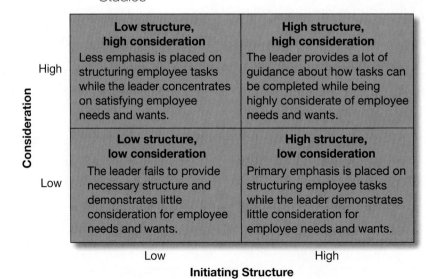

University of Michigan Studies   As in the Ohio State studies, this research sought to identify behavioral differences between effective and ineffective leaders. Researchers identified two different styles of leadership: one was employee centered; the other was job centered. These behavioral styles parallel the consideration and initiating-structure styles identified by the Ohio State group.

What Are the Takeaways from Behavioral Styles Theory?   By emphasizing leader behavior, something that is learned, the behavioral style approach makes it clear that leaders are made, not born. This is the opposite of the trait theorists' traditional assumption. Given what we know about behavior shaping and model-based training, leader behaviors can be systematically improved and developed.[32]

Behavioral styles research also revealed that there is no one best style of leadership. The effectiveness of a particular leadership style depends on the situation at hand. For instance, employees prefer structure over consideration when faced with role ambiguity. Finally, Peter Drucker, an internationally renowned management expert and consultant, recommended a set of nine behaviors (see Table 16–4) managers can focus on to improve their leadership effectiveness. The first two practices provide the knowledge leaders need. The next four help leaders convert knowledge into effective action, and the last two ensure that the whole organization feels responsible and accountable. Drucker refers to the last recommendation as a managerial rule.

Go to www.mcgrawhillconnect.com for a self-assessment to learn how ready you are to assume the leadership role.

---

table 16–4   Peter Drucker's Tips for Improving Leadership Effectiveness

1. Determine what needs to be done.

2. Determine the right thing to do for the welfare of the entire enterprise or organization.

3. Develop action plans that specify desired results, probable restraints, future revisions, check-in points, and implications for how one should spend his or her time.

4. Take responsibility for decisions.

5. Take responsibility for communicating action plans and give people the information they need to get the job done.

6. Focus on opportunities rather than problems. Do not sweep problems under the rug, and treat change as an opportunity rather than a threat.

7. Run productive meetings. Different types of meetings require different forms of preparation and different results. Prepare accordingly.

8. Think and say "we" rather than "I." Consider the needs and opportunities of the organization before thinking of your own opportunities and needs.

9. Listen first, speak last.

SOURCE: Reprinted by permission of Harvard Business Review. Recommendations were derived from "What Makes an Effective Executive," by P F Drucker, June 2004, pp 58–63. Copyright 2004 by the Harvard Business School Publishing Corporation; all rights reserved.

---

consideration Creating mutual respect and trust with followers.

initiating structure Organizing and defining what group members should be doing.

Back to the Chapter-Opening Case

Which of Peter Drucker's tips were violated by Jack Griffin?

TO THE POINT

What are the similarities and differences between Fiedler's contingency model and House's revised path-goal theory, and how can managers apply these situational theories?

Situational Theories

Situational leadership theories grew out of an attempt to explain the inconsistent findings about traits and styles. **Situational theories** propose that the effectiveness of a particular style of leader behavior depends on the situation. As situations change, different styles become appropriate. This directly challenges the idea of one best style of leadership.[33] Let us closely examine two alternative situational theories of leadership that reject the notion of one best leadership style. We conclude this section by discussing an approach you can use to implement situational theories.

 LO.4 Fiedler's Contingency Model

Fred Fiedler, an OB scholar, developed a situational model of leadership. It is the oldest and one of the most widely known models of situational leadership. He labeled the model *contingency theory* because it is based on the premise that a leader's effectiveness is contingent on the extent to which a leader's style fits or matches characteristics of the situation at hand. To understand how this matching process works, we need to consider the key leadership styles identified by Fiedler and the situational variables that constitute what Fiedler labels *situational control*. We then review relevant research and managerial implications.[34]

Leadership Styles   Fiedler believes that leaders have one dominant or natural leadership style that is resistant to change. A leader's style is described as either task-motivated or relationship-motivated. Task-motivated leaders focus on accomplishing goals, whereas relationship-motivated leaders are more interested in developing positive relationships with followers. These basic styles are similar to initiating structure/concern for production and consideration/concern for people that were previously discussed. To determine an individual's leadership style, Fiedler developed the least preferred co-worker (LPC) scale. High scores on the survey (high LPC) indicate that an individual is relationship-motivated, and low scores (low LPC) suggest a task-motivated style.

Situational Control   Situational control refers to the amount of control and influence the leader has in her or his immediate work environment. Situational control ranges from high to low. High control implies that the leader's decisions will produce predictable results because the leader has the ability to influence work outcomes. Low control implies that the leader's decisions may not influence work outcomes because the leader has very little influence. There are three dimensions of situational control: leader–member relations, task structure, and position power. These dimensions vary independently, forming eight combinations of situational control (see Figure 16–2).

The three dimensions of situational control are defined as follows:

- **Leader–member relations** reflect the extent to which the leader has the support, loyalty, and trust of the work group. This dimension is the most important component of situational control. Good leader–member relations suggest that the leader can depend on the group, thus ensuring that the work group will try to meet the leader's goals and objectives.

figure 16–2   Representation of Fiedler's Contingency Model

Situational Control	High-Control Situations			Moderate-Control Situations				Low-Control Situations
Leader-member relations	Good	Good	Good	Good	Poor	Poor	Poor	Poor
Task structure	High	High	Low	Low	High	High	Low	Low
Position power	Strong	Weak	Strong	Weak	Strong	Weak	Strong	Weak
Situation	I	II	III	IV	V	VI	VII	VIII

Optimal Leadership Style	Task-Motivated Leadership	Relationship-Motivated Leadership	Task-Motivated Leadership

SOURCE: Adapted from F E Fiedler, "Situational Control and a Dynamic Theory of Leadership," in *Managerial Control and Organizational Democracy*, ed B King, S Streufert, and F E Fiedler (New York: John Wiley & Sons, 1978), p 114.

- **Task structure** is concerned with the amount of structure contained within tasks performed by the work group. For example, a managerial job contains less structure than that of a bank teller. Because structured tasks have guidelines for how the job should be completed, the leader has more control and influence over employees performing such tasks. This dimension is the second most important component of situational control.
- **Position power** refers to the degree to which the leader has formal power to reward, punish, or otherwise obtain compliance from employees.

Linking Leadership Motivation and Situational Control   Fiedler suggests that leaders must learn to manipulate or influence the leadership situation in order to create a match between their leadership style and the amount of control within the situation at hand. These contingency relationships are depicted in Figure 16–2. The last row under the Situational Control column shows that there are eight different leadership situations. Each situation represents a unique combination of leader–member relations, task structure, and position power. Situations I, II, and III represent high-control situations. Figure 16–2 shows that task-motivated leaders are hypothesized to be most effective in situations of high control. The Real World/Real People on page 474 illustrates how Carol Bartz, Yahoo!'s CEO, used task-motivated leadership to turn around the company. We suspect that she was operating within situation III. Under conditions of moderate control (situations IV, V, VI, and VII), relationship-motivated leaders are expected to be more effective. Finally, the results orientation of task-motivated leaders is predicted to be more effective under the condition of very low control (situation VIII).

situational theories Propose that leader styles should match the situation at hand.

leader–member relations Extent that leader has the support, loyalty, and trust of the work group.

task structure Amount of structure contained within work tasks.

position power Degree to which leader has formal power.

real WORLD // **real** PEOPLE

Carol Bartz Uses Task-Motivated Leadership to Turn around Yahoo!

Not yet six weeks into the job, Yahoo Inc. Chief Executive Carol Bartz is preparing a company-wide reorganization that underscores the new CEO's belief in a more top-down managerial approach.

The plan aims to speed up decision making and give Yahoo products a more consistent appearance by consolidating certain functions that have previously been spread out across the company....

A straight-talker, Ms. Bartz has become known for stubbornly starting meetings on time, say employees. She doesn't bring her BlackBerry into meetings, according to workers who have begun leaving behind theirs as well.

She's requested briefings with staff at several levels of the organization, seeking updates on major projects and testing employees by asking, "What would you do if you were me?" say people familiar with her process.

And she hasn't shied from changing course on major projects. While Bartz's style initially helped Yahoo to overcome past problems, the board of directors was

Former Yahoo! Inc. Chief Executive Carol Bartz.

unhappy with the company's stock performance and profitability. She was fired in September 2011.

Do you think that Bartz should have been more relationship oriented given that she was only on the job for six weeks? Explain.

SOURCE: Excerpted from J E Vascellaro, "Yahoo CEO Set to Install Top-Down Management," *The Wall Street Journal*, February 23, 2009, p B1.

Takeaways from Fiedler's Model   Although research only provides partial support for this model and the LPC scale,[35] there are three key takeaways from Fiedler's model. First, this model emphasizes the point that leadership effectiveness goes beyond traits and behaviors. It is a function of the fit between a leader's style and the situational demands at hand. As a case in point, a team of researchers examined the effectiveness of 20 senior-level managers from GE who left the company for other positions. The researchers concluded that not all managers are equally suited to all business situations. The strategic skills required to control costs in the face of fierce competition are not the same as those required to improve the top line in a rapidly growing business or balance investment against cash flow to survive in a highly cyclical business. . . . We weren't surprised to find that relevant industry experience had a positive impact on performance in a new job, but that these skills didn't transfer to a new industry.[36]

This study leads to the conclusion that organizations should attempt to hire or promote people whose leadership styles *fit* or *match* situational demands.

Second, this model explains why some people are successful in some situations and not in others, such as the example of Jack Griffin in the chapter-opening case. Leaders are unlikely to be successful in all situations. If a manager is failing in a certain context, management should consider moving the individual to another situation. Don't give up on a high-potential person simply because he or she was a poor leader in one context. Finally, leaders need to modify their style to fit a situation. Leadership styles are not universally effective.

 LO.5 Path–Goal Theory

Path–goal theory was originally proposed by Robert House in the 1970s.[37] It was based on the expectancy theory of motivation discussed in Chapter 8. Recall that expectancy theory is based on the idea that motivation to exert effort increases

real WORLD // real PEOPLE

Cascade Engineering Uses the Principles of Path-Goal Theory to Help People Transition from Welfare to a Career

The Welfare-to-Career program has five key components:

1. A government case worker is on-site to assist and support participants.
2. An assessment tool is used to identify and remove barriers to employment.
3. Training and onboarding are used to help participants understand work-related norms and the "hidden rules" of different working classes (e.g., poverty versus middle class).
4. A specific career track is used to motivate workers to develop their skills.
5. A culture grounded in the values of respect and dignity is reinforced.

"Michigan Department of Human Services caseworker Joyce Gutierrez-Marsh has an office on site. She explains that while many employees lose cash assistance as their incomes rise, they receive food stamps, child care assistance and Medicaid for children and continue to be her clients. She identifies barriers to work attendance and channels clients into assistance programs to overcome those barriers."

The most common barriers are lack of child care and transportation. To accommodate these barriers, Cascade changed its attendance policy to include sick children as a legitimate reason to miss work. For transportation, the company first appealed to local government officials to extend the bus route because it stopped a quarter-mile away. The route was extended and Welfare-to-Career participants are eligible for 90 days of free bus travel. The company also created a partnership with a taxi company to help employees get home when they were asked to go home at odd times. Supervisors call the cab company, and the company pays the bill. Welfare-to-Career employees can also "take advantage of other programs, such as a $900 annual car repair benefit or a one-time $2,000 car purchase benefit."

Can Cascade's approach be used in other communities and companies?

SOURCE: Excerpted and derived from K Tyler, "From Dependence to Self-Sufficiency," *HR Magazine,* September 2010, pp 35–39.

---

as one's effort→performance→outcome expectations improve. Leader behaviors thus are expected to be acceptable when employees view them as a source of satisfaction or as paving the way to future satisfaction. In addition, leader behavior is predicted to be motivational to the extent it (1) reduces roadblocks that interfere with goal accomplishment, (2) provides the guidance and support needed by employees, and (3) ties meaningful rewards to goal accomplishment. The Real World Real People above illustrates how the basic principles of this theory are used by Cascade Engineering in Grand Rapids, Michigan, to help transition welfare recipients to gainful employment. Cascade employs 900 people, and 40 are Welfare-to-Career participants. Cascade is implementing its third Welfare-to-Work program. The first two failed, and the current one has significantly reduced the turnover of participants.

House proposed a model that describes how leadership effectiveness is influenced by the interaction between four leadership styles (directive, supportive, participative, and achievement-oriented) and a variety of contingency factors. **Contingency factors** are situational variables that cause one style of leadership to be more effective than another. Path–goal theory

This mountaineering guide in yellow is a great example of a path–goal leader. His job is to reduce roadblocks during an ascent and to provide coaching and support during the journey. Would you like to attempt this type of a hike?

contingency factors Variables that influence the appropriateness of a leadership style.

has two groups of contingency variables. They are employee characteristics and environmental factors. Five important employee characteristics are locus of control, task ability, need for achievement, experience, and need for clarity. Two relevant environmental factors are task structure (independent versus interdependent tasks) and work group dynamics. In order to gain a better understanding of how these contingency factors influence leadership effectiveness, we illustratively consider locus of control (see Chapter 5), task ability and experience, and task structure.

Employees with an internal locus of control are more likely to prefer participative or achievement-oriented leadership because they believe they have control over the work environment. Such individuals are unlikely to be satisfied with directive leader behaviors that exert additional control over their activities. In contrast, employees with an external locus tend to view the environment as uncontrollable, thereby preferring the structure provided by supportive or directive leadership. An employee with high task ability and experience is less apt to need additional direction and thus would respond negatively to directive leadership. This person is more likely to be motivated and satisfied by participative and achievement-oriented leadership. Oppositely, an inexperienced employee would find achievement-oriented leadership overwhelming as he or she confronts challenges associated with learning a new job. Supportive and directive leadership would be helpful in this situation. Finally, directive and supportive leadership should help employees experiencing role ambiguity. However, directive leadership is likely to frustrate employees working on routine and simple tasks. Supportive leadership is most useful in this context.

There have been about 50 studies testing various predictions derived from House's original model. Results have been mixed, with some studies supporting the theory and others not. House thus proposed a new version of path–goal theory in 1996 based on these results and the accumulation of new knowledge about OB.[38]

A Reformulated Theory   The revised theory is presented in Figure 16–3. There are three key changes in the new theory. First, House now believes that leadership is more complex and involves a greater variety of leader behavior. He thus identified eight categories of leadership styles or behavior (see Table 16–5).

figure 16–3   A General Representation of House's Revised Path–Goal Theory

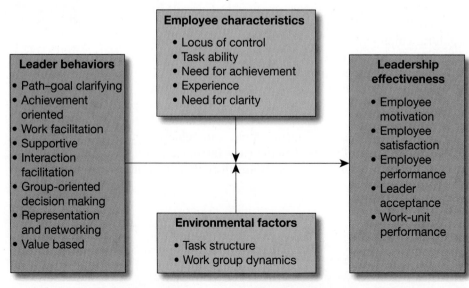

table 16–5 Categories of Leader Behavior within the Revised Path–Goal Theory

CATEGORY OF LEADER BEHAVIOR	DESCRIPTION OF LEADER BEHAVIORS
Path–goal clarifying behaviors	Clarifying employees' performance goals; providing guidance on how employees can complete tasks; clarifying performance standards and expectations; use of positive and negative rewards contingent on performance
Achievement-oriented behaviors	Setting challenging goals; emphasizing excellence; demonstrating confidence in employees' abilities
Work-facilitation behaviors	Planning, scheduling, organizing, and coordinating work; providing mentoring, coaching, counseling, and feedback to assist employees in developing their skills; eliminating roadblocks; providing resources; empowering employees to take actions and make decisions
Supportive behaviors	Showing concern for the well-being and needs of employees; being friendly and approachable; treating employees as equals
Interaction-facilitation behaviors	Resolving disputes; facilitating communication; encouraging the sharing of minority opinions; emphasizing collaboration and teamwork; encouraging close relationships among employees
Group-oriented decision-making behaviors	Posing problems rather than solutions to the work group; encouraging group members to participate in decision making; providing necessary information to the group for analysis; involving knowledgeable employees in decision making
Representation and networking behaviors	Presenting the work group in a positive light to others; maintaining positive relationships with influential others; participating in organizationwide social functions and ceremonies; doing unconditional favors for others
Value-based behaviors	Establishing a vision, displaying passion for it, and supporting its accomplishment; demonstrating self-confidence; communicating high performance expectations and confidence in others' abilities to meet their goals; giving frequent positive feedback

SOURCE: Descriptions were adapted from R J House, "Path–Goal Theory of Leadership: Lessons, Legacy, and a Reformulated Theory," *Leadership Quarterly,* 1996, pp 323–52.

The need for an expanded list of leader behaviors is supported by current research and descriptions of business leaders.

The second key change involves the role of intrinsic motivation (discussed in Chapter 9) and empowerment (discussed in Chapter 15) in influencing leadership effectiveness. House places much more emphasis on the need for leaders to foster intrinsic motivation through empowerment. Shared leadership represents the final change in the revised theory. That is, path–goal theory is based on the premise that an employee does not have to be a supervisor or manager to engage in leader behavior.

Rather, House believes that leadership is shared among all employees within an organization. More is said about shared leadership in the final section of this chapter.

Takeaways from House's Theory   There are not enough direct tests of House's revised path–goal theory using appropriate research methods and statistical procedures to draw overall conclusions. Nonetheless, there are three important takeaways from this theory. First, effective leaders possess and use more than one style of leadership. Managers are encouraged to familiarize themselves with the different categories of leader behavior outlined in path–goal theory and to try new behaviors when the situation calls for them. Consider the leader behaviors exhibited by Bob Iger, CEO of Walt Disney Company. He prefers to work behind the scenes and does not host any Disney TV productions. He is known to say hello to everyone he encounters on the Disney campus and participates in a Disney team that competes in the Malibu, California, triathalon to raise money for charity. He loves to study operational statistics and is very interested in studying and using consumers' attitudes to make decisions. Since taking over the helm at Disney, Iger patched up the rocky relationship between Pixar and Disney and ultimately purchased Pixar for $7 billion. He also resolved several contentious issues with former director Roy Disney and Comcast. Iger empowers his employees and allows them plenty of freedom to make decisions. At that same time, he holds people accountable for their work.[39] This example illustrates that Iger uses path–goal clarifying behaviors, achievement-oriented behaviors, work-facilitation behaviors, supportive behaviors, interaction-facilitation behaviors, and representation and networking behaviors.

Second, the theory offers specific suggestions for how leaders can help employees. Leaders are encouraged to clarify the paths to goal accomplishment and to remove any obstacles that may impair an employee's ability to achieve his or her goals. In so doing, managers need to guide and coach employees during the pursuit of their goals. Third, a small set of employee characteristics (i.e., ability, experience, and need for independence) and environmental factors (task characteristics of autonomy, variety, and significance) are relevant contingency factors.[40] Managers are advised to modify their leadership style to fit these various employee and task characteristics.

connect™ Go to www.mcgrawhillconnect.com for an interactive exercise to test your knowledge of House's Path–Goal Theory.

Applying Situational Theories

Although researchers and practitioners support the logic of situational leadership, the practical application of such theories has not been clearly developed. A team of researchers thus attempted to resolve this problem by proposing a general strategy that managers can use across a variety of situations. The general strategy contains five steps.[41] We explain how to implement the steps by using the examples of a head coach of a sports team and a sales manager.

1. *Identify important outcomes.* This step entails a determination of the goals the leader is trying to achieve. For example, the head coach may have goals to win or to avoid injury to key players whereas a sales manager's goals might be to increase sales by 10% or to decrease customers' complaints. It is important to identify the key goals that exist at a specific point in time.

2. *Identify relevant leadership types/behaviors.* This step requires the manager to identify the specific types of behaviors that may be appropriate for the situation at hand. The list of behaviors shown in Table 16–5 is a good starting point. A head coach in a championship game, for instance, might focus on achievement-oriented and work-facilitation behaviors. In contrast, a sales manager might find path–goal clarifying, work-facilitation, and supportive behaviors more relevant for the sales team. Don't try to use all available leadership behaviors. Rather, select the one or two that appear most helpful.

3. *Identify situational conditions.* Fiedler's contingency theory and House's path–goal theory both identify a set of potential contingency factors to consider. That said, there may be other practical considerations. For example, a star quarterback on a football team may be injured, which might require the team to adopt a different strategy toward winning the game. Similarly, managing a virtual sales team from around the world will affect the types of leadership that are most effective in this context.

4. *Match leadership to the conditions at hand.* This is the step in which research cannot provide conclusive recommendations because there simply are too

many possible situational conditions. This means that you should use your knowledge about organizational behavior to determine the best match between leadership styles/behaviors and the situation at hand. The coach whose star quarterback is injured might use supportive and values-based behaviors to instill confidence that the team can win with a different quarterback. Our virtual sales manager also might find it useful to use the empowering leadership associated with work-facilitation behaviors (see Table 16–5) and to avoid directive leadership.

5. *Determine how to make the match.* It's now time to implement the leadership style or behaviors you determined were most appropriate in step 4. There are two basic approaches you can use according to contingency theory and House's path–goal theory. You can either change the person in the leadership role or the leader can change his or her style or behavior. Returning to our examples, it is not possible to change the head coach in a championship game. This means that the head coach needs to change his or her style or behavior. In contrast, the organization employing the sales manager might move him or her to another position because the individual is too directive and does not like to empower others. Alternatively, the sales manager could change his or her behavior.

Back to the Chapter-Opening Case

Discuss how Jack Griffin could have applied the five steps to applying situational theories.

Caveat When Applying Situational Theories

Can you think of any downside to applying situational theories? Interestingly, there are. A team of OB researchers recently tested the possibility that there are unintended negative consequences when managers use a situational approach with members from a team. Study findings revealed that treating group members differently resulted in some employees feeling that they were not among the leader's "in-group" (i.e., a partnership characterized by mutual trust, respect, and liking): The concept of in-groups and out-groups is discussed later in the chapter. These negative feelings in turn had a counterproductive effect on employees' self-efficacy and subsequent group performance. The point to remember is that leaders of teams need to be careful when treating individual team members differently. There are potential pros and cons to the application of situational theories in a team context.[42]

LO.6 The Full-Range Model of Leadership: From Laissez-Faire to Transformational Leadership

One of the most recent approaches to leadership is referred to as a *full-range model of leadership*. The authors of this model, Bernard Bass and Bruce Avolio, proposed that leadership behavior varied along a continuum from laissez-faire leadership (i.e., a general failure to take responsibility for leading) to transactional leadership to transformational leadership.[43] Examples of laissez-faire leadership include avoiding conflict, surfing the Internet during work, failing to assist employees in setting performance goals, failing to give performance feedback, or being so hands-off that employees have little idea about what they should be doing. Of course, laissez-faire leadership is a terrible way for any manager to behave and should be avoided. What gender do you think engages in more laissez-faire leadership? A meta-analysis revealed that men displayed more of this type of leadership than women.[44] It is important for organizations to identify managers who lead with this style and to train and develop them to use behaviors associated with transactional and transformational leadership. Both transactional and transformational are positively related to a variety of employee attitudes and behaviors and represent different aspects of being a good leader. Let us consider these two important dimensions of leadership.

Transactional leadership focuses on clarifying employees' role and task requirements and providing followers with positive and negative rewards contingent on performance. Further, transactional leadership encompasses the fundamental managerial activities of setting goals, monitoring progress toward goal achievement, and rewarding and punishing people for their level of goal accomplishment.[45] You can see from this description that transactional leadership is based on using rewards and punishment to drive motivation and performance. Consider how Stephen Greer, founder of Hartwell Pacific, a scrap metal recycling business in Asia used transactional leadership to combat several million dollars in fraud and theft from his employees in Mexico and his operations in Asia.

Example. For Hartwell Pacific, the biggest strain was a lack of control systems. Greer was so focused on new markets that he glossed over niceties like accounting procedures, inventory audits, and reference checks for new hires. . . .

When he finally realized the extent of the fraud in his nascent empire, Greer pulled back, eventually liquidating the operation in Mexico. He also instituted a system of close oversight. He appointed local finance managers who reported directly to headquarters, creating checks and balances on local general managers. He started requiring three signatories for all company checks. He installed metal detectors to prevent theft. Once a month, the local managers flew to headquarters, where they compared revenues, costs, and overall performance. If one plant seemed to be overpaying for supplies, or if revenues seemed out of line with inventory, Greer began asking hard questions—ones he should have been asking all along.[46]

Greer's use of transactional leadership helped to correct the fraud and theft problems and the company ultimately experienced profitable growth.

In contrast, **transformational leaders** "engender trust, seek to develop leadership in others, exhibit self-sacrifice and serve as moral agents, focusing themselves and followers on objectives that transcend the more immediate needs of the work group."[47] Transformational leaders can produce significant organizational change and results because this form of leadership fosters higher levels of employee engagement, trust, commitment, and loyalty from followers than does transactional leadership. That said, however, it is important to note that transactional leadership is an essential prerequisite to effective leadership and that the best leaders learn to display both transactional and transformational leadership to various degrees. In support of this proposition, research reveals that transformational leadership leads to superior performance when it augments or adds to transactional leadership.[48] General Electric's CEO Jeff Immelt represents a good example of transformational leadership. The example that follows illustrates how Immelt is using it as a vehicle to improve the leadership talent within the company.

Example. Immelt intends to spend this year exploring new ideas, which he describes as "wallowing in it," to decide how GE should shape and measure its leaders. He has solicited management suggestions from a broad range of organizations—from Google to China's Communist Party—and sent 30 of his top people to more than

100 companies worldwide. He's holding monthly dinners with 10 executives and an external "thought leader" to debate leadership. He launched a pilot program to bring in personal coaches for high-potential talent, a practice that GE once reserved mainly for those in need of remedial work. To increase exposure to the world beyond GE, Immelt is even reconsidering the age-old rule that employees can't sit on corporate boards. "I think about it all the time," he says. "You have to be willing to change when it makes sense."[49]

LO.7 How Does Transformational Leadership Transform Followers?

Transformational leaders transform followers by creating changes in their goals, values, needs, beliefs, and aspirations. They accomplish this transformation by appealing to followers' self-concepts—namely their values and personal identity. Figure 16–4 presents a model of how leaders accomplish this transformation process.

Figure 16–4 shows that transformational leader behavior is first influenced by various individual and organizational characteristics. For example, research reveals that transformational leaders tend to have personalities that are more extraverted, agreeable, and proactive and less neurotic than nontransformational leaders. They also have higher emotional intelligence.[50] Female leaders also were

connect Go to www.mcgrawhillconnect.com for an interactive exercise to test your knowledge of transformational leadership.

figure 16–4 A Transformational Model of Leadership

SOURCE: Based in part on D A Waldman and F J Yammarino, "CEO Charismatic Leadership: Levels-of-Management and Levels-of-Analysis Effects," *Academy of Management Review,* April 1999, pp 266–85; and B Shamir, R J House, and M B Arthur, "The Motivational Effects of Charismatic Leadership: A Self-Concept Based Theory," *Organization Science,* November 1993, pp 577–94.

transactional leadership Focuses on clarifying employees' roles and providing rewards contingent on performance.

transformational leadership Transforms employees to pursue organizational goals over self-interests.

found to use transformational leadership more than male leaders.[51] It is important to note, however, that the relationship between personality traits and transformational leadership is relatively weak. This suggests that transformational leadership is less traitlike and more susceptible to managerial influence. This conclusion reinforces the notion that an individual's life experiences play a role in developing transformational leadership and that transformational leadership can be learned. Finally, Figure 16–4 shows that organizational culture influences the extent to which leaders are transformational. Cultures that are adaptive and flexible rather than rigid and bureaucratic are more likely to create environments that foster the opportunity for transformational leadership to be exhibited.

Transformational leaders engage in four key sets of leader behavior (see Figure 16–4).[52] The first set, referred to as *inspirational motivation*, involves establishing an attractive vision of the future, the use of emotional arguments, and exhibition of optimism and enthusiasm. A vision is "a realistic, credible, attractive future for your organization."[53] According to Burt Nanus, a leadership expert, the "right" vision unleashes human potential because it serves as a beacon of hope and common purpose. It does this by attracting commitment, energizing workers, creating meaning in employees' lives, establishing a standard of excellence, promoting high ideals, and bridging the gap between an organization's present problems and its future goals and aspirations. Carl-Henric Svanberg, current chairman of

British Petroleum and former CEO of Ericsson, understands the importance of establishing an organization's vision. He concluded that in large organizations "you can't just tell everyone, 'Turn left and work fast,' You have to share with them the vision you want to accomplish and get everybody on board and enthusiastic about it. When you get them to march in the same direction, you can really move mountains together."[54]

Idealized influence, the second set of leader behaviors, includes behaviors such as sacrificing for the good of the group, being a role model, and displaying high ethical standards. Home Depot's CEO Frank Blake exhibited idealized influence when he "accepted an annual pay package worth one-quarter of his predecessor's, and he is also finding creative ways to motivate employees, including giving merit awards for great customer service and assigning store workers more decision-making power."[55] Through their actions, transformational leaders like Frank Blake model the desired values, traits, beliefs, and behaviors needed to realize the vision.

Frank Blake, Home Depot's CEO, gained leadership experience at the U.S. Department of Energy and General Electric. His transformational leadership has helped the company improve profitability over the last few years.

The third set, *individualized consideration*, entails behaviors associated with providing support, encouragement, empowerment, and coaching to employees. These behaviors necessitate that leaders pay special attention to the needs of their followers and search for ways to help people develop and grow. You can do this by spending time talking with people about their interests and by identifying new learning opportunities for them. For example, Jeff Immelt, CEO of General Electric, invites one of the company's officers to his home every other Friday for a casual evening of drinks, some laughs, dinner, and conversation about world events. On Saturday, they get back together to talk about the individual's career. This "high touch" approach is a great way for Immelt to get to know his employees and to serve as a mentor.[56]

Showing interest in people by remembering their names and previous conversations are other simple ways in which you can demonstrate individualized consideration. Finally, treating people with respect and telling them the truth with compassion also represent examples of consideration.

Intellectual stimulation, the fourth set of leadership behaviors, involves behaviors that encourage employees to question the status quo and to seek innovative and creative solutions to organizational problems. As you can see, this dimension of transformational leadership pertains to encouraging employee creativity, innovation, and problem solving. The group problem-solving techniques discussed in Chapter 12 can help to stimulate employees. Further, fostering an adhocracy culture—recall our discussion in Chapter 3—will assist in creating a work environment that promotes intellectual stimulation. You can use any of the cultural embedding techniques we discussed in Chapter 3 in this pursuit.

Research and Managerial Implications

Components of the transformational model of leadership have been the most widely researched leadership topic over the last decade. Overall, relationships outlined in Figure 16–4 generally were supported by previous research. For example, a meta-analysis of 49 studies indicated that transformational leadership was positively associated with measures of leadership effectiveness and employees' job satisfaction.[57] At the organizational level, a second meta-analysis demonstrated that transformational leadership was positively correlated with organizational measures of effectiveness.[58]

Support for transformational leadership underscores six important managerial implications. First, the establishment of a positive vision of the future—inspirational motivation—should be considered a first step at applying transformational leadership. Why? Because the vision represents a long-term goal, and it is important for leaders to begin their influence attempts by gaining agreement and consensus about where the team or organization is headed. It also is critical to widely communicate the vision among the team or entire organization.[59] People can't get excited about something they don't know about or don't understand. Second, the best leaders are not just transformational; they are both transactional and transformational, and they avoid a laissez-faire or "wait-and-see" style.[60] We encourage you to use both transactional and transformational leadership.

Third, transformational leadership not only affects individual-level outcomes like job satisfaction, organizational commitment, and performance, but it also influences group dynamics and group-level outcomes.[61] Managers can thus use the four types of transformational leadership shown in Figure 16–4 as a vehicle to improve group dynamics and work-unit outcomes. This is important in today's organizations because most employees do not work in isolation. Rather, people tend to rely on the input and collaboration of others, and many organizations are structured around teams. The key point to remember is that transformational leadership transforms individuals as well as teams and work groups. We encourage you to use this to your advantage.

Fourth, transformational leadership works virtually. If you lead geographically dispersed people, then it is important to focus on how you can display the four transformational leader behaviors in your emails, tweets, webinars, and conference calls.[62] Fifth, employees at any level in an organization can be trained to be more transactional and transformational.[63] This reinforces the organizational value of developing and rolling out a combination of transactional and transformational leadership training for all employees. These programs, however, should be based on an overall corporate philosophy that constitutes the foundation of leadership development.

Finally, transformational leaders can be ethical or unethical. Whereas ethical transformational leaders enable employees to enhance their self-concepts, unethical ones select or produce obedient, dependent, and compliant followers. Top management can create and maintain ethical transformational leadership by

1. Creating and enforcing a clearly stated code of ethics.
2. Recruiting, selecting, and promoting people who display ethical behavior.
3. Developing performance expectations around the treatment of employees—these expectations can then be assessed in the performance appraisal process.
4. Training employees to value diversity.
5. Identifying, rewarding, and publicly praising employees who exemplify high moral conduct.[64]

TO THE POINT

What are the key conclusions regarding the leader–member exchange model of leadership, shared leadership, servant-leadership, and the role of being a follower?

Additional Perspectives on Leadership

This section examines four additional perspectives on leadership: leader–member exchange theory, shared leadership, servant-leadership, and a follower perspective.

LO.8 The Leader–Member Exchange (LMX) Model of Leadership

The leader–member exchange model of leadership revolves around the development of dyadic relationships between managers and their direct reports. This model is quite different from those previously discussed in that it focuses on the quality of relationships between managers and subordinates as opposed to the behaviors or traits of either leaders or followers. It also is different in that it does not assume that leader behavior is characterized by a stable or average leadership style as do the previously discussed models. In other words, most models of leadership assume a leader treats all employees in about the same way. In contrast, the LMX model is based on the assumption that leaders develop unique one-to-one relationships with each of the people reporting to them. Behavioral scientists call this sort of relationship a *vertical dyad.* The forming of vertical dyads is said to be a naturally occurring process, resulting from the leader's attempt to delegate and assign work roles. As a result of this process, two distinct types of leader–member exchange relationships are expected to evolve.[65]

One type of leader–member exchange is called the **in-group exchange**. In this relationship, leaders and followers develop a partnership characterized by reciprocal influence, mutual trust, respect and liking, and a sense of common fates. In the second type of exchange, referred to as an **out-group exchange**, leaders are characterized as overseers who fail to create a sense of mutual trust, respect, or common fate.[66]

Research Findings   If the leader–member exchange model is correct, there should be a significant relationship between the type of leader–member exchange and job-related outcomes. Research supports this prediction. For example, a positive leader–member exchange was positively associated with job satisfaction, intentions to stay employed at the company, job performance, commitment to organizational change, trust between managers and employees, procedural and distributive justice (recall our discussion in Chapter 8), willingness to help co-workers, and satisfaction with leadership.[67] Results from a recent meta-analysis of 50 studies also revealed a moderately strong, positive relationship between LMX and organizational citizenship behaviors—recall our discussion in Chapter 6.[68] You can see that a positive LMX is associated with a host of positive outcomes. Finally, studies also have identified a variety of variables that influence the quality of an LMX. For example, LMX was positively related to the extent to which employees identified with their managers and the breadth of a leader's social networks within the organization.[69]

Managerial Implications   There are three important implications associated with the LMX model of leadership. First, leaders are encouraged to establish high-performance expectations for all of their direct reports because setting high-performance standards fosters high-quality LMXs. Second, because personality and demographic similarity between leaders and followers is associated with higher LMXs, managers need to be careful that they don't create a homogeneous work environment in the spirit of having positive relationships with their direct reports. Our discussion of diversity in Chapter 2 clearly documented that there are many positive benefits of having a diverse workforce. The third implication pertains to those of us who find ourselves in a poor LMX. A management consultant offers the following tips for improving the quality of leader–member exchanges.[70]

1. Stay focused on your department's goals and remain positive about your ability to accomplish your goals. An unsupportive boss is just another obstacle to be overcome.

2. Do not fall prey to feeling powerless, and empower yourself to get things done.

3. Exercise the power you have by focusing on circumstances you can control and avoid dwelling on circumstances you cannot control.

4. Work on improving your relationship with your manager. Begin by examining the level of trust between the two of you and then try to improve it by frequently and effectively communicating. You can also increase trust by following through on your commitments and achieving your goals.

5. Use an authentic, respectful, and assertive approach to resolve differences with your manager. It also is useful to use a problem-solving approach when disagreements arise.

LO.9 Shared Leadership

A pair of OB scholars noted that "there is some speculation, and some preliminary evidence, to suggest that concentration of leadership in a single chain of command may be less optimal than shared leadership responsibility among two or more individuals in certain task environments."[71] This perspective is quite different from the previous theories and models discussed in this chapter, which assume that leadership is a vertical, downward-flowing process. In contrast, the notion of shared leadership is based on the idea that people need to share information and collaborate to get things done at work. This in turn underscores the need for employees to adopt a horizontal process of influence or leadership. **Shared leadership** is defined as "a dynamic, interactive influence process among individuals in groups for which the objective is to lead one another to the achievement of group or organizational goals or both. This influence process often involves peer, or lateral, influence and at other times involves upward or downward hierarchical influence."[72] The concept of shared leadership was first discussed in Chapter 11 when we reviewed the characteristics of high-performing teams. You may recall that *shared responsibility* is one of the eight attributes associated with high-performing teams.

Shared leadership is most likely to be needed when people work in teams, when people are involved in complex projects, and when people are doing knowledge work—work that requires voluntary contributions of intellectual capital by skilled professionals. Shared leadership also is beneficial when people are working on tasks or projects that require interdependence and creativity. Despite these recommendations, it is important to remember that people vary in the preference for shared leadership. Some of these differences are culturally based (recall our discussion in Chapter 4). For example, we conducted a consulting project with a manufacturing company in Portugal and realized that many employees preferred a directive rather than collaborative approach toward decision making and leadership.

---

in-group exchange A partnership characterized by mutual trust, respect, and liking.

out-group exchange A partnership characterized by a lack of mutual trust, respect, and liking.

shared leadership Simultaneous, ongoing, mutual influence process in which people share responsibility for leading.

The concept of shared leadership is taking hold at the highest levels in organizations. We are seeing more and more cases in which a CEO and another executive, such as a chief operating officer or chief financial officer, share the overall responsibilities of running the business. A simple way to make this work is for one leader to focus on internal matters while the other is concerned with external issues. Organizations like Goldman Sachs, Adobe, and PepsiCo are using this form of leadership because they find that two people are more likely to possess the varied abilities that are needed to run an organization. The application of shared leadership in this manner also helps organizations build a leadership pipeline for executive-level positions.

Researchers are just now beginning to explore the process of shared leadership, and results are promising. For example, shared leadership in teams was positively associated with group cohesion, group citizenship, and group effectiveness.[73] Table 16–6 contains a list of key questions and answers that managers should consider when determining how they can develop shared leadership.

Servant-Leadership

Servant-leadership is more a philosophy of managing than a testable theory. The term *servant-leadership* was coined by Robert Greenleaf in 1970. Greenleaf believes that great leaders act as servants, putting the needs of others, including employees, customers, and community, as their first priority. **Servant-leadership** focuses on increased service to others rather than to oneself.[74] Because the focus of servant-leadership is serving others over self-interest, servant-leaders are less likely to engage in self-serving behaviors that hurt others. Embedding servant-leadership

table 16–6   Key Questions and Answers to Consider When Developing Shared Leadership

KEY QUESTIONS	ANSWERS
What task characteristics call for shared leadership?	Tasks that are highly *interdependent.* Tasks that require a great deal of *creativity.* Tasks that are highly *complex.*
What is the role of the leader in developing shared leadership?	*Designing the team,* including clarifying purpose, securing resources, articulating vision, selecting members, and defining team processes. *Managing the boundaries* of the team.
How can organizational systems facilitate the development of shared leadership?	*Training and development systems* can be used to prepare both designated leaders and team members to engage in shared leadership. *Reward systems* can be used to promote and reward shared leadership. *Cultural systems* can be used to articulate and to demonstrate the value of shared leadership.
What vertical and shared leadership behaviors are important to team outcomes?	*Directive leadership* can provide task-focused directions. *Transactional leadership* can provide both personal and material rewards based on key performance metrics. *Transformational leadership* can stimulate commitment to a team vision, emotional engagement, and fulfillment of higher-order needs. *Empowering leadership* can reinforce the importance of self-motivation.
What are the ongoing responsibilities of the vertical leader?	The vertical leader needs to be able to step in and *fill voids* in the team. The vertical leader needs to continue to *emphasize the importance of the shared leadership approach,* given the task characteristics facing the team.

into an organization's culture requires actions as well as words. For example, John Donahoe, CEO of eBay, is committed to serving customers, "specifically the companies and entrepreneurs who sell goods on the site. Then he visualizes a chain of command through which the CEO can deliver what customers need. On trips around the world he takes along a Flip Video camera and films interviews with eBay sellers to share their opinions with his staff. He has even tied managers' compensation to customer loyalty, measured through regular surveys."[75]

According to Jim Stuart, cofounder of the leadership circle in Tampa, Florida, "[l]eadership derives naturally from a commitment to service. You know that you're practicing servant-leadership if your followers become wiser, healthier, more autonomous—and more likely to become servant-leaders themselves."[76] Servant-leadership is not a quick-fix approach to leadership. Rather, it is a long-term, transformational approach to life and work.

Servant-leaders have the characteristics listed in Table 16–7. An example of someone with these characteristics is Sam Palmisano, chairman and CEO of IBM. Here is what he had to say about his approach to leadership:

connect Go to www.mcgrawhillconnect.com for an interactive exercise to test your knowledge of servant leadership.

table 16–7 Characteristics of the Servant-Leader

SERVANT-LEADERSHIP CHARACTERISTICS	DESCRIPTION
1. *Listening*	Servant-leaders focus on listening to identify and clarify the needs and desires of a group.
2. *Empathy*	Servant-leaders try to empathize with others' feelings and emotions. An individual's good intentions are assumed even when he or she performs poorly.
3. *Healing*	Servant-leaders strive to make themselves and others whole in the face of failure or suffering.
4. *Awareness*	Servant-leaders are very self-aware of their strengths and limitations.
5. *Persuasion*	Servant-leaders rely more on persuasion than positional authority when making decisions and trying to influence others.
6. *Conceptualization*	Servant leaders take the time and effort to develop broader based conceptual thinking. Servant-leaders seek an appropriate balance between a short-term, day-to-day focus and a long-term, conceptual orientation.
7. *Foresight*	Servant-leaders have the ability to foresee future outcomes associated with a current course of action or situation.
8. *Stewardship*	Servant-leaders assume that they are stewards of the people and resources they manage.
9. *Commitment to the growth of people*	Servant-leaders are committed to people beyond their immediate work role. They commit to fostering an environment that encourages personal, professional, and spiritual growth.
10. *Building community*	Servant-leaders strive to create a sense of community both within and outside the work organization.

SOURCE: These characteristics and descriptions were derived from L C Spears, "Introduction: Servant-Leadership and the Greenleaf Legacy," in *Reflections on Leadership: How Robert K Greenleaf's Theory of Servant-Leadership Influenced Today's Top Management Thinkers*, ed L C Spears (New York: John Wiley & Sons, 1995), pp 1–14.

servant-leadership Focuses on increased service to others rather than to oneself.

Not only do employees *like* servant-leaders, like Sam Palmisano of IBM, but research suggests they work hard for them, too.

Example. Over the course of my IBM career I've observed many CEOs, heads of state, and others in positions of great authority. I've noticed that some of the most effective leaders don't make themselves the center of attention. They are respectful. They listen. This is an appealing personal quality, but it's also an effective leadership attribute. Their selflessness makes the people around them comfortable. People open up, speak up, contribute. They give those leaders their very best.[77]

Researchers have just begun to develop measures of servant-leadership and to examine relationships between this type of leadership and various outcomes. In support of Greenleaf's ideas, servant-leadership was found to be positively associated with employees' performance, organizational commitment, job satisfaction, creativity, organizational citizenship behaviors, and perceptions of justice. Servant-leadership also was negatively related to counterproductive work behavior.[78] These results suggest that managers would be well served by using the servant-leadership characteristics shown in Table 16–7.

LO.10   The Role of Followers in the Leadership Process

All of the previous theories discussed in this chapter have been leader-centric. That is, they focused on understanding leadership effectiveness from the leader's point of view. We conclude this chapter by discussing the role of followers in the leadership process. Although very little research has been devoted to this topic, it is an important issue to consider because the success of both leaders and followers is contingent on the dynamic relationship among the people involved.[79]

We begin our discussion by noting that both leaders and followers are closely linked. You cannot lead without having followers, and you cannot follow without having leaders. The point is that each needs the other, and the quality of the relationship determines how we behave as followers. This is why it is important for both leaders and followers to focus on developing a mutually rewarding and beneficial relationship. The Real World/Real People on page 489 summarizes Nancy Lublin's view on this mutually reinforcing relationship. Lublin was founder of Dress for Success and CEO of DoSomething.

Followers vary in terms of the extent to which they commit, comply, and resist a leader's influence attempts. For example, one researcher identified three types of followers: helpers, independents, and rebels. *"Helpers* show deference and comply with the leadership; *independents* distance themselves from the leadership and show less compliance; and *rebels* show divergence from the leader and are at least compliant. Among other types of followers, moderate in compliance, are *diplomats, partisans*, and *counselors.*"[80] Leaders obviously want followers who are productive, reliable, honest, cooperative, proactive, and flexible. Leaders do not benefit from followers who hide the truth, withhold information, fail to generate ideas, are unwilling to collaborate, provide inaccurate feedback, or are unwilling to take the lead on projects and initiatives.[81]

In contrast, research shows that followers seek, admire, and respect leaders who foster three emotional responses in others: Followers want organizational leaders to create feelings of *significance* (what one does at work is important and meaningful), *community* (a sense of unity encourages people to treat others with respect and dignity and to work together in pursuit of organizational goals), and *excitement* (people are engaged and feel energy at work).[82]

Go to www.mcgrawhillconnect.com for a video case on leadership after the Hurricane Katrina disaster.

real WORLD // real PEOPLE

Nancy Lublin Believes That Her Followers Make Her Successful

We've overdone this whole leadership/founder/entrepreneur thing. And we're not spending nearly enough time crediting the folks who turn all that visionary stuff into tangible reality....

We degrade the very idea of followers—lemmings!—yet the world needs people who can follow intelligently. I am not talking about mindless armies that march in formation and shoot if their leader points down a dark hallway. The key word is "intelligently." Good followers ask good questions. They probe their leaders. They crunch the numbers to ensure that their visionary boss's gorgeous plan actually works....

Honoring good followers isn't just a nice thing—it's necessary. It's the sanest, smartest way to run your company, for-profit or not. We have to recognize that your bright ideas—and mine—would go nowhere without the doers. Failing to do so will make us collectively poorer, not just in spirit but in money.

What does it take to be a good follower?

SOURCE: Excerpted from N Lublin, "Let's Hear It for the Little Guys," *Fastcompany*, April 2010, p 33.

A pair of OB experts developed a four-step process for followers to use in managing the leader–follower relationship.[83] First, it is critical for followers to understand their boss. Followers should attempt to gain an appreciation for their manager's leadership style, interpersonal style, goals, expectations, pressures, and strengths and weaknesses. One way of doing this is to ask your manager to answer the following seven questions:[84]

1. How would you describe your leadership style? Does your style change when you are under pressure?
2. When would you like me to approach you with questions or information? Are there any situations that are off-limits (e.g., a social event)?
3. How do you want me to communicate with you?
4. How do you like to work?
5. Are there behaviors or attitudes that you will not tolerate? What are they?
6. What is your approach toward giving feedback?
7. How can I help you?

Second, followers need to understand their own style, needs, goals, expectations, and strengths and weaknesses. The next step entails conducting a gap analysis between the understanding a follower has about his or her boss and the understanding the follower has about him- or herself. With this information in mind, followers are ready to proceed to the final step of developing and maintaining a relationship that fits both parties' needs and styles.

This final step requires followers to build on mutual strengths and to adjust or accommodate the leader's divergent style, goals, expectations, and weaknesses.[85] For example, a follower might adjust his or her style of communication in response to the boss's preferred method for receiving information. Other adjustments might be made in terms of decision making. If the boss prefers a participative approach, then followers should attempt to involve their manager in all decisions regardless of the follower's decision-making style—recall our discussion of decision-making styles in Chapter 12. Good use of time and resources is another issue for followers to consider. Most managers are pushed for time, energy, and resources and are more likely to appreciate followers who save rather than cost them time and energy. Followers should not use up their manager's time discussing trivial matters.

There are two final issues to consider. First, a follower may not be able to accommodate a leader's style, expectations, or weaknesses and may have to seek a transfer or quit his or her job to reconcile the discrepancy. We recognize that there are personal and ethical trade-offs that one may not be willing to make when managing the leader–follower relationship. Second, we can all enhance our boss's leadership effectiveness and our employer's success by becoming better followers. Remember, it is in an individual's best interest to be a good follower because leaders need and want competent employees.

Summary of Key Concepts

1. *Define the term* leadership, *and explain the difference between leading and managing.* Leadership is defined as a process in which an individual influences a group of individuals to achieve a common goal. Although leadership and management overlap, each entails a unique set of activities or functions. Managers typically perform functions associated with planning, investigating, organizing, and control, and leaders deal with the interpersonal aspects of a manager's job. Table 16–2 summarizes the differences between leading and managing. All told, organizational success requires a combination of effective leadership and management.

2. *Review trait theory research and the takeaways from this theoretical perspective.* Historical leadership research did not support the notion that effective leaders possessed unique traits from followers. More recent research showed that effective leaders possessed the following traits: task competence, interpersonal competence, intuition, traits of character, biophysical traits, and personal traits. In contrast, bad leaders displayed the following characteristics: incompetent, rigid, intemperate, callous, corrupt, insular, and evil. Research also demonstrated that men and women exhibited different styles of leadership. The takeaways from trait theory are that (*a*) we can no longer ignore the implications of leadership traits; traits influence leadership effectiveness; (*b*) organizations may want to include personality and trait assessments into their selection and promotion processes; and (*c*) management development programs can be used to enhance employees' leadership traits.

3. *Explain behavioral styles theory and its takeaways.* The thrust of behavioral styles theory is to identify the leader behaviors that directly affect work-group effectiveness. Researchers at Ohio State uncovered two key leadership behaviors: consideration and initiating structure. These behaviors are similar to the employee-centered and job-centered behaviors uncovered by researchers at the University of Michigan. The takeaways from this theoretical perspective are as follows: (*a*) leaders are made, not born; (*b*) there is no one best style of leadership; (*c*) the effectiveness of a particular style depends on the situation at hand; and (*d*) managers are encouraged to apply Drucker's tips for effective leadership.

4. *Explain, according to Fiedler's contingency model, how leadership style interacts with situational control, and discuss the takeaways from this model.* Fiedler believes leader effectiveness depends on an appropriate match between leadership style and situational control. Leaders are either task motivated or relationship motivated. Situation control is composed of leader–member relations, task structure, and position power. Task-motivated leaders are effective under situations of both high and low control. Relationship-motivated leaders are more effective when they have moderate situational control. The three takeaways are (*a*) leadership effectiveness goes beyond traits and behaviors, (*b*) leaders are unlikely to be successful in all situations, and (*c*) leaders need to modify their style to fit a situation.

5. *Discuss House's revised path–goal theory and its takeaways.* There are three key changes in the revised path–goal theory. Leaders now are viewed as exhibiting eight categories of leader behavior (see Table 16–5) instead of four. In turn, the effectiveness of these styles depends on various employee characteristics and environmental factors. Second, leaders are expected to spend more effort fostering intrinsic motivation through empowerment. Third, leadership is not limited to people in managerial roles. Rather, leadership is shared among all employees within an organization. There are three takeaways: (*a*) effective leaders possess and use more than one style of leadership, (*b*) the theory offers specific suggestions for how leaders can help employees, and (*c*) managers are advised to modify their leadership style to fit relevant contingency factors.

6. *Describe the difference between laissez-fair, transactional, and transformational leadership.* Laissez-faire leadership is the absence of leadership. It represents a general failure to take responsibility for leading. Transactional leadership focuses on clarifying employees' role and task requirements and providing followers with positive and negative rewards contingent on performance. Transformational leaders motivate employees to pursue organizational goals above their own self-interests. Transactional and transformational leadership are both important for organizational success.

7. *Discuss how transformational leadership transforms followers and work groups.* Individual characteristics and organizational culture are key precursors of transformational leadership, which comprise four sets of leader behavior. These leader behaviors in turn positively affect followers' and work-group goals, values, beliefs, aspirations, and motivation. These positive

effects are then associated with a host of preferred outcomes.

8. *Explain the leader–member exchange model of leadership.* The LMX model revolves around the development of dyadic relationships between managers and their direct reports. These leader–member exchanges qualify as either in-group or out-group relationships. Research supports this model of leadership.

9. *Review the concept of shared leadership and the practical principles of servant-leadership.* Shared leadership involves a simultaneous, ongoing, mutual influence process in which individuals share responsibility for leading regardless of formal roles and titles. This type of leadership is most likely to be needed when people work in teams, when people are involved in complex projects, and when people are doing knowledge work. Shared

leadership also is beneficial when people are working on tasks or projects that require interdependence and creativity. Servant-leadership is more a philosophy than a testable theory. It is based on the premise that great leaders act as servants, putting the needs of others, including employees, customers, and community, as their first priority.

10. *Describe the follower's role in the leadership process.* Followers can use a four-step process for managing the leader–follower relationship. Followers need to understand their boss and themselves. They then conduct a gap analysis between the understanding they have about their boss and themselves. The final step requires followers to build on mutual strengths and to adjust or accommodate the leader's divergent style, goals, expectations, and weaknesses.

Key Terms

Leadership, 462

Leader trait, 465

Implicit leadership theory, 466

Leadership prototype, 466

Consideration, 470

Initiating structure, 470

Situational theories, 472

Leader–member relations, 472

Task structure, 473

Position power, 473

Contingency factors, 475

Transactional leadership, 480

Transformational leadership, 480

In-group exchange, 484

Out-group exchange, 484

Shared leadership, 485

Servant-leadership, 486

OB in Action Case Study

Lynn Tilton Uses Her Leadership to Turn Around Failing Companies[86]

Earlier this year, private-equity chief Lynn Tilton flew to Detroit to try to improve sales at one of her auto-parts companies. She got a cool reception from Ford Motor Co.'s purchasing chief, Tony Brown, who asked if she was like other private-equity chiefs that "strip and flip" their companies.

"You must be mistaken," she shot back. "It's only men that I strip and flip. My companies I hold long and close to my heart."

With her platinum blond hair, tight leather skirts and penchant for racy remarks, Ms. Tilton has a talent for getting people's attention. Yet behind the glam facade is a sophisticated distressed-debt investor and manufacturing tycoon who has quickly become one of the richest self-made women in America.

Through her New York-based holding company, Patriarch Partners, Ms. Tilton owns all or parts of 74 companies with revenues of more than $8 billion and 120,000 employees. By most measures, Patriarch is now the largest woman-owned business in America.

Ms. Tilton, 52 years old, built her fortune from an unlikely corner of the economy: down-and-out industrial firms. Her strategy is to buy manufacturers headed for the scrap heap and bring them back to life with new

management teams and products. In the process, she's become an unlikely crusader for America's rust belt.

"The key to America's future is manufacturing," she says. "We simply have to become a country that can make things again." . . .

Ms. Tilton also has had her share of mistakes. After buying American LaFrance, the fire truck maker, she drove down revenue by more than 50% in an effort to improve profits. Four years later, she still is trying to turn the company around.

"That was a purchase I made more with my heart than my head," she said.

Ms. Tilton has the added distraction of her personality. Her office uniform usually includes five-inch stilettos, an eight-carat diamond necklace and the occasional black leather jumpsuit. Her office walls are filled with whips and handcuffs sent to her by friends, Hashemite daggers given to her by Middle Eastern royals, New Age paintings and a portrait of her stretched across the hood of a black Mercedes. Ms. Tilton makes no apologies for her unconventional look.

"I am all woman," she says. "Sometimes it makes men uncomfortable, sure. But in business and in life, I have to remain faithful to my inner truth. In the end,

I'd hope people judge me on my accomplishments and intelligence."

Ms. Tilton started on Wall Street as a single mother, working 15-hour days and putting herself through Columbia's business school. She had graduated from Yale as a nationally ranked college tennis player and aspiring poet, and married her college sweetheart. Soon after starting work on Wall Street, she got divorced and plunged into her work . . .

In 2000, she founded Patriarch, named after her late father. Her plan was to trade debt with her own money. Yet after buying two giant portfolios of distressed debt, she realized the only way to succeed was to take control of the companies in the portfolio. Suddenly, Ms. Tilton had gone from a debt investor to the accidental chief executive of dozens of failed companies. Her turnarounds were so profitable that she went on to buy more companies . . .

She sleeps only a few hours a night and sips a homemade concoction of clay, salt and chlorophyll. She often stays up late reading science fiction on her Kindle.

Walking down the manufacturing line at her MD Helicopter plant in Arizona on a recent afternoon, Ms. Tilton looked out of place in her shimmering dress and heels. Yet she quickly bonded with workers with her earthy jokes and detailed knowledge of metal alloys and machine tools.

"Workers really take to Lynn," said Duane Lugdon, a United Steelworkers union staffer who led tense negotiations with Ms. Tilton at the Maine paper plant. "She's just human and honest with people. I don't say that about many CEOs."

Her personal involvement in each company—she's still CEO of MD—is a blessing and a curse, former employees say. They say employee churn at Patriarch is high because of Ms. Tilton's tough personality.

"I'm a benevolent dictator," Ms. Tilton says. "I like to control things. What we do, the distressed area, is not for the faint of heart."

Questions for Discussion

1. Use Table 16–2 to evaluate the extent to which Lynn Tilton displayed the characteristics associated with being a good leader and good manager.
2. Which different positive and negative leadership traits and styles were displayed by Tilton? Cite examples.
3. To what extent does Tilton display situational approaches toward leadership? Explain.
4. Which of the four types of transformational leadership behavior were displayed by Tilton? Provide examples.
5. Would you like to work for Lynn Tilton? Explain why or why not.
6. What did you learn about leadership from this case?

Legal/Ethical Challenge

Is It Ethical to Use Subversive Approaches to Influence Others?

"Last week, National Public Radio's chief executive [Vivian Schiller] and senior fundraiser [Ron Schiller] resigned after off-the-cuff remarks were made to conservative activists posing as potential donors."[87] The Schillers are unrelated. The potential donors, headed by James O'Keefe, met with Ron Schiller at a posh restaurant for lunch under the guise that they wanted to donate $5 million as representatives from a Muslim organization. O'Keefe secretly recorded the interview and later released a doctored video clip that portrayed NPR in a very bad light. Schiller made negative and damaging comments about the Republican Party in general and the Tea Party in particular. You can imagine how this video was received by politicians, particularly those that vote on funding for National Public Radio (NPR).

A reporter from the *Washington Post* described the video as "selective and deceptive." He stated that "O'Keefe's final product excludes explanatory context, exaggerates [Ron] Schiller's tolerance for Islamist radicalism and attributes sentiments to Schiller that are actually quotes by others— all the hallmarks of a hit piece." The reporter concluded that "O'Keefe did not merely leave a false impression; he manufactured an elaborate lie. . . . The stingers bought access with fake money. There is no ethical canon or tradition that would excuse such deception on the part of a professional journalist."[88]

The video led some government officials to call for major, if not total funding cuts to NPR, which would threaten the organization's very existence. The end result is that the U.S. Senate voted in March 2011 to block public radio stations from spending federal money on programming. It appears that O'Keefe's influence attempts had some success.[89]

Not everyone agrees that O'Keefe did anything wrong. Some think that subversive techniques are a good way to keep people accountable. After all, TV programs like *20/20* have used hidden cameras for years to catch people doing bad things. The subversive trend is growing. For example, "the subversive approach has become so popular that the Yes Men, anti-corporate jokers who have made two critically acclaimed movies, recently opened the Yes Lab, which trains others in the art of dirty work." Mike Bonanno, who co-founded Yes Men, concluded that "with mainstream media being defunded, there is less real reporting out there and more people are resorting to these kinds of tactics to get the work out on stuff that should be obvious."[90] Further, "O'Keefe defenders contend he is not really a journalist but a new breed of 'citizen journalist.' This can be defined as the simultaneous demands for journalistic respect and for release from journalistic standards, including a commitment to honesty."[91]

What do you think should be done about James O'Keefe?

1. Although O'Keefe did not violate any laws, he should be punished. His behavior was unethical. He lied about his identity to Ron Schiller and edited the video to present false impressions about NPR. His subversive actions also led to a negative vote about funding for public radio.

2. O'Keefe didn't break any laws, so he should be left alone. He actually is providing a service to the public.

What should be done about citizen journalism?

1. Given today's technology, we need regulations to govern this aspect of modern life. If people like James O'Keefe want to do journalistic work on their own, then they should be held to the same standards as professionals.

2. Wake up and smell the coffee. The only way to expose people like Ron Schiller is to use subversive techniques. I have no problem with what O'Keefe did. Besides, others are doing the same thing.

Web Resources

For study material and exercises that apply to this chapter, visit our website at **www.mhhe.com/kreitner10e**

chapter 17

Organizational Design, Effectiveness, and Innovation

Learning Objectives

When you finish studying the material in this chapter, you should be able to:

LO.1 Describe the four characteristics common to all organizations, and explain the difference between closed and open systems.

LO.2 Define the term *learning organization.*

LO.3 Review the factors that hinder an organization's ability to learn from success and failure.

LO.4 Describe seven basic ways organizations are structured.

LO.5 Discuss Burns and Stalker's findings regarding mechanistic and organic organizations.

LO.6 Identify when each of the seven organization structures is the right fit.

LO.7 Describe the four generic organizational effectiveness criteria.

LO.8 Discuss the difference between innovation, invention, creativity, and integration.

LO.9 Review the myths about innovation.

LO.10 Explain the model of innovation.

How Can Companies Modify Their Meetings to Boost Innovation?

In the downturn, some small-business owners are looking for more creative ways to make conference-room time as efficient as possible, an effort they hope will ultimately trickle down to the company's bottom line.

Many managers say fostering participation is a major challenge, particularly when the attendees with valuable ideas are too reserved or timid to speak up. Without their contributions the meetings are less productive.

Dixon Schwabl Advertising in Rochester, New York, tried to lower the inhibitions of its 82 employees by arming them with water guns, which workers are instructed to bring to all meetings. Anyone who passes a negative comment at the meeting is bound to get wet.

"It helps them be more comfortable because no one will be criticized or scrutinized," says Lauren Dixon, the marketing and advertising firm's chief executive. . . .

Other entrepreneurs are relying on technology to propel the meetings and keep the employees engaged.

Managers at Russell Construction Co, introduced a new device at a recent quarterly meeting that calculates the average salary of those in attendance and determines exactly how much the meeting is costing the company based on those figures.

"I don't think people thought of time as an expense before," says Angelo Bagby, director of marketing and client relations for the 70-employee firm, which is based in Davenport, Iowa.

That initial 90-minute meeting cost the firm roughly $5,000 . . . since then, employees have used the device at smaller group meetings, helping to shave off as much as $100 per meeting, Ms. Bagby estimates.

Other small businesses are using special software to hold interactive meetings that end with tangible outlines and focus points.

AscendWorks LLC, a consulting firm in Austin, Texas, is using a program called Mindjet Catalyst that allows employees to write out the talking points of the meeting as they are being discussed. They can then easily manipulate the text, organizing it by category and subcategory.

"It's like thinking out loud, except it's on a screen," syas AscendWorks President Don Dalrymple.

Finis Price, a lawyer in Louisville, Kentucky, uses a visualization technology called Papershow to similarly engage his two paralegals, who work remotely.

"If I couldn't verbally describe something, I'd just have to say, 'You'll see what I mean after I send it," says Mr Price of his meetings prior to purchasing the technology last year. "Then, they'd call and inevitably have questions about it."[1]

The chapter-opening case highlights the relationship between organizational design and the use of technology in affecting innovation in small firms. The same relationships are important in large organizations. DuPont's innovative efforts, for example, have resulted in obtaining nearly 40% of its 2009 revenues from products introduced within the last five years. This helped DuPont's stock to increase 41% in 2010.[2] A pair of management experts echoed the importance of innovation by concluding "sooner or later, all businesses, even the most successful, run out of room to grow. Faced with this unpleasant reality, they are compelled to reinvent themselves periodically. The ability to pull off this difficult feat—to jump from the maturity stage of one business to the growth stage of the next—is what separates high performers from those whose times at the top is all too brief."[3]

The overall goal of this chapter is to provide you with a solid foundation for understanding how organizational design influences organizational effectiveness and innovation. We begin by defining the term *organization,* discussing important dimensions of organization charts, and contrasting views of organizations as closed or open systems. Our attention then turns to the various ways organizations are designed, from traditional divisions of work to more recent, popular ideas about lowering barriers between departments and companies. Next, we discuss the contingency approach to designing organizations. We then explore various criteria for assessing an organization's effectiveness, and conclude by discussing the topic of organizational innovation.

TO THE POINT

What are the four characteristics of organizational structure, and what are the key conclusions regarding closed and open systems and a learning organization?

LO.1 Organizations: Definition and Perspectives

As a necessary springboard for this chapter, we need to formally define the term *organization,* clarify the meaning of organization charts, and explore two open-system perspectives of organizations.

What Is an Organization?

According to Chester I Barnard's classic definition cited in Chapter 1, an **organization** is "a system of consciously coordinated activities or forces of two or more persons."[4] Embodied in the *conscious coordination* aspect of this definition are four common denominators of all organizations: coordination of effort, a common goal, division of labor, and a hierarchy of authority.[5] Organization theorists refer to these factors as the organization's *structure.*

Coordination of effort is achieved through formulation and enforcement of policies, rules, and regulations. Division of labor occurs when the common goal is pursued by individuals performing separate but related tasks. The hierarchy of authority, also called the chain of command, is a control mechanism dedicated to making sure the right people do the right things at the right time. Historically, managers have maintained the integrity of the hierarchy of authority by adhering to the unity of command principle. The **unity of command principle** specifies that each employee should report to only one manager. Otherwise, the argument goes, inefficiency would prevail because of conflicting orders and lack of personal accountability. (Indeed, these are problems in today's more fluid and flexible organizations based on innovations such as cross-functional, self-managed, and virtual teams.) Managers in the hierarchy of authority also administer rewards and punishments. When operating in concert, the four definitional factors—coordination of effort, a common goal, division of labor, and a hierarchy of authority—enable an organization to come to life and function.

figure 17–1   Sample Organization Chart for a Hospital (executive and director levels only)

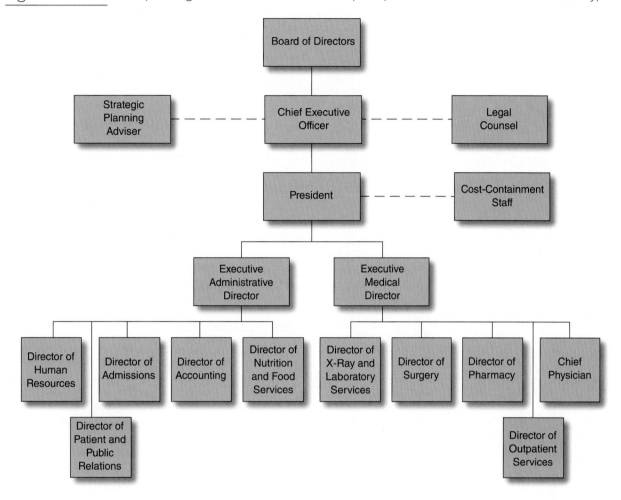

Organization Charts

An **organization chart** is a graphic representation of formal authority and division of labor relationships. To the casual observer, the term *organization chart* means the family tree–like pattern of boxes and lines posted on workplace walls. Within each box one usually finds the names and titles of current position holders. To organization theorists, however, organization charts reveal much more. The partial organization chart in Figure 17–1 reveals four basic dimensions of organizational structure: (1) hierarchy of authority (who reports to whom), (2) division of labor, (3) spans of control, and (4) line and staff positions.

Hierarchy of Authority   As Figure 17–1 illustrates, there is an unmistakable hierarchy of authority. Working from bottom to top, the 10 directors report to the two executive directors who report to the president who reports to the chief executive officer. Ultimately, the chief executive officer answers to the hospital's

connect™ Go to www.mcgrawhillconnect.com for an interactive exercise to test your knowledge of organizational charts.

---

organization System of consciously coordinated activities of two or more people.

unity of command principle Each employee should report to a single manager.

organization chart Boxes-and-lines illustration showing chain of formal authority and division of labor.

real WORLD // real PEOPLE

Companies Have Different Views about the Optimum Span of Control

Consider Pepsico Inc's Gemesa cookie business in Mexico as a case in point. There, workers have been briefed on company goals and processes so that they do more themselves to keep production running smoothly. New pay systems reward productivity, quality, service and teamwork while penalizing underperformance. That promotes efficiency, Pepsico says, while letting managers function more as coaches of self-motivating teams.

Gemesa last year ran its factories with 56 employees per boss, Pepsico says, instead of the 12:1 ratio that prevailed in the mid-1990s. The changes have helped Gemesa improve its business results, the company adds. . . .

Not all companies are eager to give bosses more subordinates. Sun Microsystems prefers work teams of 10 people or fewer, says Ann Bamesberger, vice president, Open Work Services group, at the Santa Clara, California, computer company.

Sun lately has put more energy into redesigning work environments, so that teams can expand and contract

more easily as projects evolve, says Ms Bamesberger. Among those initiatives: better support for engineers who sometimes work from home and flexible seating so that growing teams can fit in new members without losing proximity.

One boss with more than two dozen people reporting to her is Cindy Zollinger, president of Cornerstone Research, a litigation-consulting firm.

"I don't really manage them in a typical way," Ms Zollinger says. "They largely run themselves. I help them in dealing with obstacles they face, or in making the most of opportunities that they find."

Do you think an individual can effectively manage 24 employees? Explain.

SOURCE: Excerpted from G Anders, "Overseeing More Employees—with Fewer Managers," *The Wall Street Journal*, March 24, 2008, p B6.

The "king" chess piece represents the top of the hierarchy in a game of chess. The chess pieces can also be viewed as an organization of sorts because the movement of pieces are coordinated to obtain the end-goal of capturing the opponent's king.

board of directors. The chart in Figure 17–1 shows strict unity of command up and down the line. A formal hierarchy of authority also delineates the official communication network and speaks volumes about compensation. Research shows that there is an increasing wage gap between layers over time. That is, the difference in pay between successive layers tends to increase over time.[6]

Division of Labor   In addition to showing the chain of command, the sample organization chart indicates extensive division of labor. Immediately below the hospital's president, one executive director is responsible for general administration while another is responsible for medical affairs. Each of these two specialities is further subdivided as indicated by the next layer of positions. At each successively lower level in the organization, jobs become more specialized.

Spans of Control   The **span of control** refers to the number of people reporting directly to a given manager. Spans of control can range from narrow to wide. For example, the president in Figure 17–1 has a narrow span of control of two. (Staff assistants usually are not included in a manager's span of control.) The executive administrative director in Figure 17–1 has a wider span of control of five. Historically, spans of 7 to 10 people were considered best. More recently, however, corporate restructuring and improved communication technologies have increased the typical span of control.[7] Despite years of debate, organization theorists and senior executives have not arrived at a consensus regarding the ideal span of control (see Real World/Real People above).

Generally, the narrower the span of control, the closer the supervision and the higher the administrative costs as a result of a higher manager-to-worker ratio. Recent emphasis on empowering employees and administrative efficiency dictates spans of control as wide as possible but guarding against inadequate supervision and lack of coordination. Wider spans also complement the trend toward greater worker autonomy and participation.

Line and Staff Positions   The organization chart in Figure 17–1 also distinguishes between line and staff positions. Line managers such as the president, the two executive directors, and the various directors occupy formal decision-making positions within the chain of command. Line positions generally are connected by solid lines on organization charts. Dotted lines indicate staff relationships. **Staff personnel** do background research and provide technical advice and recommendations to their **line managers,** who have the authority to make decisions. For example, the cost-containment specialists in the sample organization chart merely advise the president on relevant matters. Apart from supervising the work of their own staff assistants, they have no line authority over other organizational members. Modern trends such as cross-functional teams and matrix structures, which are discussed later in this chapter, are blurring the distinction between line and staff.

An Open-System Perspective of Organizations

To better understand how organizational models have evolved over the years, we need to know the difference between closed and open systems. A **closed system** is said to be a self-sufficient entity. It is "closed" to the surrounding environment. In contrast, an **open system** depends on constant interaction with the environment for survival. The distinction between closed and open systems is a matter of degree. Because every worldly system is partly closed and partly open, the key question is: How great a role does the environment play in the functioning of the system? For instance, a battery-powered clock is a relatively closed system. Once the battery is inserted, the clock performs its time-keeping function hour after hour until the battery goes dead. The human body, on the other hand, is a highly open system because it requires a constant supply of life-sustaining oxygen from the environment. Nutrients also are imported from the environment. Open systems are capable of self-correction, adaptation, and growth, thanks to characteristics such as homeostasis and feedback control.

Historically, management theorists downplayed the environment as they used closed-system thinking to characterize organizations as either well-oiled machines or highly disciplined military units. They believed rigorous planning and control would eliminate environmental uncertainty. But that proved unrealistic. Drawing on the field of general systems theory that emerged during the 1950s, organization theorists suggested a more dynamic model for organizations.[8] The resulting open-system model likened organizations to the human body. Accordingly, the model in Figure 17–2 reveals the organization to be a living organism that transforms inputs into various outputs. The outer boundary of the organization is permeable. People, information, capital, and goods and services move back and forth across this boundary. Moreover, each of the five organizational subsystems—goals and values, technical, psychosocial, structural, and managerial—is dependent on the others. Feedback about such things as sales and customer satisfaction or dissatisfaction enables the organization to self-adjust and survive despite uncertainty and change. In effect, the organization is alive.

This aerial shot of a boat sitting on top of a building in Japan is a good example of an open-system. The tsunami in Japan caused open-system effects like this throughout Japan. The tsunami is feared to have killed over 10,000 people.

span of control The number of people reporting directly to a given manager.

staff personnel Provide research, advice, and recommendations to line managers.

line managers Have authority to make organizational decisions.

closed system A relatively self-sufficient entity.

open system Organism that must constantly interact with its environment to survive.

figure 17–2 The Organization as an Open System

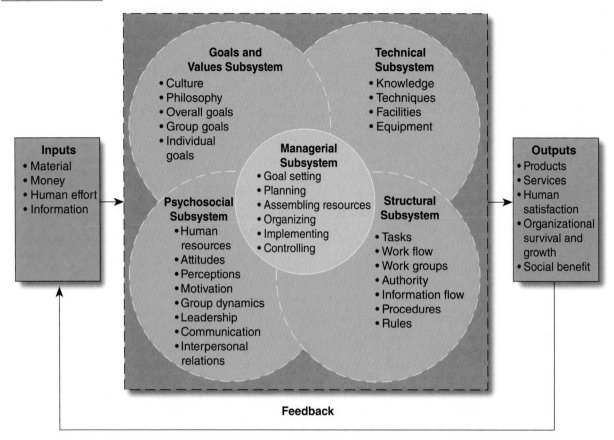

SOURCE: This model is a combination of Figures 5–2 and 5–3 in F E Kast and J E Rosenzweig, *Organization and Management: A Systems and Contingency Approach,* 4th ed (New York: McGraw-Hill, 1986), pp 112, 114. Copyright © 1986. Reprinted with permission of the McGraw-Hill Companies, Inc.

The 2011 tragedy in Japan is a good example of an open system. The crisis started with an earthquake, which led to a tsunami, and then to a nuclear accident. Open systems effects then caused many different problems for the Japanese people (e.g., nuclear exposure, food shortages, contaminated water, death, and destruction) as well as for organizations located in Japan, such as Walmart.[9] "Of its 414 Seiyu stores—as Walmart's Japanese chain is called—24 were in the Sendai and Fukushima area in northern Japan, close to the epicenter. Stores were trashed as goods fell off shelves during the temblor. A massive power outage ensued. Two stores suffered extensive damage. Close to 2,000 employees worked in the stricken region and were unaccounted for."[10] The effects of open systems also go beyond physical and geographical boundaries. For example, Ford Motor Company "halted all new orders for trucks, SUVs and cars in 'tuxedo black' and a handful of other hues due to shortages of some pigments made in Japan."[11]

 LO.2 Learning Organizations

In recent years, organizational theorists have extended the open-system model by adding a "brain" to the "living body." Organizations are said to have humanlike cognitive functions, such as the abilities to perceive and interpret, solve problems, store information, and learn from experience. Today, managers read and hear a good deal about learning organizations and team mental models. Peter Senge, a professor at the Massachusetts Institute of Technology, popularized the term *learning organization* in his best-selling book *The Fifth Discipline.* He described a learning organization as "a group of people working together to collectively enhance their capacities to create results that they truly care about."[12] A practical interpretation of these ideas results in the following definition. A **learning organization** is one that proactively creates, acquires, and transfers knowledge and that changes its behavior on the basis of new knowledge and insights.[13] The creation of a learning organization requires that organizational members use team mental models. A **team mental model** represents team members' "shared, organized understanding and mental representation of knowledge about key elements of the team's relevant environment."[14]

Learning organizations actively try to infuse their organizations, and associated team mental models, with new ideas and information. They do this by constantly scanning their external environments, hiring new talent and expertise when needed, and devoting significant resources to train and develop their employees. Next, new knowledge must be transferred throughout the organization. Learning organizations strive to reduce structural, process, and interpersonal barriers to the sharing of information, ideas, and knowledge among organizational members. They also focus on learning from both success and failure.

LO.3 Learning from Success   Success provides the *opportunity* to learn what an organization did right in terms of accomplishing a goal or implementing a project. We italicized the word *opportunity* because there are three key factors that distract or impede learning from success.[15] The first is the self-serving bias discussed in Chapter 7. This bias reflects the tendency to take more personal responsibility for success than failure and can lead managers to assume that success was due to their insights and talents and not to random events or external factors outside of management's control. The second pertains to the decision-making bias of overconfidence, which was reviewed in Chapter 12. This bias leads to the inflated perception that management is better than it actually is, which in turn can cause managers to "dismiss new innovations, dips in customer satisfaction, and increases in quality problems, and to make overly risky moves." The final distracter pertains to the natural tendency of "not asking why" we succeeded at something. "Success is commonly interpreted as evidence not only that your existing strategy and practices work but also that you have all the knowledge and information you need," along with the necessary skills. The takeaway from this discussion is that managers can learn from success by avoiding these learning traps. It also is important to remember that short-term success will not guarantee long-term success. This means that it is important to be vigilant about studying the causes of success over time.[16]

Learning from Failure   A G Lafley, CEO of Procter & Gamble from 2000 to 2009, believes that managers can learn from their mistakes and failures. He told a reporter from *Harvard Business Review* that he made plenty of mistakes and that he had "my fair share of failure. But you have to get past the disappointment and the blame and really understand what happened and why it happened. And then, more important, decide what you have learned and what you are going to do differently next time."[17] Lafley's views on learning certainly contributed to P&G's success under his leadership: "sales doubled, profits quadrupled, and P&G's market value increased by more than $100 billion."[18]

Lafley's success begs the question of why more organizations and managers don't make it a point to learn from failure. Why do you think this happens? Some

---

learning organization Proactively creates, acquires, and transfers knowledge throughout the organization.

team mental model Team members' shared understanding and knowledge about their work environment.

table 17–1 Factors that Detract from an Organization's Ability to Learn from Failure

FACTOR	DESCRIPTION AND RECOMMENDATION
1. The blame game	The tendency to blame failure on a person rather than on internal processes, systems, or external events.
2. The inability to recognize that failures are not created equal	Failures range from preventable (e.g., a person did not follow an accepted procedure or process) to noncontrollable (e.g., Ford's inability to produce black-colored cars because it could not get the needed materials from Japan during the 2011 crisis). It takes more time and effort to learn from failures caused by complex systems.
3. Not having a learning culture	People are afraid to point out or discuss failures. Managers are encouraged to create a psychologically safe culture that encourages employees to spot and discuss potential failures. It is critical to focus on processes and systems rather than on people.
4. Not detecting the lead indicators of failure	Analysis of failures focuses on people rather than on processes. Organizations are encouraged to identify and measure the status of short-term factors that lead to long-term success.
5. The self-serving bias	The tendency to blame failure on others or external events. It is important to consider the extent to which the causes of failure are controllable. It also is more beneficial to focus on controllable causes.
6. The reluctance to experiment	When people are uncertain about the causes of failure they are reluctant to experiment with different solutions. Conduct experiments and accept the idea that failure is part of the improvement process.

SOURCE: Based on A C Edmonson, "Strategies for Learning from Failure," *Harvard Business Review,* April 2011, pp 48–55.

experts suggest that the reason stems from our being programmed during childhood to believe that failure is bad and should be avoided. After all, who wants to talk about their weaknesses and failures? Although people may not like to talk about their failures, many managers believe that learning from failure is pretty easy. You simply need to ask people involved to meet and reflect on what went wrong and then encourage them to avoid these trappings on future projects. Unfortunately, this simplistic approach is unlikely to produce significant learning according to Amy Edmondson, professor at Harvard Business School.

Professor Edmonson studied organizational failures for 20 years and concluded that there are a host of factors that deter the extent to which organizations learn from failure (see Table 17–1).[19] She recommends that organizations focus on overcoming the barriers shown in Table 17–1 in order to maximize learning from failure. We conclude by noting results from a recent study on organizational learning. The researchers wanted to know if organizations learn more from success or failure. What do you think? Results indicated that organizations learned from both success and failure, but learning was stronger and longer lasting when it was based on failure.[20]

Creating a Learning Infrastructure

Professor Edmondson proposed the following four-step process for developing a learning infrastructure:

Example. First, organizations that focus on execution-as-learning use the best knowledge obtainable (which is understood to be a moving target) to inform the design of specific process guidelines. Second, they enable their employees to collaborate by making information available when and where it's needed. Third, they

real WORLD // real PEOPLE

Admiral Thad Allen Changed Mental Models When Dealing with the Aftermath of Hurricane Katrina

Here is what Admiral Allen said to an interviewer from the *Harvard Business Review* in response to a question about how leaders create unity of effort when responding to a crisis with multiple constituents.

"I'm a big fan of Peter Senge . . . who talks about learning organizations and the use of mental models. You have to understand at a very large, macro level what the problem is that you're dealing with and what needs to be done to achieve the effects you want—and you have to be able to communicate that.

With Katrina, it was clear to me after about 24 hours in New Orleans that we weren't dealing only with a natural disaster. Had the levees not collapsed, ground zero for Hurricane Katrina would have been Bay St Lous and Waverland, Mississippi, which basically got wiped off the map. But when the levees were breached and New Orleans flooded, it became a different event, and I'm not sure we recognized that as a nation. We were still treating the entire issue as if it were just a hurricane."

Admiral Allen went on to explain how the initial mental model of "hurricane" needed to be changed because it was impeding progress in dealing with the crisis. For example, under the hurricane response the federal government released resources to the local government, which was problematic because there was no functional local government during this period. Allen thus reframed the mission or mental model to one of "mass effect." This led to a new response in which the federal government and US military started to combine efforts to provide security, remove water from the city, conduct house-to-house searches, and so on.

Why did the mental model associated with "hurricanes" lead to an ineffective response from the federal government?

SOURCE: Excerpted from "You Have to Lead from Everywhere," *Harvard Business Review*, November 2010, p 77.

---

routinely capture process data to discover how work is really being done. Finally, they study these data in an effort to find ways to improve.[21]

You can see that this process requires the use of evidence-based decision making, which was discussed in Chapter 12. Following this four-step process should encourage employees to view learning as a daily activity. Retired Coast Guard Admiral Thad Allen is a good example of someone who tried to create a learning organization when he was directing the federal response to hurricanes Katrina and Rita (see Real World/Real People above).

Organization Design

Organizational design is defined as "the structures of accountability and responsibility used to develop and implement strategies, and the human resource practices and information and business processes that activate those structures."[22] The general idea behind the study of organizational design is that organizations are more effective or successful when their structure supports the execution of corporate strategies. This in turn has led researchers, consultants, and managers to consider how organizations might best structure themselves.[23] Many managers underestimate the complexity of this task. Consider the case of Yahoo!.

◀ ·······················

TO THE POINT
What are the similarities and differences between the seven basic ways organizations are structured?
·······················

organizational design A structure of accountability and responsibility that an organization uses to execute its strategies.

Just as an organization's structure should fit with its vision and strategies, so to must a building's structure match the vision of an architect or designer. This new building in Frankfurt, Germany, is being constructed for the European Central Bank (ECB).

Example. In December 2006, then CEO Terry Semel announced a sweeping reorganization of the company, replacing Yahoo's product-aligned structure with one focused on users and advertiser customers. Seven product units were merged into a group called Advertisers and Publishers. A unit dubbed Technology would provide infrastructure for the two new operating groups. The idea was to accelerate growth by exploiting economies of scope across Yahoo's rich collection of audience and advertiser products. Semel's team had thought they'd carefully defined roles and responsibilities under the new structure, but decision making and execution quickly became bogged down. Audience demanded tailored solutions that Technology could not provide at a reasonable cost. . . . In response, Yahoo executives created new roles and management levels to coordinate the units. The organization ballooned to 12 layers, product development slowed as decisions stalled, and overhead costs increased.[24]

Yahoo! clearly adopted the wrong organizational design. Unfortunately, changes in organizational design, such as the one at Google, frequently produce bad results.

For example, a McKinsey & Company survey of 1,890 executives revealed that only 8% experienced positive results after making structural changes. This finding is consistent with a study of 57 reorganizations by consulting firm Bain & Company. Results revealed that most reorgs had no effect, and some led to lower organizational performance.[25] What then is a manager supposed to do about determining the best organizational design?

While there is no simple answer to this question, you will never be able to address this issue without an understanding of the different types of structure that exist. This section thus provides an overview of seven fundamental types of organizational structures. The following section then attempts to help you determine when these structures may be most effective.[26]

LO.4 Traditional Designs

Organizations defined by a traditional approach tend to have functional, divisional, and/or matrix structures. Each of these structures relies on a vertical hierarchy and attempts to define clear departmental boundaries and reporting relationships. Let us consider each type of structure.

Functional Structure   A functional structure groups people according to the business functions they perform, for example, manufacturing, marketing, and finance. A manager is responsible for the performance of each of these functions, and employees tend to identify strongly with their particular function, such as sales or engineering. The organization chart in Figure 17–1 illustrates a functional structure. Responsibility at this hospital is first divided into administrative and medical functions, and within each category, directors are responsible for each of the functions. This arrangement puts together people who are experts in the same or similar activities. Thus, as a small company grows and hires more production workers, salespeople, and accounting staff, it typically groups them together with a supervisor who understands their function.

Divisional Structure   In a divisional structure, the organization groups together activities related to outputs, such as type of product or type (or location) of customer. For example, General Electric has four businesses (major product divisions): GE Technology Infrastructure, GE Finance, GE Energy Infrastructure, and GE Consumer & Industrial. These major business areas are subdivided further into either product or geographic divisions.[27] The people in a division can become experts at making a particular type of product or serving the particular needs of their customer group or geographic area. Typically, each division has a functional structure. Some organizations have concluded that using a functional or divisional structure divides people too much, ultimately creating silos within the organization. This in turn detracts from the extent to which employees collaborate and share best practices across functions. One way to address this problem while still focusing on hierarchy is to create a matrix structure.

Matrix Structure   Organizations use matrix structures when they need stronger horizontal alignment or cooperation in order to meet their goals. For example, Hachette Filipacchi Media, the world's largest magazine publisher, is restructuring its US operations into a matrix structure. CEO Alain Lemarchand is doing this because he wants to create greater integration and collaboration between three chief brands of women's titles and the functions of editorial, ad sales, business development, and event marketing.[28] A matrix structure combines a vertical structure with an equally strong horizontal overlay. This generally combines functional and divisional chains of command to form a grid with two command structures, one shown vertically by function, and the other shown horizontally, by product line, brand, customer group, or geographic region. In the example shown in Figure 17–3, Ford might set up vice presidents for each functional group and project managers for each make of car. Employees would

figure 17–3 Matrix Structure

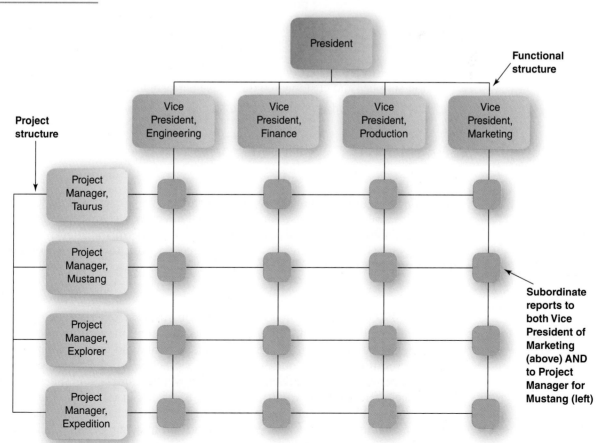

report to two managers: one in charge of the function they perform and the other in charge of the project they are working on.

Matrix organizations historically received a bad reputation for being too complex and confusing. The reality is that it takes much more collaboration and integration to effectively implement this structure. Jay Galbraith, an expert on matrix structures, noted that matrix structures frequently fail because management fails to create complementary and reinforcing changes to the organization's IT systems, human resource procedures (e.g., performance appraisals, rewards, selection criteria), planning and budgeting processes, organizational culture, internal processes, and so on. He concluded that "organization structures do not fail; managements fail at implementation."[29] This type of structure increasingly is being used by companies expanding into international markets.

Focus on Collaboration: Horizontal Design

The traditional approach of dividing up work according to functions, products, and customers is dissatisfying to managers who want to focus on bringing people together, without internal boundaries keeping them apart. If you want people to share knowledge and continually improve the way things are done, you need to create an environment in which collaboration feels easy and natural. Many organizations with this viewpoint have emphasized horizontal relationships among people who are working on shared tasks more than on vertical relationships in a traditional organizational design.

This horizontal approach to organizational design tends to focus on work processes. A process consists of every task and responsibility needed to meet a customer need, such as developing a new product or filling a customer order. Completing a process requires input from people in different functions, typically organized into a cross-functional team (described in Chapter 11). Thus, teamwork is a feature of organizations designed horizontally. Two experts in organization design have identified five principles for designing a horizontal organization:

1. Organize around complete workflow processes rather than tasks.
2. Flatten hierarchy and use teams to manage everything.
3. Appoint process team leaders to manage internal team processes.
4. Let supplier and customer contact drive performance.
5. Provide required expertise from outside the team as required.[30]

Designs That Open Boundaries between Organizations

While the horizontal organization aims to break down barriers within organizations, some structures are based on the idea that not even barriers between organizations are always ideal. Sometimes organizations can perform better by creating structures in which they can pool their resources to work toward a shared goal. This strategic approach results in structures that are called hollow, modular, or virtual.

Hollow Structure   A hollow organization results from strategic application of the trend toward outsourcing. The organization's managers identify core competencies—functions the organization can do better and more profitably than other organizations. It then outsources noncore processes to vendors who can do them cheaper or faster. An athletic shoe company, for example, might decide that it can excel at developing new designs, owing to its design talent and knowledge of the market. Then it might find outsourcing partners to handle other activities such as manufacturing, order taking, shipping, and managing employee benefits.

The more processes that are outsourced, the more the resulting organization is "hollow"—and focused on what it does best. Furniture company Herman Miller goes outside the organization for design expertise. CEO Brian Walker explains the advantages:

Example. This external network ensures that we are always taking a fresh look at problems faced by our customers without subjecting it to our own filters. If you have only an internal design staff, even an enormously talented one, you are inherently limited by their existing world view and experiences. Our ability to tap into a broader outside network lets us . . . get a fresh perspective on existing or emerging problems.[31]

Herman Miller also uses other organizations for manufacturing; Walker says the company is "more . . . an integrator than a manufacturer," which makes it less resistant to new product ideas because it doesn't have to change manufacturing processes itself.

A hollow structure is useful when an organization is faced with strong price competition and there are enough companies to perform the required outsourced processes.

Modular Structure   A modular organization, like a hollow organization, uses outsourcing. But instead of outsourcing processes, it outsources parts of a product, such as components of a jet or subroutines of a software program. The modular organization is responsible for ensuring that the parts meet quality requirements, that the parts arrive in a timely fashion, and that the organization is capable of efficiently combining the parts into the final whole. This design is useful when a company can identify product modules and create design interfaces that allow it to assemble parts into a working order. A well-known example is Boeing, in its production of the 787 Dreamliner. Modular structures are used in other industries such as automobile manufacturing, bicycle production, home appliances, consumer electronics, and software development.

Virtual Structure   Finally, an organization may identify partners to create a virtual organization, "a company outside a company created specifically to respond to an exceptional market opportunity that is often temporary."[32] Just as "virtual memory" in a computer causes it to seem as if it has more memory, so a virtual organization does more than what its founding organization could do with the resources within the organization's boundaries. The organization identifies partners with the needed talents and negotiates an agreement in which the participants typically work in separate facilities. Instead of relying heavily on face-to-face meetings, however, members of virtual organizations send e-mail and voice-mail messages, exchange project information over the Internet, and convene videoconferences among dispersed participants (recall our discussion of virtual teams in Chapter 11). Information technology clearly enables virtual organizations to work toward common goals, such as developing a new product or entering a new market. For instance, virtual organizations can help in developing cell phones for the US market.

AT&T and Verizon dominate the market for wireless service to such a degree that phone producers must work with them to create compatible products and to develop a pipeline for selling them. Nokia, which had trouble gaining market share in the United States, shifted its strategy "to develop phones in partnership with US carriers, in part by assigning 300 product developers each to AT&T and Verizon."[33] Salespeople and

Nokia uses a virtual organization design in developing and producing its phones.

R&D personnel also are assigned to work with particular wireless carriers. In general, a virtual organization demands flexibility, and managers must be able to lead and motivate people in separate locations. This structure is valuable for organizations that want to grow through partnerships with other companies.[34]

Back to the Chapter-Opening Case

Assume you are working on a project within a matrix structure and that some of the project team members are working virtually. Explain how you might use the types of technology discussed in the case to improve planning sessions between project team members.

TO THE POINT

What are the key learning points regarding mechanistic and organic organizations, and when should managers use each of the seven basic organizational structures?

The Contingency Approach to Designing Organizations

According to the **contingency approach to organization design,** organizations tend to be more effective when they are structured to fit the demands of the situation. The purpose of this section is to extend the previous one by introducing you to the contingency approach to organization design. We review a landmark study, drawing a distinction between centralized and decentralized decision making, and then discuss when each of seven organization designs previously discussed is most likely to be effective.

 LO.5 Mechanistic versus Organic Organizations

A landmark contingency design study was reported by a pair of British behavioral scientists, Tom Burns and G M Stalker. In the course of their research, they drew a very instructive distinction between what they called mechanistic and organic organizations. **Mechanistic organizations** are rigid bureaucracies with strict rules, narrowly defined tasks, and top-down communication. A mechanistic organization generally would have one of the traditional organization designs described earlier in this chapter and a hierarchical culture—see the discussion of culture types in Chapter 3. The "orderliness" of this structure is expected to produce reliability and consistency in internal processes, thereby resulting in higher efficiency, quality, and timeliness. You can imagine how valuable this type of structure might be for a company in the nuclear power industry where mistakes and errors can be catastrophic. It is important to note that being mechanistic does not mean that an organization should not be responsive to employee and customer feedback. Toyota, a company noted for being more mechanistic, fell into this trap and ended up with a recall involving faulty accelerator pedals and rusted spare-tire-carriers (see Real World/Real People on page 509).

Oppositely, **organic organizations** are flexible networks of multitalented individuals who perform a variety of tasks. An example is Eileen Fisher, Inc, which designs and manufactures women's clothing. The company's leadership includes Susan Schor, who—in the words of founder Eileen Fisher—"came in and created her own place:" heading all aspects of "people and culture," including employee development, social consciousness, human resources, and internal communications. Schor's accomplishments include crafting an organizational structure in which all employees work in teams run by facilitators and "no one reports to anyone. Instead, we 'connect into' someone else."[35] These qualities of an organic organization are easiest to maintain with the lowered boundaries of horizontal and virtual organizations. Internet technology and social media has made such arrangements

real WORLD // real PEOPLE

Has Toyota Become Too Mechanistic?

The *shusa* or chief engineer at Toyota wields much power and authority. This individual has "complete responsibility for a vehicle, beginning with its conception and sometimes lasting through its entire sales life." The *shusa* is accountable for the success of a vehicle and defines its intended market. They also are responsible for meeting goals related to cost, weight, performance, and quality. There are 38 *shusas* at Toyota and they are "highly respected and are granted near-absolute authority." You can see the mechanistic nature of Toyota's structure.

The role of *sushas* within Toyota's structure came under scrutiny when Katusake Watanabe was president from 2005–2009. Watanabe told the *sushas* to increase profitability by aggressively cutting costs. They pursued this goal with vigor around the world. "When they cut too deeply, feedback was not quick to reach them." . . .

"When Toyota customers began to raise questions about the quality of their vehicles, either because they performed unsafely or just looked cheap, Toyota brushed off the complaints and delayed finding solutions. Some current and former Toyota executives in the US came to believe that the *shusas* were responsible for the company's defensiveness. They thought the *shusas* deflected questions about quality and were reluctant to take the problems to top management because they feared losing face." . . .

"As the company grew, its Japanese leaders never relinquished the iron grip they exercised over the company's operations . . . and continued to make all important decisions in Japan. Instead of globalizing, Toyota colonized."

Why did a mechanistic structure cause problems at Toyota?

SOURCE: Excerpted from A Taylor III, "How Toyota Lost Its Way," *Fortune,* July 26, 2010, p 110.

---

more practical by enabling individuals to develop networks of people with whom they can readily share information as needed.[36]

Back to the Chapter-Opening Case

1. Will Dixon Schwabl Advertising's approach toward running meetings result in a more mechanistic or organic organization? Explain your rationale.
2. Would a mechanistic or organic organization be more likely to foster innovation?

A Matter of Degree   Importantly, as illustrated in Table 17–2, each of the mechanistic-organic characteristics is a matter of degree. Organizations tend to be relatively mechanistic or relatively organic. Pure types are rare because divisions, departments, or units in the same organization may be more or less mechanistic or organic. From an employee's standpoint, which organization structure would you prefer?

Different Approaches to Decision Making   Decision making tends to be centralized in mechanistic organizations and decentralized in organic organizations. **Centralized decision making** occurs when key decisions are made by top

contingency approach to organization design Creating an effective organization–environment fit.

mechanistic organizations Rigid, command-and-control bureaucracies.

organic organizations Fluid and flexible networks of multitalented people.

centralized decision making Top managers make all key decisions.

table 17–2 Characteristics of Mechanistic and Organic Organizations

CHARACTERISTIC	MECHANISTIC ORGANIZATION		ORGANIC ORGANIZATION
1. Task definition and knowledge required	Narrow; technical	→	Broad; general
2. Linkage between individual's contribution and organization's purpose	Vague or indirect	→	Clear or direct
3. Task flexibility	Rigid; routine	→	Flexible; varied
4. Specification of techniques, obligations, and rights	Specific	→	General
5. Degree of hierarchical control	High	→	Low (self-control emphasized)
6. Primary communication pattern	Top-down	→	Lateral (between peers)
7. Primary decision-making style	Authoritarian	→	Democratic; participative
8. Emphasis on obedience and loyalty	High	→	Low

SOURCE: Adapted from discussion in T Burns and G M Stalker, *The Management of Innovation* (London: Tavistock, 1961), pp 119–25.

management. Carol Bartz, Yahoo's former CEO, for example, decided to implement a more top-down style of management because she wanted to make the company more efficient.[37] **Decentralized decision making** occurs when important decisions are made by middle- and lower-level managers. Generally, centralized organizations are more tightly controlled while decentralized organizations are more adaptive to changing situations. Semco, a Brazilian manufacturer, turned to a more decentralized structure when it needed to spark dramatic change. Ricardo Semler became CEO when Semco was headed for bankruptcy; he eliminated most senior-management jobs and pushed decision making down to lower levels of self-managed teams. The outcomes have been promising.

Example. The move initially caused inefficiencies and higher costs but eventually allowed low-level innovation to flourish. . . . Inventory backlogs have eased, product lines have expanded, and sales have jumped. . . . After the company's reorganization, revenues climbed from $4 million to $212 million.[38]

Experts on the subject warn against extremes of centralization or decentralization. The challenge is to achieve a workable balance between the two extremes. A management consultant put it this way:

Example. The modern organization in transition will recognize the pull of two polarities: a need for greater centralization to create low-cost shared resources; and a need to improve market responsiveness with greater decentralization. Today's winning organizations are the ones that can handle the paradox and tensions of both pulls. These are the firms that analyze the optimum organizational solution in each particular circumstance, without prejudice for one type of organization over another. The result is, almost invariably, a messy mixture of decentralized units sharing cost-effective centralized resources.[39]

Centralization and decentralization are not an either–or proposition; they are an and–also balancing act.

Practical Research Insights   When they classified a sample of actual companies as either mechanistic or organic, Burns and Stalker discovered one type was not superior to the other. Each type had its appropriate place, depending on the environment. When the environment was relatively stable and certain, the successful organizations tended to be mechanistic. Organic organizations tended to be the successful ones when the environment was unstable and uncertain.[40]

Another interesting finding comes from a study of 42 voluntary church organizations. As the organizations became more mechanistic (more bureaucratic) the intrinsic motivation of their members decreased. Mechanistic organizations apparently undermined the volunteers' sense of freedom and self-determination. Additionally, the researchers believe their findings help explain why bureaucracy tends to feed on itself: "A mechanistic organizational structure may breed the need for a more extremely mechanistic system because of the reduction in intrinsically motivated behavior."[41] Thus, bureaucracy begets greater bureaucracy.

Most recently, field research in two factories, one mechanistic and the other organic, found expected communication patterns. Command-and-control (downward) communication characterized the mechanistic factory. Consultative or participative (two-way) communication prevailed in the organic factory.[42]

Both Mechanistic and Organic Structures Have Their Places   Although achievement-oriented students of organizational behavior (OB) typically express a distaste for mechanistic organizations, not all organizations or subunits can or should be organic. For example, McDonald's could not achieve its admired quality and service standards without extremely mechanistic restaurant operations. Imagine the food and service you would get if McDonald's employees used their own favorite ways of doing things and worked at their own pace. On the other hand, mechanistic structure alienates some employees because it erodes their sense of self-control.

connect™ Go to www.mcgrawhillconnect.com for an interactive exercise to test your knowledge of organizational design.

connect™ Go to www.mcgrawhillconnect.com for a self-assessment to determine your preferred organizational structure.

LO.6 Getting the Right Fit

All of the organization structures described in this chapter are used today because each structure has advantages and disadvantages that make it appropriate in some cases. For example, the clear roles and strict hierarchy of an extremely mechanistic organization are beneficial when careful routines and a set of checks and balances are important, as at a nuclear power facility. In a fast-changing environment with a great deal of uncertainty, an organization would benefit from a more organic structure that lowers boundaries between functions and organizations. Let us consider each of the seven basic organization designs.

A functional structure can save money by grouping together people who need similar materials and equipment. Quality standards can be maintained because supervisors understand what department members do and because people in the same function develop pride in their specialty. Workers can devote more of their time to what they do best. These benefits are easiest to realize in a stable environment, where the organization doesn't depend on employees to coordinate their efforts to solve varied problems. Today, fewer organizations see their environment as stable, so more are moving away from strictly functional structures.

Building a puzzle requires the pieces to fit with each other. The same is true about organizational performance. Organizations are more effective when the organizational design fits with the organization's vision and strategies. Creating this fit is not easy in today's constantly changing economic environment.

decentralized decision making
Lower-level managers are empowered to make important decisions.

Divisional structures increase employees' focus on customers and products. Managers have the flexibility to make decisions that affect several functions in order to serve customer needs. This enables the organization to move faster if a new customer need arises or if a competitor introduces an important product. However, duplicating functions in each division can add to costs, so this structure may be too expensive for some organizations. Also, divisions sometimes focus on their own customer groups or products to the exclusion of the company's overall mission. Ford Motor Company has struggled to unify its geographic and brand divisions to save money by sharing design, engineering, and manufacturing. Managers of geographic divisions have introduced new car models on different time lines and insisted that their customers want different features.[43] In contrast, geographic divisions have helped McDonald's grow by freeing managers to introduce menu items and décor that locals appreciate.[44]

A matrix structure tries to combine the advantages of functional and divisional structures. This advantage is also the structure's main drawback: it violates the unity of command principle, described previously in the chapter. Employees have to balance the demands of a functional manager and a product or project manager. When they struggle with this balance, decision making can slow to a crawl, and political behavior can overpower progress. Employees' role clarity also may be reduced. The success of a matrix organization, therefore, requires superior managers who communicate extensively, foster commitment and collaboration, manage conflict, and negotiate effectively to establish goals and priorities consistent with the organization's strategy.[45] This conclusion underscores the importance of considering the organization's culture prior to adopting a matrix structure. As discussed in Chapter 3, clan and adhocracy cultures, which endorse values related to flexibility and discretion, are more consistent with the requirements of a matrix structure. One organization that has made matrix structures work for decades is Procter & Gamble. To manage 138,000 employees in more than 80 countries, the company has a matrix structure in which global business units are responsible for a brand's development and production, while market development organizations focus on the customer needs for particular regions and the way the brands can meet those needs. Employees have to meet objectives both for the brand and for the market, with different managers responsible for each.[46]

Horizontal designs generally improve coordination and communication in organizations. Cross-functional teams can arrive at creative solutions to problems that arise in a fast-changing environment. Teams can develop new products faster and more efficiently than can functions working independently in a traditional structure. Horizontal designs also encourage knowledge sharing. However, because lines of authority are less clear, managers must be able to share responsibility for the organization's overall performance, build commitment to a shared vision, and influence others even when they lack direct authority. This type of structure is a good fit when specialization is less important than the ability to respond to varied or changing customer needs. It requires employees who can rise to the challenges of empowerment. A horizontal design is a good fit for Research in Motion (RIM) because it builds on employees' deep product and customer knowledge. All employees use the company's BlackBerry pocket computers, so they know what works and what doesn't. RIM's chief executive maintains that because employees know the details of what makes the BlackBerry work, they are well positioned to continue improving it: "We didn't just buy an operating system from one company and a radio technology from another, and then have them assembled somewhere in Asia. We actually built the whole thing. . . . I don't mind investing in it because I know there's a return."[47] RIM applies that knowledge by creating teams to brainstorm new ideas in every aspect of the company's operations.

Finally, organizations that open their boundaries to become hollow, modular, or virtual can generate superior returns by focusing on what they do best.[48] Like functional organizations, they tap people in particular specialties, who may be more expert than the generalists of a divisional or horizontal organization. The downside of these structures is that organizations give up expertise and control in the functions or operations that are outsourced. Still, like divisional and horizontal organizations, they can focus on customers or products, leaving their partners to focus on their own specialty area. In India, when Tata Motors wanted to develop a $2,500 compact car, it decided its own engineers needed assistance, so Tata adopted a modular structure. Each of its suppliers tackled designing particular components to be as inexpensive as possible while still meeting quality standards, and Tata focused on coordinating their work.[49] An example of a successful hollow organization is one global manufacturer that shifted its focus to developing products and contracted with outsourcing firms to make the products in the manufacturer's own facilities, handling the process from ordering materials to shipping the finished product. The arrangement maintained quality while cutting labor costs by 40% by avoiding inefficiency and duplication of work.[50]

The success of organizations that work across boundaries depends on managers' ability to get results from people over whom they do not have direct formal authority by virtue of their position in the organization. Boeing, for example, has been embarrassed by its setbacks in manufacturing the Dreamliner from components provided by a network of suppliers, which did not always meet their commitments to Boeing. Also, individuals in these organizations may not have the same degree of commitment as do employees of a traditional organization, so motivation and leadership may be more difficult. Therefore, these designs are the best fit when organizations have suitable partners they trust; when efficiency is very important; when the organization can identify functions, processes, or product components to outsource profitably; and in the case of a virtual organization, when the need to be met is temporary. In a study of managers in 20 organizations that extensively collaborate with other companies, these efforts most often succeeded in companies that select and train for teamwork skills, invest in processes that promote collaboration, set up tools and systems for sharing information, and treat collaboration as one of the company's ongoing programs requiring leadership.[51] Another recent study of 177 international strategic alliances further showed that open structures work best when there is a high level of trust between partnering organizations.[52]

Organizational Effectiveness (and the Threat of Decline)

▶ · · · · · · · · · · · · · · · · · ·

TO THE POINT
What are the similarities and differences among the four generic effectiveness criteria, and how can managers prevent organizational decline?

· · · · · · · · · · · · · · · · · ·

How effective are you? If someone asked you this apparently simple question, you would likely ask for clarification before answering. For instance, you might want to know if they were referring to your grade point average, annual income, actual accomplishments, ability to get along with others, public service, or perhaps something else entirely. So it is with modern organizations. Effectiveness criteria abound.

Assessing organizational effectiveness is an important topic for an array of people, including managers, job hunters, stockholders, government agencies, and OB specialists. The purpose of this section is to introduce a widely applicable and useful model of organizational effectiveness; we also will deal with the related problem of organizational decline.

LO.7 Generic Organizational-Effectiveness Criteria

A good way to better understand this complex subject is to consider four generic approaches to assessing an organization's effectiveness (see Figure 17–4). These effectiveness criteria apply equally well to large or small and profit or not-for-profit organizations. Moreover, as denoted by the overlapping circles in Figure 17–4,

figure 17–4 Four Ways to Assess Organizational Effectiveness

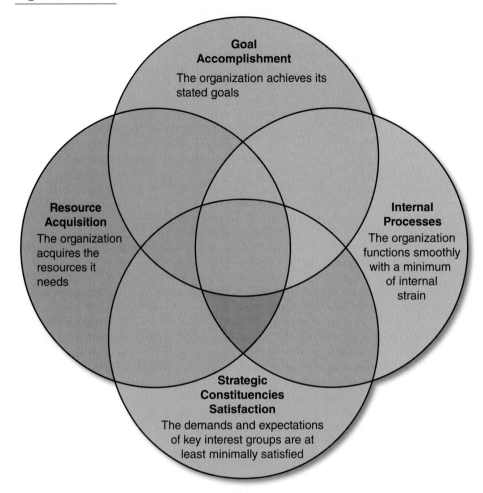

Goal Accomplishment

The organization achieves its stated goals

Resource Acquisition

The organization acquires the resources it needs

Internal Processes

The organization functions smoothly with a minimum of internal strain

Strategic Constituencies Satisfaction

The demands and expectations of key interest groups are at least minimally satisfied

SOURCES: Adapted from discussion in K Cameron, "Critical Questions in Assessing Organizational Effectiveness," *Organizational Dynamics,* Autumn 1980, pp 66–80; and K S Cameron, "Effectiveness as Paradox: Consensus and Conflict in Conceptions of Organizational Effectiveness," *Management Science,* May 1986, pp 539–53.

Go to www.mcgrawhillconnect.com for an interactive exercise to test your knowledge of the generic organizational effectiveness criteria.

the four effectiveness criteria can be used in various combinations. The key thing to remember is "no single approach to the evaluation of effectiveness is appropriate in all circumstances or for all organization types."[53] What do Coca-Cola and France Télécom, for example, have in common, other than being large profit-seeking corporations? Because a multidimensional approach is required, we need to look more closely at each of the four generic effectiveness criteria.

Goal Accomplishment   Goal accomplishment is the most widely used effectiveness criterion for organizations. Key organizational results or outputs are compared with previously stated goals or objectives. Deviations, either plus or minus, require corrective action. This is simply an organizational variation of the personal goal-setting process discussed in Chapter 9. Effectiveness, relative to the criterion of goal accomplishment, is gauged by how well the organization meets or exceeds its goals.

Productivity improvement, involving the relationship between inputs and outputs, is a common organization-level goal. Goals also may be set for organizational efforts such as minority recruiting, sustainability, customer satisfaction, employee satisfaction, quality improvement, and output. For example, Hyundai currently has capacity to produce 5.8 million cars and trucks and has established the goal of growing capacity to 6.5 million units by 2012. The company also is putting the goal of vehicle quality at the top of its list of strategic goals. Hyundai "developed a two-part quality target it calls GQ 3-3-5-5, as Joon-Sang Kim, executive vice president of Hyundai-Kia's Quality Division, explained in an interview. Hyundai aims to finish in the top three in actual quality within three years as measured by Power's dependability survey—and to finish in the top five in perceived quality in five years."[54] Given today's competitive pressures and e-business revolution, *innovation* and *speed* are very important organizational goals for many companies.

Resource Acquisition   This second criterion relates to inputs rather than outputs. An organization is deemed effective in this regard if it acquires necessary factors of production such as raw materials, labor, capital, and managerial and technical expertise. Charitable organizations such as the Salvation Army and United Way judge their effectiveness in terms of how much money they raise from private and corporate donations.

Internal Processes   This dimension of effectiveness focuses on "what the organization must excel at" to effectively meet its financial objectives and customers' expectations. A team of researchers have identified four critical high-level internal processes that managers are encouraged to measure and manage. These processes influence productivity, efficiency, quality, safety, and a host of other internal metrics. The processes include organizational activities associated with (1) innovation, (2) customer service and satisfaction, (3) operational excellence, and (4) being a good corporate citizen.[55] Companies tend to adopt continuous improvement programs, recall our discussion of TQM in Chapter 1, in pursuit of improving their internal processes. Consider what Hyundai has done to improve the quality of its internal processes.

Example.   It installed Six Sigma at its engineering center to measure its improvement. It made quality a cross-functional responsibility, with involvement from procurement, finance, and sales and marketing. It enlisted outside suppliers and put them together with designers and engineers to work out problems before they occurred. Quality oversight meetings, which had been poorly attended, became must-go events after Chairman Chung began to show up for twice-monthly gatherings.[56]

Strategic Constituencies Satisfaction   Organizations both depend on people and affect the lives of people. Consequently, many consider the satisfaction of key interested parties to be an important criterion of organizational effectiveness.

A **strategic constituency** is any group of individuals who have some stake in the organization—for example, resource providers, users of the organization's products or services, producers of the organization's output, groups whose cooperation is essential for the organization's survival, or those whose lives are significantly affected by the organization.[57]

Strategic constituencies (or *stakeholders*) generally have competing or conflicting interests.[58] For instance, customers at gas pumps were not cheering when gas companies raised the price of gasoline in 2011 in response to unrest in the

strategic constituency Any group of people with a stake in the organization's operation or success.

figure 17–5 A Sample Stakeholder Audit Identifying Strategic Constituencies

SOURCE: From N C Roberts et al., "The Stakeholder Audit Goes Public," *Organizational Dynamics*, Winter 1989. © 1989. Reprinted with permission from Elsevier.

Middle East. Strategic constituents or stakeholders can be identified systematically through a stakeholder audit.

A **stakeholder audit** enables management to identify all parties significantly impacted by the organization's performance (see Figure 17–5). Conflicting interests and relative satisfaction among the listed stakeholders can then be dealt with.

A never-ending challenge for management is to strike a workable balance among strategic constituencies so as to achieve at least minimal satisfaction on all fronts.

Multiple Effectiveness Criteria: Some Practical Guidelines

Experts on the subject recommend a multidimensional approach to assessing the effectiveness of modern organizations. This means no single criterion is appropriate for all stages of the organization's life cycle. Nor will a single criterion satisfy competing stakeholders. Well-managed organizations mix and match effectiveness criteria to fit the unique requirements of the situation. For example, Irdeto Holdings, which provides content protection for pay TV and video recordings, decided on a structural change after determining that sales were growing fastest in Asia, which already accounted for almost 40% of the company's revenues. To meet business goals for serving this important geographic market, Irdeto's executives decided to convert the company's Beijing office into a second headquarters (the first headquarters is located near Amsterdam). This change serves an important constituency—Asian customers—but raised concerns with Amsterdam employees. Responding to that second constituency, Irdeto's CEO, Graham Kill, announced plans to build a new Amsterdam office building and explained that employees can enjoy an exciting career path if they are willing to rotate between the two headquarters cities. Management also has had to address internal processes, especially in developing Chinese managers to take initiative in decision making and to think about issues affecting the entire corporation, not just Asian markets.[59]

Managers need to identify and seek input from strategic constituencies. This information, when merged with the organization's stated mission and philosophy, enables management to derive an appropriate *combination* of effectiveness criteria. The following guidelines are helpful in this regard:

- *The goal accomplishment approach* is appropriate when "goals are clear, consensual, time-bounded, measurable."[60]
- *The resource acquisition approach* is appropriate when inputs have a traceable effect on results or output. For example, the amount of money the World Wildlife Fund receives through donations dictates the level of services provided.
- *The internal processes approach* is appropriate when organizational performance is strongly influenced by specific processes (e.g., cross-functional teamwork).
- *The strategic constituencies approach* is appropriate when powerful stakeholders can significantly benefit or harm the organization.

Keeping these basic concepts of organizational effectiveness in mind, we turn our attention to preventing organizational decline.

What Are the Warning Signs of Ineffectiveness?

What do Circuit City, Lehman Brothers, Blockbuster, General Motors, Chrysler, and A&P have in common? They all declared bankruptcy within the last few years. Do you think top management in these companies had measures of effectiveness such as total revenue, profit, or market share that shed light on their future demise? Evidence suggests that they did.[61] This implies that managers may need to look for lead indicators of ineffectiveness that show up long before poor performance shows up in measures of effectiveness. Fortunately, researchers have identified such a list.

Short of illegal conduct, there are 16 early warning signs of organizational decline:

1. Excess personnel.
2. Tolerance of incompetence.
3. Cumbersome administrative procedures.
4. Disproportionate staff power (e.g., technical staff specialists politically overpower line managers, whom they view as unsophisticated and too conventional).
5. Replacement of substance with form (e.g., the planning process becomes more important than the results achieved).
6. Scarcity of clear goals and decision benchmarks.
7. Fear of embarrassment and conflict (e.g., formerly successful executives may resist new ideas for fear of revealing past mistakes).
8. Loss of effective communication.
9. Outdated organizational structure.[62]
10. Increased scapegoating by leaders.
11. Resistance to change.
12. Low morale.

McGraw Hill **connect** Go to www.mcgrawhillconnect.com for a video case on organizational design at One Smooth Stone.

stakeholder audit Systematic identification of all parties likely to be affected by the organization.

13. Special interest groups are more vocal.

14. Decreased innovation.

15. Unwillingness to experiment with new ideas.

16. Poor track record of execution.[63]

Managers who monitor these early warning signs of organizational decline are better able to take corrective action in a timely and effective manner. However, research has uncovered a troublesome perception tendency among entrenched top management teams. In companies where there had been little if any turnover among top executives, there was a tendency to attribute organizational problems to *external* causes (e.g., competition, the government, technology shifts). Oppositely, *internal* attributions tended to be made by top management teams with *many* new members. Thus, proverbial "new blood" at the top appears to be a good insurance policy against misperceiving the early-warning signs of organizational decline.

LO.8 Organizational Innovation

IBM, Google, Microsoft, Procter & Gamble, GE, Tata, Chrysler, Carlsberg, Banner Health, HP, Ford, Boeing, and Pixar all have something in common—the desire to innovate. The health care industry, for example, is under intense pressure to innovate given the need to provide high-quality care at a reasonable cost to a growing number of people.[64] This trend should not be surprising given that technological innovation is a key source of productivity and economic growth.[65] **Innovation** "is the creation of something new that makes money; it finds a pathway to the consumer."[66] This definition highlights two key aspects of innovation. First, innovation is different from *invention,* which entails the creation of something new, and *creativity,* which was defined in Chapter 12 as a process of developing something new or unique. The former CEO of Procter & Gamble A G Lafley discussed this distinction in an interview with *Business Week:* "You need creativity and invention, but until you can connect that creativity to the customer in the form of a product or service that meaningfully changes their lives, I would argue you don't have innovation." He uses the example of diapers to make his case. "We invented a material back in the 60s that would absorb a lot of water. Until we converted it into a Pampers disposable baby diaper, it was just a new kind of material. We created this entirely new product category, and that created an industry."[67] Second, innovation also is different from *integration,* which involves actions associated with getting multiple people, units, departments, functions, or sites to work together in pursuit of a goal, idea, or project.[68] As you will learn in this section, successful innovation relies on invention, creativity, and integration.

We are discussing the topic of innovation in this chapter because it is an organizational issue. That is, innovation requires us to integrate concepts pertaining to individual behavior, groups and social processes, and organizational processes (recall the topical model of OB shown in Figure 1–5). It is important to have a good understanding about innovation because it serves as the gasoline that fuels the economic engine of companies and countries alike. Interestingly, the United States' standing as an innovative nation has been falling over the last decade. A study by the Boston Consulting Group and the National Association of Manufacturers revealed that the United States is the eighth most innovative country in the world, behind (1) Singapore, (2) South Korea, (3) Switzerland, (4) Iceland, (5) Ireland, (6) Hong Kong, and (7) Finland. Another recent study further showed that US companies were planning to decrease their spending on innovation in 2009 and to reduce its importance as a strategic priority.[69] Time will tell whether or not this was a good decision.

real WORLD // real PEOPLE

IBM Is a Model of Innovation

IBM's CEO, Sam Palmisano, is remaking the company by innovating. The company had 5,896 patents in 2010, and it was ranked as the 12th most admired company in the world by *Fortune*. Palmisano takes a long-term view in running the company, and he is a strong believer in using research to determine future market trends.

"The company maintains nine research labs around the world and seven 'collaboratories' it has built with customers like Beijing center to develop high-tech railroads. In addition to business-related projects like developing new series for Indian mobile-phone operators, IBM funds experiments such as material research that may develop new products. But Palmisano sees even those super-technical 'blue-sky' projects as critical to understanding where he needs to take IBM, and how he should organize its assets and businesses.

Once a year, in a knock-down, drag-out marathon of a discussion, he spends a day with lab directors predicting the future and adjusting corporate strategy to address it. You don't dare show up unprepared, lab directors say, because he understands your work and he has his own position on its value. This session is where he can observe chip improvements that will change the way IBM markets and sells servers, for example.

Why is IBM so successful at innovating?

SOURCE: Excerpted from "IBM," *Fortune*, March 21, 2011, pp 117, 123.

To guide our investigation into how organizations can be more innovative, this section discusses myths about innovation and presents a model of innovation.

LO.9 Myths about Innovation

We would like to dispel two myths about innovation. The first focuses on the notion that innovation involves an epiphany or eureka moment. In other words, some people think that innovation is a spur-of-the-moment thing in which an idea is hatched, such as Isaac Newton discovering gravity after being hit on the head by an apple while sitting under a tree. This is a nice story, but it does not represent reality. Others conceive innovation as something that occurs when a person is in the right place at the right time. Nothing could be further from the truth. Innovation does not occur like a thunderbolt. Rather, it is a time-consuming activity that takes hard work and dedication.

Jack and Suzy Welch note that "it emerges incrementally, in bits and chugs, forged by a mixed bag of co-workers from up, down, and across an organization, sitting and wrangling it out in the trenches."[70] Innovation is hard work and requires an investment in time and resources. IBM is a good example (see Real World/ Real People above). "For 17 years running, Big Blue has been granted more US patents than any other applicant." In 2009, IBM spent $6 billion on R&D, which amounts to 6% of IBM's nearly $100 billion in total revenue.[71]

Apple's former CEO Steve Jobs once was asked, "How do you systematize innovation?" He answered,

Apple's iPhone is one of the most innovative products of the 21st century. What do you foresee being the next innovative product released by Apple?

---

innovation Creation of something new that is used by consumers.

"You don't."[72] The second myth is that innovation can be systematized. If it could, everyone would do it. There simply are too many challenges associated with innovation that make its success unpredictable. These challenges are discussed when we review a model of innovation in the next section.

LO.10 A Model of Innovation

Innovation is not a static event. Rather, it is a dynamic process that ebbs and flows over time and can lead to many potential benefits, including revenue growth, new products and services, lower costs, improved products and services, and improved processes. These benefits can manifest in both the short and long term. Honda Motor, for example, is investing millions in robotics research that is not expected to pay off for quite some time. It invented a robot that can follow four mental commands. "Honda says it foresees consumer applications—thinking a car trunk open, for instance. But R&D director Yasuhisa Arai concedes that 'practical uses are still way in the future.'"[73]

The process of growing a tree is a useful metaphor for understanding how organizations can become more innovative. Seeds are the starting point for growing trees. Over time, seeds evolve into strong trunks with the proper water, oxygen, nutrients, and sunlight. A healthy trunk enables a tree to survive and produce a canopy for all to enjoy its beauty, shade, or pollination. Innovation follows a similar process. You will learn that experts have uncovered six seeds of innovation that organizations can use to begin the process of becoming more innovative. These seeds will not produce innovation, however, unless an organization effectively manages a set of key challenges. Managing the seeds and challenges of innovation produces the trunk of innovation. Finally, innovation also needs special nutrients to help it grow, prosper, and deliver intended benefits. These nutrients include the proper organizational culture, leadership, people, and execution. Figure 17–6 shows that there are three components that influence the benefits of innovation: seeds of innovation, challenges of innovation, and nutrients of innovation. Let us consider each component.

Seeds of Innovation **Seeds of innovation** represent the starting point of organizational innovation. After studying hundreds of innovations, an expert identified six seeds of innovation.[74] They are

1. *Hard work in a specific direction.* Most innovations come from dedicated people diligently working to solve a well-defined problem. This hard work can span many years.

2. *Hard work with direction change.* Innovations frequently occur when people change their approach toward solving a problem. In other words, hard work closes some doors and opens others.

3. *Curiosity and experimentation.* Innovations can begin when people are curious about something of interest, and experimentation is used to test for the viability of curious ideas.[75] This seed of innovation requires an organizational culture that supports experimentation. The founder of Intuit, Scott Cook, recognizes this conclusion and is trying to create a culture of innovation by reinforcing the belief that "failing is perfectly fine. Whatever happens, he tells his staff, you're doing right because you've created evidence, which is better than anyone's intuition. He says the organization is buzzing with experiments."[76]

4. *Wealth and money.* Innovations frequently occur because an organization or an individual simply wants to make money. Fiat's being near bankruptcy, for instance, drove the company to look for innovative ways to cut costs and

figure 17–6   A Model of Innovation

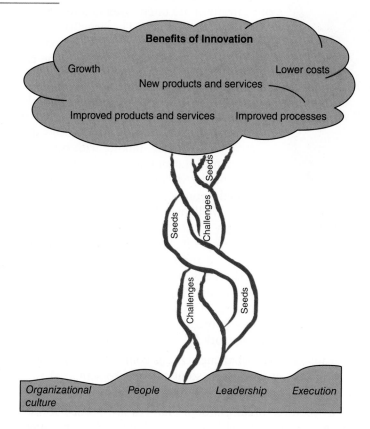

grow market share in the United States. This is the reason Fiat took a stake in Chrysler in return for releasing small-car technology.[77]

5. *Necessity.* Many innovations grow from the desire to achieve something or to complete a task that is needed to accomplish a broader goal. For example, "Xerox hired two researchers the company calls 'innovation managers' who will hunt for inventions and products from Indian startups that Xerox might adapt for North America. And Hewlett-Packard is using its research lab in India to see how it can migrate Web-interface applications for mobile phones in Asia and Africa to developed markets."[78]

6. *Combination of seeds.* Many innovations occur as a result of multiple factors.

For example, Google tries to fuel innovation by allowing employees to spend 20% of their time on projects outside of their main job. This strategy allows employee curiosity to meld with hard work to produce new products.

Back to the Chapter-Opening Case

Which of the seeds of innovation were used by the companies featured in the case? Provide examples.

---

seeds of innovation Starting point
of organizational innovation.

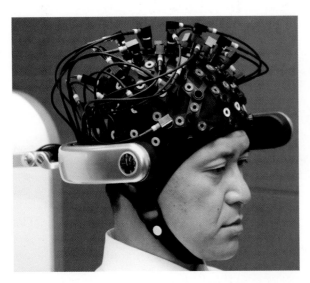

Honda's robotics research is looking to literally tap into our brains for new products.

Challenges of Innovation   Figure 17–6 illustrates that the challenges of innovation and the seeds of innovation are interwoven in a dynamic relationship that unfolds over time. The benefits of innovation are less likely to occur if these two components of innovation are not effectively integrated.[79] The challenges include the following:

1. *Find an idea.* An idea is needed to create something new, and people can get ideas from many different sources: concentrated thinking, past experience, daydreaming, reading, talking with others, or intuition. Nathan Myhrvold, founder of Intellectual Ventures, a company devoted to investing in new ideas, has a dual approach toward finding new ideas. He said that "We'll invest in existing ideas. Someone will have already invented something; they won't know what to do with it. We'll take a controlling investment in that idea and say maybe we can figure out what to do with it. But we also generate ideas ourselves. We try to pick a topic, pick a really important problem within that topic, do some homework on it, then get a set of experts who know something of the topic. But also experts who know something other than that. We've got about 100 people in our inventory network."[80]

2. *Develop a solution.* This challenge entails coming up with a model or prototype of a product or a workable solution to a problem.

3. *Sponsorship and funding.* Innovations require resources and someone to champion whatever organizational changes are needed to develop a new product or service. Tata Motors, for example, has committed billions of dollars to research and development.

4. *Reproduction.* The company must figure out how to profitably make the new product or deliver a new service.

5. *Reach your potential customer.* Many innovations fail because the company cannot figure out how to get the new product or service in the hands of consumers. Some experts recommend the use of job mapping. Job mapping "breaks down the task the customer wants done into a series of discrete process steps. By de-constructing a job from beginning to end, a company gains a complete view of all the points at which a customer might desire more help from a product or service—namely, at each step in the job."[81] Job mapping helps companies determine how customers might best use new products and services.

6. *Beat your competitors.* Remember that other companies may be pursuing the same breakthroughs. It is better to focus on a smaller number of innovations.

7. *Timing.* Customers must be ready for the new product or service and employees must be prepared to make whatever changes are necessary to turn the innovation into reality. The timing of the innovation needs to be considered.

8. *Keep the lights on.* Organizations must still make money while they are pursuing innovation. It is important to stay focused on keeping current customers happy while engaging in innovative activities.

Nutrients of Innovation   Organizations are more likely to experience the benefits of innovation when the dynamic interplay between the seeds and challenges of innovation are supported and reinforced by the nutrients of innovation: an organization's culture, leadership, people, and ability to execute. For example, a recent meta-analysis revealed that innovation was positively associated with market, adhocracy, and clan cultures—recall our discussion in Chapter 3.[82] GE already has put this research finding into use in a training program called "Leadership, Innovation, and Growth." Teams attending the training complete an internal assessment regarding the extent to which the culture is supportive of creativity. Participants then use the results to discuss how they might make the work environment more innovation friendly.[83] Research also showed that transformational leadership was helpful in creating innovative alliances between companies and in encouraging employees' creativity.[84]

Moreover, research identified several employee characteristics that can help organizations innovate. For example, innovation was positively associated with the individual characteristics associated with creativity, the level of skills and abilities possessed by people, employees' self-efficacy for innovation, and the quality of the relationship between managers and employees. Employees also were more innovative when they expected to receive positive outcomes for being innovative.[85] Finally, the ability to execute ultimately makes or breaks an organization's attempts at bringing new products and services to market. Why?

Consider the definition of **execution.**

Example. Execution is a systematic process of rigorously discussing hows and whats, questioning, tenaciously following through, and ensuring accountability. It includes making assumptions about the business environment, assessing the organization's capabilities, linking strategy to operations and the people who are going to implement the strategy, synchronizing those people and their various disciplines, and linking rewards to outcomes. It also includes mechanisms for changing assumptions as the environment changes and upgrading the company's capabilities to meet the challenges of an ambitious strategy. In its most fundamental sense, execution is a systematic way of exposing reality and acting on it.[86]

This definition highlights that execution requires organizations to effectively manage people, groups, and organizational processes and systems in the pursuit of innovation. In the end, the innovation process must be managed. John Donahoe, EBay's CEO, commented on the relationship between innovation and execution during an interview for the *Harvard Business Review.* In response to the question "So what's your biggest challenge now, execution or innovation?" he replied, "I think it's the intersection of the two. We have to keep innovating, but we have to execute at scale, and the challenge is how to balance the pace of change in the eyes of the consumer. Existing users often don't like the changes initially, because they're used to a certain way of shopping, yet new users do like them."[87] This example highlights that the consumer ultimately determines what is and what is not an innovative product or service.

execution Process of discussing hows and whats, questioning, following through, and ensuring accountability.

Summary of Key Concepts

1. *Describe the four characteristics common to all organizations, and explain the difference between closed and open systems.* They are coordination of effort (achieved through policies and rules), a common goal (a collective purpose), division of labor (people performing separate but related tasks), and a hierarchy of authority (the chain of command). Closed systems, such as a battery-powered clock, are relatively self-sufficient. Open systems, such as the human body, are highly dependent on the environment for survival. Organizations are said to be open systems.

2. *Define the term learning organization.* A learning organization is one that proactively creates, acquires, and transfers knowledge and changes its behavior on the basis of new knowledge and insights.

3. *Review the factors that hinder an organization's ability to learn from success and failure.* There are three factors that distract learning from success: the self-serving bias, overconfidence, and the natural tendency of "not asking why." Table 17–1 identifies six factors that inhibit learning from failure.

4. *Describe seven basic ways organizations are structured.* Traditional designs include (*a*) functional structures, in which work is divided according to function; (*b*) divisional structures, in which work is divided according to product or customer type or location; and (*c*) matrix structures, with dual-reporting structures based on product and function. Organizations also may be designed (*d*) horizontally, with cross-functional teams responsible for entire processes. Organization design also may reduce barriers between organizations, becoming (*e*) hollow organizations, which outsource functions; (*f*) modular organizations, which outsource the production of a product's components; or (*g*) virtual organizations, which temporarily combine the efforts of members of different companies in order to complete a project.

5. *Discuss Burns and Stalker's findings regarding mechanistic and organic organizations.* British researchers Burns and Stalker found that mechanistic (bureaucratic, centralized) organizations tended to be effective in stable situations. In unstable situations, organic (flexible, decentralized) organizations were more effective. These findings underscored the need for a contingency approach to organization design.

6. *Identify when each of the seven organization structures is the right fit.* Mechanistic organizations and functional structures may be necessary when tight control

is important and the environment is stable. Organic organizations allow for innovation in a rapidly changing environment. Divisional structures are a good fit when the organization needs deep knowledge of varied customer groups and the ability to respond to customer demands quickly. A matrix organization can deliver the advantages of functional and divisional structures if the company has superior managers who communicate extensively, foster commitment and collaboration, and negotiate effectively to establish goals and priorities consistent with the organization's strategy.

A horizontal design is a good fit when specialization is less important than the ability to respond to varied or changing customer needs. Hollow, modular, and virtual designs are best when organizations have suitable partners they trust; efficiency is very important; the organization can identify functions, processes, or product components to outsource; and in the case of a virtual organization, when the need to be met is temporary.

7. *Describe the four generic organizational effectiveness criteria.* They are goal accomplishment (satisfying stated objectives), resource acquisition (gathering the necessary productive inputs), internal processes (building and maintaining healthy organizational systems), and strategic constituencies satisfaction (achieving at least minimal satisfaction for all key stakeholders).

8. *Discuss the difference between innovation, invention, creativity, and integration.* Innovation is creating something new, that is commercialized. In contrast, invention is simply the creation of something new and creativity is the process of developing something new or unique. Integration involves actions associated with getting multiple people, units, departments, functions, or sites to work together in pursuit of a goal, idea, or project. Innovation relies on invention, creativity, and integration.

9. *Review the myths of innovation.* There are two key myths about innovation. The first is the myth that innovation involves an epiphany or eureka moment. The second is that innovation can be systematized.

10. *Explain the model of innovation.* Innovation is a dynamic process that involves the simultaneous effects of seeds of innovation and challenges of innovation. That said, the benefits of innovation only occur when the interaction between seeds and challenges is nurtured by the nutrients of innovation, which include organizational culture, leadership, people, and execution.

Key Terms

Organization, 496

Unity of command principle, 496

Organization chart, 497

Span of control, 498

Staff personnel, 499

Line managers, 499

Closed system, 499

Open system, 499

Learning organization, 501

OB in Action Case Study

Experts Propose a Process for Increasing Innovation[88]

Most great ideas for enhancing corporate growth and profits aren't discovered in the lab late at night, or in the isolation of the executive suite. They come from the people who daily fight the company's battles, who serve the customers, explore new markets and fend off the competition.

In other words, the employees.

Companies that have successfully made innovation part of their regular continuing strategy did so by harnessing the creative energies and the insights of their employees across functions and ranks. That's easy to say. But how, exactly, did they do it? One powerful answer, we found, is in what we like to call innovation communities.

Every company does it a little differently, but innovation communities typically grow from a seed planted by senior management—a desire for a new product, market or business process. A forum of employees then work together to make desire a reality.

Innovation communities tackle projects too big, too risky and too expensive to be pursued by individual operating units. They can be created with little additional cost, because no consultants are needed. After all, those in the midst of the fray already know most of the details relevant to the project. . . .

Innovation communities are a way of giving new shape and purpose to knowledge that your employees already possess. The detailed discussions that take place, led by senior managers, often represent a company's most productive and economical engine for increased profits.

Here, then, are seven key characteristics that we have identified as being part of successful innovation communities.

CREATE THE SPACE TO INNOVATE. Line managers and employees occupied with operational issues normally don't have the time to sit around and discuss ideas that lead to cross-organizational innovation. Innovation communities create a space in which employees from across the organization can exchange ideas. . . .

Each year at food retailer Supervalu Inc, 35 to 40 mid- and director-level managers break up into four teams to discuss strategic issues suggested by executives in the different business units. The managers discuss issues outside their own areas of expertise and work on their leadership development at the same time. Over periods of five to six months, they hold electronic meetings at least weekly and meet in person at least five to six times, all while continuing to perform their regular duties. . . .

GET A BROAD VARIETY OF VIEWPOINTS. It's essential to involve people from different functions, locations and ranks, not only for their unique perspectives, but also to ensure buy-in throughout the company afterward. Innovation communities focus on creating enthusiasm as well as new products. At Honda Motor Co, innovation groups in the US draw members from sales, engineering and development, and from different business units across North America. Some companies, like General Electric Co, involve customers and business clients in the new-product discussions as well. . . .

CREATE A CONVERSATION BETWEEN SENIOR MANAGEMENT AND PARTICIPANTS. By definition, innovation communities can't work in isolation: To create sustainable cross-organizational innovation, it's important that ideas flow to senior managers. If they don't, innovations will tend to have limited, local effects that don't benefit the organization as a whole. . . .

But establishing effective strategic conservations is perhaps the most challenging factor for the success of innovation communities. For example, they require that truth be allowed to speak to power. If participants are inhibited, ideas that result are likely to be limited in impact, affecting a few units instead of the entire organization.

Discussion shouldn't be without limits. Senior managers should set the topics and keep discussions on course, because "blue-sky" conversations, while fun, generally waste time. . . .

PARTICIPANTS SHOULD BE PULLED TO JOIN, NOT PUSHED. Members need to be enthusiastic about participating. Employees can't be forced to reveal their thoughts or be imaginative.

Immediate rewards, like cash, usually drive people to focus on winning the prize instead of following the often-twisting but ultimately satisfying path to successful innovation. Instead, try explaining how the forum's work has the potential to benefit the organization, its customers, or broader social goals.

Another incentive: Make it clear that participation in innovation communities will be helpful for career advancement.

TAPPING UNUSED TALENT AND ENERGY KEEPS PRODUCT-DEVELOPMENT COSTS LOW. One reason these forums are economical is because they tap into unused energy. An innovation community sends a message that senior management is listening and that employees will benefit from participating. In many cases potential contributors are just waiting to be asked.

Permanent structures aren't required and productivity needn't suffer. Innovation-community leaders and teams participate for a limited time as they must continue to perform their regular roles.

COLLATERAL BENEFITS CAN BE AS IMPORTANT AS THE INNOVATIONS THEMSELVES. Innovation communities promote learning on both a personal and organizational level by bringing people together to exchange ideas. The repeated discussions and problem-solving missions can give rise to valuable social networks that lead to further exchanges of ideas in the future. . . .

MEASUREMENT IS KEY. Innovation communities are sustainable only if they can produce demonstrable value. Otherwise senior management loses interest.

All of the organizations we've noted try to gauge the success of their communities, based on how many ideas are implemented and with what results.

Questions for Discussion

1. How do innovation communities promote an open system?
2. How would the use of innovation communities help companies to learn from both success and failure? Discuss.
3. What type of organizational structure is represented by the use of innovation communities? Explain your rationale.
4. To what extent does the process to create innovative communities rely on the characteristics of organic organizations? Provide examples.
5. To what extent is the process of creating innovative communities consistent with the model of innovation?
6. How does the process of creating innovative communities overcome the challenges of innovation? Explain.

Legal/Ethical Challenge

One of the Fastest Growing Businesses Involves Spying on Consumers? Is This Ethical?[89]

Many companies believe that the use of sophisticated software that tracks our internet behavior is an innovative way to get information that can be used to increase their revenue.

"Hidden inside Ashley Hayes-Beaty's computer, a tiny file helps gather personal details about her, all to be put up for sale for a tenth of a penny. The file consists of a single code . . . that secretly identifies her as a 26-year-old female in Nashville, Tennessee.

The code knows that her favorite movies include *The Princess Bride, 50 First Dates,* and *10 Things I Hate About You.* It knows she enjoys the *Sex and the City* series. It knows she browses entertainment news and likes to take quizzes."

Upon learning about the file, Ashley concluded it was "eerily correct." Ms Hayes behavior is being monitored without her knowledge or permission by Lotame Solutions Inc. The company uses special software called a "beacon" to track what people type on websites. "Lotame packages that data into profiles about individuals, without determining a person's name, and sells the profiles to companies seeking customers." That said, Eric Porres, Lotame's chief marketing officer, indicated that the profile can be segmented "all the way down to one person." Lotame also

claimed that you can remove yourself from their system, assuming you even know that you are being tracked by the system.

"The information that companies gather is anonymous, in the sense that Internet users are identified by a number assigned to their computer, not by a specific person's name."

Many companies are unaware that their websites were tagged with beacons and that intrusive files were being attached to anyone who visited their website. The courts have not ruled on the legality of these complex tracking procedures.

How do you feel about the practice of someone tracking your Internet behavior without your approval or awareness?

1. Give me a break, this is the Internet age. Tracking is fair game and it provides useful information to companies so they can target products that meet our needs. Besides, you can get off Latame's system if you don't want to be tracked. Further, tracking can be

used to catch pedophiles and other types of criminal behavior.

2. I can accept the idea of tracking, but companies like Latame should get our approval before they start collecting data.

3. This is an invasion of privacy, and it should be disallowed by the courts.

4. I am against any attempts to police what goes on when we use the Internet.

Web Resources

For study material and exercises that apply to this chapter, visit our website at **www.mhhe.com/kreitner10e**

chapter 18

Managing Change and Stress

 Learning Objectives

When you finish studying the material in this chapter, you should be able to:

LO.1   Discuss the external and internal forces that create the need for organizational change.

LO.2   Describe Lewin's change model and the systems model of change.

LO.3   Discuss Kotter's eight steps for leading organizational change.

LO.4   Define *organization development* (OD), and explain the OD process.

LO.5   Explain the dynamic model of resistance to change.

LO.6   Discuss the key recipient and change agent characteristics that cause resistance to change.

LO.7   Identify alternative strategies for overcoming resistance to change.

LO.8   Define the term *stress,* and describe the model of occupational stress.

LO.9   Discuss the stress moderators of social support, hardiness, and Type A behavior.

LO.10 Review the four key stress-reduction techniques and the components of a holistic approach toward stress reduction.

Is the Metaphor of a Burning Platform a Good Way to Initiate Organizational Change?

Nokia's CEO Stephen Elop used the metaphor of a burning platform to rally employees around the need to change. He did this because the company needs to make difficult changes to catch up with Apple's iPhone and smartphones that use Google's Android software. For example, Elop plans to cut 1,800 jobs while simultaneously increasing the speed and delivery of new products to the market. Elop believes that "Nokia has been characterized as an organization where it is too hard to get things done," and "the changing market dynamics demand that we must improve our ability to aggressively lead through changes in our environment." The company also plans to streamline its service organization.

Elop started the change process by sending an e-mail to all employees, which relayed the story of a man working on an oil platform in the North Sea. The story describes the man's predicament of standing on the platform with flames and smoke all around him. The man had to make a quick decision about whether to jump off the platform into the dark, cold Atlantic waters or to stay aboard and try to fight the fire. The man decided to jump, survived the fall, and was later rescued. He told fellow employees he would not normally jump into frigid waters, but he was facing an unparalleled situation and jumping seemed to provide his best chances of survival. The "burning platform" caused a radical change in behavior according to the man.

Elop then told employees that "We too, are standing on a 'burning platform,' and we must decide how we are going to change our behavior." He believes that Nokia

has "multiple points of scorching heat that are fueling a blazing fire around us. For example, there is intense heat coming from our competitors, more rapidly than we ever expected. Apple disrupted the market by redefining the smartphone and attracting developers to a closed, but very powerful ecosystem."

And then there is Android. In about two years, Android created a platform that attracts applications developers, service providers, and hardware manufacturers. Android came in at the high end, they are now winning the mid-range, and quickly they are going downstream to phones under €100. Google has become a gravitational force, drawing much of the industry's innovation to its core."

The board of directors fully supports Elop and they are pushing him to move forward with the proposed changes. Nokia has since introduced its new line of smartphones and plans to ship new devices based on the MeeGo operating system.

Will employees embrace the proposed changes and radically change their behavior? Only time will tell. Elop, however, sent the message that he believes in Nokia's employees. He concluded his burning platform e-mail by saying, "Nokia, our platform is burning. We are working on a path forward—a path to rebuild our market leadership. When we share the new strategy . . . it will be a huge effort to transform our company. But, I believe that together, we can face the challenges ahead of us. Together, we can choose to define our future."[1]

Worldwide competition and rapid changes in technology are creating tremendous pressure on organizations to change. The chapter-opening case, for example, illustrated how Nokia's CEO took a proactive approach toward leading change in the company. Other well-known companies such as GE, Intel, Toyota, and Pepsi have similarly implemented corporatewide change initiatives to help compete in the marketplace.[2] We don't expect the need to change to go away any time soon. For example, IBM's annual survey of 1,541 CEOs, general managers, and senior public-sector leaders from 60 countries and 33 industries led to the conclusion that "incremental changes are no longer sufficient in a world that is operating in fundamentally different ways." These executives believe that life in general is becoming more complex and that managing complexity will differentiate those firms that survive in the long term.[3]

Furthermore, any type of change, whether it be product driven, personal, or organizational, is likely to encounter resistance even when it represents an appropriate course of action. Even when employees don't actively resist a change, the goal of the change might not be realized if employees feel so negative about it that absenteeism and turnover rise. Peter Senge, a well-known expert on the topic of organizational change, made the following comment about organizational change during an interview with *Fast Company* magazine:

Example. When I look at efforts to create change in big companies over the past 10 years, I have to say that there's enough evidence of success to say that change is possible—and enough evidence of failure to say that it isn't likely.[4]

If Senge is correct, then it is all the more important for current and future managers to learn how they can successfully implement organizational change.

This final chapter was written to help you navigate the journey of change. Specifically, we discuss the forces that create the need for organization change, models of planned change, resistance to change, and how you can better manage the stress associated with organizational change.

LO.1 Forces of Change

TO THE POINT

What are the external and internal forces for organizational change?

How do organizations know when they should change? What cues should an organization look for? Although there are no clear-cut answers to these questions, cues signaling the need for change are found by monitoring the forces for change.

Organizations encounter many different forces for change. These forces come from external sources outside the organization and from internal sources. This section examines the forces that create the need for change. Awareness of these forces can help managers determine when they should consider implementing an organizational change. The external and internal forces for change are presented in Figure 18–1.

This burning oil platform in the Timor Sea off the coast of Western Australia resulted in an oil leak that lasted 10 weeks. These types of accidents can create a strong force to change policies and practices regarding safety.

External Forces

External forces for change originate outside the organization. Because these forces have global effects, they may cause an organization to question the essence of what business it is in and the process by which products and services are produced. Let us now consider the four key external forces for change: demographic characteristics, technological advancements, market changes, and social and political pressures.

Demographic Characteristics   Chapter 2 provided a detailed discussion of demographic changes occurring in the US workforce. You

figure 18–1 The External and Internal Forces for Change

External Forces

Demographic Characteristics
• Age
• Education
• Skill level
• Gender
• Immigration

Technological Advancements
• Manufacturing automation
• Information technology

Shareholder, Customer, and Market Changes
• Changing customer preferences
• Domestic and international competition
• Mergers and acquisitions

Social and Political Pressures
• War
• Values
• Leadership

Internal Forces

Human Resource Problems/Prospects
• Unmet needs
• Job dissatisfaction
• Absenteeism and turnover
• Productivity
• Participation/suggestions

Managerial Behavior/Decisions
• Conflict
• Leadership
• Reward systems
• Structural reorganization

The need for change

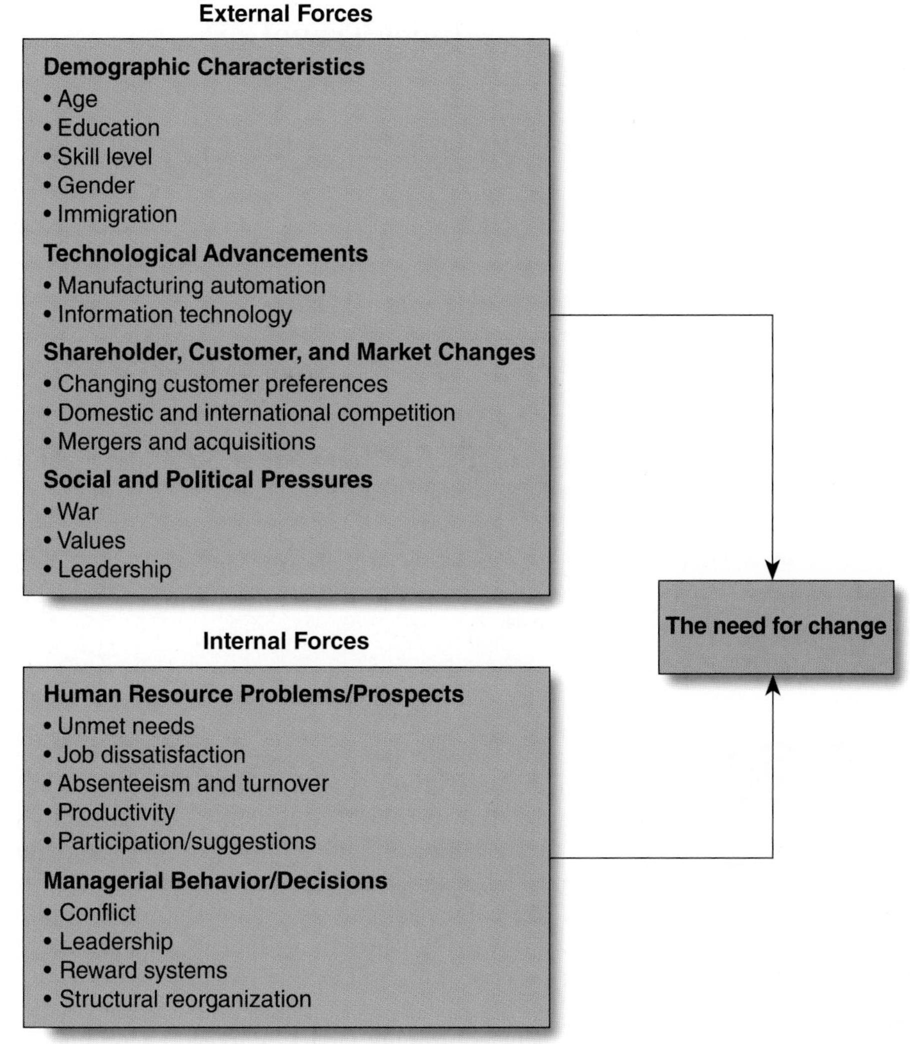

learned that organizations are changing employment benefits and aspects of the work environment in order to attract, motivate, and retain diverse employees.[5] Organizations also are changing the way in which they design and market their products and services and design their store layouts based on generational differences. For example, Ken Romanzi, North American chief operating officer for Ocean Spray Cranberries Inc, told a *Wall Street Journal* reporter that "we don't do anything to remind boomers that they are getting older."[6] Further, persistently higher unemployment levels among young people around the world is creating a strong force for change by governments and organizations alike. For example, experts believe that much of the current unrest in the Middle East is being fueled by a younger population that cannot find meaningful employment opportunities.[7]

Technological Advancements Both manufacturing and service organizations are increasingly using technology as a means to improve productivity, competitiveness, and customer service while also cutting costs. For example, more

external forces for change Originate outside the organization.

real WORLD // real PEOPLE

Telepresence Enhances Collaboration and Reduces Travel by Linking People around the Globe

"Telepresence has even come to the coffee break: Four of Cisco's European offices have wall-size telepresence screens constantly on in the office canteen, so that co-workers hundreds of miles apart can 'meet' there for a drink.

'You're able to virtualize people and resources,' says Marthin De Beer, the Cisco executive who led the development of the company's telepresence offerings, in an interview conducted between two telepresence suites. De Beer now spends much of his time in a suite at Cisco's San Jose headquarters, clicking from one distant locale to another as if flipping through TV channels. 'I'm frequently in five or six cities a day, and it would be impossible to get on that many planes,' he says. 'Rarely a day goes by when I'm not in at least three or four telepresence meetings.'"

While these systems are growing in popularity, the cost is prohibiting wide-scale application. That said, Autodesk has 20 telepresence rooms, and social network game developer Zynga uses them to coordinate interactions between designers and programmers around the world. The CBS show *The Good Wife* also uses telepresence suites to conduct bicoastal writers' meetings. Hospitals also use this technology to link remote doctors with patients.

What are the pros and cons of holding a meeting in a telepresence suite?

SOURCE: Excerpted from D Bennett, "I'll Have My Robots Talk to Your Robots," *Bloomberg Businessweek,* February 21–February 27, 2011, p 54.

This meeting is being run with the use of videoconferencing. Telepresence is a more sophisticated application of this type of technology. Have you ever participated in a videoconference?

and more companies are using social networking as standard recruiting tools, and HR professionals indicate that they expect to use them more frequently in the future.[8] Information technology is enabling more and more forms of self-service, from Internet stores and banks for customers to online help for employees who want to learn about their benefits packages. **Telepresence** is a good example of a technology that enables organizations to change the way they deliver products, coordinate virtual workers, encourage employee collaboration, improve communication, and increase productivity. It represents an advanced form of videoconferencing and robotics that in combination makes virtual conversations seem like they are taking place in one location. These systems, which can cost upwards of $300,000 are used by companies such as Bank of America, PepsiCo, Procter & Gamble, and Royal Dutch Shell. They have been found to help companies significantly cut their travel expenses (see Real World/Real People above) and to improve communications among employees and customers.[9]

Shareholder, Customer, and Market Changes   Shareholders have become more involved with pressing for organizational change in response to ethical lapses from senior management and anger over executives' compensation packages. Companies such as Amgen, Schering-Plough, and Prudential Financial, for example, have gone as far as using Web surveys to obtain shareholder feedback about pay practices. Aflac has taken this trend one step further by becoming the first US company to allow shareholders to have a say on pay. Say on pay means that shareholders actually provide the deciding vote on executives' compensation practices.[10] Increasing customer sophistication is requiring organizations to deliver higher value in their products and services. Customers are simply demanding more now than they did in the past. Moreover, customers are more likely to shop elsewhere if they do not get what they want because of lower customer switching costs. This has led more and more companies to seek customer feedback about a wide range of issues in order to retain and attract customers. For example, General Motors has made it a point to seek customer feedback in the design and marketing of its vehicles and McDonald's actively collects information about consumer preferences and tastes and uses it to revise the menu. This led McDonald's to create more chicken offerings. The company now sells almost as much chicken as beef and its chicken sales are twice those of its leading competitors combined.[11]

With respect to market changes, companies are experiencing increased pressure to obtain more productivity because global competition is fierce. Swings in the economic cycle also spur a need to change in response to surging or falling demand for products, requiring companies to produce more or survive on less.

Social and Political Pressures   These forces are created by social and political events. For example, widespread concern about the impact of climate change and rising energy costs have been important forces for change in almost every industry around the world. Companies have gone "green," looking for ways to use less energy themselves and to sell products that consume less energy and are safer to use. For example, Esquel, one of the world's largest producers of premium cotton shirts, received pressure from retail customers such as Nike and Marks & Spencer to improve its environmental and social performance. These retail stores want Esquel to produce more cotton organically. This is very difficult to do because most of Esquel's cotton comes from "Xinjiang, an arid province in northwestern China that depends mainly on underground sources of water. The traditional method of irrigation there was to periodically flood the fields—an inefficient approach that created a perfect breeding ground for insects and diseases. Heavy pesticide use was a necessity." This pressure ultimately caused Esquel to closely work with farms to implement sustainable farming techniques. "For example, it assisted them in adopting drip irrigation to decrease their water use and in establishing natural pest- and disease-control programs such as breeding disease-resistant strains of cotton, to reduce reliance on pesticides. (The new variety of cotton plants also produced stronger fiber, resulting in less scrap during fabric manufacturing then conventional cotton did.)[12]

Political events also can create substantial change. For example, the wars in Iraq and Afghanistan created tremendous opportunities for defense contractors and organizations like Halliburton that are involved in rebuilding the country. Although it is difficult for organizations to predict changes in political forces, many organizations hire lobbyists and consultants to help them detect and respond to social and political changes.

Internal Forces

Internal forces for change come from inside the organization. These forces may be subtle, such as low job satisfaction, or can manifest in outward signs, such as low productivity, conflict, or strikes. Internal forces for change come from both human resource problems and managerial behavior/decisions.

Human Resource Problems/Prospects   These problems stem from employee perceptions about how they are treated at work and the match between individual and organization needs and desires. Chapter 6 highlighted the relationship between an employee's unmet needs and job dissatisfaction. Dissatisfaction

---

telepresence Communicating with the most advanced videoconferencing systems.

internal forces for change Originate inside the organization.

is a symptom of an underlying employee problem that should be addressed. For example, employees from 3M, Sony, and Caterpillar factories in France took senior managers hostage in response to dissatisfaction with the benefits being received by laid-off workers. Chinese employees from Honda Motor and Toyota Motor also shocked management by striking in response to labor issues. Honda ultimately decided to increase salaries to a level that "would be roughly double the average amount paid to a factory worker in India or 33% higher than that in Thailand. Such higher labor costs would make it difficult for Honda to compete with vehicles exported from these countries by rivals including Toyota, which has a plant in Thailand, and Nissan Motor and Suzuki Motor, which have plants in India."[13] Unusual or high levels of absenteeism and turnover also represent forces for change. Organizations might respond to these problems by using the various approaches to job design discussed in Chapter 8; by reducing employees' role conflict, overload, and ambiguity (recall our discussion in Chapter 10); and by removing the different stressors discussed in the final section of this chapter. Prospects for positive change stem from employee participation and suggestions.

Managerial Behavior/Decisions   Excessive interpersonal conflict between managers and their subordinates is a sign that change is needed. Both the manager and the employee may need interpersonal skills training, or the two individuals may simply need to be separated. For example, one of the parties might be transferred to a new department. Inappropriate leader behaviors such as inadequate direction or support may result in human resource problems requiring change. As discussed in Chapter 16, leadership training is one potential solution for this problem. Finally, managerial decisions are a powerful force for change. Consider the case of Johnson & Johnson (J&J). The company has voluntarily recalled more than 50 products since 2010 and the 2010 annual report contained "eight pages detailing government criminal and civil investigations and thousands of private lawsuits covering a wide range of drugs, device, and business practices." A recent article in *Bloomberg Businessweek* suggested that cost-cutting decisions made by management along with a decentralized structure may be the root causes of these problems. J&J's CEO William Weldon believes that these issues are being blown out of proportion because most product-related problems originated at only 3 of 120 manufacturing facilities. Weldon believes that the company still puts patients ahead of profits and shareholders and he has no intention of stepping down because of the product recalls. The company is currently focused on fixing its manufacturing problems.[14]

Back to the **Chapter-Opening Case**

What external and internal forces for change were putting pressure on Nokia to change?

TO THE POINT

How do Lewin's model of change, a systems model of change, and Kotter's model explain the change process, and how does the process of organizational development unfold?

Models and Dynamics of Planned Change

American managers are criticized for emphasizing short-term, quick-fix solutions to organizational problems. When applied to organizational change, this approach is doomed from the start. Quick-fix solutions do not really solve underlying problems, and they have little staying power. This leads to the conclusion that organizational change should be viewed as a natural, normal, and constant characteristic of organizational life. This is what Amy Lessack, Wachovia senior vice president of enterprise learning, had to say about organizational change:

Example. Change management is not an event for us, it's something we do every day. It is embedded in the work we do, so every time we do learning design or talk to clients or to the business, we talk about change—how it's impacting employees and leaders, how to lead that change, and how can we partner with the business to help employees work through the changes.[15]

Researchers and managers alike have tried to identify effective ways to manage the change process given its importance for organizational survival. This section sheds light on their insights. After discussing different types of organizational changes, we review Lewin's change model, a systems model of change, Kotter's eight steps for leading organizational change, and organizational development.

Types of Change

A useful three-way typology of change is displayed in Figure 18–2.[16] This typology is generic because it relates to all sorts of change, including both administrative and technological changes. Adaptive change is lowest in complexity, cost, and uncertainty. It involves reimplementation of a change in the same organizational unit at a later time or imitation of a similar change by a different unit. For example, an adaptive change for a department store would be to rely on 12-hour days during the annual inventory week. The store's accounting department could imitate the same change in work hours during tax preparation time. Adaptive changes are not particularly threatening to employees because they are familiar.

Innovative changes fall midway on the continuum of complexity, cost, and uncertainty. An experiment with flexible work schedules by a farm supply warehouse company qualifies as an innovative change if it entails modifying the way other firms in the industry already use it. Unfamiliarity, and hence greater uncertainty, make fear of change a problem with innovative changes.

At the high end of the continuum of complexity, cost, and uncertainty are radically innovative changes. Changes of this sort are the most difficult to implement and tend to be the most threatening to managerial confidence and employee job security. At the same time, however, radically innovative changes potentially realize the greatest benefits. Importantly, radical changes must be supported by an organization's culture. Organizational change is more likely to fail if it is inconsistent with any of the three levels of organizational culture: observable artifacts, espoused values, and basic assumptions (see the discussion in Chapter 3).

Mc Graw Hill **connect** ™ Go to www.mcgrawhillconnect.com for a self-assessment to help determine how ready an organization is for change.

figure 18–2 A Generic Typology of Organizational Change

LO.2 Lewin's Change Model

Most theories of organizational change originated from the landmark work of social psychologist Kurt Lewin. Lewin developed a three-stage model of planned change that explained how to initiate, manage, and stabilize the change process.[17] The three stages are unfreezing, changing, and refreezing. Before reviewing each stage, it is important to highlight the assumptions underlying this model:[18]

1. The change process involves learning something new, as well as discontinuing current attitudes, behaviors, or organizational practices.
2. Change will not occur unless there is motivation to change. This is often the most difficult part of the change process.
3. People are the hub of all organizational changes. Any change, whether in terms of structure, group process, reward systems, or job design, requires individuals to change.
4. Resistance to change is found even when the goals of change are highly desirable.
5. Effective change requires reinforcing new behaviors, attitudes, and organizational practices.

Let us now consider the three stages of change.

One thousand ice sculptures were left to melt on the steps of Berlin's Concert Hall. The point of the exhibition was to underscore the earth's melting ice poles and to unfreeze people's views about global warming.

Unfreezing   The focus of this stage is to create the motivation to change. In doing so, individuals are encouraged to replace old behaviors and attitudes with those desired by management. Managers can begin the unfreezing process by disconfirming the usefulness or appropriateness of employees' present behaviors or attitudes. In other words, employees need to become dissatisfied with the old way of doing things. Managers frequently create the motivation for change by presenting data regarding levels of effectiveness, efficiency, or customer satisfaction. This helps employees understand the need for change. For example, declines in the stock price and same-store sales of Starbucks, along with the reappointment of Howard Schultz as CEO of the company he once built into an internationally known brand, signaled a need for change in how Starbucks operated. Schultz concluded that "the company had been hitting a home run in terms of growth every single year, but I could smell that things were wrong. We weren't creating a soulful, romantic experience anymore: We'd lost sight of the experience around the coffee, and we were too focused on ringing the register."[19]

To unfreeze the organization, Schultz began by apologizing to Starbucks employees about managerial decisions that led to the company's predicament. He then closed every store for retraining at a cost of $6 million. He then sent every store manager to New Orleans, which cost $30 million, for meetings and social bonding by having them volunteer in the Ninth Ward.[20]

Benchmarking is a technique that can be used to help unfreeze an organization. **Benchmarking** "describes the overall process by which a company compares its performance with that of other companies, then learns how the strongest-performing companies achieve their results."[21] For example, one company for which we consulted discovered through benchmarking that its costs to develop software were twice as high as the best companies in the industry, and the time it took to get a new product to market was four times longer than the benchmarked organizations. These data were ultimately used to unfreeze employees' attitudes and motivate people to change the organization's internal processes in order to remain competitive. Managers also need to devise ways to reduce the barriers to change during this stage.

Changing   This is the stage in which organizational change takes place. This change, whether large or small, is undertaken to improve some process, procedure, product, service, or outcome of interest to management. Because change involves learning and doing things differently, this stage entails providing employees with new information, new behavioral models, new processes or procedures, new equipment, new technology, or new ways of getting the job done. How does management know what to change?

There is no simple answer to this question. Organizational change can be aimed at improvement or growth, or it can focus on solving a problem such as poor customer service or low productivity. Change also can be targeted at different levels in an organization. For example, sending managers to leadership training programs can be a solution to improving individuals' job satisfaction and productivity. In contrast, installing new information technology may be the change required to increase work group productivity and overall corporate profits. The point to keep in mind is that change should be targeted at some type of desired end result. The systems model of change, which is the next model to be discussed, provides managers with a framework to diagnose the target of change.

Refreezing   The goal of this stage is to support and reinforce the change. Change is supported by helping employees integrate the changed behavior or attitude into their normal way of doing things. This is accomplished by first giving employees the chance to exhibit the new behaviors or attitudes. Once exhibited, positive reinforcement is used to encourage the desired change. Additional coaching and modeling also are used at this point to reinforce the stability of the change. Extrinsic rewards, particularly monetary incentives (recall our discussion in Chapter 9), are frequently used for this purpose.

Putting Lewin's Theory into Action   The Real World/Real People on page 538 illustrates the application of Lewin's theory to a call center that received negative evaluations from customers. Managers examined customer feedback and concluded that customers were unhappy about being rushed off the phone without having their concerns resolved. The focus of the change effort was to encourage employees to become more customer focused.

A Systems Model of Change

A systems approach takes a "big picture" perspective of organizational change. It is based on the notion that any change, no matter how large or small, has a cascading effect throughout an organization.[22] For example, promoting an individual to a new work group affects the group dynamics in both the old and new groups. Similarly, creating project or work teams may necessitate the need to revamp compensation practices. These examples illustrate that change creates additional change. Today's solutions are tomorrow's problems.

A systems model of change offers managers a framework or model to use for diagnosing *what* to change and for determining *how* to evaluate the success of a change effort. To further your understanding about this model, we first describe its components and then discuss a brief application. The four main components of

benchmarking Process by which a company compares its performance with that of high-performing organizations.

real WORLD // real PEOPLE

Application of Lewin's Model: Creating Customer Focus within a Call Center

1. *Unfreezing:* Managers hold a meeting with all telephone representatives. During the meeting, customer survey results are discussed. Additionally, lost customer estimates are translated into dollars and cents so that telephone representatives can see how poor customer service results in overall company performance and lost jobs.

2. *Change:* After the meeting, telephone representatives are provided with customer service training that involves role-playing and group discussions. This allows the representatives to experience "poor" service and "good" service. Representatives are instructed to take their time with calls and to make sure they address all customer needs. A new peer support system is created whereby representatives spend 15 minutes every shift listening to other calls and providing feedback and support. Mirrors are placed on every call station so that representatives can make

sure they "end the call with a smile." This becomes an unofficial slogan for the center.

3. *Refreezing:* The old compensation system rewarded representatives based on the number of calls made per hour. Clearly, this old system would not support the desired changes so the compensation system is changed. Representatives are now paid on an hourly rate and bonuses are based on customer satisfaction surveys. Additionally, the employees have the opportunity to nominate each other for "customer service guru of the week." The honor comes with a silly hat and certificate.

Would you do anything differently to improve customer service?

SOURCE: Excerpted from J H Mills, K Dye, and A J Mills, *Understanding Organizational Change* (New York: Routledge, 2009).

---

a systems model of change are inputs, strategic plans, target elements of change, and outputs (see Figure 18–3).

Inputs   All organizational changes should be consistent with an organization's mission, vision, and resulting strategic plan. A **mission statement** represents the "reason" an organization exists, and an organization's *vision* is a long-term goal that describes "what" an organization wants to become. Consider how the difference between mission and vision affects organizational change. Your university probably has a mission to educate people. This mission does not necessarily imply anything about change. It simply defines the university's overall purpose. In contrast, the university may have a vision to be recognized as the "best" university in the country. This vision requires the organization to benchmark itself against other world-class universities and to create plans for achieving the vision. For example, the vision of the W P Carey School of Business at Arizona State University is to be among the top 25 business schools in the world. An assessment of an organization's internal strengths and weaknesses against its environmental opportunities and threats (SWOT) is another key input within the systems model. This SWOT analysis is a key component of the strategic planning process.

Strategic Plans   A strategic plan outlines an organization's long-term direction and the actions necessary to achieve planned results. Among other things, strategic plans are based on results from a SWOT—strengths, weaknesses, opportunities, and threats—analysis. This analysis aids in developing an organizational strategy to attain desired goals such as profits, customer satisfaction, quality, adequate return on investment, and acceptable levels of turnover and employee satisfaction and commitment.

mission statement Summarizes "why" an organization exists.

figure 18–3 A Systems Model of Change

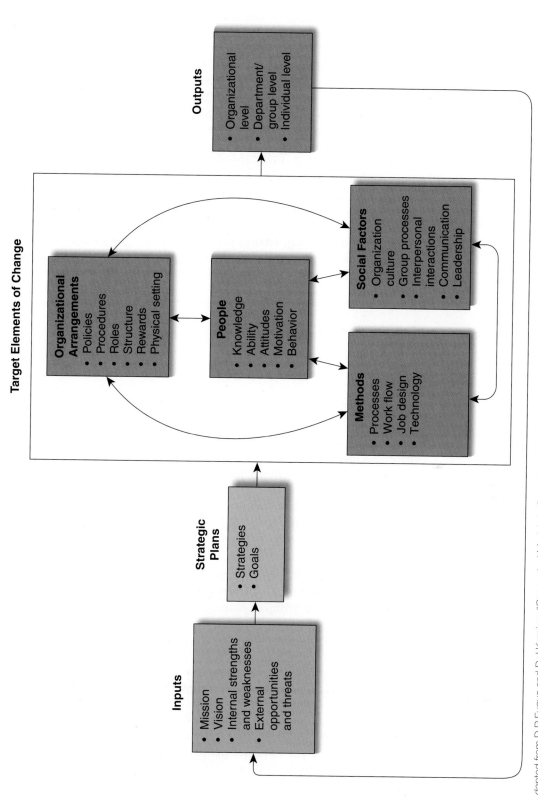

SOURCES: Adapted from D R Fuqua and D J Kurpius, "Conceptual Models in Organizational Consultation," *Journal of Counseling and Development*, July–August 1993, pp 602–18; and D A Nadler and M L Tushman, "Organizational Frame Bending: Principles for Managing Reorientation," *Academy of Management Executive*, August 1989, pp 194–203.

Target Elements of Change   **Target elements of change** are the components of an organization that may be changed. They essentially represent change levers that managers can push and pull to influence various aspects of an organization. The choice of which lever to pull, however, is based on a diagnosis of a problem, or problems, or the actions needed to accomplish a goal: A problem exists when managers are not obtaining the results they desire. The target elements of change are used to diagnose problems and to identify change-related solutions.

As shown in Figure 18–3, there are four targeted elements of change: organizational arrangements, social factors, methods, and people. Each target element of change contains a subset of more detailed organizational features. For instance, the "social factors" component includes consideration of an organization's culture, group processes, interpersonal interactions, communication, and leadership. There are two final issues to keep in mind about the target elements of change shown in Figure 18–3. First, the double-headed arrows connecting each target element of change convey the message that change ripples across an organization. For example, changing a reward system to reinforce team rather than individual performance (an organizational arrangement) is likely to impact organizational culture (a social factor). Second, the "people" component is placed in the center of the target elements of change box because all organizational change ultimately impacts employees. Organizational change is more likely to succeed when managers proactively consider the impact of change on its employees.

Back to the Chapter-Opening Case

If you were Stephen Elop, which of the target elements of change would you use to create change within Nokia? Explain your rationale.

Outputs   Outputs represent the desired end results of a change. Once again, these end results should be consistent with an organization's strategic plan. Figure 18–3 indicates that change may be directed at the organizational level, department/group level, or individual level. Change efforts are more complicated and difficult to manage when they are targeted at the organizational level. This occurs because organizational-level changes are more likely to affect multiple target elements of change shown in the model.

Applying the Systems Model of Change   There are two different ways to apply the systems model of change. The first is as an aid during the strategic planning process. Once a group of managers have determined their vision and strategic goals, the target elements of change can be considered when developing action plans to support the accomplishment of goals. For example, following the merger of Adolph Coors Company and Molson, the management team of Molson Coors Brewing established goals of cutting costs by $180 million, making Coors Light a global brand, and developing new high-end brands of beer. Target elements of change have included strengthening shared values of the predecessor companies (social factors), keeping production and distribution employees focused on their existing functions (motivation, a people factor), creating a general-management development program (another people factor), and establishing a subsidiary to specialize in new products (organizational arrangements).[23]

The second application involves using the model as a diagnostic framework to determine the causes of an organizational problem and to propose solutions. We highlight this application by considering a consulting project in which we used the model. We were contacted by the CEO of a software company and asked to figure out why the presidents of three divisions were not collaborating with each other—the problem. It turned out that two of the presidents submitted a proposal for the same $4 million project from a potential customer. Our client did not get the work because the customer was appalled at having received two proposals from the same company; hence the CEO's call to us. We decided to interview employees by using a structured set of questions that pertained to each of the target elements of change. For instance, we asked employees to comment on the extent to which the reward system, organizational culture, work flow, and physical setting contributed to collaboration across divisions. The interviews taught us that the lack of collaboration among the division presidents was due to the reward system (an organizational arrangement), a competitive culture and poor communications (social factors), and poor work flow (a methods factor). Our recommendation was to change the reward systems, restructure the organization, and redesign the work flow.

 LO.3 Kotter's Eight Steps for Leading Organizational Change

John Kotter, an expert in leadership and change management, believes that organizational change typically fails because senior management makes a host of implementation errors. Kotter proposed an eight-step process for leading change (see Table 18–1) based on these errors.[24] Unlike the systems model of change, this model is not diagnostic in orientation. Its application will not help managers to diagnose

table 18–1   Steps to Leading Organizational Change

STEP	DESCRIPTION
1. Establish a sense of urgency	Unfreeze the organization by creating a compelling reason for why change is needed.
2. Create the guiding coalition	Create a cross-functional, cross-level group of people with enough power to lead the change.
3. Develop a vision and strategy	Create a vision and strategic plan to guide the change process.
4. Communicate the change vision	Create and implement a communication strategy that consistently communicates the new vision and strategic plan.
5. Empower broad-based action	Eliminate barriers to change, and use target elements of change to transform the organization. Encourage risk taking and creative problem solving.
6. Generate short-term wins	Plan for and create short-term "wins" or improvements. Recognize and reward people who contribute to the wins.
7. Consolidate gains and produce more change	The guiding coalition uses credibility from short-term wins to create more change. Additional people are brought into the change process as change cascades throughout the organization. Attempts are made to reinvigorate the change process.
8. Anchor new approaches in the culture	Reinforce the changes by highlighting connections between new behaviors and processes and organizational success. Develop methods to ensure leadership development and succession.

SOURCE: The steps were developed by J P Kotter, *Leading Change* (Boston: Harvard Business School Press, 1996).

target elements of change Components of an organization that may be changed.

real WORLD // real PEOPLE

MasterCard Implements Kotter's Model

To increase the urgency for change (step 1), in November 2007, a getAbstract Chat hosted by Chief Marketing Officer Larry Flanagan involved close to a thousand MasterCard employees via a global teleconference of the key themes of Dr Kotter's work and their application to the company. . . .

The Guiding Team (step 2) consists of CMO Flanagan and his communication team; Valerie Gelb, chief sales development officer and an early adapter; and the GTM&D team, supported by the ISB trainers. "While we focus on creating a culture of change, we allow each business unit to assemble the correct guiding team for each individual change initiative," says Ann Schulte, VP, Learning and Development, who leads GTM&D's MasterCard University. . . .

MasterCard's vision (step 3), reveals Matthew Breitfelder, VP, Management & Leadership Development, is "To be ready, willing, and able to change as the need arises." The company's broad communication efforts (step 4)—including intranet coverage of the change initiatives—have been enhanced through its strategic partnership with Worldwide Communications (its internal marketing and advertising team). "We have empowered action (step 5) by providing all MasterCard employees access to these concepts through a variety of means. . . ."

As for producing short-term wins (step 6), Schulte says, "While we are early in our process, we already can see improvements in the ways in which teams think about and plan for change. We are beginning to build a common 'language' around change." Adds Breitfelder, "We know we have to keep the momentum going (step 7), so we spend time with teams helping them see the end goal but also making sure they remember the reason why this work is so important."

Making these changes sustainable (step 8) does not occur by coincidence. "Following each LBC session, the participants have a detailed action plan that prepares them to not only launch their initiative, but to sustain early gains," Ray says. "The GTM&D team follows up with business unit teams, providing guidance, monitoring progress against action plans, and serving as 'group mentors,' all aimed at making the changes a permanent part of our culture."

To what extent was MasterCard deficient in following Kotter's steps? Explain.

SOURCE: Excerpted from "MasterCard Worldwide: Taking Charge of Change," *Training Magazine*, June 2008, pp 30–36.

---

what needs to be changed. Rather, this model is more like Lewin's model of change in that it prescribes how managers should sequence or lead the change process.

Kotter's eight steps, shown in Table 18–1, subsume Lewin's model of change. The first four steps represent Lewin's "unfreezing" stage. Steps 5, 6, and 7 represent "changing," and step 8 corresponds to "refreezing." The value of Kotter's steps is that it provides specific recommendations about behaviors that managers need to exhibit to successfully lead organizational change. It is important to remember that Kotter's research reveals that it is ineffective to skip steps and that managers most often make mistakes at the beginning.[25] For instance, Yahoo! co-founder and former CEO Jerry Yang was partially unsuccessful in creating change at Yahoo! because "he was slow to consolidate redundant businesses (two photo-sharing properties, multiple social-media sites) and failed to explain the strategy behind his Get Google objective."[26] These errors pertain to steps one and three. The Real World/Real People above provides an example of how MasterCard's Global Talent Management and Development (GTM&D) group used Kotter's model.

Go to www.mcgrawhillconnect.com for an interactive exercise to test your knowledge of Kotter's eight steps for leading organizational change.

LO.4 Creating Change through Organization Development

Organization development (OD) is different from the previously discussed models of change. OD does not entail a structured sequence as proposed by Lewin and Kotter, but it does possess the same diagnostic focus associated with the systems model of change. That said, OD is much broader in orientation than any of the previously discussed models. Specifically, a pair of experts in this field of study and practice defined **organization development** as follows:

Example. OD consists of planned efforts to help persons work and live together more effectively, over time, in their organizations. These goals are achieved by applying behavioral science principles, methods, and theories adapted from the fields of psychology, sociology, education, and management.[27]

As you can see from this definition, OD constitutes a set of techniques or interventions that are used to implement "planned" organizational change aimed at increasing "an organization's ability to improve itself as a humane and effective system." OD techniques or interventions apply to each of the change models discussed in this section. For example OD is used during Lewin's "changing" stage. It also is used to identify and implement targeted elements of change within the systems model of change. Finally, OD might be used during Kotter's steps 1, 3, 5, 6, and 7. Finally, OD is put into practice by change agents. A **change agent** is someone who is a catalyst in helping organizations to deal with old problems in new ways. Change agents can be external consultants or internal employees. In this section, we briefly review how OD works and its research and practical implications.[28]

How OD Works   OD change agents follow a medical-like model. They approach the organization as if it were a "sick" patient, "diagnose" its ills, prescribe and implement an "intervention," and "evaluate" progress. If the evaluation reveals that positive change has not occurred, this information provides feedback that is used to refine the diagnosis and/or consider the extent to which the intervention was effectively implemented (see Figure 18–4). Let us consider the components of the OD process shown in Figure 18–4.

1. *Diagnosis: What is the problem and its causes?* Change agents use a combination of interviews, surveys, meetings, written materials, and direct observation to determine the problem and its associated causes. We recommend using the target elements of change in the systems model of change as a vehicle to develop diagnostic questions aimed at identifying causes. For example, you might ask, "To what extent does the structure or reward system contribute to the problem?"

2. *Intervention: What can be done to solve the problem?* The treatment or intervention represents the changes being made to solve the problem. Treatments are selected based on the causes of the problem. For example, if the cause of low quality is poor teamwork, then team building (see Chapter 11) might be used as the

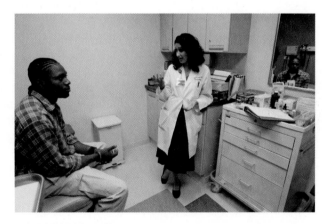

Dr. Roopal Kundu is talking with Emmanual Agbarah about his treatments to prevent "razor bumps." Organizational change agents similarly use a medical model to diagnose and solve and organization's "ills" or problems.

---

organization development A set of techniques or tools used to implement planned organizational change.

change agent Individual who is a catalyst in helping organizations to implement change.

figure 18–4 The OD Process

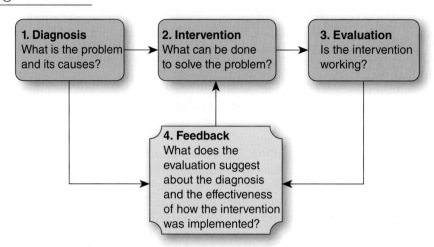

SOURCE: Adapted from W L French and C H Bell Jr, *Organization Development: Behavioral Interventions for Organizational Improvement* (Englewood Cliffs, NJ: Prentice Hall, 1978).

intervention. In contrast, managers might be sent to some type of leadership training if bad leadership is the cause of low quality (see Chapter 16). The key thing to remember is that there is not one "set" of intervention techniques that apply to all situations. Rather, you can use any number of interventions based on theories and models you studied in this book. A contingency approach allows you to select the intervention that seems best suited for the problem and causes at hand.

3. *Evaluation: Is the intervention working?* Evaluation requires the organization to develop measures of effectiveness—recall our discussion of organizational effectiveness in Chapter 17. The proper measure depends on the problem. For example, measures of voluntary turnover and productivity would be appropriate if the problem involved employee turnover and productivity, respectively. If possible, the final evaluation should be based on comparing measures of effectiveness obtained before and after the intervention.

4. *Feedback: What does the evaluation suggest about the diagnosis and the effectiveness of how the intervention was implemented?* If the evaluation reveals that the intervention worked, then the OD process is complete and the change agent can consider how best to "refreeze" the changes. Oppositely, a negative evaluation means one of two things: (1) either the initial diagnosis was wrong or (2) the intervention was not effectively implemented. Negative evaluations generally require the change agent to collect more information about steps 1 and 2 in the OD process shown in Figure 18–4.

Back to the Chapter-Opening Case

How might Stephen Elop evaluate the success of organizational change at Nokia? What measures would you use?

OD Research and Practical Implications Before discussing OD research, note that OD-related interventions produced the following insights:

- A meta-analysis of 18 studies indicated that employee satisfaction with change was higher when top management was highly committed to the change effort.[29]

- A meta-analysis of 52 studies provided support for the systems model of organizational change. Specifically, varying one target element of change created changes in other target elements. Also, there was a positive relationship between individual behavior change and organizational-level change.[30]

- A meta-analysis of 126 studies demonstrated that multifaceted interventions using more than one OD technique were more effective in changing job attitudes and work attitudes than interventions that relied on only one human process or technostructural approach.[31]

- A survey of 1,700 firms from China, Japan, the United States, and Europe revealed that (1) US and European firms used OD interventions more frequently than firms from China and Japan and (2) some OD interventions are culture free and some are not.[32]

There are four practical implications derived from this research. First, planned organizational change works. However, management and change agents are advised to rely on multifaceted interventions. As indicated elsewhere in this book, goal setting, feedback, recognition and rewards, training, participation, and challenging job design have good track records relative to improving performance and satisfaction. Second, change programs are more successful when they are geared toward meeting both short-term and long-term results. Managers should not engage in organizational change for the sake of change. Change efforts should produce positive results. Third, organizational change is more likely to succeed when top management is truly committed to the change process and the desired goals of the change program. This is particularly true when organizations pursue large-scale transformation. Finally, the effectiveness of OD interventions is affected by cross-cultural considerations. Managers and OD consultants should not blindly apply an OD intervention that worked in one country to a similar situation in another country.

Understanding and Managing Resistance to Change

> ◀ ······················
> ## TO THE POINT
> What are the key causes of resistance to change, and how can managers reduce it?
> ······················

No matter how technically or administratively perfect a proposed change may be, people make or break it because organizational change represents a form of influence. That is, organizational change is management's attempt to have employees behave, think, or perform differently. Viewing change from this perspective underscores what we discussed about influence techniques and outcomes in Chapter 15. You may recall that resistance is one of the three possible influence outcomes; the other two are commitment and compliance. This perspective has led many people to conclude that resistance to change represents a failed influence attempt by a change agent. Interestingly, recent research indicates a need to rethink this interpretation.

Past research on resistance has been based on the assumption that "change agents are doing the right and proper things while change recipients throw up unreasonable obstacles or barriers intent on 'doing in' or 'screwing up' the change. . . . Accordingly, change agents are portrayed as undeserving victims of the irrational and dysfunctional response of change recipients."[33] This is why resistance is viewed as a negative outcome that is caused by irrational and self-serving recipients. While this can be true, it is equally likely that resistance is caused by two other key factors: the change agent's characteristics, actions, inactions, and perceptions and the quality of the relationship between change agents and change recipients. This section is based on the premise that resistance is a natural form of employee feedback and that it can serve a useful purpose. Managers are encouraged to understand the causes of resistance if they are to effectively manage change.[34] Accordingly, this section presents a model that outlines the causes of resistance and practical ways of overcoming resistance to change.

figure 18–5 A Dynamic Model of Resistance to Change

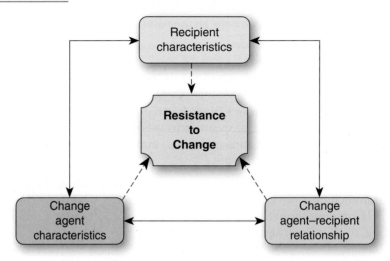

 LO.5 Causes of Resistance to Change

Resistance to change is an emotional/behavioral response to real or imagined threats to an established work routine. Resistance can be as subtle as passive resignation and as overt as deliberate sabotage. Figure 18–5 presents a model of resistance that illustrates the relationship among the three key causes of resistance. The model conceives resistance as a dynamic interaction between these three sources as opposed to being caused solely by irrational and stubborn recipients of change. For example, recipient resistance is partly based on their perceptions of change, which are very much influenced by the attitudes and behaviors exhibited by change agents and the level of trust between change agents and recipients. Similarly, change agents' actions and perceptions are affected by the recipients' actions and inactions and the quality of relationships with recipients. Let us consider each source of resistance.

 LO.6 Recipient Characteristics   Recipient characteristics include a variety of individual differences (see Chapter 5) possessed by recipients. They also represent the actions (e.g., engaging in new behaviors) or inactions (e.g., failing to engage in new behaviors) displayed by recipients. Finally, recipient perceptions of change (e.g., "This change is unfair because I am being asked to do more with no increase in pay") also contribute to resistance. Six of the key recipient characteristics are discussed below:[35]

1. *An individual's predisposition toward change.* This predisposition is highly personal and deeply ingrained. It is an outgrowth of how one learns to handle change and ambiguity as a child. While some people are distrustful and suspicious of change, others see change as a situation requiring flexibility, patience, and understanding.[36] For example, **resilience to change,** which represents a composite characteristic reflecting high self-esteem, optimism, and an internal locus of control, was positively associated with recipients' willingness to accommodate or accept a specific organizational change.[37] The US Army is taking this research one step further. The Army designed a series of courses to help military personnel become more resilient to the demands of modern warfare, which is characterized by "demanding missions, extreme climates, sleep deprivation, cultural dissonance, physical fatigue, prolonged separation from family, and the ever-present threat of serious bodily injury or death."[38] The ultimate goal of this training is to make sure that military personnel are psychologically fit for the challenges of war.

2. *Surprise and fear of the unknown.* When innovative or radically different changes are introduced without warning, affected employees become fearful of the implications. The same is true when managers announce new goals without spelling out specific plans for how the goals will be achieved. Imagine how you would feel if your boss stated that your department was going to increase sales by 25% without hiring any new employees. Failing to set expectations around a change effort or the setting of new goals is a key contributor to resistance.[39]

3. *Fear of failure.* Intimidating changes on the job can cause employees to doubt their capabilities. Self-doubt erodes self-confidence and cripples personal growth and development. Recall our discussion about self-efficacy in Chapter 5.

4. *Loss of status and/or job security.* Administrative and technological changes that threaten to alter power bases or eliminate jobs generally trigger strong resistance. For example, most corporate restructuring involves the elimination of managerial jobs. One should not be surprised when middle managers resist restructuring and participative management programs that reduce their authority and status.

5. *Peer pressure.* Someone who is not directly affected by a change may actively resist it to protect the interests of his or her friends and co-workers.

6. *Past success.* Success can breed complacency. It also can foster a stubbornness to change because people come to believe that what worked in the past will work in the future. Decades ago the Green Revolution alleviated hunger in Asia and Latin America by equipping farmers with more productive strains of wheat and rice. But in the words of Usha Tuteja, who heads the Agricultural Economics Research Center at Delhi University, "People got complacent." Governments, believing that the problem of feeding a growing population had been solved, stopped funding agricultural research. Unfortunately, today new challenges have again made food supply a major problem, and the solutions will require years of investment in further research.[40]

Change Agent Characteristics   As true for recipients, this cause includes a variety of individual differences (e.g., the big five personality dimensions discussed in Chapter 5) possessed by change agents. For example, one of us recently served as a change agent for a Scandinavian company and encountered resistance from some employees because they had negative views and stereotypes of Americans. Change agent characteristics also represent the actions or inactions displayed by change agents. For example, a change agent who fails to communicate with employees or is perceived as instituting unfair policies is likely to create resistance from recipients. Finally, resistance is a function of the change agent's perceptions of why employees are behaving the way they are in the face of organizational change. A change agent, for instance, might interpret employees' questions as a form of resistance when in fact the questions represent honest attempts at clarifying the change process. Five of the key change agent characteristics are discussed below:

1. *Decisions that disrupt cultural traditions or group relationships.* Whenever individuals are transferred, promoted, or reassigned, cultural and group dynamics are thrown into disequilibrium. It would be similar to your being

resistance to change Emotional/behavioral response to real or imagined work changes.

resilience to change Composite personal characteristic reflecting high self-esteem, optimism, and an internal locus of control.

moved from one team to another during the middle of a semester. Resistance would increase because of the uncertainty associated with dealing with new team members and their expectations.

2. *Personality conflicts.* Just as a friend can get away with telling us something we would resent hearing from an adversary, the personalities of change agents can breed resistance. Change agents that display any of the traits of bad leadership discussed in Chapter 16 are likely to engender resistance from recipients.

3. *Lack of tact or poor timing.* Undue resistance can occur because change agents introduce change in an insensitive manner or at an awkward time. Proposed organizational changes are more likely to be accepted by others when change agents effectively explain or "sell" the value of their proposed changes. This can be done by explaining how a proposed change is strategically important to an organization's success.

4. *Leadership style.* Research shows that people are less likely to resist change when the change agent uses transformational leadership (see Chapter 16).[41]

5. *Failing to legitimize change.* Change must be internalized by recipients before it will be truly accepted. Active, honest communication and reinforcing reward systems are needed to make this happen. This recommendation underscores the need for change agents to communicate with recipients in a way that considers employees' point-of-view and perspective. It also is important for change agents to explain how change will lead to positive personal and organizational benefits. This requires that change agents have a clear understanding about how recipients' jobs will change and how they will be rewarded.[42] For example, an employee is unlikely to support a change effort that is perceived as requiring him or her to work longer with more pressure without a commensurate increase in pay.

Change Agent–Recipient Relationship   In general, resistance is reduced when change agents and recipients have a positive, trusting relationship. Trust, as discussed in Chapter 11, involves reciprocal faith in others' intentions and behavior. Mutual mistrust can doom to failure an otherwise well-conceived change. Mistrust encourages secrecy, which begets deeper mistrust. Managers who trust their employees make the change process an open, honest, and participative affair. Employees who, in turn, trust management are more willing to expend extra effort and take chances with something different. In support of this conclusion, a study of employees from the oil and banking industries showed that a high-quality relationship between managers and direct reports was associated with less resistance to change.[43]

 LO.7 Alternative Strategies for Overcoming Resistance to Change

We previously noted that resistance is a form of feedback and managers need to understand why it is occurring before trying to overcome it. This can be done by considering the extent to which the three sources of resistance shown in Figure 18–5 are contributing to the problem. Consider employee characteristics as an example. Employees are more likely to resist when they perceive that the personal costs of change overshadow the benefits. If this is the case, then managers are advised to (1) provide as much information as possible to employees about the change, (2) inform employees about the reasons/rationale for the change, (3) conduct meetings to address employees' questions regarding the change, and (4) provide employees the opportunity to discuss how the proposed change might affect them. Using these recommendations also will improve the agent–recipient relationship because they enhance the level of trust between the parties.

real WORLD // real PEOPLE

Hospitals Work to Overcome Docs' Resistance to Using PCs

The US government has offered $27 billion in incentives for hospitals to convert to electronic medical records. "But performing such tasks as entering orders for medication and taking patients' medical histories by computer requires significant changes in work habits." For example, a survey of 150 hospital executives revealed that 79% were concerned about how to best train doctors and staff to properly use the records.

"To get doctors and care givers—some of whom are skeptical about the ability of electronic records to improve productivity or patient care—on board, hospitals are taking a range of approaches, including offering training any hour of the day or night, converting vacant buildings into training facilities and using computer programs to get physicians up to speed quickly."

One resister to this approach is the fact that "many physicians aren't fans of large classroom settings. 'No one likes to feel that they're not masters of the material, and they're frankly uncomfortable about being perceived as less than masterful,' says George Reynolds, chief information officer at Children's Hospital & Medical Center."

Doctors also don't like to be trained by nonphysicians, and they like trainers to come to them rather than vice versa. This can get quite expensive and inconvenient for those delivering the training. The training also can require a lot of time away from the job, which increases employee resistance. For example, labor and delivery nurses at Anne Arundel Health System required about 24 hours of training.

In the end, hospital administrators agree that it is "crucial to get key physicians behind the effort early." These physicians can play an important role in informally convincing their colleagues to "step up" and commit to taking the training.

What else can hospital administrators do to reduce resistance to change?

SOURCE: Excerpted from K Hobson, "Getting Docs to Use PCs," *The Wall Street Journal,* March 15, 2011, p B5.

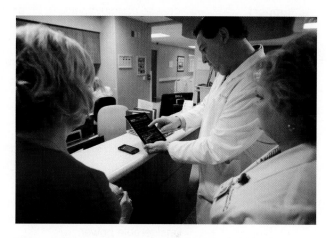

These doctors at Northwest Medical Center in Margate, Florida, are using an iPad app to review medical tests from a patient.

The Real World/Real People above illustrates how hospital administrators are using these recommendations to encourage medical doctors to incorporate PCs into their medical practice.

Moreover, Figure 18–5 cautions managers not to assume that people are consciously resisting change. Resistance has a cause and, according to John Kotter's research of more than 100 companies, the cause generally involves some obstacle in the work environment. He noted that obstacles in the organization's structure or in a "performance appraisal system [that] makes people choose between the new vision and their own self-interests" impeded change more than an individual's direct resistance.[44] This perspective implies that it is important for management to obtain employee feedback about any obstacles that may be affecting their ability or willingness to accept change. In the end, change agents should not be afraid to modify the targeted elements of change or their approach toward change based on employee resistance. If people are resisting for valid reasons, then a new change initiative is needed.

In addition to these suggestions, employee participation in the change process is another generic approach for reducing resistance. That said, however, organizational change experts have criticized the tendency to treat participation as a cure-all for resistance to change. They prefer a contingency approach because resistance can take many forms and, furthermore, because situational factors

table 18–2 Six Strategies for Overcoming Resistance to Change

APPROACH	COMMONLY USED IN SITUATIONS	ADVANTAGES	DRAWBACKS
Education + communication	Where there is a lack of information or inaccurate information and analysis.	Once persuaded, people will often help with the implementation of the change.	Can be very time-consuming if lots of people are involved.
Participation + involvement	Where the initiators do not have all the information they need to design the change and where others have considerable power to resist.	People who participate will be committed to implementing change, and any relevant information they have will be integrated into the change plan.	Can be very time-consuming if participators design an inappropriate change.
Facilitation + support	Where people are resisting because of adjustment problems.	No other approach works as well with adjustment problems.	Can be time-consuming, expensive, and still fail.
Negotiation + agreement	Where someone or some group will clearly lose out in a change and where that group has considerable power to resist.	Sometimes it is a relatively easy way to avoid major resistance.	Can be too expensive in many cases if it alerts others to negotiate for compliance.
Manipulation + co-optation	Where other tactics will not work or are too expensive.	It can be a relatively quick and inexpensive solution to resistance problems.	Can lead to future problems if people feel manipulated.
Explicit + implicit coercion	Where speed is essential and where the change initiators possess considerable power.	It is speedy and can overcome any kind of resistance.	Can be risky if it leaves people mad at the initiators.

SOURCE: Reprinted by permission of *Harvard Business Review.* Exhibit from "Choosing Strategies for Change," by J P Kotter and L A Schlesinger, March/April 1979. Copyright 1979 by the Harvard Business School Publishing Corporation; all rights reserved.

 Go to www.mcgrawhillconnect.com for a video case on change management at Louisville Slugger.

vary (see Table 18–2). As shown in Table 18–2, Participation + Involvement does have its place, but it takes time that is not always available. Also as indicated in Table 18–2, each of the other five methods has its situational niche, advantages, and drawbacks. For example, Manipulation + Co-optation may appear to be a negative approach, but it works in the right context. We once used co-optation, which involves giving a resistor a desirable role in the change process, in order to motivate the individual to endorse the change process. This approach ultimately led to a modification in the change process and the resistor's final endorsement. In short, there is no universal strategy for overcoming resistance to change. Managers need a complete repertoire of change strategies.[45]

LO.8 Dynamics of Stress

TO THE POINT

What are the key conclusions regarding the model of occupational stress, stress moderators, and stress reduction techniques?

The final section of this book deals with a topic that is common to all of us—stress. Whether you are a student, working professional, or professor, we all experience stress on a daily basis. Although stress is caused by many factors, researchers conclude that stress triggers one of two basic reactions: active fighting or passive flight (running away or acceptance), the so-called **fight-or-flight response**.[46] Physiologically, this stress response is a biochemical "passing gear" involving hormonal changes that mobilize the body for extraordinary demands.

Imagine how our prehistoric ancestors responded to the stress associated with a charging saber-toothed tiger. To avoid being eaten, they could stand their ground and fight the beast or run away. In either case, their bodies would have been energized by an identical hormonal change, involving the release of adrenaline into the bloodstream.

In today's hectic urbanized and industrialized society, charging beasts have been replaced by problems such as deadlines, roommate problems, student loans, conflicts with team members, information overload, technology, traffic congestion, noise and air pollution, family problems, and work overload. As with our ancestors, our response to stress may or may not trigger negative side effects, including headaches, ulcers, insomnia, heart disease, high blood pressure, strokes, insomnia, allergies, skin disorders, and mental illness.[47] The same stress response that helped our prehistoric ancestors survive has too often become a factor that seriously impairs our daily lives.

Because stress and its consequences are manageable, it is important for you to learn about occupational stress. After defining stress, this section provides an overview of the dynamics associated with stress by presenting a model of occupational stress, discussing moderators of occupational stress, and reviewing the effectiveness of several stress-reduction techniques.

Defining Stress

To an orchestra violinist, stress may stem from giving a solo performance before a big audience. While heat, smoke, and flames may represent stress to a firefighter, delivering a speech or presenting a lecture may be stressful for those who are shy. In short, stress means different things to different people. Managers need a working definition.

Formally defined, **stress** is "an adaptive response, mediated by individual characteristics and/or psychological processes, that is a consequence of any external action, situation, or event that places special physical and/or psychological demands upon a person."[48] This definition is not as difficult as it seems when we reduce it to three interrelated dimensions of stress: (1) environmental demands, referred to as stressors, that produce (2) an adaptive response that is influenced by (3) individual differences.

Hans Selye, considered the father of the modern concept of stress, pioneered the distinction between stressors and the stress response. Moreover, Selye emphasized that both positive and negative events can trigger an identical stress response that can be beneficial or harmful. He referred to stress that is positive or produces a positive outcome as **eustress.** Receiving an award in front of a large crowd or successfully completing a difficult work assignment both are examples of stressors that produce eustress. He also noted that

- Stress is not merely nervous tension.
- Stress can have positive consequences.
- Stress is not something to be avoided.
- The complete absence of stress is death.[49]

These points make it clear that stress is inevitable. Efforts need to be directed at managing stress, not at somehow escaping it altogether.

---

fight-or-flight response To either confront stressors or try to avoid them.

stress Behavioral, physical, or psychological response to stressors.

eustress Stress that is good or produces a positive outcome.

A Model of Occupational Stress

Figure 18–6 presents an instructive model of occupational stress. The model shows that an individual initially appraises four types of stressors. This appraisal then motivates an individual to choose a coping strategy aimed at managing stressors, which, in turn, produces a variety of outcomes. The model also specifies several individual differences that moderate the stress process. A moderator is a variable that causes the relationship between two variables—such as stressors and cognitive appraisal—to be stronger for some people and weaker for others. Three key moderators are discussed in the next section. Let us now consider the remaining components of this model in detail.

Stressors   **Stressors** are environmental factors that produce stress. Stated differently, stressors are a prerequisite to experiencing the stress response. Figure 18–6 shows the four major types of stressors: individual, group, organizational, and extraorganizational. Individual-level stressors are those directly associated with a person's job duties. The most common examples of individual stressors are job demands, work overload, role conflict, role ambiguity, everyday hassles, perceived control over events occurring in the work environment, and job characteristics.[50]

figure 18–6   A Model of Occupational Stress

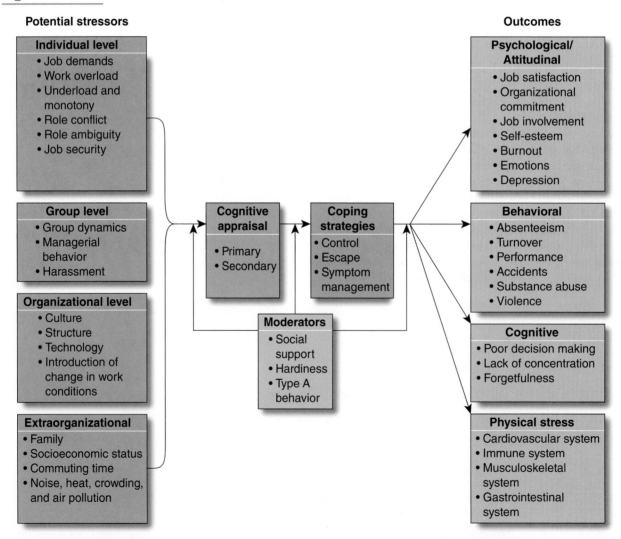

Losing one's job is another important individual-level stressor. Job loss is a very stressful event that is associated with decreased psychological and physical well-being. That said, recent research shows that psychological well-being is lower for people with really bad jobs than it is for unemployed individuals.[51] Finally, sleep-related issues are important stressors. Research shows that most people need about seven hours of sleep per night and that alertness, energy, performance, creativity, and thinking are related to how refreshed an employee feels when starting his or her workday.[52]

Group-level stressors are caused by group dynamics (recall our discussion in Chapter 10) and managerial behavior. Managers create stress for employees by (1) exhibiting inconsistent behaviors, (2) failing to provide support, (3) showing lack of concern, (4) providing inadequate direction, (5) creating a high-productivity environment, and (6) focusing on negatives while ignoring good performance. Sexual harassment experiences and bullying represent other group-level stressors.

Organizational stressors affect large numbers of employees. Organizational culture, which was discussed in Chapter 3, is a prime example. For instance, a high-pressure environment that fuels employee fear about performing up to standard can increase the stress response. The increased use of information technology is another source of organizational stress according to an international survey of 1,700 professionals. Results reveal that 59% of the respondents are overloaded and stressed by the amount of information they process at work. Unfortunately, a majority of these individuals report coping with this stressor by either deleting or ignoring work information.[53] We don't recommend this coping strategy. Finally, the air quality and ventilation found throughout an organization can represent organizational-level stressors. The World Health Organization, for instance, reports that roughly 30% of all new and remodeled buildings have problems related to air quality, and air quality is associated with a variety of conditions such as headaches, dizziness, and the ability to concentrate.[54]

Extraorganizational stressors are those caused by factors outside the organization. For instance, in Chapter 6 we discussed how conflicts associated with balancing one's career and family life are stressful. Socioeconomic status is another extraorganizational stressor. Stress is higher for people with lower socioeconomic status, which represents a combination of (1) economic status, as measured by income; (2) social status, assessed by education level; and (3) work status, as indexed by occupation. These stressors are likely to become more important in the future. In support of this conclusion, the American Psychological Association's national survey revealed that the majority of Americans cited money, work, and the economy as their biggest stressors.[55]

Cognitive Appraisal of Stressors

Cognitive appraisal reflects an individual's overall perception or evaluation of a situation or stressor. It is an important component within the stress process because people interpret the same stressors differently. For example, some of our students view a challenging assignment as an opportunity to showcase their talents, whereas others perceive it as a threat to achieving their desired grade in the class.

Figure 18–6 shows that people make two types of appraisals when evaluating the potential impact of stressors on their lives: primary and secondary appraisals.[56] A **primary appraisal** results in categorizing a situation or stressor as irrelevant, positive, or stressful. Stress appraisals are obviously the most important in terms of our current discussion because they imply that a situation or stressor is perceived as harmful, threatening, or challenging.

stressors Environmental factors that produce stress.

primary appraisal Determining whether a stressor is irrelevant, positive, or stressful.

A **secondary appraisal** occurs only in response to a stressful primary appraisal and entails an assessment of what might and can be done to reduce the level of perceived stress. During this evaluation a person considers which coping strategies are available and which ones are most likely to help resolve the situation at hand. Ultimately, the combination of an individual's primary and secondary appraisal influences the choice of coping strategies used to reduce stress.

Coping Strategies   Coping strategies are characterized by the specific behaviors and cognitions used to cope with a situation. People use a combination of three approaches to cope with stressors and stress (see Figure 18–6). The first, called a **control strategy,** consists of using behaviors and cognitions to directly anticipate or solve problems. A control strategy has a take-charge tone. Examples include talking to your professor or boss about workload if you feel overwhelmed with your responsibilities, and confronting someone who is spreading negative rumors. Results from a meta-analysis of 34 studies indicated that control coping was positively related to overall health outcomes.[57] People are more apt to use control coping when they possess high self-esteem, self-efficacy, and problem-solving skills.[58]

Researchers have uncovered a very useful control-oriented strategy that can be used by everyone. It is called **psychological detachment,** and is defined as not being involved in work-related activities, thoughts, or feelings during nonwork time.[59] These activities can include making phone calls, answering e-mail, thinking about projects and activities that must be completed in the near term, and just plain thinking and talking about people at work. The good news is that psychological detachment is positively associated with life satisfaction and psychological well-being, and negatively with emotional exhaustion and psychosomatic complaints.[60] We thus recommend that you try to detach from your work-related responsibilities while at home. This can be done by simply reserving a time period in which you will not engage in any work-related activities or thoughts. And yes, we know that this is easier to say than it is to do.

In contrast to tackling the problem head-on, an **escape strategy** amounts to avoiding the problem. Behaviors and cognitions are used to avoid or escape situations. Individuals use this strategy when they passively accept stressful situations or avoid them by failing to confront the cause of stress (an obnoxious co-worker, for instance). Finally, a **symptom management strategy** consists of using methods such as relaxation, meditation, medication, or exercise to manage the symptoms of occupational stress. A vacation, for example, can be a good way to reduce the symptoms of stress. Other people may drink or take drugs to reduce stress. In contrast, one of this book's authors snuggles with his golden retriever while the other pets his cats to relieve stress.

Stress Outcomes   Theorists contend stress has psychological/attitudinal, behavioral, cognitive, and physical health consequences or outcomes. A large body of research supports the negative effects of perceived stress on many aspects of our lives. Workplace stress is negatively related to job satisfaction, organizational commitment, organizational citizenship behavior, positive emotions, and performance, and positively with emotional exhaustion, burnout, absenteeism, and turnover.[61] Research also shows that stress is associated with negative behaviors such as yelling and verbal abuse and violence toward others. It also is associated with the frequency of drinking and taking illicit drugs.[62] These stress outcomes are very costly to individuals and organizations alike. Finally, ample evidence supports the conclusion that stress negatively affects our physical and psychological health. Stress contributes to the following physical and mental health problems: lessened ability to ward off illness and infection, high blood pressure, coronary artery disease, tension headaches, back pain, diarrhea, constipation, and psychological well-being.[63] In fact, it's stressful to even think about all of these problems!

LO.9 Moderators of Occupational Stress

Moderators, once again, are variables that cause the relationships between stressors, perceived stress, and outcomes to be weaker for some people and stronger for others. Managers with a working knowledge of important stress moderators can confront employee stress in the following ways:

1. Awareness of moderators helps identify those most likely to experience stress and its negative outcomes. Stress-reduction programs then can be formulated for high-risk employees.

2. Moderators, in and of themselves, suggest possible solutions for reducing negative outcomes of occupational stress.

Keeping these objectives in mind, we will examine three important moderators: social support, hardiness, and Type A behavior.

Social Support

Talking with a friend or taking part in a bull session can be comforting during times of fear, stress, or loneliness. For a variety of reasons, meaningful social relationships help people do a better job of handling stress.

Social support is the amount of perceived helpfulness derived from social relationships. Importantly, social support is determined by both the quantity and quality of an individual's social relationships. We receive four types of social support from others:

- *Esteem support.* Providing information that a person is accepted and respected despite any problems or inadequacies.
- *Informational support.* Providing help in defining, understanding, and coping with problems.
- *Social companionship.* Spending time with others in leisure and recreational activities.
- *Instrumental support.* Providing financial aid, material resources, or needed services.[64]

Research shows that social support is negatively related to physiological processes and mortality. In other words, people with low social support tend to have poorer cardiovascular and immune system functioning and tend to die earlier than those with strong social support networks. Further, social support protects against the perception of stress, depression, psychological problems, pregnancy complications, anxiety, loneliness, high blood pressure, and a variety of other ailments. In contrast, negative social support, which amounts to someone undermining another person, negatively affects one's mental health.[65] We are well advised to avoid people who try to undermine us.

Social support research highlights two practical recommendations. First, managers are advised to keep employees informed about external and internal social support systems. Internally, managers can use all four forms of social support when employees experience a personal crisis. Coping with a divorce is a good example. Second, participative management programs and company-sponsored

secondary appraisal Assessing what might and can be done to reduce stress.

control strategy Coping strategy that directly confronts or solves problems.

psychological detachment Not being involved in work-related activities, thoughts, or feelings during nonwork time.

escape strategy Coping strategy that avoids or ignores stressors and problems.

symptom management strategy Coping strategy that focuses on reducing the symptoms of stress.

social support Amount of helpfulness derived from social relationships.

real WORLD // real PEOPLE

Recommendations for Improving Relationships with Others

1. Share more about yourself. Be willing to open up about what is going on in your life. This increases trust between you and others and enables them to provide the type of support you need.
2. Set aside time each day to talk with those you care about. You might consider setting a time limit for the conversation so that both parties have ample time to speak. This is important when one of you is talkative and the other isn't.
3. Spend time talking outdoors. Being outdoors reduces stress by itself. Walking and talking also reduces the need for eye contact, which sometimes can help talking about sensitive or emotional issues.
4. Turn off the electronics. Too many of us try to communicate with others while multitasking with

some type of electronic device. Devote your time with another individual to that person and that person only. In other words, stay in the moment and don't allow electronics to become a distraction. This practice shows that you are solely focused on the individual with whom you are communicating.
5. Make an effort to meet new people. You can expand your social support system by extending yourself to someone you would like to meet.

SOURCE: Based in part on E Bernstein, "Making 2011 the Year of Great Relationships," *The Wall Street Journal,* December 28, 2010, pp D1, D3.

activities that make employees feel they are an important part of an extended family can be rich sources of social support. Employees need time and energy to adequately maintain their social relationships. If organizational demands are excessive, employees' social relationships and support networks will suffer, resulting in stress-related illness and decreased performance.

If the above discussion motivates you to focus on the state of your interpersonal relationships, then you will enjoy reading the Real World/Real People above. It provides recommendations for improving your interactions with friends, family, and co-workers.

Hardiness   Suzanne Kobasa, a behavioral scientist, identified a collection of personality characteristics that neutralize occupational stress. This collection of characteristics, referred to as **hardiness,** involves the ability to perceptually or behaviorally transform negative stressors into positive challenges. Hardiness embraces the personality dimensions of commitment, locus of control, and challenge.[66]

Social support helps us deal with the ups and downs of life. A simple touch can be very comforting to someone in need.

Commitment reflects the extent to which an individual is involved in whatever he or she is doing. Committed people have a sense of purpose and do not give up under pressure because they tend to invest themselves in the situation. As discussed in Chapter 5, individuals with an *internal locus of control* believe they can influence the events that affect their lives. People possessing this trait are more likely to foresee stressful events, thereby reducing their exposure to anxiety-producing situations. Moreover, their perception of being in control leads "internals" to use proactive coping strategies. *Challenge* is represented by the belief that change is a normal part of life. Hence, change is seen as an opportunity for growth and development rather than a threat to security.

Research supports the moderating influence of hardiness on the stress process.[67] This in turn has led to the development of organizational training and development programs that strengthen the characteristics of commitment, personal control, and challenge. For example, a team of researchers developed a hardiness training program based on this recommendation and tested it on a group of students and working adults. Results revealed that students' grade point average, retention, and health improved after the training. Training also resulted in increased performance, job satisfaction, and health for the working adults.[68] The hardiness concept also meshes nicely with job design. Enriched jobs are likely to fuel the hardiness components of commitment and challenge. A final application of the hardiness concept is as a diagnostic tool. Employees scoring low on hardiness would be good candidates for stress-reduction programs.

Type A Behavior Pattern   According to Meyer Friedman and Ray Rosenman (the cardiologists who isolated the Type A syndrome in the 1950s):

Example. **Type A behavior pattern** is an action-emotion complex that can be observed in any person who is aggressively involved in a chronic, incessant struggle to achieve more and more in less and less time, and if required to do so, against the opposing efforts of other things or persons. It is not psychosis or a complex of worries or fears or phobias or obsessions, but a socially acceptable—indeed often praised—form of conflict. Persons possessing this pattern also are quite prone to exhibit a free-floating but, extraordinarily well-rationalized hostility. As might be expected, there are degrees in the intensity of this behavior pattern.[69]

While labeling Type A behavior as "hurry sickness," Friedman and Rosenman noted that Type A individuals frequently tend to exhibit most of the behaviors listed in Table 18–3.

Because Type A behavior is a matter of degree, it is measured on a continuum. This continuum has the hurried, competitive Type A behavior pattern at one end and the more relaxed Type B behavior pattern at the other. Let us now consider the pros and cons of being Type A. OB research has demonstrated that Type A employees tend to be more productive than their Type B co-workers. For instance, Type A behavior yielded a significant and positive correlation with 766 students' grade point averages, the quantity and quality of 278 university professors' performance, and sales performance of 222 life insurance brokers.[70] On the other hand, Type A behavior is associated with some negative consequences. A meta-analysis of 729 studies revealed that Type A individuals had higher cardiovascular hyperactivity (e.g., heart rates, diastolic blood pressure, and systolic blood pressure) than Type B people. In turn, this hyperactivity was associated with heart disease and cardiac mortality.[71] Type A people also showed greater cardiovascular activity when they encountered the following situations:

1. Receipt of positive or negative feedback.
2. Receipt of verbal harassment or criticism.
3. Tasks requiring mental as opposed to physical work.[72]

---

hardiness Personality characteristic that neutralizes stress.

Type A behavior pattern Aggressively involved in a chronic, determined struggle to accomplish more in less time.

table 18–3 Type A Characteristics

1. Hurried speech; explosive accentuation of key words.

2. Tendency to walk, move, and eat rapidly.

3. Constant impatience with the rate at which most events take place (e.g., irritation with slow-moving traffic and slow-talking and slow-to-act people).

4. Strong preference for thinking of or doing two or more things at once (e.g., reading this text and doing something else at the same time).

5. Tendency to turn conversations around to personally meaningful subjects or themes.

6. Tendency to interrupt while others are speaking to make your point or to complete their train of thought in your own words.

7. Guilt feelings during periods of relaxation or leisure time.

8. Tendency to be oblivious to surroundings during daily activities.

9. Greater concern for things worth *having* than with things worth *being*.

10. Tendency to schedule more and more in less and less time; a chronic sense of time urgency.

11. Feelings of competition rather than compassion when faced with another Type A person.

12. Development of nervous tics or characteristic gestures.

13. A firm belief that success is due to the ability to get things done faster than the other guy.

14. A tendency to view and evaluate personal activities and the activities of other people in terms of "numbers" (e.g., number of meetings attended, telephone calls made, visitors received).

SOURCE: Adapted from M Friedman and R H Rosenman, *Type A Behavior and Your Heart* (Greenwich, CT: Fawcett Publications, 1974), pp 100–2.

Unfortunately for Type A individuals, these situations are frequently experienced at work. A second meta-analysis of 83 studies further demonstrated that the hard-driving and competitive aspects of Type A are related to coronary heart disease, but the speed and impatience and job involvement aspects are not. This meta-analysis also showed that feelings of anger, hostility, and aggression were more strongly related to heart disease than was Type A behavior.[73] Do these results signal the need for Type A individuals to quit working so hard? Not necessarily. First off, the research indicated that feelings of anger, hostility, and aggression were more detrimental to our health than being Type A. We should all attempt to reduce these negative emotions. Second, researchers have developed stress-reduction techniques to help Type A people pace themselves more realistically and achieve better balance in their lives; they are discussed in the next section. Management can help Type A people, however, by not overloading them with work despite their apparent eagerness to take an ever-increasing workload. Managers need to actively help rather than unthinkingly exploit Type A individuals.

LO.10 Stress-Reduction Techniques

Stress is costly to individuals, groups, and organizations as a whole. The American Institute of Stress, for instance, estimates that work stress costs US industries about $300 billion a year. It thus is not surprising that organizations are increasingly implementing a variety of stress-reduction programs to help employees cope with modern-day stress.[74]

table 18–4   Stress-Reduction Techniques

TECHNIQUE	DESCRIPTION	ASSESSMENT
Muscle relaxation	Uses slow, deep breathing and systematic muscle tension reduction.	Inexpensive and easy to use; may require a trained professional to implement.
Biofeedback	A machine is used to train people to detect muscular tension; muscle relaxation is then used to alleviate this symptom of stress.	Expensive due to costs of equipment; however, equipment can be used to evaluate effectiveness of other stress-reduction programs.
Meditation	The relaxation response is activated by redirecting one's thoughts away from oneself; a four-step procedure is used to attain a passive stress-free state of mind.	Least expensive, simple to implement, and can be practiced almost anywhere.
Cognitive restructuring	Irrational or maladaptive thoughts are identified and replaced with those that are rational or logical.	Expensive because it requires a trained psychologist or counselor.
Holistic wellness	A broad, interdisciplinary approach that goes beyond stress reduction by advocating that people strive for personal wellness in all aspects of their lives.	Involves inexpensive but often behaviorally difficult lifestyle changes.

There are many different stress-reduction techniques available. The four most frequently used approaches are muscle relaxation, biofeedback, meditation, and cognitive restructuring. Each method involves somewhat different ways of coping with stress (see Table 18–4). Although research supports the positive benefits of all these techniques, a meta-analysis of 55 stress management interventions demonstrated that cognitive restructuring was most effective.[75] Professor Martin Seligman, known as the father of positive psychology, developed a five-step process of cognitive restructuring that focuses on getting people to stop thinking pessimistically about an event or problem. He called it the ABCDEs, and it is illustrated below.[76]

- **A**—Name the event or problem. (For example: My roommate is going to move out, and I can't afford to pay the rent by myself.)
- **B**—List your beliefs about the event or problem. (I don't have any prospects for a new roommate, and I may have to move. I might have to move back home and quit school. I could ask my parents for money, but they really can't afford to pay my rent. I could move to a lower priced single apartment in a bad area of town.)
- **C**—Identify the consequences of your beliefs. (I'm going to move back home for spring semester and will return in the fall.)
- **D**—Formulate a disputation of your beliefs. It is important to remember that pessimistic thoughts are generally overreactions, so the first step is to correct inaccurate or distorted thoughts. (I have not studied my expenses closely, and I may be able to afford the apartment. Even if I can't afford the apartment right now, I could get a part-time job which would cover the additional expenses. I could advertise on Craig's list or the student newspaper for a new roommate. I don't have to accept a bad roommate, but worst case scenario is that I have to carry the added expenses for one semester.)

Connect™   Go to www.mcgrawhillconnect.com for an interactive exercise to test your knowledge of the stress reduction techniques.

- **E**—Describe how energized and empowered you feel at the moment. (I'm motivated to find a new roommate and get a part-time job. I have taken care of myself throughout college and there is no reason I can't continue to resolve this short-term problem.)

Seligman's research reveals that this technique works quite well over time. The key is to stay with your ABCDEs and not to expect "instantaneous" results. Try it next time you encounter an event or problem that is stressing you out.

Despite the positive results of all four stress reduction techniques, some researchers advise organizations not to implement them. They rationalize that these techniques relieve *symptoms* of stress rather than eliminate stressors themselves.[77] Thus, they conclude that organizations are using a Band-Aid approach to stress reduction.

This recommendation has led to the creation of much broader approaches toward stress reduction. Two of the broadest approaches entail the use of employee assistance programs and for individuals to use a holistic wellness approach. Let us consider each of these approaches toward stress reduction.

Employee Assistance Programs (EAPs)   **Employee assistance programs** consist of a broad array of programs aimed at helping employees to deal with personal problems such as substance abuse, health-related problems, family and marital issues, and other problems that negatively affect their job performance. EAPs are typically provided by employers or in combination with unions. Employees use these services as part of their benefit package. Alternatively, referral-only EAPs simply provide managers with telephone numbers that they can distribute to employees in need of help. Employees then pay for these services themselves.

Holistic Wellness Approach   A **holistic wellness approach** encompasses and goes beyond stress reduction by advocating that individuals strive for "a harmonious and productive balance of physical, mental, and social well-being brought about by the acceptance of one's personal responsibility for developing and adhering to a health promotion program."[78] While the costs of a wellness program vary, a 2009 survey of 121 mid-size US companies revealed that the average cost was 2% of the company's total annual health care claim dollars.[79] The benefits, however, far exceed the costs. For example, Johnson & Johnson found that the company's wellness program saved $250 million on health care costs in the last 10 years. These savings amount to a return of $2.71 for every dollar spend on the program.[80] These results in combination with findings from a meta-analysis of 17 studies suggest that organizations should consider the benefits of wellness programs. Meta-analytic findings revealed that employee participation in wellness programs was positively associated with job satisfaction and negatively with absenteeism.[81] Five dimensions of a holistic wellness approach are as follows:

1. *Self-responsibility.* Take personal responsibility for your wellness (e.g., quit smoking, moderate your intake of alcohol, wear your seat belt, and eat less food). As a case in point, experts estimate that 50 to 70% of all diseases are caused by lifestyle choices under our control.[82]

2. *Nutritional awareness.* Because we are what we eat, try to increase your consumption of foods high in fiber, vitamins, and nutrients—such as fresh fruits and vegetables, poultry, and fish—while decreasing those high in sugar and fat. Experts recommend that you eat a daily serving of walnuts and strawberries. The walnuts will lower your blood pressure and strawberries provide vitamin C and other important antioxidants.[83]

3. *Stress reduction and relaxation.* Use techniques to relax and reduce the symptoms of stress.

real WORLD // real PEOPLE

Ohio Health and IBM Use Incentives to Encourage People to Participate in Wellness Programs

Ohio Health, a central Ohio hospital chain, last year embarked on a program that paid employees to wear pedometers and get paid for walking. They more they walk, the more they win. Ohio Health set the maximum reward for its step-counting program at $500. . . . Half of the 9,000 employees at the chain's five main hospitals signed up, more than $377,000 in rewards have already been paid out, and many workers tell of weight loss and a sudden need for slimmer clothes. . . .

IBM's worksite wellness program is often called a model, with roughly half of the work force earning at least $150 a year for taking part. The company rewards employees for doing 12-week Web-based health programs.

SOURCE: Excerpted from "Employees Earn Cash for Exercising More," *The Wall Street Journal*, June 2, 2010, p D3.

---

4. *Physical fitness.* Exercise regularly to maintain strength, flexibility, endurance, and a healthy body weight. A review of employee fitness programs indicated that they were a cost-effective way to reduce medical costs, absenteeism, turnover, and occupational injuries. Because many people do not like to exercise, more companies have begun to use incentives as vehicles to motivate employees to exercise. Experts estimate that about 53% of large companies offer incentives for participating in wellness programs.[84] Consider the approaches used by OhioHealth and IBM (see Real World/Real People above).

5. *Environmental sensitivity.* Be aware of your environment and try to identify the stressors that are causing your stress. A control coping strategy might be useful to eliminate stressors.

employee assistance programs Help employees to resolve personal problems that affect their productivity.

holistic wellness approach Advocates personal responsibility for healthy living.

Summary of Key Concepts

1. *Discuss the external and internal forces that create the need for organizational change.* Organizations encounter both external and internal forces for change. There are five key external forces for change: demographic characteristics, technological advancements, customer and market changes, social and political pressures, and organizational crises. Internal forces for change come from both human resource problems and managerial behavior/decisions.

2. *Describe Lewin's change model and the systems model of change.* Lewin developed a three-stage model of planned change that explained how to initiate, manage, and stabilize the change process. The three stages were unfreezing, which entails creating the motivation to change; changing; and stabilizing change through refreezing. A systems model of change takes a big picture perspective of change. It focuses on the interaction among the key components of change. The three main components of change are inputs, target elements of change, and outputs. The target elements of change represent the components of an organization that may be changed. They include organizational arrangements, social factors, methods, and people.

3. *Discuss Kotter's eight steps for leading organizational change.* John Kotter believes that organizational change fails owing to one or more of eight common errors. He proposed eight steps that organizations should follow to overcome these errors. The eight steps are (*a*) establish a sense of urgency, (*b*) create the guiding coalition, (*c*) develop a vision and strategy, (*d*) communicate the change vision, (*e*) empower broad-based action, (*f*) generate short-term wins, (*g*) consolidate gains and produce more change, and (*h*) anchor new approaches in the culture.

4. *Define organization development (OD), and explain the OD process.* Organization development is a set of tools or techniques that are used to implement planned organizational change. OD is broader in focus and has a diagnostic focus. OD is guided by a four-step process. The steps are (*a*) diagnosis, (*b*) intervention, (*c*) evaluation, and (*d*) feedback.

5. *Explain the dynamic model of resistance to change.* The model contradicts the traditional assumption that resistance to change is caused by irrational and self-serving recipients. Rather, resistance is viewed as being caused by the dynamic interactions among three key sources of resistance. They are recipient characteristics, change agent characteristics, and the quality of the change agent–recipient relationships. Managers need to consider all three sources of resistance when trying to manage resistance to change.

6. *Discuss the key recipient and change agent characteristics that cause resistance to change.* There are six key recipient characteristics. They are (*a*) an individual's predisposition toward change, (*b*) surprise and fear of the unknown, (*c*) fear of failure, (*d*) loss of status and/ or job security, (*e*) peer pressure, and (*f*) past success. The five key change agent characteristics include the following: (*a*) decisions that disrupt cultural traditions or group relationships, (*b*) personality conflicts, (*c*) lack of tact or poor timing, (*d*) leadership style, and (*e*) failing to legitimize change.

7. *Identify alternative strategies for overcoming resistance to change.* The first step is to use the dynamic model of resistance to diagnose the causes of employee resistance. The second is to consider characteristics in the work environment that may represent obstacles to change. These obstacles then need to be eliminated. Finally, managers can adopt one or more of the generic strategies for overcoming resistance to change. They are education + communication, participation + involvement, facilitation + support, negotiation + agreement, manipulation + co-optation, and explicit + implicit coercion. Each has its situational appropriateness and advantages and drawbacks.

8. *Define the term* stress *and describe the model of occupational stress.* Stress is an adaptive reaction to environmental demands or stressors that triggers a fight-or-flight response. This response creates hormonal changes that mobilize the body for extraordinary demands. According to the occupational model of stress, the stress process begins when an individual cognitively appraises stressors. This appraisal then motivates an individual to choose a coping strategy aimed at reducing stressors, which, in turn, results in a variety of stress outcomes.

9. *Discuss the stress moderators of social support, hardiness, and Type A behavior.* People use each of these moderators to help reduce the impact of stressors that are appraised as harmful, threatening, or challenging. Social support represents the amount of perceived helpfulness derived from social relationships. People use four types of support (esteem, informational, social, and instrumental) to reduce the impact of stress. Hardiness is a collection of personality characteristics that neutralize stress. It includes the characteristics of commitment, locus of control, and challenge. The Type A behavior pattern is characterized by someone who is aggressively involved in a chronic, determined struggle to accomplish more and more in less and less time. Management can help Type A individuals by not overloading them with work despite their apparent eagerness to take on an ever-increasing workload.

10. *Review the four key stress-reduction techniques and the components of a holistic approach toward stress reduction.* The four key stress-reduction techniques are muscle relaxation, biofeedback, meditation, and cognitive restructuring. Cognitive restructuring was found to be the most effective technique. A holistic approach toward wellness goes beyond stress-reduction techniques by advocating that people strive for a harmonious balance among physical, mental, and social well-being. This approach to stress management has five key components: self-responsibility, nutritional awareness, stress reduction and relaxation, physical fitness, and environmental sensitivity.

Key Terms

External forces for change, 530

Telepresence, 532

Internal forces for change, 533

Benchmarking, 536

Mission statement, 538

Target elements of change, 540

Organization development, 543

Change agent, 543

Resistance to change, 546

Resilience to change, 546

Fight-or-flight response, 550

Stress, 551

Eustress, 551

Stressors, 552

Primary appraisal, 553

Secondary appraisal, 554

Control strategy, 554

Psychological detachment, 554

Escape strategy, 554

Symptom management strategy, 554

Social support, 555

Hardiness, 556

Type A behavior pattern, 557

Employee assistance programs, 560

Holistic wellness approach, 560

OB in Action Case Study

HCL Technologies Transforms Itself to Compete with the Big IT Services Firms[85]

Vineet Nayar, CEO of HCL Technologies, a Delhi-based IT services provider, was interviewed by the *Harvard Business Review* regarding the company's transformation. His interview is summarized in this case.

Although the company's revenues were growing by about 30% a year, it was losing market share and mindshare. Competitors were growing at the rate of 40% or 50% a year, and the IT services industry was changing rapidly. Customers didn't want to work with an undifferentiated service provider that offered discrete services; they wanted long-term partners that would provide end-to-end services. Could HCL become such a company?

History will tell you it did. By 2009 HCL had changed its business model, nearly tripled its annual revenues, doubled its market capitalization, been ranked India's best employer by Hewitt—and pioneered a unique management culture that I call Employees First, Customers Second (EFCS).

How did I do this? I didn't. One hundred senior managers and 55,000 employees, the people of our company, accomplished the transformation. . . .

I realized that no one would jump into the future until the organization acknowledged that we needed to do so. So I spent the first few weeks of my tenure visiting HCL's offices around the world, meeting senior managers in small groups and at larger gatherings. I discussed the company's current situation—Point A, I call it. . . .

I also met with customers during my travels, and it was from them that a potential Point B—where we should land—began to take shape. What struck me was that customers didn't talk much about our products, services, or technologies; they spoke mostly about HCL's employees. The value the company offered lay in the interface between customers and frontline employees—that was our value zone.

However, we weren't organized as if that was the case. HCL was a traditional pyramid, in which frontline people were accountable to a hierarchy of managers. The hierarchy usually made it more difficult for employees to add value. . . .

I had told everyone that we would set a strategy collaboratively—and I meant it. In July 2005 I convened a meeting of our top 100 managers and proposed that HCL transform itself from an IT services vendor into an end-to-end global IT services partner that could compete against the likes of IBM, Accenture, and EDS. . . .

The "Yes, buts . . ." took three forms. Some managers feared that by taking on the major global players, we would forsake the position we had built over the past decade and would lose everything. Others raised issues I hadn't thought of, asking, for example, "The IT analyst favor the established players—how can we get them to recommend HCL?" A third group supported the proposed strategy and was exasperated with the status quo. These

managers wanted us to act boldly, and often to ignore others' objections.

I said very little during these discussions. . . . Three days of debate later, we agreed to adopt the strategy I had proposed. Everyone was on board—at least in theory.

During this period I also held informal meetings with frontline employees, engaging them in discussions about the kind of company they wanted to work for and how they saw their jobs. These meetings became more formal in 2006, with a series of companywide meetings we called Directions. (We still hold them.) They involve thousands of employees and take place in large venues around the world. . . .

Transformation requires action, not just words, but I don't believe in large-scale technology initiatives or massive reorganizations. We triggered change at HCL through small-scale catalysts. . . .

Sharing financial data. At the time, employees had access to the financial information that pertained to their projects but didn't know how either their business unit or the organization was doing. Nor could they compare the performance of their team to that of others. We decided to share financial data extensively, within and across groups. . . .

The smart service desk. I set up an online system that allows anyone in the organization to lodge a complaint or make a suggestion by opening a ticket. We have a defined process for handling tickets . . . and the employee who opened the ticket determines whether its resolution is satisfactory. Not only does the system help resolve issues, but it effectively puts managers in the service of frontline employees.

The comprehensive 360-degree. Although HCL had a 360-degree performance review system in place, employees rarely reviewed managers because they didn't know what they stood to gain by doing so. I decided to allow anyone who had provided feedback to a manager to see the results. . . . I knew I couldn't force managers to make their reviews public; I could only encourage them to do so. The best way to do that was to lead by example. In 2006 I posted the results of my 360-degree appraisal on the intranet for all the company to see. Most managers followed suit. . . .

The online planning process. Rather than reviewing the business plans of my 100 managers, as had been the case earlier, I asked managers to make video recordings summarizing their plans and post them on an online portal, where other managers could review them, share feedback, and discuss changes. This made a difference in how managers formulated and communicated ideas. Consequently, plans became more specific and executable. . . .

I wanted passion. We developed a new survey, the Employee Passion Indicative Count, to identify the drivers of passion in the workplace. This led to the creation of Employees First Councils, groups that focus on specific passions, from art and music to philanthropy and social responsibility. The councils help employees break down the barriers between their personal and professional lives and bring more meaning to their work. These groups had one unexpected benefit: Some sprang up around business issues, such as cloud computing, which channeled personal passion into company innovation. . . .

The most difficult decision to make about transformation is when to start. We began when HCL was still growing at a healthy clip. We may appear to have been early, but I'm convinced that if we hadn't made our move, HCL wouldn't be so successful today.

Questions for Discussion

1. What were the external and internal forces for change at HCL?

2. To what extent did Vineet Nayar follow the change models proposed by Lewin and Kotter? Explain.

3. Which of the target elements of change within the systems model of change were affected by the changes at HCL?

4. What did Vineet Nayar do to overcome resistance to change? Could he have done anything differently? Explain.

5. What did this case teach you about organizational change? Discuss.

Legal/Ethical Challenge

Is There an Ethical Way to Implement Downsizing without Hurting Your Best Employees?[86]

Intel has restructured and eliminated about 10,500 jobs during the past 20 months. The company decided to make these cuts owing to declining revenue and market share. Intel used a quantitative approach in making the cuts. That is, the company studied workforce demographics and determined what areas were most in need of cuts and then reassigned people based on where they might best contribute to the company's future plans. The managerial ranks were reduced the most. Corporate executives are pleased with the process because the company is now more profitable and competitive.

In contrast, some employees believe that the company "botched the restructuring in ways that have harmed morale, employee development and long-term leadership quality." Interviews with employees uncovered complaints that "Intel disregarded employees' passions in reorganizing, squandered the talents of HR specialists and unwisely shifted leadership training efforts from lower-level managers to upper-level executives." Disgruntled employees believe that Intel did not consider employees' interests during the restructuring. An internal memo obtained by Workforce Management indicated that senior management knew they would be losing quality employees. The memo states: "We know we are losing good people in this move. But we have too many managers, and this manager reduction is necessary to improve our decision making and communication and to resize the company. In addition, since we need to become a leaner company and are limiting job openings, redeploying their skills, as individual contributors or as managers, is not a reasonable option."

Solving the dilemma: How would you have handled the layoffs at Intel?

1. Intel's approach sounds logical to me. Revenues are up, and the company just unveiled a new processing chip that *Time* called the best invention of the year. You can't make everyone happy when you let go more than 10,000 people.

2. Downsizing solely by the numbers is bad. Management should have accommodated employees' passions and interests when restructuring, even if it resulted in fewer cuts than desired. In the long run, this will lead to higher employee satisfaction and performance.

3. It sounds like the criticisms are being leveled by people who don't like their new assignments. They should quit complaining and be happy that they are still employed.

4. I am not sure that there is an optimum approach. It is impossible to balance the short-term goal of reducing costs while maintaining a positive work environment in which people are doing the type of work they are passionate about.

5. Invent other interpretations or options. Discuss.

Web Resources

For study material and exercises that apply to this chapter, visit our website at **www.mhhe.com/kreitner10e**

Photo Credits

CHAPTER 1

Page 4: © Isaaz Brekken/The New York Times/Redux; page 8: Women in the Relay Assembly Test Room, ca. 1930. Western Electric Company Hawthorne Studies Collection. Baker Library Historical Collections. Harvard Business School.; page 15: © Saul Loeb/AFP/Getty Images; page 17: © Sajjad Hussain/AFP/Getty Images; page 20: © Mario Tama/Getty Images; page 23: © Jon T. Fritz/MCT via Getty Images.

CHAPTER 2

Page 38: © Fabrice Dimier/Bloomberg via Getty Images; page 40: © Joe Raedle/Getty Images; page 41: Courtesy of CareFirst BlueCross BlueShield; page 44: AP Photo/Lisa Poole; page 48: © Michaela Rehle/Reuters; page 49: © Patrick Ryan/Getty Images; page 54: Courtesy of General Electric.

CHAPTER 3

Page 64: © Joe Raedle/Getty Images; page 68: © Tim Boyle/Getty Images; page 71: © Jacob Kepler/Bloomberg via Getty Images; page 76: © Jared McMillen/Aurora Photos/Corbis; page 77: © Noah Seelam/AFP/Getty Images; page 84: © Karen Bleier/AFP/Getty Images.

CHAPTER 4

Page 90: © Robert Kreitner; page 95: © Joe Kohen/WireImage/Getty Images; page 102: © Robert Kreitner; page 105: © Michael Newman/PhotoEdit; page 106: Courtesy of Margaret A. Sova; page 110: © John Gress/Reuters/Corbis.

CHAPTER 5

Page 122: © Justin Sullivan/Getty Images; page 126: © David Deal Photography; page 129: © Patrik Stollarz/AFP/Getty Images; page 136: © Big Cheese Photo/Jupiter Images; page 139: © David Young-Wolff/Stone/Getty Images; page 145: © Erik S. Lesser/Bloomberg via Getty Images.

CHAPTER 6

Page 153: © Chris Jackson/Getty Images; page 154: AP Photo/Richard Drew; page 157: © E. Dygas/Getty Images; page 161: AP Photo/Tuscaloosa News, Dusty Compton; page 166: © Brendan Hoffman/Bloomberg via Getty Images.

CHAPTER 7

Page 184: © Matthew Totton/Alamy; page 185: Image Courtesy of The Advertising Archives; page 192: AP Photo/David J. Phillip; page 194: Reprinted with permission of the Society for Human Resource Management (www.shrm.org), Alexandria, VA, publisher of *HR Magazine*. © SHRM; page 196: © Jon Kopaloff/FilmMagic; page 200: AP Photo/Eric Francis.

CHAPTER 8

Page 208: © Andrew Harrer/Bloomberg via Getty Images; page 212: © Christopher J. Morris/Corbis; page 215: © STR/AFP/Getty Images; page 222: © Bill Pugliano/Getty Images; page 223: Paul Sakuma/AP/dapd; page 229: © Monty Rakusen/Cultura/Getty Images; page 230: © Matthias Tunger/Digital Vision/Getty Images.

CHAPTER 9

Page 240: © Fred Prouser/Reuters/Corbis; page 243: © Dilip Vishwanat/Getty Images; page 244: AP Photo/Mark Humphrey; page 251: © Justin Sullivan/Getty Images; page 254: © Michael A. Foley/MAF Photography; page 256: Courtesy of Margaret A. Sova; page 260: © Imagebroker/Alamy.

CHAPTER 10

Page 271: © David Madison/Stone/Getty; page 275: © Paul Burns/Blend Images/Getty Images; page 279: © TRBfoto/Blend Images/Getty Images; page 283: © Klaus Tiedge/Corbis; page 286: © The McGraw-Hill Companies, Inc./Lars A. Niki, photographer; page 292: © John Giustina/Iconica/Getty Images.

CHAPTER 11

Page 303: © 2008 Thomas Del Brase Photography/Getty Images; page 305: © Margaret A. Sova; page 310: © Chris Crisman/Redux; page 313: Zero Creatives Cultura/Newscom; page 317: © Robert Kreitner; page 322: © Caroll Taveras.

CHAPTER 12

Page 331: © Ramin Talaie/Bloomberg via Getty Images; page 334: © David McNew/Getty Images; page 337: U.S. Coast Guard via Getty Images; page 339: © m42/m42/ZUMA Press/Newscom; page 344: © David Paul Morris/Bloomberg via Getty Images; page 351 (top): AP Photo/Richard Drew; page 351 (bottom): © Tom Merton/Getty Images.

CHAPTER 13

Page 367: © Chris Buck/Corbis Outline; page 370: © Tokyo Electric Power Company/ZUMA Press/Corbis; page 372: © Prakash Singh/AFP/Getty Images; page 377: AP Photo/Michel Euler; page 382: © Fox Photos/Getty Images; page 385: © Margaret A. Sova.

CHAPTER 14

Page 399: © Juice Images/Cultura/Getty Images; page 402: © Mohammed Abed/AFP/Getty Images; page 406: © Dominique Faget/AFP/Getty Images; page 414: © Purestock/Getty Images; page 419: © Brian Kersey/Getty Images; page 422: © Blend Images/Inti St Clair/Getty Images.

CHAPTER 15

Page 432: © Brendan McDermid/Reuters/Corbis; page 435: © Lightchaser Photography/ABACAUSA.COM/Newscom; page 438: © Andrew Harrer/Bloomberg via Getty Images; page 442: © AAGAMIA/Riser/Getty Images; page 448: © Chris Haston/NBC TV/The Kobal Collection; page 453: © Matthew Staver/Bloomberg via Getty Images.

CHAPTER 16

Page 466: © Mark Peterson/Redux; page 468: AP Photo/Alastair Grant; page 474: © Josep Lago/AFP/Getty Images; page 475: © Ocean/Corbis; page 482: © Daniel Acker/Bloomberg via Getty Images; page 488: AP Photo/Gautam Singh.

CHAPTER 17

Page 498: © Gregor SchusterPhotographer's Choice RF/Getty Images; page 499: © Yomiuri Shimbun/AFP/Getty Images; page 504: © Frank Rumpenhorst/AFP/Getty Images; page 507: © Nokia/Newscom; page 511: © Tom Grill/Photographer's Choice RF/Getty Images; page 519: AP Photo/PRNewsFoto/Apple; page 522: AP Photo/Koji Sasahara.

CHAPTER 18

Page 530: © HO/Reuters/Corbis; page 532: © B. Busco/Photographer's Choice/Getty Images; page 536: © John MacDougall/AFP/Getty Images; page 543: AP Photo/Jeff Roberson; page 549: © Mily Michot/Miami Herald/MCT via Getty Images; page 556: © Purestock/Getty Images.

Endnotes

CHAPTER 1

[1] Excerpted from T Hsieh, *Delivering Happiness: A Path to Profits, Passion, and Purpose* (New York: Business Plus, 2010), pp 157–58.

[2] Data from M Moskowitz, R Levering, and C Tkaczyk, "100 Best Companies to Work For," *Fortune,* February 7, 2011, p 93. For more see, D Brady, "Hard Choices: Tony Hsieh," *Bloomberg Businessweek,* May 31–June 6, 2010, p 88, and http://about.zappos.com/.

[3] Based on J Pfeffer, *The Human Equation: Building Profits by Putting People First* (Boston: Harvard Business School Press, 1998); and J Pfeffer and J F Veiga, "Putting People First for Organizational Success," *Academy of Management Executive,* May 1999, pp 37–48.

[4] Data from Pfeffer and Veiga, "Putting People First for Organizational Success," p 47. Also see C A O'Reilly and J Pfeffer, *Hidden Value: How Great Companies Achieve Extraordinary Results with Ordinary People* (Boston: Harvard Business School Press, 2000); J Combs, Y Liu, A Hall, and D Ketchen, "How Much Do High-Performance Work Practices Matter? A Meta-Analysis of Their Effects on Organizational Performance," *Personnel Psychology,* Autumn 2006, pp 501–28; and K W Mossholder, H A Richardson, and R P Settoon, "Human Resource Systems and Helping in Organizations: A Relational Perspective," *Academy of Management Review,* January 2011, pp 33–52.

[5] J Pfeffer, "Building Sustainable Organizations: The Human Factor," *Academy of Management Perspectives,* February 2010, p 36. Also see C Chuang and H Liao, "Strategic Human Resource Management in Service Context: Taking Care of Business by Taking Care of Employees and Customers," *Personnel Psychology,* Spring 2010, pp 153–96.

[6] "Layoffs Pack Punch to 'Surviving' Employees," *HR Magazine,* February 2009, p 18.

[7] Excerpted from M Boyle, "Cutting Costs without Cutting Jobs," *BusinessWeek,* March 9, 2009, p 55. Also see J Pfeffer, "Lay Off the Layoffs," *Newsweek,* February 15, 2010, pp 32–37; P Davidson, "Cuts in Hours vs. Cuts in Jobs," *USA Today,* February 25, 2010, p 1B; and G Colvin, "How Are Most Admired Companies Different? They Invest in People and Keep Them Employed—Even in a Downturn," *Fortune,* March 22, 2010, p 82.

[8] See D A Kaplan, "#1 SAS: The Best Company to Work For," *Fortune,* February 8, 2010, pp 56–64; and L Buchanan, "A Little Enlightened Self-Interest," *Inc.,* June 2010, pp 56–60.

[9] C I Barnard, *The Functions of the Executive* (Cambridge, MA: Harvard University Press, 1938), p 73.

[10] F Zakaria, "The Education of Paul Wolfowitz," *Newsweek,* March 28, 2005, p 37.

[11] See, for example, M V Copeland, "Intel's Cultural Anthropologist," *Fortune,* September 27, 2010, pp 25–26.

[12] Data from J B Miner, "The Rated Importance, Scientific Validity, and Practical Usefulness of Organizational Behavior Theories: A Quantitative Review," *Academy of Management Learning and Education,* September 2003, pp 250–68. Also see W F Cascio and H Aguinis, "Research in Industrial and Organizational Psychology from 1963 to 2007: Changes, Choices, and Trends," *Journal of Applied Psychology,* September 2008, pp 1062–81.

[13] E E Lawler III, *Treat People Right! How Organizations and Individuals Can Propel Each Other into a Virtuous Spiral of Success* (San Francisco: Jossey-Bass, 2003), p 19.

[14] Excerpted from J Welch and S Welch, "Growing Up but Staying Young," *BusinessWeek,* December 11, 2006, p 112.

[15] B S Lawrence, "Historical Perspective: Using the Past to Study the Present," *Academy of Management Review,* April 1984, p 307.

[16] See L T Benjamin Jr, "Hugo Munsterberg's Attack on the Application of Scientific Psychology," *Journal of Applied Psychology,* March 2006, pp 414–25.

[17] Evidence indicating that the original conclusions of the famous Hawthorne studies were unjustified may be found in R G Greenwood, A A Bolton, and R A Greenwood, "Hawthorne a Half Century Later: Relay Assembly Participants Remember," *Journal of Management,* Fall–Winter 1983, pp 217–31; and R H Franke and J D Kaul, "The Hawthorne Experiments: First Statistical Interpretation," *American Sociological Review,* October 1978, pp 623–43. For a positive interpretation of the Hawthorne studies, see J A Sonnenfeld, "Shedding Light on the Hawthorne Studies," *Journal of Occupational Behaviour,* April 1985, pp 111–30.

[18] See M Parker Follett, *Freedom and Coordination* (London: Management Publications Trust, 1949).

[19] See D McGregor, *The Human Side of Enterprise* (New York: McGraw-Hill, 1960).

[20] A Fox, "Raising Engagement," *HR Magazine,* May 2010, pp 35–36; Also see B L Rich, J A LePine, and E R Crawford, "Job Engagement: Antecedents and Effects on Job Performance," *Academy of Management Journal,* June 2010, pp 617–35.

[21] See D W Organ, "Elusive Phenomena," *Business Horizons,* March–April 2002, pp 1–2.

[22] See, for example, R Zemke, "TQM: Fatally Flawed or Simply Unfocused?" *Training,* October 1992, p 8.

[23] R O Crockett, "Six Sigma Pays Off at Motorola," *BusinessWeek,* December 4, 2006, p 50. Also see T Minton-Eversole, "Lean Overtakes Six Sigma," *HR Magazine,* April 2010, p 14.

[24] J McGregor, "The Performance Paradox," *Fast Company,* April 2005, pp 29–30. Also see R Zeidner, "Questing for Quality," *HR Magazine,* July 2010, pp 25–28.

[25] M Sashkin and K J Kiser, *Putting Total Quality Management to Work* (San Francisco: Berrett-Koehler, 1993), p 39.

[26] R J Schonberger, "Total Quality Management Cuts a Broad Swath—Through Manufacturing and Beyond," *Organizational Dynamics,* Spring 1992, p 18. Also see B Gray, "Fine Tuning Market Oriented Practices," *Business Horizons,* July–August 2010, pp 371–83.

[27] Based on C Hui, S S K Lam, and J Schaubroeck, "Can Good Citizens Lead the Way in Providing Quality Service? A Field Quasi Experiment," *Academy of Management Journal,* October 2001, pp 988–95.

[28] Deming's landmark work is W E Deming, *Out of the Crisis* (Cambridge, MA: MIT, 1986). Also see S Miller, "Pioneer of Quality Control Kept Searching For 'A Better Way' to Make and Manage," *The Wall Street Journal,* March 8, 2008, p A7.

[29] See M Trumbull, "What Is Total Quality Management?" *The Christian Science Monitor,* May 3, 1993, p 12; J Hillkirk, "World-Famous Quality Expert Dead at 93," *USA Today,* December 21, 1993, pp 1B–2B; and O Port, "The Kings of Quality," *BusinessWeek,* August 30, 2004, p 20.

[30] Based on discussion in M Walton, *Deming Management at Work* (New York: Putnam/Perigee, 1990).

[31] Ibid., p 20.

[32] Adapted from D E Bowen and E E Lawler III, "Total Quality-Oriented Human Resources Management," *Organizational Dynamics,* Spring 1992, pp 29–41.

[33] For details, see T J Douglas and W Q Judge Jr, "Total Quality Management Implementation and Competitive Advantage: The Role of Structural Control and Exploration," *Academy of Management Journal,* February 2001, pp 158–69; and K B Hendricks and V R Singhal, "The Long-Run Stock Price Performance of Firms with Effective TQM Programs," *Management Science,* March 2001, pp 359–68.

34 S Silke Carty, "So Ends a Love Affair Gone Bad," *USA Today*, July 8, 2010, p 3B.

35 Data from www.internetworldstats.com/stats.htm (accessed January 24, 2011).

36 See G T Lumpkin and G G Dess, "E-Business Strategies and Internet Business Models: How the Internet Adds Value," *Organizational Dynamics*, no. 2, 2004, pp 161–73.

37 M J Mandel and R D Hof, "Rethinking the Internet," *BusinessWeek*, March 26, 2001, p 118.

38 See D Kirkpatrick, *The Facebook Effect: The Inside Story of the Company That Is Connecting the World* (New York: Simon & Schuster, 2010); and B Stone, "Sell Your Friends," *Bloomberg Businessweek*, September 27–October 3, 2010, pp 64–72.

39 D MacMillan, "Innovator: Amit Kapur," *Bloomberg Businessweek*, November 29–December 5, 2010, p 46.

40 See "It's Not Sci-Fi, It's (Augmented) Reality," *Fortune*, March 22, 2010, p 27; K Bell, "Will the Internet Destroy Us?" *Harvard Business Review*, December 2010): 138–139; P Burrows, "Will Video Kill The Internet, Too?" *Bloomberg Businessweek*, December 6–12, 2010, pp 43–44; F Gillette, "Innovator: Evan Ratliff," *Bloomberg Businessweek*, January 24–30, 2011, p 39.

41 D Tapscott, *Grown Up Digital: How the Net Generation Is Changing Your World* (New York: McGraw-Hill, 2009), p 96. Also see the interview with Tapscott in A D Wright, "Millennials: 'Bathed in Bits,'" *HR Magazine*, July 2010, pp 40–41.

42 See H Dolezalek, "Virtual Leaders," *Training*, May 2009, pp 40–42; and Y Lee, "Tele-terminating, Terminating Employees Abroad, Recruiting Diversity," *HR Magazine*, June 2010, p 31.

43 For details on these trends, see K Dychtwald, T J Erickson, and R Morison, *Workforce Crisis: How to Beat the Coming Shortage of Skills and* Talent (Boston: Harvard Business School Press, 2006); D A Kaplan, "The STEM Challenge," *Fortune*, June 14, 2010, p 25; and J C Meister and K Willyerd, *The 2020 Workplace: How Innovative Companies Attract, Develop, and Keep Tomorrow's Employees Today* (New York: Harper Business, 2010).

44 B E Becker, M A Huselid, and D Ulrich, *The HR Scorecard: Linking People, Strategy, and Performance* (Boston: Harvard Business School Press, 2001), p 4. Also see M Weinstein, "How's Your Human Capital ROI?" *Training*, February 2010, p 12; T H Davenport, J Harris, and J Shapiro, "Competing on Talent Analytics," *Harvard Business Review*, October 2010, pp 52–58; and R E Ployhart and T P Moliterno, "Emergence of the Human Capital Resource: A Multilevel Model," *Academy of Management Review*, January 2011, pp 127–150.

45 Drawn from "Poll Identifies Top Challenges for HR During Next 10 Years," *HR Magazine*, November 2010, p 80. Also see "Research: 2010's Top Research Findings," *HR Magazine*, January 2011, p 9.

46 See www.intel.com/education/index.htm?iid=intel_edu+body_ initiative.

47 See "North Carolina Girl Wins Intel Prize," *USA Today*, March 3, 2008, p 7; D J Der Bedrosian, "Intel Science Talent Search Crowns 10 Promising Young Scientists," *USA Today*, March 12, 2009, p 7D; and "Why Do We Support Science Competitions? Because We All Win," Special Advertising Section, *Harvard Business Review*, May 2010, pp 113–15.

48 Inspired by P S Adler and S Kwon, "Social Capital: Prospects for a New Concept," *Academy of Management Review*, January 2002, pp 17–40. Also see S Hamm, "The Globe is IBM's Classroom," *BusinessWeek*, March 23–30, 2009, pp 56–57; A Fox, "Pave the Way for Volunteers," *HR Magazine*, June 2010, pp 70–74; and C Garton, "Companies Give in Kind, If Not in Cash," *USA Today*, August 9, 2010, pp 1B–2B.

49 L Prusak and D Cohen, "How to Invest in Social Capital," *Harvard Business Review*, June 2001, p 93. Also see B L Fredrickson, M A Cohn, K A Coffey, J Pek, and S M Finkel, "Open Hearts Build Lives: Positive Emotions, Induced through Loving-Kindness Meditation, Build Consequential Personal Resources," *Journal of Personality and Social Psychology*, November 2008, pp 1045–62.

50 Data from "What Makes a Job OK," *USA Today*, May 15, 2000, p 1B.

51 Based on E D Heaphy and J E Dutton, "Positive Social Interactions and the Human Body at Work: Linking Organizations and Physiology," *Academy of Management Review*, January 2008, pp 137–62.

52 J Covert and T Sattersten, "Learning from Heroes," *Harvard Business Review*, March 2009, p 24. Also see M T Hansen, "The Future Manager Is T-Shaped," *HR Magazine*, January 2010, p 60; R Barker, "No, Management Is *Not* a Profession," *Harvard Business Review*, July–August 2010, pp 52–60; and F R David, M E David, and F R David, "What Are Business Schools Doing for Business Today?" *Business Horizons*, January–February 2011, pp 51–62.

53 Excerpted from B O'Keefe, "Meet the CEO of the Biggest Company on Earth," *Fortune*, September 27, 2010, p 88.

54 See, for example, H Mintzberg, "Managerial Work: Analysis from Observation," *Management Science*, October 1971, pp B97–B110. Also see N Fondas, "A Behavioral Job Description for Managers," *Organizational Dynamics*, Summer 1992, pp 47–58.

55 See L B Kurke and H E Aldrich, "Mintzberg Was Right!: A Replication and Extension of *The Nature of Managerial Work*," *Management Science*, August 1983, pp 975–84.

56 Validation studies can be found in E Van Velsor and J B Leslie, *Feedback to Managers, Volume II: A Review and Comparison of Sixteen Multi-Rater Feedback Instruments* (Greensboro, NC: Center for Creative Leadership, 1991); F Shipper, "A Study of the Psychometric Properties of the Managerial Skill Scales of the Survey of Management Practices," *Educational and Psychological Measurement*, June 1995, pp 468–79; and C L Wilson, *How and Why Effective Managers Balance Their Skills: Technical, Teambuilding, Drive* (Columbia, MD: Rockatech Multimedia Publishing, 2003).

57 See F Shipper, "Mastery and Frequency of Managerial Behaviors Relative to Sub-Unit Effectiveness," *Human Relations*, April 1991, pp 371–88.

58 Ibid.

59 Data from F Shipper, "A Study of Managerial Skills of Women and Men and Their Impact on Employees' Attitudes and Career Success in a Nontraditional Organization," paper presented at the Academy of Management Meeting, August 1994, Dallas, Texas. The same outcome for on-the-job studies is reported in A H Eagly and B T Johnson, "Gender and Leadership Style: A Meta-Analysis," *Psychological Bulletin*, September 1990, pp 233–56.

60 For instance, see J B Rosener, "Ways Women Lead," *Harvard Business Review*, November–December 1990, pp 119–25; and C Lee, "The Feminization of Management," *Training*, November 1994, pp 25–31.

61 A similar finding is reported in J Kornik, "Bosses Say They're Great: Employees Not So Sure," *Training*, October 2006, p 20.

62 Based on F Shipper and J E Dillard Jr, "A Study of Impending Derailment and Recovery of Middle Managers across Career Stages," *Human Resource Management*, Winter 2000, pp 331–45. Also see R I Sutton, *Good Boss, Bad Boss: How to Be the Best . . . and Learn from he Worst* (New York: Business Plus, 2010); J K Summers, T P Munyon, A A Perryman, and G R Ferris, "Dysfunctional Executive Behavior: What Can Organizations Do?" *Business Horizons*, November–December 2010, pp 581–90; L A Hill and K Lineback, "Are You a Good Boss or a Great One?" *Harvard Business Review*, January–February 2011, pp 124–31.

63 See S Overman, "HR Trendbook 2011: Workforce Trends," *HR Magazine*, December 2010, p 75.

64 See G M Parker, *Team Players and Teamwork: New Strategies for Developing Successful Collaboration*, 2nd ed (San Francisco: Jossey-Bass, 2008); and A M L Raes, M G Heijltjes, U Glunk, and R A Roe, "The Interface of the Top Management Team and Middle Managers: A Process Model," *Academy of Management Review*, January 2011, pp 102–26.

[65] G Hamel, "Moon Shots for Management," *Harvard Business Review,* February 2009, p 92. Also see G Hamel with B Breen, *The Future of Management* (Boston: Harvard Business School Press, 2007).

[66] As quoted in P LaBarre, "The Industrial Revolution," *Fast Company,* November 2003, pp 116, 118. Also see N Bloom and J Van Reenen, "Why Do Management Practices Differ across Firms and Countries?" *Journal of Economic Perspectives,* Winter 2010, pp 203–224.

[67] See N Varchaver, "Long Island Confidential," *Fortune,* November 27, 2006, pp 172–86.

[68] See D R Dalton and C M Dalton, "Corporate Governance in the Post Sarbanes-Oxley Period: Compensation Disclosure and Analysis (CD&A)," *Business Horizons,* March–April 2008, pp 85–92.

[69] See J Bandler, N Varchaver, and D Burke, "How Bernie Did It," *Fortune,* May 11, 2009, pp 51–71; K McCoy, "As Victims Cheer, 'Evil' Madoff Gets 150 Years," *USA Today,* June 30, 2009, pp 1A–2A; and D Lieberman and M Krantz, "Goldman Sachs Concedes Mistake, Settles SEC Suit," *USA Today,* July 16, 2010, pp 1B–2B.

[70] See R Parloff, "Wall Street: It's Payback Time," *Fortune,* January 19, 2009, pp 56–69.

[71] T M Jones, "Corporate Social Responsibility Revisited, Redefined," *California Management Review,* Spring 1980, pp 59–60. Also see P A Heslin and J D Ochoa, "Understanding and Developing Strategic Corporate Social Responsibility," *Organizational Dynamics,* April–June 2008, pp 125–44; A Delios, "How Can Organizations Be Competitive but Dare to Care?" *Academy of Management Perspectives,* August 2010, pp 25–36; and G B Sprinkle and L A Maines, "The Benefits and Costs of Corporate Social Responsibility," *Business Horizons,* September-October 2010, pp 445–453.

[72] See J Pfeffer, "Shareholders First? Not So Fast," *Harvard Business Review,* July 8, 2009, pp 90–91; and R M Murphy, "Why Doing Good Is Good for Business," *Fortune,* February 8, 2010, pp 90–95.

[73] See, for example, J Welch and S Welch, "The Real Verdict on Business," *BusinessWeek,* June 12, 2006, p 100; and M E Porter and M R Kramer, "Creating Shared Value," *Harvard Business Review,* January–February 2011, pp 62–77.

[74] A B Carroll, "Managing Ethically with Global Stakeholders: A Present and Future Challenge," *Academy of Management Executive,* May 2004, p 118.

[75] Ibid., pp 117–18.

[76] E Levenson, "Citizen Nike," *Fortune,* November 24, 2008, p 166.

[77] D Callahan, *The Cheating Culture: Why More Americans Are Doing Wrong to Get Ahead* (Orlando: Harcourt, 2004), pp 19–20.

[78] Data from A R Carey and S Ward, "Is America Corrupt?" *USA Today,* January 12, 2011, p 1A.

[79] Based on T Jackson, "Cultural Values and Management Ethics: A 10-Nation Study," *Human Relations,* October 2001, pp 1267–1302. Also see S A Stumpf and P Chaudhry, "Country Matters: Executives Weigh In on the Causes and Counter Measures of Counterfeit Trade," *Business Horizons,* May–June 2010, pp 305–314.

[80] Results can be found in "HR Poll Results," http://hr2.blr.com/index.cfm/Nav/11.0.0.0/Action/Poll_Question/qid/170, accessed April 8, 2005. Also see J J Kish-Gephart, D A Harrison, and L K Treviño, "Bad Apples, Bad Cases, and Bad Barrels: Meta-Analytic Evidence About Sources of Unethical Decisions at Work," *Journal of Applied Psychology,* January 2010, pp 1–31.

[81] Based on L K Treviño, G R Weaver, and M E Brown, "It's Lovely at the Top: Hierarchical Levels, Identities, and Perceptions of Organizational Ethics," *Business Ethics Quarterly,* April 2008, pp 233–52.

[82] Results can be found in Matthew Boyle, "By the Numbers: Liar Liar!" *Fortune,* May 26, 2003, p 44.

[83] P Babcock, "Spotting Lies," *HR Magazine,* October 2003, p 47. Also see D Macsai, ". . . And I Invented Velcro," *BusinessWeek,* August 4, 2008, p 15.

[84] Data from N Byrnes, "Profiles in Pilfering," *BusinessWeek,* October 13, 2008, p 16.

[85] "Say No: International Anti-Corruption Day," *Fast Company,* January 2009, p 44.

[86] Supporting research can be found in J B Cullen, K P Parboteeah, and M Hoegl, "Cross-National Differences in Managers' Willingness to Justify Ethically Suspect Behaviors: A Test of Institutional Anomie Theory," *Academy of Management Journal,* June 2004, pp 411–21. Also see the debate in L D Ordonez, M E Schweitzer, A D Galinsky, and M H Bazerman, "Goals Gone Wild: The Systematic Side Effects of Overprescribing Goal Setting," *Academy of Management Perspectives,* February 2009, pp 6–16; and E A Locke and G P Latham, "Has Goal Setting Gone Wild, or Have Its Attackers Abandoned Good Scholarship?" *Academy of Management Perspectives,* February 2009, pp 17–23.

[87] See B J Tepper, "When Managers Pressure Employees to Behave Badly: Toward a Comprehensive Response," *Business Horizons,* November–December 2010, pp 591–98.

[88] S Jayson, "Teens Face Up to Ethics Choices—If You Can Believe Them," *USA Today,* December 6, 2006, p 6D.

[89] Ibid. Also see D O Neubaum, M Pagell, J A Drexler Jr, F M McKee-Ryan, and E Larson, "Business Education and Its Relationship to Student Personal Moral Philosophies and Attitudes toward Profits: An Empirical Response to Critics," *Academy of Management Learning and Education,* March 2009, pp 9–24.

[90] Data and quotation from S Jayson, "Teens Say Bullying Is Widespread," *USA Today,* October 26, 2010, p 1A.

[91] See Chapter 6 in K Hodgson, *A Rock and a Hard Place: How to Make Ethical Business Decisions When the Choices Are Tough* (New York: AMACOM, 1992), pp 66–77.

[92] See R M Fulmer, "The Challenge of Ethical Leadership," *Organizational Dynamics,* August 2004, pp 307–17; S Ambec and P Lanoie, "Does It Pay to Be Green? A Systematic Overview," *Academy of Management Perspectives,* November 2008, pp 45–62; J L Goolsby, D A Mack, and J Campbell Quick, "Winning by Staying in Bounds: Good Outcomes from Positive Ethics," *Organizational Dynamics,* July–September 2010, pp 248–57; and D Meinert, "Strong Ethical Culture Helps Bottom Line," *HR Magazine,* December 2010, p 21.

[93] Results can be found in "Tarnished Employment Brands Affect Recruiting," *HR Magazine,* November 2004, pp 16, 20.

[94] Adapted in part from W E Stead, D L Worrell, and J Garner Stead, "An Integrative Model for Understanding and Managing Ethical Behavior in Business Organizations," *Journal of Business Ethics,* March 1990, pp 233–42. Also see D Lange, "A Multidimensional Conceptualization of Organizational Corruption Control," *Academy of Management Review,* July 2008, pp 710–29; and J DesJardins, *An Introduction to Business Ethics,* 3rd ed (New York: McGraw-Hill, 2009).

[95] L W Fry and J W Slocum Jr, "Maximizing the Triple Bottom Line through Spiritual Leadership," *Organizational Dynamics,* January–March 2008, pp 86–96.

[96] For an excellent review of integrity testing, see D S Ones and C Viswesvaran, "Integrity Testing in Organizations," in *Dysfunctional Behavior in Organizations: Violent and Deviant Behavior,* ed R W Griffin et al. (Stamford, CT: JAI Press, 1998), pp 243–76. Also see J McGregor, "Background Checks That Never End," *BusinessWeek,* March 20, 2006, p 40.

[97] See K M Gilley, C J Robertson, and T C Mazur, "The Bottom-Line Benefits of Ethics Code Commitment," *Business Horizons,* January–February 2010, pp 31–37.

[98] Guidelines for conducting ethics training are discussed by K Tyler, "Do the Right Thing," *HR Magazine,* February 2005, pp 99–101; and C Kincaid, "The Right Stuff," *Training,* March–April 2009, pp 34–36.

[99] See G Beenen and J Pinto, "Resisting Organizational-Level Corruption: An Interview With Sherron Watkins," *Academy of*

Management Learning and Education, June 2009, pp 275–89. Also see P Eisler, "Whistle-Blowers' Rights Get Second Look," *USA Today*, March 15, 2010, p 6A; J Biskupic, "Supreme Court Restricts Whistle-Blower Lawsuits," *USA Today*, March 31, 2010, p 7A; and J Westbrook, "Whistleblowers Get a Raise," *Bloomberg Businessweek*, August 2–8, 2010, pp 31–32.

100 Based on S J Reynolds, "Moral Attentiveness: Who Pays Attention to Moral Aspects of Life?" *Journal of Applied Psychology,* September 2008, pp 1027–41.

101 As quoted in D Jones, "Military a Model for Execs," *USA Today,* June 9, 2004, p 4B. Also see B George with P Sims, *True North: Discover Your Authentic Leadership* (San Francisco: Jossey-Bass, 2007).

102 Complete discussion of this technique can be found in J E Hunter, F L Schmidt, and G B Jackson, *Meta-Analysis: Cumulating Research Findings across Studies* (Beverly Hills, CA: Sage Publications, 1982); J E Hunter and F L Schmidt, *Methods of Meta-Analysis: Correcting Error and Bias in Research Findings* (Newbury Park, CA: Sage Publications, 1990); H Le, I Oh, J Shaffer, and F Schmidt, "Implications of Methodological Advances for the Practice of Personnel Selection: How Practitioners Benefit from Meta-Analysis," *Academy of Management Perspectives,* August 2007, pp 6–15; and I Oh, F L Schmidt, J A Shaffer, and H Le, "The Graduate Management Admission Test (GMAT) Is Even More Valid Than We Thought: A New Development in Meta-Analysis and Its Implications for the Validity of the GMAT," *Academy of Management Learning and Education,* December 2008, pp 563–70.

103 Limitations of meta-analysis technique are discussed in P Bobko and E F Stone-Romero, "Meta-Analysis May Be Another Useful Tool, but It Is Not a Panacea, in *Research in Personnel and Human Resources Management,* vol. 16, ed G R Ferris (Stamford, CT: JAI Press, 1998), pp 359–97; and J Carey, "When Medical Studies Collide," *BusinessWeek,* August 6, 2007, p 38.

104 Excerpted from J Fox, "What Is It That Only I Can Do?" *Harvard Business Review*, January–February 2011, pp 120–21.

105 As quoted in J Chu, "Forget $100 Million. Michelle Rhee Wants to Spend a Billion!" *Fast Company*, Februrary 2011, p 97.

CHAPTER 2

1 Excerpted from J J Hensley, "Officer Is Awarded More Than $600,000," *The Arizona Republic,* October 30, 2010, pp B1, B6.

2 B Leonard, "Survey: 10% of Employees Report Harassment at Work," *HR Magazine,* October 2010, p 18.

3 See A Zimmerman and N Koppel, "Bias Suit Advances Against Wal-Mart," *The Wall Street Journal,* April 27, 2010, pp A1, A6; and J Bravin and A Zimmerman, "Wal-Mart Case Tests Class Rules," *The Wall Street Journal,* December 7, 2010, P B1.

4 H Collingwood, "Who Handles a Diverse Work Force Best?" *Working Women,* February 1996, p 25.

5 See K Gurchiek, "EEOC Addresses Religious Discrimination," *HR Magazine,* September 2008, p 21.

6 See M Moskowitz, R Levering, and C Tkaczyk, "100 Best Companies to Work For," *Fortune,* February 8, 2010, pp 75–88.

7 Results can be found in D A Harrison, D A Kravitz, D M Mayer, L M Leslie, and D Lev-Arey, "Understanding Attitudes toward Affirmative Action Programs in Employment: Summary and Meta-Analysis of 35 Years of Research," *Journal of Applied Psychology,* September 2006, pp 1013–36.

8 For a thorough review of relevant research, see M E Heilman, "Affirmative Action: Some Unintended Consequences for Working Women," in *Research in Organizational Behavior,* vol. 16, ed B M Staw and L L Cummings (Greenwich, CT: JAI Press, 1994), pp 125–69.

9 Results from this study can be found in M E Heilman, W S Battle, C E Keller, and R A Lee, "Type of Affirmative Action Policy: A

Determinant of Reactions to Sex-Based Preferential Selection?" *Journal of Applied Psychology,* April 1998, pp 190–205.

10 The survey process is described in "About the Diversity Top 50 Companies for Diversity," May 6, 2010, http://www.diversityinc.com/article/7570/.

11 A M Morrison, *The New Leaders: Guidelines on Leadership Diversity in America* (San Francisco, CA: Jossey-Bass, 1992), p 78.

12 Excerpted from "No. 1 Johnson & Johnson." Retrieved December 27, 2010, from http://www.diversityinc.com/article/5449/Mo-1-Johnson—Johnson/.

13 Results can be found in A A Cannella Jr, J-H Park, and H-U Lee, "Top Management Team Functional Background Diversity and Firm Performance: Examining the Roles of Team Member Colocation and Environmental Uncertainty," *Academy of Management Journal,* August 2008, pp 768–84.

14 These trends are discussed in J C Meister and K Willyers, *The 2020 Workplace* (New York: HarperCollins, 2010); and "Illiteracy—Major U.S. Problem." Retrieved December 27, 2010, from http://www.enotalone.com/article/19273.html.

15 See J E O'Neill, "Washington's Equal Pay Obsession," *The Wall Street Journal,* November 16, 2010, P A19; and K S Lyness and D E Thompson, "Above the Glass Ceiling: A Comparison of Matched Samples of Female and Male Executives," *Journal of Applied Psychology,* June 1997, pp 359–75.

16 Results can be found in N M Carter and C Silva, "Women in Management: Delusions of Progress," *Harvard Business Review,* March 2010, pp 19–21.

17 These conclusions were based on A H Eagly and L L Carli, *Through the Labyrinth* (Boston: Harvard Business School Press, 2007); O'Neill, "Washington's Equal Pay Obsession"; and S Miller, "'Motherhood Gap' Explains Differences in Gender Wages," *HR Magazine,* October 28, 2010, p 19.

18 These statistics were obtained from "Women CEOs of the Fortune 1000," November 2010, http://www.catalyst.org/publication/322/women-ceos-of-the-fortune-1000.

19 See M J Perry, "Carpe Diem," February 2009, http://mjperry.blogspot.com/2009/02/degree-gap-will-continue-to-widen.html; "Women in Management in the United States, 1950–Present," April 2010, http://www.catalyst.org/publication/207/women-in-management-1950-present; "Women in the Board Room and in the President's Office: What Differences Does It Make?" Retrieved December 29, 2010, from http://www.agb.org/events/annual-meeting/2011/2011-agb-national-conference-trusteeship/sessions/women-board-room-and-pr; and L Jones, "8th Circuit Lags in Female Appointees," May 31, 2010, http://www.law.com/jsp/nlj/PubArticleNLJ.jsp?id=1202458929880&slreturn=1&hbxlogin=1.

20 Eagly and Carli, pp 26–27.

21 *The American Heritage Dictionary* (New York: Bantam Dell, 2004), p 475.

22 See Bureau of Labor Statistics, "Employed Persons by Occupation, Race, Hispanic or Latino Ethnicity, and Sex," accessed February 5, 2009, www.bls.gov.

23 See U.S. Equal Employment Opportunity Commission, "Race-Based Charges FY 1997–FY 2009." Retrieved December 29, 2010, from http://www.eeoc.gov/eeoc/statistics/enforcement/race.cfm.

24 See D-W Carmen, B D Proctor, and J C Smith, U.S. Census Bureau, Current Population Reports, P60-238, *Income, Poverty, and Health Insurance Coverage in the United States: 2009, Table 1-Income and Earnings Summary Measures by Selected Characteristics: 2008 and 2009,* http://www.census.gov/prod/2010pubs/p60-238.pdf.

25 See T DeAngelis, "Unmasking 'Racial Micro Aggressions,'" *Harvard Business Review,* February 2009, pp 42–46; and D R Avery, P F McKay, and D C Wilson, "What Are the Odds? How Demographic Similarity Affects the Prevalence of Perceived Employment Discrimination," *Journal of Applied Psychology,* March 2008, pp 235–49.

26 See "U.S. Census Bureau, Current Population Survey, 2009 Annual Social and Economic Supplement," April 2010, http://www.census.gov/hhes/socdemo/education/data/cps/2009/tables.html; and Bureau of Labor Statistics, "Education Projections," May 27, 2010, http://www.bls.gov.emp/ep_chart-001.htm.

27 See S Miller, "Skills Critical for a Changing Workforce," *HR Magazine,* August 2008, p 24; N Anderson, "High-School Graduation Rates Up in U.S.," *The Arizona Republic,* December 15, 2010, p A21; and "Illiteracy—Major U.S. Problem," January 20, 2009, http://www.enotalone.com/article/19273.html.

28 "Facts on Literacy," *National Literacy Facts,* August 27, 1998, www.svs.net/wpci/Litfacts.htm.

29 The New Commission on the Skills of the American Workforce, *Tough Choices or Tough Times* (San Francisco, CA: Jossey-Bass, 2007), pp xvi, xvii.

30 See R Strack, J Baier, and A Fahlander, "Managing Demographic Risk," *Harvard Business Review,* February 2008, pp 119–28.

31 H Jones, "CEOs Now Find That Principles and Profits Can Mix Well," *The Wall Street Journal,* November 22, 2010, p R5.

32 See A Joshi, J C Dencker, G Franz, and J J Martocchio, "Unpacking Generational Identities in Organizations," *Academy of Management Review,* July 2010, pp 392–414.

33 For details, see T W H Ng and D C Feldman, "The Relationship of Age to Ten Dimensions of Job Performance," *Journal of Applied Psychology,* March 2008, pp 392–423.

34 T W H Ng and D C Feldman, "The Relationships of Age with Job Attitudes: A Meta-Analysis," *Personnel Psychology,* Autumn 2010, pp 677–718.

35 See "Demographics of Sexual Orientation," Retrieved December 30, 2010, from http://en.wikipedia.org/wiki/Demographics_of_sexual_orientation; and L Visconti, "You're Gay? You're Fired!" Retrieved December 28, 2010, from http://www.diversityinc.com/article/8206/Youre-Gay-Youre-Fired/.

36 R E Fassinger, S L Shullman, and M R Stevenson, "Toward an Affirmative Lesbian, Gay, Bisexual, and Transgender Leadership Program," *American Psychologist,* April 2010, pp 201–15.

37 These examples can be found in Moskowitz, Levering, and Tkaczyk, pp 75–88.

38 S J Wells, "Say Hola! to the Majority Minority," *HR Magazine,* September 2008, p 38.

39 See R Rashid, "The Battle for Female Talent in Emerging Markets," *Harvard Business Review,* May 2010, pp 101–6.

40 C Hymowitz, "Women Tell Women: Life in the Top Jobs Is Worth the Effort," *The Wall Street Journal,* November 20, 2006, p B1.

41 See Eagly and Carli, pp 26–27.

42 See H Ibarra, N M Carter, and C Silva, "Why Men Still Get More Promotions Than Women," *Harvard Business Review,* September 2010, pp 80–85; and "Programs for Female Leaders Scarce," *HR Magazine,* December 2010, p 22.

43 L Lowen, "Breaking the Grass Ceiling: Women Playing Golf," *About.com,* http://womenissues.about.com, February 28, 2008.

44 See S R Ezzedeen and K G Ritchey, "Career and Family Strategies of Executive Women: Revisiting the Quest to 'Have It All,'" *Organizational Dynamics,* October–December 2009, pp 270–80; and L Kellaway, "Breaking the Glass Ceiling Begins at Home," *Financial Times,* November 22, 2010, p 12.

45 A H Eagly and J L Chin, "Diversity and Leadership in a Changing World," *American Psychologist,* April 2010, pp 216–24; and J V Sanchez-Hucles and D D Davis, "Women and Women of Color in Leadership," *American Psychologist,* April 2010, pp 171–81.

46 S Boehle, "Voices of Opportunity," *Training,* January 2009, p 39.

47 D A Thomas, "The Truth about Mentoring Minorities: Race Matters," *Harvard Business Review,* April 2001, p 107.

48 See B Mirza, "Build Employee Skills, Help Nonprofits," *HR Magazine,* October 2008, p 30.

49 Details of this program can be found at C H Loch, F J Sting, N Bauer, and H Mauermann, "How BMW Is Defusing the Demographic Time Bomb," *Harvard Business Review,* March 2010, pp 99–102.

50 These recommendations were taken from G M McEvoy and M J Blahana, "Engagement or Disengagement? Older Workers and the Looming Labor Shortage," *Business Horizons,* September–October 2001, p 50.

51 R R Hastings, "Do Younger Employees Sabotage Boomers?" *HR Magazine,* October 2008, p 33.

52 T J Erickson, "Task, Not Time: Profile of a Gen Y Job," *Harvard Business Review,* February 2008, p 19.

53 P O'Connell, "What's Eating Gen X," *BusinessWeek,* September 1, 2008, p 62.

54 See the related discussion in L Gratton, "The End of the Middle Manager," *Harvard Business Review,* January–February 2011, p 36; and A D Wright, "'Millennials' Bathed in Bits," *HR Magazine,* July 2010, pp 40–41.

55 Examples are discussed in L Gerdes, "The Best Places to Launch a Career," *BusinessWeek,* September 15, 2008, pp 37–46.

56 D van Knippenberg, C K W De Dreu, and A C Homan, "Work Group Diversity and Group Performance: An Integrative Model and Research Agenda," *Journal of Applied Psychology,* December 2004, p 1009.

57 See ibid., pp 1008–22; and S E Jackson and A Joshi, "Diversity in Social Context: A Multi-Attribute, Multilevel Analysis of Team Diversity and Sales Performance," *Journal of Organizational Behavior,* September 2004, pp 675–702.

58 J L Berdahl and C Moore, "Workplace Harassment: Double Jeopardy for Minority Women," *Journal of Applied Psychology,* March 2006, pp 426–36.

59 See Jackson and Joshi, pp 675–702.

60 Results can be found in K Bezrukova, C S Spell, and J L Perry, "Violent Splits or Health Divides? Coping with Injustice Through Faultlines," *Personnel Psychology,* Autumn 2010, pp 719–51; J M Sacco and N Schmitt, "A Dynamic Multilevel Model of Demographic Diversity and Misfit Effects," *Journal of Applied Psychology,* March 2005, pp 203–31; and H Liao and A Joshi, "Sticking Out Like a Sore Thumb: Employee Dissimilarity and Deviance at Work," *Personnel Psychology,* Winter 2004, pp 969–1000.

61 van Knippenberg, De Dreu, and Homan, p 1009.

62 These conclusions were derived from Jackson and Joshi, "Diversity in Social Context."

63 See J Wegge, C Roth, B Neubach, K-H Schmidt, and R Kanfer, "Age and Gender Diversity as Determinants of Performance and Health in a Public Organization: The Role of Task Complexity and Group Size," *Journal of Applied Psychology,* November 2008, 1301–13; and Jackson and Joshi, "Diversity in Social Context."

64 See S Schulz-Hardt, F C Brodbeck, A Mojzisch, R Kerschreiter, and D Frey, "Group Decision Making in Hidden Profile Situations: Dissent as a Facilitator for Decision Quality," *Journal of Personality and Social Psychology,* December 2006, pp 1080–93.

65 See R Moss-Kanter, *The Change Masters* (New York: Simon and Schuster, 1983).

66 See K Y Williams, "Demography and Diversity in Organizations: A Review of 100 Years of Research," in *Research in Organizational Behavior,* vol. 20, ed B M Staw and L L Cummings (Greenwich, CT: JAI Press, 1998), pp 77–140.

67 J N Choi and T Sy, "Group-Level Organizational Citizenship Behavior: Effects of Demographic Faultlines and Conflict in Small Work Groups," *Journal of Organizational Behavior,* October 2010,

pp 1032–1054; and Bezrukova, Spell, and Perry, "Violent Splits or Health Divides? Coping with Injustice Through Faultlines."

68 D C Lau and J K Murnighan, "Demographic Diversity and Faultlines: The Compositional Dynamics of Organizational Groups," *Academy of Management Review,* April 1998, p 328.

69 See ibid; and A H Van De Ven, R W Rogers, J P Bechara, and K Sun, "Organizational Diversity, Integration and Performance," *Journal of Organizational Behavior,* April 2008, pp 335–54.

70 Supportive results can be found in M C Triana, M F García, and A Colella, "Managing Diversity: How Organizational Efforts to Support Diversity Moderate the Effects of Perceived Racial Discrimination on Affective Commitment," *Personnel Psychology,* Winter 2010, pp 817–43.

71 These barriers were taken from discussions in M Loden, *Implementing Diversity* (Burr Ridge, IL: Irwin, 1996); and "Link Diversity to Business Goals for Best Results," *HR Focus,* January 2010, pp 5–8.

72 J A Gonzalez and A DeNisi, "Cross-Level Effects of Demography and Diversity Climate on Organizational Attachment and Firm Effectiveness," *Journal of Organizational Behavior,* January 2009, p 24.

73 See ibid., pp 21–40.

74 See Y Lee, "Electronic Harassment, Recruiters' Sources, Global Benefits," *HR Magazine,* September 2010, p 24.

75 See the related results in L Torres and D Rollock, "Acculturation and Depression among Hispanics: The Moderating Effect of Intercultural Competence," *Cultural Diversity and Ethnic Minority Psychology,* January 2007, pp 10–17.

76 G Colvin, "Lafley and Immelt: In Search of Billions," *Fortune,* December 11, 2006, pp 70–72.

77 This discussion is based on R R Thomas Jr, *Redefining Diversity* (New York: AMACOM, 1996); and R R Thomas Jr., *World Class Diversity Management: A Strategic Approach* (San Francisco: Berrett-Koehler, 2010).

78 D J Gaiter, "Eating Crow: How Shoney's, Belted by a Lawsuit, Found the Path to Diversity," *The Wall Street Journal,* April 16, 1996, pp A, A11.

79 P Dass and B Parker, "Strategies for Managing Human Resource Diversity: From Resistance to Learning," *Academy of Management Executive,* May 1999, p 69.

80 Gaiter, pp A, A11.

81 E White, "Fostering Diversity to Aid Business," *The Wall Street Journal,* May 20, 2006, p B3.

82 Excerpted from C Tuna, "Initiative Moves Women Up Corporate Ladder," *The Wall Street Journal,* October 20, 2008, p B4. Copyright © 2008 by Dow Jones & Company, Inc. Reproduced with permission of Dow Jones & Company, Inc. via Copyright Clearance Center.

83 D Cadrain, "The Marijuana Exception," *HR Magazine,* November 2010, pp 40–41.

CHAPTER 3

1 C Barrett, "Talking Southwest Culture," *Spirit,* May 2008, p 12.

2 These companies are discussed in M Moskowitz , R Levering, and C Tkaczyk, "The 100 Best Companies to Work For," *Fortune,* February 8, 2010, pp 75–88.

3 C-H Chuang and H Liao, "Strategic Human Resource Management in Service Context: Taking Care of Employees and Customers," *Personnel Psychology,* Spring 2010, pp 153–196.

4 E H Schein, "Culture: The Missing Concept in Organization Studies," *Administrative Science Quarterly,* June 1996, p 236.

5 Excerpted from J McGregor, "The 2008 Winners," *Business Week,* March 3, 2008, p 49.

6 H Walters, "Google Did," *Bloomberg Businessweek,* May 16, 2010, p 60.

7 S H Schwartz, "Universals in the Content and Structure of Values: Theoretical Advances and Empirical Tests in 20 Countries," in *Advances in Experimental Social Psychology,* ed M P Zanna (New York: Academic Press, 1992), p 4.

8 A Fox, "Get in the Business of Being Green," *HR Magazine,* June 2008, pp 45–46.

9 See T L Friedman, "Yes, They Could. So They Did," *New York-Times.com,* February 14, 2009, www.nytimes. com/2009/02/15/opinion/15friedman.html.

10 See G Colvin, "Who's to Blame at BP?" *Fortune,* July 26, 2010, p 60; and "US Sues BP, 8 Other Companies in Gulf Oil Spill," retrieved January 3, 2011, from http://news.yahoo.com/s/ap/us_golf_oil_spill.

11 A Ignatius, "'We Had to Own the Mistakes,'" *Harvard Business Review,* July–August 2010, p 111.

12 Results are discussed in "Executing Ethics," *Training,* March 2007, p 8. Also see D Meinert, "Strong Ethical Culture Helps Bottom Line," *HR Magazine,* December 2010, p 21.

13 A L Kristof-Brown, R D Zimmerman, and E C Johnson, "Consequences of Individuals' Fit at Work: A Meta-Analysis of Person-Job, Person-Organization, Person-Group, and Person-Supervisor Fit," *Personnel Psychology,* Summer 2005, p 281.

14 See ibid., pp 281–342; and J P Meyer, T D Hecht, H Gill, and L Toplonytsky, "Person-Organization (Culture) Fit and Employee Commitment Under Conditions of Organization Change: A Longitudinal Study," *Journal of Vocational Behavior,* June 2010, pp 458–73.

15 M Bolch, "Closing the Sale," *HR Magazine,* October 2008, p 88.

16 Statistics and data contained in the Southwest Airlines example can be found in the "Southwest Airlines Fact Sheet," updated November 7, 2010, http://www.southwest.com/html/about-southwest/history/fact-sheet.html.

17 "Southwest Airlines Careers," retrieved February 2009 from http://www. southwest.com.

18 Southwest's mission statement can be found in "The Mission of Southwest Airlines," retrieved December 2008 from http://www .southwest.com.

19 See C Ostroff, A Kinicki, and M Tamkins, "Organizational Culture and Climate," in *Handbook of Psychology,* vol 12, ed W C Borman, D R Ilgen, and R J Klimoski (New York: Wiley and Sons, 2003), pp 565–93.

20 A thorough description of the CVF is provided in K S Cameron, R E Quinn, J Degraff, and A V Thakor, *Competing Values Leadership* (Northampton, MA: Edward Elgar, 2006).

21 Excerpted from K R Spors, "Top Small Workplaces 2008," *The Wall Street Journal,* October 13, 2008, p R4.

22 See Moskowitz, Levering, and Tkaczyk, pp 75–88; and M Jarman, "The Wheels Keep Turning at Discount Tire," *The Arizona Republic,* January 2, 2011, pp D1, D3.

23 Zappos is discussed in P O'Connell and J Larrere, "Develop Great Leaders," *Leadership Excellence,* April 2010, pp 12–13.

24 T Kelley and M F Cortez, "AstraZeneca's Risky Bet on Drug Discovery," *Bloomberg Businessweek,* January 3–9, 2011, p 21.

25 See M Arndt and B Einhorn, "The 50 Most Innovative Companies," *Bloomberg Businessweek,* April 25, 2010, p 39; and "Leadership with Trust," retrieved January 4, 2011, from http://www.tata.com/aboutus/sub_index.aspx?sectid=8hOk5Qq3EfQ=.

26 B Stone, "Will Richard Branson's Virgin America Fly?" *Bloomberg Businessweek,* January 3–9, 2011, pp 64–68.

27 D Welch, D Kiley, and M Ihlwan, "My Way or the Highway at Hyundai," *BusinessWeek,* March 17, 2008, pp 48–51.

[28] J D Rockoff, "J&J Lapses Are Cited in Drugs for Kids," *The Wall Street Journal,* May 27, 2010, p B1; and J S Lublin, "Some CEOs Face Big Repair Jobs in 2011," *The Wall Street Journal,* January 4, 2011, p B6.

[29] M Gunther, "3M's Innovation Revival," *Fortune,* September 27, 2010, pp 73–76.

[30] Results can be found in C Hartnell, Y Ou, and A Kinicki, "Organizational Culture and Organizational Effectiveness: A Meta-Analytic Investigation of the Competing Values Framework's Theoretical Suppositions," *Journal of Applied Psychology,* in press. Also see S A Sackman, "Culture and Performance," in *The Handbook of Organizational Culture and Climate,* 2nd ed, ed N M Ashkanasy, C P M Wilderom, and M F Peterson, (Los Angeles: Sage, 2011), pp 188–224.

[31] Mergers are discussed by L Tepedino and M Watkins, "Be a Master of Mergers and Acquisitions," *HR Magazine,* June 2010, pp 53–56.

[32] See C A Hartnell and F O Walumbwa, "Transformational Leadership and Organizational Culture," in *The Handbook of Organizational Culture and Climate,* 2nd ed, ed N M Ashkanasy, C P M Wilderom, and M F Peterson (Los Angeles: Sage, 2011), pp 225–48; and E F Goldman and A Casey, "Building a Culture that Encourages Strategic Thinking," *Journal of Leadership and Organizational Studies,* May 2010, pp 119–28.

[33] D W Young, "The Six Levers for Managing Organizational Culture," in *Readings in Organizational Behavior,* ed J A Wagner III and J R Hollenbeck (New York: Routledge, 2010), pp 533–46.

[34] W Disney, quoted in B Nanus, *Visionary Leadership: Creating a Compelling Sense of Direction for Your Organization* (San Francisco, CA: Jossey-Bass, 1992), p 28; reprinted from B Thomas, *Walt Disney: An American Tradition* (New York: Simon & Schuster, 1976), p 247.

[35] D-A Durbin, "Ford Cuts Part of Culture Shift," *The Arizona Republic,* January 24, 2006, p D3.

[36] The mechanisms were based on material contained in E H Schein, "The Role of the Founder in Creating Organizational Culture," *Organizational Dynamics,* Summer 1983, pp 13–28.

[37] J Collins, "The Secret of Enduring Greatness," *Fortune,* May 5, 2008, pp 73–76.

[38] A Fox, "Don't Let Silos Stand in the Way," *HR Magazine,* May 2010, p 51.

[39] See M Kimes, "Fluor's Corporate Crime Fighter," *Fortune,* February 16, 2009, p 26.

[40] D Moss, "Triage: Methodically Developing Its Employees," *HR Magazine,* July 2007, p 45.

[41] L Freifeld, "Highway to Health," *Training,* May 2009, pp 52–53.

[42] V Elmer, "How Storytelling Spurs Success," *Fortune,* December 6, 2010, pp 75–76.

[43] C Hymowitz, "New CEOs May Spur Resistance if They Try to Alter Firm's Culture," *The Wall Street Journal,* August 13, 2007, p B1.

[44] G Chazan and D Mattioli, "BP Links Pay to Safety in 4th Quarter," *The Wall Street Journal,* October 19, 2010, p B5.

[45] Fox, p 51.

[46] These examples are explored in B Roberts, "Social Networking at the Office," *HR Magazine,* March 2008, pp 81–83.

[47] J Van Maanen, "Breaking In: Socialization to Work," in *Handbook of Work, Organization, and Society,* ed R Dubin (Chicago: Rand-McNally, 1976), p 67.

[48] "Best Practices & Outstanding Initiatives: Pricewaterhouse Coopers: 101: PwC Internship Experience," *Training,* February 2010, p 104.

[49] See B Roberts, "Manage Candidates Right from the Start," *HR Magazine,* October 2008, pp 73–76.

[50] See J M Phillips, "Effects of Realistic Job Previews on Multiple Organizational Outcomes: A Meta-Analysis," *Academy of Management Journal,* December 1998, pp 673–90.

[51] Onboarding programs are discussed T Arnold, "Ramping Up Onboarding," *HR Magazine,* May 2010, pp 75–76; and K Fritz, M Kaestner, and M Bergman, "Coca-Cola Enterprises Invests in On-Boarding at the Front Lines to Benefit the Bottom Line," *Global Business and Organizational Excellence,* May–June 2010, pp 15–22.

[52] M Weinstein, "ADP's ABCS of Training," *Training,* February 2010, pp 34–38.

[53] H R Rafferty, "Social Media Etiquette: Communicate Behavioral Expectations," March 24, 2010, http://www.shrm.org.hrdisciplines/technology/Articles/Pages/SocialMediaEtiquette.aspx.

[54] Excerpted from S Reed, "The Stealth Oil Giant," *BusinessWeek,* January 14, 2008, p 45.

[55] See M M Smith, "Recognition ROI . . . Now More Than Ever," *HR Magazine: Special Advertisement Supplement—The Power of Incentives, HR Magazine,* 2008, pp 87–94.

[56] See J P Slattery, T T Selvarajan, and J E Anderson, "Influences of New Employee Development Practices on Temporary Employee Work-Related Attitudes," *Human Resource Development Quarterly,* 2006, pp 279–303.

[57] See E H Offstein and R L Dufresne, "Building Strong Ethics and Promoting Positive Character Development: The Influence of HRM at the United States Military Academy at West Point," *Human Resource Management,* Spring 2007, pp 95–114.

[58] J Fan and J P Wanous, "Organizational and Cultural Entry: A New Type of Orientation Program for Multiple Boundary Crossings," *Journal of Applied Psychology,* November 2008, pp 1390–1400.

[59] R Levering and M Moskowitz, "The 100 Best Companies to Work For: And the Winners Are . . .," *Fortune,* January 23, 2006, p 94.

[60] A review of stage model research can be found in B E Ashforth, *Role Transitions in Organizational Life: An Identity-Based Perspective* (Mahwah, NJ: Lawrence Erlbaum Associates, 2001).

[61] For a thorough review of research on the socialization of diverse employees with disabilities, see A Colella, "Organizational Socialization of Newcomers with Disabilities: A Framework for Future Research," in *Research in Personnel and Human Resources Management,* ed G R Ferris (Greenwich, CT: JAI Press, 1996), pp 351–417.

[62] This definition is based on the network perspective of mentoring proposed by M Higgins and K Kram, "Reconceptualizing Mentoring at Work: A Developmental Network Perspective," *Academy of Management Review,* April 2001, pp 264–88.

[63] See T D Allen, L T Eby, M L Poteet, and E Lentz, "Career Benefits Associated with Mentoring for Protégés: A Meta-Analysis," *Journal of Applied Psychology,* February 2004, pp 127–36; and D E Chandler and L Eby, "When Mentoring Goes Bad," *The Wall Street Journal,* May 24, 2010, pp R1, R3.

[64] Career functions are discussed in detail in K Kram, *Mentoring of Work: Developmental Relationships in Organizational Life* (Glenview, IL: Scott, Foresman, 1985).

[65] T J DeLong, J J Gabarro, and R J Lees, "Why Mentoring Matters in a Hypercompetitive World," *Harvard Business Review,* January 2008, pp 115–21.

[66] This discussion is based on Higgins and Kram, pp 264–88.

[67] See ibid., pp 264–88.

[68] See L T Eby, J R Durley, S C Evans, and B R Ragins, "Mentors' Perceptions of Negative Mentoring Experiences: Sale Development and Nomological Validation," *Journal of Applied Psychology,* March 2008, pp 358–73.

69 See Chandler and Eby, "When Mentoring Goes Bad;" and S Wang, E D Tomlinson, and R A Noe, "The Role of Mentor Trust and Protégé Internal Locus of Control in Formal Mentoring Relationships," *Journal of Applied Psychology,* March 2010, pp 358–67.

70 See T Gutner, "Finding Anchors in the Storm: Mentors," *The Wall Street Journal,* January 27, 2009, p D4.

71 A Pomeroy, "Internal Mentors and Coaches Are Popular," *HR Magazine,* September 2007, p 12.

72 Excerpted from K Linebaugh and J Bennett, "Marchionne Upends Chrysler's Ways," *The Wall Street Journal,* January 12, 2010, pp B1–B2.

73 Excerpted from J Silver-Greenberg, "The Credit-Card Blowup Ahead," *BusinessWeek,* October 20, 2008, pp 24–25.

CHAPTER 4

1 Adapted and excerpted from A Kedem, "Focus on Israel," *Training,* January 2010, p 14.

2 See P Engardio, G Smith, and J Sasseen, "Refighting NAFTA," *BusinessWeek,* March 31, 2008, pp 56–59; S A Stumpf and P Chaudhry, "Country Matters: Executives Weigh In on the Causes and Counter Measures of Counterfeit Trade," *Business Horizons,* May–June 2010, pp 305–14; and F Balfour and T Culpan, "Chairman Gou," *Bloomberg Businessweek,* September 13–19, 2010, pp 58–69.

3 R Zeidner, "Uncovering Offshoring's Invisible Costs," *HR Magazine,* January 2009, p 26. Also see M Boyle, "Mapping the iPod Economy," *BusinessWeek,* November 3, 2008, p 30.

4 See S de Treville and L Trigeorgis, "It May Be Cheaper to Manufacture at Home," *Harvard Business Review,* October 2010, pp 84–87; B Einhorn and K Gokhale, "India Outsourcers Feel Unloved in the US," *Bloomberg Businessweek,* November 8–14, 2010, pp 16, 18; M Yun and K Chu, "Philippines May Answer Call: Nation Passes India in Call-Center Jobs," *USA Today,* January 10, 2011, pp 1B–2B; and O Bertrand, "What Goes Around, Comes Around: Effects of Offshore Outsourcing on the Export Performance of Firms," *Journal of International Business Studies,* February–March 2011, pp 334–44.

5 D J Lynch, "Developing Nations Poised to Challenge USA as King of the Hill," *USA Today,* February 8, 2007, p 2B. Also see R Foroohar and M Liu, "It's China's World: We're Just Living in It," *Newsweek,* March 22, 2010, pp 36–39; S Prasso, "American Made . . . Chinese Owned," *Fortune,* May 24, 2010, pp 84–92; M Gunther, "The World's New Economic Landscape," *Fortune,* July 26, 2010, pp 104–6; and I S Fish, "The China Threat," *Newsweek,* January 24, 2011, pp 28–29.

6 W W Maddux, A D Galinsky, and C T Tadmar, "Be a Better Manager: Live Abroad," *Harvard Business Review,* September 2010, p 24.

7 Data from M A Carpenter, W G Sanders, and H B Gregersen, "Bundling Human Capital with Organizational Context: The Impact of International Assignment Experience on Multinational Firm Performance and CEO Pay," *Academy of Management Journal,* June 2001, pp 493–511. Also see H Lin and S Hou, "Managerial Lessons from the East: An Interview with Acer's Stan Shih," *Academy of Management Perspectives,* November 2010, pp 6–16.

8 Data from L Petrecca, "Low-Profile Nestlé Leader Aims High," *USA Today,* October 25, 2010, p 5B.

9 See G Hofstede, A V Garibaldi de Hilal, S Malvezzi, B Tanure, and H Vinken, "Comparing Regional Cultures within a Country: Lessons from Brazil," *Journal of Cross-Cultural Psychology,* May 2010, pp 336–52.

10 See U Zander and L Zander, "Opening the Grey Box: Social Communities, Knowledge and Culture in Acquisitions," *Journal of International Business Studies,* January 2010, pp 27–37.

11 See T Cappellen and M Janssens, "Enacting Global Careers: Organizational Career Scripts and the Global Economy as Co-existing Career Referents," *Journal of Organizational Behavior,* July 2010, pp 687–706; and M Harvey, H Mayerhofer, L Hartmann, and M Moeller, "Corralling the 'Horses' to Staff the Global Organization of 21st Century," *Organizational Dynamics,* July–September 2010, pp 258–68.

12 See W A Haviland, H E L Prins, B McBride, and D Walrath, *Cultural Anthropology: The Human Challenge,* 13th ed (Florence, KY: Wadsworth, 2010).

13 M Mabry, "Pin a Label on a Manager—and Watch What Happens," *Newsweek,* May 14, 1990, p 43.

14 Ibid. Also see M Munoz and M Segura, "Focus on the Philippines," *Training,* June 2009, p 18.

15 M Javidan and R J House, "Cultural Acumen for the Global Manager: Lessons from Project GLOBE," *Organizational Dynamics,* Spring 2001, p 292 (emphasis added).

16 For instructive discussion, see J S Black, H B Gregersen, and M E Mendenhall, *Global Assignments: Successfully Expatriating and Repatriating International Managers* (San Francisco: Jossey-Bass, 1992), ch 2.

17 F Trompenaars and C Hampden-Turner, *Riding the Waves of Culture: Understanding Cultural Diversity in Global Business,* 2nd ed (New York: McGraw-Hill, 1998), pp 6–7. The concept of "cultural mosaic" is discussed in G T Chao and H Moon, "The Cultural Mosaic: A Metatheory for Understanding the Complexity of Culture," *Journal of Applied Psychology,* November 2005, pp 1128–40. Also see K Leung, R Bhagat, N R Buchan, M Erez, and C B Gibson, "Beyond National Culture and Culture-Centricism: A Reply to Gould and Grein (2009)," *Journal of International Business Studies,* January 2011, pp 177–81.

18 As quoted in *BusinessWeek,* August 25–September 1, 2008, p 44.

19 Based on A K Leung and C Chiu, "Multicultural Experience, Idea Receptiveness, and Creativity," *Journal of Cross-Cultural Psychology,* September–November 2010, pp 723–41.

20 As quoted in "How Cultures Collide," *Psychology Today,* July 1976, p 69.

21 Market research by a cultural anthropologist is discussed in E Pooley, "Charged for Battle," *Bloomberg Businessweek,* January 3–9, 2011, pp 48–56.

22 J Main, "How to Go Global—and Why," *Fortune,* August 28, 1989, p 73.

23 W D Marbach, "Quality: What Motivates American Workers?" *BusinessWeek,* April 12, 1993, p 93.

24 See G A Sumner, *Folkways* (New York: Ginn, 1906).

25 As quoted in C Levinson, "In Kirkuk, Ethnic Tension Simmers," *USA Today,* August 14, 2008, p 2A.

26 D A Heenan and H V Perlmutter, *Multinational Organization Development* (Reading, MA: Addison-Wesley, 1979), p 17.

27 Data from R Kopp, "International Human Resource Policies and Practices in Japanese, European, and United States Multinationals," *Human Resource Management,* Winter 1994, pp 581–99.

28 Fareed Zakaria, *The Post-American World* (New York: W W Norton, 2008), p 46. Also see R J Crisp and R N Turner, "Cognitive Adaptation to the Experience of Social and Cultural Diversity," *Psychological Bulletin,* December 2010, pp 1–25.

29 Data from M B Marklein, "College Study Abroad Suffers a Dip," *USA Today,* November 15, 2010, p 3A. Also see D Bolton and R Nie, "Creating Value in Transnational Higher Education: The Role of Stakeholder Management," *Academy of Management Learning and Education,* December 2010, pp 701–14.

30 See R R McCrae, A Terracciano, A Realo, and J Allik, "Interpreting GLOBE Societal Practices Scales," *Journal of Cross-Cultural Psychology,* November 2008, pp 805–10.

31 J S Osland and A Bird, "Beyond Sophisticated Stereotyping: Cultural Sensemaking in Context," *Academy of Management Executive,* February 2000, p 67.

[32] "Fujio Mitarai: Canon," *BusinessWeek,* January 14, 2002, p 55.

[33] See P C Earley and E Mosakowski, "Toward Culture Intelligence: Turning Cultural Differences into a Workplace Advantage," *Academy of Management Executive,* August 2004, pp 151–57; P C Earley and E Mosakowski, "Cultural Intelligence," *Harvard Business Review,* October 2004, pp 139–46; and K Ng, L Van Dyne, and S Ang, "From Experience to Experiential Learning: Cultural Intelligence as a Learning Capability for Global Leader Development," *Academy of Management Learning and Education,* December 2010, pp 511–26.

[34] D C Thomas and K Inkson, *Cultural Intelligence: Living and Working Globally*, 2nd ed (San Francisco: Berrett-Koehler, 2009), p 16.

[35] See K A Crowne, "What Leads to Cultural Intelligence?" *Business Horizons,* September–October 2008, pp 391–99.

[36] J Porter, "How to Stand Out in the Global Crowd," *BusinessWeek,* November 24, 2008, pp 52, 54.

[37] See "How Cultures Collide," pp 66–74, 97; and M Munter, "Cross-Cultural Communication for Managers," *Business Horizons,* May–June 1993, pp 69–78.

[38] S Reed, "Meet the Master of Mideast Buyouts," *BusinessWeek,* March 10, 2008, p 70.

[39] The German management style is discussed in R Stewart, "German Management: A Challenge to Anglo-American Managerial Assumptions," *Business Horizons,* May–June 1996, pp 52–54.

[40] I Adler, "Between the Lines," *Business Mexico,* October 2000, p 24. Also see I Cantú de La Torre and L Cantú Licón, "Focus on Mexico," *Training,* February 2009, p 20.

[41] The tips were excerpted from R Drew, "Working with Foreigners," *Management Review,* September 1999, p 6.

[42] For background, see Javidan and House, "Cultural Acumen for the Global Manager," pp 289–305; the entire Spring 2002 issue of *Journal of World Business;* R J House, P J Hanges, M Javidan, P W Dorfman, and V Gupta, eds, *Culture, Leadership, and Organizations: The GLOBE Study of 62 Societies* (Thousand Oaks, CA: Sage, 2004); and www.thunderbird.edu/wwwfiles/ms/globe/.

[43] R House, M Javidan, P Hanges, and P Dorfman, "Understanding Cultures and Implicit Leadership Theories across the Globe: An Introduction to Project GLOBE," *Journal of World Business,* Spring 2002, p 4. For a critical view of GLOBE, see P Brewer and S Venaik, "GLOBE Practices and Values: A Case of Diminishing Marginal Utility?" *Journal of International Business Studies,* October–November 2010, pp 1316–24.

[44] Adapted from the list in ibid., pp 5–6. Also see M Javidan, G K Stahl, F Brodbeck, and C P M Wilderom, "Cross-Border Transfer of Knowledge: Cultural Lessons from Project GLOBE," *Academy of Management Executive,* May 2005, pp 59–76; and D A Waldman, M Sully de Luque, N Washburn, R J House, et al., "Cultural and Leadership Predictors of Corporate Social Responsibility Values of Top Management: A GLOBE Study of 15 Countries," *Journal of International Business Studies,* November 2006, pp 823–37.

[45] See M Javidan, "Forward-Thinking Cultures," *Harvard Business Review,* July–August 2007, p 20; and N Orkin, "Focus on Singapore," *Training,* January 2009, p 16.

[46] As quoted in J Reingold, "Secrets of Their Success," *Fortune,* November 24, 2008, p 162. For more detail, see M Gladwell, *Outliers: The Story of Success* (New York: Little, Brown, 2008), ch 7. Also see R Yu, "Korean Air Upgrades Service, Image," *USA Today,* August 24, 2009, pp 1B–2B.

[47] See D Oyserman, H M Coon, and M Kemmelmeier, "Rethinking Individualism and Collectivism: Evaluation of Theoretical Assumptions and Meta-Analyses," *Psychological Bulletin,* January 2002, pp 3–72; B Erdogan and R C Liden, "Collectivism as a Moderator of Responses to Organizational Justice: Implications for Leader-Member Exchange and Ingratiation," *Journal of Organizational Behavior,* February 2006, pp 1–17; and A Hwang and A M Francesco, "The Influence of Individualism-Collectivism and Power Distance on Use of Feedback Channels and Consequences for Learning," *Academy of Management Learning and Education,* June 2010, pp 243–57.

[48] M Edwards, "As Good as It Gets," *AARP: The Magazine,* November–December 2004, p 48.

[49] See table in ibid., p 49.

[50] Data from Trompenaars and Hampden-Turner, *Riding the Waves of Culture,* ch 5. For related research, see E G T Green and J Deschamps, "Variation of Individualism and Collectivism within and between 20 Countries," *Journal of Cross-Cultural Psychology,* May 2005, pp 321–39; and S Begley, "You Can Blame the Bugs," *Newsweek,* April 14, 2008, p 41.

[51] As quoted in E E Schultz, "Scudder Brings Lessons to Navajo, Gets Some of Its Own," *The Wall Street Journal,* April 29, 1999, p C12.

[52] Trompenaars and Hampden-Turner, p 56.

[53] For interesting reading, see P Zimbardo and J Boyd, *The Time Paradox: The New Psychology of Time That Will Change Your Life* (New York: Free Press, 2008).

[54] As quoted in D W Dowling, "The Best Advice I Ever Got," *Harvard Business Review,* May 2008, p 21. Also see the role of monochronic time in J Graham, "Google Starts Searching Before You Finish Typing," *USA Today,* September 9, 2010, p 1B.

[55] S Smith, "A Pirate's Life," *Newsweek,* June 26, 2006, p 45.

[56] R W Moore, "Time, Culture, and Comparative Management: A Review and Future Direction," in *Advances in International Comparative Management,* vol. 5, ed S B Prasad (Greenwich, CT: JAI Press, 1990), pp 7–8.

[57] S Reed and R Tuttle, "Qatar on the Cusp," *Bloomberg Businessweek,* March 22–29, 2010, p 53.

[58] J Deschenaux, "Less Time for Lunch," *HR Magazine,* June 2008, p 125.

[59] See E T Hall, *The Hidden Dimension* (Garden City, NY: Doubleday, 1966).

[60] "How Cultures Collide," p 72.

[61] See C L Grossman, "Young Adults Today Are a 'Less Religious' Bunch," *USA Today,* February 17, 2010, p 10B; S Prothero, "A World Apart on the Muslim Veil," *USA Today,* August 2, 2010, p 9A; and C L Grossman, "How America Sees God," *USA Today,* October 7, 2010, pp 1A–2A.

[62] Results adapted from and value definitions quoted from S R Safranski and I-W Kwon, "Religious Groups and Management Value Systems," in *Advances in International Comparative Management,* vol 3, ed R N Farner and E G McGoun (Greenwich, CT: JAI Press, 1988), pp 171–83.

[63] Ibid., p 180.

[64] N J Adler with A Gundersen, *International Dimensions of Organizational Behavior,* 5th ed (Mason, OH: Thomson SouthWestern, 2008), p 13 (emphasis added). Another good resource book is D C Thomas, *Cross-Cultural Management: Essential Concepts,* 2nd ed (Thousand Oaks, CA: Sage, 2008).

[65] Drawn from F F Chen, "What Happens if We Compare Chopsticks with Forks? The Impact of Making Inappropriate Comparisons in Cross-Cultural Research," *Journal of Personality and Social Psychology,* November 2008, pp 1005–18. Also see R L Tung and A Verbeke, "Beyond Hofstede and GLOBE: Improving the Quality of Cross-Cultural Research," *Journal of International Business Studies,* October–November 2010, pp 1259–74; and P D Ellis, "Effect Sizes and the Interpretation of Research Results in International Business," *Journal of International Business Studies,* December 2010, pp 1581–88.

[66] M Javidan and R J House, "Leadership and Cultures around the World: Findings from GLOBE—An Introduction to the Special Issue," *Journal of World Business,* Spring 2002, p 1.

67 For complete details, see G Hofstede, *Culture's Consequences: International Differences in Work-Related Values,* abridged ed (Newbury Park, CA: Sage, 1984); G Hofstede, "The Interaction between National and Organizational Value Systems," *Journal of Management Studies,* July 1985, pp 347–57; and G Hofstede, "Management Scientists Are Human," *Management Science,* January 1994, pp 4–13. Also see B L Kirkman, K B Lowe, and C B Gibson, "A Quarter Century of *Culture's Consequences:* A Review of Empirical Research Incorporating Hofstede's Cultural Values Framework," *Journal of International Business Studies,* May 2006, pp 285–320; R Fischer, C M Vauclair, J R J Fontaine, and S H Schwartz, "Are Individual-Level and Country-Level Value Structures Different? Testing Hofstede's Legacy With the Schwartz Value Survey," *Journal of Cross-Cultural Psychology,* March 2010, pp 135–51; and V Taras, B L Kirkman, and P Steel, "Examining the Impact of *Culture's Consequences*: A Three-Decade, Multilevel, Meta-Analytic Review of Hofstede's Cultural Value Dimensions," *Journal of Applied Psychology,* May 2010, pp 405–39.

68 A similar conclusion is presented in the following replication of Hofstede's work: A Merritt, "Culture in the Cockpit: Do Hofstede's Dimensions Replicate?" *Journal of Cross-Cultural Psychology,* May 2000, pp 283–301. Also see K Gilbert and S Cartwright, "Cross-Cultural Consultancy Initiatives to Develop Russian Managers: An Analysis of Five Western Aid-Funded Programs," *Academy of Management Learning and Education,* December 2008, pp 504–18.

69 For related reading, see M Javidan, P W Dorfman, M Sully de Luque, and R J House, "In the Eye of the Beholder: Cross Cultural Lessons in Leadership from Project GLOBE," *Academy of Management Perspectives,* February 2006, pp 67–90; G B Graen, "In the Eye of the Beholder: Cross-Cultural Lesson in Leadership from Project GLOBE: A Response Viewed from the Third Culture Bonding (TCB) Model of Cross-Cultural Leadership," *Academy of Management Perspectives,* November 2006, pp 95–101; R J House, M Javidan, P W Dorfman, and M Sully de Luque, "A Failure of Scholarship: Response to George Graen's Critique of GLOBE," *Academy of Management Perspectives,* November 2006, pp 102–14; P Caligiuri and I Tarique, "Predicting Effectiveness in Global Leadership Activities," *Journal of World Business,* July 2009, pp 336–46; and A McDonnell, R Lamare, P Gunnigle, and J Lavelle, Developing Tomorrow's Leaders—Evidence of Global Talent Management in Multinational Enterprises," *Journal of World Business,* April 2010, pp 150–60.

70 J Guyon, "David Whitwam," *Fortune,* July 26, 2004, p 174.

71 N Bloom and J Van Reenen, "Why Do Management Practices Differ Across Firms and Countries?" *Journal of Economic Perspectives,* Winter 2010, p 207. Also see J Yu and S Zaheer, "Building a Process Model of Local Adaptation of Practices: A Study of Six Sigma Implementation in Korean and US Firms," *Journal of International Business Studies,* April 2010, pp 475–99; and J J Lawler, S Chen, P Wu, J Bae, and B Bai, "High-Performance Work Systems in Foreign Subsidiaries of American Multinationals: An Institutional Model," *Journal of International Business Studies,* February–March 2011, pp 202–20.

72 Data from www.siemens.com/about/en/worldwide.htm; and R Weiss and B Kammel, "How Siemens Got Its *Geist* Back," *Bloomberg Businessweek,* January 31–February 6, 2011, pp 18–20.

73 See M Chen and D Miller, "West Meets East: Toward an Ambicultural Approach to Management," *Academy of Management Perspectives,* November 2010, pp 17–24.

74 J Welch and S Welch, "Red Flags for the Decade Ahead," *BusinessWeek,* May 19, 2008, p 82. Also see P Davidson, "US Job Hunters Eye Other Nations' Help Wanted Ads," *USA Today,* November 16, 2009, p 1B.

75 Data from J Clark, "New Travel Rules Set Off Confusion, Rush for Passports," *USA Today,* January 19, 2007, p 3D; and *NBC Nightly News,* January 27, 2007.

76 J S Black and H B Gregersen, "The Right Way to Manage Expats," *Harvard Business Review,* March–April 1999, p 53. A more optimistic picture is presented in R L Tung, "American Expatriates Abroad: From Neophytes to Cosmopolitans," *Journal of World Business,* Summer 1998, pp 125–44. Also see M A Clouse and M D

Watkins, "Three Keys to Getting an Overseas Assignment Right," *Harvard Business Review,* October 2009, pp 115–119.

77 Data from G S Insch and J D Daniels, "Causes and Consequences of Declining Early Departures from Foreign Assignments," *Business Horizons,* November–December 2002, pp 39–48. Also see G Chen, B L Kirkman, K Kim, C I C Farh, and S Tangirala, "When Does Cross-Cultural Motivation Enhance Expatriate Effectiveness? A Multilevel Investigation of the Moderating Roles of Subsidiary Support and Cultural Distance," *Academy of Management Journal,* October 2010, pp 1110–30.

78 S Dallas, "Rule No. 1: Don't Diss the Locals," *BusinessWeek,* May 15, 1995, p 8. Also see L S Paine, "The China Rules," *Harvard Business Review,* June 2010, pp 103–8.

79 P Capell, "Employers Seek to Trim Pay for US Expatriates," April 16, 2005, www.careerjournal.com. Also see E Krell, "Evaluating Returns on Expatriates," *HR Magazine,* March 2005, pp 60–65.

80 These insights come from Tung, "American Expatriates Abroad"; R L Tung, "Female Expatriates: The Model Global Manager?" *Organizational Dynamics,* no. 3, 2004, pp 243–53; A Varma, S M Toh, and P Budhwar, "A New Perspective on the Female Expatriate Experience: The Role of Host Country National Categorization," *Journal of World Business,* June 2006, pp 112–20; M Janssens, T Cappellen, and P Zanoni, "Successful Female Expatriates as Agents: Positioning Oneself through Gender, Hierarchy, and Culture," *Journal of World Business,* June 2006, pp 133–48; and A Pomeroy, "Outdated Policies Hinder Female Expats," *HR Magazine,* December 2006, p 16.

81 E Levenson, "Leaders of the Pack," *Fortune,* October 16, 2006, p 189.

82 "The Best Managers: Irene Rosenfeld," *BusinessWeek,* January 19, 2009, p 41.

83 J S Lublin, "Younger Managers Learn Global Skills," *The Wall Street Journal,* March 31, 1992, p B1.

84 See P C Earley, "Intercultural Training for Managers: A Comparison of Documentary and Interpersonal Methods," *Academy of Management Journal,* December 1987, pp 685–98.

85 Based on J O Okpara and J D Kabongo, "Cross-Cultural Training and Expatriate Adjustment: A Study of Western Expatriates in Nigeria," *Journal of World Business,* January 2011, pp 22–30. Also see D Holtbrügge and A T Mohr, "Cultural Determinants of Learning Style Preferences," *Academy of Management Learning and Education,* December 2010, pp 622–37.

86 E Iwata, "Time to Cut Back, Hunker Down," *USA Today,* February 20, 2008, p 6B. Also see V Harnish, "Step Right Up! Don't Miss the Biggest Opportunity in History!" *Fortune,* July 26, 2010, p 54.

87 Data from "USA Today Snapshots: Learning the Lingo," *USA Today,* January 26, 2006, p 1A.

88 Data from A R Carey and S Ward, "What Are the Most Common Foreign Languages Taught in US Schools?" *USA Today,* February 16, 2010, p 1A.

89 Data from "Diverse Landscape of Newest Americans," *USA Today,* December 4, 2006, p 8A. For interesting reading, see H Hitchings, *The Secret Life of Words: How English Became English* (New York: Farrar, Straus and Giroux, 2008).

90 See E Marx, *Breaking through Culture Shock: What You Need to Succeed in International Business* (London: Nicholas Brealey Publishing, 2001). Also see M Javidan, M Teagarden and D Bowen, "Making It Overseas," *Harvard Business Review,* April 2010, pp 109–13.

91 See M Lazarova, M Westman, and M A Shaffer, "Elucidating the Positive Side of the Work-Family Interface on International Assignments: A Model of Expatriate Work and Family Performance," *Academy of Management Review,* January 2010, pp 93–117; and C I C Farh, K M Bartol, D L Shapiro, and J Shin, "Networking Abroad: A Process Model of How Expatriates Form Support Ties to Facilitate Adjustment," *Academy of Management Review,* July 2010, pp 434–54.

[92] K L Miller, "How a Team of Buckeyes Helped Honda Save a Bundle," *BusinessWeek,* September 13, 1993, p 68.

[93] B Newman, "For Ira Caplan, Re-Entry Has Been Strange," *The Wall Street Journal,* December 12, 1995, p A12.

[94] See Black, Gregersen, and Mendenhall, p 227.

[95] Ibid., pp 226–27.

[96] See L Albright, "How Can My Company Best Retain Repatriated Employees?" *HR Magazine,* March 2008, p 35; A Andors, "Happy Returns," *HR Magazine,* March 2010, pp 61–63; and P Tharenou and N Caulfield, "Will I Stay or Will I Go? Explaining Repatriation by Self-Initiated Expatriates," *Academy of Management Journal,* October 2010, pp 1009–28.

[97] E Meyer and E Yi Shen, "China Myths, China Facts," *Harvard Business Review,* January–February 2010, p 24.

[98] "Bribery Rampant, Increasing in Russia," *USA Today,* October 28, 2010, p 6A.

[99] Excerpted from M V Gratchev, "Making the Most of Cultural Differences," *Harvard Business Review,* October 2001, pp 28, 30. For relevant background information, see R Farzad, "Drop Russia, Add Indonesia: The Debate Is On," *Bloomberg Businessweek,* November 22–28, 2010, pp 21–22; and D Brady, "Hard Choices: William Browder," *Bloomberg Businessweek,* January 10–16, 2011, p 80.

CHAPTER 5

[1] Data from www.facebook.com/press/info.php?statistics.

[2] Excerpted from D Kirkpatrick, *The Facebook Effect: The Inside Story of the Company That Is Connecting the World* (New York: Simon & Schuster, 2010), p 20.

[3] S Sternberg, "The Genome: Big Advances, Many Questions," *USA Today,* July 8, 2010, p 2A. *Note:* Population statistic updated from 6 to 7 billion.

[4] D Seligman, "The Trouble with Buyouts," *Fortune,* November 30, 1992, p 125.

[5] See J Schramm, "HR's Challenging Next Decade," *HR Magazine,* November 2010, p 96; and M R Hamdani and M R Buckley, "Diversity Goals: Reframing the Debate and Enabling a Fair Evaluation," *Business Horizons,* January–February 2011, pp 33–40.

[6] See H Ibarra and R Barbulescu, "Identity as Narrative: Prevalence, Effectiveness, and Consequences of Narrative Identity Work in Macro Work Role Transitions," *Academy of Management Review,* January 2010, pp 135–54; and R E Johnson, C Chang, and L Yang, "Commitment and Motivation at Work: The Relevance of Employee Identity and Regulatory Focus," *Academy of Management Review,* April 2010, pp 226–45.

[7] Drawn from E Porter, "Mirror, Mirror on the Wall," *Best Friends Magazine,* January–February 2007, pp 8–9.

[8] Data from "If We Could Do It Over Again," *USA Today,* February 19, 2001, p 4D.

[9] As quoted in G Colvin, "Star Power," *Fortune,* February 6, 2006, p 56.

[10] V Gecas, "The Self-Concept," in *Annual Review of Sociology,* ed R H Turner and J F Short Jr (Palo Alto, CA: Annual Reviews, 1982), vol 8, p 3. Also see R E Johnson, C C Rosen, and P E Levy, "Getting to the Core of Core Self-Evaluation: A Review and Recommendations," *Journal of Organizational Behavior,* April 2008, pp 391–413; and S W Farmer and L Van Dyne, "The Idealized Self and the Situated Self as Predictors of Employee Work Behaviors," *Journal of Applied Psychology,* May 2010, pp 503–16.

[11] L Festinger, *A Theory of Cognitive Dissonance* (Stanford, CA: Stanford University Press, 1957), p 3. Self-awareness cognitions in a practical context are discussed in K Sulkowicz, "Analyze This," *BusinessWeek,* April 21, 2008, p 17.

[12] Based in part on a definition found in Gecas, "The Self-Concept." Also see D L Ferris, H Lian, D J Brown, F X J Pang, and L M Keeping, "Self-Esteem and Job Performance: The Moderating Role of Self-Esteem Contingencies," *Personnel Psychology,* Autumn 2010, pp 561–93.

[13] See N Hellmich, "For Women, Bad Hair Days Are No Joke," *USA Today,* April 13, 2010, p 10B; D Brady, "Out of Work, Not Out of Oomph," *Bloomberg Businessweek,* September 13–19, 2010, pp 51–52; and S Jayson, "Youths Prefer Praise to Sex, Booze," *USA Today,* January 11, 2011, p 3A.

[14] H W Marsh, "Positive and Negative Global Self-Esteem: A Substantively Meaningful Distinction or Artifacts?" *Journal of Personality and Social Psychology,* April 1996, p 819.

[15] Ibid.

[16] Based on D A Stinson et al., "The Cost of Lower Self-Esteem: Testing a Self- and Social-Bonds Model of Health," *Journal of Personality and Social Psychology,* March 2008, pp 412–28; S M McCrea, "Self-Handicapping, Excuse Making, and Counterfactual Thinking: Consequences for Self-Esteem and Future Motivation," *Journal of Personality and Social Psychology,* August 2008, pp 274–92; and U Orth, R W Robins, and B W Roberts, "Low Self-Esteem Prospectively Predicts Depression in Adolescence and Young Adulthood," *Journal of Personality and Social Psychology,* September 2008, pp 695–708.

[17] U Orth, K H Trzesniewski, and R W Robins, "Self-Esteem Development from Young Adulthood to Old Age: A Cohort-Sequential Longitudinal Study," *Journal of Personality and Social Psychology,* April 2010, p 645.

[18] E Diener and M Diener, "Cross-Cultural Correlates of Life Satisfaction and Self-Esteem," *Journal of Personality and Social Psychology,* April 1995, p 662. Also see R A Brown, "Perceptions of Psychological Adjustment, Achievement Outcomes, and Self-Esteem in Japan and America," *Journal of Cross-Cultural Psychology,* January 2010, pp 51–61; and R W Tafarodi, S C Shaughnessy, S Yamaguchi, and A Murakoshi, "The Reporting of Self-Esteem in Japan and Canada," *Journal of Cross-Cultural Psychology,* January 2011, pp 155–64.

[19] Based on data in F L Smoll, R E Smith, N P Barnett, and J J Everett, "Enhancement of Children's Self-Esteem through Social Support Training for Youth Sports Coaches," *Journal of Applied Psychology,* August 1993, pp 602–10.

[20] W J McGuire and C V McGuire, "Enhancing Self-Esteem by Directed-Thinking Tasks: Cognitive and Affective Positivity Asymmetries," *Journal of Personality and Social Psychology,* June 1996, p 1124.

[21] See M Elias, "Study: Today's Youth Think Quite Highly of Themselves," *USA Today,* November 19, 2008, p 7D.

[22] Data from P Coy, "The Competition Issue: The Poll," *BusinessWeek,* August 21–28, 2006, p 46.

[23] See G Chen, S M Gully, and D Eden, "General Self-Efficacy and Self-Esteem: Toward Theoretical and Empirical Distinction between Correlated Self-Evaluations," *Journal of Organizational Behavior,* May 2004, pp 375–95.

[24] M E Gist, "Self-Efficacy: Implications for Organizational Behavior and Human Resource Management," *Academy of Management Review,* July 1987, p 472. Also see A Bandura, "Self-Efficacy: Toward a Unifying Theory of Behavioral Change," *Psychological Review,* March 1977, pp 191–215; S Ellis, Y Ganzach, E Castle, and G Sekely, "The Effect of Filmed Versus Personal After-Event Reviews on Task Performance: The Mediating and Moderating Role of Self-Efficacy," *Journal of Applied Psychology,* January 2010, pp 122–31; and A M Schmidt, and R P DeShon, "The Moderating Effects of Performance Ambiguity on the Relationship Between Self-Efficacy and Performance," *Journal of Applied Psychology,* May 2010, pp 572–81.

[25] Based on D H Lindsley, D A Brass, and J B Thomas, "Efficacy-Performance Spirals: A Multilevel Perspective," *Academy of*

Management Review, July 1995, pp 645–78. Also see J B Vancouver and L N Kendall, "When Self-Efficacy Negatively Relates to Motivation and Performance in a Learning Context," *Journal of Applied Psychology,* September 2006, pp 1146–153.

26 See, for example, V Gecas, "The Social Psychology of Self-Efficacy," in *Annual Review of Sociology,* ed W R Scott and J Blake (Palo Alto, CA: Annual Reviews, 1989), vol 15, pp 291–316; C K Stevens, A G Bavetta, and M E Gist, "Gender Differences in the Acquisition of Salary Negotiation Skills: The Role of Goals, Self-Efficacy, and Perceived Control," *Journal of Applied Psychology,* October 1993, pp 723–35; D Eden and Y Zuk, "Seasickness as a Self-Fulfilling Prophecy: Raising Self-Efficacy to Boost Performance at Sea," *Journal of Applied Psychology,* October 1995, pp 628–35; S M Jex, P D Bliese, S Buzzell, and J Primeau, "The Impact of Self-Efficacy on Stressor-Strain Relations: Coping Style as an Explanatory Mechanism," *Journal of Applied Psychology,* June 2001, pp 401–9; C A Shields, L B Brawley, and T I Lindover, "Self-Efficacy as a Mediator of the Relationship between Causal Attributions and Exercise Behavior," *Journal of Applied Social Psychology,* November 2006, pp 2785–802; and E C Dierdorff, E A Surface, and K G Brown, "Frame-of-Reference Training Effectiveness: Effects of Goal Orientation and Self-Efficacy on Affective, Cognitive, Skill-Based, and Transfer Outcomes," *Journal of Applied Psychology,* November 2010, pp 1181–91.

27 G Toppo, "A Solution to How to Teach Math: Subtract," *USA Today,* March 13, 2008, p 6D.

28 Data from A D Stajkovic and F Luthans, "Self-Efficacy and Work-Related Performance: A Meta-Analysis," *Psychological Bulletin,* September 1998, pp 240–61.

29 As quoted in G Colvin, "How One CEO Learned to Fly," *Fortune,* October 30, 2006, p 100.

30 M Snyder and S Gangestad, "On the Nature of Self-Monitoring: Matters of Assessment, Matters of Validity," *Journal of Personality and Social Psychology,* July 1986, p 125.

31 As quoted in K Sulkowicz, "Me, Me, Me, Me, Me," *BusinessWeek,* April 23, 2007, p 14.

32 Data from D V Day, D J Schleicher, A L Unckless, and N J Hiller, "Self-Monitoring Personality at Work: A Meta-Analytic Investigation of Construct Validity," *Journal of Applied Psychology,* April 2002, pp 390–401.

33 Data from M Kilduff and D V Day, "Do Chameleons Get Ahead? The Effects of Self-Monitoring on Managerial Careers," *Academy of Management Journal,* August 1994, pp 1047–60. Similar findings are reported in O Brafman and R Brafman, "To Vulnerable Go the Spoils," *Bloomberg Businessweek,* June 14–20, 2010, pp 71–73.

34 Data from D B Turban and T W Dougherty, "Role of Protégé Personality in Receipt of Mentoring and Career Success," *Academy of Management Journal,* June 1994, pp 688–702.

35 See F Luthans, "Successful vs. Effective Managers," *Academy of Management Executive,* May 1988, pp 127–32.

36 M G Pratt, "To Be or Not to Be? Central Questions in Organizational Identification," in *Identity in Organizations,* ed D A Whetten and P C Godfrey (Thousand Oaks, CA: Sage Publications, 1998), p 172. Also see G Petriglieri and J Petriglieri, "Identity Workspaces: The Case of Business Schools," *Academy of Management Learning and Education,* March 2010, pp 44–60; J E Dutton, L M Roberts, and J Bednar, "Pathways for Positive Identity Construction at Work: Four Types of Positive Identity and the Building of Social Resources," *Academy of Management Review,* April 2010, pp 265–93; and D Cooper and S M B Thatcher, "Identification in Organizations: The Role of Self-Concept Orientations and Identification Motives," *Academy of Management Review,* October 2010, pp 516–38.

37 R Levering and M Moskowitz, "Fortune 100 Best Companies to Work For," *Fortune,* January 22, 2007, p 108. Also see B Burlingham, "What Am I, If Not My Business?" *Inc.,* November 2010, pp 86–95.

38 C Fishman, "What if You'd Worked at Enron?" *Fast Company,* May 2002, pp 104, 106.

39 See E E Umphress, J B Bingham, and M S Mitchell, "Unethical Behavior in the Name of the Company: The Moderating Effect of Organizational Identification and Positive Reciprocity Beliefs on Unethical Pro-organizational Behavior," *Journal of Applied Psychology,* July 2010, pp 769–80.

40 For a good overview, see L R James and M D Mazerolle, *Personality in Work Organizations* (Thousand Oaks, CA: Sage Publications, 2002). Also see P J Rentfrow, "Statewide Differences in Personality," *American Psychologist,* September 2010, pp 548–58.

41 See W Bleidom, C Kandler, U R Hülsheger, R Riemann, A Angleitner, and F M Spinath, "Nature and Nurture of the Interplay Between Personality Traits and Major Life Goals," *Journal of Personality and Social Psychology,* August 2010, pp 366–79; P Beston, "Peace of Mind: The Battle," *The Wall Street Journal,* August 20, 2010, p W4; and S Shane, N Nicolaou, L Cherkas, and T D Spector, "Genetics, the Big Five, and the tendency to Be Self-Employed," *Journal of Applied Psychology,* November 2010, pp 1154–62.

42 Data from M C Ashton, K Lee, and L R Goldberg, "A Historical Analysis of 1,710 English Personality-Descriptive Adjectives," *Journal of Personality and Social Psychology,* November 2004, pp 707–21.

43 The landmark report is J M Digman, "Personality Structure: Emergence of the Five-Factor Model," *Annual Review of Psychology,* vol 41, 1990, pp 417–40. Also see M R Barrick and M K Mount, "Autonomy as a Moderator of the Relationships between the Big Five Personality Dimensions and Job Performance," *Journal of Applied Psychology,* February 1993, pp 111–18.

44 C J Ferguson, "A Meta-Analysis of Normal and Disordered Personality Across the Life Span," *Journal of Personality and Social Psychology,* April 2010, p 659.

45 Based on S E Hampson and L R Goldberg, "A First Large Cohort Study of Personality Trait Stability over the 40 Years between Elementary School and Midlife," *Journal of Personality and Social Psychology,* October 2006, pp 763–79.

46 Data from S V Paunonen et al., "The Structure of Personality in Six Cultures," *Journal of Cross-Cultural Psychology,* May 1996, pp 339–53; and K Yoon, F Schmidt, and R Ilies, "Cross-Cultural Construct Validity of the Five-Factor Model of Personality among Korean Employees," *Journal of Cross-Cultural Psychology,* May 2002, pp 217–35.

47 J Allik and R R McCrae, "Escapable Conclusions: Toomela (2003) and the Universality of Trait Structure," *Journal of Personality and Social Psychology,* August 2004, p 261. Also see D P Schmitt, J Allik, R R McCrae, and V Benet-Martinez, "The Geographic Distribution of Big Five Personality Traits," *Journal of Cross-Cultural Psychology,* March 2007, pp 173–212; and D P Schmitt, A Realo, M Voracek, and J Allik, "Why Can't a Man Be More Like a Woman? Sex Differences in Big Five Personality Traits across 55 Cultures," *Journal of Personality and Social Psychology,* January 2008, pp 168–82.

48 Based on B De Raad, et al., "Only Three Factors of Personality Description Are Fully Replicable Across Languages: A Comparison of 14 Trait Taxonomies," *Journal of Personality and Social Psychology,* January 2010, pp 160–73 Also see J Allik, et al., "How People See Others Is Different from How People See Themselves: A Replicable Pattern Across Cultures," *Journal of Personality and Social Psychology,* November 2010, pp 870–82.

49 See M R Barrick and M K Mount, "The Big Five Personality Dimensions and Job Performance: A Meta-Analysis," *Personnel Psychology,* Spring 1991, pp 1–26. Also see R P Tett, D N Jackson, and M Rothstein, "Personality Measures as Predictors of Job Performance: A Meta-Analytic Review," *Personnel Psychology,* Winter 1991, pp 703–42.

50 Barrick and Mount, p 18. For more research on conscientiousness, see A Minbashian, R E Wood, and N Beckmann, "Task-Contingent Conscientiousness as a Unit of Personality at Work," *Journal of Applied Psychology,* September 2010, pp 793–806.

51 Based on S J Perry, L A Witt, L M Penney, and L Atwater, "The Downside of Goal-Focused Leadership: The Role of Personality in Subordinate Exhaustion," *Journal of Applied Psychology*, November 2010, pp 1145–53; H Le, et al., "Too Much of a Good Thing: Curvilinear Relationships Between Personality Traits and Job Performance," *Journal of Applied* Psychology, January 2011, pp 113–33; and A M Cianci, H J Klein, and G H Seijts, "The Effect of Negative Feedback on Tension and Subsequent Performance: The Main and Interaction Effects of Goal Content and Conscientiousness," *Journal of Applied Psychology*, July 2010, pp 618–30.

52 See H Zhao and S E Seibert, "The Big Five Personality Dimensions and Entrepreneurial Status: A Meta-Analytical Review," *Journal of Applied Psychology,* March 2006, pp 259–71. Also see S A Woods and S E Hampson, "Predicting Adult Occupational Environments from Gender and Childhood Personality Traits," *Journal of Applied Psychology*, November 2010, pp 1045–57.

53 Based on S E Seibert and M L Kraimer, "The Five-Factor Model of Personality and Career Success," *Journal of Vocational Behavior,* February 2001, pp 1–21.

54 J M Crant, "Proactive Behavior in Organizations," *Journal of Management,* 2000, p 439. Also see N Li, J Liang, and J M Crant, "The Role of Proactive Personality in Job Satisfaction and Organizational Citizenship Behavior: A Relational Perspective," *Journal of Applied Psychology*, March 2010, pp 395–404; and G J Greguras and J M Diefendorff, "Why Does Proactive Personality Predict Employee Life Satisfaction and Work Behaviors? A Field Investigation of the Mediating Role of the Self-Concordance Model," *Personnel Psychology,* Autumn 2010, pp 539–60.

55 For an excellent overview, see J B Rotter, "Internal versus External Control of Reinforcement: A Case History of a Variable," *American Psychologist,* April 1990, pp 489–93. Also see S Wang, E C Tomlinson, and R A Noe, "The Role of Mentor Trust and Protégé Internal Locus of Control in Formal Mentoring Relationships," *Journal of Applied Psychology*, March 2010, pp 358–67; and Q Wang, N A Bowling, and K J Eschleman, "A Meta-Analytic Examination of Work and General Locus of Control," *Journal of Applied Psychology*, July 2010, pp 761–68.

56 See A Norenzayan and A Lee, "It Was Meant to Happen: Explaining Cultural Variations in Fate Attributions," *Journal of Personality and Social Psychology*, May 2010, pp 702–20.

57 Crant, "Proactive Behavior in Organizations," pp 439–41.

58 A M Grant, F Gino, and D A Hofmann, "The Hidden Advantages of Quiet Bosses," *Harvard Business Review*, December 2010, p 28.

59 See A Murphy Paul, *The Cult of Personality: How Personality Tests Are Leading Us to Miseducate Our Children, Mismanage Our Companies, and Misunderstand Ourselves* (New York: Free Press, 2004).

60 As quoted in H Dolezalek, "Tests on Trial," *Training,* April 2005, p 34. Also see D A Kaplan, "Death to the SAT!!!" *Fortune*, November 1, 2010, p 32; and D Zielinski, "Effective Assessments," *HR Magazine*, January 2011, pp 61–64.

61 For details, see S Komar, D J Brown, C Robie, and J A Komar, "Faking and the Validity of Conscientiousness: A Monte Carlo Investigation," *Journal of Applied Psychology,* January 2008, pp 140–54.

62 R N Landers, P R Sackett, and K A Tuzinski, "Retesting After Initial Failure, Coaching Rumors, and Warnings Against Faking in Online Personality Measures for Selection," *Journal of Applied Psychology,* January 2011, pp 202–210.

63 As quoted in V O'Connell, "Test for Dwindling Retail Jobs Spawns a Culture of Cheating," *The Wall Street Journal,* January 7, 2009, pp A1, A10.

64 As quoted in A Smith, "Experts: Tests, Job Steering Raise Flags," *HR Magazine,* June 2008, p 36. Also see H Aguinis, S A Culpepper, and C A Pierce, "Revival of Test Bias Research in Preemployment Testing," *Journal of Applied Psychology*, July 2010, pp 648–80; and

T Minton-Eversole, "Avoiding Bias in Pre-Employment Testing," *HR Magazine*, December 2010, pp 77–80.

65 For details, see H J Foldes, E E Duehr, and D S Ones, "Group Differences in Personality: Meta-Analyses Comparing Five U.S. Racial Groups," *Personnel Psychology,* Autumn 2008, pp 579–616.

66 J Kullman, " 'Wii' Bit of Technology Aids Medical Education," *ASU Insight,* February 22, 2008, pp 1, 6.

67 M B Marcus, "Americans of All Races Don't Get Enough Sleep," *USA Today*, March 8, 2010, p 8D.

68 M Healy and K Gelles, "What's Robbing You of a Good Night's Sleep?" *USA Today,* May 13, 2010, p 1D.

69 See M Healy, "Sleep Matters for a Healthy Heart," *USA Today,* December 24, 2008, p 6D; C M Barnes and J R Hollenbeck, "Sleep Deprivation and Decision-Making Teams: Burning the Midnight Oil or Playing with Fire?" *Academy of Management Review,* January 2009, pp 56–66; C Binnewies, S Sonnentag, and E J Mojza, "Daily Performance at Work: Feeling Recovered in the Morning as a Predictor of Day-Level Job Performance," *Journal of Organizational Behavior,* January 2009, pp 67–93; and M Healy, "Plenty of Sleep May Help Prevent Colds," *USA Today,* January 13, 2009, p 4D.

70 L J Epstein, "The Surprising Toll of Sleep Deprivation," *Newsweek*, June 28-July 5, 2010, p 75. Also see M B Marcus, "To Sleep Well, Perchance to Achieve," *USA Today,* August 12, 2010, p 4D; and Jet Lag Causes Long-Term Changes in the Brain," *South China Morning Post,* November 29, 2010, p C6.

71 A Pomeroy, "Sleep Deprivation and Medical Errors," *HR Magazine,* February 2002, p 42.

72 See K Fackelmann, "Americans Skip Sleep to Make Time for Leisure Activities," *USA Today,* August 30, 2007, p 7D.

73 As quoted in A Weintraub, "Napping Your Way to the Top," *BusinessWeek,* November 27, 2006, pp 98–99.

74 J Hoffman, "Sleeping On the Job," *Bloomberg Businessweek,* August 30–September 5, 2010, p 84. Also see R Strickgold, "The Simplest Way to Reboot Your Brain," *Harvard Business Review*, October 2009, p 36.

75 For interesting reading on intelligence, see D Lubinski, R M Webb, M J Morelock, and C P Benbow, "Top 1 in 10,000: A 10-Year Follow-Up of the Profoundly Gifted," *Journal of Applied Psychology,* August 2001, pp 718–29; and L T Benjamin Jr, "The Birth of American Intelligence Testing," *Monitor on Psychology,* January 2009, pp 20–21.

76 For an excellent overview of intelligence, including definitional distinctions and a historical perspective of the IQ controversy, see R A Weinberg, "Intelligence and IQ," *American Psychologist*, February 1989, pp 98–104. Also see G Toppo, "Poverty Dramatically Affects Children's Brains," USA Today, December 8, 2008, p 4D; S Begley, "Sex, Race and IQ: Off Limits?" Newsweek, April 20, 2009, p 53; and S Kanazawa, "Evolutionary Psychology and Intelligence Research," *American Psychologist*, May–June 2010, pp 279–89.

77 See Weinberg, "Intelligence and IQ"; and W A Walker and C Humphries, "Starting the Good Life in the Womb," *Newsweek,* September 17, 2007, pp 56, 58.

78 B Azar, "People Are Becoming Smarter—Why?" *APA Monitor,* June 1996, p 20. Also see K Baker, "Why Do IQ Scores Vary By Nation?" *Newsweek,* August 2, 2010, p 14; S Begley, "Can You Build a Better Brain?" *Newsweek*, January 10–17, 2011, pp 40–45; and S Begley, "Get Smarter: A Group of Thinkers Explains How," *Newsweek,* January 24, 2011, p 42.

79 See D Lubinski, "Introduction to the Special Section on Cognitive Abilities: 100 Years after Spearman's (1904) 'General Intelligence, Objectively Determined and Measured,'" *Journal of Personality and Social Psychology,* January 2004, pp 96–111; and R Gilkey and C Kilts, "Cognitive Fitness," *Harvard Business Review,* November 2007, pp 53–66.

80 See F L Schmidt and J E Hunter, "Employment Testing: Old Theories and New Research Findings," *American Psychologist,*

October 1981, p 1128; J W B Lang, M Kersting, U R Hülsheger, and J Lang, "General Mental Ability, Narrower Cognitive Abilities, and Job Performance: The Perspective of the Nested-Factors Model of Cognitive Abilities," *Personnel Psychology*, Autumn 2010, pp 595–640; and M A Maltarich, A J Nyberg, and G Reilly, "A Conceptual and Empirical Analysis of the Cognitive Ability-Voluntary Turnover Relationship," *Journal of Applied Psychology*, November 2010, pp 1058–70.

81 See H Gardner, *Frames of Mind: The Theory of Multiple Intelligences*, 10th anniversary ed (New York: Basic Books, 1993); H Gardner, *Intelligence Reframed: Multiple Intelligences for the 21st Century* (New York: Basic Books, 2000); and H Gardner, *Five Minds for the Future* (Boston: Harvard Business School Press, 2009).

82 For a good overview of Gardner's life and work, see M K Smith, "Howard Gardner and Multiple Intelligences," *Encyclopedia of Informal Education*, 2002, www.infed.org/thinkers/gardner.htm. Also see B Fryer, "The Ethical Mind: A Conversation with Psychologist Howard Gardner," *Harvard Business Review*, March 2007, pp 51–56.

83 See D A Shepherd and D F Kuratko, "The Death of an Innovative Project: How Grief Recovery Enhances Learning," *Business Horizons*, September–October 2009, pp 451–58; D Ariely, "The Long-Term Effects of Short-Term Emotions," *Harvard Business Review*, January-February 2010, p 38; T Menon and L Thompson, "Envy at Work," *Harvard Business Review*, April 2010, pp 74–79; and J S Lerner and K Shonk, "How Anger Poisons Decision Making," *Harvard Business Review*, September 2010, p 26.

84 D Kirkpatrick, "Microsoft after Gates," *Fortune*, July 7, 2008, p 118.

85 G Anders, "John Chambers after the Deluge," *Fast Company*, July 2001, p 108.

86 R S Lazarus, *Emotion and Adaptation* (New York: Oxford University Press, 1991), p 6. Also see P Kuppens, A Realo, and E Diener, "The Role of Positive and Negative Emotions in Life Satisfaction Judgment across Nations," *Journal of Personality and Social Psychology*, July 2008, pp 66–75; and M J Burke, et al., "The Dread Factor: How Hazards and Safety Training Influence Learning and Performance," *Journal of Applied Psychology*, January 2011, pp 46–70.

87 Based on discussion in R D Arvey, G L Renz, and T W Watson, "Emotionality and Job Performance: Implications for Personnel Selection," in *Research in Personnel and Human Resources Management*, vol 16, ed G R Ferris (Stamford, CT: JAI Press, 1998), pp 103–47. Also see S G Young and K Hugenberg, "Mere Social Categorization Modulates Identification of Facial Expressions of Emotions," *Journal of Personality and Social Psychology*, December 2010, pp 964–77; and C Harmon-Jones, B J Schmeichel, E Mennit, and E Harmon-Jones, "The Expression of Determination: Similarities Between Anger and Approach-Related Positive Affect," *Journal of Personality and Social Psychology*, January 2011, pp 172–81.

88 Based on L Van Boven, J Kane, P A McGraw, and J Dale, "Feeling Close: Emotional Intensity Reduces Perceived Psychological Distance," *Journal of Personality and Social Psychology*, June 2010, pp 872–85.

89 J A Byrne and H Timmons, "Tough Times," *BusinessWeek*, October 29, 2001, p 66. Also see B M Wilkowski, M D Robinson, and W Troop-Gordon, "How Does Cognitive Control Reduce Anger and Aggression? The Role of Conflict Monitoring and Forgiveness Processes," *Journal of Personality and Social Psychology*, May 2010, pp 830–40; and D L Shapiro, "Relational Identity Theory: A Systematic Approach for Transforming the Emotional Dimension of Conflict," *American Psychologist*, October 2010, pp 634–45.

90 J McGregor, "#1 Taryn Rose," *Fast Company*, May 2005, p 69.

91 D Goleman, *Emotional Intelligence* (New York: Bantam Books, 1995), p 34. For more, see J Antonakis, N M Ashkanasy, and M T Dasborough, "Does Leadership Need Emotional Intelligence?" *The Leadership Quarterly*, April 2009, pp 247–61; T DeAngelis, "Social Awareness + Emotional Skills = Successful Kids," *Monitor on Psychology*, April 2010, pp 46–49; and "Interaction: When Emotional Reasoning Trumps IQ," *Harvard Business Review*, December 2010, pp 20–21.

92 Based on D L Joseph and D A Newman, "Emotional Intelligence: An Integrative Meta-Analysis and Cascading Model," *Journal of Applied Psychology*, January 2010, pp 54–78.

93 Based on P D Harms and M Credé, "Emotional Intelligence and Transformational and Transactional Leadership: A Meta-Analysis," *Journal of Leadership and Organizational Studies*, no 1, 2010, pp 5–17.

94 Data from S D Pugh, "Service with a Smile: Emotional Contagion in the Service Encounter," *Academy of Management Journal*, October 2001, pp 1018–27; and P Totterdell, S Kellett, K Teuchmann, and R B Briner, "Evidence of Mood Linkage in Work Groups," *Journal of Personality and Social Psychology*, June 1998, pp 1504–15. Also see M Conlin, "Mad Men: A Little Anger Is a Good Thing," *BusinessWeek*, December 7, 2009, p 57.

95 N M Ashkanasy and C S Daus, "Emotion in the Workplace: The New Challenge for Managers," *Academy of Management Executive*, February 2002, p 79. Also see C K Lam, X Huang, and O Janssen, "Contextualizing Emotional Exhaustion and Positive Emotional Display. The Signaling Effects of Supervisors' Emotional Exhaustion and Service Climate," *Journal of Applied Psychology*, March 2010, pp 368–76; and U M Dholakia, "Why Employees Can Wreck Promotional Offers," *Harvard Business Review*, January–February 2011, p 28.

96 For details, see C Jones and M T Moore, "Flight Attendant Strikes a Nerve," *USA Today*, August 11, 2010, pp 1A–2A; and D Leonard, "Mad as Hell," *Bloomberg Businessweek*, August 16–29, 2010, pp 5–6.

97 Data from A M Kring and A H Gordon, "Sex Differences in Emotions: Expressions, Experience, and Physiology," *Journal of Personality and Social Psychology*, March 1998, pp 686–703.

98 As quoted in B Schlender, "The Bill & Warren Show," *Fortune*, July 20, 1998, p 52. Also see T A Judge, R Ilies, and N Dimotakis, "Are Health and Happiness the Product of Wisdom? The Relationship of General Mental Ability to Education and Occupational Attainment, Health, and Well-Being," *Journal of Applied Psychology*, May 2010, pp 454–68; E M Hallowell, "What Brian Science Tells Us About How to Excel," *Harvard Business Review*, December 2010, pp 123–29; M B Marklein, "Poll: Best Shot at Success is Pinned on Schooling," *USA Today*, January 6, 2011, p 4A; and A Morriss, R J Ely, and F X Frei, "Stop Holding Yourself Back," *Harvard Business Review*, January–February 2011, pp 160–63.

99 As quoted in H Mackay, "Always Follow the Advice of Dr. Lou," *The Arizona Republic*, January 18, 2009, p D2. Also see Coach John Wooden's "pyramid of success" in J Wooden and S Jamison, *Wooden on Leadership* (New York: McGraw-Hill, 2005), p 2; and M Goldsmith with M Reiter, *What Got You Here Won't Get You There: How Successful People Become Even More Successful* (New York: Hyperion, 2007).

100 F Luthans, C M Youssef, and B J Avolio, *Psychological Capital: Developing the Human Competitive Edge* (Oxford, UK: Oxford University Press, 2007), p 3 (emphasis added). Also see F Luthans, J B Avey, and J L Patera, "Experimental Analysis of a Web-Based Training Intervention to Develop Positive Psychological Capital," *Academy of Management Learning and Education*, June 2008, pp 209–21. For background reading on positive psychology, see M E P Seligman and M Csikszentmihalyi, "Positive Psychology: An Introduction," *American Psychologist*, January 2000, pp 5–14. Also see S H Harrison, D M Sluss, and B E Ashforth, "Curiosity Adapted the Cat: The Role of Trait Curiosity in Newcomer Adaptation," *Journal of Applied Psychology*, January 2011, pp 211–20.

101 C Burritt, "Home Depot's Fix-It Lady," *Bloomberg Businessweek*, January 17–23, 2011, pp 66–67. Also see M D Seery, A E Holman, and R C Silver, "Whatever Does Not Kill Us: Cumulative Lifetime Adversity, Vulnerability, and Resilience," *Journal of Personality and Social Psychology*, December 2010, pp 1025–41.

102 M Gladwell, *Outliers: The Story of Success* (New York: Little, Brown, 2008), pp 38–41. Also see M B Marklein, "First Two Years of College Wasted?" *USA Today*, January 18, 2011, p 3A.

[103] G Colvin, *Talent Is Overrated: What Really Separates World-Class Performers from Everybody Else* (New York: Penguin, 2008), p 66 (emphasis added). Also see A Beard, "Life's Work: Annie Lennox," *Harvard Business Review*, October 2010, p 152.

[104] S D Meglio, "How No 1 Keeps Getting Better," *USA Today*, March 21, 2008, p 2A.

[105] For more, see R Wiseman, *The Luck Factor: The Four Essential Principles* (New York: Miramax, 2004); D H Pink, "How to Make Your Own Luck," *Fast Company*, July 2003. pp 78–82; B Sherwood, *The Survivors Club: The Secrets and Science that Could Save Your Life* (New York: Grand Central Publishing, 2009); and www .richardwiseman.com.

[106] Robert Solomon, as quoted in D Vera and A Rodriguez-Lopez, "Strategic Virtues: Humility as a Source of Competitive Advantage," *Organizational Dynamics*, no 4, 2004, pp 394–95. Also see D A Ready, J A Conger, and L A Hill, "Are You a High Potential?" *Harvard Business Review*, June 2010, pp 78–84.

[107] Robert Solomon, as quoted in Vera and Rodriguez-Lopez, "Strategic Virtues," p 395.

[108] Reprinted by permission of *Harvard Business Review*. Excerpt from "The Best Advice I Ever Got," by D W Dowling, June 2008. Copyright 2008 by the Harvard Business School Publishing Corporation; all rights reserved.

[109] Excerpted from F J Flynn, "Guilt-Ridden People Make Great Leaders," *Harvard Business Review*, January–February 2011, p 30.

CHAPTER 6

[1] Excerpted and derived from J Shambora, "From Leverage to Corkage," *Fortune*, December 6, 2010, p 80.

[2] Schwartz's theory is discussed in S H Schwartz, "Universals in the Content and Structure of Values: Theoretical Advances and Empirical Tests in 20 Countries," in *Advances in Experimental Social Psychology*, ed M Zanna (New York: Academic Press, 1992), pp 1–65.

[3] A Bardi and S H Schwartz, "Values and Behavior: Strength and Structure of Relations," *Personality and Social Psychology Bulletin*, October 2003, p 1208.

[4] Ibid., pp 1207–20; and J A Lee, G N Soutar, and J Sneddon, "Personal Values and Social Marketing: Some Research Suggestions," *Journal of Research for Consumers*," 2010, pp 1–4.

[5] See Bardi and Schwartz, "Values and Behavior: Strength and Structure of Relations"; and S T Lyons, C A Higgins, and L Duxbury, "Work Values: Development of a New Three-Dimensional Structure Based on Confirmatory Smallest Space Analysis," *Journal of Organizational Behavior*, October 2010, pp 969–1002.

[6] K Helliker, "You Might as Well Face It: You're Addicted to Success," *The Wall Street Journal*, February 10, 2009, p D1.

[7] This example was derived from D Lieberman, "L.A. Times' Publisher Forced Out Over Refusal to Cut Staff," *USA Today*, October 6, 2006, p 1B.

[8] For a thorough discussion of person-culture fit, see A L Kristof-Brown, R D Zimmerman, and E C Johnson, "Consequences of Individuals' Fit at Work: A Meta-Analysis of Person-Job, Person-Organization, Person-Group, and Person-Supervisor Fit," *Personnel Psychology*, Summer 2005, pp 281–342.

[9] Supportive results can be found in ibid.; and J P Meyer, T D Hecht, H Gill, and L Toplonytsky, "Person-Organization (Culture) Fit and Employee Commitment Under Conditions of Organization Change: A Longitudinal Study," *Journal of Vocational Behavior*, June 2010, pp 458–73.

[10] P L Perrewé and W A Hochwarter, "Can We Really Have It All? The Attainment of Work and Family Values," *Current Directions in Psychological Science*, February 2001, p 31.

[11] See M Wang, S Liu, Y Zhan, and J Shi, "Daily Work-Family Conflict and Alcohol Use: Testing the Cross-Level Moderation Effects of Peer Drinking Norms and Social Support," *Journal of Applied Psychology*, March 2010, pp 377–86; and P Wang, J J Lawler, and K Shi, "Work–Family Conflict, Self-Efficacy, Job Satisfaction, and Gender: Evidences from Asia," *Journal of Leadership & Organizational Studies*, May 2010, pp 298–308.

[12] See S R Ezzedeen and K G Ritchey, "Career and Family Strategies of Executive Women: Revisiting the Quest to 'Have It All,'" *Organizational Dynamics*, October–December 2009, pp 270–80; and F M Cheung and D F Halpern, "Women at the Top," *American Psychologist*, April 2010, pp 182–93.

[13] See M Moskowitz, R Levering, and C Tkaczyk, "100 Best Companies to Work For," *Fortune*, February 8, 2010, p 80.

[14] "Flexible Work Plans Key to Retention," *HR Magazine*, December 2010, p 105.

[15] See D A Major, T D Fletcher, D D Davis, and L M Germano, "The Influence of Work–Family Culture and Workplace Relationships on Work Interference with Family: A Multilevel Model," *Journal of Organizational Behavior*, October 2008, pp 881–97; and D P Bhave, A Kramer, and T M Glomb, "Work–Family Conflict in Work Groups: Social Information Processing, Support, and Demographic Dissimilarity," *Journal of Applied Psychology*, January 2010, pp 145–58.

[16] See J M Twenge, S M Campbell, B J Hoffman, and C E Lance, "Generational Differences in Work Values: Leisure and Extrinsic Values Increasing, Social and Intrinsic Values Decreasing," *Journal of Management*, September 2010, pp 1117–42; and J M Twenge, "A Review of the Empirical Evidence on Generational Differences in Work Attitudes," *Journal of Business Strategy*, June 2010, pp 201–10.

[17] See J M Hoobler, J Hu, and M Wilson, "Do Workers Who Experience Conflict between the Work and Family Domains Hit a 'Glass Ceiling?': A Meta-Analytic Examination," *Journal of Vocational Behavior*, December 2010, pp 481–94; and G N Powell and J H Greenhaus, "Sex, Gender, and the Work-to-Family Interface: Exploring Negative and Positive Interdependencies," *Academy of Management Journal*, June 2010, pp 513–34.

[18] L B Hammer, E E Kossek, W K Anger, T Bodner, and K L Zimmerman, "Clarifying Work–Family Intervention Processes: The Roles of Work–Family Conflict and Family-Supportive Supervisor Behaviors," *Journal of Applied Psychology*, January 2011, pp 134–50.

[19] See Moskowitz, Levering, and Tkaczyk, p 88.

[20] These results are discussed in L Winerman, "A Healthy Mind, a Longer Life," *Monitor on Psychology*, November 2006, pp 42–44.

[21] See D A Harrison, D A Newman, and P L Roth, "How Important Are Job Attitudes? Meta-Analytic Comparisons of Integrative Behavioral Outcomes and Time Sequences," *Academy of Management Journal*, April 2006, pp 305–25; and M Riketta, "The Causal Relation between Job Attitudes and Performance: A Meta-Analysis of Panel Studies," *Journal of Applied Psychology*, March 2008, pp 472–81.

[22] M Fishbein and I Ajzen, *Belief, Attitude, Intention and Behavior: An Introduction to Theory and Research* (Reading, MA: Addison-Wesley Publishing, 1975), p 6.

[23] Research on attitudes is thoroughly discussed by A P Brief, *Attitudes in and around Organizations* (Thousand Oaks, CA: Sage, 1998), pp 49–84.

[24] For details about this theory, see L Festinger, *A Theory of Cognitive Dissonance* (Stanford, CA: Stanford University Press, 1957).

[25] See B M Staw and J Ross, "Stability in the Midst of Change: A Dispositional Approach to Job Attitudes," *Journal of Applied Psychology*, August 1985, pp 469–80.

[26] Data from P S Visser and J A Krosnick, "Development of Attitude Strength over the Life Cycle: Surge and Decline," *Journal of Personality and Social Psychology*, December 1998, pp 389–410.

[27] This example is discussed in C Levinson and M Bradley, "Mubarak Digs in as Mobs Battle Police," *The Wall Street Journal*, January 29–30, 2011, pp A1, A12.

[28] I Ajzen, "The Theory of Planned Behavior," *Organizational Behavior and Human Decision Processes,* vol 50 (1991), p 188.
29 See R P Steel and N K Ovalle II, "A Review and Meta-Analysis of Research on the Relationship between Behavioral Intentions and Employee Turnover," *Journal of Applied Psychology,* November 1984, pp 673–86.

[30] Results can be found in M R Barrick and R D Zimmerman, "Reducing Voluntary Turnover through Selection," *Journal of Applied Psychology,* January 2005, pp 159–66.

[31] Drawn from I Ajzen and M Fishbein, *Understanding Attitudes and Predicting Social Behavior* (Englewood Cliffs, NJ: Prentice Hall, 1980); J Zikic, "Job Search and Social Cognitive Theory: The Role of Career-Related Activities," *Journal of Vocational Behavior,* February 2009, pp 117–27; F A White, M A Charles, and J K Nelson, "The Role of Persuasive Arguments in Changing Affirmative Action Attitudes and Expressed Behavior in Higher Education," *Journal of Applied Psychology,* November 2008, pp 1271–86; M-F Chen and P-J Tung, "The Moderating Effect of Perceived lack of Facilities on Consumers," *Environment and Behavior,* November 2010, pp 824–44; L Luo, "Attitudes Toward Older People and Coworkers' Intention to Work with Older Employees: A Taiwanese Study," *The International Journal of Aging & Human Development,* 2010, pp 305–322; and P W Hom and C L Hulin, "A Competitive Test of the Prediction of Reenlistment by Several Models," *Journal of Applied Psychology,* February 1981, pp 23–39.

[32] Supportive research is presented in T L Webb and P Sheeran, "Does Changing Behavioral Intentions Engender Behavior Change: A Meta-Analysis of the Experimental Evidence," *Psychological Bulletin,* March 2006, pp 249–68.

[33] "Top Small Workplaces 2008," *The Wall Street Journal,* October 13, 2008, p 5.

[34] L Yerkes, *Fun Works: Creating Places Where People Love to Work* (San Francisco, CA: Berrett-Koehler, 2001), p 73.

[35] J P Meyer and L Herscovitch, "Commitment in the Workplace: Toward a General Model," *Human Resource Management Review,* Autumn 2001, p 301.

[36] J P Meyer and N J Allen, "A Three-Component Conceptualization of Organizational Commitment," *Human Resource Management Review,* Spring 1991, p 67.

[37] See B Joo, "Organizational Commitment for knowledge workers: The Role of Perceived Organizational Learning Culture, Leader-Member Exchange Quality, and Turnover Intention," *Human Resource Development Quarterly,* Spring 2010, pp 69–85; B Joo and S Park, "Career Satisfaction, Organizational Commitment, and Turnover Intention: The Effects of Goal Orientation, Organizational Learning Culture and Developmental Feedback," *Leadership & Organization Development,* 2010, pp 482–500; and R E Johnson, D Chang, and L-Q Yang, "Commitment and Motivation at Work: The Relevance of Employee Identity and Regulatory Focus," *Academy of Management Review,* April 2010, pp 226–45.

[38] "Top Small Workplaces 2008," p R9.

[39] This definition was provided by D M Rousseau, "Psychological and Implied Contracts in Organizations," *Employee Responsibilities and Rights Journal,* June 1989, pp 121–39.

[40] See T W H Ng, D C Feldman, and S S K Lam, "Psychological Contract Breaches, Organizational Commitment, and Innovation-Related Behaviors: A Latent Growth Modeling Approach," *Journal of Applied Psychology,* July 2010, pp 744–51; and T Dulac, J A-M Coyle-Shariro, D J Henderson, and S J Wayne, "Not All Responses to Breach Are the Same: The Interconnection of Social Exchange and Psychological Contract Processes in Organizations," *Academy of Management Journal,* December 2008, pp 1079–98.

[41] Results can be found in N P Podsakoff, J A LePine, and M A LePine, "Differential Challenge Stressor–Hindrance Stressor Relationships with Job Attitudes, Turnover Intentions, Turnover, and Withdrawal Behavior: A Meta-Analysis," *Journal of Applied Psychology,* March 2007, pp 438–54.

[42] Results can be found in M Riketta, "Attitudinal Organizational Commitment and Job Performance: A Meta-Analysis," *Journal of Organizational Behavior,* March 2002, pp 257–66.

[43] Results can be found in R W Griffeth, P W Hom, and S Gaertner, "A Meta-Analysis of Antecedents and Correlates of Employee Turnover: Update, Moderator Tests, and Research Implications for the Next Millennium," *Journal of Management,* 2000, pp 463–88.

[44] These examples were discussed by Moskowitz, Levering, and Tkaczyk, pp 77 and 88.

[45] R Levering and M Moskowitz, "The 100 Best Companies to Work For," *Fortune,* January 24, 2005, p 84.

[46] R Levering and M Moskowitz, "The 100 Best Companies to Work For," *Fortune,* 2009, p 75.

[47] W A Kahn, "Psychological Conditions of Personal Engagement and Disengagement at Work," *Academy of Management Journal,* December 1990, p 695.

[48] W A Macy, B Schneider, K M Barbera, and S A Young, *Employee Engagement: Tools for Analysis, Practice, and Competitive Advantage* (West Sussex, United Kingdom: Wiley-Blackwell, 2009), p 20.

[49] See W H Macey and B Schneider, "The Meaning of Employee Engagement," *Industrial and Organizational Psychology,* March 2008, pp 3–30.

[50] C A Hartnell, A Y Ou, and A Kinicki, "Organizational Culture and Organizational Effectiveness: A Meta-Analytic Investigation of the Competing Values Framework's Theoretical Suppositions," *Journal of Applied Psychology,* in press; and C D'Angela, "In Post-Recession World, Recognition Boosts Recovery," *The Power of Incentives: Special Advertising Supplement in HR Magazine,* September 2010, pp 93–97.

[51] See M Moskowitz, R Levering, and C Tkaczyk, "100 Best Companies to Work For," *Fortune,* February 7, 2011, p 95.

[52] See Kahn, "Psychological Conditions of Personal Engagement and Disengagement at Work."

[53] See B Schneider and K B Paul, "In the Company We Trust," *HR Magazine,* January 2011, pp 40–43; and P Yeramyan, "Building the (Workplace) Ties that Bind," *Fortune,* December 6, 2010, p 78.

[54] See B L Rich, J A Lepine, and E R Crawford, "Job Engagement: Antecedents and Effects on Job Performance," *Academy of Management Journal,* June 2010, pp 617–35; J S Stoner and V C Gallagher, "Who Cares? The Role of Job Involvement in Psychological Contract Violation," *Journal of Applied Social Psychology,* June 2010, pp 1490–1514.

[55] R Zeidner, "Questing for Quality," *HR Magazine,* July 2010, p 27.

[56] See J K Harter, F L Schmidt, and T L Hayes, "Business-Unit-Level Relationship between Employee Satisfaction, Employee Engagement, and Business Outcomes: A Meta-Analysis," *Journal of Applied Psychology,* April 2002, pp 268–79.

[57] See J Robison, "Building Engagement in This Economic Crisis," *Gallup Management Journal,* February 19, 2009, http://gmj.gallup.com/content/115213/Building-Engagement-Economic-Crisis.aspx.

[58] See Rich, Lepine, and Crawford, "Job Engagement: Antecedents and Effects on Job Performance;" D Fairhurst and J O'Connor, "Employee Well-Being: Taking Engagement and Performance to the Next Level," retrieved April 13, 2010, from towerswatson.com; and B Schneider, W H Macey, and K M Barbera, "Driving Customer Satisfaction and Financial Success Through Employee Engagement," *People & Strategy,* 2009, pp 22–27.

[59] See J Robison, "How the Ritz-Carlton Manages the Mystique," *Gallup Management Journal,* December 11, 2008, http://gmj.gallup.com/content/112906.

[60] Results can be found in "Generation Gap: On Their Bosses, Millennials Happier Than Boomers," *The Wall Street Journal,* November 15, 2010, p B6; and J Schramm, "Post-Recession Job Dissatisfaction," *HR Magazine,* July 2010, p 88.

[61] For a review of the development of the JDI, see P C Smith, L M Kendall, and C L Hulin, *The Measurement of Satisfaction in Work and Retirement* (Skokie, IL: Rand-McNally, 1969).

[62] S Miller, "HR, Employees Vary on Job Satisfaction," *HR Magazine,* August 2007, p 32.

[63] For a review of need satisfaction models, see E F Stone, "A Critical Analysis of Social Information Processing Models of Job Perceptions and Job Attitudes," in *Job Satisfaction: How People Feel about Their Jobs and How It Affects Their Performance,* ed C J Cranny, P Cain Smith, and E F Stone (New York: Lexington Books, 1992), pp 21–52.

[64] See J P Wanous, T D Poland, S L Premack, and K S Davis, "The Effects of Met Expectations on Newcomer Attitudes and Behaviors: A Review and Meta-Analysis," *Journal of Applied Psychology,* June 1992, pp 288–97.

[65] "Top Small Workplaces 2008," p 8.

[66] Results can be found in J Cohen-Charash and P E Spector, "The Role of Justice in Organizations: A Meta-Analysis," *Organizational Behavior and Human Decision Processes,* November 2001, pp 278–321.

[67] N A Bowling, E A Hendricks, and S H Wagner, "Positive and Negative Affectivity and Facet Satisfaction: A Meta-Analysis," *Journal of Business Strategy,* December 2008, pp 115–25.

[68] See R D Arvey, T J Bouchard Jr, N L Segal, and L M Abraham, "Job Satisfaction: Environmental and Genetic Components," *Journal of Applied Psychology,* April 1989, pp 187–92; and S A Shane, *How Your Genes Affect Your Work Life* (Cary, NC: Oxford University Press, 2010).

[69] See C Dormann and D Zapf, "Job Satisfaction: A Meta-Analysis of Stabilities," *Journal of Organizational Behavior,* August 2001, pp 483–504.

[70] P Wakeman, "The Good Life and How to Get It," *Inc.,* February 2001, p 50.

[71] See A J Kinicki, F M McKee-Ryan, C A Schriesheim, and K P Carson, "Assessing the Construct Validity of the Job Descriptive Index: A Review and Meta-Analysis," *Journal of Applied Psychology,* February 2002, pp 14–32.

[72] See Brown, "A Meta-Analysis and Review of Organizational Research on Job Involvement."

[73] D W Organ, "The Motivational Basis of Organizational Citizenship Behavior," in *Research in Organizational Behavior,* ed B M Staw and L L Cummings (Greenwich, CT: JAI Press, 1990), p 46.

[74] Results can be found in B J Hoffman, C A Blair, J P Meriac, and D J Woehr, "Expanding the Criterion Domain? A Quantitative Review of the OCB Literature," *Journal of Applied Psychology,* March 2007, pp 555–66.

[75] See N P Podsakoff, S W Whiting, P M Podsakoff, and B D Blume, "Individual- and Organizational-Level Consequences of Organizational Citizenship Behaviors: A Meta-Analysis," *Journal of Applied Psychology,* January 2009, pp 122–41; and D S Whitman, D L Van Rooy, and C Viswesvaran, "Satisfaction, Citizenship Behaviors, and Performance in Work Units: A Meta-Analysis of Collective Relations," *Personnel Psychology,* Spring 2010, pp 41–81.

[76] Results can be found in P W Hom and A J Kinicki, "Toward a Greater Understanding of How Dissatisfaction Drives Employee Turnover," *Academy of Management Journal,* October 2001, pp 975–87.

[77] See the related discussion in S Lau, "Positive Turnover, Disability Awareness, Employee Selection Guidelines," *HR Magazine,* January 2011, p 20.

[78] Y Lermusiaux, "Calculating the High Cost of Employee Turnover," accessed April 15, 2005, www.ilogos.com/en/expertviews/articles/strategic/200331007_YL.html.

[79] See ibid. An automated program for calculating the cost of turnover can be found at "Calculate Your Turnover Costs," accessed February 28, 2009, www.keepemployees.com/turnovercalc.htm.

[80] Results can be found in Griffeth, Hom, and Gaertner, pp 463–88.

[81] See A Nyberg, "Retaining Your High Performers: Moderators of the Performance-Job Satisfaction-Voluntary Turnover Relationship," *Journal of Applied Psychology,* May 2010, pp 440–53; and M A Maltarich, A J. Nyberg, and G Reilly, "A Conceptual and Empirical Analysis of the Cognitive Ability-Voluntary Turnover Relationship," *Journal of Applied Psychology,* November 2010, pp 1058–70.

[82] See J McGregor, "Giving Back to Your Stars," *Fortune,* November 1, 2010, pp 53–54; and J Martin and C Schmidt, "How to Keep Your Top Talent," *Harvard business Review,* May 2010, pp 54–61.

[83] J Light, "Keeping 'Overqualifieds' on Board," *The Wall Street Journal,* November 15, 2010, p B6.

[84] Results can be found in Podsakoff, LePine, and LePine, pp 438–54.

[85] See A Novotney, "Boosting Morale," *Monitor on Psychology,* December 2010, pp 32–34; C Fritz, M Yankelevich, A Zarubin, and P Barger, "Happy, Healthy, and Productive: The Role of Detachment From Work During Nonwork Time," *Journal of Applied Psychology,* September 2010, pp 977–83; and S Sonnentag, C Binnewies, and E J Mojza, "Staying Well and Engaged When Demands Are High: The Role of Psychological Detachment," *Journal of Applied Psychology,* September 2010, pp 965–76.

[86] The various models are discussed in T A Judge, C J Thoresen, J E Bono, and G K Patton, "The Job Satisfaction–Job Performance Relationship: A Qualitative and Quantitative Review," *Psychological Bulletin,* May 2001, pp 376–407.

[87] Results can be found in ibid.

[88] Results can be found in Whitman, Van Rooy, and C Viswesvaran, "Satisfaction, Citizenship Behaviors, and Performance in Work Units: A Meta-Analysis of Collective Relations." Also see R G Netemeyer, J G Maxham III, and D R Lichtenstein, "Store Manager Performance and Satisfaction: Effects on Store Employee Performance and Satisfaction, Store Customer Satisfaction, and Store Customer Spending Growth," *Journal of Applied Psychology,* May 2010, pp 530–45.

[89] See P E Spector and S Fox, "Theorizing About the Deviant Citizen: An Attributional Explanation of the Interplay of Organizational Citizenship and Counterproductive Work Behavior," *Human Resource Management Review,* June 2010, pp 132–43; and K Tyler, "Helping Employees Cool It," *HR Magazine,* April 2010, pp 53–55.

[90] M Conlin, "To Catch a Corporate Thief," *BusinessWeek,* February 16, 2009, p 52.

[91] See B Leonard, "Survey: 10% of Employees Report Harassment at Work," *HR Magazine,* October 2010, p 18; and B Mirza, "Attorneys Advise Action to Prevent Bullying at Work," *HR Magazine,* 2010, p 16.

[92] See B J Tepper, C A Henle, L S Lambert, R A Giacalone, and M K Duffy, "Abusive Supervision and Subordinates' Organization Deviance," *Journal of Applied Psychology,* July 2008, pp 721–32.

[93] C Hymowitz, "Bosses Have to Learn How to Confront Troubled Employees," *The Wall Street Journal,* April 23, 2007, p B1.

[94] Ibid.

[95] B W Roberts, P D Harms, A Caspi, and T E Moffitt, "Predicting the Counterproductive Employee in a Child-to-Adult Prospective Study," *Journal of Applied Psychology,* September 2007, pp 1427–36.

[96] See P E Spector and J A Bauer, and S Fox, "Measurement Artifacts in the Assessment of Counterproductive Work Behavior and Organizational Citizenship Behavior: Do We Know What We Think We Know?" *Journal of Applied Psychology,* July 2010, pp 781–90; and L R Bolton, L K Becker, and L K Barber, "Big Five Trait Predictions of Differential Counterproductive Work Behavior Dimensions," *Personality and Individual Differences,* October 2010, pp 537–41.

[97] S Dilchert, D S Ones, R D Davis, and C D Rostow, "Cognitive Ability Predicts Objectively Measured Counterproductive Work Behaviors," *Journal of Applied Psychology,* May 2007, pp 616–27.

98 J R Detert, L K Treviño, E R Burris, and M Andiappan, "Managerial Modes of Influence and Counterproductivity in Organizations: A Longitudinal Business-Unit-Level Investigation," *Journal of Applied Psychology,* July 2007, pp 993–1005.

99 J McGregor, "Keeping Talent in the Fold," *BusinessWeek,* November 3, 2008, pp 51–52.

100 Excerpted from M Dale, "Suit: District Used Webcams on Students in Their Homes," *The Arizona Republic,* February 19, 2010, p A3.

CHAPTER 7

1 Excerpted from P Lencioni, "The Power of Saying 'We Blew It,'" *Bloomberg Businessweek,* February 22, 2010, p 84.

2 See "Bernard Madoff, January 5, 2011. Retrieved January 10, 2011, from http://en.wikipedia.org/wiki/Bernard_Madoff.

3 See L Winerman, "Screening Surveyed," *Monitor on Psychology,* January 2006, pp 28–29.

4 S T Fiske and S E Taylor, *Social Cognition,* 2nd ed (Reading, MA: Addison-Wesley Publishing, 1991), pp 1–2.

5 The negative bias was examined by A Weinberg and G Hajcak, "Beyond Good and Evil: The Time-Course of Neural Activity Elicited by Specific Picture Content," *Emotion,* December 2010, pp 767–82.

6 V Harnish, "Stop Doing These Five Business Killers Now: Here's How to Get Your Life in Order," *Fortune,* December 6, 2010, p 71.

7 E Rosch, C B Mervis, W D Gray, D M Johnson, and P Boyes-Braem, "Basic Objects in Natural Categories," *Cognitive Psychology,* July 1976, p 383.

8 Results can be found in M Rotundo, D-H Nguyen, and P R Sackett, "A Meta-Analytic Review of Gender Differences in Perceptions of Sexual Harassment," *Journal of Applied Psychology,* October 2001, pp 914–22.

9 For a thorough discussion about the structure and organization of memory, see L R Squire, B Knowlton, and G Musen, "The Structure and Organization of Memory," in *Annual Review of Psychology,* ed L W Porter and M R Rosenzweig (Palo Alto, CA: Annual Reviews, 1993), vol 44, pp 453–95.

10 See M R Barrick, B W Swider, and G L Stewart, "Initial Evaluations in the Interview: Relationships with Subsequent Interviewer Evaluations and Employment Offers," *Journal of Applied Psychology,* November 2010, pp 1163–72.

11 Implicit cognition is discussed by C E Drake, K K Kellum, K G Wilson, J B Luoma, J H Weinstein, and C H Adams, "Examining the Implicit Relational Assessment Procedure: Four Preliminary Studies," *The Psychological Record,* Winter 2010, pp 81–100.

12 See M Orey, "White Men Can't Help It," *BusinessWeek,* May 15, 2006, pp 54, 57.

13 Details of this study can be found in C K Stevens, "Antecedents of Interview Interactions, Interviewers' Ratings, and Applicants' Reactions," *Personnel Psychology,* Spring 1998, pp 55–85.

14 See R C Mayer and J H Davis, "The Effect of the Performance Appraisal System on Trust for Management: A Field Quasi-Experiment," *Journal of Applied Psychology,* February 1999, pp 123–36.

15 Results can be found in W H Bommer, J L Johnson, G A Rich, P M Podsakoff, and S B Mackenzie, "On the Interchangeability of Objective and Subjective Measures of Employee Performance: A Meta-Analysis," *Personnel Psychology,* Autumn 1995, pp 587–605.

16 The effectiveness of rater training was supported by D V Day and L M Sulsky, "Effects of Frame-of-Reference Training and Information Configuration on Memory Organization and Rating Accuracy," *Journal of Applied Psychology,* February 1995, pp 158–67.

17 Results can be found in J S Phillips and R G Lord, "Schematic Information Processing and Perceptions of Leadership in Problem-Solving Groups," *Journal of Applied Psychology,* August 1982, pp 486–92; and D D Cremer, M V Dijke, and D M Mayer, "Cooperating When 'You' and 'I' are Treated Fairly: The Moderating Role of Leader Prototypicality," *Journal of Applied Psychology,* November 2010, pp 1121–33.

18 See M Beck, "Conquering Fear," *The Wall Street Journal,* January 4, 2011, pp D1, D2; and W Darr and G Johns, "Work Strain, Health, and Absenteeism: A Meta-Analysis," *Journal of Occupational Health Psychology,* October 2008, pp 293–318.

19 See E C Baig, "Survey Offers a 'Sneak Peek' into Net Surfers' Brains," *USA Today,* March 27, 2006, p 4B.

20 S Power, "Mickey Mouse, Nike Give Advice on Air Security," *The Wall Street Journal,* January 24, 2002, p B4.

21 C M Judd and B Park, "Definition and Assessment of Accuracy in Social Stereotypes," *Psychological Review,* January 1993, p 110.

22 For a discussion of stereotype accuracy, see T R Cain, J T Crawford, K Harber, and F Cohen, "The Unbearable Accuracy of Stereotypes," in *Handbook of Prejudice, Stereotyping, and Discrimination,* ed T D Nelson (New York: Psychology Press, 2009), pp 199–225.

23 Stereotype formation and maintenance is discussed by M L Pelley, J S Reimers, G Calvini, R Spears, T Beesley, and R A Murphy, "Stereotype Formation: Biased by Association," *Journal of Experimental Psychology,* February 2010, pp 138–61.

24 See E L Paluck and D P Green, "Prejudice Reduction: What Works? A Review and Assessment of Research and Practice," *Annual Review of Psychology,* 2009, pp 339–67.

25 See J V Sanchez-Hucles and D D Davis, "Women and Women of Color in Leadership," *American Psychologist,* April 2010, pp 171–81; and S Bruckmüller and N R Branscombe, "How Women End Up On the 'Glass Cliff,'" *Harvard Business Review,* January–February 2011, p 26.

26 See J D Olian, D P Schwab, and Y Haberfeld, "The Impact of Applicant Gender Compared to Qualifications on Hiring Recommendations: A Meta-Analysis of Experimental Studies," *Organizational Behavior and Human Decision Processes,* April 1988, pp 180–95.

27 Results from the meta-analyses are discussed in K P Carson, C L Sutton, and P D Corner, "Gender Bias in Performance Appraisals: A Meta-Analysis," paper presented at the 49th Annual Academy of Management Meeting, Washington, DC: 1989. Results from the field study can be found in T J Maurer and M A Taylor, "Is Sex by Itself Enough? An Exploration of Gender Bias Issues in Performance Appraisal," *Organizational Behavior and Human Decision Processes,* November 1994, pp 231–51.

28 J Landau, "The Relationship of Race and Gender to Managers' Ratings of Promotion Potential," *Journal of Organizational Behavior,* July 1995, pp 391–400.

29 K S Lyness and M E Heilman, "When Fit Is Fundamental: Performance Evaluations and Promotions of Upper-Level Female and Male Managers," *Journal of Applied Psychology,* July 2006, pp 777–85.

30 For a review of this research, see R A Posthuma and M A Campion, "Age Stereotypes in the Workplace: Common Stereotypes, Moderators, and Future Research Directions," *Journal of Management,* February 2009, pp 158–88.

31 S R Rhodes, "Age-Related Differences in Work Attitudes and Behavior: A Review and Conceptual Analysis," *Psychological Bulletin,* March 1983, pp 328–67.

32 See T W H Ng and D C Feldman, "The Relationship of Age to Ten Dimensions of Job Performance," *Journal of Applied Psychology,* March 2008, pp 392–423.

33 B J Avolio, D A Waldman, and M A McDaniel, "Age and Work Performance in Nonmanagerial Jobs: The Effects of Experience and Occupational Type," *Academy of Management Journal,* June 1990, pp 407–22.

34 D H Powell, "Aging Baby Boomers: Stretching Your Workforce Options," *HR Magazine,* July 1998, p 83.

35 Results can be found in R W Griffeth, P W Hom, and S Gaertner, "A Meta-Analysis of Antecedents and Correlates of Employee Turnover: Update, Moderator Tests, and Research Implications for the Next Millennium," *Journal of Management,* 2000, pp 463–88.

36 See J J Martocchio, "Age-Related Differences in Employee Absenteeism: A Meta-Analysis," *Psychology and Aging,* December 1989, pp 409–14.

37 T DeAngelis, "Unmasking 'Racial MicroAggressions,'" *Monitor on Psychology,* February 2009, p 44.

38 Ibid., p 43.

39 See S M Colarelli, D A Poole, K Unterborn, and G C D'Souza, "Racial Prototypicality, Affirmative Action, and Hiring Decisions in a Multiracial World," *International Journal of Selection and Assessment,"* June 2010, pp 166–73; and E B King and A S Ahmad, "An Experimental Field Study of Interpersonal Discrimination Toward Muslim Job Applicants," *Personnel Psychology,* Winter 2010, pp 881–906.

40 See "About Tiger Woods," retrieved January 11, 2011, from http://web.tigerwoods.com/aboutTiger/bio.

41 Results from these studies can be found in A I Huffcutt and P L Roth, "Racial Group Differences in Employment Interview Evaluations," *Journal of Applied Psychology,* April 1998, pp 179–89; and T-R Lin, G H Dobbins, and J-L Farh, "A Field Study of Race and Age Similarity Effects on Interview Ratings in Conventional and Situational Interviews," *Journal of Applied Psychology,* June 1992, pp 363–71.

42 See D A Waldman and B J Avolio, "Race Effects in Performance Evaluations: Controlling for Ability, Education, and Experience," *Journal of Applied Psychology,* December 1991, pp 897–901; and E D Pulakos, L A White, S H Oppler, and W C Borman, "Examination of Race and Sex Effects on Performance Ratings," *Journal of Applied Psychology,* October 1989, pp 770–80.

43 H-H D Nguyen and A M Ryan, "Does Stereotype Threat Affect Test Performance of Minorities and Women? A Meta-Analysis of Experimental Evidence," *Journal of Applied Psychology,* November 2008, p 1314.

44 See ibid., pp 1314–34; and J Owens and D S Massey, "Stereotype Threat and College Academic Performance: A Latent Variable Approach," *Social Science Research,* January 2011, pp 150–66.

45 See "Economic News Release: Employment Situation Summary Table A. Household data, seasonally adjusted," *Bureau of Labor Statistics.* Retrieved on January 11, 2011, from http://www.bls.gov/news .release/empsit.a.htm; and "Unemployment Rate for People With Disabilities Continues to Rise, Part One." Retrieved January 11, 2011, from http://www.socialsecuritydisabilitylosangeles.com/2011/ 11/unemployment-rate-for-people . . .

46 See "New Monthly Data Series on the Employment Status of People with a Disability," US Bureau of Labor Statistics. Last modified February 6, 2009, http://data.bls.gov/cgi-bin/print.pl/cps/ cpsdisability.htm.

47 The ADA and its associated accommodation requirements are discussed by J A Segal, "ADA Game Changer," *HR Magazine,* June 2010, pp 121–26.

48 See Day and Sulsky, "Effects of Frame-of-Reference Training and Information Configuration on Memory Organization and Rating Accuracy."

49 See D M Owens, "Hiring Employees with Autism," *HR Magazine,* June 2010, pp 84–90. Also see L Albright, "Positive Turnover, Disability Awareness, Employee Selection Guidelines," *HR Magazine,* January 2011, p 21.

50 R Rosenthal and L Jacobson, *Pygmalion in the Classroom: Teacher Expectation and Pupils' Intellectual Development* (New York: Holt, Rinehart & Winston, 1968). Also see C Haimerl and S Fries,

"Self-Fulfilling Prophecies in Media-Based Learning: Content Relevance Moderates Quality Expectation Effects on Academic Achievement," *Learning and Instruction,* December 2010, pp 498–510.

51 D B McNatt, "Ancient Pygmalion Joins Contemporary Management: A Meta-Analysis of the Result," *Journal of Applied Psychology,* April 2000, pp 314–22. Also see T Inamori and F Analoui, "Beyond Pygmalion Effect: The Role of Managerial Perception," *Journal of Management Development,* 2010, pp 306–21.

52 G Natanovich and D Eden, "Pygmalion Effects among Outreach Supervisors and Tutors: Extending Sex Generalizability," *Journal of Applied Psychology,* November 2008, pp 1382–89.

53 See ibid; and X M Bezuijen, P T van den Berg, K van Dam, and H Thierry, "Pygmalion and Employee Learning: The Role of Leader Behaviors," *Journal of Management,* October 2009, pp 1248–67.

54 The Golem effect is defined and investigated by O B Davidson and D Eden, "Remedial Self-Fulfilling Prophecy: Two Field Experiments to Prevent Golem Effects among Disadvantaged Women," *Journal of Applied Psychology,* June 2000, pp 386–98.

55 The role of positive expectations at Google is discussed by A Lashinsky, "Search and Joy," *Fortune,* January 22, 2007, pp 70–82.

56 See R Courtny, "Believe You Can Succeed and It's Likely You Will." Retrieved January 11, 2011, from http://www.leadershippundit .com/2011/01/believe-you-can-succeed-and-its-likely-you-will/; and M Beck, "Conquering Fear," *The Wall Street Journal,* January 4, 2011, pp D1, D2.

57 Kelley's model is discussed in detail in H H Kelley, "The Processes of Causal Attribution," *American Psychologist,* February 1973, pp 107–28.

58 See J Reb and G J Greguras, "Understanding Performance Ratings: Dynamic Performance, Attributions, and Rating Purpose," *Journal of Applied Psychology,* January 2010, pp 213–20.

59 Examples can be found in C Meyer and A Schwager, "Understanding Customer Experience," *Harvard Business Review,* February 2007, pp 117–26; and M S Hershcovis and J Barling, "Comparing Victim Attributions and Outcomes for Workplace Aggression and Sexual Harassment," *Journal of Applied Psychology,* September 2010, pp 874–88.

60 B Leonard, "A Seldom-Seen World of Work," *HR Magazine,* June 2010, p 82.

61 I Choi, R E Nisbett, and A Norenzayan, "Causal Attribution across Cultures: Variation and Universality," *Psychological Bulletin,* January 1999, pp 47–63.

62 G Kolev, "The Stock Market Bubble, Shareholders' Attribution Bias and Excessive Top CEO Pay," *The Journal of Behavioral Finance,* April 2008, pp 62–71.

63 R J Grossman, "What to Do About Substance Abuse," *HR Magazine,* November 2010, pp 33–38.

64 J Metcalfe, "Recruiting Phone Calls at Center of NCAA Hearing," *The Arizona Republic,* August 13, 2010, p C7.

65 See J Metcalfe, "NCAA Bans Arizona State University from 2011 Postseason," December 15, 2010, http://www.azcentral.com/sports/ articles/2010/12/12/20101215ncaa-bans-arizona-state-asu.

66 Results can be found in E W K Tsang, "Self-Serving Attributions in Corporate Annual Reports: A Replicated Study," *Journal of Management Studies,* January 2002, pp 51–65.

67 T S Duval and P J Silvia, "Self-Awareness, Probability of Improvement, and the Self-Serving Bias," *Journal of Personality and Social Psychology,* January 2002, pp 49–61.

68 Ibid., p 58.

69 Details may be found in S E Moss and M J Martinko, "The Effects of Performance Attributions and Outcome Dependence on Leader Feedback Behavior following Poor Subordinate Performance," *Journal of Organizational Behavior,* May 1998,

pp 259–74; and E C Pence, W C Pendleton, G H Dobbins, and J A Sgro, "Effects of Causal Explanations and Sex Variables on Recommendations for Corrective Actions Following Employee Failure," *Organizational Behavior and Human Performance,* April 1982, pp 227–40.

70 See M O'Neill, "Luck, or Hard Work?" *Forbes,* February 26, 2007, p 38.

71 See D Konst, R Vonk, and R V D Vlist, "Inferences about Causes and Consequences of Behavior of Leaders and Subordinates," *Journal of Organizational Behavior,* March 1999, pp 261–71.

72 See M Miserandino, "Attributional Retraining as a Method of Improving Athletic Performance," *Journal of Sport Behavior,* August 1998, pp 286–97.

73 Excerpted from J. Lublin, "A Question to Make a Monkey of You," *The Wall Street Journal,* February 3, 2009, p D4.

74 Excerpted from N Timiraos, "Seeing the Allure of 'Can Pay, Won't Pay,'" *The Wall Street Journal,* December 29, 2010, p A4.

CHAPTER 8

1 Excerpted from S Banchero, "Teachers Lose Jobs Over Test Scores," *The Wall Street Journal,* July 24, 2010, p A3; W McGuran, "Giving Lousy Teachers the Boot," *The Wall Street Journal,* July 27, 2010, p A17; and R Whitmire, "Can Rhee's Reforms Work Without Rhee's Toughness?" *The Washington Post,* January 21, 2011, http://www.washingtonpost.com/wp-dyn/content/article/2011/01/21 0AR2011012105238.ht.

2 T R Mitchell, "Motivation: New Direction for Theory, Research, and Practice," *Academy of Management Review,* January 1982, p 81.

3 A review of content and process theories of motivation is provided by "Motivation in Today's Workplace: The Link to Performance," *Research Quarterly,* Second Quarter 2010, pp 1–9. Published by the Society For Human Resource Management.

4 For a complete description of Maslow's theory, see A H Maslow, "A Theory of Human Motivation," *Psychological Review,* July 1943, pp 370–96.

5 See W B Swann Jr, C Chang-Schneider, and K L McClarty, "Do People's Self-Views Matter?" *American Psychologist,* February–March 2007, pp 84–94.

6 Applications of Maslow's theory are found in M Hofman, "The Idea That Saved My Company," *Inc.,* October 2007, www.inc.com; and C Conley, *How Great Companies Get Their Mojo from Maslow* (San Francisco, CA: Jossey-Bass, 2007).

7 For a complete review of ERG theory, see C P Alderfer, *Existence, Relatedness, and Growth: Human Needs in Organizational Settings* (New York: Free Press, 1972).

8 L Buchanan, "Managing One-to-One," *Inc.,* October 2001, p 87.

9 H A Murray, *Explorations in Personality* (New York: John Wiley & Sons, 1938), p 164.

10 See K G Shaver, "The Entrepreneurial Personality Myth," *Business and Economic Review,* April–June 1995, pp 20–23.

11 A Beard, "Life's Work," *Harvard Business Review,* July–August 2010, p 172.

12 See S W Spreier, M H Fontaine, and R L Malloy, "Leadership Run Amok," *Harvard Business Review,* June 2006, pp 72–82.

13 See H Heckhausen and S Krug, "Motive Modification," in *Motivation and Society,* ed A J Stewart (San Francisco, CA: Jossey-Bass, 1982).

14 Results can be found in D B Turban and T L Keon, "Organizational Attractiveness: An Interactionist Perspective," *Journal of Applied Psychology,* April 1993, pp 184–93.

15 Quoted in Spreier, Fontaine, and Malloy, p 2.

16 See "Byrraju Ramalinga Raju," Wikipedia, last updated January 27, 2011, http:wikipedia.org.

17 See F Herzberg, B Mausner, and B B Snyderman, *The Motivation to Work* (New York: John Wiley & Sons, 1959).

18 See J Flint, "How to Be A Player," *Bloomberg Businessweek,* January 24–January 30, 2011, pp 108–9.

19 F Herzberg, "One More Time: How Do You Motivate Employees?" *Harvard Business Review,* January–February 1968, p 56.

20 For a thorough review of research on Herzberg's theory, see C C Pinder, *Work Motivation: Theory, Issues, and Applications* (Glenview, IL: Scott, Foresman, 1984).

21 See R G Satter and J Lawless, "WikiLeaks Supporters Protest Via Cyberattacks," *The Arizona Republic,* December 10, 2010, p A15.

22 The comparison process was discussed by S T Fiske, "Envy Up, Scorn Down: How Comparison Divides Us," *American Psychologist,* November 2010, pp 698–706.

23 See P Bamberger and E Belogolovsky, "The Impact of Pay Secrecy on Individual Task Performance," *Personnel Psychology,* Winter 2010, pp 965–96; and M C Bolino and W H Turnley, "Old Faces, New Places: Equity Theory in Cross-Cultural Contexts," *Journal of Organizational Behavior,* January 2008, pp 29–50.

24 N Koppel and V O'Connell, "Pay Gap Widens at Big Law Firms As Partners Chase Star Attorneys," *The Wall Street Journal,* February 8, 2011, p A1.

25 Responses to inequity were examined by D P Skarlicki and D E Rupp, "Dual Processing and Organizational Justice: The Role of Rational Versu Experiential Processing in Third-Party Reactions to Workplace Mistreatment," *Journal of Applied Psychology,* September 2010, pp 944–52; and J Goodstein and K Aquino, "And Restorative Justice for All: Redemption, Forgiveness, and Reintegration in Organizations," *Journal of Organizational Behavior,* May 2010, pp 624–28.

26 J Bernoff and T Schadler, "Empowered," *Harvard Business Review,* July–August 2010, pp 95–101.

27 For a thorough review of organizational justice theory and research, see R Cropanzano, D E Rupp, C J Mohler, and M Schminke, "Three Roads to Organizational Justice," in *Research in Personnel and Human Resources Management,* vol 20, ed G R Ferris (New York: JAI Press, 2001), pp 269–329.

28 J A Colquitt, D E Conlon, M J Wesson, C O L H Porter, and K Y Ng, "Justice at the Millennium: A Meta-Analytic Review of 25 Years of Organizational Justice Research," *Journal of Applied Psychology,* June 2001, p 426.

29 Results from these studies can be found in N E Fassina, D A Jones, and K L Uggerslev, "Meta-Analytic Tests of Relationships between Organizational Justice and Citizenship Behavior: Testing Agent-System and Shared-Variance Models," *Journal of Organizational Behavior,* August 2008, pp 805–28; Y Cohen-Charash and P E Spector, "The Role of Justice in Organizations: A Meta-Analysis," *Organizational Behavior and Human Decision Processes,* November 2001, pp 278–321; Colquitt, Conlon, Wesson, Porter, and Ng, p 426; and M S Hershcovis, N Turner, J Barling, K A Arnold, K E Dupré, M Inness, M M LeBlanc, and N Sivanathan, "Predicting Workplace Aggression: A Meta-Analysis," *Journal of Applied Psychology,* January 2007, pp 228–38.

30 For recent studies of justice, see D De Cremer, J Brockner, A Fishman, M van Dijke, W van Olffen, and D M Mayer, "When Do Procedural Fairness and Outcome Fairness Interact to Influence Employees' Work Attitudes and Behaviors? The Moderating Effect of Uncertainty," *Journal of Applied Psychology,* March 2010, pp 291–304; and O Janssen, C K Lam, and X Huang, "Emotional Exhaustion and Job Performance: The Moderating Roles of Distributive Justice and Positive Affect," *Journal of Organizational Behavior,* August 2010, pp 787–809.

31 Results from this study were reported in K Gurchiek, "Show Workers Their Value, Study Says," *HR Magazine,* October 2006, p 40.

[32] E Thornton, "Managing through a Crisis: The New Rules," *BusinessWeek,* January 19, 2009, pp 30–34.

[33] The impact of groups on justice perceptions was investigated by D A Jones and D P Skarlicki, "The Effects of Overhearing Peers to Discuss an Authority's Fairness Reputation on Reactions to Subsequent Treatment," *Journal of Applied Psychology,* March 2005, pp 363–72.

[34] "Discrimination Suit Filed Against FedEx," *The Arizona Republic,* September 16, 2010, p X.

[35] Climate for justice was studied by S Tangirala and R Ramanujam, "Employee Silence on Critical Work Issues: The Cross Level Effects of Procedural Justice Climate," *Personnel Psychology,* Spring 2008, pp 37–68.

[36] See V H Vroom, *Work and Motivation* (New York: John Wiley & Sons, 1964).

[37] E E Lawler III, *Motivation in Work Organizations* (Belmont, CA: Wadsworth, 1973), p 45.

[38] See C C Pinder, *Work Motivation* (Glenview, IL: Scott, Foresman, 1984), ch 7.

[39] B Becht, "Building a Company Without Borders," *Harvard Business Review,* April 2010, p 106.

[40] "Federal Express's Fred Smith," *Inc.,* October 1986, p 38.

[41] Results can be found in W van Eerde and H Thierry, "Vroom's Expectancy Models and Work-Related Criteria: A Meta-Analysis," *Journal of Applied Psychology,* October 1996, pp 575–86.

[42] See J Cameron and W D Pierce, *Rewards and Intrinsic Motivation: Resolving the Controversy* (Alberta, Canada: Cameron and Pierce, 2002); K L Scott, J D Shaw, and M K Duffy, "Merit Pay Raises and Organization-Based Self-Esteem," *Journal of Organizational Behavior,* October 2008, pp 967–80.

[43] M Dewhurst, M Gulhridge, and W Mohr, "Motivating People: Getting Beyond Money," *McKinsey&Company,* November 2009, http://www.mckinseyquarterly.com/ghost.aspx?ID=/Organizatin/Talent/Motivating_peo. Also see E Krell, "All For Incentives, Incentives for All," *HR Magazine,* January 2011, pp 35–38.

[44] See S Terlep, "GM Rethinks Pay for Unionized Workers," *The Wall Street Journal,* January 12, 2011, p B6; and S Terlep, "GM's Profit Sharing Largest Amount Ever," *The Wall Street Journal,* February 9, 2011, p B2.

[45] L Scott, "Grocery Bagger Set Course to Be President of Bashas'," *The Arizona Republic,* February 11, 2007, p D2.

[46] E A Locke, K N Shaw, L M Saari, and G P Latham, "Goal Setting and Task Performance: 1969–1980," *Psychological Bulletin,* July 1981, p 126.

[47] The case of multiple goals is discussed by J B Vancouver, J M Weinhardt, and A M Schmidt, "A Formal, Computational Theory of Multiple-Goal Pursuit: Integrating Goal-Choice and Goal-Striving Processes," *Journal of Applied Psychology,* November 2010, pp 985–1008.

[48] R Weiss and B Kammel, "How Siemens Got Its Geist Back," *Bloomberg Businessweek,* January 31–February 6, 2011, pp 18–20.

[49] M Frese, S I Krauss, N Keith, S Escher, R Grabarkiewicz, S T Luneng, C Heers, J Unger, and C Friedrich, "Business Owners' Action Planning and Its Relationship to Business Success in Three African Countries," *Journal of Applied Psychology,* November 2007, pp 1481–98.

[50] See G P Latham and E A Locke, "Enhancing the Benefits and Overcoming the Pitfalls of Goal Setting," *Organizational Dynamics,* November 2006, pp 332–40.

[51] See E A Locke and G P Latham, *A Theory of Goal Setting and Task Performance* (Englewood Cliffs, NJ: Prentice Hall, 1990).

[52] D Morisano, J B Hirsh, J B Peterson, R O Pihl, and B M Shore, "Setting, Elaborating, and Reflecting on Personal Goals Improves Academic Performance," *Journal of Applied Psychology,* March 2010, pp 255–64.

[53] Supportive results can be found in S E Humphrey, J D Nahrgang, and F P Morgeson, "Integrating Motivational, Social, and Contextual Work Design Features: A Meta-Analytic Summary and Theoretical Extension of the Work Design Literature," *Journal of Applied Psychology,* September 2007, pp 1332–56.

[54] See J J Donovan and D J Radosevich, "The Moderating Role of Goal Commitment on the Goal Difficulty-Performance Relationship: A Meta-Analytic Review and Critical Reanalysis," *Journal of Applied Psychology,* April 1998, pp 308–15.

[55] See Latham and Locke, "Enhancing the Benefits and Overcoming the Pitfalls of Goal Setting."

[56] See "It's a Balancing Act," *Training,* May 2009, p 10.

[57] J L Bowditch and A F Buono, *A Primer on Organizational Behavior* (New York: John Wiley & Sons, 1985), p 210.

[58] A review of these approach is provided by S Hornung, D M Rousseau, J Glaser, P Angerer, and M Weigl, "Beyond Top-Down and Bottom-Up Work Redesign: Customizing Job Content Through Idiosyncratic Deals," *Journal of Organizational Behavior,* February 2010, pp 187–215; and G R Oldham and J R Hackman, "Not What It Was and Not What It Will Be: The Future of Job Design," *Journal of Organizational Behavior,* February 2010, pp 463–79.

[59] G D Babcock, *The Taylor System in Franklin Management,* 2nd ed (New York: Engineering Magazine Company, 1917), p 31.

[60] For a thorough discussion, see F B Copley, *Frederick W Taylor: The Principles of Scientific Management* (New York: Harper & Brothers, 1911).

[61] See the related discussion in S Wagner-Tsukamoto, "An Institutional Economic Reconstruction of Scientific Management: On the Lost Theoretical Logic of Taylorism," *Academy of Management Review,* January 2007, pp 105–17; and P R Lawrence, "The Key Job Design Problem Is Still Taylorism," *Journal of Organizational Behavior,* February 2010, pp 412–21.

[62] This type of program was developed and tested by M A Campion and C L McClelland, "Follow-Up and Extension of the Interdisciplinary Costs and Benefits of Enlarged Jobs," *Journal of Applied Psychology,* June 1993, pp 339–51.

[63] M Moskowitz, R Levering, and C Tkaczyk, "100 Best Companies to Work For," *Fortune,* p 96.

[64] J R Hackman, G R Oldham, R Janson, and K Purdy, "A New Strategy for Job Enrichment," *California Management Review,* Summer 1975, p 58.

[65] Definitions of the job characteristics were adapted from J R Hackman and G R Oldham, "Motivation through the Design of Work: Test of a Theory," *Organizational Behavior and Human Performance,* August 1976, pp 250–79.

[66] See Humphrey, Nahrgang, and Morgeson, pp 1332–56.

[67] See ibid; and D J Holman, C M Axtell, C A Sprigg, P Totterdell, and T D Wall, "The Mediating Role of Job Characteristics In Job Redesign Interventions: A Serendipitous Quasi-Experiment," *Journal of Organizational Behavior,* January 2010, pp 84–105.

[68] Moskowitz, Levering, and Tkaczyk, p 93.

[69] Productivity studies are reviewed in R E Kopelman, *Managing Productivity in Organizations* (New York: McGraw-Hill, 1986).

[70] A Wrzesniewski and J E Dutton, "Crafting a Job: Revisioning Employees As Active Crafters of Their Work," *Academy of Management Review,* April 2001, p 179.

[71] See J M Berg, A Wrzesniewski, and J E Dutton, "Perceiving and Responding to Challenges in Job Crafting at Different Ranks: When Proactivity Requires Adaptivity," *Journal of Organizational Behavior,* February 2010, pp 158–86.

72 Hornung, Rousseau, Glaser, Angerer, and Weigl, p 188.

73 See T Hopke, "Go Ahead, Take a Few Months Off," *HR Magazine,* September 2010, pp 71–74; and "RSM McGladrey," *Wikipedia,* last updated December 6, 2010, http://en.wikipedia.org/wiki/RSM_McGladrey.

74 Hornung, Rousseau, Glaser, Angerer, and Weigl, pp 187–215.

75 J Welch and S Welch, "An Employee Bill of Rights," *BusinessWeek,* March 16, 2009, p 72.

76 Excerpted from B. Conaty, "Cutbacks: Don't Neglect the Survivors," *Bloomberg Businessweek,* January 11, 2010, p 68.

77 Excerpted from M Kimes, "Nomenclature: Your Swiss Bank May Be Getting Kickbacks," *Fortune,* February 16, 2009, p 19.

CHAPTER 9

1 M Moskowitz, R Levering, and C Tkaczyk, "The List: 100 Best Companies to Work For," *Fortune,* February 7, 2011, p 95.

2 Quoted and adapted from D A Kaplan, "Undercover Employee: A Day on the Job at Three Best Companies," *Fortune,* February 7, 2011, p 84.

3 B Tulgan, "The Under-Management Epidemic," *HR Magazine,* October 2004, p 119.

4 S Meisinger, "Management Holds Key to Employee Engagement," *HR Magazine,* February 2008, p 8.

5 See K Gurchiek, "Report Ties Coaching Strategies to Business," *HR Magazine,* July 2010, p 75; T H Davenport, J Harris, and J Shapiro, "Competing on Talent Analytics," *Harvard Business Review,* October 2010, pp 52–58; J A Segal, "Performance Management Blunders," *HR Magazine,* November 2010, pp 75–78; and C M Plump, "Dealing with Problem Employees: A Legal Guide for Employers," *Business Horizons,* November–December 2010, pp 607–18.

6 This distinction is drawn from G P Latham, J Almost, S Mann, and C Moore, "New Developments in Performance Management," *Organizational Dynamics,* no 1, 2005, pp 77–87.

7 See A Fox, "Curing What Ails Performance Reviews," *HR Magazine,* January 2009, pp 52–56; "A Bad Review for Performance Reviews," *HR Magazine,* May 2010, p 28; K W Platts and M Sobótka, "When the Uncountable Counts: An Alternative to Monitoring Employee Performance," *Business Horizons,* July–August 2010, pp 349–57; and "Rave Reviews," *Training,* September–October 2010, p 7.

8 As quoted in P B Brown, "What I Know Now," *Fast Company,* April 2005, p 104. Also see B Roberts, "Close-Up on Screening," *HR Magazine,* February 2011, pp 22–29; and D Meinert, "Seeing Behind the Mask," *HR Magazine,* February 2011, pp 30–37.

9 See M Weinstein, "Holding On to Talent?" *Training,* March-April 2010, p 12.

10 Adapted and quoted from "ThermoSTAT," *Training,* July–August 2003, p 16.

11 Based on W R Boswell, J B Bingham, and A J S Colvin, "Aligning Employees through 'Line of Sight,'" *Business Horizons,* November–December 2006, pp 499–509. Also see E Patton, "What Are the Characteristics of Good Strategic Objectives?" *HR Magazine,* April 2010, p 23.

12 C J Loomis, "The Bloomberg," *Fortune,* April 16, 2007, p 68.

13 G H Seijts and G P Latham, "Learning versus Performance Goals: When Should Each Be Used?" *Academy of Management Executive,* February 2005, pp 126–27. See the following instructive ongoing debate about goal setting: L D Ordóñez, M E Schweitzer, A D Galinsky, and M H Bazerman, "Goals Gone Wild: The Systematic Side Effects of Overprescribing Goal Setting," *Academy of Management Perspectives,* February 2009, pp 6–16; E A Locke and G P Latham, "Has Goal Setting Gone Wild, or Have Its Attackers Abandoned Good Scholarship?" *Academy of Management Perspectives,*

February 2009, pp 17–23; L D Ordóñez, M E Schweitzer, A D Galinsky, and M H Bazerman, "On Good Scholarship, Goal Setting, and Scholars Gone Wild," *Academy of Management Perspectives,* August 2009, pp 82–87; and G P Latham and E A Locke, "Science and Ethics: What Should Count as Evidence Against the Use of Goal Setting?" *Academy of Management Perspectives,* August 2009, pp 88–91.

14 D Morisano, J B Hirsh, J B Peterson, R O Pihl, and B M Shore, "Setting, Elaborating, and Reflecting on Personal Goals Improves Academic Performance," *Journal of Applied Psychology,* March 2010, p 255.

15 Thorough discussions of MBO are provided by P F Drucker, *The Practice of Management* (New York: Harper, 1954); and P F Drucker, "What Results Should You Expect? A User's Guide to MBO," *Public Administration Review,* January–February 1976, pp 12–19. Also see A M Kantrow, "Why Read Peter Drucker?" *Harvard Business Review,* November 2009, pp 72–82.

16 As quoted in M Kimes, "How Do I Groom and Keep Talented Employees?" *Fortune,* November 10, 2008, p 26.

17 Results from both studies can be found in R Rodgers and J E Hunter, "Impact of Management by Objectives on Organizational Productivity," *Journal of Applied Psychology,* April 1991, pp 322–36; and R Rodgers, J E Hunter, and DL Rogers, "Influence of Top Management Commitment on Management Program Success," *Journal of Applied Psychology,* February 1993, pp 151–55.

18 D Foust, "Why Did IndyMac Implode?" *BusinessWeek,* August 4, 2008, p. 24. Also see L M Bacon, "Study: Soldiers Go to Extremes to Meet Army's Weight Rules," *The Arizona Republic,* December 12, 2010, p A30.

19 For a good overview, see G P Latham and E A Locke, "Enhancing the Benefits and Overcoming the Pitfalls of Goal Setting," *Organizational Dynamics,* no 4, 2006, pp 332–40.

20 Based on J A Colquitt and M J Simmering, "Conscientiousness, Goal Orientation, and Motivation to Learn during the Learning Process: A Longitudinal Study," *Journal of Applied Psychology,* August 1998, pp 654–65.

21 D VandeWalle, S P Brown, W L Cron, and J W Slocum Jr, "The Influence of Goal Orientation and Self-Regulated Tactics on Sales Performance: A Longitudinal Field Test," *Journal of Applied Psychology,* April 1999, p 250. Also see G H Seijts, G P Latham, K Tasa, and B W Latham, "Goal Setting and Goal Orientation: An Integration of Two Different Yet Related Literatures," *Academy of Management Journal,* April 2004, pp 227–39; and C L Porath and T S Bateman, "Self-Regulation: From Goal Orientation to Job Performance," *Journal of Applied Psychology,* January 2006, pp 185–86.

22 For more, see Y Gong and J Fan, "Longitudinal Examination of the Role of Goal Orientation in Cross-Cultural Adjustment," *Journal of Applied Psychology,* January 2006, pp 176–84; S C Payne, S S Youngcourt, and J M Beaubien, "A Meta-Analytic Examination of the Goal Orientation Nomological Net," *Journal of Applied Psychology,* January 2007, pp 128–50; and C Porter, J W Webb, and C I Gogus, "When Goal Orientations Collide: Effects of Learning and Performance Orientation on Team Adaptability in Response to Workload Imbalance," *Journal of Applied Psychology,* September 2010, pp 935–43.

23 As quoted in "The Best Managers," *BusinessWeek,* January 19, 2009, p 41.

24 See J McGregor, "Giving Back to Your Stars," *Fortune,* November 1, 2010, pp 53–54.

25 Drawn from M Koo and A Fishbach, "Climbing the Goal Ladder: How Upcoming Actions Increase Level of Aspiration," *Journal of Personality and Social Psychology,* July 2010, pp 1–13.

26 E A Locke and G P Latham, *Goal Setting: A Motivational Technique That Works!* (Englewood Cliffs, NJ: Prentice Hall, 1984), p 79. Also see K S Cravens, E G Oliver, and J S Stewart, "Can a Positive Approach to Performance Evaluation Help Accomplish Your Goals?" *Business Horizons,* May–June 2010, pp 269–79.

27 See E A Locke, "Linking Goals to Monetary Incentives," *Academy of Management Executive,* November 2004, pp 130–33.

28 K Tyler, "One Bad Apple," *HR Magazine,* December 2004, p 85.

29 See E G Love, D W Love, and G B Northcraft, "Is the End in Sight? Student Regulation on In-Class and Extra-Credit Effort in Response to Performance Feedback," *Academy of Management Learning and Education,* March 2010, pp 81–97.

30 Data from "500 Largest U.S. Corporations," *Fortune,* May 3, 2010, p F-46.

31 As quoted in C Fishman, "Fred Smith," *Fast Company,* June 2001, p F-54.

32 C D Lee, "Feedback, Not Appraisal," *HR Magazine,* November 2006, p 111. Also see M Rosenthal, "Performance Review 201," *Training,* July–August 2010, p 44.

33 Both the definition of feedback and the functions of feedback are based on discussion in D R Ilgen, C D Fisher, and M S Taylor, "Consequences of Individual Feedback on Behavior in Organizations," *Journal of Applied Psychology,* August 1979, pp 349–71; and R E Kopelman, *Managing Productivity in Organizations: A Practical People-Oriented Perspective* (New York: McGraw-Hill, 1986), p 175.

34 See P C Earley, G B Northcraft, C Lee, and T R Lituchy, "Impact of Process and Outcome Feedback on the Relation of Goal Setting to Task Performance," *Academy of Management Journal,* March 1990, pp 87–105.

35 Data from A N Kluger and A DeNisi, "The Effects of Feedback Interventions on Performance: A Historical Review, a Meta-Analysis, and a Preliminary Feedback Intervention Theory," *Psychological Bulletin,* March 1996, pp 254–84. Also see G Morse, "Feedback Backlash," *Harvard Business Review,* October 2004, p 28.

36 Data from K D Harber, "Feedback to Minorities: Evidence of a Positive Bias," *Journal of Personality and Social Psychology,* March 1998, pp 622–28.

37 See T Matsui, A Okkada, and T Kakuyama, "Influence of Achievement Need on Goal Setting, Performance, and Feedback Effectiveness," *Journal of Applied Psychology,* October 1982, pp 645–48.

38 S J Ashford, "Feedback-Seeking in Individual Adaptation: A Resource Perspective," *Academy of Management Journal,* September 1986, pp 465–87. Also see D B Fedor, R B Rensvold, and S M Adams, "An Investigation of Factors Expected to Affect Feedback Seeking: A Longitudinal Field Study," *Personnel Psychology,* Winter 1992, pp 779–805; and M F Sully De Luque and S M Sommer, "The Impact of Culture on Feedback-Seeking Behavior: An Integrated Model and Propositions," *Academy of Management Review,* October 2000, pp 829–49.

39 See D B Turban and T W Dougherty, "Role of Protégé Personality in Receipt of Mentoring and Career Success," *Academy of Management Journal,* June 1994, pp 688–702.

40 See C Unkelbach, K Fielder, M Bayer, M Stegmuller, and D Danner, "Why Positive Information Is Processed Faster: The Density Hypothesis," *Journal of Personality and Social Psychology,* July 2008, pp 36–49.

41 For complete details, see P M Podsakoff and J L Farh, "Effects of Feedback Sign and Credibility on Goal Setting and Task Performance," *Organizational Behavior and Human Decision Processes,* August 1989, pp 45–67.

42 W S Silver, T R Mitchell, and M E Gist, "Responses to Successful and Unsuccessful Performance: The Moderating Effect of Self-Efficacy on the Relationship between Performance and Attributions," *Organizational Behavior and Human Decision Processes,* June 1995, p 297. Also see A P Tolli and A M Schmidt, "The Role of Feedback, Causal Attributions, and Self-Efficacy in Goal Revision," *Journal of Applied Psychology,* May 2008, pp 692–701.

43 J M Kouzes and B Z Posner, *Credibility: How Leaders Gain and Lose It, Why People Demand It* (San Francisco, CA: Jossey-Bass,

1993), p 25. For research support, see A J Kinicki, G E Prussia, B Wu, and F M McKee-Ryan, "A Covariance Structure Analysis of Employees' Response to Performance Feedback," *Journal of Applied Psychology,* December 2004, pp 1057–69. Also see J Pfeffer, *What Were They Thinking? Unconventional Wisdom about Management* (Boston: Harvard Business School Press, 2007), pp 104–6.

44 See K Leung, S Su, and M W Morris, "When Is Criticism *Not* Constructive? The Roles of Fairness Perceptions and Dispositional Attributions in Employee Acceptance of Critical Supervisory Feedback," *Human Relations,* September 2001, pp 1123–54; and the discussion of how an artist handles criticism in K Bell, "Life's Work: Richard Serra," *Harvard Business Review,* March 2010, p 132.

45 Based on discussion in Ilgen, Fisher, and Taylor, pp 367–68. Also see A M O'Leary-Kelly, "The Influence of Group Feedback on Individual Group Member Response," in *Research in Personnel and Human Resources Management,* vol 16, ed G R Ferris (Stamford, CT: JAI Press, 1998), pp 255–94.

46 See P C Earley, "Computer-Generated Performance Feedback in the Magazine-Subscription Industry," *Organizational Behavior and Human Decision Processes,* February 1988, pp 50–64.

47 See M De Gregorio and C D Fisher, "Providing Performance Feedback: Reactions to Alternate Methods," *Journal of Management,* December 1988, pp 605–16.

48 For details, see R A Baron, "Countering the Effects of Destructive Criticism: The Relative Efficacy of Four Interventions," *Journal of Applied Psychology,* June 1990, pp 235–45. Also see A Maingault, "Q: I'm Trying to Help a Manager Who Inadvertently Destroys Morale When Providing Criticism," *HR Magazine,* May 2008, p 36.

49 C O Longenecker and D A Gioia, "The Executive Appraisal Paradox," *Academy of Management Executive,* May 1992, p 18.

50 See M Carson, "Saying It Like It Isn't: The Pros and Cons of 360-Degree Feedback," *Business Horizons,* September–October 2006, pp 395–402; T van Rensburg and G Prideaux, "Turning Professionals into Managers Using Multisource Feedback," *Journal of Management Development,* no 6, 2006, pp 561–71; and J T Polzer, "Making Diverse Teams Click," *Harvard Business Review,* July–August 2008, pp 20–21.

51 J W Smither, M London, and R R Reilly, "Does Performance Improve Following Multisource Feedback? A Theoretical Model, Meta-Analysis, and Review of Empirical Findings," *Personnel Psychology,* Spring 2005, p 33. Also see F Shipper, R C Hoffman, and D M Rotondo, "Does the 360 Feedback Process Create Actionable Knowledge Equally across Cultures?" *Academy of Management Learning and Education,* March 2007, pp 33–50.

52 S Kolhatkar and S V Bhaktavatsalam, "The Colossus of Wall Street," *Bloomberg Businessweek,* December 13–19, 2010, p 67.

53 D E Coates, "Don't Tie 360 Feedback to Pay," *Training,* September 1998, pp 68–78. Also see "Full-Circle Assessments," *Training,* November–December 2010, p 7; and S Brutus and M B L Donia, "Improving the Effectiveness of Students in Groups with a Centralized Peer Evaluation System," *Academy of Management Learning and Education,* December 2010, pp 652–62.

54 For more on coaching, see S Kochanowski, C F Seifert, and G Yukul, "Using Coaching to Enhance the Effects of Behavioral Feedback to Managers," *Journal of Leadership and Organizational Studies,* no 4, 2010, pp 363–69; R T Whipple, "Stop the Enabling," *HR Magazine,* September 2010, pp 114–15; and E de Haan, C Bertie, A Day, and C Sills, "Clients' Critical Moments of Coaching: Toward a 'Client Model' of Executive Coaching," *Academy of Management Learning and Education,* December 2010, pp 607–21.

55 See J E Core and W R Guay, "Is CEO Pay Too High and Are Incentives Too Low? Wealth-Based Contracting Framework," *Academy of Management Perspectives,* February 2010, pp 5–19; A G Lafley, "Executive Pay: Time for CEOs to Take a Stand," *Harvard Business Review,* May 2010, p 40; J Silver-Greenberg and A Leondis, "How Much Is a CEO Worth?" *Bloomberg Businessweek,* May 10–16, 2010, pp 70–71; and B George, "Executive Pay: Rebuilding Trust in an Era of Rage," *Bloomberg Businessweek,* September 13–19, 2010, p 56.

56 "The Stat," *BusinessWeek,* October 4, 2004, p 16. Also see S Highhouse, M J Zickar, and M Yankelevich, "Would You Work If You Won the Lottery? Tracking Changes in the American Work Ethic," *Journal of Applied Psychology*, March 2010, pp 349–57.

57 See, for example, S Kerr with G Rifkin, *Reward Systems: Does Yours Measure Up?* (Boston: Harvard Business Press, 2009).

58 See D Brady, "Hard Choices: Joe Torre," *Bloomberg Businessweek*, June 21–27, 2010, p 96; J Shambora, "From Leverage to Corkage," *Fortune*, December 6, 2010, p 80; and K Nicholas, "Where the Wild Things Are," *Bloomberg Businessweek*, January 17–23, 2011, p 74.

59 List adapted from J L Pearce and R H Peters, "A Contradictory Norms View of Employer–Employee Exchange," *Journal of Management,* Spring 1985, pp 19–30. Also see T A Judge, and D M Cable, "When It Comes to Pay, Do the Thin Win? The Effects of Weight on Pay for Men and Women," *Journal of Applied Psychology*, January 2011, pp 95–112.

60 B Hindo, "Rewiring Westinghouse," *BusinessWeek,* May 19, 2008, p 49.

61 R Levering and M Moskowitz, "100 Best Companies to Work For: And the Winners Are . . .," *Fortune,* February 2, 2009, pp 67–78.

62 See K W Thomas, *Intrinsic Motivation at Work: Building Energy and Commitment* (San Francisco, CA: Berrett-Koehler Publishers, 2000). Also see A M Grant, "Does Intrinsic Motivation Fuel the Prosocial Fire? Motivational Synergy in Predicting Persistence, Performance, and Productivity," *Journal of Applied Psychology,* January 2008, pp 48–58.

63 See E L Deci and R M Ryan, "The 'What' and 'Why' of Goal Pursuits: Human Needs and Self-Determination of Behavior," *Psychological Inquiry,* December 2000, pp 227–68.

64 This study is summarized by S Ellingwood, "On a Mission," *Gallup Management Journal,* Winter 2001, pp 6–7.

65 R Randazzo, "Nuclear Watchdog," *The Arizona Republic*, November 2, 2008, p D1.

66 M Littman, "Best Bosses Tell All," *Working Woman,* October 2000, p 55.

67 A Carter, "Lighting a Fire under Campbell," *BusinessWeek,* December 4, 2006, p 96. Also see P Post, "The Note," *Training*, September–October 2010, p 44.

68 D R Spitzer, "Power Rewards: Rewards That Really Motivate," *Management Review,* May 1996, p 47. Also see B Schwartz, "The Dark Side of Incentives," *Businessweek*, November 23, 2009, p 84; and J Berry, "Tough Tests," *The Arizona Republic*, January 30, 2011, pp D1–D2.

69 List adapted from discussion in Spitzer, "Power Rewards," pp 45–50.

70 "Performance-Based Pay Plans," *HR Magazine,* June 2004, p 22. Also see S Miller, "Pay Incentives Planned to Limit Post-Recession Flight," *HR Magazine*, July 2010, p 11.

71 For arguments against incentive compensation, see B W Heineman Jr, "The Fatal Flaw in Pay for Performance," *Harvard Business Review,* June 2008, pp 31, 34; W F Cascio and P Cappelli, "Lessons from the Financial Services Crisis," *HR Magazine,* January 2009, pp 46–50; and D Heath and C Heath, "The Curse of Incentives," *Fast Company,* February 2009, pp 48–49.

72 Data from D Kiley, "Crafty Basket Makers Cut Downtime, Waste," *USA Today,* May 10, 2001, p 3B.

73 See S Ladd, "May the Sales Force Be with You," *HR Magazine*, September 2010, pp 105–7.

74 N J Perry, "Here Come Richer, Riskier Pay Plans," *Fortune,* December 19, 1988, p 51. Also see E Krell, "All for Incentives, Incentives for All," *HR Magazine*, January 2011, pp 34–38.

75 Data from M Bloom and G T Milkovich, "Relationships among Risk, Incentive Pay, and Organizational Performance," *Academy of Management Journal,* June 1998, pp 283–97.

76 For details, see G D Jenkins Jr, N Gupta, A Mitra, and J D Shaw, "Are Financial Incentives Related to Performance? A Meta-Analytic Review of Empirical Research," *Journal of Applied Psychology,* October 1998, pp 777–87. Also see S J Peterson and F Luthans, "The Impact of Financial and Nonfinancial Incentives on Business-Unit Outcomes over Time," *Journal of Applied Psychology,* January 2006, pp 156–65.

77 See M J Mandel, "Those Fat Bonuses Don't Seem to Boost Performance," *BusinessWeek*, January 8, 1990, p 26; S F O'Byrne and S D Young, "Why Executive Pay Is Failing," *Harvard Business Review*, June 2006, p 28; and A Pomeroy, "Pay for Performance Is Working, Says a New Study," *HR Magazine*, January 2007, pp 14, 16.

78 Based on discussion in R Ricklefs, "Whither the Payoff on Sales Commissions?" *The Wall Street Journal,* June 6, 1990, p B1.

79 "Performance-Based Pay Plans," p 22.

80 For a model profit-sharing plan, see F Koller, *Spark: How Old-Fashioned Values Drive a Twenty-First Century Corporation—Lessons from Lincoln Electric's Unique Guaranteed Employment Program* (New York: PublicAffairs, 2010).

81 See B E Litzky, K A Eddleston, and D L Kidder, "The Good, the Bad, and the Misguided: How Managers Inadvertently Encourage Deviant Behaviors," *Academy of Management Perspectives,* February 2006, pp 91–103.

82 See E L Thorndike, *Educational Psychology: The Psychology of Learning, Vol. II* (New York: Columbia University Teachers College, 1913).

83 Discussion of an early behaviorist who influenced Skinner's work can be found in P J Kreshel, "John B Watson at J Walter Thompson: The Legitimation of 'Science' in Advertising," *Journal of Advertising,* no 2, 1990, pp 49–59. More recent discussions involving behaviorism include M R Ruiz, "B F Skinner's Radical Behaviorism: Historical Misconstructions and Grounds for Feminist Reconstructions," *Psychology of Women Quarterly,* June 1995, pp 161–79; J A Nevin, "Behavioral Economics and Behavioral Momentum," *Journal of the Experimental Analysis of Behavior,* November 1995, pp 385–95; and H Rachlin, "Can We Leave Cognition to Cognitive Psychologists? Comments on an Article by George Loewenstein," *Organizational Behavior and Human Decision Processes,* March 1996, pp 296–99.

84 For discussion, see J W Donahoe, "The Unconventional Wisdom of B F Skinner: The Analysis-Interpretation Distinction," *Journal of the Experimental Analysis of Behavior,* September 1993, pp 453–56.

85 See B F Skinner, *The Behavior of Organisms* (New York: Appleton-Century-Crofts, 1938).

86 For modern approaches to respondent behavior, see B Azar, "Classical Conditioning Could Link Disorders and Brain Dysfunction, Researchers Suggest," *APA Monitor,* March 1999, p 17.

87 For interesting discussions of Skinner and one of his students, see M B Gilbert and T F Gilbert. "What Skinner Gave Us," *Training,* September 1991, pp 42–48; and "HRD Pioneer Gilbert Leaves a Pervasive Legacy," *Training,* January 1996, p 14. Also see F Luthans and R Kreitner, *Organizational Behavior Modification and Beyond: An Operant and Social Learning Approach* (Glenview, IL: Scott, Foresman, 1985).

88 Based on A M Grant and F Gino, "A Little Thanks Goes a Long Way: Explaining Why Gratitude Expressions motivate Prosocial Behavior," *Journal of Personality and Social Psychology*, June 2010, pp 946–55. Also see S Berinato, "Success Gets into Your Head—and Changes It," *Harvard Business Review*, January–February 2010, p 28.

89 Data from J Yang and A Gonzalez, "Most Preferred Forms of Recognition at Workplace," *USA Today,* May 4, 2009, p 1B. Also see N Lublin, "Two Little Words," *Fast Company,* November 2010, p 56.

90 R Levering and M Moskowitz, "100 Best Companies to Work For: And the Winners Are . . .," *Fortune,* February 2, 2009, pp 67–78.

91 Research on punishment is reported in L E Atwater, D A Waldman, J A Carey, and P Cartier, "Recipient and Observer Reactions to Discipline: Are Managers Experiencing Wishful Thinking?" *Journal*

of Organizational Behavior, May 2001, pp 249–70; and T K Peng and M F Peterson, "Nation, Demographic, and Attitudinal Boundary Conditions on Leader Social Rewards and Punishments in Local Governments," *Journal of Organizational Behavior,* January 2008, pp 95–117.

92 See C B Ferster and B F Skinner, *Schedules of Reinforcement* (New York: Appleton-Century-Crofts, 1957).

93 See L M Saari and G P Latham, "Employee Reactions to Continuous and Variable Ratio Reinforcement Schedules Involving a Monetary Incentive," *Journal of Applied Psychology,* August 1982, pp 506–8.

94 P Brinkley-Rogers and R Collier, "Along the Colorado, the Money's Flowing," *The Arizona Republic,* March 4, 1990, p A12.

95 J M O'Brien, "Zappos Knows How to Kick It," *Fortune,* February 2, 2009, p 58.

96 K Gurchiek, "'New Collar' Workers Choose Hourly Careers," *HR Magazine,* September 2008, p 24.

97 N Lublin, "Something Special," *Fast Company,* June 2010, p 40.

98 See D Jones, "Training Workers the SeaWorld Way," *USA Today,* August 21, 2006, p 3B; E Zlomek, "Zookeeper: People, Like Animals, Relish Fast Rewards," *The Arizona Republic,* May 30, 2009, p D1; and J Lloyd, "His Cats Know All the Tricks," *USA Today,* October 5, 2009, p 7D.

99 Data from K L Alexander, "Continental Airlines Soars to New Heights," *USA Today,* January 23, 1996, p 4B; and M Knez and D Simester, "Making Across-the-Board Incentives Work," *Harvard Business Review,* February 2002, pp 16–17.

100 Excerpted from D W Dowling, "Conversation: DineEquity Chairman and CEO Julia A. Stewart on Leaders as Teachers," *Harvard Business Review,* March 2009, p 29.

101 Excerpted from P Davidson, "Employees Work More to Meet Demand," *USA Today,* June 21, 2010, p 3B.

CHAPTER 10

1 Excerpted from R I Sutton, *Good Boss, Bad Boss: How to Be the Best . . . and Learn from the Worst* (New York: Business Plus, 2010), pp 246–47.

2 Drawn from C O Longenecker, M J Neubert, and L S Fink, "Causes and Consequences of Managerial Failure in Rapidly Changing Organizations," *Business Horizons,* March–April 2007, pp 145–55.

3 Data from M Moskowitz, R Levering, and C Tkaczyk, "100 Best Companies to Work For," *Fortune,* February 7, 2011, p 96.

4 See P S Adler and S Kwon, "Social Capital: Prospects for a New Concept," *Academy of Management Review,* January 2002, pp 17–40; and J Savage and S Kanazawa, "Social Capital and the Human Psyche: Why Is Social Life 'Capital'?" *Sociological Theory,* September 2004, pp 504–24. Research about a threat to building social capital can be found in T W H Ng and D C Feldman, "The Effects of Organizational Embeddedness on Development of Social Capital and Human Capital," *Journal of Applied Psychology,* July 2010, pp 696–712.

5 D Goleman, *Social Intelligence: The New Science of Human Relationships* (New York: Bantam, 2006); and D Goleman and R Boyatzis, "Social Intelligence and the Biology of Leadership," *Harvard Business Review,* September 2008, pp 74–81.

6 Excerpted and adapted from M Porter, "How Big Business Can Help Itself by Helping Its Neighbors," *Bloomberg Businessweek,* May 31–June 6, 2010, p 56.

7 See G Morse, "Health Care Needs a New Kind of Hero," *Harvard Business Review,* April 2010, pp 60–61; D S D Rue, C M Barnes, and F P Morgeson, "Understanding the Motivational Contingencies of Team Leadership," *Small Group Research,* October 2010, pp 621–51;

and A M L Raes, M G Heijljes, U Glunk, and R A Roe, "The Interface of the Top-Management Team and Middle Managers: A Process Model," *Academy of Management Review,* January 2011, pp 102–26.

8 This definition is based in part on one found in D Horton Smith, "A Parsimonious Definition of 'Group': Toward Conceptual Clarity and Scientific Utility," *Sociological Inquiry,* Spring 1967, pp 141–67. For a debate about whether or not just two people can be considered a group, see R L Moreland, "Are Dyads Really Groups?" *Small Group Research,* April 2010, pp 251–67; and K D Williams, "Dyads Can Be Groups (and Often Are)," *Small Group Research,* April 2010, pp 268–74.

9 E H Schein, *Organizational Psychology,* 3rd ed (Englewood Cliffs, NJ: Prentice Hall, 1980), p 145.

10 Data and quote from J Yang and V Salazar, "Inviting Co-workers to Wedding," *USA Today,* September 22, 2010, p 1B. Also see J Stein, "The Secret Cult of Office Smokers," *Bloomberg Businessweek,* May 10–16, 2010, pp 73–77.

11 See L Petrecca, "Hiring Family or Friends Can Be Boon or Bust," *USA Today,* October 11, 2010, p 6B.

12 J Castro, "Mazda U," *Time,* October 20, 1986, p 65.

13 Data from J Yang and K Gelles, "Workplace Friendships," *USA Today,* April 13, 2010, p 1B.

14 See M Giglio, "The Keystroke Revolution," *Newsweek,* February 7, 2011, pp 25–27.

15 www.pcmag.com/encyclopedia_term/0,2542,t=social+ networr king&i=55316,00.asp, accessed February 7, 2009.

16 Data from S Jayson, "A Few Wrinkles Are Etching Facebook, Other Social Sites," *USA Today,* January 15, 2009, p 9D.

17 See R McDermott and D Archibald, "Harnessing Your Staff's Informal Networks," *Harvard Business Review,* March 2010, pp 82–89; M Weinstein, "Are You LinkedIn?" *Training,* September–October 2010, pp 30–33; and M Weinstein, "Verizon Connects to Success," *Training,* January–February 2011, pp 40–42.

18 J Welch and S Welch, "From the Old, Something New," *BusinessWeek,* November 20, 2006, p 124.

19 For an instructive overview of five different theories of group development, see J P Wanous, A E Reichers, and S D Malik, "Organizational Socialization and Group Development: Toward an Integrative Perspective," *Academy of Management Review,* October 1984, pp 670–83.

20 See B W Tuckman, "Developmental Sequence in Small Groups," *Psychological Bulletin,* June 1965, pp 384–99; and B W Tuckman and M A C Jensen, "Stages of Small-Group Development Revisited," *Group & Organization Studies,* December 1977, pp 419–27. Also see G Seijts and J Gandz, "Gaining a Competitive Edge through Rapid Team Formation and Development," *Organizational Dynamics,* October–December 2009, pp 261–69.

21 For details, see C Cleveland, J Blascovich, C Gangi, and L Finez, "When Good Teammates Are Bad: Physiological Threat on Recently Formed Teams," *Small Group Research,* February 2011, pp 3–31.

22 Based on J R Rentsch, L A Delise, E Salas, and M P Letsky, "Facilitating Knowledge Building in Teams: Can a New Team Training Strategy Help? *Small Group Research,* October 2010, pp 505–23.

23 For related research, see J C Biesanz, S G West, and A Millevoi, "What Do You Learn about Someone over Time? The Relationship between Length of Acquaintance and Consensus and Self-Other Agreement in Judgments of Personality," *Journal of Personality and Social Psychology,* January 2007, pp 119–35; and R I Swaab, K W Phillips, D Diermeier, and V H Medvec, "The Pros and Cons of Dyadic Side Conversations in Small Groups," *Small Group Research,* June 2008, pp 372–90.

24 Based on B L Riddle, C M Anderson, and M M Martin, "Small Group Socialization Scale: Development and Validity," *Small Group Research,* October 2000, pp 554–72; and M Van Vugt and C M Hart,

"Social Identity as Social Glue: The Origins of Group Loyalty," *Journal of Personality and Social Psychology,* April 2004, pp 585–98.

25 L N Jewell and H J Reitz, *Group Effectiveness in Organizations* (Glenview, IL: Scott, Foresman, 1981), p 19.

26 Based on J F McGrew, J G Bilotta, and J M Deeney, "Software Team Formation and Decay: Extending the Standard Model for Small Groups," *Small Group Research,* April 1999, pp 209–34.

27 Ibid., p 232.

28 Ibid., p 231.

29 D Davies and B C Kuypers, "Group Development and Interpersonal Feedback," *Group & Organization Studies,* June 1985, p 194.

30 Ibid., pp 184–208.

31 C J G Gersick, "Marking Time: Predictable Transitions in Task Groups," *Academy of Management Journal,* June 1989, pp 274–309.

32 D K Carew, E Parisi-Carew, and K H Blanchard, "Group Development and Situational Leadership: A Model for Managing Groups," *Training and Development Journal,* June 1986, pp 48–49. For evidence linking leadership and group effectiveness, see G R Bushe and A L Johnson, "Contextual and Internal Variables Affecting Task Group Outcomes in Organizations," *Group & Organization Studies,* December 1989, pp 462–82.

33 See T J Erickson, "The Leaders We Need Now," *Harvard Business Review,* May 2010, pp 63–66; and R H Schaffer, "Mistakes Leaders Keep Making," *Harvard Business Review,* September 2010, pp 86–91.

34 For related reading, see M Jokisaari and J Nurmi, "Change in Newcomers' Supervisor Support and Socialization Outcomes After Organizational Entry," *Academy of Management Journal,* June 2009, pp 527–44; and J T Arnold, "Ramping Up Onboarding," *HR Magazine,* May 2010, pp 75–78.

35 G Graen, "Role-Making Processes within Complex Organizations," in *Handbook of Industrial and Organizational Psychology,* ed M D Dunnette (Chicago: Rand-McNally, 1976), p 1201.

36 Data from D S Chiaburu and D A Harrison, "Do Peers Make the Place? Conceptual Synthesis and Meta-Analysis of Coworker Effects on Perceptions, Attitudes, OCBs, and Performance," *Journal of Applied Psychology,* September 2008, pp 1082–1103.

37 G L Miles, "Doug Danforth's Plan to Put Westinghouse in the 'Winner's Circle,'" *BusinessWeek,* July 28, 1986, p 75.

38 Data and quote from "Great Expectations," *Training,* January–February 2011, p 12.

39 Schein, p 198.

40 A Romano and T Dokoupil, "Men's Lib," *Newsweek,* September 27, 2010, pp 45. Also see G N Powell and J H Greenhaus, "Sex, Gender, and the Work-to-Family Interface: Exploring Negative and Positive Interdependencies," *Academy of Management Journal,* June 2010, pp 513–34; S Shellenbarger, "A New White-Collar Juggle," *The Wall Street Journal,* August 18, 2010, p D3; and J C Santora and M Esposito, "Dual Family Earners: Do Role Overload and Stress Treat Them as Equals?" *Academy of Management Perspectives,* November 2010, pp 92–93.

41 Schein, p 198. Four types of role ambiguity are discussed in M A Eys and A V Carron, "Role Ambiguity, Task Cohesion, and Task Self-Efficacy," *Small Group Research,* June 2001, pp 356–73.

42 D Heath and C Heath, "Tase the Haze," *Fast Company,* September 2010, pp 46, 48.

43 Drawn from M Peterson et al., "Role Conflict, Ambiguity, and Overload: A 21-Nation Study," *Academy of Management Journal,* April 1995, pp 429–52.

44 Based on Y Fried, H A Ben-David, R B Tiegs, N Avital, and U Yeverechyahu, "The Interactive Effect of Role Conflict and Role Ambiguity on Job Performance," *Journal of Occupational and Organizational Psychology,* March 1998, pp 19–27.

45 R R Blake and J Srygley Mouton, "Don't Let Group Norms Stifle Creativity," *Personnel,* August 1985, p 28.

46 A Dunkin, "Pepsi's Marketing Magic: Why Nobody Does It Better," *BusinessWeek,* February 10, 1986, p 52.

47 For related research, see G M Wittenbaum, H C Shulman, and M E Braz, "Social Ostracism in Task Groups: The Effects of Group Composition," *Small Group Research,* June 2010, pp 330–53; I R Pinto, J M Marques, J M Levine, and D Abrams, "Membership Status and Subjective Group Dynamics: Who Triggers the Black Sheep Effect?" *Journal of Personality and Social Psychology,* July 2010, pp 107–19; and C D Parks and A B Stone, "The Desire to Expel Unselfish Members from the Group," *Journal of Personality and Social Psychology,* August 2010, pp 303–10.

48 D C Feldman, "The Development and Enforcement of Group Norms," *Academy of Management Review,* January 1984, pp 50–52. Also see E K Kelan and R D Jones, "Gender and the MBA," *Academy of Management Learning and Education,* March 2010, pp 26–43.

49 Feldman, "The Development and Enforcement of Group Norms." Also see D Abrams, G R de Moura, J M Marques, and P Hutchison, "Innovation Credit: When Can Leaders Oppose Their Group's Norms?" *Journal of Personality and Social Psychology,* September 2008, pp 662–78.

50 See R G Netemeyer, M W Johnston, and S Burton, "Analysis of Role Conflict and Role Ambiguity in a Structural Equations Framework," *Journal of Applied Psychology,* April 1990, pp 148–57; and G W McGee, C E Ferguson Jr, and A Seers, "Role Conflict and Role Ambiguity: Do the Scales Measure These Two Constructs?" *Journal of Applied Psychology,* October 1989, pp 815–18.

51 See S E Jackson and R S Schuler, "A Meta-Analysis and Conceptual Critique of Research on Role Ambiguity and Role Conflict in Work Settings," *Organizational Behavior and Human Decision Processes,* August 1985, pp 16–78.

52 Based on C S Crandall, A Eshleman, and L O'Brien, "Social Norms and the Expression and Suppression of Prejudice: The Struggle for Internalization," *Journal of Personality and Social Psychology,* March 2002, pp 359–78. Also see L Ashburn-Nardo, K A Morris, and S A Goodwin, "The Confronting Prejudiced Responses (CPR) Model: Applying CPR in Organizations," *Academy of Management Learning and Education,* September 2008, pp 332–42.

53 See B Weber and G Hertel, "Motivation Gains of Inferior Group Members: A Meta-Analytic Review," *Journal of Personality and Social Psychology,* December 2007, pp 973–93; and M C Schilpzand, D M Herold, and C E Shalley, "Members' Openness to Experience and Teams' Creative Performance," *Small Group Research,* February 2011, pp 55–76.

54 See K D Benne and P Sheats, "Functional Roles of Group Members," *Journal of Social Issues,* Spring 1948, pp 41–49. For an alternative typology, see T V Mumford, C H Van Iddekinge, F P Morgeson, and M A Campion, "The Team Role Test: Development and Validation of a Team Role Knowledge Situational Judgment Test," *Journal of Applied Psychology,* March 2008, pp 250–67.

55 See G P Latham and E A Locke, "Enhancing the Benefits and Overcoming the Pitfalls of Goal Setting," *Organizational Dynamics,* no 4, 2006, pp 332–40.

56 A Zander, "The Value of Belonging to a Group in Japan," *Small Group Behavior,* February 1983, pp 7–8. Also see C Lin and S Yamaguchi, "Under What Conditions Do People Feel Face-Loss? Effects of the Presence of Others and Social Roles on the Perception of Losing Face in Japanese Culture," *Journal of Cross-Cultural Psychology,* January 2011, pp 120–24.

57 Data from M Vella, "InData," *BusinessWeek,* April 28, 2008, p 58. Also see P R Laughlin, E C Hatch, J S Silver, and L Boh, "Groups Perform Better Than the Best Individuals on Letters-to-Numbers Problems: Effects of Group Size," *Journal of Personality and Social Psychology,* April 2006, pp 644–51; and J L Yang, "The Power of Number 4.6," *Fortune,* June 12, 2006, p 122.

58 For example, see B Grofman, S L Feld, and G Owen, "Group Size and the Performance of a Composite Group Majority: Statistical

Truths and Empirical Results," *Organizational Behavior and Human Performance*, June 1984, pp 350–59.

59 See P Yetton and P Bottger, "The Relationships among Group Size, Member Ability, Social Decision Schemes, and Performance," *Organizational Behavior and Human Performance,* October 1983, pp 145–59.

60 This copyrighted exercise may be found in J Hall, "Decisions, Decisions, Decisions," *Psychology Today,* November 1971, pp 51–54, 86, 88.

61 Yetton and Bottger, p 158.

62 Based on R B Gallupe, A R Dennis, W H Cooper, J S Valacich, L M Bastianutti, and J F Nunamaker Jr, "Electronic Brainstorming and Group Size," *Academy of Management Journal,* June 1992, pp 350–69. Also see J Barauh and P B Paulus, "Effects of Training on Idea Generation in Groups," *Small Group Research,* October 2008, pp 523–41.

63 Data from E Salas, D Rozell, B Mullen, and J E Driskell, "The Effect of Team Building on Performance: An Integration," *Small Group Research,* June 1999, pp 309–29.

64 Drawn from B Mullen, C Symons, L-T Hu, and E Salas, "Group Size, Leadership Behavior, and Subordinate Satisfaction," *Journal of General Psychology,* April 1989, pp 155–69. Also see B Ogungbamila, A Ogungbamila, and G A Adetula, "Effects of Team Size and Work Team Perception on Workplace Commitment: Evidence from 23 Production Teams," *Small Group Research,* December 2010, pp 725–45.

65 D S Carlson, K M Kacmar, and D Whitten, "What Men Think They Know about Executive Women," *Harvard Business Review,* September 2006, p 28. Also see T A Judge and B A Livingston, "Is the Gap More Than Gender? A Longitudinal Analysis of Gender, Gender Role Orientation, and Earnings," *Journal of Applied Psychology,* September 2008, pp 994–1012; and G N Powell, "The Gender and Leadership Wars," *Organizational Dynamics,* January–March 2011, pp 1–9.

66 G L Stewart, S L Dustin, M R Barrick, and T C Darnold, "Exploring the Handshake in Employment Interviews," *Journal of Applied Psychology,* September 2008, p 1145.

67 See L Smith-Lovin and C Brody, "Interruptions in Group Discussions: The Effects of Gender and Group Composition," *American Sociological Review,* June 1989, pp 424–35.

68 L Karakowsky, K McBey, and D L Miller, "Gender, Perceived Competence, and Power Displays: Examining Verbal Interruptions in a Group Context," *Small Group Research,* August 2004, p 407. Also see E W Morrison, S L Wheeler-Smith, and D Kamdar, "Speaking Up in Groups: A Cross-Level Study of Group Voice Climate and Voice," *Journal of Applied Psychology,* January 2011, pp 183–91.

69 E M Ott, "Effects of the Male–Female Ratio at Work," *Psychology of Women Quarterly,* March 1989, p 53.

70 "Daily Downer," *Training,* April 2005, p 12. Also see J Swartz, "Will Hurd's Sexual-Harassment Scandal Tarnish HP?" *USA Today,* August 9, 2010, p 1B; B Leonard, "Survey: 10% of Employees Report Harassment at Work," *HR Magazine,* October 2010, p 18; and D Leinwand, "Navy Captain Loses Carrier Job Over Racy Videos," *USA Today,* January 5, 2011, p 4A.

71 M Elias, "15% of Female Veterans Tell of Sexual Trauma," *USA Today,* October 28, 2008, p 6D.

72 J L Berdahl and C Moore, "Workplace Harassment: Double Jeopardy for Minority Women," *Journal of Applied Psychology,* March 2006, p 426. Also see J L Raver and L H Nishii, "Once, Twice, or Three Times as Harmful? Ethnic Harassment, Gender Harassment, and Generalized Workplace Harassment," *Journal of Applied Psychology,* March 2010, pp 236–54.

73 See D Leinwand, "Survey: 1 in 5 Teens 'Sext' Despite Risks," *USA Today,* June 24, 2009, p 3A; and S Jayson, "Teens Say Bullying is Widespread," *USA Today,* October 26, 2010, p 1A.

74 Data from B A Gutek, A Groff Cohen, and A M Konrad, "Predicting Social-Sexual Behavior at Work: A Contact Hypothesis," *Academy of Management Journal,* September 1990, pp 560–77. Also see S Morgan, "The End of the Office Affair?" *Bloomberg Businessweek*, September 20–26, 2010, pp 73–75.

75 Data from M Rotundo, D Nguyen, and P R Sackett, "A Meta-Analytic Review of Gender Differences in Perceptions of Sexual Harassment," *Journal of Applied Psychology,* October 2001, pp 914–22. Also see N A Bowling and T A Beehr, "Workplace Harassment from the Victim's Perspective: A Theoretical Model and Meta-Analysis," *Journal of Applied Psychology,* September 2006, pp 998–1012; and M S Hershcovis and J Barling, "Comparing Victim Attributions and Outcomes for Workplace Aggression and Sexual Harassment," *Journal of Applied Psychology*, September 2010, pp 874–88.

76 S J South, C M Bonjean, W T Markham, and J Corder, "Female Labor Force Participation and the Organizational Experiences of Male Workers," *Sociological Quarterly,* Summer 1983, p 378.

77 R R Hirschfeld, M H Jordan, H S Field, W F Giles, and A A Armenakis, "Teams' Female Representation and Perceived Potency as Inputs to Team Outcomes in a Predominantly Male Field Setting," *Personnel Psychology,* Winter 2005, p 893. Also see P Raghubir and A Valenzuela, "Male-Female Dynamics in Groups: A Field Study of the Weakest Link," *Small Group Research,* February 2010, pp 41–70.

78 B T Thornton, "Sexual Harassment, 1: Discouraging It in the Work Place," *Personnel,* April 1986, p 18.

79 See J Deschenaux, "EEOC: Train Managers on Harassment," *HR Magazine,* May 2008, p 26.

80 See J L Goolsby, D A Mack, and J C Quick, "Winning by Staying in Bounds: Good Outcomes from Positive Ethics," *Organizational Dynamics,* July–September 2010, pp 248–57; and P T Leeson, "Opportunism and Organization Under the Black Flag," *Organizational Dynamics,* January–March 2011, pp 34–42.

81 For additional information, see S E Asch, *Social Psychology* (Englewood Cliffs, NJ: Prentice Hall, 1952), ch 16. Also see G D Reeder, A E Monroe, and J B Pryor, "Impressions of Milgram's Obedient Teachers: Situational Cues Inform Inferences about Motives and Traits," *Journal of Personality and Social Psychology,* July 2008, pp 1–17.

82 See T P Williams and S Sogon, "Group Composition and Conforming Behavior in Japanese Students," *Japanese Psychological Research,* no 4, 1984, pp 231–34; T Amir, "The Asch Conformity Effect: A Study in Kuwait," *Social Behavior and Personality,* no 2, 1984, pp 187–90; and Y Takano and S Sogon, "Are Japanese More Collectivistic Than Americans," *Journal of Cross-Cultural Psychology,* May 2008, pp 237–50.

83 Data from R Bond and P B Smith, "Culture and Conformity: A Meta-Analysis of Studies Using Asch's (1952b, 1956) Line Judgment Task," *Psychological Bulletin,* January 1996, pp 111–37.

84 J L Roberts and E Thomas, "Enron's Dirty Laundry," *Newsweek,* March 11, 2002, p 26. Also see G Farrell, "Pride at Root of Skilling's Downfall," *USA Today,* October 24, 2006, p 3B.

85 Sutton, p 148. Also see K R Morrison and D T Miller, "Distinguishing between Silent and Vocal Minorities: Not All Deviants Feel Marginal," *Journal of Personality and Social Psychology,* May 2008, pp 871–82; and P Bordia, S L D Restubog, and R L Tang, "When Employees Strike Back: Investigating Mediating Mechanisms between Psychological Contract Breach and Workplace Deviance," *Journal of Applied Psychology,* September 2008, pp 1104–17.

86 I L Janis, *Groupthink,* 2nd ed (Boston: Houghton Mifflin, 1982), p 9. Alternative models are discussed in K Granstrom and D Stiwne, "A Bipolar Model of Groupthink: An Expansion of Janis's Concept," *Small Group Research,* February 1998, pp 32–56; and A R Flippen, "Understanding Groupthink from a Self-Regulatory Perspective," *Small Group Research,* April 1999, pp 139–65. For comprehensive coverage of groupthink, see the entire February–March 1998 issue of *Organizational Behavior and Human Decision Processes* (12 articles).

[87] Ibid. For an alternative model, see R J Aldag and S Riggs Fuller, "Beyond Fiasco: A Reappraisal of the Groupthink Phenomenon and a New Model of Group Decision Processes," *Psychological Bulletin,* May 1993, pp 533–52. Also see A A Mohamed and F A Wiebe, "Toward a Process Theory of Groupthink," *Small Group Research,* August 1996, pp 416–30.

[88] N Byrnes and J Sasseen, "Board of Hard Knocks," *BusinessWeek,* January 22, 2007, pp 37–38. Also see N Rajagopalan and Y Zhang, "Recurring Failures in Corporate Governance: A Global Disease?" *Business Horizons,* November–December 2009, pp 545–52; and R C Pozen, "The Case for Professional Boards," *Harvard Business Review,* December 2010, pp 50–58.

[89] Details of this study may be found in M R Callaway and J K Esser, "Groupthink: Effects of Cohesiveness and Problem-Solving Procedures on Group Decision Making," *Social Behavior and Personality,* no. 2, 1984, pp 157–64. Also see C R Leana, "A Partial Test of Janis's Groupthink Model: Effects of Group Cohesiveness and Leader-Behavior on Defective Decision Making," *Journal of Management,* Spring 1985, pp 5–17; and G Moorhead and J R Montanari, "An Empirical Investigation of the Groupthink Phenomenon," *Human Relations,* May 1986, pp 399–410. A more modest indirect effect is reported in J N Choi and M U Kim, "The Organizational Application of Groupthink and Its Limitations in Organizations," *Journal of Applied Psychology,* April 1999, pp 297–306.

[90] Adapted from discussion in Janis, ch 11.

[91] See M C Gentile, "Keeping Your Colleagues Honest," *Harvard Business Review,* March 2010, pp 114–17; R Tedlow, "Toyota Was in Denial. How About You?" *Bloomberg Businessweek,* April 19, 2010, p 76; and F J Flynn and S S Wiltermuth, "Who's With Me? False Consensus, Brokerage, and Ethical Decision Making in Organizations," *Academy of Management Journal,* October 2010, pp 1074–89.

[92] Based on discussion in B Latane, K Williams, and S Harkins, "Many Hands Make Light the Work: The Causes and Consequences of Social Loafing," *Journal of Personality and Social Psychology,* June 1979, pp 822–32; and D A Kravitz and B Martin, "Ringelmann Rediscovered: The Original Article," *Journal of Personality and Social Psychology,* May 1986, pp 936–41. Also see A Jassawalla, H Sashittal, and A Malshe, "Students' Perceptions of Social Loafing: Its Antecedents and Consequences in Undergraduate Business Classroom Teams," *Academy of Management Learning and Education,* March 2009, pp 42–54.

[93] See J A Shepperd, "Productivity Loss in Performance Groups: A Motivation Analysis," *Psychological Bulletin,* no. 1, 1993, pp 67–81; R E Kidwell Jr and N Bennett, "Employee Propensity to Withhold Effort: A Conceptual Model to Intersect Three Avenues of Research," *Academy of Management Review,* July 1993, pp 429–56; and S J Karau and K D Williams, "Social Loafing: Meta-Analytic Review and Theoretical Integration," *Journal of Personality and Social Psychology,* October 1993, pp 681–706.

[94] See S J Zaccaro, "Social Loafing: The Role of Task Attractiveness," *Personality and Social Psychology Bulletin,* March 1984, pp 99–106; J M Jackson and K D Williams, "Social Loafing on Difficult Tasks: Working Collectively Can Improve Performance," *Journal of Personality and Social Psychology,* October 1985, pp 937–42; and J M George, "Extrinsic and Intrinsic Origins of Perceived Social Loafing in Organizations," *Academy of Management Journal,* March 1992, pp 191–202.

[95] For complete details, see K Williams, S Harkins, and B Latane, "Identifiability as a Deterrent to Social Loafing: Two Cheering Experiments," *Journal of Personality and Social Psychology,* February 1981, pp 303–11.

[96] See J M Jackson and S G Harkins, "Equity in Effort: An Explanation of the Social Loafing Effect," *Journal of Personality and Social Psychology,* November 1985, pp 1199–206.

[97] Both studies are reported in S G Harkins and K Szymanski, "Social Loafing and Group Evaluation," *Journal of Personality and Social Psychology,* June 1989, pp 934–41. Also see R Hoigaard, R Safvenbom, and F E Tonnessen, "The Relationship between Group Cohesion, Group Norms, and Perceived Social Loafing in Soccer Teams," *Small Group Research,* June 2006, pp 217–32.

[98] Data from J A Wagner III, "Studies of IndividualismCollectivism: Effects on Cooperation in Groups," *Academy of Management Journal,* February 1995, pp 152–72. Also see R C Liden, S J Wayne, R A Jaworski, and N Bennett, "Social Loafing: A Field Investigation," *Journal of Management,* no. 2, 2004, pp 285–304.

[99] Based on M J Pearsall, M S Christian, and A P J Ellis, "Motivating Interdependent Teams: Individual Rewards, Shared Rewards, or Something in Between?" *Journal of Applied Psychology,* January 2010, pp 183–91.

[100] For more, see R E Kidwell, "Loafing in the 21st Century: Enhanced Opportunities—and Remedies—for Withholding Job Effort in the New Workplace," *Business Horizons,* November–December 2010, pp 543–52.

[101] Reprinted by permission of *Harvard Business Review,* "Unmasking Manly Men," by R J Ely and D Meyerson, August 2008. Copyright 2008 by the Harvard Business School Publishing Corporation; all rights reserved.

[102] Excerpted from J Sandberg, "My Boss Wants to Be My Online Friend," *The Arizona Republic,* July 14, 2007, p D3.

[103] Adapted and quoted from J Yang and K Gelles, "Is It Smart to Keep Personal and Professional Lives Separate?" *USA Today,* April 14, 2010, p 1B.

CHAPTER 11

[1] Excerpted from A Gostick and C Elton, *The Orange Revolution* (New York: Free Press, 2010), pp 114–15.

[2] J Welch and S Welch, "Company Man or Free Agent," *BusinessWeek,* February 12, 2007, p 106. Also see M de Rond, "Lessons from the Oxford and Cambridge Boat Race," *Harvard Business Review,* September 2008, p 28; and E Catmull, "How Pixar Fosters Collective Creativity," *Harvard Business Review,* September 2008, pp 64–72.

[3] Data from "Workforce Readiness and the New Essential Skills," SHRM *Workplace Visions,* no 2, 2008, Table 3, p 5.

[4] As quoted in A Fisher, "How to Get Hired by a 'Best' Company," *Fortune,* February 4, 2008, p 96.

[5] J R Katzenbach, and D K Smith, *The Wisdom of Teams: Creating the High-Performance Organization* (New York: HarperBusiness, 1999), p 45.

[6] See J Welch and S Welch, "Team Building: Wrong and Right," *BusinessWeek,* November 24, 2008, p 130.

[7] J R Katzenbach and D K Smith, "The Discipline of Teams," *Harvard Business Review,* March–April 1993, p 112 (emphasis added).

[8] A Gardiner, "Perfect Fit: Holtz Leads East Carolina Revival," *USA Today,* September 12, 2008, p 8C.

[9] "A Team's-Eye View of Teams," *Training,* November 1995, p 16.

[10] See E Sundstrom, K P DeMeuse, and D Futrell, "Work Teams," *American Psychologist,* February 1990, pp 120–33.

[11] For an alternative typology of teams, see S G Scott and Walter O Einstein, "Strategic Performance Appraisal in Team-Based Organizations: One Size Does Not Fit All," *Academy of Management Executive,* May 2001, pp 107–16. Also see M J Pearsall, A P J Ellis, and B S Bell, "Building the Infrastructure: The Effects of Role Identification Behaviors on Team Cognition Development and Performance," *Journal of Applied Psychology,* January 2010, pp 192–200; J Farh, C Lee and C I C Farh, "Task Conflict and Team Creativity: A Question of How Much and When," *Journal of Applied Psychology,* November 2010, pp 1173–80; and A M L Raes, M G Heijltjes, U Glunk, and R A Roe, "The Interface of the Top Management Team and Middle Managers: A Process Model," *Academy of Management Review,* January 2011, pp 102–26.

[12] S Hamm and K Hall, "Perfect: The Quest to Design the Ultimate Portable PC," *BusinessWeek,* February 25, 2008, p 45. Also see

G R Bushe, "When People Come and Go," *The Wall Street Journal,* August 23, 2010, p R6.

[13] For example, see A Zimmerman, "Wal-Mart's Emergency-Relief Team Girds for Hurricane Gustav," *The Wall Street Journal,* August 30, 2008, p A3; and S Sternberg, "Saved by 96 Minutes of CPR," *USA Today,* March 3, 2011, pp 1D–2D.

[14] P King, "What Makes Teamwork Work?" *Psychology Today,* December 1989, p 16.

[15] See J A LePine, R F Piccolo, C L Jackson, J E Mathieu, and J R Saul, "A Meta-Analysis of Teamwork Processes: Tests of a Multidimensional Model and Relationship with Team Effectiveness Criteria," *Personnel Psychology,* Summer 2008, pp 273–307; L A DeChurch, and J R Mesmer-Magnus, "The Cognitive Underpinnings of Effective Teamwork: A Meta-Analysis," *Journal of Applied Psychology,* January 2010, pp 32–53; and M R Haas, "The Double-Edged Swords of Autonomy and External Knowledge: Analyzing Team Effectiveness in a Multinational Organization," *Academy of Management Journal,* October 2010, pp 989–1008.

[16] Based on A M Christie and J Barling, "Beyond Status: Relating Status Inequality to Performance and Health in Teams," *Journal of Applied Psychology,* September 2010, pp 920–34.

[17] "Collaboration Provides Edge," *The Arizona Republic,* April 10, 2005, p 2. Also see T H Lee, "Turning Doctors into Leaders," *Harvard Business Review,* April 2010, pp 50–58.

[18] See M Bolch, "Rewarding the Team," *HR Magazine,* February 2007, pp 91–93.

[19] P Burrows, "Cisco's Comeback," *BusinessWeek,* November 24, 2003, p 124.

[20] See C O L H Porter, C I Gogus, and R C Yu, "When Does Teamwork Translate Into Improved Team Performance? A Resource Allocation Perspective," *Small Group Research,* April 2010, pp 221–48; H Van Mierlo and A Kleingeld, "Goals, Strategies, and Group Performance: Some Limits of Goal Setting in Groups," *Small Group Research,* October 2010, pp 524–55; and T L Griffith and J E Sawyer, "Multilevel Knowledge and Team Performance," *Journal of Organizational Behavior,* October 2010, pp 1003–31.

[21] As quoted in P B Brown, "What I Know Now," *Fast Company,* January 2005, p 96. Also see G Hirst, D Van Knippenberg, and J Zhou, "A Cross-Level Perspective on Employee Creativity: Goal Orientation, Team Learning Behavior, and Individual Creativity," *Academy of Management Journal,* April 2009, pp 280–93.

[22] J Vesterman, "From Wharton to War," *Fortune,* June 12, 2006, p 108.

[23] For more on team effectiveness, see S Sonnentag and J Volmer, "Individual-Level Predictors of Task-Related Teamwork Processes: The Role of Expertise and Self-Efficacy in Team Meetings," *Group and Organization Management,* February 2009, pp 37–66.

[24] For more, see D Coutu, "Why Teams Don't Work," *Harvard Business Review,* May 2009, pp 99–105.

[25] P Raeburn, "Whoops! Wrong Patient," *BusinessWeek,* June 17, 2002, p 85. Also see G Morse, "Health Care Needs a New Kind of Hero," *Harvard Business Review,* April 2010, pp. 60–61.

[26] See C M Christensen, M Marx, and H H Stevenson, "The Tools of Cooperation and Change," *Harvard Business Review,* October 2006, pp 73–80.

[27] J Gordon, "Redefining Elegance," *Training,* March 2007, p 20.

[28] See A Kohn, "How to Succeed without Even Vying," *Psychology Today,* September 1986, pp 27–28. Sports psychologists discuss "cooperative competition" in S Sleek, "Competition: Who's the Real Opponent?" *APA Monitor,* July 1996, p 8.

[29] As quoted in M C Meaney, "Seeing Beyond the Woman: An Interview with a Pioneering Academic and Board Member," *The McKinsey Quarterly,* September 2008, pp 7–8.

[30] As reported in J C Santora and M Esposito, "Do Competitive Work Environments Help or Hurt Employees?" *Academy of Management Perspectives,* February 2010, pp 81–82.

[31] D W Johnson, G Maruyama, R Johnson, D Nelson, and L Skon, "Effects of Cooperative, Competitive, and Individualistic Goal Structures on Achievement: A Meta-Analysis," *Psychological Bulletin,* January 1981, pp 56–57. An alternative interpretation of the foregoing study that emphasizes the influence of situational factors can be found in J L Cotton and M S Cook, "Meta-Analysis and the Effects of Various Reward Systems: Some Different Conclusions from Johnson et al.," *Psychological Bulletin,* July 1982, pp 176–83.

[32] R Zemke, "Office Spaces," *Training,* May 2002, p 24. Also see A Fox, "Don't Let Silos Stand in the Way," *HR Magazine,* May 2010, pp 50–51.

[33] S W Cook and M Pelfrey, "Reactions to Being Helped in Cooperating Interracial Groups: A Context Effect," *Journal of Personality and Social Psychology,* November 1985, p 1243. Also see G K Stahl, M L Maznevski, A Voigt, and K Jonsen, "Unraveling the Effects of Cultural Diversity in Teams: A Meta-Analysis of Research on Multicultural Work Groups," *Journal of International Business Studies,* May 2010, pp 690–709.

[34] See A J Stahelski and R A Tsukuda, "Predictors of Cooperation in Health Care Teams," *Small Group Research,* May 1990, pp 220–33.

[35] See M E Porter and M R Kramer, "Creating Shared Value," *Harvard Business Review,* January–February 2011, pp 62–77.

[36] H El Nasser and P Overberg, "Census Response: 71% and Counting," *USA Today,* April 21, 2010, p 1A.

[37] Data and quote from R Zeidner, "Employees Trust Managers More Than Top Brass," *HR Magazine,* October 2008, p 10. Also see D Jones, "CEO," *USA Today,* June 23, 2009, pp 1B–2B.

[38] J Barbian, "Short Shelf Life," *Training,* June 2002, p 52.

[39] See J O'Toole and W Bennis, "What's Needed Next: A Culture of Candor," *Harvard Business Review,* June 2009, pp 54–61; M Yakovleva, R R Reilly, and R Werko, "Why Do We Trust? Moving Beyond Individual to Dyadic Perceptions," *Journal of Applied Psychology,* January 2010, pp 79–91; and J P MacDuffie, "Inter-Organizational Trust and the Dynamics of Distrust," *Journal of International Business Studies,* January 2011, pp 35–47.

[40] B Schneider and K B Paul, "In the Company We Trust," *HR Magazine,* January 2011, p 41.

[41] H Mackay, "Truth or Consequences," www.harveymackay.com/columns/column_this_week.cfm. Accessed March 6, 2009.

[42] See E C Tomlinson and R C Mayer, "The Role of Causal Attribution Dimensions in Trust Repair," *Academy of Management Review,* January 2009, pp 85–104; N Gillespie and G Dietz, "Trust Repair after an Organization-Level Failure," *Academy of Management Review,* January 2009, pp 127–45; and P H Kim, K T Dirks, and C D Cooper, "The Repair of Trust: A Dynamic Bilateral Perspective and Multilevel Conceptualization," *Academy of Management Review,* July 2009, pp 401–422.

[43] R C Mayer, J H Davis, and F D Schoorman, "An Integrative Model of Organizational Trust," *Academy of Management Review,* July 1995, p 715.

[44] J D Lewis and A Weigert, "Trust as a Social Reality," *Social Forces,* June 1985, p 970. Also see R F Hurley, "The Decision to Trust," *Harvard Business Review,* September 2006, pp 55–62.

[45] M Powell, "Betrayal," *Inc.,* April 1996, p 24.

[46] Adapted from F Bartolomé, "Nobody Trusts the Boss Completely—Now What?" *Harvard Business Review,* March–April 1989, pp 135–42. Also see D Seidman, "Building Trust by Trusting," *BusinessWeek,* September 7, 2009, p 76; P Lencioni, "The Power of Saying 'We Blew It,'" *Bloomberg Businessweek,* February 22, 2010, p 84; and M V Copeland, "A Sick CEO's Full Disclosure," *Fortune,* October 18, 2010, pp 47–52.

47 S M R Covey with R R Merrill, *The Speed of Trust: The One Thing That Changes Everything* (New York: Free Press, 2006), p 45 (emphasis added). For recent research, see M L Frazier, P D Johnson, M Gavin, J Gooty, and D B Snow, "Organizational Justice, Trustworthiness, and Trust: A Multifoci Examination," *Group and Organization Management,* February 2010, pp 39–76; S Wong and W F Boh, "Leveraging the Ties of Others to Build a Reputation for Trustworthiness Among Peers," *Academy of Management Journal,* February 2010, pp 129–48; and B A De Jong and T Elfring, "How Does Trust Affect the Performance of Ongoing Teams? The Mediating Role of Reflexivity, Monitoring, and Effort," *Academy of Management Journal,* June 2010, pp 535–49.

48 W Foster Owen, "Metaphor Analysis of Cohesiveness in Small Discussion Groups," *Small Group Behavior,* August 1985, p 416.

49 This distinction is based on discussion in A Tziner, "Differential Effects of Group Cohesiveness Types: A Clarifying Overview," *Social Behavior and Personality,* no 2, 1982, pp 227–39.

50 Based on L Van Boven, J Kane, P A McGraw, and J Dale, "Feeling Close: Emotional Intensity Reduces Perceived Psychological Distance," *Journal of Personality and Social Psychology,* June 2010, pp 872–85.

51 B Mullen and C Copper, "The Relation between Group Cohesiveness and Performance: An Integration," *Psychological Bulletin,* March 1994, p 224.

52 Ibid. Additional research evidence is reported in M I Norton, J H Frost, and D Ariely, "Less Is More: The Lure of Ambiguity, or Why Familiarity Breeds Contempt," *Journal of Personality and Social Psychology,* January 2007, pp 97–105.

53 Based on B Mullen, T Anthony, E Salas, and J E Driskell, "Group Cohesiveness and Quality of Decision Making: An Integration of Tests of the Groupthink Hypothesis," *Small Group Research,* May 1994, pp 189–204. Also see M C Andrews, K M Kacmar, G L Blakely, and N S Bucklew, "Group Cohesion as an Enhancement to the Justice-Affective Commitment Relationship," *Group and Organization Management,* December 2008, pp 736–55.

54 G L Miles, "The Plant of Tomorrow Is in Texas Today," *Business-Week,* July 28, 1986, p 76.

55 See, for example, P Jin, "Work Motivation and Productivity in Voluntarily Formed Work Teams: A Field Study in China," *Organizational Behavior and Human Decision Processes,* 1993, pp 133–55. Also see S Reysen, "Construction of a New Scale: The Reysen Likability Scale," *Social Behavior and Personality,* no 2, 2005, pp 201–8.

56 Based on discussion in E E Lawler III and S A Mohrman, "Quality Circles: After the Honeymoon," *Organizational Dynamics,* Spring 1987, pp 42–54.

57 See D L Duarte and N Tennant Snyder, *Mastering Virtual Teams: Strategies, Tools, and Techniques,* 3rd ed (San Francisco, CA: Jossey-Bass, 2006); and J Cordery, C Soo, B Kirkman, and B Rosen, "Leading Parallel Global Virtual Teams: Lessons from Alcoa," *Organizational Dynamics,* July–September 2009, pp 204–16.

58 J Yang and K Gelles, "Working Remotely vs. In the Office," *USA Today,* June 10, 2008, p 1B.

59 B Williamson, "Managing at a Distance," *BusinessWeek,* July 27, 2009, p 64. Also see "Mobile Workforce: Concerns and Benefits," *HR Magazine,* February 2011, p 14; and D Dahl, "Want a Job? Let the Bidding Begin. A Radical Take on the Virtual Company," *Inc.,* March 2011, pp 93–96.

60 Based on P Bordia, N DiFonzo, and A Chang, "Rumor as Group Problem Solving: Development Patterns in Informal Computer-Mediated Groups," *Small Group Research,* February 1999, pp 8–28.

61 See K A Graetz, E S Boyle, C E Kimble, P Thompson, and J L Garloch, "Information Sharing in Face-to-Face, Teleconferencing, and Electronic Chat Groups," *Small Group Research,* December 1998, pp 714–43.

62 Based on F Niederman and R J Volkema, "The Effects of Facilitator Characteristics on Meeting Preparation, Set Up, and Implementation," *Small Group Research,* June 1999, pp 330–60; and B Whitworth, B Gallupe, and R McQueen, "Generating Agreement in Computer-Mediated Groups," *Small Group Research,* October 2001, pp 625–65.

63 Based on J J Sosik, B J Avolio, and S S Kahai, "Inspiring Group Creativity: Comparing Anonymous and Identified Electronic Brainstorming," *Small Group Research,* February 1998, pp 3–31. Also see S S Kahai, J J Sosik, and B J Avolio, "Effects of Participative and Directive Leadership in Electronic Groups," *Group and Organization Management,* February 2004, pp 67–105.

64 Based on M M Montoya-Weiss, A P Massey, and M Song, "Getting It Together: Temporal Coordination and Conflict Management in Global Virtual Teams," *Academy of Management Journal,* December 2001, pp 1251–62.

65 J Hyatt, "A Surprising Truth about Geographically Dispersed Teams," *MIT Sloan Management Review,* Summer 2008, pp 5–6.

66 B Dumaine, "Who Needs a Boss?" *Fortune,* May 7, 1990, p 52.

67 Adapted from Table 1 in V U Druskat and J V Wheeler, "Managing from the Boundary: The Effective Leadership of Self-Managing Work Teams," *Academy of Management Journal,* August 2003, pp 435–57.

68 See J I Cash Jr, M J Earl, and R Morison, "Teaming Up to Crack Innovation Enterprise Integration," *Harvard Business Review,* November 2008, pp 90–100.

69 L Freifeld, "Top Young Trainers 2010," *Training,* July–August 2010, p 37. Cross-functional teamwork is discussed in H Walters, "Google Did," *Bloomberg Businessweek,* May 10–16, 2010, pp 56–62.

70 Excerpted from "Fast Talk," *Fast Company,* February 2004, p 50.

71 See "1996 Industry Report: What Self-Managing Teams Manage," *Training,* October 1996, p 69.

72 For a preview of the future workplace, see L C. Lancaster and D Stillman, *The M-Factor: How the Millennial Generation Is Rocking the Workplace* (New York: HarperCollins, 2010).

73 Based on P S Goodman, R Devadas, and T L Griffith Hughson, "Groups and Productivity: Analyzing the Effectiveness of Self-Managing Teams," in *Productivity in Organizations,* ed J P Campbell, R J Campbell, and Associates (San Francisco, CA: Jossey-Bass, 1998), pp 295–327. Also see S Kauffeld, "Self-Directed Work Groups and Team Competence," *Journal of Occupational and Organizational Psychology,* March 2006, pp 1–21; and K A Smith-Jentsch, J A Cannon-Bowers, S L Tannenbaum, and E Salas, "Guided Team Self-Correction: Impacts on Team Mental Models, Processes, and Effectiveness," *Small Group Research,* June 2008, pp 303–27.

74 Drawn from V Rousseau and C Aubé, "Team Self-Managing Behaviors and Team Effectiveness: The Moderating Effect of Task Routineness," *Group and Organization Management,* December 2010, pp 751–81.

75 See C Douglas and W L Gardner, "Transition to Self-Directed Work Teams: Implications of Transition Time and Self-Monitoring for Managers' Use of Influence Tactics," *Journal of Organizational Behavior,* February 2004, pp 47–65.

76 J M O'Brien, "Team Building in Paradise," *Fortune,* May 26, 2008, p 113. Also see T Wayne, "Should Your Trainer Look Like This?" *Bloomberg Businessweek,* August 30–September 5, 2010, pp 81–83; and L Freifeld, "Paddle to Collaborate," *Training,* November–December 2010, p 6.

77 See S McChrystal, "Step Up for Your Country," *Newsweek,* January 31, 2011, pp 36–39.

78 As quoted in C Tkaczyk, "Keeping Creatives Happy," *Fortune,* March 16, 2009, p 40. Also see K Wehrum, "Hello, Conference Room A! An Office Where Employees Rock," *Inc.,* November 2010, pp 115–16.

79 See S Prokesch, "How GE Teaches Teams to Lead Change," *Harvard Business Review,* January 2009, pp 99–106; and B Burn, "Teambuilding Dilemma," *Training,* September–October 2010, p 42.

[80] See J Brett, K Behfar, and M C Kern, "Managing Multicultural Teams," *Harvard Business Review,* November 2006, pp 83–91.

[81] S Bucholz and T Roth, *Creating the High-Performance Team* (New York: John Wiley & Sons, 1987), p xi.

[82] Ibid., p 14. Also see K Gurchiek, "Report Ties Coaching Strategies to Business," *HR Magazine,* July 2010, p 75.

[83] P King, "What Makes Teamwork Work?" *Psychology Today,* December 1989, p 17. For related discussion and research, see P F Skilton and K J Dooley, "The Effects of Repeat Collaboration on Creative Abrasion," *Academy of Management Review,* January 2010, pp 118–34; and A Wiedow and U Konradt, "Two-Dimensional Structure of Team Process Improvement: Team Reflection and Team Adaptation," *Small Group Research,* February 2011, pp 32–54.

[84] For more, see D L Kirkpatrick and J D Kirkpatrick, *Evaluating Training Programs: The Four Levels,* 3rd ed (San Francisco, CA: Berrett-Koehler, 2006); and L Freifeld, "50 Years for Four Levels," *Training,* October–November 2009, pp 38–39. Also see T Sitzmann, K Ely, K G Brown, and K N Bauer, "Self-Assessment of Knowledge: A Cognitive Learning or Affective Measure?" *Academy of Management Learning and Education,* June 2010, pp 169–91; K V Mann, "Self-Assessment: The Complex Process of Determining 'How We Are Doing'—A Perspective from Medical Education," *Academy of Management Learning and Education,* June 2010, pp 305–13; and B M Moskal, "Self-Assessments: What Are Their Valid Uses?" *Academy of Management Learning and Education,* June 2010, pp 314–20.

[85] J M O'Brien, "Zappos Knows How to Kick It," *Fortune,* February 2, 2009, p 58.

[86] For related research, see C B Gibson, C D Cooper, and J A Conger, "Do You See What We See? The Complex Effects of Perceptual Distance between Leaders and Teams," *Journal of Applied Psychology,* January 2009, pp 62–76; S W J Kozlowski, D Watola, J M Jensen, B Kim, and I Botero, "Developing Adaptive Teams: A Theory of Dynamic Leadership," in *Team Effectiveness in Complex Organizations,* ed E Sales, G F Goodwin, and C S Burke (New York: Routledge Academic, 2009); and T L Pittinsky, "A Two-Dimensional Model of Intergroup Leadership," *American Psychologist,* April 2010, pp 194–200.

[87] L A Hill, "Becoming the Boss," *Harvard Business Review,* January 2007, p 54. Also see L A Hill and K Lineback, "Are You a Good Boss—Or a Great One?" *Harvard Business Review,* January–February 2011, pp 124–31.

[88] Based on V K Gupta, R Huang, and S Niranjan, "A Longitudinal Examination of the Relationship Between Team Leadership and Performance," *Journal of Leadership and Organizational Studies,* November 2010, pp. 335–50.

[89] Drawn from D S DeRue, C M Barnes, and F P Morgeson, "Understanding the Motivational Contingencies of Team Leadership," *Small Group Research,* October 2010, pp 621–51.

[90] J B Wu, A S Tsui, and A J Kinicki, "Consequences of Differentiated Leadership in Groups," *Academy of Management Journal,* February 2010, p 103.

[91] Excerpted from D Zielinski, "Building a Better HR Team," *HR Magazine,* August 2010, pp 65–68.

[92] J Stein, "Where the Copy Machine Never Jams," *Bloomberg Businessweek,* June 28–July 4, 2010, pp 74–75.

CHAPTER 12

[1] Excerpted from B Stone, P Burrows, and D MacMillan, "Google Once and Future CEO, Larry Page, on His Plan for Growth—and the Star Deputies Who Have to Make It Happen," *Bloomberg Businessweek,* January 31–February 6, 2011 pp 51–52.

[2] D Brady, "Etc. Hard Choices," *Bloomberg Businessweek,* February 7–February 13, 2011, p 92.

[3] Strengths and weaknesses of the rational model are discussed by M H Bazerman, *Judgment in Managerial Decision Making* (Hoboken, NJ: John Wiley & Sons, 2006).

[4] J L Lang, "Mattel's CEO Recalls a Rough Summer," *Fortune,* January 22, 2008, http://cnn.money.com (interview with Bob Eckert).

[5] See M V Copeland, "Reed Hastings: Leader of the Pack," *Fortune,* December 6, 2010, pp 121–30.

[6] This study was conducted by P C Nutt, "Expanding the Search for Alternatives during Strategic Decision Making," *Academy of Management Executive,* November 2004, pp 13–28.

[7] Yang, "Mattel's CEO recalls a Rough Summer."

[8] H A Simon, "Rational Decision Making in Business Organizations," *American Economic Review,* September 1979, p 510.

[9] These conclusions were proposed by R Brown, *Rational Choice and Judgment* (Hoboken, NJ: John Wiley & Sons, 2005), p 9.

[10] Results can be found in J P Byrnes, D C Miller, and W D Schafer, "Gender Differences in Risk Taking: A Meta-Analysis," *Psychological Bulletin,* May 1999, pp 367–83.

[11] Bounded rationality is discussed by A R Memati, A M Bhatti, M Maqsal, I Mansoor, and F Naveed, "Impact of Resource Based View and Resource Dependence Theory on Strategic Decision Making," *International Journal of Business Management,* December 2010, pp 110–15; and H A Simon, *Administrative Behavior,* 2nd ed (New York: Free Press, 1957).

[12] These conclusions were excerpted from "Poor Decisions Hurt Company Performance," *HR Magazine,* February 2007, p 16.

[13] The model is discussed in detail in M D Cohen, J G March, and J P Olsen, "A Garbage Can Model of Organizational Choice," *Administrative Science Quarterly,* March 1981, pp 1–25.

[14] Ibid, p 2.

[15] See G Fioretti and A Lomi, "Passing the Buck in the Garbage Can Model of Organizational Choice," *Computational and Mathematical Organization Theory,* June 2010, pp 113–43; and A Styhre, L Wikmalm, S Olilla, and J Roth, "Garbage-Can Decision Making and the Accommodation of Uncertainty in New Drug Development Work," *Creativity and Innovation Management,* June 2010, pp 134–46.

[16] See A Carter, "Lighting a Fire Under Campbell," *BusinessWeek,* December 4, 2006, pp 96, 99.

[17] An example of a garbage can process can be found in K A Strassel, "Mr. Fairness," *The Wall Street Journal,* August 7–8, 2010, p A11.

[18] See D J Snowden and M E Boone, "A Leader's Framework for Decision Making," *Harvard Business Review,* November 2007, pp 69–76.

[19] See P M Tingling and M J Brydon, "Is Decision-Based Evidence Making Necessarily Bad?" *MIT Sloan Management Review,* Summer 2010, pp 71–76.

[20] Biases associated with using shortcuts in decision making are discussed by A Tversky and D Kahneman, "Judgment under Uncertainty: Heuristics and Biases," *Science,* September 1974, pp 1124–31.

[21] See L Landro, "What the Doctor Missed," *The Wall Street Journal,* September 28, 2010, pp D1, D4.

[22] Results can be found in R A Lowe and A A Ziedonis, "Overoptimism and the Performance of Entrepreneurial Firms," *Management Science,* February 2006, pp 173–86.

[23] See B Borenstein, "Disasters Often Stem from Hubris," *The Arizona Republic,* July 12, 2010, p A4.

[24] This scenario was taken from Bazerman, p 41.

[25] M Spector and J S Lublin, "Blockbuster Asks for More Cash," *The Wall Street Journal,* January 18, 2011, p B1.

[26] See J Ross and B M Staw, "Organizational Escalation and Exit: Lessons from the Shoreham Nuclear Power Plant," *Academy of Management Journal,* August 1993, pp 701–32; and G Pan and L Shan, "Transition to IS Project De-Escalation: An Exploration into Management Executives' Influence Behaviors," *IEEE Transactions on Engineering Management,* February 2011, pp 109–23.

[27] The definition comes from J Pfeffer and R I Sutton, "Evidence-Based Management," *Harvard Business Review,* January 2006, p 112. Case applications can be found in S Birk, "The Evidence-Based Road," *Healthcare Executive,* July–August 2010, pp 28–36.

[28] The model was proposed by R B Briner, D Denyer, and D M Rousseau, "Evidence-Based Management: Concept Cleanup Time?" *Academy of Management Perspectives,* November 2009, pp 19–32.

[29] The following definitions and discussion were derived from Tingling and Brydon, pp 71–76.

[30] The quotes and discussion were based on J Pfeffer and R I Sutton, "Profiting from Evidence-Based Management," *Strategy & Leadership* 34, no 2 (2006): 35–42.

[31] For details, see E T Anderson and D Simester, "Every Company Can Profit from Testing Customers' Reactions to Changes. Here's How to Get Started," *Harvard Business Review,* March 2011, pp 99–105.

[32] See D Meinert, "Top Performers Boast Analytics Over Intuition," *HR Magazine,* February 2011, p 18; and D Rich, "Power of Predictive Analytics," *Malaysian Business,* December 1, 2010, p 66.

[33] K Naughton, "The Happiest Man in Detroit," *Bloomberg Businessweek,* February 7 – February 13, 2011, p 68.

[34] From Pfeffer and Sutton, "Evidence-Based Management." Also see J Griffin, "Who's Responsible for Analytics?" *Information Management,* January 1, 2011, p 29.

[35] This definition was derived from A J Rowe and R O Mason, *Managing with Style: A Guide to Understanding, Assessing and Improving Decision Making* (San Francisco, CA: Jossey-Bass, 1987).

[36] The discussion of styles was based on material contained in ibid.

[37] Excerpted from B Gimbel, "Keeping Planes Apart," *Fortune,* June 27, 2005, p 112.

[38] B Bremner and D Roberts, "A Billion Tough Sells," *BusinessWeek,* March 20, 2006, p 44.

[39] Y I Kane and P Dvorak, "Howard Stringer, Japanese CEO," *The Wall Street Journal,* March 3–4, 2007, pp A1, A6.

[40] See M Gupta, A Brantley, and V P Jackson, "Product Involvement as a Predictor of Generation Y Consumer Decision Making Styles," *The Business Review,* Summer 2010, pp 28–33; and S S Wang, "Why So Many People Can't Make Decisions," *The Wall Street Journal,* September 28, 2010, pp D1, D2.

[41] L Lehrer, *How We Decide* (Boston: Houghton Mifflin, 2009).

[42] D Kahneman and G Klein, "Conditions for Intuitive Expertise: A Failure to Disagree," *American Psychologist,* September 2009, p 519.

[43] See R Lange and J Houran, "A Transliminal View of Intuitions in the Workplace," *North American Journal of Psychology,* December 2010, pp 501–16.

[44] Excerpted from C C Miller and R D Ireland, "Intuition in Strategic Decision Making: Friend or Foe in the Fast-Paced 21st Century," *Academy of Management Executive,* February 2005, p 20.

[45] See Kahneman and Klein, pp 515–26.

[46] See E Dane and M G Pratt, "Exploring Intuition and Its Role in Managerial Decision Making," *Academy of Management Review,* January 2007, pp 33–54.

[47] N M Tichy and W G Bennis, "Making Judgment Calls: The Ultimate Act of Leadership," *Harvard Business Review,* October 2007, p 99.

[48] See Kahneman and Klein, pp 515–26.

[49] See *Ethics Resource Center,* 2010, "Reporting: Who's Telling You What You Need to Know, Who Isn't, and What You Can Do About It," retrieved March 5, 2011, from www.ethics.org/nbes; and *Ethics Resource Center,* 2010, "Ethics and Employee Engagement," retrieved March 5, 2011, from www.ethics.org/nbes.

[50] The decision tree and resulting discussion are based on C E Bagley, "The Ethical Leader's Decision Tree," *Harvard Business Review,* February 2003, pp 18–19.

[51] Details of this example can be found in E E Schultz and T Francis, "Financial Surgery: How Cuts in Retiree Benefits Fatten Companies' Bottom Lines," *The Wall Street Journal,* March 1, 2004, p A1.

[52] See L Langlois and C Lapointe, "Can Ethics be Learned?" *Journal of Educational Administration,* November 2010, pp 147–63; and R Müller, K Spang, and S Ozcan, "Cultural Differences in Decision Making in Project Teams," *International Journal of Managing Projects in Business,* 2009, pp 70–93.

[53] Excerpted from "Top Small Workplaces 2008," *The Wall Street Journal,* October 13, 2008, p R4.

[54] Results can be found in C K W De Dreu and M A West, "Minority Dissent and Team Innovation: The Importance of Participation in Decision Making," *Journal of Applied Psychology,* December 2001, pp 1191–201.

[55] G Park and R P DeShon, "A Multilevel Model of Minority Opinion Expression and Team Decision-making Effectiveness," *Journal of Applied Psychology,* September 2010, pp 824–33.

[56] These guidelines were derived from G P Huber, *Managerial Decision Making* (Glenview, IL: Scott, Foresman, 1980), p 149.

[57] G W Hill, "Group versus Individual Performance: Are N+1 Heads Better Than One?" *Psychological Bulletin,* May 1982, p 535.

[58] R Adams and D Ferreira, "Moderation in Groups: Evidence from Betting on Ice Break-Ups in Alaska," *The Review of Economic Studies,* July 2010, pp 882–913.

[59] Supporting results can be found in J Hedlund, D R Ilgen, and J R Hollenbeck, "Decision Accuracy in Computer-Mediated versus Face-to-Face Decision-Making Teams," *Organizational Behavior and Human Decision Processes,* October 1998, pp 30–47.

[60] See J R Winquist and J R Larson Jr, "Information Pooling: When It Impacts Group Decision Making," *Journal of Personality and Social Psychology,* February 1998, pp 371–77.

[61] G M Parker, *Team Players and Teamwork: The New Competitive Business Strategy* (San Francisco, CA: Jossey-Bass, 1990).

[62] These recommendations were obtained from ibid.

[63] See A F Osborn, *Applied Imagination: Principles and Procedures of Creative Thinking,* 3rd ed (New York: Scribners, 1979).

[64] P Sanders, "Boeing Brings in Old Hands, Gets an Earful," *The Wall Street Journal,* July 19, 2010, pp B1, B5. Also see K German, "Boeing Resumes Dreamliner Testing," December 23, 2010, http://news.cnet.com/8301-11386_3-20026583-76.html.

[65] See J Castaldo, "Getting Drowned Out by the Brainstorm," *Canadian Business,* July 19, 2010, p 91; and K Girotra and C Terwiesch, "Idea Generation and the Quality of the Best Idea," *Management Science,* April 2010, pp 591–605.

[66] A summary of brainstorming research is provided by R C Litchfield, "Brainstorming Reconsidered: A Goal-Based View," *Academy of Management Review,* July 2008, pp 649–68.

[67] These recommendations and descriptions were derived from B Nussbaum, "The Power of Design," *BusinessWeek,* May 17, 2004, pp 86–94.

[68] An application of the NGT can be found in S Lloyd, "Applying the Nominal Group Technique to Specify the Domain of a Construct," *Qualitative Market Research,* January 2011, pp 105–21.

[69] See L Thompson, "Improving the Creativity of Organizational Work Groups," *Academy of Management Executive,* February 2003, pp 96–109.

[70] See N C Dalkey, D L Rourke, R Lewis, and D Snyder, *Studies in the Quality of Life: Delphi and Decision Making* (Lexington, MA: Lexington Books: D C Heath and Co, 1972).

[71] An application of the Delphi technique can be found in A Graefe and J S Armstrong, "Comparing Face-to-Face Meetings, Nominal Groups, Delphi and Prediction Markets on an Estimating Task," *International Journal of Forecasting,* January–March 2011, pp 183–95.

[72] See P Dvorak, "Best Buy Taps 'Prediction Market'; Imaginary Stocks Let Workers Forecast Whether Retailer's Plans Will Meet Goals," *The Wall Street Journal,* September 16, 2008, p B1.

[73] See K Maher, "Wal-Mart Seeks New Flexibility in Worker Shifts," *The Wall Street Journal,* January 3, 2007, pp A1, A11.

[74] M Weinstein, "So Happy Together," *Training,* May 2006, p 38.

[75] Supportive results can be found in S S Lam and J Schaubroeck, "Improving Group Decisions by Better Polling Information: A Comparative Advantage of Group Decision Support Systems," *Journal of Applied Psychology,* August 2000, pp 565–73.

[76] This definition was adapted from one provided by R K Scott, "Creative Employees: A Challenge to Managers," *Journal of Creative Behavior,* First Quarter 1995, pp 64–71.

[77] E Werner, "Obama Urges Budget Deal," *The Arizona Republic,* March 6, 2011, p A10.

[78] T A Matherly and R E Goldsmith, "The Two Faces of Creativity," *Business Horizons,* September–October 1985, p 9.

[79] See S H Harrison, D M Sluss, and B E Ashforth, "Curiosity Adapted the Cat: The Role of Trait Curiosity in Newcomer Adaptation," *Journal of Applied Psychology,* January 2011, pp 211–20.

[80] Personality and creativity were investigated by M Baer and G R Oldham, "The Curvilinear Relations between Experienced Creative Time Pressure and Creativity: Moderating Effects of Openness to Experience and Support for Creativity," *Journal of Applied Psychology,* July 2006, pp 963–70; and X Zhang and K M Bartol, "The Influence of Creative Process Engagement on Employee Creative Performance and Overall Job Performance: A Curvilinear Assessment," *Journal of Applied Psychology,* September 2010, pp 862–73.

[81] J M Higgins, "Innovate or Evaporate: Seven Secrets of Innovative Corporations," *The Futurist,* September–October 1995, p 46.

[82] See C A Hartnell, A Y Ou, and A Kinicki, "Organizational Culture and Organizational Effectiveness: A Meta-Analytic Investigation of the Competing Values Framework's Theoretical Suppositions," *Journal of Applied Psychology,* in press.

[83] See C M Pearson and S A Sommer, "Infusing Creativity Into Crisis Management: An Essential Approach Today," *Organizational Dynamics,* January–March 2011, pp 27–33; J-L Farh, C Lee, and C I C Farh, "Task Conflict and Team Creativity: A Question of How Much and When," *Journal of Applied Psychology,* November 2010, pp 1173–80; and K Byron, S Khazanchi, and D Nazarian, "The Relationship Between Stressor and Creativity: A Meta-Analysis Examining Competing Theoretical Models," *Journal of Applied Psychology,* January 2010, pp 201–12.

[84] See A-C Wang and B-S Cheng, "When Does Benevolent Leadership Lead to Creativity? The Moderating Role of Creative Role Identity and Job Autonomy," *Journal of Organizational Behavior,* January 2010, pp 106–21; and S Khazanchi and S S Masterson, "Who and What is Fair Matters: A Multi-Foci Social Exchange Model of Creativity," *Journal of Organizational Behavior,* January 2011, pp 86–106.

[85] J Y Kim, "A Lifelong Battle against Disease," *US News & World Report,* November 19, 2007, pp 62, 64.

[86] Quoted on pp 48–49 of D Coutu, "Creativity Step by Step," *Harvard Business Review,* April 2008, pp 47–51 (interview with Twyla Tharp).

[87] See J Lehrer, "Bother Me, I'm Thinking," *The Wall Street Journal,* February 19–20, 2011, p C12.

[88] Details of this study can be found in M Basadur, "Managing Creativity: A Japanese Model," *Academy of Management Executive,* May 1992, pp 29–42.

[89] These recommendations were derived from E Catmull, "How Pixar Fosters Collective Creativity," *Harvard Business Review,* September 2008, pp 65–72; "Keeping Creatives Happy," *Fortune,* March 16, 2009, p 40 (interview with Jeffrey Katzenberg); and L Tischler, "A Designer Takes on His Biggest Challenge Ever," *Fast Company,* February 2009, pp 78–83.

[90] See A Oke, N Munshi, and F O Walumbwa, "The Influence of Leadership on Innovation Processes and Activities," *Organizational Dynamics,* January–March 2009, pp 64–72.

[91] D A Peluso, "Preserving Employee Know-How," *HR Magazine,* May 2010, p 99.

[92] Excerpted from R Gold, "Rig's Final Hours Probed," *The Wall Street Journal,* July 19, 2010, pp A1, A4.

[93] Excerpted from M C Gentile, "Keeping Your Colleagues Honest," *Harvard Business Review,* March 2010, p 114.

CHAPTER 13

[1] Excerpted from J Sandberg, "Avoiding Conflicts: The Too-Nice Boss Makes Matters Worse," *The Wall Street Journal,* February 26, 2008.

[2] D Tjosvold, *Learning to Manage Conflict: Getting People to Work Together Productively* (New York: Lexington Books, 1993), p xi.

[3] Ibid., pp xi–xii. Also see G J Kilduff, H A Elfenbein, and B M Staw, "The Psychology of Rivalry: A Relationally Dependent Analysis of Competition," *Academy of Management Journal,* October 2010, pp 943–69, and A Vance and A Ricadela, "HP Cancels *The Board And the Beautiful,*" *Bloomberg Businessweek,* January 31–February 6, 2011, pp 33–34.

[4] J A Wall Jr and R Robert Callister, "Conflict and Its Management," *Journal of Management,* no 3 (1995), p 517. Also see M Sheehan, "Understanding Opposition," *Harvard Business Review,* February 2008, p 21.

[5] Wall and Callister, p 544.

[6] D Stead, "The Big Picture," *BusinessWeek,* January 8, 2007, p 11.

[7] See R R Vallacher, P T Coleman, A Nowak, and L Bui-Wrzosinska, "Rethinking Intractable Conflict: The Perspective of Dynamical Systems," *American Psychologist,* May–June 2010, pp 262–78; and D L Shapiro, "Relational Identity Theory: A Systematic Approach for Transforming the Emotional Dimension of Conflict," *American Psychologist,* October 2010, pp 634–45.

[8] K Cloke and J Goldsmith, *Resolving Conflicts at Work: A Complete Guide for Everyone on the Job* (San Francisco, CA: Jossey-Bass, 2000), pp 25, 27, 29. Also see R Lipsyte, " 'Jock Culture' Permeates Life," *USA Today,* April 10, 2008, p 11A.

[9] D Brady, "It's All Donald, All the Time," *BusinessWeek,* January 22, 2007, p 51.

[10] C Day, "Learn to Love the Spotlight," *Fortune,* November 10, 2008, p 36. Also see B Pike, "Dealing with Difficult Participants," *Training,* March–April 2011, p 40.

[11] Cloke and Goldsmith, pp 31–32.

[12] Data from L Petrecca, "Bullying in Workplace Is Common, Hard to Fix," *USA Today,* December 28, 2010, pp 1B–2B. Also see E Kim and T M Glomb, "Get Smarty Pants: Cognitive, Personality, and Victimization," *Journal of Applied Psychology,* September 2010,

pp 889–901; D Levine, "Investigation of Bullying, Job Analyses, Dual Career Ladders," *HR Magazine,* November 2010, p 20; and A R Wheeler, J R B Halbesleben, and K Shanine, "Eating Their Cake and Everyone Else's Cake, Too: Resources as the Main Ingredient to Workplace Bullying," *Business Horizons,* November–December 2010, pp 553–60.

13 See D Cadrain, "Campus Violence Reveals Background Screening Flaws," *HR Magazine,* May 2010, p 13, S Whitson, "Checking Passive Aggression," *HR Magazine,* June 2010, pp 115–16; and A C Klotz and M R Buckley, "'Where Everybody Knows Your Name': Lessons from Small Business about Preventing Workplace Violence," *Business Horizons,* November–December 2010, pp 571–79.

14 S P Robbins, "'Conflict Management' and 'Conflict Resolution' Are Not Synonymous Terms," *California Management Review,* Winter 1978, p 70. Also see P S Hempel, Z Zhang, and D Tjosvold, "Conflict Management between and within Teams for Trusting Relationships and Performance in China," *Journal of Organizational Behavior,* January 2009, pp 41–65.

15 Excerpted from K Sulkowicz, "Analyze This," *BusinessWeek,* September 29, 2008, p 19. Also see S A Joni and D Beyer, "How to Pick a Good Fight," *Harvard Business Review,* December 2009, pp 48–57.

16 Excerpted from T Ursiny, *The Coward's Guide to Conflict: Empowering Solutions for Those Who Would Rather Run Than Fight* (Naperville, IL: Sourcebooks, 2003), p 27.

17 See D Jones, "Could Insecurity Be the Secret to CEOs' Success?" *USA Today,* February 1, 2007, pp 1B–2B.

18 Adapted in part from discussion in A C Filley, *Interpersonal Conflict Resolution* (Glenview, IL: Scott, Foresman, 1975), pp 9–12; and B Fortado, "The Accumulation of Grievance Conflict," *Journal of Management Inquiry,* December 1992, pp 288–303. For a situation with many of these antecedents of conflict, see M Adams, "Pilots Have Much to Lose during Mergers," *USA Today,* March 10, 2008, p 3B.

19 Adapted from discussion in Tjosvold, *Learning to Manage Conflict,* pp 12–13. Also see K A Jehn, S Rispens, and S M B Thatcher, "The Effects of Conflict Asymmetry on Work Group and Individual Outcomes," *Academy of Management Journal,* June 2010, pp 596–616.

20 P Wingert, "Give Peace a Chance," *Newsweek,* December 13, 2010, p 43.

21 L Gardenswartz and A Rowe, *Diverse Teams at Work: Capitalizing on the Power of Diversity* (New York: McGraw-Hill, 1994), p 32.

22 Excerpted from F Keenan, "EMC: Turmoil at the Top?" *BusinessWeek,* March 11, 2002; www.businessweek.com/magazine/content/02_10/b3773092.htm; accessed March 28, 2011.

23 For updates, see S Hamm, "The Fine Art of Tech Mergers," *BusinessWeek,* July 10, 2006, pp 70, 72; and A Vance, "EMC Wants R-E-S-P-E-C-T," *Bloomberg Businessweek,* January 24–30, 2011, pp 33–34.

24 C M Pearson and C L Porath, "On the Nature, Consequences, and Remedies of Workplace Incivility: No Time for 'Nice'? Think Again," *Academy of Management Executive,* February 2005, p 7. Also see C L Porath and C M Pearson, "The Cost of Bad Behavior," *Organizational Dynamics,* January-March 2010, pp 64–71; S Page, "Poll: Less Civility Seen as Political Disputes Heat Up," *USA Today,* April 22, 2010, p 4A.

25 C Farrell, "Is the Workplace Getting Raunchier?" *BusinessWeek,* March 17, 2008, p 19.

26 Data and quote from J Yang and S Ward, "USA Today Snapshots," *USA Today,* September 15, 2008, p 1B.

27 See P Post, "Rude Awakening," *Training,* January 2010, p 40; and M Weinstein, "Tips to Neutralize Toxic Personalities," *Training,* March–April 2010, p 13.

28 P Falcone, "Days of Contemplation," *HR Magazine,* February 2007, p 107.

29 Data from D Stamps, "Yes, Your Boss Is Crazy," *Training,* July 1998, pp 35–39. Also see S S Wang, "Mental Illness, Redefined," *The Wall Street Journal,* February 10, 2010, p A3; A Andors, "Dispel the Stigma of Mental Illness," *HR Magazine,* October 2010, pp 83–86; and M Harvey, M Moeller, H Sloan III, and A Williams, "*Business Horizons,*" November–December 2010, pp 561–70.

30 See L P Postol, "ADAAA Will Result in Renewed Emphasis on Reasonable Accommodations," SHRM *Legal Report,* January 2009, pp 1–6; R J Grossman, "What to Do About Substance Abuse," *HR Magazine,* November 2010, pp 32–38; and D Cadrain, "The Marijuana Exception," *HR Magazine,* November 2010, pp 40–42.

31 Drawn from J C McCune, "The Change Makers," *Management Review,* May 1999, pp 16–22.

32 Based on discussion in C W Leach et al., "Group-Level Self-Definition and Self-Investment: A Hierarchical (Multicomponent) Model of In-Group Identification," *Journal of Personality and Social Psychology,* July 2008, pp 144–65; J Gillispie and J H Chrispeels, "Us and Them," *Small Group Research,* August 2008, pp 397–437; A C Homan, J R Hollenbeck, S E Humphrey, D Van Knippenberg, D R Ilgen, and G A Van Kleef, "Facing Differences with an Open Mind: Openness to Experience, Salience of Intragroup Differences, and Performance of Diverse Work Groups," *Academy of Management Journal,* December 2008, pp 1204–22; and A B Dessel, "Effects of Intergroup Dialogue: Public School Teachers and Sexual Orientation Prejudice," *Small Group Research,* October 2010, pp 556–92.

33 See T F Pettigrew and L R Tropp, "A Meta-Analytic Test of Intergroup Contact Theory," *Journal of Personality and Social Psychology,* May 2006, pp 751–83.

34 G Labianca, D J Brass, and B Gray, "Social Networks and Perceptions of Intergroup Conflict: The Role of Negative Relationships and Third Parties," *Academy of Management Journal,* February 1998, p 63 (emphasis added).

35 For example, see S C Wright, A Aron, T McLaughlin-Volpe, and S A Ropp, "The Extended Contact Effect: Knowledge of Cross-Group Friendships and Prejudice," *Journal of Personality and Social Psychology,* July 1997, pp 73–90; and E Page-Gould, R Mendoza-Denton, and L R Tropp, "With a Little Help from My Cross-Group Friend: Reducing Anxiety in Intergroup Contexts through Cross-Group Friendship," *Journal of Personality and Social Psychology,* November 2008, pp 1080–94.

36 See A Karacanta and J Fitness, "Majority Support for Minority Out-Groups: The Roles of Compassion and Guilt," *Journal of Applied Social Psychology,* November 2006, pp 2730–49; D A Butz and E A Plant, "Perceiving Outgroup Members as Unresponsive: Implications for Approach-Related Emotions, Intentions, and Behavior," *Journal of Personality and Social Psychology,* December 2006, pp 1066–79; and C M Fiol, M G Pratt, and E J O'Connor, "Managing Intractable Identity Conflicts," *Academy of Management Review,* January 2009, pp 32–55.

37 See "Developing Your Global Know-How," *Harvard Business Review,* March 2011, pp 70–75.

38 See M Alexander and H Korine, "When You Shouldn't Go Global," *Harvard Business Review,* December 2008, pp 70–77; C M Dalton, "Strategic Alliances: There Are Battles and There Is War," *Business Horizons,* March–April 2009, pp 105–8; and S Green, "The Would-Be Pioneer," *Harvard Business Review,* April 2011, pp 124–26.

39 "Negotiating South of the Border," *Harvard Management Communication Letter,* August 1999, p 12.

40 Excerpted from A Rosenbaum, "Testing Cultural Waters," *Management Review,* July–August 1999, p 43.

41 See R L Tung, "American Expatriates Abroad: From Neophytes to Cosmopolitans," *Journal of World Business,* Summer 1998, pp 125–44.

42 See K A Crowne, "What Leads to Cultural Intelligence?" *Business Horizons,* September–October 2008, pp 391–99; and N Goodman, "Cultivating Cultural Intelligence," *Training,* March–April 2011, p 38.

43 See J Weiss and J Hughes, "What Collaboration? Accept— and Actively Manage—Conflict," *Harvard Business Review,* March 2005, pp 92–101; G Colvin, "The Wisdom of Dumb Questions," *Fortune,* June 27, 2005, p 157; and B Frisch, "When Teams Can't Decide," *Harvard Business Review,* November 2008, pp 121–26.

44 R A Cosier and C R Schwenk, "Agreement and Thinking Alike: Ingredients for Poor Decisions," *Academy of Management Executive,* February 1990, p 71. Also see J P Kotter, "Combating Complacency," *BusinessWeek,* September 15, 2008, pp 54–55.

45 For example, see "Facilitators as Devil's Advocates," *Training,* September 1993, p 10.

46 Good background reading on devil's advocacy can be found in C R Schwenk, "Devil's Advocacy in Managerial Decision Making," *Journal of Management Studies,* April 1984, pp 153–68.

47 See L Buchanan, "Armed with Data: How the Military Can Help You Learn from Your Mistakes," *Inc,* March 2009, pp 98, 100.

48 See D M Schweiger, W R Sandberg, and P L Rechner, "Experiential Effects of Dialectical Inquiry, Devil's Advocacy, and Consensus Approaches to Strategic Decision Making," *Academy of Management Journal,* December 1989, pp 745–72.

49 See J S Valacich and C Schwenk, "Devil's Advocacy and Dialectical Inquiry Effects on Face-to-Face and Computer-Mediated Group Decision Making," *Organizational Behavior and Human Decision Processes,* August 1995, pp 158–73.

50 As quoted in D Jones, "CEOs Need X-Ray Vision in Transition," *USA Today,* April 23, 2001, p 4B.

51 Based on C K W De Dreu and M A West, "Minority Dissent and Team Innovation: The Importance of Participation in Decision Making," *Journal of Applied Psychology,* December 2001, pp 119–201. Also see P Shachaf, "Cultural Diversity and Information and Communication Technology Impacts on Global Virtual Teams: An Exploratory Study," *Information and Management,* March 2008, pp 131–42; and H P Sims Jr, S Faraj, and S Yun, "When Should a Leader Be Directive or Empowering? How to Develop Your Own Situational Theory of Leadership," *Business Horizons,* March–April 2009, pp 149–58.

52 A statistical validation for this model can be found in M A Rahim and N R Magner, "Confirmatory Factor Analysis of the Styles of Handling Interpersonal Conflict: First-Order Factor Model and Its Invariance across Groups," *Journal of Applied Psychology,* February 1995, pp 122–32. Also see M A Rahim, *Managing Conflict in Organizations* (Westport, CT: Greenwood Publishing Group, 2001); and D Bargal, "Group Processes to Reduce Intergroup Conflict," *Small Group Research,* February 2008, pp 42–59.

53 See D Ebenstein, "Removing 'Personal' from Interpersonal Tension," *Training,* September 2009, p 48.

54 M A Rahim, "A Strategy for Managing Conflict in Complex Organizations," *Human Relations,* January 1985, p 84.

55 For an alternative approach, see H Ren and B Gray, "Repairing Relationship Conflict: How Violation Types and Culture Influence the Effectiveness of Restoration Rituals," *Academy of Management Review,* January 2009, pp 105–26.

56 "Female Officers Draw Fewer Brutality Suits," *USA Today,* May 2, 2002, p 3A. Also see K Tyler, "Helping Employees Cool It," *HR Magazine,* April 2010, pp 53–55; B M Wilkowski, M D Robinson, and W Troop-Gordon, "How Does Cognitive Control Reduce Anger and Aggression? The Role of Conflict Monitoring and Forgiveness Processes," *Journal of Personality and Social Psychology,* May 2010, pp 830–40; and E Bernstein, "This Loved One Will Explode in Five, Four . . .," *The Wall Street Journal,* December 14, 2010, pp D1, D3.

57 P Ruzich, "Triangles: Tools for Untangling Interpersonal Messes," *HR Magazine,* July 1999, p 129. Also see P Falcone, "Avoid Preemptive Strikes," *HR Magazine,* May 2007, pp 101–4.

58 M Orey, "Fear of Firing," *BusinessWeek,* April 23, 2007, p 54.

59 For background, see P S Nugent, "Managing Conflict: Third-Party Interventions for Managers," *Academy of Management Executive,* February 2002, pp 139–54; F P Phillips, "Ten Ways to Sabotage Dispute Management," *HR Magazine,* September 2004, pp 163–68; and R Zeidner, "What's Important about Dispute Resolution?" *HR Magazine,* September 2008, p 10.

60 See M Bordwin, "Do-It-Yourself Justice," *Management Review,* January 1999, pp 56–58; and E Jensen, D Wagner, and D FitzGerald, "Mediators Help Take Bite Out of Dog Disputes," *USA Today,* March 16, 2009, p 3A.

61 B Morrow and L M Bernardi, "Resolving Workplace Disputes," *Canadian Manager,* Spring 1999, p 17. For related research, see J M Brett, M Olekalns, R Friedman, N Goates, C Anderson, and C Cherry Lisco, "Sticks and Stones: Language, Face, and Online Dispute Resolution," *Academy of Management Journal,* February 2007, pp 85–99.

62 Adapted from discussion in K O Wilburn, "Employment Disputes: Solving Them Out of Court," *Management Review,* March 1998, pp 17–21; and Morrow and Bernardi, "Resolving Workplace Disputes," pp 17–19, 27. Also see W H Ross and D E Conlon, "Hybrid Forms of Third-Party Dispute Resolution: Theoretical Implications of Combining Mediation and Arbitration," *Academy of Management Review,* April 2000, pp 416–27.

63 Wilburn, p 19. Also see J Hanley, "Transformative Mediation," *HR Magazine,* April 2010, pp 64–65.

64 For background on this contentious issue, see S Armour, "Arbitration's Rise Raises Fairness Issue," *USA Today,* June 12, 2001, pp 1B–2B; T J Heinsz, "The Revised Uniform Arbitration Act: An Overview," *Dispute Resolution Journal,* May–July 2001, pp 28–39; and J B Thelen, "Manager Who Refused to Sign Agreement Must Arbitrate," *HR Magazine,* January 2007, p 111.

65 For example, see M G Danaher, "Employee's Arbitration Victory Had Limits," *HR Magazine,* March 2007, p 116.

66 See R E Jones and B H Melcher, "Personality and the Preference for Modes of Conflict Resolution," *Human Relations,* August 1982, pp 649–58.

67 See R A Baron, "Reducing Organizational Conflict: An Incompatible Response Approach," *Journal of Applied Psychology,* May 1984, pp 272–79.

68 See G A Youngs Jr, "Patterns of Threat and Punishment Reciprocity in a Conflict Setting," *Journal of Personality and Social Psychology,* September 1986, pp 541–46.

69 For more details, see V D Wall Jr and L L Nolan, "Small Group Conflict: A Look at Equity, Satisfaction, and Styles of Conflict Management," *Small Group Behavior,* May 1987, pp 188–211. Also see S M Farmer and J Roth, "Conflict-Handling Behavior in Work Groups: Effects of Group Structure, Decision Processes, and Time," *Small Group Research,* December 1998, pp 669–713.

70 K J Behfar, R S Peterson, E A Mannix, and W M K Trochim, "The Critical Role of Conflict Resolution in Teams: A Close Look at the Links between Conflict Type, Conflict Management Strategies, and Team Outcomes," *Journal of Applied Psychology,* January 2008, p 185. The first student to read this and e-mail r.kreitner@cox.net before December 31, 2013, will receive a $100 grant for being a serious scholar.

71 Based on B Richey, H J Bernardin, C L Tyler, and N McKinney, "The Effects of Arbitration Program Characteristics on Applicants' Intentions toward Potential Employers," *Journal of Applied Psychology,* October 2001, pp 1006–13.

72 See M E Schnake and D S Cochran, "Effect of Two Goal-Setting Dimensions on Perceived Intraorganizational Conflict," *Group & Organization Studies,* June 1985, pp 168–83. Also see O Janssen, E Van De Vliert, and C Veenstra, "How Task and Person Conflict Shape the Role of Positive Interdependence in Management Teams," *Journal of Management,* no. 2, 1999, pp 117–42.

73 Drawn from L H Chusmir and J Mills, "Gender Differences in Conflict Resolution Styles of Managers: At Work and at Home," *Sex Roles,* February 1989, pp 149–63.

[74] See K K Smith, "The Movement of Conflict in Organizations: The Joint Dynamics of Splitting and Triangulation," *Administrative Science Quarterly,* March 1989, pp 1–20.

[75] Based on C Tinsley, "Models of Conflict Resolution in Japanese, German, and American Cultures," *Journal of Applied Psychology,* April 1998, pp 316–23; and S M Adams, "Settling Cross-Cultural Disagreements Begins with 'Where' Not 'How,'" *Academy of Management Executive,* February 1999, pp 109–10.

[76] S Covey, "7 Ways to Come Together," *USA Weekend,* January 15–17, 2010, p 6.

[77] Based on a definition in M A Neale and M H Bazerman, "Negotiating Rationally: The Power and Impact of the Negotiator's Frame," *Academy of Management Executive,* August 1992, pp 42–51. Also see D Malhotra, "When Contracts Destroy Trust," *Harvard Business Review,* May 2009, p 25.

[78] For example, see L P Barovick, "Sharing the Pain," *HR Magazine,* November 2010, pp 51–54.

[79] Data and quote from J Yang and K Carter, "USA Today Snapshots," *USA Today,* March 9, 2009, p 1B.

[80] M H Bazerman and M A Neale, *Negotiating Rationally* (New York: Free Press, 1992), p 16. Also see M Kaplan, "How to Negotiate Anything," *Money,* May 2005, pp 117–19; D Malhotra, G Ku, and J K Murnighan, "When Winning Is Everything," *Harvard Business Review,* May 2008, pp 78–86; and E T Amanatullah, M W Morris, and J R Curhan, "Negotiators Who Give Too Much? Unmitigated Communion, Relational Anxieties, and Economic Costs in Distributive and Integrative Bargaining," *Journal of Personality and Social Psychology,* September 2008, pp 723–38.

[81] Good win–win negotiation strategies can be found in R R Reck and B G Long, *The Win–Win Negotiator: How to Negotiate Favorable Agreements That Last* (New York: Pocket Books, 1987); R Fisher and W Ury, *Getting to YES: Negotiating Agreement without Giving In* (Boston: Houghton Mifflin, 1981); and R Fisher and D Ertel, *Getting Ready to Negotiate: The Getting to YES Workbook* (New York: Penguin Books, 1995). Also see B Spector, "An Interview with Roger Fisher and William Ury," *Academy of Management Executive,* August 2004, pp 101–108; B Booth and M McCredie, "Taking Steps toward 'Getting to Yes' at Blue Cross and Blue Shield of Florida," *Academy of Management Executive,* August 2004, pp 109–12; and N Brodsky, "The Paranoia Moment. Are They Stalling? Is This Deal about to Fall Apart?" *Inc,* April 2007, pp 67–68.

[82] See L R Weingart, E B Hyder, and M J Prietula, "Knowledge Matters: The Effect of Tactical Descriptions on Negotiation Behavior and Outcome," *Journal of Personality and Social Psychology,* June 1996, pp 1205–17.

[83] For more, see L E Metcalf, A Bird, M Shankarmahesh, Z Aycan, J Larimo, and D D Valdelamar, "Cultural Tendencies in Negotiation: A Comparison of Finland, India, Mexico, Turkey, and the United States," *Journal of World Business,* December 2006, pp 382–94; and L A Liu, C H Chua, and G K Stahl, "Quality of Communication Experience: Definition, Measurement, and Implications for Intercultural Negotiations," *Journal of Applied Psychology,* May 2010, pp 469–87.

[84] Drawn from "How to Negotiate Effectively," *Inc Guidebook, Inc,* November 2010, pp 65–68.

[85] M Latz, "Great Negotiators Research, Weigh Feelings," *The Arizona Republic,* December 2, 2010, p D2. For related research, see S S Wiltermuth and M A Neale, "Too Much Information: The Perils of Nondiagnostic Information in Negotiations," *Journal of Applied Psychology,* January 2011, pp 192–201.

[86] For supporting evidence, see J K Butler Jr, "Trust Expectations, Information Sharing, Climate of Trust, and Negotiation Effectiveness and Efficiency," *Group and Organization Management,* June 1999, pp 217–38.

[87] See D R Dalton and C M Dalton, "On the *Many* Limitations of Threat in Negotiation, as Well as Other Contexts," *Business Horizons,* March–April 2009, pp 109–115.

[88] D R Dalton and C M Dalton, "Trips and Tips for Negotiation Self-Defense: Forewarned is Forearmed," *Business Horizons,* January–February 2011, pp 63–72.

[89] Based on R L Pinkley, T L Griffith, and G B Northcraft, "'Fixed Pie' a la Mode: Information Availability, Information Processing, and the Negotiation of Suboptimal Agreements," *Organizational Behavior and Human Decision Processes,* April 1995, pp 101–12.

[90] Based on A E Walters, A F Stuhlmacher, and L L Meyer, "Gender and Negotiator Competitiveness: A Meta-Analysis," *Organizational Behavior and Human Decision Processes,* October 1998, pp 1–29.

[91] Based on B Barry and R A Friedman, "Bargainer Characteristics in Distributive and Integrative Negotiation," *Journal of Personality and Social Psychology,* February 1998, pp 345–59.

[92] For more, see J P Forgas, "On Feeling Good and Getting Your Way: Mood Effects on Negotiator Cognition and Bargaining Strategies," *Journal of Personality and Social Psychology,* March 1998, pp 565–77.

[93] Data from B Campbell and M M Marx, "Toward More Effective Stakeholder Dialogue: Applying Theories of Negotiation to Policy and Program Evaluation," *Journal of Applied Social Psychology,* December 2006, pp 2834–63.

[94] Drawn from J M Brett and T Okumura, "Inter- and Intracultural Negotiation: US and Japanese Negotiators," *Academy of Management Journal,* October 1998, pp 495–510.

[95] R A Clay, "Meeting Emotions Head On," *Monitor on Psychology,* May 2010, p 78. (Emphasis added.) Also see D Ariely, "In Praise of The Handshake," *Harvard Business Review,* March 2011, p 40.

[96] W Johnson, "I Lost the Friendship, Along with a Painful Amount of Money," *Harvard Business Review,* April 2011, p 115.

[97] Excerpted from K Sulkowicz, "Sparring Execs Need a Time Out," *BusinessWeek,* December 18, 2006, p 18.

CHAPTER 14

[1] D Brady, "Etc. Hard Choices: Brian Dunn," *Bloomberg Businessweek,* December 6–12, 2010, p 104.

[2] S Martin, "More Companies Put iPads to Work," *USA Today,* March 2, 2011, p 1B.

[3] See B Kowitt, "Building the (Workplace) Ties That Bind," *Fortune,* December 6, 2010, p 78.

[4] Data from G Naik, "A Hospital Races to Learn Lessons of Ferrari Pit Stop," *The Wall Street Journal,* November 14, 2006, pp A1, A10.

[5] Based on "Why Am I Here," *Training,* April 2006, p 13. For a similar interpretation, see D Robb, "From the Top," *HR Magazine,* February 2009, pp 61–63.

[6] "3Rs or 4 Cs?" *Training,* July–August 2010, p 8.

[7] J L Bowditch and A F Buono, *A Primer on Organizational Behavior,* 4th ed (New York: John Wiley & Sons, 1997), p 120. For an alternative perspective, see U Hasson, "I Can Make Your Brain Look Like Mine," *Harvard Business Review,* December 2010, pp 32–33.

[8] Data from H Hitchings, *The Secret Life of Words: How English Became English* (New York: Farrar, Straus and Giroux, 2008), p 7.

[9] G A Fowler, "In China's Offices, Foreign Colleagues Might Get an Earful," *The Wall Street Journal,* February 13, 2007, p B1. Also see L Kramer, "How French Innovators Are Putting the 'Social' Back in Social Networking," *Harvard Business Review,* October 2010, pp 121–24; and C Schmidt, "The Battle for China's Talent," *Harvard Business Review,* March 2011, pp 25–27.

[10] See "Developing Your Global Know-How," *Harvard Business Review,* March 2011, pp 70–75; and N Goodman, "Cultivating Cultural Intelligence," *Training,* March–April 2011, p 38.

[11] See A Damast, "For Communication Skills, the Play's the Thing," *BusinessWeek,* April 7, 2008, p 92; and M Weinstein, "Mane Event," *Training,* March–April 2009, pp 20–24.

[12] See B Schneider and K B Paul, "In the Company We Trust," *HR Magazine,* January 2011, pp 40–43.

[13] See R R Hastings, "Poll Finds Mistrust among Racial Groups," *HR Magazine,* February 2008, p 26.

[14] For a thorough discussion of these barriers, see C R Rogers and F J Roethlisberger, "Barriers and Gateways to Communication," *Harvard Business Review,* July–August 1952, pp 46–52.

[15] Ibid., p 47.

[16] Excerpted from J Sandberg, "'It Says Press Any Key. Where's the Any Key?'" *The Wall Street Journal,* February 20, 2007, p B1.

[17] See B Levisohn, "Techie Charm School," *BusinessWeek,* August 25–September 1, 2008, p 13.

[18] L Petrecca, "More Grads Use Social Media to Job Hunt," *USA Today,* April 5, 2011, p 1B.

[19] S Reed, "Youth Unemployment Shakes the Arab World," *Bloomberg Businessweek,* January 24–30, 2011, pp 13–14.

[20] See F Ajami, "Demise of the Dictators," *Newsweek,* February 14, 2011, pp 18–27.

[21] M V Copeland, "Google: The Search Party Is Over," *Fortune,* August 16, 2010, p 61.

[22] Results can be found in J D Johnson, W A Donohue, C K Atkin, and S Johnson, "Communication, Involvement, and Perceived Innovativeness," *Group and Organization Management,* March 2001, pp 24–52; and B Davenport Sypher and T E Zorn Jr, "Communication-Related Abilities and Upward Mobility: A Longitudinal Investigation," *Human Communication Research,* Spring 1986, pp 420–31.

[23] See M Weinstein, "Mind Your Manners," Training, July–August 2009, pp 24–29; and T Wayne, "Etiquette School for Dummies," *Bloomberg Businessweek,* October 18–24, 2010, pp 89–91.

[24] J Swartz, "Yahoo's New CEO Finds Plenty on Her Plate," *USA Today,* January 15, 2009, p 3B; J Swartz, "Bartz Inherited Tough Situation at Yahoo," *USA Today,* September 8, 2011, p 2B.

[25] These recommendations were adapted from J Yadegaran, "Just Say 'No,'" *The Arizona Republic,* September 14, 2006, p E3.

[26] W D St. John, "You Are What You Communicate," *Personnel Journal,* October 1985, p 40. Also see S Baker, "Reading the Body Language of Leadership," *BusinessWeek,* March 23–30, 2009, p 48.

[27] This statistic was reported in R O Crockett, "The 21st Century Meeting," *BusinessWeek,* February 26, 2007, pp 72–79.

[28] A study of decoding nonverbal cues was conducted by E L Cooley, "Attachment Style and Decoding of Nonverbal Cues," *North American Journal of Psychology,* 2005, pp 25–33. Also see T Murphy, "Coffee Kinesiology," *Bloomberg Businessweek,* October 25–31, 2010, pp 106–7; and T Murphy, "Airport Semiotics," *Bloomberg Businessweek,* January 10–16, 2011, pp 76–77.

[29] H Mackay, "Words Whisper; Body Language Roars," *The Arizona Republic,* March 30, 2008, p D2.

[30] L Talley, "Body Language: Read It and Weep," *HR Magazine,* July 2010, p 64.

[31] Based on J A Hall, "Male and Female Nonverbal Behavior," in *Multichannel Integrations of Nonverbal Behavior,* ed A W Siegman and S Feldstein (Hillsdale, NJ: Lawrence Erlbaum, 1985), pp 195–226.

[32] See B Kachka, "Etiquette 101," *Condé Nast Traveler,* April 2008, pp 112–18; and S Pika, E Nicoladis, and P Marentette, "How to Order a Beer: Cultural Differences in the Use of Conventional Gestures for Numbers," *Journal of Cross-Cultural Psychology,* no 1, 2009, pp 70–80.

[33] Results can be found in Hall, pp 195–226.

[34] See J A Russell, "Facial Expressions of Emotion: What Lies beyond Minimal Universality?" *Psychological Bulletin,* November 1995, pp 379–91. Also see B Azar, "A Case for Angry Men and Happy Women," *Monitor on Psychology,* April 2007, pp 18–19.

[35] Norms for cross-cultural eye contact are discussed by C Engholm, *When Business East Meets Business West: The Guide to Practice and Protocol in the Pacific Rim* (New York: John Wiley & Sons, 1991). Also seen G Ward and Y Al Bayyari, "American and Arab Perceptions of an Arabic Turn-Taking Cue," *Journal of Cross-Cultural Psychology,* March 2010, pp 270–75.

[36] These recommendations were adapted from those in P Preston, "Nonverbal Communication: Do You Really Say What You Mean?" *Journal of Healthcare Management,* March–April 2005, pp 83–86.

[37] As quoted in M Gunther, "Best Buy Wants Your Junk," *Fortune,* December 7, 2009, p 97.

[38] See R D Ramsey, "Ten Things That Never Change for Supervisors," *SuperVision,* April 2007, pp 16–18; "CEOs Emphasize Listening to Employees," *HR Magazine,* January 2007, p 14; and M Marchetti, "Listen to Me!" *Sales and Marketing Management,* April 2007, p 12.

[39] The discussion of listening styles is based on "5 Listening Styles," www.crossroadsinstitute.org/listyle.html, accessed May 5, 2005; and J Condrill, "What Is Your Listening Style?" *Authors Den.Com,* July 7, 2005, www.authorsden.com/visit/viewarticle. asp?id=18707.

[40] As quoted in J Weber, "Against the Grain," *BusinessWeek,* January 12, 2009, p 37. Also see D W Dowling, "Maureen Chiquet: The Best Advice I Ever Got," *Harvard Business Review,* November 2008, p 30.

[41] These recommendations were excerpted from J Jay, "On Communicating Well," *HR Magazine,* January 2005, pp 87–88. Also see myth No 5 in V Harnish, "Five Business Myths to Ditch Now," *Fortune,* January 17, 2011, p 45.

[42] D Tannen, "The Power of Talk: Who Gets Heard and Why," *Harvard Business Review,* September–October 1995, p 139. Also see D Tannen, *You Just Don't Understand: Women and Men in Conversation* (New York: Ballantine Books, 1990).

[43] See M Dainton and E D Zelley, *Applying Communication Theory for Professional Life: A Practical Introduction* (Thousand Oaks, CA: Sage, 2005); and E Bernstein, "She Talks a Lot, He Listens a Little," *The Wall Street Journal,* November 16, 2010, pp D1, D4.

[44] This definition was taken from J C Tingley, *Genderflex: Men and Women Speaking Each Other's Language at Work* (New York: American Management Association, 1994), p 16.

[45] Tannen, pp 147–48. Also see G N Powell, "The Gender and Leadership Wars," *Organizational Dynamics,* January–February 2011, pp 1–9; and A Joyner, "Damning with Praise," *Inc,* February 2011, p 28.

[46] J R Detert, E R Burris, and D A Harrison, "Debunking Four Myths About Employee Silence," *Harvard Business Review,* June 2010, p 26. Also see V Venkataramani and S Tangirala, "When and Why Do Central Employees Speak Up? An Examination of Mediating and Moderating Variables," *Journal of Applied Psychology,* May 2010, pp 582–91; and "Most Employees Don't Speak Up," *HR Magazine,* September 2010, p 22.

[47] See L Grensing-Pophal, "To Ask or Not to Ask," *HR Magazine,* February 2009, pp 53–55; M Kimes, "How Can I Get Candid Feedback from My Employees?" *Fortune,* April 13, 2009, p 24; and "How Often Should Exit Interview Results Be Presented to Senior Managers? What Should Be Reported?" *HR Magazine,* July 2010, p 23.

[48] As quoted in M Krantz, "There's Definitely Life After Taxes at Intuit," *USA Today,* March 15, 2010, p 3B. For practical advice and examples, see M Marquardt, *Leading with Questions: How Leaders Find the Right Solutions by Knowing What to Ask* (San Francisco, CA: Jossey-Bass, 2005); and S Freeman, "Ask the 'Dumb' Questions," *USA Today,* January 13, 2009, p 11A.

[49] J Yang and S Ward, "USA Today Snapshots," *USA Today,* February 26, 2008, p 1B.

50 J Yang and V Salazar, "USA Today Snapshots," *USA Today,* November 20, 2008, p 1B. Also see the first Q&A in "Ask Inc: Tough Questions, Smart Answers," *Inc,* January–February 2009, pp 104–5.

51 V Harnish, "Five Ways to Get Your Strategy Right," *Fortune,* April 11, 2011, p 42.

52 These recommendations were taken from N H Woodward, "Doing Town Hall Meetings Better," *HR Magazine,* December 2006, p 70. Also see J L Yang, "What's the Secret to Running Great Meetings?" *Fortune,* October 27, 2008, p 26; N Morgan, "How to Become an Authentic Speaker," *Harvard Business Review,* November 2008, pp 115–19; and S B Fink, "Address the Human Side of M&As," *Training,* March–April 2009, p 16.

53 Excerpted from L Szabo, "Checklist Reduces Surgery Deaths," *USA Today,* January 15, 2009, p 8D.

54 For more, see L Sussman, "Disclosure, Leaks, and Slips: Issues and Strategies for Prohibiting Employee Communication," *Business Horizons,* July–August 2008, pp 331–39; B Newstead and L Lanzerotti, "Can You Open-Source Your Strategy?" *Harvard Business Review,* October 2010, p 32; and B Helm, "Spy Games," *Inc,* April 2011, pp 75–83.

55 G Labianca, "It's Not 'Unprofessional' to Gossip at Work," *Harvard Business Review,* September 2010, p 28. Also see K M Kniffin and D S Wilson, "Evolutionary Perspectives on Workplace Gossip: Why and How Gossip Can Serve Groups," *Group and Organization Management,* April 2010, pp 150–76; and G Michelson, A van Iterson, and K Waddington, "Gossip in Organizations: Contexts, Consequences, and Controversies," *Group and Organization Management,* August 2010, pp 371–90.

56 Drawn from S M Crampton, J W Hodge, and J M Mishra, "The Informal Communication Network: Factors Influencing Grapevine Activity," *Public Personnel Management,* Winter 1998, pp 569–84; J Yang and V Salazar, "What Is the Most Taboo Topic to Discuss at Work?" *USA Today,* June 17, 2008, p 1B; and C Mills, "Experiencing Gossip: The Foundations for a Theory of Embedded Organizational Gossip," *Group and Organization Management,* April 2010, pp 213–40.

57 J Yang and S Parker, "Top Managers Don't Appreciate Office Gossip," *USA Today,* December 24, 2008, p 1B.

58 J McGregor, "Mining the Office Chatter," *BusinessWeek,* May 19, 2008, p 54.

59 Management by walking around is discussed by T Peters and N Austin, *A Passion for Excellence: The Leadership Difference* (New York: Random House, 1985).

60 L Dulye, "Get Out of Your Office," *HR Magazine,* July 2006, p 99.

61 These recommendations were adapted from ibid., pp 100–1.

62 Data from J M O'Brien, "Zappos Knows How to Kick It," *Fortune,* February 2, 2009, pp 54–60.

63 R Levering and M Moskowitz, "And the Winners Are . . .," *Fortune,* February 2, 2009, pp 67–78.

64 R L Daft and R H Lengel, "Information Richness: A New Approach to Managerial Behavior and Organizational Design," in *Research in Organizational Behavior,* ed B M Staw and L L Cummings (Greenwich, CT: JAI Press, 1984), p 196.

65 For good discussion, see A M Kaplan and M Haenlein, "Users of the World, Unite! The Challenges and Opportunities of Social Media," *Business Horizons,* January–February 2010, pp 59–68.

66 Details of this example are provided in L Grensing-Pophal, "Spread the Word—Correctly," *HR Magazine,* March 2005, pp 83–88. Also see P Post, "The Note," *Training,* September–October 2010, p 44.

67 See E Binney, "Is E-Mail the New Pink Slip?" *HR Magazine,* November 2006, pp 32, 38; and D M Cable and K Y T Yu, "Managing Job Seekers' Organizational Image Beliefs: The Role of Media Richness and Media Credibility," *Journal of Applied Psychology,* July 2006, pp 828–40.

68 See B Barry and I S Fulmer, "The Medium and the Message: The Adaptive Use of Communication Media in Dyadic Influence," *Academy of Management Review,* April 2004, pp 272–92; and A F Simon, "Computer-Mediated Communication: Task Performance and Satisfaction," *The Journal of Social Psychology,* June 2006, pp 349–79.

69 See R E Rice and D E Shook, "Relationships of Job Categories and Organizational Levels to Use of Communication Channels, Including Electronic Mail: A Meta-Analysis and Extension," *Journal of Management Studies,* March 1990, pp 195–229.

70 For digital innovations, see "It's Not Sci-Fi, It's (Augmented) Reality," *Fortune,* March 22, 2010, p 27; A Vance, "The Power of the Cloud," *Bloomberg Businessweek,* March 7–13, 2011, pp 52–59; and "Sign Language," *Fortune,* March 21, 2011, p 45.

71 A Fisher, "E-Mail Is for Liars," *Fortune,* November 24, 2008, p 57.

72 A Pentland, "How Social Networks Network Best," *Harvard Business Review,* February 2009, p 37. Also see B Barton, "Are We Losing Empathy?" *USA Today,* October 20, 2010, p 9A; and M Rosenwald, "The Antisocial Network," *Bloomberg Businessweek,* March 7–13, 2011, pp 82–83.

73 J Swartz, "Communications Overload," *USA Today,* February 2, 2011, p 1B. Also see V Elmer, "Why You Need a *Career Curator,*" *Fortune,* July 5, 2010, pp 33–34; and D Meinert, "Too Much Information," *HR Magazine,* January 2011, p 19.

74 Data from www.ic3.gov/media/2011/110224.aspx; accessed April 7, 2011. Also see D MacMillan, "Washington's Web Cop Turns Up the Heat," *Bloomberg Businessweek,* July 12–18, 2010, pp 39–40.

75 R Zeidner, "Out of the Breach," *HR Magazine,* August 2008, p 39. Also see B Acohido, "Social-Media Tools Used to Target Corporate Secrets," *USA Today,* March 31, 2011, pp 1B–2B.

76 See K Wehrum, "When IT Workers Attack: How to Prevent Tech Sabotage," *Inc,* April 2009, pp 132, 134; J Swartz, "Privacy Breached in Facebook Apps," *USA Today,* October 19, 2010, p 2B; and J Bennett, "Privacy is Dead," *Newsweek,* November 1, 2010, pp 40–41.

77 D Tapscott, *Grown Up Digital: How the Net Generation Is Changing Your World* (New York: McGraw-Hill, 2009), p 36. Also see S Terbush, "Twitter, Facebook, Blogs—Young Adults Are Active 'Social Animals,'" *USA Today,* February 21, 2011, p 5D.

78 J L Yang, "How to Get a Job," *Fortune,* April 13, 2009, p 51.

79 See P Burrows, "Virtual Meetings for Real-World Budgets," *Bloomberg Businessweek,* August 9–15, 2010, pp 36–37; A Schwartz, "Bring Your Robot to Work Day," *Fast Company,* November 2010, pp 72–74; and J Swartz, "SocialEyes Delivers Group Video Chat," *USA Today,* February 28, 2011, p 2B.

80 Data from E Reed, "Telecommuting by the Numbers," *HR Magazine,* September 2008, p 61. For another survey, see J Schramm, "At Work in a Virtual World," *HR Magazine,* June 2010, p 152.

81 M Conlin, "Home Offices: The New Math," *BusinessWeek,* March 9, 2009, p 66. Also see J Swartz, "No Place Like Home for Start-Ups," *USA Today,* April 28, 2010, p 3B.

82 J A Pearce II, "Successful Corporate Telecommuting with Technology Considerations for Late Adopters," *Organizational Dynamics,* January–March 2009, p 17.

83 Data from "The Virtual Workforce," *BusinessWeek,* March 5, 2007, p 6; and T D Golden, J F Veiga, and Z Simsek, "Telecommuting's Differential Impact of Work-Family Conflict: Is There No Place Like Home?" *Journal of Applied Psychology,* November 2006, pp 1240–50. Also see R Zeidner, "Home Is Where the Productivity Is," *HR Magazine,* July 2010, p 20.

84 M Conlin, "Telecommuting: Out of Sight, Yes. Out of Mind, No," *BusinessWeek,* February 18, 2008, p 60.

85 Results are reported in K Gurchiek, "Telecommuting Could Hold Back Careers," *HR Magazine,* March 2007, p 34.

86 T D Golden, J F Veiga, and R N Dino, "The Impact of Professional Isolation on Teleworker Job Performance and Turnover Intentions: Does Time Spent Teleworking, Interacting Face-to-Face, or Having Access to Communication-Enhancing Technology Matter?" *Journal of Applied Psychology,* November 2008, p 1412. Also see M Chafkin, "Freelancer Tony Bacigalupo Longed for Co-Workers," *Inc,* October 2010, pp 67–68.

87 C R Stoner, P Stephens, and M K McGowan, "Connectivity and Work Dominance: Panacea or Pariah?" *Business Horizons,* January–February 2009, p 67. Also see B Roberts, "Mobile Workforce Management? There Are Apps for That," *HR Magazine,* March 2011, pp 67–70.

88 See B Levisohn, "Write On, Dood," *BusinessWeek,* August 4, 2008, p 16; P Welch, "Txting Away Ur Education," *USA Today,* June 23, 2009, p 11A; and D Baron, *A Better Pencil: Readers, Writers, and the Digital Revolution* (New York: Oxford University Press, 2009).

89 L Stone, "Living with Continuous Partial Attention," *Harvard Business Review,* February 2007, p 28. N L Reinsch Jr, J W Turner, and C H Tinsley, "Multicommunicating: A Practice Whose Time Has Come?" *Academy of Management Review,* April 2008, pp 391–403.

90 Data from A R Carey and S Ward, "How Many E-mail Accounts Do You Have?" *USA Today,* March 16, 2011, p 1A. Also see B Stone, "Dear E-Mail: Die Already. Love, Facebook," *Bloomberg Businessweek,* November 22–28, 2010, pp 50, 52.

91 Based on K Byron, "Carrying Too Heavy a Load? The Communication and Miscommunication of Emotion by Email," *Academy of Management Review,* April 2008, pp 309–27 and C E Naquin, T R Kurtzberg, and L Y Belkin, "The Finer Points of Lying Online: E-mail Versus Pen and Paper," *Journal of Applied Psychology,* March 2010, pp 387–94.

92 B Roberts, "Stay Ahead of the Technology Use Curve," *HR Magazine,* October 2008, p 58. Also see W P Smith and F Tabak, "Monitoring Employee E-Mails: Is There Any Room for Privacy?" *Academy of Management Perspectives,"* November 2009, pp 33–48; and J Deschenaux, "New Jersey: Employee E-Mail With Attorney Is Private," *HR Magazine,* May 2010, p 20.

93 M Kessler, "Fridays Turning E-mail Free," *The Arizona Republic,* October 7, 2007, p D3. Also see P Kemp, "10 Ways to Reduce E-Mail Overload," *Harvard Business Review,* September 2009, p 88.

94 Data A R Carey and J Snider, "Replacing Land-Line Phones with Cellphones," *USA Today,* April 7, 2009, p 1A; S Jayson, "2010: The Year We Stopped Talking," *USA Today,* December 30, 2010, pp 1A–2A; and J Graham, "More Companies Shrink Sites," *USA Today,* March 30, 2011, p 3B.

95 See W Koch, "More Teens Caught Up in 'Sexting,'" *USA Today,* March 12, 2009, p 1A; J Michaels, "Cellphones Put to 'Unnerving' Use in Gaza," *USA Today,* January 14, 2009, p 4A; and A R Carey and S Ward, "What Experienced U.S. Business Travelers Most Wish Other Travelers Knew About," *USA Today,* June 15, 2010, p 1A.

96 R Petrancosta, "There's a Reason We Can't Text and Drive: Science," *USA Today,* June 30, 2010, p 11A. Also see L Copeland, "Most Teens Still Driving While Distracted," *USA Today,* August 2, 2010, p 7A.

97 Data for this list drawn in order from: L Fabel, "The Business of Facebook," *Fast Company,* April 2011, p 128; S Berfield, "Dueling Your Facebook Friends for a New Job," *Bloomberg Businessweek,* March 7–13, 2011, pp 35–36; L Szabo, "Teens Share Internet Injury Videos," *USA Today,* February 21, 2011, p 3A; http://blog.twitter.com/2011/03/numbers.html (accessed April 8, 2011); A D Wright, "More Employees Visit Social Sites While Working," *HR Magazine,* September 2010, p 21; A R Carey and P Trap, "How Honest Are You on Your Social Networking Sites?" *USA Today,* January 3, 2011, p 1A; and J Yang and S Ward, "Does Your Company Audit and Monitor Postings to Social-Networking Sites?" *USA Today,* February 23, 2010, p 1B.

98 M Conlin and D MacMillan, "Managing the Tweets," *BusinessWeek,* June 1, 2009, pp 20–21. Also see M Weinstein, "Are You LinkedIn?" *Training,* September–October 2010, pp 30–33; A M Kaplan and M Haenlein, "The Early Bird Catches the News: Nine Things You Should Know About Micro-blogging," *Business Horizons,* March–April 2011, pp 105–13; and A Vance, "Trouble at the Virtual Water Cooler," *Bloomberg Businessweek,* May 2–8, 2011, pp 31–32.

99 Reprinted from R King, "Go Ahead, Use Facebook," August 25–September 1, 2008, issue of *BusinessWeek* by special permission. Copyright © 2009 by The McGraw-Hill Companies. Seven Twitter tools are discussed in R Scoble, "Brand New Day," *Fast Company,* May 2009, p 52.

100 L Petrecca, "Feel Like Someone's Watching? You're Right." *USA Today,* March 17, 2010, p 1B.

CHAPTER 15

1 Excerpted from E Lopatto, "Takeda's Anti-Cancer Crusader," *Bloomberg Businessweek,* March 21–27, 2011, pp 57–58.

2 Quotes and data from J Yang and V Salazar, "USA Today Snapshots," *USA Today,* February 10, 2009, p 1B. Also see K Tyler, "Preparing for Impact," *HR Magazine,* March 2011, pp 53–56.

3 H Malcolm and C Sokoloff, "Values, Human Relations, and Organization Development," in *The Emerging Practice of Organizational Development,* ed W Sikes, A Drexler, and J Gant (San Diego, CA: University Associates, 1989), p 64.

4 As quoted in "The World's Most Influential Companies," *BusinessWeek,* December 22, 2008, p 44. For more of Hamel's ideas, see G Hamel, "Moon Shots for Management," *Harvard Business Review,* February 2009, pp 91–98.

5 See D Kipnis, S M Schmidt, and I Wilkinson, "Intraorganizational Influence Tactics: Explorations in Getting One's Way," *Journal of Applied Psychology,* August 1980, pp 440–52. Also see C A Schriesheim and T R Hinkin, "Influence Tactics Used by Subordinates: A Theoretical and Empirical Analysis and Refinement of the Kipnis, Schmidt, and Wilkinson Subscales," *Journal of Applied Psychology,* June 1990, pp 246–57; G Yukl and C M Falbe, "Influence Tactics and Objectives in Upward, Downward, and Lateral Influence Attempts," *Journal of Applied Psychology,* April 1990, pp 132–40; and G Yukl and B Tracey, "Consequences of Influence Tactics Used with Subordinates, Peers, and the Boss," in *Organizational Influence Processes,* 2nd ed, ed L W Porter, H L Angle, and R W Allen (Armonk, NY: M E Sharpe, 2003), pp 96–116.

6 Based on Table 1 in G Yukl, C M Falbe, and J Y Youn, "Patterns of Influence Behavior for Managers," *Group and Organization Management,* March 1993, pp 5–28. An additional influence tactic is presented in B P Davis and E S Knowles, "A Disrupt-Then-Reframe Technique of Social Influence," *Journal of Personality and Social Psychology,* February 1999, pp 192–99. Also see K Savani, M W Morris, N V R Naidu, S Kumar, and N V Berlia, "Cultural Conditioning: Understanding Interpersonal Accommodation in India and the United States in Terms of the Modal Characteristics of Interpersonal Influence Situations," *Journal of Personality and Social Psychology,* January 2011, pp 84–102.

7 For comprehensive coverage, see L W Porter, H L Angle, and R W Allen, eds, *Organizational Influence Processes,* 2nd ed (Armonk, NY: M E Sharpe, 2003); and The Society for Human Resource Management and Harvard Business School Press, *The Essentials of Power, Influence, and Persuasion* (Boston: Harvard Business School Press, 2006). Also see R Barnett, "I Deserve a Raise. Do I Dare Ask for One?" *Fortune,* July 5, 2010, p 36.

8 Excerpted from A Weintraub, "Making Her Mark at Merck," *BusinessWeek,* January 8, 2007, p 65. Also see B Azar, "More Powerful Persuasion," *Monitor on Psychology,* April 2010, pp 36, 38; M Hofman, "What Are You Talking About?" *Inc,* March 2011, p 8; and Z Tormala, "Experts Are More Persuasive When They're Less Certain," *Harvard Business Review,* March 2011, pp 32–33.

9 Based on discussion in G Yukl, H Kim, and C M Falbe, "Antecedents of Influence Outcomes," *Journal of Applied Psychology,* June 1996, pp 309–17.

[10] Data from ibid.

[11] Data from G Yukl and J B Tracey, "Consequences of Influence Tactics Used with Subordinates, Peers, and the Boss," *Journal of Applied Psychology,* August 1992, pp 525–35. Also see C M Falbe and G Yukl, "Consequences for Managers of Using Single Influence Tactics and Combinations of Tactics," *Academy of Management Journal,* August 1992, pp 638–52.

[12] Data from R A Gordon, "Impact of Ingratiation on Judgments and Evaluations: A Meta-Analytic Investigation," *Journal of Personality and Social Psychology,* July 1996, pp 54–70.

[13] Based on J D Westphal and I Stern, "Flattery Will Get You Everywhere (Especially if You Are a Male Caucasian): How Ingratiation, Boardroom Behavior, and Demographic Minority Status Affect Additional Board Appointments at US Companies," *Academy of Management Journal,* April 2007, pp 267–88; and N Byrnes, "Profiles in Sycophancy," *BusinessWeek,* August 13, 2007, p 12.

[14] Data from Yukl, Kim, and Falbe, pp 309–17

[15] Based on R T Sparrowe, B W Soetjipto, and M L Kraimer, "Do Leaders' Influence Tactics Relate to Members' Helping Behavior? It Depends on the Quality of the Relationship," *Academy of Management Journal,* December 2006, pp 1194–208. Also see F A White, M A Charles, and J K Nelson, "The Role of Persuasive Arguments in Changing Affirmative Action Attitudes and Expressed Behavior in Higher Education," *Journal of Applied Psychology,* November 2008, pp 1271–86.

[16] Data from B J Tepper, R J Eisenbach, S L Kirby, and P W Potter, "Test of a Justice-Based Model of Subordinates' Resistance to Downward Influence Attempts," *Group and Organization Management,* June 1998, pp 144–60.

[17] J E Driskell, B Olmstead, and E Salas, "Task Cues, Dominance Cues, and Influence in Task Groups," *Journal of Applied Psychology,* February 1993, p 51. No gender bias was found in H Aguinis and S K R Adams, "Social-Role versus Structural Models of Gender and Influence Use in Organizations: A Strong Inference Approach," *Group and Organization Management,* December 1998, pp 414–46.

[18] See P P Fu et al., "The Impact of Societal Cultural Values and Individual Social Beliefs on the Perceived Effectiveness of Managerial Influence Strategies: A Meso Approach," *Journal of International Business Studies,* July 2004, pp 284–305. Also see C Anderson, S E Spataro, and F J Flynn, "Personality and Organizational Culture as Determinants of Influence," *Journal of Applied Psychology,* May 2008, pp 702–10.

[19] B Moses, "You Can't Make Change; You Have to Sell It," *Fast Company,* April 1999, p 101. Also see S Jayson, "The Ugly Truth: Good Looks Make You Richer, Happier," *USA Today,* March 30, 2011, p 2B; and F Gino and G P Pisano, "Why Leaders Don't Learn from Success," *Harvard Business Review,* April 2011, pp 68–74.

[20] See J Pfeffer, *Power: Why Some People Have It—and Others Don't* (New York: Harper Business, 2010); J Pfeffer, "Power Play," *Harvard Business Review,* July–August 2010, pp 84–92; and I McGugan, "The Goldman Doctrine," *Bloomberg Businessweek,* April 11–17, 2011, pp 86–87.

[21] D Tjosvold, "The Dynamics of Positive Power," *Training and Development Journal,* June 1984, p 72. Also see D Tjosvold and B Wisse, eds, *Power and Interdependence in Organizations* (Cambridge, UK: Cambridge University Press, 2009).

[22] M W McCall Jr, *Power, Influence, and Authority: The Hazards of Carrying a Sword,* Technical Report No. 10 (Greensboro, NC: Center for Creative Leadership, 1978), p 5. For an excellent discussion, see J O Hagberg, *Real Power: Stages of Personal Power in Organizations,* 3rd ed (Salem, WI: Sheffield Publishing, 2003).

[23] D Weimer, "Daughter Knows Best," *BusinessWeek,* April 19, 1999, pp 132, 134. Also see "How to Stage a Coup," *Inc,* March 2005, p 52.

[24] For an update, see C L Bernick, "When Your Culture Needs a Makeover," *Harvard Business Review,* June 2001, pp 53–61.

[25] L H Chusmir, "Personalized versus Socialized Power Needs among Working Women and Men," *Human Relations,* February 1986, p 149. Also see R I Sutton, "The Boss as Human Shield," *Harvard Business Review,* September 2010, pp 106–9.

[26] R I Sutton, "Are You Being a Jerk Again?" *BusinessWeek,* August 25–September 1, 2008, p 52. Also see C J Torelli and S Shavitt, "Culture and Concepts of Power," *Journal of Personality and Social Psychology,* October 2010, pp 703–23.

[27] As quoted in L Buchanan, "That's Quite a Story: How I Did It," *Inc,* November 2006, p 113.

[28] Based on D W Cantor and T Bernay, *Women in Power: The Secrets of Leadership* (Boston: Houghton Mifflin, 1992). Also see J Shambora and B Kowitt, "50 Most Powerful Women," *Fortune,* October 18, 2010, pp 129–34.

[29] S Sandberg, "Changing the World, One Job at a Time," *Newsweek,* October 13, 2008, p 68.

[30] See J R P French and B Raven, "The Bases of Social Power," in *Studies in Social Power,* ed D Cartwright (Ann Arbor: University of Michigan Press, 1959), pp 150–67.

[31] R Saunderson, "Changing Minds," *Training,* March-April 2011, pp 42–43.

[32] G Edmondson, "Power Play at VW," *BusinessWeek,* December 4, 2006, p 45.

[33] See, for example, C H Nelson Jr. and L Tyson, "HR Undercover," *HR Magazine,* October 2010, pp 107–10.

[34] Data from J R Larson Jr, C Christensen, A S Abbott, and T M Franz, "Diagnosing Groups: Charting the Flow of Information in Medical Decision-Making Teams," *Journal of Personality and Social Psychology,* August 1996, pp 315–30.

[35] See A Pentland, "We Can Measure the Power of Charisma," *Harvard Business Review,* January–February 2010, pp 34–35; B Stone and P Burrows, "The Essence of Apple," *Bloomberg Businessweek,* January 24–30, 2011, pp 6–8; and J Sonnenfeld, "The Genius Dilemma," *Newsweek,* January 31, 2011, pp 12–17. For an interesting new research thrust, see D A Waldman, P A Balthazard, and S J Peterson, "Leadership and Neuroscience: Can We Revolutionize the Way That Inspirational Leaders Are Identified and Developed?" *Academy of Management Perspectives,* February 2011, pp 60–74.

[36] Excerpted from the first Q&A with J Welch and S Welch, "It's Not about Empty Suits," *BusinessWeek* October 16, 2006, p 100.

[37] Details may be found in Chusmir, "Personalized versus Socialized Power Needs among Working Women and Men," pp 149–59. For a review of research on individual differences in the need for power, see R J House, "Power and Personality in Complex Organizations," in *Research in Organizational Behavior,* ed B M Staw and L L Cummings (Greenwich, CT: JAI Press, 1988), pp 305–57.

[38] B Filipczak, "Is It Getting Chilly in Here?" *Training,* February 1994, p 27.

[39] Data from J Onyx, R Leonard, and K Vivekananda, "Social Perception of Power: A Gender Analysis," *Perceptual and Motor Skills,* February 1995, pp 291–96.

[40] P M Podsakoff and C A Schriesheim, "Field Studies of French and Raven's Bases of Power: Critique, Reanalysis, and Suggestions for Future Research," *Psychological Bulletin,* May 1985, p 388. Also see C A Schriesheim, T R Hinkin, and P M Podsakoff, "Can Ipsative and Single-Item Measures Produce Erroneous Results in Field Studies of French and Raven's (1950) Five Bases of Power? An Empirical Investigation," *Journal of Applied Psychology,* February 1991, pp 106–14.

[41] See T R Hinkin and C A Schriesheim, "Relationships between Subordinate Perceptions and Supervisor Influence Tactics and Attributed Bases of Supervisory Power," *Human Relations,* March 1990, pp 221–37.

[42] W Clark, "The Potency of Persuasion," *Fortune,* November 12, 2007, p 48. Also see A J Ferguson, M E Ormiston, and H Moon,

"From Approach to Inhibition: The Influence of Power on Responses to Poor Performance," *Journal of Applied Psychology,* March 2010, pp 305–20.

⁴³ Based on P A Wilson, "The Effects of Politics and Power on the Organizational Commitment of Federal Executives," *Journal of Management,* Spring 1995, pp 101–18. For related research, see D Carney, "Powerful People Are Better Liars," *Harvard Business Review,* May 2010, pp 32–33; M Segalla, "Find the Real Power in Your Organization," *Harvard Business Review,* May 2010, pp 34–35; and J K Maner, and N L Mead, "The Essential Tension Between Leadership and Power: When Leaders Sacrifice Group Goals for the Sake of Self-Interest," *Journal of Personality and Social Psychology,* September 2010, pp 482–97.

⁴⁴ As quoted in W A Randolph and M Sashkin, "Can Organizational Empowerment Work in Multinational Settings?" *Academy of Management Executive,* February 2002, p 104 (emphasis added). Also see H P Sims Jr, S Faraj, and S Yun, "When Should a Leader Be Directive or Empowering? How to Develop Your Own Situational Theory of Leadership," *Business Horizons,* March–April 2009, pp 149–58; and L B Cattaneo and A R Chapman, "The Process of Empowerment: A Model for Use in Research and Practice," *American Psychologist,* October 2010, pp 646–59.

⁴⁵ R M Hodgetts, "A Conversation with Steve Kerr," *Organizational Dynamics,* Spring 1996, p 71. Also see J Bernoff and T Schadler, "Empowered," *Harvard Business Review,* July-August 2010, p 95.

⁴⁶ A Fox, "Raising Engagement," *HR Magazine,* May 2010, p 39. Also see "How May We Help You?" *Inc,* March 2011, p 63.

⁴⁷ J Welch and S Welch, "Why Your Office Isn't Like Google's," *BusinessWeek,* August 25–September 1, 2008, p 100.

⁴⁸ L Shaper Walters, "A Leader Redefines Management," *Christian Science Monitor,* September 22, 1992, p 14. Also see A D Amar, C Hentrich, and V Hlupic, "To Be a Better Leader, Give Up Authority," *Harvard Business Review,* December 2009, pp 22–24; and L Wiseman and G McKeown, "Bringing Out the Best in Your People," *Harvard Business Review,* May 2010, pp 117–21.

⁴⁹ For a 15-item empowerment scale, see Table 1 on p 103 of B P Niehoff, R H Moorman, G Blakely, and J Fuller, "The Influence of Empowerment and Job Enrichment on Employee Loyalty in a Downsizing Environment," *Group and Organization Management,* March 2001, pp 93–113.

⁵⁰ F Vogelstein, "Star Power: Greg Brown, Motorola," *Fortune,* February 6, 2006, p 57.

⁵¹ For an extended discussion of this model, see M Sashkin, "Participative Management Is an Ethical Imperative," *Organizational Dynamics,* Spring 1984, pp 4–22.

⁵² Drawn from X Huang, Joyce Iun, A Liu, and Y Gong, "Does Participative Leadership Enhance Work Performance by Inducing Empowerment or Trust? The Differential Effects on Managerial and Nonmanagerial Subordinates," *Journal of Organizational Behavior,* January 2010, pp 122–43.

⁵³ D Lieberman, "Hammer Determined to Extend Cable Reach," *USA Today,* March 23, 2009, p 6B. Also see the practical tips in J Hempel, "Putting Ads Into Apps," *Fortune,* July 26, 2010, p 16.

⁵⁴ For more on delegation, see L Bossidy, "The Job No CEO Should Delegate," *Harvard Business Review,* March 2001, pp 46–49; and S Sanghi, "Good Delegation Means Setting Objectives, Getting Results," *The Arizona Republic,* August 1, 2010, p D5.

⁵⁵ See S Gazda, "The Art of Delegating," *HR Magazine,* January 2002, pp 75–78; and J W Womack, "Delegating = Developing Leadership," *Training,* November–December 2010, p 6.

⁵⁶ M Memmott, "Managing Government Inc," *USA Today,* June 28, 1993, p 2B. Also see R C Ford and C P Heaton, "Lessons from Hospitality That Can Serve Anyone," *Organizational Dynamics,* Summer 2001, pp 30–47.

⁵⁷ R Kreitner, *Management,* 11th ed (Boston: Houghton Mifflin Harcourt, 2009), p 254.

⁵⁸ Drawn from G Yukl and P P Fu, "Determinants of Delegation and Consultation by Managers," *Journal of Organizational Behavior,* March 1999, pp 219–32. Also see Z X Chen and S Aryee, "Delegation and Employee Work Outcomes: An Examination of the Cultural Context of Mediating Processes in China," *Academy of Management Journal,* February 2007, pp 226–38.

⁵⁹ See D Moyer, "Broken Trust," *Harvard Business Review,* April 2009, p 120; and B Schneider and K B Paul, "In the Company We Trust," *HR Magazine,* January 2011, pp 40–43.

⁶⁰ M Frese, W Kring, A Soose, and J Zempel, "Personal Initiative at Work: Differences between East and West Germany," *Academy of Management Journal,* February 1996, p 38 (emphasis added). Also see D N Den Hartog and F D Belschak, "Personal Initiative, Commitment and Affect at Work," *Journal of Occupational and Organizational Psychology,* December 2007, pp 601–22; and R Bledow and M Frese, "A Situational Judgment Test of Personal Initiative and Its Relationship to Performance," *Personnel Psychology,* Summer 2009, pp 229–58.

⁶¹ See W A Randolph, "Re-thinking Empowerment: Why Is It So Hard to Achieve?" *Organizational Dynamics,* Fall 2000, pp 94–107.

⁶² Results can be found in B D Cawley, L M Keeping, and P E Levy, "Participation in the Performance Appraisal Process and Employee Reactions: A Meta-Analytic Review of Field Investigations," *Journal of Applied Psychology,* August 1998, pp 615–33.

⁶³ Results are contained in J A Wagner III, C R Leana, E A Locke, and D M Schweiger, "Cognitive and Motivational Frameworks in US Research on Participation: A Meta-Analysis of Primary Effects," *Journal of Organizational Behavior,* 1997, pp 49–65.

⁶⁴ Based on A Srivastava, K M Bartol, and E A Locke, "Empowering Leadership in Management Teams: Effects on Knowledge Sharing, Efficacy, and Performance," *Academy of Management Journal,* December 2006, pp 1239–251.

⁶⁵ Based on J P Guthrie, "High-Involvement Work Practices, Turnover, and Productivity: Evidence from New Zealand," *Academy of Management Journal,* February 2001, pp 180–90.

⁶⁶ Based on M Workman and W Bommer, "Redesigning Computer Call Center Work: A Longitudinal Field Experiment," *Journal of Organizational Behavior,* May 2004, pp 317–37.

⁶⁷ Based on C D Zatzick and R D Iverson, "High-Involvement Management and Workforce Reduction: Competitive Advantage or Disadvantage?" *Academy of Management Journal,* October 2006, pp 999–1015.

⁶⁸ Based on X Zhang and K M Bartol, "Linking Empowering Leadership and Employee Creativity: The Influence of Psychological Empowerment, Intrinsic Motivation, and Creative Process Involvement," *Academy of Management Journal,* February 2010, pp 107–28; and E Lamm and J R Gordon, "Empowerment, Predisposition to Resist Change, and Support for Organizational Change," *Journal of Leadership and Organizational Studies,* no 4, 2010, pp 426–37.

⁶⁹ W A Randolph, "Navigating the Journey to Empowerment," *Organizational Dynamics,* Spring 1995, p 31. For more on empowerment, see B Burlingham, "How Has It Come to This?" *Inc,* February 2008, pp 102–9; S Mantere and E Vaara, "On the Problem of Participation in Strategy: A Critical Discursive Perspective," *Organization Science,* March–April 2008, pp 341–58; and F Kiel, "Flaws in the Selfish-Worker Theory," *BusinessWeek,* October 6, 2008, p 78.

⁷⁰ See www.nbc.com/The_Office, accessed April 25, 2011.

⁷¹ D J Burrough, "Office Politics Mirror Popular TV Program," *The Arizona Republic,* February 4, 2001, p EC1.

⁷² L B MacGregor Serven, *The End of Office Politics as Usual* (New York: American Management Association, 2002), p 5. Also see J Hempel, "Trouble @ Twitter," *Fortune,* May 2, 2011, pp 66–76.

⁷³ Quotes and data from J Yang and K Simmons, "USA Today Snapshots," *USA Today,* November 17, 2008, p 1B.

⁷⁴ M G McIntyre, *Secrets to Winning at Office Politics: How to Achieve Your Goals and Increase Your Influence at Work* (New

York: St. Martin's Griffin: 2005), p 160. For more practical tips, see C Hawley, *100+ Tactics for Office Politics,* 2nd ed (Hauppauge, NY: Barron's Educational Series, 2008).

[75] Data from M Weinstein, "Training Today: Q&A," *Training,* January–February 2007, p 7. Also see M Conlin, "Make Yourself Into a Rainmaker," *Money,* September 2010, p 36; J Kehoe, "How to Save Good Ideas," *Harvard Business Review,* October 2010, pp 129–132; and E Pofeldt, "Step Up Your Career This Year," *Money,* January–February 2011, p 40.

[76] R W Allen, D L Madison, L W Porter, P A Renwick, and B T Mayes, "Organizational Politics: Tactics and Characteristics of Its Actors," *California Management Review,* Fall 1979, p 77.

[77] Drawn from P M Fandt and G R Ferris, "The Management of Information and Impressions: When Employees Behave Opportunistically," *Organizational Behavior and Human Decision Processes,* February 1990, pp 140–58.

[78] First four based on discussion in D R Beeman and T W Sharkey, "The Use and Abuse of Corporate Politics," *Business Horizons,* March–April 1987, pp 26–30. For supportive evidence, see C C Rosen, P E Levy, and R J Hall, "Placing Perceptions of Politics in the Context of the Feedback Environment, Employee Attitudes, and Job Performance," *Journal of Applied Psychology,* January 2006, pp 211–20.

[79] A Raia, "Power, Politics, and the Human Resource Professional," *Human Resource Planning,* no 4, 1985, p 203.

[80] As quoted in A J DuBrin, "Career Maturity, Organizational Rank, and Political Behavioral Tendencies: A Correlational Analysis of Organizational Politics and Career Experience," *Psychological Reports,* October 1988, p 535. Also see D A Ready, J A Conger, and L A Hill, "Are You a High Potential?" *Harvard Business Review,* June 2010, pp 78–84.

[81] This three-level distinction comes from A T Cobb, "Political Diagnosis: Applications in Organizational Development," *Academy of Management Review,* July 1986, pp 482–96. Also see R Cross, A Cowen, L Vertucci, and R J Thomas, "Leading in a Connected World: How Effective Leaders Drive Results Through Networks," *Organizational Dynamics,* April–June 2009, pp 93–105.

[82] L Baum, "The Day Charlie Bradshaw Kissed off Transworld," *BusinessWeek,* September 29, 1986, p 68. Also see C J Loomis, "How the HP Board KO'd Carly," *Fortune,* March 7, 2005, pp 99–102; and B Worthen and J S Lublin, "Hurd Deal Inflamed Directors at H-P," *The Wall Street Journal,* August 16, 2010, pp A1–A2.

[83] See H Ibarra and M Hunter, "How Leaders Create and Use Networks," *Harvard Business Review,* January 2007, pp 40–47; N Anand and J A Conger, "Capabilities of the Consummate Networker," *Organizational Dynamics,* no 1, 2007, pp 13–27; and R Cross and R J Thomas, "How Top Talent Uses Networks and Where Rising Stars Get Trapped," *Organizational Dynamics,* April–June 2008, pp 165–80.

[84] Drawn from J T Arnold, "Employee Networks," *HR Magazine,* June 2006, pp 145–52.

[85] Allen et al., "Organizational Politics," p 77. Also see D C Treadway, W A Hochwarter, C J Kacmar, and G R Ferris, "Political Will, Political Skill, and Political Behavior," *Journal of Organizational Behavior,* May 2005, pp 229–45.

[86] See B Fryer, "When Your Colleague Is a Saboteur," *Harvard Business Review,* November 2008, pp 41–45; and E Spitznagel, "How to Play Hooky in the Afternoon," *Bloomberg Businessweek,* April 4–10, 2011, p 96.

[87] A Rao, S M Schmidt, and L H Murray, "Upward Impression Management: Goals, Influence Strategies, and Consequences," *Human Relations,* February 1995, p 147.

[88] See W H Turnley and M C Bolino, "Achieving Desired Images While Avoiding Undesired Images: Exploring the Role of Self-Monitoring in Impression Management," *Journal of Applied Psychology,* April 2001, pp 351–60.

[89] Data from "Dressing for Success," *USA Today,* October 24, 2006, p 1B.

[90] "CEOs of Tomorrow," *BusinessWeek,* May 11, 2009, p 36.

[91] See S J Wayne and G R Ferris, "Influence Tactics, Affect, and Exchange Quality in Supervisor-Subordinate Interactions: A Laboratory Experiment and Field Study," *Journal of Applied Psychology,* October 1990, pp 487–99. For another version, see Table 1 (p 246) in S J Wayne and R C Liden, "Effects of Impression Management on Performance Ratings: A Longitudinal Study," *Academy of Management Journal,* February 1995, pp 232–60. Also see M C Bolino, J A Varela, B Bande, and W H Turnley, "The Impact of Impression-Management Tactics on Supervisor Ratings of Organizational Citizenship Behavior," *Journal of Organizational Behavior,* May 2006, pp 281–97.

[92] M E Mendenhall and C Wiley, "Strangers in a Strange Land: The Relationship between Expatriate Adjustment and Impression Management," *American Behavioral Scientist,* March 1994, pp 605–20.

[93] T E Becker and S L Martin, "Trying to Look Bad at Work: Methods and Motives for Managing Poor Impressions in Organizations," *Academy of Management Journal,* February 1995, p 191.

[94] Ibid., p 181. Also see M K Duffy, D C Ganster, and M Pagon, "Social Undermining in the Workplace," *Academy of Management Journal,* April 2002, pp 331–51; and M K Duffy, J D Shaw, B J Tepper, and K L Scott, "The Moderating Roles of Self-Esteem and Neuroticism in the Relationship between Group and Individual Undermining Behavior," *Journal of Applied Psychology,* September 2006, pp 1066–77.

[95] Adapted from Becker and Martin, "Trying to Look Bad at Work," pp 180–81.

[96] J Sandberg, "The Art of Showing Pure Incompetence at an Unwanted Task," *The Wall Street Journal,* April 17, 2008, p B1.

[97] Data from G R Ferris, D D Frink, D P S Bhawuk, J Zhou, and D C Gilmore, "Reactions of Diverse Groups to Politics in the Workplace," *Journal of Management,* no. 1, 1996, pp 23–44. For other findings from the same database, see G R Ferris, D D Frink, M C Galang, J Zhou, K M Kacmar, and J L Howard, "Perceptions of Organizational Politics: Prediction, Stress-Related Implications, and Outcomes," *Human Relations,* February 1996, pp 233–66. Also see C C Cruz, L R Gómez-Mejia, and M Becerra, "Perceptions of Benevolence and the Design of Agency Contracts: CEO-TMT Relationships in Family Firms," *Academy of Management Journal,* February 2010, pp 69–89.

[98] A Drory and D Beaty, "Gender Differences in the Perception of Organizational Influence Tactics," *Journal of Organizational Behavior,* May 1991, pp 256–57.

[99] Based on L A Witt, T F Hilton, and W A Hochwarter, "Addressing Politics in Matrix Teams," *Group and Organization Management,* June 2001, pp 230–47. Also see C Chang, C C Rosen, and P E Levy, "The Relationship between Perceptions of Organizational Politics and Employee Attitudes, Strain, and Behavior: A Meta-Analytic Examination," *Academy of Management Journal,* August 2009, pp 779–801.

[100] D A Buchanan, "You Stab My Back, I'll Stab Yours: Management Experience and Perceptions of Organizational Political Behaviour," *British Journal of Management,* March 2008, p 49. Also see C Porath and C Pearson, "How Toxic Colleagues Corrode Performance," *Harvard Business Review,* April 2009, p 24.

[101] S A Akimoto and D M Sanbonmatsu, "Differences in Self-Effacing Behavior between European and Japanese Americans," *Journal of Cross-Cultural Psychology,* March 1999, pp 172–73.

[102] A Zaleznik, "Real Work," *Harvard Business Review,* January–February 1989, p 60.

[103] As quoted in D Lieberman, "Kraft Sees Benefits as Consumers Stay Home," *USA Today,* December 11, 2008, p 4B. Also see S Whitson, "Checking Passive Aggression," *HR Magazine,* June 2010, pp 115–16; D J Ketchen and M R Buckley, "Divas at Work: Dealing

with Drama Kings and Queens in Organizations," *Business Horizons,* November–December 2010, pp 599–606; and T Murphy, "Lunch Theater," *Bloomberg Businessweek,* April 11–17, 2011, pp 78–79.

104 D Rauch, "You're Driving Us Crazy. You've Got to Back Off," *Harvard Business Review,* April 2011, p 56.

105 J Fleming and L Schwarz, "Must I Save My Snooty Co-Worker from Making a Big Career Gaffe?" *Money,* April 2008, p 30.

CHAPTER 16

1 Excerpted from R Adams and L Schuker, "Time Inc.'s CEO Shown the Door," *The Wall Street Journal,* February 18, 2011, p B1.

2 The four commonalities were identified by P G Northouse, *Leadership: Theory and Practice,* 4th ed (Thousand Oaks, CA: Sage Publications, 2007), p 3. Also see A J Kinicki, K J L Jacobson, B M Galvin, and G E Prussia, "A Multilevel Systems Model of Leadership," *Journal of Leadership & Organizational Studies,* in press.

3 Ibid.

4 B Kellerman, "Leadership—Warts and All," *Harvard Business Review,* January 2004, p 45.

5 B M Bass and R Bass, *The Bass Handbook of Leadership: Theory, Research, and Managerial Applications,* 4th ed (New York: Free Press, 2008), p 654.

6 For a discussion about the differences between leading and managing, see Bass and Bass, *The Bass Handbook of Leadership,* pp 651–81.

7 See P Sellers, "The Next JetBlue," *Fortune,* July 26, 2010, pp 97–100.

8 See B Stone and P Burrows, "Opening Remarks: The Essence of Apple," *Bloomberg Businessweek,* January 24–January 20, 2011, pp 6–8; and P Ingrassia, "Ford's Renaissance Man," *The Wall Street Journal,* February 27–28, 2010, p A13.

9 For a summary, see Bass and Bass, pp 103–35.

10 See R Smith, "After 3 Years Pandit Comes Into His Own," *The Wall Street Journal,* December 11–12, 2011, pp B1, B3.

11 Implicit leadership theory is discussed by Bass and Bass, pp 46–78; and J S Mueller, J A Goncalo, and D Kamdar, "Recognizing Creative Leadership: Can Creative Idea Expression Negatively Relate to Perceptions of Leadership Potential?" *Journal of Experimental Social Psychology,* in press.

12 Results can be found in R G Lord, C L De Vader, and G M Alliger, "A Meta-Analysis of the Relation between Personality Traits and Leadership Perceptions: An Application of Validity Generalization Procedures," *Journal of Applied Psychology,* August 1986, pp 402–10.

13 See A H Eagly and J L Chin, "Diversity and Leadership in a Changing World," *American Psychologist,* April 2010, pp 216–24; and D D Cremer, M van Dijke, and D M Mayer, "Cooperating When 'You' and 'I' Are Treated Fairly: The Moderating Role of Leader Prototypicality," *Journal of Applied Psychology,* November 2010, pp 1121–33.

14 Results can be found in J M Kouzes and B Z Posner, *The Leadership Challenge* (San Francisco, CA: Jossey-Bass, 1995).

15 R S Nadler, *Leading with Emotional Intelligence* (New York: McGraw-Hill, 2011).

16 See D L Joseph and D A Newman, "Emotional Intelligence: An Integrative Meta-Analysis and Cascading Model, "*Journal of Applied Psychology,* January 2010, pp 54–78; and J Antonakis, N M Ashkanasy, and M T Dasborough, "Does Leadership Need Emotional Intelligence?" *The Leadership Quarterly,* April 2009, pp 247–61.

17 Results can be found in T A Judge, J E Hono, R Ilies, and M W Gerhardt, "Personality and Leadership: A Qualitative and Quantitative Review," *Journal of Applied Psychology,* August 2002, pp 765–80.

18 See T A Judge, A E Colbert, and R Ilies, "Intelligence and Leadership: A Quantitative Review and Test of Theoretical Propositions," *Journal of Applied Psychology,* June 2004, pp 542–52.

19 Kellerman's research can be found in B Kellerman, *Bad Leadership* (Boston: Harvard Business School Press, 2004).

20 "Nokia CEO's Letter to Employees," February 9, 2011, http://timesofindia.indiatimes.com/tech/news/telecom/Nokia-CEOs-letter-to-employees/art...

21 The trait definitions were quoted from ibid., pp 40–46. Some of the personal examples were taken from "The Worst Managers," *BusinessWeek,* January 19, 2009, p 42.

22 See A Morriss, R J Ely, and F X Frei, "Stop Holding Yourself Back," *Harvard Business Review,* January–February 2011, pp 160–64; and L Wiseman and G McKeown, "Bringing Out the Best In Your People," *Harvard Business Review,* May 2010, pp 117–21.

23 Gender and the emergence of leaders was examined by A H Eagly and S J Karau, "Gender and the Emergence of Leaders: A Meta-Analysis," *Journal of Personality and Social Psychology,* May 1991, pp 685–710; and R Ayman and K Korabik, "Leadership: Why Gender and Culture Matter," *American Psychologist,* April 2010, pp 157–70.

24 See A H Eagly, S J Karau, and B T Johnson, "Gender and Leadership Style among School Principals: A Meta-Analysis," *Educational Administration Quarterly,* February 1992, pp 76–102.

25 Supportive findings are contained in J M Twenge, "Changes in Women's Assertiveness in Response to Status and Roles: A Cross-Temporal Meta-Analysis, 1931–1993," *Journal of Personality and Social Psychology,* July 2001, pp 133–45.

26 For a summary of this research, see H Ibarra and O Obodaru, "Women and Vision Thing," *Harvard Business Review,* January 2009, pp 62–70.

27 D Zielinski, "Effective Assessments," *HR Magazine,* January 2011, pp 61–64.

28 See J Helyar and C Hymowitz, "Companies & Industries: The Recession Is Gone, and The CEO Could Be Next," *Bloomberg Businessweek,* February 7–February 13, 2011, pp 24–26; and "What Happened to Your Future Leaders?" *Training,* February 2010, p 11.

29 See N Doss, "Fast Food: East Meets West at Hamburger University," *Bloomberg Businessweek,* January 31–February 6, 2011, pp 22–23; and H Dolezalek, "Talent Scout," *Training,* February 2010, pp 52–56.

30 This research is summarized and critiqued by Bass and Bass, pp 497–538.

31 Results can be found in T A Judge, R F Piccolo, and R Ilies, "The Forgotten Ones? The Validity of Consideration and Initiating Structure in Leadership Research," *Journal of Applied Psychology,* February 2004, pp 36–51.

32 See S T Hannah and B J Avolio, "Ready or Not: How Do We Accelerate the Developmental Readiness of Leaders?" *Journal of Organizational Behavior,* November 2010, pp 1181–87; and J M Leigh, E R Shapiro, and S H Penney, "Developing Diverse, Collaborative Leaders: An Empirical Program Evaluation," *Journal of Leadership & Organizational Studies,* November 2010, pp 370–79.

33 Situational theories are discussed by Bass and Bass, pp 497–538.

34 For more on this theory, see F E Fiedler, "A Contingency Model of Leadership Effectiveness," in *Advances in Experimental Social Psychology,* vol 1, ed L Berkowitz (New York: Academic Press, 1964); and F E Fiedler, *A Theory of Leadership Effectiveness* (New York: McGraw-Hill, 1967).

35 See L H Peters, D D Hartke, and J T Pohlmann, "Fiedler's Contingency Theory of Leadership: An Application of the Meta-Analyses Procedures of Schmidt and Hunter," *Psychological Bulletin,* March 1985, pp 274–85; and C A Schriesheim, B J Tepper, and L A Tetrault, "Least Preferred Co-worker Score, Situational Control, and

Leadership Effectiveness: A Meta-Analysis of Contingency Model Performance Predictions," *Journal of Applied Psychology,* August 1994, pp 561–73.

[36] B Groysberg, A N McLean, and N Nohria, "Are Leaders Portable?" *Harvard Business Review,* May 2006, pp 95, 97.

[37] For more detail on this theory, see R J House, "A Path–Goal Theory of Leader Effectiveness," *Administrative Science Quarterly,* September 1971, pp 321–38.

[38] This research is summarized by R J House, "Path–Goal Theory of Leadership: Lessons, Legacy, and a Reformulated Theory," *The Leadership Quarterly,* Autumn 1996, pp 323–52.

[39] See R Siklos, "Bob Iger Rocks Disney," *Fortune,* January 19, 2009, pp 80–86.

[40] Results can be found in P M Podsakoff, S B MacKenzie, M Ahearne, and W H Bommer, "Searching for a Needle in a Haystack: Trying to Identify the Illusive Moderators of Leadership Behaviors," *Journal of Management,* 1995, pp 422–70.

[41] The steps were developed by H P Sims Jr, S Faraj, and S Yun, "When Should a Leader Be Directive or Empowering? How to Develop Your Own Situational Theory of Leadership," *Business Horizons,* March–April 2009, pp 149–58.

[42] See J B Wu, A S Tsui, and A J Kinicki, "Consequences of Differentiated Leadership in Groups," *Academy of Management Journal,* February 2010, pp 90–106.

[43] For a complete description of this theory, see B J Avolio and B M Bass, *A Manual for Full-Range Leadership Development* (Binghamton, NY: Center for Leadership Studies, 1991). The manual is now published by www.mindgarden.com.

[44] Results can be found in A H Eagly, M C Johannesen-Schmidt, and M L van Engen, "Transformational, Transactional, and Laissez-Faire Leadership Styles: A Meta-Analysis Comparing Women and Men," *Psychological Bulletin,* June 2003, pp 569–91.

[45] A definition and description of transactional leadership is provided by Bass and Bass, pp 618–48.

[46] Excerpted from D McGinn, "Battling Back from Betrayal," *Harvard Business Review,* December 2010, p 131.

[47] U R Dumdum, K B Lowe, and B J Avolio, "A Meta-Analysis of Transformational and Transactional Leadership Correlates of Effectiveness and Satisfaction: An Update and Extension," in *Transformational and Charismatic Leadership: The Road Ahead,* ed B J Avolio and F J Yammarino (New York: JAI Press, 2002), p 38.

[48] Supportive research is summarized by Bass and Bass, pp 618–48.

[49] Excerpted from D Brady, "Can GE Still Manage?" *Bloomberg Businessweek,* April 25, 2010, p 28.

[50] Supportive results can be found in P D Harms and M Credé, "Emotional Intelligence and Transformational and Transactional Leadership: A Meta-Analysis," *Journal of Leadership & Organizational Studies,* February 2010, pp 5–17; and J E Bono and T A Judge, "Personality and Transformational and Transactional Leadership: A Meta-Analysis," *Journal of Applied Psychology,* October 2004, pp 901–10.

[51] See Eagly, Johannesen-Schmidt, and van Engen.

[52] These definitions are derived from R Kark, B Shamir, and C Chen, "The Two Faces of Transformational Leadership: Empowerment and Dependency," *Journal of Applied Psychology,* April 2003, pp 246–55.

[53] B Nanus, *Visionary Leadership* (San Francisco, CA: Jossey-Bass, 1992), p 8.

[54] T Bisoux, "Making Connections," *BizEd,* January–February 2009, p 22. Also see "Carl-Henric Svanberg," *The New York Times,* March 16, 2011, http://topics.nytimes.com/top/reference/timestopics/people/s/carlhenric_svanberg/index.ht...

[55] J Reingold, "Meet Your New Leader," *Fortune,* November 24, 2008, p 146.

[56] See Brady, p 28.

[57] Results can be found in U R Dumdum, K B Lowe, and B J Avolio, "A Meta-Analysis of Transformational and Transactional Leadership Correlates of Effectiveness and Satisfaction: An Update and Extension," in *Transactional and Charismatic Leadership: The Road Ahead,* ed B J Avolio and F J Yammarino (New York: JAI, 2002), pp 35–66.

[58] See K B Lowe, K G Kroeck, and N Sivasubramaniam, "Effectiveness Correlates of Transformational and Transactional Leadership: A Meta-Analytic Review of the MLQ Literature," *The Leadership Quarterly,* 1996, pp 385–425.

[59] Visionary leadership is studied by C A Hartnell and F O Walumbwa, "Transformational Leadership and Organizational Culture," in *The Handbook of Organizational Culture and Climate,* 2nd ed, ed N M Ashkanasy, C P M Wilderom, and M F Peterson (Thousand Oaks, CA: Sage, 2011), pp 225–48; and M A Griffin, S K Parker, and C M Mason, "Leader Vision and the Development of Adaptive and Proactive Performance: A Longitudinal Study," *Journal of Applied Psychology,* January 2010, pp 174–82.

[60] Supportive results can be found in T A Judge and R F Piccolo, "Transformational and Transactional Leadership: A Meta-Analytic Test of Their Relative Validity," *Journal of Applied Psychology,* October 2004, pp 755–68.

[61] X-H Wang and J M Howell, "Exploring the Dual-Level Effects of Transformational Leadership on Followers," *Journal of Applied Psychology,* November 2010, pp 1134–44.

[62] T Whitford and S A Moss, "Transformational Leadership in Distributed Work Groups: The Moderating Role of Follower Regulatory Focus and Goal Orientation," *Communication Research,* December 2009, pp 810–37.

[63] See A J Towler, "Effects of Charismatic Influence Training on Attitudes, Behavior, and Performance," *Personnel Psychology,* Summer 2003, pp 363–81; and M Frese and S Beimel, "Action Training for Charismatic Leadership: Two Evaluations of Studies of a Commercial Training Module on Inspirational Communication of a Vision," *Personnel Psychology,* Autumn 2003, pp 671–97.

[64] These recommendations were derived from J M Howell and B J Avolio, "The Ethics of Charismatic Leadership: Submission or Liberation?" *Academy of Management Executive,* May 1992, pp 43–54.

[65] See F Dansereau Jr, G Graen, and W Haga, "A Vertical Dyad Linkage Approach to Leadership within Formal Organizations," *Organizational Behavior and Human Performance,* February 1975, pp 46–78; and K S Wilson, H-P Sin, and D E Conlon, "What About the Leader in Leader-Member Exchange? The Impact of Resource Exchanges and Substitutability on the Leader," *Academy of Management Review,* July 2010, pp 358–72.

[66] These descriptions were taken from D Duchon, S G Green, and T D Taber, "Vertical Dyad Linkage: A Longitudinal Assessment of Antecedents, Measures, and Consequences," *Journal of Applied Psychology,* February 1986, pp 56–60.

[67] Supportive results can be found in B Erodogan and T N Bauer, "Differentiated Leader-Member Exchanges: The Buffering Role of Justice Climate," *Journal of Applied Psychology,* November 2010, pp 1104–20; and L W Hughes, J B Avey, and D R Nixon, "Relationships Between Leadership and Followers' Quitting Intentions and Job Search Behaviors," *Journal of Leadership & Organizational Studies,* November 2010, pp 351–62.

[68] Results can be found in R Ilies, J D Nahrgang, and F P Morgeson, "Leader–Member Exchange and Citizenship Behaviors: A Meta-Analysis," *Journal of Applied Psychology,* January 2007, pp 269–77.

[69] See V Venkataramani, S G Green, and D J Schleicher, "Well-Connected Leaders: The Impact of Leaders' Social Network Ties on LMX and Members' Work Attitudes," *Journal of Applied Psychology,* November 2010, pp 1071–84; R Eisenberger, G Karagonlar, F Stinglhamber, P Neves, T E Becker, M G Gonzalez-Morales, and M Steiger-Mueller, "Leader-Member Exchange and Affective

Organizational Commitment: The Contribution of Supervisor's Organizational Embodiment," *Journal of Applied Psychology,* November 2010, pp 1085–1103.

[70] These recommendations were derived from G C Mage, "Leading Despite Your Boss," *HR Magazine,* September 2003, pp 139–44.

[71] R J House and R N Aditya, "The Social Scientific Study of Leadership Quo Vadis?" *Journal of Management,* 1997, p 457.

[72] C L Pearce and J A Conger, "All Those Years Ago: The Historical Underpinnings of Shared Leadership," in *Shared Leadership: Reframing the Hows and Whys of Leadership,* ed C L Pearce and J A Conger (Thousand Oaks, CA: Sage, 2002), p 1.

[73] This research is summarized in B J Avolio, J J Sosik, D I Jung, and Y Berson, "Leadership Models, Methods, and Applications," in *Handbook of Psychology: Industrial and Organizational Psychology,* vol. 12, ed W C Borman, D R Ilgen, and R J Klimoski (Hoboken, NJ: John Wiley & Sons, 2003), pp 277–307.

[74] An overall summary of servant-leadership is provided by L C Spears, *Reflections on Leadership: How Robert K Greenleaf's Theory of Servant-Leadership Influenced Today's Top Management Thinkers* (New York: John Wiley & Sons, 1995).

[75] D MacMillan, "Survivor: CEO Edition," *Bloomberg Businessweek,* March 1, 2010, p 35.

[76] J Stuart, *Fast Company,* September 1999, p 114.

[77] "The Best Advice I Ever Got," *Fortune,* May 12, 2008, p 74.

[78] Supportive results can be found in F O Walumbwa, C A Hartnell, and A Oke, "Servant Leadership, Procedural Justice Climate, Service Climate, Employee Attitudes, and Organizational Citizenship Behavior: A Cross-Level Investigation," *Journal of Applied Psychology,* May 2010, pp 517–29; and R C Liden, S J Wayne, H Zhao, and D Henderson, "Servant Leadership: Development of a Multidimensional Measure and Multi-Level Assessment," *The Leadership Quarterly,* April 2008, pp 161–77.

[79] The role of followers is discussed by D S DeRue and S J Ashford, "Who Will Lead and Who Will Follow? A Social Process of Leadership Identity Construction in Organizations," *Academy of Management Review,* October 2010.

[80] Bass and Bass, p 408.

[81] See L Bossidy, "What Your Leader Expects of You and What You Should Expect in Return," *Harvard Business Review,* April 2007, pp 58–65.

[82] See R Goffee and G Jones, "Followership: It's Personal, Too," *Harvard Business Review,* December 2001, p 148.

[83] This checklist was proposed by J J Gabarro and J P Kotter, "Managing Your Boss," *Harvard Business Review,* January 2005, pp 92–99.

[84] These ideas were partially based on B Dattner, "Forewarned Is Forearmed," *BusinessWeek,* September 1, 2008, p 50; and P Drucker, "Managing Oneself," *Harvard Business Review,* January 2005, pp 2–11.

[85] The following suggestions were discussed by Gabarro and Kotter, "Managing Your Boss." Also see J Banks and D Coutu, "How to Protect Your Job in a Recession," *Harvard Business Review,* September 2008, pp 113–16.

[86] Excerpted from R Frank, "Tilton Flaunts Her Style at Patriarch," *The Wall Street Journal,* January 8–9, 2011, pp B1, B17.

[87] N Justin, "Political Pranksters Keep Getting Savvier," *The Arizona Republic,* March 17, 2011, p A10.

[88] M Gerson, "No Journalism Ethic Justifies NPR Video Attack," *The Arizona Republic,* March 17, 2011, p B5.

[89] J Hook and D Yadron, "Spending Bill Passes, NPR Targeted," *The Wall Street Journal,* March 18, 2011, p A4.

[90] Justin, p A10.

[91] Gerson, p B5.

CHAPTER 17

[1] Excerpted from E Maltby, "Boring Meetings? Get Out the Water Guns," *The Wall Street Journal,* January 7, 2010, p B5.

[2] "Ellen Kullman," *Fortune,* December 6, 2010, p 139.

[3] P Nunes and T Breene, "Reinvent Your Business Before It's Too Late: Watch Out for Those S Curves," *Harvard Business Review,* January–February 2011, p 82.

[4] C I Barnard, *The Functions of the Executive* (Cambridge, MA: Harvard University Press, 1938), p 73.

[5] Drawn from E H Schein, *Organizational Psychology,* 3rd ed (Englewood Cliffs, NJ: Prentice Hall, 1980), pp 12–15.

[6] See V Smeets and F Warzynski, "Too Many Theories, Too Few Facts: What the Data Tell Us about the Link between Span of Control, Compensation, and Career Dynamics," *Labour Economics,* August 2008, pp 688–704.

[7] See G Anders, "Overseeing More Employees—With Fewer Managers," *The Wall Street Journal,* March 24, 2008, p B6.

[8] A management-oriented discussion of general systems theory can be found in K E Boulding, "General Systems Theory—The Skeleton of Science," *Management Science,* April 1956, pp 197–208. For more recent systems-related ideas, see A J Kinicki, K J L Jacobson, B M Galvin, and G E Prussia, "A Multi-Systems Model of Leadership," *Journal of Leadership & Organizational Studies,* in press.

[9] See J Bussey, "Nation Will Rebuild from Quake but Faces Other Daunting Tests," *The Wall Street Journal,* March 25, 2011, pp B1, B5; and A Dowell, "Japan: The Business Aftershocks," *The Wall Street Journal,* March 25, 2011, pp B1, B4.

[10] M Sanchanta, "Wal-Mart's Local Team Shifts Into Crisis Mode," *The Wall Street Journal,* March 25, 2011, p B1.

[11] N E Boudette and J Bennett, "Henry Ford Maxim Is Reversed," *The Wall Street Journal,* March 25, 2011, p B5.

[12] R M Fulmer and J B Keys, "A Conversation with Peter Senge: New Development in Organizational Learning," *Organizational Dynamics,* Autumn 1998, p 35.

[13] This definition was based on D A Garvin, "Building a Learning Organization," *Harvard Business Review,* July–August 1993, pp 78–91.

[14] S Mohammed, L Ferzandi, and K Hamilton, "Metaphor No More: A 15-Year Review of the Team Mental Model Construct," *Journal of Management,* July 2010, p 879.

[15] This discussion and quotes come from F Gino and G P Pisano, "Why Leaders Don't Learn from Success," *Harvard Business Review,* April 2011, pp 68–74.

[16] A Zolli and A M Healy, "Vision Statement: When Failure Looks Like Success," *Harvard Business Review,* April 2011, pp 30–31.

[17] K Dillon, "'I Think of My Failures as a Gift,'" *Harvard Business Review,* April 2011, p 86.

[18] A G Lafley, *Wikipedia.* Last updated January 13, 2011, http://en.wikipedia.org/wiki/A._G._Lafley.

[19] See A C Edmondson, "Strategies For Learning From Failure," *Harvard Business Review,* April 2011, pp 48–55.

[20] See P M Madsen and V Desai, "Failing to Learn? The Effects of Failure and Success on Organizational Learning in the Global Orbital Launch Vehicle Industry," *Academy of Management Journal,* June 2010, pp 451–76.

[21] A C Edmondson, "The Competitive Imperative of Learning," *Harvard Business Review,* July–August 2008, p 62.

[22] R Greenwood and D Miller, "Tackling Design Anew: Getting Back to the Heart of Organizational Theory," *Academy of Management Perspectives,* November 2010, p 78.

[23] Reviews of organizational design are provided by R E Miles, C C Snow, Ø D Fjeldstad, G Miles, and C Lettl, "Designing Organizations to Meet 21st-Century Opportunities and Challenges," *Organizational Dynamics,* April–June 2010, pp 93–103; and J R Galbraith, "The Multi-Dimensional and Reconfigurable Organization," *Organizational Dynamics,* April–June 2010, 115–25.

[24] M C Mankins and P Rogers, "The Decision-Driven Organization," *Harvard Business Review,* June 2010, pp 56–57.

[25] See ibid, and "Full Speed Ahead," *HR Magazine,* March 2011, p 18.

[26] The following discussion is based on N Anand and R L Daft, "What Is the Right Organization Design?" *Organizational Dynamics,* 2007, pp 329–44.

[27] "GE Businesses," Retrieved March 26, 2011, from http://www .ge.com/citizenship/about-citizenship/ge-citizneship-facts/ ge-businesses.html.

[28] See R Adams, "Hachette to Break through 'Silos' as It Restructures Women's Magazines," *The Wall Street Journal,* March 2, 2009, p B1.

[29] J R Galbraith, *Designing Matrix Organizations That Actually Work* (San Francisco, CA: Jossey-Bass, 2009), p ix.

[30] Ibid, p 332.

[31] P Lawrence, "Herman Miller's Creative Network," *BusinessWeek,* February 15, 2008, www.businessweek.com (interview with Brian Walker).

[32] Anand and Daft, p 338.

[33] D Kiley, "Nokia Starts Listening," *BusinessWeek,* May 5, 2008, p 30.

[34] See "Successfully Transitioning to a Virtual Organization: Challenges, Impact and Technology," *SHRM Research Quarterly,* First Quarter 2010, pp 1–9.

[35] A Pomeroy, "Passion, Obsession Drive the 'Eileen Fisher Way,'" *HR Magazine,* July 2007, p 55.

[36] A Bruzzese, "Employers Can Harness Social Media," *The Arizona Republic,* July 21, 2010, p CL1.

[37] See J E Vascellaro, "Bartz Remakes Yahoo's Top Ranks," *The Wall Street Journal,* February 27, 2009, p B.

[38] J Ewers, "No Ideas? You're Not Alone," *US News & World Report,* June 18, 2007, pp 50–52, quoting from p 51.

[39] P Kaestle, "A New Rationale for Organizational Structure," *Planning Review,* July–August 1990, p 22.

[40] Details of this study can be found in T Burns and G M Stalker, *The Management of Innovation* (London: Tavistock, 1961).

[41] J D Sherman and H L Smith, "The Influence of Organizational Structure on Intrinsic versus Extrinsic Motivation," *Academy of Management Journal,* December 1984, p 883.

[42] See J A Courtright, G T Fairhurst, and L E Rogers, "Interaction Patterns in Organic and Mechanistic Systems," *Academy of Management Journal,* December 1989, pp 773–802.

[43] A Taylor III, "Can This Car Save Ford?" *Fortune,* April 22, 2008, http://money.cnn.com.

[44] P Gumbel, "Big Mac's Local Flavor," *Fortune,* May 2, 2008, http:// money.cnn.com.

[45] See Galbraith, *Designing Matrix Organizations That Actually Work.*

[46] Galbraith, "The Multi-Dimensional and Reconfigurable Organization."

[47] A Hesseldahl, "BlackBerry: Innovation behind the Icon," *BusinessWeek,* April 4, 2008, www.businessweek.com.

[48] Anand and Daft, pp 333–40.

[49] M Kripalani, "Inside the Tata Nano Factory," *BusinessWeek,* May 9, 2008, www.businessweek.com.

[50] J Holland, "Innovative Outsourcing Model Saves Company Millions," *Industry Week,* April 25, 2007, www.industryweek.com.

[51] A MacCormack and T Forbath, "Learning the Fine Art of Global Collaboration," *Harvard Business Review,* January 2008, pp 24, 26.

[52] See M J Robson, C S Katsikeas, and D C Bello, "Drivers and Performance Outcomes of Trust in International Strategic Alliances: The Role of Organizational Complexity," *Organization Science,* July–August 2008, pp 647–65.

[53] K Cameron, "Critical Questions in Assessing Organizational Effectiveness," *Organizational Dynamics,* Autumn 1980, p 70.

[54] A Taylor III, "Hyundai Smokes the Competition," *Fortune,* January 18, 2010, p 69.

[55] See R S Kaplan and D P Norton, "Having Trouble with Your Strategy? Then Map It," *Harvard Business Review,* September–October 2000, pp 167–76.

[56] Taylor III, "Hyundai Smokes the Competition," pp 66, 68.

[57] Cameron, p 67.

[58] See R J Martinez and P M Norman, "Whither Reputation? The Effects of Different Stakeholders," *Business Horizons,* September–October 2004, pp 25–32.

[59] P Dvorak, "How Irdeto Split Headquarters," *The Wall Street Journal,* January 7, 2008, p B3.

[60] K S Cameron, "Effectiveness as Paradox: Consensus and Conflict in Conceptions of Organizational Effectiveness," *Management Science,* May 1986, p 542.

[61] See J Antioco, "How I Did It … Blockbuster's Former CEO on Sparring with an Activist Shareholder," *Harvard Business Review,* April 2011, pp 39–44.

[62] Excerpted from P Lorange and R T Nelson, "How to Recognize—and Avoid—Organizational Decline," *Sloan Management Review,* Spring 1987, pp 43–45.

[63] See "How eBay Developed a Culture of Experimentation," *Harvard Business Review,* March 2011, pp 93–97; and L McCreary, "Kaiser Permanente's Innovation on the Front Lines," *Harvard Business Review,* September 2010, pp 92–97.

[64] See L Landro, "The Time to Innovate Is Now," *The Wall Street Journal,* March 28, 2011, p R1; and L Landro, "Delivering Results," *The Wall Street Journal,* March 28, 2011, p R7.

[65] See D Senor and S Singer, *Start-Up Nation: The Story of Israel's Economic Miracle* (New York: Twelve, 2009).

[66] A Fisher, "America's Most Admired Companies," *Fortune,* March 17, 2008, p 66.

[67] "How P&G Plans to Clean Up," *BusinessWeek,* April 13, 2009, p 44.

[68] J I Cash Jr, M J Earl, and R Morison, "Teaming Up to Crack Innovation Enterprise Integration," *Harvard Business Review,* November 2008, pp 90–100.

[69] See "Innovation Nations," *BusinessWeek,* April 6, 2009, p 10; and R Jana, "Spending on Innovation: A Casualty of the Recession," *BusinessWeek,* April 20, 2009, p 58.

[70] J Welch and S Welch, "Finding Innovation Where It Lives," *BusinessWeek,* April 21, 2008, p 84.

[71] See S LeVine, "IBM Piles Up Patents, but Quantity Isn't King," *Bloomberg Businessweek,* January 25, 2010, p 53; and "IBM," *Fortune,* March 21, 2011, pp 116–24.

[72] Source quoted in S Berkum, *The Myths of Innovation* (Sebastopol, CA: O'Reilly Media, 2007), p 44.

[73] I Rowley, "Drive, He Thought," *BusinessWeek,* April 20, 2009, p 12.

[74] This discussion is based on Berkum.

[75] Curiosity is examined by S H Harrison, D M Sluss, and B E Ashforth, "Curiosity Adapted the Cat: The Role of Trait Curiosity in Newcomere Adaptation," *Journal of Applied Psychology,* January 2011, pp 211–20.

[76] D Ariely, "Why Business Don't Experiment," *Harvard Business Review,* April 2010, p 34.

[77] See D Kiley and C Matlack, "Fiat: On the Road Back to America," *BusinessWeek,* April 20, 2009, p 28.

[78] R Jana, "Inspiration from Emerging Economies," *BusinessWeek,* March 23 and 30, 2009, p 41.

[79] This discussion is based on Berkum.

[80] "The Next Smart Thing," *The Wall Street Journal,* March 7, 2011, p R8.

[81] L A Bettencourt, "The Customer-Centered Innovation Map," *Harvard Business Review,* May 2008, p 109.

[82] See C Hartnell, Y Ou, and A Kinicki, "Organizational Culture and Organizational Effectiveness: A Meta-Analytic Investigation of the Competing Values Framework's Theoretical Suppositions," *Journal of Applied Psychology,* in press.

[83] See S Prokesch, "How GE Teaches Teams to Lead Change," *Harvard Business Review,* January 2009, pp 99–106.

[84] See L Gumusluoglu and A Ilsev, "Transformational Leadership and Organizational Innovation: The Roles of Internal and External Support for Innovation," *Journal of Product Innovation Management,* May 2009, pp 264–75.

[85] See J N Choi and J Y Chang, "Innovation Implementation in the Public Sector: An Integration of Institutional and Collective Dynamics," *Journal of Applied Psychology,* January 2009, pp 245–53; and F Yuon and R W Woodman, "Innovative Behavior in the Work-place: The Role of Performance and Image Outcome Expectations," *Academy of Management Journal,* April 2010, pp 323–42.

[86] L Bossidy and R Charan, *Execution: The Discipline of Getting Things Done* (New York: Crown Business, 2002), p 22.

[87] How eBay Developed a Culture of Experimentation," *Harvard Business Review,* March 2011, p 96.

[88] Excerpted from J C Spender and B Strong, "Who Has Innovative Ideas? Employees," *The Wall Street Journal,* August 23, 2010, p R5.

[89] Excerpted from J Angwin, "The Web's New Gold Mine: Your Secrets," *The Wall Street Journal,* July 31–August 1, 2010, p W1.

CHAPTER 18

[1] Excerpted from G Sandstrom and C Lawton, "Nokia CEO Makes His Mark," *The Wall Street Journal,* October 22, 2010, p B3; and C Ziegler, "Nokia CEO Stephen Elop Rallies Troops in Brutally Honest 'Burning Platform' Memo?" Retrieved April 8, 2011, from http://www.engadget.com/2011/02/08/nokia-ceo-stephen-elop-rallies-troups-in-brutally-hon…

[2] See G Colvin, "Grading Jeff Immelt," *Fortune,* February 28, 2011, pp 75–80; and M Moskowitz, R Levering, and C Tkaczyk, "The 100 Best Companies to Work For," *Fortune,* February 7, 2011, pp 91–101.

[3] "Capitalizing on Complexity," IBM Corporation, May 2010.

[4] A M Webber, "Learning for a Change," *Fast Company,* May 1999, p 180.

[5] See "Training Top 125," *Training,* January–February 2011, pp 54–93.

[6] E Byron, "How to Market to an Aging Boomer: Flattery, Subter-fuge and Euphemism," *The Wall Street Journal,* February 2, 2011, pp A1, A12.

[7] P Coy, "A Message from the Street," *Bloomberg Businessweek,* February 7–February 13, 2011, pp 58–65.

[8] See "Social Networking Comes to Fore as Regular Recruiting Tool," *HR Trendbook HR Magazine,* 2011, p 63.

[9] See D Bennett, "I'll Have My Robots Talk to Your Robots," *Bloomberg Businessweek,* February 21–February 27, 2011, pp 52–61.

[10] See P Dvorak, "Companies Seek Shareholder Input on Pay Prac-tices," *The Wall Street Journal,* April 6, 2009, p B4.

[11] See D Welch, "For Dan Akerson, A Magic Moment to Remake GM," *Bloomberg Business Week,* January 24–January 30, 2011, pp 21–22; and J Shambora, A Lashinsky, B Gimbel, and J Schlosser, "A View from the Top," *Fortune,* March 16, 2009, p 110.

[12] H L Lee, "Don't Tweak Your Supply Chain—Rethink It End to End," *Harvard Business Review,* October 2010, pp 64–65.

[13] Y Takahashi, "Strikes in China Roil Honda's Strategy," *The Wall Street Journal,* June 24, 2010, p B3.

[14] See D Voreacos, A Nussbaum, and G Farrell, "Johnson & Johnson Fights to Clear Its Once-Trusted Name," *Bloomberg Businessweek,* April 4–April 10, 2011, pp 64–71; and A Nussbaum and D Voreacos, "J&J CEO Weldon Has 'No Plans' to Retire, Focuses on Recalls," *Bloomberg Businessweek,* April 9, 2011. Retrieved from http://www.businessweek.com/news/2011-03-18/j-j-ceo-weldon-has-no-plans-to-retire.focu…

[15] L Wheeler, "Change Every Day," *Training,* October 2008, p 51.

[16] This three-way typology of change was adapted from discussion in P C Nutt, "Tactics of Implementation," *Academy of Management Journal,* June 1986, pp 230–61.

[17] For a thorough discussion of the model, see K Lewin, *Field Theory in Social Science* (New York: Harper & Row, 1951); and J Helms, K Dye, and A J Mills, *Understanding Organizational Change* (New York: Routledge, 2009) pp 39–55.

[18] These assumptions are discussed in E H Schein, *Organizational Psychology,* 3rd ed (Englewood Cliffs, NJ: Prentice Hall, 1980).

[19] D Brady, "Etc. Hard Choices: Howard Schultz," *Bloomberg Businessweek,* April 4–April 10, 2011, p 102.

[20] See ibid.

[21] C Goldwasser, "Benchmarking: People Make the Process," *Management Review,* June 1995, p 40.

[22] See D Shaner, *The Seven Arts of Change* (New York: Union Square Press, 2010).

[23] Details of this example can be found in D Kesmodel, "How 'Chief Beer Taster' Blended Molson, Coors," *The Wall Street Journal,* October 1, 2007, pp B1, B5.

[24] These errors are discussed in J P Kotter, "Leading Change: When Transformation Efforts Fail," *Harvard Business Review,* January 2007, pp 96–103.

[25] See L Freifeld, "Changes with Penguins," *Training,* June 2008, pp 24–28; and J P Kotter, "Transformation," *Leadership Excellence,* December 2008, p 20.

[26] J Fortt, "Yahoo's Taskmaster," *Fortune,* April 27, 2009, p 83.

[27] P G Hanson and B Lubin, "Answers to Questions Frequently Asked about Organization Development," in *The Emerging Practice of Organization Development,* ed W Sikes, A Drexler, and J Grant (Alexandria, VA: NTL Institute, 1989), p 16.

[28] Reviews of organizational development are provided by L Martins, "Organizational Change and Development," *Handbook of Industrial and Organizational Psychology,* 2011, pp 691–728.

[29] See R Rodgers, J E Hunter, and D L Rogers, "Influence of Top Management Commitment on Management Program Success," *Journal of Applied Psychology,* February 1993, pp 151–55.

[30] Results can be found in P J Robertson, D R Roberts, and J I Porras, "Dynamics of Planned Organizational Change: Assessing Empirical Support for a Theoretical Model," *Academy of Management Journal,* June 1993, pp 619–34.

[31] Results from the meta-analysis can be found in G A Neuman, J E Edwards, and N S Raju, "Organizational Development Interventions: A Meta-Analysis of Their Effects on Satisfaction and Other Attitudes," *Personnel Psychology,* Autumn 1989, pp 461–90.

[32] Results can be found in C-M Lau and H-Y Ngo, "Organization Development and Firm Performance: A Comparison of Multinational and Local Firms," *Journal of International Business Studies,* First Quarter 2001, pp 95–114.

[33] J D Ford, L W Ford, and A D'Amelio, "Resistance to Change: The Rest of the Story," *Academy of Management Review,* April 2008, p 362.

[34] See J D Ford and L W Ford, "Stop Blaming Resistance to Change and Start Using It," *Organizational Dynamics,* January–March 2010, pp 24–36.

[35] Adapted from R J Marshak, *Covert Processes at Work* (San Francisco, CA: Berrett-Koehler Publishers, 2006); and A S Judson, *Changing Behavior in Organizations: Minimizing Resistance to Change* (Cambridge, MA: Blackwell, 1991).

[36] An individual's predisposition to change was investigated by E Lamm and J R Gordon, "Empowerment, Predisposition to Resist Change, and Support for Organizational Change," *Journal of Leadership & Organizational Studies,* November 2010, pp 426–37.

[37] Research regarding resilience is discussed by K Kersting, "Resilience: The Mental Muscle Everyone Has," *Monitor on Psychology,* April 2005, pp 32–33.

[38] R Cornum, M D Matthews, and M E P Seligman, "Comprehensive Soldier Fitness," *American Psychologist,* January 2011, p 4; Also see K J Reivich, M E P Seligman, and S McBride, "Master Resilience Training in the US Army," *American Psychologist,* January 2011, pp 25–34.

[39] See R H Schaffer, "Mistakes Leaders Keep Making," *Harvard Business Review,* September 2010, pp 86–91.

[40] L Goering, "Land of Plenty No Longer," *Chicago Tribune,* May 20, 2008, sec 1, p 8.

[41] See D M Harold, D B Fedor, S Caldwell, and Y Liu, "The Effects of Transformational and Change Leadership on Employees' Commitment to Change: A Multilevel Study," *Journal of Applied Psychology,* March 2008, pp 346–57.

[42] See R H Miles, "Accelerating Corporate Transformations (Don't Lose Your Nerve!)," *Harvard Business Review,* January–February 2010, pp 69–75.

[43] See S A Furst and D M Cable, "Employee Resistance to Organizational Change: Managerial Influence Tactics and Leader-Member Exchange," *Journal of Applied Psychology,* March 2008, pp 453–62.

[44] J P Kotter, "Leading Change: Why Transformation Efforts Fail," *Harvard Business Review,* 1995, p 64.

[45] J P Kotter and L A Schlesinger, "Choosing Strategies for Change," *Harvard Business Review,* July–August 2008, pp 130–39.

[46] The stress response is thoroughly discussed by H Selye, *Stress without Distress* (New York: J B Lippincott, 1974).

[47] See T A Wright, "The Role of Psychological Well-Being in Job Performance, Employee Retention and Cardiovascular Health," *Organizational Dynamics,* January–March 2010, pp 13–23.

[48] J M Ivancevich and M T Matteson, *Stress and Work: A Managerial Perspective* (Glenview, IL: Scott, Foresman, 1980), pp 8–9.

[49] See Selye.

[50] See J D Nahrgang, F P Morgeson, and D A Hoffman, "Safety at Work: A Meta-Analytic Investigation of the Link Between Job Demands, Job Resources, Burnout, Engagement, and Safety Outcomes," *Journal of Applied Psychology,* January 2011, pp 71–94; and S Ohly and C Fritz, "Work Characteristics, Challenge Appraisal, Creativity, and Proactive Behavior: A Multi-level Study," *Journal of Organizational Behavior,* May 2010, pp 543–65.

[51] F M McKee-Ryan, Z Song, C R Wanberg, and A J Kinicki, "Psychological and Physical Well-Being during Unemployment: A Meta-Analytic Study," *Journal of Applied Psychology,* January 2005, pp 53–76; and P Butterworth, L S Leach, L Strazdins, S C Olesen, B Rodgers, and D H Broom, "The Psychosocial Quality of Work Determines Whether Employment Has Benefits for Mental Health: Results from a Longitudinal National Household Panel Study," *Occupational & Environmental Medicine,* March 14, 2011, http://oem.bmj.com/content/early/2011/02/26/oem.2010.059030.abstract?sid=716907ef-4e

[52] See C Binnewies, S Sonnentag, and E J Mojza, "Daily Performance at Work: Feeling Recovered in the Morning as a Predictor of Day-Level Job Performance," *Journal of Organizational Behavior,* January 2009, pp 67–93.

[53] "Too Much Information," *HR Magazine,* January 2011, p 19.

[54] The issue of environmental conditions is discussed by A Bruzzese, "Is the Building Making You 'Sick' of Work?" *The Arizona Republic,* January 29, 2005, p D3.

[55] See R A Clay, "Stressed in America," *Monitor on Psychology,* January 2011, pp 60–61.

[56] The discussion of appraisal is based on R S Lazarus and S Folkman, *Stress, Appraisal, and Coping* (New York: Springer Publishing, 1984).

[57] Results are presented in J A Penley, J Tomaka, and J S Wiebe, "The Association of Coping to Physical and Psychological Health Outcomes: A Meta-Analytic Review," *Journal of Behavioral Medicine,* December 2002, pp 551–609.

[58] See J D Kammeyer-Mueller, T A Judge, and B A Scott, "The Role of Core Self-Evaluations in the Coping Process," *Journal of Applied Psychology,* January 2009, pp 177–95.

[59] This definition was modified from C Fritz, M Yankelevich, A Zarubin, and P Barger, "Happy, Health, and Productive: The Role of Detachment From Work During Nonwork Time," *Journal of Applied Psychology,* September 2010, pp 977–83.

[60] See ibid; S Sonnentag, C Binnewies, and E J Mojza, "Staying Well and Engaged When Demands Are High: The Role of Psychological Detachment," *Journal of Applied Psychology,* September 2010, pp 965–76; and C Fritz, S Sonnentag, P E Spector, and J A McInroe, "The Weekend Matters: Relationships between Stress Recovery and Affective Experiences," *Journal of Organizational Behavior,* November 2010, pp 1137–62.

[61] Supportive results can be found in R Ilies, N Dimotakis, and I E De Pater, "Psychological and Physiological Reactions to High Workloads: Implications for Well-Being," *Personnel Psychology,* Summer 2010, pp 407–36; and E R Crawford, J A LePine, and B L Rich, "Linking Job Demands and Resources to Employee Engagement and Burnout: A Theoretical Extension and Meta-Analytic Test," *Journal of Applied Psychology,* September 2010, pp 834–48.

[62] See M R Frone, "Are Work Stressors Related to Employee Substance Use? The Importance of Temporal Context in Assessments of Alcohol and Illicit Drug Use," *Journal of Applied Psychology,* January 2008, pp 199–206.

[63] Supportive results can be found in Wright, "The Role of Psychological Well-Being in Job Performance, Employee Retention and Cardiovascular Health;" and P Steel, J Schmidt, and J Shultz, "Refining the Relationship between Personality and Subjective Well-Being," *Psychological Bulletin,* January 2008, pp 138–61; and G E Miller, E Chen, and E S Zhou, "If It Goes Up, Must It Come Down? Chronic Stress and the Hypothalamic-Pituitary-Adrenocortical Axis in Humans," *Psychological Bulletin,* January 2007, pp 25–45.

[64] Types of support are discussed by S Cohen and T A Wills, "Stress, Social Support, and the Buffering Hypothesis," *Psychological Bulletin,* September 1985, pp 310–57.

[65] See W Arnold, "Studies Show Friendships May Be Factor in Keeping Us Alive," *The Arizona Republic,* March 5, 2011, p Z15; and R Ilies, M D Johnson, T A Judge, and J Keeney, "A Within-Individual Study of Interpersonal Conflict as a Work Stressor: Dispositional and Situational Moderators," *Journal of Organizational Behavior,* January 2011, pp 44–64.

[66] This pioneering research is presented in S C Kobasa, "Stressful Life Events, Personality, and Health: An Inquiry into Hardiness," *Journal of Personality and Social Psychology,* January 1979, pp 1–11.

[67] See S C Kobasa, S R Maddi, and S Kahn, "Hardiness and Health: A Prospective Study," *Journal of Personality and Social Psychology,* January 1982, pp 168–77.

[68] Results from this study are discussed in S R Maddi, "On Hardiness and Other Pathways to Resilience," *American Psychologist,* April 2005, pp 261–62.

[69] M Friedman and R H Rosenman, *Type A Behavior and Your Heart* (Greenwich, CT: Fawcett Publications, 1974), p 84. (Boldface added.)

[70] See C Lee, L F Jamieson, and P C Earley, "Beliefs and Fears and Type A Behavior: Implications for Academic Performance and Psychiatric Health Disorder Symptoms," *Journal of Organizational Behavior,* March 1996, pp 151–77; S D Bluen, J Barling, and W Burns, "Predicting Sales Performance, Job Satisfaction, and Depression by Using the Achievement Strivings and Impatience–Irritability Dimensions of Type A Behavior," *Journal of Applied Psychology,* April 1990, pp 212–16; and M S Taylor, E A Locke, C Lee, and M E Gist, "Type A Behavior and Faculty Research Productivity: What Are the Mechanisms?" *Organizational Behavior and Human Performance,* December 1984, pp 402–18.

[71] Results are contained in Y Chida and M Hamer, "Chronic Psychological Factors and Acute Physiological Responses to Laboratory-Induced Stress in Healthy Populations: A Quantitative Review of 30 Years of Investigations," *Psychological Bulletin,* November 2008, pp 829–85.

[72] See S A Lyness, "Predictors of Differences between Type A and B Individuals in Heart Rate and Blood Pressure Reactivity," *Psychological Bulletin,* September 1993, pp 266–95.

[73] See T Q Miller, T W Smith, C W Turner, M L Guijarro, and A J Hallet, "A Meta-Analytic Review of Research on Hostility and Physical Health," *Psychological Bulletin,* March 1996, pp 322–48.

[74] See S J Wells, "Finding Wellness's Return on Investment," *HR Magazine,* June 2008, pp 75–84.

[75] Results are presented in K M Richardson and H R Rothstein, "Effects of Occupational Stress Management Intervention Programs: A Meta-Analysis," *Journal of Occupational Health Psychology,* January 2008, pp 69–93.

[76] These steps were based on a discussion in L Dzubow, "Optimism 101," *The Oprah Magazine,* April 2011, p 130.

[77] See D C Ganster, B T Mayes, W E Sime, and G D Tharp, "Managing Organizational Stress: A Field Experiment," *Journal of Applied Psychology,* October 1982, pp 533–42.

[78] R Kreitner, "Personal Wellness: It's Just Good Business," *Business Horizons,* May–June 1982, p 28.

[79] S J Wells, "Navigating the Expanding Wellness Industry," *HR Magazine,* March 2011, pp 45–50.

[80] See L L Berry, A M Mirabito, and W B Baun, "What's the Hard Return on Employee Wellness Programs?" *Harvard Business Review,* December 2010, pp 104–12.

[81] See K M Parks and L A Steelman, "Organizational Wellness Programs: A Meta-Analysis," *Journal of Occupational Health Psychology,* January 2008, pp 58–68.

[82] This statistic was reported in "Meeting the Challenge of Motivating Employees to Embrace Wellness," *HR Magazine,* May 2005, pp 15–17.

[83] See "New Year, New You," *USA Weekend,* December 31–January 2, 2011, pp 6–8.

[84] See R Zeidner, "Health Incentives' Financial Rewards Spur Buy-In, Not Necessarily Results," *HR Magazine,* June 2010, p 25.

[85] Excerpted from V Nayar, "A Maverick CEO Explains How He Persuaded His Team to Leap Into the Future," *Harvard Business Review,* June 2010, pp 110–13.

[86] This case is based on material contained in E Frauenheim, "Culture Crash: Lost in the Shuffle," *Workforce Management,* January 14, 2008, pp 1, 12–17.

Glossary/Subject Index

A

Abilities *Stable characteristics responsible for a person's maximum physical or mental performance. See also* Competence

development of, 135
explanation of, **135**
intelligence and cognitive, 136–138
major mental, 137–138
need for sleep and, 135–136
types of, 137
Absenteeism, 48
Accountability, 26
Achievement needs, 209

Action plans *Outlines the activities or tasks that need to be accomplished in order to obtain a goal.*

explanation of, **224, 225**
goal setting and, 223
Action teams, 302, 303
Active listening, 407–408. *See also* **Listening**
Adaptive change, 535

Adhocracy culture *A culture that has an external focus and values flexibility,* **70, 71**

Advice teams, 302, 303
Affective commitment, 164, 166

Affective component *The feelings or emotions one has about an object or situation,* **158, 159**

Affiliation need, 209

Affirmative action *Focuses on achieving equality of opportunity in an organization,* **36, 37**

African Americans, 41–42. *See also* Minorities
Age. *See* Older employees
Age stereotypes, 190–191
Aggressive communication style, 404
Agreeableness, 131

Alternative dispute resolution (ADR) *Avoiding costly lawsuits by resolving conflicts informally or through mediation or arbitration.*

explanation of, 382–**383**
techniques for, 383–384
Ambiguity, 280–282, 341–342

Americans with Disabilities Act (ADA) *Prohibits discrimination against the disabled,* 139, 374

Analytical style of decision making, 342–343
Anchoring bias, 336

Anticipatory socialization phase *Occurs before an individual joins an organization, and involves the information people learn about different careers, occupations, professions, and organizations,* 77–78

Arbitration, 384
Artifacts, 63

Asch effect *Giving in to a unanimous but wrong opposition,* **290–291**

Asian Americans, 41–42
Assertive communication style, 404–405
Assertiveness, 99, 100
Assimilation, 55
Assumptions, 65

Attention *Being consciously aware of something or someone,* **182, 183**

Attitudes *Learned predisposition toward a given object.*

behavior and, 160–162
collision between reality and, 158–159
components of, 158
explanation of, **158, 159**
overview of, 157–158
stability of, 159–160
work, 162–168
Attribution
explanation of, 197
managerial applications for, 200–201
model of, 198–199
tendencies related to, 199–200
Authority, hierarchy of, 497–498
Autonomy, 24
Availability heuristic, 335
Avoiding, as conflict-handling style, 382

B

Baby Boomers, 43–45

Behavioral component *How one intends or expects to act toward someone or something,* **158, 159**

Behavioral style of decision making, 343
Behavioral styles theory
explanation of, 463, 470
implications of, 471
Ohio State studies on, 470
University of Michigan studies on, 471
Behaviorism, 256
Behavior shaping, 260, 261

Benchmarking *Process by which a company compares its performance with that of high-performing organizations,* **536–537**

Bias, in decision making, 335–338
Bodily-kinesthetic intelligence, 138
Body movements, 405–406

Bounded rationality *Constraints that restrict rational decision making,* **333**

Brainstorming *Process to generate a quantity of ideas,* **353**

Buddhists, 104

C

Callousness, 468
Career planning, 53

Case studies *In-depth study of a single person, group, or organization,* **27**

Catholics, 104

Causal attributions *Suspected or inferred causes of behavior.*

attribution tendencies and, 199–200
explanation of, **197**
managerial applications for, 200–201
model of, 198–199
Cell phones, 424–425

Centralized decision making *Top managers make all key decisions,* **509–510**

Central tendency, 189
Change. *See also* Organizational change
adaptive, 535
external forces for, 530–533
innovative, 535
internal forces for, 533–534
Kotter's steps for leading, 541–542
Lewin's model of planned, 536–538
organizational development to create, 542–545
radically innovative, 535
resilience to, 546
resistance to, 545–550
systems model of, 537–541
target elements of, 539–541

Change agents *Individual who is a catalyst in helping organizations to implement change.*

characteristics of, 547–548
explanation of, **543**
relationship between recipients and, 548

Change and acquisition phase *Requires employees to master tasks and roles and to adjust to work group values and norms,* **79**

Changing stage (Lewin), 537
Charisma, 439

Name/Company Index

Page numbers followed by n refer to notes.